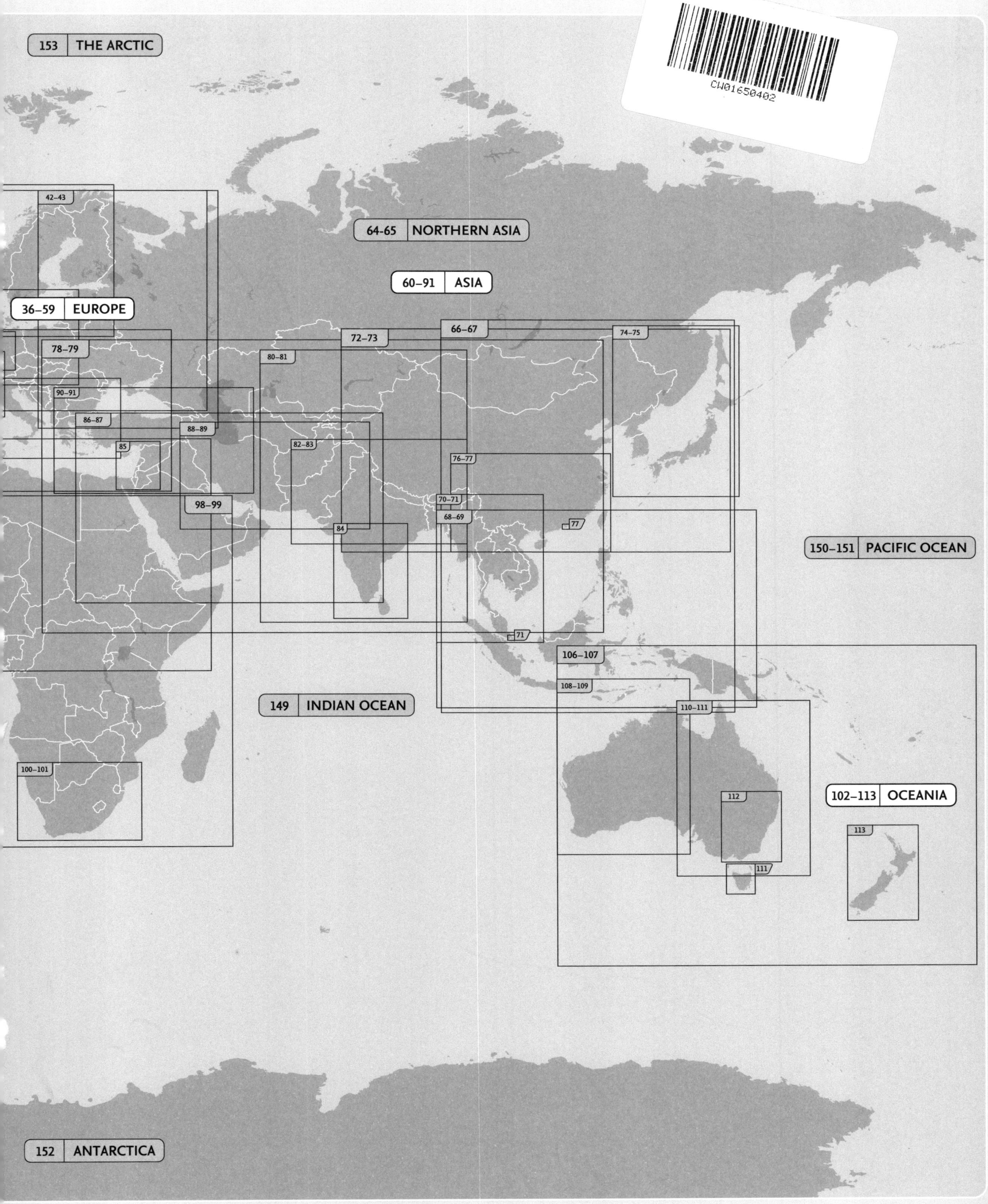
153 THE ARCTIC
42–43
64-65 NORTHERN ASIA
60–91 ASIA
36–59 EUROPE
72–73
66–67
74–75
78–79
80–81
90–91
86–87
88–89
85
82–83
76–77
70–71
68–69
77
98–99
84
150–151 PACIFIC OCEAN
71
106–107
108–109
149 INDIAN OCEAN
110–111
100–101
112
102–113 OCEANIA
113
111
152 ANTARCTICA

Find your map

Contents

Africa		92–101
Landscapes		92–93
Countries		94–95
Northern Africa	1:16 000 000	96–97
Inset: Cape Verde	1:16 000 000	
Central and Southern Africa	1:16 000 000	98–99
South Africa	1:5 000 000	100–101

Oceania		102–113
Landscapes		102–103
Countries		104–105
Australia, New Zealand and Southwest Pacific	1:20 000 000	106–107
Western Australia	1:8 000 000	108–109
Eastern Australia	1:8 000 000	110–111
Inset: Tasmania	1:8 000 000	
Southeast Australia	1:5 000 000	112
New Zealand	1:5 250 000	113

North America		114–137
Landscapes		114–115
Countries		116–117
Canada	1:16 000 000	118–119
Western Canada	1:7 000 000	120–121
Eastern Canada	1:7 000 000	122–123
United States of America	1:12 000 000	124–125
Western United States	1:7 000 000	126–127
Inset: Hawaiian Islands	1:7 000 000	
Southwest United States	1:3 500 000	128–129
Central United States	1:7 000 000	130–131
Eastern United States	1:7 000 000	132–133
Northeast United States	1:3 500 000	134–135
Central America and the Caribbean	1:14 000 000	136–137

South America		138–145
Landscapes		138–139
Countries		140–141
Northern South America	1:14 000 000	142–143
Inset: Galapagos Islands	1:14 000 000	
Southern South America	1:14 000 000	144
Southeast Brazil	1:7 000 000	145

Oceans and Poles		146–153
Features		146–147
Atlantic Ocean and Indian Ocean	1:50 000 000	148–149
Pacific Ocean	1:50 000 000	150–151
Antarctica	1:26 000 000	152
The Arctic	1:26 000 000	153

World Statistics	154–160
Index	161–239
Acknowledgements	240

Map Symbols and Time Zones

Southern Europe

Japan

Antarctica

Settlements

Population	National capital	Administrative capital	Other city or town
over 10 million	BEIJING	Karachi	New York
5 million to 10 million	LONDON	Tianjin	Santos
1 million to 5 million	KĀBUL	Sydney	Kaohsiung
500 000 to 1 million	BANGUI	Trujillo	Amritsar
100 000 to 500 000	WELLINGTON	Mansa	Apucarana
50 000 to 100 000	PORT OF SPAIN	Potenza	Arecibo
10 000 to 50 000	MALABO	Chinhoyi	Ceres
under 10 000	VALLETTA	Ati	Venta

Built-up area

Relief

Contour intervals and layer colours

Height metres	feet
5000	16404
3000	9843
2000	6562
1000	3281
500	1640
200	656
0	0
below sea level	
0	0
200	656
2000	6562
4000	13124
6000	19686
Depth	

1234 Summit
height in metres

-123 Spot height
height in metres

123 Ocean deep
depth in metres

Boundaries

- International boundary
- Disputed international boundary or alignment unconfirmed
- Disputed territory boundary
- Administrative boundary
- Ceasefire line
- UN Buffer zone

Miscellaneous

- National park
- Reserve or Regional park
- Site of specific interest
- Wall

Land and sea features

- Desert
- Oasis
- Lava field
- Marsh
- 1234 Volcano
  height in metres
- Ice cap or Glacier
- Escarpment
- Coral reef
- 1234 Pass
  height in metres

Lakes and rivers

- Lake
- Impermanent lake
- Salt lake or lagoon
- Impermanent salt lake
- Dry salt lake or salt pan
- 123 Lake height
  surface height above sea level, in metres
- River
- Impermanent river or watercourse
- Waterfall
- Dam
- Barrage

Transport

- Motorway (tunnel; under construction)
- Main road (tunnel; under construction)
- Secondary road (tunnel; under construction)
- Track
- Main railway (tunnel; under construction)
- Secondary railway (tunnel; under construction)
- Other railway (tunnel; under construction)
- Canal
- Main airport
- Regional airport

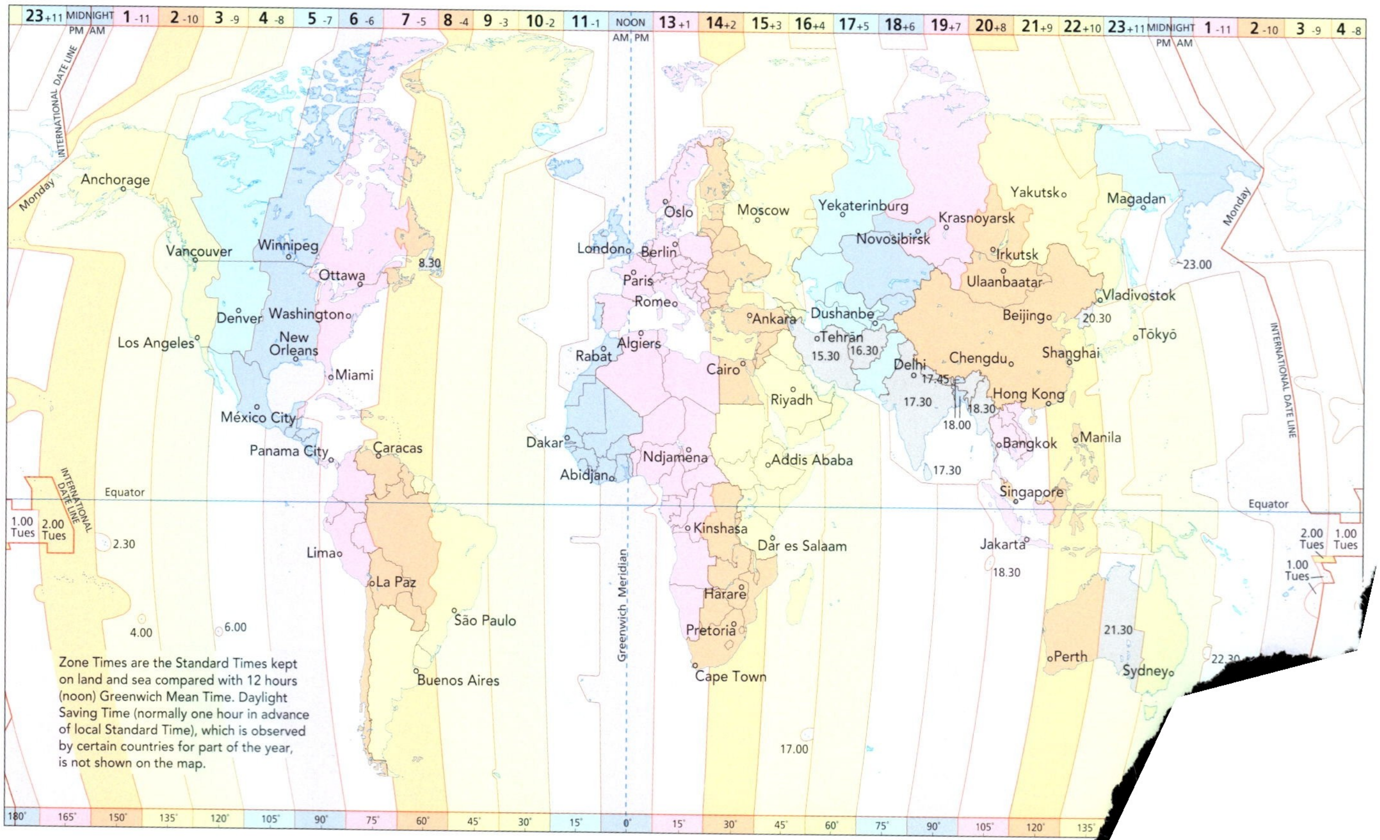

Zone Times are the Standard Times kept on land and sea compared with 12 hours (noon) Greenwich Mean Time. Daylight Saving Time (normally one hour in advance of local Standard Time), which is observed by certain countries for part of the year, is not shown on the map.

Collins

WORLD ATLAS

REFERENCE EDITION

Contents

Title	Scale	Page
Map Symbols and Time Zones		4
World States and Territories		5–9
World		**10–35**
Countries		10–11
Landscapes		12–13
Earthquakes and Volcanoes		14–15
Climate and Weather		16–17
Land Cover		18–19
Population		20–21
Urbanization and Cities		22–23
Communications		24–25
Social Indicators		26–27
Economy and Wealth		28–29
Conflict		30–31
Global Issues		32–33
Environmental Threats		34–35
Europe		**36–59**
Landscapes		36–37
Countries		38–39
Northern Europe	1:10 000 000	40–41
Western Russia	1:7 500 000	42–43
Scandinavia and the Baltic States	1:5 000 000	44–45
Inset: Iceland	1:6 000 000	
Inset: Faroe Islands	1:5 000 000	
Northwest Europe	1:5 000 000	46–47
England and Wales	1:2 000 000	48–49
Scotland	1:2 000 000	50
Inset: Shetland Islands	1:2 000 000	
Ireland	1:2 000 000	51
Belgium, Netherlands, Luxembourg and Northwest Germany	1:2 000 000	52–53
Southern Europe and the Mediterranean	1:10 000 000	54–55
France	1:5 000 000	56
Spain and Portugal	1:5 000 000	57
Italy and the Balkans	1:5 000 000	58–59
Asia		**60–91**
Landscapes		60–61
Countries		62–63
Northern Asia	1:20 000 000	64–65
Eastern and Southeast Asia	1:20 000 000	66–67
Southeast Asia	1:15 000 000	68–69
Myanmar, Thailand, Peninsular Malaysia and Indo-China	1:7 000 000	70–71
Inset: Singapore	1:550 000	
Eastern Asia	1:15 000 000	72–73
Japan, North Korea and South Korea	1:7 000 000	74–75
Southeast China	1:7 000 000	76–77
Inset: Hong Kong	1:700 000	
Central and Southern Asia	1:20 000 000	78–79
Southern Asia	1:13 000 000	80–81
Northern India, Nepal, Bhutan and Bangladesh	1:7 000 000	82–83
Southern India and Sri Lanka	1:7 000 000	84
Middle East	1:3 000 000	85
Southwest Asia	1:13 000 000	86–87
The Gulf, Iran, Afghanistan and Pakistan	1:7 000 000	88–89
Eastern Mediterranean, the Caucasus and Iraq	1:7 000 000	90–91

The Alps

Paris, France

Europe	Area sq km	Area sq miles	Population	Capital	Languages ('de facto' speakers over one per cent of population)	Religions ('de facto' adherents over one per cent of population)	Currency
ALBANIA	28 748	11 100	2 897 000	Tirana	Albanian, Greek	Sunni Muslim, Albanian Orthodox, Roman Catholic	Lek
ANDORRA	465	180	70 000	Andorra la Vella	Spanish, Catalan, French	Roman Catholic	Euro
AUSTRIA	83 855	32 377	8 545 000	Vienna	German, Croatian, Turkish	Roman Catholic, Protestant	Euro
BELARUS	207 600	80 155	9 496 000	Minsk	Belarusian, Russian	Belarusian Orthodox, Roman Catholic	Belarusian rouble
BELGIUM	30 520	11 784	11 299 000	Brussels	Dutch (Flemish), French (Walloon), German	Roman Catholic, Protestant	Euro
BOSNIA AND HERZEGOVINA	51 130	19 741	3 810 000	Sarajevo	Bosnian, Serbian, Croatian	Sunni Muslim, Serbian Orthodox, Roman Catholic, Protestant	Convertible mark
BULGARIA	110 994	42 855	7 150 000	Sofia	Bulgarian, Turkish, Romany, Macedonian	Bulgarian Orthodox, Sunni Muslim	Lev
CROATIA	56 538	21 829	4 240 000	Zagreb	Croatian, Serbian	Roman Catholic, Serbian Orthodox, Sunni Muslim	Kuna
CZECHIA (CZECH REPUBLIC)	78 864	30 450	10 543 000	Prague	Czech, Moravian, Slovak	Roman Catholic, Protestant	Koruna
DENMARK	43 075	16 631	5 669 000	Copenhagen	Danish	Protestant	Danish krone
ESTONIA	45 200	17 452	1 313 000	Tallinn	Estonian, Russian	Protestant, Estonian and Russian Orthodox	Euro
FINLAND	338 145	130 559	5 503 000	Helsinki	Finnish, Swedish, Sami languages	Protestant, Greek Orthodox	Euro
FRANCE	543 965	210 026	64 395 000	Paris	French, German dialects, Italian, Arabic, Breton	Roman Catholic, Protestant, Sunni Muslim	Euro
GERMANY	357 022	137 849	80 689 000	Berlin	German, Turkish	Protestant, Roman Catholic	Euro
GREECE	131 957	50 949	10 955 000	Athens	Greek	Greek Orthodox, Sunni Muslim	Euro
HUNGARY	93 030	35 919	9 855 000	Budapest	Hungarian	Roman Catholic, Protestant	Forint
ICELAND	102 820	39 699	329 000	Reykjavík	Icelandic	Protestant	Icelandic króna
IRELAND	70 282	27 136	4 688 000	Dublin	English, Irish	Roman Catholic, Protestant	Euro
ITALY	301 245	116 311	59 798 000	Rome	Italian	Roman Catholic	Euro
KOSOVO	10 908	4 212	1 805 000	Prishtinë (Priština)	Albanian, Serbian	Sunni Muslim, Serbian Orthodox	Euro
LATVIA	64 589	24 938	1 971 000	Rīga	Latvian, Russian	Protestant, Roman Catholic, Russian Orthodox	Euro
LIECHTENSTEIN	160	62	38 000	Vaduz	German	Roman Catholic, Protestant	Swiss franc
LITHUANIA	65 200	25 174	2 878 000	Vilnius	Lithuanian, Russian, Polish	Roman Catholic, Protestant, Russian Orthodox	Euro
LUXEMBOURG	2 586	998	567 000	Luxembourg	Letzeburgish, German, French	Roman Catholic	Euro
MACEDONIA (F.Y.R.O.M.)	25 713	9 928	2 078 000	Skopje	Macedonian, Albanian, Turkish	Macedonian Orthodox, Sunni Muslim	Macedonian denar
MALTA	316	122	419 000	Valletta	Maltese, English	Roman Catholic	Euro
MOLDOVA	33 700	13 012	4 069 000	Chișinău	Romanian, Ukrainian, Gagauz, Russian	Romanian Orthodox, Russian Orthodox	Moldovan leu
MONACO	2	1	38 000	Monaco-Ville	French, Monegasque, Italian	Roman Catholic	Euro
MONTENEGRO	13 812	5 333	626 000	Podgorica	Serbian (Montenegrin), Albanian	Montenegrin Orthodox, Sunni Muslim	Euro
NETHERLANDS	41 526	16 033	16 925 000	Amsterdam/The Hague	Dutch, Frisian	Roman Catholic, Protestant, Sunni Muslim	Euro
NORWAY	323 878	125 050	5 211 000	Oslo	Norwegian, Sami languages	Protestant, Roman Catholic	Norwegian krone
POLAND	312 683	120 728	38 612 000	Warsaw	Polish, German	Roman Catholic, Polish Orthodox	Złoty
PORTUGAL	88 940	34 340	10 350 000	Lisbon	Portuguese	Roman Catholic, Protestant	Euro
ROMANIA	237 500	91 699	19 511 000	Bucharest	Romanian, Hungarian	Romanian Orthodox, Protestant, Roman Catholic	Romanian leu
RUSSIA	17 075 400	6 592 849	143 457 000	Moscow	Russian, Tatar, Ukrainian, other local languages	Russian Orthodox, Sunni Muslim, Protestant	Russian rouble
SAN MARINO	61	24	32 000	San Marino	Italian	Roman Catholic	Euro
SERBIA	77 453	29 904	7 046 000	Belgrade	Serbian, Hungarian	Serbian Orthodox, Roman Catholic, Sunni Muslim	Serbian dinar
SLOVAKIA	49 035	18 933	5 426 000	Bratislava	Slovak, Hungarian, Czech	Roman Catholic, Protestant, Orthodox	Euro
SLOVENIA	20 251	7 819	2 068 000	Ljubljana	Slovene, Croatian, Serbian	Roman Catholic, Protestant	Euro
SPAIN	504 782	194 897	46 122 000	Madrid	Spanish, Castilian, Catalan, Galician, Basque	Roman Catholic	Euro
SWEDEN	449 964	173 732	9 779 000	Stockholm	Swedish, Sami languages	Protestant, Roman Catholic	Swedish krona
SWITZERLAND	41 293	15 943	8 299 000	Bern	German, French, Italian, Romansch	Roman Catholic, Protestant	Swiss franc
UKRAINE	603 700	233 090	44 824 000	Kiev	Ukrainian, Russian	Ukrainian Orthodox, Ukrainian Catholic, Roman Catholic	Hryvnia
UNITED KINGDOM	243 609	94 058	64 716 000	London	English, Welsh, Gaelic	Protestant, Roman Catholic, Muslim	Pound sterling
VATICAN CITY	0.5	0.2	800	Vatican City	Italian	Roman Catholic	Euro

Dependent and disputed territories	Territorial status	Area sq km	Area sq miles	Population	Capital	Languages	Religions	Currency
Azores	Autonomous Region of Portugal	2 300	888	247 413	Ponta Delgada	Portuguese	Roman Catholic, Protestant	Euro
Crimea	Disputed Territory	27 000	10 400	2 348 600	Simferopol'	Ukrainian, Russian	Russian Orthodox, Sunni Muslim	Russian rouble
Faroe Islands	Self-governing Danish Territory	1 399	540	48 000	Tórshavn	Faroese, Danish	Protestant	Danish krone
Gibraltar	United Kingdom Overseas Territory	7	3	32 000	Gibraltar	Engllish, Spanish	Roman Catholic, Protestant, Sunni Muslim	Gibraltar pound
Guernsey	United Kingdom Crown Dependency	78	30	65 000	St Peter Port	English, French	Protestant, Roman Catholic	Pound sterling
Isle of Man	United Kingdom Crown Dependency	572	221	88 000	Douglas	English	Protestant, Roman Catholic	Pound sterling
Jersey	United Kingdom Crown Dependency	116	45	101 000	St Helier	English, French	Protestant, Roman Catholic	Pound sterling
Transnistria	Disputed Territory	4 200	1 622	...	Tiraspol	Russian, Ukrainian, Moldovan	Eastern Orthodox, Roman Catholic	Transnistrian rouble, Moldovan leu

World

States and Territories

Cyprus, eastern Mediterranean

Angkor, Cambodia

Asia	Area sq km	Area sq miles	Population	Capital	Languages ('de facto' speakers over one per cent of population)	Religions ('de facto' adherents over one per cent of population)	Currency
AFGHANISTAN	652 225	251 825	32 527 000	Kābul	Dari, Pashto (Pashtu), Uzbek, Turkmen	Sunni Muslim, Shi'a Muslim	Afghani
ARMENIA	29 800	11 506	3 018 000	Yerevan	Armenian, Kurdish	Armenian Orthodox	Dram
AZERBAIJAN	86 600	33 436	9 754 000	Baku	Azeri, Armenian, Russian, Lezgian	Shi'a Muslim, Sunni Muslim, Russian and Armenian Orthodox	Azerbaijani manat
BAHRAIN	691	267	1 377 000	Manama	Arabic, English	Shi'a Muslim, Sunni Muslim, Christian	Bahraini dinar
BANGLADESH	143 998	55 598	160 996 000	Dhaka	Bengali, English	Sunni Muslim, Hindu	Taka
BHUTAN	46 620	18 000	775 000	Thimphu	Dzongkha, Nepali, Assamese	Buddhist, Hindu	Ngultrum, Indian rupee
BRUNEI	5 765	2 226	423 000	Bandar Seri Begawan	Malay, English, Chinese	Sunni Muslim, Buddhist, Christian	Bruneian dollar
CAMBODIA	181 035	69 884	15 578 000	Phnom Penh	Khmer	Buddhist, Roman Catholic, Sunni Muslim	Riel
CHINA	9 606 802	3 709 186	1 383 925 000	Beijing	Mandarin (Putonghua), Wu, Cantonese, Hsiang, regional languages	Confucian, Taoist, Buddhist, Christian, Sunni Muslim	Yuan, HK dollar**, Macau pataca
CYPRUS	9 251	3 572	1 165 000	Nicosia	Greek, Turkish, English	Greek Orthodox, Sunni Muslim	Euro
EAST TIMOR (TIMOR-LESTE)	14 874	5 743	1 185 000	Dili	Portuguese, Tetun, English	Roman Catholic	United States dollar
GEORGIA	69 700	26 911	4 000 000	Tbilisi	Georgian, Russian, Armenian, Azeri, Ossetian, Abkhaz	Georgian Orthodox, Russian Orthodox, Sunni Muslim	Lari
INDIA	3 166 620	1 222 632	1 311 051 000	New Delhi	Hindi, English, many regional languages	Hindu, Sunni Muslim, Shi'a Muslim, Sikh, Christian	Indian rupee
INDONESIA	1 919 445	741 102	257 564 000	Jakarta	Indonesian, other local languages	Sunni Muslim, Protestant, Roman Catholic, Hindu, Buddhist	Rupiah
IRAN	1 648 000	636 296	79 109 000	Tehrān	Farsi, Azeri, Kurdish, regional languages	Shi'a Muslim, Sunni Muslim	Iranian rial
IRAQ	438 317	169 235	36 423 000	Baghdād	Arabic, Kurdish, Turkmen	Shi'a Muslim, Sunni Muslim, Christian	Iraqi dinar
ISRAEL	20 770	8 019	8 064 000	Jerusalem (Yerushalayim) (El Quds)*	Hebrew, Arabic	Jewish, Sunni Muslim, Christian, Druze	Shekel
JAPAN	377 727	145 841	126 573 000	Tōkyō	Japanese	Shintoist, Buddhist, Christian	Yen
JORDAN	89 206	34 443	7 595 000	'Ammān	Arabic	Sunni Muslim, Christian	Jordanian dinar
KAZAKHSTAN	2 717 300	1 049 155	17 625 000	Astana	Kazakh, Russian, Ukrainian, German, Uzbek, Tatar	Sunni Muslim, Russian Orthodox, Protestant	Tenge
KUWAIT	17 818	6 880	3 892 000	Kuwait	Arabic	Sunni Muslim, Shi'a Muslim, Christian, Hindu	Kuwaiti dinar
KYRGYZSTAN	198 500	76 641	5 940 000	Bishkek	Kyrgyz, Russian, Uzbek	Sunni Muslim, Russian Orthodox	Kyrgyz som
LAOS	236 800	91 429	6 802 000	Vientiane	Lao, other local languages	Buddhist, traditional beliefs	Kip
LEBANON	10 452	4 036	5 851 000	Beirut	Arabic, Armenian, French	Shi'a Muslim, Sunni Muslim, Christian	Lebanese pound
MALAYSIA	332 965	128 559	30 331 000	Kuala Lumpur/Putrajaya	Malay, English, Chinese, Tamil, other local languages	Sunni Muslim, Buddhist, Hindu, Christian, traditional beliefs	Ringgit
MALDIVES	298	115	364 000	Male	Divehi (Maldivian)	Sunni Muslim	Rufiyaa
MONGOLIA	1 565 000	604 250	2 959 000	Ulan Bator	Khalka (Mongolian), Kazakh, other local languages	Buddhist, Sunni Muslim	Tugrik (tögrög)
MYANMAR (BURMA)	676 577	261 228	53 897 000	Nay Pyi Taw	Burmese, Shan, Karen, other local languages	Buddhist, Christian, Sunni Muslim	Kyat
NEPAL	147 181	56 827	28 514 000	Kathmandu	Nepali, Maithili, Bhojpuri, English, other local languages	Hindu, Buddhist, Sunni Muslim	Nepalese rupee
NORTH KOREA	120 538	46 540	25 155 000	P'yŏngyang	Korean	Traditional beliefs, Chondoist, Buddhist	North Korean won
OMAN	309 500	119 499	4 491 000	Muscat	Arabic, Baluchi, Indian languages	Ibadhi Muslim, Sunni Muslim	Omani rial
PAKISTAN	881 888	340 497	188 925 000	Islamabad	Urdu, Punjabi, Sindhi, Pashto (Pashtu), English, Balochi	Sunni Muslim, Shi'a Muslim, Christian, Hindu	Pakistani rupee
PALAU	497	192	21 000	Melekeok (Ngerulmud)	Palauan, English	Roman Catholic, Protestant, traditional beliefs	United States dollar
PHILIPPINES	300 000	115 831	100 699 000	Manila	English, Filipino, Tagalog, Cebuano, other local languages	Roman Catholic, Protestant, Sunni Muslim, Aglipayan	Philippine peso
QATAR	11 437	4 416	2 235 000	Doha	Arabic	Sunni Muslim	Qatari riyal
RUSSIA	17 075 400	6 592 849	143 457 000	Moscow	Russian, Tatar, Ukrainian, other local languages	Russian Orthodox, Sunni Muslim, Protestant	Russian rouble
SAUDI ARABIA	2 200 000	849 425	31 540 000	Riyadh	Arabic	Sunni Muslim, Shi'a Muslim	Saudi Arabian rial
SINGAPORE	639	247	5 604 000	Singapore	Chinese, English, Malay, Tamil	Buddhist, Taoist, Sunni Muslim, Christian, Hindu	Singapore dollar
SOUTH KOREA	99 274	38 330	50 293 000	Seoul	Korean	Buddhist, Protestant, Roman Catholic	South Korean won
SRI LANKA	65 610	25 332	20 715 000	Sri Jayewardenepura Kotte	Sinhalese, Tamil, English	Buddhist, Hindu, Sunni Muslim, Roman Catholic	Sri Lankan rupee
SYRIA	185 180	71 498	18 502 000	Damascus	Arabic, Kurdish, Armenian	Sunni Muslim, Shi'a Muslim, Christian	Syrian pound
TAIWAN+	36 179	13 969	23 462 000	Taipei (Taibei)	Mandarin (Putonghua), Min, Hakka, other local languages	Buddhist, Taoist, Confucian, Christian	New Taiwan dollar
TAJIKISTAN	143 100	55 251	8 482 000	Dushanbe	Tajik, Uzbek, Russian	Sunni Muslim	Somoni
THAILAND	513 115	198 115	67 959 000	Bangkok	Thai, Lao, Chinese, Malay, Mon-Khmer languages	Buddhist, Sunni Muslim	Baht
TURKEY	779 452	300 948	78 666 000	Ankara	Turkish, Kurdish	Sunni Muslim, Shi'a Muslim	Lira
TURKMENISTAN	488 100	188 456	5 374 000	Aşgabat (Ashgabad)	Turkmen, Uzbek, Russian	Sunni Muslim, Russian Orthodox	Turkmen manat
UNITED ARAB EMIRATES	77 700	30 000	9 157 000	Abu Dhabi (Abū , aby)	Arabic, English	Sunni Muslim, Shi'a Muslim	United Arab Emirates dirham
UZBEKISTAN	447 400	172 742	29 893 000	Toshkent (Tashkent)	Uzbek, Russian, Tajik, Kazakh	Sunni Muslim, Russian Orthodox	Uzbek som
VIETNAM	329 565	127 246	93 448 000	Ha Nôi (Hanoi)	Vietnamese, Thai, Khmer, Chinese, other local languages	Buddhist, Taoist, Roman Catholic, Cao Dai, Hoa Hao	Dong
YEMEN	527 968	203 850	26 832 000	Şan'ā'	Arabic	Sunni Muslim, Shi'a Muslim	Yemeni rial

Dependent and disputed territories	Territorial status	Area sq km	Area sq miles	Population	Capital	Languages	Religions	Currency
Abkhazia	Disputed territory	8 700	3 359	...	Sokhumi (Aq''a)	Abkhaz, Russian, Georgian	Abkhaz Orthodox, Sunni Muslim	Russian rouble, Abkhaz apsar
Christmas Island	Australian External Territory	135	52	2 240	The Settlement	English	Buddhist, Sunni Muslim, Protestant, Roman Catholic	Australian dollar
Cocos (Keeling) Islands	Australian External Territory	14	5	590	West Island	English	Sunni Muslim, Christian	Australian dollar
Gaza	Disputed territory	363	140	1 820 000	Gaza	Arabic	Sunni Muslim, Shi'a Muslim	Israeli shekel
Nagorno-Karabakh	Disputed territory	6 000	2 317	149 000	Xankändi (Stepanakert)	Armenian	Armenian Orthodox	Armenian dram
South Ossetia	Disputed territory	4 000	1 544	...	Tskhinvali	Ossetian, Russian, Georgian	Eastern Orthodox	Russian rouble
West Bank	Disputed territory	5 860	2 263	2 862 000		Arabic, Hebrew	Sunni Muslim, Jewish, Shi'a Muslim, Christian	Jordanian dinar, Israeli shekel

+China claims Taiwan as its 23rd province

*De facto capital. Disputed

**Hong Kong dollar

Victoria Falls, Zambia/Zimbabwe

Africa	Area sq km	Area sq miles	Population	Capital	Languages ('de facto' speakers over one per cent of population)	Religions ('de facto' adherents over one per cent of population)	Currency
ALGERIA	2 381 741	919 595	39 667 000	Algiers (Alger)	Arabic, French, Berber	Sunni Muslim	Algerian dinar
ANGOLA	1 246 700	481 354	25 022 000	Luanda	Portuguese, Bantu, other local languages	Roman Catholic, Protestant, traditional beliefs	Kwanza
BENIN	112 620	43 483	10 880 000	Porto-Novo	French, Fon, Yoruba, Adja, other local languages	Traditional beliefs, Roman Catholic, Sunni Muslim	CFA franc*
BOTSWANA	581 370	224 468	2 262 000	Gaborone	English, Setswana, Shona, other local languages	Traditional beliefs, Protestant, Roman Catholic	Pula
BURKINA FASO	274 200	105 869	18 106 000	Ouagadougou	French, Moore (Mossi), Fulani, other local languages	Sunni Muslim, traditional beliefs, Roman Catholic	CFA franc*
BURUNDI	27 835	10 747	11 179 000	Bujumbura	Kirundi (Hutu, Tutsi), French	Roman Catholic, traditional beliefs, Protestant	Burundian franc
CAMEROON	475 442	183 569	23 344 000	Yaoundé	French, English, Fang, Bamileke, other local languages	Roman Catholic, traditional beliefs, Sunni Muslim, Protestant	CFA franc*
CAPE VERDE	4 033	1 557	521 000	Praia	Portuguese, creole	Roman Catholic, Protestant	Cape Verdean escudo
CENTRAL AFRICAN REPUBLIC	622 436	240 324	4 900 000	Bangui	French, Sango, Banda, Baya, other local languages	Protestant, Roman Catholic, traditional beliefs, Sunni Muslim	CFA franc*
CHAD	1 284 000	495 755	14 037 000	Ndjamena	Arabic, French, Sara, other local languages	Sunni Muslim, Roman Catholic, Protestant, traditional beliefs	CFA franc*
COMOROS	1 862	719	788 000	Moroni	Shikomor (Comorian), French, Arabic	Sunni Muslim, Roman Catholic	Comorian franc
CONGO	342 000	132 047	4 620 000	Brazzaville	French, Kongo, Monokutuba, other local languages	Roman Catholic, Protestant, traditional beliefs, Sunni Muslim	CFA franc*
CONGO, DEM. REP. OF THE	2 345 410	905 568	77 267 000	Kinshasa	French, Lingala, Swahili, Kongo, other local languages	Christian, Sunni Muslim	Congolese franc
CÔTE D'IVOIRE (IVORY COAST)	322 463	124 504	22 702 000	Yamoussoukro	French, creole, Akan, other local languages	Sunni Muslim, Roman Catholic, traditional beliefs, Protestant	CFA franc*
DJIBOUTI	23 200	8 958	888 000	Djibouti	Somali, Afar, French, Arabic	Sunni Muslim, Christian	Djiboutian franc
EGYPT	1 001 450	386 660	91 508 000	Cairo (Al Qāhirah)	Arabic	Sunni Muslim, Coptic Christian	Egyptian pound
EQUATORIAL GUINEA	28 051	10 831	845 000	Malabo	Spanish, French, Fang	Roman Catholic, traditional beliefs	CFA franc*
ERITREA	117 400	45 328	5 228 000	Asmara	Tigrinya, Tigre	Sunni Muslim, Coptic Christian	Nakfa
ETHIOPIA	1 133 880	437 794	99 391 000	Addis Ababa	Oromo, Amharic, Tigrinya, other local languages	Ethiopian Orthodox, Sunni Muslim, traditional beliefs	Birr
GABON	267 667	103 347	1 725 000	Libreville	French, Fang, other local languages	Roman Catholic, Protestant, traditional beliefs	CFA franc*
THE GAMBIA	11 295	4 361	1 991 000	Banjul	English, Malinke, Fulani, Wolof	Sunni Muslim, Protestant	Dalasi
GHANA	238 537	92 100	27 410 000	Accra	English, Hausa, Akan, other local languages	Christian, Sunni Muslim, traditional beliefs	Cedi
GUINEA	245 857	94 926	12 609 000	Conakry	French, Fulani, Malinke, other local languages	Sunni Muslim, traditional beliefs, Christian	Guinean franc
GUINEA-BISSAU	36 125	13 948	1 844 000	Bissau	Portuguese, crioulo, other local languages	Traditional beliefs, Sunni Muslim, Christian	CFA franc*
KENYA	582 646	224 961	46 050 000	Nairobi	Swahili, English, other local languages	Christian, traditional beliefs	Kenyan shilling
LESOTHO	30 355	11 720	2 135 000	Maseru	Sesotho, English, Zulu	Christian, traditional beliefs	Loti, S. African rand
LIBERIA	111 369	43 000	4 503 000	Monrovia	English, creole, other local languages	Traditional beliefs, Christian, Sunni Muslim	Liberian dollar
LIBYA	1 759 540	679 362	6 278 000	Tripoli	Arabic, Berber	Sunni Muslim	Libyan dinar
MADAGASCAR	587 041	226 658	24 235 000	Antananarivo	Malagasy, French	Traditional beliefs, Christian, Sunni Muslim	Ariary
MALAWI	118 484	45 747	17 215 000	Lilongwe	Chichewa, English, other local languages	Christian, traditional beliefs, Sunni Muslim	Malawian kwacha
MALI	1 240 140	478 821	17 600 000	Bamako	French, Bambara, other local languages	Sunni Muslim, traditional beliefs, Christian	CFA franc*
MAURITANIA	1 030 700	397 955	4 068 000	Nouakchott	Arabic, French, other local languages	Sunni Muslim	Ouguiya
MAURITIUS	2 040	788	1 273 000	Port Louis	English, creole, Hindi, Bhojpurī, French	Hindu, Roman Catholic, Sunni Muslim	Mauritian rupee
MOROCCO	446 550	172 414	34 378 000	Rabat	Arabic, Berber, French	Sunni Muslim	Moroccan dirham
MOZAMBIQUE	799 380	308 642	27 978 000	Maputo	Portuguese, Makua, Tsonga, other local languages	Traditional beliefs, Roman Catholic, Sunni Muslim	Metical
NAMIBIA	824 292	318 261	2 459 000	Windhoek	English, Afrikaans, German, Ovambo, other local languages	Protestant, Roman Catholic	Namibian dollar
NIGER	1 267 000	489 191	19 899 000	Niamey	French, Hausa, Fulani, other local languages	Sunni Muslim, traditional beliefs	CFA franc*
NIGERIA	923 768	356 669	182 202 000	Abuja	English, Hausa, Yoruba, Ibo, Fulani, other local languages	Sunni Muslim, Christian, traditional beliefs	Naira
RWANDA	26 338	10 169	11 610 000	Kigali	Kinyarwanda, French, English	Roman Catholic, traditional beliefs, Protestant	Rwandan franc
SÃO TOMÉ AND PRÍNCIPE	964	372	190 000	São Tomé	Portuguese, creole	Roman Catholic, Protestant	Dobra
SENEGAL	196 720	75 954	15 129 000	Dakar	French, Wolof, Fulani, other local languages	Sunni Muslim, Roman Catholic, traditional beliefs	CFA franc*
SEYCHELLES	455	176	96 000	Victoria	English, French, creole	Roman Catholic, Protestant	Seychelles rupee
SIERRA LEONE	71 740	27 699	6 453 000	Freetown	English, creole, Mende, Temne, other local languages	Sunni Muslim, traditional beliefs	Leone
SOMALIA	637 657	246 201	10 787 000	Mogadishu	Somali, Arabic	Sunni Muslim	Somali shilling
SOUTH AFRICA	1 219 090	470 693	54 490 000	Bloemfontein/ Cape Town/Pretoria	Afrikaans, English, nine official other local languages	Protestant, Roman Catholic, Sunni Muslim, Hindu	Rand
SOUTH SUDAN	644 329	248 775	12 340 000	Juba	English, Arabic, Dinka, Nuer, other local languages	Traditional beliefs, Christian	South Sudanese pound
SUDAN	1 861 484	718 725	40 235 000	Khartoum	Arabic, Dinka, Nubian, Beja, Nuer, other local languages	Sunni Muslim, traditional beliefs, Christian	Sudanese pound (Sudani)
SWAZILAND	17 364	6 704	1 287 000	Mbabane	Swazi, English	Christian, traditional beliefs	Lilangeni, South African rand
TANZANIA	945 087	364 900	53 470 000	Dodoma	Swahili, English, Nyamwezi, other local languages	Shi'a Muslim, Sunni Muslim, traditional beliefs, Christian	Tanzanian shilling
TOGO	56 785	21 925	7 305 000	Lomé	French, Ewe, Kabre, other local languages	Traditional beliefs, Christian, Sunni Muslim	CFA franc*
TUNISIA	164 150	63 379	11 254 000	Tunis	Arabic, French	Sunni Muslim	Tunisian dinar
UGANDA	241 038	93 065	39 032 000	Kampala	English, Swahili, Luganda, other local languages	Roman Catholic, Protestant, Sunni Muslim, traditional beliefs	Ugandan shilling
ZAMBIA	752 614	290 586	16 212 000	Lusaka	English, Bemba, Nyanja, Tonga, other local languages	Christian, traditional beliefs	Zambian kwacha
ZIMBABWE	390 759	150 873	15 603 000	Harare	16 official languages including English, Shona and Ndebele	Christian, traditional beliefs	US dollar and other currencies

Dependent and disputed territories	Territorial status	Area sq km	Area sq miles	Population	Capital	Languages	Religions	Currency
Canary Islands	Autonomous Community of Spain	7 447	2 875	...	Santa Cruz de Tenerife/Las Palmas	Spanish	Roman Catholic	Euro
Madeira	Autonomous Region of Portugal	779	301	259 000	Funchal	Portuguese	Roman Catholic, Protestant	Euro
Mayotte	French Overseas Department	373	144	240 000	Dzaoudzi	French, Mahorian	Sunni Muslim, Christian	Euro
Réunion	French Overseas Department	2 551	985	861 000	St-Denis	French, creole	Roman Catholic	Euro
St Helena, Ascension and Tristan da Cunha	United Kingdom Overseas Territory	410	158	5 793	Jamestown	English	Protestant, Roman Catholic	St Helena pound
Somaliland	Disputed territory	140 000	54 054	3 850 000	Hargeysa	Somali, Arabic, English	Sunni Muslim	Somaliland shilling
Western Sahara	Disputed territory (Morocco)	266 000	102 703	573 000	Laâyoune	Arabic	Sunni Muslim	Moroccan dirham

*Communauté Financière Africaine franc

World
States and Territories

Mataiva Atoll, Tuamotu Archipelago, French Polynesia

Uluru (Ayers Rock), Australia

Oceania		Area sq km	Area sq miles	Population	Capital	Languages ('de facto' speakers over one per cent of population)	Religions ('de facto' adherents over one per cent of population)	Currency
AUSTRALIA		7 692 024	2 969 907	23 969 000	Canberra	English, Italian, Greek	Protestant, Roman Catholic, Orthodox	Australian dollar
FIJI		18 330	7 077	892 000	Suva	English, Fijian, Hindi	Christian, Hindu, Sunni Muslim	Fijian dollar
KIRIBATI		717	277	112 000	Bairiki	Gilbertese, English	Roman Catholic, Protestant	Australian dollar
MARSHALL ISLANDS		181	70	53 000	Delap-Uliga-Djarrit	English, Marshallese	Protestant, Roman Catholic	United States dollar
MICRONESIA, FEDERATED STATES OF		701	271	526 000	Palikir	English, Chuukese, Pohnpeian, other local languages	Roman Catholic, Protestant	United States dollar
NAURU		21	8	10 000	Yaren (de facto capital)	Nauruan, English	Protestant, Roman Catholic	Australian dollar
NEW ZEALAND		270 534	104 454	4 529 000	Wellington	English, Maori	Protestant, Roman Catholic	New Zealand dollar
PAPUA NEW GUINEA		462 840	178 704	7 619 000	Port Moresby	English, Tok Pisin (creole), other local languages	Protestant, Roman Catholic, traditional beliefs	Kina
SAMOA		2 831	1 093	193 000	Apia	Samoan, English	Protestant, Roman Catholic	Tala
SOLOMON ISLANDS		28 370	10 954	584 000	Honiara	English, creole, local languages	Protestant, Roman Catholic	Solomon Islands dollar
TONGA		748	289	106 000	Nuku'alofa	Tongan, English	Protestant, Roman Catholic	Pa'anga
TUVALU		25	10	9 916	Vaiaku	Tuvaluan, English	Protestant	Australian dollar
VANUATU		12 190	4 707	265 000	Port Vila	English, Bislama (creole), French	Protestant, Roman Catholic, traditional beliefs	Vatu

Dependent territories		Territorial status	Area sq km	Area sq miles	Population	Capital	Languages	Religions	Currency
American Samoa		United States Unincorporated Territory	197	76	56 000	Fagatogo	Samoan, English	Protestant, Roman Catholic	United States dollar
Cook Islands		Self-governing New Zealand Territory	293	113	21 000	Avarua	English, Maori	Protestant, Roman Catholic	New Zealand dollar
French Polynesia		French Overseas Country	3 265	1 261	283 000	Papeete	French, Tahitian, other Polynesian languages	Protestant, Roman Catholic	CFP franc*
Guam		United States Unincorporated Territory	541	209	170 000	Hagåtña (Agana)	Chamorro, English, Tapalog	Roman Catholic	United States dollar
New Caledonia		French Overseas Collectivity	19 058	7 358	263 000	Nouméa	French, other local languages	Roman Catholic, Protestant, Sunni Muslim	CFP franc*
Niue		Self-governing New Zealand Overseas Territory	258	100	1 610	Alofi	English, Niuean	Christian	New Zealand dollar
Norfolk Island		Australian External Territory	35	14	2 302	Kingston	English	Protestant, Roman Catholic	Australian Dollar
Northern Mariana Islands		United States Commonwealth	477	184	55 000	Capitol Hill	English, Chamorro, other local languages	Roman Catholic	United States dollar
Pitcairn Islands		United Kingdom Overseas Territory	45	17	49	Adamstown	English	Protestant	New Zealand dollar
Tokelau		New Zealand Overseas Territory	10	4	1 250		English, Tokelauan	Christian	New Zealand dollar
Wallis and Futuna		French Overseas Collectivity	274	106	13 000	Matā'utu	French, Wallisian, Futunian	Roman Catholic	CFP franc*

*Franc des Comptoirs Français du Pacifique

Queenstown and Lake Wakatipu, New Zealand

World
States and Territories

Liberty Island, New York, USA

Cuba, Caribbean Sea

North America	Area sq km	Area sq miles	Population	Capital	Languages ('de facto' speakers over one per cent of population)	Religions ('de facto' adherents over one per cent of population)	Currency
ANTIGUA AND BARBUDA	442	171	92 000	St John's	English, creole	Protestant, Roman Catholic	East Caribbean dollar
THE BAHAMAS	13 939	5 382	388 000	Nassau	English, creole	Protestant, Roman Catholic	Bahamian dollar
BARBADOS	430	166	284 000	Bridgetown	English, creole	Protestant, Roman Catholic	Barbadian dollar
BELIZE	22 965	8 867	359 000	Belmopan	English, Spanish, Mayan, creole	Roman Catholic, Protestant	Belizean dollar
CANADA	9 984 670	3 855 103	35 940 000	Ottawa	English, French, other local languages	Roman Catholic, Protestant, Eastern Orthodox, Jewish	Canadian dollar
COSTA RICA	51 100	19 730	4 808 000	San José	Spanish	Roman Catholic, Protestant	Costa Rican colón
CUBA	110 860	42 803	11 390 000	Havana	Spanish	Roman Catholic, Protestant	Cuban peso
DOMINICA	750	290	73 000	Roseau	English, creole	Roman Catholic, Protestant	East Caribbean dollar
DOMINICAN REPUBLIC	48 442	18 704	10 528 000	Santo Domingo	Spanish, creole	Roman Catholic, Protestant	Dominican peso
EL SALVADOR	21 041	8 124	6 127 000	San Salvador	Spanish	Roman Catholic, Protestant	United States dollar
GRENADA	378	146	107 000	St George's	English, creole	Roman Catholic, Protestant	East Caribbean dollar
GUATEMALA	108 890	42 043	16 343 000	Guatemala City	Spanish, Mayan languages	Roman Catholic, Protestant	Quetzal
HAITI	27 750	10 714	10 711 000	Port-au-Prince	French, creole	Roman Catholic, Protestant, Voodoo	Gourde
HONDURAS	112 088	43 277	8 075 000	Tegucigalpa	Spanish, Amerindian languages	Roman Catholic, Protestant	Lempira
JAMAICA	10 991	4 244	2 793 000	Kingston	English, creole	Protestant, Roman Catholic	Jamaican dollar
MEXICO	1 972 545	761 604	127 017 000	Mexico City	Spanish, Amerindian languages	Roman Catholic, Protestant	Mexican peso
NICARAGUA	130 000	50 193	6 082 000	Managua	Spanish, Amerindian languages	Roman Catholic, Protestant	Córdoba
PANAMA	77 082	29 762	3 929 000	Panama City	Spanish, English, Amerindian languages	Roman Catholic, Protestant, Sunni Muslim	Balboa
ST KITTS AND NEVIS	261	101	56 000	Basseterre	English, creole	Protestant, Roman Catholic	East Caribbean dollar
ST LUCIA	616	238	185 000	Castries	English, creole	Roman Catholic, Protestant	East Caribbean dollar
ST VINCENT AND THE GRENADINES	389	150	109 000	Kingstown	English, creole	Protestant, Roman Catholic	East Caribbean dollar
TRINIDAD AND TOBAGO	5 130	1 981	1 360 000	Port of Spain	English, creole, Hindi	Roman Catholic, Hindu, Protestant, Sunni Muslim	Trinidad and Tobago dollar
UNITED STATES OF AMERICA	9 826 635	3 794 085	321 774 000	Washington DC	English, Spanish	Protestant, Roman Catholic, Sunni Muslim, Jewish	United States dollar

Dependent territories	Territorial status	Area sq km	Area sq miles	Population	Capital	Languages	Religions	Currency
Anguilla	United Kingdom Overseas Territory	155	60	15 000	The Valley	English	Protestant, Roman Catholic	East Caribbean dollar
Aruba	Self-governing Netherlands Territory	193	75	104 000	Oranjestad	Papiamento, Dutch, English	Roman Catholic, Protestant	Arubian florin
Bermuda	United Kingdom Overseas Territory	54	21	62 000	Hamilton	English	Protestant, Roman Catholic	Bermuda dollar
Cayman Islands	United Kingdom Overseas Territory	259	100	60 000	George Town	English	Protestant, Roman Catholic	Cayman Islands dollar
Curaçao	Self-governing Netherlands territory	444	171	157 000	Willemstad	Dutch, Papiamento	Roman Catholic, Protestant	Netherlands Antillean guilder
Greenland	Self-governing Danish Territory	2 175 600	840 004	56 000	Nuuk	Greenlandic, Danish	Protestant	Danish krone
Guadeloupe	French Overseas Department	1 780	687	468 000	Basse-Terre	French, creole	Roman Catholic	Euro
Martinique	French Overseas Department	1 079	417	396 000	Fort-de-France	French, creole	Roman Catholic, traditional beliefs	Euro
Montserrat	United Kingdom Overseas Territory	100	39	5 125	Brades (Temporary capital)	English	Protestant, Roman Catholic	East Caribbean dollar
Puerto Rico	United States Commonwealth	9 104	3 515	3 683 000	San Juan	Spanish, English	Roman Catholic, Protestant	United States dollar
St Pierre and Miquelon	French Territorial Collectivity	242	93	6 288	St-Pierre	French	Roman Catholic	Euro
Turks and Caicos Islands	United Kingdom Overseas Territory	430	166	34 000	Grand Turk	English	Protestant	United States dollar
Virgin Islands (U.K.)	United Kingdom Overseas Territory	153	59	30 000	Road Town	English	Protestant, Roman Catholic	United States dollar
Virgin Islands (U.S.A.)	United States Unincorporated Territory	352	136	106 000	Charlotte Amalie	English, Spanish	Protestant, Roman Catholic	United States dollar

South America	Area sq km	Area sq miles	Population	Capital	Languages ('de facto' speakers over one per cent of population)	Religions ('de facto' adherents over one per cent of population)	Currency
ARGENTINA	2 766 889	1 068 302	43 417 000	Buenos Aires	Spanish, Italian, Amerindian languages	Roman Catholic, Protestant	Argentinian peso
BOLIVIA	1 098 581	424 164	10 725 000	La Paz/Sucre	Spanish, Quechua, Aymara	Roman Catholic, Protestant, Baha'i	Boliviano
BRAZIL	8 514 879	3 287 613	207 848 000	Brasília	Portuguese	Roman Catholic, Protestant	Real
CHILE	756 945	292 258	17 948 000	Santiago	Spanish, Amerindian languages	Roman Catholic, Protestant	Chilean peso
COLOMBIA	1 141 748	440 831	48 229 000	Bogotá	Spanish, Amerindian languages	Roman Catholic, Protestant	Colombian peso
ECUADOR	272 045	105 037	16 144 000	Quito	Spanish, Quechua, and other Amerindian languages	Roman Catholic	US dollar
GUYANA	214 969	83 000	767 000	Georgetown	English, creole, Amerindian languages	Protestant, Hindu, Roman Catholic, Sunni Muslim	Guyanese dollar
PARAGUAY	406 752	157 048	6 639 000	Asunción	Spanish, Guaraní	Roman Catholic, Protestant	Guaraní
PERU	1 285 216	496 225	31 377 000	Lima	Spanish, Quechua, Aymara	Roman Catholic, Protestant	Nuevo sol
SURINAME	163 820	63 251	543 000	Paramaribo	Dutch, Surinamese, English, Hindi	Hindu, Roman Catholic, Protestant, Sunni Muslim	Surinamese dollar
URUGUAY	176 215	68 037	3 432 000	Montevideo	Spanish	Roman Catholic, Protestant, Jewish	Uruguayan peso
VENEZUELA	912 050	352 144	31 108 000	Caracas	Spanish, Amerindian languages	Roman Catholic, Protestant	Bolívar

Dependent territories	Territorial status	Area sq km	Area sq miles	Population	Capital	Languages	Religions	Currency
Falkland Islands	United Kingdom Overseas Territory	12 170	4 699	2 903	Stanley	English	Protestant, Roman Catholic	Falkland Islands pound
French Guiana	French Overseas Department	90 000	34 749	269 000	Cayenne	French, creole	Roman Catholic	Euro

World
Countries

The current pattern of the world's countries and territories is a result of a long history of exploration, colonialism, conflict and politics. The fact that there are currently 196 independent countries in the world – the most recent, South Sudan, only being created in July 2011 – illustrates the significant political changes which have occurred since 1950 when there were only eighty-two. There has been a steady progression away from colonial influences over the last fifty years, although many dependent overseas territories remain.

The shapes of countries and the pattern of international boundaries reflect both physical and political processes. Some borders follow natural features – rivers, mountain ranges, etc. – others are defined according to political agreement or as a result of war. Some are still subject to dispute between two or more countries, and many remain undefined on the ground.

Facts

- The longest single continuous land border stretches for 6 416 kilometres between Canada and the USA
- Both China and Russia have land borders with 14 different countries
- Vatican City, the smallest independent country, was created in 1929 as an enclave within Rome, the capital of Italy
- All countries of the world are members of the United Nations except Kosovo, Taiwan and Vatican City

Internet Links

United Nations	www.un.org
Foreign and Commonwealth Office	www.fco.gov.uk
International Boundaries Research Unit	www.dur.ac.uk/ibru
Permanent Committee on Geographical Names	www.pcgn.org.uk
U.S. Board on Geographic Names	geonames.usgs.gov

Abbreviation Key

A.	ANDORRA	HUN.	HUNGARY	ROM.	ROMANIA
AL.	ALBANIA	ISR.	ISRAEL	RU.	RUSSIA
ARM.	ARMENIA	JOR.	JORDAN	S.	SERBIA
AUST.	AUSTRIA	K.	KOSOVO	SL.	SLOVENIA
AZER.	AZERBAIJAN	L.	LUXEMBOURG	SLA.	SLOVAKIA
B.	BURUNDI	LAT.	LATVIA	SUR.	SURINAME
BE.	BENIN	LEB.	LEBANON	SW.	SWITZERLAND
BEL.	BELGIUM	LITH.	LITHUANIA	T.	TOGO
B.H.	BOSNIA AND HERZEGOVINA	M.	MONTENEGRO	TAJIK.	TAJIKISTAN
BULG.	BULGARIA	MA.	MACEDONIA	TURKM.	TURKMENISTAN
CR.	CROATIA	MOL.	MOLDOVA	U.A.E.	UNITED ARAB EMIRATES
CZ.	CZECHIA (CZECH REPUBLIC)	NETH.	NETHERLANDS	U.K.	UNITED KINGDOM
EST.	ESTONIA	N.Z.	NEW ZEALAND	U.S.A.	UNITED STATES OF AMERICA
GEOR.	GEORGIA	R.	RWANDA	UZBEK.	UZBEKISTAN

Aerial view of the **Vatican City**, the world's smallest country by both population and area.

International boundaries in the sea shown on this map indicate ownership of islands and island groups only. They do not infer the alignments of legal maritime boundaries.

World extremes

Countries			
Largest country (area)	**Russia**	17 075 400 sq km	6 592 849 sq miles
Smallest country (area)	**Vatican City**	0.5 sq km	0.2 sq miles
Largest country (population)	**China**	1 383 925 000	
Smallest country (population)	**Vatican City**	800	
Most densely populated country	**Monaco**	19 000 per sq km	38 000 per sq mile
Least densely populated country	**Mongolia**	1.8 per sq km	4.7 per sq mile
Capitals			
Largest national capital (population)	**Tōkyō, Japan**	38 197 000	
Smallest national capital (population)	**Melekeok, (Ngerulmud) Palau**	391	
Most northerly national capital	**Reykjavík, Iceland**	64° 08'N	
Most southerly national capital	**Wellington, New Zealand**	41° 18'S	
Highest national capital	**La Paz, Bolivia**	3 636 m	11 910 ft

The Earth's physical features, both on land and on the sea bed, closely reflect its geological structure. The current shapes of the continents and oceans have evolved over millions of years. Movements of the tectonic plates which make up the Earth's crust have created some of the best-known and most spectacular features. The processes which have shaped the Earth continue today with earthquakes, volcanoes, erosion, climatic variations and man's activities all affecting the Earth's landscapes.

The total topographic range of the Earth's surface is nearly 20 000 metres, from the highest point Mount Everest, to the lowest point in the Mariana Trench. Major mountain ranges include the Himalaya, the Andes and the Rocky Mountains, each of which give rise to some of the world's greatest rivers. In contrast, the deserts of the Sahara, Australia, the Arabian Peninsula and the Gobi cover vast areas and each provide unique landscapes.

Greenland, the world's largest island, located almost entirely within the Arctic Circle.

Internet Links	
United Nations Environment Programme	www.unep.org
IUCN The International Union for Conservation of Nature	www.iucn.org
NASA Visible Earth	visibleearth.nasa.gov
NASA Earth Observatory	earthobservatory.nasa.gov
Earth Resources Observation and Science	edc.usgs.gov

Earth's dimensions

Mass	5.974 x 10^{21} tonnes
Total area	509 450 000 sq km / 196 698 645 sq miles
Land area	149 450 000 sq km / 57 702 645 sq miles
Water area	360 000 000 sq km / 138 996 000 sq miles
Volume	1 083 207 x 10^6 cubic km / 259 911 x 10^6 cubic miles
Equatorial diameter	12 756 km / 7 927 miles
Polar diameter	12 714 km / 7 900 miles
Equatorial circumference	40 075 km / 24 903 miles
Meridional circumference	40 008 km / 24 861 miles

Facts

- Approximately 10% of the Earth's land surface is permanently covered by ice
- The Pacific Ocean is larger than all the continents' land areas combined
- The world's highest waterfall, 979 metres high, is Angel Falls, Venezuela
- 52% of the Earth's land surface is below 500 metres
- The mean elevation of the Earth's land surface is 840 metres
- Lake Baikal is the world's deepest lake with a maximum depth of 1 642 metres

World's physical features

Highest mountains			Largest islands		
Mt Everest, China/Nepal	8 848 m	29 028 ft	Greenland, North America	2 175 600 sq km	839 999 sq miles
K2, China/Pakistan	8 611 m	28 251 ft	New Guinea, Oceania	808 510 sq km	312 166 sq miles
Kangchenjunga, India/Nepal	8 586 m	28 169 ft	Borneo, Asia	745 561 sq km	287 861 sq miles
Lhotse, China/Nepal	8 516 m	27 939 ft	Madagascar, Africa	587 040 sq km	226 656 sq miles
Makalu, China/Nepal	8 463 m	27 765 ft	Baffin Island, North America	507 451 sq km	195 927 sq miles
Longest rivers			**Largest lakes**		
Nile, Africa	6 695 km	4 160 miles	Caspian Sea, Asia/Europe	371 000 sq km	143 243 sq miles
Amazon, South America	6 516 km	4 049 miles	Lake Superior, North America	82 100 sq km	31 699 sq miles
Yangtze, Asia	6 380 km	3 965 miles	Lake Victoria, Africa	68 870 sq km	26 591 sq miles
Mississippi-Missouri, North America	5 969 km	3 709 miles	Lake Huron, North America	59 600 sq km	23 012 sq miles
Ob'-Irtysh, Asia	5 568 km	3 460 miles	Lake Michigan, North America	57 800 sq km	22 317 sq miles

World

Earthquakes and Volcanoes

Earthquakes and volcanoes hold a constant fascination because of their power, their beauty, and the fact that they cannot be controlled or accurately predicted. Our understanding of these phenomena relies mainly on the theory of plate tectonics. This defines the Earth's surface as a series of 'plates' which are constantly moving relative to each other, at rates of a few centimetres per year. As plates move against each other enormous pressure builds up and when the rocks can no longer bear this pressure they fracture, and energy is released as an earthquake. The pressures involved can also melt the rock to form magma which then rises to the Earth's surface to form a volcano. The distribution of earthquakes and volcanoes therefore relates closely to plate boundaries. In particular, most active volcanoes and much of the Earth's seismic activity are centred on the 'Ring of Fire' around the Pacific Ocean.

Facts

- Over 900 earthquakes of magnitude 5.0 or greater occur every year
- An earthquake of magnitude 8.0 releases energy equivalent to 1 billion tons of TNT explosive
- Ground shaking during an earthquake in Alaska in 1964 lasted for 3 minutes
- Indonesia has more than 120 volcanoes and over 30% of the world's active volcanoes
- Volcanoes can produce very fertile soil and important industrial materials and chemicals

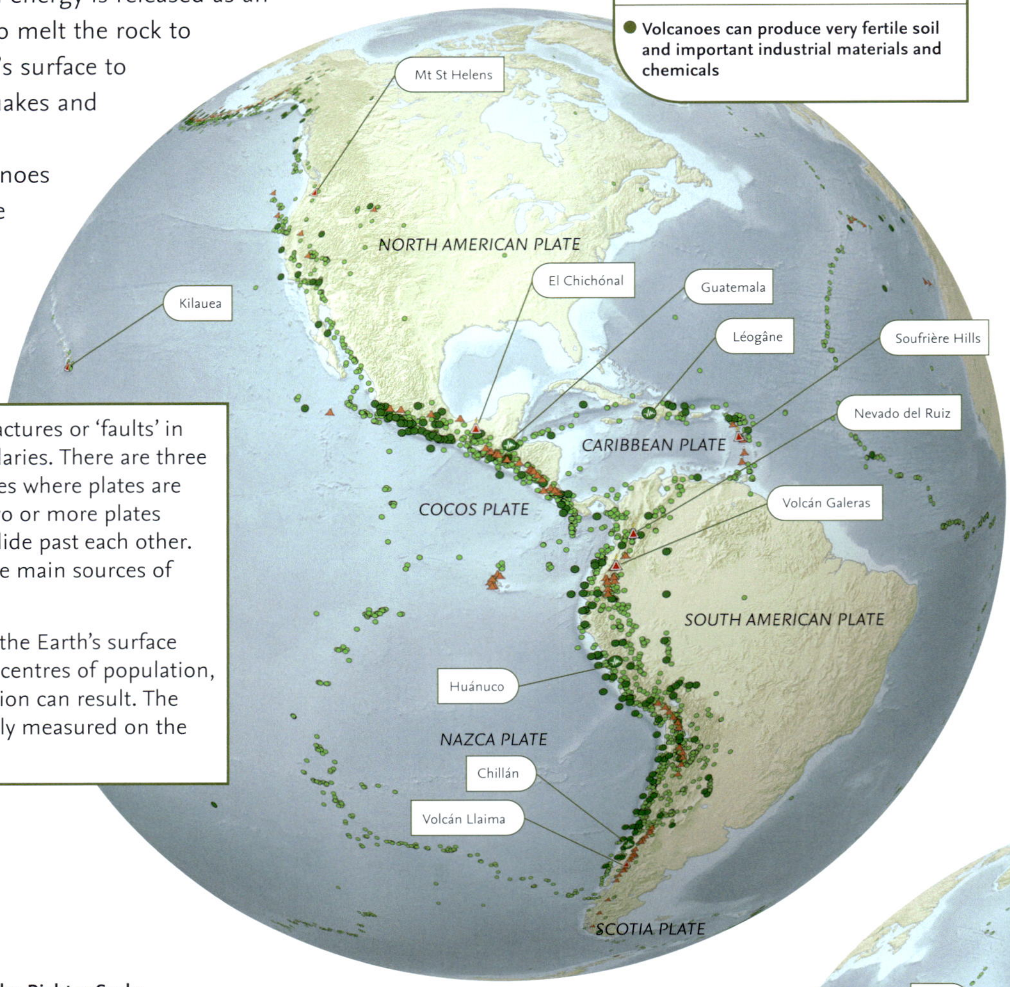

Earthquakes

Earthquakes are caused by movement along fractures or 'faults' in the Earth's crust, particularly along plate boundaries. There are three types of plate boundary: constructive boundaries where plates are moving apart; destructive boundaries where two or more plates collide; conservative boundaries where plates slide past each other. Destructive and conservative boundaries are the main sources of earthquake activity.

The epicentre of an earthquake is the point on the Earth's surface directly above its source. If this is near to large centres of population, and the earthquake is powerful, major devastation can result. The size, or magnitude, of an earthquake is generally measured on the Richter Scale.

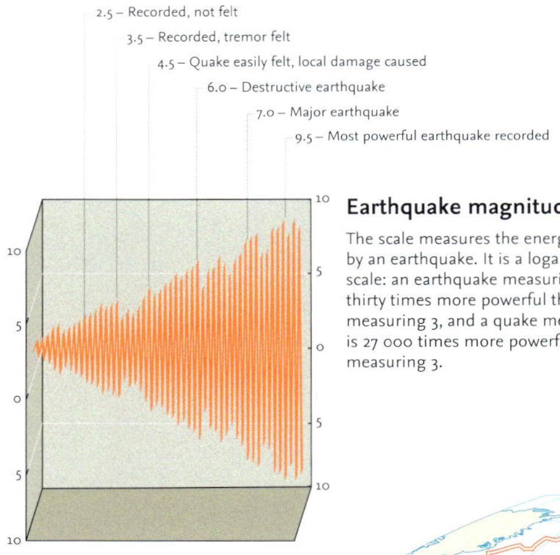

Earthquake magnitude – the Richter Scale

The scale measures the energy released by an earthquake. It is a logarithmic scale: an earthquake measuring 4 is thirty times more powerful than one measuring 3, and a quake measuring 6 is 27 000 times more powerful than one measuring 3.

Plate boundaries

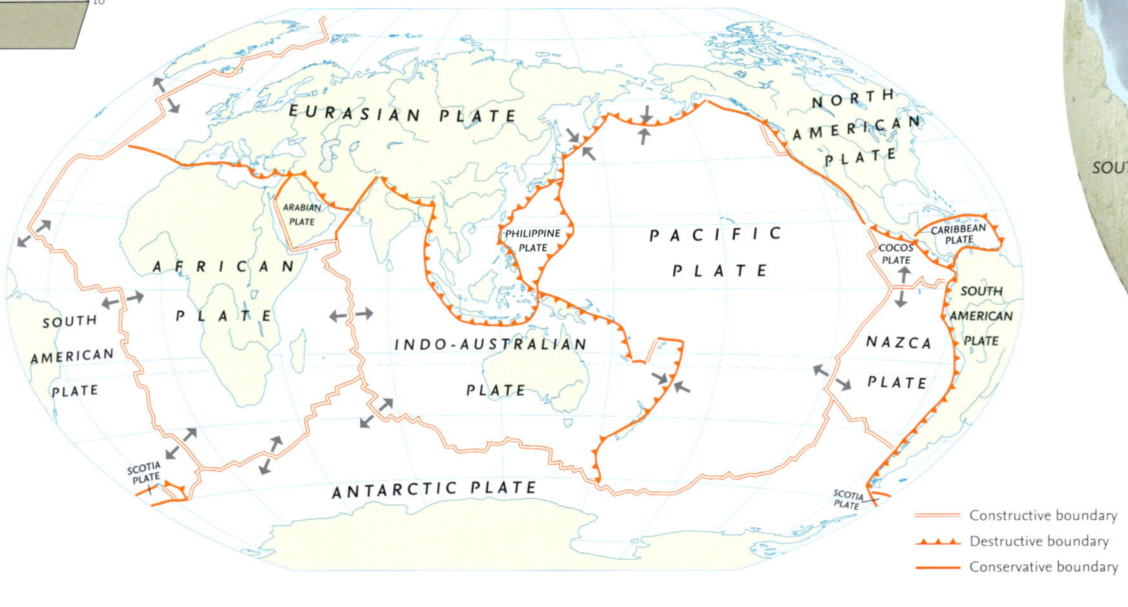

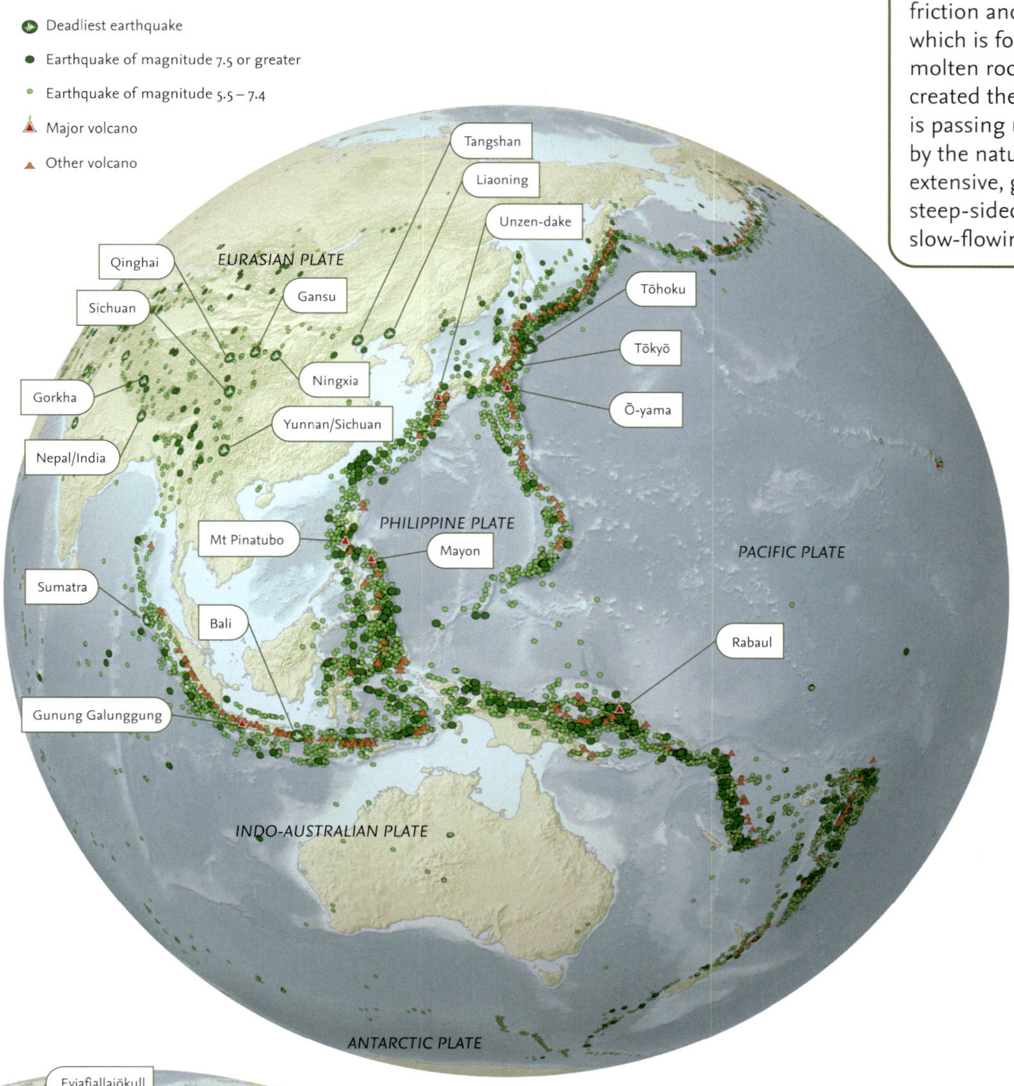

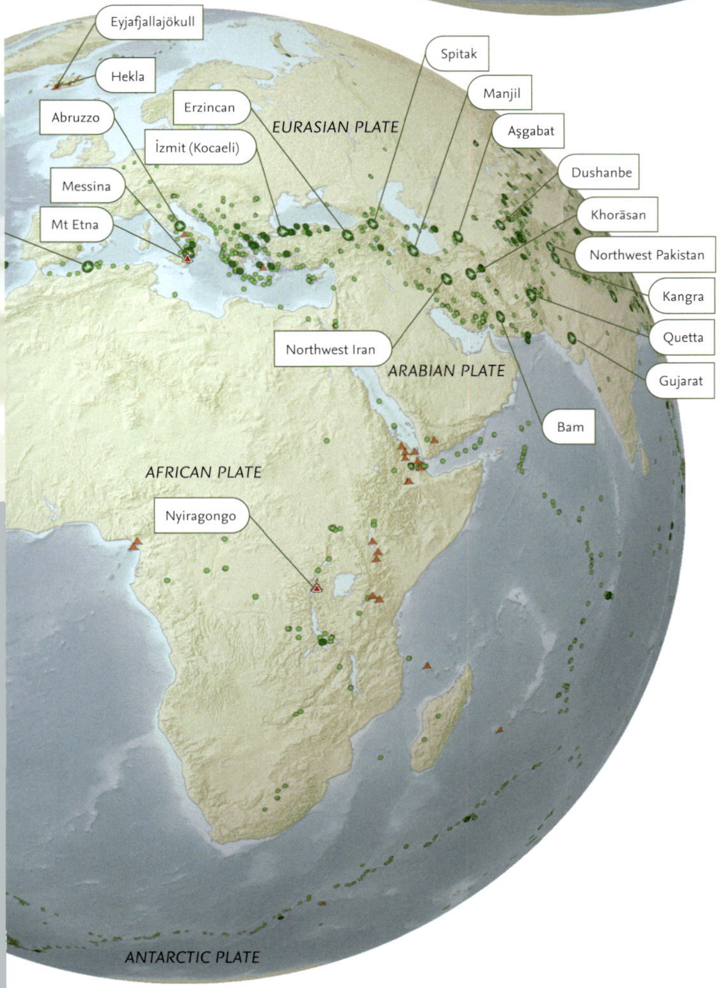

Volcanoes

The majority of volcanoes occur along destructive plate boundaries in the 'subduction zone' where one plate passes under another. The friction and pressure causes the rock to melt and to form magma which is forced upwards to the Earth's surface where it erupts as molten rock (lava) or as particles of ash or cinder. This process created the numerous volcanoes in the Andes, where the Nazca Plate is passing under the South American Plate. Volcanoes can be defined by the nature of the material they emit. 'Shield' volcanoes have extensive, gentle slopes formed from free-flowing lava, while steep-sided 'continental' volcanoes are created from thicker, slow-flowing lava and ash.

Major volcanic eruptions 1980–2014

Volcano	Country	Date
Mt St Helens	USA	1980
El Chichónal	Mexico	1982
Gunung Galunggung	Indonesia	1982
Kilauea	Hawaii, USA	1983
Ō-yama	Japan	1983
Nevado del Ruiz	Colombia	1985
Mt Pinatubo	Philippines	1991
Unzen-dake	Japan	1991
Mayon	Philippines	1993
Volcán Galeras	Colombia	1993
Volcán Llaima	Chile	1994
Rabaul	Papua New Guinea	1994
Soufrière Hills	Montserrat	1997
Hekla	Iceland	2000
Mt Etna	Italy	2001
Nyiragongo	Dem. Rep. of the Congo	2002
Eyjafjallajökull	Iceland	2010

Deadliest earthquakes since 1900

Year	Location	Deaths
1905	**Kangra,** India	19 000
1907	west of **Dushanbe,** Tajikistan	12 000
1908	**Messina,** Italy	110 000
1915	**Abruzzo,** Italy	35 000
1917	**Bali,** Indonesia	15 000
1920	**Ningxia Province,** China	200 000
1923	**Tōkyō,** Japan	142 807
1927	**Qinghai Province,** China	200 000
1932	**Gansu Province,** China	70 000
1933	**Sichuan Province,** China	10 000
1934	**Nepal/India**	10 700
1935	**Quetta,** Pakistan	30 000
1939	**Chillán,** Chile	28 000
1939	**Erzincan,** Turkey	32 700
1948	**Aşgabat,** Turkmenistan	19 800
1962	northwest **Iran**	12 225
1970	**Huánuco Province,** Peru	66 794
1974	**Yunnan** and **Sichuan Provinces,** China	20 000
1975	**Liaoning Province,** China	10 000
1976	central **Guatemala**	22 778
1976	**Tangshan,** Hebei Province, China	255 000
1978	**Khorāsan Province,** Iran	20 000
1980	**Chlef,** Algeria	11 000
1988	**Spitak,** Armenia	25 000
1990	**Manjil,** Iran	50 000
1999	**İzmit (Kocaeli),** Turkey	17 000
2001	**Gujarat,** India	20 000
2003	**Bam,** Iran	26 271
2004	off **Sumatra,** Indian Ocean	> 225 000
2005	northwest **Pakistan**	74 648
2008	**Sichuan Province,** China	> 60 000
2009	**Abruzzo** region, Italy	308
2009	**Sumatra,** Indonesia	> 1 100
2010	**Léogâne,** Haiti	222 570
2011	**Tōhoku,** Japan	15 891
2015	**Gorkha,** Nepal	8 831

Internet Links

USGS Earthquake Hazards Program	**earthquake.usgs.gov**
USGS Volcano Hazards Program	**volcanoes.usgs.gov**
British Geological Survey	**www.bgs.ac.uk**
NASA Natural Hazards	**earthobservatory.nasa.gov/NaturalHazards**
Volcano World	**volcano.oregonstate.edu**

The climate of a region is defined by its long-term prevailing weather conditions. Classification of Climate Types is based on the relationship between temperature and humidity and how these factors are affected by latitude, altitude, ocean currents and winds. Weather is the specific short term condition which occurs locally and consists of events such as thunderstorms, hurricanes, blizzards and heat waves. Temperature and rainfall data recorded at weather stations can be plotted graphically and the graphs shown here, typical of each climate region, illustrate the various combinations of temperature and rainfall which exist worldwide for each month of the year. Data used for climate graphs are based on average monthly figures recorded over a minimum period of thirty years.

World Statistics: see pages **154–160**

Major climate regions, ocean currents and sea surface temperatures

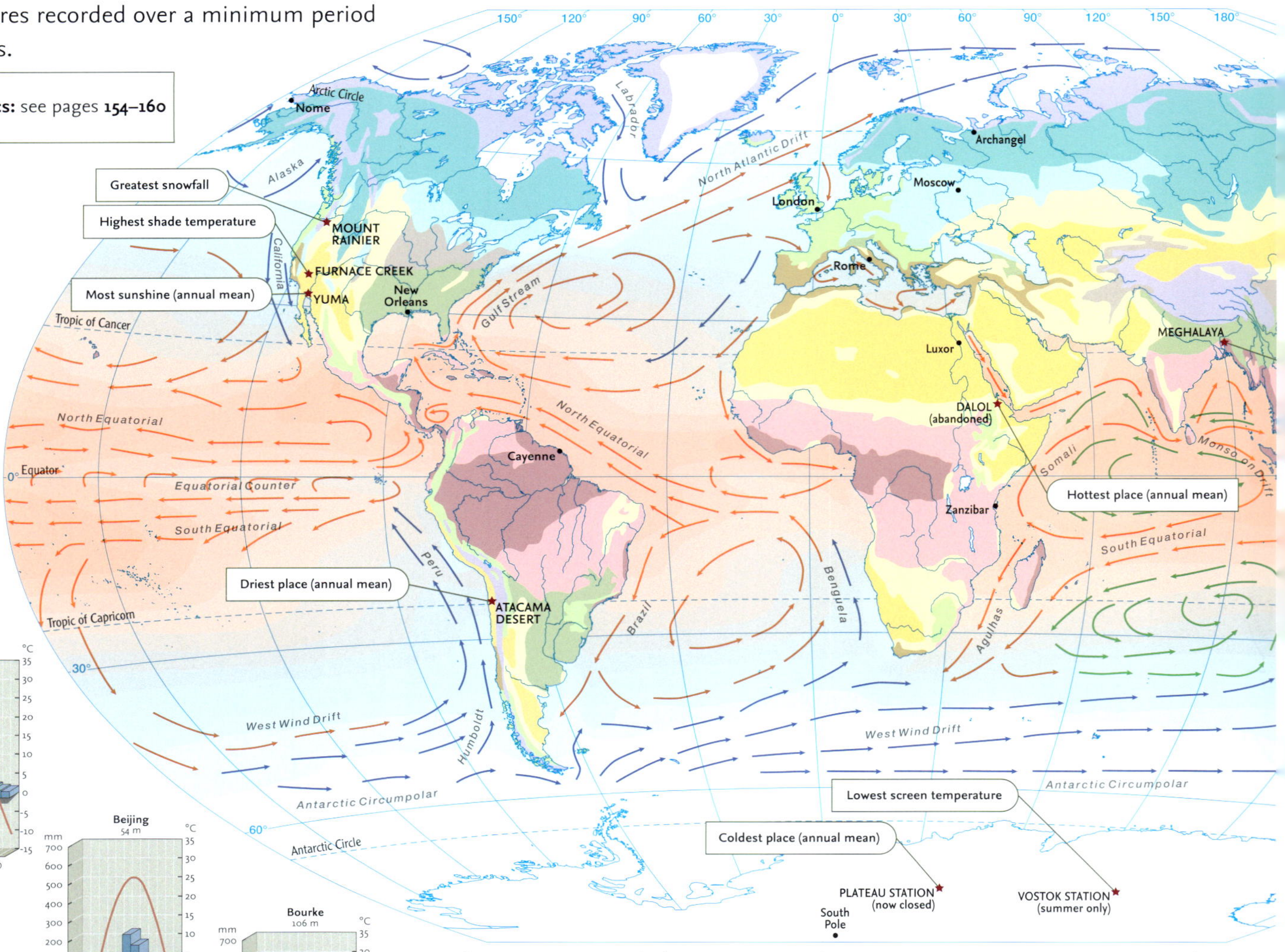

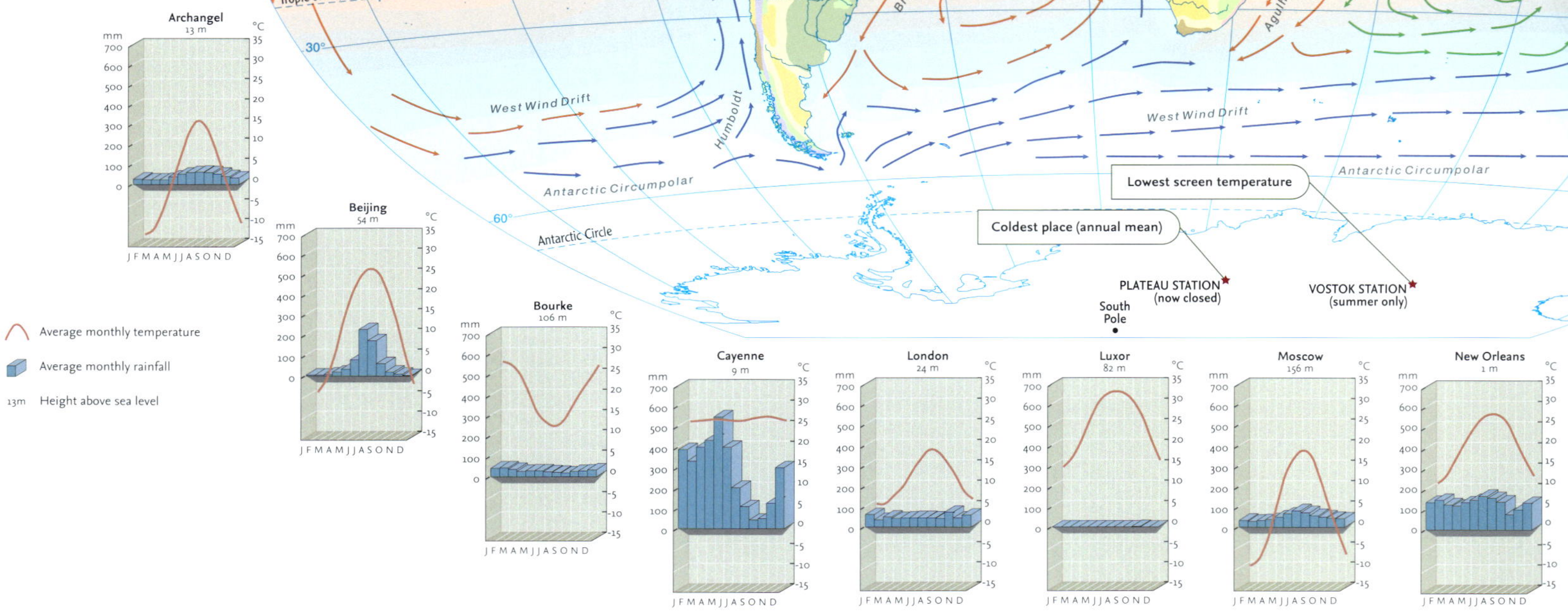

Climate change

The temperatures in 2015 were the warmest on record with a global average 0.9 °C above the 20th century average. Globally fifteen of the sixteen hottest years have been recorded this century. Most of this warming is caused by human activities which result in a build-up of greenhouse gases, mainly carbon dioxide, allowing heat to be trapped within the atmosphere. Carbon dioxide emissions have increased since the beginning of the industrial revolution due to burning of fossil fuels, increased urbanization, population growth, deforestation and industrial pollution.

Annual climate indicators such as number of frost-free days, length of growing season, heat wave frequency, number of wet days, length of dry spells and frequency of weather extremes are used to monitor climate change. The map opposite shows how future changes in temperature will not be spread evenly around the world. Some regions will warm faster than the global average, while others will warm more slowly. The Arctic is warming twice as fast as other areas mainly due to ice melting and there being less to reflect sunlight to keep the surface cool.

Facts

- Arctic Sea ice thickness has declined 40% in the last 40 years
- El Niño and La Niña episodes occur at irregular intervals of 2–7 years
- Sea levels are rising by one centimetre per decade
- Precipitation in the northern hemisphere is increasing
- Droughts have increased in frequency and intensity in parts of Asia and Africa

Projection of global temperatures 2090–2099

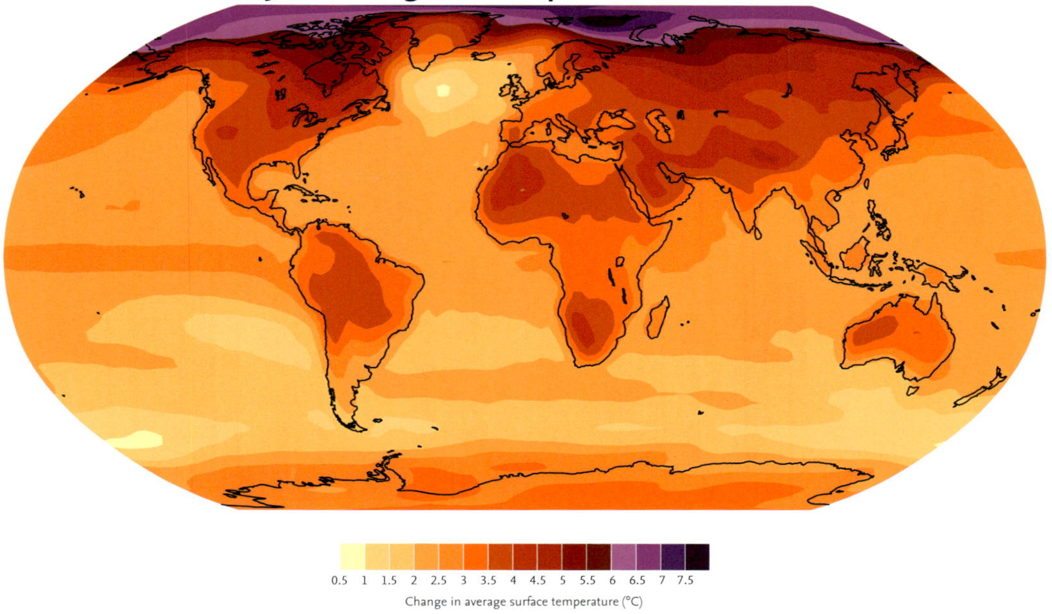

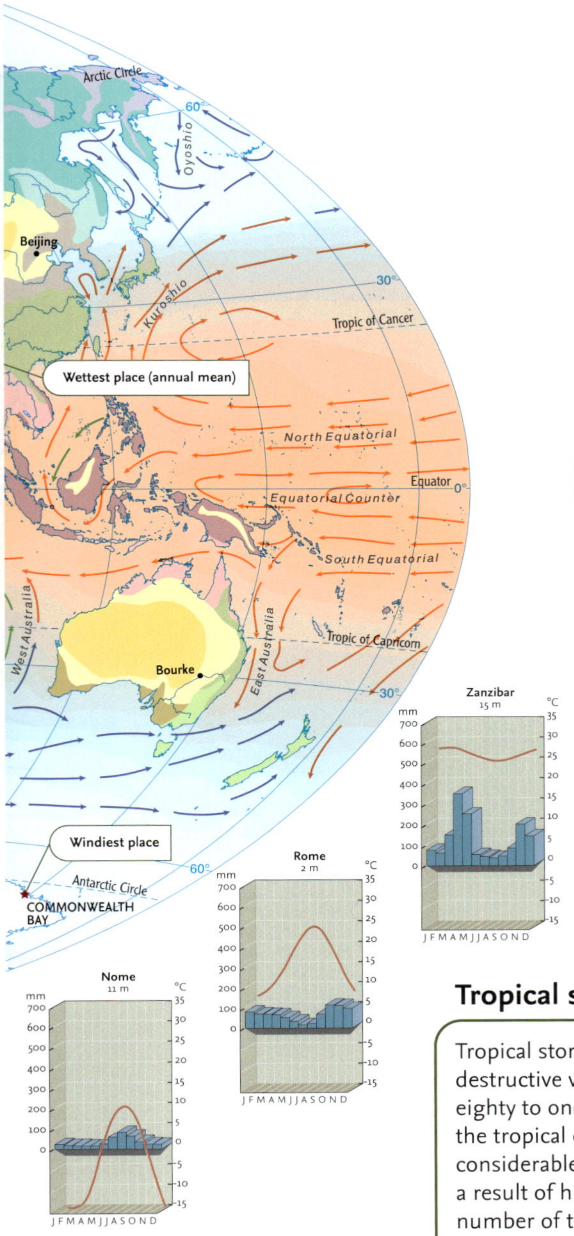

Tracks of tropical storms

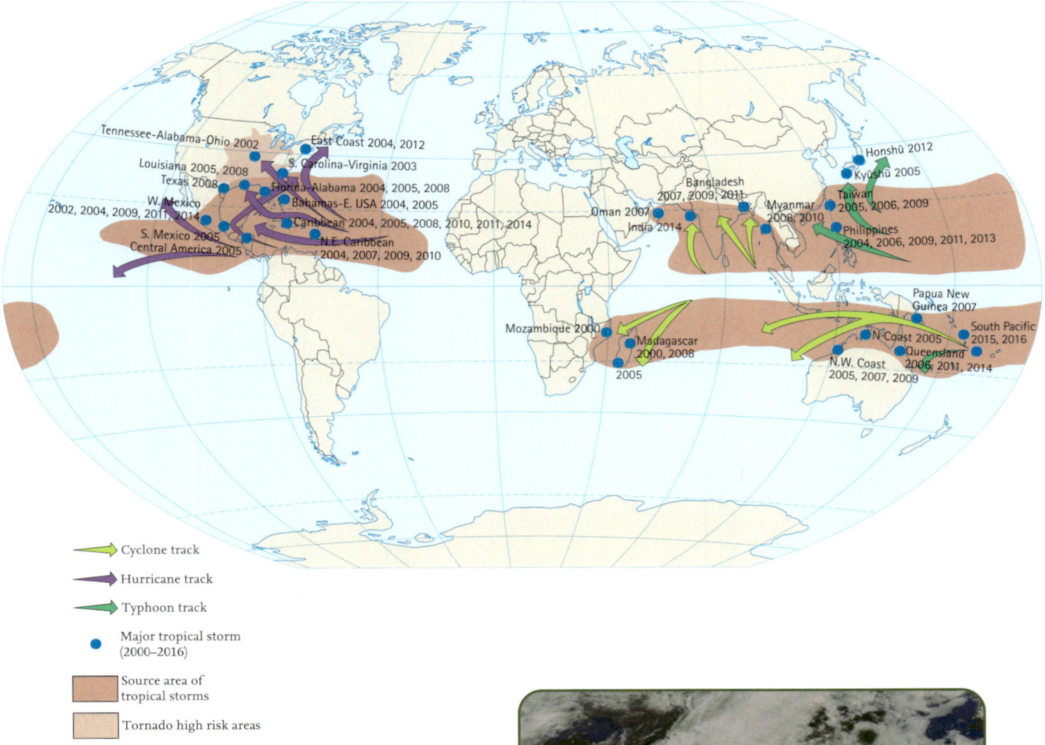

Tropical storms

Tropical storms are among the most powerful and destructive weather systems on Earth. Of the eighty to one hundred which develop annually over the tropical oceans, many make landfall and cause considerable damage to property and loss of life as a result of high winds and heavy rain. Although the number of tropical storms is projected to decrease, their intensity, and therefore their destructive power, is likely to increase.

Hurricane Sandy off the east coast of the USA, October 2012.

Weather extremes

Highest shade temperature	**56.7 °C/134 °F** Furnace Creek, Death Valley, California, USA (July 1913)
Hottest place - annual mean	**34.4 °C/93.9 °F** Dalol, Ethiopia
Driest place - annual mean	**0.1 mm/0.004 inches** Atacama Desert, Chile
Most sunshine - annual mean	**90%** Yuma, Arizona, USA (over 4000 hours)
Lowest screen temperature	**-89.2 °C/-128.6 °F** Vostok Station, Antarctica (July 1983)
Coldest place - annual mean	**-56.6 °C/-69.9 °F** Plateau Station, Antarctica
Wettest place - annual mean	**11 873 mm/467.4 inches** Meghalaya, India
Greatest snowfall	**31 102 mm/1 224.5 inches** Mount Rainier, Washington, USA (February 1971 – February 1972)
Windiest place	**322 km per hour/200 miles per hour** (in gales) Commonwealth Bay, Antarctica

Internet Links

Met Office	**www.metoffice.gov.uk**
BBC Weather Centre	**www.bbc.co.uk/weather**
National Oceanic and Atmospheric Administration	**www.noaa.gov**
National Climatic Data Center	**www.ncdc.noaa.gov**
United Nations World Meteorological Organization	**www.wmo.int**

World
Land Cover

The oxygen- and water-rich environment of the Earth has helped create a wide range of habitats. Forest and woodland ecosystems form the predominant natural land cover over most of the Earth's surface. Tropical rainforests are part of an intricate land-atmosphere relationship that is disturbed by land cover changes. Forests in the tropics are believed to hold most of the world's bird, animal, and plant species. Grassland, shrubland and deserts collectively cover most of the unwooded land surface, with tundra on frozen subsoil at high northern latitudes. These areas tend to have lower species diversity than most forests, with the notable exception of Mediterranean shrublands, which support some of the most diverse floras on the Earth. Humans have extensively altered most grassland and shrubland areas, usually through conversion to agriculture, burning and introduction of domestic livestock. They have had less immediate impact on tundra and true desert regions, although these remain vulnerable to global climate change.

Land cover

The land cover map shown here was developed at Boston University in Boston, MA, U.S.A. using data from the Moderate-resolution Imaging-Spectroradiometer (MODIS) instrument aboard NASA's Terra satellite. The high resolution (ground resolution of 1km) of the imagery used to compile the data set and map allows detailed interpretation of land cover patterns across the world. Important uses include managing forest resources, improving estimates of the Earth's water and energy cycles, and modelling climate change.

Urban, Tōkyō, capital of Japan and the largest city in the world.

Internet Links

World Resources Institute	www.wri.org
World Conservation Monitoring Centre	www.unep-wcmc.org
United Nations Environment Programme (UNEP)	www.unep.org
IUCN, International Union for Conservation of Nature	www.iucn.org
MODIS Land Cover Group at Boston University	www.bu.edu/lcsc

Cropland, near Consuegra, Spain.

Barren/Shrubland, Mojave Desert, California, United States of America.

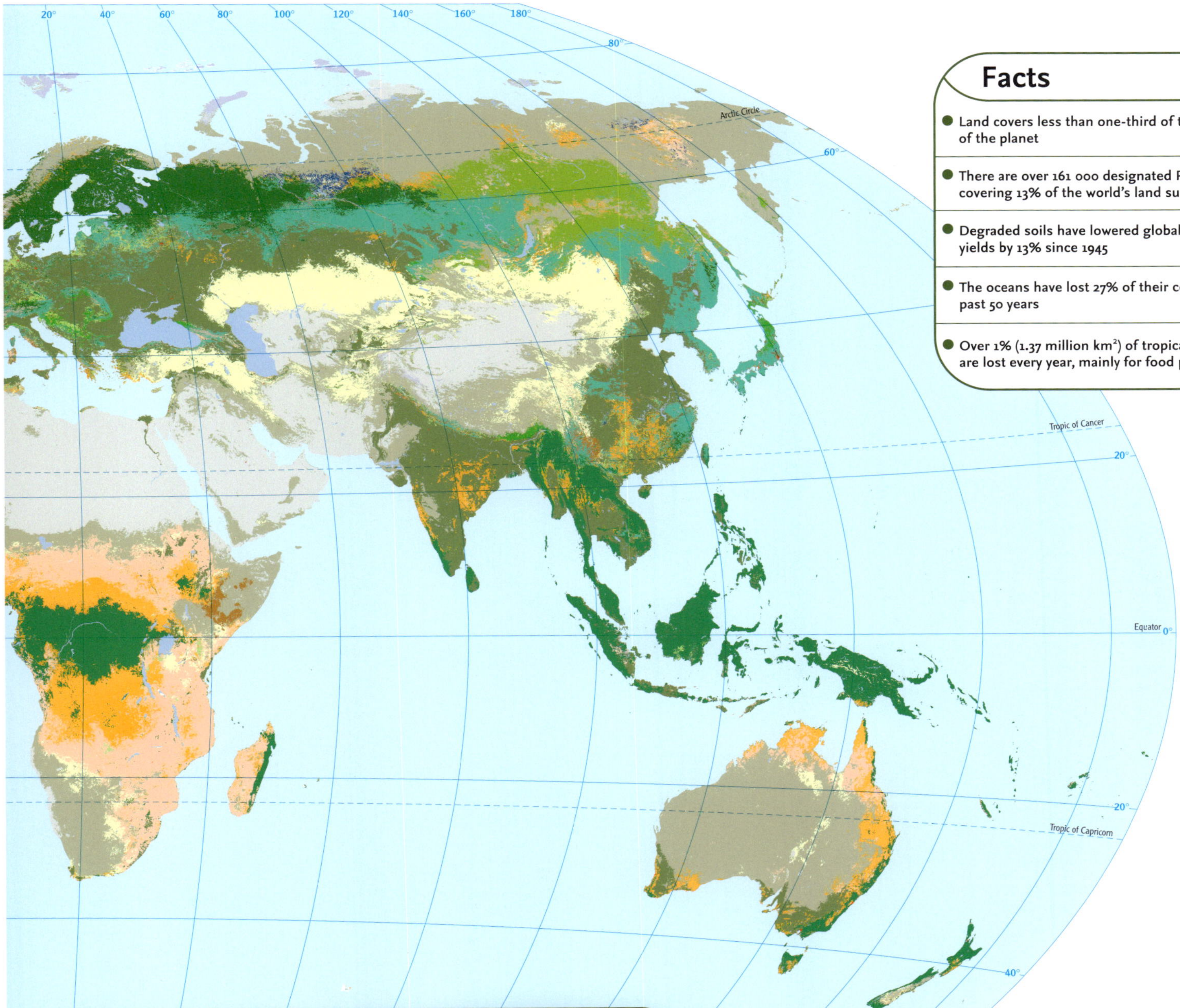

Facts

- Land covers less than one-third of the total surface of the planet
- There are over 161 000 designated Protected Areas covering 13% of the world's land surface
- Degraded soils have lowered global agricultural yields by 13% since 1945
- The oceans have lost 27% of their coral in the past 50 years
- Over 1% (1.37 million km²) of tropical forests are lost every year, mainly for food production

Land cover composition and change

The continents all have different characteristics. There are extensive croplands in North America and eastern Europe, while south of the Sahara are belts of grass/shrubland which are at risk from desertification. Tropical forests are not pristine areas either as they show signs of human activity in deforestation of land for crops or grazing.

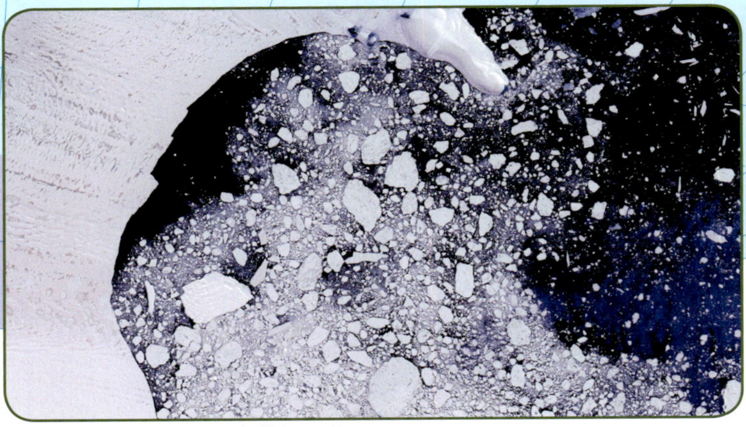

Snow and ice, Larsen Ice Shelf, Antarctica.

World

Population

After increasing very slowly for most of human history, world population more than doubled in the last half century. Whereas world population did not pass the one billion mark until 1804 and took another 123 years to reach two billion in 1927, it then added the third billion in 33 years, the fourth in 14 years and the fifth in 13 years. Just twelve years later on October 12, 1999 the United Nations announced that the global population had reached the six billion mark, with seven billion being reached only eleven years later, on October 31, 2011. It is expected that another two billion people will have been added to the world's population by 2043.

World Statistics: see pages **154–160**

World population distribution

Population density (2005), continental populations (2013) and continental population change (2010–2015)

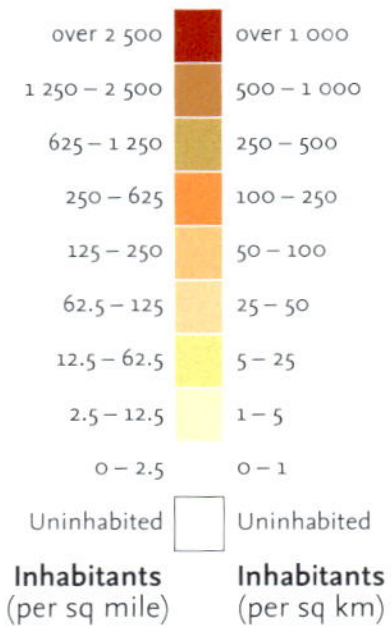

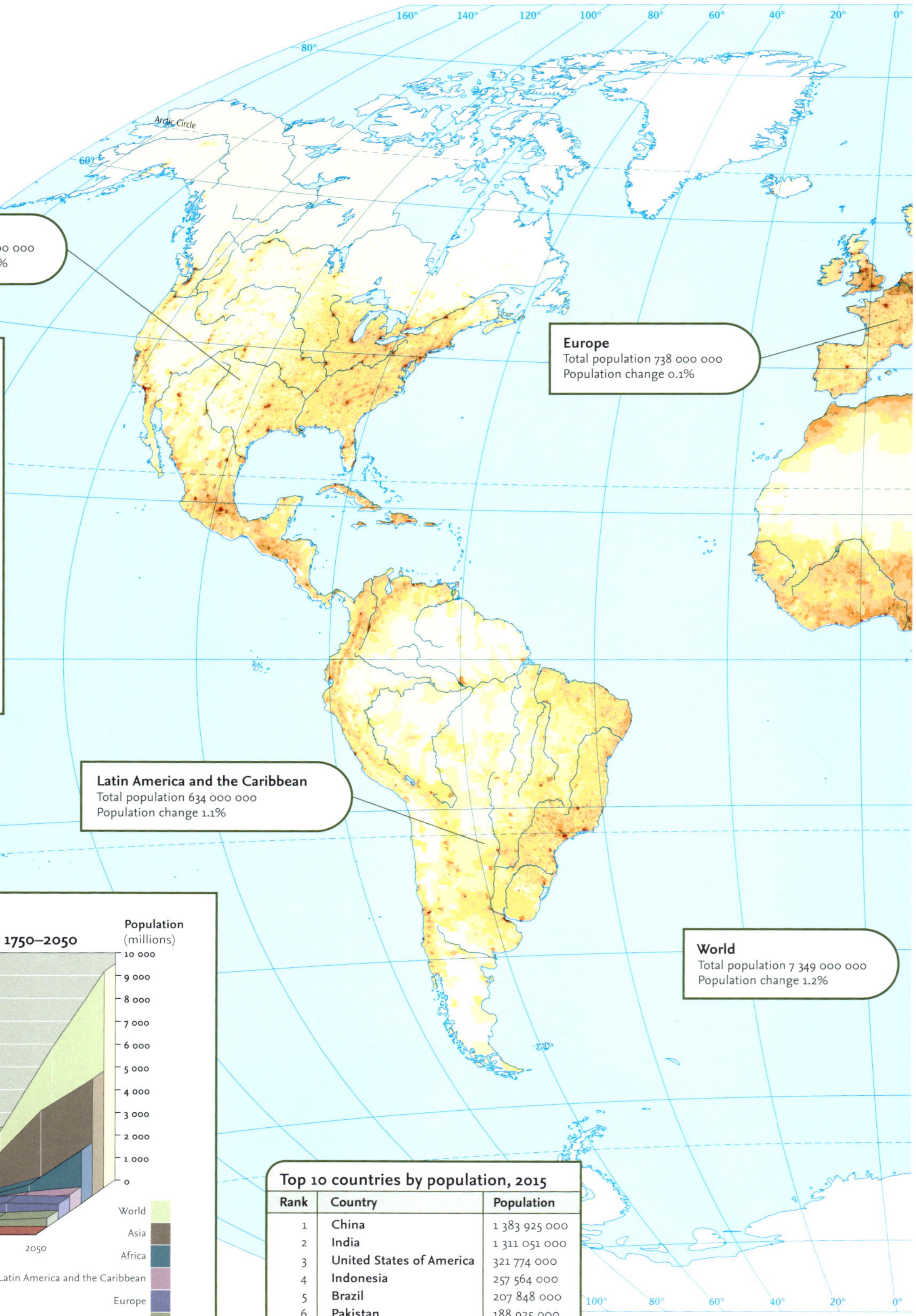

World population change

Population growth since 1950 has been spread very unevenly between the continents. While overall numbers have been growing rapidly since 1950, a massive 89 per cent increase has taken place in the less developed regions, especially southern and eastern Asia. In contrast, Europe's population level has been almost stationary and is expected to decrease in the future. India and China alone are responsible for over one-third of current growth. Most of the highest rates of growth are to be found in Sub-Saharan Africa and, until population growth is brought under tighter control, the developing world in particular will continue to face enormous problems of supporting a rising population.

World population growth, 1750–2050

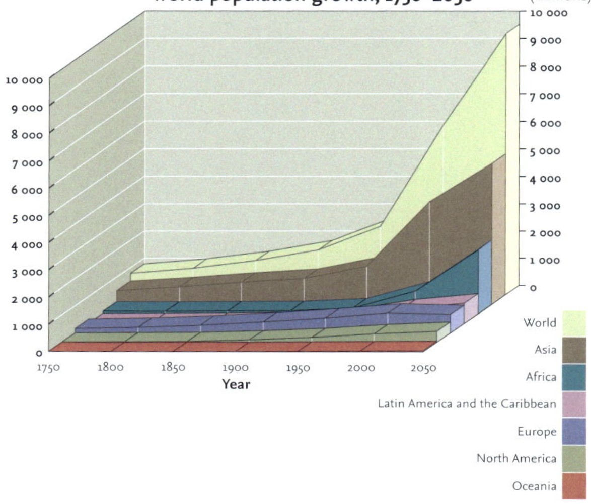

Top 10 countries by population, 2015

Rank	Country	Population
1	China	1 383 925 000
2	India	1 311 051 000
3	United States of America	321 774 000
4	Indonesia	257 564 000
5	Brazil	207 848 000
6	Pakistan	188 925 000
7	Nigeria	182 202 000
8	Bangladesh	160 996 000
9	Russia	143 457 000
10	Mexico	127 017 000

The island nation of **Singapore,** the world's second most densely populated country.

Kuna Indians inhabit this congested island off the north coast of Panama.

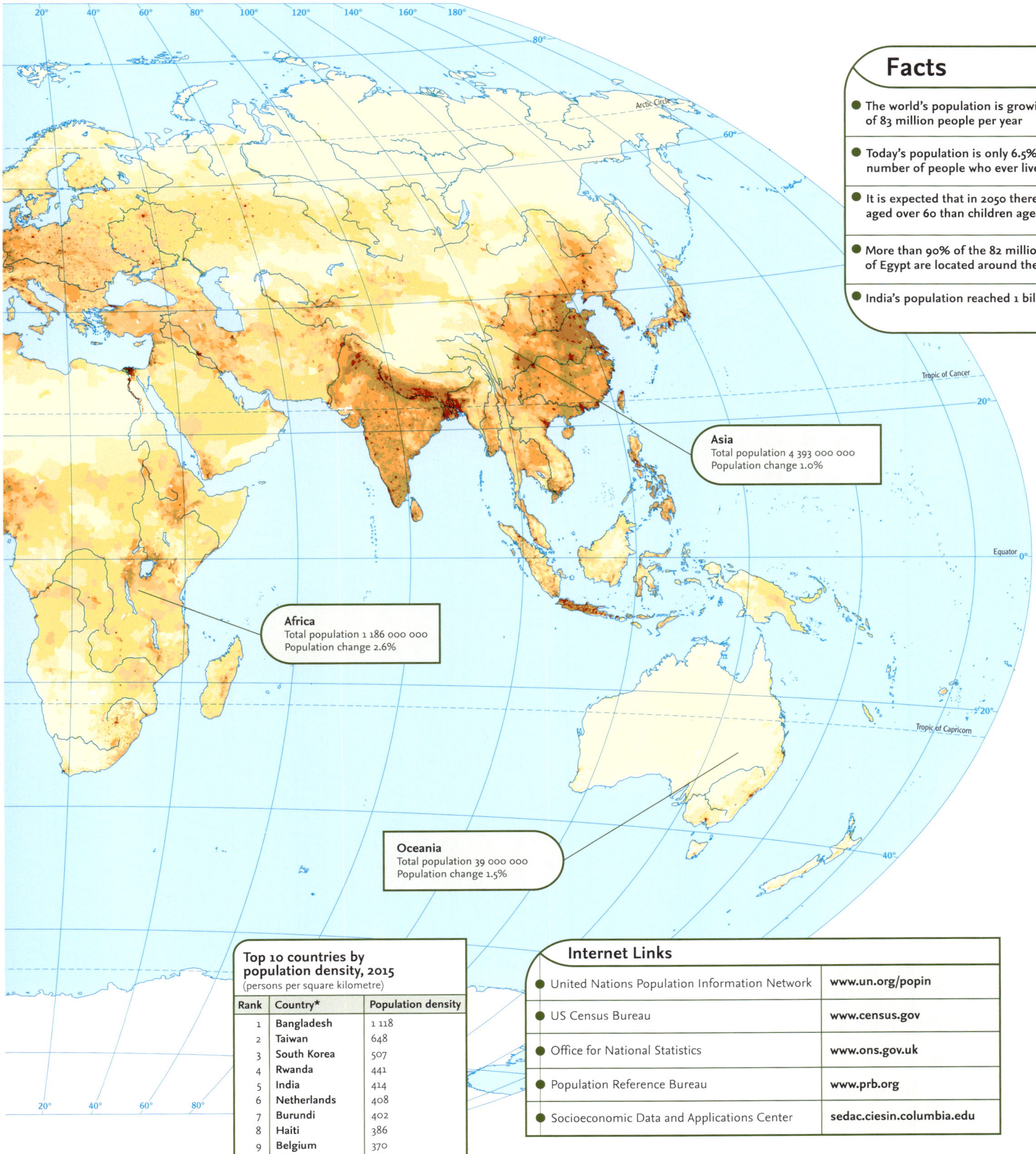

Facts

- The world's population is growing at an annual rate of 83 million people per year
- Today's population is only 6.5% of the total number of people who ever lived on the Earth
- It is expected that in 2050 there will be more people aged over 60 than children aged less than 14
- More than 90% of the 82 million inhabitants of Egypt are located around the River Nile
- India's population reached 1 billion in August 1999

Top 10 countries by population density, 2015

(persons per square kilometre)

Rank	Country*	Population density
1	Bangladesh	1 118
2	Taiwan	648
3	South Korea	507
4	Rwanda	441
5	India	414
6	Netherlands	408
7	Burundi	402
8	Haiti	386
9	Belgium	370
10	Philippines	336

*Only countries with a population of over 10 million are considered

Internet Links

United Nations Population Information Network	**www.un.org/popin**
US Census Bureau	**www.census.gov**
Office for National Statistics	**www.ons.gov.uk**
Population Reference Bureau	**www.prb.org**
Socioeconomic Data and Applications Center	**sedac.ciesin.columbia.edu**

World

Urbanization and Cities

The world is becoming increasingly urban but the level of urbanization varies greatly between and within continents. At the beginning of the twentieth century only fourteen per cent of the world's population was urban and by 1950 this had increased to thirty per cent. In the more developed regions and in Latin America and the Caribbean over seventy per cent of the population is urban while in Africa and Asia the figure is forty per cent. In recent decades urban growth has increased rapidly to over fifty per cent and in 2015 there are more than 500 cities with over 1 000 000 inhabitants. It is in the developing regions that the most rapid increases are taking place and it is expected that by 2030 over half of urban dwellers worldwide will live in Asia. Migration from the countryside to the city in the search for better job opportunities is the main factor in urban growth.

World Statistics: see pages **154–160**

Characteristic high-rise urban development **Hong Kong,** China.

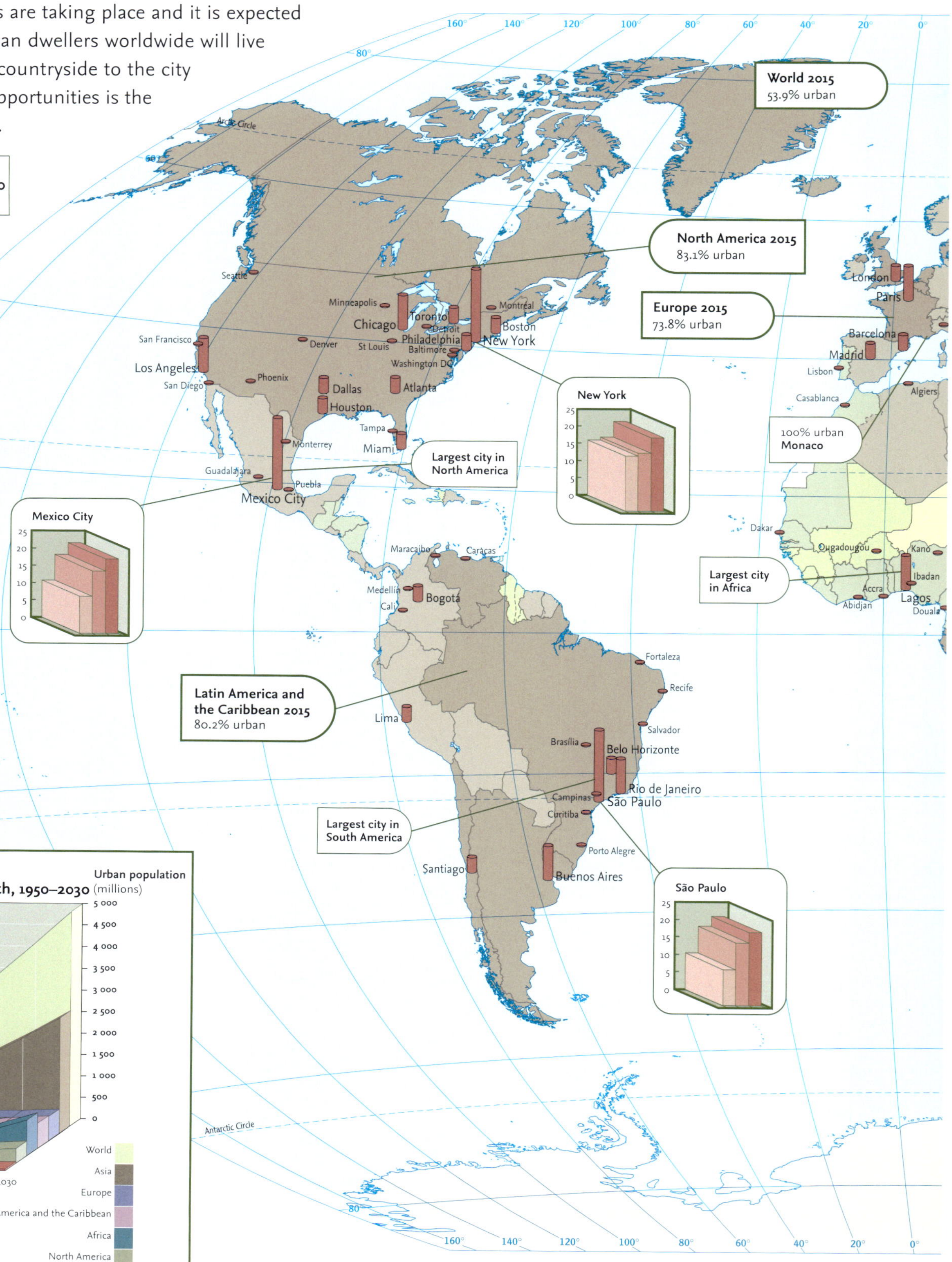

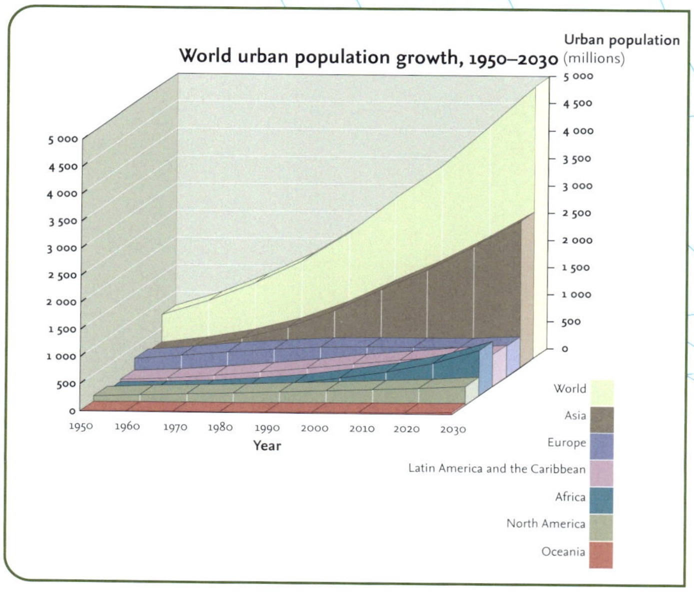

Level of urbanization and the world's largest cities

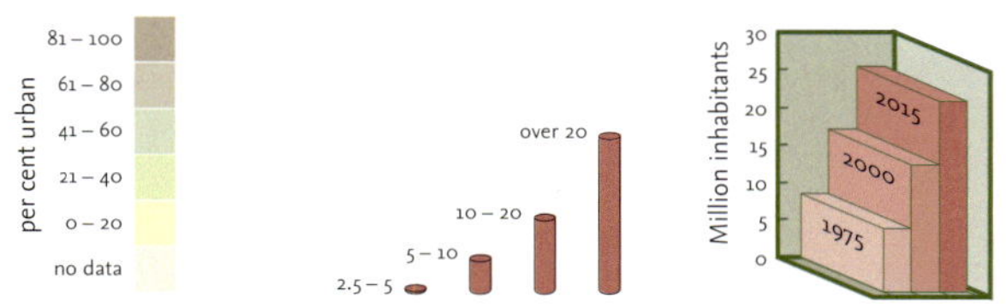

Megacities

There are currently sixty-nine cities in the world with over 5 000 000 inhabitants. Twenty-nine of these, often referred to as megacities, have over 10 000 000 inhabitants and one has over 30 000 000. Tōkyō, with 38 197 000 inhabitants, has remained the world's largest city since 1970 and is likely to remain so for the next decade. Other cities over 20 000 000 inhabitants in 2015 are Mumbai, São Paulo, Delhi, Shanghai, New York and Mexico City. Sixteen of the world's megacities are in Asia.

Facts

- From mid-2009, cities occupying less than 2% of the Earth's land surface housed over 50% of the human population
- Urban growth rates in Africa are the highest in the world
- Antarctica is uninhabited and most settlements in the Arctic regions have less than 5 000 inhabitants
- In 2015 India will have 56 cities with over one million inhabitants
- London was the first city to reach a population of over 5 million

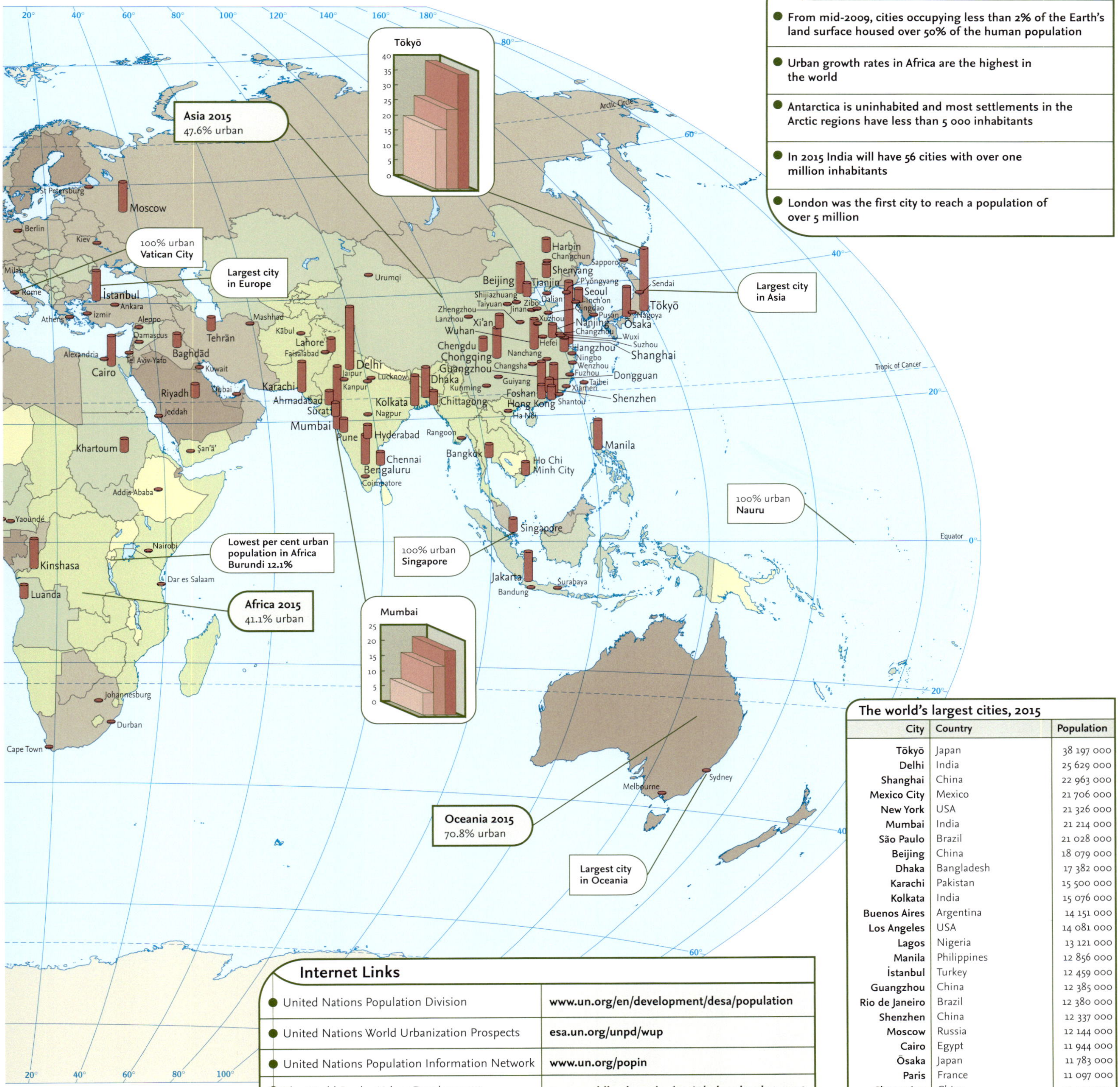

The world's largest cities, 2015

City	Country	Population
Tōkyō	Japan	38 197 000
Delhi	India	25 629 000
Shanghai	China	22 963 000
Mexico City	Mexico	21 706 000
New York	USA	21 326 000
Mumbai	India	21 214 000
São Paulo	Brazil	21 028 000
Beijing	China	18 079 000
Dhaka	Bangladesh	17 382 000
Karachi	Pakistan	15 500 000
Kolkata	India	15 076 000
Buenos Aires	Argentina	14 151 000
Los Angeles	USA	14 081 000
Lagos	Nigeria	13 121 000
Manila	Philippines	12 856 000
İstanbul	Turkey	12 459 000
Guangzhou	China	12 385 000
Rio de Janeiro	Brazil	12 380 000
Shenzhen	China	12 337 000
Moscow	Russia	12 144 000
Cairo	Egypt	11 944 000
Ōsaka	Japan	11 783 000
Paris	France	11 097 000
Chongqing	China	11 054 000
Jakarta	Indonesia	10 470 000

Internet Links

United Nations Population Division	www.un.org/en/development/desa/population
United Nations World Urbanization Prospects	esa.un.org/unpd/wup
United Nations Population Information Network	www.un.org/popin
The World Bank - Urban Development	www.worldbank.org/en/topic/urbandevelopment
City Population	www.citypopulation.de

Increased availability and ownership of telecommunications equipment over the last thirty years has aided the globalization of the world economy. Over half of the world's fixed telephone lines have been installed since 1987, and the majority of the world's Internet hosts have come on line since 1997. Cellular subscribers, particularly using digital technologies, are increasing much more rapidly than fixed telephone lines as in many countries they are a more practical option. Mobile broadband subscribers have now overtaken fixed broadband subscribers in all regions.

Internet users have been increasing rapidly since 1991 when there were only 4.4 million, with many large jumps especially in the last ten years, to 2 497 million in 2012, a figure that is more than double that of 2005. However, access levels vary, with approximately twenty countries still with less than 3 per cent Internet penetration.

Facts

- The first transatlantic telegraph cable came into operation in 1858
- In 2014, forty percent of the world's population were using the Internet
- The Falkland Islands have the world's highest density of Internet subscribers
- In 2011, 45 percent of Internet users were below the age of twenty-five

Broadband subscribers

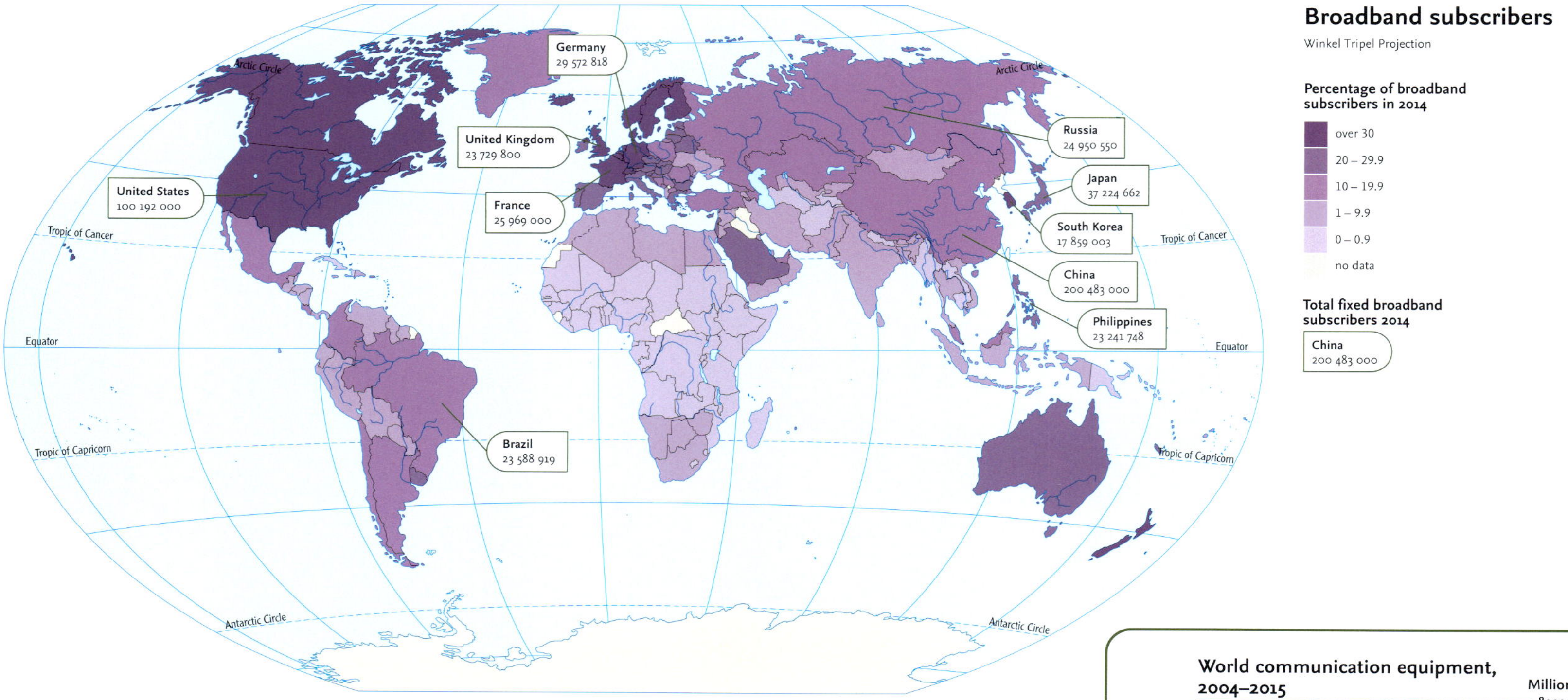

The Internet

Broadband connections for access to the Internet are relatively recent, but in that short time huge developments have been made in the technology and access speeds have shown a steady rise which is still continuing. Broadband access has had an impact on the delivery of electronic services in many areas such as health, education and finance. Mobile broadband (or mobile Internet) is wireless high-speed Internet access available through a portable modem device on a laptop computer and increasingly widely on hand-held tablets and mobile cellular telephones. In 2005 all regions with broadband access showed at least 64 per cent of all subscriptions were for fixed broadband. By 2008 almost all regions showed mobile broadband subscriptions had overtaken fixed as the technology improved and users were offered more options.

Top Broadband Economies 2014

Countries with the highest broadband penetration rate – subscribers per 100 inhabitants

	Top Economies – Fixed Broadband	Rate
1	Monaco	46.8
2	Switzerland	46.0
3	Denmark	41.4
4	Netherlands	41.0
5	Liechtenstein	40.3
6	France	40.2
7	South Korea	38.8
8	Norway	38.1
9	United Kingdom	37.4
10	San Marino	37.0

	Top Economies – Mobile Broadband	Rate
1	Singapore	156.1
2	Kuwait	139.8
3	Finland	138.5
4	Bahrain	126.2
5	Japan	121.4
6	Estonia	117.0
7	Sweden	116.3
8	Denmark	115.8
9	United Arab Emirates	114.0
10	Australia	112.2

World communication equipment, 2004–2015

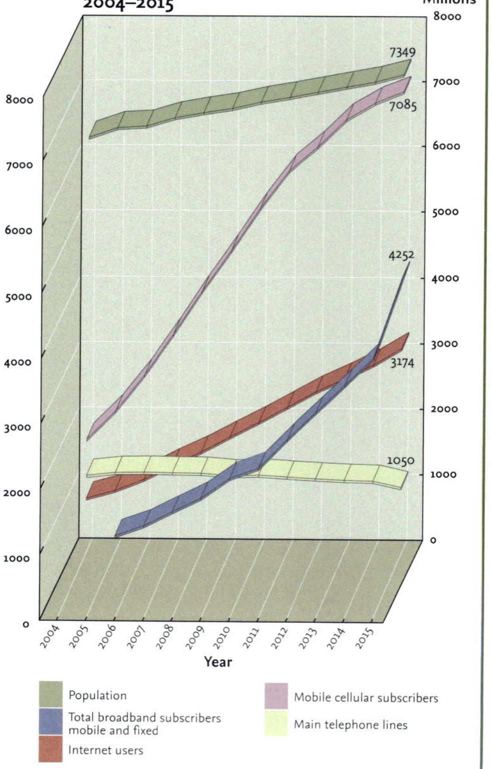

Mobile phone subscribers

Winkel Tripel Projection

Cellular mobile subscribers per 100 inhabitants 2014

- over 150
- 120 – 150
- 90 – 119.9
- 60 – 89.9
- 30 – 59.9
- 0 – 29.9
- no data

Total mobile phone subscribers 2014 Top ten countries

China
Total mobile phone subscribers
1 286 093 000

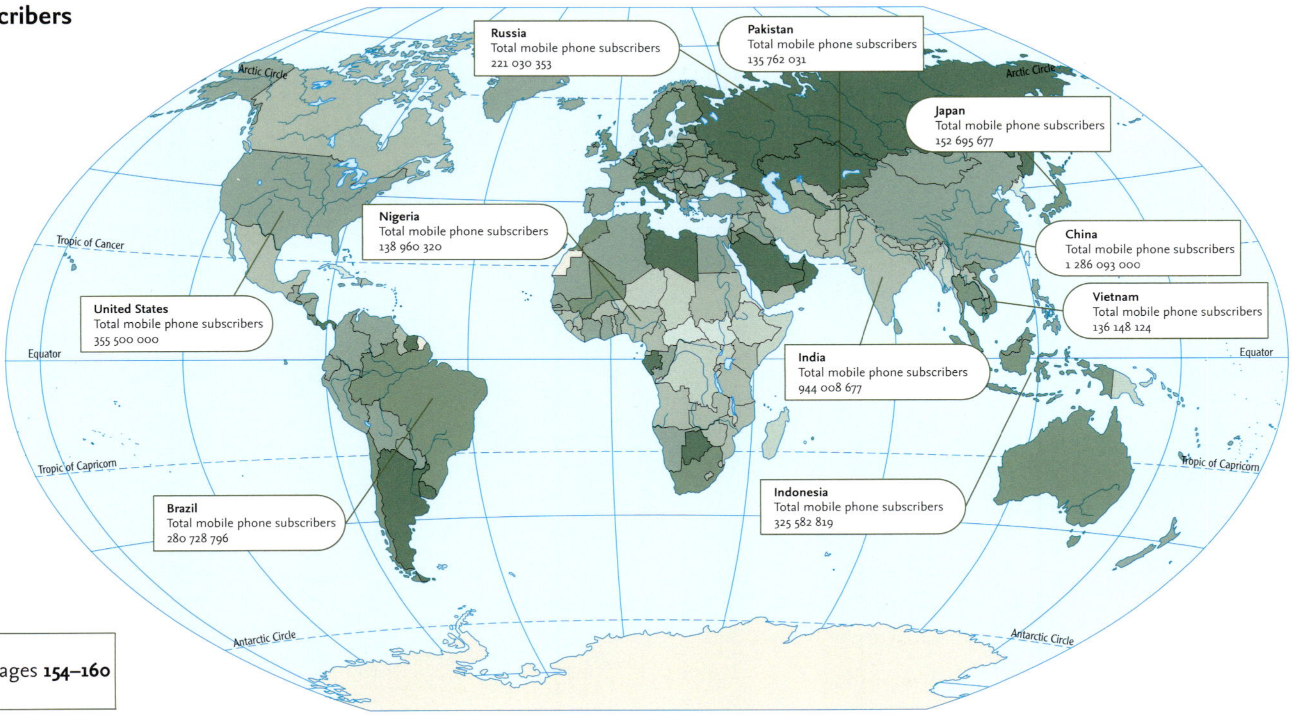

World Statistics: see pages **154–160**

Mobile phone subscribers

In 2014, there were almost seven billion mobile cellular subscribers and it was estimated that out of every one hundred people, ninety-six of them owned a mobile. One area showing a recent change with the development of new mobile cellular technology, is mobile broadband where subscribers are now more than triple the number of fixed broadband subscribers in all regions. The total number of Short Message Service (SMS) or text messages sent globally tripled between 2007 and 2010 to over 6 trillion messages, around 200 000 every second. Many phone packages now include "unlimited" free text messages encouraging many shorter messages to be sent.

Internet Links

OECD Organisation for Economic Co-operation and Development	**www.oecd.org**
TeleGeography	**www.telegeography.com**
International Telecommunication Union	**www.itu.int**

Fixed telephone lines

Winkel Tripel Projection

Telephone lines per 100 inhabitants 2014

- over 50.0
- 35.0 – 50.0
- 15.0 – 34.9
- 10.0 – 14.9
- 5.0 – 9.9
- 1.0 – 4.9
- 0 – 0.9
- no data

Total telephone lines 2014 Top ten countries

China
Total telephone lines
249 430 000

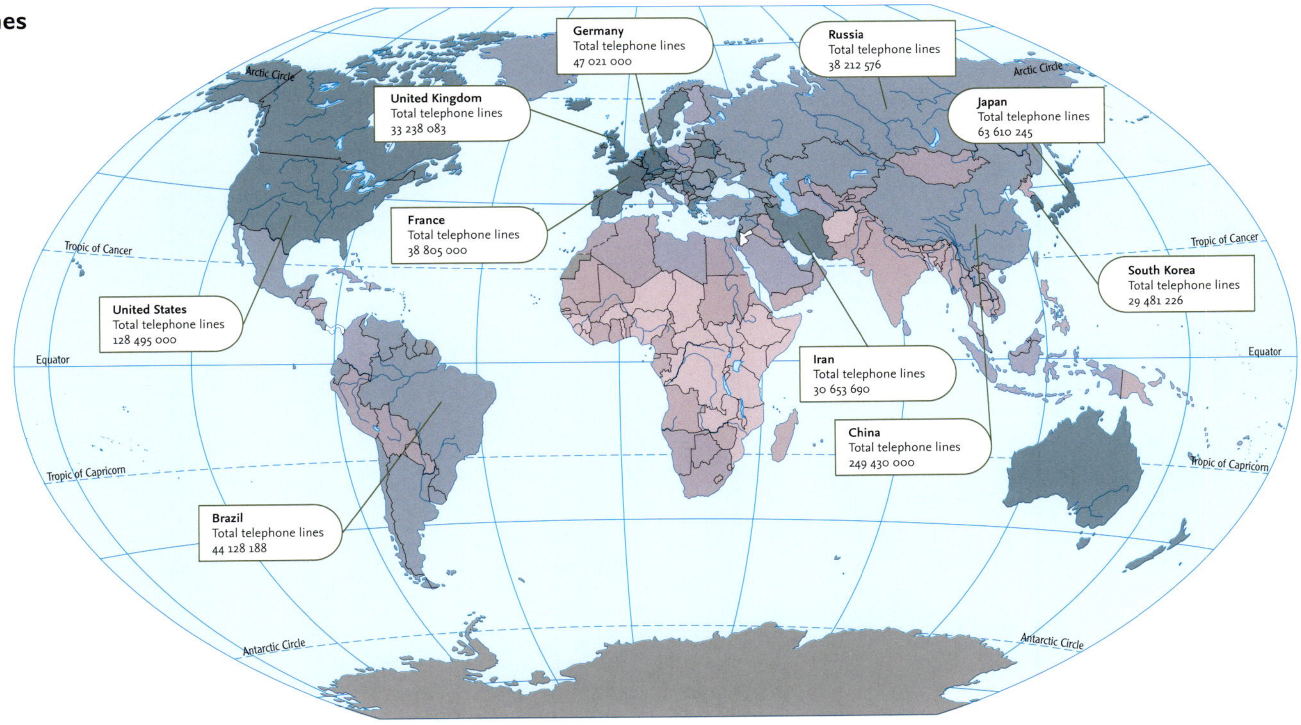

World

Social Indicators

Countries are often judged on their level of economic development, but national and personal wealth are not the only measures of a country's status. Numerous other indicators can give a better picture of the overall level of development and standard of living achieved by a country. The availability and standard of health services, levels of educational provision and attainment, levels of nutrition, water supply, life expectancy and mortality rates are just some of the factors which can be measured to assess and compare countries.

While nations strive to improve their economies, and hopefully also to improve the standard of living of their citizens, the measurement of such indicators often exposes great discrepancies between the countries of the 'developed' world and those of the 'less developed' world. They also show great variations within continents and regions and at the same time can hide great inequalities within countries.

World Statistics: see pages **154–160**

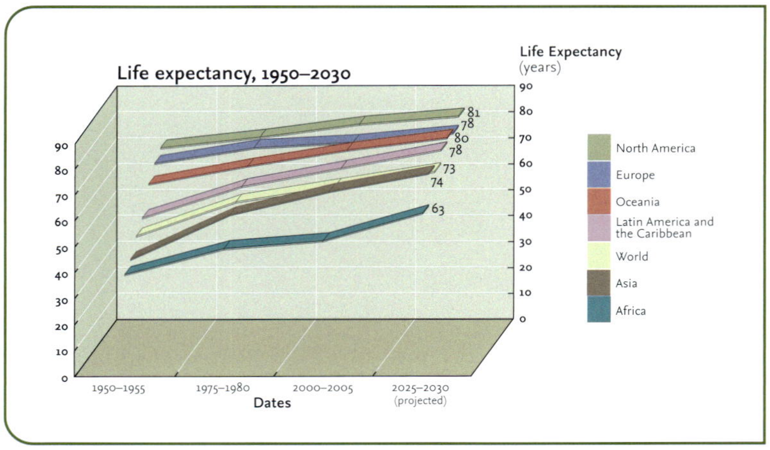

Internet Links

United Nations Development Programme	**www.undp.org**
World Health Organization	**www.who.int**
United Nations Statistics Division	**unstats.un.org**
United Nations Millennium Development Goals Indicators	**www.un.org/millenniumgoals**

Under-five mortality rate, 2015 and life expectancy by continent, 2015–2020

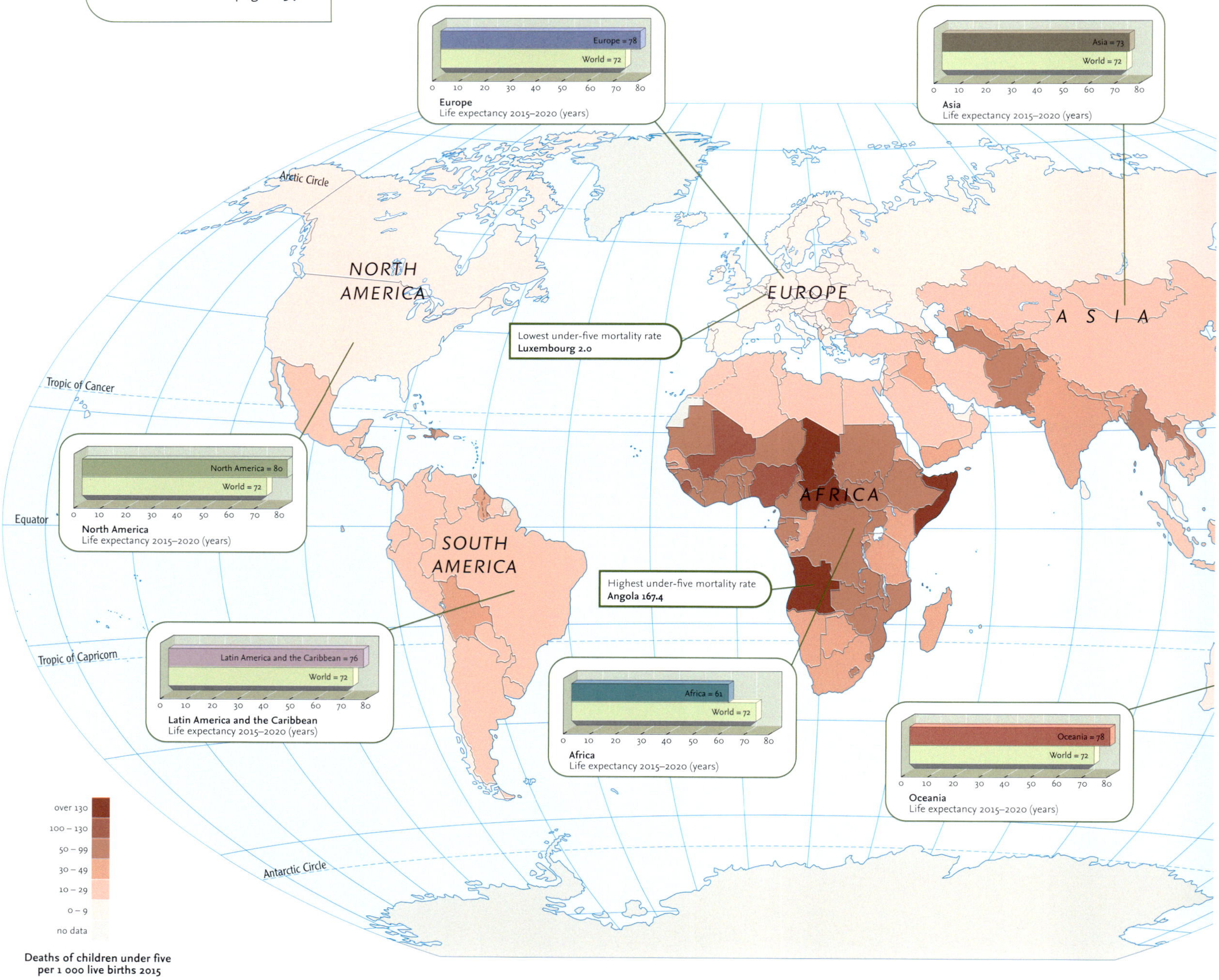

Facts

- All of the 7 countries with under-5 mortality rates of more than 100 per 1000 live births, are in Africa
- Many western countries believe they have achieved satisfactory levels of education and no longer closely monitor levels of literacy
- Children born in Nepal have only a 12% chance of their birth being attended by trained health personnel; for most European countries the figure is 100%
- The illiteracy rate among young women in the Middle East and north Africa is almost twice the rate for young men

Health and education

Perhaps the most important indicators used for measuring the level of national development are those relating to health and education. Both of these key areas are vital to the future development of a country, and if there are concerns in standards attained in either (or worse, in both) of these, then they may indicate fundamental problems within the country concerned. The ability to read and write (literacy) is seen as vital in educating people and encouraging development, while easy access to appropriate health services and specialists is an important requirement in maintaining satisfactory levels of basic health.

Adult Literacy rate

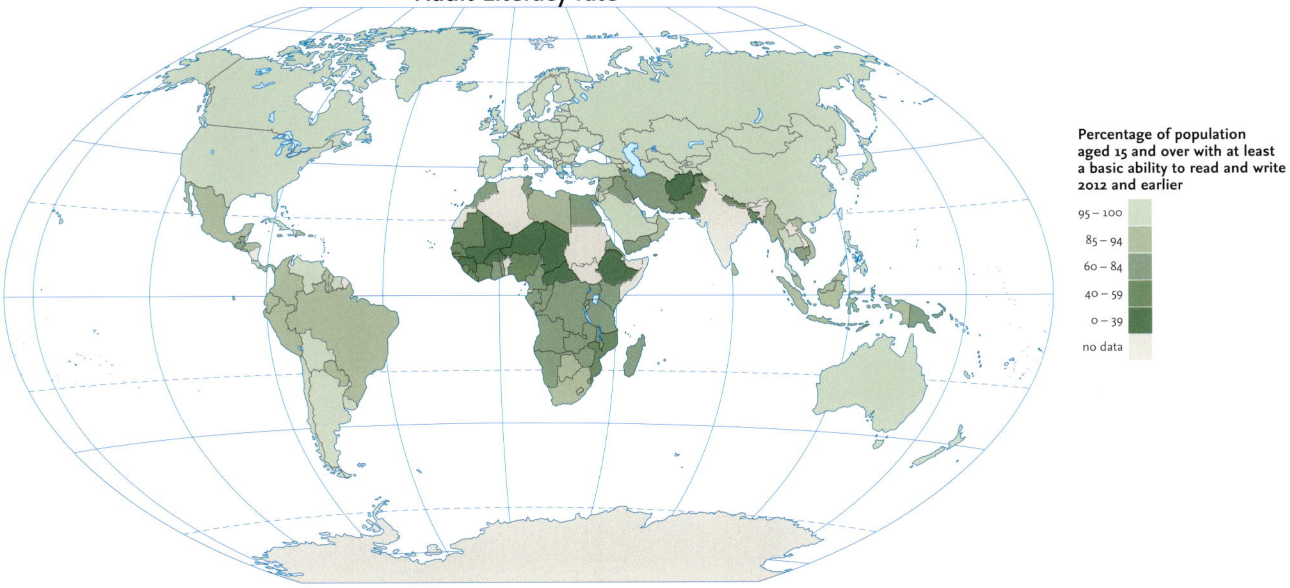

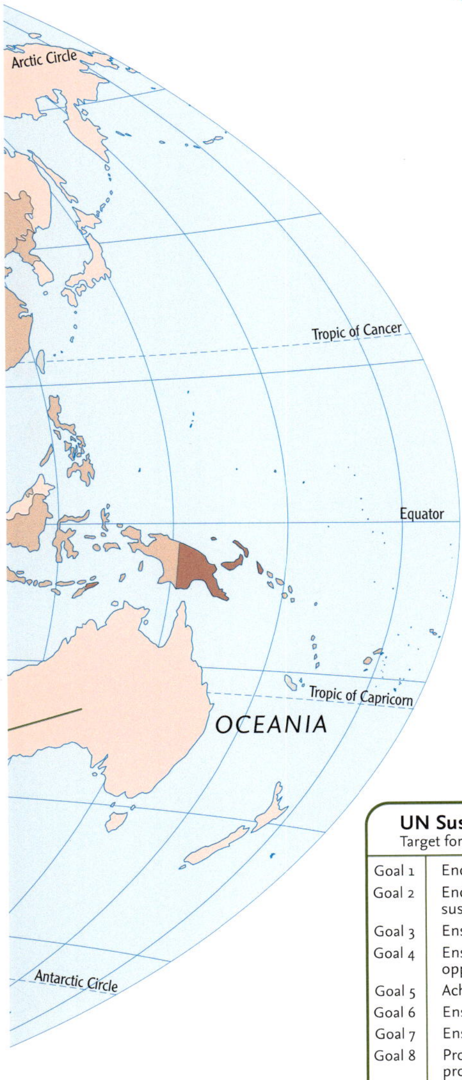

Doctors per 100 000 people

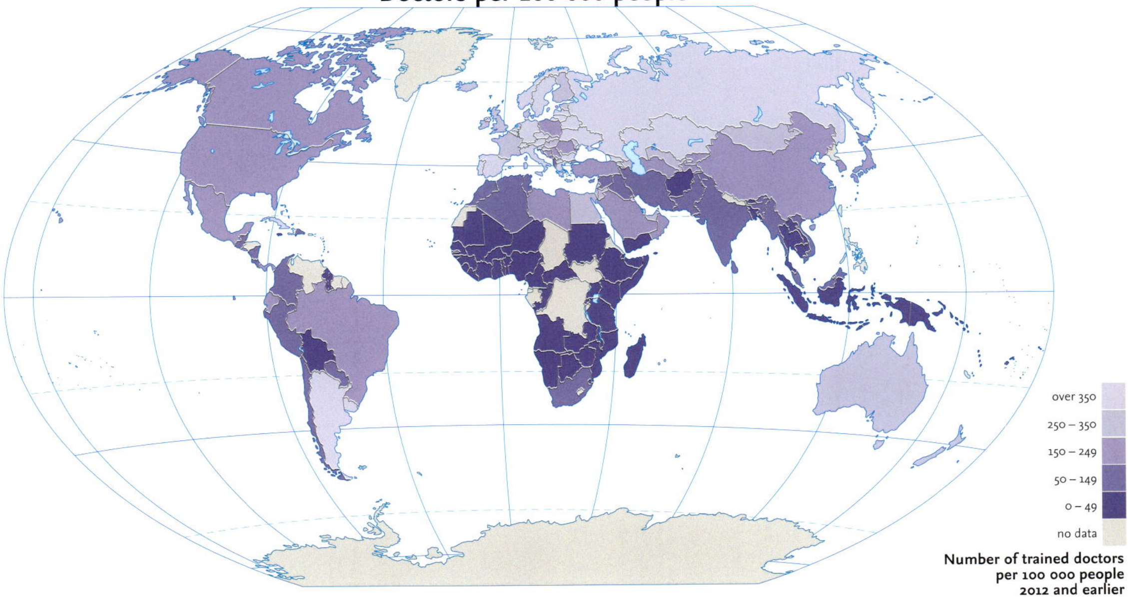

UN Sustainable Development Goals

Target for these to be reached is 2030

Goal 1	End poverty in all its forms everywhere	Goal 10	Reduce inequality within and among countries
Goal 2	End hunger, achieve food security and improved nutrition and promote sustainable agriculture	Goal 11	Make cities and human settlements inclusive, safe, resilient and sustainable
Goal 3	Ensure healthy lives and promote well-being for all at all ages	Goal 12	Ensure sustainable consumption and production patterns
Goal 4	Ensure inclusive and equitable quality education and promote lifelong learning opportunities for all	Goal 13	Take urgent action to combat climate change and its impacts
Goal 5	Achieve gender equality and empower all women and girls	Goal 14	Conserve and sustainably use the oceans, seas and marine resources for sustainable development
Goal 6	Ensure availability and sustainable management of water and sanitation for all	Goal 15	Protect, restore and promote sustainable use of terrestrial ecosystems, sustainably manage forests, combat desertification, and halt and reverse land degradation and halt biodiversity loss
Goal 7	Ensure access to affordable, reliable, sustainable and modern energy for all	Goal 16	Promote peaceful and inclusive societies for sustainable development, provide access to justice for all and build effective, accountable and inclusive institutions at all levels
Goal 8	Promote sustained, inclusive and sustainable economic growth, full and productive employment and decent work for all	Goal 17	Strengthen the means of implementation and revitalize the global partnership for sustainable development
Goal 9	Build resilient infrastructure, promote inclusive and sustainable industrialization and foster innovation		

World
Economy and Wealth

The globalization of the economy is making the world appear a smaller place. However, this shrinkage is an uneven process. Countries are being included in and excluded from the global economy to differing degrees. The wealthy countries of the developed world, with their market-led economies, access to productive new technologies and international markets, dominate the world economic system. Great inequalities exist between and within countries. There may also be discrepancies between social groups within countries due to gender and ethnic divisions. Differences between countries are evident by looking at overall wealth on a national and individual level.

Many of the world's largest financial institutions are to be found in the City of London.

World Statistics: see pages **154–160**

Poverty and inequality

In 2005, 25 per cent of the population of low- and middle-income economies lived in extreme poverty. With continued growth of average incomes, that number was expected to fall to less than 900 million by 2015. Even then there will be more than 2 billion people living on less than $2.00 a day or $730 a year. The greatest number of the extreme poor live in the large, lower-middle income economies of Asia – India and China – which together account for almost half of the people living in extreme poverty. But these are fast growing economies, where poverty rates have been falling rapidly. The highest rates of poverty are found in Sub-Saharan Africa, where economic growth was slowest in the 1990s and the regional poverty rate has only recently fallen below 50 per cent and was expected to reach 36 per cent by 2015. Since the mid-1990s, income inequality, as measured by the Gini index, has increased in slightly more than half of developing countries with available data.

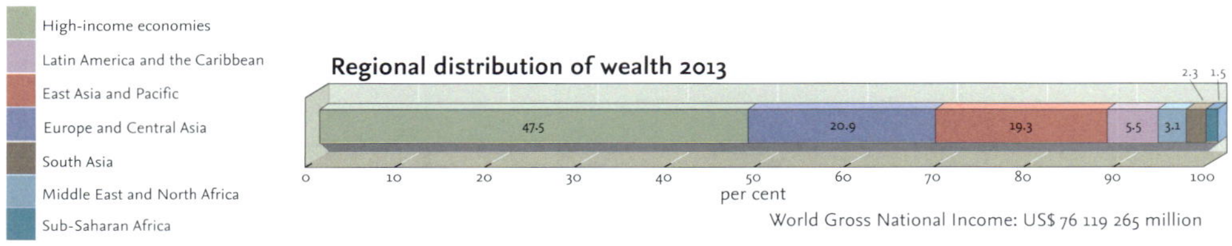

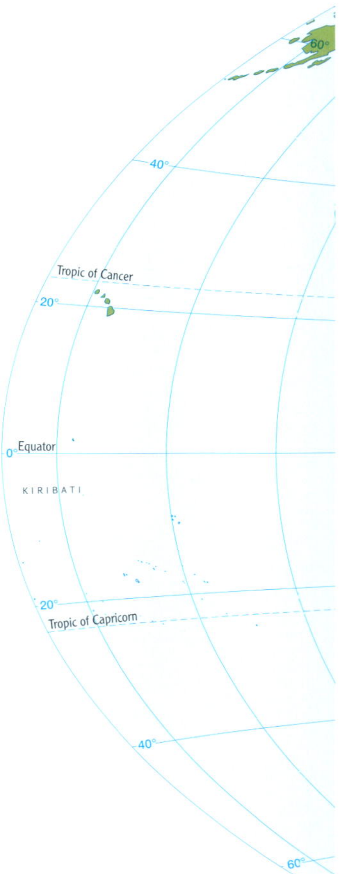

Income inequality

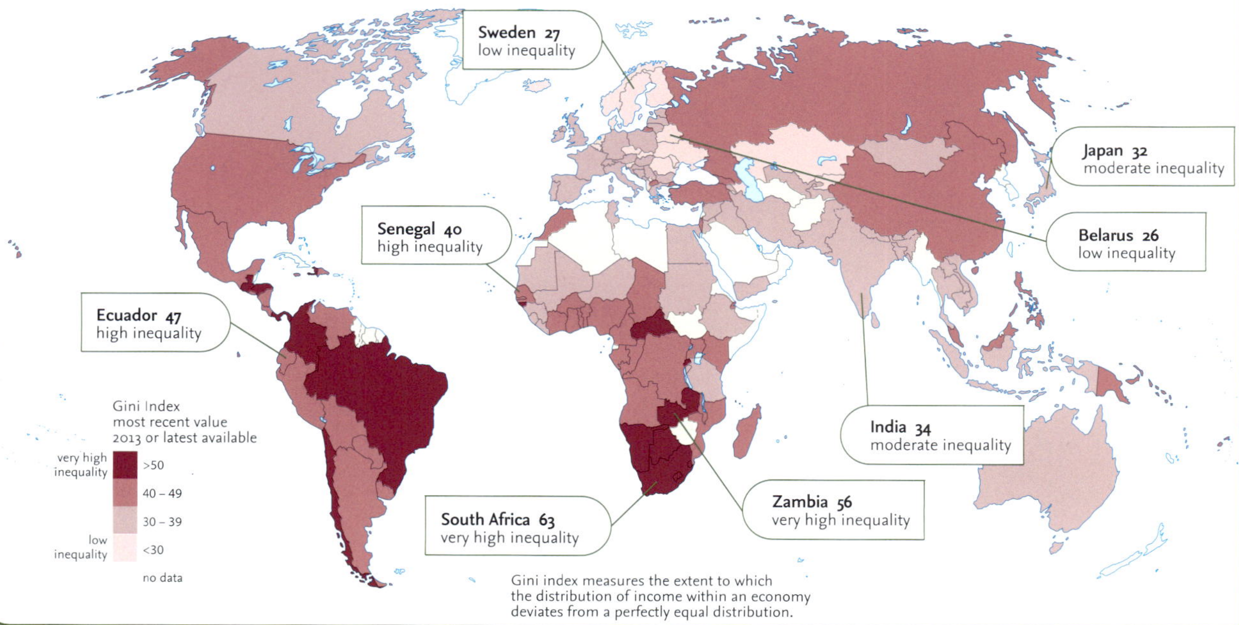

Facts

- The City, one of 33 London boroughs, is the world's largest financial centre and contains Europe's biggest stock market
- 40 percent of the world's population earns only 5% of the world's wealth
- During the second half of the 20th century rich countries gave over US$1 trillion in aid
- For every £1 in grant aid to developing countries, more than £25 comes back in debt repayments
- On average, The World Bank distributes US$40 billion each year between 100 countries

Rural village, **Malawi** – most of the world's poorest countries are in Africa.

Gross National Income per capita

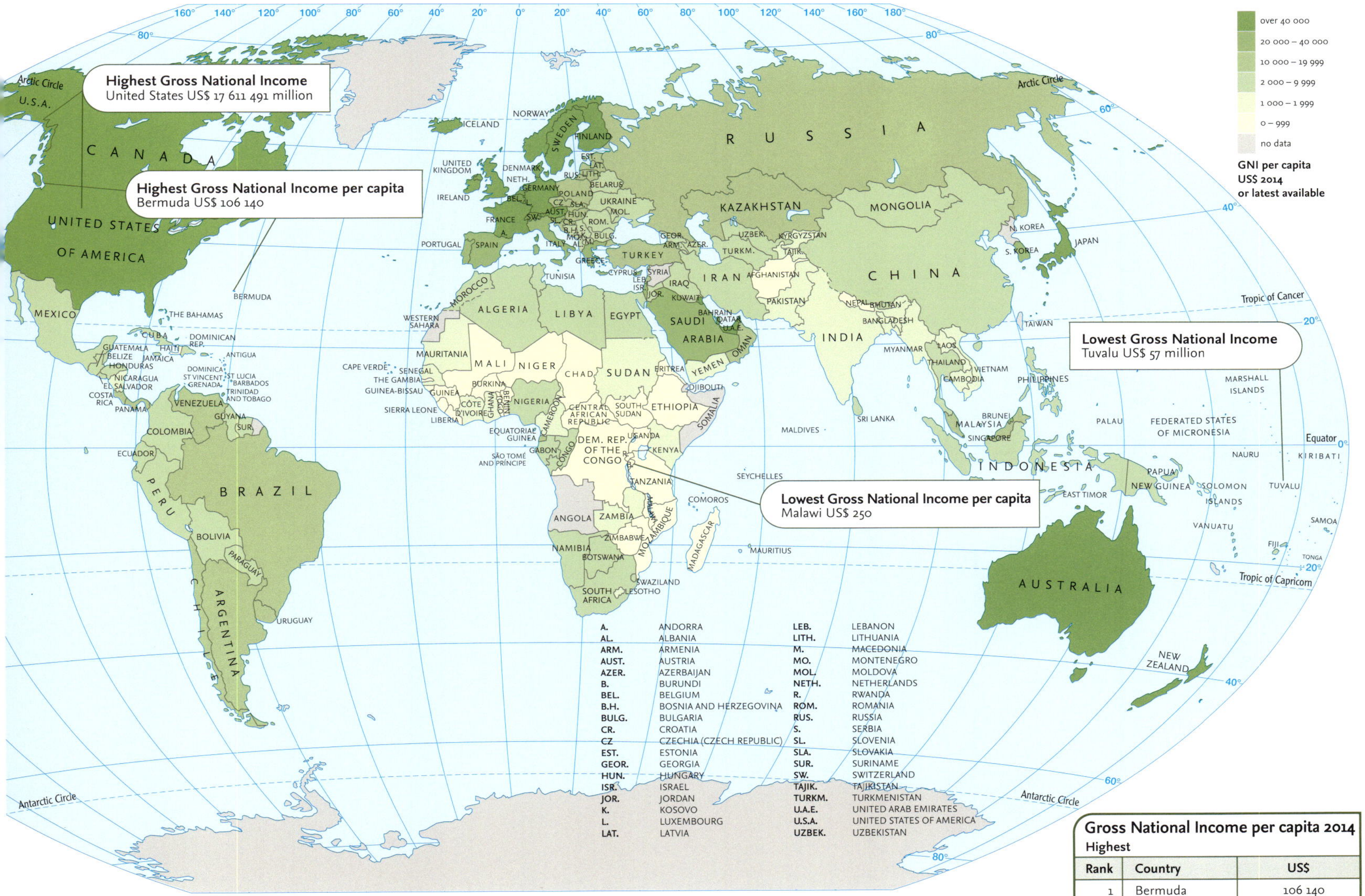

Measuring wealth

One of the indicators used to determine a country's wealth is its Gross National Income (GNI). This gives a broad measure of an economy's performance. This is the value of the final output of goods and services produced by a country plus net income from non-resident sources. The total GNI is divided by the country's population to give an average figure of the GNI per capita. From this it is evident that the developed countries dominate the world economy with the United States having the highest GNI. China is a rapidly growing world economic player with the second highest GNI figure and a relatively high GNI per capita (US$7 400) in proportion to its huge population.

Internet Links

United Nations Statistics Division	**unstats.un.org**
The World Bank	**www.worldbank.org**
International Monetary Fund	**www.imf.org**
OECD Organisation for Economic Co-operation and Development	**www.oecd.org**

Gross National Income per capita 2014

Highest

Rank	Country	US$
1	Bermuda	106 140
2	Norway	103 620
3	Qatar	92 200
4	Switzerland	84 720
5	Luxembourg	75 960
6	Australia	64 600
7	Sweden	61 570
8	Denmark	61 330
9	USA	55 230
10	Singapore	55 150

Lowest

Rank	Country	US$
178	Eritrea	480
179	Guinea	470
180	The Gambia	460
181	Madagascar	440
182	Niger	410
183	Dem. Rep. of the Congo	380
184	Liberia	370
185	Central African Republic	320
186	Burundi	270
187	Malawi	250

World
Conflict

Geo-political issues shape the countries of the world and the current political situation in many parts of the world reflects a long history of armed conflict. Since the Second World War conflicts have been fairly localized, but there are numerous 'flash points' where factors such as territorial claims, ideology, religion, ethnicity and access to resources can cause friction between two or more countries. Such factors also lie behind the recent growth in global terrorism.

Military expenditure can take up a disproportionate amount of a country's wealth – South Sudan, with a Gross Domestic Product (GDP) per capita of US$1 115 spends nearly ten per cent of its total GDP on military activity. There is an encouraging trend towards wider international cooperation, mainly through the United Nations (UN) and the North Atlantic Treaty Organization (NATO), to prevent escalation of conflicts and on peacekeeping missions.

Military spending 2014, and conflicts since 1946

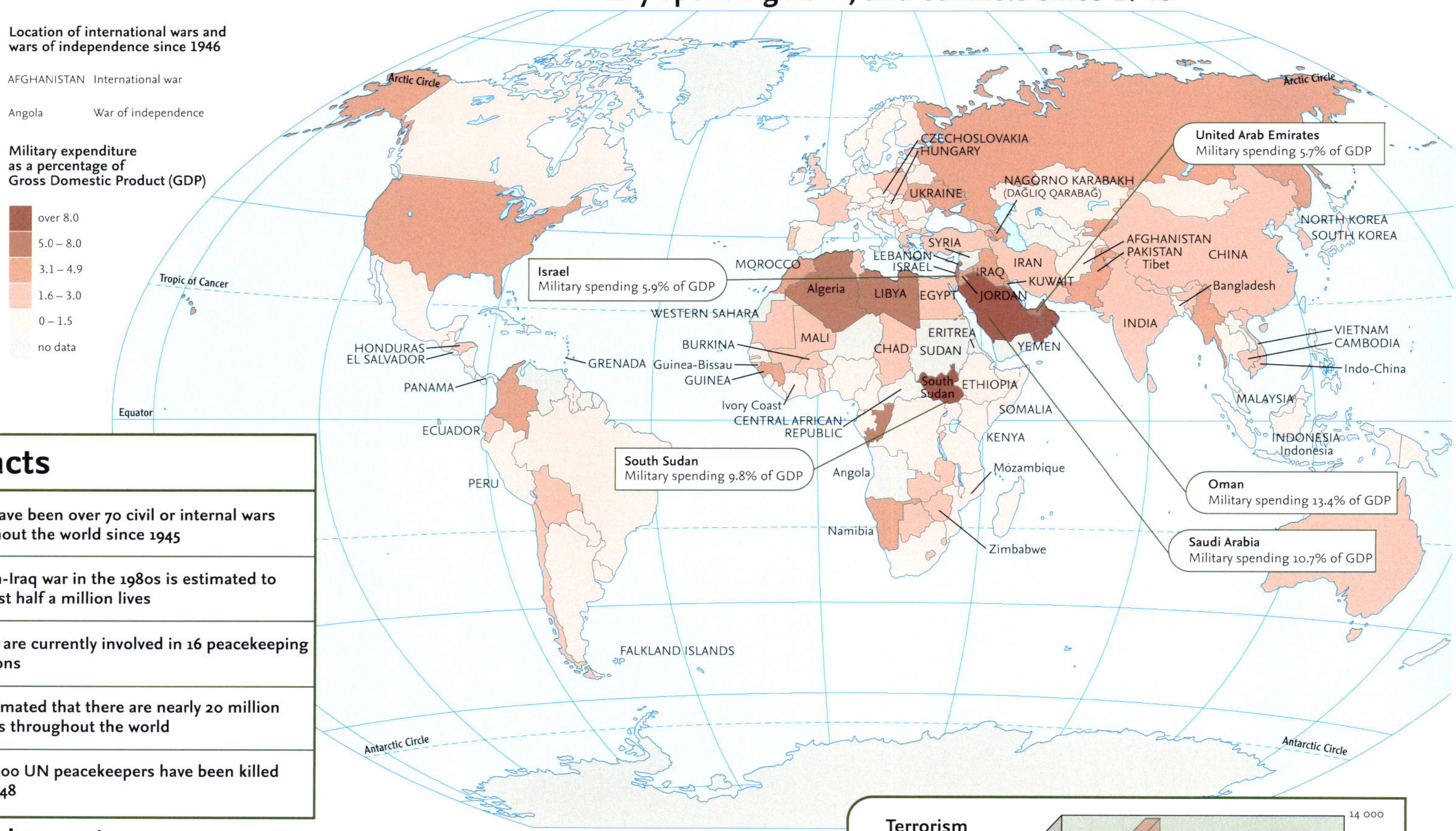

Facts

- There have been over 70 civil or internal wars throughout the world since 1945
- The Iran-Iraq war in the 1980s is estimated to have cost half a million lives
- The UN are currently involved in 16 peacekeeping operations
- It is estimated that there are nearly 20 million refugees throughout the world
- Over 3 300 UN peacekeepers have been killed since 1948

Global terrorism

Terrorism is defined by the United Nations as "All criminal acts directed against a State and intended or calculated to create a state of terror in the minds of particular persons or a group of persons or the general public". The world has become increasingly concerned about terrorism and the possibility that terrorists could acquire and use nuclear, chemical and biological weapons. One common form of terrorist attack is suicide bombing. Pioneered by Tamil secessionists in Sri Lanka, it has been widely used by Palestinian groups fighting against Israeli occupation of the West Bank and Gaza. In recent years it has also been used by the Al Qaida network in its attacks on the western world. Suicide bombings have also been used in Iraq and Afghanistan. The most recent terrorist organisation to be designated as such by the United Nations and many countries around the world is the Islamic State, also known as ISIS or ISIL. It is renowned for internet and social media propaganda, for the beheadings of civilians, journalists, soldiers and aid workers, and for the deliberate destruction of cultural heritage sites.

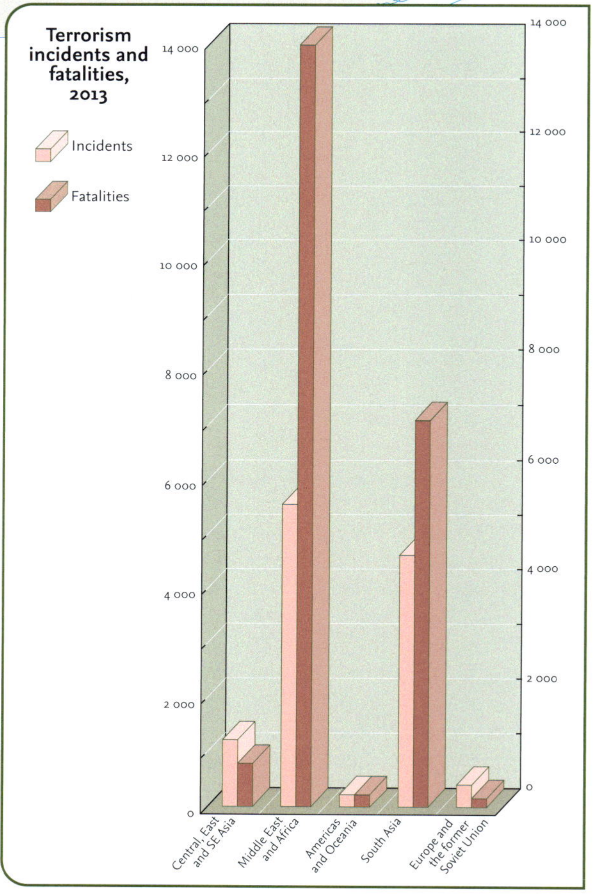

Internet Links

United Nations Peacekeeping	www.un.org/en/peacekeeping
United Nations Refugee Agency	www.unhcr.org
NATO	www.nato.int
BBC News	www.bbc.co.uk/news
International Boundaries Research Unit	www.dur.ac.uk/ibru
Peace Research Institute Oslo	www.prio.org

United Nations peacekeeping

United Nations peacekeeping was developed by the Organization as a way to help countries torn by conflict create the conditions for lasting peace. The first UN peacekeeping mission was established in 1948, when the Security Council authorized the deployment of UN military observers to the Middle East to monitor the Armistice Agreement between Israel and its Arab neighbours. Since then, there have been a total of 69 UN peacekeeping operations around the world.

UN peacekeeping goals were primarily limited to maintaining ceasefires and stabilizing situations on the ground, so that efforts could be made at the political level to resolve the conflict by peaceful means. Today's peacekeepers undertake a wide variety of complex tasks, from helping to build sustainable institutions of governance, to human rights monitoring, to security sector reform, to the disarmament, demobilization and reintegration of former combatants.

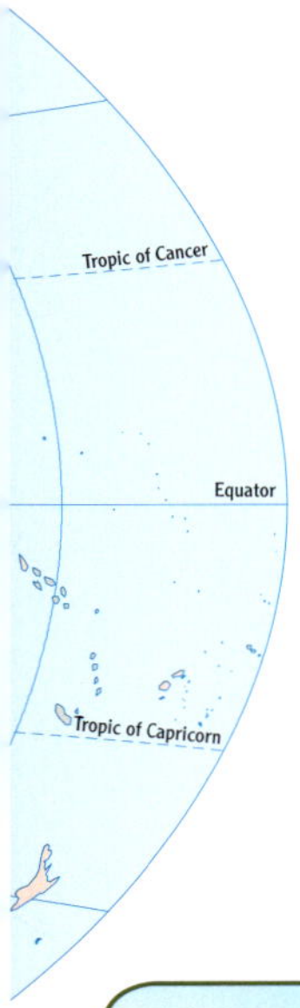

United Nations peacekeeping operations 1948–2016

Current peacekeeping operations are named on the map

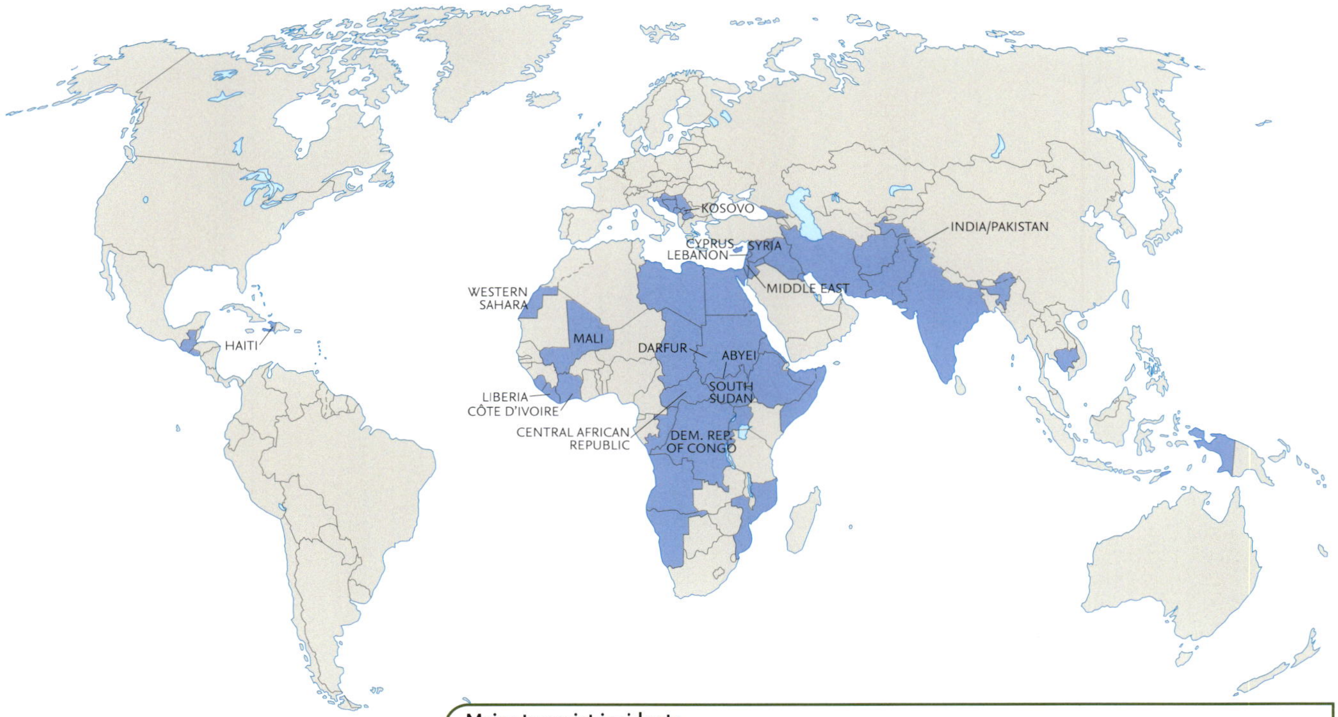

Many refugees from **Myanmar** (Burma) live in villages in Thailand.

Major terrorist incidents

Date	Location	Summary	Killed	Injured
December 1988	**Lockerbie, Scotland**	Airline bombing	270	5
March 1995	**Tōkyō, Japan**	Sarin gas attack on subway	12	5 510
April 1995	**Oklahoma City, USA**	Bomb in the Federal building	168	over 800
August 1998	**Nairobi, Kenya and Dar es Salaam, Tanzania**	US Embassy bombings	225	over 4 000
August 1998	**Omagh, Northern Ireland**	Town centre bombing	29	220
September 2001	**New York and Washington D.C., USA**	Airline hijacking and crashing	3 018	over 6 200
October 2002	**Bali, Indonesia**	Car bomb outside nightclub	202	over 200
October 2002	**Moscow, Russia**	Theatre siege	170	over 600
March 2004	**Bāghdad and Karbalā', Iraq**	Suicide bombing of pilgrims	181	over 400
March 2004	**Madrid, Spain**	Train bombings	191	1 800
September 2004	**Beslan, Russia**	School siege	385	over 700
July 2005	**London, UK**	Underground and bus bombings	56	700
July 2005	**Sharm ash Shaykh, Egypt**	Bombs at tourist sites	88	200
July 2006	**Mumbai, India**	Train bombings	209	700
August 2007	**Qahtaniya, Iraq**	Suicide bombing in town centres	796	over 1 500
November 2008	**Mumbai, India**	Coordinated shootings at eight sites	183	over 300
October 2011	**Mogadishu, Somalia**	Suicide truck bomb	139	over 90
March 2012	**Zinjibar, Yemen**	Army base attack	210	n/a
September 2013	**Nairobi, Kenya**	Shopping centre attack	72	201
May 2014	**Gamboru and Ngala, Nigeria**	Attack on market	310	n/a
April 2015	**Garissa, Kenya**	College shooting	147	79
November 2015	**Paris, France**	Attacks at six sites	130	368
March 2016	**Brussels, Belgium**	Bombings at three sites	32	340

Terrorist incidents

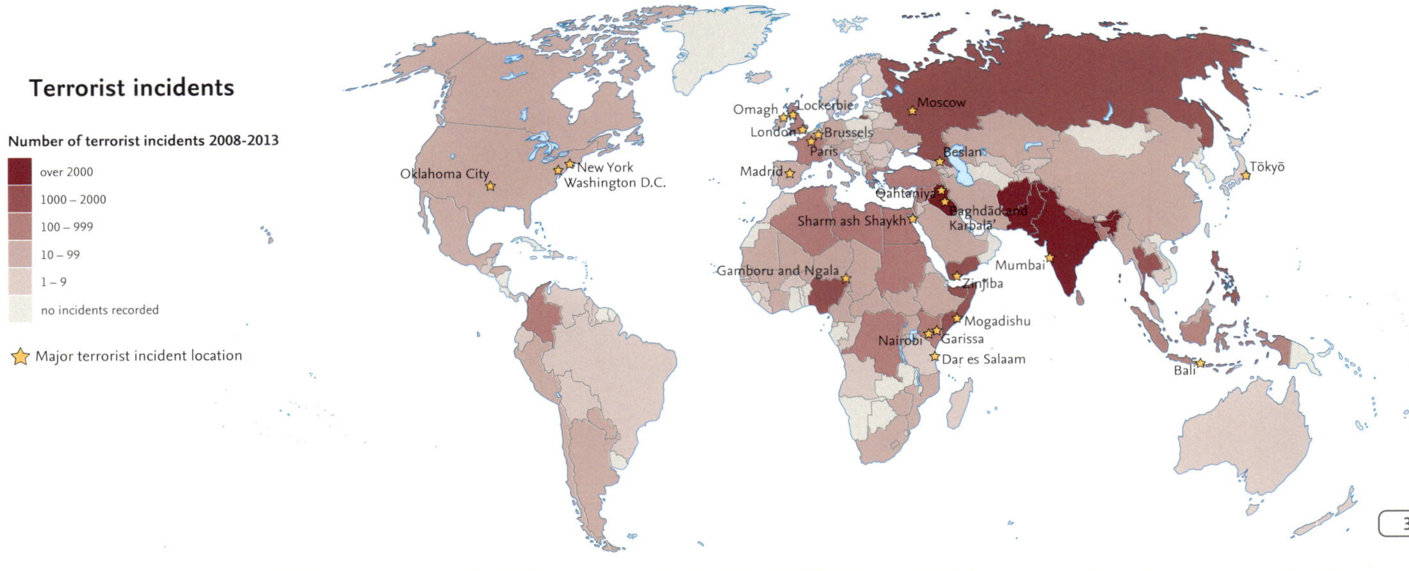

With the process of globalization has come an increased awareness of, and direct interest in, issues which have global implications. Social issues can now affect large parts of the world and can impact on large sections of society. Perhaps the current issues of greatest concern are those of national security, including the problem of international terrorism, health, crime and natural resources. The three social issues highlighted here reflect this and are of immediate concern.

The international drugs trade, and the crimes commonly associated with it, can impact on society and individuals in devastating ways; scarcity of water resources and lack of access to safe drinking water can have major economic implications and cause severe health problems; and the AIDS epidemic is having disastrous consequences in large parts of the world, particularly in sub-Saharan Africa.

The drugs trade

The international trade in illegal drugs is estimated to be worth over US$400 billion. While it may be a lucrative business for the criminals involved, the effects of the drugs on individual users and on society in general can be devastating. Patterns of drug production and abuse vary, but there are clear centres for the production of the most harmful drugs – the opiates (opium, morphine and heroin) and cocaine. The 'Golden Triangle' of Laos, Myanmar and Thailand, and western South America respectively are the main producing areas for these drugs. Significant efforts are expended to counter the drugs trade, and there have been signs recently of downward trends in the production of heroin and cocaine.

The **opium poppy** is the plant from which opium is extracted.

The international drugs trade

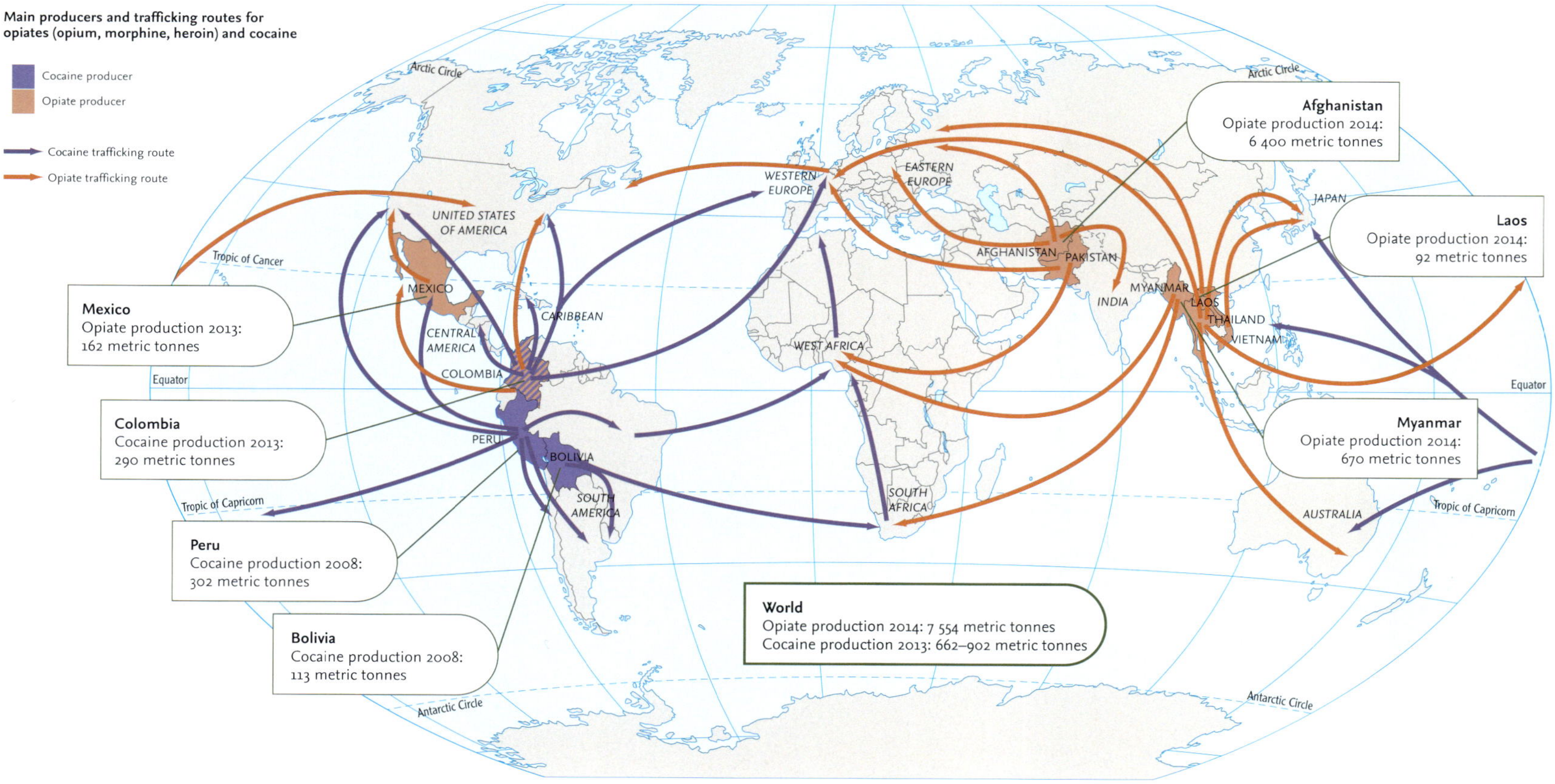

AIDS epidemic

With 35 million people living with HIV/AIDS (Human Immunodeficiency Virus/Acquired Immune Deficiency Syndrome) and more than 20 million deaths from the disease, the AIDS epidemic poses one of the biggest threats to public health. The UNAIDS project estimated that 2.1 million people were newly infected in 2013 and that 1.5 million AIDS sufferers died. This is nearly one half the number of infections than the peak of 3.2 million in 1997. As well as the death count itself, there are millions of living African children, between the ages of 10 and 17, that have been orphaned as a result of the disease. Treatment to prevent HIV transmission to babies has resulted in 33 per cent drop in infections.

Facts

- The majority of people infected with HIV, if not treated, develop signs of AIDS within 8 to 10 years
- Agriculture uses 70 per cent of all the water taken from aquifers, streams and lakes
- Nearly 4 million people die each year from water-related diseases such as cholera and dysentery
- Estimates suggest that 243 million people consume illegal drugs around the world

Population living with HIV/AIDS, 2013

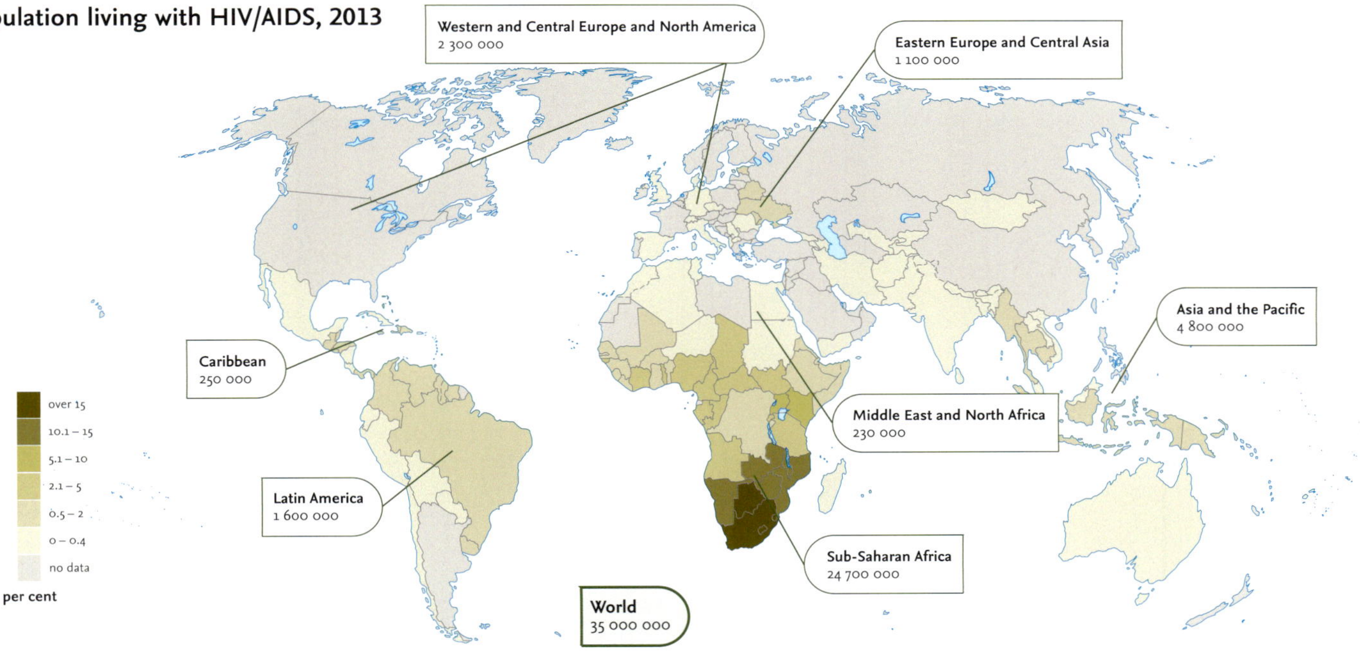

Water resources

Water is one of the fundamental requirements of life, and yet in some countries it is becoming more scarce due to increasing population and climate change. Safe drinking water, basic hygiene, health education and sanitation facilities are often virtually nonexistent for impoverished people in developing countries throughout the world. WHO/UNICEF estimate that the combination of these conditions results in over 4 000 deaths every day, most of these being children. Currently, 1.8 billion people drink untreated water and expose themselves to serious health risks, while political struggles over diminishing water resources are increasingly likely to be the cause of international conflict.

Domestic use of **untreated water** in Varanasi, India

Access to safe water, 2015

Percentage of population with access to improved drinking water

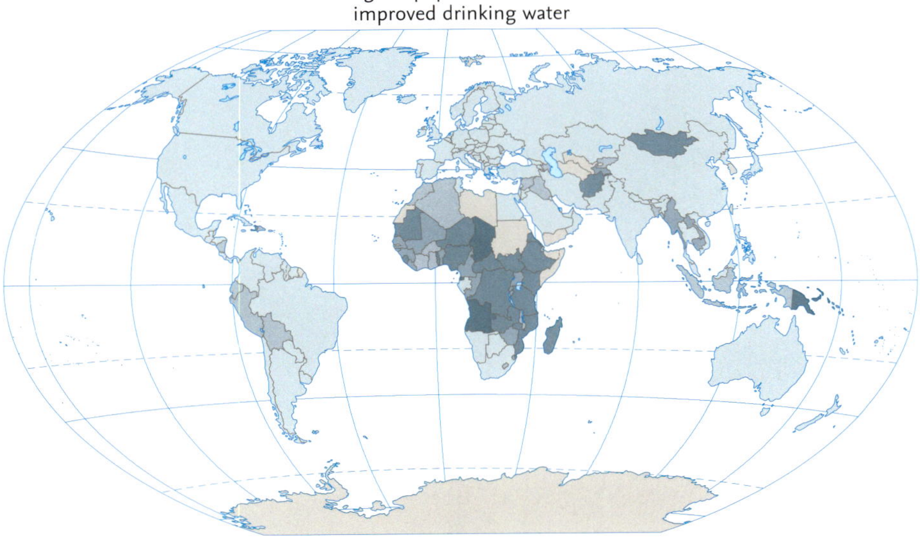

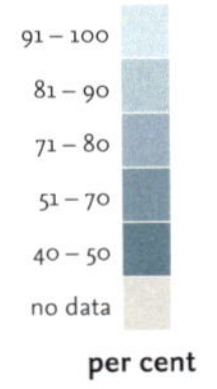

Internet Links

UNESCO	**www.unesco.org**
UNAIDS	**www.unaids.org**
WaterAid	**www.wateraid.org.uk**
World Health Organization	**www.who.int**
UNODC United Nations Office on Drugs and Crime	**www.unodc.org**

The Earth has a rich and diverse environment which is under threat from both natural and man-induced forces. Forests and woodland form the predominant natural land cover with tropical rain forests – currently disappearing at alarming rates – believed to be home to the majority of animal and plant species. Grassland and scrub tend to have a lower natural species diversity but have suffered the most impact from man's intervention through conversion to agriculture, burning and the introduction of livestock. Wherever man interferes with existing biological and environmental processes degradation of that environment occurs to varying degrees. This interference also affects inland water and oceans where pollution, over-exploitation of marine resources and the need for fresh water has had major consequences on land and sea environments.

Facts

- The Sundarbans stretching across the Ganges delta is the largest area of mangrove forest in the world, covering 10 000 square kilometres (3 861 square miles) and forming an important ecological area, home to 260 species of birds, the Bengal tiger and other threatened species
- Over 90 000 square kilometres of precious tropical forest and wetland habitats are lost each year
- The surface level of the Dead Sea has fallen by more than 35 metres over the last 50 years
- Climate change and mismanagement of land areas can lead to soils becoming degraded and semi-arid grasslands becoming deserts – a process known as desertification

Environmental change

Whenever natural resources are exploited by man, the environment is changed. Approximately half the area of post-glacial forest has been cleared or degraded, and the amount of old-growth forest continues to decline. Desertification caused by climate change and the impact of man can turn semi-arid grasslands into arid desert. Regions bordering tropical deserts, such as the Sahel region south of the Sahara and regions around the Thar Desert in India, are most vulnerable to this process. Coral reefs are equally fragile environments, and many are under threat from coastal development, pollution and over-exploitation of marine resources.

Water resources in certain parts of the world are becoming increasingly scarce and competition for water is likely to become a common cause of conflict. The Aral Sea in central Asia was once the world's fourth largest lake but it now ranks only sixteenth after shrinking by more than 51 000 square kilometres since the 1960s. This shrinkage has been due to climatic change and to the diversion, for farming purposes, of the major rivers which feed the lake. The change has had a devastating effect on the local fishing industry and the exposure of chemicals on the lake bed has caused health problems for the local population.

Deforestation and the creation of the **Itaipu Dam** on the Paraná river in Brazil have had a dramatic effect on the landscape and ecosystems of this part of South America. Some forest on the right of the images lies within Iguaçu National Park and has been protected from destruction.

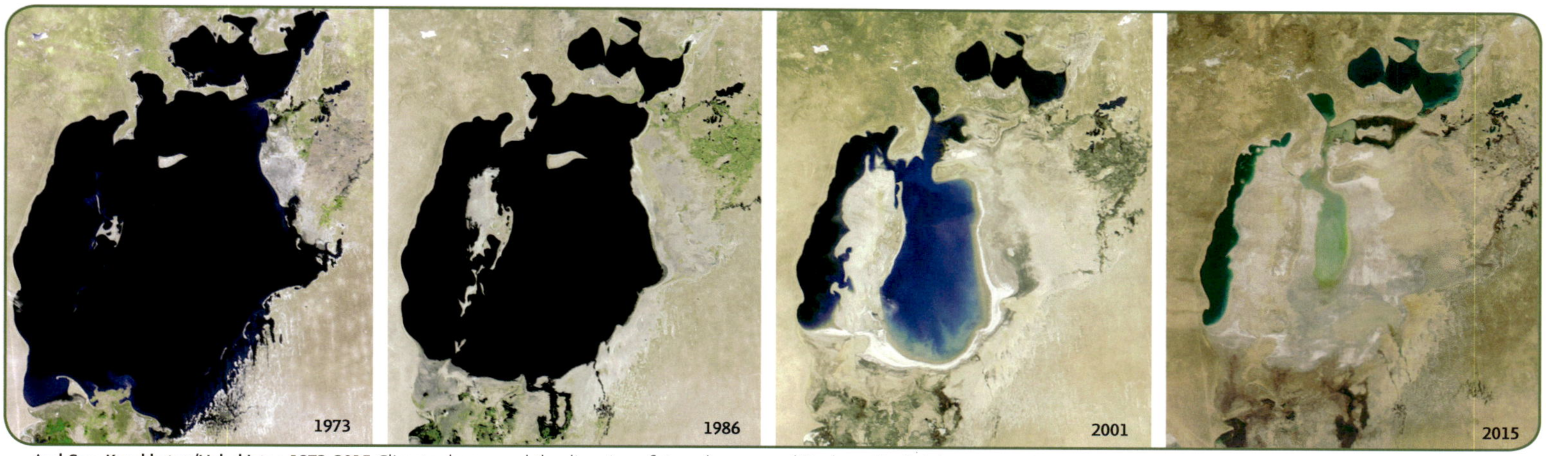

Aral Sea, Kazakhstan/Uzbekistan 1973-2015 Climate change and the diversion of rivers have caused its dramatic shrinkage.

Environmental Impacts

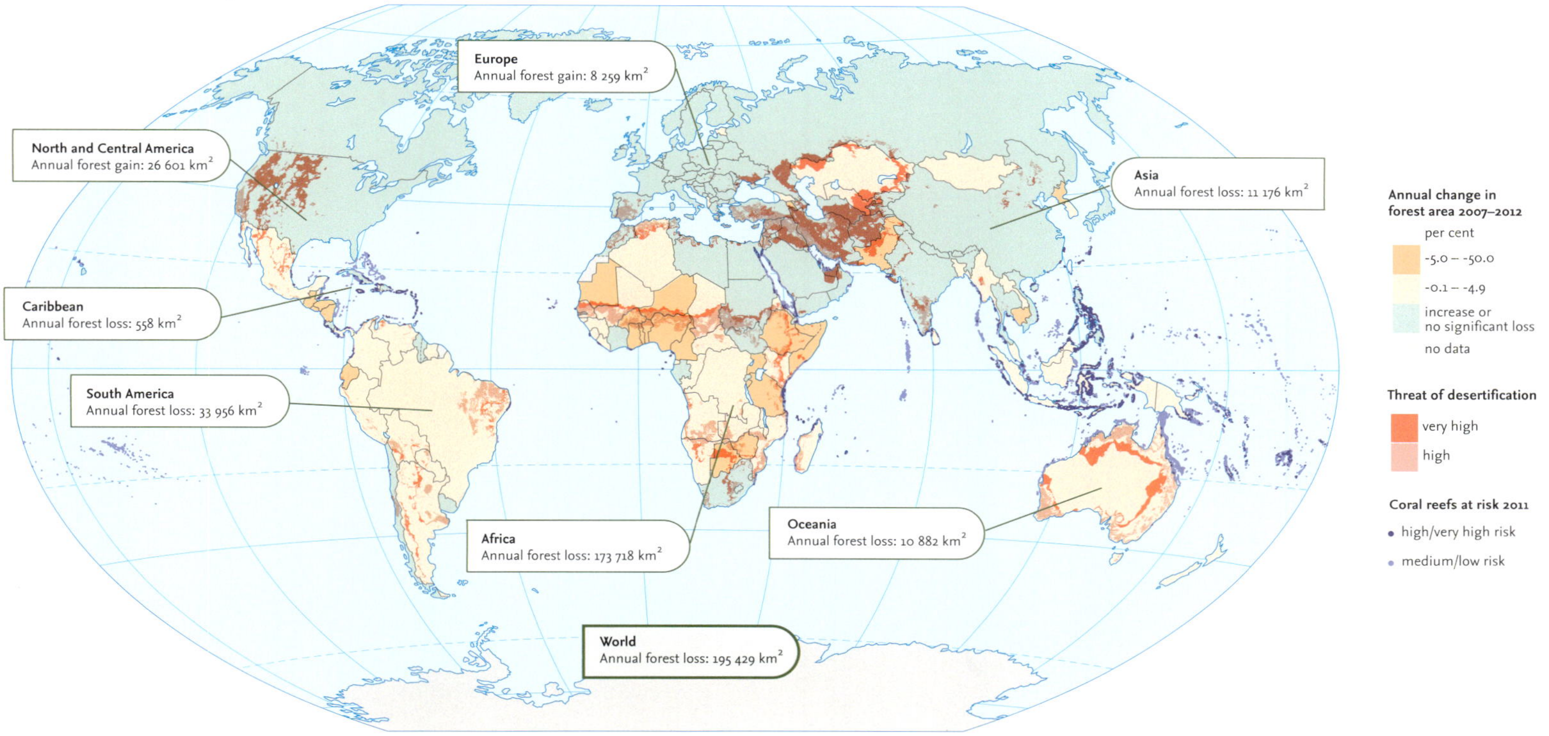

Internet links	
United Nations Environment Programme (UNEP)	**www.unep.org**
IUCN International Union for Conservation of Nature	**www.iucn.org**
UNESCO World Heritage	**whc.unesco.org**

Environmental protection

Top 10 protected areas by size

Rank	Protected area	Country	Size (sq km)	Designation
1	Natural Park of the Coral Sea	New Caledonia, France	1 292 967	Marine Protected Area
2	South Georgia and South Sandwich Islands Marine Protected Area	South Georgia and South Sandwich Islands, United Kingdom	1 070 000	Marine Protected Area
3	Coral Sea Reserve	Australia	989 842	Marine Protected Area
4	Northeast Greenland	Greenland	972 000	National Park
5	Rub' al-Khālī	Saudi Arabia	640 000	Wildlife Management Area
6	Chagos Marine Protected Area	BIOT, United Kingdom	640 000	Marine Protected Area
7	Kermadec Islands Marine Reserve	New Zealand	469 276	Marine Protected Area
8	Phoenix Islands Protected Area	Kiribati	410 500	Marine Protected Area
9	Papahānaumokuākea Marine National Monument	United States	362 075	Marine Protected Area
10	Great Barrier Reef Marine Park	Australia	348 700	Marine Protected Area

Great Barrier Reef, Australia, the world's seventh largest protected area.

Europe
Landscapes

Europe, the westward extension of the Asian continent and the second smallest of the world's continents, has a remarkable variety of physical features and landscapes. The continent is bounded by mountain ranges of varying character – the highlands of Scandinavia and northwest Britain, the Pyrenees, the Alps, the Carpathian Mountains, the Caucasus and the Ural Mountains. Two of these, the Caucasus and Ural Mountains, define the eastern limits of Europe, with the Black Sea and the Bosporus defining its southeastern boundary with Asia.

Across the centre of the continent stretches the North European Plain, broken by some of Europe's greatest rivers, including the Volga and the Dnieper and containing some of its largest lakes. To the south, the Mediterranean Sea divides Europe from Africa. The Mediterranean region itself has a very distinct climate and landscape.

Facts

- The Danube flows through 7 countries and has 7 different name forms
- Lakes cover almost 10% of the total land area of Finland
- The Strait of Gibraltar, separating the Atlantic Ocean from the Mediterranean Sea and Europe from Africa, is only 13 kilometres wide at its narrowest point
- The highest mountain in the Alps is Mont Blanc, 4 810 metres, on the France/Italy border

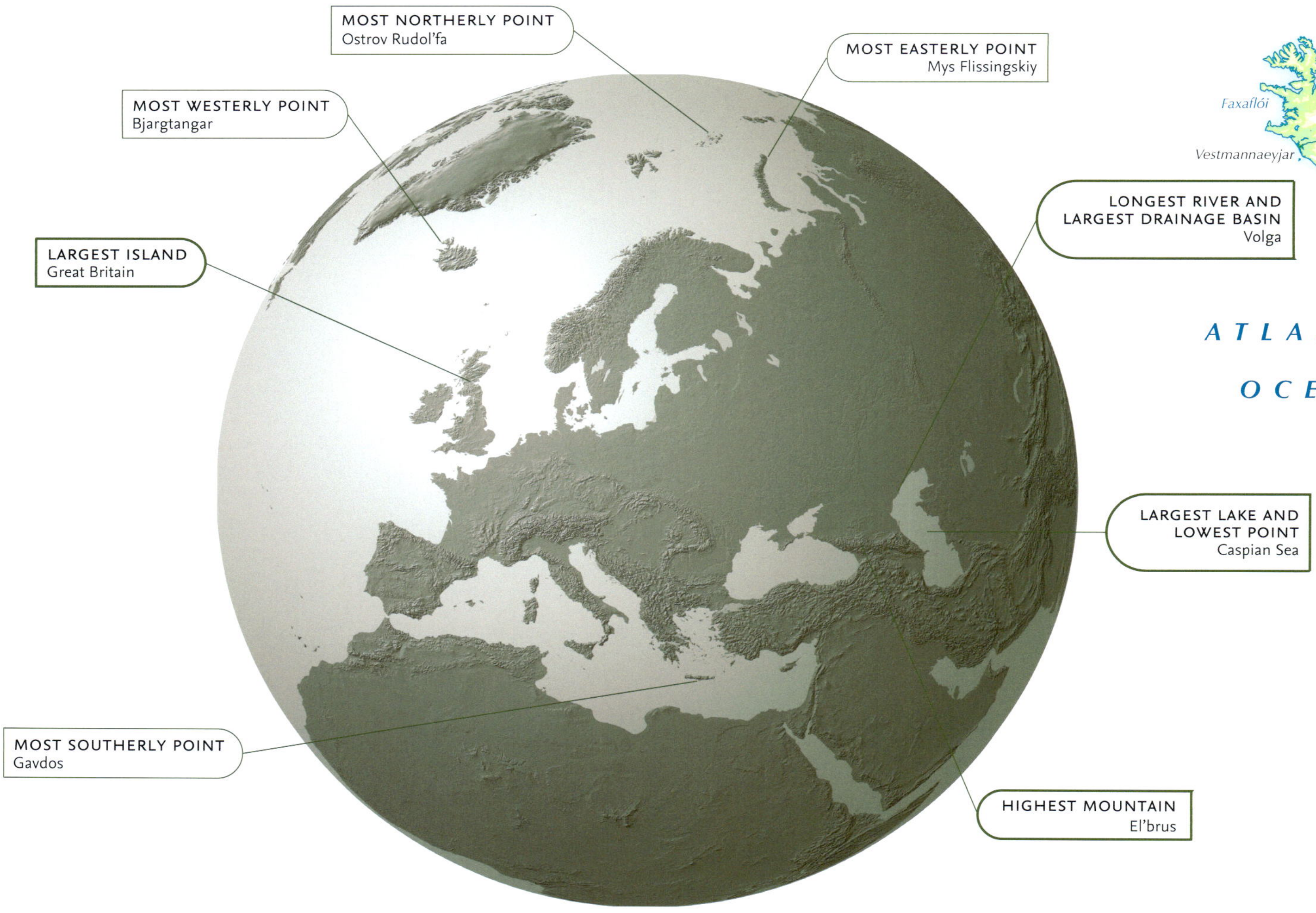

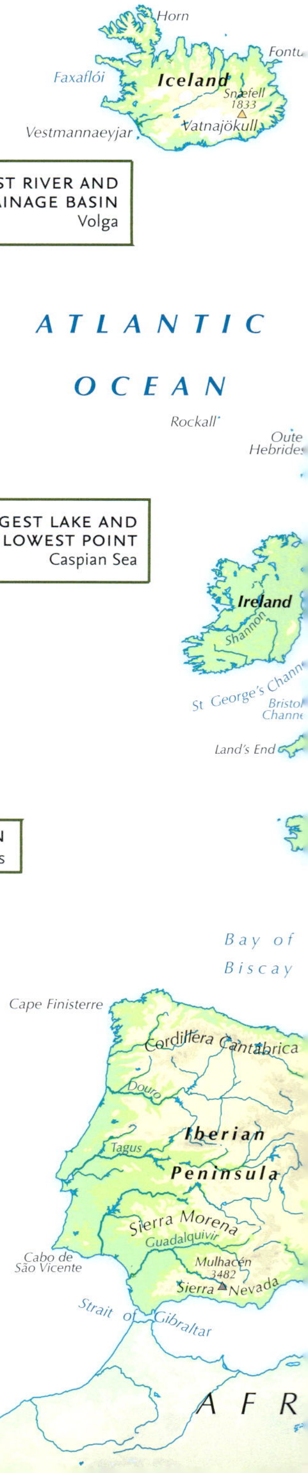

Europe's greatest physical features

Highest mountain	El'brus, Russia	5 642 metres	18 510 feet
Longest river	Volga, Russia	3 688 km	2 292 miles
Largest lake	Caspian Sea	371 000 sq km	143 243 sq miles
Largest island	Great Britain, United Kingdom	218 476 sq km	84 354 sq miles
Largest drainage basin	Volga, Russia	1 380 000 sq km	532 818 sq miles

Europe's extent

TOTAL LAND AREA	9 908 599 sq km / 3 825 710 sq miles
Most northerly point	Ostrov Rudol'fa, Russia
Most southerly point	Gavdos, Crete, Greece
Most westerly point	Bjargtangar, Iceland
Most easterly point	Mys Flissingskiy, Russia

Iceland in winter, one of Europe's largest islands.

Internet Links

NASA Visible Earth	**visibleearth.nasa.gov**
European Space Agency	**www.esa.int**
European Environment Agency	**www.eea.europa.eu**
Alpine mountaineering	**www.alpine-club.org.uk**

Europe
Countries

The predominantly temperate climate of Europe has led to it becoming the most densely populated of the continents. It is highly industrialized, and has exploited its great wealth of natural resources and agricultural land to become one of the most powerful economic regions in the world.

The current pattern of countries within Europe is a result of numerous and complicated changes throughout its history. Ethnic, religious and linguistic differences have often been the cause of conflict, particularly in the Balkan region which has a very complex ethnic pattern. Current boundaries reflect, to some extent, these divisions which continue to be a source of tension. The historic distinction between 'Eastern' and 'Western' Europe is no longer made, following the collapse of Communism and the break up of the Soviet Union in 1991.

Facts

- The European Union was founded by six countries: Belgium, France, Germany, Italy, Luxembourg, and the Netherlands. It now has 28 members
- The newest member of the European Union, Croatia, joined in 2013
- Europe has the two smallest independent countries in the world – Vatican City and Monaco
- Vatican City is an independent country entirely within the city of Rome, and is the centre of the Roman Catholic Church

Bosporus, Turkey, a narrow strait of water which separates Europe from Asia.

Europe's capitals

Largest capital (population)	Moscow, Russia	12 144 000
Smallest capital (population)	Vatican City	800
Most northerly capital	Reykjavík, Iceland	64° 39'N
Most southerly capital	Valletta, Malta	35° 54'N
Highest capital	Andorra la Vella, Andorra	1 029 metres 3 376 feet

Europe's countries

Largest country (area)	Russia	17 075 400 sq km	6 592 849 sq miles
Smallest country (area)	Vatican City	0.5 sq km	0.2 sq miles
Largest country (population)	Russia	143 457 000	
Smallest country (population)	Vatican City	800	
Most densely populated country	Monaco	19 000 per sq km	38 000 per sq mile
Least densely populated country	Iceland	3 per sq km	8 per sq mile

Internet Links

European Union	europa.eu/
UK Foreign and Commonwealth Office	www.fco.gov.uk
CIA World Factbook	www.cia.gov/library/publications/the-world-factbook/index.html

Conic Equidistant Projection

1:10 000 000
0 100 200 300 400 miles
0 100 200 300 400 500 600 km

Barents Sea
White Sea
Kola Peninsula
Lake Ladoga
Onezhskoye Ozero
Gulf of Finland
Gulf of Riga
Bothnia
FINLAND
ESTONIA
LATVIA
LITHUANIA
BELARUS
UKRAINE
MOLDOVA
ROMANIA
RUSSIA
KAZAKHSTAN
HELSINKI
TALLINN
RIGA
VILNIUS
MINSK
KIEV
CHIȘINĂU
WARSAW
MOSCOW
St Petersburg
Ural Mountains
Timanskiy Kryazh
Central Russian Upland
Caspian Sea
Sea of Azov
CRIMEA
Caspian Lowland
Volgograd
Nizhniy Novgorod
Kazan'
Samara
Perm'
Ufa
Archangel
Murmansk
Odessa
Kharkiv
Rostov-na-Donu
Astrakhan'
Saratov
Voronezh
Yaroslavl'
Vologda
Syktyvkar
Ukhta
Vorkuta
Izhevsk
Kirov
Penza
Krasnodar
Ul'yanovsk
Tol'yatti
Orenburg
Lapland
Hiiumaa
Saaremaa
Arctic Circle
← 64
↓ 55

Europe
Northern Europe

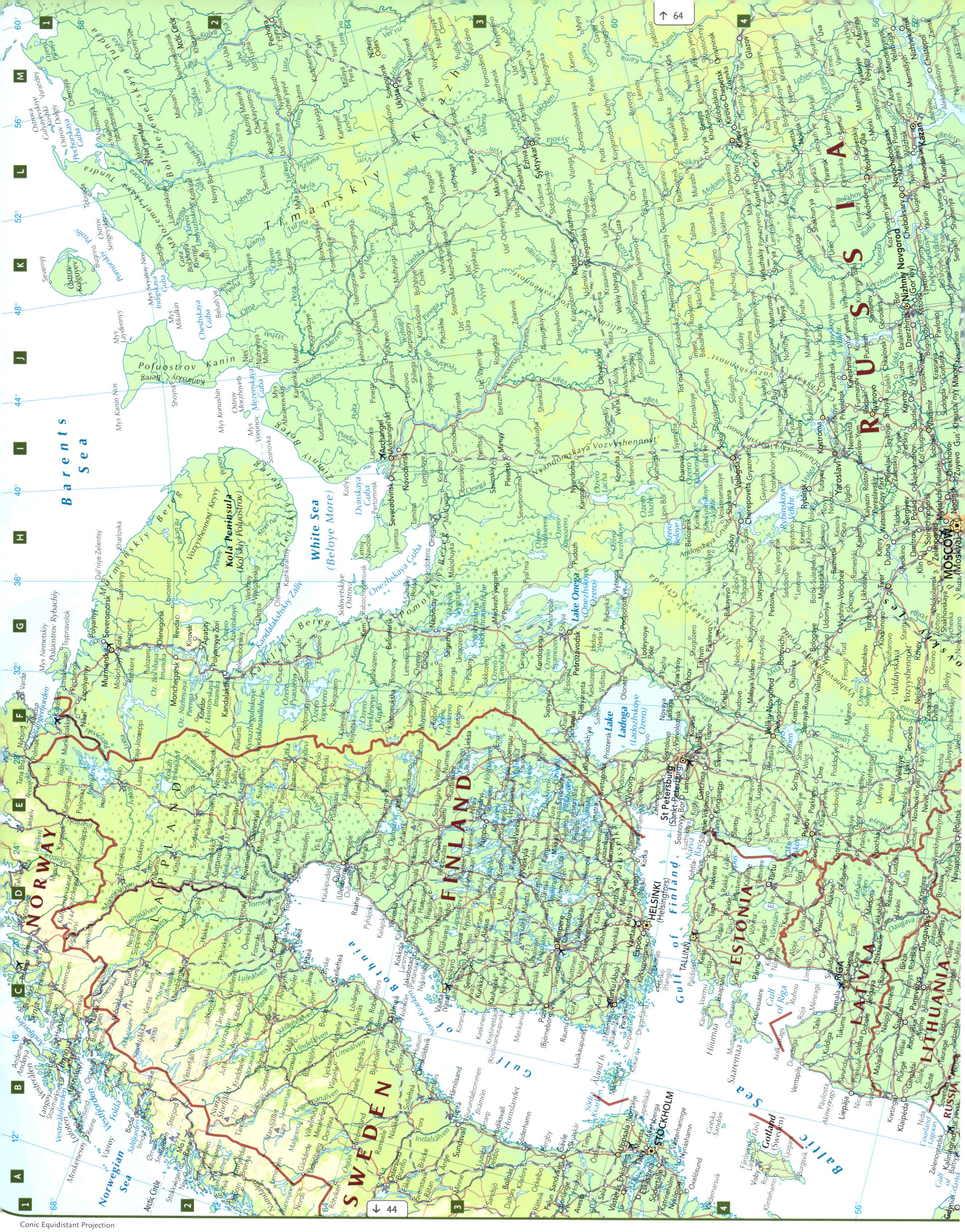

Conic Equidistant Projection

1:7 500 000

0 100 200 300 miles

0 100 200 300 400 500 km

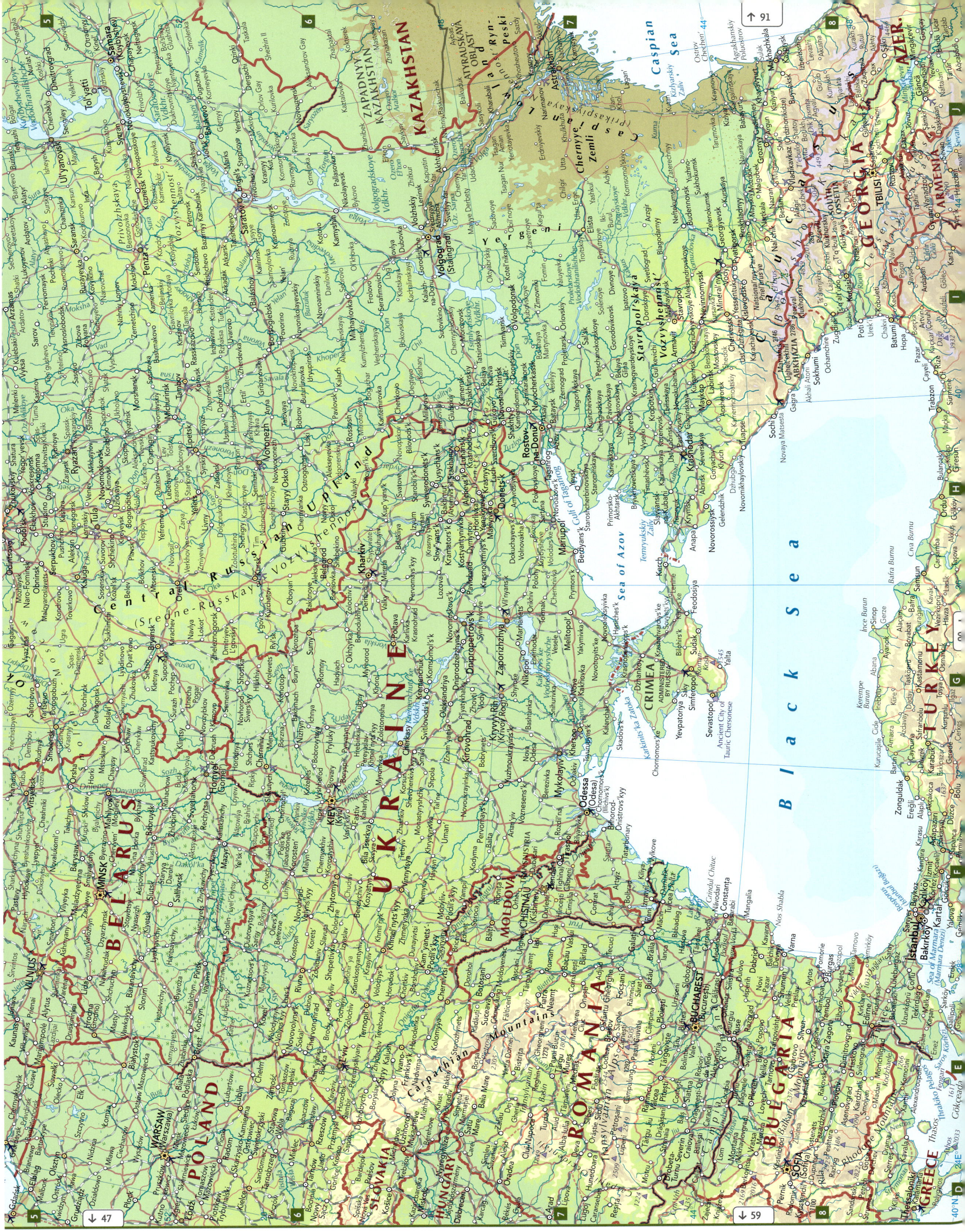
KAZAKHSTAN
ZAPADNYY KAZAKHSTAN
ATYRAUSKAYA OBLAST'
Caspian Sea
Caspian Lowland
Chernyye Zemli
Yergeni
Volgograd (Stalingrad)
Astrakhan'
Saratov
Samara (Kuybyshev)
Tol'yatti
Penza
Voronezh
Tambov
Lipetsk
Tula
Ryazan'
Central Russian Upland
Belgorod
Kharkiv
Kursk
Bryansk
Smolensk
Kaluga
Obninsk
Rostov-na-Donu
Krasnodar
Stavropol'
Stavropol'skaya Vozvyshennost'
Sochi
Novorossiysk
Sea of Azov
Black Sea
CRIMEA
Sevastopol'
Simferopol'
Yalta
Kerch
Donets'k
Luhans'k
Mariupol'
Zaporizhzhya
Dnipropetrovs'k
Kryvyy Rih
Odesa (Odessa)
Mykolayiv
Kherson
Poltava
UKRAINE
KIEV (Kyiv)
Chernihiv
Zhytomyr
Vinnytsya
L'viv
BELARUS
MINSK
Homyel'
Mahilyow
Vitsyebsk
VILNIUS
Hrodna
Brest
POLAND
WARSAW (Warszawa)
Lublin
Łódź
Białystok
Gdańsk
SLOVAKIA
HUNGARY
MOLDOVA
CHIŞINĂU (Kishinev)
ROMANIA
BUCHAREST (Bucureşti)
Carpathian Mountains
Transylvanian Alps
Constanța
BULGARIA
SOFIA (Sofiya)
Varna
Burgas
Plovdiv
Rhodope Mountains
GREECE
Thessaloniki
TURKEY
İstanbul
Sea of Marmara
Samsun
Trabzon
Sinop
Zonguldak
GEORGIA
TBILISI
ARMENIA
AZER.
ABKHAZIA
SOUTH OSSETIA
Caucasus
Batumi
Sokhumi
Groznyy
Nal'chik
Vladikavkaz
Makhachkala
Elista
Ancient City of Tauric Chersonese
ADMINISTERED BY RUSSIA

↑ 91
↓ 47
↓ 59

Europe
Western Russia

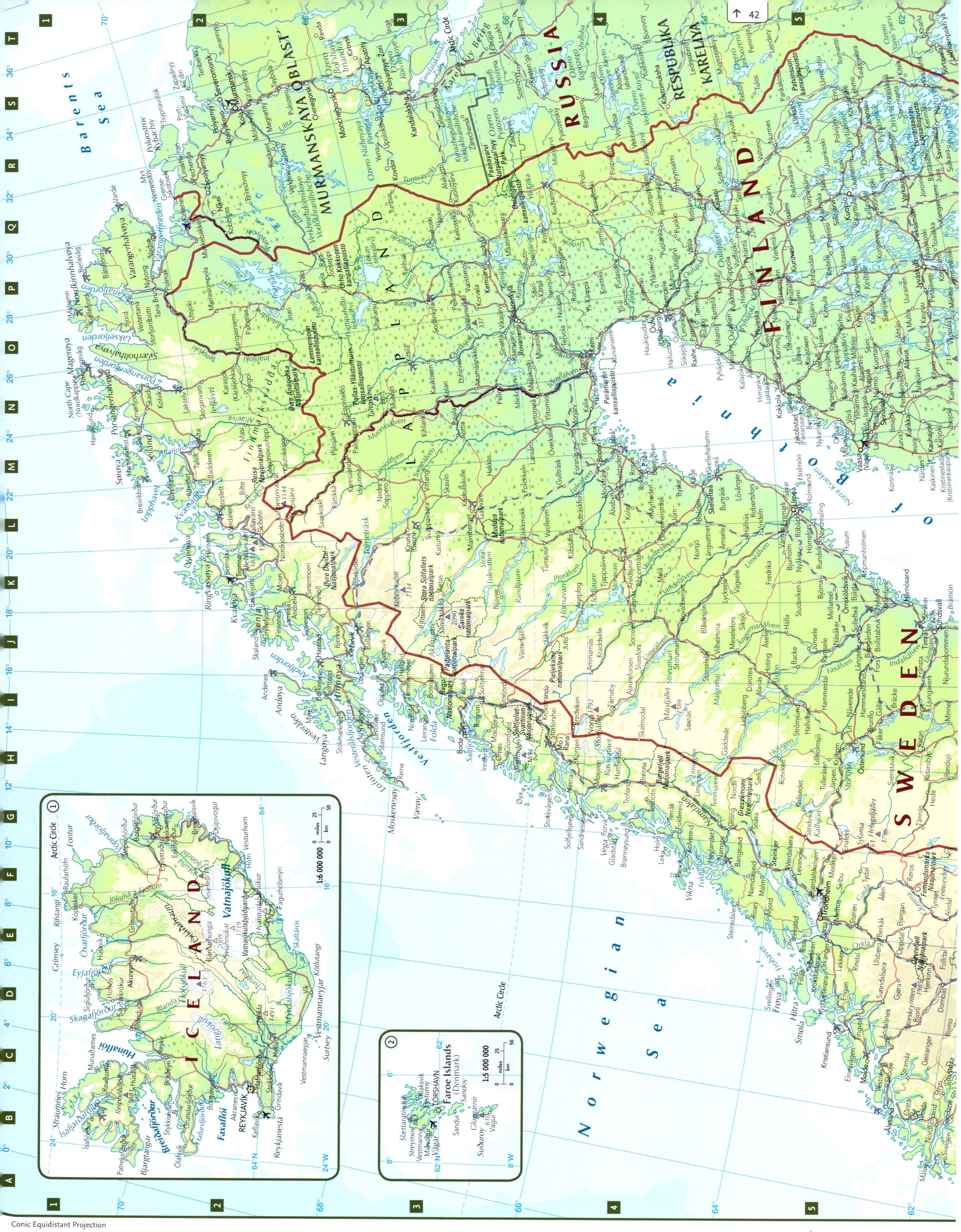

42

Conic Equidistant Projection

1:5 000 000 — 0, 50, 100, 150 miles; 0, 50, 100, 150, 200, 250 km

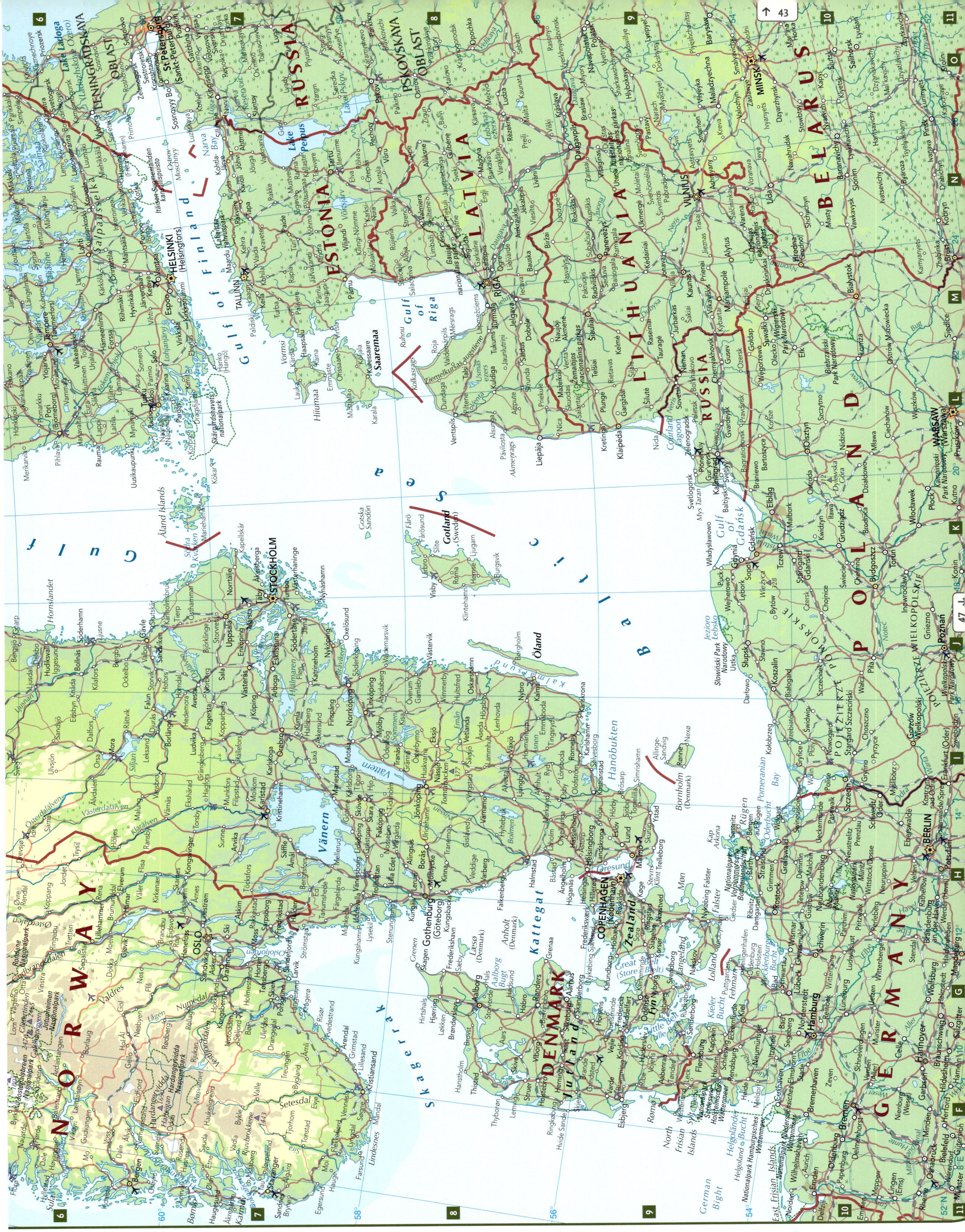
NORWAY
DENMARK
GERMANY
POLAND
LITHUANIA
LATVIA
ESTONIA
RUSSIA
BELARUS
Baltic Sea
Gulf of Finland
Gulf of Riga
Gulf of Bothnia
Skagerrak
Kattegat
OSLO
STOCKHOLM
HELSINKI (Helsingfors)
TALLINN
RIGA
VILNIUS
MINSK
WARSAW (Warszawa)
BERLIN
COPENHAGEN
St Petersburg (Sankt-Peterburg)
Gotland (Sweden)
Öland
Saaremaa
Hiiumaa
Bornholm (Denmark)
Zealand
Jutland
Åland Islands

↑ 43

47

Europe

Scandinavia and the Baltic States

Conic Equidistant Projection

1:5 000 000

0 50 100 150 miles

0 50 100 150 200 250 km

NORWAY
SWEDEN
ESTONIA
LATVIA
LITHUANIA
RUSSIA
DENMARK
POLAND
GERMANY
CZECHIA (CZECH REPUBLIC)
SLOVAKIA
AUSTRIA
HUNGARY
SWITZERLAND
LIECHTENSTEIN
ITALY
SLOVENIA
CROATIA
SERBIA
Skagerrak
Kattegat
Baltic Sea
Gulf of Riga
Gulf of Gdańsk
German Bight
Jutland
Zealand
Gotland
Öland
Bornholm (Denmark)
COPENHAGEN (København)
BERLIN
WARSAW (Warszawa)
PRAGUE (Praha)
VIENNA (Wien)
BRATISLAVA
BUDAPEST
BAVARIA
ALSACE
LORRAINE
Harz
Sudety
Erzgebirge
Böhmer Wald
Vosges
Jura
Hamburg
Munich (München)
Gothenburg (Göteborg)

45
43
58

Europe
Northwest Europe

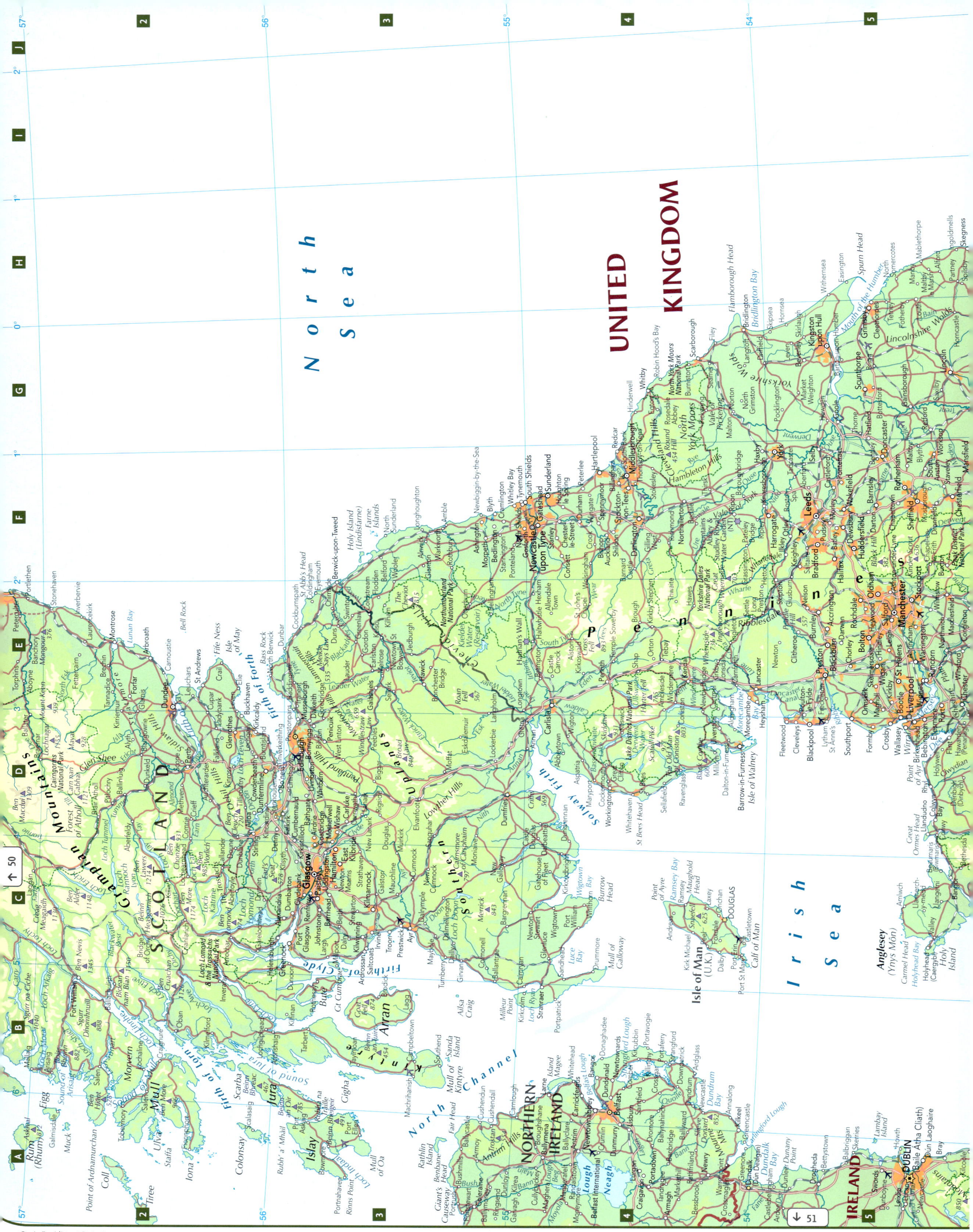
North Sea
UNITED KINGDOM
SCOTLAND
NORTHERN IRELAND
IRELAND
Irish Sea
North Channel
Firth of Clyde
Firth of Forth
Firth of Lorn
Solway Firth
Grampian Mountains
Southern Uplands
Pennines
Isle of Man (U.K.)
Anglesey (Ynys Môn)
Glasgow
Edinburgh
Newcastle upon Tyne
Leeds
Manchester
Liverpool
Belfast
DUBLIN (Baile Átha Cliath)
DOUGLAS
Conic Equidistant Projection

1:2 000 000

0	25	50	75		miles
0	25	50	75	100	125 km

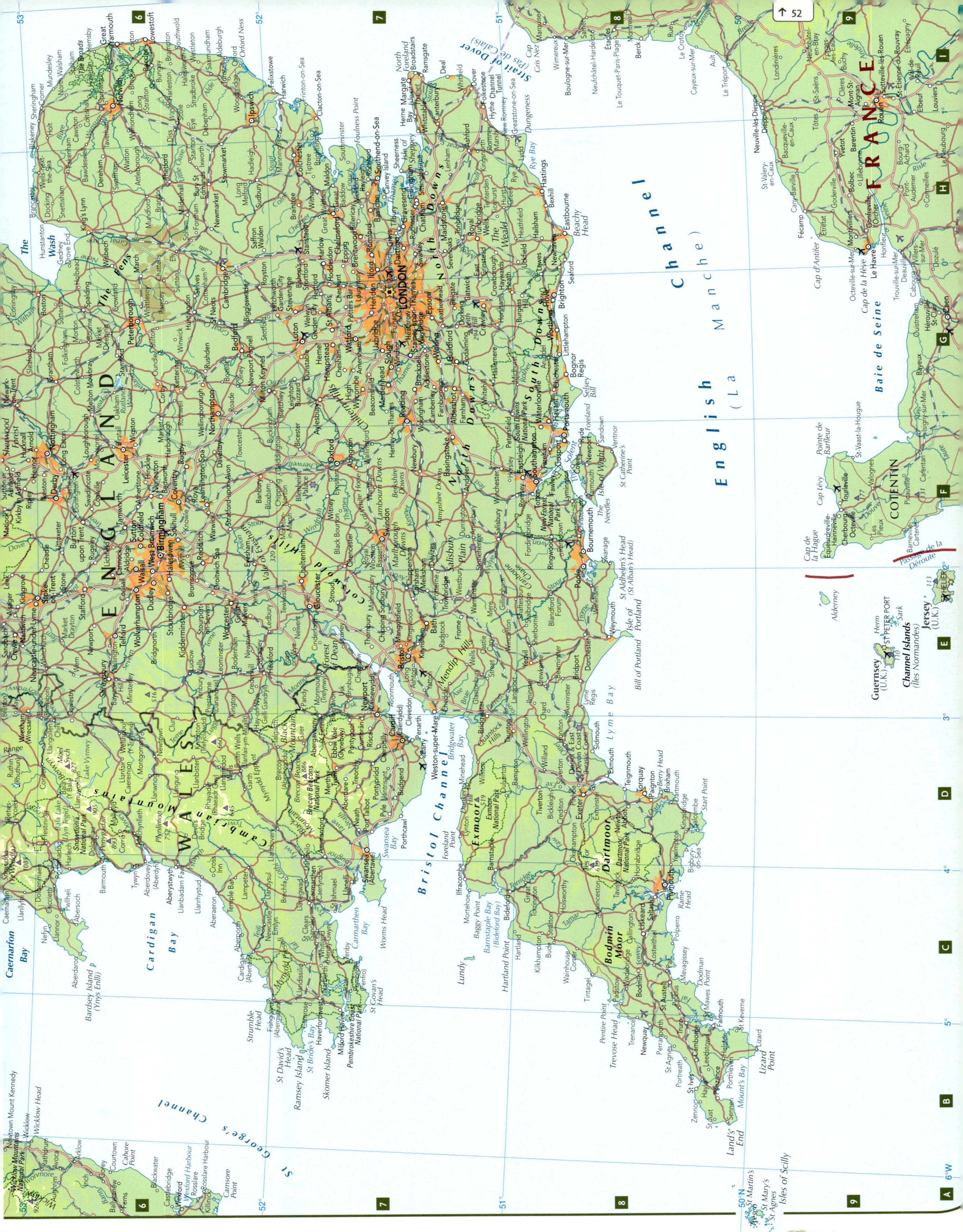
ENGLAND
WALES
FRANCE
English Channel
(La Manche)
Bristol Channel
St George's Channel
Cardigan Bay
Caernarfon Bay
Strait of Dover
(Pas de Calais)
Baie de Seine
LONDON
Birmingham
Manchester
Bristol
Cardiff
Southampton
Plymouth
Norwich
Cambridge
Oxford
Brighton
Exeter
Swansea
Ipswich
Channel Islands
(Îles Normandes)
Guernsey
(U.K.)
Jersey
(U.K.)
Alderney
Sark
Isle of Wight
Isles of Scilly
Land's End
Lizard Point
Dartmoor
Exmoor
Bodmin Moor
Cambrian Mountains
Cotswold Hills
The Wash
The Fens
COTENTIN
Le Havre
Rouen
Cherbourg
Caen
↑ 52

Europe

England and Wales

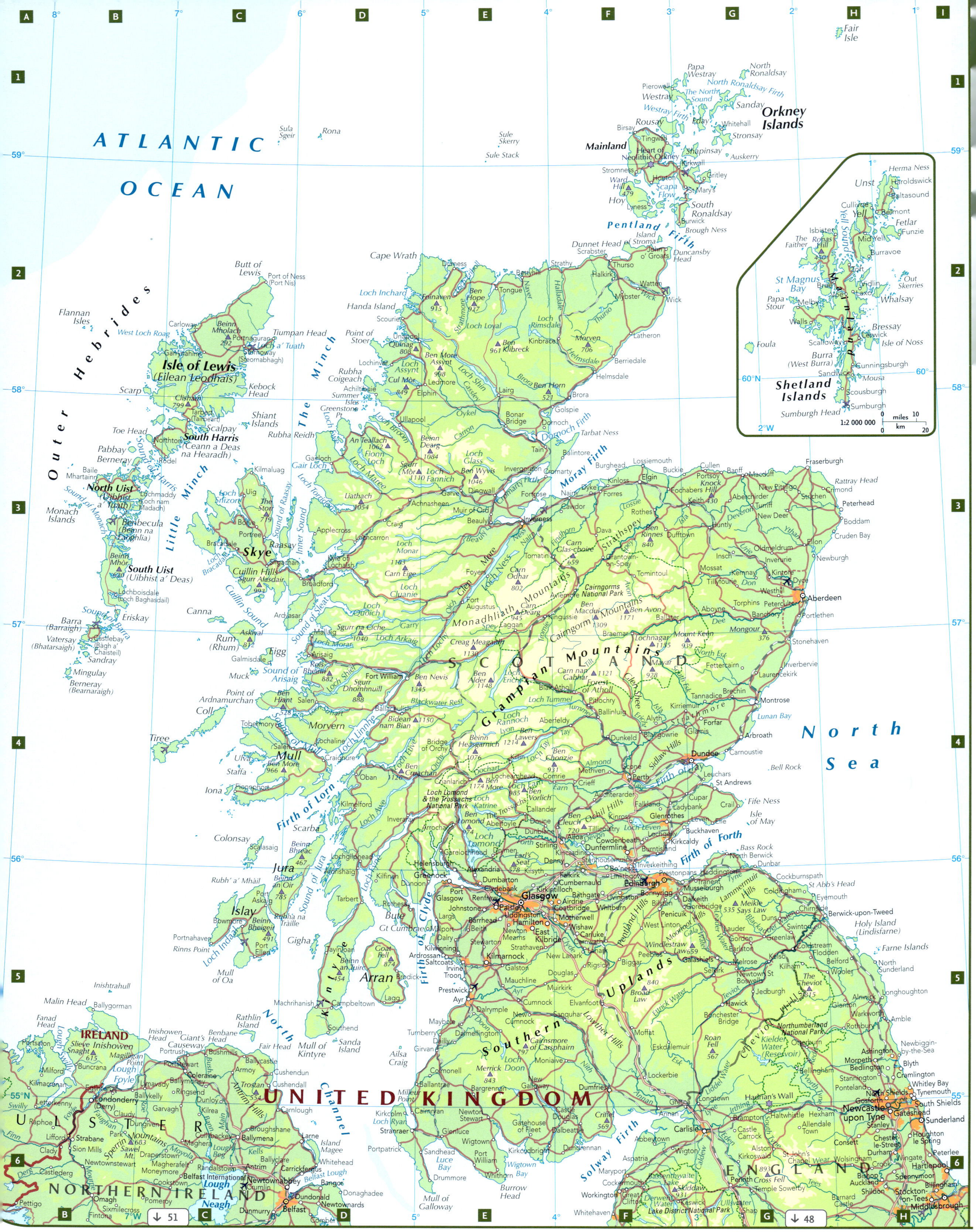

Europe
Scotland

1:2 000 000

0 25 50 75 miles
0 25 50 75 100 125 km

Conic Equidistant Projection

1:2 000 000

0 25 50 75 miles

0 25 50 75 100 125 km

Europe

Ireland

North Sea
UNITED KINGDOM
ENGLAND
NETHERLANDS
BELGIUM
LUXEMBOURG
FRANCE
West Frisian Islands
Waddenzee
IJsselmeer
Markermeer
AMSTERDAM
THE HAGUE ('s-Gravenhage) (Den Haag)
Rotterdam
Utrecht
Eindhoven
Groningen
Leeuwarden
Antwerp
Ghent (Gent)
BRUSSELS (Brussel/Bruxelles)
Liège
Namur
Charleroi
LUXEMBOURG
Lille
Amiens
Reims
Metz
Nancy
PARIS
Rouen
Norwich
Ipswich
Strait of Dover (Pas de Calais)
NORD-PAS-DE-CALAIS
PICARDY
NORMANDIE
ÎLE-DE-FRANCE
CHAMPAGNE-ARDENNE
ALSACE, CHAMPAGNE-ARDENNE ET LORRAINE
FLANDRE
ARTOIS
HAINAUT
THIÉRACHE
Ardennes
Eifel
SAARLAND
Köln
Düsseldorf
Essen
Aachen
49
Conic Equidistant Projection

1:2 000 000

0 25 50 75 miles

0 25 50 75 100 125 km

GERMANY
CZECHIA (CZECH REPUBLIC)
SCHLESWIG-HOLSTEIN
MECKLENBURG-VORPOMMERN
NIEDERSACHSEN
BRANDENBURG
SACHSEN-ANHALT
NORDRHEIN-WESTFALEN
HESSEN
THÜRINGEN
SACHSEN
RHEINLAND-PFALZ
BADEN-WÜRTTEMBERG
BAVARIA
BAYERN
HAMBURG
BREMEN
BERLIN
Hamburg
Bremen
Hannover
Magdeburg
Leipzig
Dortmund
Frankfurt am Main
Wiesbaden
Mainz
Mannheim
Nuremberg (Nürnberg)
Stuttgart
Erfurt
Braunschweig
Wolfsburg
Göttingen
Kassel
Würzburg
Regensburg
Heidelberg
Karlsruhe
Osnabrück
Oldenburg
OSTFRIESLAND
AMMERLAND
LÜNEBURGER HEIDE
ALTMARK
PRIGNITZ
UCKERMARK
ZAUCHE
Fläming
GOLDENE AUE
Thüringer Wald
Erzgebirge
Krušné hory
Fichtelgebirge
Oberpfälzer Wald
Böhmer Wald
Bayerischer Wald
Fränkische Alb
Fränkische Schweiz
Hohe Rhön
Spessart
ODENWALD
Taunus
Westerwald
Teutoburger Wald
Wiehengebirge
MÜNSTER LAND
TECKLENBURGER LAND
BERGISCHES LAND
OBERWALDER LAND
Harz
↑ 45
→ 47
↓ 56

Conic Equidistant Projection

1:10 000 000
0 100 200 300 400 miles
0 100 200 300 400 500 600 km

↑ 41
→ 86
↓ 97
Baltic Sea
RUSSIA
BELARUS
POLAND
WARSAW
MINSK
UKRAINE
KIEV
RUSSIA
MOLDOVA
CHIȘINĂU
SLOVAKIA
BRATISLAVA
VIENNA
HUNGARY
BUDAPEST
ROMANIA
BUCHAREST
CROATIA
ZAGREB
BOSNIA AND HERZEGOVINA
SARAJEVO
SERBIA
BELGRADE
MONTENEGRO
PODGORICA
KOSOVO
PRISHTINË
ALBANIA
TIRANA
MACEDONIA
SKOPJE
BULGARIA
SOFIA
GREECE
ATHENS
TURKEY
ANKARA
Istanbul
CRIMEA
ADMINISTERED BY RUSSIA
Sea of Azov
Black Sea
Aegean Sea
Ionian Sea
Mediterranean Sea
Caucasus (Bol'shoy Kavkaz)
Carpathian Mountains
Transylvanian Alps
Dinaric Alps
Balkan Mts
Rhodope Mts
Taurus Mountains
Central Russian Upland
Cyclades (Kyklades)
Dodecanese (Dodekanisa)
Ionian Islands
Crete (Kriti)
CYPRUS
NICOSIA
SYRIA
DAMASCUS
LEBANON
BEIRUT
ISRAEL
JERUSALEM
Tel Aviv-Yafo
JORDAN
'AMMAN
EGYPT
CAIRO (Al Qahirah)
Alexandria (Al Iskandariyah)
Sinai
LIBYA
Benghazi
Gulf of Sirte (Khalīj Surt)
MALTA
VALLETTA
Malta Channel
SAUDI ARABIA
Red Sea
Qattara Depression (Munkhafaḑ al Qaţţārah)
Libyan Plateau (Ad Diffah)
CZECHIA (CZECH REP.)
PRAGUE
AUSTRIA
SLOVENIA
LJUBLJANA

↑ 47
↑ 58
↑ 46

Conic Equidistant Projection

Europe
France

1:5 000 000

0 50 100 150 miles
0 50 100 150 200 250 km

Conic Equidistant Projection

1:5 000 000 — 0, 50, 100, 150 miles; 0, 50, 100, 150, 200, 250 km

Europe
Spain and Portugal

↑ 47
← 56
↓ 96

Conic Equidistant Projection

1:5 000 000 — 0 50 100 150 miles; 0 50 100 150 200 250 km

43
90
UKRAINE
MOLDOVA
CHIŞINĂU (Kishinev)
ROMANIA
BUCHAREST (Bucureşti)
BUDAPEST
SERBIA
BELGRADE (Beograd)
VOJVODINA
KOSOVO
PRISHTINE (Priština)
MONTENEGRO
PODGORICA
ALBANIA
TIRANA (Tiranë)
MACEDONIA (F.Y.R.O.M.)
SKOPJE
BULGARIA
SOFIA (Sofiya)
GREECE
ATHENS (Athina)
TURKEY
İstanbul
İzmir (Smyrna)
Bursa
Antalya
Odessa (Odesa)
CRIMEA
ADMINISTERED BY RUSSIA
Black Sea
Aegean Sea
Ionian Islands
Sea
Sea of Marmara (Marmara Denizi)
Mirtoo Pelagos
Kritiko Pelagos
Thrakiko Pelagos
Cyclades (Kyklades)
Dodecanese (Dodekanisa)
Peloponnese
Crete (Kriti)
Rhodes (Rodos)
Lesbos (Lesvos)
Chios
Evvoia
Corfu (Kerkyra)
Cephalonia (Kefallonia)
Zakynthos (Zante)
Lefkada
Carpathian Mountains
Transylvanian Alps
Balkan Mountains
Rhodope Mountains
Pindus Mountains
Danube
Thessaloniki
Varna
Burgas
Constanţa
Cluj-Napoca
Timişoara
Plovdiv
Niš
Patras
Larisa
Ioannina

Asia
Landscapes

Asia is the world's largest continent and occupies almost one-third of the world's total land area. Stretching across approximately 165° of longitude from the Mediterranean Sea to the easternmost point of the Russian Federation on the Bering Strait, it contains the world's highest and lowest points and some of the world's greatest physical features. Its mountain ranges include the Himalaya, Hindu Kush, Karakoram and the Ural Mountains and its major rivers – including the Yangtze, Tigris-Euphrates, Indus, Ganges and Mekong – are equally well-known and evocative.

Asia's deserts include the Gobi, the Taklimakan, and those on the Arabian Peninsula, and significant areas of volcanic and tectonic activity are present on the Kamchatka Peninsula, in Japan, and on Indonesia's numerous islands. The continent's landscapes are greatly influenced by climatic variations, with great contrasts between the islands of the Arctic Ocean and the vast Siberian plains in the north, and the tropical islands of Indonesia.

The **Yangtze,** China, Asia's longest river, flowing into the East China Sea near Shanghai.

Internet Links

NASA Visible Earth	**visibleearth.nasa.gov**
NASA Earth Observatory	**earthobservatory.nasa.gov**
Peakware World Mountain Encyclopedia	**www.peakware.com**
Mountaineering	**www.alpine-club.org.uk**

Asia's physical features

Highest mountain	Mt Everest, China/Nepal	8 848 metres	29 028 feet
Longest river	Yangtze, China	6 380 km	3 965 miles
Largest lake	Caspian Sea	371 000 sq km	143 243 sq miles
Largest island	Borneo	745 561 sq km	287 861 sq miles
Largest drainage basin	Ob'-Irtysh, Kazakhstan/Russia	2 990 000 sq km	1 154 439 sq miles
Lowest point	Dead Sea, Israel/Jordan	-428 metres	-1 404 feet

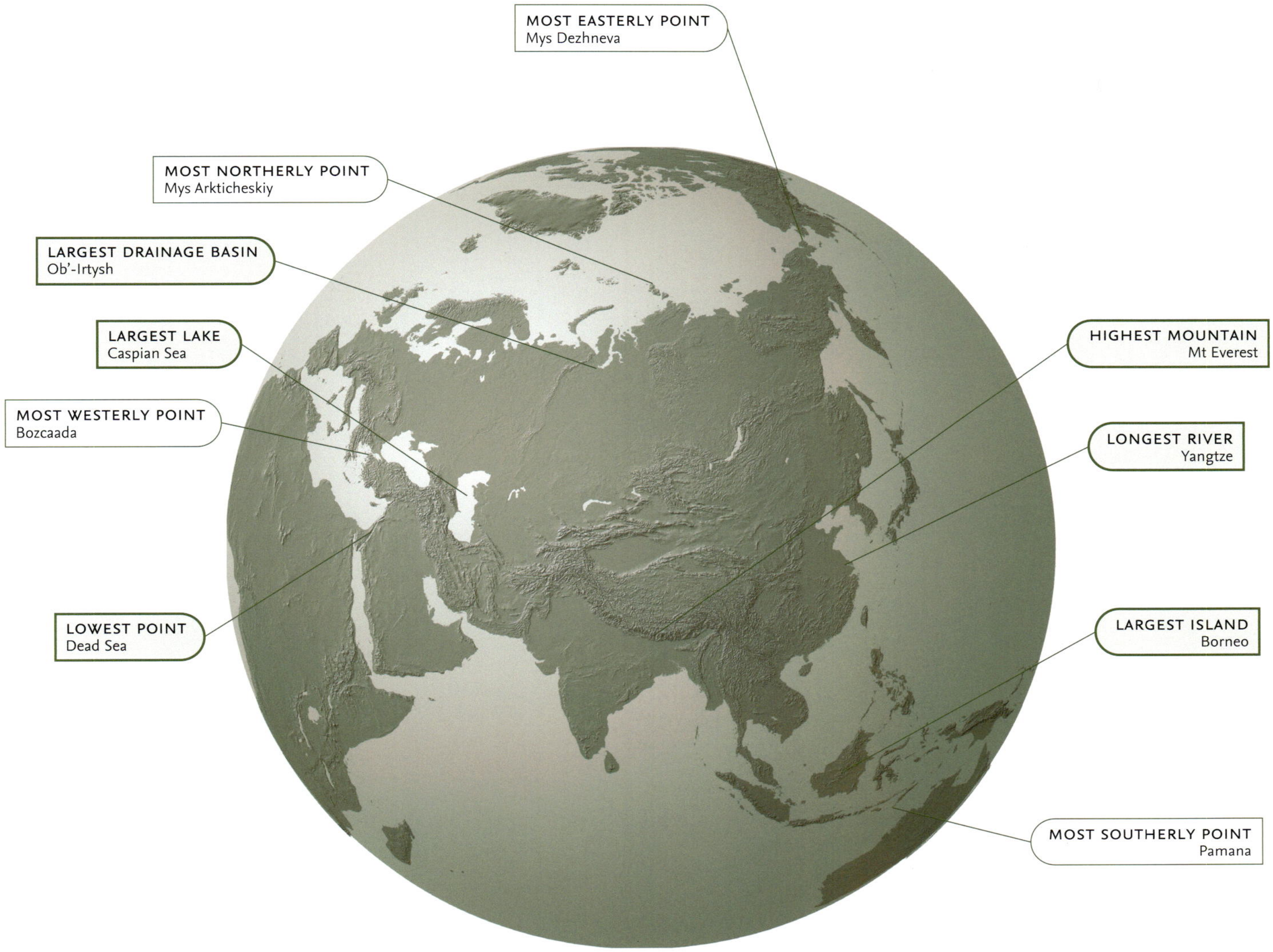

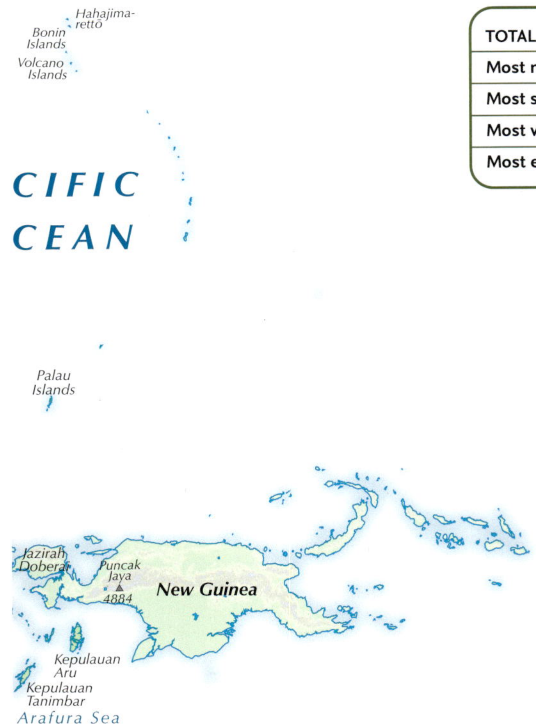

Asia's extent

TOTAL LAND AREA	45 036 492 sq km / 17 388 686 sq miles
Most northerly point	Mys Arkticheskiy, Russia
Most southerly point	Pamana, Indonesia
Most westerly point	Bozcaada, Turkey
Most easterly point	Mys Dezhneva, Russia

Facts

- **90 of the world's 100 highest mountains are in Asia**
- **The Indonesian archipelago is made up of over 13 500 islands**
- **The height of the land in Nepal ranges from 60 metres to 8 848 metres**
- **The deepest lake in the world is Lake Baikal, Russia, with a maximum depth of 1 642 metres**

Caspian Sea, Europe/Asia, the world's largest expanse of inland water.

With approximately sixty per cent of the world's population, Asia is home to numerous cultures, people groups and lifestyles. Several of the world's earliest civilizations were established in Asia, including those of Sumeria, Babylonia and Assyria. Cultural and historical differences have led to a complex political pattern, and the continent has been, and continues to be, subject to numerous territorial and political conflicts – including the current disputes in the Middle East and in Jammu and Kashmir.

Separate regions within Asia can be defined by the cultural, economic and political systems they support. The major regions are: the arid, oil-rich, mainly Islamic southwest; southern Asia with its distinct cultures, isolated from the rest of Asia by major mountain ranges; the Indian- and Chinese-influenced monsoon region of southeast Asia; the mainly Chinese-influenced industrialized areas of eastern Asia; and Soviet Asia, made up of most of the former Soviet Union.

Timor island in southeast Asia, on which East Timor, Asia's newest independent state, is located.

Internet Links

UK Foreign and Commonwealth Office	www.fco.gov.uk
CIA World Factbook	www.cia.gov/library/publicaions/the-world-factbook/index.html
Asian Development Bank	www.adb.org
Association of Southeast Asian Nations (ASEAN)	www.asean.org
Asia-Pacific Economic Cooperation	www.apec.org

Asia's countries

Largest country (area)	Russia	17 075 400 sq km	6 592 849 sq miles
Smallest country (area)	Maldives	298 sq km	115 sq miles
Largest country (population)	China	1 383 925 000	
Smallest country (population)	Palau	21 000	
Most densely populated country	Singapore	8 469 per sq km	21 911 per sq mile
Least densely populated country	Mongolia	2 per sq km	5 per sq mile

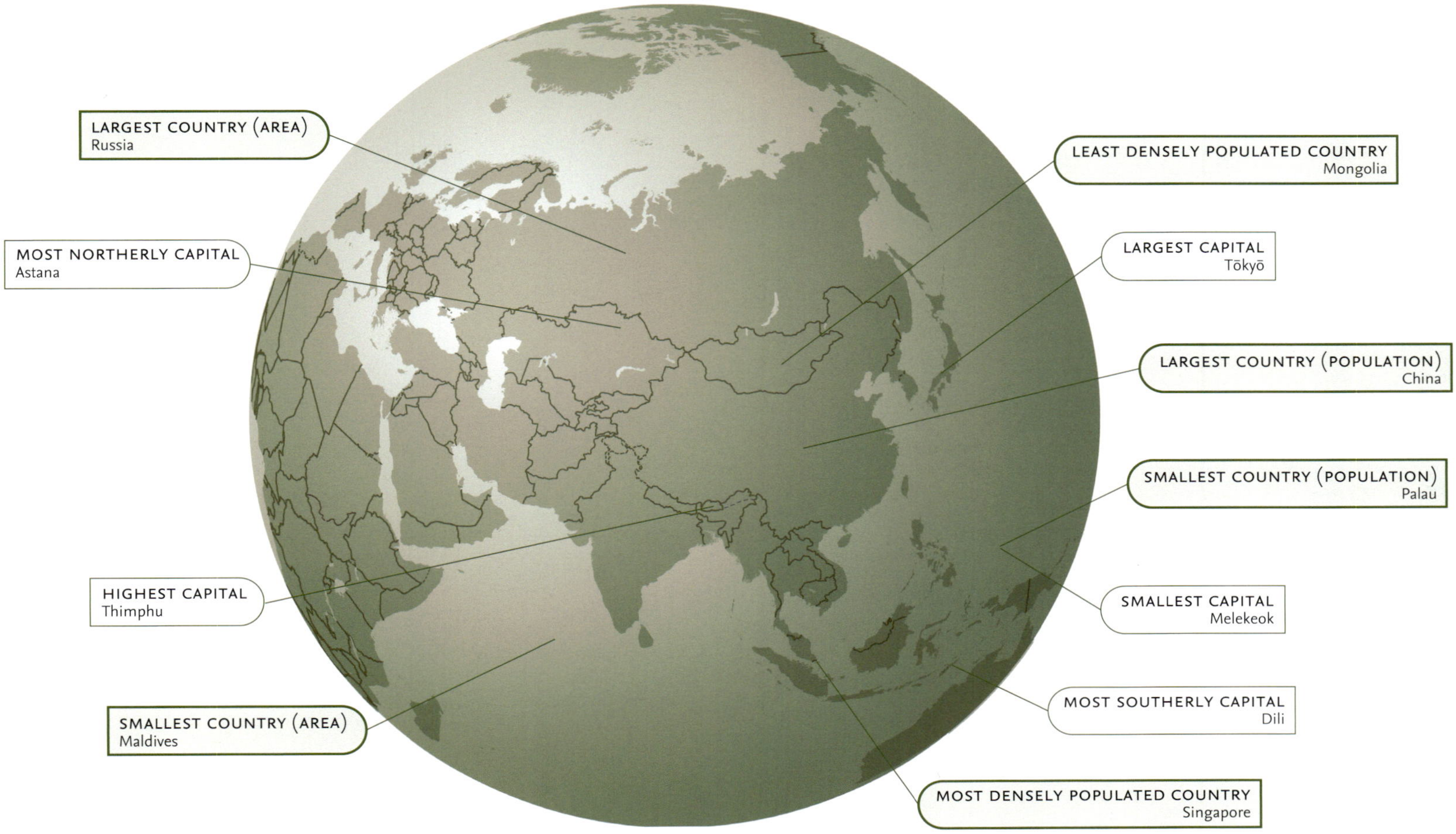

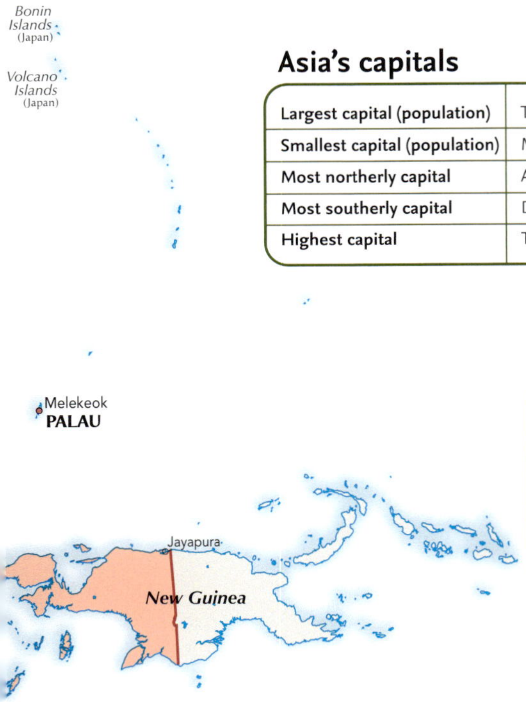

Asia's capitals

Largest capital (population)	Tōkyō, Japan	38 197 000	
Smallest capital (population)	Melekeok, Palau	391	
Most northerly capital	Astana, Kazakhstan	51° 10'N	
Most southerly capital	Dili, East Timor	8° 35'S	
Highest capital	Thimphu, Bhutan	2 423 metres	7 949 feet

Facts

- Over 60% of the world's population live in Asia
- Asia has 11 of the world's 20 largest cities
- The Korean peninsula was divided into North Korea and South Korea in 1948 approximately along the 38th parallel

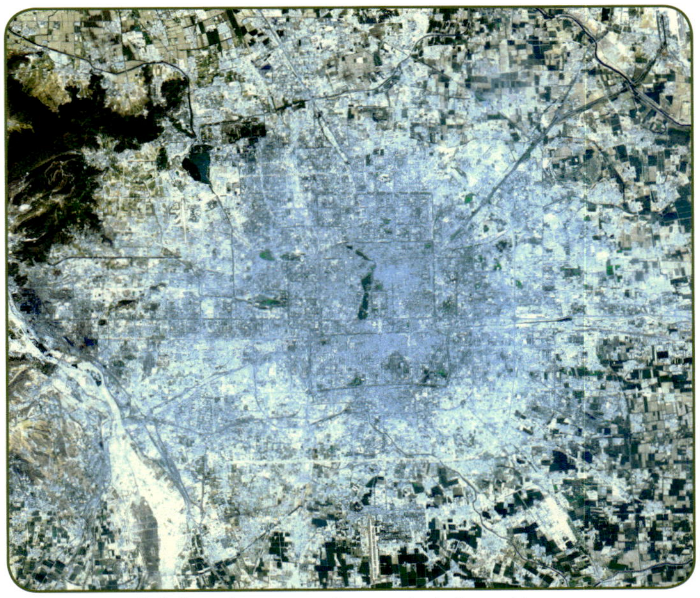

Beijing, capital of China, the most populous country in the world.

Conic Equidistant Projection

1:20 000 000

miles 0 200 400 600

km 0 200 400 600 800 1000

OCEAN
Severnaya Zemlya
East Siberian Sea
(Vostochno-Sibirskoye More)
New Siberia Islands
(Novosibirskiye Ostrova)
Laptev Sea
(More Laptevykh)
Chukchi Sea
Wrangel Island
Bering Sea
Bering Strait
Arctic Circle
U.S.A.
Aleutian Islands
Central Siberian Plateau
(Sredne Sibirskoye Ploskogor'ye)
SIBERIA
Khrebet Cherskogo
Kolymskoye Nagor'ye
Verkhoyanskiy Khrebet
Stanovoy Khrebet
Sea of Okhotsk
(Okhotskoye More)
Kamchatka Peninsula
(Poluostrov Kamchatka)
Petropavlovsk-Kamchatskiy
Magadan
Yakutsk
Lena
Sakhalin
Kuril Islands
(Kuril'skiye Ostrova)
ADMINISTERED BY RUSSIA, CLAIMED BY JAPAN
La Pérouse Strait
PACIFIC OCEAN
Hokkaido
Sapporo
JAPAN
Sea of Japan
(East Sea)
TOKYO
Yokohama
Nagoya
Kyoto
Osaka
Kobe
Hiroshima
Fukuoka
Sendai
Khabarovsk
Vladivostok
Irkutsk
Lake Baikal
Ulan-Ude
Chita
ULAN BATOR
(Ulaanbaatar)
MONGOLIA
Gobi Desert
CHINA
INNER MONGOLIA
BEIJING
(Peking)
Tianjin
Harbin
Changchun
Shenyang
Dalian
Bo Hai
Yellow Sea
(Huang Hai)
NORTH KOREA
P'YONGYANG
SOUTH KOREA
SEOUL
Busan
Da Hinggan Ling
Xiao Hinggan Ling
Sikhote-Alin'
Vostochnyy Sayan
↑ 118
↓ 66

Albers Conic Equal Area Projection

1:20 000 000

0 200 400 600 miles

0 200 400 600 800 1000 km

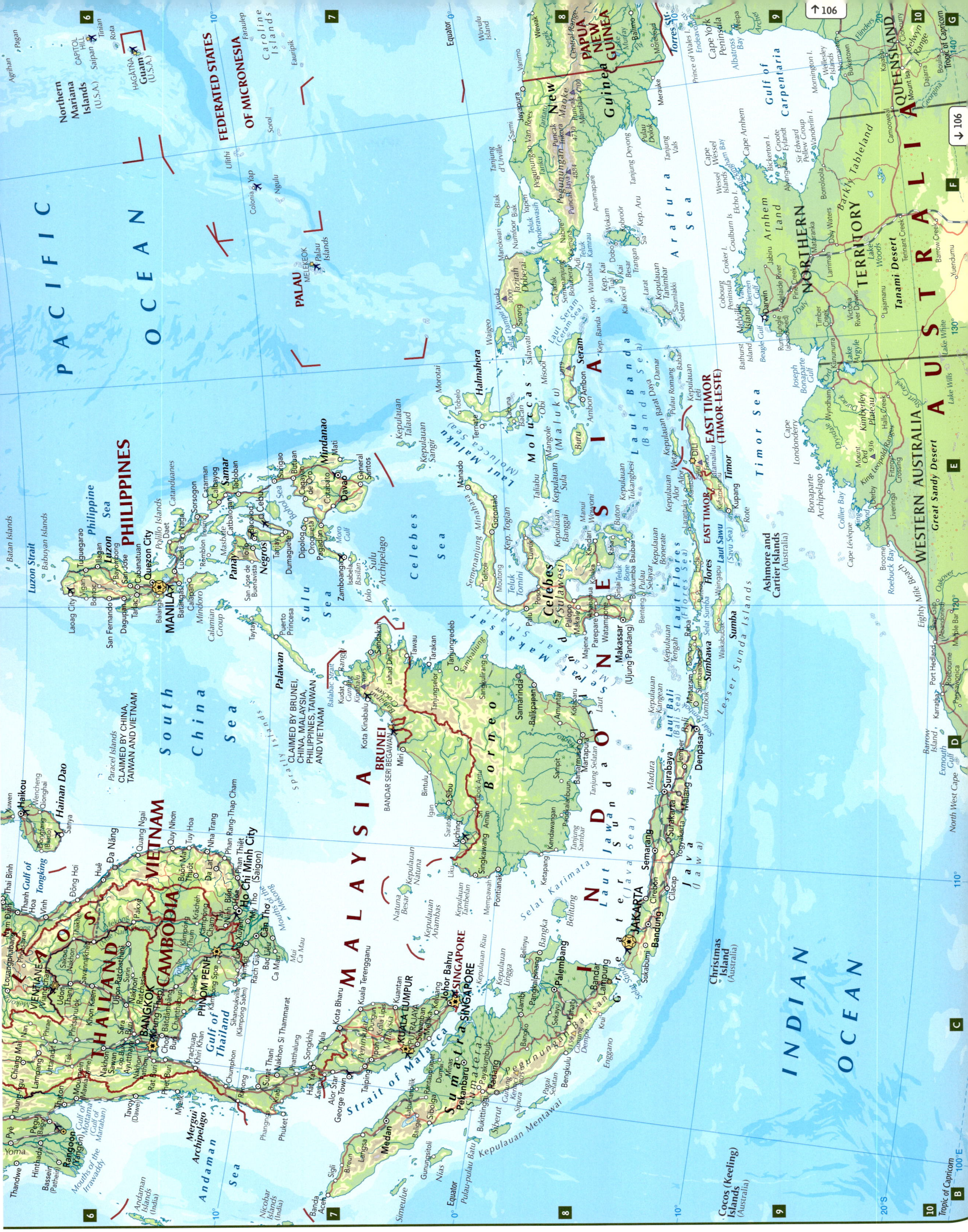
PACIFIC OCEAN
PHILIPPINES
MANILA
Philippine Sea
South China Sea
VIETNAM
THAILAND
BANGKOK
CAMBODIA
PHNOM PENH
LAOS
VIENTIANE
Gulf of Thailand
Gulf of Tongking
Hainan Dao
MALAYSIA
KUALA LUMPUR
SINGAPORE
BRUNEI
BANDAR SERI BEGAWAN
Borneo
Sumatera
Java Sea
JAKARTA
INDONESIA
Celebes Sea
Celebes (Sulawesi)
Sulu Sea
Banda Sea
Arafura Sea
Timor Sea
EAST TIMOR (TIMOR-LESTE)
DILI
PAPUA NEW GUINEA
New Guinea
PALAU
FEDERATED STATES OF MICRONESIA
Northern Mariana Islands (U.S.A.)
Guam (U.S.A.)
INDIAN OCEAN
Andaman Sea
Strait of Malacca
AUSTRALIA
WESTERN AUSTRALIA
NORTHERN TERRITORY
QUEENSLAND
Gulf of Carpentaria
Christmas Island (Australia)
Cocos (Keeling) Islands (Australia)
Ashmore and Cartier Islands (Australia)
Equator
Tropic of Capricorn
↑ 106
↓ 106

Mercator Projection

1:15 000 000

0 200 400 miles

0 200 400 600 800 km

PACIFIC OCEAN
PHILIPPINES
TAIWAN
The People's Republic of China claims Taiwan as its 23rd province
TAIPEI (Taipei)
Keelung (Jilong)
Hsinchu (Xinzhu)
Fengyuan
Hualien (Hualian)
Changhua
Chiayi (Jiayi)
Tainan
T'aitung (Táidong)
Kaohsiung (Gaoxiong)
Lan Yu
Bashi Channel
Ryukyu Islands (Nansei-shotō) (Japan)
Sakishima-shotō
Ishigaki
Yaeyama-rettō
Okino-Daitō-jima
Kita-Iō-jima
Volcano Islands (Kazan-rettō) (Japan)
Minami-Iō-jima
Tropic of Cancer
Okino-Tori-shima (Japan)
Farallon de Pajaros (Uracas)
Maug Islands
Asuncion
Agrihan
Pagan
Alamagan
Guguan
Sarigan
Anatahan
Farallon de Medinilla
Northern Mariana Islands (U.S.A.)
CAPITOL HILL
Saipan
Tinian
Aguijan
Rota
HAGÅTÑA
Guam (U.S.A.)
Itbayat
Batan Islands
Batan
Luzon Strait
Babuyan
Calayan
Babuyan Islands
Fuga
Babuyan Channel
Laoag City
Vigan
Bangued
Tuguegarao
Ilagan
Bontoc
San Fernando
Santiago
Bayombong
Baguio
Dagupan
Baler
San Jose
Cabanatuan
Tarlac
Olongapo
Quezon City
MANILA
Luzon
Philippine Sea
Polillo Islands
Balanga
Nasugbu
San Pablo
Batangas
Lucena
Calapan
Daet
Naga
Catanduanes
Virac
Legazpi
Sorsogon
Iriga
Irosin
Mindoro
Mamburao
Roxas
Sibuyan Sea
Romblon
Masbate
Calbayog
Catbalogan
Samar
Tacloban
Leyte
Ormoc
Panay
Roxas
Iloilo
Bacolod
Negros
Cebu
Bohol
Bohol Sea
Surigao
Dinagat
Siargao
Tandag
Butuan
Cagayan de Oro
Iligan
Ozamis
Dipolog
Oroquieta
Malaybalay
Bislig
Mindanao
Davao
Mati
Pagadian
Cotabato
Zamboanga
Moro Gulf
Isabela
Basilan
Jolo
Sulu Archipelago
Digos
General Santos
Malita
Cape San Agustin
Sarangani Islands
Dumaguete
Tanjay
Cauayan
Dumaran
Cuyo Islands
Culion
Mindoro Strait
Sea
Kepulauan Nanusa
Karakelong
Kepulauan Talaud
Salibabu
Niampak
Kaburuang
Tahuna
Sangir
Siau
Kepulauan Sangir
Tahulandang
Celebes Sea
Manado
Bitung
Tondano
Kotamobagu
Gorontalo
Semenanjung Minahasa
Tolitoli
Taman Nasional Bogani Nani Wartabone
Moutong
Marisa
Teluk Tomini
Kepulauan Togian
Togian
Ampana
Batudaka
Luwuk
Poso
Kolonedale
Kepulauan Banggai
Banggai
Taliabu
Kepulauan Sula
Mangole
Celebes (Sulawesi)
Palopo
Kolaka
Kendari
Wawonii
Buton
Raha
Muna
Bone
Watampone
Sinjai
Bulukumba
Baubau
Wangiwangi
Kepulauan Tukangbesi
Benteng
Pulau Selayar
Laut Flores (Flores Sea)
Kep. Bonerate
Tanjung Kapondai
Komba
Kalabahi
Kepulauan Alor
Alor
Wetar
Flores
Lomblen
Solor
Ende
Ruteng
Sumba
Waingapu
Laut Sawu (Savu Sea)
Savu
Raijua
Rote
Kupang
Timor
Soe
Kefamenanu
Atambua
DILI
Foho Tatamailau
EAST TIMOR
EAST TIMOR (TIMOR-LESTE)
Tutuala
Selat Wetar
Kepulauan Leti
Kepulauan Barat Daya
Damar
Pulau Romang
Moa
Kepulauan Babar
Babar
Sermata
Selaru
Yamdena
Kepulauan Tanimbar
Larat
Molu
Timor Sea
Ashmore and Cartier Islands (Australia)
Morotai
Daruba
Tanjung Sopi
Tanjung Lelai
Tobelo
Akelamo
Halmahera
Ternate
Laut Maluku (Molucca Sea)
Gebe
Laut Halmahera (Halmahera Sea)
Waigeo
Selat Dampir
Sorong
Salawati
Kep. Raja Ampat
Misoöl
Tg Libobo
Labuha
Bacan
Obi
Moluccas (Maluku)
Fogi
Buru
Ambelau
Ambon
Seram
Laut Seram (Ceram Sea)
Wahai
Manusela
Kep. Pisang
Tg Winsop
Fakfak
Semenanjung
Bomberai
Kaimana
Teluk Kamrau
Nusawulan
Kepulauan Gorong
Kepulauan Watubela
Kepulauan Banda
Kepulauan Lucipara
Laut Banda (Banda Sea)
Kepulauan Tayandu
Kai Besar
Kai Kecil
Tual
Kepulauan Kai
Dobo
Benjina
Kola
Wokam
Kobroör
Trangan
Kepulauan Aru
Workai
Arafura Sea
Jazirah Doberai
Manokwari
Sajam
Kwoka
Kairoini
Numfoor
Supiori
Biak
Yapen
Serui
Rumberpon
Maswaar
Taman Nasional Teluk Cenderawasih
Nabire
Teluk Cenderawasih
Tembagapura
Amamapare
Pegunungan Maoke
Puncak Jaya
Tanjung d'Urville
Teba
Sarmi
Ansudu
Demta
Jayapura
Pegunungan Van Rees
Taman Nasional Lorentz
Mulia
Puncak Trikora
Puncak Mandala
Puncak Yamin
Agats
New Guinea
Tanjung Deyong
Pembre
Yomuka
Pulau Dolok
Komoran
Tanjung Vals
Merauke
Mombum
Kumbe
Vanimo
Sissano
Bewani
Lumi
Aitape
Amanab
Green River
Ambunti
Wewak
Maprik
Pagwi
Watam
Sepik
Schouten Islands
Bismarck Sea
Manam I.
Karkar Island
Madang
Mount Kanangio
Central Ra.
Kobiago
Lake Kopiago
Tari
Wabag
Mount Hagen
Mendi
Mount Wilhelm
Goroka
Bismarck Ra.
Kratke Ra.
PAPUA NEW GUINEA
Lake Murray
Komako
Kikori
Baimuru
Kerema
Balimo
Gulf of Papua
Kiwai Island
Daru
Tais
Sibidiri
Morehead
Weam
Bula
Boigu I.
Torres Strait
Badu Island
Moa Island
Prince of Wales Island
Endeavour Strait
Cape York
Jardine River National Park
Great Barrier Reef Marine Park (Far North Section)
Cape Grenville
Mapoon
Bramwell
Ashmore Reefs
PORT MORESBY
Kwikila
Hood Point
Abau
Bereina
Hisiu
Kokoda
Mount Victoria
Popondetta
Cape Nelson
Owen Stanley Ra.
Morobe
Cape Ward Hunt
Bulolo
Wau
Lae
Finschhafen
Kandrian
New Britain
Walingai
Wasum
Anepmete
Umboi
Long I.
Dampier Str.
Nukuhu
Witu Islands
Bismarck Sea
Admiralty Islands
Manus Island
Kabuli
Lorengau
Rambutyo Island
St Matthias Group
Tabalo
Mussau Island
Bismarck Archipelago
Ninigo Group
Aua Island
Wuvulu Island
Hermit Islands
Pelleluhu Is
Ngeruangel
PALAU
MELEKEOK
Koror
Eil Malk
Angaur
Palau Islands
Sonsorol Islands
Pulo Anna
Merir
Tobi
Helen
Helen Reef
Colonia
Yap
Ngulu
Ulithi
Fais
Sorol
FEDERATED STATES OF MICRONESIA
Gaferut
Faraulep
West Fayu
Pikelot
Namonuito
Olimarao
Lamotrek
Elato
Satawal
Puluwat
Pulap
Pulusuk
Woleai
Ifalik
Eauripik
Caroline Islands
Equator
Garig Gunak Barlu National Park
Cape Van Diemen
Milikapiti
Dundas Str.
Melville I.
Bathurst Island
Mitchell Point
Croker Island
Cobourg Peninsula
Goulburn Is
Maningrida
Elcho I.
Wessel Islands
Cape Wessel
AUSTRALIA
↓ 110
→ 106
125°
130°
135°
140°
145°
25°
20°
15°
10°
5°
0°
G
H
I
J
K
L
1
2
3
4
5
6
7
8
9

Asia

Southeast Asia

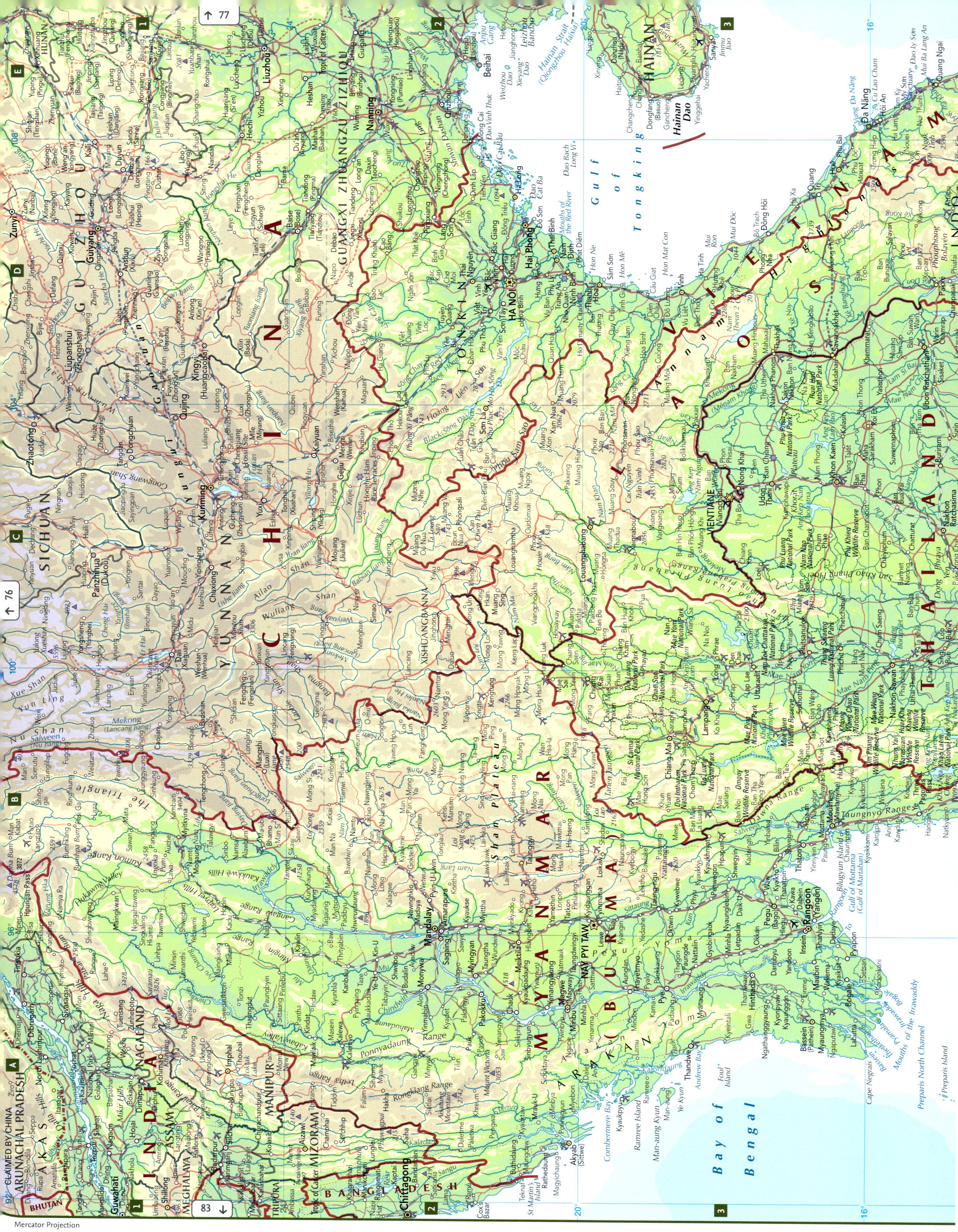

↑ 77
↑ 76
83 ↓

Mercator Projection

1:7 000 000

0 100 200 miles
0 100 200 300 400 km

CAMBODIA
CHINA
MALAYSIA
SINGAPORE
INDONESIA
Gulf of Thailand
South China Sea
Andaman Sea
Strait of Malacca
INDIAN OCEAN
Mergui Archipelago
Andaman Islands (India)
Nicobar Islands (India)
Peninsular Malaysia
Borneo
BANGKOK (Krung Thep)
PHNOM PENH
Ho Chi Minh City (Saigon)
KUALA LUMPUR
Medan
Bight of Bangkok
Mouths of the Mekong

↑ 64
← 80
↓ 68

Albers Conic Equal Area Projection

1:15 000 000

0 200 400 miles

0 200 400 600 800 km

↑ 65
↓ 81
MONGOLIA
NEI MONGOL ZIZHIQU (INNER MONGOLIA)
HEILONGJIANG
JILIN
LIAONING
NORTH KOREA
SOUTH KOREA
JAPAN
TAIWAN
PHILIPPINES
HEBEI
SHANXI
SHANDONG
SHAANXI
HENAN
JIANGSU
ANHUI
HUBEI
HUNAN
JIANGXI
ZHEJIANG
FUJIAN
GUANGDONG
GUANGXI ZHUANGZU ZIZHIQU
BEIJING
TIANJIN
SHANGHAI
P'YŎNGYANG
SEOUL
TŌKYŌ
TAIPEI
Harbin
Changchun
Shenyang
Dalian
Qingdao
Nanjing
Wuhan
Hangzhou
Guangzhou
Hong Kong (Xianggang)
Shenzhen (Bao'an)
Vladivostok
Khabarovsk
Sapporo
Sendai
Nagoya
Ōsaka
Hiroshima
Fukuoka
Busan (Pusan)
Hokkaidō
Honshū
Shikoku
Kyūshū
Sakhalin
Hainan Dao
Sea of Okhotsk (Okhotskoye More)
Sea of Japan (East Sea)
Yellow Sea (Huang Hai)
Bo Hai
East China Sea (Dong Hai)
South China Sea
PACIFIC OCEAN
Ryukyu Islands (Nansei-shotō) (Japan)
Kuril Islands (Kuril'skiye Ostrova)
ADMINISTERED BY RUSSIA, CLAIMED BY JAPAN
The People's Republic of China claims Taiwan as its 23rd province
MILITARY DEMARCATION LINE 1953
Tropic of Cancer
Bonin Islands (Ogasawara-shotō) (Japan)
Volcano Islands (Kazan-rettō) (Japan)
Luzon Strait
Bashi Channel
Taiwan Strait
Korea Strait
La Pérouse Strait

Conic Equidistant Projection

1:7 000 000

0 100 200 miles

0 100 200 300 400 km

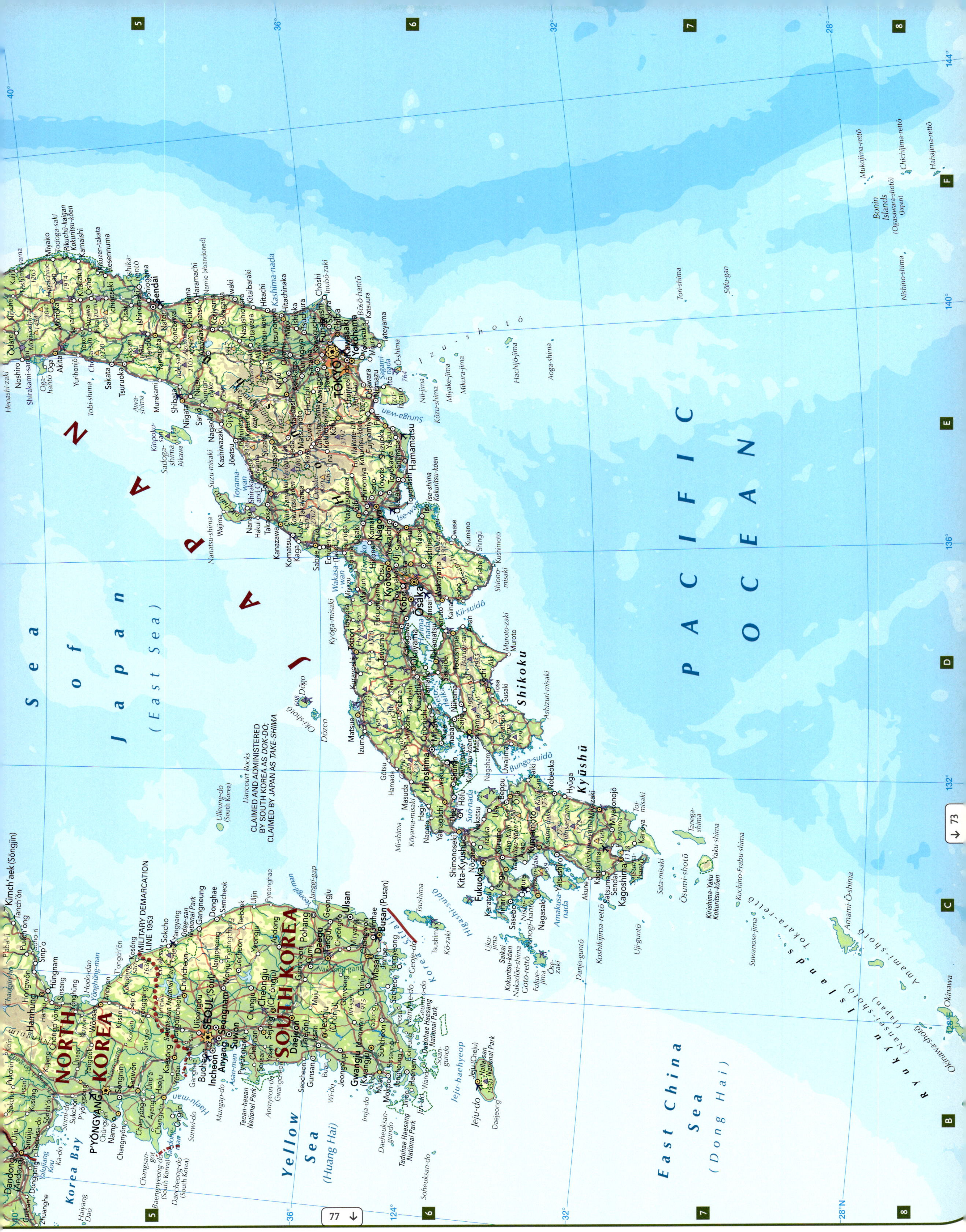
Sea of Japan
(East Sea)
JAPAN
PACIFIC OCEAN
East China Sea
(Dong Hai)
Yellow Sea
(Huang Hai)
Korea Bay
NORTH KOREA
SOUTH KOREA
P'YŎNGYANG
SEOUL (Sŏul)
TŌKYŌ
Ōsaka
Kyōto
Nagoya
Kōbe
Hiroshima
Fukuoka
Kita-Kyūshū
Sendai
Niigata
Yokohama
Kawasaki
Busan (Pusan)
Daegu
Incheon
Daejeon
Gwangju
Ulsan
Shikoku
Kyūshū
Honshū
Bonin Islands
(Ogasawara-shotō)
(Japan)
Ryukyu Islands
(Nansei-shotō)
(Japan)
Izu-shotō
Amami-shotō
Okinawa-shotō
Tokara-rettō
Ōsumi-shotō
Jeju-do
Jeju-haehyeop
Korea Strait
Tsushima
Oki-shotō
Dōgo
Ulleung-do
(South Korea)
Liancourt Rocks
CLAIMED AND ADMINISTERED BY SOUTH KOREA AS DOK-DO;
CLAIMED BY JAPAN AS TAKE-SHIMA
MILITARY DEMARCATION LINE 1953
Sado-ga-shima
Hachijō-jima
Tanega-shima
Yaku-shima
Kashima-nada
Suruga-wan
Sagami-nada
Ise-wan
Kii-suidō
Bungo-suidō
Toyama-wan
Wakasa-wan
77
73

Conic Equidistant Projection

1:7 000 000

0 100 200 miles

0 100 200 300 400 km

Yellow Sea
(Huang Hai)
East China Sea
(Dong Hai)
South China Sea
Taiwan Strait
SHANDONG
HENAN
ANHUI
JIANGSU
HUBEI
HUNAN
JIANGXI
ZHEJIANG
FUJIAN
GUANGDONG
GUANGXI ZHUANGZU ZIZHIQU
HAINAN
TAIWAN
Hainan Dao
Shanghai
Nanjing
Hangzhou
Wuhan
Changsha
Nanchang
Fuzhou
Guangzhou
Hong Kong (Xianggang)
HONG KONG (XIANGGANG)
MACAO (AOMEN)
Shenzhen
Xiamen (Amoy)
TAIPEI (Taibei)
Kaohsiung (Gaoxiong)
Zhengzhou
Xi'an
Nanning
Haikou
Tropic of Cancer
The People's Republic of China claims Taiwan as its 23rd province
GUANGDONG
SHENZHEN SPECIAL ECONOMIC ZONE
HONG KONG (XIANGGANG)
Kowloon
South China Sea

↑ 73
↓ 69

Albers Conic Equal Area Projection

1:20 000 000

0 200 400 600 miles

0 200 400 600 800 1000 km

RUSSIA
MONGOLIA
CHINA
KYRGYZSTAN
TAJIKISTAN
NEPAL
BHUTAN
BANGLADESH
INDIA
MYANMAR (BURMA)
THAILAND
LAOS
VIETNAM
CAMBODIA
MALAYSIA
SINGAPORE
INDONESIA
SRI LANKA
MALDIVES
Gobi Desert
Tarim Basin (Tarim Pendi)
Taklimakan Desert (Taklimakan Shamo)
Plateau of Tibet (Qingzang Gaoyuan)
Tien Shan
Altai Mountains
Kunlun Shan
Altun Shan
Qaidam Pendi
Saryarka
Kazakh Steppe
Betpakdala
INNER MONGOLIA
XINJIANG
TIBET
Bay of Bengal
Andaman Sea
South China Sea
Gulf of Thailand
Gulf of Tongking
Strait of Malacca
Laccadive Sea
Coromandel Coast
Malabar Coast
Mouths of the Ganges
Mouths of the Irrawaddy
Mouths of the Mekong
Andaman Islands (India)
Nicobar Islands (India)
Lakshadweep (Laccadive Islands) (India)
Ten Degree Channel
Nine Degree Channel
Eight Degree Channel
ULAN BATOR (Ulaanbaatar)
BEIJING (Peking)
ISLAMABAD
KATHMANDU
THIMPHU
DHAKA (Dacca)
NEW DELHI
NAY PYI TAW
VIENTIANE
HA NOI
BANGKOK
PHNOM PENH
KUALA LUMPUR
PUTRAJAYA
SRI JAYEWARDENEPURA KOTTE
BISHKEK
ASTANA (Akmola)
Almaty (Alma-Ata)
Mumbai (Bombay)
Kolkata (Calcutta)
Chennai (Madras)
Bengaluru (Bangalore)
Hyderabad
Delhi
Karachi
Chongqing
Chengdu
Wuhan
Xi'an
Lanzhou
Kunming
Guangzhou
Hong Kong
Shenzhen
Ho Chi Minh City (Saigon)
Chittagong
Colombo
Tianjin
Bo Hai
70°
80°
90°
100°
110°
120°
G
H
I
J
K
L
1
2
3
4
5
6
65
66
67
81

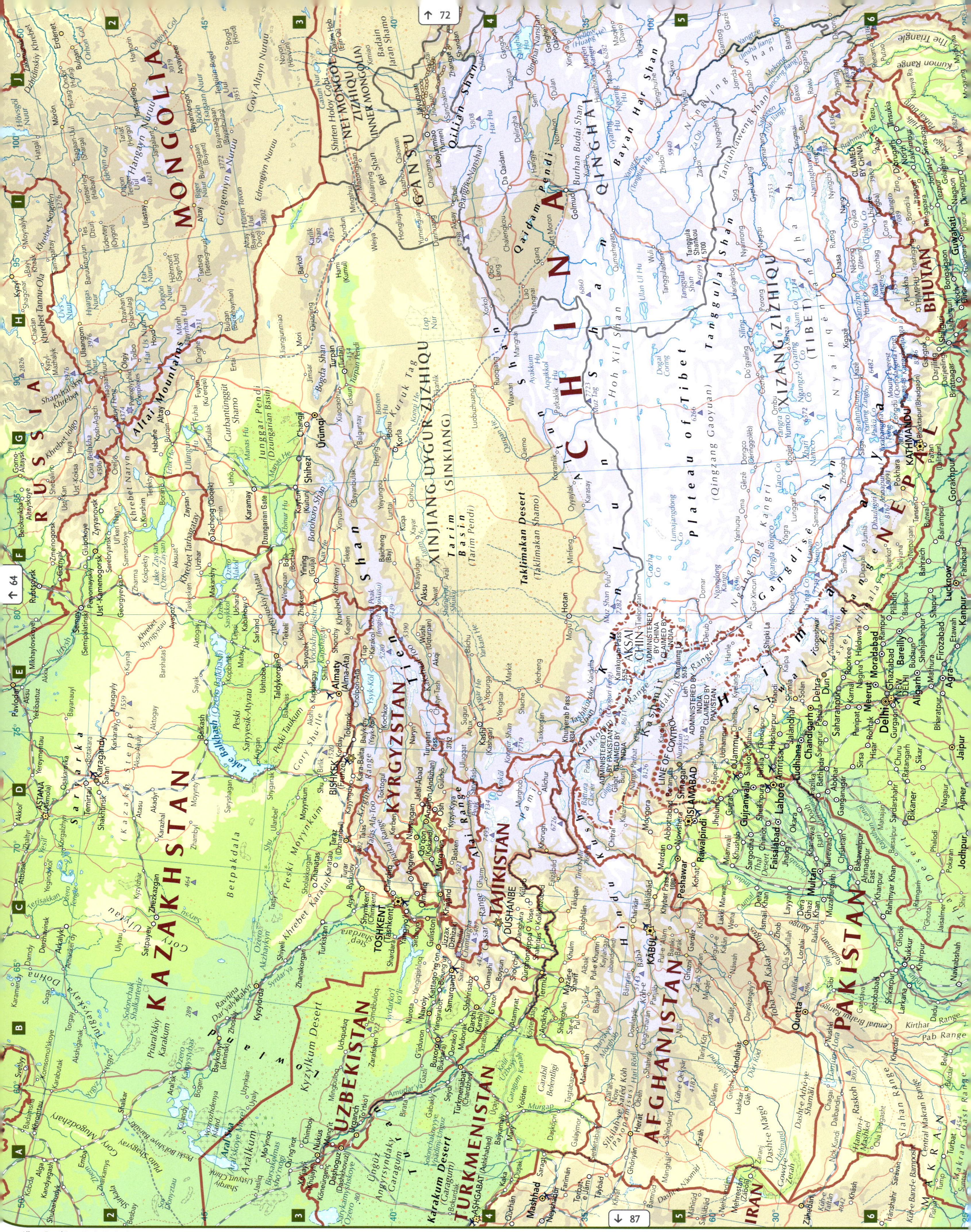

Albers Equal Area Conic Projection

1:13 000 000

0 100 200 300 400 500 miles

0 100 200 300 400 500 600 700 800 km

↑ 68

INDIA
BANGLADESH
MYANMAR (BURMA)
SRI LANKA
MALDIVES
INDONESIA
Bay of Bengal
Arabian Sea
Laccadive Sea
Andaman Sea
INDIAN OCEAN
Mumbai (Bombay)
Kolkata (Calcutta)
Chennai (Madras)
Bengaluru (Bangalore)
Hyderabad
Karachi
DHAKA (Dacca)
Chittagong
NAY PYI TAW
Rangoon (Yangon)
Mandalay
Colombo
SRI JAYEWARDENEPURA KOTTE
MALE
Lakshadweep (Laccadive Islands) (India)
Andaman Islands (India)
Nicobar Islands (India)
Nine Degree Channel
Eight Degree Channel
Ten Degree Channel
One and a Half Degree Channel
Tropic of Cancer
Equator
Malabar Coast
Coromandel Coast
Mouths of the Ganges
Mouths of the Indus
Gulf of Mannar
Palk Strait
Gulf of Khambhat
Gulf of Kachchh

Asia
Southern Asia

Conic Equidistant Projection

1:7 000 000

0 100 200 miles

0 100 200 300 400 km

Asia

Northern India, Nepal, Bhutan and Bangladesh

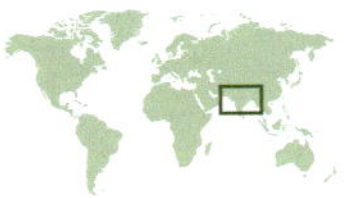

Conic Equidistant Projection

Asia

Southern India and Sri Lanka

1:7 000 000

0 100 200 miles

0 100 200 300 400 km

Conic Equidistant Projection

1:3 000 000

0	25	50	75	100	miles			
0	25	50	75	100	125	150	175	km

Asia
Middle East

Albers Conic Equal Area Projection

1:13 000 000

0	100	200	300	400	500	miles
0	100 200	300 400	500	600 700	800	km

KAZAKHSTAN
UZBEKISTAN
TURKMENISTAN
KYRGYZSTAN
TAJIKISTAN
AFGHANISTAN
PAKISTAN
INDIA
CHINA
NEPAL
OMAN
UNITED ARAB EMIRATES
XINJIANG UYGUR ZIZHIQU (SINKIANG)
XIZANG ZIZHIQU (TIBET)
Taklimakan Desert (Taklimakan Shamo)
Tarim Basin (Tarim Pendi)
Kunlun Shan
Hindu Kush
Himalaya
Karakum Desert (Peski Karakumy)
Turan Lowland
Dasht-e Kavir
Dasht-e Lut
Thar Desert
Arabian Sea
Gulf of Oman
Strait of Hormuz
Gulf of Kachchh
Gulf of Khambhat
Rann of Kachchh
Lakshadweep (Laccadive Islands) (India)
Socotra (Suquṭrā) (Yemen)
Nine Degree Channel
Malabar Coast
AKSAI CHIN
LINE OF CONTROL
TOSHKENT (Tashkent)
DUSHANBE
KABUL
ISLAMABAD
NEW DELHI
ASGABAT (Ashkhabad)
MUSCAT (Masqat)
ABU DHABI (Abū Ẓaby)
Karachi
Mumbai (Bombay)
Delhi
Lahore
Bengaluru (Bangalore)
Hyderabad
Ahmadabad
Samarqand
Kandahar
Herat
Mashhad
Quetta
Multan
Peshawar
Rawalpindi
Srinagar
Jaipur
Lucknow
Kanpur
Nagpur
Pune (Poona)
Surat
Kochi (Cochin)
Thiruvananthapuram (Trivandrum)
↑ 80
→ 80
→ 81
H I J K L M N O
1 2 3 4 5 6 7 8
55° 60° 65° 70° 75° 80° 85°

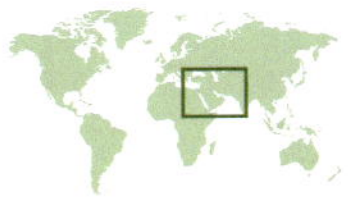

Asia
Southwest Asia

Conic Equidistant Projection

1:7 000 000

0 100 200 miles

0 100 200 300 400 km

UZBEKISTAN
TAJIKISTAN
KYRGYZSTAN
CHINA
XINJIANG UYGUR ZIZHIQU
AFGHANISTAN
PAKISTAN
INDIA
BALOCHISTAN
SINDH
PUNJAB
RAJASTHAN
GUJARAT
HARYANA
KHYBER PAKHTUNKHWA
TRIBAL AREAS
GILGIT-BALTISTAN
JAMMU AND KASHMIR
ADMINISTERED BY PAKISTAN, CLAIMED BY INDIA
ADMINISTERED BY INDIA, CLAIMED BY PAKISTAN
Arabian Sea
Gulf of Kachchh
Mouths of the Indus
Rann of Kachchh
Hindu Kush
Karakoram Range
Pamir
Sulaiman Range
Central Makran Range
Kirthar Range
Thar Desert
DUSHANBE
KĀBUL
ISLAMABAD
Rawalpindi
Peshawar
Lahore
Amritsar
Faisalabad
Multan
Quetta
Karachi
Hyderabad
Kandahār
Herāt
Mashhad
Mazār-e Sharīf
Srinagar
Jammu
Ahmadabad
Vadodara (Baroda)
Jodhpur
Bikaner
Rajkot
Jamnagar
Zāhedān
Gwādar
Samarqand
Qarshi
Türkmenabat
Mary
Jiddah
Kohat
Sargodha
Gujranwala
Sialkot
Bahawalpur
Sukkur
Larkana
Jacobabad
Dera Ghazi Khan
Dera Ismail Khan
Rahimyar Khan
Zhob
Khorugh
Kulob
Termiz
Kunduz
Jalālābād
Gardēz
Ghaznī
Farāh
Zaranj
Lashkar Gāh

↑ 80
→ 82

Administrative divisions in Russia numbered on the map:
1. RESPUBLIKA KALMYKIYA-KHALM'G-TANGCH (G1)
2. RESPUBLIKA DAGESTAN (G2)
3. CHECHENSKAYA RESPUBLIKA (G2)
4. RESPUBLIKA INGUSHETIYA (G2)
5. RESPUBLIKA SEVERNAYA OSETIYA-ALANIYA (G2)
6. KABARDINO-BALKARSKAYA RESPUBLIKA (F2)
7. KARACHAYEVO-CHERKESSKAYA RESPUBLIKA (F2)
8. RESPUBLIKA ADYGEYA (F1)
↑ 43
← 59
← 97
↓ 97
ROMANIA
BUCHAREST (Bucureşti)
SERBIA
KOSOVO
PRISHTINE (Priština)
BULGARIA
SOFIA (Sofiya)
MACEDONIA (F.Y.R.O.M.)
SKOPJE
GREECE
ATHENS (Athina)
Thessaloniki
Aegean Sea
Lesbos (Lesvos)
Evvoia
Cyclades (Kyklades)
Crete (Kriti)
Rhodes (Rodos)
Kritiko Pelagos
Myrtoo Pelagos
Black Sea
UKRAINE
Simferopol'
Sevastopol'
Yevpatoriya
CRIMEA ADMINISTERED BY RUSSIA
Krasnodar
Novorossiysk
TURKEY
ANKARA
Istanbul
İzmir (Smyrna)
Bursa
Konya
Antalya
Adana
Gaziantep
Samsun
Anadolu
Kapadokya
Pisidia
Taurus Mountains
Köroğlu Dağları
Zonguldak
Eskişehir
Kayseri
Sivas
Malatya
Antalya Körfezi
Aleppo (Halab)
Homs
Hamāh
SYRIA
DAMASCUS (Dimashq)
LEBANON
BEIRUT (Beyrouth)
Tripoli (Trâblous)
CYPRUS
NICOSIA (Lefkosia)
ADMINISTERED AS NORTHERN CYPRUS
Limassol (Lemesos)
Larnaca
Paphos (Pafos)
Mediterranean Sea
ISRAEL
JERUSALEM
Tel Aviv-Yafo
Haifa (Hefa)
WEST BANK
GAZA
JORDAN
'AMMĀN
SAUDI ARABIA
EGYPT
CAIRO (Al Qāhirah)
Alexandria (Al Iskandarīyah)
Port Said (Būr Sa'īd)
Suez
Gulf of Suez
Gulf of Aqaba
Red Sea
Sinai
Qattara Depression (Munkhafad al Qaţţārah)
Western Desert
Eastern Desert
Great Sand Sea
LIBYA
Darnah
Tubruq
Marsá Maţrūḩ
Conic Equidistant Projection

1:7 000 000

0 100 200 miles

0 100 200 300 400 km

Asia

Eastern Mediterranean, the Caucasus and Iraq

Africa
Landscapes

Some of the world's greatest physical features are in Africa, the world's second largest continent. Variations in climate and elevation give rise to the continent's great variety of landscapes. The Sahara, the world's largest desert, extends across the whole continent from west to east, and covers an area of over nine million square kilometres. Other significant African deserts are the Kalahari and the Namib. In contrast, some of the world's greatest rivers flow in Africa, including the Nile, the world's longest, and the Congo.

The Great Rift Valley is perhaps Africa's most notable geological feature. It stretches for nearly 3 000 kilometres from Jordan, through the Red Sea and south to Mozambique, and contains many of Africa's largest lakes. Significant mountain ranges on the continent are the Atlas Mountains and the Ethiopian Highlands in the north, the Ruwenzori in east central Africa, and the Drakensberg in the far southeast.

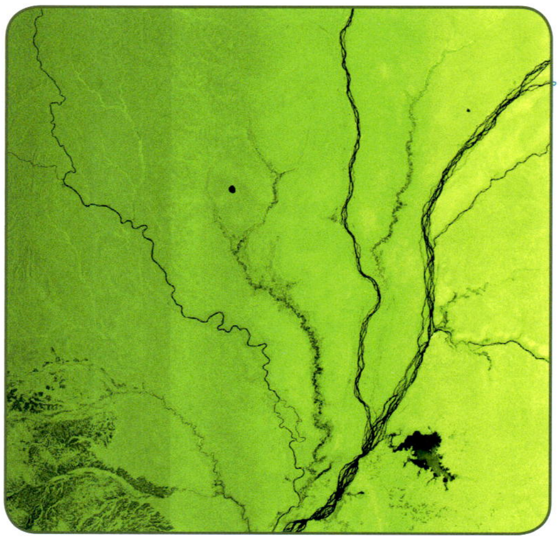

The confluence of the Ubangi and Africa's second longest river, the **Congo**.

Africa's extent

TOTAL LAND AREA	30 343 578 sq km / 11 715 655 sq miles
Most northerly point	La Galite, Tunisia
Most southerly point	Cape Agulhas, South Africa
Most westerly point	Santo Antão, Cape Verde
Most easterly point	Raas Xaafuun, Somalia

Internet Links

NASA Visible Earth	**visibleearth.nasa.gov**
NASA Astronaut Photography	**eol.jsc.nasa.gov**
Peace Parks Foundation	**www.peaceparks.org**

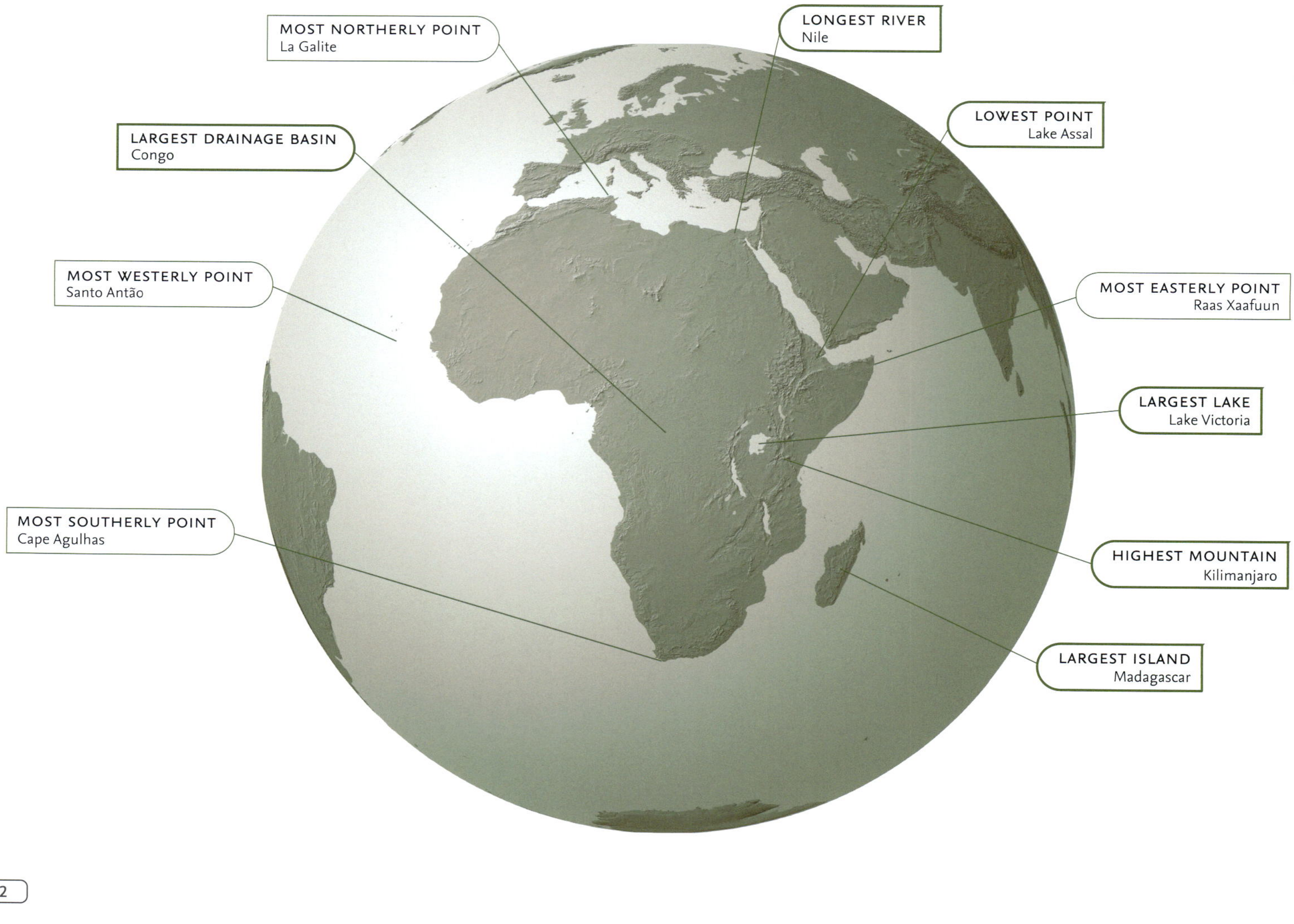

Lake Victoria, Africa's largest lake, and Lake Albert lie within Africa's Great Rift Valley.

Africa's physical features

Highest mountain	Kilimanjaro, Tanzania	5 892 metres	19 330 feet
Longest river	Nile	6 695 km	4 160 miles
Largest lake	Lake Victoria	68 870 sq km	26 591 sq miles
Largest island	Madagascar	587 040 sq km	226 656 sq miles
Largest drainage basin	Congo, Congo/Dem. Rep. Congo	3 700 000 sq km	1 428 570 sq miles
Lowest point	Lake Assal, Djibouti	-156 metres	-512 feet

Facts

- The Atlas Mountains are part of the same geological system as the Alps
- Lake Chad has shrunk by almost 95% over the last 40 years
- The Suez Canal, linking the Mediterranean Sea to the Red Sea, is 163 kilometres long and opened in 1869
- The Sahara desert covers 9 million square kilometres, approximately 30% of Africa's total land area
- Lake Assal in Djibouti is one of the saltiest lakes in the world

Africa
Countries

Africa is a complex continent, with over fifty independent countries and a long history of political change. It supports a great variety of ethnic groups, with the Sahara creating the major divide between Arab and Berber groups in the north and a diverse range of groups, including the Yoruba and Masai, in the south.

The current pattern of countries in Africa is a product of a long and complex history, including the colonial period, which saw European control of the vast majority of the continent from the fifteenth century until widespread moves to independence began in the 1950s. Despite its great wealth of natural resources, Africa is by far the world's poorest continent. Many of its countries are heavily dependent upon foreign aid and many are also subject to serious political instability.

Facts

- Africa has over 1 000 linguistic and cultural groups
- Only Liberia and Ethiopia have remained free from colonial rule throughout their history
- Over 30% of the world's minerals, and over 46% of the world's diamonds, come from Africa
- 9 of the 10 poorest countries in the world are in Africa

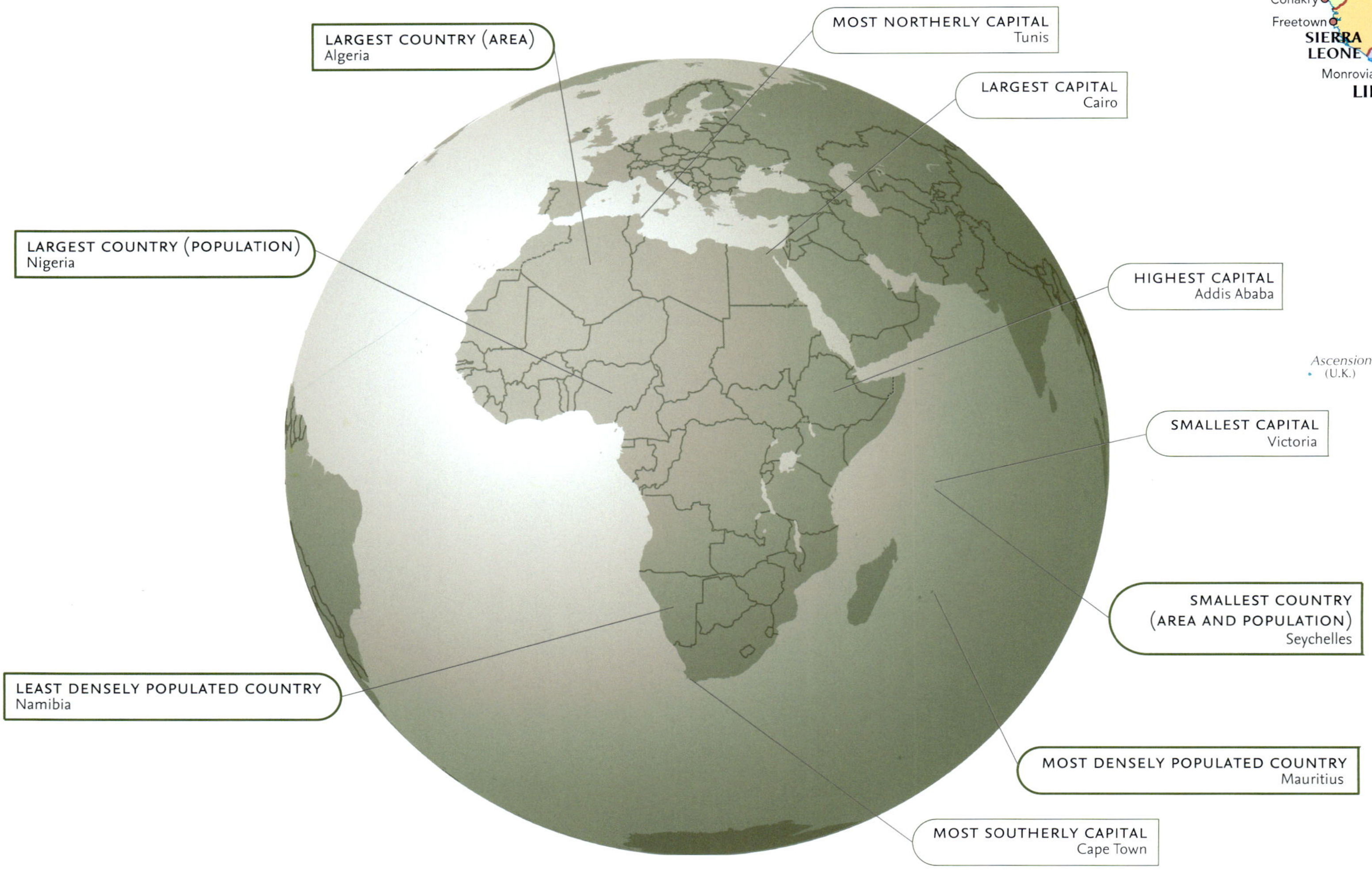

Internet Links

UK Foreign and Commonwealth Office	**www.fco.gov.uk**
CIA World Factbook	**www.cia.gov/library/publications/the-world-factbook/index.html**
Southern African Development Community	**www.sadc.int**
African Union (AU)	**www.au.int**

Cape Town, legislative capital of the Republic of South Africa and the most southerly African capital city.

Africa's capitals

Largest capital (population)	Cairo, Egypt	11 944 000	
Smallest capital (population)	Victoria, Seychelles	26 000	
Most northerly capital	Tunis, Tunisia	36° 46'N	
Most southerly capital	Cape Town, South Africa	33° 57'S	
Highest capital	Addis Ababa, Ethiopia	2 408 metres	7 900 feet

Africa's countries

Largest country (area)	Algeria	2 381 741 sq km	919 595 sq miles
Smallest country (area)	Seychelles	455 sq km	176 sq miles
Largest country (population)	Nigeria	182 202 000	
Smallest country (population)	Seychelles	96 000	
Most densely populated country	Mauritius	610 per sq km	1 579 per sq mile
Least densely populated country	Namibia	3 per sq km	7 per sq mile

Lambert Azimuthal Equal Area Projection

1:16 000 000
0 200 400 miles
0 200 400 600 800 km

55
98
99
Mediterranean Sea
Sicily
ITALY
MALTA
VALLETTA
Malta Channel
Palermo
Reggio di Calabria
Catania
Syracuse
ATHENS (Athina)
GREECE
Crete (Kriti)
Rhodes (Rodos)
Dodecanese
TURKEY
Konya
Adana
Antalya
Gaziantep
Mersin
CYPRUS
NICOSIA (Lefkoşa)
Limassol
SYRIA
Aleppo (Halab)
Hamah
Homs
LEBANON
BEIRUT (Beyrouth)
DAMASCUS (Dimashq)
Syrian Desert
Haifa
Tel Aviv-Yafo
JERUSALEM
ISRAEL
AMMAN
JORDAN
IRAQ
BAGHDAD
Mosul
An Najaf
Basra
Euphrates
IRAN
KUWAIT
KUWAIT (Al Kuwayt)
Sea
SAUDI ARABIA
RIYADH (Ar Riyad)
Tropic of Cancer
An Nafud
Medina (Al Madinah)
Jeddah (Jiddah)
Mecca (Makkah)
Ha'il
Buraydah
Ad Dahna
YEMEN
SAN'A
Aden ('Adan)
Gulf of Aden
Hodeidah (Al Hudaydah)
TRIPOLI (Tarabulus)
Misratah
Gulf of Sirte (Khalij Surt)
Benghazi
Tubruq
LIBYA
Libyan Desert
Great Sand Sea
Cyrenaica
AS SARIR
Rebiana Sand Sea (Ramlat Rabyanah)
Tibesti
Murzuq
Sabha
Alexandria (Al Iskandariyah)
CAIRO (Al Qahirah)
Giza
Port Said
Suez
EGYPT
Western Desert
Eastern Desert
Qattara Depression
Siwa
Luxor
Aswan
Lake Nasser
Red Sea
Sinai
HALAIB TRIANGLE
Nubian Desert
Port Sudan
Wadi Halfa
SUDAN
KHARTOUM
Omdurman
Atbara
El Obeid
Jebel Marra
Darfur
Nile
CHAD
NDJAMENA
Lake Chad
Abéché
Ennedi
Erg du Djourab
Dépression du Mourdi
de Bilma
ERITREA
ASMARA
Massawa
Dahlak Archipelago
DJIBOUTI
Gulf of Aden
SOMALILAND
Berbera
Hargeysa
ETHIOPIA
ADDIS ABABA (Adis Abeba)
Lake Tana
Bahir Dar
Gonder
OGADEN
SOMALIA
MOGADISHU (Muqdisho)
Kismaayo
Equator
INDIAN OCEAN
SOUTH SUDAN
Juba
Wau
Malakal
Sudd
Lotikipi Plain
KENYA
NAIROBI
Lake Turkana
Mombasa
Malindi
Lamu
Garissa
UGANDA
KAMPALA
Lake Victoria
Entebbe
Mount Kenya
RWANDA
KIGALI
BURUNDI
BUJUMBURA
TANZANIA
Arusha
Mwanza
CENTRAL AFRICAN REPUBLIC
BANGUI
Bouar
Bambari
DEMOCRATIC REPUBLIC OF THE CONGO
Kisangani
Congo Basin
Mbandaka
CONGO
Ouesso
Ouaddaï
Great Rift Valley
Mwanza
Musoma
Shinyanga
Bukavu

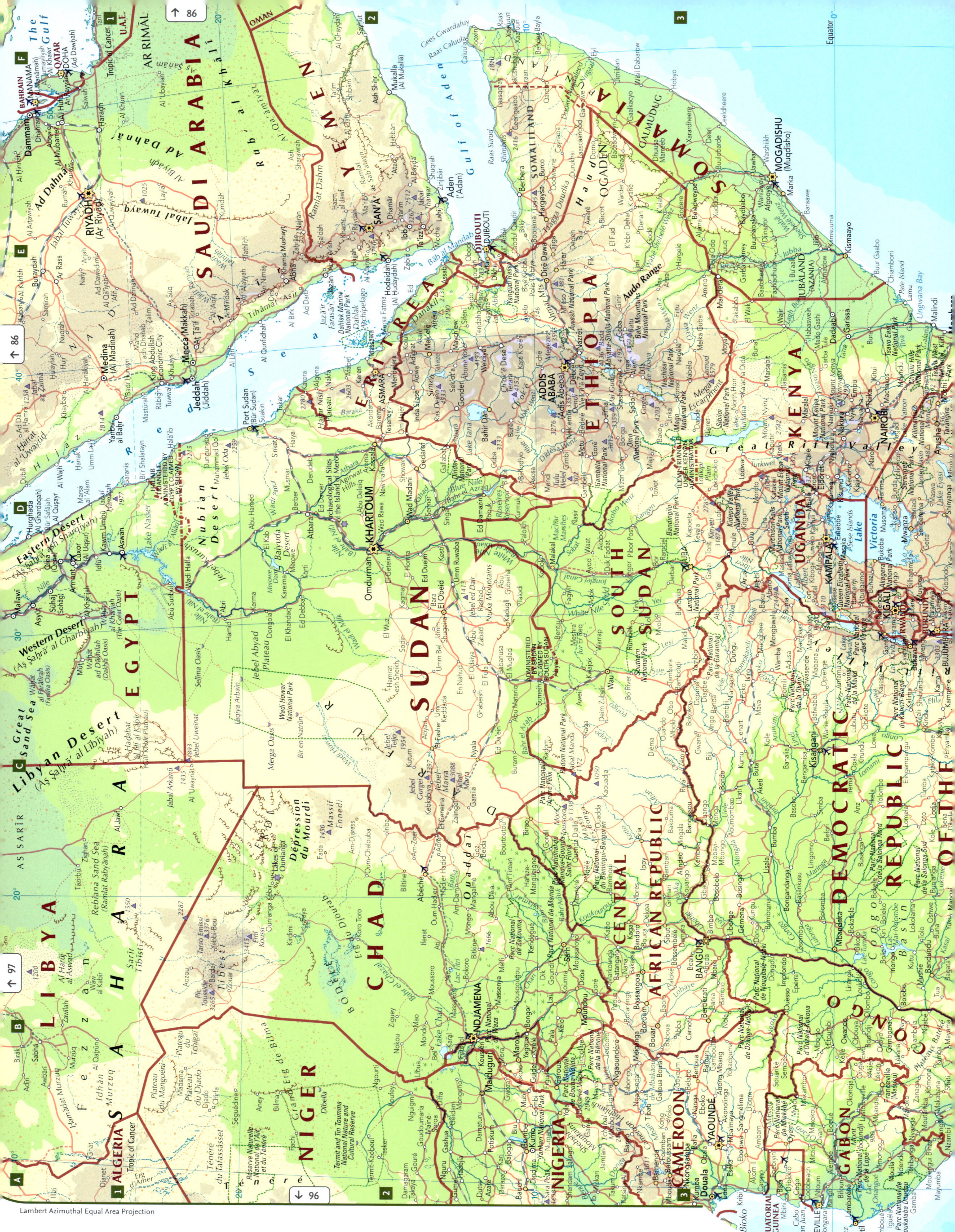
SAUDI ARABIA
YEMEN
OMAN
SOMALIA
ETHIOPIA
ERITREA
DJIBOUTI
SUDAN
SOUTH SUDAN
EGYPT
LIBYA
CHAD
NIGER
NIGERIA
CAMEROON
CENTRAL AFRICAN REPUBLIC
DEMOCRATIC REPUBLIC OF THE
KENYA
UGANDA
RWANDA
BURUNDI
GABON
EQUATORIAL GUINEA
ALGERIA
QATAR
BAHRAIN
U.A.E.
RIYADH (Ar Riyāḍ)
SAN'A'
KHARTOUM
ADDIS ABABA (Ādīs Ābeba)
MOGADISHU (Muqdisho)
NAIROBI
KAMPALA
KIGALI
BUJUMBURA
N'DJAMENA
BANGUI
YAOUNDÉ
LIBREVILLE
DOHA (Ad Dawhah)
MANAMA
DJIBOUTI
ASMARA
JUBA
Red Sea
Gulf of Aden
Lake Victoria
Libyan Desert (Aş Şaḩrā' al Lībīyah)
Western Desert
Eastern Desert
Nubian Desert
Great Sand Sea
SAHARA
Rub' al Khālī
Tibesti
Congo Basin
Great Rift Valley
Tropic of Cancer
Equator
Lambert Azimuthal Equal Area Projection
1:16 000 000
0 200 400 miles
0 200 400 600 800 km

CONGO
TANZANIA
ANGOLA
ZAMBIA
MALAWI
MOZAMBIQUE
ZIMBABWE
BOTSWANA
NAMIBIA
SOUTH AFRICA
LESOTHO
SWAZILAND
MADAGASCAR
COMOROS
INDIAN OCEAN
ATLANTIC OCEAN
Mozambique Channel
Kalahari Desert
Namib Desert
KINSHASA
BRAZZAVILLE
LUANDA
DODOMA
Dar es Salaam
LUSAKA
LILONGWE
HARARE
WINDHOEK
GABORONE
PRETORIA
MAPUTO
MASERU
BLOEMFONTEIN
CAPE TOWN
Durban
ANTANANARIVO
MORONI
Tropic of Capricorn

Lambert Azimuthal Equal Area Projection

1:5 000 000

0 50 100 150 miles

0 50 100 150 200 250 km

ZIMBABWE
MOZAMBIQUE
SWAZILAND
LESOTHO
CENTRAL
KGATLENG
LIMPOPO
MPUMALANGA
GAUTENG
WEST
FREE STATE
KWAZULU-NATAL
EASTERN CAPE
GRIQUALAND
EAST
GAZA
INHAMBANE
MAPUTO
INDIAN
OCEAN
Drakensberg
GABORONE
PRETORIA
(Tshwane)
Johannesburg
Soweto
Vereeniging
BLOEMFONTEIN
MASERU
MBABANE
MAPUTO
Matola
Pietermaritzburg
Durban
Port Shepstone
East London
Port Elizabeth
Mafeteng
Welkom
Polokwane
(Pietersburg)
Richards Bay
Tropic of Capricorn
Kruger
National
Park
Great Limpopo
Transfrontier
Park
Parque Nacional
de Banhine
Lake St Lucia
Kosi Bay
Lake Sibayi
Cape Hermes
Coffee Bay
Port Edward
South Sand Bluff
Great Fish Point
Cape Recife
Algoa
Bay
Beacon Bay
Xai-Xai
Chongoene
Inhambane
Ponta da Barra
Cabo de Santa Maria
Península
Inhaca
22°
24°
26°
28°
30°
32°
34°
36°
H
I
J
K
L
M
1
2
3
4
5
6
7
8

Oceania

Landscapes

Oceania comprises Australia, New Zealand, New Guinea and the islands of the Pacific Ocean. It is the smallest of the world's continents by land area. Its dominating feature is Australia, which is mainly flat and very dry. Australia's western half consists of a low plateau, broken in places by higher mountain ranges, which has very few permanent rivers or lakes. The narrow, fertile coastal plain of the east coast is separated from the interior by the Great Dividing Range, which includes the highest mountain in Australia.

The numerous Pacific islands of Oceania are generally either volcanic in origin or consist of coral. They can be divided into three main regions - Micronesia, north of the equator between Palau and the Gilbert islands; Melanesia, stretching from mountainous New Guinea to Fiji; and Polynesia, covering a vast area of the eastern and central Pacific Ocean.

Princess Chatlotte Bay, on the east coast of Cape York Peninsula and the Claremont Isles National Park.

Facts

- Australia's Great Barrier Reef is the world's largest coral reef and stretches for over 2 000 kilometres
- The highest point of Tuvalu is less than 5 metres above sea level
- New Zealand lies directly on the boundary between the Pacific and Indo-Australian tectonic plates
- The Mariana Trench in the Pacific Ocean contains the earth's deepest point – Challenger Deep, 10 920 metres below sea level

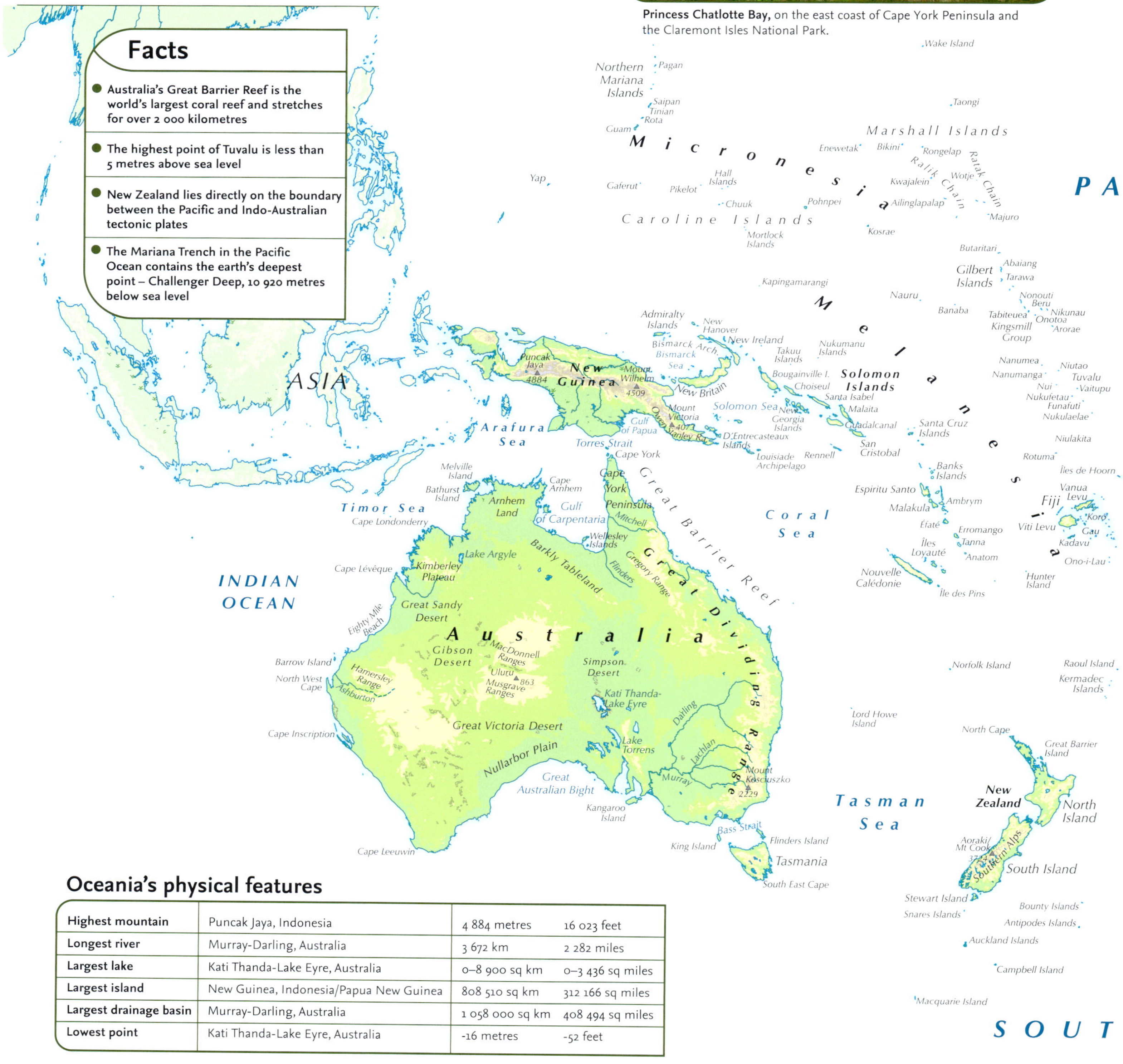

Oceania's physical features

Highest mountain	Puncak Jaya, Indonesia	4 884 metres	16 023 feet
Longest river	Murray-Darling, Australia	3 672 km	2 282 miles
Largest lake	Kati Thanda-Lake Eyre, Australia	0–8 900 sq km	0–3 436 sq miles
Largest island	New Guinea, Indonesia/Papua New Guinea	808 510 sq km	312 166 sq miles
Largest drainage basin	Murray-Darling, Australia	1 058 000 sq km	408 494 sq miles
Lowest point	Kati Thanda-Lake Eyre, Australia	-16 metres	-52 feet

Internet Links

NASA Visible Earth	**visibleearth.nasa.gov**
NASA Astronaut Photography	**eol.jsc.nasa.gov**
Great Barrier Reef Marine Park Authority	**www.gbrmpa.gov.au**

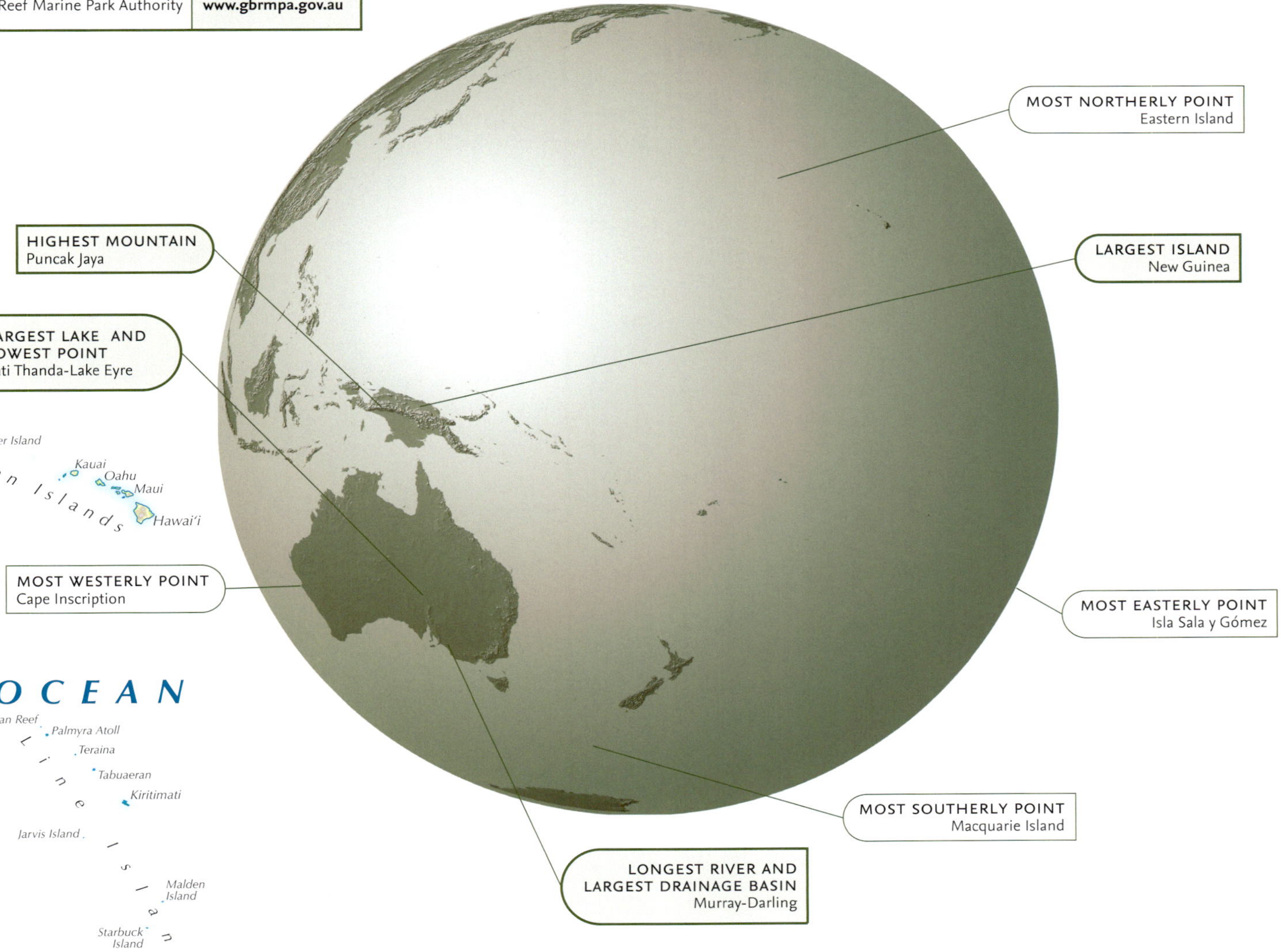

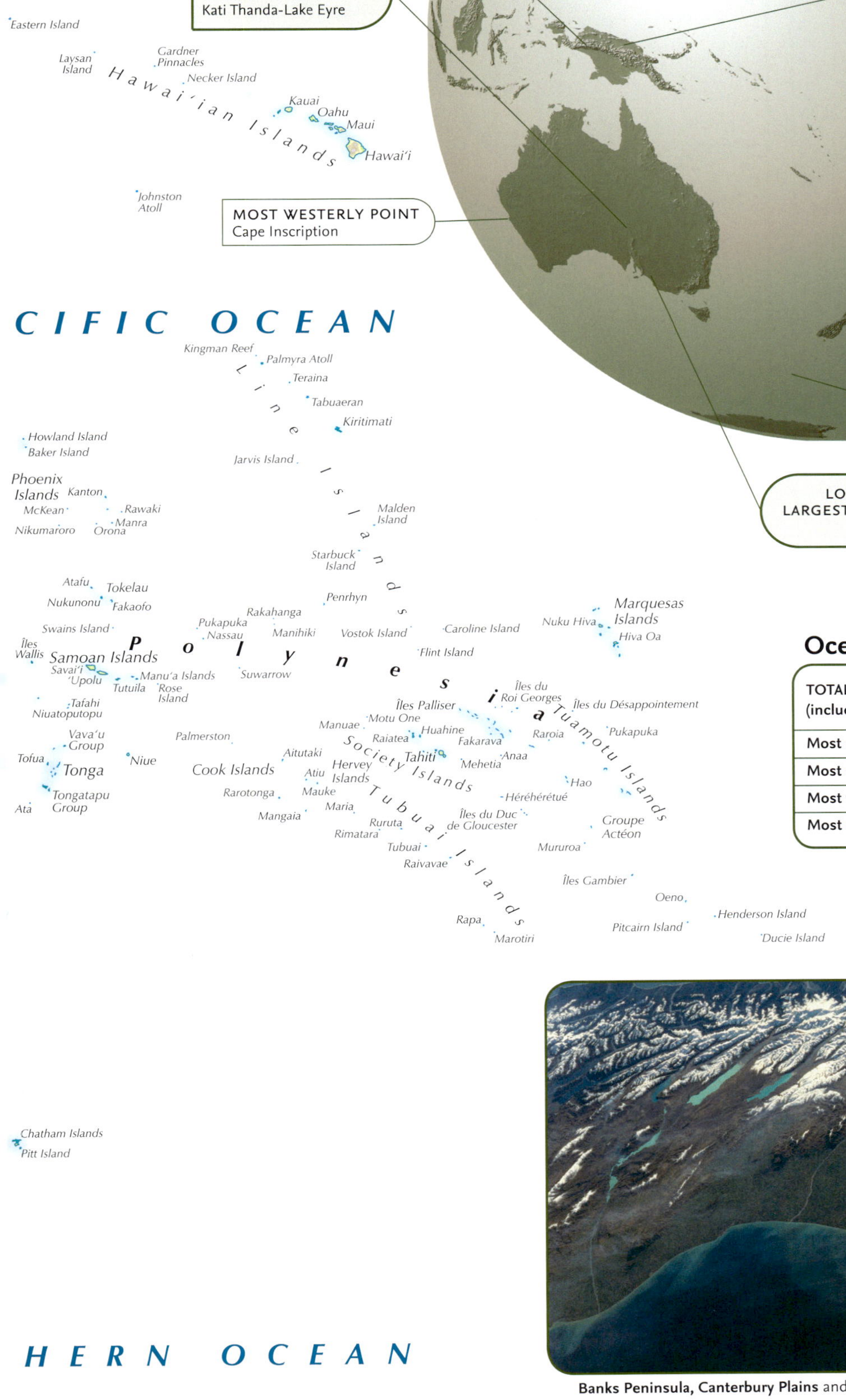

Oceania's extent

TOTAL LAND AREA (includes New Guinea and Pacific Island nations)	8 844 516 sq km / 3 414 868 sq miles
Most northerly point	Eastern Island, North Pacific Ocean
Most southerly point	Macquarie Island, South Pacific Ocean
Most westerly point	Cape Inscription, Australia
Most easterly point	Isla Sala y Gómez, South Pacific Ocean

Banks Peninsula, Canterbury Plains and the **Southern Alps,** South Island, New Zealand.

Oceania
Countries

Stretching across almost the whole width of the Pacific Ocean, Oceania has a great variety of cultures and an enormously diverse range of countries and territories. Australia, by far the largest and most industrialized country in the continent, contrasts with the numerous tiny Pacific island nations which have smaller, and more fragile economies based largely on agriculture, fishing and the exploitation of natural resources.

The division of the Pacific island groups into the main regions of Micronesia, Melanesia and Polynesia – often referred to as the South Sea islands – broadly reflects the ethnological differences across the continent. There is a long history of colonial influence in the region, which still contains dependent territories belonging to Australia, France, New Zealand, the UK and the USA.

Nouméa, capital of the French dependency of New Caledonia in the southern Pacific Ocean.

Facts

- Over 91% of Australia's population live in urban areas
- The Maori name for New Zealand is Aotearoa, meaning 'land of the long white cloud'
- Auckland, New Zealand, has the largest Polynesian population of any city in Oceania
- Over 800 different languages are spoken in Papua New Guinea

Internet Links

UK Foreign and Commonwealth Office	www.fco.gov.uk
CIA World Factbook	www.cia.gov/library/publications/the-world-factbook/index.html
Geoscience Australia	www.ga.gov.au

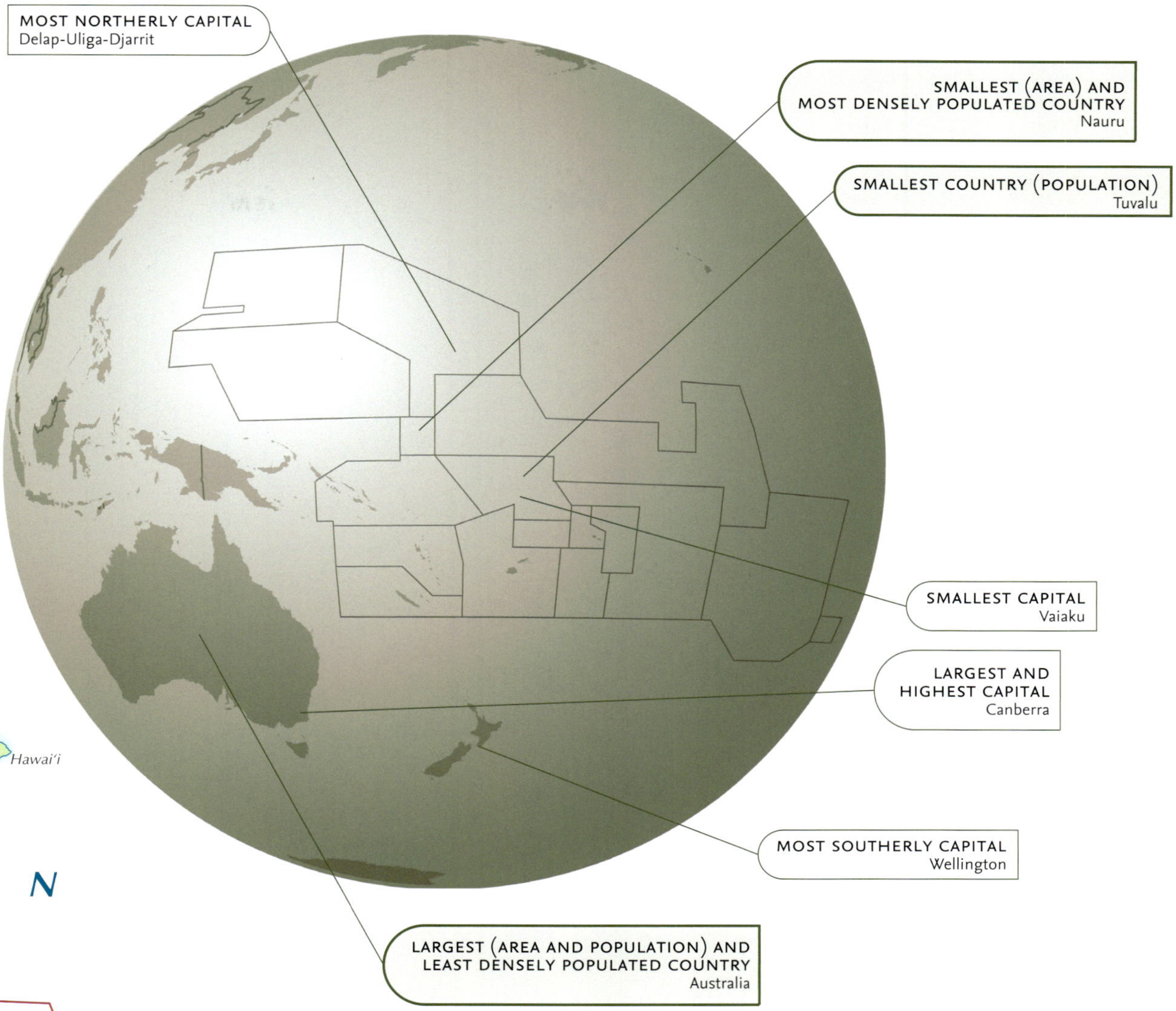

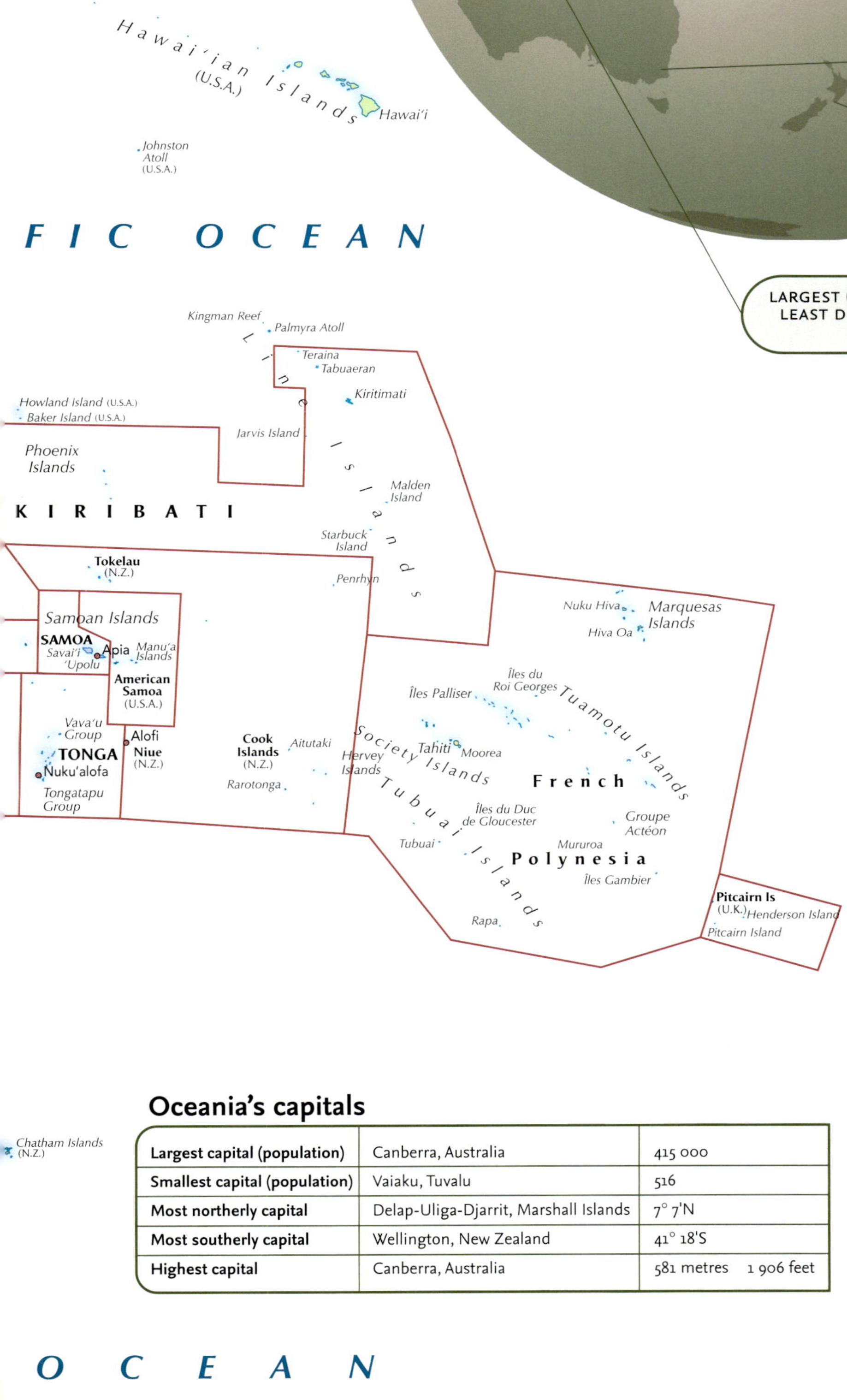

Oceania's countries

Largest country (area)	Australia	7 692 024 sq km	2 969 907 sq miles
Smallest country (area)	Nauru	21 sq km	8 sq miles
Largest country (population)	Australia	23 969 000	
Smallest country (population)	Tuvalu	9 916	
Most densely populated country	Nauru	476 per sq km	1 250 per sq mile
Least densely populated country	Australia	3 per sq km	8 per sq mile

Oceania's capitals

Largest capital (population)	Canberra, Australia	415 000	
Smallest capital (population)	Vaiaku, Tuvalu	516	
Most northerly capital	Delap-Uliga-Djarrit, Marshall Islands	7° 7'N	
Most southerly capital	Wellington, New Zealand	41° 18'S	
Highest capital	Canberra, Australia	581 metres	1 906 feet

Wellington, capital of New Zealand.

Lambert Azimuthal Equal Area Projection

1:20 000 000 — 0, 200, 400, 600 miles; 0, 200, 400, 600, 800, 1000 km

Oceania

Australia, New Zealand and Southwest Pacific

Lambert Azimuthal Equal Area Projection

1:8 000 000

0 100 200 300 miles
0 100 200 300 400 500 km

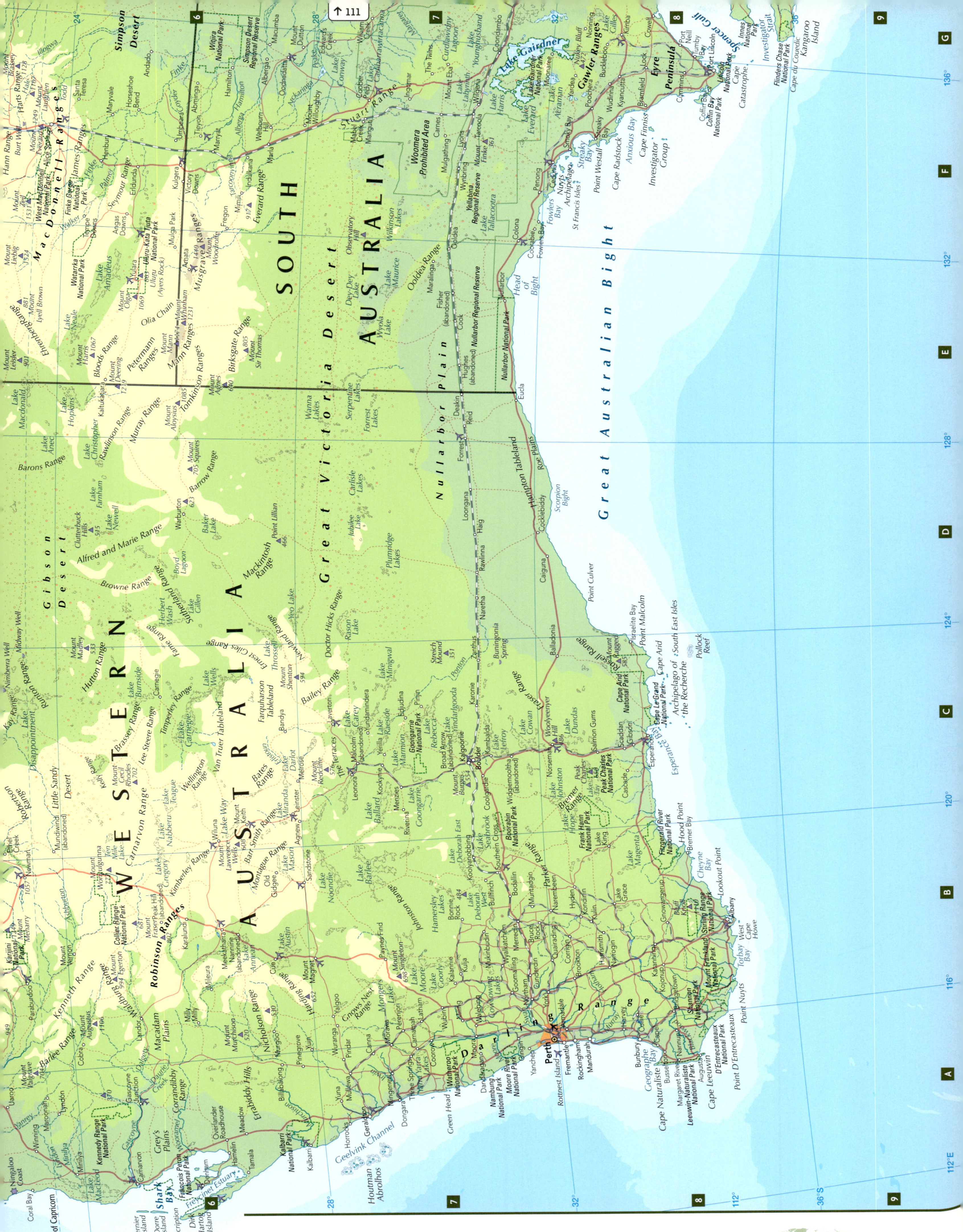

↑ 111
WESTERN AUSTRALIA
SOUTH AUSTRALIA
Great Victoria Desert
Nullarbor Plain
Great Australian Bight
Gibson Desert
Little Sandy Desert
Simpson Desert
MacDonnell Ranges
Darling Range
Perth
Fremantle
Rottnest Island
Mandurah
Bunbury
Geographe Bay
Cape Naturaliste
Cape Leeuwin
Albany
Esperance
Kalgoorlie
Boulder
Coolgardie
Geraldton
Houtman Abrolhos
Shark Bay
Dirk Hartog Island
Carnarvon
Ningaloo Coast
Tropic of Capricorn
Eyre Peninsula
Lake Gairdner
Gawler Ranges
Spencer Gulf
Kangaroo Island
Nuyts Archipelago
Archipelago of the Recherche
Hampton Tableland
Eucla
Ceduna
Uluru-Kata Tjuta National Park
Musgrave Ranges
Everard Range
Woomera Prohibited Area
Nullarbor National Park
Nullarbor Regional Reserve
Alice Springs
24°
28°
32°
36°S
112°E
116°
120°
124°
128°
132°
136°

Oceania
Western Australia

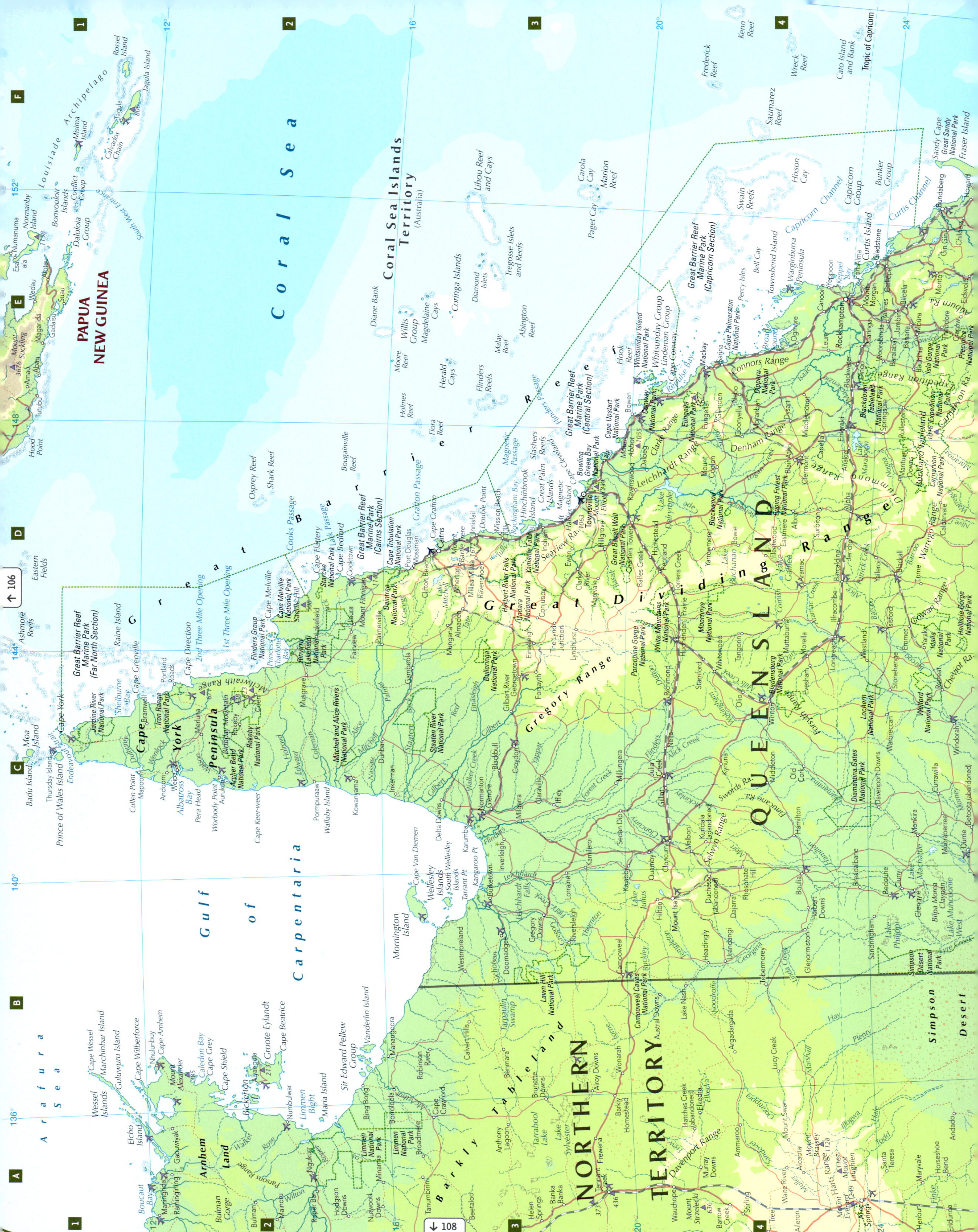

Lambert Azimuthal Equal Area Projection

1:8 000 000

0	100	200	300	miles	
0	100	200	300	400	500 km

AUSTRALIA
SOUTH AUSTRALIA
NEW SOUTH WALES
VICTORIA
QUEENSLAND
TASMANIA
Tasman Sea
Bass Strait
Great Australian Bight
Spencer Gulf
Gulf St Vincent
Kangaroo Island
Eyre Peninsula
Lake Eyre
Lake Torrens
Lake Gairdner
Simpson Desert
Sturt Stony Desert
Strzelecki Desert
Great Dividing Range
Flinders Ranges
Grey Range
Darling Downs
Adelaide
Melbourne
Sydney
Brisbane
Canberra
Hobart
Newcastle
Geelong
Wollongong
Gold Coast
Launceston
AUSTRALIAN CAPITAL TERRITORY
JERVIS BAY TERRITORY
↓ 109

QUEENSLAND
AUSTRALIA
NEW SOUTH WALES
VICTORIA
AUSTRALIAN CAPITAL TERRITORY
JERVIS BAY TERRITORY
Tasman Sea
Bass Strait
Darling Downs
Brisbane
Gold Coast
Newcastle
Sydney
Wollongong
CANBERRA
Melbourne
Geelong
Bendigo
Ballarat
Dubbo
Tamworth
Wagga Wagga
Albury
Toowoomba
Port Macquarie
Coffs Harbour
Moreton Island
North Stradbroke Island
Cape Byron
Port Phillip Bay
Wilson's Promontory
Cape Otway
Cape Howe
Lambert Azimuthal Equal Area Projection

Oceania

Southeast Australia

1:5 000 000

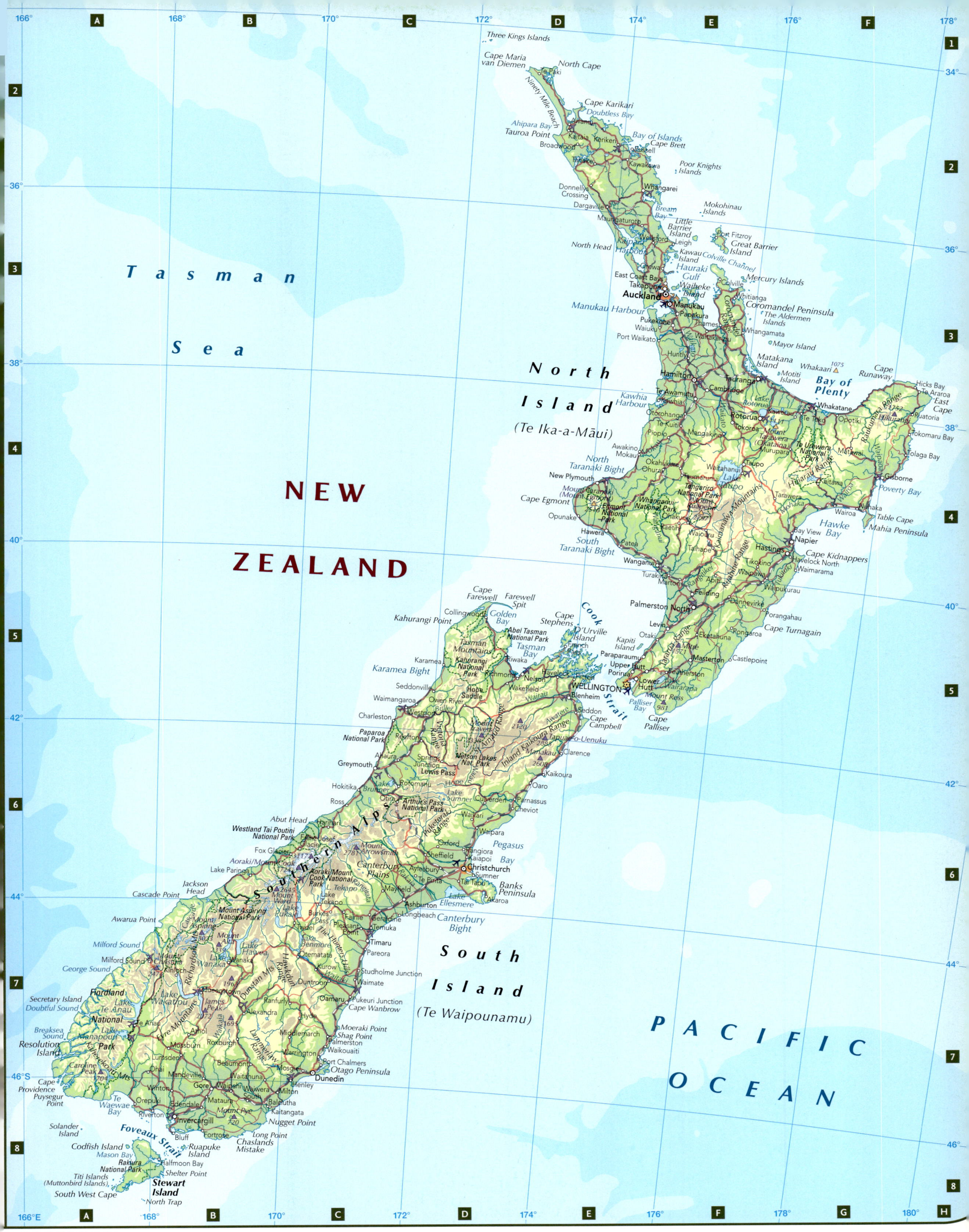

Conic Equidistant Projection

1:5 250 000

0 50 100 150 miles

0 50 100 150 200 250 km

Oceania

New Zealand

North America
Landscapes

North America, the world's third largest continent, supports a wide range of landscapes from the Arctic north to sub-tropical Central America. The main physiographic regions of the continent are the mountains of the west coast, stretching from Alaska in the north to Mexico and Central America in the south; the vast, relatively flat Canadian Shield; the Great Plains which make up the majority of the interior; the Appalachian Mountains in the east; and the Atlantic coastal plain.

These regions contain some significant physical features, including the Rocky Mountains, the Great Lakes – three of which are amongst the five largest lakes in the world – and the Mississippi-Missouri river system which is the world's fourth longest river. The Caribbean Sea contains a complex pattern of islands, many volcanic in origin, and the continent is joined to South America by the narrow Isthmus of Panama.

Internet Links

NASA Visible Earth	**visibleearth.nasa.gov**
U.S. Geological Survey	**www.usgs.gov**
Natural Resources Canada	**www.nrcan.gc.ca/home**
Satellite imagery	**www.geo-airbusds.com**

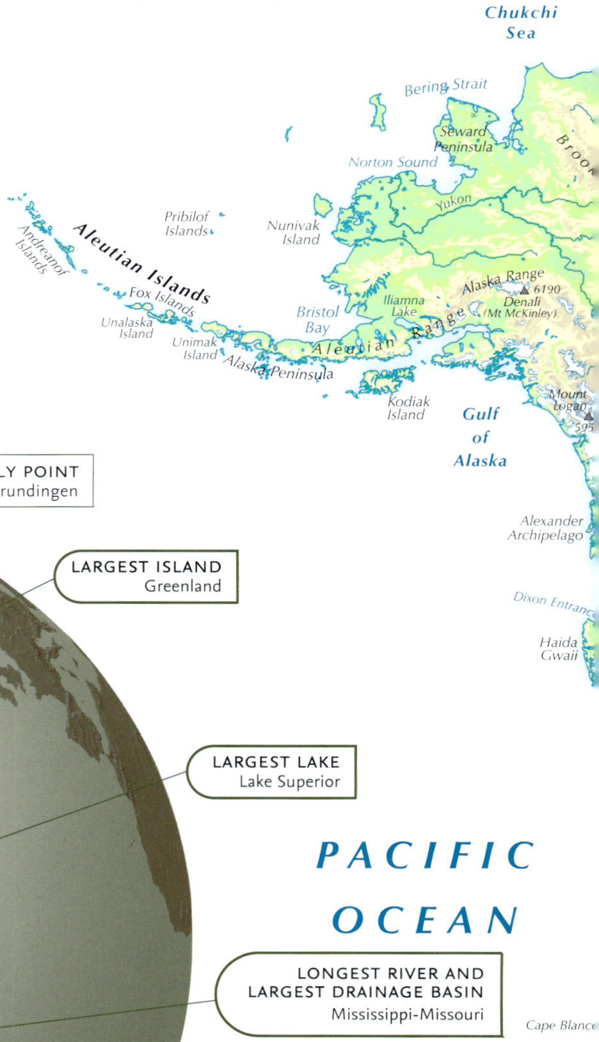

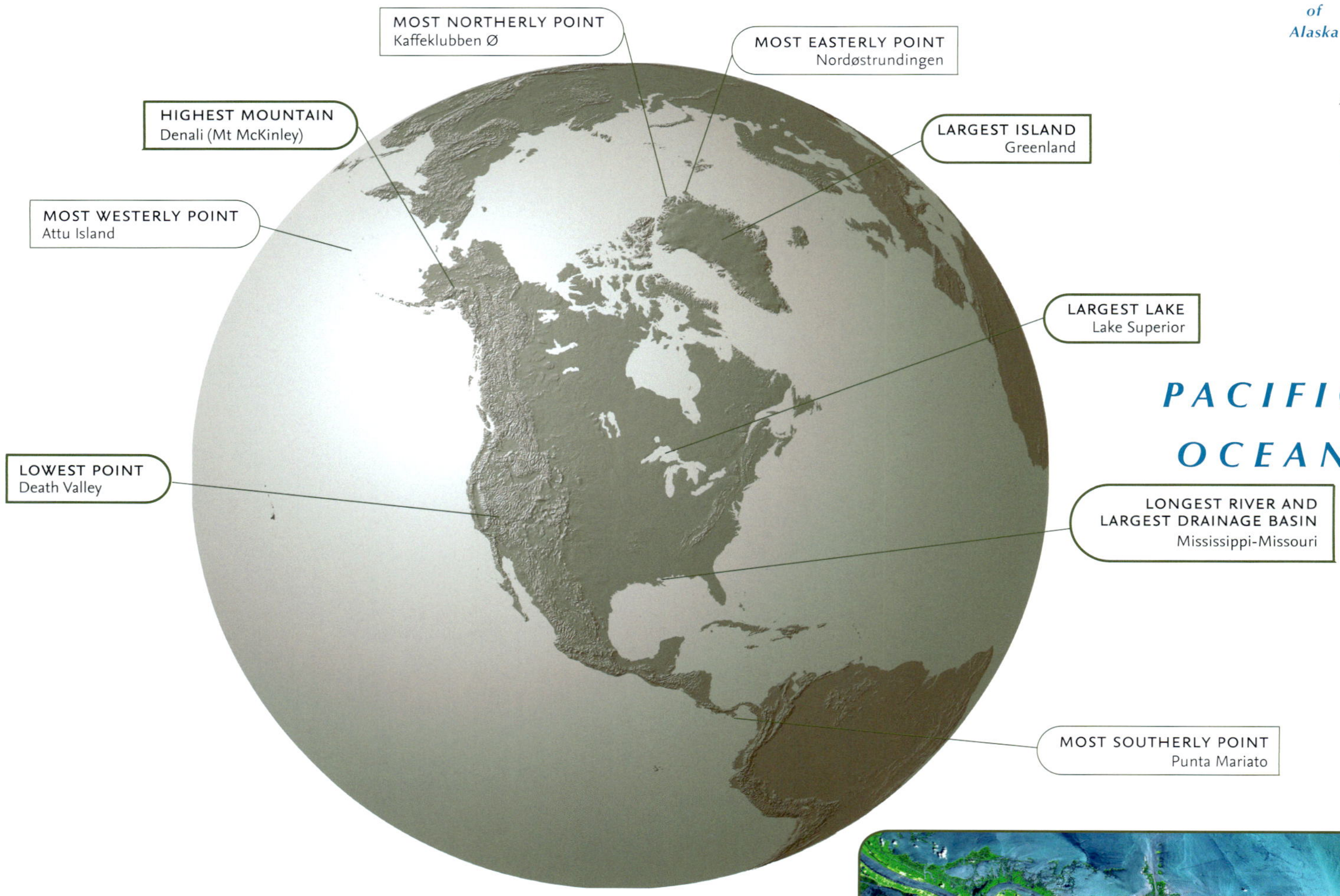

North America's longest river system, the **Mississippi-Missouri,** flows into the Gulf of Mexico through the Mississippi Delta.

North America's physical features

Highest mountain	Denali (Mt McKinley), USA	6 190 metres	20 310 feet
Longest river	Mississippi-Missouri, USA	5 969 km	3 709 miles
Largest lake	Lake Superior, Canada/USA	82 100 sq km	31 699 sq miles
Largest island	Greenland	2 175 600 sq km	839 999 sq miles
Largest drainage basin	Mississippi-Missouri, USA	3 250 000 sq km	1 254 825 sq miles
Lowest point	Death Valley, USA	-86 metres	-282 feet

North America's extent

TOTAL LAND AREA (including Hawai'ian Islands)	24 680 331 sq km / 9 529 076 sq miles
Most northerly point	Kaffeklubben Ø, Greenland
Most southerly point	Punta Mariato, Panama
Most westerly point	Attu Island, USA
Most easterly point	Nordøstrundingen, Greenland

The **Panama Canal,** Panama, linking the Pacific Ocean to the Atlantic Ocean.

Facts

- Devon Island, Canada, is the world's largest uninhabited island
- Canada has the longest coastline of any country in the world
- Lake Superior is the world's largest freshwater lake
- Over 320 000 square kilometres of the USA is protected for conservation purposes

North America

Countries

North America has been dominated economically and politically by the USA since the nineteenth century. Before that, the continent was subject to colonial influences, particularly of Spain in the south and of Britain and France in the east. The nineteenth century saw the steady development of the western half of the continent. The wealth of natural resources and the generally temperate climate were an excellent basis for settlement, agriculture and industrial development which has led to the USA being the richest nation in the world today.

Although there are twenty-three independent countries and fourteen dependent territories in North America, Canada, Mexico and the USA have approximately eighty-five per cent of the continent's population and eighty-eight per cent of its land area. Large parts of the north remain sparsely populated, while the most densely populated areas are in the northeast USA, and the Caribbean.

North America's capitals

Largest capital (population)	Mexico City, Mexico	21 706 000	
Smallest capital (population)	Roseau, Dominica	15 000	
Most northerly capital	Ottawa, Canada	45° 25'N	
Most southerly capital	Panama City, Panama	8° 56'N	
Highest capital	Mexico City, Mexico	2 300 metres	7 546 feet

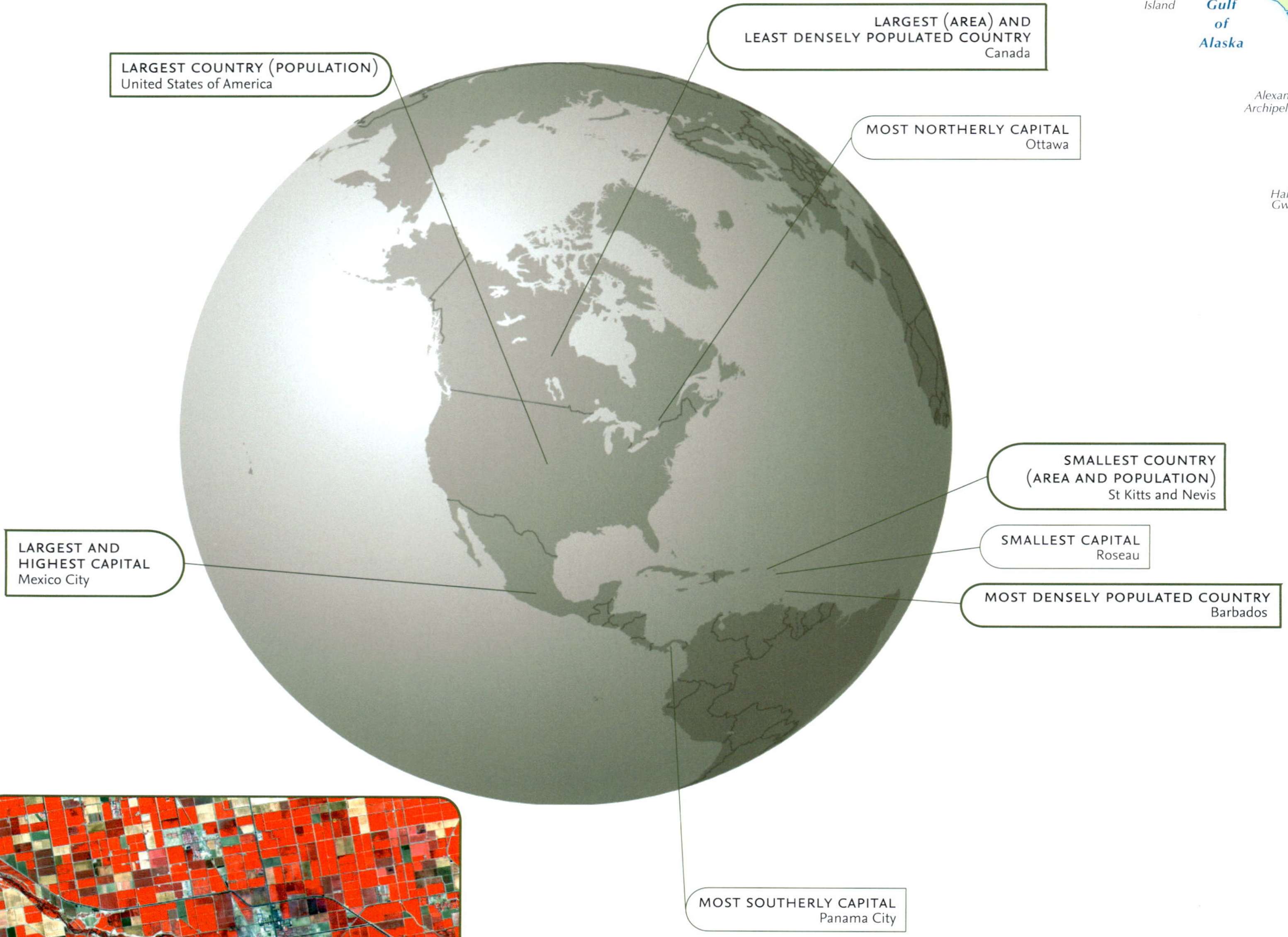

False-colour satellite image of the **Mexico-USA** boundary at Mexicali.

North America's countries

Largest country (area)	Canada	9 984 670 sq km	3 855 103 sq miles
Smallest country (area)	St Kitts and Nevis	261 sq km	101 sq miles
Largest country (population)	United States of America	321 774 000	
Smallest country (population)	St Kitts and Nevis	56 000	
Most densely populated country	Barbados	663 per sq km	1 717 per sq mile
Least densely populated country	Canada	4 per sq km	9 per sq mile

Internet Links

UK Foreign and Commonwealth Office	www.fco.gov.uk
CIA World Factbook	www.cia.gov/library/publications/the-world-factbook/index.html
U.S. Board on Geographic Names	geonames.usgs.gov
NASA Astronaut Photography	eol.jsc.nasa.gov

The Bahamas, a chain of islands in the North Atlantic Ocean, lying southeast of Florida, USA.

Facts

- The Panama Canal, opened in 1914, cut the journey between the Atlantic and the Pacific by over 14 000 km
- Mexico City is the highest city in North America and houses approximately 18% of Mexico's population
- The state of Alaska was bought by the USA from Russia in 1867
- The territory of Nunavut is Canada's newest administrative division, created in 1999 from the eastern part of Northwest Territories

Lambert Conformal Conic Projection

1:16 000 000

0 200 400 miles

0 200 400 600 800 km

Greenland (Kalaallit Nunaat) (Denmark)
ICELAND
REYKJAVÍK
Baffin Bay
Davis Strait
Denmark Strait
Labrador Sea
Hudson Bay
Hudson Strait
James Bay
Foxe Basin
Baffin Island
Ellesmere Island
Devon Island
Queen Elizabeth Islands
Parry Islands
NUNAVUT
CANADA
Péninsule d'Ungava
QUÉBEC
ONTARIO
MANITOBA
NEWFOUNDLAND AND LABRADOR
Newfoundland
NEW BRUNSWICK
NOVA SCOTIA
PRINCE EDWARD I.
Gulf of St Lawrence
Île d'Anticosti
St Pierre and Miquelon (France)
ATLANTIC OCEAN
Gulf of Maine
Lake Superior
Lake Michigan
Lake Huron
Lake Erie
Lake Ontario
Lake Winnipeg
OTTAWA
Montréal
Québec
Toronto
Winnipeg
Halifax
St John's
Chicago
Detroit
Boston
New York
MINNESOTA
WISCONSIN
MICHIGAN
IOWA
NEW YORK
PENNSYLVANIA
MAINE
AMERICA
States in the U.S.A. numbered on the map:
1. CONNECTICUT (K5)
2. MASSACHUSETTS (K5)
3. NEW HAMPSHIRE (K5)
4. RHODE ISLAND (K5)
5. VERMONT (K5)

↓ 125

North America
Canada

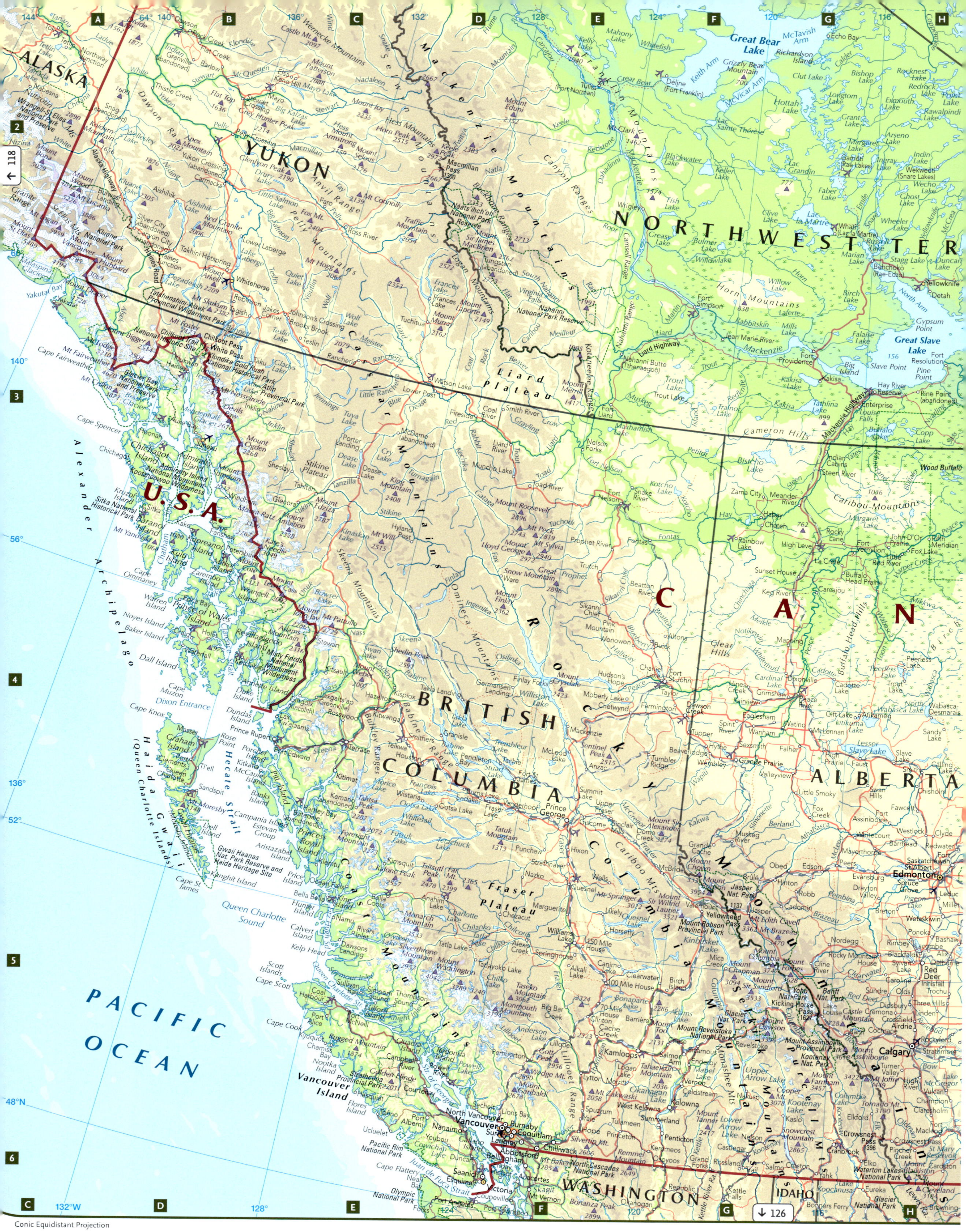
ALASKA
YUKON
NORTHWESTER
BRITISH COLUMBIA
ALBERTA
U.S.A.
C A N
PACIFIC OCEAN
WASHINGTON
IDAHO
Great Bear Lake
Great Slave Lake
Mackenzie Mountains
Cassiar Mountains
Rocky Mountains
Coast Mountains
Columbia Mountains
Liard Plateau
Fraser Plateau
Stikine Plateau
Caribou Mountains
Alexander Archipelago
Haida Gwaii (Queen Charlotte Islands)
Hecate Strait
Dixon Entrance
Queen Charlotte Sound
Vancouver Island
Whitehorse
Yellowknife
Fort Nelson
Fort St John
Dawson Creek
Grande Prairie
Prince Rupert
Prince George
Edmonton
Red Deer
Calgary
Kamloops
Kelowna
Vancouver
Nanaimo
Victoria
← 118
↓ 126

Conic Equidistant Projection

1:7 000 000

↑ 118
→ 122
↓ 130

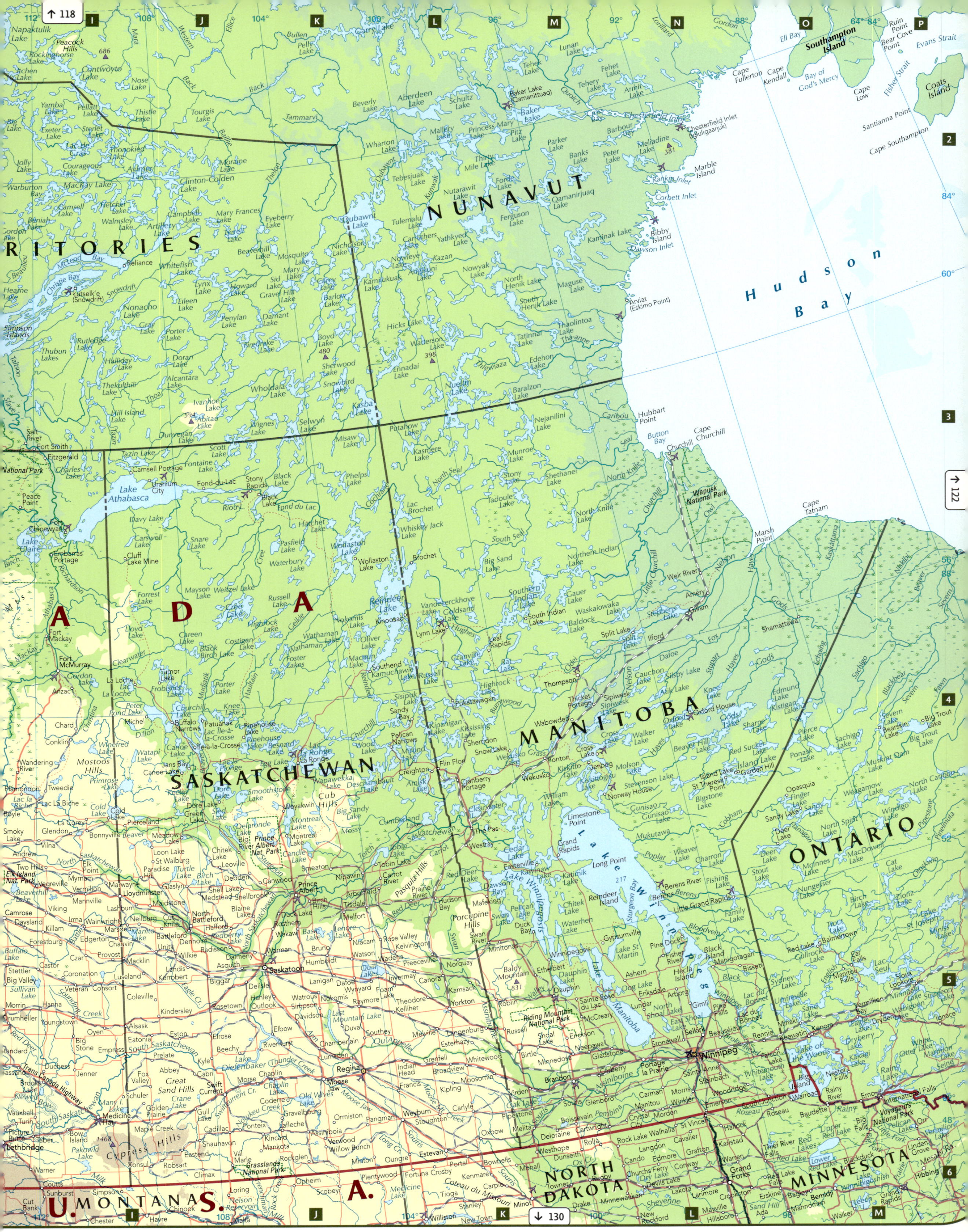
NUNAVUT
RITORIES
A
D
A
SASKATCHEWAN
MANITOBA
ONTARIO
Hudson Bay
NORTH DAKOTA
MINNESOTA
U. MONTANA S.
A.
Southampton Island
Coats Island
Lake Athabasca
Reindeer Lake
Lake Winnipeg
Lake Winnipegosis
Lake Manitoba
Winnipeg
Regina
Saskatoon
Brandon
Churchill
The Pas
Thompson
Baker Lake (Qamanittuaq)
Chesterfield Inlet (Igluligaarjuk)
Rankin Inlet
Arviat (Eskimo Point)
Prince Albert
Moose Jaw
Swift Current
Medicine Hat
Lethbridge
Lloydminster
Flin Flon
Fort McMurray
Wapusk National Park
Riding Mountain National Park
Prince Albert Nat. Park
Grasslands National Park
Voyageurs National Park
Cypress Hills
Porcupine Hills
Cape Churchill
Cape Tatnam
Nelson
Churchill
Saskatchewan
North Saskatchewan
South Saskatchewan
Trans-Canada Highway

Conic Equidistant Projection

1:7 000 000

0 100 200 miles

0 100 200 300 400 km

Labrador Sea
Ungava Bay
Torngat Mountains National Park Reserve
NEWFOUNDLAND AND LABRADOR
Labrador
Smallwood Reservoir
Lake Melville
Mealy Mountains
Churchill Falls
Happy Valley-Goose Bay
Hopedale
Nain
Cartwright
Strait of Belle Isle
Belle Isle
Cape Bauld
St Anthony
Long Range Mountains
Gros Morne National Park
Corner Brook
Gander
Bonavista Bay
Trinity Bay
Avalon Peninsula
St John's
Cape Race
Placentia Bay
Burin Peninsula
Fortune Bay
St Pierre and Miquelon (France)
ST-PIERRE
Cape Ray
Channel-Port-aux-Basques
Cabot Strait
St George's Bay
QUÉBEC
Réservoir Manicouagan
Sept-Îles
Île d'Anticosti
Gulf of St Lawrence
Détroit de Jacques-Cartier
Détroit d'Honguedo
Péninsule de la Gaspésie
Monts Notre-Dame
Gaspé
Îles de la Madeleine
Chicoutimi
Lac St-Jean
Québec
Trois-Rivières
Sherbrooke
St Lawrence
NEW BRUNSWICK
Fredericton
Saint John
Moncton
Bathurst
Miramichi
Edmundston
Bay of Fundy
PRINCE EDWARD ISLAND
Charlottetown
Northumberland Strait
NOVA SCOTIA
Halifax
Dartmouth
Sydney
Cape Breton Island
Cape Breton Highlands National Park
Yarmouth
Cape Sable
Sable Island National Park Reserve
Sable Island
ATLANTIC OCEAN
MAINE
Bangor
Augusta
Portland
Mt Katahdin
Acadia National Park
Gulf of Maine
VERMONT
Burlington
NEW HAMPSHIRE
Mt Washington
Manchester
Concord
Portsmouth
Lowell
Salem

North America
Eastern Canada

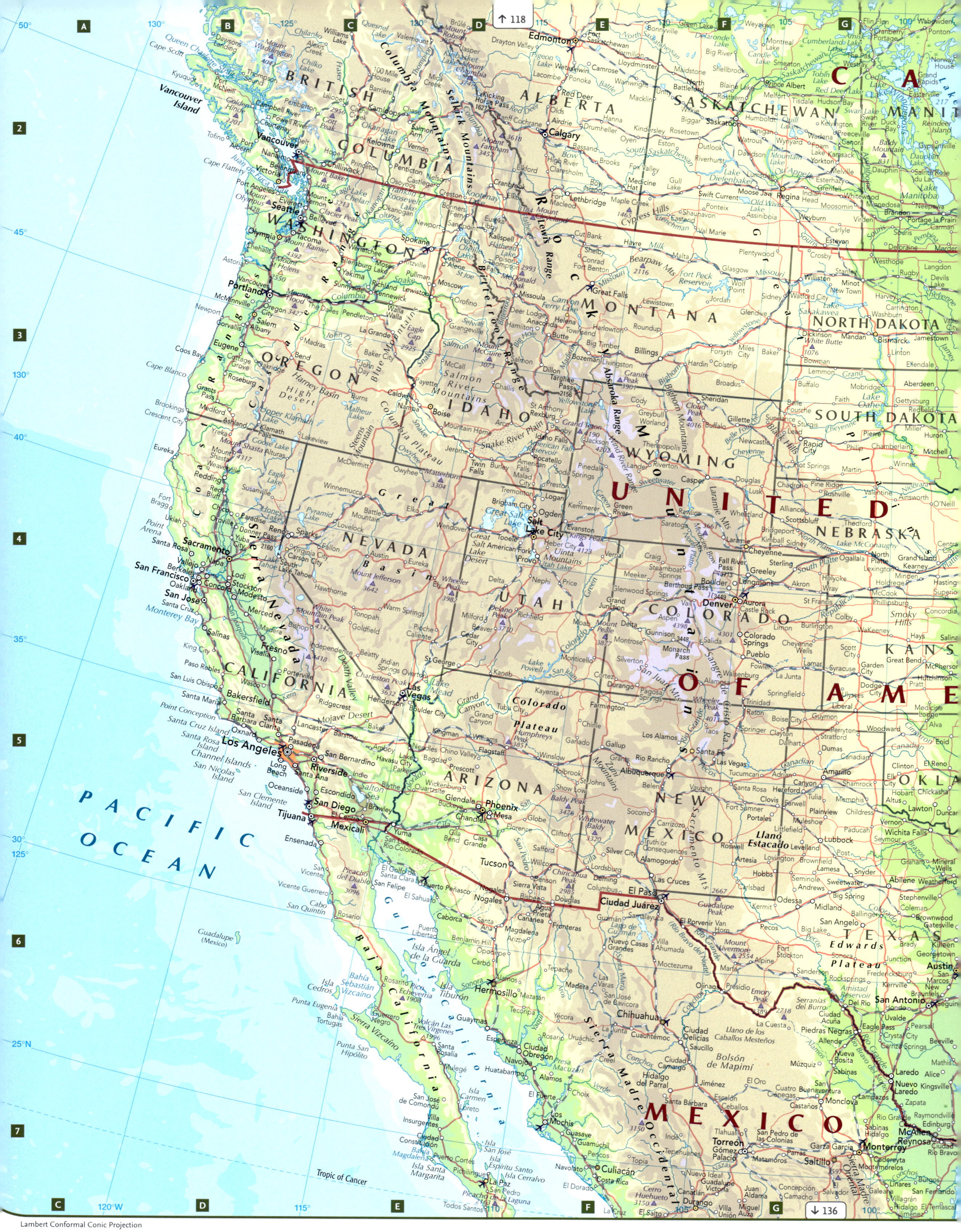

Lambert Conformal Conic Projection

1:12 000 000

miles	0	100	200	300	400			
km	0	100	200	300	400	500	600	700

↑ 119

CANADA
UNITED STATES OF AMERICA
ONTARIO
QUÉBEC
NEW BRUNSWICK
NOVA SCOTIA
PRINCE EDWARD ISLAND
MAINE
VERMONT
NEW HAMPSHIRE
MASSACHUSETTS
CONNECTICUT
RHODE ISLAND
NEW YORK
NEW JERSEY
PENNSYLVANIA
DELAWARE
MARYLAND
WASHINGTON D.C.
VIRGINIA
WEST VIRGINIA
NORTH CAROLINA
SOUTH CAROLINA
GEORGIA
FLORIDA
ALABAMA
MISSISSIPPI
LOUISIANA
TENNESSEE
KENTUCKY
OHIO
INDIANA
ILLINOIS
MICHIGAN
WISCONSIN
MINNESOTA
IOWA
MISSOURI
ARKANSAS
Lake Superior
Lake Michigan
Lake Huron
Lake Erie
Lake Ontario
James Bay
Gulf of St Lawrence
Gulf of Maine
Appalachian Mountains
Allegheny Mountains
Cumberland Plateau
Ozark Plateau
ATLANTIC OCEAN
Gulf of Mexico
Straits of Florida
Great Bahama Bank
THE BAHAMAS
CUBA
Tropic of Cancer
New York
Chicago
Philadelphia
Boston
Washington
Atlanta
Detroit
Toronto
Montréal
Ottawa
Québec
Miami
Houston
Dallas
New Orleans
Memphis
Nashville
St Louis
Minneapolis
Milwaukee
Pittsburgh
Cleveland
Indianapolis
Jacksonville
Tampa
Orlando
Charlotte
Richmond
Baltimore
Buffalo
Winnipeg
Nassau

↓ 137

North America
United States of America

Lambert Conformal Conic Projection

1:7 000 000

0 100 200 miles

0 100 200 300 400 km

PACIFIC OCEAN
CALIFORNIA
ARIZONA
NEW MEXICO
TEXAS
MEXICO
SONORA
CHIHUAHUA
SINALOA
DURANGO
BAJA CALIFORNIA
BAJA CALIFORNIA SUR
Gulf of California
HAWAII (U.S.A.)

North America

Western United States

126

CALIFORNIA
NEVADA
UNITED STATES OF
BAJA CAL
PACIFIC OCEAN
San Francisco
Oakland
San Jose
Sacramento
Fresno
Bakersfield
Los Angeles
San Diego
Tijuana
Reno
Carson City
Redding
Stockton
Modesto
Santa Barbara
Riverside
San Bernardino
Sacramento Valley
San Joaquin Valley
Sierra Nevada
Coast Ranges
Diablo Range
Santa Lucia Range
Mojave Desert
Death Valley
Monterey Bay
Santa Barbara Channel
Channel Islands
San Pedro Channel
Santa Catalina Island
San Clemente Island
San Nicolas Island
Santa Rosa Island
Santa Cruz Island
Gulf of Santa Catalina
Lake Tahoe
Point Conception
Point Arena
Cape Mendocino
Lambert Conformal Conic Projection

1:3 500 000 — 0, 50, 100 miles; 0, 50, 100, 150, 200 km

UTAH
COLORADO
ARIZONA
NEW MEXICO
UNITED STATES OF AMERICA
MEXICO
SONORA
Great Salt Lake
Great Salt Lake Desert
Salt Lake City
Provo
Grand Junction
Las Vegas
Henderson
Flagstaff
Phoenix
Mesa
Glendale
Tempe
Tucson
Yuma
Mexicali
Lake Mead
Lake Powell
Colorado Plateau
Grand Canyon
Painted Desert
Sonoran Desert
Uinta Mountains
San Juan Mountains
Zion National Park
Bryce Canyon National Park
Arches National Park
Canyonlands National Park
Capitol Reef National Park
Mesa Verde National Park
Petrified Forest National Park
Great Basin National Park
Saguaro National Park
Joshua Tree National Park
Grand Staircase-Escalante National Monument
Organ Pipe Cactus National Monument
Chiricahua National Monument
Mogollon Plateau
↑ 127
↓ 136

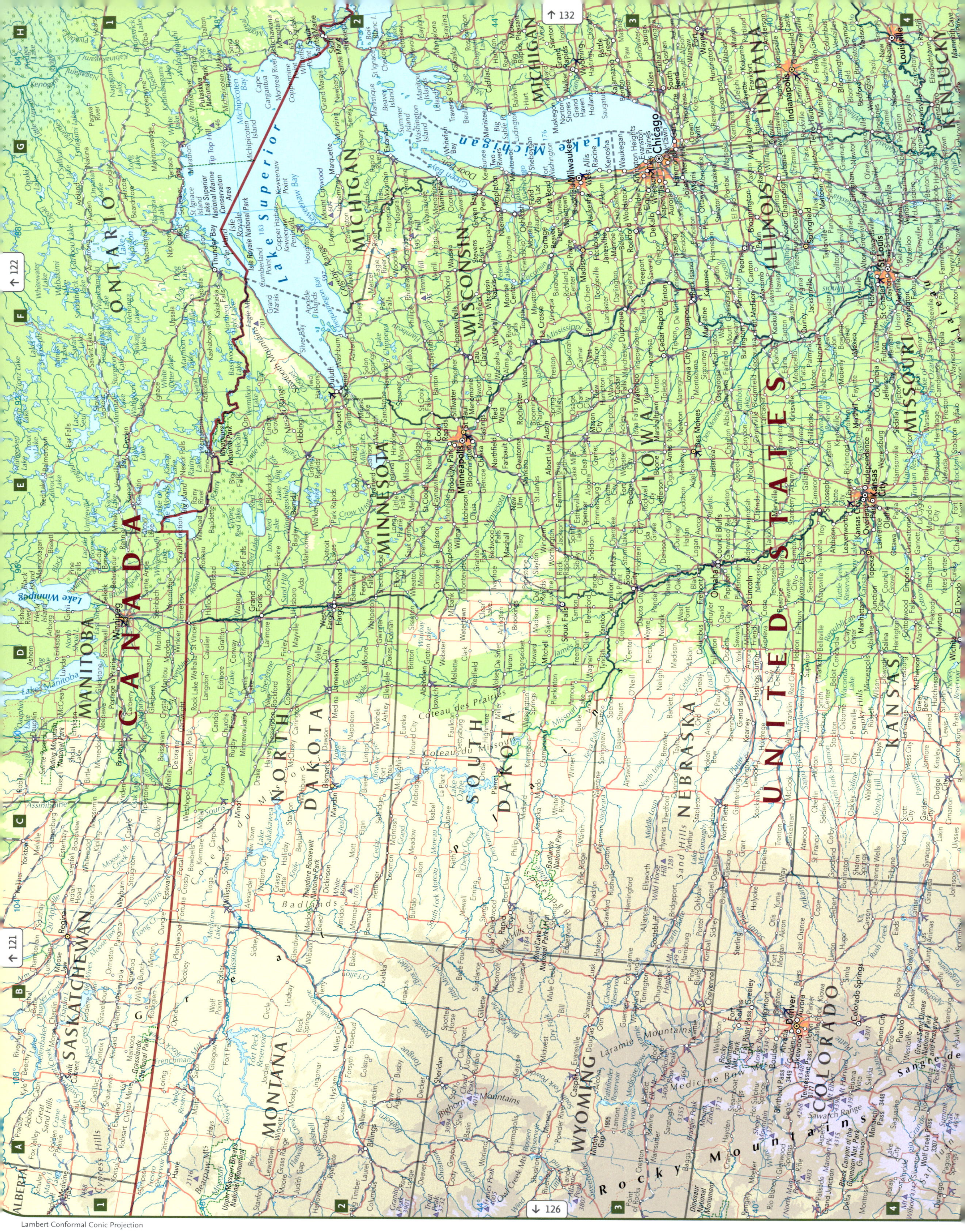

↑ 132
↑ 122
↑ 121
↓ 126

Lambert Conformal Conic Projection

1:7 000 000

↑ 133
↓ 127
↓ 136
OF AMERICA
TENNESSEE
ALABAMA
MISSISSIPPI
ARKANSAS
LOUISIANA
OKLAHOMA
TEXAS
NEW MEXICO
FLORIDA
MEXICO
CHIHUAHUA
COAHUILA
NUEVO LEÓN
TAMAULIPAS
DURANGO
ZACATECAS
Gulf of Mexico
Tropic of Cancer

North America
Central United States

CANADA
QUÉBEC
ONTARIO
UNITED STATES
NEW BRUNSWICK
MAINE
VERMONT
NEW HAMPSHIRE
NEW YORK
PENNSYLVANIA
NEW JERSEY
MARYLAND
WEST VIRGINIA
VIRGINIA
NORTH CAROLINA
KENTUCKY
TENNESSEE
OHIO
INDIANA
ILLINOIS
MICHIGAN
WISCONSIN
MINNESOTA
IOWA
MISSOURI
Lake Superior
Lake Michigan
Lake Huron
Lake Erie
Lake Ontario
Georgian Bay
Gulf of Maine
Chesapeake Bay
OTTAWA
WASHINGTON D.C.
Montréal
Québec
Toronto
Boston
New York
Philadelphia
Baltimore
Pittsburgh
Cleveland
Detroit
Chicago
Milwaukee
Indianapolis
Columbus
Cincinnati
Louisville
Nashville
St Louis
Buffalo
Richmond
Virginia Beach
States in the U.S.A. numbered on the map:
1. CONNECTICUT (F3)
2. DELAWARE (F4)
3. MASSACHUSETTS (F3)
4. RHODE ISLAND (G3)
↑ 123
↑ 122
↓ 130

Lambert Conformal Conic Projection

1:7 000 000

ATLANTIC OCEAN
THE BAHAMAS
Gulf of Mexico
OF AMERICA
SOUTH CAROLINA
GEORGIA
ALABAMA
MISSISSIPPI
FLORIDA
CUBA
MEXICO
Turks and Caicos Islands (U.K.)
Straits of Florida
Great Bahama Bank
Yucatan Channel
Tropic of Cancer

North America
Eastern United States

Lambert Conformal Conic Projection

1:3 500 000

0 50 100 miles

0 50 100 150 200 km

CANADA
QUÉBEC
OTTAWA
Lake Ontario
NEW YORK
VERMONT
NEW HAMPSHIRE
MAINE
MASSACHUSETTS
CONNECTICUT
RHODE ISLAND
PENNSYLVANIA
NEW JERSEY
DELAWARE
MARYLAND
VIRGINIA
WASHINGTON
New York
Boston
Philadelphia
Baltimore
Richmond
Buffalo
Rochester
Syracuse
Albany
Hartford
Providence
Bridgeport
Allentown
Virginia Beach
Adirondack Mountains
Catskill Mountains
Green Mountains
White Mountains
Long Island
Long Island Sound
Gulf of Maine
Cape Cod
Massachusetts Bay
Chesapeake Bay
Delaware Bay
ATLANTIC
OCEAN
↑ 123

North America

Northeast United States

Lambert Conformal Conic Projection

1:14 000 000

0	200	400	miles
0	200	400	600	800 km

North America

Central America and the Caribbean

South America
Landscapes

South America is a continent of great contrasts, with landscapes varying from the tropical rainforests of the Amazon Basin, to the Atacama Desert, the driest place on earth, and the sub-Antarctic regions of southern Chile and Argentina. The dominant physical features are the Andes, stretching along the entire west coast of the continent and containing numerous mountains over 6 000 metres high, and the Amazon, which is the second longest river in the world and has the world's largest drainage basin.

The Altiplano is a high plateau lying between two of the Andes ranges. It contains Lake Titicaca, the world's highest navigable lake. By contrast, large lowland areas dominate the centre of the continent, lying between the Andes and the Guiana and Brazilian Highlands. These vast grasslands stretch from the Llanos of the north through the Selvas and the Gran Chaco to the Pampas of Argentina.

Confluence of the **Amazon** and **Negro** rivers at Manaus, northern Brazil.

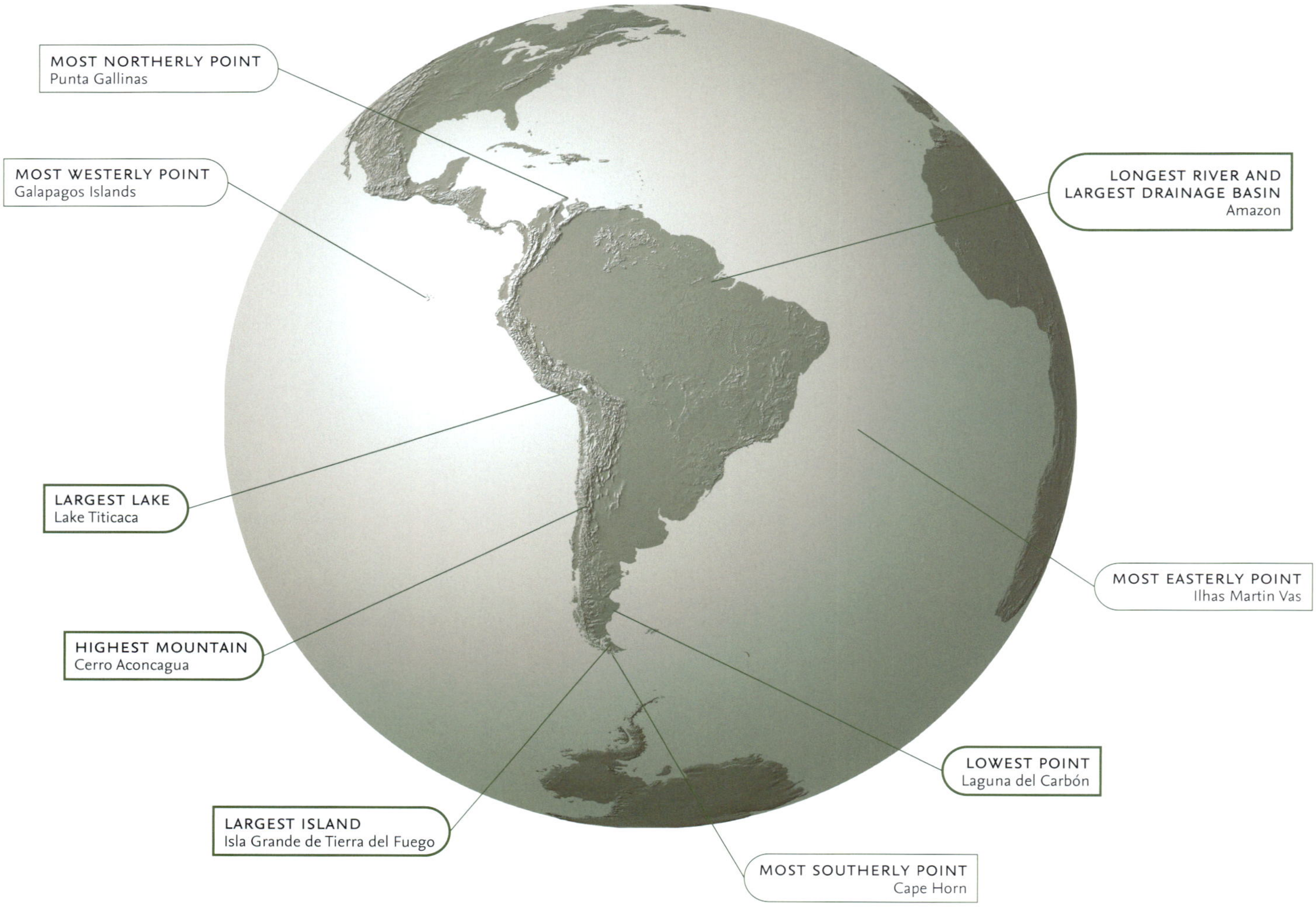

South America's physical features

Highest mountain	Cerro Aconcagua, Argentina	6 959 metres	22 831 feet
Longest river	Amazon	6 516 km	4 049 miles
Largest lake	Lake Titicaca, Bolivia/Peru	8 340 sq km	3 220 sq miles
Largest island	Isla Grande de Tierra del Fuego, Argentina/Chile	47 000 sq km	18 147 sq miles
Largest drainage basin	Amazon	7 050 000 sq km	2 722 005 sq miles
Lowest point	Laguna del Carbón, Argentina	-105 metres	-345 feet

Internet Links

NASA Visible Earth	**visibleearth.nasa.gov**
NASA Astronaut Photography	**eol.jsc.nasa.gov**
World Rainforest Information Portal	**www.ran.org**
Peakware World Mountain Encyclopedia	**www.peakware.com**

Isla Grande de Tierra del Fuego, South America's largest island, situated at the southernmost tip of the continent.

South America's extent

TOTAL LAND AREA	17 815 420 sq km / 6 878 534 sq miles
Most northerly point	Punta Gallinas, Colombia
Most southerly point	Cape Horn, Chile
Most westerly point	Galagapos Islands, Ecuador
Most easterly point	Ilhas Martin Vas, Atlantic Ocean

Facts

- Water flow along the Amazon is over 1 500 times that of the River Thames
- Cerro Aconcagua, 6 959 metres, is the highest point in the western hemisphere
- The Amazon rainforest supports approximately half of all the world's living species
- The Pantanal in Brazil is the largest area of wetland in the world
- The world's driest desert is the Atacama, where only 1mm of rain may fall as infrequently as once every 5–20 years

South America
Countries

French Guiana, a French Department, is the only remaining territory under overseas control on a continent which has seen a long colonial history. Much of South America was colonized by Spain in the sixteenth century, with Britain, Portugal and the Netherlands each claiming territory in the northeast of the continent. This colonization led to the conquering of ancient civilizations, including the Incas in Peru. Most countries became independent from Spain and Portugal in the early nineteenth century.

The population of the continent reflects its history, being composed primarily of indigenous Indian peoples and mestizos – reflecting the long Hispanic influence. There has been a steady process of urbanization within the continent, with major movements of the population from rural to urban areas. The majority of the population now lives in the major cities and within 300 kilometres of the coast.

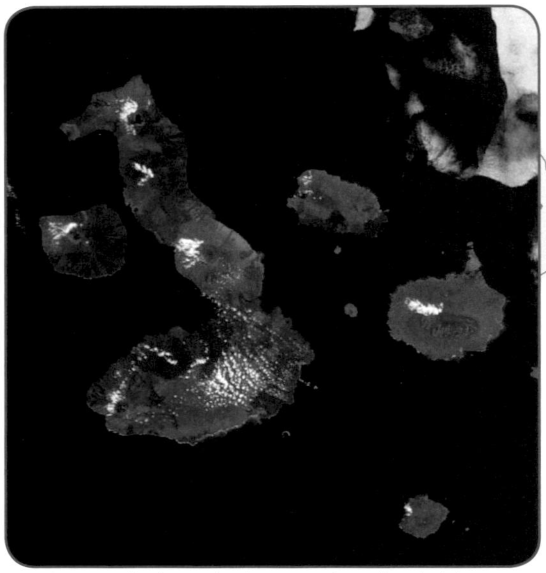

Galapagos Islands, an island territory of Ecuador which lies on the equator in the eastern Pacific Ocean over 900 kilometres west of the coast of Ecuador.

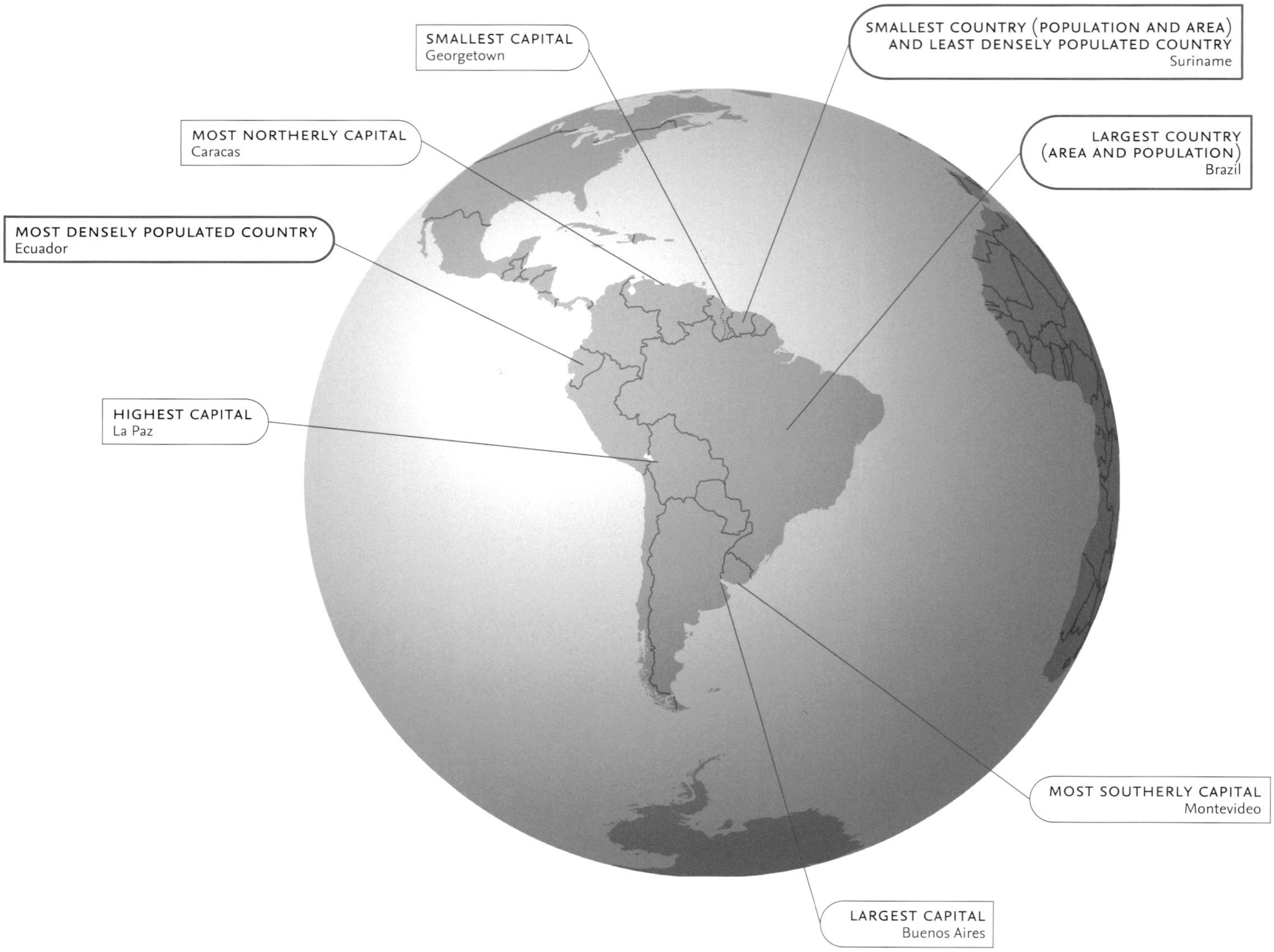

South America's countries

Largest country (area)	Brazil	8 514 879 sq km	3 287 613 sq miles
Smallest country (area)	Suriname	163 820 sq km	63 251 sq miles
Largest country (population)	Brazil	207 848 000	
Smallest country (population)	Suriname	543 000	
Most densely populated country	Ecuador	58 per sq km	150 per sq mile
Least densely populated country	Suriname	3 per sq km	9 per sq mile

Internet Links

UK Foreign and Commonwealth Office	**www.fco.gov.uk**
CIA World Factbook	**www.cia.gov/library/publications/the-world-factbook/index.html**
Caribbean Community (Caricom)	**www.caricom.org**
Latin American Network Information Center	**lanic.utexas.edu**

South America's capitals

Largest capital (population)	Buenos Aires, Argentina	14 151 000
Smallest capital (population)	Georgetown, Guyana	124 000
Most northerly capital	Caracas, Venezuela	10° 28'N
Most southerly capital	Montevideo, Uruguay	34° 52'S
Highest capital	La Paz, Bolivia	3 630 metres 11 909 feet

Facts

- South America is often referred to as 'Latin America', reflecting the historic influences of Spain and Portugal
- The largest city in each South American country is the capital, except in Brazil and Ecuador
- South America has only two landlocked countries – Bolivia and Paraguay
- Chile is over 4 000 kilometres long but has an average width of only 177 kilometres

Falkland Islands, an overseas UK territory in the South Atlantic Ocean.

Lambert Azimuthal Equal Area Projection

1:14 000 000 (0–400 miles; 0–800 km)

ATLANTIC OCEAN
GUYANA
SURINAME
French Guiana
BRAZIL
PARAGUAY
GEORGETOWN
PARAMARIBO
CAYENNE
BRASÍLIA
Mouths of the Amazon
Brazilian Highlands
Equator
Belém
São Luís
Fortaleza (Ceará)
Natal
João Pessoa
Recife (Pernambuco)
Maceió
Aracaju
Salvador (Bahia)
Vitória
Belo Horizonte
Rio de Janeiro
São Paulo
Campinas
Goiânia
Cuiabá
Campo Grande
Teresina
Macapá
Santarém
Imperatriz
Uberlândia
Montes Claros
Ilhéus
Campos dos Goytacazes
Cabo Frio
Cabo de São Roque
Cabo de São Tomé
Cabo Orange
Fernando de Noronha (Brazil)
Ilha da Trindade (Brazil)
Ilha de Marajó
Baía de Marajó
Ilhas de São João
Serra do Cachimbo
Serra dos Carajás
Serra do Roncador
Serra Geral de Goiás
Serra do Espinhaço
Chapada Diamantina
Tumucumaque
↓ 144

South America
Northern South America

Lambert Azimuthal Equal Area Projection

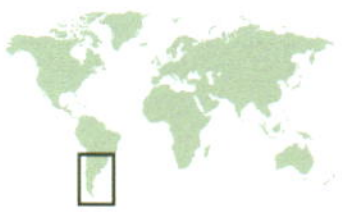

South America

Southern South America

1:14 000 000

0 200 400 miles

0 200 400 600 800 km

↑ 143

← 144

Lambert Azimuthal Equal Area Projection

1:7 000 000

0 100 200 miles

0 100 200 300 400 km

South America

Southeast Brazil

Oceans and Poles

Features

Between them, the world's oceans and polar regions cover approximately seventy per cent of the Earth's surface. The oceans contain ninety-six per cent of the Earth's water and a vast range of flora and fauna. They are a major influence on the world's climate, particularly through ocean currents. The Arctic and Antarctica are the coldest and most inhospitable places on the Earth. They both have vast amounts of ice which, if global warming continues, could have a major influence on sea level across the globe.

Our understanding of the oceans and polar regions has increased enormously over the last twenty years through the development of new technologies, particularly that of satellite remote sensing, which can generate vast amounts of data relating to, for example, topography (both on land and the seafloor), land cover and sea surface temperature.

The oceans

The world's major oceans are the Pacific, the Atlantic and the Indian Oceans. The Arctic Ocean is generally considered as part of the Atlantic, and the Southern Ocean, which stretches around the whole of Antarctica is usually treated as an extension of each of the three major oceans.

One of the most important factors affecting the earth's climate is the circulation of water within and between the oceans. Differences in temperature and surface winds create ocean currents which move enormous quantities of water around the globe. These currents re-distribute heat which the oceans have absorbed from the sun, and so have a major effect on the world's climate system. El Niño is one climatic phenomenon directly influenced by these ocean processes.

Internet Links

National Oceanic and Atmospheric Administration	www.noaa.gov
National Oceanography Centre, Southampton	www.soc.soton.ac.uk
British Antarctic Survey	www.bas.ac.uk
Scott Polar Research Institute (SPRI)	www.spri.cam.ac.uk
The National Snow and Ice Data Center (NSIDC)	nsidc.org

Facts

- If all of Antarctica's ice melted, world sea level would rise by more than 60 metres
- The Arctic Ocean produces up to 50 000 icebergs per year
- The Mid-Atlantic Ridge in the Atlantic Ocean is the earth's longest mountain range
- The world's greatest tidal range – 21 metres – is in the Bay of Fundy, Nova Scotia, Canada
- The Circumpolar current in the Southern Ocean carries 125 million cubic metres of water per second

Polar regions

Although a harsh climate is common to the two polar regions, there are major differences between the Arctic and Antarctica. The North Pole is surrounded by the Arctic Ocean, much of which is permanently covered by sea ice, while the South Pole lies on the huge land mass of Antarctica. This is covered by a permanent ice cap which reaches a maximum thickness of over four kilometres. Antarctica has no permanent population, but Europe, Asia and North America all stretch into the Arctic region which is populated by numerous ethnic groups. Antarctica is subject to the Antarctic Treaty of 1959 which does not recognize individual land claims and protects the continent in the interests of international scientific cooperation.

Arctic Ocean profile

Cross-section of the Arctic Ocean from northwest Canada to northwest Russia

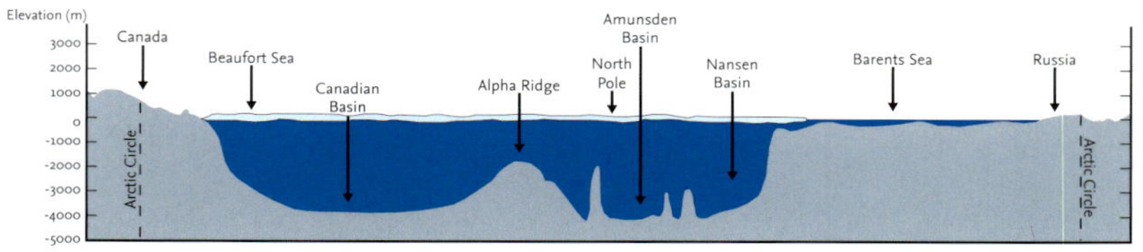

Antarctic profile

Cross-section of West Antarctica from the Ronne Ice Shelf to the Ross Ice Shelf

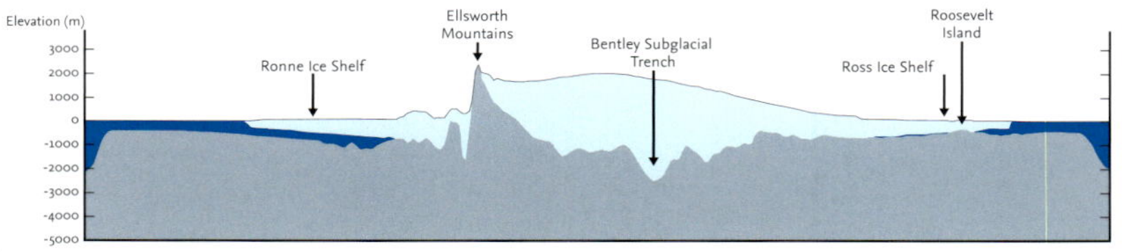

Antarctica's physical features

Highest mountain: Mt Vinson	4 897 m	16 066 ft
Total land area (excluding ice shelves)	12 093 000 sq km	4 669 107 sq miles
Ice shelves	1 559 000 sq km	601 930 sq miles
Exposed rock	49 000 sq km	18 919 sq miles
Lowest bedrock elevation (Bentley Subglacial Trench)	2 496 m below sea level	8 189 ft below sea level
Maximum ice thickness (Astrolabe Subglacial Basin)	4 776 m	15 669 ft
Mean ice thickness (including ice shelves)	1 859 m	6 099 ft
Volume of ice sheet (including ice shelves)	25 400 000 cubic km	6 094 628 cubic miles

The **Antarctic Peninsula** and the **Larsen Ice Shelf** in western Antarctica.

Lambert Azimuthal Equal Area Projection

1:50 000 000

0 500 1000 1500 miles
0 500 1000 1500 2000 2500 km

RUSSIA
KAZAKHSTAN
MONGOLIA
CHINA
Gobi Desert
Plateau of Tibet
Himalaya
UZBEKISTAN
TURKMENISTAN
AFGHANISTAN
PAKISTAN
INDIA
NEPAL
BANGLADESH
MYANMAR (BURMA)
THAILAND
CAMBODIA
MALAYSIA
INDONESIA
PHILIPPINES
JAPAN
TURKEY
IRAN
IRAQ
SAUDI ARABIA
Arabian Peninsula
OMAN
YEMEN
EGYPT
SUDAN
SOUTH SUDAN
CHAD
ETHIOPIA
SOMALIA
KENYA
TANZANIA
DEMOCRATIC REPUBLIC OF THE CONGO
ANGOLA
ZAMBIA
ZIMBABWE
MOZAMBIQUE
NAMIBIA
BOTSWANA
SOUTH AFRICA
MADAGASCAR
AUSTRALIA
MOSCOW
BEIJING
TOKYO
SEOUL
DELHI
KARACHI
Mumbai
Kolkata
DHAKA
BANGKOK
JAKARTA
MANILA
TEHRAN
BAGHDAD
RIYADH
CAIRO
KHARTOUM
ADDIS ABABA
NAIROBI
KINSHASA
CAPE TOWN
PRETORIA
ANTANANARIVO
Caspian Sea
Black Sea
Mediterranean Sea
Red Sea
Arabian Sea
Bay of Bengal
South China Sea
PACIFIC OCEAN
INDIAN OCEAN
Somali Basin
Mascarene Basin
Madagascar Basin
Mid-Indian Basin
Mid-Indian Ridge
Carlsberg Ridge
Chagos-Laccadive Ridge
Ninetyeast Ridge
Southwest Indian Ridge
Southeast Indian Ridge
West Australian Basin
Crozet Basin
Crozet Plateau
Agulhas Basin
Agulhas Plateau
Natal Basin
Kerguelen Plateau
French Southern and Antarctic Lands
Antarctic Basin
Australian-Antarctic Basin
East Antarctica
ANTARCTICA

Atlantic Ocean
Indian Ocean

International boundaries in the sea shown on this map indicate ownership of islands and island groups only. They do not infer the alignments of legal maritime boundaries.

Lambert Azimuthal Equal Area Projection

1:50 000 000

0	500	1000	1500	miles		
0	500	1000	1500	2000	2500	km

CANADA
UNITED STATES OF AMERICA
MEXICO
ATLANTIC OCEAN
PACIFIC OCEAN
Gulf of Alaska
Rocky Mountains
Coast Mountains
Edmonton
Calgary
Vancouver
Seattle
Portland
Sacramento
San Francisco
San Jose
Los Angeles
San Diego
Las Vegas
Salt Lake City
Denver
Phoenix
El Paso
Dallas
Houston
San Antonio
Austin
Oklahoma City
Chicago
Minneapolis
Detroit
Toronto
OTTAWA
Montreal
Boston
New York
Philadelphia
WASHINGTON D.C.
Pittsburgh
Atlanta
Charlotte
Jacksonville
Orlando
Miami
Tampa
New Orleans
Memphis
Nashville
St Louis
Gulf of Mexico
Monterrey
Guadalajara
MEXICO CITY
Puebla
Acapulco
HAVANA
CUBA
THE BAHAMAS
NASSAU
HAITI
PORT-AU-PRINCE
DOMINICAN REPUBLIC
SANTO DOMINGO
JAMAICA
KINGSTON
Caribbean Sea
BELIZE
GUATEMALA
GUATEMALA CITY
EL SALVADOR
SAN SALVADOR
HONDURAS
TEGUCIGALPA
NICARAGUA
MANAGUA
COSTA RICA
SAN JOSE
PANAMA
PANAMA CITY
COLOMBIA
BOGOTA
Medellín
Cali
Barranquilla
Cartagena
Maracaibo
CARACAS
VENEZUELA
GUYANA
GEORGETOWN
SURINAME
PARAMARIBO
CAYENNE
French Guiana
ECUADOR
QUITO
Guayaquil
PERU
LIMA
BRAZIL
BRASÍLIA
Manaus
Belém
Rio de Janeiro
Sao Paulo
Salvador
BOLIVIA
LA PAZ
SUCRE
PARAGUAY
ASUNCIÓN
URUGUAY
MONTEVIDEO
BUENOS AIRES
ARGENTINA
SANTIAGO
Valparaíso
Córdoba
Equator
Tropic of Cancer
Tropic of Capricorn
Mid-Atlantic Ridge
Sargasso Sea
Northeast Pacific Basin
East Pacific Rise
Galapagos Islands
Galapagos Rise
Gallego Rise
Peru Basin
Nazca Ridge
Chile Basin
Roggeveen Basin
Challenger Fracture Zone
Pacific-Antarctic Ridge
Southeast Pacific Basin
Amundsen Abyssal Plain
Bellingshausen Sea
Drake Passage
Cape Horn
Falkland Islands
Argentine Basin
Argentine Rise
Mornington Abyssal Plain
French Polynesia
PAPEETE
Tahiti
Marquesas Islands
Tuamotu Islands
Pitcairn Islands
ADAMSTOWN
Easter Island
Honolulu
Hawai'i
Kiritimati
Tiki Basin
West Antarctica
Marie Byrd Land
Antarctic Circle
Antarctic Peninsula

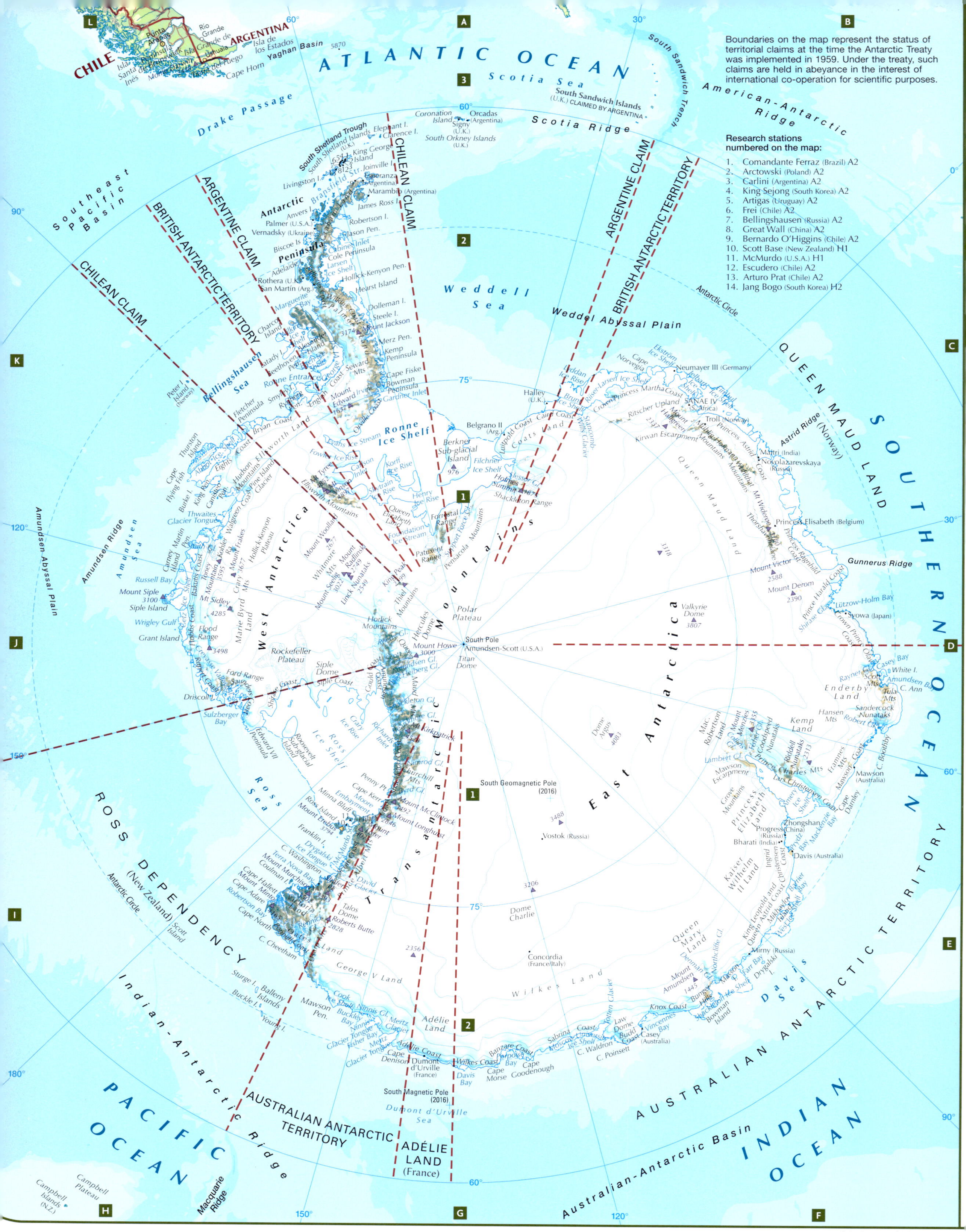

Polar Stereographic Projection

Antarctica

1:26 000 000
0 200 400 600 800 1000 miles
0 200 400 600 800 1000 1200 1400 1600 km

Polar Stereographic Projection

1:26 000 000

0 200 400 600 800 1000 miles

0 200 400 600 800 1000 1200 1400 1600 km

The Arctic

World
Statistics

See page 160 for explanatory table and sources

	Population							Economy					
	Total population	Population change (%)	% urban	Total fertility	Population by age (%) 0–14	Population by age (%) 65 or over	2050 projected population	Total Gross National Income (GNI) (US$M)	GNI per capita (US$)	Debt service ratio (% GNI)	Total debt service (US$)	Aid receipts (% GNI)	Military spending (% GDP)
WORLD	7 349 472 000	1.2	53.4	2.5	26.2	8.1	9 725 148 000	78 399 394	10 799	...	...	0.6	2.3
AFGHANISTAN	32 527 000	2.4	26.3	4.8	44.9	2.4	55 955 000	21 395	680	0.2	38 035 000	23.0	1.3
ALBANIA	2 897 000	-0.1	56.4	1.8	18.9	12.1	2 710 000	12 875	4 450	2.6	334 434 000	2.1	1.3
ALGERIA	39 667 000	1.8	70.1	2.9	28.2	5.8	56 461 000	213 784	5 490	0.1	298 308 000	0.1	5.6
ANDORRA	70 000	1.2	85.6	...	...	...	72 000	3 284	43 270	...	...	...	...
ANGOLA	25 022 000	3.1	43.3	6.1	47.9	2.3	65 473 000	...	...	...	7 303 904 000	0.2	...
ANTIGUA AND BARBUDA	92 000	1.0	24.2	2.1	24.6	7.1	114 000	1 209	13 300	...	...	0.2	...
ARGENTINA	43 417 000	0.9	91.6	2.3	25.3	10.8	55 445 000	579 220	13 480	...	...	0.0	0.9
ARMENIA	3 018 000	0.2	62.8	1.5	18.7	10.6	2 729 000	12 083	4 020	11.8	1 436 204 000	2.3	3.9
AUSTRALIA	23 969 000	1.6	89.3	1.9	18.7	14.7	33 496 000	1 516 201	64 600	...	...	...	1.8
AUSTRIA	8 545 000	0.6	65.9	1.4	14.3	18.6	8 846 000	423 906	49 600	...	...	...	0.8
AZERBAIJAN	9 754 000	1.3	54.4	2.0	22.0	5.6	10 963 000	72 425	7 600	2.5	1 791 147 000	0.3	4.6
THE BAHAMAS	388 000	1.4	82.8	1.9	21.1	8.0	489 000	8 037	20 980	...	...	...	...
BAHRAIN	1 377 000	0.9	88.7	2.1	21.2	2.4	1 822 000	28 424	21 060	...	...	...	4.4
BANGLADESH	160 996 000	1.2	33.5	2.2	30.0	5.0	202 209 000	171 250	1 080	0.9	1 740 720 000	1.3	0.0
BARBADOS	284 000	0.5	31.6	1.8	19.4	13.8	282 000	4 311	15 310	...	...	..	...
BELARUS	9 496 000	0.0	76.3	1.6	15.8	14.0	8 125 000	69 533	7 340	7.2	5 342 376 000	0.2	1.3
BELGIUM	11 299 000	0.4	97.8	1.8	16.9	18.0	12 527 000	530 558	47 240	...	...	...	1.0
BELIZE	359 000	2.3	44.1	2.6	33.1	3.8	588 000	1 496	4 350	...	91 973 000	..	1.0
BENIN	10 880 000	2.6	43.5	4.8	42.5	2.9	22 549 000	9 472	890	1.1	105 024 000	6.9	1.0
BHUTAN	775 000	1.5	37.9	2.0	27.4	5.0	950 000	1 811	2 370	4.5	82 792 000	7.4	...
BOLIVIA	10 725 000	1.6	68.1	3.0	32.9	6.3	15 963 000	30 344	2 870	3.2	995 658 000	2.1	1.9
BOSNIA AND HERZEGOVINA	3 810 000	-0.1	39.6	1.3	13.6	15.0	3 069 000	18 482	4 840	4.3	813 280 000	3.4	1.0
BOTSWANA	2 262 000	0.9	57.2	2.8	32.2	3.5	3 389 000	16 067	7 240	0.4	55 828 000	0.6	2.4
BRAZIL	207 848 000	0.8	85.4	1.8	23.5	7.6	238 270 000	2 429 720	11 790	2.5	59 895 313 000	0.0	1.4
BRUNEI	423 000	1.3	76.9	1.9	23.5	4.2	546 000	15 133	37 320	...	...	...	3.1
BULGARIA	7 150 000	-0.5	73.6	1.5	14.0	19.7	5 154 000	55 042	7 620	10.4	5 772 714 000	...	1.5
BURKINA FASO	18 106 000	2.8	29.0	5.5	45.8	2.4	42 789 000	12 278	700	0.7	91 488 000	9.0	1.6
BURUNDI	11 179 000	3.1	11.8	5.9	44.6	2.5	28 668 000	2 880	270	0.9	29 180 000	16.2	2.0
CAMBODIA	15 578 000	1.8	20.5	2.6	31.8	4.0	22 545 000	15 595	1 020	1	165 062 000	5.0	1.7
CAMEROON	23 344 000	2.5	53.8	4.7	42.8	3.2	48 362 000	30 763	1 350	1.4	444 977 000	2.6	1.3
CANADA	35 940 000	1.1	81.7	1.6	16.0	15.7	44 136 000	1 835 099	51 630	...	...	...	1.0
CAPE VERDE (CABO VERDE)	521 000	0.9	64.8	2.3	30.0	4.7	707 000	1 772	3 450	2.5	43 645 000	12.9	0.5
CENTRAL AFRICAN REPUBLIC	4 900 000	2.0	39.8	4.3	39.4	3.9	8 782 000	1 559	320	0.9	15 525 000	34.1	...
CHAD	14 037 000	3.0	22.3	6.2	48.0	2.5	35 131 000	13 292	980	0.9	125 660 000	2.9	2.8
CHILE	17 948 000	0.9	89.4	1.8	20.5	10.7	21 601 000	264 761	14 910	...	...	0.1	2.0
CHINA	1 383 925 000	0.5	54.4	1.6	17.2	9.2	1 357 042 000	10 096 966	7 400	0.5	51 736 841 000	0.0	1.9
COLOMBIA	48 229 000	1.3	76.2	1.9	24.7	6.8	54 927 000	380 998	7 970	3.6	13 233 040 000	0.3	3.1
COMOROS	788 000	2.4	28.2	4.5	40.5	2.8	1 502 000	605	790	0.1	592 000	11.4	...
CONGO	4 620 000	2.5	65.0	4.9	42.6	3.6	10 732 000	12 256	2 720	2.6	303 851 000	0.9	5.0
CONGO, DEM. REPUBLIC OF THE	77 267 000	2.7	42.0	6.0	46.2	3.0	195 277 000	28 730	380	1.4	410 141 000	8.3	1.0
COSTA RICA	4 808 000	1.3	75.9	1.8	22.7	8.6	5 759 000	48 140	10 120	7.2	3 464 431 000	0.1	0.0
CÔTE D'IVOIRE (IVORY COAST)	22 702 000	2.4	53.5	5.0	42.7	3.0	48 797 000	32 196	1 450	5.1	1 672 574 000	2.8	1.5
CROATIA	4 240 000	-0.5	58.7	1.5	15.0	18.6	3 554 000	55 017	12 980	...	...	..	1.6
CUBA	11 390 000	-0.1	77.0	1.6	16.6	13.6	10 339 000	66 620	5 880	...	...	..	...
CYPRUS	1 165 000	1.0	67.0	1.4	16.7	12.6	1 402 000	22 519	26 370	...	...	...	1.5
CZECHIA (CZECH REPUBLIC)	10 543 000	0.0	73.0	1.5	14.8	17.5	9 965 000	193 121	18 350	...	...	...	1.0
DENMARK	5 669 000	0.4	87.5	1.7	17.1	18.5	6 299 000	345 784	61 330	...	...	...	1.2
DJIBOUTI	888 000	1.5	77.3	3.2	33.0	4.1	1 186 000	...	...	...	41 480 000	..	...
DOMINICA	73 000	0.5	69.3	...	...	...	74 000	501	6 930	3.8	19 292 000	3.0	...
DOMINICAN REPUBLIC	10 528 000	1.2	78.1	2.5	30.3	6.5	13 238 000	62 862	6 040	5.3	3 239 166 000	0.3	0.7
EAST TIMOR (TIMOR-LESTE)	1 185 000	2.7	32.1	5.1	42.3	5.5	2 162 000	3 244	2 680	...	...	6.4	2.1
ECUADOR	16 144 000	1.5	63.5	2.5	29.3	6.5	23 013 000	96 845	6 090	4	4 001 602 000	0.2	2.9
EGYPT	91 508 000	1.6	43.1	3.3	33.0	5.2	151 111 000	287 683	3 210	2	5 994 632 000	1.3	1.7
EL SALVADOR	6 127 000	0.7	66.3	1.9	27.6	8.0	6 390 000	23 935	3 920	5.2	1 246 732 000	0.4	0.9
EQUATORIAL GUINEA	845 000	2.7	39.8	4.8	39.4	2.9	1 816 000	8 379	10 210	...	...	0.0	1.1
ERITREA	5 228 000	3.2	22.2	4.3	42.8	2.6	10 421 000	2 313	480	...	46 287 000	2.2	...
ESTONIA	1 313 000	-0.3	67.6	1.5	15.8	18.5	1 129 000	24 994	19 010	...	...	...	1.9
ETHIOPIA	99 391 000	2.5	19.0	4.4	42.1	3.5	188 455 000	53 621	550	1.4	767 725 000	6.6	0.7
FIJI	892 000	0.7	53.4	2.6	28.8	5.6	924 000	4 314	4 870	1.2	51 551 000	2.3	1.0
FINLAND	5 503 000	0.5	84.1	1.8	16.3	19.8	5 752 000	264 554	48 440	...	...	...	1.3
FRANCE	64 395 000	0.4	79.3	2.0	18.5	18.7	71 137 000	2 844 284	42 950	...	...	...	2.2
GABON	1 725 000	2.3	86.9	3.9	37.3	5.2	3 164 000	16 401	9 720	2.6	421 033 000	0.7	1.1
THE GAMBIA	1 991 000	3.2	59.0	5.7	46.3	2.3	4 981 000	878	460	5.3	43 385 000	12.7	1.7
GEORGIA	4 000 000	0.4	53.5	1.8	17.2	14.1	3 483 000	16 742	4 490	11.4	1 871 172 000	3.4	2.5

Social Indicators					Environment				Communications				
Child mortality rate	Life expectancy	Literacy rate (%)	Access to safe water (%)	Doctors per 100 000 people	Forest area (%)	Annual change in forest area (%)	Protected land area (%)	CO_2 emissions (metric tonnes per capita)	Main telephone lines per 100 people	Cellular phone subscribers per 100 people	Fixed broadband subscribers per 100 people	International dialling code	Time zone
42.5	**71.5**	**85.2**	**91.0**	**154**	**31.0**	**-0.1**	**14**	**4.9**	**15.1**	**96.9**	**10.6**	**...**	**...**
91.1	60.4	31.7	55.3	27	2.1	0.0	0	0.4	0.3	74.9	0	93	+4.5
14.0	77.8	97.2	95.1	115	28.2	-0.2	11	1.6	7.4	105.5	6.6	355	+1
25.5	74.8	...	83.6	121	0.6	-0.6	7	3.3	7.8	92.9	4	213	+1
2.8	...	...	100.0	400	34.0	0.0	10	6.0	47.7	82.6	35.9	376	+1
156.9	52.3	70.8	49.0	17	46.7	-0.2	12	1.4	1.3	63.5	0.4	244	+1
8.1	75.9	98.9	97.9	...	22.3	0.0	10	5.8	21.9	132.1	11.8	1 268	-4
12.5	76.2	98.0	99.1	386	10.6	-0.8	7	4.6	23	158.8	15.6	54	-3
14.1	74.7	99.7	100.0	270	8.9	-1.5	8	1.7	19.2	115.9	9.1	374	+4
3.8	82.3	...	100.0	327	19.2	-0.6	13	16.5	38.9	131.2	27.7	61	+8 to +10.5
3.5	81.3	...	100.0	483	47.3	0.1	24	7.8	38.2	151.9	27.7	43	+1
31.7	70.8	99.8	87.0	340	11.3	0.0	7	3.6	18.9	110.9	19.9	994	+4
12.1	75.2	...	98.4	282	51.4	0.0	14	5.2	32.8	82.3	20.2	1 242	-5
6.2	76.7	94.6	100.0	92	0.7	3.3	3	17.9	21.2	173.3	21.4	973	+3
37.6	71.6	59.7	86.9	36	11.0	-0.2	5	0.4	0.6	80	2	880	+6
13.0	75.5	...	99.7	181	19.4	0.0	0	5.6	52.9	128.7	27.2	1 246	-4
4.6	73	99.6	99.7	393	42.9	0.5	8	6.7	48.5	122.5	28.8	375	+2
4.1	80.6	...	100.0	489	22.5	0.2	23	8.8	40.7	114.3	36	32	+1
16.5	70.1	...	99.5	83	60.2	-0.7	37	1.7	6.7	50.7	2.9	501	-6
99.5	59.5	...	77.9	6	39.6	-1.1	26	0.5	1.8	99.7	0.4	229	+1
32.9	69.5	...	100.0	26	85.8	0.3	28	0.8	3.1	82.1	3.3	975	+6
38.4	68.3	94.5	90.0	47	52.2	-0.5	21	1.6	8.1	96.3	1.6	591	-4
5.4	76.4	98.3	99.9	193	42.8	0.0	1	6.2	22.2	91.3	14.2	387	+1
43.6	64.4	87.3	96.2	34	19.6	-1.0	37	2.3	8.3	167.3	1.6	267	+2
16.4	74.4	91.5	98.1	189	61.6	-0.4	26	2.2	21.8	139	11.7	55	-2 to -5
10.2	78.8	96.1	...	144	71.4	-0.5	44	24.4	11.4	110.1	7.1	673	+8
10.4	75.4	98.4	99.4	387	37.2	1.5	37	6.7	25.3	137.7	20.7	359	+2
88.6	58.6	...	82.3	5	20.2	-1.0	15	0.1	0.7	71.7	0	226	UTC
81.7	56.7	86.9	75.9	...	6.6	-1.0	5	0.0	0.2	30.5	0	257	+2
28.7	68.2	73.9	75.5	17	55.7	-1.2	26	0.3	2.3	132.7	0.4	855	+7
87.9	55.5	71.3	75.6	8	41.2	-1.1	11	0.3	4.6	75.7	0.1	237	+1
4.9	82	...	99.8	207	34.1	0.0	9	14.1	46.2	81	35.4	1	-3.5 to -8
24.5	73.1	85.3	91.7	31	21.3	0.4	2	0.9	11.6	121.8	3.4	238	-1
130.1	50.7	36.8	68.5	5	36.2	-0.1	18	0.1	0	24.5	..	236	+1
138.7	51.6	38.2	50.8	...	9.0	-0.7	17	0.0	0.2	39.8	0.1	235	+1
8.1	81.5	96.7	99.0	103	21.9	0.2	19	4.6	19.2	133.3	14.1	56	-4
10.7	75.8	95.1	95.5	194	22.6	1.4	17	6.7	17.9	92.3	14.4	86	+8
15.9	74	93.6	91.4	147	54.3	-0.2	21	1.6	14.7	113.1	10.3	57	-5
73.5	63.3	76.6	90.1	...	1.2	-9.7	10	0.2	3.1	50.9	0.2	269	+3
45.0	62.3	79.3	76.5	10	65.6	-0.1	30	0.5	0.4	108.1	0	242	+1
98.3	58.7	75.0	52.4	...	67.7	-0.2	12	0.1	0	53.5	0	243	+1 & +2
9.7	79.4	97.4	97.8	111	51.9	0.9	27	1.7	17.8	143.8	10.5	506	-6
92.6	51.6	41.0	81.9	14	32.7	0.0	23	0.3	1.2	106.2	0.6	225	UTC
4.3	77.3	99.1	99.6	300	34.4	0.2	14	4.8	36.7	104.4	23	385	+1
5.5	79.4	99.8	94.9	672	27.6	1.3	12	3.2	11.2	22.5	0.1	53	-5
2.7	80.1	98.7	100.0	233	18.8	0.0	41	6.7	28.4	96.3	21.1	357	+2
3.4	78.3	...	100.0	362	34.5	0.1	22	10.4	18.6	129.5	27.9	420	+1
3.5	80.5	...	100.0	349	12.9	0.4	18	7.2	33.2	125.9	41.3	45	+1
65.3	62	...	90.0	23	0.2	0.0	0	0.6	2.5	32.4	2.3	253	+3
21.2	...	...	...	...	58.8	-0.6	22	1.7	24.3	127.5	15.8	1 767	-4
30.9	73.5	90.9	84.7	149	40.8	0.0	19	2.2	11.6	78.9	5.7	1 809	-4
52.6	68.3	58.3	71.9	7	48.4	-1.4	9	0.2	0.3	119.4	0.1	670	+9
21.6	75.9	93.3	86.9	172	38.1	-1.9	24	2.4	15.3	103.9	8.3	593	-5
24.0	71.1	75.1	99.4	283	0.1	0.9	11	2.6	7.6	114.3	3.7	20	+2
16.8	72.8	86.8	93.8	160	13.4	-1.5	8	1.1	14.9	144	5	503	-6
94.1	57.6	94.8	47.9	...	57.1	-0.7	21	8.9	1.9	66.4	0.5	240	+1
46.5	63.7	71.6	57.8	...	15.1	-0.3	5	0.1	1	6.4	0	291	+3
2.9	77.2	99.9	99.6	324	51.8	-0.3	21	14.0	31.7	160.7	28.9	372	+2
59.2	64	...	57.3	2	12.0	-1.1	18	0.1	0.8	31.6	0.5	251	+3
22.4	70.1	...	95.7	43	55.9	0.3	4	1.4	8.5	98.8	1.4	679	+12
2.3	81.1	...	100.0	291	72.9	0.0	15	10.2	11.7	139.7	32.3	358	+2
4.3	82.4	...	100.0	319	29.3	0.3	25	5.2	60	101.2	40.2	33	+1
50.8	64.4	82.3	93.2	...	85.4	0.0	20	1.4	1.1	171.4	0.6	241	+1
68.9	60.2	53.2	90.2	4	47.8	0.4	5	0.2	2.9	119.6	0.1	220	UTC
11.9	74.7	99.7	100.0	427	39.4	-0.1	4	1.8	25.4	124.9	12.2	995	+4

World

Statistics

See page 160 for explanatory table and sources

	Population							Economy					
	Total population	Population change (%)	% urban	Total fertility	Population by age (%) 0–14	65 or over	2050 projected population	Total Gross National Income (GNI) (US$M)	GNI per capita (US$)	Debt service ratio (% GNI)	Total debt service (US$)	Aid receipts (% GNI)	Military spending (% GDP)
GERMANY	80 689 000	0.3	75.1	1.4	13.0	21.1	74 513 000	3 853 623	47 590	...	...	...	1.2
GHANA	27 410 000	2.1	53.4	4.2	38.9	3.4	50 071 000	42 653	1 590	2.1	778 640 000	3.0	0.5
GREECE	10 955 000	-0.6	77.7	1.3	14.6	20.9	9 705 000	250 095	22 810	...	...	...	2.3
GRENADA	107 000	0.4	35.6	2.1	26.6	7.1	110 000	841	7 910	3	25 493 000	4.6	...
GUATEMALA	16 343 000	2.5	51.1	3.2	37.1	4.8	27 754 000	55 005	3 430	3.6	2 058 290 000	0.5	0.4
GUINEA	12 609 000	2.5	36.7	5.0	42.7	3.1	27 486 000	5 773	470	1.2	76 381 000	9.1	3.8
GUINEA-BISSAU	1 844 000	2.4	48.6	4.8	41.0	3.1	3 564 000	995	550	0.2	1 989 000	10.6	2.1
GUYANA	767 000	0.5	28.5	2.6	29.8	4.9	806 000	3 000	3 940	2.1	65 655 000	4.9	1.3
HAITI	10 711 000	1.4	57.4	3.0	34.2	4.6	14 189 000	8 651	820	0.3	24 382 000	12.4	0.0
HONDURAS	8 075 000	2.0	54.1	2.4	32.5	4.7	11 217 000	18 085	2 270	3.9	701 959 000	3.3	1.6
HUNGARY	9 855 000	-0.3	70.8	1.4	14.5	17.5	8 318 000	131 595	13 340	...	...	...	0.9
ICELAND	329 000	1.2	94.0	1.9	20.4	13.3	389 000	15 005	46 350	...	...	...	...
INDIA	1 311 051 000	1.2	32.4	2.4	29.2	5.5	1 705 333 000	2 027 964	1 570	4.6	92 518 516 777	0.1	2.5
INDONESIA	257 564 000	1.2	53.0	2.5	28.0	5.1	322 237 000	923 738	3 630	5.4	46 356 059 000	0.0	0.8
IRAN	79 109 000	1.3	72.9	1.7	23.5	5.0	92 219 000	548 968	7 120	...	506 167 000	..	2.3
IRAQ	36 423 000	2.5	69.4	4.6	41.1	3.1	83 652 000	227 343	6 530	...	...	0.6	4.3
IRELAND	4 688 000	0.3	63.0	2.0	21.6	12.7	5 789 000	214 711	46 520	...	...	...	0.5
ISRAEL	8 064 000	1.9	92.1	3.1	27.8	11.0	12 610 000	290 180	35 320	...	...	...	5.9
ITALY	59 798 000	1.8	68.8	1.4	13.8	22.0	56 513 000	2 102 247	34 580	...	...	...	1.5
JAMAICA	2 793 000	0.2	54.6	2.0	24.2	9.0	2 710 000	14 014	5 150	11.4	1 542 786 000	..	0.9
JAPAN	126 573 000	-0.2	93.0	1.4	12.9	25.7	107 411 000	5 339 076	42 000	...	...	...	1.0
JORDAN	7 595 000	2.3	83.4	3.4	35.8	3.8	11 717 000	34 070	5 160	3.9	1 395 649 000	7.6	4.3
KAZAKHSTAN	17 625 000	1.5	53.3	2.7	26.1	6.7	22 447 000	204 800	11 850	16	31 170 530 000	0.0	1.1
KENYA	46 050 000	2.7	25.2	4.3	42.1	2.8	95 505 000	58 086	1 290	2	1 237 038 000	4.4	1.3
KIRIBATI	112 000	1.5	44.2	3.7	35.0	3.7	178 000	326	2 950	...	...	35.1	...
KOSOVO	1 805 000	0.3	...	2.1	...	...	...	7 275	3 990	2	152 659 000	7.8	0.7
KUWAIT	3 892 000	3.2	98.3	2.1	22.5	1.9	5 924 000	185 026	49 300	...	...	...	3.6
KYRGYZSTAN	5 940 000	2.0	35.6	3.2	31.0	4.2	8 248 000	7 318	1 250	5.6	401 960 000	8.7	3.4
LAOS	6 802 000	1.8	37.6	3.0	35.1	3.8	10 172 000	11 078	1 660	3.1	357 268 000	4.2	...
LATVIA	1 971 000	-1.1	67.4	1.5	14.6	19.3	1 593 000	30 413	15 250	...	...	...	1.0
LEBANON	5 851 000	1.0	87.7	1.7	24.1	8.1	5 610 000	45 600	10 030	7.2	3 306 124 000	1.8	5.0
LESOTHO	2 135 000	1.1	26.8	3.2	36.3	4.2	2 987 000	2 804	1 330	1.6	40 922 000	4.0	2.2
LIBERIA	4 503 000	2.4	49.3	4.7	42.6	3.0	9 436 000	1 637	370	1	17 378 000	43.9	0.7
LIBYA	6 278 000	0.8	78.4	2.5	29.7	4.5	8 375 000	48 974	7 820	...	...	0.5	8.0
LIECHTENSTEIN	38 000	0.7	14.3	1.5	...	...	43 000	...	...	...	...	...	...
LITHUANIA	2 878 000	-1.0	66.5	1.6	14.5	18.6	2 375 000	45 185	15 410	...	...	...	0.9
LUXEMBOURG	567 000	2.3	89.9	1.6	16.7	14.0	803 000	42 256	75 960	...	...	...	0.4
MACEDONIA (F.Y.R.O.M.)	2 078 000	0.1	57.0	1.5	17.1	12.0	1 938 000	10 686	5 150	8.9	977 515 000	1.9	1.1
MADAGASCAR	24 235 000	2.8	34.5	4.4	42.0	2.8	55 294 000	10 403	440	0.9	95 919 000	5.7	0.7
MALAWI	17 215 000	2.8	16.1	5.1	45.4	3.4	43 155 000	4 180	250	1.6	65 301 000	22.8	1.3
MALAYSIA	30 331 000	1.6	74.0	1.9	25.0	5.6	40 725 000	332 507	11 120	4	12 947 893 000	0.0	1.5
MALDIVES	364 000	1.9	44.5	2.1	27.6	4.7	494 000	2 570	6 410	2.9	76 984 000	0.9	...
MALI	17 600 000	3.0	39.1	6.2	47.5	2.6	45 404 000	11 038	650	0.8	87 371 000	10.6	1.8
MALTA	419 000	0.9	95.3	1.4	14.8	18.7	411 000	8 889	21 000	...	...	...	...
MARSHALL ISLANDS	53 000	0.3	72.4	...	...	...	67 000	232	4 390	...	...	..	...
MAURITANIA	4 068 000	2.4	59.3	4.6	40.3	3.2	8 049 000	5 033	1 270	4.6	220 978 000	5.4	2.9
MAURITIUS	1 273 000	0.2	39.8	1.4	19.8	9.1	1 249 000	12 149	9 630	28.5	3 512 427 000	0.4	0.3
MEXICO	127 017 000	1.2	79.0	2.2	28.1	6.3	163 754 000	1 237 533	9 870	4.1	52 242 252 000	0.1	0.7
MICRONESIA, FED. STATES OF	526 000	0.3	22.4	3.2	34.6	4.2	690 000	333	3 200	...	...	..	...
MOLDOVA	4 069 000	-0.1	44.9	1.3	15.8	9.9	3 243 000	9 090	2 560	6.7	591 208 000	5.9	0.3
MONACO	38 000	0.6	100.0	...	...	...	44 000	...	...	...	...	...	...
MONGOLIA	2 959 000	1.5	71.2	2.7	27.9	4.0	4 028 000	12 458	4 280	12.2	1 361 263 000	2.8	0.9
MONTENEGRO	626 000	0.1	63.8	1.7	18.9	13.3	574 000	4 549	7 320	5.8	270 878 000	2.2	1.5
MOROCCO	34 378 000	1.5	59.7	2.5	27.3	6.1	43 696 000	105 831	3 070	4.5	4 799 518 000	2.2	3.7
MOZAMBIQUE	27 978 000	2.4	31.9	5.4	45.5	3.3	65 544 000	16 421	600	1.1	176 837 000	12.8	1.0
MYANMAR (BURMA)	53 897 000	0.9	33.6	2.2	28.1	5.2	63 575 000	68 129	1 270	0.1	62 035 000	2.2	3.7
NAMIBIA	2 459 000	1.9	45.7	3.5	36.9	3.5	4 322 000	13 531	5 630	...	...	1.7	4.2
NAURU	10 000	...	...	...	...	...	11 000	...	...	...	...	..	...
NEPAL	28 514 000	1.2	18.2	2.2	33.5	5.4	36 159 000	20 643	730	1.1	226 524 000	4.4	1.6
NETHERLANDS	16 925 000	0.3	89.9	1.7	16.7	17.7	17 602 000	874 591	51 860	...	...	...	1.2
NEW ZEALAND	4 529 000	1.5	86.3	1.9	20.3	14.4	5 607 000	185 214	41 070	...	...	...	1.1
NICARAGUA	6 082 000	1.4	58.5	2.3	30.5	5.0	7 863 000	11 264	1 870	6.5	744 028 636	3.7	0.7
NIGER	19 899 000	3.9	18.5	7.6	50.4	2.6	72 238 000	7 838	410	0.7	59 054 000	11.4	...
NIGERIA	182 202 000	2.8	46.9	5.7	44.1	2.7	398 508 000	526 467	2 970	0.1	702 825 000	0.5	0.4
NORTH KOREA	25 155 000	0.5	60.7	2.0	21.4	9.6	26 907 000	...	...	...	...	..	...
NORWAY	5 211 000	1.1	80.2	1.8	18.1	16.0	6 658 000	532 277	103 620	...	...	...	1.5

Social Indicators					Environment				Communications				
Child mortality rate	Life expectancy	Literacy rate (%)	Access to safe water (%)	Doctors per 100 000 people	Forest area (%)	Annual change in forest area (%)	Protected land area (%)	CO_2 emissions (metric tonnes per capita)	Main telephone lines per 100 people	Cellular phone subscribers per 100 people	Fixed broadband subscribers per 100 people	International dialling code	Time zone
3.7	80.8	...	100.0	389	31.8	0.0	48	8.9	56.9	120.4	35.8	49	+1
61.6	61.3	71.5	88.7	10	20.7	-2.2	15	0.4	1	114.8	0.3	233	UTC
4.6	81.3	97.5	100.0	617	30.7	0.8	35	7.6	46.9	110.3	28.4	30	+2
11.8	73.4	...	96.6	...	50.0	0.0	2	2.4	25.7	110.2	18.3	1 473	-4
29.1	71.7	77.0	92.8	93	33.1	-1.5	31	0.7	10.8	106.6	2.7	502	-6
93.7	58.7	25.3	76.8	10	26.3	-0.5	28	0.2	0	72.1	0	224	UTC
92.5	55.2	57.8	79.3	5	71.2	-0.5	16	0.1	0.3	63.5	0.1	245	UTC
39.4	66.4	85.0	98.3	21	77.2	0.0	5	2.4	19.9	70.5	5.6	592	-4
69.0	62.7	...	57.7	...	3.6	-0.8	0	0.2	0.4	64.7	0	509	-5
20.4	73.1	85.5	91.2	...	44.3	-2.2	21	1.1	6.4	93.5	1.4	504	-6
5.9	75.9	99.0	100.0	308	22.6	0.5	23	4.9	30.3	118.1	27.3	36	+1
2.0	82.1	...	100.0	348	0.3	3.3	20	5.9	51.5	111.1	35.9	354	UTC
47.7	68	69.3	94.1	70	23.1	0.2	5	1.7	2.1	74.5	1.2	91	+5.5
27.2	68.9	92.8	87.4	20	51.4	-0.7	15	2.3	10.4	128.8	1.2	62	+7 to +9
15.5	75.4	83.6	96.2	89	6.8	0.0	7	7.8	39.1	87.8	9.5	98	+3.5
32.0	69.4	79.3	86.6	61	1.9	0.0	0	4.2	5.6	94.9	..	964	+3
3.6	81.2	...	97.9	267	11.0	1.2	14	7.9	43.2	105.1	26.9	353	UTC
4.0	82.2	...	100.0	334	7.1	-0.1	17	9.0	37.1	121.5	27.2	972	+2
3.5	82.7	99.1	100.0	376	31.6	0.9	22	6.7	33.7	154.3	23.5	39	+1
15.7	75.7	87.9	93.8	41	31.0	-0.1	16	2.9	9.1	107.4	5.4	1 876	-5
2.7	83.6	...	100.0	230	68.6	0.0	17	9.3	50.1	120.2	29.3	81	+9
17.9	74.1	97.9	96.9	256	1.1	0.0	...	3.6	5	147.8	4.7	962	+2
14.1	71.6	99.7	92.9	362	1.2	-0.2	3	15.8	26.2	172.2	12.9	7	+5 & +6
49.4	61.6	...	63.2	20	6.1	-0.3	12	0.3	0.4	73.8	0.2	254	+3
55.9	66	...	66.9	38	15.0	0.0	22	0.6	8.9	17.4	1.2	686	+12 to +14
...	71.1	...	...	...	...	...	...	...	..	..	..	381	+1
8.6	74.6	95.6	99.0	270	0.4	2.4	18	28.1	14.2	218.4	1.4	965	+3
21.3	70.4	99.2	90.0	197	5.1	1.9	6	1.2	7.9	134.5	4.2	996	+6
66.7	66.1	...	75.7	18	67.6	-0.5	17	0.2	13.4	67	0.2	856	+7
7.9	74.2	99.9	99.3	358	54.3	0.3	19	3.8	19.6	116.8	24.7	371	+2
8.3	79.4	...	99.0	320	13.4	0.1	1	4.7	19.4	88.3	22.8	961	+2
90.2	49.7	75.8	81.8	...	1.5	0.5	1	1.1	2	85	0.1	266	+2
69.9	60.8	...	75.6	1	44.3	-0.7	3	0.2	0.2	73.4	0.1	231	UTC
13.4	71.7	90.3	...	190	0.1	0.0	0	6.2	11.3	161.1	1	218	+1
...	82.3	...	...	...	43.1	0.0	43	1.4	48.5	109.3	42	423	+1
5.2	74	99.8	96.6	412	34.7	0.4	17	4.5	19.5	147	26.7	370	+2
1.9	82.2	...	100.0	290	33.5	0.0	40	20.9	50.5	149.5	34.8	352	+1
5.5	75.3	97.6	99.4	263	39.9	0.5	7	4.5	18.2	105.5	16.8	389	+1
49.6	65.1	64.5	51.5	16	21.4	-0.5	5	0.1	1.1	41.2	0.1	261	+3
64.0	62.7	61.3	90.2	2	33.6	-1.0	18	0.1	0.4	33.5	0.1	265	+2
7.0	74.7	93.1	98.2	120	61.7	-0.4	18	7.9	14.6	148.8	10.1	60	+8
8.6	76.8	...	98.6	142	3.0	0.0	...	3.3	6.1	189.4	5.6	960	+5
114.7	58	33.6	77.0	8	10.1	-0.6	6	0.1	1	149.1	0	223	UTC
6.4	81.7	93.3	100.0	349	0.9	0.0	22	6.0	53.6	127	35.2	356	+1
36.0	...	...	94.6	44	70.2	0.0	3	2.0	4.5	29.4	2.6	692	+12
84.7	63	...	57.9	13	0.2	-2.0	1	0.6	1.3	94.2	0.2	222	UTC
13.5	74.2	89.2	99.9	...	17.3	0.1	4	3.1	29.8	132.2	14.6	230	+4
13.2	76.7	94.0	96.1	210	33.2	-0.2	13	3.9	17.8	82.2	10.5	52	-5 to -8
34.7	69.1	...	89.0	18	91.7	0.0	4	1.2	6.8	..	3	691	+10 & +11
15.8	71.5	99.2	88.4	298	12.0	1.2	4	1.4	35.2	108	14.7	373	+2
3.5	...	...	100.0	717	...	...	36	...	133	88.5	46.8	377	+1
22.4	69.5	98.3	64.4	284	6.9	-0.7	14	6.9	7.9	105.1	6.8	976	+7 & +8
4.7	76.2	98.4	99.7	211	40.4	0.0	15	4.1	26.5	163	16.7	382	+1
27.6	74	67.1	85.4	62	11.5	0.2	22	1.7	7.4	131.7	3	212	UTC
78.5	55	50.6	51.1	4	49.1	-0.5	18	0.1	0.3	69.8	0.1	258	+2
50.0	65.9	92.8	80.6	61	47.7	-1.0	7	0.2	1	54	0.3	95	+6.5
45.4	64.7	...	91.0	37	8.7	-1.0	43	1.2	7.8	113.8	1.8	264	+1
...	...	...	...	...	...	...	...	...	...	...	...	674	+12
35.8	69.6	59.6	91.6	...	25.4	0.0	16	0.2	3	81.9	0.9	977	+5.75
3.8	81.3	...	100.0	286	10.8	0.0	20	10.1	41.3	116.4	40.8	31	+1
5.7	81.4	...	100.0	274	31.3	-0.1	27	7.1	40.6	112.1	31	64	+12 & +12.75
22.1	74.8	...	87.0	...	24.7	-2.1	31	0.8	5.5	114.6	2.5	505	-6
95.5	61.5	15.5	58.2	2	0.9	-1.0	17	0.1	0.6	44.4	0	227	+1
108.8	52.8	51.1	68.5	40	9.0	-4.0	14	0.5	0.1	77.8	0	234	+1
24.9	70.1	100.0.	99.7	...	45.0	-2.1	2	3.0	4.7	11.2	..	850	+8.5
2.6	81.8	...	100.0	428	28.0	0.8	16	9.2	21.2	116.1	38.8	47	+1

World
Statistics

See page 160 for explanatory table and sources

	Population							Economy					
	Total population	Population change (%)	% urban	Total fertility	Population by age (%) 0–14	Population by age (%) 65 or over	2050 projected population	Total Gross National Income (GNI) (US$M)	GNI per capita (US$)	Debt service ratio (% GNI)	Total debt service (US$)	Aid receipts (% GNI)	Military spending (% GDP)
OMAN	4 491 000	7.8	77.2	2.8	21.1	2.5	5 844 000	65 921	16 870	...	...	..	13.4
PAKISTAN	188 925 000	1.6	38.3	3.6	35.2	4.5	309 640 000	258 311	1 400	2.3	5 947 830 000	1.4	3.5
PALAU	21 000	0.9	86.5	...	...	...	28 000	234	11 110	...	...	9.7	...
PANAMA	3 929 000	1.6	66.3	2.4	27.5	7.4	5 599 000	43 064	11 130	3.2	1 401 124 000	-0.4	0.0
PAPUA NEW GUINEA	7 619 000	2.1	13.0	3.8	37.5	3.0	13 240 000	16 724	2 240	7.1	1 165 245 000	..	0.7
PARAGUAY	6 639 000	1.7	59.4	2.5	30.6	5.9	8 895 000	28 803	4 400	9.3	2 714 653 000	0.2	1.4
PERU	31 377 000	1.3	78.3	2.5	28.2	6.7	41 899 000	196 931	6 360	2.6	5 065 622 000	0.2	1.4
PHILIPPINES	100 699 000	1.7	44.5	3.0	32.2	4.5	148 260 000	347 458	3 500	1.8	6 096 397 000	0.2	1.1
POLAND	38 612 000	-0.1	60.6	1.3	14.9	15.0	33 136 000	520 138	13 680	...	...	...	1.9
PORTUGAL	10 350 000	-0.6	62.9	1.2	14.2	20.4	9 216 000	222 126	21 360	...	...	...	1.8
QATAR	2 235 000	4.5	99.2	2.0	15.3	1.2	3 205 000	200 262	92 200	...	...	...	...
ROMANIA	19 511 000	-0.4	54.4	1.4	15.6	16.9	15 207 000	189 513	9 520	12.6	24 622 485 000	...	1.4
RUSSIA	143 457 000	0.2	73.9	1.7	16.4	13.2	128 599 000	1 930 634	13 220	...	...	...	4.6
RWANDA	11 610 000	2.7	27.8	3.9	41.4	2.7	21 187 000	7 885	700	0.7	56 702 000	13.3	1.2
ST KITTS AND NEVIS	56 000	1.1	32.0	...	...	...	68 000	820	14 920	...	...	..	...
ST LUCIA	185 000	0.7	18.5	1.9	23.5	8.9	207 000	1 333	7 260	2.7	37 064 000	1.3	...
ST VINCENT AND THE GRENADINES	109 000	0.0	50.2	2.0	24.8	7.2	109 000	723	6 610	4.3	31 247 000	1.3	...
SAMOA	193 000	0.8	19.3	4.1	37.5	5.2	241 000	778	4 060	2.5	19 063 000	12.0	...
SAN MARINO	32 000	0.6	94.2	...	...	...	33 000	...	...	...	...	...	...
SÃO TOMÉ AND PRÍNCIPE	190 000	2.5	64.5	4.6	42.9	3.2	353 000	312	1 670	4.1	13 655 000	11.6	...
SAUDI ARABIA	31 540 000	1.9	82.9	2.8	28.8	2.8	46 059 000	759 271	25 140	...	...	...	10.7
SENEGAL	15 129 000	2.9	43.4	5.1	43.8	3.0	36 223 000	15 361	1 050	2.3	359 629 000	7.2	1.5
SERBIA	7 046 000	-0.5	55.5	1.4	16.5	16.6	7 331 000	41 505	5 820	19.7	8 296 307 000	0.9	2.1
SEYCHELLES	96 000	1.8	53.6	2.3	23.2	6.8	100 000	1 291	14 120	...	...	0.7	2.4
SIERRA LEONE	6 453 000	1.8	39.6	4.6	42.7	2.7	11 392 000	4 410	700	0.8	34 801 000	20.9	1.0
SINGAPORE	5 604 000	1.3	100.0	1.3	15.9	11.1	6 681 000	301 633	55 150	...	...	...	3.1
SLOVAKIA	5 426 000	0.1	53.8	1.3	15.1	13.5	4 892 000	96 200	17 750	...	...	...	1.0
SLOVENIA	2 068 000	0.1	49.7	1.6	14.6	17.6	1 942 000	48 625	23 580	...	...	...	1.0
SOLOMON ISLANDS	584 000	2.1	21.9	4.0	39.8	3.4	992 000	1 048	1 830	1.6	17 372 000	18.1	...
SOMALIA	10 787 000	2.9	39.1	6.5	46.9	2.8	27 030 000	...	...	0	35 000	..	0.0
SOUTH AFRICA	54 490 000	1.6	64.3	2.4	29.5	5.0	65 540 000	367 201	6 800	2.9	10 035 454 000	0.3	1.1
SOUTH KOREA	50 293 000	0.4	82.4	1.2	14.3	12.7	50 593 000	1 365 797	27 090	...	...	...	2.6
SOUTH SUDAN	12 340 000	3.8	18.6	5.0	42.4	3.5	25 855 000	11 609	970	...	...	20.0	9.8
SPAIN	46 122 000	-0.5	79.4	1.3	14.9	18.4	44 840 000	1 366 027	29 390	...	...	...	1.2
SRI LANKA	20 715 000	0.8	18.3	2.1	24.8	8.9	20 836 000	71 360	3 440	3.4	2 490 324 000	0.7	2.6
SUDAN	40 235 000	2.1	33.6	4.4	40.9	3.3	80 284 000	67 285	1 710	0.4	260 725 000	1.2	...
SURINAME	543 000	0.9	66.1	2.4	27.1	6.8	624 000	5 358	9 950	...	...	..	...
SWAZILAND	1 287 000	1.4	21.3	3.3	37.6	3.5	1 792 000	4 512	3 550	0.7	30 235 000	2.7	1.8
SWEDEN	9 779 000	0.9	85.7	1.9	17.1	19.6	11 881 000	596 941	61 570	...	...	...	1.1
SWITZERLAND	8 299 000	1.2	73.8	1.5	14.8	17.8	10 019 000	693 726	84 720	...	...	...	0.7
SYRIA	18 502 000	2.0	57.3	3.0	36.8	3.9	34 902 000	...	...	...	213 000	..	...
TAIWAN	23 462 000	...	...	...	...	...	...	...	...	...	...	...	...
TAJIKISTAN	8 482 000	2.4	26.7	3.5	34.9	3.1	14 288 000	8 948	1 080	4.6	419 012 000	3.9	1.1
TANZANIA	53 470 000	3.0	30.9	5.1	45.2	3.2	137 136 000	46 375	920	0.5	251 780 000	5.5	1.0
THAILAND	67 959 000	0.3	49.2	1.5	18.0	10.1	62 452 000	391 696	5 780	3.9	14 974 717 000	0.1	1.4
TOGO	7 305 000	2.6	39.5	4.6	42.4	2.8	15 681 000	4 047	570	1.5	59 679 000	5.1	1.8
TONGA	106 000	0.4	23.6	3.7	37.0	5.9	140 000	449	4 260	1.5	6 640 000	18.0	...
TRINIDAD AND TOBAGO	1 360 000	0.2	8.6	1.8	20.8	9.2	1 291 000	27 185	20 070	...	...	..	0.7
TUNISIA	11 254 000	1.0	66.6	2.2	23.3	7.5	13 476 000	46 537	4 230	4.1	1 928 073 000	..	1.9
TURKEY	78 666 000	1.2	72.9	2.1	25.9	7.4	95 819 000	822 450	10 830	7.1	55 900 086 000	0.4	2.2
TURKMENISTAN	5 374 000	1.3	49.7	2.3	28.4	4.1	6 555 000	42 544	8 020	0.1	55 705 000	0.1	...
TUVALU	9 916	0.2	58.8	...	...	...	11 000	57	5 720	...	...	..	...
UGANDA	39 032 000	3.3	15.8	5.8	48.3	2.5	101 873 000	25 303	670	0.4	98 519 000	6.3	1.2
UKRAINE	44 824 000	-0.3	69.5	1.5	14.6	15.3	35 117 000	152 065	3 560	13.7	17 878 190 000	1.1	3.1
UNITED ARAB EMIRATES	9 157 000	1.1	85.3	1.8	13.8	1.0	12 789 000	405 225	44 600	...	...	...	5.7
UNITED KINGDOM	64 716 000	0.6	82.3	1.8	17.7	17.5	75 361 000	2 801 499	43 390	...	...	...	2.0
UNITED STATES OF AMERICA	321 774 000	0.7	81.4	1.9	19.1	14.4	388 865 000	17 611 491	55 230	...	...	...	3.5
URUGUAY	3 432 000	0.3	95.2	2.0	21.6	14.3	3 667 000	55 915	16 350	...	...	0.2	1.5
UZBEKISTAN	29 893 000	1.6	36.3	2.2	28.5	4.6	37 126 000	64 266	2 090	1.4	887 704 000	0.5	...
VANUATU	265 000	2.2	25.8	3.3	36.8	4.1	476 000	819	3 160	1	7 852 000	..	...
VATICAN CITY	800	...	...	...	...	...	824	...	...	...	...	...	...
VENEZUELA	31 108 000	1.5	88.9	2.4	28.4	6.1	41 562 000	373 257	12 500	...	...	0.0	...
VIETNAM	93 448 000	1.1	33.0	2.0	23.1	6.6	112 783 000	171 905	1 890	3.8	6 716 374 000	2.4	2.3
YEMEN	26 832 000	2.3	34.0	4.2	40.7	2.7	47 170 000	33 319	1 300	...	305 611 000	..	...
ZAMBIA	16 212 000	3.3	40.5	5.4	46.1	2.9	42 975 000	26 396	1 680	1.6	410 375 000	3.9	1.6
ZIMBABWE	15 603 000	3.1	32.5	3.9	41.6	3.0	29 615 000	12 821	840	25.3	3 308 351 000	6.0	2.6

Social Indicators					Environment				Communications				
Child mortality rate	Life expectancy	Literacy rate (%)	Access to safe water (%)	Doctors per 100 000 people	Forest area (%)	Annual change in forest area (%)	Protected land area (%)	CO_2 emissions (metric tonnes per capita)	Main telephone lines per 100 people	Cellular phone subscribers per 100 people	Fixed broadband subscribers per 100 people	International dialling code	Time zone
11.6	77.1	86.9	93.4	243	0.0	0.0	11	20.2	9.6	157.8	4.5	968	+4
81.1	66.2	56.8	91.4	83	2.1	-2.4	11	0.9	2.6	73.3	1.1	92	+5
16.4	...	99.5	...	138	87.6	0.0	16	10.9	33.8	90.6	9.4	680	+9
17.0	77.6	94.1	94.7	165	43.4	-0.4	21	2.6	15	158.1	7.9	507	-5
57.3	62.6	63.3	40.0	6	62.8	-0.5	3	0.7	1.9	44.9	0.2	675	+10 & +11
20.5	72.9	93.9	98.0	123	43.4	-1.0	6	0.8	5.4	105.6	2.4	595	-4
16.9	74.5	93.8	86.7	113	52.9	-0.2	19	1.8	9.9	103.6	5.7	51	-5
28.0	68.3	95.4	91.8	...	26.1	0.7	11	0.9	3.1	111.2	23.2	63	+8
5.2	77.3	99.8	98.3	222	30.7	0.3	34	8.3	12.6	148.9	18.9	48	+1
3.6	80.7	94.5	100.0	410	37.8	0.1	22	4.7	43.2	112.1	25.7	351	UTC
8.0	78.6	97.5	100.0	774	0.0	...	3	44.0	18.4	145.8	9.9	974	+3
11.1	75.1	98.6	100.0	245	28.9	0.6	19	4.2	21.1	105.9	18.5	40	+2
9.6	70.4	99.7	96.9	431	49.4	0.0	11	12.6	26.8	155.1	17.5	7	+2 to +12
41.7	64	68.3	76.1	6	18.4	2.5	11	0.1	0.4	64	0	250	+2
10.5	...	...	98.3	...	42.3	0.0	4	5.1	35.4	118.6	25.6	1 869	-4
14.3	75	...	96.3	11	77.0	0.0	17	2.3	17.9	102.6	15.4	1 758	-4
18.3	72.9	...	95.1	...	68.9	0.3	11	2.2	21.9	105.2	14.9	1 784	-4
17.5	73.5	99.0	99.0	48	60.4	0.0	7	1.3	6.1	55.5	1.1	685	+13
2.9	...	...	...	510	0.0	...	...	...	58.8	118.8	37	378	+1
47.3	66.4	69.5	97.1	...	28.1	0.0	...	0.6	3.4	64.9	0.6	239	UTC
14.5	74.3	94.4	97.0	249	0.5	0.0	31	18.1	12.3	179.6	23.4	966	+3
47.2	66.4	42.8	78.5	6	43.6	-0.5	25	0.6	2.1	98.8	0.7	221	UTC
6.7	75.5	98.0	99.2	211	32.1	1.9	6	6.8	37.3	122.1	15.6	381	+1
13.6	73.2	94.0	95.7	107	88.5	0.0	42	6.8	22.7	162.2	12.7	248	+4
120.4	50.9	45.7	62.6	2	37.2	-0.7	10	0.2	0.3	76.7	..	232	UTC
2.7	82.6	96.5	100.0	195	3.3	0.0	5	4.3	36.2	146.9	26.7	65	+8
7.3	76.7	...	100.0	332	40.2	0.0	36	6.4	16.8	116.9	21.8	421	+1
2.6	80.5	99.7	99.5	252	62.4	0.2	55	7.5	37.1	112.1	26.6	386	+1
28.1	67.9	...	80.8	22	78.7	-0.3	2	0.4	1.3	65.8	0.2	677	+11
136.8	55.4	...	...	4	10.5	-1.1	1	0.1	0.5	50.9	0.6	252	+3
40.5	57.2	93.7	93.2	78	7.6	0.0	6	9.3	6.9	149.2	3.2	27	+2
3.4	82.2	...	...	214	63.8	-0.1	6	11.8	59.5	115.7	38.8	82	+9
92.6	55.7	26.8	58.7	...	...	...	...	...	0	24.5	0	211	+3
4.1	83.1	98.1	100.0	495	37.1	1.0	29	5.8	40.6	107.8	27.3	34	+1
9.8	74.8	91.2	95.6	68	29.2	-0.8	22	0.7	12.5	103.2	2.6	94	+5.5
70.1	63.5	74.3	...	28	...	-0.1	...	0.3	1.1	72.2	0.1	249	+3
21.3	71.2	94.7	94.8	...	94.6	0.0	15	3.6	15.6	170.6	8.5	597	-3
60.7	48.9	83.1	74.1	17	33.2	0.8	3	0.9	3.5	72.3	0.4	268	+2
3.0	82	...	100.0	393	69.2	0.0	15	5.5	39.2	127.8	34.1	46	+1
3.9	82.8	...	100.0	405	31.6	0.4	26	4.6	53.6	136.7	42.5	41	+1
12.9	70.1	85.5	90.1	146	2.7	1.3	1	2.7	16.5	63.9	2.3	963	+2
...	...	...	...	...	...	...	...	...	...	...	...	886	+8
44.8	69.6	99.8	73.8	192	2.9	0.0	5	0.4	5.2	95.1	0.1	992	+5
48.7	64.9	79.0	55.6	3	36.8	-1.2	32	0.2	0.3	62.8	0.2	255	+3
12.3	74.4	96.4	97.8	39	37.2	0.1	19	4.5	8.5	144.4	8.5	66	+7
78.4	59.7	60.4	63.1	5	4.9	-5.8	25	0.3	0.8	64.6	0.2	228	UTC
16.7	72.8	99.4	99.6	56	12.5	0.0	16	1.0	11.3	64.3	1.7	676	+13
20.4	70.4	98.9	95.1	118	43.9	-0.3	33	37.1	21.5	147.3	17.6	1 868	-4
14.0	74.1	79.7	97.7	122	6.7	1.7	5	2.4	8.5	128.5	4.5	216	+1
13.5	75.2	95.3	100.0	171	15.0	1.1	2	4.4	16.5	94.8	11.7	90	+2
51.4	65.6	99.7	...	239	8.8	0.0	3	12.2	11.8	135.8	0	993	+5
27.1	...	...	97.7	109	33.3	0.0	2	...	15.2	38.4	9.1	688	+12
54.6	58.5	70.2	79.0	12	14.1	-2.7	11	0.1	0.8	52.4	0.3	256	+3
9.0	71.2	99.7	96.2	354	16.8	0.3	4	6.3	24.6	144.1	9.3	380	+2 & +4 (Crimea)
6.8	77.4	...	99.6	253	3.8	0.3	18	20.4	22.3	178.1	11.6	971	+4
4.2	81.1	...	100.0	281	12.0	0.3	28	7.1	52.4	123.6	37.4	44	UTC
6.5	78.9	...	99.2	245	33.3	0.1	14	17.0	39.8	110.2	31.1	1	-5 to -10
10.1	77	98.4	99.7	374	10.5	2.8	3	2.3	31.7	160.8	24.6	598	-3
39.1	68.3	99.5	...	253	7.7	-0.1	3	3.9	8.6	78.4	1.9	998	+5
27.5	71.9	84.0	94.5	12	36.1	0.0	4	0.6	2.2	60.4	1.8	678	+11
...	...	...	...	...	...	0.0	...	...	...	...	...	39	+1
14.9	74.2	94.8	93.1	...	51.8	-0.6	53	6.4	25.3	99	7.8	58	-4
21.7	75.6	93.5	97.6	119	45.4	1.1	6	2.0	6	147.1	6.5	84	+7
41.9	63.8	67.6	...	20	1.0	0.0	1	0.9	4.7	68.5	1.4	967	+3
64.0	60	...	65.4	17	66.1	-0.3	38	0.2	0.8	67.3	0.1	260	+2
70.7	57.5	83.6	76.9	8	38.7	-2.0	27	0.7	2.3	80.8	1	263	+2

Definitions

Indicator	Definition
Population	
Total population	Interpolated mid-year population, 2015.
Population change	Population growth (annual %), 2014.
% urban	Urban population as a percentage of the total population, 2014.
Total fertility	Average number of children a woman will have during her child-bearing years, 2014.
Population by age	Percentage of population in age groups 0–14 and 65 or over, 2014.
2050 projected population	Projected total population for the year 2050.
Economy	
Total Gross National Income (GNI)	The sum of value added to the economy by all resident producers plus taxes, less subsidies, plus net receipts of primary income from abroad. Data are in U.S. dollars (millions), 2014 or latest available. Formerly known as Gross National Product (GNP).
GNI per capita	Gross National Income per person in U.S. dollars using the World Bank Atlas method, 2014 or latest available.
Debt service ratio	Debt service as a percentage of GNI, 2014.
Total debt service	Sum of principal repayments and interest paid on long-term debt, interest paid on short-term debt and repayments to the International Monetary Fund (IMF), 2014.
Aid receipts	Aid received as a percentage of GNI from the Development Assistance Committee (DAC) countries of the Organization for Economic Co-operation and Development (OECD), 2014.
Military spending	Military-related spending, including recruiting, training, construction and the purchase of military supplies and equipment, as a percentage of Gross Domestic Product (GDP), 2014.
Social Indicators	
Child mortality rate	Number of deaths of children aged under 5 per 1 000 live births, 2015.
Life expectancy	Average life expectancy, at birth in years, male and female, 2014.
Adult literacy rate	Percentage of population aged 15 or over with at least a basic ability to read and write, 2013 and earlier.
Access to safe water	Percentage of population using improved drinking water, 2015.
Doctors	Number of trained doctors per 100 000 people, 2013 and earlier.
Environment	
Forest area	Percentage of total land area covered by forest, 2012.
Change in forest area	Average annual percentage change in forest area, 2005-2010.
Protected land area	Percentage of total land area designated as protected land, 2012.
CO_2 emissions	Emissions of carbon dioxide from the burning of fossil fuels and the manufacture of cement, divided by the population, expressed in metric tons per capita, 2011.
Communications	
Telephone lines	Main (fixed) telephone lines per 100 inhabitants, 2014.
Cellular phone subscribers	Cellular mobile subscribers per 100 inhabitants, 2014.
Fixed broadband subscribers	Fixed broadband subscribers per 100 inhabitants, 2014.
International dialling code	The country code prefix to be used when dialling from another country.
Time zone	Time difference in hours between local standard time and Coordinated Universal Time.

Main Statistical Sources	Internet Links
● United Nations Department of Economic and Social Affairs (UDESA) World Population Prospects: The 2010 Revision. World Urbanization Prospects: The 2009 Revision.	www.un.org/esa/population/unpop
● UNESCO Education Data Centre	stats.uis.unesco.org
● UN Human Development Report 2011	hdr.undp.org
● World Bank World Development Indicators online	www.worldbank.org/data
● OECD: Development Co-operation Report 2011	www.oecd.org
● UNICEF: The State of the World's Children 2011	www.unicef.org
● Food and Agriculture Organization (FAO) of the UN: Global Forest Resources Assessment 2010	www.fao.org
● World Resources Institute Biodiversity and Protected Areas Database	www.wri.org
● International Telecommunications Union (ITU)	www.itu.int

Introduction to the index

The index includes all names shown on the reference maps in the atlas. Each entry includes the country or geographical area in which the feature is located, a page number and an alphanumeric reference. Additional entry details and aspects of the index are explained below.

Name forms

The names policy in this atlas is generally to use local name forms which are officially recognized by the governments of the countries concerned. Rules established by the Permanent Committee on Geographical Names for British Official Use (PCGN) are applied to the conversion of non-roman alphabet names, for example in the Russian Federation, into the roman alphabet used in English.

However, English conventional name forms are used for the most well-known places for which such a form is in common use. In these cases, the local form is included in brackets on the map and appears as a cross-reference in the index. Other alternative names, such as well-known historical names or those in other languages, may also be included in brackets on the map and as cross-references in the index. All country names and those for international physical features appear in their English forms. Names appear in full in the index, although they may appear in abbreviated form on the maps.

Referencing

Names are referenced by page number and by grid reference. The grid reference relates to the alphanumeric values which appear on the edges of each map. These reflect the graticule on the map – the letter relates to longitude divisions, the number to latitude divisions. Names are generally referenced to the largest scale map page on which they appear. For large geographical features, including countries, the reference is to the largest scale map on which the feature appears in its entirety, or on which the majority of it appears.

Rivers are referenced to their lowest downstream point – either their mouth or their confluence with another river. The river name will generally be positioned as close to this point as possible.

Alternative names

Alternative names appear as cross-references and refer the user to the index entry for the form of the name used on the map.

For rivers with multiple names - for example those which flow through several countries - all alternative name forms are included within the main index entries, with details of the countries in which each form applies.

Administrative qualifiers

Administrative divisions are included in entries to differentiate duplicate names - entries of exactly the same name and feature type within the one country - where these division names are shown on the maps. In such cases, duplicate names are alphabetized in the order of the administrative division names.

Additional qualifiers are included for names within selected geographical areas, to indicate more clearly their location.

Descriptors

Entries, other than those for towns and cities, include a descriptor indicating the type of geographical feature. Descriptors are not included where the type of feature is implicit in the name itself, unless there is a town or city of exactly the same name.

Insets

Where relevant, the index clearly indicates [inset] if a feature appears on an inset map.

Alphabetical order

The Icelandic characters Þ and þ are transliterated and alphabetized as 'Th' and 'th'. The German character ß is alphabetized as 'ss'. Names beginning with Mac or Mc are alphabetized exactly as they appear. The terms Saint, Sainte, etc, are abbreviated to St, Ste, etc, but alphabetized as if in the full form.

Numerical entries

Entries beginning with numerals appear at the beginning of the index, in numerical order. Elsewhere, numerals are alphabetized before 'a'.

Permuted terms

Names beginning with generic geographical terms are permuted - the descriptive term is placed after, and the index alphabetized by, the main part of the name. For example, Mount Everest is indexed as Everest, Mount; Lake Superior as Superior, Lake. This policy is applied to all languages. Permuting has not been applied to names of towns, cities or administrative divisions beginning with such geographical terms. These remain in their full form, for example, Lake Isabella, USA.

Gazetteer entries

Selected entries have been extended to include gazetteer-style information. Important geographical facts which relate specifically to the entry are included within the entry.

Abbreviations

admin. dist.	administrative district	IA	Iowa	Pak.	Pakistan
admin. div.	administrative division	ID	Idaho	Para.	Paraguay
admin. reg.	administrative region	IL	Illinois	P.E.I.	Prince Edward Island
Afgh.	Afghanistan	imp. l.	impermanent lake	pen.	peninsula
AK	Alaska	IN	Indiana	Phil.	Philippines
AL	Alabama	Indon.	Indonesia	plat.	plateau
Alg.	Algeria	is	islands	P.N.G.	Papua New Guinea
AR	Arkansas	Kazakh.	Kazakhstan	Port.	Portugal
Arg.	Argentina	KS	Kansas	pref.	prefecture
aut. comm.	autonomous community	KY	Kentucky	prov.	province
aut. reg.	autonomous region	Kyrg.	Kyrgyzstan	pt	point
aut. rep.	autonomous republic	l.	lake	Qld	Queensland
AZ	Arizona	LA	Louisiana	Que.	Québec
Azer.	Azerbaijan	lag.	lagoon	r.	river
b.	bay	Lith.	Lithuania	reg.	region
Bangl.	Bangladesh	Lux.	Luxembourg	res.	reserve
B.C.	British Columbia	MA	Massachusetts	resr	reservoir
B.I.O.T.	British Indian Ocean Territory	Madag.	Madagascar	RI	Rhode Island
Bol.	Bolivia	Madh. Prad.	Madhya Pradesh	S.	South, Southern
Bos. & Herz.	Bosnia and Herzegovina	Mahar.	Maharashtra	S.A.	South Australia
Bulg.	Bulgaria	Man.	Manitoba	Sask.	Saskatchewan
c.	cape	MD	Maryland	SC	South Carolina
CA	California	ME	Maine	SD	South Dakota
Cent. Afr. Rep.	Central African Republic	Mex.	Mexico	Sing.	Singapore
chan.	channel	MI	Michigan	Switz.	Switzerland
CO	Colorado	MN	Minnesota	Tajik.	Tajikistan
Col.	Colombia	MO	Missouri	Tanz.	Tanzania
CT	Connecticut	Moz.	Mozambique	Tas.	Tasmania
DC	District of Columbia	MS	Mississippi	terr.	territory
DE	Delaware	MT	Montana	Thai.	Thailand
Dem. Rep. Congo	Democratic Republic of the Congo	mt.	mountain	TN	Tennessee
depr.	depression	mts	mountains	Trin. and Tob.	Trinidad and Tobago
des.	desert	mun.	municipality	Turkm.	Turkmenistan
disp. terr.	disputed territory	N.	North, Northern	TX	Texas
Dom. Rep.	Dominican Republic	nat. park	national park	U.A.E.	United Arab Emirates
E.	East, Eastern	N.B.	New Brunswick	U.K.	United Kingdom
Equat. Guinea	Equatorial Guinea	NC	North Carolina	Ukr.	Ukraine
esc.	escarpment	ND	North Dakota	U.S.A.	United States of America
est.	estuary	NE	Nebraska	UT	Utah
Eth.	Ethiopia	Neth.	Netherlands	Uttar Prad.	Uttar Pradesh
Fin.	Finland	Nfld and Lab.	Newfoundland and Labrador	Uzbek.	Uzbekistan
FL	Florida	NH	New Hampshire	VA	Virginia
for.	forest	NJ	New Jersey	Venez.	Venezuela
Fr. Guiana	French Guiana	NM	New Mexico	Vic.	Victoria
Fr. Polynesia	French Polynesia	N.S.	Nova Scotia	vol.	volcano
F.Y.R.O.M.	Former Yugoslav Republic of Macedonia	N.S.W.	New South Wales	vol. crater	volcanic crater
g.	gulf	N.T.	Northern Territory	VT	Vermont
GA	Georgia	NV	Nevada	W.	West, Western
Guat.	Guatemala	N.W.T.	Northwest Territories	WA	Washington
hd	headland	NY	New York	W.A.	Western Australia
HI	Hawaii	N.Z.	New Zealand	WI	Wisconsin
Hima. Prad.	Himachal Pradesh	OH	Ohio	WV	West Virginia
hist. area	historical area	OK	Oklahoma	WY	Wyoming
H.K.	Hong Kong	Ont.	Ontario	Y.T.	Yukon
Hond.	Honduras	OR	Oregon		
i.	island	PA	Pennsylvania		

1

1st Three Mile Opening *sea chan.* Australia 110 D2
2nd Three Mile Opening *sea chan.* Australia 110 C2
5 de Outubro Angola *see* Xá-Muteba
9 de Julio Arg. 144 D5
25 de Mayo *Buenos Aires* Arg. 144 D5
25 de Mayo *La Pampa* Arg. 144 C5
70 Mile House Canada 120 F5
100 Mile House Canada 120 F5
150 Mile House Canada 120 F4

A

Aabenraa Denmark 45 F9
Aachen Germany 52 G4
Aalborg Denmark 45 F8
Aalborg Bugt *b.* Denmark 45 G8
Aalen Germany 53 K6
Aalesund Norway *see* Ålesund
Aaley Lebanon *see* Aley
Aalo India 83 H3
Aalst Belgium 52 E4
Aanaar Fin. *see* Inari
Aarhus Denmark 45 G8
Aarlen Belgium *see* Arlon
Aars Denmark 45 F8
Aarschot Belgium 52 E4
Aasiaat Greenland 119 M3
Aath Belgium *see* Ath
Aba China 76 D1
Aba Dem. Rep. Congo 98 D3
Aba Nigeria 96 D4
Abacaxis *r.* Brazil 143 G4
Ābādān Iran 88 C4
Abadan Turkm. 88 E2
Ābādeh Iran 88 D4
Ābādeh Ţashk Iran 88 D4
Abadla Alg. 54 D5
Abaeté Brazil 145 B2
Abaetetuba Brazil 143 I4
Abagnar Qi China *see* Xilinhot
Abaiang *atoll* Kiribati 150 H5
Abajo Peak U.S.A. 129 I3
Abakaliki Nigeria 96 D4
Abakan Russia 72 G2
Abakanskiy Khrebet *mts* Russia 72 F2
Abalak Niger 96 D3
Abana Turkey 90 D2
Abancay Peru 142 D6
Abariringa *atoll* Kiribati *see* Kanton
Abarkūh Iran 88 D4
Abarkūh, Kavīr-e *des.* Iran 88 D4
Abarshahr Iran *see* Neyshābūr
Abashiri Japan 74 G3
Abashiri-wan *b.* Japan 74 G3
Abasolo Mex. 131 D7
Abau P.N.G. 110 E1
Abaya, Lake Eth. 98 D3
Ābaya Hāyk' *l.* Eth. *see* Abaya, Lake
Ābay Wenz *r.* Eth./Sudan *see* Blue Nile
Abaza Russia 72 G2
Abba Cent. Afr. Rep. 98 B3
'Abbāsābād *Eşfahān* Iran 88 D3
'Abbāsābād *Semnān* Iran 88 E2
Abbasanta *Sardinia* Italy 58 C4
Abbatis Villa France *see* Abbeville
Abbe, Lake Djibouti/Eth. 86 F7
Abbeville France 52 B4
Abbeville *AL* U.S.A. 133 C6
Abbeville *GA* U.S.A. 133 D6
Abbeville *LA* U.S.A. 131 E6
Abbeville *SC* U.S.A. 133 D5
Abbey Canada 121 I5
Abbeyfeale Ireland 51 C5
Abbeytown U.K. 48 D4
Abborrträsk Sweden 44 K4
Abbot, Mount Australia 110 D4
Abbot Ice Shelf Antarctica 152 K2
Abbotsford Canada 120 F5
Abbott *NM* U.S.A. 127 G5
Abbott *VA* U.S.A. 134 E5
Abbottabad Pak. 89 I3
'Abd al 'Azīz *hill* Syria 91 F3
'Abd al Kūrī *i.* Yemen 86 H7
'Abd Allah, Khawr *sea chan.* Iraq/Kuwait 88 C4
Abd al Ma'asīr *well* Saudi Arabia 85 D4
Ābdānān Iran 88 B3
'Abdollāhābād Iran 88 D3
Abdulino Russia 41 Q5
Abéché Chad 97 F3
Ab-e Garm, Chashmeh-ye *spring* Iran 88 E3
Abellinum Italy *see* Avellino
Abel Tasman National Park N.Z. 113 D5
Abengourou Côte d'Ivoire 96 C4
Åbenrå Denmark *see* Aabenraa
Abensberg Germany 53 L6
Abeokuta Nigeria 96 D4
Aberaeron U.K. 49 C6
Aberchirder U.K. 50 G3
Abercorn Zambia *see* Mbala
Abercrombie *r.* Australia 112 D4
Aberdare U.K. 49 D7
Aberdaron U.K. 49 C6
Aberdaugleddau U.K. *see* Milford Haven
Aberdeen Australia 112 E4
Aberdeen *H.K.* China 77 [inset]
Aberdeen S. Africa 100 G7
Aberdeen U.K. 50 G3
Aberdeen U.S.A. 130 D2
Aberdeen Lake Canada 121 L1
Aberdovey U.K. 49 C6
Aberdyfi U.K. *see* Aberdovey
Aberfeldy U.K. 50 F4
Aberford U.K. 48 F5
Aberfoyle U.K. 50 E4
Abergavenny U.K. 49 D7
Abergwaun U.K. *see* Fishguard
Aberhonddu U.K. *see* Brecon
Abermaw U.K. *see* Barmouth
Abernathy U.S.A. 131 C5
Aberporth U.K. 49 C6
Abersoch U.K. 49 C6
Abertawe U.K. *see* Swansea
Aberteifi U.K. *see* Cardigan
Aberystwyth U.K. 49 C6
Abeshr Chad *see* Abéché
Abez' Russia 41 S2
Ābgāh Iran 89 E5
Abhā Saudi Arabia 86 F6
Abhar Iran 88 C2
Abiad, Bahr el *r.* Africa *see* White Nile

▶Abidjan Côte d'Ivoire 96 C4
Former capital of Côte d'Ivoire (Ivory Coast).

Abijatta-Shalla National Park Eth. 98 D3
Ab-i-Kavīr *salt flat* Iran 88 E3
Abilene *KS* U.S.A. 130 D4
Abilene *TX* U.S.A. 131 D5
Abingdon U.K. 49 F7
Abingdon U.S.A. 134 D5
Abington Reef Australia 110 E3
Abinsk Russia 90 E1
Abitau Lake Canada 121 J2
Abitibi, Lake Canada 122 E4
Abkhazia *disp. terr.* Georgia 91 F2
Āb Khūrak Iran 88 E3
Abminga Australia 109 F6
Abnūb Egypt 90 C6
Åbo Fin. *see* Turku
Abohar India 82 C3
Aboisso Côte d'Ivoire 96 C4
Aboite U.S.A. 134 C3
Abomey Benin 96 D4
Abongabong, Gunung *mt.* Indon. 71 B6
Abong Mbang Cameroon 96 E4
Abou Déia Chad 97 E3
Abovyan Armenia 91 G2
Aboyne U.K. 50 G3
Abqaiq Saudi Arabia 88 C5
Abraham's Bay Bahamas 133 F8
Abramovskiy, Mys *pt* Russia 42 I2
Abrantes Port. 57 B4
Abra Pampa Arg. 144 C2
Abreojos, Punta *pt* Mex. 127 E8
'Abri Sudan 86 D5
Abrolhos Bank *sea feature* S. Atlantic Ocean 148 F7
Abruzzo, Lazio e Molise, Parco Nazionale d' *nat. park* Italy 58 E4
Absaroka Range *mts* U.S.A. 126 F3
Abtar, Jabal al *hills* Syria 85 C2
Abtsgmünd Germany 53 J6
Abū aḑ Ḑuhūr Syria 85 C2
Abū al Abyaḑ *i.* U.A.E. 88 D5
Abū al Ḩusayn, Qā' *imp. l.* Jordan 85 D3
Abū 'Alī *i.* Saudi Arabia 88 C5
Abū 'Āmūd, Wādī *watercourse* Jordan 85 C4
Abū 'Arīsh Saudi Arabia 86 F6
Abu 'Aweigîla *well* Egypt *see* Abū 'Uwayqilah
Abu Deleiq Sudan 86 D6

▶Abu Dhabi U.A.E. 88 D5
Capital of the United Arab Emirates.

Abū Du'ān Syria 85 D1
Abu Gubeiha Sudan 86 D7
Abū Ḩafnah, Wādī *watercourse* Jordan 85 D3
Abu Haggag Egypt *see* Ra's al Ḩikmah
Abū Ḩallūfah, Jabal *hill* Jordan 85 C4
Abu Hamed Sudan 86 D6

▶Abuja Nigeria 96 D4
Capital of Nigeria.

Abū Jifān *well* Saudi Arabia 88 B5
Abū Jurdhān Jordan 85 B4
Abū Kamāl Syria 91 F4
Abu Matariq Sudan 97 F3
Abumombazi Dem. Rep. Congo 98 C3
Abu Musa *i.* The Gulf *see* Abū Mūsá, Jazīreh-ye
Abū Mūsá, Jazīreh-ye *i.* The Gulf 88 D5
Abunā *r.* Bol. 142 E5
Abunā Brazil 142 E5
Ābune Yosēf *mt.* Eth. 86 E7
Abū Nujaym Libya 97 E1
Abū Qa'ţūr Syria 85 C2
Abū Rawthah, Jabal *mt.* Egypt 85 B5
Aburo *mt.* Dem. Rep. Congo 98 D3
Abu Road India 79 G4
Abū Rujmayn, Jabal *mts* Syria 85 D2
Abu Rûtha, Gebel *mt.* Egypt *see* Abū Rawthah, Jabal
Abū Sawādah *well* Saudi Arabia 88 C5
Abu Simbil Egypt *see* Abū Sunbul
Abū Sunbul Egypt 86 D5
Abū Ţarfā', Wādī *watercourse* Egypt 85 A5
Abut Head *hd* N.Z. 113 C6
Abū 'Uwayqilah *well* Egypt 85 B4
Abu Zabad Sudan 86 C7
Abū Ẓaby U.A.E. *see* Abu Dhabi
Abūzam Iran 88 C4
Abū Zanīmah Egypt 90 D5
Abu Zenîma Egypt *see* Abū Zanīmah
Abyad Sudan 86 C7
Abyaḑ, Jabal al *mts* Syria 85 C2
Abyār al Ḩakīm *well* Libya 90 A5
Abydos Australia 108 B5
Abyei Sudan 86 C8
Abyssinia *country* Africa *see* Ethiopia
Academician Vernadskiy *research station* Antarctica *see* Vernadsky
Academy Bay Russia *see* Akademii, Zaliv
Acadia *prov.* Canada *see* Nova Scotia
Acadia National Park U.S.A. 132 G2
Açailândia Brazil 143 I5
Acamarachi *mt.* Chile *see* Pili, Cerro
Acampamento de Caça do Mucusso Angola 99 C5
Acandí Col. 142 C2
A Cañiza Spain 57 B2
Acaponeta Mex. 136 C4
Acapulco Mex. 136 E5
Acapulco de Juárez Mex. *see* Acapulco
Acará Brazil 143 I4
Acarai Mountains *hills* Brazil/Guyana 143 G3
Acaraú Brazil 143 J4
Acaray, Represa de *resr* Para. 144 E3
Acarigua Venez. 142 E2
Acatlán Mex. 136 E5
Accho Israel *see* 'Akko
Accomac U.S.A. 135 H5
Accomack U.S.A. *see* Accomac

▶Accra Ghana 96 C4
Capital of Ghana.

Accrington U.K. 48 E5
Ach *r.* Germany 53 L6
Achacachi Bol. 142 E7
Achaguas Venez. 142 E2
Achalpur India 82 D5
Achampet India 84 C2
Achan Russia *see* Bolon'
Achayvayam Russia 65 S3
Acheng China 74 B3
Achhota India 84 D1
Achicourt France 52 C4
Achill Ireland 51 C4
Achillbeg Island Ireland 51 C4
Achill Island Ireland 51 B4
Achiltibuie U.K. 50 D2
Achim Germany 53 J1
Achinsk Russia 64 K4
Achit Russia 41 R4
Achit Nuur *l.* Mongolia 80 H2
Achkhoy-Martan Russia 91 G2
Achna Cyprus 85 A2
Achnasheen U.K. 50 D3
Acıgöl *l.* Turkey 59 M6
Acıpayam Turkey 59 M6
Acireale *Sicily* Italy 58 F6
Ackerman U.S.A. 131 F5
Ackley U.S.A. 130 E3
Acklins Island Bahamas 133 F8
Acle U.K. 49 I6

▶Aconcagua, Cerro *mt.* Arg. 144 B4
Highest mountain in South America.

Acopiara Brazil 143 K5
Açores *terr.* N. Atlantic Ocean *see* Azores
Açores, Arquipélago dos *terr.* N. Atlantic Ocean *see* Azores
A Coruña Spain 57 B2
Acquaviva delle Fonti Italy 58 G4
Acqui Terme Italy 58 C2
Acra U.S.A. 135 H2
Acragas *Sicily* Italy *see* Agrigento
Acraman, Lake *salt flat* Australia 111 A7
Acre *r.* Brazil 142 E6
Acre Israel *see* 'Akko
Acre, Bay of Israel *see* Haifa, Bay of
Acri Italy 58 G5
Ács Hungary 47 Q7
Actaeon Group *is* Fr. Polynesia *see* Actéon, Groupe
Actéon, Groupe *is* Fr. Polynesia 151 K7
Acton Canada 134 E2
Acton U.S.A. 128 D4
Açungui Brazil 145 A4
Acunum Acusio France *see* Montélimar
Ada *MN* U.S.A. 130 D2
Ada *OH* U.S.A. 134 D3
Ada *OK* U.S.A. 131 D5
Ada *WI* U.S.A. 134 B2
Adabazar Turkey *see* Adapazarı
Adaja *r.* Spain 57 D3
Adalia Turkey *see* Antalya
Adam Oman 87 I5
Adam, Mount *hill* Falkland Is 144 E8
Adamantina Brazil 145 A3
Adams *IN* U.S.A. 134 C4
Adams *KY* U.S.A. 134 D4
Adams *MA* U.S.A. 135 I2
Adams *NY* U.S.A. 135 G2
Adams, Mount U.S.A. 126 C3
Adams Center U.S.A. 135 G2
Adams Lake Canada 120 G5
Adams Mountain U.S.A. 120 D4
Adam's Peak Sri Lanka 84 D5
Adams Peak U.S.A. 128 C2

▶Adamstown Pitcairn Is 151 L7
Capital of the Pitcairn Islands.

'Adan Yemen *see* Aden
Adana Turkey 85 B1
Adana *prov.* Turkey 85 B1
Adana Yemen *see* Aden
Adapazarı Turkey 59 N4
Adare Ireland 51 D5
Adare, Cape Antarctica 152 H2
Adavale Australia 111 D5
Ad Dabbah Sudan *see* Ed Debba
Ad Ḑabbīyah *well* Saudi Arabia 88 C5
Ad Dafinah Saudi Arabia 86 F5
Ad Dahnā' *des.* Saudi Arabia 86 G5
Ad Dakhla W. Sahara *see* Dakhla
Ad Damir Sudan *see* Ed Damer
Ad Dammām Saudi Arabia *see* Dammam
Addanki India 84 C3
Ad Dār al Ḩamrā' Saudi Arabia 86 E4
Ad Darb Saudi Arabia 86 F6
Ad Dawādimī Saudi Arabia 86 F5
Ad Dawḩah Qatar *see* Doha
Ad Dawr Iraq 91 F4
Ad Daww *plain* Syria 85 C2
Ad Dayr Iraq 91 G5
Ad Dibdibah *plain* Saudi Arabia 88 B5
Ad Ḑiffah *plat.* Egypt *see* Libyan Plateau
Ad Dir'īyah Saudi Arabia 97 H2

▶Addis Ababa Eth. 98 D3
Capital of Ethiopia.

Addison U.S.A. 135 G2
Ad Dīwānīyah Iraq 91 G5
Addlestone U.K. 49 G7
Addo Elephant National Park S. Africa 101 G7
Addoo Atoll Maldives *see* Addu Atholhu
Addu Atholhu Maldives 81 D12
Ad Duqm Oman 87 I6
Ad Duwayd *well* Saudi Arabia 91 F5
Ad Duwaym Sudan *see* Ed Dueim
Ad Duwayris *well* Saudi Arabia 88 C6
Adegaon India 82 D5
Adel *GA* U.S.A. 133 D6
Adel *IA* U.S.A. 130 E3

▶Adelaide Australia 111 B7
Capital of South Australia.

Adelaide *r.* Australia 108 E3
Adelaide Bahamas 133 E7
Adelaide Island Antarctica 152 L2
Adelaide River Australia 108 E3
Adele Island Australia 108 C3
Adélie Coast Antarctica 152 G2
Adélie Land *reg.* Antarctica 152 G2
Adelong Australia 112 D5
Aden Yemen 86 F7
Aden, Gulf of Somalia/Yemen 86 G7
Adena U.S.A. 134 E3
Adenau Germany 52 G4
Adendorf Germany 53 K1
Aderbissinat Niger 96 D3
Aderno *Sicily* Italy *see* Adrano
Adesar India 82 B5
Adhan, Jabal *mt.* U.A.E. 88 E5
Adh Dhāyūf *well* Saudi Arabia 91 G6
'Adhfā' *well* Saudi Arabia 91 F5
'Ādhirīyāt, Jibāl al *mts* Jordan 85 C4
Adi *i.* Indon. 69 I7
Ādī Ārk'ay Eth. 86 E7
Adige *r.* Italy 58 E2
Ādīgrat Eth. 98 D2
Adilabad India 84 C2
Adilcevaz Turkey 91 F3
Adin U.S.A. 126 C4
Adīrī Libya 97 E2
Adirondack Mountains U.S.A. 135 H1
Ādīs Ābeba Eth. *see* Addis Ababa
Adi Ugri Eritrea *see* Mendefera
Adıyaman Turkey 90 E3
Adjud Romania 59 L1
Adjuntas, Presa de las *resr* Mex. 131 D8
Adlavik Islands Canada 123 K3
Admiralty Island Canada 119 H3
Admiralty Island U.S.A. 120 C3
Admiralty Island National Monument-Kootznoowoo Wilderness *nat. park* U.S.A. 120 C3
Admiralty Islands P.N.G. 69 L7
Ado-Ekiti Nigeria 96 D4
Adok South Sudan 86 D8
Adolfo L. Mateos Mex. 127 E8
Adolphus U.S.A. 134 B5
Adonara *i.* Indon. 108 C2
Adoni India 84 C3
Adorf (Diemelsee) Germany 53 I3
Adorf/Vogtland Germany 53 M4
Ado-Tymovo Russia 74 F2
Adour *r.* France 56 D5
Adra Spain 57 E5
Adramyttium Turkey *see* Edremit
Adramyttium, Gulf of Turkey *see* Edremit Körfezi
Adrano *Sicily* Italy 58 F6
Adrar Alg. 96 C2
Adrar *hills* Mali *see* Ifôghas, Adrar des
Adrar, Dahr *hills* Mauritania 96 B3
Adré Chad 97 F3
Adrian *MI* U.S.A. 134 C3
Adrian *TX* U.S.A. 131 C5
Adrianople Turkey *see* Edirne
Adrianopolis Turkey *see* Edirne
Adriatic Sea Europe 58 E2
Adua Eth. *see* Ādwa
Adunara *i.* Indon. *see* Adonara
Adusa Dem. Rep. Congo 98 C3
Aduwa Eth. *see* Ādwa
Adverse Well Australia 108 C5
Ādwa Eth. 98 D2
Adycha *r.* Russia 65 O3
Adyk Russia 43 J7
Adzopé Côte d'Ivoire 96 C4
Aegean Sea Greece/Turkey 59 K5
Aegina *i.* Greece *see* Aigina
Aegyptus *country* Africa *see* Egypt
Aela Jordan *see* Al 'Aqabah
Aelana Jordan *see* Al 'Aqabah
Aelia Capitolina Israel/West Bank *see* Jerusalem
Aelönlaplap *atoll* Marshall Is *see* Ailinglaplap
Aenus Turkey *see* Enez
Aerzen Germany 53 J2
Aesernia Italy *see* Isernia
A Estrada Spain 57 B2
Afabet Eritrea 86 E6
Afanas'yevo Russia 42 L4
Affreville Alg. *see* Khemis Miliana
Afghānestān *country* Asia *see* Afghanistan
Afghanistan *country* Asia 89 G3
Afgooye Somalia 98 E3
'Afīf Saudi Arabia 86 F5
Afiun Karahissar Turkey *see* Afyon
Åfjord Norway 44 G5
Aflou Alg. 54 E5
Afmadow Somalia 98 E3
Afogados da Ingazeira Brazil 143 K5
A Fonsagrada Spain 57 C2
Afonso Cláudio Brazil 145 C3
Āfrēra *vol.* Eth. 86 F7
Africa Nova *country* Africa *see* Tunisia
'Afrīn Syria 85 C1
'Afrīn, Nahr *r.* Syria/Turkey 85 C1
Afşin Turkey 90 E3
Afsluitdijk *barrage* Neth. 52 F2
Afton U.S.A. 126 F4
Afuá Brazil 143 H4
'Afula Israel 85 B3
Afyon Turkey 59 N5
Afyonkarahisar Turkey *see* Afyon
Aga Germany 53 M4
Agadès Niger *see* Agadez
Agadez Niger 96 D3
Agadir Morocco 96 C1
Agalega Islands Mauritius 149 L6
Agana Guam *see* Hagåtña
Agara Georgia 91 F2
Agartala India 83 G5
Agashi India 84 B2
Agate Canada 122 E4
Agathe France *see* Agde
Agathonisi *i.* Greece 59 L6
Agats Indon. 69 J8
Agatti *i.* India 84 B4
Agboville Côte d'Ivoire 96 C4
Ağcabädi Azer. 91 G2
Ağdam (abandoned) Azer. 91 G3
Ağdaş Azer. 91 G2
Agdash Azer. *see* Ağdaş
Agde France 56 F5
Agdzhabedi Azer. *see* Ağcabädi
Agedabia Libya *see* Ajdābiyā
Agen France 56 E4
Aggeneys S. Africa 100 D5
Aggteleki *nat. park* Hungary 47 R6
Aghil Dawan China 82 D1
Agiabampo Mex. 127 F8
Agiguan *i.* N. Mariana Is *see* Aguijan
Ağın Turkey 90 E3
Aginskoye Russia 72 G1
Aginum France *see* Agen
Agios Dimitrios Greece 59 J6
Agios Efstratios *i.* Greece 59 K5
Agios Georgios *i.* Greece 59 J6
Agios Nikolaos Greece 59 K7
Agios Theodoros Cyprus 85 B2
Agiou Orous, Kolpos *b.* Greece 59 J4
Agirwat Hills Sudan 86 E6
Agisanang S. Africa 101 G4
Agnes, Mount *hill* Australia 109 E6
Agnew Australia 109 C6
Agnibilékrou Côte d'Ivoire 96 C4
Agnita Romania 59 K2
Agniye-Afanas'yevsk Russia 74 E2
Agra India 82 D4
Agrakhanskiy Poluostrov *pen.* Russia 91 G2
Agram Croatia *see* Zagreb
Ağrı Turkey 91 F3
Agria Gramvousa *i.* Greece 59 J7
Ağrı Dağı *mt.* Turkey *see* Ararat, Mount
Agrigan *i.* N. Mariana Is *see* Agrihan
Agrigento *Sicily* Italy 58 E6
Agrigentum *Sicily* Italy *see* Agrigento
Agrihan *i.* N. Mariana Is 69 L3
Agrinio Greece 59 I5
Agropoli Italy 58 F4
Agryz Russia 41 Q4
Ağsu Azer. 91 H2
Agua, Volcán de *vol.* Guat. 136 F6
Água Clara Brazil 144 F2
Aguadilla Puerto Rico 137 K5
Agua Escondida Arg. 144 C5
Agua Fria *r.* U.S.A. 129 G5
Agua Fria National Monument *nat. park* U.S.A. 129 G4
Aguanaval *r.* Mex. 131 C7
Aguanga U.S.A. 128 E5
Aguanish *r.* Canada 123 J4
Aguapeí *r.* Brazil 145 A3
Agua Prieta Mex. 127 F7
Aguaro-Guariquito, Parque Nacional *nat. park* Venez. 142 E2
Aguascalientes Mex. 136 D4
Águas Lindas de Goiás Brazil 145 A1
Agudos Brazil 145 A3
Águeda Port. 57 B3
Aguemour *reg.* Alg. 96 D2
Aguié Niger 96 D3
Aguijan *i.* N. Mariana Is 69 L4
Aguilar U.S.A. 127 G5
Aguilar de Campoo Spain 57 D2
Águilas Spain 57 F5

▶Agulhas, Cape S. Africa 100 E8
Most southerly point of Africa.

Agulhas Basin *sea feature* Southern Ocean 149 J9
Agulhas Negras *mt.* Brazil 145 B3
Agulhas Plateau *sea feature* Southern Ocean 149 J8
Agulhas Ridge *sea feature* S. Atlantic Ocean 148 I8
Ağva Turkey 59 M4
Agvali Russia 91 G2
Ahaggar *plat.* Alg. 96 D2
Ahaggar, Tassili oua-n- *plat.* Alg. 96 D2
Āhangarān Iran 89 F3
Ahar Iran 88 B2
Ahaura N.Z. 113 C6
Ahaus Germany 52 H2
Ahipara Bay N.Z. 113 D2
Ahiri India 84 D2
Ahklun Mountains U.S.A. 118 B4
Ahlen Germany 53 H3
Ahmadabad India 82 C5
Aḩmadābād Iran 89 E3
Aḩmad al Bāqir, Jabal *mt.* Jordan 85 B5
Ahmadī Iran 88 E5
Ahmadnagar India 84 B2
Ahmadpur East Pak. 89 H4
Ahmar Mountains *mts* Eth. 98 E3
Ahmedabad India *see* Ahmadabad
Ahmednagar India *see* Ahmadnagar
Ahorn Germany 53 K4
Ahr *r.* Germany 52 H4
Ahram Iran 88 C4
Ahrensburg Germany 53 K1
Āhtäri Fin. 44 N5
Ahtme Estonia 45 O7
Ahu China 77 H1
Āhū Iran 88 C4
Ahun France 56 F3
Ahuzhen China *see* Ahu
Ahvāz Iran 88 C4
Ahwa India 84 B1
Ahwāz Iran *see* Ahvāz
Ai-Ais Namibia 100 C4
Ai-Ais Hot Springs and Fish River Canyon Park *nature res.* Namibia 100 C4
Ai-Ais/Richtersveld Transfrontier Park Namibia/S. Africa 100 C5
Aībak Afgh. 89 H2
Aichwara India 82 D4
Aid U.S.A. 134 D4
Aigialousa Cyprus 85 B2
Aigina *i.* Greece 59 J6
Aigio Greece 59 J5
Aigle de Chambeyron *mt.* France 56 H4
Aigüestortes i Estany de Sant Maurici, Parc Nacional d' *nat. park* Spain 57 G2
Ai He *r.* China 74 B4
Aihua China *see* Yunxian
Aihui China *see* Heihe
Aijal India *see* Aizawl
Aikawa Japan 75 E5
Aiken U.S.A. 133 D5
Ailao Shan *mts* China 76 D3
Aileron Australia 108 F5
Ailinglabelab *atoll* Marshall Is *see* Ailinglaplap
Ailinglaplap *atoll* Marshall Is 150 H5
Ailly-sur-Noye France 52 C5
Ailsa Craig Canada 134 E2
Ailsa Craig *i.* U.K. 50 D5
Ailt an Chorráin Ireland 51 D3
Aimorés, Serra dos *hills* Brazil 145 C2
Aïn Beïda Alg. 58 B7
'Aïn Ben Tili Mauritania 96 C2
'Aïn Dâlla *spring* Egypt *see* 'Ayn Dāllah
Aïn Defla Alg. 57 H5
Aïn Deheb Alg. 57 G6
Aïn el Hadjel Alg. 57 H6
'Aïn el Maqfi *spring* Egypt *see* 'Ayn al Maqfī
Aïn el Melh Alg. 57 I6
Aïn Mdila *well* Alg. 58 B7
Aïn-M'Lila Alg. 54 F4
Aïn Oussera Alg. 57 H6
Ain Salah Alg. *see* In Salah
Aïn Sefra Alg. 54 D5
Ainsworth U.S.A. 130 D3
Aintab Turkey *see* Gaziantep
Aïn Taya Alg. 57 H5
Aïn Tédélès Alg. 57 G6
Aïn Temouchent Alg. 57 F6
'Ain Tibaghbagh *spring* Egypt *see* 'Ayn Tabaghbugh
'Ain Timeira *spring* Egypt *see* 'Ayn Tumayrah
'Ain Zeitûn Egypt *see* 'Ayn az Zaytūn
Aiquile Bol. 142 E7
Air *i.* Indon. 71 D7
Aïr, Massif de l' *mts* Niger 96 D3
Airaines France 52 B5
Airdrie Canada 120 H5
Airdrie U.K. 50 F5
Aire *r.* France 52 E5
Aire, Canal d' France 52 C4
Aire-sur-l'Adour France 56 D5
Air Force Island Canada 119 K3
Airpanas Indon. 108 D1
Aisatung Mountain Myanmar 70 A2
Aisch *r.* Germany 53 L5
Aishihik Canada 120 B2
Aishihik Lake Canada 120 B2
Aisne *r.* France 52 C5
Aïssa, Djebel *mt.* Alg. 54 D5
Aitamännikkö Fin. 44 N3
Aitana *mt.* Spain 57 F4
Aït Benhaddou *tourist site* Morocco 54 C5
Aiterach *r.* Germany 53 M6
Aitkin U.S.A. 130 E2
Aiud Romania 59 J1
Aix France *see* Aix-en-Provence
Aix-en-Provence France 56 G5
Aix-la-Chapelle Germany *see* Aachen
Aix-les-Bains France 56 G4
Aíyina *i.* Greece *see* Aigina
Aíyion Greece *see* Aigio
Aizawl India 83 H5
Aizkraukle Latvia 45 N8
Aizpute Latvia 45 L8
Aizuwakamatsu Japan 75 E5
Ajaccio *Corsica* France 56 I6
Ajanta India 84 B1
Ajanta Range *hills* India *see* Sahyadriparvat Range
Ajaureforsen Sweden 44 I4
Ajax Canada 134 F2
Ajayameru India *see* Ajmer
Ajban U.A.E. 88 D5
Ajdābiyā Libya 97 F1
a-Jiddét *des.* Oman *see* Ḩarāsīs, Jiddat al
Ajjer, Tassili n' *plat.* Alg. 96 D2
'Ajlūn Jordan 85 B3
'Ajman U.A.E. 88 D5
Ajmer India 82 C4
Ajmer-Merwara India *see* Ajmer
Ajnala India 82 C3
Ajo U.S.A. 129 G5
Ajo, Mount U.S.A. 129 G5
Ajrestān Afgh. 89 G3
Ajyyap Turkm. 88 D2
Akademii, Zaliv *b.* Russia 74 E1
Akademii Nauk, Khrebet *mt.* Tajik. *see* Akademiyai Fanho, Qatorkŭhi
Akademiyai Fanho, Qatorkŭhi *mt.* Tajik. 89 H2
Akadyr Kazakh. 80 D2
Akagera National Park Rwanda 98 D4
Akalkot India 84 C2
Akama, Akra *c.* Cyprus *see* Arnauti, Cape
Akamagaseki Japan *see* Shimonoseki
Akan Kokuritsu-kōen *nat. park* Japan 74 G4
Akaroa N.Z. 113 D6
Akas *reg.* India 76 B3
'Akāshāt Iraq 91 E4
Akbarābād Iran 91 I5
Akbarpur *Uttar Prad.* India 82 E4
Akbarpur *Uttar Prad.* India 83 E4
Akbaytal, Pereval *pass* Tajik. 89 I2
Akbaytal Pass Tajik. *see* Akbaytal, Pereval
Akbez Turkey 85 C1
Akçadağ Turkey 90 E3
Akçakale Turkey 85 D1
Akçakoca Turkey 59 N4
Akçakoca Dağları *mts* Turkey 59 N4
Akçakoyunlu Turkey 85 C1
Akçalı Dağları *mts* Turkey 85 A1
Akchâr *reg.* Mauritania 96 B3
Akchi Kazakh. *see* Akshi
Akdağlar *mts* Turkey 59 M6
Akdağmadeni Turkey 90 D3
Akdere Turkey 85 A1
Akelamo Indon. 69 H6
Åkersberga Sweden 45 K7
Akersloot Neth. 52 E2
Aketi Dem. Rep. Congo 98 C3
Akgyr Erezi *hills* Turkm. 88 D1
Akhali-Afoni Georgia *see* Akhali Atoni
Akhali Atoni Georgia 91 F2
Akhḑar, Al Jabal al *mts* Libya 97 F1
Akhḑar, Jabal *mts* Oman 88 E6
Akhisar Turkey 59 L5
Akhnoor India 82 C2
Akhsu Azer. *see* Ağsu

Akhta Armenia see Hrazdan
Akhtarīn Syria 85 C1
Akhtubinsk Russia 43 J6
Akhty Russia 91 G2
Akhtyrka Ukr. see Okhtyrka
Aki Japan 75 D6
Akiéni Gabon 98 B4
Akimiski Island Canada 122 E3
Akishma r. Russia 74 D1
Akita Japan 75 F5
Akjoujt Mauritania 96 B3
Akkajaure l. Sweden 44 J3
Akkerman Ukr. see Bilhorod-Dnistrovs'kyy
Akkeshi Japan 74 G4
'Akko Israel 85 B3
Akkol' Akmolinskaya Oblast' Kazakh. 80 D1
Akkol' Atyrauskaya Oblast' Kazakh. 43 K7
Akku Kazakh. 80 E1
Akkul' Kazakh. see Akkol'
Akkuş Turkey 90 E2
Akkyr, Gory hills Turkm. see Akgyr Erezi
Aklavik Canada 118 E3
Aklera India 82 D4
Ak-Mechet Kazakh. see Kyzylorda
Akmeņrags pt Latvia 45 L8
Akmeqit China 82 D1
Akmola Kazakh. see Astana
Akmolinsk Kazakh. see Astana
Akobo South Sudan 97 G4
Akobo Wenz r. Eth./South Sudan 98 D3
Akokan Niger 96 D3
Akola India 84 C1
Akom II Cameroon 96 E4
Akonolinga Cameroon 96 E4
Akordat Eritrea 86 E6
Akören Turkey 90 D3
Akot India 82 D5
Akpatok Island Canada 123 I1
Akqi China 80 E3
Akra, Jabal mt. Syria/Turkey see Aqra', Jabal al
Akranes Iceland 44 [inset 1]
Åkrehamn Norway 45 D7
Akrérèb Niger 96 D3
Akron CO U.S.A. 130 C3
Akron IN U.S.A. 134 B3
Akron OH U.S.A. 134 E3
Akrotiri Bay Cyprus 85 A2
Akrotirion Bay Cyprus see Akrotiri Bay
Akrotiriou, Kolpos b. Cyprus see Akrotiri Bay
Akrotiri Sovereign Base Area military base Cyprus 85 A2
Aksai Chin terr. Asia 82 D2
Aksaray Turkey 90 D3
Aksay China 80 H4
Aksay Kazakh. 41 Q5
Ak-Say r. Kyrg. 87 M1
Aksay Russia 43 H7
Akşehir Turkey 59 N5
Akşehir Gölü l. Turkey 59 N5
Akseki Turkey 90 C3
Aksha Russia 73 K2
Akshi Kazakh. 80 E3
Akshiganak Kazakh. 80 B2
Akshukyr Kazakh. 91 H2
Aksu China 80 F3
Aksu Kazakh. 80 E1
Aksu r. Tajik. see Oqsu
Aksu r. Turkey 59 N6
Aksuat Kazakh. 80 F2
Aksu-Ayuly Kazakh. 80 D2
Aksubayevo Russia 43 K5
Āksum Eth. 86 E7
Aktag mt. China 83 F1
Aktas Dağı mt. Turkey 91 G3
Aktau Kazakh. 78 E2
Akto China 89 J2
Aktobe Kazakh. 78 E1
Aktogay Karagandinskaya Oblast' Kazakh. 80 E2
Aktogay Vostochnyy Kazakhstan Kazakh. 80 E2
Aktsyabrski Belarus 43 F5
Aktyubinsk Kazakh. see Aktobe
Akulivik Canada 119 K3
Akune Japan 75 C6
Akure Nigeria 96 D4
Akuressa Sri Lanka 84 D5
Akureyri Iceland 44 [inset 1]
Akusha Russia 43 J8
Akwanga Nigeria 96 D4
Akxokesay China 83 G1
Akyab Myanmar 70 A2
Akyatan Gölü salt l. Turkey 85 B1
Akyazı Turkey 59 N4
Akzhaykyn, Ozero salt l. Kazakh. 80 C3
Ål Norway 45 F6
'Alā, Jabal al hills Syria 85 C2
Alabama r. U.S.A. 133 C6
Alabama state U.S.A. 133 C5
Alabaster AL U.S.A. 133 C5
Alabaster MI U.S.A. 134 D1
Al 'Abṭīyah well Iraq 91 G5
Alaca Turkey 90 D2
Alacahan Turkey 90 E3
Alaçam Turkey 90 D2
Alaçam Dağları mts Turkey 59 M5
Alacant Spain see Alicante
Alaçatı Turkey 59 L5
Aladağ Turkey 90 D3
Ala Dağlar mts Turkey 91 F3
Ala Dağları mts Turkey 90 D3
Al 'Adam Libya 90 A5
Al Aflāj reg. Saudi Arabia 88 B6
Alag Hu l. China 76 C1
Alagir Russia 91 G2
Alagoinhas Brazil 145 D1
Alahärmä Fin. 44 M5
Al Aḥmadī Kuwait 88 C4
Alai Range mts Asia 89 H2
Ālaivān Iran 88 D3
Ālājah Syria 85 B2
Alajärvi Fin. 44 M5
Al 'Ajrūd well Egypt 85 B4
Alakanuk U.S.A. 118 B3
Al Akhḍar Saudi Arabia 90 E5
Alakol', Ozero salt l. Kazakh. 80 F2
Ala Kul salt l. Kazakh. see Alakol', Ozero
Alakurtti Russia 44 Q3
Al 'Alamayn Egypt 90 C5
Al 'Alayyah Saudi Arabia 86 F6
Alama Somalia 98 E3
Alamagan i. N. Mariana Is 69 L3
Alamaguan i. N. Mariana Is see Alamagan
Al 'Amārah Iraq 91 G5
'Alam ar Rūm, Ra's pt Egypt 90 B5
'Alāmarvdasht watercourse Iran 88 D4
Alameda U.S.A. 128 B3
'Alam el Rûm, Râs pt Egypt see 'Alam ar Rūm, Ra's
Al Amghar waterhole Iraq 91 G5
Al 'Āmirīyah Egypt 90 C5
Alamítos, Sierra de los mt. Mex. 131 C7
Alamo GA U.S.A. 133 D5
Alamo NV U.S.A. 129 F3
Alamo Dam U.S.A. 129 G4
Alamogordo U.S.A. 127 G6
Alamo Heights U.S.A. 131 D6
Alamos Sonora Mex. 127 F7
Alamos Sonora Mex. 127 F8
Alamos r. Mex. 131 C7
Alamos, Sierra mts Mex. 127 F8
Alamosa U.S.A. 127 G5
Alamos de Peña Mex. 127 G7
Alampur India 84 C3
Alan Myanmar see Aunglan
Alanäs Sweden 44 I4
Åland is Fin. see Åland Islands
Aland r. Germany 53 L1
Aland India 84 C2
Åland Islands Fin. 45 K6
Alando China 76 B2
Alandur India 84 D3
Alanson U.S.A. 134 C1
Alanya Turkey 90 D3
Alaplı Turkey 59 N4
Alappuzha India 84 C4
Alapuzha India see Alappuzha
Al 'Aqabah Jordan 85 B5
'Alāqahdārī Gēlān Afgh. 89 G3
'Alāqahdārī Gulistān Afgh. 89 F3
'Alāqahdārī Shāh Jōy Afgh. 89 G3
'Alāqahdārī Shumūlzaī Afgh. 89 G4
'Alāqahdārī-ye Kirān wa Munjān Afgh. 89 H2
Al 'Aqīq Saudi Arabia 86 F5
Al 'Arabīyah as Sa'ūdīyah country Asia see Saudi Arabia
Alarcón, Embalse de resr Spain 57 E4
Al 'Arīsh Egypt 85 A4
Al Arṭāwīyah Saudi Arabia 86 G4
Alas, Selat sea chan. Indon. 108 B2
Alaşehir Turkey 59 M5
Alashiya country Asia see Cyprus
Al Ashmūnayn Egypt 90 C6
Alaska state U.S.A. 118 D3
Alaska, Gulf of U.S.A. 118 D4
Alaska Highway Canada/U.S.A. 120 A2
Alaska Peninsula U.S.A. 118 B4
Alaska Range mts U.S.A. 118 D3
Älät Azer. 91 H3
Alat Uzbek. see Olot
Alataw Shankou pass China/Kazakh. see Dzungarian Gate
Al Atwā' well Saudi Arabia 91 F5
Alatyr' Russia 43 J5
Alatyr' r. Russia 43 J5
Alausí Ecuador 142 C4
Alaverdi Armenia 91 G2
Alavieska Fin. 44 N4
'Alavījeh Iran 88 C3
Alavus Fin. 44 M5
Alawbum Myanmar 70 B1
Alawoona Australia 111 C7
Alay Kyrka Toosu mts Asia see Alai Range
Al 'Ayn Oman 88 E6
Al 'Ayn U.A.E. 88 D5
Alayskiy Khrebet mts Asia see Alai Range
Al 'Azīzīyah Iraq 91 G4
Al 'Azīzīyah Libya 55 G5
Al Azraq al Janūbī Jordan 85 C4
Alba Italy 58 C2
Alba U.S.A. 134 C1
Al Bāb Syria 85 C1
Albacete Spain 57 F4
Al Badī' Saudi Arabia 88 B6
Al Bādiyah al Janūbīyah hill Iraq 91 G5
Al Baḥrayn country Asia see Bahrain
Alba Iulia Romania 59 J1
Al Bajā' well U.A.E. 88 C5
Albājī Iran 88 C4
Al Bakhrā well Saudi Arabia 88 B5
Albanel, Lac l. Canada 123 G4
Albania country Europe 59 H4
Albany Australia 109 B8
Albany r. Canada 122 E3
Albany GA U.S.A. 133 C6
Albany IN U.S.A. 134 C3
Albany KY U.S.A. 134 C5
Albany MO U.S.A. 130 E3
▶Albany NY U.S.A. 135 I2
Capital of New York state.
Albany OH U.S.A. 134 D4
Albany OR U.S.A. 126 C3
Albany TX U.S.A. 131 D5
Albany Downs Australia 112 D1
Al Bāridah hills Saudi Arabia 85 D5
Al Başrah Iraq see Basra
Al Baṭḥa' marsh Iraq 91 G5
Al Bāṭinah reg. Oman 88 E5
Albatross Bay Australia 110 C2
Albatross Island Australia 111 [inset]
Al Bawīṭī Egypt 90 C5
Al Bayḍā' Libya 86 B3
Al Bayḍā' Yemen 86 G7
Albemarle U.S.A. 133 D5
Albemarle Sound sea chan. U.S.A. 132 E5
Albenga Italy 58 C2
Alberche r. Spain 57 D4
Alberga Australia 111 A5
Alberga watercourse Australia 111 A5
Albergaria-a-Velha Port. 57 B3
Albert Australia 112 C4
Albert France 52 C5
Albert, Lake Dem. Rep. Congo/Uganda 98 D3
Albert, Parc National nat. park Dem. Rep. Congo see Virunga, Parc National des
Alberta prov. Canada 120 H4
Alberta U.S.A. 135 G5
Albert Kanaal canal Belgium 52 F4
Albert Lea U.S.A. 130 E3
Albert Nile r. South Sudan/Uganda 97 G4
Alberto de Agostini, Parque Nacional nat. park Chile 144 B8
Alberton S. Africa 101 I4
Alberton U.S.A. 126 E3
Albert Town Bahamas 133 F8
Albertville Dem. Rep. Congo see Kalemie
Albertville France 56 H4
Albertville U.S.A. 133 C5
Albestroff France 52 G6
Albi France 56 F5
Albia U.S.A. 130 E3
Al Biḍah des. Saudi Arabia 88 C5
Albina Suriname 143 H2
Albino Italy 58 C2
Albion CA U.S.A. 128 B2
Albion IL U.S.A. 130 F4
Albion IN U.S.A. 134 C3
Albion MI U.S.A. 134 C2
Albion NE U.S.A. 130 D3
Albion NY U.S.A. 135 F2
Albion PA U.S.A. 134 E3
Al Biqā' valley Lebanon see El Béqaa
Al Bi'r Saudi Arabia 90 E5
Al Birk Saudi Arabia 86 F6
Al Biyāḍh reg. Saudi Arabia 86 G5
Alborán, Isla de i. Spain 57 E6
Alboran Sea sea Europe 57 E5
Ålborg Denmark see Aalborg
Ålborg Bugt b. Denmark see Aalborg Bugt
Albro Australia 110 D4
Al Budayyi' Bahrain 88 C5
Albufeira Port. 57 B5
Al Buḥayrāt al Murrah lakes Egypt see Bitter Lakes
Albuquerque U.S.A. 127 G6
Al Burayj Syria 85 C2
Al Buraymī Oman 88 D5
Al Burdī Libya 90 B5
Al Burj Jordan 85 B5
Alburquerque Spain 57 C4
Albury Australia 112 C6
Al Buşayrah Syria 91 F4
Al Busayṭā' plain Saudi Arabia 85 D4
Al Bushūk well Saudi Arabia 88 B4
Alcácer do Sal Port. 57 B4
Alcalá de Henares Spain 57 E3
Alcalá la Real Spain 57 E5
Alcamo Sicily Italy 58 E6
Alcañiz Spain 57 F3
Alcántara Spain 57 C4
Alcantara Lake Canada 121 I2
Alcaraz Spain 57 E4
Alcázar de San Juan Spain 57 E4
Alcazarquivir Morocco see Ksar el Kebir
Alchevs'k Ukr. 43 H6
Alcobaça Brazil 145 D2
Alcoi Spain see Alcoy-Alcoi
Alcoota Australia 108 F5
Alcova U.S.A. 126 G4
Alcoy Spain see Alcoy-Alcoi
Alcoy-Alcoi Spain 57 F4
Alcúdia Spain 57 H4
Aldabra Islands Seychelles 99 E4
Aldan Russia 65 N4
Aldan r. Russia 65 N3
Al Dayyen Qatar 88 C5
Alde r. U.K. 49 I6
Aldeboarn Neth. 52 F1
Aldeburgh U.K. 49 I6
Alder Creek U.S.A. 135 H2
Alderney i. Channel Is 49 E9
Alder Peak U.S.A. 128 C4
Aldershot U.K. 49 G7
Al Dhafrah reg. U.A.E. 88 D6
Aldingham U.K. 48 D4
Aldridge U.K. 49 F6
Aleg Mauritania 96 B3
Alegre Espírito Santo Brazil 145 C3
Alegre Minas Gerais Brazil 145 B2
Alegrete Brazil 144 E3
Alegros Mountain U.S.A. 129 I4
Aleksandra, Mys hd Russia 74 E1
Aleksandriya Ukr. see Oleksandriya
Aleksandro-Nevskiy Russia 43 I5
Aleksandropol Armenia see Gyumri
Aleksandrov Russia 42 H4
Aleksandrov Gay Russia 43 K6
Aleksandrovsk Russia 41 R4
Aleksandrovsk Ukr. see Zaporizhzhya
Aleksandrovskiy Russia see Aleksandrovsk
Aleksandrovskoye Russia 91 F1
Aleksandrovsk-Sakhalinskiy Russia 74 F2
Aleksandry, Zemlya i. Russia 64 F1
Alekseyevka Akmolinskaya Oblast' Kazakh. see Akkol'
Alekseyevka Vostochnyy Kazakhstan Kazakh. see Terekty
Alekseyevka Amurskaya Oblast' Russia 74 B1
Alekseyevka Belgorodskaya Oblast' Russia 43 H6
Alekseyevka Belgorodskaya Oblast' Russia 43 H6
Alekseyevskaya Russia 43 I6
Alekseyevskoye Russia 42 K5
Aleksin Russia 43 H5
Aleksinac Serbia 59 I3
Alèmbé Gabon 98 B4
Ålen Norway 44 G5
Alençon France 56 E2
Alenquer Brazil 143 H4
'Alenuihāhā Channel U.S.A. 127 [inset]
Alep Syria see Aleppo
Aleppo Syria 85 C1
Alert Canada 119 L1
Alerta Peru 142 D6
Alès France 56 G4
Aleşd Romania 59 J1
Aleshki Ukr. see Tsyurupyns'k
Aleşkirt Turkey see Eleşkirt
Alessandria Italy 58 C2
Alessio Albania see Lezhë
Ålesund Norway 44 E5
Aleutian Basin sea feature Bering Sea 150 H2
Aleutian Islands U.S.A. 118 A4
Aleutian Range mts U.S.A. 118 C4
Aleutian Trench sea feature N. Pacific Ocean 150 I2
Alevina, Mys c. Russia 65 Q4
Alevişik Turkey see Samandağı
Alexander U.S.A. 130 C2
Alexander, Kap c. Greenland see Ullersuaq
Alexander, Mount hill Australia 110 B2
Alexander Archipelago is U.S.A. 120 B3
Alexander Bay b. Namibia/S. Africa 100 C5
Alexander Bay S. Africa 100 C5
Alexander City U.S.A. 133 C5
Alexander Island Antarctica 152 L2
Alexandra Australia 112 B6
Alexandra N.Z. 113 B7
Alexandra, Cape S. Georgia 144 I8
Alexandra Channel India 71 A4
Alexandra Land i. Russia see Aleksandry, Zemlya
Alexandreia Greece 59 J4
Alexandretta Turkey see İskenderun
Alexandria Afgh. see Ghaznī
Alexandria Canada 135 H1
Alexandria Egypt 90 C5
Alexandria Romania 59 K3
Alexandria S. Africa 101 H7
Alexandria Turkm. see Mary
Alexandria U.K. 50 E5
Alexandria IN U.S.A. 134 C3
Alexandria KY U.S.A. 134 C4
Alexandria LA U.S.A. 131 E6
Alexandria VA U.S.A. 135 G4
Alexandria Arachoton Afgh. see Kandahār
Alexandria Areion Afgh. see Herāt
Alexandria Bay U.S.A. 135 H1
Alexandria Prophthasia Afgh. see Farāh
Alexandrina, Lake Australia 111 B7
Alexandroupoli Greece 59 K4
Alexis r. Canada 123 K3
Alexis Creek Canada 120 F4
Aley Lebanon 85 B3
Aleyak Iran 88 E2
Aleysk Russia 72 E2
Alf Germany 52 H4
Al Farwānīyah Kuwait 88 B4
Al Fas Morocco see Fès
Al Fatḥah Iraq 91 F4
Al Fāw Iraq 91 H5
Al Fayyūm Egypt 90 C5
Alfeld (Leine) Germany 53 J3
Alfenas Brazil 145 B3
Alford U.K. 48 H5
Alfred ME U.S.A. 135 J2
Alfred NY U.S.A. 135 G2
Alfred and Marie Range hills Australia 109 D6
Al Fujayrah U.A.E. see Fujairah
Al Fuqahā' Libya 97 E2
Al Furāt r. Asia see Euphrates
Alga Kazakh. 80 A2
Ålgård Norway 45 D7
Algarrobo del Aguilla Arg. 144 C5
Algarve reg. Port. 57 B5
Algeciras Spain 57 D5
Algemesí Spain 57 F4
Algena Eritrea 86 E6
Alger Alg. see Algiers
Alger U.S.A. 134 C1
▶Algeria country Africa 96 C2
Largest country in Africa and 10th largest in the world.
Algérie country Africa see Algeria
Algermissen Germany 53 J2
Algha Kazakh. see Alga
Al Ghāfāt Oman 88 E6
Al Ghammās Iraq 91 G5
Al Ghardaqah Egypt see Hurghada
Al Ghawr plain Jordan/West Bank 85 B4
Al Ghayḍah Yemen 86 H6
Alghero Sardinia Italy 58 C4
Al Ghurdaqah Egypt see Hurghada
Al Ghuwayr well Qatar 88 C5
▶Algiers Alg. 57 H5
Capital of Algeria.
Algoa Bay S. Africa 101 G7
Algoma U.S.A. 134 B1
Algona U.S.A. 130 E3
Algonac U.S.A. 134 D2
Algonquin Park Canada 135 F1
Algonquin Provincial Park Canada 135 F1
Algorta Spain 57 E2
Algueirao Moz. see Hacufera
Al Habakah well Saudi Arabia 91 F5
Al Ḥabbānīyah Iraq 91 F4
Al Ḥadaqah well Saudi Arabia 88 B4
Al Ḥadd Bahrain 88 C5
Al Hadhālīl plat. Saudi Arabia 91 F5
Al Ḥadīthah Iraq 91 F4
Al Ḥadīthah Saudi Arabia 85 C4
Al Ḥaḍr Iraq see Hatra
Al Ḥafār well Saudi Arabia 91 F5
Al Ḥaffah Syria 85 C2
Al Ḥajar al Gharbī mts Oman 88 E5
Al Ḥajar ash Sharqī mts Oman 88 E6
Al Ḥamād plain Asia 90 E5
Alhama de Murcia Spain 57 F5
Al Ḥamar Saudi Arabia 88 B6
Al Ḥamdānīyah Syria 85 C2
Al Ḥamīdīyah Syria 85 B2
Al Ḥammām Egypt 90 C5
Al Ḥanākīyah Saudi Arabia 86 F5
Al Haniyah esc. Iraq 91 G5
Al Hariq Saudi Arabia 88 B6
Al Ḥarrah Egypt 90 C5
Al Harūj al Aswad hills Libya 97 E2
Al Hasa reg. Saudi Arabia 88 C5
Al Ḥasakah Syria 91 F3
Al Hawi salt pan Saudi Arabia 85 D5
Al Ḥawīyah Saudi Arabia 86 F5
Al Hawjā' Saudi Arabia 90 E5
Al Ḥawṭah reg. Saudi Arabia 88 B6
Al Ḥayy Iraq 91 G4
Al Ḥayz Egypt 90 C5
Al Hazīm Jordan 85 C4
Al Ḥazm Saudi Arabia 90 E5
Al Ḥibāk des. Saudi Arabia 87 H6
Al Hījānah Syria 85 C3
Al Ḥillah Iraq see Hillah
Al Ḥillah Saudi Arabia 86 G5
Al Ḥinnāh Saudi Arabia 98 E1
Al Ḥinw mt. Saudi Arabia 85 D4
Al Hirrah well Saudi Arabia 88 C6
Al Hīshah Syria 85 D1
Al Ḥismā plain Saudi Arabia 90 D5
Al Ḥiṣn Jordan 85 B3
Al Hoceima Morocco 57 E6
Al Hoceima, Baie d' b. Morocco 57 E6
Al Ḥudaydah Yemen see Hodeidah
Al Ḥufrah reg. Saudi Arabia 90 E5
Al Hufūf Saudi Arabia 86 G4
Al Hūj hills Saudi Arabia 90 E5
Al Husayfin Oman 88 E5
Al Huwwah Saudi Arabia 88 B6
Ali China 82 D2
'Alīābād Afgh. 89 H2
'Alīābād Golestān Iran 88 D2
'Alīābād Hormozgān Iran 88 D4
'Alīābād Khorāsān-e Jonūbī Iran 89 F4
'Alīābād, Kūh-e mt. Iran 88 C3
'Alīābād-e Marān Iran 88 B2
'Ali 'Addé Djibouti 86 F7
Aliağa Turkey 59 L5
Aliakmonas r. Greece 59 J4
Alibag India 84 B2
Alicante Spain 57 F4
Alice r. Australia 110 C2
Alice watercourse Australia 110 D5
Alice U.S.A. 131 D7
Alice, Punta pt Italy 58 G5
Alice Springs Australia 109 F5
Alice Town Bahamas 133 E7
Aliceville U.S.A. 131 F5
Alichur Tajik. 89 I2
Alichur r. Tajik. 89 I2
Alick Creek r. Australia 110 C4
Alifu Atoll Maldives see Ari Atholhu
Al Ifẓī'iyah i. U.A.E. 88 C5
Aliganj India 82 D4
Aligarh Rajasthan India 82 D4
Aligarh Uttar Prad. India 82 D4
Alīgūdarz Iran 88 C3
Alihe China 74 A2
'Alījūq, Kūh-e mt. Iran 88 C4
'Alī Khēl Afgh. 89 H3
Al Imārāt al 'Arabīyah at Muttaḥidah country Asia see United Arab Emirates
Alimia i. Greece 59 L6
Alindao Cent. Afr. Rep. 98 C3
Alingsås Sweden 45 H8
Aliova r. Turkey 59 M5
Alipura India 82 D4
Alipur Duar India 83 G4
Alirajpur India 82 C5
Al 'Irāq country Asia see Iraq
Al 'Īsāwīyah Saudi Arabia 85 C4
Al Iskandarīyah Egypt see Alexandria
Al Iskandarīyah Iraq 91 G4
Al Ismā'īlīyah Egypt 90 D5
Al Ismā'īlīyah governorate Egypt 85 A4
Aliveri Greece 59 K5
Aliwal North S. Africa 101 H6
Alix Canada 120 H4
Al Jafr Jordan 85 C4
Al Jāfūrah des. Saudi Arabia 88 C5
Al Jaghbūb Libya 90 B5
Al Jahrah Kuwait 88 B4
Al Jarāwī well Saudi Arabia 85 D4
Al Jauf Saudi Arabia see Dawmat al Jandal
Al Jawb reg. Saudi Arabia 88 C6
Al Jawf Libya 97 F2
Al Jawsh Libya 96 E1
Al Jaza'ir country Africa see Algeria
Al Jaza'ir Alg. see Algiers
Aljezur Port. 57 B5
Al Jībān reg. Saudi Arabia 88 C5
Al Jil well Iraq 91 F5
Al Jilh esc. Saudi Arabia 88 B5
Al Jithāmīyah Saudi Arabia 91 F6
Al Jīzah Egypt see Giza
Al Jīzah Jordan 85 B4
Al Jubayl hills Saudi Arabia 88 B5
Al Jubaylah Saudi Arabia 88 B5
Al Jufrah Libya 97 E2
Al Julayqah well Saudi Arabia 88 C5
Al Jumaylīyah Qatar 88 C5
Aljustrel Port. 57 B5
Al Juwayf depr. Syria 85 C3
Al Kahfah Ash Sharqīyah Saudi Arabia 88 C5
Al Kahfah Ḥā'il Saudi Arabia 86 F4
Alkali Lake Canada 120 F5
Al Karak Jordan 85 B4
Al Kāẓimīyah Iraq 91 G4
Al Khābūrah Oman 88 E6
Al Khalīl West Bank see Hebron
Al Khāliṣ Iraq 91 G4
Al Khamāsīn Saudi Arabia 86 F5
Al Khārijah Egypt 86 D4
Al Kharj reg. Saudi Arabia 88 B6
Al Kharrārah Qatar 88 C5
Al Kharrūbah Egypt 85 A4
Al Khaṣab Oman 88 E5
Al Khatam reg. U.A.E. 88 D5
Al Khawkhah Yemen 86 F7
Al Khawr Qatar 88 C5
Al Khizāmī well Saudi Arabia 88 C5
Al Khums Libya 97 E1
Al Khunfah sand area Saudi Arabia 90 E5
Al Khunn Saudi Arabia 98 E1
Al Kifl Iraq 91 G4
Al Kir'ānah Qatar 88 C5
Al Kiswah Syria 85 C3
Alkmaar Neth. 52 E2
Al Kūbrī Egypt 85 A4
Al Kūfah Iraq 91 G4
Al Kumayt Iraq 91 G4
Al Kuntillah Egypt 85 B5
Al Kusūr hills Saudi Arabia 85 D4
Al Kūt Iraq 91 G4
Al Kuwayt country Asia see Kuwait
Al Kuwayt Kuwait see Kuwait
Al Labbah plain Saudi Arabia 91 F5
Al Lādhiqīyah Syria see Latakia
Allagadda India 84 C3
Allahabad India 83 E4
Al Lajā lava field Syria 85 C3
Allakaket U.S.A. 118 C3
Allakh-Yun' Russia 65 O3
Allanmyo Myanmar see Aunglan
Allanridge S. Africa 101 H4
Allapalli India 84 D2
'Allāqī, Wādī al watercourse Egypt 86 D5
'Allâqi, Wâdi el watercourse Egypt see 'Allāqī, Wādī al
Allardville Canada 123 I5
Alldays S. Africa 101 I2
Allegan U.S.A. 134 C2
Allegheny r. U.S.A. 134 F3
Allegheny Mountains U.S.A. 134 D5
Allegheny Reservoir U.S.A. 135 F3
Allen, Lough l. Ireland 51 D3
Allendale U.S.A. 133 D5
Allendale Town U.K. 48 E4
Allende Coahuila Mex. 131 C6
Allende Nuevo León Mex. 131 C7
Allendorf (Lumda) Germany 53 I4
Allenford Canada 134 E1
Allenstein Poland see Olsztyn
Allensville U.S.A. 134 B5
Allentown U.S.A. 135 H3
Alleppey India see Alappuzha
Aller r. Germany 53 J2
Alliance NE U.S.A. 130 C3
Alliance OH U.S.A. 134 E3
Al Lībīyah country Africa see Libya
Allier r. France 56 F3
Al Lihābah well Saudi Arabia 88 B5
Allinge-Sandvig Denmark 45 I9
Al Liṣāfah well Saudi Arabia 88 B5
Al Lisān pen. Jordan 85 B4
Alliston Canada 134 F1
Al Līth Saudi Arabia 86 F5
Al Liwā' oasis U.A.E. 88 D6
Alloa U.K. 50 F4
Allons U.S.A. 134 C5
Allora Australia 112 F2
Allur India 84 D3
Alluru Kottapatnam India 84 D3
Al Lussuf well Iraq 91 F5
Alma Canada 123 H4
Alma MI U.S.A. 134 C2
Alma NE U.S.A. 130 D3
Alma WI U.S.A. 130 F2
Al Ma'ānīyah Iraq 91 F5
Alma-Ata Kazakh. see Almaty
Almada Port. 57 B4
Al Madāfi' plat. Saudi Arabia 90 E5
Al Ma'danīyāt well Iraq 91 G5
Almaden Australia 110 D3
Almadén Spain 57 D4
Al Madīnah Saudi Arabia see Medina
Al Mafraq Jordan 85 C3
Al Maghrib country Africa see Morocco
Al Maghrib reg. U.A.E. 88 D6
Al Maḥajjah depr. Saudi Arabia 90 E6
Al Mahākīk reg. Saudi Arabia 88 C6
Al Maḥwīt Yemen 86 F6
Al Malsūnīyah reg. Saudi Arabia 88 C5
Almalyk Uzbek. see Olmaliq
Al Manadir reg. Oman 88 D6
Al Manāmah Bahrain see Manama
Al Manjūr well Saudi Arabia 88 B6
Almanor, Lake U.S.A. 128 C1
Almansa Spain 57 F4
Al Manṣūrah Egypt 90 C5
Almanzor mt. Spain 57 D3
Al Mariyyah U.A.E. 88 D6
Al Marj Libya 97 F1
Almas, Rio das r. Brazil 145 A1
Al Maṭarīyah Egypt 90 D5
▶Almaty Kazakh. 80 E3
Former capital of Kazakhstan.
Al Mawşil Iraq see Mosul
Al Mayādīn Syria 91 F4
Al Mazār Egypt 85 A4
Almaznyy Russia 65 M3
Almeirim Brazil 143 H4
Almeirim Port. 57 B4
Almelo Neth. 52 G2
Almenara Brazil 145 C2
Almendra, Embalse de resr Spain 57 C3
Almendralejo Spain 57 C4
Almere Neth. 52 F2
Almería Spain 57 E5
Almería, Golfo de b. Spain 57 E5
Al'met'evsk Russia see Al'met'yevsk
Al'met'yevsk Russia 41 Q5
Älmhult Sweden 45 I8
Almina, Punta pt Spain 57 D6
Al Mindak Saudi Arabia 86 F5
Al Minyā Egypt 90 C5
Almirós Greece see Almyros
Al Mish'āb Saudi Arabia 88 C4
Almodôvar Port. 57 B5
Almond r. U.K. 50 F4
Almont U.S.A. 134 D2
Almonte Spain 57 C5
Almora India 82 D3
Al Mu'ayzīlah hill Saudi Arabia 85 D5
Al Mubarrez Saudi Arabia 86 G4
Al Muḍaibī Oman 87 I5
Al Muḍairib Oman 88 E6
Al Muharraq Bahrain 88 C5
Al Mukallā Yemen see Mukalla
Al Mukhā Yemen see Mocha
Al Mukhaylī Libya 86 B3
Al Munbaṭiḥ des. Saudi Arabia 88 C6
Almuñécar Spain 57 E5
Al Muqdādīyah Iraq 91 G4
Al Mūrītānīyah country Africa see Mauritania
Al Murūt well Saudi Arabia 91 E5
Almus Turkey 90 E2
Al Musannāh ridge Saudi Arabia 88 B4
Al Musayyib Iraq 91 G4
Al Muwaqqar Jordan 85 C4
Almyros Greece 59 J5
Almyrou, Ormos b. Greece 59 K7
Alnwick U.K. 48 F3
▶Alofi Niue 107 J3
Capital of Niue.
Aloja Latvia 45 N8
Alon Myanmar 70 A2

Alongshan China 74 A2
Alonnisos i. Greece 59 J5
Alor i. Indon. 108 D2
Alor, Kepulauan is Indon. 108 D2
Alor Setar Malaysia see Alor Star
Alor Star Malaysia 71 C6
Alost Belgium see Aalst
Aloysius, Mount Australia 109 E6
Alozero (abandoned) Russia 44 Q4
Alpen Germany 52 G3
Alpena U.S.A. 134 D1
Alpercatas, Serra das hills Brazil 143 J5
Alpha Australia 110 D4
Alpha Ridge sea feature Arctic Ocean 153 A1
Alpine AZ U.S.A. 129 I5
Alpine NY U.S.A. 135 G2
Alpine TX U.S.A. 131 C6
Alpine WY U.S.A. 126 F4
Alpine National Park Australia 112 C6
Alps mts Europe 56 H4
Al Qa'āmīyāt reg. Saudi Arabia 86 G6
Al Qaddāḥīyah Libya 97 E1
Al Qadmūs Syria 85 C2
Al Qaffāy i. U.A.E. 88 D5
Al Qāhirah Egypt see Cairo
Al Qā'īyah Saudi Arabia 86 F5
Al Qā'īyah well Saudi Arabia 88 B5
Al Qalībah Saudi Arabia 90 E5
Al Qāmishlī Syria 91 F3
Al Qar'ah Libya 90 B5
Al Qar'ah well Saudi Arabia 88 B5
Al Qar'ah lava field Syria 85 C3
Al Qardāḥah Syria 85 C2
Al Qarqar Saudi Arabia 85 C4
Al Qaryatayn Syria 85 C2
Al Qaṣab Ar Riyāḍ Saudi Arabia 88 B5
Al Qaṣab Ash Sharqīyah Saudi Arabia 88 C6
Al Qaṭīf Saudi Arabia 88 C5
Al Qaṭn Yemen 86 G6
Al Qaṭrānah Jordan 85 C4
Al Qaṭrūn Libya 97 E2
Al Qayṣūmah well Saudi Arabia 91 F5
Alqueva, Barragem de resr Port. 57 C4
Al Qumur country Africa see Comoros
Al Qunayṭirah (abandoned) Syria 85 B3
Al Qunfidhah Saudi Arabia 86 F6
Al Qurayyāt Saudi Arabia 85 C4
Al Qurnah Iraq 91 G5
Al Quṣaymah Egypt 85 B4
Al Quṣayr Egypt 86 D4
Al Quṣayr Syria 85 C2
Al Qūṣīyah Egypt 90 C6
Al Qūṣūrīyah Saudi Arabia 88 B6
Al Quṭayfah Syria 85 C3
Al Quwayi' Saudi Arabia 88 B6
Al Quwayīyah Saudi Arabia 86 G5
Al Quwayrah Jordan 85 B5
Al Rabbād reg. U.A.E. 88 D6
Alroy Downs Australia 110 B3
Alsace admin. reg. France see Alsace, Champagne-Ardenne et Lorraine
Alsace reg. France 56 H2
Alsace, Champagne-Ardenne et Lorraine admin. reg. France 52 F5
Alsager U.K. 49 E5
Al Samīt well Iraq 91 F5
Alsask Canada 121 I5
Alsatia reg. France see Alsace
Alsek r. U.S.A. 120 B3
Alsfeld Germany 53 J4
Alsleben (Saale) Germany 53 L3
Alston U.K. 48 E4
Alstonville Australia 112 F2
Alsunga Latvia 45 L8
Alta Norway 44 M2
Alta, Mount N.Z. 113 B7
Altaelva r. Norway 44 M2
Altafjorden sea chan. Norway 44 M1
Alta Floresta Brazil 143 G5
Altai Mountains Asia 72 F3
Altamaha r. U.S.A. 133 D6
Altamira Brazil 143 H4
Altamura Italy 58 G4
Altan Xiret China 73 J5
Altar r. Mex. 127 F7
Altar, Desierto de des. Mex. 129 F6
Altavista U.S.A. 134 F5
Altay China 80 G2
Altay Govĭ-Altay Mongolia 80 H3
Altay Govĭ-Altay Mongolia 80 I2
Altayskiy Khrebet mts Asia see Altai Mountains
Altayskoye Russia 80 G1
Altdorf Switz. 56 I3
Altea Spain 57 F4
Alteidet Norway 44 M1
Altenahr Germany 52 G4
Altenberge Germany 53 H2
Altenburg Germany 53 M4
Altenkirchen (Westerwald) Germany 53 H4
Altenqoke China 83 H1
Altın Köprü Iraq 91 G4
Altınoluk Turkey 59 L5
Altınözü Turkey 85 C1
Altıntaş Turkey 59 N5
Altiplano plain Bol. 142 E7
Altmark reg. Germany 53 L2
Altmühl r. Germany 53 L6
Alto, Monte hill Italy 58 D2
Alto Chicapa Angola 99 B5
Alto Garças Brazil 143 H7
Alto Madidi, Parque Nacional nat. park Bol. 142 E6
Alton CA U.S.A. 128 A1
Alton IL U.S.A. 130 F4
Alton MO U.S.A. 131 F4
Alton NH U.S.A. 135 J2
Altona Canada 120 F3
Altoona U.S.A. 135 F3
Alto Paraíso de Goiás Brazil 145 B1
Alto Parnaíba Brazil 143 I5
Alto Taquari Brazil 143 H7
Altötting Germany 47 N6
Altrincham U.K. 48 E5
Alt Schwerin Germany 53 M1
Altūn Kūbrī Iraq see Altin Köprü
Altun Shan mts China 80 G4
Alturas U.S.A. 126 C4
Altus U.S.A. 131 D5
Al 'Ubaylah Saudi Arabia 98 F1
Alucra Turkey 90 E2
Alūksne Latvia 45 O8
Alūm Iran 88 C3
Alum Bridge U.S.A. 134 E4
Al 'Uqaylah Libya 97 E1
Al 'Uqaylah Saudi Arabia see An Nabk
Al Uqṣur Egypt see Luxor
Alur India 84 C3
Al 'Urayq des. Saudi Arabia 90 E5
Al 'Urdun country Asia see Jordan
Alur Setar Malaysia see Alor Star
Ālūt Iran 88 B3
Aluva India 84 C4
Al 'Uwayjā' well Saudi Arabia 88 C6
Al 'Uwaynāt Libya 86 B5
Al 'Uwayqīlah Saudi Arabia 91 F5
Al 'Uzayr Iraq 91 G5
Alva U.S.A. 131 D4
Alvand, Kūh-e mt. Iran 88 C3
Alvarães Brazil 142 F4
Alvaton U.S.A. 134 B5
Alvdal Norway 44 G5
Älvdalen Sweden 45 I6
Alvesta Sweden 45 I8
Ålvik Norway 45 E6
Alvik Sweden 44 J5
Alvin U.S.A. 131 E6
Alvorada do Norte Brazil 145 B1
Älvsbyn Sweden 44 L4
Al Wafrah Kuwait 88 B4
Al Wajh Saudi Arabia 86 E4
Al Wakrah Qatar 88 C5
Al Waqbá well Saudi Arabia 88 B4
Alwar India 82 D4
Al Warī'ah Saudi Arabia 86 G4
Al Wāṭiyah well Egypt 90 B5
Alwaye India see Aluva
Al Widyān plat. Iraq/Saudi Arabia 91 F4
Al Wusayṭ well Saudi Arabia 88 B4
Alxa Youqi China see Ehen Hudag
Alxa Zuoqi China see Bayan Hot
Al Yamāmah Saudi Arabia 88 B5
Al Yaman country Asia see Yemen
Alyangula Australia 110 B2
Al Ya'rūbīyah Syria 91 F3
Al Yāsāt i. U.A.E. 88 C5
Alyth U.K. 50 F4
Alytus Lith. 45 N9
Alzette r. Lux. 52 G5
Alzey Germany 53 I5
Amacayacu, Parque Nacional nat. park Col. 142 D4
Amadeus, Lake salt flat Australia 109 E6
'Amādīyah/Amêdî Iraq 91 F3
Amadjuak Lake Canada 119 K3
Amadora Port. 57 B4
Amakusa-nada b. Japan 75 C6
Åmål Sweden 45 H7
Amalia S. Africa 101 G4
Amaliada Greece 59 I6
Amalner India 82 C5
Amamapare Indon. 69 J7
Amambaí Brazil 144 E2
Amambaí, Serra de hills Brazil/Para. 144 E2
Amami-Ō-shima i. Japan 75 C7
Amami-shotō is Japan 75 C8
Amamula Dem. Rep. Congo 98 C4
Amanab P.N.G. 69 K7
Amankeldi Kazakh. see Amankel'dy
Amankel'dy Kazakh. 80 C1
Amantea Italy 58 G5
Amapá Brazil 143 H3
Amarante Brazil 143 J5
Amarapura Myanmar 70 B2
Amareleja Port. 57 C4
Amargosa Brazil 145 D1
Amargosa watercourse U.S.A. 128 E3
Amargosa Desert U.S.A. 128 E3
Amargosa Range mts U.S.A. 128 E3
Amargosa Valley U.S.A. 128 E3
Amarillo U.S.A. 131 C5
Amarillo, Cerro mt. Arg. 144 C4
Amarkantak India 83 E5
Amarpur India 82 E5
Amasia Turkey see Amasya
Amasra Turkey 90 D2
Amassine W. Sahara 96 B2
Amasya Turkey 90 D2
Amata Australia 109 E6
Amatulla India 83 H4
Amau P.N.G. 110 E1
Amay Belgium 52 F4
Amazar Russia 74 A1
Amazar r. Russia 74 A1

►Amazon r. S. America 142 F4
Longest river and largest drainage basin in South America and 2nd longest river in the world.
Also known as Amazonas or Solimões

Amazon, Mouths of the Brazil 143 I3
Amazonas r. S. America see Amazon
Amazon Cone sea feature S. Atlantic Ocean 148 E5
Amazônia, Parque Nacional nat. park Brazil 143 G4
Ambajogai India 84 C2
Ambala India 82 D3
Ambalangoda Sri Lanka 84 D5
Ambalavao Madag. 99 E6
Ambam Cameroon 98 B3
Ambar Iran 88 E4
Ambarchik Russia 65 R3
Ambarnyy Russia 44 R4
Ambasa India see Ambassa
Ambasamudram India 84 C4
Ambassa India 83 G5
Ambathala Australia 111 D5
Ambato Ecuador 142 C4
Ambato Boeny Madag. 99 E5
Ambato Finandrahana Madag. 99 E6
Ambatolampy Madag. 99 E5
Ambatomainty Madag. 99 E5
Ambatondrazaka Madag. 99 E5
Ambejogai India see Ambajogai
Ambelau i. Indon. 69 H7
Ambeno enclave East Timor see Ocussi
Amberg Germany 53 L5
Ambergris Caye i. Belize 136 G5
Ambérieu-en-Bugey France 56 G4
Amberley Canada 134 E1
Ambgaon India 84 D1
Ambianum France see Amiens
Ambikapur India 83 E5
Ambilobe Madag. 99 E5
Ambition, Mount Canada 120 D3
Amble U.K. 48 F3
Ambler U.S.A. 118 C3
Ambleside U.K. 48 E4
Amblève r. Belgium 52 F4
Ambo India 83 F5
Amboasary Madag. 99 E6
Ambodifotatra Madag. 99 E5
Ambohimahasoa Madag. 99 E6
Ambohitra mt. Madag. 99 E5
Amboina Indon. see Ambon
Ambon Indon. 69 H7
Ambon i. Indon. 69 H7
Amboró, Parque Nacional nat. park Bol. 142 F7
Ambositra Madag. 99 E6
Ambovombe Madag. 99 E6
Amboy U.S.A. 129 F4
Ambre, Cap d' c. Madag. see Bobaomby, Tanjona
Ambrim i. Vanuatu see Ambrym
Ambriz Angola 99 B4
Ambrizete Angola see N'zeto
Ambrosia Lake U.S.A. 129 J4
Ambrym i. Vanuatu 107 G3
Ambunti P.N.G. 69 K7
Ambur India 84 C3
Am-Dam Chad 97 F3
Amded, Oued watercourse Alg. 96 D2
Am-Djarass Chad 97 F3
Amdo China see Lharigarbo
Ameland i. Neth. 52 F1
Amelia Court House U.S.A. 135 G5
Amenia U.S.A. 135 I3
Amer, Erg d' des. Alg. 98 A1
Amereli India see Amreli
American, North Fork r. U.S.A. 128 C2
Americana Brazil 145 B3
American-Antarctic Ridge sea feature S. Atlantic Ocean 148 G9
American Falls U.S.A. 126 E4
American Falls Reservoir U.S.A. 126 E4
American Fork U.S.A. 129 H1

►American Samoa terr. S. Pacific Ocean 107 J3
United States Unincorporated Territory.

Americus U.S.A. 133 C5
Amersfoort Neth. 52 F2
Amersfoort S. Africa 101 I4
Amersham U.K. 49 G7
Amery Canada 121 M3
Amery Ice Shelf Antarctica 152 E2
Ames U.S.A. 130 E3
Amesbury U.K. 49 F7
Amesbury U.S.A. 135 J2
Amet India 82 C4
Amethi India 83 E4
Amfissa Greece 59 J5
Amga Russia 65 O3
Amgalang China 73 L3
Amgu Russia 74 E3
Amguid Alg. 96 D2
Amgun' r. Russia 74 E1
Amherst Canada 123 I5
Amherst Myanmar see Kyaikkami
Amherst MA U.S.A. 135 I2
Amherst OH U.S.A. 134 D3
Amherst VA U.S.A. 134 F5
Amherstburg Canada 134 D2
Amherst Island Canada 135 G1
Amiata, Monte mt. Italy 58 D3
Amida Turkey see Diyarbakır
Amidon U.S.A. 130 C2
Amiens France 52 C5
'Amīj, Wādī watercourse Iraq 91 F4
Amik Ovası marsh Turkey 85 C1
Amīnābād Iran 88 D4
Amindivi atoll India see Amini
Amindivi Islands India 84 B4
Amini atoll India 84 B4
Amino Eth. 98 E3
Aminuis Namibia 100 D2
Amīr, Band-e l. Afgh. 89 G3
Amīrābād Īlām Iran 88 B3
Amīrābād Yazd Iran 88 E3
Amirante Islands Seychelles 149 L6
Amirante Trench sea feature Indian Ocean 149 L6
Amisk Lake Canada 121 K4
Amistad, Represa de resr Mex./U.S.A. see Amistad Reservoir
Amistad Reservoir Mex./U.S.A. 131 C6
Amisus Turkey see Samsun
Amite U.S.A. 131 F6
Amity Point Australia 112 F1
Amla India 82 D5
Amlapura Indon. see Karangasem
Amlash Iran 88 C2
Amlekhganj Nepal 83 F4
Åmli Norway 45 F7
Amlia Island U.S.A. 118 A4
Amlwch U.K. 48 C5

►'Ammān Jordan 85 B4
Capital of Jordan.

Ammanazar Turkm. 88 D2
Ammanford U.K. 49 D7
Ämmänsaari Fin. 44 P4
'Ammār, Tall hill Syria 85 C3
Ammarnäs Sweden 44 J4
Ammaroo Australia 110 A4
Ammassalik Greenland see Tasiilaq
Ammerland reg. Germany 53 H1
Ammern Germany 53 K3
Ammochostos Cyprus see Famagusta
Ammochostos Bay Cyprus 85 B2
Amne Machin Range mts China see A'nyêmaqên Shan
Amnok-kang r. China/N. Korea see Yalu Jiang
Āmol Iran 88 D2
Amorbach Germany 53 J5
Amorgos i. Greece 59 K6
Amory U.S.A. 131 F5
Amos Canada 122 F4
Amourj Mauritania 96 C3
Amoy China see Xiamen
Ampani India 84 D2
Ampanihy Madag. 99 E6
Ampara Sri Lanka 84 D5
Amparo Brazil 145 B3
Ampasimanolotra Madag. 99 E5
Amphitheatre Australia 112 A6
Amphitrite Group is Paracel Is 68 E3
Ampoa Indon. 69 G7
'Amrah, Qaṣr tourist site Jordan 85 C4
Amraoti India see Amravati
Amravati India 84 C1
Amrawad India 82 D5
Amreli India 82 B5
Amri Pak. 89 H5
Amring India 83 H4
'Amrīt Syria 85 B2
Amritsar India 82 C3
Amroha India 82 D3
Amsden U.S.A. 134 D3
Åmsele Sweden 44 K4
Amstelveen Neth. 52 E2

►Amsterdam Neth. 52 E2
Official capital of the Netherlands.

Amsterdam S. Africa 101 J4
Amsterdam U.S.A. 135 H2
Amsterdam, Île i. Indian Ocean 149 N8
Amstetten Austria 47 O6
Am Timan Chad 97 F3
Amudar'ya r. Asia 89 F2
Amudaryo r. Asia see Amudar'ya
Amund Ringnes Island Canada 119 I2
Amundsen, Mount Antarctica 152 F2
Amundsen Abyssal Plain sea feature Southern Ocean 152 J2
Amundsen Basin sea feature Arctic Ocean 153 H1
Amundsen Bay Antarctica 152 D2
Amundsen Coast Antarctica 152 J1
Amundsen Glacier Antarctica 152 I1
Amundsen Gulf Canada 118 F2
Amundsen Ridges sea feature Southern Ocean 152 J2
Amundsen-Scott research station Antarctica 152 C1
Amundsen Sea Antarctica 152 K2
Amuntai Indon. 68 F7
Amur r. China/Russia 74 D2
also known as Heilong Jiang (China)
'Amur, Wadi watercourse Sudan 86 D6
Amuro-Baltiysk Russia 74 B1
Amur Oblast admin. div. Russia see Amurskaya Oblast'
Amursk Russia 74 E2
Amurskaya Oblast' admin. div. Russia 74 C1
Amurskiy Liman strait Russia 74 F1
Amurzet Russia 74 C3
Amvrosiyivka Ukr. 43 H7
Amyderya r. Asia see Amudar'ya
Am-Zoer Chad 97 F3
An Myanmar 70 A3
Anaa atoll Fr. Polynesia 151 K7
Anabanua Indon. 69 G7
Anabar r. Russia 65 M2
Anacapa Island U.S.A. 128 D4
Anaconda U.S.A. 126 E3
Anacortes U.S.A. 126 C2
Anadarko U.S.A. 131 D5
Anadolu reg. Turkey 90 D3
Anadolu Dağları mts Turkey 90 E2
Anadyr' Russia 65 S3
Anadyr, Gulf of Russia see Anadyrskiy Zaliv
Anadyrskiy Zaliv b. Russia 65 T3
Anafi i. Greece 59 K6
Anagé Brazil 145 C1
'Ānah Iraq 91 F4
Anaheim U.S.A. 128 E5
Anahim Lake Canada 120 E4
Anáhuac Mex. 131 C7
Anahuac U.S.A. 131 E6
Anaimalai Hills India 84 C4
Anai Mudi mt. India 84 C4
Anaiteum i. Vanuatu see Anatom
Anajás Brazil 143 I4
Anakie Australia 110 D4
Analalava Madag. 99 E5
Anamã Brazil 142 F4
Anambas, Kepulauan is Indon. 71 D7
Anamosa U.S.A. 130 F3
Anamur Turkey 85 A1
Anan Japan 75 D6
Anand India 82 C5
Anandapur India 83 F5
Anantapur India 84 C3
Ananthapur India see Anantapur
Anantnag India 82 C2
Anant Peth India 82 D4
Anantpur India see Anantapur
Ananyev Ukr. see Anan'yiv
Anan'yiv Ukr. 43 F7
Anapa Russia 90 E1
Anápolis Brazil 145 A2
Anār Fin. see Inari
Anār Iran 88 D4
Anār Darah Afgh. 89 F3
Anatahan i. N. Mariana Is 69 L3
Anatajan i. N. Mariana Is see Anatahan
Anatom i. Vanuatu 107 G4
Añatuya Arg. 144 D3
Anaypazari Turkey see Gülnar
An Baile Breac Ireland 51 B6
An Bun Beag Ireland 51 D2
Anbūr-e Kālārī Iran 88 D5
Anbyon N. Korea 75 B5
Ancenis France 56 D3
Anchorage U.S.A. 118 D3
Anchorage Island atoll Cook Is see Suwarrow
Anchor Bay U.S.A. 134 D2
Anchuthengu India 84 C4
Anci China see Langfang
Ancient City of Tauric Chersonese tourist site Ukr. 43 G7
Ancient Villages of Northern Syria tourist site Syria 85 C1
An Clochán Liath Ireland 51 D3
An Cóbh Ireland see Cobh
Ancona Italy 58 E3
Ancón de Sardinas, Bahía de b. Col. 142 C3
Ancud, Golfo de g. Chile 144 B6
Ancyra Turkey see Ankara
Anda Heilong. China 74 B3
Anda Heilong. China see Daqing
Andacollo Chile 144 B4
Andado Australia 110 A5
Andahuaylas Peru 142 D6
Andal India 83 F5
Åndalsnes Norway 44 E5
Andalucía aut. comm. Spain 57 D5
Andalusia aut. comm. Spain see Andalucía
Andalusia U.S.A. 133 C6
Andaman Basin sea feature Indian Ocean 149 O5
Andaman Islands India 71 A4
Andaman Sea Indian Ocean 71 A5
Andaman Strait India 71 A4
Andamooka Australia 111 B6
Andapa Madag. 99 E5
Andarāb, Darah-ye reg. Afgh. 89 H3
Ande China 76 E4
Andegavum France see Angers
Andelle r. France 52 B5
Andenes Norway 44 J2
Andenne Belgium 52 F4
Andéramboukane Mali 96 D3
Anderlecht Belgium 52 E4
Andermatt Switz. 56 I3
Andernos-les-Bains France 56 D4
Anderson r. Canada 118 F3
Anderson AK U.S.A. 118 D3
Anderson IN U.S.A. 134 C3
Anderson SC U.S.A. 133 D5
Anderson TX U.S.A. 131 E6
Anderson Bay Australia 111 [inset]
Anderson Lake Canada 120 F5
Andes mts S. America 144 C4
Andfjorden sea chan. Norway 44 J2
Andhíparos i. Greece see Antiparos
Andhra Lake India 84 B2
Andhra Pradesh state India 84 C2
Andijon Uzbek. 80 D3
Andikíthira i. Greece see Antikythira
Andilamena Madag. 99 E5
Andilanatoby Madag. 99 E5
Andīmeshk Iran 88 C3
Andímilos i. Greece see Antimilos
Andípsara i. Greece see Antipsara
Andırın Turkey 90 E3
Andirlangar China 83 E1
Andizhan Uzbek. see Andijon
Andkhōy Afgh. 89 G2
Andoany Madag. 99 E5
Andoas Peru 142 C4
Andogskaya Gryada hills Russia 42 H4
Andol India 84 C2
Andong China see Dandong
Andong S. Korea 75 C5
Andongwei China 77 H1
Andoom Australia 110 C2
Andorra country Europe 57 G2

►Andorra la Vella Andorra 57 G2
Capital of Andorra.

Andorra la Vieja Andorra see Andorra la Vella
Andover U.K. 49 F7
Andover NY U.S.A. 135 G2
Andover OH U.S.A. 134 E3
Andøya i. Norway 44 I2
Andrade U.S.A. 129 F5
Andradina Brazil 145 A3
Andranomavo Madag. 99 E5
Andranopasy Madag. 99 E6
Andreanof Islands U.S.A. 150 I2
Andreapol' Russia 42 G4
Andreas Isle of Man 48 C4
André Félix, Parc National nat. park Cent. Afr. Rep. 98 C3
Andrelândia Brazil 145 B3
Andrew Canada 121 H4
Andrew Bay Myanmar 70 A3
Andrews SC U.S.A. 133 E5
Andrews TX U.S.A. 131 C5
Andria Italy 58 G4
Androka Madag. 99 E6
Andropov Russia see Rybinsk
Andros i. Bahamas 133 E7
Andros i. Greece 59 K6
Androscoggin r. U.S.A. 135 K2
Andros Town Bahamas 133 E7
Andrott i. India 84 B4
Andselv Norway 44 K2
Andújar Spain 57 D4
Andulo Angola 99 B5
Anec, Lake salt flat Australia 109 E5
Äneen-Kio terr. N. Pacific Ocean see Wake Island
Anéfis Mali 96 D3
Anegada, Bahía b. Arg. 144 D6
Anegada Passage Virgin Is (U.K.) 137 L5
Aného Togo 96 D4
Aneityum i. Vanuatu see Anatom
'Aneiza, Jabal hill Iraq see 'Unayzah, Jabal
Anemourion tourist site Turkey 85 A1
Anepmete P.N.G. 69 L8
Anet France 52 B6
Anetchom, Île i. Vanuatu see Anatom
Aneto mt. Spain 57 G2
Änewetak atoll Marshall Is see Enewetak
Aney Niger 96 E3
Aneytioum, Île i. Vanuatu see Anatom
Anfu China 77 G3
Angalarri r. Australia 108 E3
Angamos, Punta pt Chile 144 B2
Ang'angxi China 74 A3

►Angara r. Russia 72 G1
Part of the Yenisey-Angara-Selenga, 3rd longest river in Asia.

Angarsk Russia 72 I2
Angas Downs Australia 109 F6
Angatuba Brazil 145 A3
Angaur i. Palau 69 I5
Ånge Sweden 44 I5
Angel, Salto waterfall Venez. see Angel Falls
Ángel de la Guarda, Isla i. Mex. 127 E7

►Angel Falls waterfall Venez. 142 F2
Highest waterfall in the world.

Ängelholm Sweden 45 H8
Angellala Creek r. Australia 112 C1
Angels Camp U.S.A. 128 C2
Ångermanälven r. Sweden 44 J5
Angers France 56 D3
Angikuni Lake Canada 121 L2
Angiola U.S.A. 128 D4
Angkor tourist site Cambodia 71 C4
Angledool Australia 112 C2
Anglesea Australia 112 B7
Anglesey i. U.K. 48 C5
Angleton U.S.A. 131 E6
Anglo-Egyptian Sudan country Africa see Sudan
Angmagssalik Greenland see Tasiilaq
Ang Mo Kio Sing. 71 [inset]
Ango Dem. Rep. Congo 98 C3
Angoche Moz. 99 D5
Angol Chile 144 B5
Angola country Africa 99 B5
Angola IN U.S.A. 134 C3
Angola NY U.S.A. 134 F2
Angola Basin sea feature S. Atlantic Ocean 148 H7
Angora Turkey see Ankara
Angostura Mex. 127 F8
Angoulême France 56 E4
Angra dos Reis Brazil 145 B3
Angren Uzbek. 80 D3
Ang Thong Thai. 71 C4
Anguang China 74 A3

►Anguilla terr. West Indies 137 L5
United Kingdom Overseas Territory.

Anguilla Cays is Bahamas 133 E8
Anguille, Cape Canada 123 K5
Angul India 84 E1
Angus Canada 134 F1
Angutia Char i. Bangl. 83 G5
Anholt i. Denmark 45 G8
Anhua China 77 F2
Anhui prov. China 77 H1
Anhumas Brazil 143 H7
Anhwei prov. China see Anhui
Aniak U.S.A. 118 C3
Aniakchak National Monument and Preserve nat. park U.S.A. 118 C4
Anin Myanmar 70 B4
Anitápolis Brazil 145 A4
Anıtlı Turkey 85 A1
Aniva Russia 74 F3
Aniva, Mys c. Russia 74 F3
Aniva, Zaliv b. Russia 74 F3
Anizy-le-Château France 52 D5
Anjadip i. India 84 B3
Anjengo India see Anchuthengu
Anji China 77 H2
Anjīr Āvand Iran 88 D3
Anjoman Iran 88 E3
Anjou reg. France 56 D3
Anjouan i. Comoros see Ndzuani
Anjozorobe Madag. 99 E5
Anjuman reg. Afgh. 89 H3
Anjuthengu India see Anchuthengu
Ankang China 77 F1

►Ankara Turkey 90 D3
Capital of Turkey.

Ankaratra mt. Madag. 99 E5
Ankazoabo Madag. 99 E6
Ankeny U.S.A. 130 E3
An Khê Vietnam 71 E4
Ankleshwar India 82 C5
Anklesvar India see Ankleshwar
Ankola India 84 B3
Ankou China 76 E1
An Lôc Vietnam 71 D5
Anlong China 76 E3
Anlu China 77 G2
Anmoore U.S.A. 134 E4
An Muileann gCearr Ireland see Mullingar
Anmyeon-do i. S. Korea 75 B5
Ann, Cape Antarctica 152 D2
Ann, Cape U.S.A. 135 J2
Anna Russia 43 I6
Anna, Lake U.S.A. 135 G4
Anna, Pulo i. Palau 69 I6
Annaba Alg. 58 B6
Annaberg-Buchholz Germany 53 N4
An Nābiyah Yemen 86 F7
An Nabk Saudi Arabia 85 C4
An Nabk Syria 85 C2
An Nafūd des. Saudi Arabia 91 F5
An Najaf Iraq 91 G5
Annalee r. Ireland 51 E3
Annalong U.K. 51 G3
Annam reg. Vietnam 68 D3
Annam Highlands mts Laos/Vietnam 70 D3
Annan U.K. 50 F6
Annan r. U.K. 50 F6
'Annān, Wādī al watercourse Syria 85 D2
Annandale U.S.A. 135 G4
Anna Plains Australia 108 C4

►Annapolis U.S.A. 135 G4
Capital of Maryland.

Annapurna Conservation Area nature res. Nepal 83 F3

►Annapurna I mt. Nepal 83 E3
10th highest mountain in Asia and the world.

Ann Arbor U.S.A. 134 D2
Anna Regina Guyana 143 G2
An Nás Ireland see Naas
An Nāṣirīyah Iraq 91 G5
Annean, Lake salt flat Australia 109 B6
Anne Arundel Town U.S.A. see Annapolis
Annecy France 56 H4

Anne Marie Lake Canada 123 J3
Annen Neth. 52 G1
Annette Island U.S.A. 120 D4
An Nimārah Syria 85 C3
An Nimāş Saudi Arabia 86 F6
Anning China 76 D3
Anniston U.S.A. 133 C5
Annobón i. Equat. Guinea 96 D5
Annonay France 56 G4
An Nu'mānīyah Iraq 91 G4
Anonima atoll Micronesia see Namonuito
Anorontany, Tanjona hd Madag. 99 E5
Ano Viannos Greece see Viannos
Anpu Gang b. China 77 F4
Anqing China 77 H2
Anren China 77 G3
Ans Belgium 52 F4
Ansbach Germany 53 K5
Anser Group is Australia 112 C7
Anshan China 74 A4
Anshun Guizhou China 76 E3
Anshun Sichuan China 76 D2
Ansley U.S.A. 130 D3
Anson U.S.A. 131 D5
Anson Bay Australia 108 E3
Ansongo Mali 96 D3
Ansonville Canada 122 E4
Ansted U.S.A. 134 E4
Ansudu Indon. 69 J7
Antabamba Peru 142 D6
Antakya Turkey 85 C1
Antalaha Madag. 99 F5
Antalya Turkey 59 N6
Antalya prov. Turkey 85 A1
Antalya Körfezi g. Turkey 59 N6

▶Antananarivo Madag. 99 E5
Capital of Madagascar.

An tAonach Ireland see Nenagh

▶Antarctica 152
Most southerly and coldest continent, and the continent with the highest average elevation.

Antarctic Peninsula Antarctica 152 L2
Antas r. Brazil 145 A5
An Teallach mt. U.K. 50 D3
Antelope Island U.S.A. 129 G1
Antelope Range mts U.S.A. 128 E2
Antequera Spain 57 D5
Anthony Lagoon Australia 110 A3
Anti-Atlas mts Morocco 54 C6
Antibes France 56 H5
Anticosti, Île d' i. Canada 123 J4
Anticosti Island Canada see Anticosti, Île d'
Antifer, Cap d' c. France 49 H9
Antigo U.S.A. 130 F2
Antigonish Canada 123 J5
Antigua i. Antigua and Barbuda 137 L5
Antigua country West Indies see Antigua and Barbuda
Antigua and Barbuda country West Indies 137 L5
Antikythira i. Greece 59 J7
Antikythiro, Steno sea chan. Greece 59 J7
Anti Lebanon mts Lebanon/Syria see Sharqī, Jabal ash
Antimilos i. Greece 59 K6
Antimony U.S.A. 129 H2
An tInbhear Mór Ireland see Arklow
Antioch Turkey see Antakya
Antioch U.S.A. 128 C2
Antiocheia ad Cragum tourist site Turkey 85 A1
Antiochia Turkey see Antakya
Antiparos i. Greece 59 K6
Antipodes Islands N.Z. 107 H6
Antipsara i. Greece 59 K5
Antium Italy see Anzio
Antlers U.S.A. 131 E5
Antofagasta Chile 144 B2
Antofagasta de la Sierra Arg. 144 C3
Antofalla, Volcán vol. Arg. 144 C3
Antoing Belgium 52 D4
Antonine Wall tourist site U.K. 50 E5
António Enes Moz. see Angoche
Antri India 82 D4
Antrim U.K. 51 F3
Antrim Hills U.K. 51 F2
Antrim Plateau Australia 108 E4
Antropovo Russia 42 I4
Antsalova Madag. 99 E5
Antseranana Madag. see Antsirañana
Antsirabe Madag. 99 E5
Antsirañana Madag. 99 E5
Antsla Estonia 45 O8
Antsohihy Madag. 99 E5
Anttis Sweden 44 M3
Anttola Fin. 45 O6
An Tuc Vietnam see An Khê
Antwerp Belgium 52 E3
Antwerp U.S.A. 135 H1
Antwerpen Belgium see Antwerp
An Uaimh Ireland see Navan
Anuc, Lac l. Canada 122 G2
Anuchino Russia 74 D4
Anugul India see Angul
Anupgarh India 82 C3
Anuradhapura Sri Lanka 84 D4
Anveh Iran 88 D5
Anvers Island Antarctica 152 L2
Anvik U.S.A. 118 B3
Anvil Range mts Canada 120 C2
Anxi China 77 H3
Anxiang China 77 G2
Anxious Bay Australia 109 F8
Anyang Guangxi China see Du'an
Anyang Henan China 73 K5
Anyang S. Korea 75 B5
A'nyêmaqên Shan mts China 76 C1
Anyuan Jiangxi China 77 G3
Anyuan Jiangxi China 77 G3
Anyue China 76 E2
Anyuy r. Russia 74 E2
Anyuysk Russia 65 R3
Anzac Alta Canada 121 I3
Anzac B.C. Canada 120 F4
Anzhero-Sudzhensk Russia 64 J4
Anzi Dem. Rep. Congo 98 C4
Anzio Italy 58 E4
Aoba i. Vanuatu 107 G3
Aoga-shima i. Japan 75 E6
Ao Kham, Laem pt Thai. 71 B5
Aomen China see Macao
Aomen aut. reg. China see Macao
Aomen Tebie Xingzhengqu aut. reg. China see Macao
Aomori Japan 74 F4
Ao Phang Nga National Park Thai. 71 B5

▶Aoraki/Mount Cook mt. N.Z. 113 C6
Highest mountain in New Zealand.

Aoraki/Mount Cook National Park N.Z. 113 C6
Aôral, Phnum mt. Cambodia 71 D4
Aorangi mt. N.Z. see Aoraki/Mount Cook
Aosta Italy 58 B2
Aotearoa country Oceania see New Zealand
Aouk, Bahr r. Cent. Afr. Rep./Chad 97 E4
Aoukâr reg. Mali/Mauritania 96 C2
Aoulef Alg. 96 D2
Aoussard W. Sahara 96 B2
Aozou Chad 97 E2
Apa r. Brazil 144 E2
Apache Creek U.S.A. 129 I5
Apache Junction U.S.A. 129 H5
Apaiang atoll Kiribati see Abaiang
Apalachee Bay U.S.A. 133 C6
Apalachicola U.S.A. 133 C6
Apalachicola r. U.S.A. 133 C6
Apalachin U.S.A. 135 G2
Apamea Turkey see Dinar
Apaporis r. Col. 142 E4
Aparecida do Tabuado Brazil 145 A3
Aparima N.Z. see Riverton
Aparri Phil. 150 E4
Apatity Russia 44 R3
Apatzingán Mex. 136 D5
Ape Latvia 45 O8
Apeldoorn Neth. 52 F2
Apelern Germany 53 J2
Apennines mts Italy 58 C2
Apensen Germany 53 J1
Apex Mountain Canada 120 B2
Api mt. Nepal 82 E3
Api i. Vanuatu see Épi
Apia atoll Kiribati see Abaiang

▶Apia Samoa 107 I3
Capital of Samoa.

Apiacas, Serra dos hills Brazil 143 G6
Apiaí Brazil 145 A4
Apishapa r. U.S.A. 130 C4
Apiti N.Z. 113 E4
Apizolaya Mex. 131 C7
Apkhazeti disp. terr. Georgia see Abkhazia
Aplao Peru 142 D7
Apo, Mount vol. Phil. 69 H5
Apoera Suriname 143 G2
Apolda Germany 53 L3
Apollo Bay Australia 112 A7
Apollonia Bulg. see Sozopol
Apolo Bol. 142 E6
Aporé Brazil 145 A2
Aporé r. Brazil 145 A2
Apostelens Tommelfinger mt. Greenland 119 N3
Apostle Islands U.S.A. 130 F2
Apostolos Andreas, Cape Cyprus 85 B2
Apoteri Guyana 143 G3
Apozai Pak. 89 H4
Appalachian Mountains U.S.A. 134 D5
Appalla i. Fiji see Kabara
Appennino mts Italy see Apennines
Appennino Abruzzese mts Italy 58 E3
Appennino Tosco-Emiliano mts Italy 58 D3
Appennino Umbro-Marchigiano mts Italy 58 E3
Appingedam Neth. 52 G1
Applecross U.K. 50 D3
Appleton MN U.S.A. 130 D2
Appleton WI U.S.A. 134 A1
Apple Valley U.S.A. 128 E4
Appomattox U.S.A. 135 F5
Aprilia Italy 58 E4
Aprunyi India 76 B2
Apsheronsk Russia 91 E1
Apsheronskaya Russia see Apsheronsk
Apsley Canada 135 F1
Apt France 56 G5
Apucarana Brazil 145 A3
Apucarana, Serra da hills Brazil 145 A3
Apuka Russia 65 R3
Apulum Romania see Alba Iulia
Aq"a Georgia see Sokhumi
'Aqaba Jordan see Al 'Aqabah
'Aqaba, Gulf of Asia 90 D5
'Aqaba, Wâdi el watercourse Egypt see 'Aqabah, Wādī al
'Aqabah, Birkat al well Iraq 88 A4
'Aqabah, Wādī al watercourse Egypt 85 A4
Aqadyr Kazakh. see Akadyr
Aqdoghmish r. Iran 88 B2
Aqköl Akmolinskaya Oblast' Kazakh. see Akkol'
Aqköl Atyrauskaya Oblast' Kazakh. see Akkol'
Aqmola Kazakh. see Astana
Aqqan China 83 F1
Aqqikkol Hu salt l. China 83 G1
Aqra', Jabal al mt. Syria/Turkey 85 B2
'Aqran hill Saudi Arabia 85 D4
Aqsay Kazakh. see Aksay
Aqsayqin terr. China see Aksai Chin
Aqshī Kazakh. see Akshi
Aqshuqyr Kazakh. see Akshukyr
Aqsū Kazakh. see Aksu
Aqsūat Kazakh. see Aksuat
Aqsū-Ayuly Kazakh. see Aksu-Ayuly
Aqtaū Kazakh. see Aktau
Aqtöbe Kazakh. see Aktobe
Aqtoghay Kazakh. see Aktogay
Aquae Grani Germany see Aachen
Aquae Gratianae France see Aix-les-Bains
Aquae Sextiae France see Aix-en-Provence
Aquae Statiellae Italy see Acqui Terme
Aquarius Mountains U.S.A. 129 G4
Aquarius Plateau U.S.A. 129 H3
Aquidauana Brazil 144 E2
Aquiles Mex. 127 G7
Aquincum Hungary see Budapest
Aquiry r. Brazil see Acre
Aquisgranum Germany see Aachen
Aquitaine reg. France 56 D5
Aquitania reg. France see Aquitaine
Aqzhayqyn Köli salt l. Kazakh. see Akzhaykyn, Ozero
Ara India see Arrah
Āra Ārba Eth. 98 E3
'Arab Afgh. 89 G4
Arab, Bahr el watercourse Sudan 97 F4
'Arab, Khalîg el b. Egypt see 'Arab, Khalīj al
'Arab, Khalīj al b. Egypt 90 C5
'Arabah, Wādī al watercourse Israel/Jordan 85 B5
Arabian Basin sea feature Indian Ocean 149 M5
Arabian Gulf Asia see The Gulf
Arabian Peninsula Asia 86 G5
Arabian Sea Indian Ocean 87 K6
Araç Turkey 90 D2
Araça r. Brazil 142 F4
Aracaju Brazil 143 K6
Aracati Brazil 143 K4
Aracatu Brazil 145 C1
Araçatuba Brazil 145 A3
Aracena Spain 57 C5
Aracruz Brazil 145 C2
Araçuaí Brazil 145 C2
Araçuaí r. Brazil 145 C2
'Arad Israel 85 B4
Arad Romania 59 I1
'Arādah U.A.E. 88 D6
Arafura Sea Australia/Indon. 106 D2
Arafura Shelf sea feature Australia/Indon. 150 E6
Aragarças Brazil 143 H7
Aragón r. Spain 57 F2
Araguaçu Brazil 145 A1
Araguaia r. Brazil 145 A1
Araguaia, Parque Nacional do nat. park Brazil 143 H6
Araguaiana Brazil 145 A1
Araguaína Brazil 143 I5
Araguari Brazil 145 A2
Araguari r. Brazil 143 H3
Araguatins Brazil 143 I5
Araí Brazil 145 B1
'Arâif el Naga, Gebel hill Egypt see 'Urayf an Nāqah, Jabal
Araioses Brazil 143 J4
Arak Alg. 96 D2
Ārāk Iran 88 C3
Arak Syria 85 D2
Arakan reg. Myanmar 70 A2
Arakan Yoma mts Myanmar 70 A2
Arakkonam India 84 C3
Araks r. Azer. see Araz
Araku India 84 D2
Aral China 80 F3
Aral Kazakh. see Aral'sk
Aral Tajik. see Vose'
Aralkum des. Kazakh./Uzbek. 80 A3

▶Aral Sea salt l. Kazakh./Uzbek. 80 A3
4th largest lake in Asia.

Aral'sk Kazakh. 80 B2
Aral'skoye More salt l. Kazakh./Uzbek. see Aral Sea
Aralsor, Ozero l. Kazakh. 43 K6
Aral Tengizi salt l. Kazakh./Uzbek. see Aral Sea
Aramac Australia 110 D4
Aramac Creek watercourse Australia 110 D4
Aramah plat. Saudi Arabia 88 B5
Aramberri Mex. 131 D7
Aramia r. P.N.G. 69 K8
Aran r. India 84 C2
Aranda de Duero Spain 57 E3
Arandai Indon. 69 I7
Aranđelovac Serbia 59 I2
Arandis Namibia 100 B2
Arang India 83 E5
Arani India 84 C3
Aran Islands Ireland 51 C4
Aranjuez Spain 57 E3
Aranos Namibia 100 D3
Aransas Pass U.S.A. 131 D7
Arantangi India 84 C4
Aranuka atoll Kiribati 107 H1
Aranyaprathet Thai. 71 C4
Arao Japan 75 C6
Araouane Mali 96 C3
Arapaho U.S.A. 131 D5
Arapgir Turkey 90 E3
Arapiraca Brazil 143 K5
Arapis, Akra pt Greece see Arapis, Akrotirio
Arapis, Akrotirio pt Greece 59 K4
Arapkir Turkey see Arapgir
Arapongas Brazil 145 A3
Araquari Brazil 145 A4
'Ar'ar Saudi Arabia 91 F5
Araranguá Brazil 145 A5
Araraquara Brazil 145 A3
Araras Brazil 143 H5
Ararat Armenia 91 G3
Ararat Australia 112 A6
Ararat, Mount 91 G3
Araria India 83 F4
Araripina Brazil 143 J5
Aras r. Azer. see Araz
Aras Turkey 91 F3
Arataca Brazil 145 D1
Arauca Col. 142 D2
Arauca r. Venez. 142 E2
Aravalli Range mts India 82 C4
Aravete Estonia 45 N7
Arawa P.N.G. 106 F2
Araxá Brazil 145 B2
Araxes r. Azer. see Araz
Arayıt Dağı mt. Turkey 59 N5
Araz r. Azer. 91 H2
also spelt Araks (Armenia), Aras (Turkey), formerly known as Araxes
Arbailu Iraq see Arbīl/Hewlêr
Arbela Iraq see Arbīl/Hewlêr
Arberth U.K. see Narberth
Arbīl/Hewlêr Iraq 91 G3
Arboga Sweden 45 I7
Arborfield Canada 121 K4
Arborg Canada 121 L5
Arbroath U.K. 50 G4
Arbuckle U.S.A. 128 B2
Arbū-ye Shamālī, Dasht-e des. Afgh. 89 F4
Arcachon France 56 D4
Arcade U.S.A. 135 F2
Arcadia FL U.S.A. 133 D7
Arcadia LA U.S.A. 131 E5
Arcadia MI U.S.A. 134 B1
Arcanum U.S.A. 134 C4
Arcata U.S.A. 126 B4
Arc Dome mt. U.S.A. 128 E2
Arcelia Mex. 136 D5
Archaeological Sites of the Island of Meroe tourist site Sudan 97 G3
Archangel Russia 42 I2
Archer r. Australia 67 G9
Archer Bend National Park Australia 110 C2
Archer City U.S.A. 131 D5
Arches National Park U.S.A. 129 I2
Archipel-de-Mingan, Réserve du Parc National de l' nat. park Canada 123 J4
Archipiélago Los Roques, Parque Nacional nat. park Venez. 142 E1
Ärçivan Azer. 91 H3
Arckaringa watercourse Australia 111 A6
Arco U.S.A. 126 E4
Arcos Brazil 145 B3
Arcos de la Frontera Spain 57 D5
Arctic Bay Canada 119 J2
Arctic Institute Islands Russia see Arkticheskogo Instituta, Ostrova
Arctic Mid-Ocean Ridge sea feature Arctic Ocean 153 H1
Arctic Ocean 153 B1
Arctic Red r. Canada 118 E3
Arctowski research station Antarctica 152 A2
Arda r. Bulg. 59 L4
also known as Ardas (Greece)
Ardabīl Iran 88 C2
Ardahan Turkey 91 F2
Ardakān Iran 88 D3
Årdalstangen Norway 45 E6
Ardara Ireland 51 D3
Ardas r. Bulg. see Arda
Ard aş Şawwān plain Jordan 85 C4
Ardatov Nizhegorodskaya Oblast' Russia 43 I5
Ardatov Respublika Mordoviya Russia 43 J5
Ardee Ireland 51 F4
Ardennes plat. Belgium 52 F5
Ardennes, Canal des France 52 E5
Arden Town U.S.A. 128 C2
Arderin hill Ireland 51 E4
Ardestān Iran 88 D3
Ardglass U.K. 51 G3
Ardila r. Port. 57 C4
Ardlethan Australia 112 C5
Ardmore U.S.A. 131 D5
Ardnamurchan, Point of U.K. 50 C4
Ardon Russia 91 G2
Ardrishaig U.K. 50 D4
Ardrossan U.K. 50 E5
Ardvasar U.K. 50 D3
Areia Branca Brazil 143 K4
Arel Belgium see Arlon
Arelas France see Arles
Arelate France see Arles
Aremberg hill Germany 52 G4
Arena, Point U.S.A. 128 B2
Arenas de San Pedro Spain 57 D3
Arendal Norway 45 F7
Arendsee (Altmark) Germany 53 L2
Areopoli Greece 59 J6
Arequipa Peru 142 D7
Arere Brazil 143 H4
Arévalo Spain 57 D3
Arezzo Italy 58 D3
'Arfajah well Saudi Arabia 85 D4
Argadargada Australia 110 B4
Arganda del Rey Spain 57 E3
Argel Alg. see Algiers
Argentan France 56 D2
Argentario, Monte hill Italy 58 D3
Argentera, Cima dell' mt. Italy 58 B2
Argenthal Germany 53 H5

▶Argentina country S. America 144 C5
2nd largest and 3rd most populous country in South America and 8th largest in the world.

Argentine Abyssal Plain sea feature S. Atlantic Ocean 148 E9
Argentine Basin sea feature S. Atlantic Ocean 148 F8
Argentine Republic country S. America see Argentina
Argentine Rise sea feature S. Atlantic Ocean 148 E8
Argentino, Lago l. Arg. 144 B8
Argenton-sur-Creuse France 56 E3
Argentoratum France see Strasbourg
Argeş r. Romania 59 L2
Arg-e Zārī Afgh. 89 G3
Arghandāb Rōd r. Afgh. 89 G4
Argi r. Russia 74 C1
Argolikos Kolpos b. Greece 59 J6
Argos Greece 59 J6
Argos U.S.A. 134 B3
Argostoli Greece 59 I5
Arguis Spain 57 F2
Argun' r. China/Russia 73 M2
Argun Russia 91 G2
Argungu Nigeria 96 D3
Argus, Dome ice feature Antarctica 152 E1
Argus Range mts U.S.A. 128 E4
Argyle Canada 123 I6
Argyle, Lake Australia 108 E4
Argyrokastron Albania see Gjirokastër
Ar Horqin Qi China see Tianshan
Århus Denmark see Aarhus
Ariah Park Australia 112 C5
Ariamsvlei Namibia 100 D5
Ariana Tunisia see L'Ariana
Ariano Irpino Italy 58 F4
Ari Atholhu Maldives 81 D11
Aribinda Burkina Faso 96 C3
Arica Chile 142 D7
Arid, Cape Australia 109 C8
Arigza China 76 C1
Arīḥā Syria 85 C2
Arīḥā West Bank see Jericho
Arikaree r. U.S.A. 130 C3
Arima Trin. and Tob. 137 L6
Ariminum Italy see Rimini
Arinos Brazil 145 B1
Aripuanã Brazil 143 G6
Aripuanã r. Brazil 142 F5
Ariquemes Brazil 142 F5
Aris Namibia 100 C2
Arisaig U.K. 50 D4
Arisaig, Sound of sea chan. U.K. 50 D4
'Arīsh, Wādī al watercourse Egypt 85 A4
Aristazabal Island Canada 120 D4
Arixang China see Wenquan
Ariyalur India 84 C4
Arizaro, Salar de salt flat Arg. 144 C2
Arizona Arg. 144 C5
Arizona state U.S.A. 127 F6
Arizpe Mex. 127 F7
'Arjah Saudi Arabia 86 F5
Arjasa Indon. 68 F8
Arjeplog Sweden 44 J3
Arjuni Chhattisgarh India 84 D1
Arjuni Mahar. India 82 E5
Arkadak Russia 43 I6
Arkadelphia U.S.A. 131 E5
Arkaig, Loch l. U.K. 50 D4
Arkalyk Kazakh. 80 C1
Arkansas r. U.S.A. 131 F5
Arkansas state U.S.A. 131 E5
Arkansas City AR U.S.A. 131 F5
Arkansas City KS U.S.A. 131 D4
Arkanū, Jabal mt. Libya 86 B5
Arka Tag mts China 83 G1
Arkell, Mount Canada 120 C2
Arkhangel'sk Russia see Archangel
Arkhara Russia 74 C2
Arkhipovka Russia 74 D4
Árki i. Greece see Arkoi
Arklow Ireland 51 F5
Arkoi i. Greece 59 L6
Arkona Canada 134 E2
Arkona, Kap c. Germany 47 N3
Arkonam India see Arakkonam
Arkport U.S.A. 135 G2

▶Arkticheskiy, Mys c. Russia 153 E1
Most northerly point of Asia.

Arkticheskogo Instituta, Ostrova is Russia 64 J2
Arkul' Russia 42 K4
Arlandag mt. Turkm. 88 D2
Arles France 56 G5
Arli, Parc National de l' nat. park Burkina Faso 96 D3
Arlington S. Africa 101 H5
Arlington NY U.S.A. 135 I3
Arlington OH U.S.A. 134 D3
Arlington SD U.S.A. 130 D2
Arlington VA U.S.A. 135 G4
Arlington Heights U.S.A. 134 A2
Arlit Niger 96 D3
Arlon Belgium 52 F5
Arm r. Canada 121 J5
Armadale Australia 109 A8
Armagh U.K. 51 F3
Arma Konda mt. India 84 D2
Armant Egypt 86 D4
Armavir Armenia 91 G2
Armavir Russia 91 F1
Armenia country Asia 91 G2
Armenia Col. 142 C3
Armenopolis Romania see Gherla
Armeria Mex. 136 D5
Armidale Australia 112 E3
Armington U.S.A. 126 F3
Armit Lake Canada 121 N1
Armori India 84 D1
Armour U.S.A. 130 D3
Armoy U.K. 51 F2
Armstrong r. Australia 108 E4
Armstrong Canada 122 C4
Armstrong, Mount Canada 120 C2
Armstrong Island Cook Is see Rarotonga
Armu r. Russia 74 E3
Armur India 84 C2
Armutçuk Dağı mts Turkey 59 L5
Armyanskaya S.S.R. country Asia see Armenia
Arnaoutis, Cape Cyprus see Arnauti, Cape
Arnaud r. Canada 123 H2
Arnauti, Cape Cyprus 85 A2
Årnes Norway 45 G6
Arnett U.S.A. 131 D4
Arnhem Neth. 52 F3
Arnhem, Cape Australia 110 B2
Arnhem Land reg. Australia 108 F3
Arniston S. Africa 100 E8
Arno r. Italy 58 D3
Arno Bay Australia 111 B7
Arnold U.K. 49 F5
Arnold's Cove Canada 123 L5
Arnon r. Jordan see Mawjib, Wādī al
Arnprior Canada 135 G1
Arnsberg Germany 53 I3
Arnstadt Germany 53 K4
Arnstein Germany 53 J5
Arnstorf Germany 53 M6
Aroab Namibia 100 D4
Aroland Canada 122 D4
Arolsen Germany 53 J3
Aroma Sudan 86 E6
Arona Italy 58 C2
Arorae i. Kiribati 107 H2
Arore i. Kiribati see Arorae
Aros r. Mex. 127 F7
Arossi i. Solomon Is see Makira
Arqalyq Kazakh. see Arkalyk
Arquipélago da Madeira aut. reg. Port. 96 B1
Arrabury Australia 111 C5
Arrah India 83 F4
Arraias Brazil 145 B1
Arraias, Serra de hills Brazil 145 B1
Ar Ramādī Iraq 91 F4
Ar Ramlah Jordan 85 B5
Ar Ramthā Jordan 85 C3
Arran i. U.K. 50 D5
Arranmore Island Ireland 51 D3
Ar Raqqah Syria 85 D2
Arras France 52 C4
Ar Rass Saudi Arabia 86 F4
Ar Rastan Syria 85 C2
Ar Rayyān Qatar 88 C5
Arrecife Canary Is 96 B2
Arretium Italy see Arezzo
Arriagá Mex. 136 F5
Ar Rifā'ī Iraq 91 G5
Ar Riḩāb salt flat Iraq 91 G5
Ar Rimāl reg. Saudi Arabia 98 F1
Arrington U.S.A. 135 F5
Ar Riyāḑ Saudi Arabia see Riyadh
Arrochar U.K. 50 E4
Arrojado r. Brazil 145 B1
Arrow, Lough l. Ireland 51 D3
Arrowsmith, Mount N.Z. 113 C6
Arroyo Grande U.S.A. 128 C4
Ar Rubay'iyah Saudi Arabia 88 B5
Ar Rummān Jordan 85 B3
Ar Ruq'ī well Saudi Arabia 88 B4
Ar Ruşayfah Jordan 85 C3
Ar Rustāq Oman 88 E6
Ar Ruţbah Iraq 91 F4
Ar Ruwaydah Saudi Arabia 88 B5
Ar Ruwayḑah Saudi Arabia 88 B6
Ar Ruwayḑah Syria 85 C2
Års Denmark see Aars
Ars Iran 88 B2
Arseno Lake Canada 120 H1
Arsen'yev Russia 74 D3
Arsk Russia 42 K4
Arta Greece 59 I5
Artem Russia 74 D4
Artemisa Cuba 133 D8
Artemivs'k Ukr see Bakhmut
Artemovsk Ukr. see Artemivs'k
Artenay France 56 E2
Artesia AZ U.S.A. 129 I5
Artesia NM U.S.A. 127 G6
Arthur Canada 134 E2
Arthur NE U.S.A. 130 C3
Arthur TN U.S.A. 134 D5
Arthur, Lake U.S.A. 134 E3
Arthur's Pass National Park N.Z. 113 C6
Arthur's Town Bahamas 133 F7
Arti Russia 41 R4
Artigas research station Antarctica 152 A2
Artigas Uruguay 144 E4
Art'ik Armenia 91 F2
Artillery Lake Canada 121 I2
Artisia Botswana 101 H3
Artois reg. France 52 B4
Artois, Collines d' hills France 52 B4
Artos Dağı mt. Turkey 91 F3
Artova Turkey 90 E2
Artsakh disp. terr. Azer. see Nagorno-Karabakh
Artsiz Ukr. see Artsyz
Artsyz Ukr. 59 M2
Artur de Paiva Angola see Kuvango
Arturo Prat research station Antarctica 152 A2
Artux China 80 E4
Artvin Turkey 91 F2
Artyk Turkm. 88 E2
Aru, Kepulauan is Indon. 108 F1
Arua Uganda 98 D3
Aruanã Brazil 145 A1

▶Aruba terr. West Indies 137 K6
Self-governing Netherlands territory.

Arumã Brazil 142 F4
Arunachal Pradesh state India 83 H4
Arundel U.K. 49 G8
Arun Gol r. China see Arun He
Arun He r. China 74 B3
Arun Qi China see Naji
Aruppukkottai India 84 C4
Arusha Tanz. 98 D4
Aruwimi r. Dem. Rep. Congo 98 C3
Arvada U.S.A. 126 G5
Arvagh Ireland 51 E4
Arvayheer Mongolia 80 J2
Arviat Canada 121 M2
Arvidsjaur Sweden 44 K4
Arvika Sweden 45 H7
Arvonia U.S.A. 135 F5
Arwā' Saudi Arabia 88 B6
Arwād, Jazīrat i. Syria 85 B2
Arwala Indon. 108 D1
Arxan China 73 L3
Aryanah Tunisia see L'Ariana
Āryānshahr Iran 88 E3
Arys Kazakh. 80 C3
Arzamas Russia 43 I5
Arzanah i. U.A.E. 88 D5
Arzberg Germany 53 M4
Arzew Alg. 57 F6
Arzgir Russia 91 G1
Arzila Morocco see Asilah
Aš Czechia 53 M4
Asaba Nigeria 96 D4
Asad, Buḩayrat al resr Syria 85 D1
Asadābād Afgh. 89 H3
Asadābād Iran 88 C3
Asahi-dake vol. Japan 74 F4
Asahikawa Japan 74 F4
'Asal Egypt 85 A5
Āsalē l. Eth. 98 E2
Asālem Iran 88 C2
'Asalūyeh Iran 88 D5
Asan-man b. S. Korea 75 B5
Asansol India 83 F5
Āsayita Eth. 98 E2
Asbach Germany 53 H4
Asbestos Mountains S. Africa 100 F5
Asbury Park U.S.A. 135 H3
Ascalon Israel see Ashqelon
Ascea Italy 58 F4
Ascensión Bol. 142 F7
Ascensión Mex. 127 G7
Ascension atoll Micronesia see Pohnpei

▶Ascension i. S. Atlantic Ocean 148 H6
Part of St Helena, Ascension and Tristan da Cunha.

Ascensión, Bahía de la b. Mex. 137 G5
Aschaffenburg Germany 53 J5
Ascheberg Germany 53 H3
Aschersleben Germany 53 L3
Ascoli Piceno Italy 58 E3
Asculum Italy see Ascoli Piceno
Asculum Picenum Italy see Ascoli Piceno
Ascutney U.S.A. 135 I2
Āseb Eritrea see Assab
Åseda Sweden 45 I8
Åsele Sweden 44 J4
Asenovgrad Bulg. 59 K3
Aşfar, Jabal al mt. Jordan 85 C3
Aşfar, Tall al hill Syria 85 C3

▶Aşgabat Turkm. 88 E2
Capital of Turkmenistan.

Asha Russia 41 R5
Ashāwī, Mishāsh al well Saudi Arabia 88 C5
Ashburn U.S.A. 133 D6
Ashburton watercourse Australia 108 A5
Ashburton N.Z. 113 C6
Ashburton Range hills Australia 108 F4
Ashdod Israel 85 B4
Ashdown U.S.A. 131 E5
Asheboro U.S.A. 132 E5
Asher U.S.A. 131 D5
Ashern Canada 121 L5
Asheville U.S.A. 132 D5
Asheweig r. Canada 122 D3
Ashford Australia 112 E2
Ashford U.K. 49 H7
Ash Fork U.S.A. 129 G4
Ashgabat Turkm. see Aşgabat
Ashibetsu Japan 74 F4
Ashikaga Japan 75 E5
Ashington U.K. 48 F3
Ashizuri-misaki pt Japan 75 D6
Ashkelon Israel see Ashqelon
Ashkhabad Turkm. see Aşgabat
Ashkum U.S.A. 134 B3
Ashkun reg. Afgh. 89 H3
Ashland AL U.S.A. 133 C5
Ashland ME U.S.A. 132 G2
Ashland NH U.S.A. 135 J2
Ashland OH U.S.A. 134 D3
Ashland OR U.S.A. 126 C4
Ashland VA U.S.A. 135 G5
Ashland WI U.S.A. 130 F2
Ashland City U.S.A. 134 B5
Ashley Australia 112 D2
Ashley MI U.S.A. 134 C2
Ashley ND U.S.A. 130 D2

▶Ashmore and Cartier Islands terr. Australia 108 C3
Australian External Territory.

Ashmore Reef Australia 108 C3
Ashmore Reefs Australia 110 D1
Ashmyany Belarus 45 N9
Ashqelon Israel 85 B4
Ash Shabakah Iraq 91 F5
Ash Shaddādah Syria 91 F3
Ash Shallūfah Egypt 85 A4
Ash Sham Syria see Damascus
Ash Shanāfīyah Iraq 91 G5
Ash Shaqīq well Saudi Arabia 91 F5
Ash Sharāh mts Jordan 85 B4
Ash Sharawrah Saudi Arabia 86 G6
Ash Shāriqah U.A.E. see Sharjah
Ash Sharqāṭ Iraq 91 F4
Ash Shaṭrah Iraq 91 G5
Ash Shaṭṭ Egypt 85 A5
Ash Shawbak Jordan 85 B4
Ash Shaybānī well Saudi Arabia 91 F5
Ash Shaykh Ibrāhīm Syria 85 D2
Ash Shiblīyāt hill Saudi Arabia 85 C5
Ash Shiḥr Yemen 86 G7
Ash Shu'āybah Saudi Arabia 91 F6
Ash Shu'bah Saudi Arabia 86 F4
Ash Shurayf Saudi Arabia see Khaybar
Ashta India 82 D5
Ashtabula U.S.A. 134 E3
Ashtarak Armenia 91 G2
Ashti Mahar. India 82 D5
Ashti Mahar. India 84 B2
Ashti Mahar. India 84 C2
Āshtīān Iran 88 C3
Ashton S. Africa 100 E7
Ashton U.S.A. 126 F3
Ashton-under-Lyne U.K. 48 E5
Ashuanipi r. Canada 123 I3
Ashuanipi Lake Canada 123 I3
Ashur Iraq see Ash Sharqāṭ
Ashville U.S.A. 133 C5
Ashwaubenon U.S.A. 134 A1
Asi r. Asia see 'Āṣī, Nahr al
'Āṣī r. Lebanon/Syria see Orontes
'Āṣī, Nahr al r. Asia 90 E3
also known as Asi or Orontes
Āsīā Bak Iran 88 C3
Asifabad India 84 C2
Asika India 84 E2
Asilah Morocco 57 C6
Asinara, Golfo dell' b. Sardinia Italy 58 C4
Asino Russia 64 J4
Asipovichy Belarus 43 F5
Asīr Iran 88 D5
'Asīr reg. Saudi Arabia 86 F5
Asisium Italy see Assisi
Askale Pak. 82 C2
Aşkale Turkey 91 F3
Asker Norway 45 G7
Askersund Sweden 45 I7
Askim Norway 45 G7
Askī Mawşil Iraq 91 F3
Askino Russia 41 R4
Askival hill U.K. 50 C4
Asl Egypt see 'Asal
Aslanköy r. Turkey 85 B1
Āsmār reg. Afgh. 89 H3

▶Asmara Eritrea 86 E6
Capital of Eritrea.

Āsmera Eritrea see Asmara
Åsnen l. Sweden 45 I8
Aso-Kuju Kokuritsu-kōen nat. park Japan 75 C6
Asonli India 76 B2
Asop India 82 C4
Asori Indon. 69 J7
Āsosa Eth. 98 D2
Asotin U.S.A. 126 D3
Aspang-Markt Austria 47 P7
Aspatria U.K. 48 D4
Aspen U.S.A. 126 G5
Asperg Germany 53 J6
Aspermont U.S.A. 131 C5
Aspiring, Mount N.Z. 113 B7
Aspro, Cape Cyprus 85 A2
Aspromonte, Parco Nazionale dell' nat. park Italy 58 F5
Aspron, Cape Cyprus see Aspro, Cape
Aspur India 89 I6
Asquith Canada 121 J4
As Sa'an Syria 85 C2
Assab Eritrea 86 F7
As Sabsab well Saudi Arabia 88 C5
Assad, Lake resr Syria see Asad, Buḥayrat al
Aş Şadr U.A.E. 88 D5
Aş Şafā lava field Syria 85 C3
Aş Şafāqis Tunisia see Sfax
Aş Şaff Egypt 90 C5
Aş Safīrah Syria 85 C1
Aş Şaḥrā' al Gharbīyah des. Egypt see Western Desert
Aş Şaḥrā' ash Sharqīyah des. Egypt see Eastern Desert
Assake-Audan, Vpadina depr. Kazakh./Uzbek. 91 J2

▶'Assal, Lac Djibouti 86 F7
Lowest point in Africa.

'Assal, Lac l. Djibouti see 'Assal, Lac
Aş Şāliḥīyah Syria 91 F4
As Sallūm Egypt 90 B5
As Salmān Iraq 91 G5
As Salṭ Jordan 85 B3
Assam state India 83 G4
Assamakka Niger 96 D3
As Samāwah Iraq 91 G5
As Samrā' Jordan 85 C3
Aş Şanām reg. Saudi Arabia 86 H5
As Sarīr reg. Libya 97 F2
Assateague Island U.S.A. 135 H4
As Sawādah reg. Saudi Arabia 88 B6
Assayeta Eth. see Āsayita
As Sayḥ Saudi Arabia 88 B6
Assen Neth. 52 G1
Assenede Belgium 52 D3
Assesse Belgium 52 F4
As Sidrah Libya 97 E1
As Sīfah Oman 88 E6
Assigny, Lac l. Canada 123 I3
As Sikak Saudi Arabia 88 C5
Assiniboia Canada 121 J5
Assiniboine r. Canada 121 L5
Assiniboine, Mount Canada 118 G4
Assis Brazil 145 A3
Assisi Italy 58 E3
Aßlar Germany 53 I4
Aş Şubayḥīyah Kuwait 88 B4
Aş Şufayrī well Saudi Arabia 88 B4
As Sukhnah Syria 85 D2
As Sulaymānīyah/Slêmānî Iraq 91 G4
As Sulaymī Saudi Arabia 86 F4
Aş Şulb reg. Saudi Arabia 88 C5
Aş Şummān plat. Saudi Arabia 88 B5
Aş Şummān plat. Saudi Arabia 88 C6
As Sūq Saudi Arabia 86 F5
As Sūrīyah country Asia see Syria
Aş Şuwar Syria 91 F4
As Suwaydā' Syria 85 C3
As Suways Egypt see Suez
As Suways governorate Egypt 85 A4
Assynt, Loch l. U.K. 50 D2
Astacus Turkey see İzmit
Astakida i. Greece 59 L7
Astakos Greece 59 I5
Astalu Island Pak. see Astola Island

▶Astana Kazakh. 80 D1
Capital of Kazakhstan.

Āstāneh-ye Ashrafīyeh Iran 88 C2
Astara Azer. 91 H3
Āstārā Iran 86 G2
Asterābād Iran see Gorgān
Asti Italy 58 C2
Astillero Peru 142 E6
Astin Tag mts China see Altun Shan
Astipálaia i. Greece see Astypalaia
Astola Island Pak. 89 F5
Astor r. Pak. 89 I3
Astorga Spain 57 C2
Astoria U.S.A. 126 C3
Åstorp Sweden 45 H8
Astrabad Iran see Gorgān
Astrakhan' Russia 43 K7
Astrakhan' Bazar Azer. see Cälilabad
Astravyets Belarus 45 N9
Astrida Rwanda see Butare
Asturias aut. comm. Spain 57 C2
Asturias, Principado de aut. comm. Spain see Asturias
Asturica Augusta Spain see Astorga
Astypalaia i. Greece 59 L6
Asuncion i. N. Mariana Is 69 L3

▶Asunción Para. 144 E3
Capital of Paraguay.

'Āşūr, Tall mt. West Bank 85 B4
Aswad Oman 88 E5
Aswân Egypt see Aswān
Aswān Egypt 86 D5
Asyāḥ, Safrā' al esc. Saudi Arabia 88 A5
Asyūt Egypt see Asyūṭ
Asyūṭ Egypt 90 C6
Ata i. Tonga 107 I4
Atacama, Desierto de des. Chile see Atacama Desert
Atacama, Salar de salt flat Chile 144 C2

▶Atacama Desert Chile 144 C3
Driest place in the world.

Atafu atoll Tokelau 107 I2
Atafu i. Tokelau 150 I6
'Aṭā'iṭah, Jabal al mt. Jordan 85 B4
Atakent Turkey 85 B1
Atakpamé Togo 96 D4
Atalándi Greece see Atalanti
Atalanti Greece 59 J5
Atalaya Peru 142 D6
Ataléia Brazil 145 C2
Atambua Indon. 108 D2
Atamyrat Turkm. 89 G2
Ataniya Turkey see Adana
Atanur India 84 C2
'Ataq Yemen 86 G7
Atâr Mauritania 96 B2
Atari Pak. 89 I4
Atascadero U.S.A. 128 C4
Ātashān Iran 88 D3
Atasu Kazakh. 80 D2
Ataúro, Ilha de i. East Timor 108 D2
Atáviros mt. Greece see Atavyros
Atavyros mt. Greece 59 L6
Atayurt Turkey 85 A1
Atbara Sudan 86 D6
Atbara r. Sudan 86 D6
Atbasar Kazakh. 80 C1
Atchison U.S.A. 130 E4
Atebubu Ghana 96 C4
Ateransk Kazakh. see Atyrau
Atessa Italy 58 F3
Ath Belgium 52 D4
Athabasca r. Canada 121 I3
Athabasca, Lake Canada 121 I3
Athalia U.S.A. 134 D4
'Athāmīn, Birkat al well Iraq 88 A4
Atharan Hazari Pak. 89 I4
Athboy Ireland 51 F4
Athenae Greece see Athens
Athenry Ireland 51 D4
Athens Canada 135 H1

▶Athens Greece 59 J6
Capital of Greece.

Athens AL U.S.A. 133 C5
Athens GA U.S.A. 133 D5
Athens MI U.S.A. 134 C2
Athens OH U.S.A. 134 D4
Athens PA U.S.A. 135 G3
Athens TN U.S.A. 132 C5
Athens TX U.S.A. 131 E5
Atherstone U.K. 49 F6
Atherton Australia 110 D3
Athies France 52 C5
Athina Greece see Athens
Athínai Greece see Athens
Athleague Ireland 51 D4
Athlone Ireland 51 E4
Athnā', Wādī al watercourse Jordan 85 D3
Athni India 84 B2
Athol N.Z. 113 B7
Athol U.S.A. 135 I2
Atholl, Forest of reg. U.K. 50 E4
Athos mt. Greece 59 K4
Ath Thamad Egypt 85 B5
Ath Thawrah Syria 85 D2
Ath Thāyat mt. Saudi Arabia 85 C5
Ath Thumāmī well Saudi Arabia 88 B5
Athy Ireland 51 F5
Ati Chad 97 E3
Aṭīābād Iran 88 E3
Atico Peru 142 D7
Atikameg Canada 120 H4
Atikameg r. Canada 122 E3
Atik Lake Canada 121 M4
Atikokan Canada 119 I5
Atikonak Lake Canada 123 I3
Atīsh Khānah, Kōh-e hill Afgh. 89 F3
Atka Russia 65 Q3
Atka Island U.S.A. 118 A4
Atkarsk Russia 43 J6
Atkri Indon. 69 I7

▶Atlanta GA U.S.A. 133 C5
Capital of Georgia.

Atlanta IN U.S.A. 134 B3
Atlanta MI U.S.A. 134 C1
Atlantic IA U.S.A. 130 E3
Atlantic NC U.S.A. 133 E5
Atlantic City U.S.A. 135 H4
Atlantic-Indian-Antarctic Basin sea feature S. Atlantic Ocean 148 H10
Atlantic-Indian Ridge sea feature Southern Ocean 148 H9

▶Atlantic Ocean 148
2nd largest ocean in the world.

Atlantic Peak U.S.A. 126 F4
Atlantis S. Africa 100 D7
Atlas Méditerranéen mts Alg. see Atlas Tellien
Atlas Mountains Africa 54 C5
Atlas Saharien mts Alg. 54 E5
Atlas Tellien mts Alg. 57 H6
Atlin Lake Canada 120 C3
Atmakur India 84 C3
Atmore U.S.A. 133 C6
Atocha Bol. 142 E8
Atoka U.S.A. 131 D5
Atouat mt. Laos 70 D3
Atouila, Erg des. Mali 96 C2
Atqan China see Aqqan
Atrak r. Iran/Turkm. see Atrek
Atrato r. Col. 142 C2
Atrek r. Iran/Turkm. 88 D2
also known as Atrak, alt. Etrek
Atropatene country Asia see Azerbaijan
Atsonupuri, Vulkan vol. Russia 74 G3
Aṭ Ṭafīlah Jordan 85 B4
Aṭ Ṭā'if Saudi Arabia 86 F5
Attalea Turkey see Antalya
Attalia Turkey see Antalya
At Tamīmī Libya 90 A4
Attapu Laos 70 D4
Attawapiskat Canada 122 E3
Attawapiskat r. Canada 122 E3
Attawapiskat Lake Canada 122 D3
Aṭ Ṭawīl mts Saudi Arabia 91 E5
At Taysīyah plat. Saudi Arabia 91 F5
Attendorn Germany 53 H3
Attersee l. Austria 47 N7
Attica IN U.S.A. 134 B3
Attica NY U.S.A. 135 F2
Attica OH U.S.A. 134 D3
Attigny France 52 E5
Attikamagen Lake Canada 123 I3
Attila Line Cyprus 85 A2
Attleborough U.K. 49 I6
Attopeu Laos see Attapu
Attu Greenland 119 M3
Aṭ Ṭubayq reg. Saudi Arabia 85 C5

▶Attu Island U.S.A. 65 S4
Most westerly point of North America.

At Tünisīyah country Africa see Tunisia
Aṭ Ṭūr Egypt 90 D5
Attur India 84 C4
Aṭ Ṭuwayyah well Saudi Arabia 91 F6
Atuk Mountain hill U.S.A. 118 A3
Åtvidaberg Sweden 45 I7
Atwater U.S.A. 128 C3
Atwood U.S.A. 130 C4
Atwood Lake U.S.A. 134 E3
Atyashevo Russia 43 J5
Atyrau Kazakh. 78 E2
Atyraū admin. div. Kazakh. see Atyrauskaya Oblast'
Atyrau Oblast admin. div. Kazakh. see Atyrauskaya Oblast'
Atyrauskaya Oblast' admin. div. Kazakh. 41 Q6
Aua Island P.N.G. 69 K7
Aub Germany 53 K5
Aubagne France 56 G5
Aubange Belgium 52 F5
Aubenas France 56 G4
Aubergenville France 52 B6
Auboué France 52 F5
Aubrey Cliffs mts U.S.A. 129 G4
Aubry Lake Canada 118 F3
Auburn r. Australia 111 E5
Auburn Canada 134 E2
Auburn AL U.S.A. 133 C5
Auburn CA U.S.A. 128 C2
Auburn IN U.S.A. 134 C3
Auburn KY U.S.A. 134 B5
Auburn ME U.S.A. 135 J1
Auburn NE U.S.A. 130 E3
Auburn NY U.S.A. 135 G2
Auburn Range hills Australia 110 E5
Aubusson France 56 F4
Auch France 56 E5
Auche Myanmar 70 B1
Auchterarder U.K. 50 F4

▶Auckland N.Z. 113 E3
5th most populous city in Oceania.

Auckland Islands N.Z. 107 G7
Auden Canada 122 D4
Audenarde Belgium see Oudenaarde
Audo Range mts Eth. 98 E3
Audruicq France 52 C4
Audubon U.S.A. 130 E3
Aue Germany 53 M4
Auerbach Germany 53 M4
Auerbach in der Oberpfalz Germany 53 L5
Auersberg mt. Germany 53 M4
Augathella Australia 111 D5
Augher U.K. 51 E3
Aughnacloy U.K. 51 F3
Aughrim Ireland 51 F5
Augrabies S. Africa 100 E5
Augrabies Falls S. Africa 100 E5
Augrabies Falls National Park S. Africa 100 E5
Au Gres U.S.A. 134 D1
Augsburg Germany 47 M6
Augusta Australia 109 A8
Augusta Sicily Italy 58 F6
Augusta AR U.S.A. 131 F5
Augusta GA U.S.A. 133 D5
Augusta KY U.S.A. 134 C4

▶Augusta ME U.S.A. 135 K1
Capital of Maine.

Augusta MT U.S.A. 126 E3
Augusta Auscorum France see Auch
Augusta Taurinorum Italy see Turin
Augusta Treverorum Germany see Trier
Augusta Vindelicorum Germany see Augsburg
Augusto de Lima Brazil 145 B2
Augustus, Mount Australia 109 B6
Auke Bay U.S.A. 120 C3
Aukštaitijos nacionalinis parkas nat. park Lith. 45 O9
Aulavik National Park Canada 118 G2
Auld, Lake salt flat Australia 108 C5
Auliye Ata Kazakh. see Taraz
Aulnoye-Aymeries France 52 D4
Aulon Albania see Vlorë
Ault France 52 B4
Aumale Alg. see Sour el Ghozlane
Aumale France 52 B5
Aundh India 84 B2
Aundhi India 84 D1
Aunglan Myanmar 70 A3
Auob watercourse Namibia/S. Africa 100 E4
Aupaluk Canada 123 H2
Aur i. Malaysia 71 D7
Aura Fin. 45 M6
Auraiya India 82 D4
Aurangabad Bihar India 83 F4
Aurangabad Mahar. India 84 B2
Aure r. France 49 F9
Aurich Germany 53 H1
Aurigny i. Channel Is see Alderney
Aurilândia Brazil 145 A2
Aurillac France 56 F4
Aurora CO U.S.A. 126 G5
Aurora IL U.S.A. 134 A3
Aurora MO U.S.A. 131 E4
Aurora NE U.S.A. 130 D3
Aurora UT U.S.A. 129 H2
Aurora Island Vanuatu see Maéwo
Aurukun Australia 110 C2
Aus Namibia 100 C4
Au Sable U.S.A. 134 D1
Au Sable Point U.S.A. 134 D1
Auskerry i. U.K. 50 G1
Austin IN U.S.A. 134 C4
Austin MN U.S.A. 130 E3
Austin NV U.S.A. 128 E2

▶Austin TX U.S.A. 131 D6
Capital of Texas.

Austin, Lake salt flat Australia 109 B6
Austintown U.S.A. 134 E3
Austral Downs Australia 110 B4
Australes, Îles is Fr. Polynesia see Tubuai Islands

▶Australia country Oceania 106 C4
Largest and most populous country in Oceania and 6th largest in the world.

Australian-Antarctic Basin sea feature S. Atlantic Ocean 150 C9
Australian Antarctic Territory reg. Antarctica 152 G2
Australian Capital Territory admin. div. Australia 112 D5
Australian Convict Sites tourist site Australia 111 D9
Austria country Europe 47 N7
Austvågøy i. Norway 44 I2
Autazes Brazil 143 G4
Autesiodorum France see Auxerre
Authie r. France 52 B4
Autti Fin. 44 O3
Auvergne reg. France 56 F4
Auvergne, Monts d' mts France 56 F4
Auxerre France 56 F3
Auxi-le-Château France 52 C4
Auxonne France 56 G3
Auyuittuq National Park Canada 119 L3
Auzangate, Nevado mt. Peru 142 D6
Ava MO U.S.A. 131 E4
Ava NY U.S.A. 135 H2
Āvaj Iran 88 C3
Avallon France 56 F3
Avalon U.S.A. 128 D5
Avalon Peninsula Canada 123 L5
Avān Iran 91 G3
Avarau atoll Cook Is see Palmerston
Avaré Brazil 145 A3
Avaricum France see Bourges

▶Avarua Cook Is 151 J7
Capital of the Cook Islands, on Rarotonga.

Avawam U.S.A. 134 D5
Āvāz Iran 89 F3
Aveiro Port. 57 B3
Aveiro, Ria de est. Port. 57 B3
Avellino Italy 58 F4
Avenal U.S.A. 128 C3
Avenio France see Avignon
Aversa Italy 58 F4
Avesnes-sur-Helpe France 52 D4
Avesta Sweden 45 J6
Aveyron r. France 56 E4
Avezzano Italy 58 E3
Aviemore U.K. 50 F3
Avignon France 56 G5
Ávila Spain 57 D3
Avilés Spain 57 D2
Avion France 52 C4
Avis U.S.A. 135 G3
Avlama Dağı mt. Turkey 85 A1
Avlona Albania see Vlorë
Avnyugskiy Russia 42 J3
Avoca Australia 112 A6
Avoca r. Australia 112 A5
Avoca Ireland 51 F5
Avoca IA U.S.A. 130 E3
Avoca NY U.S.A. 135 G2
Avola Sicily Italy 58 F6
Avon r. England U.K. 49 E6
Avon r. England U.K. 49 E7
Avon r. England U.K. 49 F8
Avon r. Scotland U.K. 50 F3
Avon U.S.A. 135 G2
Avondale U.S.A. 129 G5
Avonmore r. Ireland 51 F5
Avonmore U.S.A. 134 F3
Avonmouth U.K. 49 E7
Avranches France 56 D2
Avre r. France 52 C5
Avsuyu Turkey 85 C1
Avuavu Solomon Is 107 G2
Avveel Fin. see Ivalo
Avvil Fin. see Ivalo
A'waj, Nahr al r. Syria 85 B3
Awakino N.Z. 113 E4
'Awālī Bahrain 88 C5
Awanui N.Z. 113 D2
Āwarē Eth. 98 E3
'Awāriḍ, Wādī al watercourse Syria 85 D2
Awarua Point N.Z. 113 B7
Āwash Eth. 98 E3
Āwash r. Eth. 98 E2
Awa-shima i. Japan 75 E5
Āwash National Park Eth. 98 D3
Awasib Mountains Namibia 100 B3
Awat China 80 F3
Awatere r. N.Z. 113 E5
Awbārī Libya 96 E2
Awbārī, Idhān des. Libya 96 E2
Awbeg r. Ireland 51 D5
'Awdah well Saudi Arabia 88 C6
'Awdah, Hawr al imp. l. Iraq 91 G5
Aw Dheegle Somalia 97 H4
Awe, Loch l. U.K. 50 D4
Aweil South Sudan 97 F4
Awka Nigeria 96 D4
Awkal Afgh. 89 F3
Axe r. England U.K. 49 D8
Axe r. England U.K. 49 E7
Axedale Australia 112 B6
Axel Heiberg Glacier Antarctica 152 I1
Axel Heiberg Island Canada 119 I2
Axim Ghana 96 C4
Axminster U.K. 49 E8
Axum Eth. see Āksum
Ay France 52 E5
Ayachi, Jbel mt. Morocco 54 D5
Ayacucho Arg. 144 E5
Ayacucho Peru 142 D6
Ayadaw Myanmar 70 A2
Ayagoz Kazakh. 80 F2
Ayaguz Kazakh. see Ayagoz
Ayakkum Hu salt l. China 83 G1
Ayaköz Kazakh. see Ayagoz
Ayan Russia 65 O4
Ayancık Turkey 90 D2
Ayang N. Korea 75 B5
Ayaş Turkey 90 D2
Aybas Kazakh. 43 K7
Aydar r. Ukr. 43 H6
Aydarko'l ko'li l. Uzbek. 80 C3
Aydere Turkm. 88 E2
Aydın Turkey 59 L6
Aydıncık Turkey 85 A1
Aydın Dağları mts Turkey 59 L5
Aýdyň Turkm. 88 D2
Āyelu vol. Eth. 86 F7
Ayer U.S.A. 135 J2
Ayers Rock hill Australia see Uluṟu
Ayeyarwady r. Myanmar see Irrawaddy
Ayila Ri'gyü mts China 82 D2
Áyios Dhimítrios Greece see Agios Dimitrios
Áyios Evstrátios i. Greece see Agios Efstratios
Áyios Nikólaos Greece see Agios Nikolaos
Áyios Yeóryios i. Greece see Agios Georgios
Aylesbury N.Z. 113 D6
Aylesbury U.K. 49 G7
Aylett U.S.A. 135 G5
Ayllón Spain 57 E3
Aylmer Ont. Canada 134 E2
Aylmer Que. Canada 135 H1
Aylmer Lake Canada 121 I1
Aymangala India 84 C3
'Ayn al 'Abd well Saudi Arabia 88 C4
'Ayn al 'Arab Syria 85 D1
'Ayn al Baidā' Saudi Arabia 85 C4
'Ayn al Bayḍā' well Syria 85 C2
'Ayn al Ghazalah well Libya 90 A4
'Ayn al Maqfī spring Egypt 90 C6
'Ayn az Zaytūn Egypt 90 B5
'Ayn Dāllah spring Egypt 90 B6
Ayní Tajik. 89 H2
'Ayn 'Īsá Syria 85 D1
'Ayn Tabaghbugh spring Egypt 90 B5
'Ayn Tumayrah spring Egypt 90 B5
Ayod South Sudan 86 D8
Ayon, Ostrov i. Russia 65 R3
'Ayoûn el 'Atroûs Mauritania 96 C3
Ayr Australia 110 D3
Ayr Canada 134 E2
Ayr U.K. 50 E5
Ayr r. U.K. 50 E5
Ayr, Point of U.K. 48 D5
Ayrancı Turkey 90 D3
Ayre, Point of Isle of Man 48 C4
Aytos Bulg. 59 L3
A Yun Pa Vietnam 71 E4
Ayutthia Thai. see Ayutthaya
Ayutthaya Thai. 71 C4
Ayvacık Turkey 59 L5
Ayvalı Turkey 90 E3
Ayvalık Turkey 59 L5
Azad Kashmir admin. div. Pak. 89 I3
Azak Russia see Azov
Azalia U.S.A. 134 C4
Azamgarh India 83 E4
Azania area Somalia 98 E3
Azaouâd reg. Mali 96 C3
Azaouagh, Vallée de watercourse Mali/Niger 96 D3
Azaran Iran see Hashtrūd
Azärbaycan country Asia see Azerbaijan
Azärbayjan country Asia see Azerbaijan
Azare Nigeria 96 E3
Azawad reg. Mali 96 C3
A'zāz Syria 85 C1
Azbine mts Niger see Aïr, Massif de l'
Azdavay Turkey 90 D2
Azerbaijan country Asia 91 G2
Azerbaydzhanskaya S.S.R. country Asia see Azerbaijan
Azhibeksor, Ozero salt l. Kazakh. 79 F1
Azhikode India 84 B4
Aziscohos Lake U.S.A. 135 J1
'Azīzābād Iran 88 E4
Aziziye Turkey see Pınarbaşı
Azogues Ecuador 142 C4

▶Azores terr. N. Atlantic Ocean 148 G3
Autonomous Region of Portugal.

Azores-Biscay Rise sea feature N. Atlantic Ocean 148 G3
Azotus Israel see Ashdod
Azov Russia 43 H7
Azov, Sea of Russia/Ukr. 43 H7
Azovs'ke More sea Russia/Ukr. see Azov, Sea of
Azovskoye More sea Russia/Ukr. see Azov, Sea of
Azraq, Bahr el r. Eth./Sudan see Blue Nile
Azraq, Qaşr al Jordan 85 C4
Azraq ash Shīshān Jordan 85 C4
Azrou Morocco 54 C5
Aztec U.S.A. 129 I3
Azuaga Spain 57 D4
Azuero, Península de pen. Panama 137 H7
Azul, Cordillera mts Peru 142 C5
Azuma-san vol. Japan 75 F5
Azur, Côte d' coastal area France 56 H5
'Azza Gaza see Gaza
Azzaba Alg. 58 B6

Az Zāhirīyah West Bank 85 B4
Az Zahrān Saudi Arabia see Dhahran
Az Zaqāzīq Egypt 90 C5
Az Zarbah Syria 85 C1
Az Zarqā' Jordan 85 C3
Az Za'tarī Jordan 85 C3
Az Za'yin Qatar see Al Dayyen
Azzeffâl hills Mauritania/W. Sahara 96 B
Az Zubayr Iraq 91 G5
Az Zuqur i. Yemen 86 F7

B

Ba, Sông r. Vietnam 71 E4
Baa Indon. 108 C2
Baabda Lebanon 85 B3
Ba'albek Lebanon 85 C2
Baan Baa Australia 112 D3
Baardheere Somalia 98 E3
Bab India 82 D4
Bābā, Kōh-e mts Afgh. 89 H3
Baba Burnu pt Turkey 59 L5
Babadağ mt. Azer. 91 H2
Babadag Romania 59 M2
Babadurmaz Turkm. 88 E2
Babaeski Turkey 59 L4
Babahoyo Ecuador 142 C4
Babai India 82 D5
Babai r. Nepal 83 E3
Bābā Kalān Iran 88 C4
Bāb al Mandab strait Africa/Asia 86 F7
Babanusa Sudan 86 C7
Babao Qinghai China see Qilian
Babao Yunnan China 76 E4
Babar i. Indon. 108 E1
Babar, Kepulauan is Indon. 108 E1
Babati Tanz. 99 D4
Babayevo Russia 42 G4
Babayurt Russia 91 G2
B'abdā Lebanon see Baabda
Bab el Mandeb, Straits of Africa/Asia see Bāb al Mandab
Babi, Pulau i. Indon. 71 B7
Babian Jiang r. China 76 D4
Babine r. Canada 120 E4
Babine Lake Canada 120 E4
Babine Range mts Canada 120 E4
Bābol Iran 88 D2
Bābolsar Iran 88 D2
Babongo Cameroon 97 E4
Baboon Point S. Africa 100 D7
Baboua Cent. Afr. Rep. 98 B3
Babruysk Belarus 43 F5
Babstovo Russia 74 D2
Babu China see Hezhou
Babuhri India 82 B4
Babusar Pass Pak. 89 I3
Babushkina, imeni Russia 42 I4
Babuyan i. Phil. 69 G3
Babuyan Channel Phil. 69 G3
Babuyan Islands Phil. 69 G3
Bacaadweyn Somalia 98 E3
Bacabal Brazil 143 J4
Bacan i. Indon. 69 H7
Bacanora Mex. 127 F7
Bacău Romania 59 L1
Baccaro Point Canada 123 I6
Bắc Giang Vietnam 70 D2
Bacha China 74 D2
Bach Ice Shelf Antarctica 152 L2
Bach Long Vi, Đao i. Vietnam 70 D2
Bachu China 80 E4
Bachuan China see Tongliang
Back r. Australia 110 C3
Back r. Canada 121 M1
Bačka Palanka Serbia 59 H2
Backbone Mountain U.S.A. 134 F4
Backbone Ranges mts Canada 120 D2
Backe Sweden 44 J5
Backstairs Passage Australia 111 B7
Bac Liêu Vietnam 71 D5
Bắc Ninh Vietnam 70 D2
Bacoachi Mex. 127 F7
Bacoachi watercourse Mex. 127 F7
Bacobampo Mex. 127 F8
Bacolod Phil. 69 G4
Bacqueville, Lac l. Canada 122 G2
Bacqueville-en-Caux France 49 H9
Bacubirito Mex. 127 G8
Bada China see Xilin
Bada mt. Eth. 98 D3
Bada i. Myanmar 71 B5
Badabaýhan Turkm. 89 F2
Bad Abbach Germany 53 M6
Badain Jaran Shamo des. China 80 J3
Badajoz Spain 57 C4
Badami India 84 B3
Badampaharh India 83 F5
Badamsha Kazakh. 80 A1
Badanah Saudi Arabia 91 F5
Badanjilin Shamo des. China see Badain Jaran Shamo
Badaojiang China see Baishan
Badarpur India 83 H4
Badaun India see Budaun
Bad Axe U.S.A. 134 D2
Bad Bederkesa Germany 53 I1
Bad Belzig Germany 53 M2
Bad Bergzabern Germany 53 H5
Bad Berleburg Germany 53 I3
Bad Bevensen Germany 53 K1
Bad Blankenburg Germany 53 L4
Bad Camberg Germany 53 I4
Badderen Norway 44 M2
Bad Driburg Germany 53 J3
Bad Düben Germany 53 M3
Bad Dürkheim Germany 53 I5
Bad Dürrenberg Germany 53 M3
Bademli Turkey see Aladağ
Bademli Geçidi pass Turkey 90 C3
Bad Ems Germany 53 H4
Baden Austria 47 P6
Baden Switz. 56 I3
Baden-Baden Germany 53 I6
Baden-Württemberg land Germany 53 I6
Bad Essen Germany 53 I2
Bad Fallingbostel Germany 53 J2
Bad Grund (Harz) Germany 53 K3
Bad Harzburg Germany 53 K3
Bad Hersfeld Germany 53 J4
Bad Hofgastein Austria 47 N7
Bad Homburg vor der Höhe Germany 53 I4
Badia Polesine Italy 58 D2
Badin Pak. 89 H5
Bad Ischl Austria 47 N7
Bādiyat ash Shām des. Asia see Syrian Desert
Bad Kissingen Germany 53 K4
Bad Königsdorff Poland see Jastrzębie-Zdrój
Bad Kösen Germany 53 L3
Bad Kötzting Germany 53 M5
Bad Kreuznach Germany 53 H5
Bad Laasphe Germany 53 I4
Badlands reg. ND U.S.A. 130 C2
Badlands reg. SD U.S.A. 130 C3
Badlands National Park U.S.A. 130 C3
Bad Langensalza Germany 53 K3
Bad Lauterberg im Harz Germany 53 K3
Bad Liebenwerda Germany 53 N3
Bad Lippspringe Germany 53 I3
Bad Marienberg (Westerwald) Germany 53 H4
Bad Mergentheim Germany 53 J5
Bad Nauheim Germany 53 I4
Badnawar India 82 C5
Badnera India 84 C1
Bad Neuenahr-Ahrweiler Germany 52 H4
Bad Neustadt an der Saale Germany 53 K4
Badnor India 82 C4
Badong China 77 F2
Ba Đông Vietnam 71 D5
Badou Togo 96 D4
Bad Pyrmont Germany 53 J3
Badrah Iraq 91 G4
Badreh Iran 88 B3
Bad Reichenhall Germany 47 N7
Badr Ḩunayn Saudi Arabia 86 E5
Bādrūd Iran 88 D3
Bad Sachsa Germany 53 K3
Bad Salzdetfurth Germany 53 K2
Bad Salzuflen Germany 53 I2
Bad Salzungen Germany 53 K4
Bad Schwalbach Germany 53 I4
Bad Schwartau Germany 47 M4
Bad Segeberg Germany 47 M4
Bad Sobernheim Germany 53 H5
Bad Staffelstein Germany 53 K4
Badu Island Australia 110 C1
Badulla Sri Lanka 84 D5
Bad Vilbel Germany 53 I4
Bad Wilsnack Germany 53 L2
Bad Windsheim Germany 53 K5
Badzhal Russia 74 D2
Badzhal'skiy Khrebet mts Russia 74 D2
Bad Zwischenahn Germany 53 I1
Bae Colwyn U.K. see Colwyn Bay
Baengnyeong-do i. S. Korea 75 B5
Baesweiler Germany 52 G4
Baeza Spain 57 E5
Bafatá Guinea-Bissau 96 B3
Baffa Pak. 89 I3
Baffin Bay sea Canada/Greenland 119 L2

▶Baffin Island Canada 119 L3
2nd largest island in North America and 5th in the world.

Bafia Cameroon 96 E4
Bafilo Togo 96 D4
Bafing r. Africa 96 B3
Bafoulabé Mali 96 B3
Bafoussam Cameroon 96 E4
Bāfq Iran 88 D4
Bafra Turkey 90 D2
Bafra Burnu pt Turkey 90 D2
Bāft Iran 88 E4
Bafwaboli Dem. Rep. Congo 98 C3
Bafwasende Dem. Rep. Congo 98 C3
Bagaha India 83 F4
Bagalkot India 84 B2
Bagalkote India see Bagalkot
Bagamoyo Tanz. 99 D4
Bagan China 76 C1
Bagan Datoh Malaysia see Bagan Datuk
Bagan Datuk Malaysia 71 C7
Bagansiapiapi Indon. 71 C7
Bagata Dem. Rep. Congo 98 B4
Bagdad U.S.A. 129 G4
Bagdarin Russia 73 K2
Bagé Brazil 144 F4
Bagenalstown Ireland 51 F5
Bagerhat Bangl. 83 G5
Bageshwar India 82 D3
Baggs U.S.A. 126 G4
Baggy Point U.K. 49 C7
Bagh India 82 C5
Bāgh, Chāh-e well Iran 88 D4
Bàgh a'Chaisteil U.K. see Castlebay
Baghak Pak. 89 G4
Baghbaghū Iran 89 F2

▶Baghdād Iraq 91 G4
Capital of Iraq.

Bāgh-e Malek Iran 88 C4
Bagherhat Bangl. see Bagerhat
Bāghīn Iran 88 E4
Baghlān Afgh. 89 H2
Baghrān Afgh. 89 G3
Bağırsak r. Turkey 85 C1
Bağırsak Deresi r. Syria/Turkey see Sājūr, Nahr
Bagley U.S.A. 130 E2
Baglung Nepal 83 E3
Bagnères-de-Luchon France 56 E5
Bago Myanmar see Pegu
Bago Phil. 69 G4
Bagong China see Sansui
Bagor India 89 I5
Bagrationovsk Russia 45 L9
Bagrax China see Bohu
Bagrax Hu l. China see Bosten Hu
Baguio Phil. 69 G3
Bagur, Cabo c. Spain see Begur, Cap de
Bagzane, Monts mts Niger 96 D3
Bahādorābād Iran 88 E4
Bahalda India 83 F5
Bahamas, The country West Indies 133 E7
Bahara Pak. 89 G5
Baharampur India 83 G4
Bahardipur Pak. 89 H5
Bahariya Oasis oasis Egypt see Baḩrīyah, Wāḩāt al
Bahau Malaysia 71 C7
Bahawalnagar Pak. 89 I4
Bahawalpur Pak. 89 H4
Bahçe Adana Turkey 85 B1
Bahçe Osmaniye Turkey 90 E3
Baher Dar Eth. see Bahir Dar
Baheri India 82 D3
Bahia Brazil see Salvador
Bahia state Brazil 145 C1
Bahía, Islas de la is Hond. 137 G5
Bahía Asunción Mex. 127 E8
Bahía Blanca Arg. 144 D5
Bahía Kino Mex. 127 F7
Bahía Laura Arg. 144 C7
Bahía Negra Para. 144 E2
Bahía Tortugas Mex. 127 E8
Bahir Dar Eth. 98 D2
Bahl India 82 C3
Bahlā Oman 88 E6
Bahomonte Indon. 69 G7
Bahraich India 83 E4
Bahrain country Asia 88 C5
Bahrain, Gulf of Asia 88 C5
Bahrāmābād Iran see Rafsanjān
Bahrām Beyg Iran 88 C2
Bahramjerd Iran 88 E4
Baḩrīyah, Wāḩāt al oasis Egypt 90 C6
Bahuaja-Sonene, Parque Nacional nat. park Peru 142 E6
Baia Mare Romania 59 J1
Baicang China 83 G3
Baicheng Jilin China 74 A3
Baicheng Xinjiang China 80 F3
Baidoa Somalia see Baydhabo
Baidoi Co l. China 83 F2
Baidu China 77 H3
Baie-aux-Feuilles Canada see Tasiujaq
Baie-Comeau Canada 123 H4
Baie-du-Poste Canada see Mistissini
Baie-St-Paul Canada 123 H5
Baie-Trinité Canada 123 I4
Baie Verte Canada 123 K4
Baiguan China see Shangyu
Baiguo Hubei China 77 G2
Baiguo Hunan China 77 G3
Baihar India 82 E5
Baihe Jilin China 74 C4
Baihe Shaanxi China 77 F1
Baiji Iraq see Bayjī

▶Baikal, Lake Russia 72 J2
Deepest lake in Asia and the world, and 2nd largest lake in Asia and 8th in the world.

Baikalu Shan mt. China 74 A1
Baikunthpur India 83 E5
Baile Átha Cliath Ireland see Dublin
Baile Átha Luain Ireland see Athlone
Baile Mhartainn U.K. 50 B3
Baile na Finne Ireland 51 D3
Băileşti Romania 59 J2
Bailey Range hills Australia 109 C7
Bailianhe Shuiku resr China 77 G2
Bailieborough Ireland 51 F4
Bailleul France 52 C4
Baillie r. Canada 121 J1
Bailong China see Hadapu
Bailong Jiang r. China 76 E1
Baima Qinghai China 76 D1
Baima Xizang China see Baxoi
Baima Jian mt. China 77 H2
Baimuru P.N.G. 69 K8
Bain r. U.K. 48 G5
Bainang China see Norkyung
Bainbridge GA U.S.A. 133 C6
Bainbridge IN U.S.A. 134 B4
Bainbridge NY U.S.A. 135 H2
Bainduru India 84 B3
Baingoin China see Porong
Baini China see Yuqing
Baiona Spain 57 B2
Baiqên China 76 D1
Baiquan China 74 B3
Bā'ir Jordan 85 C4
Bā'ir, Wādī watercourse Jordan/Saudi Arabia 85 C4
Bairab Co l. China 83 E2
Bairat India 82 D4
Baird U.S.A. 131 D5
Baird Mountains U.S.A. 118 C3

▶Bairiki Kiribati 150 H5
Capital of Kiribati, on Tarawa atoll.

Bairin Youqi China see Daban
Bairnsdale Australia 112 C6
Baise China 76 E4
Baisha Chongqing China 76 E2
Baisha Hainan China 77 F5
Baisha Sichuan China 77 F2
Baishan Guangxi China see Mashan
Baishan Jilin China 74 B4
Baishan Jilin China 74 B4
Baishanzhen China see Baishan
Baishui Shaanxi China 77 F1
Baishui Sichuan China 76 E1
Baishui Jiang r. China 76 E1
Baisogala Lith. 45 M9
Baitadi Nepal 82 E3
Baitang China 76 C1
Bai Thương Vietnam 70 D3
Baitou Shan mt. China/N. Korea 74 C4
Baixi China see Yibin
Baiyashi China see Dong'an
Baiyin China 72 I5
Baiyü China 76 C2
Baiyuda Desert Sudan 86 D6
Baja Hungary 58 H1
Baja, Punta pt Mex. 127 E7
Baja California pen. Mex. 127 E7
Baja California state Mex. 127 E7
Baja California Norte state Mex. see Baja California
Baja California Sur state Mex. 127 E8
Bajan Mex. 131 C7
Bajau i. Indon. 71 D7
Bajaur reg. Pak. 89 H3
Bajawa Indon. 108 C2
Baj Baj India 83 G5
Bājgīrān Iran 88 E2
Bajiang China 77 F3
Bājil Yemen 86 F7
Bajo Caracoles Arg. 144 B7
Bajoga Nigeria 96 E3
Bajoi China 76 D2
Bajrakot India 83 F5
Bakala Cent. Afr. Rep. 97 F4
Bakanas Kazakh. 80 E3
Bakar Pak. 89 H5
Bakel Senegal 96 B3
Baker CA U.S.A. 128 E4
Baker ID U.S.A. 126 E3
Baker LA U.S.A. 131 F6
Baker MT U.S.A. 126 G3
Baker NV U.S.A. 129 F2
Baker WV U.S.A. 135 F4
Baker, Mount vol. U.S.A. 126 C2
Baker Butte mt. U.S.A. 129 H4
Baker City U.S.A. 126 D3

▶Baker Island terr. N. Pacific Ocean 107 I1
United States Unincorporated Territory.

Baker Island U.S.A. 120 C4
Baker Lake salt flat Australia 109 D6
Baker Lake Canada 121 M1
Baker Lake l. Canada 121 M1
Baker's Dozen Islands Canada 122 F2
Bakersfield U.S.A. 128 D4
Bakersville U.S.A. 132 D4
Bâ Kêv Cambodia 71 D4
Bakhardok Turkm. see Bokurdak
Bākharz, Kūhhā-ye mts Iran 89 F3
Bakhasar India 82 B4
Bakhirevo Russia 74 C2
Bakhmach Ukr. 43 G6
Bakhma Dam Iraq see Bēkma, Sadd
Bakhmut Ukr. 43 H6
Bākhtarān Iran see Kermānshāh
Bakhtegan, Daryācheh-ye l. Iran 88 D4
Bakhtiari Country reg. Iran 88 C3
Bakı Azer. see Baku
Baki Somalia 98 E2
Bakırköy Turkey 59 M4
Bakkejord Norway 44 K2
Bakloh India 82 C2
Bako Eth. 98 D3
Bakongan Indon. 71 B7
Bakouma Cent. Afr. Rep. 98 C3
Baksan Russia 91 F2

▶Baku Azer. 91 H2
Capital of Azerbaijan.

Baku Dem. Rep. Congo 98 D3
Bakutis Coast Antarctica 152 J2
Baky Azer. see Baku
Balâ Turkey 90 D3
Bala U.K. 49 D6
Bala, Cerros de mts Bol. 142 E6
Balabac i. Phil. 68 F5
Balabac Strait Malaysia/Phil. 68 F5
Baladeh Māzandarān Iran 88 C2
Baladeh Māzandarān Iran 88 C2
Baladek Russia 74 D1
Balagar Gaole China see Bayan Ul
Balaghat India 82 E5
Balaghat Range hills India 84 B2
Bālā Ḩowz Iran 88 E4
Balaka Malawi 99 D5
Balakān Azer. 91 G2
Balakhna Russia 42 I4
Balakhta Russia 72 G1
Balaklava Australia 111 B7
Balaklava Crimea 90 D1
Balakleya Ukr. see Balakliya
Balakliya Ukr. 43 H6
Balakovo Russia 43 J5
Bala Lake l. U.K. 49 D6
Balaman India 82 E4
Balan India 82 B4
Balanda Russia see Kalininsk
Balanda r. Russia 43 J6
Balan Dağı hill Turkey 59 M6
Balanga Phil. 69 G4
Ba Lang An, Mui pt Vietnam 70 E4
Balangir India 84 D1
Balaözen r. Kazakh./Russia see Saryozen
Balarampur India see Balrampur
Bālā Shahr Iran 88 E5
Balashov Russia 43 I6
Balasore India see Baleshwar
Balaton, Lake Hungary 58 G1
Balatonboglár Hungary 58 G1
Balatonfüred Hungary 58 G1
Balbina Brazil 143 G4
Balbina, Represa de resr Brazil 143 G4
Balbriggan Ireland 51 F4
Balchik Bulg. 59 M3
Bal Chirāgh Afgh. 89 G3
Balclutha N.Z. 113 B8
Balcones Escarpment U.S.A. 131 C6
Bald Knob U.S.A. 134 E5
Bald Mountain U.S.A. 129 F3
Baldock Lake Canada 121 L3
Baldwin Canada 134 F1
Baldwin FL U.S.A. 133 D6
Baldwin MI U.S.A. 134 C2
Baldwin PA U.S.A. 134 F3
Baldy Mount Canada 126 D2
Baldy Mountain hill Canada 121 K5
Baldy Peak U.S.A. 129 I5
Bale Indon. 68 C7
Bâle Switz. see Basel
Baléa Mali 96 B3
Baleares is Spain see Balearic Islands
Baleares, Islas is Spain see Balearic Islands
Baleares Insulae is Spain see Balearic Islands
Balearic Islands is Spain 57 G4
Balearic Sea Spain 57 G3
Balears is Spain see Balearic Islands
Balears, Illes is Spain see Balearic Islands
Baleia, Ponta da pt Brazil 145 D2
Baleine, Grande Rivière de la r. Canada 122 F3
Baleine, Petite Rivière de la r. Canada 122 F3
Baleine, Rivière à la r. Canada 123 I2
Bale Mountains National Park Eth. 98 D3
Baler Phil. 69 G3
Baleshwar India 83 F5
Balestrand Norway 45 E6
Balestrieri, Punta mt. Italy 58 C4
Baléyara Niger 96 D3
Balezino Russia 41 Q4
Balfes Creek Australia 110 D4
Balfour Downs Australia 108 C5
Balgo Australia 108 D5
Balguntay China 80 G3
Bali India 82 C4
Bali i. Indon. 108 A2
Bali, Laut sea Indon. 108 A1
Balia India see Ballia
Baliapal India 83 F5
Balige Indon. 71 B7
Baliguda India 84 D1
Balıkesir Turkey 59 L5
Balīkh r. Syria/Turkey 85 D2
Balikpapan Indon. 68 F7
Balimila Reservoir India 84 D2
Balimo P.N.G. 69 K8
Balin China 74 A2
Baling Malaysia 71 C6
Balingen Germany 47 L6
Balintore U.K. 50 F3
Bali Sea Indon. see Bali, Laut
Balk Neth. 52 F2
Balkanabat Turkm. 88 D2
Balkan Mountains Bulg./Serbia 59 J3
Balkash Kazakh. 80 D2
Balkassar Pak. 89 I3
Balkh r. Afgh. 89 G2

▶Balkhash, Lake Kazakh. 80 D2
3rd largest lake in Asia.

Balkhash, Ozero l. Kazakh. see Balkhash, Lake
Balkuduk Kazakh. 43 J7
Ballachulish U.K. 50 D4
Balladonia Australia 109 C8
Balladoran Australia 112 D3
Ballaghaderreen Ireland 51 D4
Ballan Australia 112 B6
Ballangen Norway 44 J2
Ballantine U.S.A. 126 F3
Ballantrae U.K. 50 E5
Ballarat Australia 112 A6
Ballard, Lake salt flat Australia 109 C7
Ballari India 84 C3
Ballarpur India 84 C2
Ballater U.K. 50 F3
Ballé Mali 96 C3
Ballena, Punta pt Chile 144 B3
Balleny Islands Antarctica 152 H2
Ballia India 83 F4
Ballina Australia 112 F2
Ballina Ireland 51 C3
Ballinafad Ireland 51 D3
Ballinalack Ireland 51 E4
Ballinamore Ireland 51 E3
Ballinasloe Ireland 51 D4
Ballindine Ireland 51 D4
Ballinger U.S.A. 131 D6
Ballinluig U.K. 50 F4
Ballinrobe Ireland 51 C4
Ballston Spa U.S.A. 135 I2
Ballybay Ireland 51 F3
Ballybunion Ireland 51 C5
Ballycanew Ireland 51 F5
Ballycastle Ireland 51 C3
Ballycastle U.K. 51 F2
Ballyclare U.K. 51 G3
Ballyconnell Ireland 51 E3
Ballygar Ireland 51 D4
Ballygawley U.K. 51 E3
Ballygorman Ireland 51 E2
Ballyhaunis Ireland 51 D4
Ballyheigue Ireland 51 C5
Ballykelly U.K. 51 E2
Ballylynan Ireland 51 E5
Ballymacmague Ireland 51 E5
Ballymahon Ireland 51 E4
Ballymena U.K. 51 F3
Ballymoney U.K. 51 F2
Ballymote Ireland 51 D3
Ballynahinch U.K. 51 G3
Ballyshannon Ireland 51 D3
Ballyteige Bay Ireland 51 F5
Ballyvaughan Ireland 51 C4
Ballyward U.K. 51 F3
Balmartin U.K. see Baile Mhartainn
Balmer India see Barmer
Balmertown Canada 121 M5
Balmorhea U.S.A. 131 C6
Balochistan prov. Pak. 89 G4
Balombo Angola 99 B5
Balonne r. Australia 112 D2
Balotra India 82 C4
Balqash Kazakh. see Balkash
Balqash Köli l. Kazakh. see Balkhash, Lake
Balrampur India 83 E4
Balranald Australia 112 A5
Balş Romania 59 K2
Balsam Lake Canada 135 F1
Balsas Brazil 143 I5
Balta Ukr. 43 F7
Baltasound U.K. 50 [inset]
Baltay Russia 43 J5
Bălţi Moldova 43 E7
Baltic U.S.A. 134 E3
Baltic Sea g. Europe 45 J9
Balṭīm Egypt 90 C5
Balṭîm Egypt see Balṭīm
Baltimore S. Africa 101 I2
Baltimore MD U.S.A. 135 G4
Baltimore OH U.S.A. 134 D4
Baltinglass Ireland 51 F5
Baltistan reg. Pak. 82 C2
Baltiysk Russia 45 K9
Balu India 76 B3
Baluarte, Arroyo watercourse U.S.A. 131 D7
Baluch Ab well Iran 88 E4
Balumundam Indon. 71 B7
Balurghat India 83 G4
Balve Germany 53 H3
Balvi Latvia 45 O8
Balya Turkey 59 L5
Balykchy Kyrg. 80 E3
Balykshi Kazakh. 78 E2
Balyqshy Kazakh. see Balykshi
Bam Iran 88 E4
Bām Iran 88 E2
Bama China 76 E3

▶Bamako Mali 96 C3
Capital of Mali.

Bamba Mali 96 C3
Bambari Cent. Afr. Rep. 98 C3
Bambel Indon. 71 B7
Bamberg Germany 53 K5
Bamberg U.S.A. 133 D5
Bambili Dem. Rep. Congo 98 C3
Bambio Cent. Afr. Rep. 98 B3
Bamboesberg mts S. Africa 101 H6
Bamboo Creek Australia 108 C5
Bambouti Cent. Afr. Rep. 98 C3
Bambuí Brazil 145 B3
Bamda China 76 C2
Bamenda Cameroon 96 E4
Bamiantong China see Muling
Bamingui Cent. Afr. Rep. 98 C3
Bamingui-Bangoran, Parc National du nat. park Cent. Afr. Rep. 98 B3
Bâmnák Cambodia 71 D4
Bamnet Narong Thai. 70 C4
Bamor India 82 D4
Bamori India 84 C1
Bamposht reg. Iran 89 F5
Bampton U.K. 49 D8
Bampūr Iran 89 F5
Bampūr watercourse Iran 89 E5
Bamrūd Iran 89 F3
Bāmyān Afgh. 89 G3
Bamyili Australia 108 F3
Banaba i. Kiribati 107 G2
Banabuiu, Açude resr Brazil 143 K5
Banagher Ireland 51 E4
Banalia Dem. Rep. Congo 98 C3
Banamana, Lagoa l. Moz. 101 K2
Banamba Mali 96 C3
Banámichi Mex. 127 F7
Banana Australia 110 E5
Bananal, Ilha do i. Brazil 143 H6
Bananga India 71 A6
Banapur India 84 E2
Banas r. India 82 D4
Banaz Turkey 59 M5
Ban Ban Laos 70 C3
Banbān, 'Irq des. Saudi Arabia 88 B5
Banbar China see Domartang
Ban Bo Laos 70 C3
Banbridge U.K. 51 F3
Ban Bua Chum Thai. 70 C4
Ban Bua Yai Thai. 70 C4
Ban Bungxai Laos 70 D4
Banbury U.K. 49 F6
Ban Cang Vietnam 70 C2
Banc d'Arguin, Parc National du nat. park Mauritania 96 B2
Ban Channabot Thai. 70 C3
Banchory U.K. 50 G3
Bancroft Canada 135 G1
Bancroft Zambia see Chililabombwe
Banda Dem. Rep. Congo 98 C3
Banda India 82 E4
Banda, Kepulauan is Indon. 69 H7
Banda, Laut sea Indon. 69 H8
Banda Aceh Indon. 71 A6
Banda Banda, Mount Australia 112 F3
Banda Daud Shah Pak. 89 H3
Bandahara, Gunung mt. Indon. 71 B7
Bandama r. Côte d'Ivoire 96 C4
Bandān Kūh mts Iran 89 F4
Bandar India see Machilipatnam
Bandar Moz. 99 D5
Bandar Abbas Iran see Bandar-e 'Abbās
Bandarban Bangl. 83 H5
Bandar-e 'Abbās Iran 88 E5
Bandar-e Anzalī Iran 88 C2
Bandar-e Būshehr Iran 88 C4
Bandar-e Dayyer Iran 88 C5
Bandar-e Deylam Iran 88 C4
Bandar-e Emām Khomeynī Iran 88 C4
Bandar-e Ganāveh Iran 88 C4
Bandar-e Ḩeydarābād Iran 88 B2
Bandar-e Jāsk Iran 88 E5
Bandar-e Kangān Iran 88 D5
Bandar-e Lengeh Iran 88 D5
Bandar-e Māhshahr Iran 88 C4
Bandar-e Nakhīlū Iran 88 D5
Bandar-e Pahlavī Iran see Bandar-e Anzalī
Bandar-e Shāh Iran see Bandar-e Torkaman
Bandar-e Torkaman Iran 88 D2
Bandar Labuan Malaysia see Labuan
Bandar Lampung Indon. 68 D8
Bandarpunch mt. India 82 D3

▶Bandar Seri Begawan Brunei 68 E6
Capital of Brunei.

Banda Sea sea Indon. see Banda, Laut
Band-e Bābā, Silsilah-ye Kōh-e mts Afgh. 89 F3
Band-e Bamposht, Kūh-e mts Iran 89 F5
Bandeira Brazil 145 C1
Bandeirante Brazil 145 A1
Bandeiras, Pico de mt. Brazil 145 C3
Bandelierkop S. Africa 101 I2
Banderas Mex. 131 B6
Banderas, Bahía de b. Mex. 136 C4
Band-e Sar Qom Iran 88 D3
Bandhi Pak. 89 H5
Bandhogarh India 82 E5
Bandi r. India 82 C4
Bandiagara Mali 96 C3
Bandikui India 82 D4
Bandingilo National Park South Sudan 97 G4
Bandipur National Park India 84 C4
Bandırma Turkey 59 L4
Bandjarmasin Indon. see Banjarmasin
Bandon Ireland 51 D6
Bandon r. Ireland 51 D6
Ban Don Thai. see Surat Thani

Bandon U.S.A. 126 B4
Band Qīr Iran 88 C4
Bandra India 84 B2
Bandundu Dem. Rep. Congo 98 B4
Bandung Indon. 68 D8
Bandya Australia 109 C6
Bāneh Iran 88 B3
Banera India 82 C4
Banes Cuba 137 I4
Banff Canada 120 H5
Banff U.K. 50 G3
Banff National Park Canada 120 G5
Banfora Burkina Faso 96 C3
Banga Dem. Rep. Congo 99 C4
Bangalore India *see* **Bengaluru**
Bangalow Australia 112 F2
Bangaon India 83 G5
Bangar Brunei 68 F6
Bangassou Cent. Afr. Rep. 98 C3
Bangdag Co *salt l.* China 83 E2
Banggai Indon. 69 G7
Banggai, Kepulauan *is* Indon. 69 G7
Banggi *i.* Malaysia 68 F5
Banghāzī Libya *see* **Benghazi**
Banghiang, Xé *r.* Laos 70 D3
Bangka *i.* Indon. 68 D7
Bangka, Selat *sea chan.* Indon. 68 D7
Bangkalan Indon. 68 E8
Bangkaru *i.* Indon. 71 B7
Bangko Indon. 68 C7

▶**Bangkok** Thai. 71 C4
Capital of Thailand.

Bangkok, Bight of *b.* Thai. 71 C4
Bangkor China 83 F3
Bangla *state* India *see* **West Bengal**

▶**Bangladesh** *country* Asia 83 G4
5th most populous country in Asia and 8th in the world.

Bangma Shan *mts* China 76 C4
Bang Mun Nak Thai. 70 C3
Ba Ngoi Vietnam 71 E5
Bangolo Côte d'Ivoire 96 C4
Bangong Co *salt l.* China/India 82 D2
Bangor *Northern Ireland* U.K. 51 G3
Bangor *Wales* U.K. 48 C5
Bangor *ME* U.S.A. 132 G2
Bangor *MI* U.S.A. 134 B2
Bangor *PA* U.S.A. 135 H3
Bangor Erris Ireland 51 C3
Bangs, Mount U.S.A. 129 G3
Bang Saphan Yai Thai. 71 B5
Bangsund Norway 44 G4
Bangued Phil. 69 G3

▶**Bangui** Cent. Afr. Rep. 98 B3
Capital of the Central African Republic.

Bangweulu, Lake Zambia 99 C5
Banhā Egypt 90 C5
Banhine, Parque Nacional de *nat. park* Moz. 101 K2
Ban Hin Heup Laos 70 C3
Ban Houei Sai Laos *see* **Houayxay**
Ban Huai Khon Thai. 70 C3
Ban Huai Yang Thai. 71 B5
Bani, Jebel *ridge* Morocco 54 C6
Bania Cent. Afr. Rep. 98 B3
Bani-Bangou Niger 96 D3
Banifing *r.* Mali 96 C3
Banihal Pass and Tunnel India 82 C2
Banister *r.* U.S.A. 134 F5
Banī Suwayf Egypt 90 C5
Banī Walīd Libya 97 E1
Banī Wuṭayfān *well* Saudi Arabia 88 C5
Bāniyās Israel 85 B3
Bāniyās Syria 85 B2
Bani Yas *reg.* U.A.E. 88 D6
Banja Luka Bos. & Herz. 58 G2
Banjarmasin Indon. 68 E7
Banjës, Liqeni i *resr* Albania 59 I4

▶**Banjul** Gambia 96 B3
Capital of The Gambia.

Banka India 83 F4
Banka Banka Australia 108 F4
Bankapur India 84 B3
Bankass Mali 96 C3
Ban Kèngkabao Laos 70 D3
Ban Khao Yoi Thai. 71 B4
Ban Khok Kloi Thai. 71 B5
Bankilaré Niger 96 D3
Banks Island *B.C.* Canada 120 D4
Banks Island *N.W.T.* Canada 118 F2
Banks Islands Vanuatu 107 G3
Banks Lake Canada 121 M2
Banks Lake U.S.A. 126 D3
Banks Peninsula N.Z. 113 D6
Banks Strait Australia 111 [inset]
Bankura India 83 F5
Ban Lamduan Thai. 71 C4
Banlan China 77 F3
Ban Mae La Luang Thai. 70 B3
Banmaw Myanmar *see* **Bhamo**
Banmo Myanmar *see* **Bhamo**
Bann *r.* Ireland 51 F5
Bann *r.* U.K. 51 F2
Ban Nakham Laos 70 D3
Bannerman Town Bahamas 133 E7
Banning U.S.A. 128 E5
Banningville Dem. Rep. Congo *see* **Bandundu**
Ban Noi Myanmar 70 B3
Ban Nonghèt Laos 70 D3
Ban Nong Kung Thai. 70 D3
Bannu Pak. 89 H3
Bano India 83 F5
Bañolas Spain *see* **Banyoles**
Ban Phai Thai. 70 C3
Ban Phôn Laos *see* **Xékong**
Ban Phôn-Hông Laos 70 C3
Banqiao *Yunnan* China 76 C3
Banqiao *Yunnan* China 76 E3
Bansi *Bihar* India 83 F4
Bansi *Rajasthan* India 82 C4
Bansi *Uttar Prad.* India 82 D4
Bansi *Uttar Prad.* India 83 E4
Bansihari India 83 G4
Banská Bystrica Slovakia 47 Q6
Banspani India 83 F5
Bansur India 82 D4
Ban Sut Ta Thai. 70 B3
Ban Suwan Wari Thai. 70 D4
Banswara India 82 C5
Banteer Ireland 51 D5
Ban Tha Song Yang Thai. 70 B3
Banthat *mts* Cambodia/Thai. *see* **Cardamom Range**
Ban Tha Tum Thai. 70 C4
Ban Tôp Laos 70 D3
Bantry Ireland 51 C6
Bantry Bay Ireland 51 C6
Bantval India 84 B3
Ban Wang Chao Thai. 70 B3
Ban Woen Laos 70 C3
Ban Xepian Laos 70 D4
Banyak, Pulau-pulau *is* Indon. 71 B7
Ban Yang Yong Thai. 71 B4
Banyo Cameroon 96 E4
Banyoles Spain 57 H2
Banyuwangi Indon. 108 A2
Banzare Coast Antarctica 152 G2
Banzare Seamount *sea feature* Indian Ocean 149 N9
Banzart Tunisia *see* **Bizerte**
Banzkow Germany 53 L1
Banzyville Dem. Rep. Congo *see* **Mobayi-Mbongo**
Bao'an China *see* **Shenzhen**
Baochang China 73 L4
Baocheng China 76 E1
Baoding China 73 L5
Baofeng China 77 G1
Baohe China *see* **Weixi**
Baoji China 76 E1
Baokang *Hubei* China 77 F2
Baokang *Nei Mongol* China 74 A3
Bao Lac Vietnam 70 D2
Baolin China 74 C3
Bao Lôc Vietnam 71 D5
Baoqing China 74 D3
Baoro Cent. Afr. Rep. 98 B3
Baoshan China 76 C3
Baotou China 73 K4
Baoulé *r.* Mali 96 C3
Baoxing China 76 D2
Baoying China 77 H1
Baoyou China *see* **Ledong**
Bap India 82 C4
Bapatla India 84 D3
Bapaume France 52 C4
Baptiste Lake Canada 135 F1
Bapu China *see* **Meigu**
Baq'ā' *oasis* Saudi Arabia 91 F6
Baqbaq Egypt *see* **Buqbuq**
Baqên *Xizang* China 76 B1
Baqên *Xizang* China 76 B2
Baqiu China 77 G3
Ba'qūbah Iraq 91 G4
Bar Montenegro 59 H3
Bara Sudan 86 D7
Baraawe Somalia 98 E3
Bara Banki India *see* **Barabanki**
Barabanki India 82 E4
Baraboo U.S.A. 130 F3
Baracaju *r.* Brazil 145 A1
Baracaldo Spain *see* **Barakaldo**
Baracoa Cuba 137 J4
Baradá, Nahr *r.* Syria 85 C3
Baradine Australia 112 D3
Baradine *r.* Australia 112 D3
Baragarh India *see* **Bargarh**
Barahona Dom. Rep. 137 J5
Barail Range *mts* India 83 H4
Baraka *watercourse* Eritrea/Sudan 97 G3
Barakaldo Spain 57 E2
Barakī Barak Afgh. 89 H3
Baralaba Australia 110 E5
Bara Lacha La India 82 D2
Baralzon Lake Canada 121 L3
Baram India 83 F5
Baram *r.* Malaysia 68 E6
Baramati India 84 B2
Baramula India *see* **Baramulla**
Baramulla India 82 C2
Baran India 82 D4
Baran *r.* Pak. 89 H5
Bārān, Kūh-e *mts* Iran 89 F3
Barana Pak. 89 I4
Baranavichy Belarus 45 O10
Barang, Dasht-e *des.* Afgh. 89 F3
Baranikha Russia 65 R3
Baranīs Egypt 86 E5
Baranīs Egypt *see* **Baranīs**
Barannda India 82 E4
Baranof Island U.S.A. 120 C3
Baranovichi Belarus *see* **Baranavichy**
Baranowicze Belarus *see* **Baranavichy**
Baraouéli Mali 96 C3
Baraque de Fraiture *hill* Belgium 52 F4
Barasat India 83 G5
Barat Daya, Kepulauan *is* Indon. 108 D1
Baraut India 82 D3
Barbacena Brazil 145 C3
Barbados *country* West Indies 137 M6
Barbar, Gebel el *mt.* Egypt *see* **Barbar, Jabal**
Barbar, Jabal *mt.* Egypt 85 A5
Barbara Lake Canada 122 D4
Barbastro Spain 57 G2
Barbate Spain 57 D5
Barbaza Phil. 69 G4
Barberton S. Africa 101 J3
Barberton U.S.A. 134 E3
Barbezieux-St-Hilaire France 56 D4
Barbour Bay Canada 121 M2
Barbourville U.S.A. 134 D5
Barbuda *i.* Antigua and Barbuda 137 L5
Barby Germany 53 L3
Barcaldine Australia 110 D4
Barce Libya *see* **Al Marj**
Barcelona Spain 57 H3
Barcelona Venez. 142 F1
Barcelonnette France 56 H4
Barcelos Brazil 142 F4
Barchfeld Germany 53 K4
Barcino Spain *see* **Barcelona**
Barclay de Tolly *atoll* Fr. Polynesia *see* **Raroia**
Barclayville Liberia 96 C4
Barcoo *watercourse* Australia 110 C5
Barcoo Creek *watercourse* Australia *see* **Cooper Creek**
Barcoo National Park Australia *see* **Welford National Park**
Barcs Hungary 58 G2
Bärdä Azer. 91 G2
Bardaï Chad 97 E2
Bárðarbunga *mt.* Iceland 44 [inset 1]
Bardawīl, Khabrat al *salt pan* Saudi Arabia 85 D4
Bardawīl, Sabkhat al *lag.* Egypt 85 A4
Barddhaman India 83 F5
Bardejov Slovakia 43 D6
Bardera Somalia *see* **Baardheere**
Bardeskan Iran 88 E3
Bardhaman India *see* **Barddhaman**
Bardsey Island U.K. 49 C6
Bardsīr Iran 88 E4
Bárðsneshorn *pt* Iceland 40 D2
Bardstown U.S.A. 134 C5
Barduli Italy *see* **Barletta**
Bardwell U.S.A. 131 F4
Bareilly India 82 D3
Barellan Australia 112 C5
Barentin France 49 H9
Barentsburg Svalbard 64 C2
Barents Sea Arctic Ocean 42 I1
Barentu Eritrea 86 E6
Barfleur, Pointe de *pt* France 49 F9
Bargāh Iran 88 E5
Bargarh India 83 E5
Barghamad Iran 88 E2
Bargrennan U.K. 50 E5
Bargteheide Germany 53 K1
Barguna Bangl. 83 G5
Barhaj India 83 E4
Barham Australia 112 B5
Bari Italy 58 G4
Bariadi Tanz. 98 D4
Bari Doab *lowland* Pak. 89 I4
Barika Alg. 54 F4
Barinas Venez. 142 D2
Baripada India 83 F5
Bariri Brazil 145 A3
Bari Sadri India 82 C4
Barisal Bangl. 83 G5
Barisan, Pegunungan *mts* Indon. 68 C7
Barito *r.* Indon. 68 E7
Barium Italy *see* **Bari**
Barkal Bangl. 83 H5
Barkam China 76 D2
Barkan, Ra's-e *pt* Iran 88 C4
Barkava Latvia 45 O8
Bark Lake Canada 135 G1
Barkly East S. Africa 101 H6
Barkly Homestead Australia 110 A3
Barkly-Oos S. Africa *see* **Barkly East**
Barkly Tableland *reg.* Australia 110 A3
Barkly-Wes S. Africa *see* **Barkly West**
Barkly West S. Africa 100 G5
Barkol China 80 H3
Barla Turkey 59 N5
Bârlad Romania 59 L1
Bar-le-Duc France 52 F6
Barlee, Lake *salt flat* Australia 109 B7
Barlee Range *hills* Australia 109 A5
Barletta Italy 58 G4
Barlow Canada 120 B2
Barlow Lake Canada 121 K2
Barmah Forest Australia 112 B5
Barmedman Australia 112 C5
Barmen-Elberfeld Germany *see* **Wuppertal**
Barmer India 82 B4
Barm Fīrūz, Kūh-e *mt.* Iran 88 C4
Barmouth U.K. 49 C6
Barnala India 82 C3
Barnard Castle U.K. 48 F4
Barnato Australia 112 B3
Barnaul Russia 72 E2
Barnegat Bay U.S.A. 135 H4
Barnes Icecap Canada 119 K2
Barnesville *GA* U.S.A. 133 D5
Barnesville *MN* U.S.A. 130 D2
Barneveld Neth. 52 F2
Barneville-Carteret France 49 F9
Barneys Lake *imp. l.* Australia 112 B4
Barney Top *mt.* U.S.A. 129 H3
Barnsley U.K. 48 F5
Barnstable U.S.A. 135 J3
Barnstaple U.K. 49 C7
Barnstaple Bay U.K. 49 C7
Barnstorf Germany 53 I2
Baro Nigeria 96 D4
Baroda *Gujarat* India *see* **Vadodara**
Baroda *Madh. Prad.* India 82 D4
Barong China 76 C2
Barons Range *hills* Australia 109 D6
Barpathar India 76 B3
Barpeta India 83 G4
Bar Pla Soi Thai. *see* **Chon Buri**
Barques, Point Aux U.S.A. 134 D1
Barquisimeto Venez. 142 E1
Barra Brazil 143 J6
Barra *i.* U.K. 50 B4
Barra, Ponta da *pt* Moz. 101 L2
Barra, Sound of *sea chan.* U.K. 50 B3
Barraba Australia 112 E3
Barra Bonita Brazil 145 A3
Barracão do Barreto Brazil 143 G5
Barra do Bugres Brazil 143 G7
Barra do Corda Brazil 143 I5
Barra do Cuieté Brazil 145 C2
Barra do Garças Brazil 143 H7
Barra do Piraí Brazil 145 C3
Barra do São Manuel Brazil 143 G5
Barra do Turvo Brazil 145 A4
Barra Falsa, Ponta da *pt* Moz. 101 L2
Barraigh *i.* U.K. *see* **Barra**
Barra Mansa Brazil 145 B3
Barranca Peru 142 C4
Barranqueras Arg. 144 E3
Barranquilla Col. 142 D1
Barre *MA* U.S.A. 135 I2
Barre *VT* U.S.A. 135 I1
Barre des Écrins *mt.* France 56 H4
Barreiras Brazil 143 J6
Barreirinha Brazil 143 G4
Barreirinhas Brazil 143 J4
Barreiro Port. 57 B4
Barreiros Brazil 143 K5
Barren Island India 71 A4
Barren Island Kiribati *see* **Starbuck Island**
Barren River Lake U.S.A. 134 B5
Barretos Brazil 145 A3
Barrett, Mount *hill* Australia 108 D4
Barrhead Canada 120 H4
Barrhead U.K. 50 E5
Barrie Canada 134 F1
Barrier Bay Antarctica 152 E2
Barrière Canada 120 F5
Barrier Range *hills* Australia 111 C6
Barrington Canada 123 I6
Barrington, Mount Australia 112 E4
Barrington Tops National Park Australia 112 E4
Barringun Australia 112 B2
Barro Alto Brazil 145 A1
Barrocão Brazil 145 C2
Barron U.S.A. 130 F2
Barrow *r.* Ireland 51 F5
Barrow U.S.A. 118 C2
Barrow, Point *pt* U.S.A. 118 C2
Barrow Creek Australia 108 F5
Barrow-in-Furness U.K. 48 D4
Barrow Island Australia 108 A5
Barrow Range *hills* Australia 109 D6
Barrow Strait Canada 119 I2
Barr Smith Range *hills* Australia 109 C6
Barry U.K. 49 D7
Barrydale S. Africa 100 E7
Barry Mountains Australia 112 C6
Barrys Bay Canada 135 G1
Barryville U.S.A. 135 H3
Barsalpur India 82 C3
Barshatas Kazakh. 80 E2
Barshi India *see* **Barsi**
Barsi India 84 B2
Barsinghausen Germany 53 J2
Barstow U.S.A. 128 E4
Barsur India 84 D2
Bar-sur-Aube France 56 G2
Bartang Tajik. 89 H2
Barth Germany 47 N3
Bartica Guyana 143 G2
Bartın Turkey 90 D2
Bartle Frere, Mount Australia 110 D3
Bartlett U.S.A. 130 D3
Bartlett Reservoir U.S.A. 129 H5
Barton U.S.A. 135 I1
Barton-upon-Humber U.K. 48 G5
Bartoszyce Poland 47 R3
Bartow U.S.A. 133 D7
Barú, Volcán *vol.* Panama 137 H7
Barung *i.* Indon. 68 E8
Barunga Australia *see* **Bamyili**
Barun-Torey, Ozero *l.* Russia 73 L2
Barus Indon. 71 B7
Baruunturuun Mongolia 80 H2
Baruun-Urt Mongolia 73 K3
Baruva India 84 E2
Barwani India 82 C5
Barwéli Mali *see* **Baraouéli**
Barwon *r.* Australia 112 C3
Barygaza India *see* **Bharuch**
Barysaw Belarus 45 P9
Barysh Russia 43 J5
Basaga Turkm. 89 G2
Basăk, Tônlé *r.* Cambodia 71 D5
Basalt *r.* Australia 110 D3
Basalt Island *H.K.* China 77 [inset]
Basankusu Dem. Rep. Congo 98 B3
Basar India 84 C2
Basarabi Romania 59 M2
Basargechar Armenia *see* **Vardenis**
Basaseachic, Parque Nacional Cascada de *nat. park* Mex. 127 F7
Bascuñán, Cabo *c.* Chile 144 B3
Basel Switz. 56 H3
Bāsh Ābdān Afgh. 89 H2
Bashäkerd, Kūhhā-ye *mts* Iran 88 E5
Bashanta Russia *see* **Gorodovikovsk**
Bashaw Canada 120 H4
Bāshī Iran 88 C4
Bashi Channel Phil./Taiwan 69 G2
Bashmakovo Russia 43 I5
Bāsht Iran 88 C4
Bashtanka Ukr. 43 G7
Basi *Punjab* India 82 D3
Basi *Rajasthan* India 82 D4
Basia India 83 F5
Basilan *i.* Phil. 69 G5
Basildon U.K. 49 H7
Basile, Pico *mt.* Equat. Guinea 96 D4
Basin U.S.A. 126 F3
Basingstoke U.K. 49 F7
Basin Lake Canada 121 J4
Basirhat India 83 G5
Basīṭ, Ra's al *pt* Syria 85 B2
Başkale Turkey 91 G3
Baskatong, Réservoir *resr* Canada 122 G5
Baskerville, Cape Australia 108 C4
Başkomutan Tarıhı Milli Parkı *nat. park* Turkey 59 N5
Başköy Turkey 85 A1
Baskunchak, Ozero *l.* Russia 43 J6
Basle Switz. *see* **Basel**
Basmat India 84 C2
Basoko Dem. Rep. Congo 98 C3
Basol *r.* Pak. 89 G5
Basra Iraq 91 G5
Bassano Canada 121 H5
Bassano del Grappa Italy 58 D2
Bassar Togo 96 D4
Bassas da India *reef* Indian Ocean 99 D6
Bassas de Pedro Padua Bank *sea feature* India 84 B3
Bassein Myanmar 70 A3
Bassein *r.* Myanmar 70 A3
Bassenthwaite Lake U.K. 48 D4
Basse Santa Su Gambia 96 B3

▶**Basse-Terre** Guadeloupe 137 L5
Capital of Guadeloupe.

▶**Basseterre** St Kitts and Nevis 137 L5
Capital of St Kitts and Nevis.

Bassett *NE* U.S.A. 130 D3
Bassett *VA* U.S.A. 134 F5
Bassikounou Mauritania 96 C3
Bass Rock *i.* U.K. 50 G4
Bass Strait Australia 111 D8
Bassum Germany 53 I2
Basswood Lake Canada 122 C4
Båstad Sweden 45 H8
Bastheim Germany 53 K4
Basti India 83 E4
Bastia *Corsica* France 56 I5
Bastioes *r.* Brazil 143 K5
Bastogne Belgium 52 F4
Bastrop *LA* U.S.A. 131 F5
Bastrop *TX* U.S.A. 131 D6
Basuo China *see* **Dongfang**
Basutoland *country* Africa *see* **Lesotho**
Başyayla Turkey 85 A1
Bata Equat. Guinea 96 D4
Batabanó, Golfo de *b.* Cuba 137 H4
Batagay Russia 65 O3
Batala India 82 C3
Batalha Port. 57 B4
Batam Indon. 71 D7
Batam *i.* Indon. 71 D7
Batamay Russia 65 N3
Batamshy Kazakh. *see* **Badamsha**
Batan *Jiangsu* China 77 I1
Batan *Qinghai* China 76 D1
Batan *i.* Phil. 69 G2
Batang China 76 C2
Batangafo Cent. Afr. Rep. 98 B3
Batangas Phil. 69 G4
Batangtoru Indon. 71 B7
Batan Islands Phil. 69 G2
Batavia Indon. *see* **Jakarta**
Batavia *NY* U.S.A. 135 F2
Batavia *OH* U.S.A. 134 C4
Bataysk Russia 43 H7
Batchawana Mountain *hill* Canada 122 D5
Bătdâmbâng Cambodia 71 C4
Bateemeucica, Gunung *mt.* Indon. 71 A6
Batéké, Plateaux Congo 98 B4
Batemans Bay Australia 112 E5
Bates Range *hills* Australia 109 C6
Batesville *AR* U.S.A. 131 F5
Batesville *IN* U.S.A. 134 C4
Batesville *MS* U.S.A. 131 F5
Batetskiy Russia 42 F4
Bath *N.B.* Canada 123 I5
Bath *Ont.* Canada 135 G1
Bath U.K. 49 E7
Bath *ME* U.S.A. 135 K2
Bath *NY* U.S.A. 135 G2
Bath *PA* U.S.A. 135 H3
Batha *watercourse* Chad 97 E3
Bathéay Cambodia 71 D5
Bathgate U.K. 50 F5
Bathinda India 82 C3
Bathurst Australia 112 D4
Bathurst Canada 123 I5
Bathurst Gambia *see* **Banjul**
Bathurst S. Africa 101 H7
Bathurst, Cape Canada 118 F2
Bathurst, Lake Australia 112 D5
Bathurst Inlet *inlet* Canada 118 H3
Bathurst Inlet (abandoned) Canada 118 H3
Bathurst Island Australia 108 E2
Bathurst Island Canada 119 I2
Bathyz Döwlet Gorugy *nature res.* Turkm. 89 F3
Batié Burkina Faso 96 C4
Batı Menteşe Dağları *mts* Turkey 59 L6
Batı Toroslar *mts* Turkey 59 N6
Batken Kyrg. 80 D4
Bāṭlāq-e Gavkhūnī *marsh* Iran 88 D3
Batley U.K. 48 F5
Batlow Australia 112 D5
Batman Turkey 91 F3
Batna Alg. 54 F4
Batok, Bukit *hill* Sing. 71 [inset]

▶**Baton Rouge** U.S.A. 131 F6
Capital of Louisiana.

Batopilas Mex. 127 G8
Batouri Cameroon 97 E4
Batrā' *tourist site* Jordan *see* **Petra**
Batrā', Jabal al *mt.* Jordan 85 B5
Batroûn Lebanon 85 B2
Båtsfjord Norway 44 P1
Battambang Cambodia *see* **Bătdâmbâng**
Batticaloa Sri Lanka 84 D5
Batti Malv *i.* India 71 A5
Battipaglia Italy 58 F4
Battle *r.* Canada 121 I4
Battle Creek U.S.A. 134 C2
Battleford Canada 121 I4
Battle Mountain U.S.A. 128 E1
Battle Mountain *mt.* U.S.A. 128 E1
Battura Glacier Pak. 82 C1
Batu *mt.* Eth. 98 D3
Batu, Pulau-pulau *is* Indon. 68 B7
Batudaka *i.* Indon. 69 G7
Batu Gajah Malaysia 71 C6
Batum Georgia *see* **Bat'umi**
Bat'umi Georgia 91 F2
Batu Pahat Malaysia 71 C7
Batu Putih, Gunung *mt.* Malaysia 71 C6
Baturaja Indon. 68 C7
Baturité Brazil 143 K4
Batyrevo Russia 43 J5
Batys Qazaqstan *admin. div.* Kazakh. *see* **Zapadnyy Kazakhstan**
Bau *Sarawak* Malaysia 68 E6
Baubau Indon. 69 G8
Baucau East Timor 108 D2
Bauchi Nigeria 96 D3
Bauda India 84 E1
Baudette U.S.A. 130 E1
Baudh India *see* **Bauda**
Baugé-en-Anjou France 56 D3
Bauhinia Australia 110 E5
Baukau East Timor *see* **Baucau**
Bauld, Cape Canada 123 L4
Baume-les-Dames France 56 H3
Baunach *r.* Germany 53 K5
Baura Bangl. 83 G4
Bauru Brazil 145 A3
Bausendorf Germany 52 G4
Bauska Latvia 45 N8
Bautino Kazakh. 91 H1
Bautzen Germany 47 O5
Bavānāt Iran 88 D4
Bavaria *land* Germany *see* **Bayern**
Bavaria *reg.* Germany 53 L6
Bavda India 84 B2
Baviaanskloofberge *mts* S. Africa 100 F7
Bavispe *r.* Mex. 127 F7
Bavla India 82 C5
Bavly Russia 41 Q5
Baw Myanmar 70 A2
Bawal India 82 D3
Baw Baw National Park Australia 112 C6
Bawdeswell U.K. 49 I6
Bawdwin Myanmar 70 B2
Bawean *i.* Indon. 68 E8
Bawinkel Germany 53 H2
Bawlake Myanmar 70 B3
Bawolung China 76 D2
Baxi China 76 D1
Baxley U.S.A. 133 D6
Baxoi China 76 C2
Baxter Mountain U.S.A. 129 J2
Bay China *see* **Baicheng**
Bayamo Cuba 137 I4
Bayan *Heilong.* China 74 B3
Bayan *Qinghai* China 76 C1
Bayana India 82 D4
Bayan-Adarga Mongolia 73 K3
Bayanaul Kazakh. 80 E1
Bayanbulak China 80 F3
Bayanday Russia 72 J2
Bayan Gol China *see* **Dengkou**
Bayan Har Shan *mts* China 76 B1
Bayan Har Shankou *pass* China 76 C1
Bayanhongor Mongolia 80 J2
Bayan Hot China 72 J5
Bayanlū Iran 88 B3
Bayannur China 73 J4
Bayan Obo China 73 J4
Bayan Shutu China 73 K4
Bayantsagaan Mongolia 80 I2
Bayan Ul China 73 L4
Bayan-Uul Mongolia 73 K3
Bayard U.S.A. 129 I5
Bayat Turkey 59 N5
Bayāẕ Iran 88 E4
Bayāẕīyeh Iran 88 D3
Baybay Phil. 69 G4
Bayboro U.S.A. 133 E5
Bayburt Turkey 91 F2
Bay Canh, Hon *i.* Vietnam 71 D5
Bay City *MI* U.S.A. 134 D2
Bay City *TX* U.S.A. 131 D6
Baydaratskaya Guba Russia 64 H3
Baydhabo Somalia 98 E3
Bayerischer Wald *mts* Germany 47 N6
Bayerischer Wald, Nationalpark *nat. park* Germany 47 N6
Bayern *land* Germany 53 L6
Bayeux France 49 G9
Bayfield Canada 134 E2
Bayındır Turkey 59 L5
Bay Islands *is* Hond. *see* **Bahía, Islas de la**
Bayizhen China *see* **Nyingchi**
Bayjī Iraq 91 F4
Baykal, Ozero *l.* Russia *see* **Baikal, Lake**
Baykal-Amur Magistral Russia 74 C1
Baykal Range *mts* Russia *see* **Baykal'skiy Khrebet**
Baykal'skiy Khrebet *mts* Russia 73 J2
Baykan Turkey 91 F3
Bay-Khaak Russia 80 H1
Baykibashevo Russia 41 R4
Baykonur Kazakh. *see* **Baykonyr**
Baykonyr Kazakh. 80 B2
Baymak Russia 64 G4
Bay Minette U.S.A. 133 C6
Baynūna'h *reg.* U.A.E. 88 D6
Bayombong Phil. 69 G3
Bayona Spain *see* **Baiona**
Bayonne France 56 D5
Bayonne U.S.A. 135 H3
Bay Port U.S.A. 134 D2
Bayqongyr Kazakh. *see* **Baykonyr**
Bayram-Ali Turkm. *see* **Baýramaly**
Baýramaly Turkm. 89 F2
Bayramiç Turkey 59 L5
Bayreuth Germany 53 L5
Bayrūt Lebanon *see* **Beirut**
Bays, Lake of Canada 134 F1
Bay Shore *MI* U.S.A. 134 C1
Bay Shore *NY* U.S.A. 135 I3
Bay Springs U.S.A. 131 F6
Bayston Hill U.K. 49 E6
Baysun Uzbek. *see* **Boysun**
Bayt Jālā West Bank 85 B4
Bayt Lahm West Bank *see* **Bethlehem**
Baytown U.S.A. 131 E6
Bay View N.Z. 113 F4
Bayy al Kabīr, Wādī *watercourse* Libya 97 E1
Baza Spain 57 E5
Baza, Sierra de *mts* Spain 57 E5
Bāzārak Afgh. 89 G3
Bazardüzü Dağı *mt.* Azer./Russia *see* **Bazardyuzyu, Gora**
Bazardyuzyu, Gora *mt.* Azer./Russia 91 G2
Bāzār-e Māsāl Iran 88 C2
Bazarnyy Karabulak Russia 43 J5
Bazaruto, Ilha do *i.* Moz. 99 D6
Bazdar Pak. 89 G5
Bazhong China 76 E2
Bazhou China *see* **Bazhong**
Bazin *r.* Canada 122 G5
Bazmān Iran 89 F5
Bazmān, Kūh-e *mt.* Iran 89 F4
Bcharré Lebanon 85 C2
Be, Sông *r.* Vietnam 71 D5
Beach U.S.A. 130 C2
Beachy Head *hd* U.K. 49 H8
Beacon U.S.A. 135 I3
Beacon Bay S. Africa 101 H7
Beaconsfield U.K. 49 G7
Beagle, Canal *sea chan.* Arg. 144 C8
Beagle Bank *reef* Australia 108 C3
Beagle Bay Australia 108 C4
Beagle Gulf Australia 108 E3
Bealanana Madag. 99 E5
Béal an Átha Ireland *see* **Ballina**
Béal an Mhuirthead Ireland 51 C3
Béal Átha na Sluaighe Ireland *see* **Ballinasloe**

Beale, Lake India 84 B2
Beaminster U.K. 49 E8
Bear r. U.S.A. 126 E4
Bearalváhki Norway see Berlevåg
Bear Cove Point Canada 121 O2
Beardmore Canada 122 D4
Beardmore Glacier Antarctica 152 H1
Bear Island Arctic Ocean see Bjørnøya
Bear Island Canada 122 E3
Bear Lake l. Canada 122 A3
Bear Lake U.S.A. 134 B1
Bear Lake l. U.S.A. 126 F4
Bearma r. India 82 D4
Bear Mountain U.S.A. 130 C3
Bearnaraigh i. U.K. see Berneray
Bear Paw Mountain U.S.A. 126 F2
Bearpaw Mountains U.S.A. 126 F2
Bearskin Lake Canada 121 N4
Beas Dam India 82 C3
Beata, Cabo c. Dom. Rep. 137 J5
Beatrice U.S.A. 130 D3
Beatrice, Cape Australia 110 B2
Beatton r. Canada 120 F3
Beatton River Canada 120 F3
Beatty U.S.A. 128 E3
Beattyville Canada 122 F4
Beattyville U.S.A. 134 D5
Beaucaire France 56 G5
Beauchene Island Falkland Is 144 E8
Beaufort Australia 112 A6
Beaufort NC U.S.A. 133 E5
Beaufort SC U.S.A. 133 D5
Beaufort Island H.K. China 77 [inset]
Beaufort Sea Canada/U.S.A. 118 D2
Beaufort West S. Africa 100 F7
Beaulieu r. Canada 121 H2
Beauly U.K. 50 E3
Beauly r. U.K. 50 E3
Beaumaris U.K. 48 C5
Beaumont Belgium 52 E4
Beaumont N.Z. 113 B7
Beaumont MS U.S.A. 131 F6
Beaumont TX U.S.A. 131 E6
Beaune France 56 G3
Beaupréau France 56 D3
Beauquesne France 52 C4
Beauraing Belgium 52 E4
Beauséjour Canada 121 L5
Beauvais France 52 C5
Beauval France 52 C4
Beaver r. Alta/Sask. Canada 121 J4
Beaver r. Ont. Canada 122 D3
Beaver r. Y.T. Canada 120 E3
Beaver OK U.S.A. 131 C4
Beaver PA U.S.A. 134 E3
Beaver UT U.S.A. 129 G2
Beaver r. U.S.A. 129 G2
Beaver Creek Canada 153 A2
Beavercreek U.S.A. 134 C4
Beaver Creek r. MT U.S.A. 130 B1
Beaver Creek r. ND U.S.A. 130 C2
Beaver Dam KY U.S.A. 134 B5
Beaver Dam WI U.S.A. 130 F3
Beaver Falls U.S.A. 134 E3
Beaverhead Mountains U.S.A. 126 E3
Beaverhill Lake Alta Canada 121 H4
Beaver Hill Lake Canada 121 M4
Beaverhill Lake N.W.T. Canada 121 J2
Beaver Island U.S.A. 132 C2
Beaverlodge Canada 120 G4
Beaverton Canada 134 F1
Beaverton MI U.S.A. 134 C2
Beaverton OR U.S.A. 126 C3
Beawar India 82 C4
Beazley Arg. 144 C4
Bebedouro Brazil 145 A3
Bebington U.K. 48 D5
Bebra Germany 53 J4
Bêca China 76 C2
Bécard, Lac l. Canada 123 G1
Beccles U.K. 49 I6
Bečej Serbia 59 I2
Becerreá Spain 57 C2
Béchar Alg. 54 D5
Bechhofen Germany 53 K5
Bechuanaland country Africa see Botswana
Beckley U.S.A. 134 E5
Beckum Germany 53 I3
Becky Peak U.S.A. 129 F2
Bečov nad Teplou Czechia 53 M4
Bedale U.K. 48 F4
Bedburg Germany 52 G4
Bedelē Eth. 98 D3
Bedford N.S. Canada 123 J5
Bedford Que. Canada 135 I1
Bedford E. Cape S. Africa 101 H7
Bedford KwaZulu-Natal S. Africa 101 J5
Bedford U.K. 49 G6
Bedford IN U.S.A. 134 B4
Bedford KY U.S.A. 134 C4
Bedford PA U.S.A. 135 F3
Bedford VA U.S.A. 134 F5
Bedford, Cape Australia 110 D2
Bedford Downs Australia 108 D4
Bedgerebong Australia 112 C4
Bedi India 82 B5
Bedla India 82 C4
Bedlington U.K. 48 F3
Bedok Sing. 71 [inset]
Bedok Jetty Sing. 71 [inset]
Bedok Reservoir Sing. 71 [inset]
Bedourie Australia 110 B5
Bedum Neth. 52 G1
Bedworth U.K. 49 F6
Beechworth Australia 112 C6
Beechy Canada 121 J5
Beecroft Peninsula Australia 112 E5
Beed India see Bid
Beelitz Germany 53 M2
Beenleigh Australia 112 F1
Beernem Belgium 52 D3
Beersheba Israel 85 B4
Be'ér Sheva' Israel see Beersheba
Be'ér Sheva', Naḥal watercourse Israel 85 B4
Beervlei Dam S. Africa 100 F7
Beerwah Australia 112 F1
Beetaloo Australia 108 F4
Beethoven Peninsula Antarctica 152 L2
Beeville U.S.A. 131 D6
Befori Dem. Rep. Congo 98 C3
Beg, Lough l. U.K. 51 F3
Bega Australia 112 D6
Begari r. Pak. 89 H4
Begicheva, Ostrov i. Russia see Bol'shoy Begichev, Ostrov
Begur, Cap de c. Spain 57 H3
Begusarai India 83 F4
Behābād Iran 88 D4
Béhague, Pointe pt Fr. Guiana 143 H3
Behbahān Iran 88 C4
Behchokǫ̀ Canada 120 G2
Behrūsī Iran 88 D4
Behshahr Iran 88 D2
Bei'an China 74 B2
Bei'ao China see Dongtou
Beibei China 76 E2
Beichuan China see Qushan
Beida Libya see Al Bayḍā'
Beigang Taiwan 77 I4
Beiguan China see Anyang
Beihai China 77 F4
Bei Hulsan Hu salt l. China 83 H1

▶Beijing China 73 L5
Capital of China. 5th most populous city in Asia and 8th in the world.

Beijing mun. China 73 L4
Beik Myanmar see Myeik
Beilen Neth. 52 G2
Beiliu China 77 F4
Beilngries Germany 53 L5
Beiluheyan China 76 B1
Beinn an Oir hill U.K. 50 D5
Beinn an Tuirc hill U.K. 50 D5
Beinn Bheigeir hill U.K. 50 C5
Beinn Bhreac hill U.K. 50 D4
Beinn Dearg mt. U.K. 50 E3
Beinn Heasgarnich mt. U.K. 50 E4
Beinn Mholach hill U.K. 50 C2
Beinn Mhòr hill U.K. 50 B3
Beinn na Faoghlia i. U.K. see Benbecula
Beipan Jiang r. China 76 E3
Beipiao China 73 M4
Beira Moz. 99 D5

▶Beirut Lebanon 85 B3
Capital of Lebanon.

Bei Shan mts China 80 I3
Beitbridge Zimbabwe 99 C6
Beith U.K. 50 E5
Beja Port. 57 C4
Béja Tunisia 58 C6
Bejaïa Alg. 57 I5
Béjar Spain 57 D3
Beji r. Pak. 80 C6
Bekaa valley Lebanon see El Béqaa
Békés Hungary 59 I1
Békéscsaba Hungary 59 I1
Bekily Madag. 99 E6
Bēkma, Sadd dam Iraq 91 G3
Bekovo Russia 43 I5
Bekwai Ghana 96 C4
Bela India 83 E4
Bela Pak. 89 G5
Belab r. Pak. 89 H4
Bela-Bela S. Africa 101 I3
Bélabo Cameroon 96 E4
Bela Crkva Serbia 59 I2
Belagavi India 84 B3
Bel Air U.S.A. 135 G4
Belalcázar Spain 57 D4
Bělá nad Radbuzou Czechia 53 M5
Belapur India 84 B2
Belarus country Europe 43 E5
Belau country N. Pacific Ocean see Palau
Bela Vista Brazil 144 E2
Bela Vista Moz. 101 K4
Bela Vista de Goiás Brazil 145 A2
Belawan Indon. 71 B7
Belaya r. Russia 65 S3 also known as Bila
Belaya Glina Russia 43 I7
Belaya Kalitva Russia 43 I6
Belaya Kholunitsa Russia 42 K4
Belaya Tserkva Ukr. see Bila Tserkva
Belbédji Niger 96 D3
Bełchatów Poland 47 Q5
Belcher U.S.A. 134 D5
Belcher Islands Canada 122 F2
Belcoo U.K. 51 E3
Belden U.S.A. 128 C1
Belding U.S.A. 134 C2
Beleapani reef India see Cherbaniani Reef
Belebey Russia 41 Q5
Beledweyne Somalia 98 E3
Belém Brazil 143 I4
Belém Novo Brazil 145 A5
Belén Arg. 144 C3
Belen Antalya Turkey 85 A1
Belen Hatay Turkey 85 C1
Belen U.S.A. 127 G6
Belep, Îles is New Caledonia 107 G3
Belev Russia 43 H5

▶Belfast U.K. 51 G3
Capital of Northern Ireland.

Belfast U.S.A. 132 G2
Belfast Lough inlet U.K. 51 G3
Bēlfodiyo Eth. 98 D2
Belford U.K. 48 F3
Belfort France 56 H3
Belgaum India see Belagavi
Belgern Germany 53 N3
Belgian Congo country Africa see Congo, Democratic Republic of the
België country Europe see Belgium
Belgique country Europe see Belgium
Belgium country Europe 52 E4
Belgorod Russia 43 H6
Belgorod-Dnestrovskyy Ukr. see Bilhorod-Dnistrovs'kyy

▶Belgrade Serbia 59 I2
Capital of Serbia.

Belgrade ME U.S.A. 135 K1
Belgrade MT U.S.A. 126 F3
Belgrano II research station Antarctica 152 A1
Belice r. Sicily Italy 58 E6
Belinskiy Russia 43 I5
Belinyu Indon. 68 D7
Belitung i. Indon. 68 D7
Belize Angola 99 B4

▶Belize Belize 136 G5
Former capital of Belize.

Belize country Central America 136 G5
Beljak Austria see Villach
Belkina, Mys pt Russia 74 E3
Bel'kovskiy, Ostrov i. Russia 65 O2
Bell Australia 112 E1
Bell r. Australia 112 D4
Bell r. Canada 122 F4
Bella Bella Canada 120 D4
Bellac France 56 E3
Bella Coola Canada 120 E4
Bellaire U.S.A. 134 C1
Bellary India see Ballari
Bellata Australia 112 D2
Bella Unión Uruguay 144 E4
Bella Vista U.S.A. 128 B1
Bellbrook Australia 112 F3
Bell Cay reef Australia 110 E4
Belledonne mts France 56 G4
Bellefontaine U.S.A. 134 D3
Bellefonte U.S.A. 135 G3
Belle Fourche U.S.A. 130 C2
Belle Fourche r. U.S.A. 130 C2
Belle Glade U.S.A. 133 D7
Belle-Île i. France 56 C3
Belle Isle i. Canada 123 L4
Belle Isle, Strait of Canada 123 K4
Belleville Canada 135 G1
Belleville IL U.S.A. 130 F4
Belleville KS U.S.A. 130 D4
Bellevue IA U.S.A. 130 F3
Bellevue MI U.S.A. 134 C2
Bellevue OH U.S.A. 134 D3
Bellevue WA U.S.A. 126 C3
Bellin Canada see Kangirsuk
Bellingham U.K. 48 E3
Bellingham U.S.A. 126 C2
Bellingshausen research station Antarctica 152 A2
Bellingshausen Sea Antarctica 152 L2
Bellinzona Switz. 56 I3
Bellows Falls U.S.A. 135 I2
Bellpat Pak. 89 H4
Belluno Italy 58 E1
Bell Ville Arg. 144 D4
Bellville S. Africa 100 D7
Belm Germany 53 I2
Belmont Australia 112 E4
Belmont U.K. 50 [inset]
Belmont U.S.A. 135 F2
Belmonte Brazil 145 D1

▶Belmopan Belize 136 G5
Capital of Belize.

Belmore, Mount hill Australia 112 F2
Belo Madag. 99 E6
Belo Campo Brazil 145 C1
Belœil Belgium 52 D4
Belogorsk Crimea see Bilohirs'k
Belogorsk Russia 74 C2
Beloha Madag. 99 E6
Belo Horizonte Brazil 145 C2
Beloit KS U.S.A. 130 D4
Beloit WI U.S.A. 130 F3
Belokurikha Russia 80 F1
Belo Monte Brazil 143 H4
Belomorsk Russia 42 G2
Belonia India 83 G5
Belorechensk Russia 91 E1
Belorechenskaya Russia see Belorechensk
Belören Turkey 90 D3
Beloretsk Russia 64 G4
Belorussia country Europe see Belarus
Belorusskaya S.S.R. country Europe see Belarus
Belostok Poland see Białystok
Belot, Lac l. Canada 118 F3
Belo Tsiribihina Madag. 99 E5
Belovo Russia 72 F2
Beloyarskiy Russia 41 T3
Beloye, Ozero l. Russia 42 H3
Beloye More sea Russia see White Sea
Belozersk Russia 42 H3
Belpre U.S.A. 134 E4
Beltana Australia 111 B6
Belted Range mts U.S.A. 128 E3
Belton U.S.A. 131 D6
Bel'ts' Moldova see Bălți
Bel'tsy Moldova see Bălți
Belukha, Gora mt. Kazakh./Russia 80 G2
Belush'ye Russia 42 J2
Belvidere IL U.S.A. 130 F3
Belvidere NJ U.S.A. 135 H3
Belyando r. Australia 110 D4
Belyayevka Ukr. see Bilyayivka
Belyy Russia 42 G5
Belyy, Ostrov i. Russia 64 I2
Belzoni U.S.A. 131 F5
Bemaraha, Plateau du Madag. 99 E5
Bembe Angola 99 B4
Bemidji U.S.A. 130 E2
Béna Burkina Faso 96 C3
Bena Dibele Dem. Rep. Congo 98 C4
Ben Alder mt. U.K. 50 E4
Benalla Australia 112 B6
Benares India see Varanasi
Ben Arous Tunisia 58 D6
Benavente Spain 57 D2
Ben Avon mt. U.K. 50 F3
Benbane Head hd U.K. 51 F2
Benbecula i. U.K. 50 B3
Ben Boyd National Park Australia 112 E6
Benburb U.K. 51 F3
Bencha China 77 I1
Ben Chonzie hill U.K. 50 F4
Ben Cleuch hill U.K. 50 F4
Ben Cruachan mt. U.K. 50 D4
Bend U.S.A. 126 C3
Bendearg mt. S. Africa 101 H6
Bender Moldova 59 M1
Bender-Bayla Somalia 98 F3
Bendery Moldova see Bender
Bendigo Australia 112 B6
Bendoc Australia 112 D6
Bene Moz. 99 D5
Benedict, Mount hill Canada 123 K3
Benenitra Madag. 99 E6
Benešov Czechia 47 O6
Bénestroff France 52 G6
Benevento Italy 58 F4
Beneventum Italy see Benevento
Benezette U.S.A. 135 F3
Beng, Nâm r. Laos 70 C3
Bengal, Bay of sea Indian Ocean 81 G8
Bengaluru India 84 C3
Bengamisa Dem. Rep. Congo 98 C3
Bengbu China 77 H1
Benghazi Libya 97 F1
Bengkalis Indon. 71 C7
Bengkalis i. Indon. 71 C7
Bengkulu Indon. 68 C7
Bengtsfors Sweden 45 H7
Benguela Angola 99 B5
Benha Egypt see Banhā
Ben Hiant hill U.K. 50 C4
Ben Hope hill U.K. 50 E2
Ben Horn hill U.K. 50 E2
Beni r. Bol. 142 E6
Beni Dem. Rep. Congo 98 C3
Beni Nepal 83 E3
Beni Abbès Alg. 54 D5
Beniah Lake Canada 121 H2
Benidorm Spain 57 F4
Beni Hammad, Al Qal'a tourist site Alg. 57 I6
Beni Mellal Morocco 54 C5
Benin country Africa 96 D4
Benin, Bight of g. Africa 96 D4
Benin City Nigeria 96 D4
Beni Saf Alg. 57 F6
Beni Snassen, Monts des mts Morocco 57 E6
Beni Suef Egypt see Banī Suwayf
Benito, Islas is Mex. 127 E7
Benito Juárez Arg. 144 E5
Benito Juárez Mex. 129 F5
Benjamin U.S.A. 131 D5
Benjamin Constant Brazil 142 E4
Benjamín Hill Mex. 127 F7
Benjina Indon. 69 I8
Benkelman U.S.A. 130 C3
Ben Klibreck hill U.K. 50 E2
Ben Lavin Nature Reserve S. Africa 101 I2
Ben Lawers mt. U.K. 50 E4
Ben Lomond mt. Australia 112 E3
Ben Lomond hill U.K. 50 E4
Ben Lomond National Park Australia 111 [inset]
Ben Macdui mt. U.K. 50 F3
Benmara Australia 110 B3
Ben More hill U.K. 50 C4
Ben More mt. U.K. 50 E4
Benmore, Lake N.Z. 113 C7
Ben More Assynt hill U.K. 50 E2
Bennäs Fin. 44 M5
Bennetta, Ostrov i. Russia 65 P2
Bennett Island Russia see Bennetta, Ostrov
Bennett Lake Canada 120 C3
Bennettsville U.S.A. 133 E5
Ben Nevis mt. U.K. 50 D4
Bennington NH U.S.A. 135 J2
Bennington VT U.S.A. 135 I2
Benoni S. Africa 101 I4
Bénoué, Parc National de la nat. park Cameroon 97 E4
Ben Rinnes hill U.K. 50 F3
Bensheim Germany 53 I5
Benson AZ U.S.A. 129 H6
Benson MN U.S.A. 130 E2
Benta Seberang Malaysia 71 C6
Benteng Indon. 69 G8
Bentinck Island Myanmar 71 B5
Bentiu South Sudan 86 C8
Bent Jbaïl Lebanon 85 B3
Bentley U.K. 48 F5
Bento Gonçalves Brazil 145 A5
Benton AR U.S.A. 131 E5
Benton CA U.S.A. 128 D3
Benton IL U.S.A. 130 F4
Benton KY U.S.A. 131 F4
Benton LA U.S.A. 131 E5
Benton MO U.S.A. 131 F4
Benton PA U.S.A. 135 G3
Bentong Malaysia see Bentung
Benton Harbor U.S.A. 134 B2
Bentonville U.S.A. 131 E4
Bên Tre Vietnam 71 D5
Bentung Malaysia 71 C7
Benue r. Nigeria 96 D4
Benum, Gunung mt. Malaysia 71 C7
Ben Vorlich hill U.K. 50 E4
Benwee Head hd Ireland 51 C3
Benwood U.S.A. 134 E3
Ben Wyvis mt. U.K. 50 E3
Benxi Liaoning China 74 A4
Benxi Liaoning China 74 B4
Beograd Serbia see Belgrade
Béoumi Côte d'Ivoire 96 C4
Beppu Japan 75 C6
Béqaa valley Lebanon see El Béqaa
Berach r. India 82 C4
Beraketa Madag. 99 E6
Bérard, Lac l. Canada 123 H2
Berasia India 82 D5
Berat Albania 59 H4
Beravina Madag. 99 E5
Berbak, Taman Nasional nat. park Indon. 68 C7
Berber Sudan 86 D6
Berbera Somalia 98 E2
Berbérati Cent. Afr. Rep. 98 B3
Berchtesgaden, Nationalpark nat. park Germany 47 N7
Berck France 52 B4
Berdichev Ukr. see Berdychiv
Berdigestyakh Russia 65 N3
Berdyans'k Ukr. 43 H7
Berdychiv Ukr. 43 F6
Berea KY U.S.A. 134 C5
Berea OH U.S.A. 134 E3
Beregovo Ukr. see Berehove
Beregovoy Russia 74 B1
Berehove Ukr. 43 D6
Bereina P.N.G. 69 L8
Bere Island Ireland 51 C6
Bereket Turkm. 88 D2
Berekum Ghana 96 C4
Berenice Egypt see Baranīs
Berenice Libya see Benghazi
Berens r. Canada 121 L4
Berens Island Canada 121 L4
Berens River Canada 121 L4
Beresford U.S.A. 130 D3
Bereza Belarus see Byaroza
Berezino Belarus see Byerazino
Berezivka Ukr. 43 F7
Berezne Ukr. 43 E6
Bereznik Russia 42 I3
Berezniki Russia 41 R4
Berezov Russia see Berezovo
Berezovka Russia 74 B2
Berezovka Ukr. see Berezivka
Berezovo Russia 41 T3
Berezovyy Russia 74 D2
Berga Germany 53 L3
Berga Spain 57 G2
Bergama Turkey 59 L5
Bergamo Italy 58 C2
Bergby Sweden 45 J6
Bergen Germany 53 J2
Bergen Norway 45 D6
Bergen U.S.A. 135 G2
Bergen auf Rügen Germany 47 N3
Bergen op Zoom Neth. 52 E3
Bergerac France 56 E4
Bergères-lès-Vertus France 52 E6
Bergheim Germany 52 G4
Bergisches Land reg. Germany 53 H4
Bergisch Gladbach Germany 52 H4
Bergland Namibia 100 C2
Bergomum Italy see Bergamo
Bergoo U.S.A. 134 E4
Bergpark Wilhelmshöhe tourist site Germany 47 L5
Bergsjö Sweden 45 J6
Bergsviken Sweden 44 L4
Bergtheim Germany 53 K5
Bergues France 52 C4
Bergum Neth. see Burgum
Bergville S. Africa 101 I5
Berhampur India see Baharampur
Beringa, Ostrov i. Russia 65 R4
Beringen Belgium 52 F3
Beringovskiy Russia 65 S3
Bering Sea N. Pacific Ocean 65 S4
Bering Strait Russia/U.S.A. 65 U3
Berīs, Ra's pt Iran 89 F5
Berislav Ukr. see Beryslav
Berkåk Norway 44 G5
Berkane Morocco 57 E6
Berkel r. Neth. 52 G2
Berkeley U.S.A. 128 B3
Berkeley Springs U.S.A. 135 F4
Berkhout Neth. 52 F2
Berkner Sub-glacial Island Antarctica 152 A1
Berkovitsa Bulg. 59 J3
Berkshire Downs hills U.K. 49 F7
Berkshire Hills U.S.A. 135 I2
Berland r. Canada 120 G4
Berlare Belgium 52 E3
Berlevåg Norway 44 P1

▶Berlin Germany 53 N2
Capital of Germany.

Berlin land Germany 53 N2
Berlin MD U.S.A. 135 H4
Berlin NH U.S.A. 135 J1
Berlin PA U.S.A. 135 F4
Berlin Lake U.S.A. 134 E3
Bermagui Australia 112 E6
Bermejo r. Arg./Bol. 144 E3
Bermejo Bol. 142 F8
Bermen, Lac l. Canada 123 H3

▶Bermuda terr. N. Atlantic Ocean 137 L2
United Kingdom Overseas Territory.

Bermuda Rise sea feature N. Atlantic Ocean 148 D4

▶Bern Switz. 56 H3
Capital of Switzerland.

Bernalillo U.S.A. 127 G6
Bernardino de Campos Brazil 145 A3
Bernardo O'Higgins research station Antarctica 152 A2
Bernardo O'Higgins, Parque Nacional nat. park Chile 144 B7
Bernasconi Arg. 144 D5
Bernau bei Berlin Germany 53 N2
Bernburg (Saale) Germany 53 L3
Berne Germany 53 I1
Berne Switz. see Bern
Berne U.S.A. 134 C3
Berner Alpen mts Switz. 56 H3
Berneray i. Scotland U.K. 50 B3
Berneray i. Scotland U.K. 50 B4
Bernier Island Australia 109 A6
Bernina, Piz mt. Italy/Switz. 58 C1
Bernina Pass Switz. 56 J3
Bernkastel-Kues Germany 52 H5
Beroea Greece see Veroia
Beroea Syria see Aleppo
Beroroha Madag. 99 E6
Beroun Czechia 47 O6
Berounka r. Czechia 47 O6
Berovina Madag. see Beravina
Berri Australia 111 C7
Berriane Alg. 54 E5
Berridale Australia 112 D6
Berriedale U.K. 50 F2
Berrigan Australia 112 B5
Berrima Australia 112 E5
Berrouaghia Alg. 57 H5
Berry Australia 112 E5
Berry U.S.A. 134 C4
Berryessa, Lake U.S.A. 128 B2
Berry Head hd U.K. 49 D8
Berry Islands Bahamas 133 E7
Berryville U.S.A. 135 G4
Berseba Namibia 100 C4
Bersenbrück Germany 53 H2
Bertam Malaysia 71 C6
Berté, Lac l. Canada 123 H4
Berthoud Pass U.S.A. 126 G5
Bertolínia Brazil 143 J5
Bertoua Cameroon 96 E4
Bertraghboy Bay Ireland 51 C4
Beru atoll Kiribati 107 H2
Beruri Brazil 142 F4
Beruwala Sri Lanka 84 C5
Berwick Australia 112 B7
Berwick U.S.A. 135 G3
Berwick-upon-Tweed U.K. 48 E3
Berwyn hills U.K. 49 D6
Beryslav Ukr. 59 O1
Berytus Lebanon see Beirut
Besalampy Madag. 99 E5
Besançon France 56 H3
Besar, Gunung mt. Malaysia 71 C7
Besbay Kazakh. 80 A2
Beserah Malaysia 71 C7
Beshkent Uzbek. 89 G2
Besheh Iran 88 D4
Besikama Indon. 108 D2
Besitang Indon. 71 B6
Beskra Alg. see Biskra
Beslan Russia 91 G2
Besnard Lake Canada 121 J4
Besni Turkey 90 E3
Besor, Naḥal watercourse Israel 85 B4
Beşparmak Dağları mts Cyprus see Pentadaktylos Range
Bessbrook U.K. 51 F3
Bessemer U.S.A. 133 C5
Besshoky, Gora hill Kazakh. 91 I1
Besskorbnaya Russia 43 I7
Bessonovka Russia 43 J5
Betalongchhip mt. India 83 H5
Betanzos Spain 57 B2
Bet Guvrin Israel 85 B4
Bethal S. Africa 101 I4
Bethanie Namibia 100 C4
Bethany U.S.A. 130 E3
Bethel U.S.A. 123 H5
Bethel Park U.S.A. 134 E3
Bethesda U.K. 48 C5
Bethesda MD U.S.A. 135 G4
Bethesda OH U.S.A. 134 E3
Bethlehem S. Africa 101 I5
Bethlehem U.S.A. 135 H3
Bethlehem West Bank 85 B4
Bethulie S. Africa 101 G6
Béthune France 52 C4
Beti Pak. 89 H4
Betim Brazil 145 B2
Bet Lehem West Bank see Bethlehem
Betma India 82 C5
Betong Thai. 71 C6
Betoota (abandoned) Australia 110 C5
Betpakdala plain Kazakh. 80 D2
Betroka Madag. 99 E6
Bet She'an Israel 85 B3
Betsiamites Canada 123 H4
Betsiamites r. Canada 123 H4
Betsukai Japan 74 G4
Bettiah India 83 F4
Bettyhill U.K. 50 E2
Bettystown Ireland 51 F4
Betul India 82 D5
Betung Kerihun, Taman Nasional nat. park Indon. 68 E6
Betwa r. India 82 D4
Betws-y-coed U.K. 49 D5
Betzdorf Germany 53 H4
Beulah Australia 111 C7
Beulah MI U.S.A. 134 B1
Beulah ND U.S.A. 130 C2
Beult r. U.K. 49 H7
Beuthen Poland see Bytom
Bever r. Germany 53 H2
Beverley U.K. 48 G5
Beverly MA U.S.A. 135 J2
Beverly OH U.S.A. 134 E4
Beverly Hills U.S.A. 128 D4
Beverly Lake Canada 121 K1
Beverstedt Germany 53 I1
Beverungen Germany 53 J3
Beverwijk Neth. 52 E2
Bewani P.N.G. 69 K7
Bexbach Germany 53 H5
Bexhill U.K. 49 H8
Bexley, Cape Canada 118 G3
Beyce Turkey see Orhaneli
Bey Dağları mts Turkey 59 N6
Beykoz Turkey 59 M4
Beyla Guinea 96 C4
Beylagan Azer. see Beyläqan
Beyläqan Azer. 91 G3
Beyneu Kazakh. 78 E2
Beypazarı Turkey 59 N4
Beypınarı Turkey 90 E3
Beypore India 84 B4
Beyrouth Lebanon see Beirut
Beyşehir Turkey 90 C3
Beyşehir Gölü l. Turkey 90 C3
Beytonovo Russia 74 B1
Beytüşşebap Turkey 91 F3
Bezameh Iran 88 E3
Bezbozhnik Russia 42 K4
Bezhanitsy Russia 42 F4
Bezhetsk Russia 42 H4
Béziers France 56 F5
Bezmein Turkm. see Abadan
Bezwada India see Vijayawada
Bhabha India see Bhabua
Bhabhar India 82 B4
Bhabhua India see Bhabua
Bhabua India 83 E4
Bhachau India 82 B5
Bhachbhar India 82 B4
Bhadgaon Nepal see Bhaktapur
Bhadohi India 83 E4
Bhadra India 82 C3
Bhadrachalam Road Station India see Kottagudem
Bhadrak India 83 F5
Bhadrakh India see Bhadrak
Bhadravati India 84 B3
Bhag Pak. 89 G4
Bhagalpur India 83 F4
Bhainsa India 84 C2

Bhainsdehi India 82 D5
Bhairab Bazar Bangl. 83 G4
Bhairi Hol mt. Pak. 89 G5
Bhaktapur Nepal 83 F4
Bhalki India 84 C2
Bhamo Myanmar 70 B1
Bhamragarh India 84 D2
Bhandal India 82 C2
Bhandara India 82 D5
Bhanjanagar India 84 E2
Bhanrer Range hills India 82 D5
Bhaptiahi India 83 F4
Bharat country Asia see India
Bharati research station Antarctica 152 E2
Bharatpur India 82 D4
Bhareli r. India 83 H4
Bharuch India 82 C5
Bhatapara India 83 E5
Bhatarsaigh i. U.K. see Vatersay
Bhatghar Lake India 84 B2
Bhatinda India see Bathinda
Bhatnair India see Hanumangarh
Bhatpara India 83 G5
Bhaunagar India see Bhavnagar
Bhavani r. India 84 C4
Bhavani Sagar l. India 84 C4
Bhavnagar India 82 C5
Bhawana Pak. 89 I4
Bhawanipatna India 84 D2
Bhearnaraigh, Eilean i. U.K. see Berneray
Bheemavaram India see Bhimavaram
Bhekuzulu S. Africa 101 J4
Bhera Pak. 89 I3
Bhigvan India 84 B2
Bhikhna Thori Nepal 83 F4
Bhilai India 82 E5
Bhildi India 82 C4
Bhilwara India 82 C4
Bhima r. India 84 C2
Bhimar India 82 B4
Bhimavaram India 84 D2
Bhimlath India 82 E5
Bhind India 82 D4
Bhinga India 83 E4
Bhisho S. Africa 101 H7
Bhiwandi India 84 B2
Bhiwani India 82 D3
Bhogaipur India 82 D4
Bhojpur Nepal 83 F4
Bhola Bangl. 83 G5
Bhongweni S. Africa 101 I6
Bhopal India 82 D5
Bhopalpatnam India 84 D2
Bhrigukaccha India see Bharuch
Bhuban India 84 E1
Bhubaneshwar India 84 E1
Bhubaneswar India see Bhubaneshwar
Bhuj India 82 B5
Bhusawal India 82 C5
Bhutan country Asia 83 G4
Bhuttewala India 82 B4
Bia r. Ghana 96 C4
Bīabān mts Iran 88 E5
Biafo Glacier Pak. 82 C2
Biak Indon. 69 J7
Biak i. Indon. 69 J7
Biała Podlaska Poland 43 D5
Białogard Poland 47 O4
Białystok Poland 43 D5
Bianco, Monte mt. France/Italy see Blanc, Mont
Biandan Gang r. mouth China 77 I1
Bianzhao China 74 A3
Bianzhuang China see Cangshan
Biaora India 82 D5
Biarritz France 56 D5
Bi'ār Tabrāk well Saudi Arabia 88 B5
Bibai Japan 74 F4
Bibbenluke Australia 112 D6
Bibbiena Italy 58 D3
Bibby Island Canada 121 M2
Biberach an der Riß Germany 47 L6
Bibile Sri Lanka 84 D5
Biblis Germany 53 I5
Biblos Lebanon see Jbail
Bicas Brazil 145 C3
Biçer Turkey 59 N5
Bicester U.K. 49 F7
Bichabhera India 82 C4
Bicheng China see Bishan
Bichevaya Russia 74 D3
Bichi r. Russia 74 E1
Bickerton Island Australia 110 B2
Bickleigh U.K. 49 D8
Bicknell U.S.A. 134 B4
Bicuari, Parque Nacional do nat. park Angola 99 B5
Bid India 84 B2
Bida Nigeria 96 D4
Bidar India 84 C2
Biddeford U.S.A. 135 J2
Biddinghuizen Neth. 52 F2
Bidean nam Bian mt. U.K. 50 D4
Bideford U.K. 49 C7
Bideford Bay U.K. see Barnstaple Bay
Bīdokht Iran 88 E3
Bidzhan Russia 74 C3
Bié Angola see Kuito
Bié, Planalto do Angola 99 B5
Biebrzański Park Narodowy nat. park Poland 45 M10
Biedenkopf Germany 53 I4
Bielawa Poland 47 P5
Biel/Bienne Switz. 56 H3
Bielefeld Germany 53 I2
Bielitz Poland see Bielsko-Biała
Biella Italy 58 C2
Bielsko-Biała Poland 47 Q6
Bielstein hill Germany 53 J3
Bienenbüttel Germany 53 K1
Biên Hoa Vietnam 71 D5
Bienne Switz. see Biel/Bienne
Bienville, Lac l. Canada 123 G3
Bierbank Australia 112 B1
Biesiesvlei S. Africa 101 G4
Bietigheim-Bissingen Germany 53 J6
Bièvre Belgium 52 F5
Bifoun Gabon 98 B4
Big r. Canada 123 K3
Biga Turkey 59 L4
Bigadiç Turkey 59 M5
Biga Yarımadası pen. Turkey 59 L5
Big Baldy Mountain U.S.A. 126 F3
Big Bar Creek Canada 120 F5
Big Bear Lake U.S.A. 128 E4
Big Belt Mountains U.S.A. 126 F3
Big Bend Swaziland 101 J4
Big Bend National Park U.S.A. 131 C6
Bigbury-on-Sea U.K. 49 D8
Big Canyon watercourse U.S.A. 131 C6
Biger Nuur salt l. Mongolia 80 I2
Big Falls U.S.A. 130 E1
Big Fork r. U.S.A. 130 E1
Biggar Canada 121 J4
Biggar U.K. 50 F5
Biggar, Lac l. Canada 122 G4
Bigge Island Australia 108 D3
Biggenden Australia 111 F5
Bigger, Mount Canada 120 B3
Biggesee l. Germany 53 H3
Biggleswade U.K. 49 G6
Biggs U.S.A. 128 C2
Biggs Junction U.S.A. 126 C3
Big Hole r. U.S.A. 126 E3
Bighorn r. U.S.A. 126 G3
Bighorn Mountains U.S.A. 126 G3
Big Island Nunavut Canada 119 K3
Big Island N.W.T. Canada 120 G2
Big Island Ont. Canada 121 M5
Big Kalzas Lake Canada 120 C2
Big Lake l. Canada 121 H1
Big Lake U.S.A. 131 C6
Big Pine U.S.A. 128 D3
Big Pine Peak U.S.A. 128 D4
Big Raccoon r. U.S.A. 134 B4
Big Rapids U.S.A. 134 C2
Big River Canada 121 J4
Big Sable Point U.S.A. 134 B1
Big Salmon r. Canada 120 C2
Big Sand Lake Canada 121 L3
Big Sandy r. U.S.A. 126 F4
Big Sandy Lake Canada 121 J4
Big Smokey Valley U.S.A. 128 E2
Big South Fork National River and Recreation Area park U.S.A. 134 C5
Big Spring U.S.A. 131 C5
Big Stone Canada 121 I5
Big Stone Gap U.S.A. 134 D5
Bigstone Lake Canada 121 M4
Big Timber U.S.A. 126 F3
Big Trout Lake Canada 121 N4
Big Trout Lake l. Canada 121 N4
Big Valley Canada 121 H4
Big Water U.S.A. 129 H3
Bihać Bos. & Herz. 58 F2
Bihar state India 83 F4
Bihariganj India 83 F4
Bihar Sharif India 83 F4
Bihor, Vârful mt. Romania 59 J1
Bihoro Japan 74 G4
Bijagós, Arquipélago dos is Guinea-Bissau 96 B3
Bijaipur India 82 D4
Bijapur India see Vijayapura
Bījār Iran 88 B3
Bijbehara India 82 C2
Bijeljina Bos. & Herz. 59 H2
Bijelo Polje Montenegro 59 H3
Bijiang China see Zhiziluo
Bijie China 76 E3
Bijji India 84 D2
Bijnor India 82 D3
Bijnore India see Bijnor
Bijnot Pak. 89 H4
Bijrān well Saudi Arabia 88 C5
Bijrān, Khashm hill Saudi Arabia 88 C5
Bikampur India 82 C4
Bikaner India 82 C3
Bīkhūyeh Iran 88 D5
Bikin Russia 74 D3
Bikin r. Russia 74 D3
Bikini atoll Marshall Is 150 H5
Bikori Sudan 86 D7
Bikoro Dem. Rep. Congo 98 B4
Bikou China 76 E1
Bikramganj India 83 F4
Bilād Banī Bū 'Alī Oman 87 I5
Bilaigarh India 84 D1
Bilara India 82 C4
Bilaspur Chhattisgarh India 83 E5
Bilaspur Hima. Prad. India 82 D3
Biläsuvar Azer. 91 H3
Bila Tserkva Ukr. 43 F6
Bilauktaung Range mts Myanmar/Thai. 71 B4
Bilbao Spain 57 E2
Bilbays Egypt 90 C5
Bilbeis Egypt see Bilbays
Bilbo Spain see Bilbao
Bilecik Turkey 59 M4
Biłgoraj Poland 43 D6
Bilharamulo Tanz. 98 D4
Bilhaur India 82 E4
Bilhorod-Dnistrovs'kyy Ukr. 59 N1
Bili Dem. Rep. Congo 98 C3
Bilibino Russia 65 R3
Bilin Myanmar 70 B3
Bill U.S.A. 126 G4
Billabalong Australia 109 A6
Billabong Creek r. Australia see Moulamein Creek
Billericay U.K. 49 H7
Billiluna Australia 108 D4
Billingham U.K. 48 F4
Billings U.S.A. 126 F3
Billiton i. Indon. see Belitung
Bill of Portland hd U.K. 49 E8
Bill Williams r. U.S.A. 129 F4
Bill Williams Mountain U.S.A. 129 G4
Bilma Niger 96 E3
Bilma, Grand Erg de des. Niger 96 E3
Bilo r. Russia see Belaya
Biloela Australia 110 E5
Bilohirs'k Crimea 90 D1
Bilohir"ya Ukr. 43 E6
Biloku Guyana 143 G3
Biloli India 84 C2
Bilovods'k Ukr. 43 H6
Biloxi U.S.A. 131 F6
Bilpa Morea Claypan salt flat Australia 110 B5
Bilston U.K. 50 F5
Biltine Chad 97 F3
Bilto Norway 44 L2
Bilugyun Island Myanmar 70 B3
Bilyayivka Ukr. 59 N1
Bilzen Belgium 52 F4
Bima Indon. 108 B2
Bimberi, Mount Australia 112 D5
Bimbo Cent. Afr. Rep. 97 E4
Bimini Islands Bahamas 133 E7
Bimlipatam India 84 D2
Bina-Etawa India 82 D4
Binaija, Gunung mt. Indon. 67 E8
Bīnālūd, Reshteh Kūh-e mts Iran 88 E2
Binboğa Daği mt. Turkey 90 E3
Bincheng China see Binzhou
Binchuan China 76 D3
Bindebango Australia 112 C1
Bindle Australia 112 D1
Bindu Dem. Rep. Congo 99 B4
Bindura Zimbabwe 99 D5
Binéfar Spain 57 G3
Binga Zimbabwe 99 C5
Binga, Monte mt. Moz. 99 D5
Bingara Australia 112 E2
Bingaram i. India 84 B4
Bing Bong Australia 110 B2
Bingen am Rhein Germany 53 H5
Bingham U.S.A. 135 K1
Binghamton U.S.A. 135 H2
Bingmei China see Congjiang
Bingöl Turkey 91 F3
Bingol Dağı mt. Turkey 91 F3
Bingxi China see Yushan
Bingzhongluo China 76 C2
Binh Gia Vietnam 70 D2
Binika India 83 E5
Binjai Indon. 71 B7
Bin Mürkhan well U.A.E. 88 D5
Binnaway Australia 112 D3
Binpur India 83 F5
Bintan i. Indon. 71 D7
Bint Jbeil Lebanon see Bent Jbaïl
Bintulu Sarawak Malaysia 68 E6
Binxian Heilong. China 74 B3
Binxian Shaanxi China 77 F1
Binya Australia 112 C5
Binyang China 77 F4
Bin-Yauri Nigeria 96 D3
Binzhou Guangxi China see Binyang
Binzhou Heilong. China see Binxian
Binzhou Shandong China 73 L5
Bioco i. Equat. Guinea see Bioko
Biograd na Moru Croatia 58 F3
Bioko i. Equat. Guinea 96 D4
Biokovo mts Croatia 58 G3
Biquinhas Brazil 145 B2
Bir India see Bid
Bira Russia 74 D2
Bi'r Abū Jady oasis Syria 85 D1
Birāk Libya 97 E2
Birakan Russia 74 C2
Bi'r al 'Abd Egypt 85 A4
Bi'r al Ḩalbā well Syria 85 D2
Bi'r al Jifjāfah well Egypt 85 A4
Bi'r al Khamsah well Egypt 90 B5
Bi'r al Māliḩah well Egypt 85 A5
Bi'r al Mulūsi Iraq 91 F4
Bi'r al Munbaṭiḩ well Syria 85 D2
Bi'r al Qaṭrānī well Egypt 90 B5
Bi'r al Ubbayiḑ well Egypt 90 B6
Bi'r an Nuṣf well Egypt see Bi'r an Nuṣṣ
Bi'r an Nuṣṣ well Egypt 90 B5
Bir Anzarane W. Sahara 96 B2
Birao Cent. Afr. Rep. 98 C2
Bi'r ar Rābiyah well Egypt 90 B5
Birata Turkm. 89 F1
Biratnagar Nepal 83 F4
Bi'r aṭ Ṭarfāwī well Libya 90 B5
Bi'r Başīrī well Syria 85 C2
Bi'r Bayḑā' well Egypt 85 B4
Bi'r Baylī well Egypt 90 B5
Bîr Beiḍa well Egypt see Bi'r Bayḑā'
Bi'r Buṭaymān Syria 91 E3
Birch r. Canada 121 H3
Birch Hills Canada 121 J4
Birch Island Canada 120 G5
Birch Lake N.W.T. Canada 120 G2
Birch Lake Ont. Canada 121 M5
Birch Lake Sask. Canada 121 I4
Birch Mountains Canada 120 H3
Birch River U.S.A. 134 E4
Birch Run U.S.A. 134 D2
Bircot Eth. 98 E3
Birdaard Neth. see Burdaard
Bîr Dignâsh well Egypt see Bi'r Diqnāsh
Bi'r Diqnāsh well Egypt 90 B5
Bird Island N. Mariana Is see Farallon de Medinilla
Birdseye U.S.A. 129 H2
Birdsville Australia 111 B5
Birecik Turkey 90 E3
Bîr el 'Abd Egypt see Bi'r al 'Abd
Bir el Arbi well Alg. 57 I6
Bîr el Istabl well Egypt see Bi'r Iṣṭabl
Bîr el Khamsa well Egypt see Bi'r al Khamsah
Bîr el Nuṣṣ well Egypt see Bi'r an Nuṣṣ
Bîr el Obeiyiḍ well Egypt see Bi'r al Ubbayiḑ
Bîr el Qaṭrâni well Egypt see Bi'r al Qaṭrānī
Bîr el Râbia well Egypt see Bi'r ar Rābiyah
Birendranagar Nepal see Surkhet
Bir en Natrûn well Sudan 86 C6
Bireun Indon. 71 B6
Bi'r Fāḑil well Saudi Arabia 88 C6
Bi'r Fajr well Saudi Arabia 90 E5
Bi'r Fu'ād well Egypt 90 B5
Bīrg, Kūh-e mts Iran 89 F5
Bîr Gifgâfa well Egypt see Bi'r al Jifjāfah
Bi'r Ḩajal well Syria 85 D2
Bi'r Ḩasanah well Egypt 85 A4
Bi'r Ḩayzān well Saudi Arabia 90 E6
Bi'r Ibn Hirmās Saudi Arabia see Al Bi'r
Bir Ibn Juhayyim Saudi Arabia 88 C6
Birigui Brazil 145 A3
Bīrīn Syria 85 C2
Bi'r Iṣṭabl well Egypt 90 B5
Bīrjand Iran 88 E3
Bi'r Jubnī well Libya 90 B5
Birkát Hamad well Iraq 91 G5
Birkenfeld Germany 53 H5
Birkenhead U.K. 48 D5
Birkirkara Malta 58 F7
Birksgate Range hills Australia 109 E6
Bîrlad Romania see Bârlad
Bi'r Lahfān well Egypt 85 A4
Bir Lahlou W. Sahara 96 C2
Birlik Kazakh. 80 D3
Birmal reg. Afgh. 89 H3
Birmingham U.K. 49 F6
Birmingham U.S.A. 133 C5
Bîr Mogreïn Mauritania 96 B2
Bi'r Muḩaymid al Wazwaz well Syria 85 D2
Bi'r Nāḩid oasis Egypt 90 C5
Birnin-Gwari Nigeria 96 D3
Birnin-Kebbi Nigeria 96 D3
Birnin Konni Niger 96 D3
Birobidzhan Russia 74 D2
Bi'r Qaṣīr as Sirr well Egypt 90 B5
Birr Ireland 51 E4
Bi'r Rawḑ Sālim well Egypt 85 A4
Birrie r. Australia 112 C2
Birrindudu Australia 108 E4
Bîr Rôḍ Sâlim well Egypt see Bi'r Rawḑ Sālim
Birsay U.K. 50 F1
Bi'r Shalatayn Egypt 86 E5
Bîr Shalatein Egypt see Bi'r Shalatayn
Birsk Russia 41 R4
Birstall U.K. 49 F6
Birstein Germany 53 J4
Bir Talḩah well Saudi Arabia 88 B6
Birthday Mountain hill Australia 110 C2
Birtle Canada 121 K5
Biru China 76 B2
Birur India 84 B3
Bi'r Usaylīlah well Saudi Arabia 88 B6
Biruxiong China see Biru
Biržai Lith. 45 N8
Bisa India 70 A1
Bisa i. Indon. 69 H7
Bisalpur India 82 D3
Bisau India 82 C3
Bisbee U.S.A. 127 F7
Biscay, Bay of sea France/Spain 56 B4
Biscay Abyssal Plain sea feature N. Atlantic Ocean 148 H3
Biscayne National Park U.S.A. 133 D7
Biscoe Islands Antarctica 152 L2
Biscotasi Lake Canada 122 E5
Biscotasing Canada 122 E5
Bisezhai China 76 D4
Bishan China 76 E2
Bishbek Kyrg. see Bishkek
Bishenpur India see Bishnupur

▶Bishkek Kyrg. 80 D3
Capital of Kyrgyzstan.

Bishnupur Manipur India 83 H4
Bishnupur W. Bengal India 83 F5
Bishop U.S.A. 128 D3
Bishop Auckland U.K. 48 F4
Bishop Lake Canada 120 G1
Bishop's Stortford U.K. 49 H7
Bishopville U.S.A. 133 D5
Bishrī, Jabal hills Syria 85 D2
Bishui Heilong. China 74 A1
Bishui Henan China see Biyang
Biskra Alg. 54 F5
Bislig Phil. 69 H5

▶Bismarck U.S.A. 130 C2
Capital of North Dakota.

Bismarck Archipelago is P.N.G. 69 L7
Bismarck Range mts P.N.G. 69 K7
Bismarck Sea P.N.G. 69 L7
Bismark (Altmark) Germany 53 L2
Bismil Turkey 91 F3
Bismo Norway 44 F6
Bison U.S.A. 130 C2
Bispgården Sweden 44 J5
Bispingen Germany 53 K1
Bissa, Djebel mt. Alg. 57 G5
Bissagos Islands Guinea-Bissau see Bijagós, Arquipélago dos
Bissamcuttak India 84 D2

▶Bissau Guinea-Bissau 96 B3
Capital of Guinea-Bissau.

Bissaula Nigeria 96 E4
Bissett Canada 121 M5
Bistcho Lake Canada 120 G3
Bistrița Romania 59 K1
Bistrița r. Romania 59 L1
Bitburg Germany 52 G5
Bitche France 53 H5
Bithur India 82 E4
Bithynia hist. area Turkey 59 M4
Bitkine Chad 97 E3
Bitlis Turkey 91 F3
Bitola Macedonia 59 I4
Bitolj Macedonia see Bitola
Bitonto Italy 58 G4
Bitrān, Jabal hill Saudi Arabia 88 B6
Bitra Par reef India 84 B4
Bitter Creek r. U.S.A. 129 I2
Bitterfeld Germany 53 M3
Bitterfontein S. Africa 100 D6
Bitter Lakes Egypt 90 D5
Bitterroot r. U.S.A. 126 E3
Bitterroot Range mts U.S.A. 126 E3
Bitterwater U.S.A. 128 C3
Bittkau Germany 53 L2
Bitung Indon. 69 H6
Biu Nigeria 96 E3
Biwa-ko l. Japan 75 D6
Biwmaris U.K. see Beaumaris
Biyang China 77 G1
Bīye K'obē Folīs T'abīya Eth. 98 E2
Biysk Russia 72 F2
Bizana S. Africa 101 I6
Bizerta Tunisia see Bizerte
Bizerte Tunisia 58 C6

▶Bjargtangar hd Iceland 44 [inset 1]
Most westerly point of Europe.

Bjästa Sweden 44 K5
Bjelovar Croatia 58 G2
Bjerkvik Norway 44 J2
Bjerringbro Denmark 45 F8
Bjørgan Norway 44 G5
Björkliden Sweden 44 K2
Björklinge Sweden 45 J6
Bjorli Norway 44 F5
Björna Sweden 44 K5
Björneborg Fin. see Pori

▶Bjørnøya i. Arctic Ocean 64 C2
Part of Norway.

Bjurholm Sweden 44 K5
Bla Mali 96 C3
Black r. Man. Canada 121 L5
Black r. Ont. Canada 122 E4
Black r. AR U.S.A. 131 F5
Black r. AZ U.S.A. 129 H5
Black r. Vietnam 70 D2
Blackadder Water r. U.K. 50 G5
Blackall Australia 110 D5
Blackbear r. Canada 121 N4
Black Birch Lake Canada 121 J3
Black Bourton U.K. 49 F7
Blackbull Australia 110 C3
Blackburn U.K. 48 E5
Blackbutt Australia 112 F1
Black Butte mt. U.S.A. 128 B2
Black Butte Lake U.S.A. 128 B2
Black Canyon gorge U.S.A. 129 F4
Black Canyon of the Gunnison National Park U.S.A. 129 J2
Black Combe hill U.K. 48 D4
Black Creek watercourse U.S.A. 129 I4
Black Donald Lake Canada 135 G1
Blackdown Tableland National Park Australia 110 E4
Blackduck U.S.A. 130 E2
Blackfalds Canada 120 H4
Blackfoot U.S.A. 126 E4
Black Foot r. U.S.A. 126 E3
Black Forest mts Germany 47 L7
Black Hill hill U.K. 48 F5
Black Hills SD U.S.A. 124 G3
Black Hills SD U.S.A. 126 G3
Black Island Canada 121 L5
Black Lake Canada 121 J3
Black Lake l. Canada 121 J3
Black Lake l. U.S.A. 134 C1
Black Mesa mt. U.S.A. 129 I5
Black Mesa ridge U.S.A. 129 H3
Black Mountain Pak. 89 I3
Black Mountain hill U.K. 49 D7
Black Mountain AK U.S.A. 118 B3
Black Mountain CA U.S.A. 128 E4
Black Mountain KY U.S.A. 134 D5
Black Mountain NM U.S.A. 129 I5
Black Mountains hills U.K. 49 D7
Black Mountains U.S.A. 129 F4
Black Nossob watercourse Namibia 100 D2
Black Pagoda India see Konarka
Blackpool U.K. 48 D5
Black Range mts U.S.A. 129 I5
Black River MI U.S.A. 134 D1
Black River NY U.S.A. 135 H1
Black River Falls U.S.A. 130 F2
Black Rock hill Jordan see 'Unāb, Jabal al
Black Rock Desert U.S.A. 126 D4
Blacksburg U.S.A. 134 E5
Black Sea Asia/Europe 43 H8
Blacks Fork r. U.S.A. 126 F4
Blackshear U.S.A. 133 D6
Blacksod Bay Ireland 51 B3
Black Springs U.S.A. 128 D2
Blackstairs Mountains hills Ireland 51 F5
Blackstone U.S.A. 135 F5
Black Sugarloaf mt. Australia 112 E3
Black Tickle Canada 123 L3
Blackville Australia 112 E3
Blackwater Australia 110 E4
Blackwater Ireland 51 F5
Blackwater r. Ireland 51 E5
Blackwater r. Ireland/U.K. 51 F3
Blackwater watercourse U.S.A. 131 C5
Blackwater Lake Canada 120 F2
Blackwater Reservoir U.K. 50 E4
Blackwood r. Australia 109 A8
Blackwood National Park Australia 110 D4
Bladensburg National Park Australia 110 C4
Blaenavon U.K. 49 D7
Blagodarnyy Russia 91 F1
Blagoevgrad Bulg. 59 J3
Blagoveshchensk Amurskaya Oblast' Russia 74 B2
Blagoveshchensk Respublika Bashkortostan Russia 41 R4
Blaikiston, Mount Canada 120 H5
Blaine Lake Canada 121 J4
Blair U.S.A. 130 D3
Blair Athol Australia 110 D4
Blair Atholl U.K. 50 F4
Blairgowrie U.K. 50 F4
Blairsden U.S.A. 128 C2
Blairsville U.S.A. 133 D5
Blakely U.S.A. 133 C6
Blakeney U.K. 49 I6

▶Blanc, Mont mt. France/Italy 56 H4
5th highest mountain in Europe.

Blanca, Bahía b. Arg. 144 D5
Blanca, Sierra mt. U.S.A. 127 G6
Blanca Peak U.S.A. 127 G5
Blanche, Lake salt flat S.A. Australia 111 B6
Blanche, Lake salt flat W.A. Australia 108 C5
Blanchester U.S.A. 134 D4
Blanc Nez, Cap c. France 52 B4
Blanco r. Bol. 142 F6
Blanco U.S.A. 129 J3
Blanco, Cape U.S.A. 126 B4
Blanc-Sablon Canada 123 K4
Bland r. Australia 112 C4
Bland U.S.A. 134 E5
Blanda r. Iceland 44 [inset 1]
Blandford Forum U.K. 49 E8
Blanding U.S.A. 129 I3
Blanes Spain 57 H3
Blangah, Telok Sing. 71 [inset]
Blangkejeren Indon. 71 B7
Blangpidie Indon. 71 B7
Blankenberge Belgium 52 D3
Blankenheim Germany 52 G4
Blanquilla, Isla i. Venez. 142 F1
Blansko Czechia 47 P6
Blantyre Malawi 99 D5
Blarney Ireland 51 D6
Blaufelden Germany 53 J5
Blåviksjön Sweden 44 K4
Blaye France 56 D4
Blayney Australia 112 D4
Blaze, Point Australia 108 E3
Bleckede Germany 53 K1
Bleilochtalsperre resr Germany 53 L4
Blenheim Canada 134 E2
Blenheim N.Z. 113 D5
Blenheim Palace tourist site U.K. 49 F7
Blerick Neth. 52 G3
Blessington Lakes Ireland 51 F4
Bletchley U.K. 49 G6
Blida Alg. 57 H5
Blies r. Germany 53 H5
Bligh Water b. Fiji 107 H3
Blind River Canada 122 E5
Bliss U.S.A. 126 E4
Blissfield U.S.A. 134 D3
Blitta Togo 96 D4
Blocher U.S.A. 134 C4
Block Island U.S.A. 135 J3
Block Island Sound sea chan. U.S.A. 135 J3
Bloemfontein S. Africa 101 H5
Bloemhof S. Africa 101 G4
Bloemhof Dam S. Africa 101 G4
Bloemhof Dam Nature Reserve S. Africa 101 G4
Blomberg Germany 53 J3
Blönduós Iceland 44 [inset 1]
Blongas Indon. 108 B2
Bloods Range mts Australia 109 E6
Bloodsworth Island U.S.A. 135 G4
Bloodvein r. Canada 121 L5
Bloody Foreland pt Ireland 51 D2
Bloomer U.S.A. 130 F2
Bloomfield Canada 135 G2
Bloomfield IA U.S.A. 130 E3
Bloomfield IN U.S.A. 134 B4
Bloomfield MO U.S.A. 131 F4
Bloomfield NM U.S.A. 129 J3
Blooming Prairie U.S.A. 130 E3
Bloomington IL U.S.A. 130 F3
Bloomington IN U.S.A. 134 B4
Bloomington MN U.S.A. 130 E2
Bloomsburg U.S.A. 135 G3
Blossburg U.S.A. 135 G3
Blosseville Kyst coastal area Greenland 119 P3
Blouberg S. Africa 101 I2
Blouberg Nature Reserve S. Africa 101 I2
Blountstown U.S.A. 133 C6
Blountville U.S.A. 134 D5
Bloxham U.K. 49 F6
Blue r. Canada 120 D3
Blue watercourse U.S.A. 129 I5
Blue Bell Knoll mt. U.S.A. 129 H2
Blueberry r. Canada 120 F3
Blue Diamond U.S.A. 129 F3
Blue Earth U.S.A. 130 E3
Bluefield VA U.S.A. 132 D4
Bluefield WV U.S.A. 134 E5
Bluefields Nicaragua 137 H6
Blue Hills Turks and Caicos Is 133 F8
Blue Knob hill U.S.A. 135 F3
Blue Mesa Reservoir U.S.A. 129 J2
Blue Mountain hill Canada 123 K4
Blue Mountain Lake U.S.A. 135 H2
Blue Mountain Pass Lesotho 101 H5
Blue Mountains Australia 112 D4
Blue Mountains U.S.A. 126 D3
Blue Mountains National Park Australia 112 E4
Blue Nile r. Eth./Sudan 86 D6
also known as Abay Wenz (Ethiopia), Bahr el Azraq (Sudan)
Bluenose Lake Canada 118 G3
Blue Ridge GA U.S.A. 133 C5
Blue Ridge VA U.S.A. 134 F5
Blue Ridge mts U.S.A. 134 E5
Blue Stack hill Ireland 51 D3
Blue Stack Mountains hills Ireland 51 D3
Bluestone Lake U.S.A. 134 E5
Bluewater U.S.A. 129 J4
Bluff N.Z. 113 B8
Bluff U.S.A. 129 I3
Bluffdale U.S.A. 129 H1
Bluff Island H.K. China 77 [inset]
Bluff Knoll mt. Australia 109 B8
Bluffton IN U.S.A. 134 C3
Bluffton OH U.S.A. 134 D3
Blumenau Brazil 145 A4
Blustry Mountain Canada 126 C2
Blyde River Canyon Nature Reserve S. Africa 101 J3
Blyth Canada 134 E2
Blyth England U.K. 48 F3
Blyth England U.K. 48 F5
Blythe U.S.A. 129 F5
Blytheville U.S.A. 131 F5
Bø Norway 45 F7
Bo Sierra Leone 96 B4
Boa Esperança Brazil 145 B3
Bo'ai Henan China 77 G1
Bo'ai Yunnan China 76 E4
Boali Cent. Afr. Rep. 98 B3
Boalsert Neth. see Bolsward
Boane Moz. 101 K4
Boa Nova Brazil 145 C1
Boardman U.S.A. 134 E3
Boatlaname Botswana 101 G2
Boa Viagem Brazil 143 K5
Boa Vista Brazil 142 F3
Boa Vista i. Cape Verde 96 [inset]
Bobadah Australia 112 C4
Bobai China 77 F4
Bobaomby, Tanjona c. Madag. 99 E5
Bobbili India 84 D2
Bobcaygeon Canada 135 F1
Bobo-Dioulasso Burkina Faso 96 C3
Bobotov Kuk mt. Montenegro see Durmitor
Bobriki Russia see Novomoskovsk

Bobrinets Ukr. see **Bobrynets'**
Bobrov Russia **43** I6
Bobrovitsa Ukr. see **Bobrovytsya**
Bobrovytsya Ukr. **43** F6
Bobruysk Belarus see **Babruysk**
Bobrynets' Ukr. **43** G6
Bobs Lake Canada **135** G1
Bobuk Sudan **86** D7
Bobures Venez. **142** D2
Boby mt. Madag. **99** E6
Boca de Macareo Venez. **142** F2
Boca do Acre Brazil **142** E5
Boca do Jari Brazil **143** H4
Bocaiúva Brazil **145** C2
Bocaranga Cent. Afr. Rep. **98** B3
Boca Raton U.S.A. **133** D7
Bocas del Toro Panama **137** H7
Bochnia Poland **47** R6
Bocholt Germany **52** G3
Bochum Germany **53** H3
Bockenem Germany **53** K2
Bocoio Angola **99** B5
Bocoyna Mex. **127** G8
Boda Cent. Afr. Rep. **98** B3
Bodalla Australia **112** E6
Bodallin Australia **109** B7
Bodaybo Russia **65** M4
Boddam U.K. **50** H3
Bode r. Germany **53** L3
Bodega Head hd U.S.A. **128** B2
Bodélé reg. Chad **97** E3
Boden Sweden **44** L4
Bodenham U.K. **49** E6
Bodensee l. Germany/Switz. see **Constance, Lake**
Bodenteich Germany **53** K2
Bodenwerder Germany **53** J3
Bodie (abandoned) U.S.A. **128** D2
Bodinayakkanur India **84** C4
Bodmin U.K. **49** C8
Bodmin Moor moorland U.K. **49** C8
Bodø Norway **44** I3
Bodoquena Brazil **143** G7
Bodoquena, Serra da hills Brazil **144** E2
Bodrum Turkey **59** L6
Bodträskfors Sweden **44** L3
Boechout Belgium **52** E3
Boende Dem. Rep. Congo **97** F5
Bœng Méaléa Cambodia **71** D4
Boerne U.S.A. **131** D6
Boeuf r. U.S.A. **131** F6
Boffa Guinea **96** B3
Bogalay Myanmar see **Bogale**
Bogale Myanmar **70** A3
Bogale r. Myanmar **70** A4
Bogalusa U.S.A. **131** F6
Bogan r. Australia **112** C2
Bogandé Burkina Faso **96** C3
Bogan Gate Australia **112** C4
Bogani Nani Wartabone, Taman Nasional nat. park Indon. **69** G6
Boğazlıyan Turkey **90** D3
Bogcang Zangbo r. China **83** F3
Bogd Mongolia **80** J3
Bogda Shan mts China **80** G3
Bogen Kazakh. **80** B2
Boggabilla Australia **112** E2
Boggabri Australia **112** E3
Boggeragh Mountains hills Ireland **51** C5
Boghar Alg. **57** H6
Boghari Alg. see **Ksar el Boukhari**
Bognor Regis U.K. **49** G8
Bogodukhov Ukr. see **Bohodukhiv**
Bog of Allen reg. Ireland **51** E4
Bogong, Mount Australia **112** C6
Bogopol' Russia **74** D3
Bogor Indon. **68** D8
Bogoroditsk Russia **43** H5
Bogorodsk Russia **42** I4
Bogorodskoye Khabarovskiy Kray Russia **74** F1
Bogorodskoye Kirovskaya Oblast' Russia **42** K4

▶**Bogotá** Col. **142** D3
Capital of Colombia. 5th most populous city in South America.

Bogotol Russia **64** J4
Bogoyavlenskoye Russia see **Pervomayskiy**
Bogra Bangl. **83** G4
Boguchanskoye Vodokhranilishche resr Russia **65** L4
Boguchany Russia **65** K4
Boguchar Russia **43** I6
Bogué Mauritania **96** B3
Bo Hai g. China **73** L5
Bohain-en-Vermandois France **52** D5
Bohai Wan b. China **66** D4
Bohemian Forest mts Germany see **Böhmer Wald**
Böhlen Germany **53** M3
Bohlokong S. Africa **101** I5
Böhme r. Germany **53** J2
Böhmer Wald mts Germany **53** M5
Bohmte Germany **53** I2
Bohodukhiv Ukr. **43** G6
Bohol i. Phil. **69** G5
Bohol Sea Phil. **69** G5
Bohu China **80** G3
Boiaçu Brazil **142** F4
Boiba China **76** C1
Boichoko S. Africa **100** F5
Boigu Island Australia **69** K8
Boikhutso S. Africa **101** H4
Boileau, Cape Australia **108** C4
Boim Brazil **143** G4
Boipeba, Ilha i. Brazil **145** D1
Bois r. Brazil **145** A2
Bois Blanc Island U.S.A. **132** C2

▶**Boise** U.S.A. **126** D4
Capital of Idaho.

Boise City U.S.A. **131** C4
Boissevain Canada **121** K5
Boitumelong S. Africa **101** G4
Boizenburg/Elbe Germany **53** K1
Bojd Iran **88** E3
Bojnūrd Iran **88** E2
Bokaak atoll Marshall Is see **Taongi**
Bokajan India **83** H4
Bokaro India **83** F5
Bokaro Reservoir India **83** F5
Bokatola Dem. Rep. Congo **98** B4
Boké Guinea **96** B3
Bokele Dem. Rep. Congo **98** C4
Bokhara r. Australia **112** C2
Bo Kheo Cambodia see **Bâ Kêv**
Boknafjorden sea chan. Norway **45** D7
Bokoko Dem. Rep. Congo **98** C3
Bokoro Chad **97** E3
Bokovskaya Russia **43** I6
Bokspits S. Africa **100** E4
Boktor Russia **74** E2
Bokurdak Turkm. **88** E2
Bol Chad **97** E3
Bolaiti Dem. Rep. Congo **97** F5
Bolama Guinea-Bissau **96** B3
Bolangir India see **Balangir**
Bolan Pass Pak. **89** G4
Bolavén, Phouphiang plat. Laos **70** D4
Bolbec France **56** E2
Bole China **80** F3
Bole Ghana **96** C4
Boleko Dem. Rep. Congo **98** B4
Bolen Russia **74** D2
Bolgar Russia **43** K5
Bolgatanga Ghana **96** C3
Bolgrad Ukr. see **Bolhrad**
Bolhrad Ukr. **59** M2
Boli China **74** C3
Bolia Dem. Rep. Congo **98** B4
Boliden Sweden **44** L4
Bolikhamxai Laos **70** C3
Bolingbrook U.S.A. **134** A3
Bolintin-Vale Romania **59** K2
Bolívar Peru **142** C5
Bolivar NY U.S.A. **135** F2
Bolivar TN U.S.A. **131** F5
Bolívar, Pico mt. Venez. **142** D2
Bolivia Cuba **133** E8

▶**Bolivia** country S. America **142** E7
5th largest country in South America.

Bolkhov Russia **43** H5
Bollène France **56** G4
Bollnäs Sweden **45** J6
Bollon Australia **112** C2
Bollstabruk Sweden **44** J5
Bolmen l. Sweden **45** H8
Bolobo Dem. Rep. Congo **98** B4
Bologna Italy **58** D2
Bolognesi Peru **142** D5
Bologoye Russia **42** G4
Bolokanang S. Africa **101** G5
Bolomba Dem. Rep. Congo **98** B3
Bolon' Russia **74** E2
Bolpur India **83** F5
Bolsena, Lago di l. Italy **58** D3
Bol'shakovo Russia **45** L9
Bol'shaya Chernigovka Russia **41** Q5
Bol'shaya Glushitsa Russia **43** K5
Bol'shaya Imandra, Ozero l. Russia **44** R3
Bol'shaya Kovriga, Gora hill Russia **42** K2
Bol'shaya Martynovka Russia **43** I7
Bol'shaya Tsarevshchina Russia see **Volzhskiy**
Bol'shevik, Ostrov i. Russia **65** L2
Bol'shezemel'skaya Tundra lowland Russia **42** L2
Bol'shiye Barsuki, Peski des. Kazakh. **80** A2
Bol'shiye Chirki Russia **42** J3
Bol'shoy Begichev, Ostrov i. Russia **153** E2
Bol'shoye Murashkino Russia **42** J5
Bol'shoy Irgiz r. Russia **43** J6
Bol'shoy Kamen' Russia **74** D4
Bol'shoy Kavkaz mts Asia/Europe see **Caucasus**
Bol'shoy Kundysh r. Russia **42** J4
Bol'shoy Lyakhovskiy, Ostrov i. Russia **65** P2
Bol'shoy Tokmak Ukr. see **Tokmak**
Bolsward Neth. **52** F1
Bolton Canada **134** F2
Bolton U.K. **48** E5
Bolu Turkey **59** N4
Boluntay China **83** H1
Boluo China **77** G4
Bolus Head hd Ireland **51** B6
Bolvadin Turkey **59** N5
Bolzano Italy **58** D1
Boma Dem. Rep. Congo **99** B4
Bomaderry Australia **112** E5
Bombala Australia **112** D6
Bombay India see **Mumbai**
Bombay Beach U.S.A. **129** F5
Bomberai, Semenanjung pen. Indon. **69** I7
Bomboma Dem. Rep. Congo **98** B3
Bom Comércio Brazil **142** E5
Bomdila India **83** H4
Bomi China **76** B2
Bomili Dem. Rep. Congo **98** C3
Bom Jardim de Goiás Brazil **145** A2
Bom Jesus Brazil **145** A5
Bom Jesus da Gurgueia, Serra do hills Brazil **143** J5
Bom Jesus da Lapa Brazil **145** C1
Bom Jesus do Norte Brazil **145** C3
Bømlo i. Norway **45** D7
Bomokandi r. Dem. Rep. Congo **98** C3
Bom Retiro Brazil **145** A4
Bom Sucesso Brazil **145** B3
Bon, Cap c. Tunisia **58** D6
Bon, Ko i. Thai. **71** B5
Bona Alg. see **Annaba**
Bona, Mount U.S.A. **120** A2
Bonāb Āzarbāyjān-e Sharqī Iran **88** B2
Bonāb Zanjān Iran **88** C2
Bon Air U.S.A. **135** G5
Bonaire mun. West Indies **137** K6
Bonanza Peak U.S.A. **126** C2
Bonaparte Archipelago is Australia **108** D3
Bonaparte Lake Canada **120** F5
Bonar Bridge U.K. **50** E3
Bonavista Canada **123** L4
Bonavista Bay Canada **123** L4
Bonchester Bridge U.K. **50** G5
Bondo Dem. Rep. Congo **98** C3
Bondokodi Indon. **68** F8
Bondoukou Côte d'Ivoire **96** C4
Bonduel U.S.A. **134** A1
Bondyuzhskiy Russia see **Mendeleyevsk**
Bône Alg. see **Annaba**
Bone, Teluk b. Indon. **69** G8
Bönen Germany **53** H3
Bonerate, Kepulauan is Indon. **108** C1
Bo'ness U.K. **50** F4

▶**Bonete, Cerro** mt. Arg. **144** C3
3rd highest mountain in South America.

Bonga Eth. **98** D3
Bongaigaon India **83** G4
Bongandanga Dem. Rep. Congo **98** C3
Bongani S. Africa **100** F5
Bongao Phil. **68** F5
Bongba China **82** E2
Bong Co l. China **83** G3
Bongo, Massif des mts Cent. Afr. Rep. **98** C3
Bongo, Serra do mts Angola **99** B4
Bongolava mts Madag. **99** E5
Bongor Chad **97** E3
Bông Sơn Vietnam **71** E4
Bonham U.S.A. **131** D5
Bonheiden Belgium **52** E3
Boni Mali **96** C3
Bonifacio Corsica France **56** I6
Bonifacio, Bocche di strait France/Italy see **Bonifacio, Strait of**
Bonifacio, Bouches de strait France/Italy see **Bonifacio, Strait of**
Bonifacio, Strait of France/Italy **56** I6

▶**Bonin Islands** Japan **75** F8
Part of Japan.

▶**Bonn** Germany **52** H4
Former capital of Germany.

Bonna Germany see **Bonn**
Bonnåsjøen Norway **44** I3
Bonners Ferry U.S.A. **126** D2
Bonnet, Lac du resr Canada **121** M5
Bonneville France **56** H3
Bonneville Salt Flats U.S.A. **129** G1
Bonnières-sur-Seine France **52** B5
Bonnie Rock Australia **109** B7
Bonnieville U.S.A. **134** C5
Bonnyrigg U.K. **50** F5
Bonnyville Canada **121** I4
Bonobono Phil. **68** F5
Bononia Italy see **Bologna**
Bonorva Sardinia Italy **58** C4
Bonshaw Australia **112** E2
Bontebok National Park S. Africa **100** E8
Bonthe Sierra Leone **96** B4
Bontoc Phil. **69** G3
Bontosunggu Indon. **68** F8
Bontrug S. Africa **101** G7
Bonvouloir Islands P.N.G. **110** E1
Bonwapitse Botswana **101** H2
Boo, Kepulauan is Indon. **69** H7
Book Cliffs ridge U.S.A. **129** I2
Booker U.S.A. **131** C4
Boolba Australia **112** D2
Booligal Australia **112** B4
Boomer U.S.A. **134** E4
Boomi Australia **112** D2
Boon U.S.A. **134** C1
Boonah Australia **112** F1
Boone CO U.S.A. **127** G5
Boone IA U.S.A. **130** E3
Boone NC U.S.A. **132** D4
Boone Lake U.S.A. **134** D5
Boones Mill U.S.A. **134** F5
Booneville AR U.S.A. **131** E5
Booneville KY U.S.A. **134** D5
Booneville MS U.S.A. **131** F5
Böön Tsagaan Nuur salt l. Mongolia **80** I2
Boonville CA U.S.A. **128** B2
Boonville IN U.S.A. **134** B4
Boonville MO U.S.A. **130** E4
Boonville NY U.S.A. **135** H2
Boorabin National Park Australia **109** C7
Boorama Somalia **98** E3
Booroorban Australia **112** B5
Boorowa Australia **112** D5
Boort Australia **112** A6
Boothby, Cape Antarctica **152** D2
Boothia, Gulf of Canada **119** J3
Boothia Peninsula Canada **119** I2
Bootle U.K. **48** E5
Booué Gabon **98** B4
Boppard Germany **53** H4
Boqê China **83** G3
Boqueirão, Serra do hills Brazil **143** J6
Bor Czechia **53** M5
Bor Russia **42** J4
Bor Serbia **59** J2
Bor South Sudan **97** G4
Bor Turkey **90** D3
Bor, Lagh watercourse Kenya/Somalia **98** E3
Boraha, Nosy i. Madag. **99** F5
Borah Peak U.S.A. **126** E3
Borai India **84** D1
Borakalalo Nature Reserve S. Africa **101** H3
Boran Kazakh. **80** G2
Boraphet, Bung l. Thai. **70** C4
Boraphet, Nong l. Thai. see **Boraphet, Bung**
Borås Sweden **45** H8
Borasambar India **84** D1
Borāzjān Iran **88** C4
Borba Brazil **143** G4
Borborema, Planalto da plat. Brazil **143** K5
Borchen Germany **53** I3
Borçka Turkey **91** F2
Bor Dağı mt. Turkey **59** M6
Bordeaux France **56** D4
Borden Island Canada **119** G2
Borden Peninsula Canada **119** J2
Border Ranges National Park Australia **112** F2
Borðeyri Iceland **44** [inset 1]
Bordj Bou Arréridj Alg. **57** I5
Bordj Bounaama Alg. **57** G6
Bordj Flye Ste-Marie Alg. **96** C2
Bordj Messaouda Alg. **54** F5
Bordj Mokhtar Alg. **96** D2
Bordj Omar Driss Alg. see **Bordj Omer Driss**
Bordj Omer Driss Alg. **96** D2
Boreas Abyssal Plain sea feature Arctic Ocean **153** H1
Borel r. Canada **123** H2
Borgå Fin. see **Porvoo**
Borgarfjörður Iceland **44** [inset 1]
Borgarnes Iceland **44** [inset 1]
Børgefjell Nasjonalpark nat. park Norway **44** H4
Borger U.S.A. **131** C5
Borgholm Sweden **45** J8
Borgne, Lake b. U.S.A. **131** F6
Borgo San Lorenzo Italy **58** D3
Bori India **84** C1
Bori r. India **82** C5
Borislav Ukr. see **Boryslav**
Borisoglebsk Russia **43** I6
Borisov Belarus see **Barysaw**
Borisovka Russia **43** H6
Borispol' Ukr. see **Boryspil'**
Bo River South Sudan **97** F4
Borja Peru **142** C4
Borken Germany **52** G3
Borkenes Norway **44** J2
Borkovskaya Russia **42** K2
Borkum Germany **52** G1
Borkum i. Germany **52** G1
Borlänge Sweden **45** I6
Borlaug Norway **45** E6
Borlu Turkey **59** M5
Borna Germany **53** M3
Born-Berge hill Germany **53** K3
Borndiep sea chan. Neth. **52** F1
Borne Neth. **52** G2

▶**Borneo** i. Asia **68** E6
Largest island in Asia and 3rd in the world.

Bornholm i. Denmark **45** I9
Bornova Turkey **59** L5
Borodino Russia **64** J3
Borodinskoye Russia **45** P6
Borogontsy Russia **65** O3
Borohoro Shan mts China **80** F3
Borok-Sulezhskiy Russia **42** H4
Boromo Burkina Faso **96** C3
Boron U.S.A. **128** E4
Borondi India **84** D2
Boroughbridge U.K. **48** F4
Borovichi Russia **42** G4
Borovoy Kirovskaya Oblast' Russia **42** K4
Borovoy Respublika Kareliya Russia **44** R4
Borovoy Respublika Komi Russia **42** L3
Borpeta India see **Barpeta**
Borrisokane Ireland **51** D5
Borroloola Australia **110** B3
Børsa Norway **44** G5
Borşa Romania **43** E7
Borsakelmas sho'rxogi salt marsh Uzbek. **91** J2
Borshchiv Ukr. **43** E6
Borshchovochnyy Khrebet mts Russia **73** J3
Bortala China see **Bole**
Borton U.S.A. **134** B4
Borūjen Iran **88** C4
Borūjerd Iran **88** C3
Borūn Iran **88** E3
Borve U.K. **50** C3
Boryslav Ukr. **43** D6
Boryspil' Ukr. **43** F6
Borzna Ukr. **43** G6
Borzya Russia **73** L2
Bosanska Dubica Bos. & Herz. **58** G2
Bosanska Gradiška Bos. & Herz. **58** G2
Bosanska Krupa Bos. & Herz. **58** G2
Bosanski Novi Bos. & Herz. **58** G2
Bosansko Grahovo Bos. & Herz. **58** G2
Boscawen Island Tonga see **Niuatoputopu**
Bose China see **Baise**
Boseong S. Korea **75** B6
Boshof S. Africa **101** G5
Boshrū'īyeh Iran **88** E3
Bosna i Hercegovina country Europe see **Bosnia and Herzegovina**
Bosna Saray Bos. & Herz. see **Sarajevo**
Bosnia and Herzegovina country Europe **58** G2
Bosobogolo Pan salt pan Botswana **100** F3
Bosobolo Dem. Rep. Congo **98** B3
Bōsō-hantō pen. Japan **75** F6
Bosporus strait Turkey **59** M4
Bossaga Turkm. see **Basaga**
Bossangoa Cent. Afr. Rep. **98** B3
Bossembélé Cent. Afr. Rep. **98** B3
Bossier City U.S.A. **131** E5
Bossiesvlei Namibia **100** C3
Bossut, Cape Australia **108** C4
Bostān Iran **88** B4
Bostan Pak. **89** G4
Bostānābād Iran **88** B2
Bostāneh, Ra's-e pt Iran **88** D5
Bosten Hu l. China **80** G3
Boston U.K. **49** G6

▶**Boston** U.S.A. **135** J2
Capital of Massachusetts.

Boston Mountains U.S.A. **131** E5
Boston Spa U.K. **48** F5
Boswell U.S.A. **134** B3
Botad India **82** B5
Botakara Kazakh. **80** D1
Botany Bay Australia **112** E4
Botev mt. Bulg. **59** K3
Botevgrad Bulg. **59** J3
Bothaville S. Africa **101** H4
Bothnia, Gulf of Fin./Sweden **45** K6
Bothwell Canada **134** E2
Botkins U.S.A. **134** C3
Botlikh Russia **91** G2
Botoșani Romania **43** E7
Botou China **73** L5
Bô Trach Vietnam **70** D3
Botshabelo S. Africa **101** H5
Botswana country Africa **99** C6
Botte Donato, Monte mt. Italy **58** G5
Bottesford U.K. **48** G5
Bottrop Germany **52** G3
Botucatu Brazil **145** A3
Botuporã Brazil **145** C1
Botwood Canada **123** L4
Bouaflé Côte d'Ivoire **96** C4
Bouaké Côte d'Ivoire **96** C4
Bouar Cent. Afr. Rep. **98** B3
Bou Arfa Morocco **54** D5
Bouba Ndjida, Parc National de nat. park Cameroon **97** E4
Bouca Cent. Afr. Rep. **98** B3
Boucaut Bay Australia **108** F3
Bouchain France **52** D4
Boucle du Baoulé, Parc National de la nat. park Mali **96** C3
Bouctouche Canada **123** I5
Boudh India see **Bauda**
Bougaa Alg. **57** I5
Bougainville, Cape Australia **108** D3
Bougainville Island P.N.G. **106** F2
Bougainville Reef Australia **110** D2
Boughessa Mali **96** D3
Bougie Alg. see **Bejaïa**
Bougouni Mali **96** C3
Bougtob Alg. **54** E5
Bouillon Belgium **52** F5
Bouira Alg. **57** H5
Bou Izakarn Morocco **96** C2
Boujdour W. Sahara **96** B2
Boulder Australia **109** C7
Boulder CO U.S.A. **126** G4
Boulder MT U.S.A. **126** E3
Boulder UT U.S.A. **129** H3
Boulder Canyon gorge U.S.A. **129** F3
Boulder City U.S.A. **129** F4
Boulevard U.S.A. **128** E5
Boulia Australia **110** B4
Boulogne France see **Boulogne-sur-Mer**
Boulogne-Billancourt France **52** C6
Boulogne-sur-Mer France **52** B4
Boumerdès Alg. **57** H5
Bouna Côte d'Ivoire **96** C4
Bou Naceur, Jbel mt. Morocco **54** D5
Boû Nâga Mauritania **96** B3
Boundary Mountains U.S.A. **135** J1
Boundary Peak U.S.A. **128** D3
Boundiali Côte d'Ivoire **96** C4
Boundji Congo **98** B4
Boun Nua Laos **70** C2
Bountiful U.S.A. **129** H1
Bounty Islands N.Z. **107** H6
Bounty Trough sea feature S. Pacific Ocean **150** H9
Bourail New Caledonia **107** G4
Bourbon reg. France see **Bourbonnais**
Bourbon terr. Indian Ocean see **Réunion**
Bourbon U.S.A. **134** B3
Bourbonnais reg. France **56** F3
Bourem Mali **96** C3
Bouressa Mali see **Boughessa**
Bourg-Achard France **49** H9
Bourganeuf France **56** E4
Bourg-en-Bresse France **56** G3
Bourges France **56** F3
Bourget Canada **135** H1
Bourgogne reg. France see **Burgundy**
Bourgogne, Canal de France **56** G3
Bourke Australia **112** B3
Bourne U.K. **49** G6
Bournemouth U.K. **49** F8
Bourtoutou Chad **97** F3
Bou Saâda Alg. **57** I6
Bou Salem Tunisia **58** C6
Bouse U.S.A. **129** F5
Bouse Wash watercourse U.S.A. **129** F4
Boussu Belgium **52** D4
Boutilimit Mauritania **96** B3
Bouvet Island terr. S. Atlantic Ocean see **Bouvetøya**

▶**Bouvetøya** terr. S. Atlantic Ocean **148** I9
Dependency of Norway.

Bouy France **52** E5
Bova Marina Italy **58** F6
Bovenden Germany **53** J3
Bow r. Alta Canada **121** I5
Bow r. Alta Canada **126** F2
Bowa China see **Muli**
Bowbells U.S.A. **130** C1
Bowden U.S.A. **134** F4
Bowditch atoll Tokelau see **Fakaofo**
Bowen Australia **110** E4
Bowen, Mount Australia **112** D6
Bowenville Australia **112** E1
Bowers Ridge sea feature Bering Sea **150** H2
Bowie Australia **110** D4
Bowie AZ U.S.A. **129** I5
Bowie TX U.S.A. **131** D5
Bow Island Canada **121** I5
Bowling Green KY U.S.A. **134** B5
Bowling Green MO U.S.A. **130** F4
Bowling Green OH U.S.A. **134** D3
Bowling Green VA U.S.A. **135** G4
Bowling Green Bay National Park Australia **110** D3
Bowman U.S.A. **130** C2
Bowman, Mount Canada **126** C2
Bowman Island Antarctica **152** F2
Bowman Peninsula Antarctica **152** L2
Bowmore U.K. **50** C5
Bowo China see **Bomi**
Bowral Australia **112** E5
Bowser Lake Canada **120** D3
Boxberg Germany **53** J5
Box Elder U.S.A. **130** C2
Box Elder r. U.S.A. **130** C2
Boxtel Neth. **52** F3
Boyabat Turkey **90** D2
Boyana tourist site Bulg. **59** J3
Boyang China see **Poyang**
Boyd r. Australia **112** F2
Boyd Lagoon salt flat Australia **109** D6
Boyd Lake Canada **121** K2
Boydton U.S.A. **135** F5
Boyers U.S.A. **134** F3
Boykins U.S.A. **135** G5
Boyle Canada **121** H4
Boyle Ireland **51** D4
Boyne r. Ireland **51** F4
Boyne City U.S.A. **134** C1
Boysen Reservoir U.S.A. **126** F4
Boysun Uzbek. **89** G2
Boyuibe Bol. **142** F8
Böyük Qafqaz mts Asia/Europe see **Caucasus**

▶**Bozcaada** i. Turkey **59** L5
Most westerly point of Asia.

Bozdağ mt. Turkey **59** L5
Bozdağ mt. Turkey **85** C1
Boz Dağları mts Turkey **59** L5
Bozdoğan Turkey **59** M6
Bozeat U.K. **49** G6
Bozeman U.S.A. **126** F3
Bozen Italy see **Bolzano**
Bozhou China **77** G1
Bozoum Cent. Afr. Rep. **98** B3
Bozova Turkey **90** E3
Bozqūsh, Kūh-e mts Iran **88** B2
Bozüyük Turkey **59** N5
Bozyazı Turkey **85** A1
Bra Italy **58** B2
Brač i. Croatia **58** G3
Bracadale U.K. **50** C3
Bracadale, Loch b. U.K. **50** C3
Bracara Port. see **Braga**
Bracciano, Lago di l. Italy **58** E3
Bracebridge Canada **134** F1
Bräcke Sweden **44** I5
Brackenheim Germany **53** J5
Brackettville U.S.A. **131** C6
Bracknell U.K. **49** G7
Bradano r. Italy **58** G4
Bradenton U.S.A. **133** D7

▶**Brades** Montserrat **137** L5
Temporary capital of Montserrat. Plymouth was abandoned in 1997 owing to volcanic activity.

Bradford Canada **134** F1
Bradford U.K. **48** F5
Bradford OH U.S.A. **134** C3
Bradford PA U.S.A. **135** F3
Bradley U.S.A. **134** B3
Brady U.S.A. **131** D6
Brady Glacier U.S.A. **120** B3
Brae U.K. **50** [inset]
Braemar U.K. **50** F3
Braga Port. **57** B3
Bragado Arg. **144** D5
Bragança Brazil **143** I4
Bragança Port. **57** C3
Bragança Paulista Brazil **145** B3
Brahin Belarus **43** F6
Brahlstorf Germany **53** K1
Brahmanbaria Bangl. **83** G5
Brahmapur India **84** E2
Brahmaputra r. Asia **83** H4
also known as Dihang (India) or Siang (India) or Yarlung Zangbo (China) or Jamuna (Bangladesh)
Brahmaur India **82** D2
Brăila Romania **59** L2
Braine France **52** D5
Braine-le-Comte Belgium **52** E4
Brainerd U.S.A. **130** E2
Braintree U.K. **49** H7
Braithwaite Point Australia **108** F2
Brak r. S. Africa **101** I2
Brake (Unterweser) Germany **53** I1
Brakel Belgium **52** D4
Brakel Germany **53** J3
Brakwater Namibia **100** C2
Bramfield Australia **109** F8
Bramming Denmark **45** F9
Brämön i. Sweden **44** J5
Brampton Canada **134** F2
Brampton England U.K. **48** E4
Brampton England U.K. **49** I6
Bramsche Germany **53** I2
Bramwell Australia **110** C2
Brancaster U.K. **49** H6
Branch Canada **123** L5
Branco r. Brazil **142** F4
Brandberg mt. Namibia **99** B6
Brandbu Norway **45** G6
Brande Denmark **45** F9
Brandenburg land Germany **53** N2
Brandenburg U.S.A. **134** B5
Brandenburg an der Havel Germany **53** M2
Brandfort S. Africa **101** H5
Brandis Germany **53** N3
Brandon Canada **121** L5
Brandon U.K. **49** H6
Brandon MS U.S.A. **131** F5
Brandon VT U.S.A. **135** I2
Brandon Head hd Ireland **51** B5
Brandon Mountain hill Ireland **51** B5
Brandvlei S. Africa **100** E6
Braniewo Poland **47** Q3
Bransfield Strait Antarctica **152** L2
Branson U.S.A. **131** C4
Brantford Canada **134** E2
Branxton Australia **112** E4
Bras d'Or Lake Canada **123** J5
Brasil country S. America see **Brazil**
Brasil, Planalto do plat. Brazil **143** J7
Brasiléia Brazil **142** E6

▶**Brasília** Brazil **145** B1
Capital of Brazil.

Brasília de Minas Brazil **145** B2
Braslav Belarus see **Braslaw**
Braslaw Belarus **45** O9
Brașov Romania **59** K2
Brassey, Mount Australia **109** F5
Brassey Range hills Australia **109** C6
Brasstown Bald mt. U.S.A. **133** D5

▶**Bratislava** Slovakia **47** P6
Capital of Slovakia.

Bratsk Russia 72 I1
Bratskoye Vodokhranilishche *resr* Russia 72 I1
Brattleboro U.S.A. 135 I2
Braunau am Inn Austria 47 N6
Braunfels Germany 53 I4
Braunlage Germany 53 K3
Braunsbedra Germany 53 L3
Braunschweig Germany 53 K2
Brava *i.* Cape Verde 96 [inset]
Brave U.S.A. 134 E4
Bråviken *inlet* Sweden 45 J7
Bravo, Cerro *mt.* Bol. 142 F7
Bravo del Norte, Río *r.* Mex. 124 H6
Bravo del Norte, Río *r.* Mex./U.S.A. *see* Rio Grande
Brawley U.S.A. 129 F5
Bray Ireland 51 F4
Bray, Pays de *reg.* France 52 B5
Bray Island Canada 119 K3
Brazeau *r.* Canada 120 H4
Brazeau, Mount Canada 120 G4

▶Brazil *country* S. America 143 G5
Largest and most populous country in South America and 5th largest and 5th most populous in the world.

Brazil U.S.A. 134 B4
Brazil Basin *sea feature* S. Atlantic Ocean 148 G7
Brazos *r.* U.S.A. 131 E6

▶Brazzaville Congo 99 B4
Capital of Congo.

Brčko Bos. & Herz. 58 H2
Bré Ireland *see* Bray
Breadalbane Australia 110 B4
Breaksea Sound *inlet* N.Z. 113 A7
Bream Bay N.Z. 113 E2
Brechfa U.K. 49 C7
Brechin U.K. 50 G4
Brecht Belgium 52 E3
Breckenridge *MI* U.S.A. 134 C2
Breckenridge *MN* U.S.A. 130 D2
Breckenridge *TX* U.S.A. 131 D5
Břeclav Czechia 47 P6
Brecon U.K. 49 D7
Brecon Beacons *reg.* U.K. 49 D7
Brecon Beacons National Park U.K. 49 D7
Breda Neth. 52 E3
Bredasdorp S. Africa 100 E8
Bredbo Australia 112 D5
Breddin Germany 53 M2
Bredevoort Neth. 52 G3
Bredviken Sweden 44 I3
Bree Belgium 52 F3
Breed U.S.A. 134 A1
Bregenz Austria 47 L7
Breiðafjörður *b.* Iceland 44 [inset 1]
Breiðdalsvík Iceland 44 [inset 1]
Breidenbach Germany 53 I4
Breien U.S.A. 130 C2
Breitenfelde Germany 53 K1
Breitengüßbach Germany 53 K5
Breiter Luzinsee *l.* Germany 53 N1
Breivikbotn Norway 44 M1
Breizh *reg.* France *see* Brittany
Brejo Velho Brazil 145 C1
Brekstad Norway 44 F5
Bremen Germany 53 I1
Bremen *land* Germany 53 I1
Bremen *IN* U.S.A. 134 B3
Bremen *OH* U.S.A. 134 D4
Bremer Bay Australia 109 B8
Bremerhaven Germany 53 I1
Bremer Range *hills* Australia 109 C8
Bremersdorp Swaziland *see* Manzini
Bremervörde Germany 53 J1
Bremm Germany 52 H4
Brenham U.S.A. 131 D6
Brenna Norway 44 H4
Brennero, Passo di *pass* Austria/Italy *see* Brenner Pass
Brennerpaß *pass* Austria/Italy *see* Brenner Pass
Brenner Pass Austria/Italy 58 D1
Brentwood U.K. 49 H7
Brescia Italy 58 D2
Breslau Poland *see* Wrocław
Bresle *r.* France 52 B4
Brésolles, Lac *l.* Canada 123 H3
Bressanone Italy 58 D1
Bressay *i.* U.K. 50 [inset]
Bressuire France 56 D3
Brest Belarus 45 M10
Brest France 56 B2
Brest-Litovsk Belarus *see* Brest
Bretagne *reg.* France *see* Brittany
Breteuil France 52 C5
Brétigny-sur-Orge France 52 C6
Breton Canada 120 H4
Breton Sound *b.* U.S.A. 131 F6
Brett, Cape N.Z. 113 E2
Bretten Germany 53 I5
Bretton U.K. 48 E5
Breueh, Pulau *i.* Indon. 71 A6
Brevard U.S.A. 133 D5
Breves Brazil 143 H4
Brewarrina Australia 112 C2
Brewer U.S.A. 132 G2
Brewster *NE* U.S.A. 130 D3
Brewster *OH* U.S.A. 134 E3
Brewster, Kap *c.* Greenland *see* Kangikajik
Brewster, Lake *imp. l.* Australia 112 B4
Brewton U.S.A. 133 C6
Breyten S. Africa 101 I4
Breytovo Russia 42 H4
Brezhnev Russia *see* Naberezhnyye Chelny
Brezno Slovakia 47 Q6
Brezovo Bulg. 59 K3
Brezovo Polje *hill* Croatia 58 G2
Bria Cent. Afr. Rep. 98 C3
Briançon France 56 H4
Brian Head *mt.* U.S.A. 129 G3
Bribbaree Australia 112 C5
Bribie Island Australia 112 F1
Briceni Moldova 43 E6
Brichany Moldova *see* Briceni
Brichen' Moldova *see* Briceni
Bridgend U.K. 49 D7
Bridge of Orchy U.K. 50 E4
Bridgeport *CA* U.S.A. 128 D2
Bridgeport *CT* U.S.A. 135 I3
Bridgeport *IL* U.S.A. 134 B4
Bridgeport *NE* U.S.A. 130 C3
Bridger Peak U.S.A. 126 G4
Bridgeton U.S.A. 135 H4
Bridgetown Australia 109 B8

▶Bridgetown Barbados 137 M6
Capital of Barbados.

Bridgetown Canada 123 I5
Bridgeville U.S.A. 135 H4
Bridgewater Canada 123 I5
Bridgewater U.S.A. 135 H2
Bridgnorth U.K. 49 E6
Bridgton U.S.A. 135 J1
Bridgwater U.K. 49 D7
Bridgwater Bay U.K. 49 D7
Bridlington U.K. 48 G4
Bridlington Bay U.K. 48 G4
Bridport Australia 111 [inset]
Bridport U.K. 49 E8
Brie *reg.* France 56 F2
Brie-Comte-Robert France 52 C6
Brieg Poland *see* Brzeg
Briery Knob *mt.* U.S.A. 134 E4
Brig Switz. 56 H3
Brigg U.K. 48 G5
Brigham City U.S.A. 126 E4
Brightlingsea U.K. 49 I7
Brighton Canada 135 G1
Brighton U.K. 49 G8
Brighton *CO* U.S.A. 126 G5
Brighton *MI* U.S.A. 134 D2
Brighton *NY* U.S.A. 135 G2
Brighton *WV* U.S.A. 134 D4
Brignoles France 56 H5
Brikama Gambia 96 B3
Brillion U.S.A. 134 A1
Brilon Germany 53 I3
Brindisi Italy 58 G4
Brinkley U.S.A. 131 F5
Brion, Île *i.* Canada 123 J5
Brioude France 56 F4
Brisay Canada 123 H3

▶Brisbane Australia 112 F1
Capital of Queensland. 3rd most populous city in Oceania.

Brisbane Ranges National Park Australia 112 B6
Bristol U.K. 49 E7
Bristol *CT* U.S.A. 135 I3
Bristol *FL* U.S.A. 133 C6
Bristol *NH* U.S.A. 135 J2
Bristol *RI* U.S.A. 135 J3
Bristol *TN* U.S.A. 134 D5
Bristol *VT* U.S.A. 135 I1
Bristol Bay U.S.A. 118 B4
Bristol Channel *est.* U.K. 49 C7
Bristol Lake U.S.A. 129 F4
Britannia Island New Caledonia *see* Maré
British Antarctic Territory *reg.* Antarctica 152 L2
British Columbia *prov.* Canada 120 F5
British Empire Range *mts* Canada 119 J1
British Guiana *country* S. America *see* Guyana
British Honduras *country* Central America *see* Belize

▶British Indian Ocean Territory *terr.* Indian Ocean 149 M6
United Kingdom Overseas Territory.

British Solomon Islands *country* S. Pacific Ocean *see* Solomon Islands
Brito Godins Angola *see* Kiwaba N'zogi
Brits S. Africa 101 H3
Britstown S. Africa 100 F6
Brittany *reg.* France 56 C2
Britton U.S.A. 130 D2
Brive-la-Gaillarde France 56 E4
Briviesca Spain 57 E2
Brixham U.K. 49 D8
Brixia Italy *see* Brescia
Brlik Kazakh. *see* Birlik
Brno Czechia 47 P6
Broach India *see* Bharuch
Broad *r.* U.S.A. 133 D5
Broadalbin U.S.A. 135 H2
Broad Arrow (abandoned) Australia 109 C7
Broadback *r.* Canada 122 F4
Broad Bay U.K. *see* Tuath, Loch a'
Broadford Australia 112 B6
Broadford Ireland 51 D5
Broadford U.K. 50 D3
Broad Law *hill* U.K. 50 F5
Broadmere Australia 110 A3
Broad Peak China/Pak. 89 J3
Broad Sound *sea chan.* Australia 110 E4
Broadstairs U.K. 49 I7
Broadus U.S.A. 126 G3
Broadview Canada 121 K5
Broadway U.S.A. 135 F4
Broadwood N.Z. 113 D2
Brochet Canada 121 K3
Brochet, Lac *l.* Canada 121 K3
Brochet, Lac au *l.* Canada 123 H4
Brocken *mt.* Germany 53 K3
Brockman, Mount Australia 108 B5
Brockport *NY* U.S.A. 135 G2
Brockport *PA* U.S.A. 135 F3
Brockton U.S.A. 135 J2
Brockville Canada 135 H1
Brockway U.S.A. 135 F3
Brodeur Peninsula Canada 119 J2
Brodhead U.S.A. 134 C5
Brodick U.K. 50 D5
Brodnica Poland 47 Q4
Brody Ukr. 43 E6
Bröghīl, Kōtal-e Afgh. 89 I2
Broken Arrow U.S.A. 131 E4
Broken Bay Australia 112 E4
Broken Bow *NE* U.S.A. 130 D3
Broken Bow *OK* U.S.A. 131 E5
Brokenhead *r.* Canada 121 L5
Broken Hill Australia 111 C6
Broken Hill Zambia *see* Kabwe
Broken Plateau *sea feature* Indian Ocean 149 O8
Brokopondo Suriname 143 G2
Brokopondo Stuwmeer *resr* Suriname *see* Professor van Blommestein Meer
Bromberg Poland *see* Bydgoszcz
Brome Germany 53 K2
Bromsgrove U.K. 49 E6
Brønderslev Denmark 45 F8
Brønnøysund Norway 44 H4
Bronson *FL* U.S.A. 133 D6
Bronson *MI* U.S.A. 134 C3
Brooke U.K. 49 I6
Brookfield U.S.A. 134 A2
Brookhaven U.S.A. 131 F6
Brookings *OR* U.S.A. 126 B4
Brookings *SD* U.S.A. 130 D2
Brookline U.S.A. 135 J2
Brooklyn U.S.A. 134 C2
Brooklyn Park U.S.A. 130 E2
Brookneal U.S.A. 135 F5
Brooks Canada 121 I5
Brooks Brook Canada 120 C2
Brooks Range *mts* U.S.A. 118 D3
Brookston U.S.A. 134 B3
Brooksville *FL* U.S.A. 133 D6
Brooksville *KY* U.S.A. 134 C4
Brookton Australia 109 B8
Brookville *IN* U.S.A. 134 C4
Brookville *PA* U.S.A. 134 F3
Brookville Lake U.S.A. 134 C4
Broom, Loch *inlet* U.K. 50 D3
Broome Australia 108 C4
Brora U.K. 50 F2
Brora *r.* U.K. 50 F2
Brösarp Sweden 45 I9
Brosna *r.* Ireland 51 E4
Brosville U.S.A. 134 F5
Brothers *is* India 71 A5
Brough U.K. 48 E4
Brough Ness *pt* U.K. 50 G2
Broughshane U.K. 51 F3
Broughton Island Canada *see* Qikiqtarjuaq
Broughton Islands Australia 112 F4
Brovary Ukr. 43 F6
Brovinia Australia 111 E5
Brovst Denmark 45 F8
Brown City U.S.A. 134 D2
Brown Deer U.S.A. 134 B2
Browne Range *hills* Australia 109 D6
Brownfield U.S.A. 131 C5
Browning U.S.A. 126 E2
Brown Mountain U.S.A. 128 E4
Brownstown U.S.A. 134 B4
Brownsville *KY* U.S.A. 134 B5
Brownsville *PA* U.S.A. 134 F3
Brownsville *TN* U.S.A. 131 F5
Brownsville *TX* U.S.A. 131 D7
Brownwood U.S.A. 131 D6
Browse Island Australia 108 C3
Bruay-la-Buissière France 52 C4
Bruce Peninsula Canada 134 E1
Bruce Peninsula National Park Canada 134 E1
Bruce Rock Australia 109 B7
Bruchsal Germany 53 I5
Brück Germany 53 M2
Bruck an der Mur Austria 47 O7
Brue *r.* U.K. 49 E7
Bruges Belgium *see* Brugge
Brugge Belgium 52 D3
Brühl *Baden-Württemberg* Germany 53 I5
Brühl *Nordrhein-Westfalen* Germany 52 G4
Bruin *KY* U.S.A. 134 D4
Bruin *PA* U.S.A. 134 F3
Bruini India 83 I3
Bruin Point *mt.* U.S.A. 129 H2
Brûk, Wâdi el *watercourse* Egypt *see* Burūk, Wādī al
Brukkaros Namibia 100 D3
Brûlé Canada 120 G4
Brûlé, Lac *l.* Canada 123 J3
Brûly Belgium 52 E5
Brumado Brazil 145 C1
Brumath France 53 H6
Brumunddal Norway 45 G6
Brunau Germany 53 L2
Brundisium Italy *see* Brindisi
Bruneau U.S.A. 126 E4
Brunei *country* Asia 68 E6
Brunei Brunei *see* Bandar Seri Begawan
Brunette Downs Australia 110 A3
Brunflo Sweden 44 I5
Brunico Italy 58 D1
Brünn Czechia *see* Brno
Brunner, Lake N.Z. 113 C6
Bruno Canada 121 J4
Brunswick Germany *see* Braunschweig
Brunswick *GA* U.S.A. 133 D6
Brunswick *MD* U.S.A. 135 G4
Brunswick *ME* U.S.A. 135 K2
Brunswick, Península de *pen.* Chile 144 B8
Brunswick Bay Australia 108 D3
Brunswick Lake Canada 122 E4
Bruntál Czechia 47 P6
Brunt Ice Shelf Antarctica 152 B2
Bruntville S. Africa 101 J5
Bruny Island Australia 111 [inset]
Brusa Turkey *see* Bursa
Brusenets Russia 42 I3
Brushton U.S.A. 135 H1
Brusque Brazil 145 A4
Brussel Belgium *see* Brussels

▶Brussels Belgium 52 E4
Capital of Belgium.

Bruthen Australia 112 C6
Bruxelles Belgium *see* Brussels
Bruzual Venez. 142 E2
Bryan *OH* U.S.A. 134 C3
Bryan *TX* U.S.A. 131 D6
Bryan, Mount *hill* Australia 111 B7
Bryan Coast Antarctica 152 L2
Bryansk *Bryanskaya Oblast'* Russia 43 G5
Bryansk *Respublika Dagestan* Russia 91 G1
Bryant Pond U.S.A. 135 J1
Bryantsburg U.S.A. 134 C4
Bryce Canyon National Park U.S.A. 129 G3
Bryce Mountain U.S.A. 129 I5
Brynbuga U.K. *see* Usk
Bryne Norway 45 D7
Bryukhovetskaya Russia 43 H7
Brzeg Poland 47 P5
Brześć nad Bugiem Belarus *see* Brest
Bua *r.* Malawi 99 D5
Bu'aale Somalia 98 E3
Buala Solomon Is 107 F2
Buan S. Korea 75 B6
Bu'ayj *well* Saudi Arabia 88 C5
Būbiyān, Jazīrat Kuwait 88 C4
Bucak Turkey 59 N6
Bucaramanga Col. 142 D2
Buccaneer Archipelago *is* Australia 108 C4
Buchanan Liberia 96 B4
Buchanan *MI* U.S.A. 134 B3
Buchanan *VA* U.S.A. 134 F5
Buchanan, Lake *salt flat* Australia 110 D4
Buchan Gulf Canada 119 K2

▶Bucharest Romania 59 L2
Capital of Romania.

Büchen Germany 53 K1
Buchen (Odenwald) Germany 53 J5
Bucheon S. Korea 75 B5
Buchholz Germany 53 M1
Buchholz in der Nordheide Germany 53 J1
Buchon, Point U.S.A. 128 C4
Buchy France 52 B5
Bucin, Pasul *pass* Romania 59 K1
Buckambool Mountain *hill* Australia 112 B3
Bückeburg Germany 53 J2
Bücken Germany 53 J2
Buckeye U.S.A. 129 G5
Buckhannon U.S.A. 134 E4
Buckhaven U.K. 50 F4
Buckhorn Lake Canada 135 F1
Buckie U.K. 50 G3
Buckingham U.K. 49 G6
Buckingham U.S.A. 135 F5
Buckingham Bay Australia 67 F9
Buckland Tableland *reg.* Australia 110 E5
Buckleboo Australia 109 G8
Buckle Island Antarctica 152 H2
Buckley *watercourse* Australia 110 B4
Buckley Bay Antarctica 152 G2
Bucklin U.S.A. 130 D4
Buckskin Mountains U.S.A. 129 G4
Bucks Mountain U.S.A. 128 C2
Bucksport U.S.A. 123 H5
Bückwitz Germany 53 M2
București Romania *see* Bucharest
Bucyrus U.S.A. 134 D3
Buda-Kashalyova Belarus 43 F5
Budalin Myanmar 70 A2

▶Budapest Hungary 59 H1
Capital of Hungary.

Budaun India 82 D3
Budawang National Park Australia 112 E5
Budda Australia 112 B3
Budd Coast Antarctica 152 F2
Buddusò *Sardinia* Italy 58 C4
Bude U.K. 49 C8
Bude U.S.A. 131 F6
Budennovsk Russia 91 G1
Buderim Australia 112 F1
Būdīng Iran 88 E5
Büdingen Germany 53 J4
Budīyah, Jabal *hills* Egypt 85 A5
Budongquan China 83 H2
Budoni *Sardinia* Italy 58 C4
Budū, Ḥadabat al *plain* Saudi Arabia 88 C6
Budū', Sabkhat al *salt pan* Saudi Arabia 88 C6
Budweis Czechia *see* České Budějovice
Buenaventura Col. 142 C3
Buena Vista *i.* N. Mariana Is *see* Tinian
Buena Vista *CO* U.S.A. 126 G5
Buena Vista *VA* U.S.A. 134 F5
Buendía, Embalse de *resr* Spain 57 E3

▶Buenos Aires Arg. 144 E4
Capital of Argentina. 2nd most populous city in South America.

Buenos Aires, Lago *l.* Arg./Chile 144 B7
Buerarema Brazil 145 D1
Buet *r.* Canada 123 H1
Búfalo Mex. 131 B7
Buffalo *r.* Canada 120 H2
Buffalo *KY* U.S.A. 134 C5
Buffalo *MO* U.S.A. 130 E4
Buffalo *NY* U.S.A. 135 F2
Buffalo *OK* U.S.A. 131 D4
Buffalo *SD* U.S.A. 130 C2
Buffalo *TX* U.S.A. 131 D6
Buffalo *WY* U.S.A. 126 G3
Buffalo Head Hills Canada 120 G3
Buffalo Head Prairie Canada 120 G3
Buffalo Hump *mt.* U.S.A. 126 E3
Buffalo Lake *Alta* Canada 121 H4
Buffalo Lake *N.W.T.* Canada 120 H2
Buffalo Narrows Canada 121 I4
Buffels *watercourse* S. Africa 100 C5
Buffels Drift S. Africa 101 H2
Buftea Romania 59 K2
Bug *r.* Poland 47 S5
Buga Col. 142 C3
Bugaldie Australia 112 D3
Bugdaýly Turkm. 88 D2
Buggenhout Belgium 52 E3
Bugojno Bos. & Herz. 58 G2
Bugrino Russia 42 K1
Bugsuk *i.* Phil. 68 F5
Bugt China 74 A2
Bugul'ma Russia 41 Q5
Bügür China *see* Luntai
Buguruslan Russia 41 Q5
Buhera Zimbabwe 99 D5
Bühl Germany 53 I6
Buhuşi Romania 59 L1
Buick Canada 120 F3
Builth Wells U.K. 49 D6
Buin, Piz *mt.* Austria/Switz. 47 M7
Bui National Park Ghana 96 C4
Buinsk Russia 43 K5
Bū'īn Zahrā Iran 88 C3
Buitepos Namibia 100 D2
Bujanovac Serbia 59 I3

▶Bujumbura Burundi 98 C4
Capital of Burundi.

Bukachacha Russia 73 L2
Bukadaban Feng *mt.* China 83 G1
Buka Island P.N.G. 106 F2
Būkān Iran 88 B2
Būkand Iran 88 D4
Bukavu Dem. Rep. Congo 98 C4
Bukhara Uzbek. *see* Buxoro
Bukhoro Uzbek. *see* Buxoro
Bukit Baka-Bukit Raya, Taman Nasional *nat. park* Indon. 68 E7
Bukittinggi Indon. 68 C7
Bukkapatnam India 84 C3
Bukoba Tanz. 98 D4
Bükreş Romania *see* Bucharest
Būl, Kūh-e *mt.* Iran 88 D4
Bula P.N.G. 69 K8
Bülach Switz. 56 I3
Bulan *i.* Indon. 71 C7
Bulancak Turkey 90 E2
Bulandshahr India 82 D3
Bulanık Turkey 91 F3
Bulava Russia 74 F2
Bulawayo Zimbabwe 99 C6
Buldan Turkey 59 M5
Buldana India 84 C1
Buldhana India *see* Buldana
Buleda *reg.* Pak. 89 F5
Bulembu Swaziland 101 J3
Bulgan *Bulgan* Mongolia 80 J2
Bulgan *Hovd* Mongolia 80 H2
Bulgar Russia *see* Bolgar
Bulgaria *country* Europe 59 K3
Bŭlgariya *country* Europe *see* Bulgaria
Bulkley Ranges *mts* Canada 120 D4
Bullawarra, Lake *salt flat* Australia 112 A1
Bullen *r.* Canada 121 K1
Buller *r.* N.Z. 113 C5
Buller, Mount Australia 112 C6
Bulleringa National Park Australia 110 C3
Bullfinch Australia 109 B7
Bullhead City U.S.A. 129 F4
Bulli Australia 112 E5
Bullion Mountains U.S.A. 128 E4
Bullo *r.* Australia 108 E3
Bulloo Downs Australia 111 C6
Bulloo Lake *salt flat* Australia 111 C6
Büllsport Namibia 100 C3
Bully Choop Mountain U.S.A. 128 B1
Bulman Australia 108 F3
Bulman Gorge Australia 108 F3
Bulmer Lake Canada 120 F2
Buloh, Pulau *i.* Sing. 71 [inset]
Buloke, Lake *dry lake* Australia 112 A6
Bulolo P.N.G. 69 L8
Bulsar India *see* Valsad
Bultfontein S. Africa 101 H5
Bulukumba Indon. 69 G8
Bulun Russia 65 N2
Bulungu Dem. Rep. Congo 99 C4
Bulung'ur Uzbek. 89 G2
Bumba Dem. Rep. Congo 98 C3
Būmbah Libya 90 A4
Bumbah, Khalīj al *b.* Libya 90 A4
Bumhkang Myanmar 70 B1
Bumhpa Bum *mt.* Myanmar 70 B1
Buna Dem. Rep. Congo 98 B4
Buna Kenya 98 D3
Bunayyān *well* Saudi Arabia 88 C6
Bunazi Tanz. 98 D4
Bunbury Australia 109 A8
Buncrody Ireland 51 F5
Buncrana Ireland 51 E2
Bunda Tanz. 98 D4
Bundaberg Australia 110 F5
Bundaleer Australia 112 C2
Bundarra Australia 112 E3
Bundi India 82 C4
Bundjalung National Park Australia 112 F2
Bundoran Ireland 51 D3
Bundukia South Sudan 97 G4
Buner *reg.* Pak. 89 I3
Bungalaut, Selat *sea chan.* Indon. 68 B7
Bungay U.K. 49 I6
Bungendore Australia 112 D5
Bunger Hills Antarctica 152 F2
Bungle Bungle National Park Australia *see* Purnululu National Park
Bungo-suidō *sea chan.* Japan 75 D6
Bunguran, Kepulauan *is* Indon. *see* Natuna, Kepulauan
Bunguran, Pulau *i.* Indon. *see* Natuna Besar
Bunia Dem. Rep. Congo 98 D3
Buniangа Dem. Rep. Congo 98 C4
Buningonia *well* Australia 109 C7
Bunji Pak. 82 C2
Bunker Group *atolls* Australia 110 F4
Bunkeya Dem. Rep. Congo 99 C5
Bunnell U.S.A. 133 D6
Bünsum China 83 E3
Bunya Mountains National Park Australia 112 E1
Bünyan Turkey 90 D3
Bunyu *i.* Indon. 68 F6
Buôn Đôn Vietnam 71 D4
Buôn Ma Thuôt Vietnam 71 E4
Buor-Khaya, Guba *b.* Russia 65 O2
Bup *r.* China 83 F3
Buqayq Saudi Arabia *see* Abqaiq
Buqbuq Egypt 90 B5
Bura Kenya 98 D4
Buraan Somalia 98 E2
Buram Sudan 97 F3
Buran Kazakh. *see* Boran
Buranhaém *r.* Brazil 145 D2
Buranhém Brazil 145 C2
Burāq Syria 85 C3
Buray *r.* India 82 C5
Buraydah Saudi Arabia 86 F4
Burbach Germany 53 I4
Burbank U.S.A. 128 D4
Burcher Australia 112 C4
Burco Somalia 98 E3
Burdaard Neth. 52 F1
Burdalyk Turkm. 89 G2
Burdigala France *see* Bordeaux
Burdur Turkey 59 N6
Burdur Gölü *l.* Turkey 59 N6
Burdwan India *see* Barddhaman
Burē Eth. 98 D2
Bure *r.* U.K. 49 I6
Bureå Sweden 44 L4
Bureinskiy Khrebet *mts* Russia 74 D2
Bureinskiy Zapovednik *nature res.* Russia 74 D2
Burewala Pak. 89 I4
Bureya *r.* Russia 74 C2
Bureya Range *mts* Russia *see* Bureinskiy Khrebet
Burford Canada 134 E2
Burg Germany 53 L2
Burgas Bulg. 59 L3
Burgaw U.S.A. 133 E5
Burgbernheim Germany 53 K5
Burgdorf Germany 53 K2
Burgeo Canada 123 K5
Burgersdorp S. Africa 101 H6
Burgersfort S. Africa 101 J3
Burges, Mount *hill* Australia 109 C7
Burgess Hill U.K. 49 G8
Burghaun Germany 53 J4
Burghausen Germany 47 N6
Burghead U.K. 50 F3
Burgh-Haamstede Neth. 52 D3
Burgio, Serra di *hill Sicily* Italy 58 F6
Burglengenfeld Germany 53 M5
Burgos Mex. 131 D7
Burgos Spain 57 E2
Burgstädt Germany 53 M4
Burgsvik Sweden 45 K8
Burgum Neth. 52 G1
Burgundy *reg.* France 56 G3
Burhan Budai Shan *mts* China 80 H4
Burhaniye Turkey 59 L5
Burhanpur India 82 D5
Burhar-Dhanpuri India 83 E5
Buri Brazil 145 A3
Burias *i.* Phil. 69 G4
Burin Canada 123 L5
Burin Peninsula Canada 123 L5
Buriram Thai. 70 C4
Buritama Brazil 145 A3
Buriti Alegre Brazil 145 A2
Buriti Bravo Brazil 143 J5
Buritirama Brazil 143 J6
Buritis Brazil 145 B1
Burj Aziz Khan Pak. 89 G4
Burke U.S.A. 130 D3
Burke Island Antarctica 152 K2
Burke Pass N.Z. *see* Burkes Pass
Burkes Pass N.Z. 113 C7
Burkesville U.S.A. 134 C5
Burketown Australia 110 B3
Burkeville U.S.A. 135 F5
Burkina *country* Africa *see* Burkina Faso
Burkina Faso *country* Africa 96 C3
Burk's Falls Canada 122 F5
Burley U.S.A. 126 E4
Burlington Canada 134 F2
Burlington *CO* U.S.A. 130 C4
Burlington *IA* U.S.A. 130 F3
Burlington *KS* U.S.A. 130 E4
Burlington *KY* U.S.A. 134 C4
Burlington *VT* U.S.A. 135 I1
Burlington *WI* U.S.A. 134 A2
Burma *country* Asia *see* Myanmar
Burmantovo Russia 41 S3
Burnaby Canada 120 F5
Burnet U.S.A. 131 D6
Burney U.S.A. 128 C1
Burney, Monte *vol.* Chile 144 B8
Burnham U.S.A. 135 G3
Burnie Australia 111 [inset]
Burniston U.K. 48 G4
Burnley U.K. 48 E5
Burns U.S.A. 126 D4
Burnside *r.* Canada 118 H3
Burnside U.S.A. 134 C5
Burnside, Lake *salt flat* Australia 109 C6
Burns Junction U.S.A. 126 D4
Burns Lake Canada 120 E4
Burntisland U.K. 50 F4
Burnt Lake Canada *see* Brûlé, Lac
Burntwood *r.* Canada 121 L4
Burog Co *l.* China 83 F2
Buron *r.* Canada 123 H2
Burovoy Uzbek. 89 F1
Burqin China 80 G2
Burqu' Jordan 85 D3
Burqu', Qaşr *tourist site* Jordan 85 C3
Burra Australia 111 B7
Burra *i.* U.K. 50 [inset]
Burravoe U.K. 50 [inset]
Burrel Albania 59 I4
Burrel U.S.A. 128 D3
Burren *reg.* Ireland 51 C4
Burrendong, Lake Australia 112 D4
Burren Junction Australia 112 D3
Burrewarra Point Australia 112 E5
Burrinjuck Australia 112 D5
Burrinjuck Reservoir Australia 112 D5
Burro, Serranías del *mts* Mex. 131 C6
Burr Oak Reservoir U.S.A. 134 D4
Burro Creek *watercourse* U.S.A. 129 G4
Burro Peak U.S.A. 129 I5
Burrowa Pine Mountain National Park Australia 112 C6
Burrow Head *hd* U.K. 50 E6
Burrows U.S.A. 134 B3
Burrundie Australia 108 E3
Bursa Turkey 59 M4
Būr Safāga Egypt *see* Būr Safājah
Būr Safājah Egypt 86 D4
Būr Sa'īd Egypt *see* Port Said
Būr Sa'īd Egypt *see* Port Said
Būr Sa'īd *governorate* Egypt *see* Būr Sa'īd
Būr Sa'īd *governorate* Egypt 85 A4
Bürstadt Germany 53 I5
Būr Sudan Sudan *see* Port Sudan
Burt Lake U.S.A. 132 C2
Burton U.S.A. 134 D2

Burton, Lac l. Canada 122 F3
Burton upon Trent U.K. 49 F6
Burträsk Sweden 44 L4
Burt Well Australia 109 F5
Buru i. Indon. 69 H7
Burūk, Wādī al watercourse Egypt 85 A4
Burullus, Baḥra el lag. Egypt see Burullus, Lake
Burullus, Buḥayrat al lag. Egypt see Burullus, Lake
Burullus, Lake lag. Egypt 90 C5
Burultokay China see Fuhai
Burūn, Ra's pt Egypt 85 A4
Burundi country Africa 98 C4
Burunniy Russia see Tsagan Aman
Bururi Burundi 98 C4
Burwash Landing Canada 120 B2
Burwick U.K. 50 G2
Buryn' Ukr. 43 G6
Bury St Edmunds U.K. 49 H6
Burzil Pass Pak. 82 C2
Busambra, Rocca mt. Sicily Italy 58 E6
Busan S. Korea 75 C6
Busanga Dem. Rep. Congo 98 C4
Busby U.S.A. 126 G3
Buseire Syria see Al Buşayrah
Bush r. U.K. 51 F2
Bushêngcaka China 83 E2
Bushenyi Uganda 98 D4
Bushire Iran see Bandar-e Būshehr
Bushmills U.K. 51 F2
Bushnell U.S.A. 133 D6
Businga Dem. Rep. Congo 98 C3
Buşrá ash Shām Syria 85 C3
Busse Russia 74 B2
Busselton Australia 109 A8
Bussum Neth. 52 F2
Bustillos, Lago l. Mex. 127 G7
Busto Arsizio Italy 58 C2
Buta Dem. Rep. Congo 98 C3
Butare Rwanda 98 C4
Butaritari atoll Kiribati 150 H5
Bute Australia 111 B7
Bute i. U.K. 50 D5
Butedale (abandoned) Canada 120 D4
Butha-Buthe Lesotho 101 I5
Butha Qi China see Zalantun
Buthidaung Myanmar 70 A2
Butler AL U.S.A. 131 F5
Butler GA U.S.A. 133 C5
Butler IN U.S.A. 134 C3
Butler KY U.S.A. 134 C4
Butler MO U.S.A. 130 E4
Butler PA U.S.A. 134 F3
Butlers Bridge Ireland 51 E3
Buton i. Indon. 69 G7
Bütow Germany 53 M1
Butte MT U.S.A. 126 E3
Butte NE U.S.A. 130 D3
Buttelstedt Germany 53 L3
Butterworth Malaysia 71 C6
Butterworth S. Africa see Gcuwa
Buttes, Sierra mt. U.S.A. 128 C2
Buttevant Ireland 51 D5
Butt of Lewis hd U.K. 50 C2
Button Bay Canada 121 M3
Butuan Phil. 69 H5
Butuo China 76 D3
Buturlinovka Russia 43 I6
Butwal Nepal 83 E4
Butzbach Germany 53 I4
Buulobarde Somalia 98 E3
Buur Gaabo Somalia 98 E4
Buurhabaka Somalia 98 E3
Buutsagaan Mongolia 80 I2
Buxar India 83 F4
Buxoro Uzbek. 89 G2
Buxtehude Germany 53 J1
Buxton U.K. 48 F5
Buy Russia 42 I4
Buynaksk Russia 91 G2
Buyr Nuur l. Mongolia 73 L3
Büyükçekmece Turkey 90 C2
Büyük Egri Dağ mt. Turkey 85 A1
Büyükmenderes r. Turkey 59 L6
Buzancy France 52 E5
Buzău Romania 59 L2
Buzdyak Russia 41 Q5
Búzi Moz. 99 D5
Büzmeýin Turkm. see Abadan
Buzuluk Russia 41 Q5
Buzuluk r. Russia 43 I6
Buzzards Bay U.S.A. 135 J3
Byakar Bhutan see Jakar
Byala Bulg. 59 K3
Byala Slatina Bulg. 59 J3
Byalynichy Belarus 43 F5
Byarezina r. Belarus 43 F5
Byaroza Belarus 45 N10
Byblos tourist site Lebanon 85 B2
Bydgoszcz Poland 47 Q4
Byelorussia country Europe see Belarus
Byerazino Belarus 43 F5
Byers U.S.A. 126 G5
Byeshankovichy Belarus 43 F5
Byesville U.S.A. 134 E4
Bygland Norway 45 E7
Bykhaw Belarus 43 F5
Bykhov Belarus see Bykhaw
Bykle Norway 45 E7
Bykovo Russia 43 J6
Bylas U.S.A. 129 H5
Bylot Island Canada 119 K2
Byramgore Reef India 84 A4
Byrd Glacier Antarctica 152 H1
Byrdstown U.S.A. 134 C5
Byrkjelo Norway 45 E6
Byrock Australia 112 C3
Byron U.S.A. 135 J1
Byron, Cape Australia 112 F2
Byron Bay Australia 112 F2
Byron Island Kiribati see Nikunau
Byrranga, Gory mts Russia 65 K2
Byske Sweden 44 L4
Byssa Russia 74 C1
Byssa r. Russia 74 C1
Bytom Poland 47 Q5
Bytów Poland 47 P3
Byurgyutli Turkm. 88 D2
Byzantium Turkey see İstanbul

C

Ca, Sông r. Vietnam 70 D3
Caacupé Para. 144 E3
Caatinga Brazil 145 B2
Caazapá Para. 144 E3
Cabaiguán Cuba 133 E8
Caballas Peru 142 C6
Caballococha Peru 142 D4
Caballos Mesteños, Llano de los plain Mex. 131 B6
Cabanaconde Peru 142 D7
Cabanatuan Phil. 69 G3
Cabano Canada 123 H5
Cabdul Qaadir Somalia 98 E2
Cabeceira Rio Manso Brazil 143 G7
Cabeceiras Brazil 145 B1
Cabeza del Buey Spain 57 D4
Cabezas Bol. 142 F7
Cabimas Venez. 142 D1
Cabinda Angola 99 B4
Cabinda prov. Angola 99 B5
Cabinet Inlet Antarctica 152 L2
Cabinet Mountains U.S.A. 126 E2
Cabistra Turkey see Ereğli
Cabo Frio Brazil 145 C3
Cabo Frio, Ilha do i. Brazil 145 C3
Cabonga, Réservoir resr Canada 122 F5
Cabool U.S.A. 131 E4
Caboolture Australia 112 F1
Cabo Orange, Parque Nacional de nat. park Brazil 143 H3
Cabo Pantoja Peru 142 C4
Cabora Bassa, Lake resr Moz. 99 D5
Cabo Raso Arg. 144 C6
Caborca Mex. 127 E7
Cabo San Lucas Mex. 136 C4
Cabot Head hd Canada 134 E1
Cabot Strait Canada 123 J5
Cabourg France 49 G9
Cabo Verde country Africa see Cape Verde
Cabo Verde, Ilhas do is N. Atlantic Ocean 96 [inset]
Cabo Yubi Morocco see Tarfaya
Cabral, Serra do mts Brazil 145 B2
Cäbrayıl Azer. 91 G3
Cabrera, Illa de i. Spain 57 H4
Cabrera, Sierra de la mts Spain 57 C2
Cabri Canada 121 I5
Cabullona Mex. 127 F7
Caçador Brazil 145 A4
Cacagoin China see Qagca
Čačak Serbia 59 I3
Caccia, Capo c. Sardinia Italy 58 C4
Çäçe Turkm. 89 F2
Cacequi Brazil 144 F3
Cáceres Brazil 143 G7
Cáceres Spain 57 C4
Cache Creek Canada 120 F5
Cache Peak U.S.A. 126 E4
Cacheu Guinea-Bissau 96 B3
Cachi, Nevados de mts Arg. 144 C2
Cachimbo, Serra do hills Brazil 143 H5
Cachoeira Brazil 145 D1
Cachoeira Alta Brazil 145 A2
Cachoeira de Goiás Brazil 145 A2
Cachoeira do Arari Brazil 143 I4
Cachoeiro de Itapemirim Brazil 145 C3
Cacine Guinea-Bissau 96 B3
Caciporé, Cabo c. Brazil 143 H3
Cacolo Angola 99 B5
Cacongo Angola 99 B4
Cactus U.S.A. 131 C4
Caçu Brazil 145 A2
Caculé Brazil 145 C1
Čadca Slovakia 47 Q6
Cadereyta Mex. 131 C7
Cadibarrawirracanna, Lake salt flat Australia 111 A6
Cadillac Canada 121 J5
Cadillac U.S.A. 134 C1
Cadiz Phil. 69 G4
Cádiz Spain 57 C5
Cadiz IN U.S.A. 134 C4
Cadiz KY U.S.A. 132 C4
Cadiz OH U.S.A. 134 E3
Cádiz, Golfo de g. Spain 57 C5
Cadiz Lake U.S.A. 129 F4
Cadomin Canada 120 G4
Cadotte r. Canada 120 G3
Cadotte Lake Canada 120 G3
Caen France 56 D2
Caerdydd U.K. see Cardiff
Caerffili U.K. see Caerphilly
Caerfyrddin U.K. see Carmarthen
Caergybi U.K. see Holyhead
Caernarfon U.K. 49 C5
Caernarfon Bay U.K. 49 C5
Caernarvon U.K. see Caernarfon
Caerphilly U.K. 49 D7
Caesaraugusta Spain see Zaragoza
Caesarea Alg. see Cherchell
Caesarea Cappadociae Turkey see Kayseri
Caesarea Philippi Syria see Bāniyās
Caesarodunum France see Tours
Caesaromagus U.K. see Chelmsford
Caetité Brazil 145 C1
Cafayate Arg. 144 C3
Cafelândia Brazil 145 A3
Caffa Crimea see Feodosiya
Cagayan de Oro Phil. 69 G5
Cagayan de Tawi-Tawi i. Phil. 68 F5
Cagles Mill Lake U.S.A. 134 B4
Cagli Italy 58 E3
Cagliari Sardinia Italy 58 C5
Cagliari, Golfo di b. Sardinia Italy 58 C5
Çagyl Turkm. 91 I2
Cahama Angola 99 B5
Caha Mountains hills Ireland 51 C6
Cahermore Ireland 51 B6
Cahersiveen Ireland see Cahirsiveen
Cahir Ireland 51 E5
Cahirsiveen Ireland 51 B6
Cahora Bassa, Lago de resr Moz. see Cabora Bassa, Lake
Cahore Point Ireland 51 F5
Cahors France 56 E4
Cahuapanas Peru 142 C5
Cahul Moldova 59 M2
Caia Moz. 99 D5
Caiabis, Serra dos hills Brazil 143 G6
Caianda Angola 99 C5
Caiapó r. Brazil 145 A1
Caiapó, Serra do mts Brazil 145 A2
Caiapônia Brazil 145 A2
Caibarién Cuba 133 E8
Cai Bâu, Đao i. Vietnam 70 D2
Caicara Venez. 142 E2
Caicos Islands Turks and Caicos Is 137 J4
Caicos Passage Bahamas/Turks and Caicos Is 133 F8
Caidian China 77 G2
Caiguna Australia 109 D8
Caimodorro mt. Spain 57 F3
Cainnyigoin China 76 D1
Cains Store U.S.A. 134 C5
Caipe Arg. 144 C2
Caird Coast Antarctica 152 B1
Cairngorm Mountains U.K. 50 F3
Cairngorms National Park U.K. 50 F3
Cairnryan U.K. 50 D6
Cairns Australia 110 D3
Cairnsmore of Carsphairn hill U.K. 50 E5

▶Cairo Egypt 90 C5
Capital of Egypt. 2nd most populous city in Africa.

Cairo U.S.A. 133 C6
Caisleán an Bharraigh Ireland see Castlebar
Caiundo Angola 99 B5
Caiwarro (abandoned) Australia 112 B2
Caiyuanzhen China see Shengsi
Caizi Hu l. China 77 H2
Cajamarca Peru 142 C5
Cajati Brazil 145 A4
Cajuru Brazil 145 B3
Čakovec Croatia 58 G1
Çal Denizli Turkey 59 M5
Çal Hakkâri Turkey see Çukurca
Cala S. Africa 101 H6
Calabar Nigeria 96 D4
Calabogie Canada 135 G1
Calabria, Parco Nazionale della nat. park Italy 58 G5
Calafat Romania 59 J3
Calagua Mex. 127 F8
Calagurris Spain see Calahorra
Calahorra Spain 57 F2
Calai Angola 99 B5
Calais France 52 B4
Calais U.S.A. 123 I5
Calalasteo, Sierra de mts Arg. 144 C3
Calama Brazil 142 F5
Calama Chile 144 C2
Calamajué Mex. 127 E7
Calamar Col. 142 D1
Calamian Group is Phil. 68 F4
Calamocha Spain 57 F3
Calandula Angola 99 B4
Calang Indon. 71 A6
Calanques, Parc National des nat. park France 56 G5
Calapan Phil. 69 G4
Călărași Romania 59 L2
Calatayud Spain 57 F3
Calayan i. Phil. 69 G3
Calbayog Phil. 69 G4
Calbe (Saale) Germany 53 L3
Calçoene Brazil 143 H3
Calcutta India see Kolkata
Caldas da Rainha Port. 57 B4
Caldas Novas Brazil 143 I7
Calden Germany 53 J3
Calder r. Canada 120 G1
Caldera Chile 144 B3
Caldervale Australia 110 D5
Caldew r. U.K. 48 E4
Caldwell ID U.S.A. 126 D4
Caldwell KS U.S.A. 131 D4
Caldwell OH U.S.A. 134 E4
Caldwell TX U.S.A. 131 D6
Caledon r. Lesotho/S. Africa 101 H6
Caledon S. Africa 100 D8
Caledon Bay Australia 110 B2
Caledonia Canada 134 F2
Caledonia admin. div. U.K. see Scotland
Caledonia U.S.A. 135 G2
Caleta el Cobre Chile 144 B2
Calexico U.S.A. 129 F5
Calf of Man i. Isle of Man 48 C4
Calgary Canada 120 H5
Calhoun U.S.A. 134 B5
Cali Col. 142 C3
Calicut India see Kozhikode
Caliente U.S.A. 129 F3
California U.S.A. 134 F3
California state U.S.A. 127 C4
California, Gulf of g. Mex. 127 E7
California Aqueduct canal U.S.A. 128 C3
Cälilabad Azer. 91 H3
Calingasta Arg. 144 C4
Calipatria U.S.A. 129 F5
Calistoga U.S.A. 128 B2
Calkiní Mex. 136 F4
Callabonna, Lake salt flat Australia 111 C6
Callaghan, Mount U.S.A. 128 E2
Callan Ireland 51 E5
Callan r. U.K. 51 F3
Callander Canada 122 F5
Callander U.K. 50 E4
Callao Peru 142 C6
Callao U.S.A. 129 G2
Callicoon U.S.A. 135 H3
Calling Lake Canada 120 H4
Callington U.K. 49 C8
Calliope Australia 110 E5
Callipolis Turkey see Gallipoli
Calmar U.S.A. 130 F3
Caloosahatchee r. U.S.A. 133 D7
Caloundra Australia 112 F1
Caltagirone Sicily Italy 58 F6
Caltanissetta Sicily Italy 58 F6
Calucinga Angola 99 B5
Calulo Angola 99 B4
Calunga Angola 99 B5
Caluquembe Angola 99 B5
Caluula Somalia 98 F2
Caluula, Raas pt Somalia 98 F2
Calvados Chain is P.N.G. 110 F1
Calvert Hills Australia 110 B3
Calvert Island Canada 120 D5
Calvi Corsica France 56 I5
Calvià Spain 57 H4
Calvinia S. Africa 100 D6
Calvo, Monte mt. Italy 58 F4
Cam r. U.K. 49 H6
Camaçari Brazil 145 D1
Camache Reservoir U.S.A. 128 C2
Camachigama r. Canada 122 F5
Camacho Mex. 131 C7
Camacuio Angola 99 B5
Camacupa Angola 99 B5
Camagüey Cuba 137 I4
Camagüey, Archipiélago de is Cuba 137 I4
Camamu Brazil 145 D1
Camaná Peru 142 D7
Camanongue Angola 99 C5
Camapuã Brazil 143 H7
Camaquã Brazil 144 F4
Çamardı Turkey 90 D3
Camargo Bol. 142 E8
Camargue reg. France 56 G5
Camarillo U.S.A. 128 D4
Camarones Arg. 144 C6
Camarones, Bahía b. Arg. 144 C6
Camas r. U.S.A. 126 E4
Ca Mau Vietnam 71 D5
Ca Mau, Mui c. Vietnam 71 D5
Cambay India see Khambhat
Cambay, Gulf of India see Khambhat, Gulf of
Camberley U.K. 49 G7
Cambodia country Asia 71 D4
Camboriú Brazil 145 A4
Camborne U.K. 49 B8
Cambrai France 52 D4
Cambria admin. div. U.K. see Wales
Cambrian Mountains hills U.K. 49 D6
Cambridge Canada 134 E2
Cambridge N.Z. 113 E3
Cambridge U.K. 49 H6
Cambridge MA U.S.A. 135 J2
Cambridge MD U.S.A. 135 G4
Cambridge MN U.S.A. 130 E2
Cambridge NY U.S.A. 135 I2
Cambridge OH U.S.A. 134 E3
Cambridge Bay Canada 119 H3
Cambridge City U.S.A. 134 C4
Cambridge Springs U.S.A. 134 E3
Cambrien, Lac l. Canada 123 H2
Cambulo Angola 99 C4
Cambundi-Catembo Angola 99 B5
Cambuquira Brazil 145 B3
Cam Co l. China 83 E2
Camdeboo National Park S. Africa 100 G7
Camden AL U.S.A. 133 C5
Camden AR U.S.A. 131 E5
Camden NJ U.S.A. 135 H4
Camden NY U.S.A. 135 H2
Camden SC U.S.A. 133 D5
Camdenton U.S.A. 130 E4
Cameia Angola 99 C5
Cameia, Parque Nacional da nat. park Angola 99 C5
Cameron AZ U.S.A. 129 H4
Cameron LA U.S.A. 131 E6
Cameron MO U.S.A. 130 E4
Cameron TX U.S.A. 131 D6
Cameron Highlands mts Malaysia 71 C6
Cameron Hills Canada 120 G3
Cameron Island Canada 119 H2
Cameron Park U.S.A. 128 C2
Cameroon country Africa 96 E4
Cameroon, Mount vol. Cameroon see Cameroun, Mont
Cameroon Highlands slope Cameroon/Nigeria 96 E4
Caméroun country Africa see Cameroon
Cameroun, Mont vol. Cameroon 96 D4
Cametá Brazil 143 I4
Camiña Chile 142 E7
Camino Real de Tierra Adentro tourist site Mex. 131 B6
Camiri Bol. 142 F8
Camisea Peru 142 D6
Camocim Brazil 143 J4
Camooweal Australia 110 B3
Camooweal Caves National Park Australia 110 B4
Camorta i. India 81 H10
Campana Mex. 131 C7
Campana, Isla i. Chile 144 A7
Campania Island Canada 120 D4
Campbell S. Africa 100 F5
Campbell, Cape N.Z. 113 E5
Campbell, Mount hill Australia 108 E5
Campbellford Canada 135 G1
Campbell Hill hill U.S.A. 134 D3
Campbell Island N.Z. 150 H9
Campbell Lake Canada 121 J2
Campbell Plateau sea feature S. Pacific Ocean 150 H9
Campbell Range hills Australia 108 D3
Campbell River Canada 120 E5
Campbellsville U.S.A. 134 C5
Campbellton Canada 123 I5
Campbelltown Australia 112 E5
Campbeltown U.K. 50 D5
Campeche Mex. 136 F5
Campeche, Bahía de g. Mex. 136 F5
Camperdown Australia 112 A7
Câmpina Romania 59 K2
Campina Grande Brazil 143 K5
Campinas Brazil 145 B3
Campina Verde Brazil 145 A2
Campo Cameroon 96 D4
Campobasso Italy 58 F4
Campo Belo Brazil 145 B3
Campo Belo do Sul Brazil 145 A4
Campo de Diauarum Brazil 143 H6
Campo Florido Brazil 145 A2
Campo Gallo Arg. 144 D3
Campo Grande Brazil 144 F2
Campo Largo Brazil 145 A4
Campo Maior Brazil 143 J4
Campo Maior Port. 57 C4
Campo Mourão Brazil 144 F2
Campos Altos Brazil 145 B2
Campos dos Goytacazes Brazil 145 C3
Campos Novos Brazil 145 A4
Campos Sales Brazil 143 J5
Campton U.S.A. 134 D5
Câmpulung Romania 59 K2
Câmpulung Moldovenesc Romania 59 K1
Camp Verde U.S.A. 129 H4
Camrose Canada 121 H4
Camrose U.K. 49 B7
Camsell Lake Canada 121 I2
Camsell Portage Canada 121 I3
Camsell Range mts Canada 120 F2
Camulodunum U.K. see Colchester
Çan Turkey 59 L4
Ca Na, Mui hd Vietnam 71 E5
Canaã dos Carajás Brazil 143 H5
Canaan r. Canada 123 I5
Canaan U.S.A. 135 I2
Canaan Peak U.S.A. 129 H3
Canabrava Brazil 145 B2
Canacona India 84 B3

▶Canada country N. America 118 H4
Largest country in North America and 2nd in the world. 3rd most populous country in North America.

Canada Basin sea feature Arctic Ocean 153 A1
Canadian U.S.A. 131 C5
Canadian r. U.S.A. 131 E5
Canadian Abyssal Plain sea feature Antarctica 153 A1
Cañadón Grande, Sierra mts Arg. 144 C7
Canaima, Parque Nacional nat. park Venez. 142 F2
Çanakkale Turkey 59 L4
Çanakkale Boğazı strait Turkey see Dardanelles
Canalejas Arg. 144 C5
Canal-Supe, Sacred City of tourist site Peru 142 C6
Cañamares Spain 57 E3
Canandaigua U.S.A. 135 G2
Cananea Mex. 127 F7
Cananéia Brazil 145 B4
Canápolis Brazil 145 A2
Cañar Ecuador 142 C4
Canarias terr. N. Atlantic Ocean see Canary Islands
Canárias, Ilha das i. Brazil 143 J4
Canarias, Islas terr. N. Atlantic Ocean see Canary Islands
Canarreos, Archipiélago de los is Cuba 137 H4

▶Canary Islands terr. N. Atlantic Ocean 96 B2
Autonomous Community of Spain.

Canaseraga U.S.A. 135 G2
Canastota U.S.A. 135 H2
Canastra, Serra da mts Brazil 145 A1
Canastra, Serra da mts Minas Gerais Brazil 145 B2
Canatiba Brazil 145 C1
Canatlán Mex. 131 B7
Canaveral, Cape U.S.A. 133 D6
Cañaveras Spain 57 E3
Canavieiras Brazil 145 D1
Canbelego Australia 112 C3

▶Canberra Australia 112 D5
Capital of Australia and Australian Capital Territory.

Cancún Mex. 137 G4
Çandar Turkey see Kastamonu
Çandarlı Turkey 59 L5
Candela Mex. 131 C7
Candela r. Mex. 131 C7
Candelaria Mex. 127 G7
Candia Greece see Iraklion
Cândido de Abreu Brazil 145 A4
Çandır Turkey 90 D2
Candle Lake Canada 121 J4
Candlewood, Lake U.S.A. 135 I3
Cando U.S.A. 130 D1
Cane r. Australia 108 A5
Canea Greece see Chania
Canela Brazil 145 A5
Canelones Uruguay 144 E4
Cane Valley U.S.A. 134 C5
Cangallo Peru 142 D6
Cangamba Angola 99 B5
Cangandala, Parque Nacional de nat. park Angola 99 B4
Cango Caves S. Africa 100 F7
Cangola Angola 99 B4
Cangshan China 77 H1
Canguaretama Brazil 143 K5
Canguçu Brazil 144 F4
Canguçu, Serra do hills Brazil 144 F4
Cangwu China 77 F4
Cangzhou China 73 L5
Caniapiscau Canada 123 H3
Caniapiscau r. Canada 123 H2
Caniapiscau, Réservoir de l. Canada 123 H3
Caniçado Moz. see Guija
Canicattì Sicily Italy 58 E6
Canim Lake Canada 120 F5
Canindé Brazil 143 K4
Canisteo U.S.A. 135 G2
Canisteo r. U.S.A. 135 G2
Canisteo Peninsula Antarctica 152 K2
Cañitas de Felipe Pescador Mex. 131 C8
Çankırı Turkey 90 D2
Canna Australia 109 A7
Canna i. U.K. 50 C3
Cannanore India see Kannur
Cannanore Islands India 84 B4
Cannelton U.S.A. 134 B5
Cannes France 56 H5
Cannock U.K. 49 E6
Cannon Beach U.S.A. 126 C3
Cann River Australia 112 D6
Canoas Brazil 145 A5
Canõas, Rio das r. Brazil 145 A4
Canoeiros Brazil 145 B2
Canoe Lake Canada 121 I4
Canoe Lake l. Canada 121 I4
Canoinhas Brazil 145 A4
Canon City U.S.A. 127 G5
Cañon Largo watercourse U.S.A. 129 J3
Canoona Australia 110 E4
Canora Canada 121 K5
Canowindra Australia 112 D4
Canso Canada 123 J5
Canso, Cape Canada 123 J5
Cantabrian Mountains Spain see Cantábrica, Cordillera
Cantábrica, Cordillera mts Spain 57 D2
Cantábrico, Mar sea Spain 57 C2
Cantagalo Brazil 145 C3
Canterbury U.K. 49 I7
Canterbury Bight b. N.Z. 113 C7
Canterbury Plains N.Z. 113 C6
Cân Thơ Vietnam 71 D5
Cantil U.S.A. 128 E4
Canton GA U.S.A. 133 C5
Canton IL U.S.A. 130 F3
Canton MO U.S.A. 130 F3
Canton MS U.S.A. 131 F5
Canton NY U.S.A. 135 H1
Canton OH U.S.A. 134 E3
Canton PA U.S.A. 135 G3
Canton SD U.S.A. 130 D3
Canton TX U.S.A. 131 E5
Canton Island atoll Kiribati see Kanton
Cantuaria U.K. see Canterbury
Canunda National Park Australia 111 C8
Canutama Brazil 142 F5
Canutillo Mex. 131 B7
Canvey Island U.K. 49 H7
Canwood Canada 121 J4
Cany-Barville France 49 H9
Canyon U.S.A. 131 C5
Canyon City U.S.A. 126 D3
Canyon City (abandoned) Canada 120 B2
Canyondam U.S.A. 128 C1
Canyon de Chelly National Monument nat. park U.S.A. 129 I3
Canyon Ferry Lake U.S.A. 126 F3
Canyon Lake U.S.A. 129 H5
Canyonlands National Park U.S.A. 129 I2
Canyon Ranges mts Canada 120 E2
Canyons of the Ancients National Monument nat. park U.S.A. 129 I3
Canyonville U.S.A. 126 C4
Cao Bằng Vietnam 70 D2
Caocheng China see Caoxian
Caohai China see Weining
Caohe China see Qichun
Caohu China 80 F3
Caojiahe China see Qichun
Caojian China 76 C3
Caoshi China 74 B4
Caoxian China 77 G1
Caozhou China see Heze
Capac U.S.A. 134 D2
Çapakçur Turkey see Bingöl
Capanaparo r. Venez. 142 E2
Capanema Brazil 143 I4
Capão Bonito Brazil 145 A4
Caparaó, Serra do mts Brazil 145 C3
Cap-aux-Meules Canada 123 J5
Cap-de-la-Madeleine Canada 123 G5
Cape r. Australia 110 D4
Cape Arid National Park Australia 109 C8
Cape Barren Island Australia 111 [inset]
Cape Basin sea feature S. Atlantic Ocean 148 I8
Cape Breton Highlands National Park Canada 123 J5
Cape Breton Island Canada 123 J5
Cape Charles Canada 123 L3
Cape Charles U.S.A. 135 G5
Cape Coast Ghana 96 C4
Cape Coast Castle Ghana see Cape Coast
Cape Cod Bay U.S.A. 135 J3
Cape Cod National Seashore nature res. U.S.A. 135 K3
Cape Coral U.S.A. 133 D7
Cape Crawford Australia 110 A3
Cape Dorset Canada 119 K3
Cape Fanshaw U.S.A. 120 C3
Cape Fear r. U.S.A. 133 E5
Cape George Canada 123 J5
Cape Girardeau U.S.A. 131 F4
Cape Johnson Depth sea feature N. Pacific Ocean 150 E5
Cape Juby Morocco see Tarfaya
Cape Krusenstern National Monument nat. park U.S.A. 118 B3
Capel Australia 109 A8
Cape Le Grand National Park Australia 109 C8
Capelinha Brazil 145 C2
Capella Australia 110 E4
Capelle aan den IJssel Neth. 52 E3
Capelongo Angola see Kuvango
Cape May U.S.A. 135 H4
Cape May Court House U.S.A. 135 H4
Cape May Point U.S.A. 135 H4
Cape Melville National Park Australia 110 D2
Capenda-Camulemba Angola 99 B4
Cape Palmerston National Park Australia 110 E4
Cape Range National Park Australia 108 A5
Cape St George Canada 123 K4

▶Cape Town S. Africa 100 D7
Legislative capital of South Africa.

Cape Tribulation National Park Australia 110 D2
Cape Upstart National Park Australia 110 D3
Cape Verde country Africa 96 [inset]
Cape Verde Basin sea feature N. Atlantic Ocean 148 F5
Cape Verde Plateau sea feature N. Atlantic Ocean 148 F4
Cape Vincent U.S.A. 135 G1
Cape York Peninsula Australia 110 C2
Cap-Haïtien Haiti 137 J5
Capim r. Brazil 143 I4

▶**Capitol Hill** N. Mariana Is 69 L3
Capital of the Northern Mariana Islands, on Saipan.

Capitol Reef National Park U.S.A. 129 H2
Capivara, Represa *resr* Brazil 145 A3
Čapljina Bos. & Herz. 58 G3
Cappadocia *hist. area* Turkey 90 D3
Cappoquin Ireland 51 E5
Capraia, Isola di *i.* Italy 58 C3
Caprara, Punta *pt Sardinia* Italy 58 C4
Capri, Isola di *i.* Italy 58 F4
Capricorn Channel Australia 110 E4
Capricorn Group *atolls* Australia 110 F4
Caprivi Strip *reg.* Namibia 99 C5
Cap Rock Escarpment U.S.A. 131 C5
Capsa Tunisia *see* **Gafsa**
Captain Cook U.S.A. 127 [inset]
Captina *r.* U.S.A. 134 E4
Capuava Brazil 145 B4
Caquetá *r.* Col. 142 E4
Caracal Romania 59 K2

▶**Caracas** Venez. 142 E1
Capital of Venezuela.

Caraguatatuba Brazil 145 B3
Caraí Brazil 145 C2
Carajás, Serra dos *hills* Brazil 143 H5
Carales *Sardinia* Italy *see* **Cagliari**
Caralis *Sardinia* Italy *see* **Cagliari**
Carandaí Brazil 145 C3
Caransebeş Romania 59 J2
Caraquet Canada 123 I5
Caratasca, Laguna de *lag.* Hond. 137 H5
Caratinga Brazil 145 C2
Carauari Brazil 142 E4
Caravaca de la Cruz Spain 57 F4
Caravelas Brazil 145 D2
Carberry Canada 121 L5
Carbó Mex. 127 F7
Carbon, Cap *hd* Alg. 57 F6

▶**Carbón, Laguna del** *l.* Arg. 144 C7
Lowest point in South America.

Carbonara, Capo *c. Sardinia* Italy 58 C5
Carbondale *CO* U.S.A. 129 J2
Carbondale *PA* U.S.A. 135 H3
Carboneras Mex. 131 D7
Carbonia *Sardinia* Italy 58 C5
Carbonita Brazil 145 C2
Carcaixent Spain 57 F4
Carcajou Canada 120 G3
Carcajou *r.* Canada 120 D1
Carcar Phil. 69 G4
Carcassonne France 56 F5
Cardamomes, Chaîne des *mts* Cambodia/Thai. *see* **Cardamom Range**
Cardamom Hills India 84 C4
Cardamom Range *mts* Cambodia/Thai. 71 C4
Cárdenas Cuba 137 H4
Cárdenas Mex. 136 E4
Cardenyabba *watercourse* Australia 112 A2
Çardi Turkey *see* **Harmancık**
Cardiel, Lago *l.* Arg. 144 B7

▶**Cardiff** U.K. 49 D7
Capital of Wales.

Cardiff U.S.A. 135 G4
Cardigan U.K. 49 C6
Cardigan Bay U.K. 49 C6
Cardinal Lake Canada 120 G3
Cardington U.S.A. 134 D3
Cardón, Cerro *hill* Mex. 127 E8
Cardoso Brazil 145 A3
Cardoso, Ilha do *i.* Brazil 145 B4
Cardston Canada 120 H5
Careen Lake Canada 121 I3
Carei Romania 59 J1
Carentan France 56 D2
Carey U.S.A. 134 D3
Carey, Lake *salt flat* Australia 109 C7
Carey Lake Canada 121 K2
Cargados Carajos Islands Mauritius 149 L7
Carhaix-Plouguer France 56 C2
Cariacica Brazil 145 C3
Cariamanga Ecuador 142 C4
Caribbean Sea N. Atlantic Ocean 137 H5
Cariboo Mountains Canada 120 F4
Caribou *r. Man.* Canada 121 M3
Caribou *r. N.W.T.* Canada 120 E2
Caribou U.S.A. 132 G2
Caribou Lake Canada 119 J4
Caribou Mountains Canada 120 H3
Carichic Mex. 127 G8
Carignan France 52 F5
Carinda Australia 112 C3
Cariñena Spain 57 F3
Carinhanha *r.* Brazil 145 C1
Carlabhagh U.K. *see* **Carloway**
Carleton U.S.A. 134 D2
Carleton, Mount *hill* Canada 123 I5
Carletonville S. Africa 101 H4
Carlin U.S.A. 128 E1
Carlingford Lough *inlet* Ireland/U.K. 51 F3
Carlini *research station* Antarctica 152 A2
Carlinville U.S.A. 130 F4
Carlisle U.K. 48 E4
Carlisle *IN* U.S.A. 134 B4
Carlisle *KY* U.S.A. 134 C4
Carlisle *NY* U.S.A. 135 H2
Carlisle *PA* U.S.A. 135 G3
Carlisle Lakes *salt flat* Australia 109 D7
Carlit, Pic *mt.* France 56 E5
Carlos Chagas Brazil 145 C2
Carlow Ireland 51 F5
Carloway U.K. 50 C2
Carlsbad Czechia *see* **Karlovy Vary**
Carlsbad *CA* U.S.A. 128 E5
Carlsbad *NM* U.S.A. 127 G6
Carlsbad Caverns National Park U.S.A. 127 G6
Carlsberg Ridge *sea feature* Indian Ocean 149 L5
Carlson Inlet Antarctica 152 L1
Carlton U.S.A. 130 E2
Carlton Hill Australia 108 E3
Carluke U.K. 50 F5
Carlyle Canada 121 K5
Carmacks Canada 120 B2
Carmagnola Italy 58 B2
Carman Canada 121 L5
Carmana Iran *see* **Kermān**
Carmarthen U.K. 49 C7
Carmarthen Bay U.K. 49 C7
Carmaux France 56 F4
Carmel *IN* U.S.A. 134 B4
Carmel *NY* U.S.A. 135 I3
Carmel, Mount *hill* Israel 85 B3
Carmel Head *hd* U.K. 48 C5
Carmel Valley U.S.A. 128 C3
Carmen *r.* Mex. 131 B6
Carmen U.S.A. 127 F7
Carmen, Isla *i.* Mex. 127 F8
Carmen de Patagones Arg. 144 D6
Carmi U.S.A. 130 F4
Carmichael U.S.A. 128 C2
Carmo da Cachoeira Brazil 145 B3
Carmo do Paranaíba Brazil 145 B2
Carmona Angola *see* **Uíge**
Carmona Spain 57 D5
Carnac France 56 C3
Carnamah Australia 109 A7
Carnarvon Australia 109 A6
Carnarvon S. Africa 100 F6
Carnarvon National Park Australia 110 D5
Carnarvon Range *hills* Australia 109 C6
Carnarvon Range *mts* Australia 110 E5
Carn Dearg *hill* U.K. 50 E3
Carndonagh Ireland 51 E2
Carnegie Australia 109 C6
Carnegie, Lake *salt flat* Australia 109 C6
Carn Eige *mt.* U.K. 50 D3
Carnes Australia 109 F7
Carney Island Antarctica 152 J2
Carnforth U.K. 48 E4
Carn Glas-choire *hill* U.K. 50 F3
Car Nicobar *i.* India 71 A5
Carnlough U.K. 51 G3
Carn nan Gabhar *mt.* U.K. 50 F4
Carn Odhar *hill* U.K. 50 E3
Carnot Cent. Afr. Rep. 98 B3
Carnoustie U.K. 50 G4
Carnsore Point Ireland 51 F5
Carnwath U.K. 50 F5
Caro U.S.A. 134 D2
Carola Cay *reef* Australia 110 F3
Carol City U.S.A. 133 D7
Carolina Brazil 143 I5
Carolina S. Africa 101 J4
Carolina Beach U.S.A. 133 E5
Caroline Canada 120 H4
Caroline Island *atoll* Kiribati 151 J6
Caroline Islands N. Pacific Ocean 69 K5
Caroline Peak N.Z. 113 A7
Caroline Range *hills* Australia 108 D4
Carolingian Westwork and Civitas Corvey *tourist site* Germany 53 J3
Caroní *r.* Venez. 142 F2
Carp Canada 135 G1
Carpathian Mountains Europe 43 C6
Carpaţii *mts* Europe *see* **Carpathian Mountains**
Carpaţii Meridionali *mts* Romania *see* **Transylvanian Alps**
Carpaţii Occidentali *mts* Romania 59 J2
Carpentaria, Gulf of Australia 110 B2
Carpentras France 56 G4
Carpi Italy 58 D2
Carpinteria U.S.A. 128 D4
Carpio U.S.A. 130 C1
Carra, Lough *l.* Ireland 51 C4
Carraig na Siuire Ireland *see* **Carrick-on-Suir**
Carrantuohill *mt.* Ireland 51 C6
Carrara Italy 58 D2
Carrasco, Parque Nacional *nat. park* Bol. 142 F7
Carrathool Australia 112 B5
Carrhae Turkey *see* **Harran**
Carrickfergus U.K. 51 G3
Carrickmacross Ireland 51 F4
Carrick-on-Shannon Ireland 51 D4
Carrick-on-Suir Ireland 51 E5
Carrigallen Ireland 51 E4
Carrigtohill Ireland 51 D6
Carrillo Mex. 131 C7
Carrington U.S.A. 130 D2
Carrizal Mex. 127 G7
Carrizal Bajo Chile 144 B3
Carrizo U.S.A. 129 H4
Carrizo Creek *r.* U.S.A. 131 C4
Carrizo Springs U.S.A. 131 D6
Carrizo Wash *watercourse* U.S.A. 129 I4
Carrizozo U.S.A. 127 G6
Carroll U.S.A. 130 E3
Carrollton *AL* U.S.A. 131 F5
Carrollton *GA* U.S.A. 133 C5
Carrollton *IL* U.S.A. 130 F4
Carrollton *KY* U.S.A. 134 C4
Carrollton *MO* U.S.A. 130 E4
Carrollton *OH* U.S.A. 134 E3
Carrolltown U.S.A. 135 F3
Carron *r.* U.K. 50 E3
Carrot *r.* Canada 121 K4
Carrothers U.S.A. 134 D3
Carrot River Canada 121 K4
Carrowmore Lake Ireland 51 C3
Carrsville U.S.A. 135 G5
Carruthers Lake Canada 121 K2
Carry Falls Reservoir U.S.A. 135 H1
Çarşamba Turkey 90 E2
Carson *r.* U.S.A. 128 D2
Carson City *MI* U.S.A. 134 C2

▶**Carson City** *NV* U.S.A. 128 D2
Capital of Nevada.

Carson Escarpment Australia 108 D3
Carson Lake U.S.A. 128 D2
Carson Sink *l.* U.S.A. 128 D2
Carstensz Pyramid *mt.* Indon. *see* **Jaya, Puncak**
Carstensz-top *mt.* Indon. *see* **Jaya, Puncak**
Carswell Lake Canada 121 I3
Cartagena Col. 142 C1
Cartagena Spain 57 F5
Carteret Group *is* P.N.G. *see* **Kilinailau Islands**
Carteret Island Solomon Is *see* **Malaita**
Cartersville U.S.A. 133 C5
Carthage *tourist site* Tunisia 58 D6
Carthage *MO* U.S.A. 131 E4
Carthage *NC* U.S.A. 133 E5
Carthage *NY* U.S.A. 135 H2
Carthage *TX* U.S.A. 131 E5
Carthago *tourist site* Tunisia *see* **Carthage**
Carthago Nova Spain *see* **Cartagena**
Cartier Island Australia 108 C3
Cartmel U.K. 48 E4
Cartwright *Man.* Canada 121 L5
Cartwright *Nfld. and Lab.* Canada 123 K3
Caruarú Brazil 143 K5
Carúpano Venez. 142 F1
Caruthersville U.S.A. 131 F4
Carver U.S.A. 134 D5
Carvin France 52 C4
Cary U.S.A. 132 E5
Caryapundy Swamp Australia 111 C6
Casablanca Morocco 54 C5
Casa Branca Brazil 145 B3
Casa de Piedra, Embalse *resr* Arg. 144 C5
Casa Grande U.S.A. 129 H5
Casale Monferrato Italy 58 C2
Casalmaggiore Italy 58 D2
Casas Grandes Mex. 127 G7
Casca Brazil 145 A5
Cascade Australia 109 C8
Cascade *r.* N.Z. 113 B7
Cascade *ID* U.S.A. 126 D3
Cascade *MT* U.S.A. 126 F3
Cascade Point N.Z. 113 B7
Cascade Range *mts* Canada/U.S.A. 126 C4
Cascade Reservoir U.S.A. 126 D3
Cascais Port. 57 B4
Cascavel Brazil 144 F2
Casco Bay U.S.A. 135 K2
Caserta Italy 58 F4
Casey *research station* Antarctica 152 F2
Casey Bay Antarctica 152 D2
Caseyr, Raas *c.* Somalia *see* **Gwardafuy, Gees**
Cashel Ireland 51 E5
Cashmere Australia 112 D1
Casino Australia 112 F2
Casiquiare, Canal *r.* Venez. 142 E3
Casita Mex. 127 F7
Casnewydd U.K. *see* **Newport**
Caspe Spain 57 F3
Casper U.S.A. 126 G4
Caspian Lowland Kazakh./Russia 78 D2

▶**Caspian Sea** *l.* Asia/Europe 91 H1
Largest lake in Asia/Europe and the world, and lowest point in Europe.

Cass U.S.A. 134 F4
Cass *r.* U.S.A. 134 D2
Cassacatiza Moz. 99 D5
Cassadaga U.S.A. 134 F2
Cassaigne Alg. *see* **Sidi Ali**
Cassamba Angola 99 C5
Cass City U.S.A. 134 D2
Cassel France 52 C4
Casselman Canada 135 H1
Cássia Brazil 145 B3
Cassiar Mountains Canada 120 D2
Cassilândia Brazil 145 A2
Cassilis Australia 112 D4
Cassino Italy 58 E4
Cassley *r.* U.K. 50 E3
Cassongue Angola 99 B5
Cassopolis U.S.A. 134 B3
Cassville U.S.A. 131 E4
Castanhal Brazil 143 I4
Castanho Brazil 142 F5
Castaños Mex. 131 C7
Castelfranco Veneto Italy 58 D2
Castell-nedd U.K. *see* **Neath**
Castell Newydd Emlyn U.K. *see* **Newcastle Emlyn**
Castellón Spain *see* **Castellón de la Plana**
Castellón de la Plana Spain 57 F4
Castelo Branco Port. 57 C4
Castelo de Vide Port. 57 C4
Casteltermini *Sicily* Italy 58 E6
Castelvetrano *Sicily* Italy 58 E6
Castiglione della Pescaia Italy 58 D3
Castignon, Lac *l.* Canada 123 H2
Castilla y León *reg.* Spain 56 B6
Castlebar Ireland 51 C4
Castlebay U.K. 50 B4
Castlebellingham Ireland 51 F4
Castleblayney Ireland 51 F3
Castlebridge Ireland 51 F5
Castle Carrock U.K. 48 E4
Castle Cary U.K. 49 E7
Castle Dale U.S.A. 129 H2
Castlederg U.K. 51 E3
Castledermot Ireland 51 F5
Castle Dome Mountains U.S.A. 129 F5
Castle Donington U.K. 49 F6
Castle Douglas U.K. 50 F6
Castleford U.K. 48 F5
Castlegar Canada 120 G5
Castlegregory Ireland 51 B5
Castle Island Bahamas 133 F8
Castleisland Ireland 51 C5
Castlemaine Australia 112 B6
Castlemaine Ireland 51 C5
Castlemartyr Ireland 51 D6
Castle Mountain *Alta* Canada 120 H5
Castle Mountain *Y.T.* Canada 120 C1
Castle Mountain U.S.A. 128 C4
Castle Peak *hill H.K.* China 77 [inset]
Castle Peak Bay *H.K.* China 77 [inset]
Castlepoint N.Z. 113 F5
Castlepollard Ireland 51 E4
Castlerea Ireland 51 D4
Castlereagh *r.* Australia 112 C3
Castle Rock U.S.A. 126 G5
Castletown Ireland 51 E5
Castletown Isle of Man 48 C4
Castor Canada 121 I4
Castor *r.* U.S.A. 131 F4
Castor, Rivière du *r.* Canada 122 F3
Castra Regina Germany *see* **Regensburg**
Castres France 56 F5
Castricum Neth. 52 E2

▶**Castries** St Lucia 137 L6
Capital of St Lucia.

Castro Brazil 145 A4
Castro Chile 144 B6
Castro Alves Brazil 145 D1
Castro Verde Port. 57 B5
Castroville U.S.A. 128 C3
Çat Turkey 91 F3
Catacaos Peru 142 B5
Cataguases Brazil 145 C3
Catahoula Lake U.S.A. 131 E6
Çatak Turkey 91 F3
Catalão Brazil 145 B2
Çatalca Yarımadası *pen.* Turkey 59 M4
Çatal Hüyük *tourist site* Turkey 90 D3
Catalina U.S.A. 129 H5
Catalonia *aut. comm.* Spain *see* **Cataluña**
Cataluña *aut. comm.* Spain 57 G3
Catalunya *aut. comm.* Spain *see* **Cataluña**
Catamarca Arg. 144 C3
Catana *Sicily* Italy *see* **Catania**
Catanduanes *i.* Phil. 69 G4
Catanduva Brazil 145 A3
Catania *Sicily* Italy 58 F6
Catanzaro Italy 58 G5
Cataract Creek *watercourse* U.S.A. 129 G3
Catarina U.S.A. 131 D6
Catarina, Raso da *hills* Brazil 143 K5
Catarino Rodríguez Mex. 131 C7
Catarman Phil. 69 G4
Catastrophe, Cape Australia 111 A7
Catawba *r.* U.S.A. 133 D5
Cataxa Moz. 99 D5
Cat Ba, Đao *i.* Vietnam 70 D2
Catbalogan Phil. 69 G4
Catembe Moz. 101 K4
Catengue Angola 99 B5
Catete Angola 99 B4
Cathair Dónall Ireland 51 B6
Cathcart Australia 112 D6
Cathcart S. Africa 101 H7
Cathedral Peak S. Africa 101 I5
Cathedral Rock National Park Australia 112 F3
Catherine, Mount U.S.A. 129 G2
Catheys Valley U.S.A. 128 C3
Cathlamet U.S.A. 126 C3
Catió Guinea-Bissau 96 B3
Catisimiña Venez. 142 F3
Cat Island Bahamas 133 F7
Cat Lake Canada 121 N5
Catlettsburg U.S.A. 134 D4
Catoche, Cabo *c.* Mex. 133 C8
Cato Island and Bank *reef* Australia 110 F4
Catriló Arg. 144 D5
Cats, Mont des *hill* France 52 C4
Catskill U.S.A. 135 I2
Catskill Mountains U.S.A. 135 H2
Catuane Moz. 101 K4
Cauayan Phil. 69 G5
Caubvick, Mount Canada 123 J2
Cauca *r.* Col. 137 J7
Caucaia Brazil 143 K4
Caucasia Col. 142 C2
Caucasus *mts* Asia/Europe 91 F2
Cauchon Lake Canada 121 L4
Caudry France 52 D4
Câu Giat Vietnam 70 D3
Caulonia Italy 58 G5
Caungula Angola 99 B4
Cauquenes Chile 144 B5
Causapscal Canada 123 I4
Cavaglià Italy 58 C2
Cavalcante, Serra do *hills* Brazil 145 B1
Cavalier U.S.A. 130 D1
Cavan Ireland 51 E4
Çavdır Turkey 59 M6
Cave City U.S.A. 134 C5
Cave Creek U.S.A. 129 H5
Caveira *r.* Brazil 145 C1
Cavern Island Myanmar 71 B5
Cave Run Lake U.S.A. 134 D4
Caviana, Ilha *i.* Brazil 143 H3
Cawdor U.K. 50 F3
Cawnpore India *see* **Kanpur**
Cawston U.K. 49 I6
Caxias Brazil 143 J4
Caxias do Sul Brazil 145 A5
Caxito Angola 99 B4
Çay Turkey 59 N5
Cayambe, Volcán *vol.* Ecuador 142 C3
Çaybaşı Turkey *see* **Çayeli**
Çaycuma Turkey 59 O4
Çayeli Turkey 91 F2

▶**Cayenne** Fr. Guiana 143 H3
Capital of French Guiana.

Cayeux-sur-Mer France 52 B4
Çayırhan Turkey 59 N4
Cayman Brac *i.* Cayman Is 137 I5

▶**Cayman Islands** *terr.* West Indies 137 H5
United Kingdom Overseas Territory.

Cayman Trench *sea feature* Caribbean Sea 148 C4
Caynaba Somalia 98 E3
Cay Sal *i.* Bahamas 133 D8
Cay Sal Bank *sea feature* Bahamas 133 D8
Cay Santa Domingo *i.* Bahamas 133 F8
Cayucos U.S.A. 128 C4
Cayuga Canada 134 F2
Cayuga Lake U.S.A. 135 G2
Cay Verde *i.* Bahamas 133 F8
Cazê China 83 F3
Cazenovia U.S.A. 135 H2
Cazombo Angola 99 C5
Ceadâr-Lunga Moldova *see* **Ciadîr-Lunga**
Ceanannus Mór Ireland *see* **Kells**
Ceará Brazil *see* **Fortaleza**
Ceara Abyssal Plain *sea feature* S. Atlantic Ocean 148 F6
Ceatharlach Ireland *see* **Carlow**
Ceballos Mex. 131 B7
Cebu Phil. 69 G4
Cebu *i.* Phil. 69 G4
Čechy *reg.* Czechia 47 N6
Cecil Plains Australia 112 E1
Cecil Rhodes, Mount *hill* Australia 109 C6
Cecina Italy 58 D3
Cedar *r. ND* U.S.A. 130 C2
Cedar *r. NE* U.S.A. 130 D3
Cedar City U.S.A. 129 G3
Cedaredge U.S.A. 129 J2
Cedar Falls U.S.A. 130 E3
Cedar Grove U.S.A. 134 B2
Cedar Hill *NM* U.S.A. 129 J3
Cedar Hill *TN* U.S.A. 134 B5
Cedar Island U.S.A. 135 H5
Cedar Lake Canada 121 K4
Cedar Point U.S.A. 134 D3
Cedar Rapids U.S.A. 130 F3
Cedar Run U.S.A. 135 H4
Cedar Springs U.S.A. 134 C2
Cedartown U.S.A. 133 C5
Cedarville S. Africa 101 I6
Cedros Mex. 127 F8
Cedros, Cerro *mt.* Mex. 127 E7
Cedros, Isla *i.* Mex. 127 E7
Ceduna Australia 109 F8
Ceeldheere Somalia 98 E3
Ceerigaabo Somalia 98 E2
Cefalù *Sicily* Italy 58 F5
Cegléd Hungary 59 H1
Cêgnê China 76 B1
Ceheng China 76 E3
Çekerek Turkey 90 D2
Çekiçler Turkm. 88 D2
Celaya Mex. 136 D4
Celbridge Ireland 51 F4

▶**Celebes** *i.* Indon. 69 G7
4th largest island in Asia.

Celebes Basin *sea feature* Pacific Ocean 150 E5
Celebes Sea Indon./Phil. 69 G6
Celestún Mex. 136 F4
Celina *OH* U.S.A. 134 C3
Celina *TN* U.S.A. 134 C5
Celje Slovenia 58 F1
Celle Germany 53 K2
Celovec Austria *see* **Klagenfurt am Wörthersee**
Celtic Sea Ireland/U.K. 46 D5
Celtic Shelf *sea feature* N. Atlantic Ocean 148 H2
Çemenibit Turkm. 89 F3
Cenderawasih, Teluk *b.* Indon. 69 J7
Çendir *r.* Turkm. 88 D2
Centane S. Africa 101 I7
Centenary Zimbabwe 99 D5
Center *NE* U.S.A. 130 D3
Center *TX* U.S.A. 131 E6
Centereach U.S.A. 135 I3
Center Point U.S.A. 133 C5
Centerville *IA* U.S.A. 130 E3
Centerville *MO* U.S.A. 131 F4
Centerville *TX* U.S.A. 131 E6
Centerville *WV* U.S.A. 134 E4
Centrafricaine, République *country* Africa *see* **Central African Republic**
Central *admin. dist.* Botswana 101 H2
Central, Cordillera *mts* Col. 142 C3
Central, Cordillera *mts* Peru 142 C6
Central African Empire *country* Africa *see* **Central African Republic**
Central African Republic *country* Africa 98 B3
Central Brahui Range *mts* Pak. 89 G4
Central Butte Canada 126 G2
Central City U.S.A. 130 D3
Centralia *IL* U.S.A. 130 F4
Centralia *WA* U.S.A. 126 C3
Central Kalahari Game Reserve *nature res.* Botswana 100 F2
Central Kara Rise *sea feature* Arctic Ocean 153 F1
Central Makran Range *mts* Pak. 89 G5
Central Mount Stuart *hill* Australia 108 F5
Central Pacific Basin *sea feature* Pacific Ocean 150 H5
Central Provinces *state* India *see* **Madhya Pradesh**
Central Range *mts* P.N.G. 69 K7
Central Russian Upland *hills* Russia 43 H5
Central Siberian Plateau Russia 65 M3
Central Square U.S.A. 135 G2
Centre U.S.A. 133 C5
Centreville *AL* U.S.A. 133 C5
Centreville *MD* U.S.A. 135 G4
Cenxi China 77 F4
Cenyang China *see* **Hengfeng**
Ceos *i.* Greece *see* **Tzia**
Cephaloedium *Sicily* Italy *see* **Cefalù**
Cephalonia *i.* Greece 59 I5
Ceram *i.* Indon. *see* **Seram**
Ceram Sea Indon. *see* **Seram, Laut**
Cerbat Mountains U.S.A. 129 F4
Čerchov *mt.* Czechia 53 M5
Ceres Arg. 144 D3
Ceres Brazil 145 A1
Ceres S. Africa 100 D7
Ceres U.S.A. 128 C3
Céret France 56 F5
Cerezo de Abajo Spain 57 E3
Cerignola Italy 58 F4
Cerigo *i.* Greece *see* **Kythira**
Cêringgolêb China *see* **Dongco**
Çerkeş Turkey 90 D2
Çerkeşli Turkey 59 M4
Çermik Turkey 91 E3
Cernăuţi Ukr. *see* **Chernivtsi**
Cernavodă Romania 59 M2
Cerralvo, Isla *i.* Mex. 136 C4
Cërrik Albania 59 H4
Cerritos Mex. 136 D4
Cerro Azul Brazil 145 A4
Cerro de Pasco Peru 142 C6
Cerros Colorados, Embalse *resr* Arg. 144 C5
Cervantes, Cerro *mt.* Arg. 144 B8
Cervati, Monte *mt.* Italy 58 F4
Cervione *Corsica* France 56 I5
Cervo Spain 57 C2
Cesena Italy 58 E2
Cēsis Latvia 45 N8
Česká Republika *country* Europe *see* **Czech Republic**
České Budějovice Czechia 47 O6
Českomoravská vysočina *hills* Czechia 47 O6
Český Krumlov Czechia 47 O6
Český les *mts* Czechia/Germany 53 M5
Çeşme Turkey 59 L5
Cessnock Australia 112 E4
Cestos City Liberia 96 C4
Cetatea Albă Ukr. *see* **Bilhorod-Dnistrovs'kyy**
Cetinje Montenegro 58 H3
Cetraro Italy 58 F5

▶**Ceuta** N. Africa 57 D6
Autonomous Community of Spain.

Ceva-i-Ra *reef* Fiji 107 H4
Cévennes *mts* France 56 F5
Cévennes, Parc National des *nat. park* France 56 F4
Cevizli Turkey 85 C1
Cevizlik Turkey *see* **Maçka**
Ceyhan Turkey 90 D3
Ceyhan *r.* Turkey 85 B1
Ceyhan Boğazı *r. mouth* Turkey 85 B1
Ceylanpınar Turkey 91 F3
Ceylon *country* Asia *see* **Sri Lanka**
Chābahār Iran 89 F5
Chabrol *i.* New Caledonia *see* **Lifou**
Chabug China 83 E2
Chabyêr Caka *salt l.* China 83 F3
Chachapoyas Peru 142 C5
Chacharan Pak. 89 H4
Chäche Turkm. *see* **Çäçe**
Chachoengsao Thai. 71 C4
Chachro Pak. 89 H5
Chaco *r.* U.S.A. 129 I3
Chaco Boreal *reg.* Para. 144 E2
Chaco Culture National Historical Park *nat. park* U.S.A. 129 J3
Chaco Mesa *plat.* U.S.A. 129 J4

▶**Chad** *country* Africa 97 E3
5th largest country in Africa.

Chad, Lake Africa 97 E3
Chadaasan Mongolia 72 I3
Chadan Russia 80 H1
Chadibe Botswana 101 H2
Chadron U.S.A. 130 C3
Chadyr-Lunga Moldova *see* **Ciadîr-Lunga**
Chae Hom Thai. 70 B3
Chaeryŏng N. Korea 75 B5
Chae Son National Park Thai. 70 B3
Chagai Pak. 89 G4
Chagai Hills Afgh./Pak. 89 F4
Chagdo Kangri *mt.* China 83 F2
Chaghcharān Afgh. 89 G3
Chagny France 56 G3
Chagoda Russia 42 G4
Chagos Archipelago *is* B.I.O.T. 149 M6
Chagos-Laccadive Ridge *sea feature* Indian Ocean 149 M6
Chagos Trench *sea feature* Indian Ocean 149 M6
Chagoyan Russia 74 C1
Chagrayskoye Plato *plat.* Kazakh. *see* **Shagyray, Plato**
Chagyoi China 76 C2
Chāh Āb Afgh. 89 H2
Chāh Ākhvor Iran 89 E3
Chāh 'Alī Akbar Iran 88 E3
Chāhār Borj Iran 88 E2
Chāhār Kent Afgh. 89 G2
Chahbounia Alg. 57 H6
Chahchaheh Turkm. 89 F2
Chāh-e Bāzargānī Iran 88 D4
Chāh-e Dow Chāhī Iran 88 D4
Chāh-e Khoshāb Iran 88 E3
Chāh-e Rāh Iran 88 D4
Chāh Kūh Iran 88 D4
Chāh Lak Iran 88 E5
Chah Sandan Pak. 89 F4
Chaibasa India 83 F5
Chaigneau, Lac *l.* Canada 123 I3
Chainat Thai. 70 C4
Chainjoin Co *l.* China 83 F2
Chai Prakan Thai. 70 B3
Chaitén Chile 144 B6
Chai Wan *H.K.* China 77 [inset]
Chaiya Thai. 71 B5
Chaiyaphum Thai. 70 C4
Chajarí Arg. 144 E4
Chakai India 83 F4
Chak Amru Pak. 89 I3
Chakar *r.* Pak. 89 H4
Chakaria Bangl. 83 H5
Chakdarra Pak. 89 I3
Chakku Pak. 89 G5
Chakonipau, Lac *l.* Canada 123 H2
Chakoria Bangl. *see* **Chakaria**
Chakvi Georgia 91 F2
Chala Peru 142 D7
Chalatenango El Salvador 136 G6
Chaláua Moz. 99 D5
Chalaxung China 76 C1
Chalcedon Turkey *see* **Kadıköy**
Chalengkou China 80 H4
Chaleur Bay *inlet* Canada 123 I4
Chaleurs, Baie des *inlet* Canada *see* **Chaleur Bay**
Chali China 76 C2
Chaling China 77 G3
Chalisgaon India 84 B1
Chalki *i.* Greece 59 L6
Chalkida Greece 59 J5
Challakere India 84 C3
Challans France 56 D3
Challapata Bol. 142 E7

▶**Challenger Deep** *sea feature* N. Pacific Ocean 150 F5
Deepest point in the world (Mariana Trench).

Challenger Fracture Zone *sea feature* S. Pacific Ocean 150 M8
Challis U.S.A. 126 E3
Chalmette U.S.A. 131 F6

Châlons-en-Champagne France 52 E6
Châlons-sur-Marne France see Châlons-en-Champagne
Chalon-sur-Saône France 56 G3
Chālūs Iran 88 C2
Cham Germany 53 M5
Cham, Cu Lao i. Vietnam 70 E4
Cham, Kūh-e hill Iran 88 C3
Chamah, Gunung mt. Malaysia 71 C6
Chamaico Arg. 144 D5
Chamais Bay Namibia 100 B4
Chaman Pak. 78 F3
Chaman Bīd Iran 88 E2
Chamao, Khao mt. Thai. 71 C4
Chamarajanagar India 84 C4
Chamba India 82 D2
Chamba Tanz. 99 D5
Chambal r. India 82 D4
Chambas Cuba 133 E8
Chambeaux, Lac l. Canada 123 H3
Chamberlain r. Australia 108 D4
Chamberlain Canada 121 J5
Chamberlain U.S.A. 130 D3
Chamberlain Lake U.S.A. 132 G2
Chambers U.S.A. 129 I4
Chambersburg U.S.A. 135 G4
Chambers Island U.S.A. 134 B1
Chambéry France 56 G4
Chambeshi r. Zambia 99 C5
Chambi, Jebel mt. Tunisia 58 C7
Chambūk Iran 88 E3
Chamdo China see Qamdo
Chamechaude mt. France 56 G4
Chamiss Bay Canada 120 E5
Chamoli India see Gopeshwar
Chamonix-Mont-Blanc France 56 H4
Champa India 83 E5
Champagne-Ardenne admin. reg. France see Alsace, Champagne-Ardenne et Lorraine
Champagne Castle mt. S. Africa 101 I5
Champagne Humide reg. France 56 G2
Champagne Pouilleuse reg. France 56 F2
Champagnole France 56 G3
Champagny Islands Australia 108 D3
Champaign U.S.A. 130 F3
Champasak Laos 70 D4
Champdoré, Lac l. Canada 123 I3
Champhai India 83 H5
Champion Canada 120 H5
Champlain U.S.A. 135 G4
Champlain, Lake Canada/U.S.A. 135 I1
Champotón Mex. 136 F5
Chamzinka Russia 43 J5
Chana Thai. 71 C6
Chanak Turkey see Çanakkale
Chañaral Chile 144 B3
Chanda India see Chandrapur
Chandalar r. U.S.A. 118 D3
Chandausi India 82 D3
Chandbali India 83 F5
Chandeleur Islands U.S.A. 131 F6
Chanderi India 82 D4
Chandigarh India 82 D3
Chandil India 83 F5
Chandir Uzbek. 89 G2
Chandler Canada 123 I4
Chandler AZ U.S.A. 129 H5
Chandler IN U.S.A. 134 B4
Chandler OK U.S.A. 131 D5
Chandod India 82 C5
Chandos Lake Canada 135 G1
Chandpur Bangl. 83 G5
Chandpur India 82 D3
Chandragiri India 84 C3
Chandrapur India 84 C2
Chandvad India 84 B1
Chang, Ko i. Thai. 71 C4
Chang'an China 77 F1
Changane r. Moz. 101 K3
Changbai China 74 C4
Changbai Shan mts China/N. Korea 74 B4
Chang Cheng research station Antarctica see Great Wall
Changcheng China 77 F5
Changchow Fujian China see Zhangzhou
Changchow Jiangsu China see Changzhou
Changchun China 74 B4
Changchunling China 74 B3
Changde China 77 F2
Changgang China 77 G3
Changge China 77 G1
Changgo China 83 F3
Chang Hu l. China 77 G2
Changhua Taiwan 77 I3
Changhwa Taiwan see Changhua
Changi Sing. 71 [inset]
Changji China 80 G3
Changjiang China 77 F5
Chang Jiang r. China see Yangtze
Changjiang Kou China see Mouth of the Yangtze
Changjin-ho resr N. Korea 75 B4
Changkiang China see Zhanjiang
Changlang India 83 H4
Changleng China see Xinjian
Changling China 74 A3
Changlung India 87 M3
Changma China 80 I4
Changna China 83 F3
Changning Jiangxi China see Xunwu
Changning Sichuan China 76 E2
Changnyŏn N. Korea 75 B5
Ch'ang-pai Shan mts China/N. Korea see Changbai Shan
Changpu China see Suining
Changsan-got pt N. Korea 75 B5
Changsha China 77 G2
Changshan China 77 H2
Changshi China 76 E3
Changshou China 77 G2
Changshoujie China see Changshou
Changshu China 77 I2
Changtai China 77 H3
Changteh China see Changde
Changting Fujian China 77 H3
Changting Heilong. China 74 C3
Changwon S. Korea 75 C6
Changxing China 77 H2
Changyang China 77 F2
Changyŏn N. Korea 75 B5
Changyuan China 77 G1
Changzhi China 73 K5
Changzhou China 77 H2
Chañi, Nevado de mt. Arg. 144 C2
Chania Greece 59 K7
Chanion, Kolpos b. Greece 59 J7
Chankou China 76 E1
Channahon U.S.A. 134 A3
Channapatna India 84 C3
Channel Islands English Chan. 49 E9
Channel Islands U.S.A. 128 D5
Channel Islands National Park U.S.A. 128 D4
Channel-Port-aux-Basques Canada 123 K5
Channel Rock i. Bahamas 133 E8
Channel Tunnel France/U.K. 49 I7
Channing U.S.A. 131 C5
Chantada Spain 57 C2
Chanthaburi Thai. 71 C4
Chantilly France 52 C5
Chanumla India 71 A5
Chanute U.S.A. 130 E4
Chanuwala Pak. 89 I3
Chany, Ozero salt l. Russia 64 I4
Chaohu China 77 H2
Chao Hu l. China 77 H2
Chaor He r. China 74 A3
Chaowula Shan mt. China 76 C1
Chaoyang Guangdong China 77 H4
Chaoyang Heilong. China see Jiayin
Chaoyang Liaoning China 73 M4
Chaoyang Nei Mongol China 74 B2
Chaoyang Hu l. China 83 F2
Chaozhong China 74 A2
Chaozhou China 77 H4
Chapada Diamantina, Parque Nacional nat. park Brazil 145 C1
Chapada dos Veadeiros, Parque Nacional da nat. park Brazil 145 B1
Chapais Canada 122 G4
Chapak Gozār Afgh. 89 G2
Chapala, Laguna de l. Mex. 136 D4
Chāpārī, Kōtal-e Afgh. 89 G3
Chapayeva, imeni Turkm. see S. A. Nyýazow Adyndaky
Chapayevo Kazakh. 78 E1
Chapayevsk Russia 43 K5
Chapecó Brazil 144 F3
Chapecó r. Brazil 144 F3
Chapel-en-le-Frith U.K. 48 F5
Chapelle-lez-Herlaimont Belgium 52 E4
Chapeltown U.K. 48 F5
Chapleau Canada 122 E5
Chaplin Canada 121 J5
Chaplin Lake Canada 121 J5
Chaplygin Russia 43 H5
Chapman, Mount Canada 120 G5
Chapmanville U.S.A. 134 D5
Chappell U.S.A. 130 C3
Chappell Islands Australia 111 [inset]
Chapra Bihar India 83 F4
Chapra Jharkhand India see Chatra
Chaqmaqtīn, Kōl-e Afgh. 89 I2
Charagua Bol. 142 F7
Charay Mex. 127 F8
Charcas Mex. 136 D4
Charcot Island Antarctica 152 L2
Chard Canada 121 I4
Chard U.K. 49 E8
Chardara Kazakh. see Shardara
Chardara, Step' plain Kazakh. see Shardara, Step'
Chardon U.S.A. 134 E3
Chardzhev Turkm. see Türkmenabat
Chardzhou Turkm. see Türkmenabat
Charef Alg. 57 H6
Charef, Oued watercourse Morocco 54 D5
Charente r. France 56 D4
Chari r. Cameroon/Chad 97 E3
Chārī Iran 88 E4
Chārīkār Afgh. 89 H3
Chariton U.S.A. 130 E3
Chärjew Turkm. see Türkmenabat
Charkayuvom Russia 42 L2
Charkhlik China see Ruoqiang
Charleroi Belgium 52 E4
Charles, Cape U.S.A. 135 H5
Charlesbourg Canada 123 H5
Charles City IA U.S.A. 130 E3
Charles City VA U.S.A. 135 G5
Charles Hill Botswana 100 E2
Charles Lake Canada 121 I3
Charles Point Australia 108 E3
Charleston N.Z. 113 C5
Charleston IL U.S.A. 130 F4
Charleston MO U.S.A. 131 F4
Charleston SC U.S.A. 133 E5

▶Charleston WV U.S.A. 134 E4
Capital of West Virginia.

Charleston Peak U.S.A. 129 F3
Charlestown Ireland 51 D4
Charlestown IN U.S.A. 134 C4
Charlestown NH U.S.A. 135 I2
Charlestown RI U.S.A. 135 J3
Charles Town U.S.A. 135 G4
Charleville Australia 111 D5
Charleville Ireland 51 D5
Charleville-Mézières France 52 E5
Charlevoix U.S.A. 134 C1
Charlie, Dome ice feature Antarctica 152 F2
Charlie Lake Canada 120 F3
Charlotte MI U.S.A. 134 C2
Charlotte NC U.S.A. 133 D5
Charlotte TN U.S.A. 134 B5

▶Charlotte Amalie Virgin Is (U.S.A.) 137 L5
Capital of the U.S. Virgin Islands.

Charlotte Harbor b. U.S.A. 133 D7
Charlotte Lake Canada 120 E4
Charlottesville U.S.A. 135 F4

▶Charlottetown Canada 123 J5
Capital of Prince Edward Island.

Charlton Australia 112 A6
Charlton Island Canada 122 F3
Charron Lake Canada 121 M4
Charsadda Pak. 89 H3
Charshanga Turkm. see Köýtendag
Charshangngy Turkm. see Köýtendag
Charters Towers Australia 110 D4
Chartres France 56 E2
Chas India 83 F5
Chase Canada 120 G5
Chase U.S.A. 134 C2
Chase City U.S.A. 135 F5
Chashmeh Nūrī Iran 88 E3
Chashmeh-ye Palasi Iran 88 D3
Chashniki Belarus 43 F5
Chaska U.S.A. 130 E2
Chaslands Mistake c. N.Z. 113 B8
Chasŏng N. Korea 74 B4
Chasseral mt. Switz. 47 K7
Chassiron, Pointe de pt France 56 D3
Chastab, Kūh-e mts Iran 88 D3
Chāt Iran 88 D2
Chatanika U.S.A. 118 D3
Châteaubriant France 56 D3
Château-du-Loir France 56 E3
Châteaudun France 56 E2
Chateaugay U.S.A. 135 H1
Châteauguay Canada 135 I1
Châteauguay r. Canada 123 H2
Châteauguay, Lac l. Canada 123 H2
Châteaulin France 56 B2
Châteaumeillant France 56 F3
Châteauneuf-en-Thymerais France 52 B6
Châteauneuf-sur-Loire France 56 F3
Chateau Pond l. Canada 123 K3
Châteauroux France 56 E3
Château-Salins France 52 G6
Château-Thierry France 52 D5
Chateh Canada 120 G3
Châtelet Belgium 52 E4
Châtellerault France 56 E3
Chatfield U.S.A. 122 B6
Chatham Canada 134 D2
Chatham U.K. 49 H7
Chatham MA U.S.A. 135 K3
Chatham NY U.S.A. 135 I2
Chatham PA U.S.A. 135 H4
Chatham VA U.S.A. 134 F5
Chatham, Isla i. Chile 144 B8
Chatham Island N.Z. 107 I6
Chatham Island Samoa see Savai'i
Chatham Islands N.Z. 107 I6
Chatham Rise sea feature S. Pacific Ocean 150 I8
Chatham Strait U.S.A. 120 C3
Châtillon-sur-Seine France 56 G3
Chatkal Range mts Kyrg./Uzbek. 80 D3
Chatom U.S.A. 131 F6
Chatra India 83 F4
Chatra Nepal 83 F4
Chatsworth Canada 134 E1
Chatsworth U.S.A. 135 H4
Chattagam Bangl. see Chittagong
Chattanooga U.S.A. 133 C5
Chattarpur India see Chhatarpur
Chatteris U.K. 49 H6
Chattisgarh state India see Chhattisgarh
Chatturat Thai. 70 C4
Chatyr-Tash Kyrg. 80 E3
Châu Đốc Vietnam 71 D5
Chauhtan India 82 B4
Chauk Myanmar 70 A2
Chaumont France 56 G2
Chauncey U.S.A. 134 D4
Chaungzon Myanmar 70 B3
Chaunskaya Guba b. Russia 65 R3
Chauny France 52 D5
Châu Phu Vietnam see Châu Đốc
Chausy Belarus see Chavusy
Chautauqua, Lake U.S.A. 134 F2
Chauter Pak. 89 G4
Chauvin Canada 121 I4
Chavakachcheri Sri Lanka 84 D4
Chavakkad India 84 B4
Chaves Port. 57 C3
Chavigny, Lac l. Canada 122 G2
Chavusy Belarus 43 F5
Chawal r. Pak. 89 G4
Chay, Sông r. Vietnam 70 D2
Chayatyn, Khrebet ridge Russia 74 E1
Chayevo Russia 42 H4
Chaykovskiy Russia 41 Q4
Chazhegovo Russia 42 L3
Chazy U.S.A. 135 I1
Cheadle U.K. 49 F6
Cheaha Mountain hill U.S.A. 133 C5
Cheat r. U.S.A. 134 F4
Cheatham Lake U.S.A. 134 B5
Cheb Czechia 53 M4
Chebba Tunisia 58 D7
Cheboksarskoye Vodokhranilishche resr Russia 42 J5
Cheboksary Russia 42 J4
Cheboygan U.S.A. 132 C2
Chechen', Ostrov i. Russia 91 G2
Chedabucto Bay Canada 123 J5
Cheddar U.K. 49 E7
Cheduba Myanmar see Man-aung
Cheduba Island i. Myanmar see Man-aung Kyun
Chée r. France 52 E6
Cheektowaga U.S.A. 135 F2
Cheepie Australia 112 B1
Cheetham, Cape Antarctica 152 H2
Chefchaouene Morocco 57 D6
Chefoo China see Yantai
Chefornak U.S.A. 118 B3
Chefu Moz. 101 K2
Chegdomyn Russia 74 D2
Chegga Mauritania 96 C2
Chegutu Zimbabwe 99 D5
Chehalis U.S.A. 126 C3
Chehardeh Iran 88 E3
Chehel Chashmeh, Kūh-e hill Iran 88 B3
Chehel Dokhtarān, Kūh-e mt. Iran 89 F4
Chehel Pāyeh Iran 88 E4
Cheju S. Korea see Jeju
Cheju-do i. S. Korea 75 B6
Chekhov Moskovskaya Oblast' Russia 43 H5
Chekhov Sakhalinskaya Oblast' Russia 74 F3
Chekiang prov. China see Zhejiang
Chekichler Turkm. see Çekiçler
Chek Lap Kok reg. H.K. China 77 [inset]
Chekunda Russia 74 D2
Chela, Serra da mts Angola 99 B5
Chelan, Lake U.S.A. 126 C2
Cheleken Turkm. see Hazar
Cheline Moz. 101 L2
Chelkar Kazakh. see Shalkar
Chełm Poland 43 D6
Chelmer r. U.K. 49 H7
Chełmno Poland 47 Q4
Chelmsford U.K. 49 H7
Chelsea MI U.S.A. 134 C2
Chelsea VT U.S.A. 135 I2
Cheltenham U.K. 49 E7
Chelva Spain 57 F4
Chelyabinsk Russia 64 H4
Chemba Moz. 99 D5
Chêm Co l. China 82 D2
Chemnitz Germany 53 M4
Chemulpo S. Korea see Incheon
Chenab r. India/Pak. 82 B3
Chenachane, Oued watercourse Alg. 96 C2
Chenārān Iran 88 E2
Chencang China 76 E1
Chendir r. Turkm. see Çendir
Cheney U.S.A. 126 D3
Cheney Reservoir U.S.A. 130 D4
Chengalpattu India 84 D3
Chengbu China 77 F3
Chengchow China see Zhengzhou
Chengde China 73 L4
Chengdu China 76 E2
Chengele India 76 C2
Chenggong China 76 D3
Chenghai China 77 H4
Cheng Hai l. China 76 D3
Chengjiang China see Taihe
Chengjiang Fossil Site tourist site China 76 D3
Chengmai China 77 F5
Chengtu China see Chengdu
Chengwu China 77 G1
Chengxian China 76 E1
Chengxiang Chongqing China see Wuxi
Chengxiang Jiangxi China see Quannan
Chengzhong China see Ningming
Cheniu Shan i. China 77 H1
Chenkaladi Sri Lanka 84 D5
Chennai India 84 D3
Chenqing China 74 B2
Chenqingqiao China see Chenqing
Chenstokhov Poland see Częstochowa
Chenxi China 77 F3
Chenyang China see Chenxi
Chenying China see Wannian
Chenzhou China 77 G3
Cheonan S. Korea 75 B5
Cheongdo S. Korea 75 C6
Cheongju S. Korea 75 B5
Chepén Peru 142 C5
Chepes Arg. 144 C4
Chepo Panama 137 I7
Chepstow U.K. 49 E7
Cheptsa r. Russia 42 K4
Chequamegon Bay U.S.A. 130 F2
Cher r. France 56 E3
Chera state India see Kerala
Cheraw U.S.A. 133 E5
Cherbaniani Reef India 84 A3
Cherbourg-Octeville France 56 D2
Cherchell Alg. 57 H5
Cherchen China see Qiemo
Cherdakly Russia 43 K5
Cherdyn' Russia 41 R3
Chereapani reef India see Byramgore Reef
Cheremkhovo Russia 72 I2
Cheremshany Russia 74 D3
Cheremukhovka Russia 42 K4
Cherepanovo Russia 72 E2
Cherepovets Russia 42 H4
Cherevkovo Russia 42 J3
Chergui, Chott ech imp. l. Alg. 54 D5
Chéria Alg. 58 B7
Cheriton U.S.A. 135 H5
Cheriyakara, Suheli India 84 B4
Cheriyam atoll India 84 B4
Cherkassy Ukr. see Cherkasy
Cherkasy Ukr. 43 G6
Cherkessk Russia 91 F1
Cherla India 84 D2
Chernaya Russia 42 M1
Chernaya r. Russia 42 M1
Chernigov Ukr. see Chernihiv
Chernigovka Russia 74 D3
Chernihiv Ukr. 43 F6
Cherninivka Ukr. 43 H7
Chernivtsi Ukr. 43 E6
Chernobyl' Ukr. see Chornobyl'
Chernogorsk Russia 72 G2
Chernovtsy Ukr. see Chernivtsi
Chernoye More sea Asia/Europe see Black Sea
Chernushka Russia 41 R4
Chernyakhiv Ukr. 43 F6
Chernyakhovsk Russia 45 L9
Chernyanka Russia 43 H6
Chernyayevo Russia 74 B1
Chernyshevsk Russia 73 L2
Chernyshevskiy Russia 65 M3
Chernyshkovskiy Russia 43 I6
Chernyye Zemli reg. Russia 43 J7
Chernyy Irtysh r. China/Kazakh. see Ertix He
Chernyy Porog Russia 42 G3
Chernyy Yar Russia 43 J6
Cherokee U.S.A. 130 E3
Cherokee Sound Bahamas 133 E7

▶Cherrapunji India 83 G4
Highest recorded annual rainfall in the world.

Cherry Creek r. U.S.A. 130 C2
Cherry Creek Mountains U.S.A. 129 F1
Cherry Hill U.S.A. 135 H4
Cherry Island Solomon Is 107 G3
Cherry Lake U.S.A. 128 D2
Cherskiy Russia 153 C2
Cherskogo, Khrebet mts Russia 65 P3
Chertkov Ukr. see Chortkiv
Chertkovo Russia 43 I6
Cherven Bryag Bulg. 59 K3
Chervonoarmeyskoye Ukr. see Vil'nyans'k
Chervonoarmiys'k Donets'ka Oblast' Ukr. see Krasnoarmiys'k
Chervonoarmiys'k Rivnens'ka Oblast' Ukr. see Radyvyliv
Chervonograd Ukr. see Chervonohrad
Chervonohrad Ukr. 43 E6
Chervyen' Belarus 43 F5
Cherwell r. U.K. 49 F7
Cherykaw Belarus 43 F5
Chesapeake U.S.A. 135 G5
Chesapeake Bay U.S.A. 135 G4
Chesham U.K. 49 G7
Cheshire Plain U.K. 48 E5
Cheshme Vtoroy Turkm. 89 F2
Cheshskaya Guba b. Russia 42 J2
Cheshtebe Tajik. 89 I2
Cheshunt U.K. 49 G7
Chesnokovka Russia see Novoaltaysk
Chester Canada 123 I5
Chester U.K. 48 E5
Chester CA U.S.A. 128 C1
Chester IL U.S.A. 130 F4
Chester MT U.S.A. 126 F2
Chester OH U.S.A. 134 E4
Chester SC U.S.A. 133 D5
Chester r. U.S.A. 135 G4
Chesterfield U.K. 48 F5
Chesterfield U.S.A. 135 G5
Chesterfield, Îles is New Caledonia 107 F3
Chesterfield Inlet Canada 121 N2
Chesterfield Inlet inlet Canada 121 M2
Chester-le-Street U.K. 48 F4
Chestertown MD U.S.A. 135 G4
Chestertown NY U.S.A. 135 I2
Chesterville Canada 135 H1
Chestnut Ridge U.S.A. 134 F3
Chesuncook Lake U.S.A. 132 G2
Chetaïbi Alg. 58 B6
Chéticamp Canada 123 J5
Chetlat i. India 84 B4
Chetumal Mex. 136 G5
Chetwynd Canada 120 F4
Cheung Chau H.K. China 77 [inset]
Chevelon Creek r. U.S.A. 129 H4
Cheviot N.Z. 113 D6
Cheviot Hills U.K. 48 E3
Cheviot Range hills Australia 110 C5
Chevreulx r. Canada 122 G3
Cheyenne OK U.S.A. 131 D5

▶Cheyenne WY U.S.A. 126 G4
Capital of Wyoming.

Cheyenne r. U.S.A. 130 C2
Cheyenne Wells U.S.A. 130 C4
Cheyne Bay Australia 109 B8
Cheyur India 84 D3
Chezacut Canada 120 E4
Chhapra India see Chapra
Chhata India 82 D4
Chhatak Bangl. 83 G4
Chhatarpur Jharkhand India 83 F4
Chhatarpur Madh. Prad. India 82 D4
Chhatr Pak. 89 H4
Chhatrapur India 84 E2
Chhattisgarh state India 83 E5
Chhay Arêng, Stœng r. Cambodia 71 C5
Chhindwara India 82 D5
Chhitkul India see Chitkul
Chhlong Cambodia 71 D4
Chhukha Bhutan 83 G4
Chi, Lam r. Thai. 71 C4
Chi, Mae Nam r. Thai. 70 D4
Chiai Taiwan see Jiayi
Chiamboni Somalia 98 E4
Chiange Angola 99 B5
Chiang Kham Thai. 70 C3
Chiang Khan Thai. 70 C3
Chiang Mai Thai. 70 B3
Chiang Rai Thai. 70 B3
Chiang Saen Thai. 70 C2
Chiari Italy 58 C2
Chiautla Mex. 136 E5
Chiavenna Italy 58 C1
Chiayi Taiwan see Jiayi
Chiba Japan 75 F6
Chibi China 77 G2
Chibia Angola 99 B5
Chibizovka Russia see Zherdevka
Chiboma Moz. 99 D6
Chibougamau Canada 122 G4
Chibougamau, Lac l. Canada 122 G4
Chibuto Moz. 101 K3
Chibuzhang Co l. China 83 G2
Chicacole India see Srikakulam

▶Chicago U.S.A. 134 B3
4th most populous city in North America.

Chic-Chocs, Monts mts Canada 123 I4
Chichagof U.S.A. 120 B3
Chichagof Island U.S.A. 120 C3
Chichak r. Pak. 89 G5
Chichaoua Morocco 54 C5
Chichatka Russia 74 A1
Chicheng China see Pengxi
Chichester U.K. 49 G8
Chichester Range mts Australia 108 B5
Chichgarh India 84 D1
Chichibu Japan 75 E6
Chichibu-Tama Kokuritsu-kōen nat. park Japan 75 E6
Chichijima-rettō is Japan 75 F8
Chickasha U.S.A. 131 D5
Chiclana de la Frontera Spain 57 C5
Chiclayo Peru 142 C5
Chico r. Arg. 144 C6
Chico U.S.A. 128 C2
Chicomo Moz. 101 L3
Chicopee U.S.A. 135 I2
Chicoutimi Canada 123 H4
Chicualacuala Moz. 101 J2
Chidambaram India 84 C4
Chidenguele Moz. 101 L3
Chidley, Cape Canada 119 L3
Chido China see Sêndo
Chiducuane Moz. 101 L3
Chiefland U.S.A. 133 D6
Chiemsee l. Germany 47 N7
Chiengmai Thai. see Chiang Mai
Chiers r. France 52 F5
Chieti Italy 58 F3
Chifeng China 73 L4
Chifre, Serra do mts Brazil 145 C2
Chiginagak Volcano, Mount U.S.A. 118 C4
Chigu China 83 G3
Chigubo Moz. 101 K2
Chigu Co l. China 83 G3
Chihil Abdālān, Kōh-e mts Afgh. 89 G3
Chihli, Gulf of China see Bo Hai
Chihuahua Mex. 127 G7
Chihuahua state Mex. 127 G7
Chikalda India 82 D5
Chikan China 77 F4
Chikaskia r. U.S.A. 131 D4
Chikhli India 84 C1
Chikishlyar Turkm. see Çekiçler
Chikkamagaluru India 84 B3
Chikodi India 84 B2
Chilanko r. Canada 120 F4
Chilas Pak. 82 C2
Chilaw Sri Lanka 84 C5
Chilcotin r. Canada 120 F5
Childers Australia 110 F5
Childress U.S.A. 131 C5
Chile country S. America 144 B4
Chile Basin sea feature S. Pacific Ocean 151 O8
Chile Chico Chile 144 B7
Chile Rise sea feature S. Pacific Ocean 151 O8
Chilgir Russia 43 J7
Chilhowie U.S.A. 134 E5
Chilia-Nouă Ukr. see Kiliya
Chilika Lake India 84 E2
Chililabombwe Zambia 99 C5
Chilko r. Canada 120 F4
Chilko Lake Canada 120 E5
Chilkoot Pass Canada/U.S.A. 120 C3
Chilkoot Trail National Historic Site nat. park Canada 120 C3
Chillán Chile 144 B5
Chillicothe MO U.S.A. 130 E4
Chillicothe OH U.S.A. 134 D4
Chilliwack Canada 120 F5
Chilo India 82 C4
Chiloé, Isla de i. Chile 144 B6
Chiloé, Isla Grande de i. Chile see Chiloé, Isla de
Chilpancingo Mex. 136 E5
Chilpancingo de los Bravos Mex. see Chilpancingo
Chilpi Pak. 82 C1
Chiltern Hills U.K. 49 G7
Chilton U.S.A. 134 A1
Chiluage Angola 99 C4
Chilubi Zambia 99 C5
Chilung Taiwan see Jilong
Chilwa, Lake Malawi 99 D5
Chimala Tanz. 99 D4
Chimaltenango Guat. 136 F6
Chi Ma Wan H.K. China 77 [inset]
Chimay Belgium 52 E4
Chimbas Arg. 144 C4
Chimbay Uzbek. see Chimboy
Chimborazo mt. Ecuador 142 C4
Chimbote Peru 142 C5
Chimboy Uzbek. 80 A3
Chimishliya Moldova see Cimişlia
Chimkent Kazakh. see Shymkent
Chimney Rock U.S.A. 129 J3
Chimoio Moz. 99 D5
Chimtargha, Qullai mt. Tajik. 89 H2
Chimtorga, Gora mt. Tajik. see Chimtargha, Qullai

▶China country Asia 72 H5
Most populous country in Asia and the world. 2nd largest country in Asia and 4th largest in the world.

China Mex. 131 D7
China, Republic of country Asia see Taiwan
China Bakir r. Myanmar see To
China Lake CA U.S.A. 128 E4
China Lake ME U.S.A. 135 K1
Chinandega Nicaragua 136 G6
China Point U.S.A. 128 D5
Chinati Peak U.S.A. 131 B6
Chincha Alta Peru 142 C6
Chinchaga r. Canada 120 G3
Chinchilla Australia 112 E1
Chincholi India 84 C2
Chinchorro, Banco sea feature Mex. 137 G5
Chincoteague Bay U.S.A. 135 H5
Chinde Moz. 99 D5
Chindwin r. Myanmar 70 A2
Chinese Turkestan aut. reg. China see Xinjiang Uygur Zizhiqu
Chinghai prov. China see Qinghai
Chingleput India see Chengalpattu
Chingola Zambia 99 C5
Chinguar Angola 99 B5
Chinguețți Mauritania 96 B2
Chinhoyi Zimbabwe 99 D5
Chini India see Kalpa
Chining China see Jining
Chiniot Pak. 89 I4
Chinipas Mex. 127 F8
Chinīt, Stœng r. Cambodia 71 D4
Chinju S. Korea 75 C6
Chinle U.S.A. 129 I3
Chinmen Taiwan see Jinmen
Chinmen Tao i. Taiwan see Jinmen Dao
Chinnamp'o N. Korea see Namp'o
Chinnur India 84 C2
Chino Creek watercourse U.S.A. 129 G4
Chinon France 56 E3
Chinook U.S.A. 126 F2
Chinook Trough sea feature N. Pacific Ocean 150 I3
Chino Valley U.S.A. 129 G4
Chinsali Zambia 99 D5
Chin-shan China see Zhujing
Chintamani India 84 C3
Chioggia Italy 58 E2
Chios Greece 59 L5
Chios i. Greece 59 K5
Chipata Zambia 99 D5
Chipchihua, Sierra de mts Arg. 144 C6

Chiphu Cambodia 71 D5
Chipindo Angola 99 B5
Chipinga Zimbabwe see Chipinge
Chipinge Zimbabwe 99 D6
Chipley U.S.A. 133 C6
Chipman Canada 123 I5
Chippenham U.K. 49 E7
Chippewa, Lake U.S.A. 130 F2
Chippewa Falls U.S.A. 130 F2
Chipping Norton U.K. 49 F7
Chipping Sodbury U.K. 49 E7
Chipurupalle Andhra Prad. India 84 D2
Chipurupalle Andhra Prad. India 84 D2
Chiquilá Mex. 133 C8
Chiquinquirá Col. 142 D2
Chir r. Russia 43 I6
Chirada India 84 D3
Chirala India 84 D3
Chīras Afgh. 89 G3
Chirchiq Uzbek. 80 C3
Chiredzi Zimbabwe 99 D6
Chirfa Niger 96 E2
Chiricahua National Monument nat. park U.S.A. 129 I5
Chiricahua Peak U.S.A. 129 I6
Chirikof Island U.S.A. 118 C4
Chiriquí, Golfo de b. Panama 137 H7
Chiriquí, Volcán de vol. Panama see Barú, Volcán
Chirk U.K. 49 D6
Chirnside U.K. 50 G5
Chirripó mt. Costa Rica 137 H7
Chisamba Zambia 99 C5
Chisana r. U.S.A. 120 A2
Chisasibi Canada 122 F3
Chishima-retto is Russia see Kuril Islands
Chisholm Canada 120 H4
Chishtian Pak. 89 I4
Chishui Guizhou China 76 E2
Chishui Sichuan China 76 E3
Chisimaio Somalia see Kismaayo

▶Chişinău Moldova 59 M1
Capital of Moldova.

Chistopol' Russia 42 K5
Chita Russia 73 K2
Chitado Angola 99 B5
Chitaldrug India see Chitradurga
Chitalwana India 82 B4
Chitambo Zambia 99 D5
Chitato Angola 99 C4
Chitek Lake Canada 121 J4
Chitek Lake l. Canada 121 L4
Chitembo Angola 99 B5
Chitina U.S.A. 118 D3
Chitipa Malawi 99 D4
Chitkul India 82 D3
Chitobe Moz. 99 D6
Chitoor India see Chittoor
Chitor India see Chittaurgarh
Chitose Japan 74 F4
Chitradurga India 84 C3
Chitrakoot India 82 E4
Chitrakut India see Chitrakoot
Chitral Pak. 89 H3
Chitral r. Pak. 89 H3
Chitravati r. India 84 C3
Chitré Panama 137 H7
Chitrod India 82 B5
Chittagong Bangl. 83 G5
Chittaurgarh India 82 C4
Chittoor India 84 C3
Chittor India see Chittoor
Chittorgarh India see Chittaurgarh
Chittur India 84 C4
Chitungwiza Zimbabwe 99 D5
Chiume Angola 99 C5
Chivasso Italy 58 B2
Chívato, Punta pt Mex. 127 F8
Chivhu Zimbabwe 99 D5
Chixixu China 77 G4
Chizarira National Park Zimbabwe 99 C5
Chizhou China 77 H2
Chizu Japan 75 D6
Chkalov Russia see Orenburg
Chkalovsk Russia 42 I4
Chkalovskoye Russia 74 D3
Chlef Alg. 57 G5
Chlef, Oued r. Alg. 57 G5
Chloride U.S.A. 129 F4
Chlya, Ozero l. Russia 74 F1
Choa Chu Kang Sing. 71 [inset]
Choa Chu Kang hill Sing. 71 [inset]
Chobe National Park Botswana 99 C5
Chodov Czechia 53 M4
Choele Choel Arg. 144 C5
Chogar r. Russia 74 D1
Chogori Feng mt. China/Pak. see K2
Chograyskoye Vodokhranilishche resr Russia 43 J7
Choiseul i. Solomon Is 107 F2
Choix Mex. 127 F8
Chojnice Poland 47 P4
Chōkai-san vol. Japan 75 F5
Ch'ok'ē mts Eth. 98 D2
Ch'ok'ē Mountains Eth. see Ch'ok'ē
Ch'ok'ē Terara mt. Eth. 98 D2
Chokola mt. China 82 E3
Choksum China 83 F3
Chokue Moz. see Chókwè
Chokurdakh Russia 65 P2
Chókwè Moz. 101 K3
Cho La pass China 76 C2
Cholame U.S.A. 128 C4
Cholet France 56 D3
Cholpon-Ata Kyrg. 80 E3
Choluteca Hond. 137 G6
Choma Zambia 99 C5
Chomo Ganggar mt. China 83 G3
Chơ Moi Vietnam 70 D2
Chomo Lhari mt. Bhutan/China 83 G4
Chom Thong Thai. 70 B3
Chomutov Czechia 47 N5
Chon Buri Thai. 71 C4
Ch'ŏnch'ŏn N. Korea 74 B4
Chone Ecuador 142 B4
Ch'ŏngch'ŏn-gang r. N. Korea 75 B5
Chonggye China see Qonggyai
Ch'ŏngjin N. Korea 74 C4
Ch'ŏngju S. Korea see Cheongju
Chŏng Kal Cambodia 71 C4
Chongkü China 76 C2
Chonglong China see Zizhong
Chongming Dao i. China 77 I2
Chongoroi Angola 99 B5
Chŏngp'yŏng N. Korea 75 B5
Chongqing China 76 E2
Chongqing mun. China 76 E2
Chonguene Moz. 101 K3
Chongyang China 77 G2
Chongyi China 77 G3
Chongzuo China 76 E4
Chŏnju S. Korea see Jeonju
Chonos, Archipiélago de los is Chile 144 A6

▶Cho Oyu mt. China/Nepal 83 F3
6th highest mountain in Asia and the world.

Chopda India 82 C5
Chor Pak. 89 H5
Chora Sfakion Greece 59 K7
Chorley U.K. 48 E5
Chornobyl' Ukr. 43 F6
Chornomors'k Ukr. 43 F7
Chornomors'ke Crimea 59 O2
Chortkiv Ukr. 43 E6
Ch'osan N. Korea 74 B4
Chōshi Japan 75 F6
Chosŏn country Asia see South Korea
Chosŏn-minjujuŭi-inmin-konghwaguk country Asia see North Korea
Choszczno Poland 47 O4
Chota Peru 142 C5
Chota Sinchula hill India 83 G4
Choteau U.S.A. 126 E3
Choti Pak. 89 H4
Choûm Mauritania 96 B2
Chowchilla U.S.A. 128 C3
Chown, Mount Canada 120 G4
Choybalsan Mongolia 73 K3
Choyr Mongolia 73 J3
Chrétiens, Île aux i. Canada see Christian Island
Chřiby hills Czechia 47 P6
Chrisman U.S.A. 134 B4
Chrissiesmeer S. Africa 101 J4
Christchurch N.Z. 113 D6
Christchurch U.K. 49 F8
Christian, Cape Canada 119 L2
Christiana S. Africa 101 G4
Christiania Norway see Oslo
Christian Island Canada 134 E1
Christiansburg U.S.A. 134 E5
Christianshåb Greenland see Qasigiannguit
Christie Bay Canada 121 I2
Christie Island Myanmar 71 B5
Christina r. Canada 121 I3
Christina, Mount N.Z. 113 B7

▶Christmas Island terr. Indian Ocean 68 D9
Australian External Territory.

Christopher, Lake salt flat Australia 109 D6
Chrudim Czechia 47 O6
Chrysi i. Greece see Gaïdouronisi
Chrysochou Bay Cyprus 85 A2
Chrysochous, Kolpos b. Cyprus see Chrysochou Bay
Chu Kazakh. see Shu
Chuadanga Bangl. 83 G5
Chuali, Lago l. Moz. 101 K3
Chuanhui China see Zhoukou
Chuansha China 77 I2
Chubalung China 76 C2
Chubarovka Ukr. see Polohy
Chubartau Kazakh. see Barshatas
Chūbu-Sangaku Kokuritsu-kōen nat. park Japan 75 E5
Chu-ching China see Zhujing
Chuchkovo Russia 43 I5
Chuckwalla Mountains U.S.A. 129 F5
Chudniv Ukr. 43 F6
Chudovo Russia 42 F4
Chudskoye, Ozero l. Estonia/Russia see Peipus, Lake
Chugach Mountains U.S.A. 118 D3
Chūgoku-sanchi mts Japan 75 D6
Chugqênsumdo China see Jigzhi
Chuguchak China see Tacheng
Chuguyev Ukr. see Chuhuyiv
Chuguyevka Russia 74 D3
Chugwater U.S.A. 126 G4
Chuhai China see Zhuhai
Chuhuyiv Ukr. 43 H6
Chujiang China see Shimen
Chukai Malaysia see Cukai
Chukchagirskoye, Ozero l. Russia 74 E1
Chukchi Abyssal Plain sea feature Arctic Ocean 153 B1
Chukchi Peninsula Russia see Chukotskiy Poluostrov
Chukchi Plateau sea feature Arctic Ocean 153 B1
Chukchi Sea Russia/U.S.A. 65 T3
Chukhloma Russia 42 I4
Chukotskiy, Mys c. Russia 118 A3
Chukotskiy Poluostrov pen. Russia 65 T3
Chulakkurgan Kazakh. see Sholakkorgan
Chulaktau Kazakh. see Karatau
Chulasa Russia 42 J2
Chula Vista U.S.A. 128 E5
Chulucanas Peru 142 B5
Chulung Pass Pak. 82 D2
Chulym Russia 64 J4
Chumar India 82 D2
Chumbicha Arg. 144 C3
Chumda China 76 C1
Chumikan Russia 65 O4
Chum Phae Thai. 70 C3
Chumphon Thai. 71 B5
Chum Saeng Thai. 70 C4
Chunar India 83 E4
Chuncheon S. Korea 75 B5
Chunga Zambia 99 C5
Chung-hua Jen-min Kung-ho-kuo country Asia see China
Chung-hua Min-kuo country Asia see Taiwan
Chungju S. Korea 75 B5
Chungking China see Chongqing
Ch'ungmu S. Korea see Tongyeong
Chŭngsan N. Korea 75 B5
Chunian Pak. 89 I4
Chunskiy Russia 72 H1
Chunya r. Russia 65 K3
Chuôi, Hon i. Vietnam 71 D5
Chuosijia China see Guanyinqiao
Chupa Russia 44 R3
Chūplū Iran 88 B2
Chuquicamata Chile 144 C2
Chur Switz. 56 I3
Churachandpur India 83 H4
Chūrān Iran 88 D4
Churapcha Russia 65 O3
Churchill Canada 121 M3
Churchill r. Man. Canada 121 M3
Churchill r. Nfld. and Lab. Canada 123 J3
Churchill, Cape Canada 121 M3
Churchill Falls Canada 123 J3
Churchill Lake Canada 121 I4
Churchill Mountains Antarctica 152 H1
Churchill Sound sea chan. Canada 122 F2
Churchs Ferry U.S.A. 130 D1
Churchville U.S.A. 134 F4
Churia Ghati Hills Nepal 83 F4
Churu India 82 C3
Churubusco U.S.A. 134 C3
Churún-Merú waterfall Venez. see Angel Falls
Chushul India 82 D2
Chuska Mountains U.S.A. 129 I3
Chusovaya r. Russia 41 R4
Chusovoy Russia 41 R4
Chust Ukr. see Khust
Chute-des-Passes Canada 123 H4
Chutia Assam India 83 H4
Chutia Jharkhand India 83 F5
Chutung Taiwan see Zhudong
Chuuk is Micronesia 150 G5
Chuxiong China 76 D3
Chüy r. Kazakh./Kyrg. see Shu
Chuzhou Anhui China 77 H1
Chuzhou Jiangsu China 77 H1
Chymyshliya Moldova see Cimişlia
Chyulu Hills National Park Kenya 98 D4
Ciadăr-Lunga Moldova see Ciadîr-Lunga
Ciadîr-Lunga Moldova 59 M1
Ciamis Indon. 68 D8
Cianjur Indon. 68 D8
Cianorte Brazil 144 F2
Cibecue U.S.A. 129 H4
Cibolo Creek r. U.S.A. 131 D6
Cibuta, Sierra mt. Mex. 127 F7
Čićarija mts Croatia 58 E2
Cicero U.S.A. 134 B3
Cidade Velha Cape Verde 96 [inset]
Cide Turkey 90 D2
Ciechanów Poland 47 R4
Ciego de Ávila Cuba 137 I4
Ciénaga Col. 142 D1
Ciénega Mex. 131 C7
Ciénega de Flores Mex. 131 C7
Cienfuegos Cuba 137 H4
Cieza Spain 57 F4
Çiftlik Turkey see Kelkit
Cifuentes Spain 57 E3
Cigüela r. Spain 57 E4
Cihanbeyli Turkey 90 D3
Cíjara, Embalse de resr Spain 57 D4
Cilacap Indon. 68 D8
Çıldır Turkey 91 F2
Çıldır Gölü l. Turkey 91 F2
Çıldıroba Turkey 85 C1
Cilento, Vallo di Diano e Alburni, Parco Nazionale del nat. park Italy 58 F4
Cili China 77 F2
Cilician Gates pass Turkey see Gülek Boğazı
Cill Airne Ireland see Killarney
Cill Chainnigh Ireland see Kilkenny
Cill Mhantáin Ireland see Wicklow
Çilmämmetgum des. Turkm. 88 D1
Cilo Dağı mt. Turkey 91 G3
Çilov Adası i. Azer. 91 H2
Cimarron CO U.S.A. 129 J2
Cimarron KS U.S.A. 130 C4
Cimarron NM U.S.A. 127 G5
Cimarron r. U.S.A. 131 D4
Cimişlia Moldova 59 M1
Cimone, Monte mt. Italy 58 D2
Cîmpina Romania see Câmpina
Cîmpulung Romania see Câmpulung
Cîmpulung Moldovenesc Romania see Câmpulung Moldovenesc
Cina, Tanjung c. Indon. 68 C8
Çınar Turkey 91 F3
Cinca r. Spain 57 G3
Cincinnati U.S.A. 134 C4
Cinco de Outubro Angola see Xá-Muteba
Cinderford U.K. 49 E7
Çine Turkey 59 M6
Ciney Belgium 52 F4
Cintalapa Mex. 136 F5
Cinto, Monte mt. France 56 I5
Ciping China 77 G3
Circeo, Parco Nazionale del nat. park Italy 58 E4
Circle AK U.S.A. 118 D3
Circle MT U.S.A. 126 G3
Circleville OH U.S.A. 134 D4
Circleville UT U.S.A. 129 G2
Cirebon Indon. 68 D8
Cirencester U.K. 49 F7
Cirò Marina Italy 58 G5
Cirta Alg. see Constantine
Cisco (abandoned) U.S.A. 129 I2
Cisne, Islas del is Caribbean Sea 137 H5
Citlaltépetl vol. Mex. see Orizaba, Pico de
Čitluk Bos. & Herz. 58 G3
Citronelle U.S.A. 131 F6
Citrus Heights U.S.A. 128 C2
Città di Castello Italy 58 E3
Ciucaş, Vârful mt. Romania 59 K2
Ciudad Acuña Mex. 131 C6
Ciudad Altamirano Mex. 136 D5
Ciudad Bolívar Venez. 142 F2
Ciudad Camargo Mex. 131 B7
Ciudad Constitución Mex. 136 B3
Ciudad del Carmen Mex. 136 F5
Ciudad Delicias Mex. 131 B6
Ciudad de Panamá Panama see Panama City
Ciudad de Valles Mex. 136 E4
Ciudad Flores Guat. see Flores
Ciudad Guayana Venez. 142 F2
Ciudad Guerrero Mex. 127 G7
Ciudad Guzmán Mex. 136 D5
Ciudad Juárez Mex. 127 G7
Ciudad Lerdo Mex. 131 C7
Ciudad Mante Mex. 136 E4
Ciudad Obregón Mex. 127 F8
Ciudad Real Spain 57 E4
Ciudad Río Bravo Mex. 131 D7
Ciudad Rodrigo Spain 57 C3
Ciudad Trujillo Dom. Rep. see Santo Domingo
Ciudad Victoria Mex. 131 D8
Ciutadella Spain 57 H3
Cıva Burnu pt Turkey 90 E2
Cividale del Friuli Italy 58 E1
Civitanova Marche Italy 58 E3
Civitavecchia Italy 58 D3
Çivril Turkey 59 M5
Cixi China 77 I2
Cizre Turkey 91 F3
Clacton-on-Sea U.K. 49 I7
Clady U.K. 51 E3
Claire, Lake Canada 121 H3
Clairfontaine Alg. see El Aouinet
Clamecy France 56 F3
Clane Ireland 51 F4
Clanton U.S.A. 133 C5
Clanwilliam Dam S. Africa 100 D7
Clara Ireland 51 E4
Clara Island Myanmar 71 B5
Claraville Australia 110 C3
Clare N.S.W. Australia 112 A4
Clare S.A. Australia 111 B7
Clare r. Ireland 51 C4
Clare U.S.A. 134 C2
Clarecastle Ireland 51 D5
Clare Island Ireland 51 B4
Claremont U.S.A. 135 I2
Claremore U.S.A. 131 E4
Claremorris Ireland 51 D4
Clarence r. Australia 112 F2
Clarence N.Z. 113 D6
Clarence Island Antarctica 152 A2
Clarence Strait Iran see Khūran
Clarence Strait U.S.A. 120 C3
Clarence Town Bahamas 133 F8
Clarendon AR U.S.A. 131 F5
Clarendon PA U.S.A. 134 F3
Clarendon TX U.S.A. 131 C5
Clarenville Canada 123 L4
Claresholm Canada 120 H5
Clarie Coast Antarctica see Wilkes Coast
Clarinda U.S.A. 130 E3
Clarington U.S.A. 134 E4
Clarion IA U.S.A. 130 E3
Clarion PA U.S.A. 134 F3
Clarion r. U.S.A. 134 F3
Clarión, Isla i. Mex. 136 B5
Clark U.S.A. 130 D2
Clark, Mount Canada 120 F1
Clarkdale U.S.A. 129 G4
Clarkebury S. Africa 101 I6
Clarke Range mts Australia 110 D4
Clarke River Australia 110 D3
Clarke's Head Canada 123 L4
Clark Mountain U.S.A. 129 F4
Clark Point Canada 134 E1
Clarksburg U.S.A. 134 E4
Clarksdale U.S.A. 131 F5
Clarks Hill U.S.A. 134 B3
Clarksville AR U.S.A. 131 E5
Clarksville TN U.S.A. 134 B5
Clarksville TX U.S.A. 131 E5
Clarksville VA U.S.A. 135 F5
Claro r. Goiás Brazil 145 A2
Claro r. Mato Grosso Brazil 145 A1
Clashmore Ireland 51 E5
Claude U.S.A. 131 C5
Claudy U.K. 51 E3
Clavier Belgium 52 F4
Claxton U.S.A. 133 D5
Clay U.S.A. 134 E4
Clayburg U.S.A. 135 I1
Clay Center KS U.S.A. 130 D4
Clay Center NE U.S.A. 130 D3
Clay City IN U.S.A. 134 B4
Clay City KY U.S.A. 134 D5
Clayhole Wash watercourse U.S.A. 129 G3
Claypool U.S.A. 129 H5
Clay Springs U.S.A. 129 H4
Clayton DE U.S.A. 135 H4
Clayton GA U.S.A. 133 D5
Clayton MI U.S.A. 134 C3
Clayton MO U.S.A. 130 F4
Clayton NM U.S.A. 131 C4
Clayton NY U.S.A. 135 G1
Claytor Lake U.S.A. 134 E5
Clay Village U.S.A. 134 C4
Clear, Cape Ireland 51 C6
Clearco U.S.A. 134 E4
Clear Creek Canada 134 E2
Clear Creek r. U.S.A. 129 H4
Cleare, Cape U.S.A. 118 D4
Clearfield PA U.S.A. 135 F3
Clearfield UT U.S.A. 126 E4
Clear Fork Brazos r. U.S.A. 131 D5
Clear Hills Canada 120 G3
Clear Island Ireland 51 C6
Clear Lake IA U.S.A. 130 E3
Clear Lake SD U.S.A. 130 D2
Clear Lake l. CA U.S.A. 128 B2
Clear Lake l. UT U.S.A. 129 G2
Clearmont U.S.A. 126 G3
Clearwater Canada 120 G5
Clearwater r. Alta/Sask. Canada 121 I3
Clearwater r. Alta Canada 120 H4
Clearwater U.S.A. 133 D7
Clearwater Lake Canada 121 K4
Clearwater Mountains U.S.A. 126 E3
Cleaton U.S.A. 134 B5
Cleburne U.S.A. 131 D5
Cleethorpes U.K. 48 G5
Clementi Sing. 71 [inset]
Clendenin U.S.A. 134 E4
Clendening Lake U.S.A. 134 E3
Clères France 52 B5
Clerf Lux. see Clervaux
Clerke Reef Australia 108 B4
Clermont Australia 110 D4
Clermont France 52 C5
Clermont-en-Argonne France 52 F5
Clermont-Ferrand France 56 F4
Clervaux Lux. 52 G4
Cles Italy 58 D1
Clevedon U.K. 49 E7
Cleveland MS U.S.A. 131 F5
Cleveland OH U.S.A. 134 E3
Cleveland TN U.S.A. 133 C5
Cleveland UT U.S.A. 129 H2
Cleveland WI U.S.A. 134 B2
Cleveland, Cape Australia 110 D3
Cleveland, Mount U.S.A. 126 E2
Cleveland Heights U.S.A. 134 E3
Cleveland Hills U.K. 48 F4
Cleveleys U.K. 48 D5
Cleves Germany see Kleve
Clew Bay Ireland 51 C4
Clifden Ireland 51 B4
Cliff U.S.A. 129 I5
Cliffoney Ireland 51 D3
Clifton Australia 112 E1
Clifton U.S.A. 129 I5
Clifton Beach Australia 110 D3
Clifton Forge U.S.A. 134 F5
Clifton Park U.S.A. 135 I2
Climax Canada 121 I5
Climax U.S.A. 134 C2
Clinch Mountain mts U.S.A. 134 D5
Cline River Canada 120 G4
Clinton B.C. Canada 120 F5
Clinton Ont. Canada 134 E2
Clinton IA U.S.A. 130 F3
Clinton IL U.S.A. 130 F3
Clinton IN U.S.A. 134 B4
Clinton KY U.S.A. 131 F4
Clinton MI U.S.A. 134 D2
Clinton MO U.S.A. 130 E4
Clinton MS U.S.A. 131 F5
Clinton NC U.S.A. 133 E5
Clinton NJ U.S.A. 135 H3
Clinton OK U.S.A. 131 D5
Clinton-Colden Lake Canada 121 J1
Clintwood U.S.A. 134 D5

▶Clipperton, Île terr. N. Pacific Ocean 151 M5
Part of France. Most easterly point of Oceania.

Clisham hill U.K. 50 C3
Clitheroe U.K. 48 E5
Clive Lake Canada 120 G2
Cliza Bol. 142 E7
Clocolan S. Africa 101 H5
Cloghan Ireland 51 E4
Clonakilty Ireland 51 D6
Clonbern Ireland 51 D4
Cloncurry Australia 110 C4
Cloncurry r. Australia 110 C3
Clones Ireland 51 E3
Clonmel Ireland 51 E5
Clonygowan Ireland 51 E4
Cloonbannin Ireland 51 C5
Clooneagh Ireland 51 E4
Cloppenburg Germany 53 I2
Cloquet U.S.A. 130 E2
Cloquet r. U.S.A. 130 E2
Cloud Peak WY U.S.A. 124 F3
Cloud Peak WY U.S.A. 126 G3
Clova Canada 122 G4
Clover U.S.A. 129 G1
Cloverdale CA U.S.A. 128 B2
Cloverdale IN U.S.A. 134 B4
Cloverport U.S.A. 134 B5
Clovis CA U.S.A. 128 D3
Clovis NM U.S.A. 131 C5
Cloyne Canada 135 G1
Cluain Meala Ireland see Clonmel
Cluanie, Loch l. U.K. 50 D3
Cluff Lake Mine Canada 121 I3
Cluj-Napoca Romania 59 J1
Clun U.K. 49 D6
Clunes Australia 112 A6
Cluny Australia 110 B5
Cluses France 56 H3
Cluster Springs U.S.A. 135 F5
Clut Lake Canada 120 G1
Clutterbuck Head hd Canada 123 H1
Clutterbuck Hills hill Australia 109 D6
Clwydian Range hills U.K. 48 D5
Clyde Canada 120 H4
Clyde r. U.K. 50 E5
Clyde NY U.S.A. 135 G2
Clyde OH U.S.A. 134 D3
Clyde, Firth of est. U.K. 50 E5
Clydebank U.K. 50 E5
Clyde River Canada 119 L2
Côa r. Port. 57 C3
Coachella U.S.A. 128 E5
Coahuila state Mex. 131 C7
Coahuila de Zaragoza state Mex. see Coahuila
Coal r. Canada 120 E3
Coal City U.S.A. 134 A3
Coaldale (abandoned) U.S.A. 128 E2
Coalgate U.S.A. 131 D5
Coal Harbour Canada 120 E5
Coalinga U.S.A. 128 C3
Coalport U.S.A. 135 F3
Coal River Canada 120 E3
Coal Valley U.S.A. 129 F3
Coalville U.K. 49 F6
Coalville U.S.A. 129 H1
Coari Brazil 142 F4
Coari r. Brazil 142 F4
Coarsegold U.S.A. 128 D3
Coastal Plain U.S.A. 131 E6
Coast Mountains Canada 120 E4
Coast Range hills Australia 111 E5
Coast Ranges mts U.S.A. 128 B1
Coatbridge U.K. 50 E5
Coatesville U.S.A. 135 H4
Coaticook Canada 135 J1
Coats Island Canada 119 J3
Coats Land reg. Antarctica 152 A1
Coatzacoalcos Mex. 136 F5
Cobar Australia 112 B3
Cobargo Australia 112 D6
Cobden Australia 112 A7
Cobh Ireland 51 D6
Cobham r. Canada 121 M4
Cobija Bol. 142 E6
Coblenz Germany see Koblenz
Cobleskill U.S.A. 135 H2
Cobourg Peninsula Australia 108 F2
Cobra Australia 109 B6
Cobram Australia 112 B5
Coburg Germany 53 K4
Coburg Island Canada 119 K2
Coca Ecuador 142 C4
Coca Spain 57 D3
Cocalinho Brazil 145 A1
Cocanada India see Kakinada
Cochabamba Bol. 142 E7
Cochem Germany 53 H4
Cochin India see Kochi
Cochin reg. Vietnam 71 D5
Cochinos, Bahía de b. Cuba see Pigs, Bay of
Cochise U.S.A. 129 I5
Cochise Head mt. U.S.A. 129 I5
Cochrane Alta Canada 120 H5
Cochrane Ont. Canada 122 E4
Cochrane r. Canada 121 K3
Cockburn Australia 111 C7
Cockburnspath U.K. 50 G5
Cockburn Town Bahamas 133 F7
Cockburn Town Turks and Caicos Is see Grand Turk
Cockermouth U.K. 48 D4
Cocklebiddy Australia 109 D8
Cockscomb mt. S. Africa 100 G7
Coco r. Hond./Nicaragua 137 H6
Coco, Cayo i. Cuba 133 E8
Coco, Isla de i. N. Pacific Ocean 137 G7
Cocobeach Gabon 98 A3
Coco Channel India 71 A4
Cocomórachic Mex. 127 G7
Coconino Plateau U.S.A. 129 G4
Cocopara National Park Australia 112 C5
Cocos Brazil 145 B1

▶Cocos (Keeling) Islands terr. Indian Ocean 68 B9
Australian External Territory.

Cocos Basin sea feature Indian Ocean 149 O5
Cocos Ridge sea feature N. Pacific Ocean 151 O5
Cocuy, Sierra Nevada del mt. Col. 142 D2
Cod, Cape U.S.A. 135 J3
Codajás Brazil 142 F4
Coderre Canada 121 J5
Codfish Island N.Z. 113 A8
Codigoro Italy 58 E2
Cod Island Canada 123 J2
Codlea Romania 59 K2
Codó Brazil 143 J4
Codsall U.K. 49 E6
Cod's Head hd Ireland 51 B6
Cody U.S.A. 126 F3
Coeburn U.S.A. 134 D5
Coen Australia 110 C2
Coesfeld Germany 53 H3
Coeur d'Alene U.S.A. 126 D3
Coeur d'Alene Lake U.S.A. 126 D3
Coevorden Neth. 52 G2
Coffee Bay S. Africa 101 I6
Coffee Cultural Landscape of Colombia tourist site Col. 142 C2
Coffeyville U.S.A. 131 E4
Coffin Bay Australia 111 A7
Coffin Bay National Park Australia 111 A7
Coffs Harbour Australia 112 F3
Cofimvaba S. Africa 101 H7
Cognac France 56 D4
Cogo Equat. Guinea 96 D4
Coguno Moz. 101 L3
Cohoes U.S.A. 135 I2
Cohuna Australia 112 B5
Coiba, Isla de i. Panama 137 H7
Coigeach, Rubha pt U.K. 50 D2
Coihaique Chile 144 B7
Coimbatore India 84 C4
Coimbra Port. 57 B3
Coipasa, Salar de salt flat Bol. 142 E7
Coire Switz. see Chur
Colac Australia 112 A7
Colair Lake India see Kolleru Lake
Colatina Brazil 145 C2
Colbitz Germany 53 L2
Colborne Canada 135 G2
Colby U.S.A. 130 C4
Colchester U.K. 49 H7
Colchester U.S.A. 135 I3
Cold Bay U.S.A. 118 B4
Coldingham U.K. 50 G5
Colditz Germany 53 M3
Cold Lake Canada 121 I4
Cold Lake l. Canada 121 I4
Coldspring U.S.A. 131 E6
Coldstream Canada 120 G5
Coldstream U.K. 50 G5
Coldwater Canada 134 F1
Coldwater KS U.S.A. 131 D4
Coldwater MI U.S.A. 134 C3
Coldwater r. U.S.A. 131 F5
Coleambally Australia 112 B5
Colebrook U.S.A. 135 J1
Coleman r. Australia 110 C2
Coleman U.S.A. 131 D6
Çölemerik Turkey see Hakkâri
Colenso S. Africa 101 I5
Cole Peninsula Antarctica 152 L2
Coleraine Australia 111 C8
Coleraine U.K. 51 F2
Coles, Punta de pt Peru 142 D7
Coles Bay Australia 111 [inset]
Colesberg S. Africa 101 G6
Coleville Canada 121 I5
Colfax CA U.S.A. 128 C2
Colfax LA U.S.A. 131 E6
Colfax WA U.S.A. 126 D3
Colhué Huapí, Lago l. Arg. 144 C7
Coligny S. Africa 101 H4
Colima Mex. 136 D5
Colima, Nevado de vol. Mex. 136 D5

Coll *i.* U.K. **50** C4
Collado Villalba Spain **57** E3
Collarenebri Australia **112** D2
College Station U.S.A. **131** D6
Collerina Australia **112** C2
Collie *N.S.W.* Australia **112** D3
Collie *W.A.* Australia **109** B8
Collier Bay Australia **108** D4
Collier Range National Park Australia **109** B6
Collingwood Canada **134** E1
Collingwood N.Z. **113** D5
Collins U.S.A. **131** F6
Collins Glacier Antarctica **152** E2
Collinson Peninsula Canada **119** H2
Collipulli Chile **144** B5
Collmberg *hill* Germany **53** N3
Collooney Ireland **51** D3
Colmar France **56** H2
Colmenar Viejo Spain **57** E3
Colmonell U.K. **50** E5
Colne *r.* U.K. **49** H7
Cologne Germany **52** G4
Coloma U.S.A. **134** B2
Colomb-Béchar Alg. *see* **Béchar**
Colômbia Brazil **145** A3
Colombia Mex. **131** D7

▶**Colombia** *country* S. America **142** D3
2nd most populous and 4th largest country in South America.

Colombian Basin *sea feature* S. Atlantic Ocean **148** C5

▶**Colombo** Sri Lanka **84** C5
Former capital of Sri Lanka.

Colomiers France **56** E5
Colón *Buenos Aires* Arg. **144** D4
Colón *Entre Ríos* Arg. **144** E4
Colón Cuba **133** D8
Colón Panama **137** I7
Colon U.S.A. **134** C3
Colón, Archipiélago de *is* Ecuador *see* **Galapagos Islands**
Colona Australia **109** F7
Colonelganj India **83** E4
Colonel Hill Bahamas **133** F8
Colonet, Cabo *c.* Mex. **127** D7
Colônia *r.* Brazil **145** D1
Colonia Micronesia **69** J5
Colonia Agrippina Germany *see* **Cologne**
Colonia Díaz Mex. **127** F7
Colonia Julia Fenestris Italy *see* **Fano**
Colonial Heights U.S.A. **135** G5
Colonna, Capo *c.* Italy **58** G5
Colonsay *i.* U.K. **50** C4
Colorado *r.* Arg. **144** D5
Colorado *r.* Mex./U.S.A. **127** E7
Colorado *r.* U.S.A. **131** D6
Colorado *state* U.S.A. **126** G5
Colorado City *AZ* U.S.A. **129** G3
Colorado City *TX* U.S.A. **131** C5
Colorado Desert U.S.A. **128** E5
Colorado National Monument *nat. park* U.S.A. **129** I2
Colorado Plateau U.S.A. **129** I3
Colorado River Aqueduct *canal* U.S.A. **129** F4
Colorado Springs U.S.A. **126** G5
Colossae Turkey *see* **Honaz**
Colotlán Mex. **136** D4
Cölpin Germany **53** N1
Colquiri Bol. **142** E7
Colquitt U.S.A. **133** C6
Colson U.S.A. **134** D5
Colsterworth U.K. **49** G6
Colstrip U.S.A. **126** G3
Coltishall U.K. **49** I6
Colton *CA* U.S.A. **128** E4
Colton *NY* U.S.A. **135** H1
Colton (abandoned) U.S.A. **129** H2
Columbia *KY* U.S.A. **134** C5
Columbia *LA* U.S.A. **131** E5
Columbia *MD* U.S.A. **135** G4
Columbia *MO* U.S.A. **130** E4
Columbia *MS* U.S.A. **131** F6
Columbia *NC* U.S.A. **132** E5
Columbia *PA* U.S.A. **135** G3

▶**Columbia** *SC* U.S.A. **133** D5
Capital of South Carolina.

Columbia *TN* U.S.A. **132** C5
Columbia *r.* U.S.A. **126** C3
Columbia, District of *admin. dist.* U.S.A. **135** G4
Columbia, Mount Canada **120** G4
Columbia, Sierra *mts* Mex. **127** E7
Columbia City U.S.A. **134** C3
Columbia Lake Canada **120** H5
Columbia Mountains Canada **120** F4
Columbia Plateau U.S.A. **126** D3
Columbine, Cape S. Africa **100** C7
Columbus *GA* U.S.A. **133** C5
Columbus *IN* U.S.A. **134** C4
Columbus *MS* U.S.A. **131** F5
Columbus *MT* U.S.A. **126** F3
Columbus *NC* U.S.A. **133** D5
Columbus *NE* U.S.A. **130** D3
Columbus *NM* U.S.A. **127** G7

▶**Columbus** *OH* U.S.A. **134** D4
Capital of Ohio.

Columbus *TX* U.S.A. **131** D6
Columbus Grove U.S.A. **134** C3
Columbus Salt Marsh U.S.A. **128** D2
Colusa U.S.A. **128** B2
Colville N.Z. **113** E3
Colville U.S.A. **126** D2
Colville *r.* U.S.A. **118** C2
Colville Channel N.Z. **113** E3
Colville Lake Canada **118** F3
Colwyn Bay U.K. **48** D5
Comacchio Italy **58** E2
Comacchio, Valli di *lag.* Italy **58** E2
Comai China **83** G3
Comalcalco Mex. **136** F5
Comanche U.S.A. **131** D6
Comandante Ferraz *research station* Antarctica **152** A2
Comandante Salas Arg. **144** C4
Comănești Romania **59** L1
Combahee *r.* U.S.A. **133** D5
Combarbalá Chile **144** B4
Comber U.K. **51** G3
Combermere Bay Myanmar **70** A3
Combles France **52** C4
Combol *i.* Indon. **71** C7
Combomune Moz. **101** K2
Comboyne Australia **112** F3
Comencho, Lac *l.* Canada **122** G4
Comendador Dom. Rep. *see* **Elías Piña**
Comendador Gomes Brazil **145** A2
Comeragh Mountains *hills* Ireland **51** E5
Comercinho Brazil **145** C2
Cometela Moz. **101** L1
Comfort U.S.A. **131** D6
Comilla Bangl. **83** G5
Comines Belgium **52** C4
Comino, Capo *c. Sardinia* Italy **58** C4
Comitán de Domínguez Mex. **136** F5
Commack U.S.A. **135** I3
Commentry France **56** F3
Committee Bay Canada **119** J3
Commonwealth Territory *admin. div.* Australia *see* **Jervis Bay Territory**
Como Italy **58** C2
Como, Lago di Italy *see* **Como, Lake**
Como, Lake Italy **58** C2
Como Chamling *l.* China **83** G3
Comodoro Rivadavia Arg. **144** C7
Comoé, Parc National de la *nat. park* Côte d'Ivoire **96** C4
Comores *country* Africa *see* **Comoros**
Comorin, Cape India **84** C4
Comoro Islands *country* Africa *see* **Comoros**
Comoros *country* Africa **99** E5
Compiègne France **52** C5
Comprida, Ilha *i.* Brazil **145** B4
Comrat Moldova **59** M1
Comrie U.K. **50** F4
Comstock U.S.A. **131** C6
Côn, Sông *r.* Vietnam **71** E4
Cona China **83** G4

▶**Conakry** Guinea **96** B4
Capital of Guinea.

Cona Niyeo Arg. **144** C6
Conceição *r.* Brazil **145** B2
Conceição da Barra Brazil **145** D2
Conceição do Araguaia Brazil **143** I5
Conceição do Mato Dentro Brazil **145** C2
Concepción Chile **144** B5
Concepción Mex. **131** C7
Concepción *r.* Mex. **127** E7
Concepción Para. **144** E2
Concepción, Punta *pt* Mex. **127** F8
Concepción de la Vega Dom. Rep. *see* **La Vega**
Conception, Point U.S.A. **128** C4
Conception Island Bahamas **133** F8
Conchas U.S.A. **127** G6
Conchas Lake U.S.A. **127** G6
Concho U.S.A. **129** I4
Conchos *r. Chihuahua* Mex. **131** B6
Conchos *r. Nuevo León/Tamaulipas* Mex. **131** D7
Concord *CA* U.S.A. **128** B3
Concord *NC* U.S.A. **133** D5

▶**Concord** *NH* U.S.A. **135** J2
Capital of New Hampshire.

Concord *VT* U.S.A. **135** J1
Concordia *research station* Antarctica **152** G2
Concordia Arg. **144** E4
Concordiá Mex. **131** B8
Concordia Peru **142** D4
Concordia S. Africa **100** C5
Concordia *KS* U.S.A. **130** D4
Concordia *KY* U.S.A. **134** B4
Concord Peak Afgh. **89** I2
Con Cuông Vietnam **70** D3
Condamine Australia **112** E1
Condamine *r.* Australia **112** D1
Côn Đao Vietnam **71** D5
Condeúba Brazil **145** C1
Condobolin Australia **112** C4
Condom France **56** E5
Condon U.S.A. **126** C3
Cóndor, Cordillera del *mts* Ecuador/Peru **142** C4
Condroz *reg.* Belgium **52** E4
Conecuh *r.* U.S.A. **133** C6
Conegliano Italy **58** E2
Conejos Mex. **131** C7
Conejos U.S.A. **127** G5
Conemaugh *r.* U.S.A. **134** F3
Conestogo Lake Canada **134** E2
Conesus Lake U.S.A. **135** G2
Conflict Group *is* P.N.G. **110** E1
Confoederatio Helvetica *country* Europe *see* **Switzerland**
Confusion Range *mts* U.S.A. **129** G2
Congdü China **83** F3
Conghua China **77** G4
Congjiang China **77** F3
Congleton U.K. **48** E5
Congo *country* Africa **98** B4

▶**Congo** *r.* Congo/Dem. Rep. Congo **98** B4
2nd longest river in Africa and 8th in the world.
Formerly known as Zaïre.

Congo (Brazzaville) *country* Africa *see* **Congo**
Congo (Kinshasa) *country* Africa *see* **Congo, Democratic Republic of the**

▶**Congo, Democratic Republic of the** *country* Africa **98** C4
2nd largest and 4th most populous country in Africa.

Congo, Republic of the *country* Africa *see* **Congo**
Congo Basin Dem. Rep. Congo **98** C4
Congo Cone *sea feature* S. Atlantic Ocean **148** I6
Congo Free State *country* Africa *see* **Congo, Democratic Republic of the**
Congonhas Brazil **145** C3
Congress U.S.A. **129** G4
Conimbla National Park Australia **112** D4
Coningsby U.K. **49** G5
Coniston Canada **122** E5
Coniston U.K. **48** D4
Conjuboy Australia **110** D3
Conklin Canada **121** I4
Conn *r.* Canada **122** F3
Conn, Lough *l.* Ireland **51** C3
Connacht *reg.* Ireland **51** C4
Connaught *reg.* Ireland *see* **Connacht**
Conneaut U.S.A. **134** E3
Connecticut *state* U.S.A. **135** I3
Connemara *reg.* Ireland **51** C4
Connemara National Park Ireland **51** C4
Connersville U.S.A. **134** C4
Connolly, Mount Canada **120** C2
Connors Range *hills* Australia **110** E4
Conoble Australia **112** B4
Conquista Brazil **145** B2
Conrad U.S.A. **126** F2
Conrad Rise *sea feature* Southern Ocean **149** K9
Conroe U.S.A. **131** E6
Conselheiro Lafaiete Brazil **145** C3
Consett U.K. **48** F4
Consolación del Sur Cuba **133** D8
Côn Sơn, Đao *i.* Vietnam **71** D5
Consort Canada **121** I4
Constance Germany *see* **Konstanz**
Constance, Lake Germany/Switz. **47** L7
Constância dos Baetas Brazil **142** F5
Constanța Romania **59** M2
Constantia *tourist site* Cyprus *see* **Salamis**
Constantia Germany *see* **Konstanz**
Constantina Spain **57** D5
Constantine Alg. **54** F4
Constantine, Cape U.S.A. **118** C4
Constantinople Turkey *see* **İstanbul**
Constitución de 1857, Parque Nacional *nat. park* Mex. **129** F5
Consul Canada **121** I5
Contact U.S.A. **126** E4
Contamana Peru **142** C5
Contas *r.* Brazil **145** D1
Contoy, Isla *i.* Mex. **133** C8
Contria Brazil **145** B2
Contwoyto Lake Canada **121** I1
Convención Col. **142** D2
Convent U.S.A. **131** F6
Conway U.K. *see* **Conwy**
Conway *AR* U.S.A. **131** E5
Conway *ND* U.S.A. **130** D1
Conway *NH* U.S.A. **135** J2
Conway *SC* U.S.A. **133** E5
Conway, Cape Australia **110** E4
Conway, Lake *salt flat* Australia **111** A6
Conway National Park Australia **110** E4
Conway Reef Fiji *see* **Ceva-i-Ra**
Conwy U.K. **48** D5
Conwy *r.* U.K. **49** D5
Coober Pedy Australia **109** F7
Coochbehar India *see* **Koch Bihar**
Cooch Behar India *see* **Koch Bihar**
Cook Australia **109** E7
Cook, Cape Canada **120** E5
Cook, Grand Récif de *reef* New Caledonia **107** G3
Cook, Mount N.Z. *see* **Aoraki/Mount Cook**
Cookes Peak U.S.A. **127** G6
Cookeville U.S.A. **132** C4
Cookhouse S. Africa **101** G7
Cook Ice Shelf Antarctica **152** H2
Cook Inlet *sea chan.* U.S.A. **118** C3

▶**Cook Islands** *terr.* S. Pacific Ocean **150** J7
Self-governing New Zealand overseas territory.

Cooksburg U.S.A. **135** H2
Cooks Passage Australia **110** D2
Cookstown U.K. **51** F3
Cook Strait N.Z. **113** E5
Cooktown Australia **110** D2
Coolabah Australia **112** C3
Cooladdi Australia **112** B1
Coolah Australia **112** D3
Coolamon Australia **112** C5
Coolgardie Australia **109** C7
Coolibah Australia **108** E3
Coolidge U.S.A. **129** H5
Coolum Beach Australia **111** F5
Cooma Australia **112** D6
Coombah Australia **111** C7
Coonabarabran Australia **112** D3
Coonamble Australia **112** D3
Coondambo Australia **111** A6
Coondapoor India *see* **Kundapura**
Coongoola Australia **112** B1
Coon Rapids U.S.A. **130** E2
Cooper Creek *watercourse* Australia **111** B6
Cooper Mountain Canada **120** G5
Coopernook Australia **112** F3
Cooper's Town Bahamas **133** E7
Cooperstown *ND* U.S.A. **130** D2
Cooperstown *NY* U.S.A. **135** H2
Coopracambra National Park Australia **112** D6
Coorabie Australia **109** F7
Coorong National Park Australia **111** B8
Coorow Australia **109** B7
Coosa *r.* U.S.A. **133** C5
Coos Bay U.S.A. **126** B4
Coos Bay *b.* U.S.A. **126** B4
Cootamundra Australia **112** D5
Cootehill Ireland **51** E3
Cooyar Australia **112** E1
Copala Mex. **136** E5
Cope U.S.A. **130** C4
Copemish U.S.A. **134** C1

▶**Copenhagen** Denmark **45** H9
Capital of Denmark.

Copenhagen U.S.A. **135** H2
Copertino Italy **58** H4
Copeton Reservoir Australia **112** E2
Cô Pi, Phou *mt.* Laos/Vietnam **70** D3
Copiapó Chile **144** B3
Copley Australia **111** B6
Copparo Italy **58** D2
Copper Cliff Canada **122** E5
Copper Harbor U.S.A. **132** C2
Coppermine Canada *see* **Kugluktuk**
Coppermine *r.* Canada **120** H1
Coppermine Point Canada **122** D5
Copperton S. Africa **100** F5
Copp Lake Canada **120** H2
Coqên *Xizang* China **83** F3
Coqên *Xizang* China **83** F3
Coquilhatville Dem. Rep. Congo *see* **Mbandaka**
Coquille *i.* Micronesia *see* **Pikelot**
Coquille U.S.A. **126** B4
Coquimbo Chile **144** B3
Coquitlam Canada **120** F5
Corabia Romania **59** K3
Coração de Jesus Brazil **145** B2
Coracesium Turkey *see* **Alanya**
Coraki Australia **112** F2
Coral Bay Australia **109** A5
Coral Harbour Canada **119** J3
Coral Sea S. Pacific Ocean **106** F3
Coral Sea Basin S. Pacific Ocean **150** G6

▶**Coral Sea Islands Territory** *terr.* Australia **106** F3
Australian External Territory.

Corangamite, Lake Australia **112** A7
Corat Azer. **91** H2
Corbeny France **52** D5
Corbett Inlet Canada **121** M2
Corbett National Park India **82** D3
Corbie France **52** C5
Corbin U.S.A. **134** C5
Corby U.K. **49** G6
Corcaigh Ireland *see* **Cork**
Corcoran U.S.A. **128** D3
Corcovado, Golfo de *sea chan.* Chile **144** B6
Corcyra *i.* Greece *see* **Corfu**
Cordele U.S.A. **133** D6
Cordelia U.S.A. **128** B2
Cordell U.S.A. **131** D5
Cordilheiras, Serra das *hills* Brazil **143** I5
Cordillera Azul, Parque Nacional *nat. park* Peru **142** C5
Cordillera de los Picachos, Parque Nacional *nat. park* Col. **142** D3
Cordillo Downs Australia **111** C5
Cordisburgo Brazil **145** B2
Córdoba Arg. **144** D4
Córdoba *Durango* Mex. **131** C7
Córdoba *Veracruz* Mex. **136** E5
Córdoba Spain **57** D5
Córdoba, Sierras de *mts* Arg. **144** D4
Cordova Spain *see* **Córdoba**
Cordova U.S.A. **118** D3
Corduba Spain *see* **Córdoba**
Corfu *i.* Greece **59** H5
Coria Spain **57** C4
Coribe Brazil **145** B1
Coricudgy *mt.* Australia **112** E4
Corigliano Calabro Italy **58** G5
Coringa Islands Australia **110** E3
Corinium U.K. *see* **Cirencester**
Corinth Greece **59** J6
Corinth *KY* U.S.A. **134** C4
Corinth *MS* U.S.A. **131** F5
Corinth *NY* U.S.A. **135** I2
Corinth, Gulf of *sea chan.* Greece **59** J5
Corinthus Greece *see* **Corinth**
Corinto Brazil **145** B2
Cork Ireland **51** D6
Corleone *Sicily* Italy **58** E6
Çorlu Turkey **59** L4
Cormeilles France **49** H9
Cornelia S. Africa **101** I4
Cornélio Procópio Brazil **145** A3
Cornélios Brazil **145** A5
Cornell U.S.A. **130** F2
Corner Brook Canada **123** K4
Corner Inlet *b.* Australia **112** C7
Corner Seamounts *sea feature* N. Atlantic Ocean **148** E3
Corneto Italy *see* **Tarquinia**
Cornillet, Mont *hill* France **52** E5
Corning *AR* U.S.A. **131** F4
Corning *CA* U.S.A. **128** B2
Corning *NY* U.S.A. **135** G2
Cornish *watercourse* Australia **110** D4
Corn Islands *is* Nicaragua *see* **Maíz, Islas del**
Corno di Campo *mt.* Italy/Switz. **56** J3
Corno Grande *mt.* Italy **58** E3
Cornwall Canada **135** H1
Cornwallis Island Canada **119** I2
Cornwall Island Canada **119** I2
Coro Venez. **142** E1
Coroaci Brazil **145** C2
Coroatá Brazil **143** J4
Corofin Ireland **51** C5
Coromandel Brazil **145** B2
Coromandel Coast India **84** D4
Coromandel Peninsula N.Z. **113** E3
Coromandel Range *hills* N.Z. **113** E3
Corona *CA* U.S.A. **128** E5
Corona *NM* U.S.A. **127** G6
Coronado U.S.A. **128** E5
Coronado, Bahía de *b.* Costa Rica **137** H7
Coronation Canada **121** I4
Coronation Gulf Canada **118** G3
Coronation Island S. Atlantic Ocean **152** A2
Coronda Arg. **144** D4
Coronel Fabriciano Brazil **145** C2
Coronel Oviedo Para. **144** E3
Coronel Pringles Arg. **144** D5
Coronel Suárez Arg. **144** D5
Coropuna, Nudo *mt.* Peru **142** D7
Çorovodë Albania **59** I4
Corowa Australia **112** C5
Corpus Christi U.S.A. **131** D7
Corque Bol. **142** E7
Corral de Cantos *mt.* Spain **57** D4
Corrales Mex. **131** B7
Corralilla Cuba **133** D8
Corrandibby Range *hills* Australia **109** A6
Corrente Brazil **143** I6
Corrente *r. Bahia* Brazil **145** C1
Corrente *r. Minas Gerais* Brazil **145** A2
Correntes Brazil **143** H7
Correntina Brazil **145** B1
Correntina *r.* Brazil *see* **Éguas**
Corrib, Lough *l.* Ireland **51** C4
Corrientes Arg. **144** E3
Corrientes, Cabo *c.* Col. **142** C2
Corrientes, Cabo *c.* Cuba **133** C8
Corrientes, Cabo *c.* Mex. **136** C4
Corrigin Australia **109** B8
Corris U.K. **49** D6
Corry U.S.A. **134** F3
Corse *i.* France *see* **Corsica**
Corse, Cap *c. Corsica* France **56** I5
Corsham U.K. **49** E7
Corsica *i.* France **56** I5
Corsicana U.S.A. **131** D5
Corte *Corsica* France **56** I5
Cortegana Spain **57** C5
Cortes, Sea of *g.* Mex. *see* **California, Gulf of**
Cortez U.S.A. **129** I3
Cortina d'Ampezzo Italy **58** E1
Cortland U.S.A. **135** G2
Corton U.K. **49** I6
Cortona Italy **58** D3
Coruche Port. **57** B4
Çoruh Turkey *see* **Artvin**
Çoruh *r.* Turkey **91** F2
Çorum Turkey **90** D2
Corumbá Brazil **143** G7
Corumbá *r.* Brazil **145** A2
Corumbá de Goiás Brazil **145** A1
Corumbaíba Brazil **145** A2
Corumbaú, Ponta *pt* Brazil **145** D2
Corunna Spain *see* **A Coruña**
Corunna U.S.A. **134** C2
Corvallis U.S.A. **126** C3
Corvette, Lac de la *l.* Canada **122** G3
Corwen U.K. **49** D6
Corydon *IA* U.S.A. **130** E3
Corydon *IN* U.S.A. **134** B4
Coryville U.S.A. **135** F3
Cos *i.* Greece *see* **Kos**
Cosentia Italy *see* **Cosenza**
Cosenza Italy **58** G5
Coshocton U.S.A. **134** E3
Cosne-Cours-sur-Loire France **56** F3
Costa Blanca *coastal area* Spain **57** F4
Costa Brava *coastal area* Spain **57** H3
Costa de la Luz *coastal area* Spain **57** C5
Costa del Sol *coastal area* Spain **57** D5
Costa de Miskitos *coastal area* Nicaragua *see* **Mosquitos, Costa de**
Costa Marques Brazil **142** F6
Costa Rica Brazil **143** H7
Costa Rica *country* Central America **137** H6
Costa Rica Mex. **136** C4
Costa Verde *coastal area* Spain **57** C2
Costermansville Dem. Rep. Congo *see* **Bukavu**
Costești Romania **59** K2
Costigan Lake Canada **121** J3
Coswig (Anhalt) Germany **53** M3
Cotabato Phil. **69** G5
Cotagaita Bol. **142** E8
Cotahuasi Peru **142** D7
Cote, Mount U.S.A. **120** D3
Coteau des Prairies *slope* U.S.A. **130** D2
Coteau du Missouri *slope ND* U.S.A. **130** C1
Coteau du Missouri *slope SD* U.S.A. **130** C2
Côte d'Ivoire *country* Africa **96** C4
Côte Française de Somalis *country* Africa *see* **Djibouti**
Cotentin *pen.* France **49** F9
Cothi *r.* U.K. **49** C7
Cotiaeum Turkey *see* **Kütahya**
Cotiella *mt.* Spain **57** G2
Cotonou Benin **96** D4
Cotopaxi, Volcán *vol.* Ecuador **142** C4
Cotswold Hills U.K. **49** E7
Cottage Grove U.S.A. **126** C4
Cottbus Germany **47** O5
Cottenham U.K. **49** H6
Cottian Alps *mts* France/Italy **56** H4
Cottica Suriname **143** H3
Cottiennes, Alpes *mts* France/Italy *see* **Cottian Alps**
Cottonwood *AZ* U.S.A. **129** G4
Cottonwood *CA* U.S.A. **128** B1
Cottonwood *r.* U.S.A. **130** D4
Cottonwood Falls U.S.A. **130** D4
Cotulla U.S.A. **131** D6
Coubre, Pointe de la *pt* France **56** D4
Coudersport U.S.A. **135** F3
Couedic, Cape du Australia **111** B8
Coulee City U.S.A. **126** D3
Coulee Dam U.S.A. **126** D3
Coulman Island Antarctica **152** H2
Coulogne France **52** B4
Coulommiers France **52** D6
Coulonge *r.* Canada **122** F5
Coulterville U.S.A. **128** C3
Council U.S.A. **126** D3
Council Bluffs U.S.A. **130** E3
Council Grove U.S.A. **130** D4
Councillor Island Australia **111** [inset]
Counselor U.S.A. **129** J3
Coupeville U.S.A. **126** C2
Courageous Lake Canada **121** I1
Courland Lagoon *b.* Lith./Russia **45** L9
Courtenay Canada **120** E5
Courtland U.S.A. **135** G5
Courtmacsherry Ireland **51** D6
Courtmacsherry Bay Ireland **51** D6
Courtown Ireland **51** F5
Courtrai Belgium *see* **Kortrijk**
Coushatta U.S.A. **131** E5
Coutances France **56** D2
Coutts Canada **121** I5
Couture, Lac *l.* Canada **122** G2
Couvin Belgium **52** E4
Cove Fort U.S.A. **129** G2
Cove Island Canada **134** E1
Cove Mountains *hills* U.S.A. **135** F4
Coventry U.K. **49** F6
Covesville U.S.A. **135** F5
Covilhã Port. **57** C3
Covington *GA* U.S.A. **133** D5
Covington *IN* U.S.A. **134** B3
Covington *KY* U.S.A. **134** C4
Covington *LA* U.S.A. **131** F6
Covington *MI* U.S.A. **130** F2
Covington *TN* U.S.A. **131** F5
Covington *VA* U.S.A. **134** E5
Cowal, Lake *dry lake* Australia **112** C4
Cowan, Lake *salt flat* Australia **109** C7
Cowansville Canada **135** I1
Cowargarzê China **76** C1
Cowcowing Lakes *salt flat* Australia **109** B7
Cowdenbeath U.K. **50** F4
Cowell Australia **111** B7
Cowes U.K. **49** F8
Cowichan Lake Canada **120** E5
Cowley Australia **112** B1
Cowper Point Canada **119** G2
Cowra Australia **112** D4
Cox *r.* Australia **110** A2
Coxá *r.* Brazil **145** B1
Coxen Hole Hond. *see* **Roatán**
Coxilha de Santana *hills* Brazil/Uruguay **144** E4
Coxilha Grande *hills* Brazil **144** F3
Coxim Brazil **143** H7
Cox's Bazar Bangl. **83** G5
Coyame Mex. **131** B6
Coyhaique Chile *see* **Coihaique**
Coyote Lake U.S.A. **128** E4
Coyote Peak *hill* U.S.A. **129** F5
Cozhê *Xizang* China **83** F2
Cozhê *Xizang* China **83** F3
Cozie, Alpi *mts* France/Italy *see* **Cottian Alps**
Cozumel Mex. **137** G4
Cozumel, Isla de *i.* Mex. **137** G4
Craboon Australia **112** D4
Cracovia Poland *see* **Kraków**
Cracow Australia **110** E5
Cracow Poland *see* **Kraków**
Cradle Mountain Lake St Clair National Park Australia **111** [inset]
Cradock S. Africa **101** G7
Craig U.K. **50** D3
Craig *AK* U.S.A. **120** C4
Craig *CO* U.S.A. **129** J1
Craigavon U.K. **51** F3
Craigieburn Australia **112** B6
Craig Island Taiwan *see* **Mianhua Yu**
Craignure U.K. **50** D4
Craigsville U.S.A. **134** E4
Crail U.K. **50** G4
Crailsheim Germany **53** K5
Craiova Romania **59** J2
Cramlington U.K. **48** F3
Cranberry Lake U.S.A. **135** H1
Cranberry Portage Canada **121** K4
Cranborne Chase *for.* U.K. **49** E8
Cranbourne Australia **112** B7
Cranbrook Canada **120** H5
Crandon U.S.A. **130** F2
Crane Lake Canada **121** I5
Cranston *KY* U.S.A. **134** D4
Cranston *RI* U.S.A. **135** J3
Cranz Russia *see* **Zelenogradsk**
Crary Ice Rise Antarctica **152** I1
Crary Mountains Antarctica **152** J1
Crater Lake National Park U.S.A. **126** C4
Crater Peak U.S.A. **128** C1
Craters of the Moon National Monument *nat. park* U.S.A. **126** E4
Crateús Brazil **143** J5
Crato Brazil **143** K5
Crawford *CO* U.S.A. **129** J2
Crawford *NE* U.S.A. **130** C3
Crawfordsville U.S.A. **134** B3
Crawfordville *FL* U.S.A. **133** C6
Crawfordville *GA* U.S.A. **133** D5
Crawley U.K. **49** G7
Crazy Mountains U.S.A. **126** F3
Creag Meagaidh *mt.* U.K. **50** E4
Crécy-en-Ponthieu France **52** B4
Credenhill U.K. **49** E6
Crediton U.K. **49** D8
Cree *r.* Canada **121** J3
Creel Mex. **127** G8
Cree Lake Canada **121** J3
Creemore Canada **134** E1
Creighton Canada **121** K4
Creil France **52** C5
Creil Neth. **52** F2
Crema Italy **58** C2
Cremlingen Germany **53** K2
Cremona Canada **120** H5
Cremona Italy **58** D2
Crépy-en-Valois France **52** C5
Cres *i.* Croatia **58** F2
Crescent U.S.A. **126** C4
Crescent City *CA* U.S.A. **126** B4
Crescent City *FL* U.S.A. **133** D6
Crescent Group *is* Paracel Is **68** E3
Crescent Head Australia **112** F3
Crescent Junction U.S.A. **129** I2
Crescent Valley U.S.A. **128** E1
Cressy Australia **112** A7
Crestline U.S.A. **134** D3
Creston Canada **120** G5
Creston *IA* U.S.A. **130** E3
Creston *WY* U.S.A. **126** G4
Crestview U.S.A. **133** C6
Creswick Australia **112** A6
Creta *i.* Greece *see* **Crete**
Crete *i.* Greece **59** K7
Crete U.S.A. **130** D3
Creus, Cap de *c.* Spain **57** H2
Creuse *r.* France **56** E3
Creußen Germany **53** L5
Creutzwald France **52** G5
Creuzburg Germany **53** K3
Crevasse Valley Glacier Antarctica **152** J1
Crewe U.K. **49** E5
Crewe U.S.A. **135** F5

Crewkerne U.K. 49 E8
Crianlarich U.K. 50 E4
Criccieth U.K. 49 C6
Criciúma Brazil 145 A5
Crieff U.K. 50 F4
Crifell hill U.K. see Criffel
Criffel hill U.K. 50 F6
Crikvenica Croatia 58 F2
Crillon, Mount U.S.A. 120 B3
Crimea disp. terr. Europe 55 K2
Crimmitschau Germany 53 M4
Crimond U.K. 50 H3
Crisfield U.S.A. 135 H5
Cristalândia Brazil 143 I6
Cristalina Brazil 145 B2
Cristalino r. Brazil see Mariembero
Cristóbal Colón, Pico mt. Col. 142 D1
Crixás Brazil 145 A1
Crixás Açu r. Brazil 145 A1
Crixás Mirim r. Brazil 145 A1
Crna Gora country Europe see Montenegro
Crni Vrh mt. Serbia 59 J2
Črnomelj Slovenia 58 F2
Croagh Patrick hill Ireland 51 C4
Croajingolong National Park Australia 112 D6
Croatia country Europe 58 G2
Crocker, Banjaran mts Malaysia 68 E6
Crockett U.S.A. 131 E6
Crofton KY U.S.A. 134 B5
Crofton NE U.S.A. 130 D3
Croghan U.S.A. 135 H2
Croisilles France 52 C4
Croker, Cape Canada 134 E1
Croker Island Australia 108 F2
Cromarty U.K. 50 E3
Cromarty Firth est. U.K. 50 E3
Cromer U.K. 49 I6
Crook U.K. 48 F4
Crooked Harbour b. H.K. China 77 [inset]
Crooked Island Bahamas 133 F8
Crooked Island H.K. China 77 [inset]
Crooked Island Passage Bahamas 133 F8
Crookston U.S.A. 130 D2
Crooksville U.S.A. 134 D4
Crookwell Australia 112 D5
Croom Ireland 51 D5
Croppa Creek Australia 112 E2
Crosby U.K. 48 D5
Crosby MN U.S.A. 130 E2
Crosby ND U.S.A. 130 C1
Crosbyton U.S.A. 131 C5
Cross Bay Canada 121 M2
Cross City U.S.A. 133 D6
Cross Fell hill U.K. 48 E4
Crossfield Canada 120 H5
Crossgar U.K. 51 G3
Crosshaven Ireland 51 D6
Cross Inn U.K. 49 C6
Cross Lake Canada 121 L4
Cross Lake l. Canada 121 L4
Cross Lake l. U.S.A. 135 G2
Crossmaglen U.K. 51 F3
Crossman Peak U.S.A. 129 F4
Crossville U.S.A. 132 C5
Crotch Lake Canada 135 G1
Croton Italy see Crotone
Crotone Italy 58 G5
Crouch r. U.K. 49 H7
Crow r. Canada 120 E3
Crow Agency U.S.A. 126 G3
Crowal watercourse Australia 112 C3
Crowborough U.K. 49 H7
Crowdy Bay National Park Australia 112 F3
Crowell U.S.A. 131 D5
Crowland U.K. 49 G6
Crowley U.S.A. 131 E6
Crowley, Lake U.S.A. 128 D3
Crown Point IN U.S.A. 134 B3
Crownpoint U.S.A. 129 I4
Crown Point NY U.S.A. 135 I2
Crown Prince Olav Coast Antarctica 152 D2
Crown Princess Martha Coast Antarctica 152 B1
Crows Nest Australia 112 F1
Crowsnest Pass Canada 120 H5
Crowsnest Pass pass Canada 120 H5
Crow Wing r. U.S.A. 130 E2
Croydon Australia 110 C3
Crozet U.S.A. 135 F4
Crozet, Îles is Indian Ocean 149 L9
Crozet Basin sea feature Indian Ocean 149 M8
Crozet Plateau sea feature Indian Ocean 149 K8
Crozon France 56 B2
Cruces Cuba 133 D8
Cruden Bay U.K. 50 H3
Cruillas Mex. 131 D7
Crum U.S.A. 134 D5
Crumlin U.K. 51 F3
Crusheen Ireland 51 D5
Cruz Alta Brazil 144 F3
Cruz del Eje Arg. 144 D4
Cruzeiro Brazil 145 B3
Cruzeiro do Sul Brazil 142 D5
Cry Lake Canada 120 D3
Crysdale, Mount Canada 120 F4
Crystal U.S.A. 129 I3
Crystal City Canada 121 L5
Crystal City U.S.A. 131 D6
Crystal Falls U.S.A. 130 F2
Crystal Lake U.S.A. 134 A2
Crystal River U.S.A. 133 D6
Csongrád Hungary 59 I1
Cửa Lớn, Sông r. Vietnam 71 D5
Cuamba Moz. 99 D5
Cuando r. Angola/Zambia 99 C5
Cuangar Angola 99 B5
Cuango Angola 99 B4
Cuanza r. Angola 99 B4
Cuatro Ciénegas Mex. 131 C7
Cuauhtémoc Mex. 127 G7
Cuba NM U.S.A. 127 G5
Cuba NY U.S.A. 135 F2

▶Cuba country West Indies 137 H4
5th largest island and 5th most populous country in North America.

Cubal Angola 99 B5
Cubango r. Angola/Namibia 99 C5
Cubatão Brazil 145 B3
Cub Hills Canada 121 J4
Çubuk Turkey 90 D2
Cucapa, Sierra mts Mex. 129 F5
Cuchi Angola 99 B5
Cuchilla Grande hills Uruguay 144 E4
Cucuí Brazil 142 E3
Cucurpe Mex. 127 F7
Cúcuta Col. 142 D2
Cudal Australia 112 D4
Cuddalore India 84 C4
Cuddapah India see Kadapa
Cuddeback Lake U.S.A. 128 E4
Cue Australia 109 B6
Cuéllar Spain 57 D3
Cuemba Angola 99 B5
Cuenca Ecuador 142 C4
Cuenca Spain 57 E3
Cuenca, Serranía de mts Spain 57 E3
Cuencamé Mex. 131 C7
Cuernavaca Mex. 136 E5
Cuero U.S.A. 131 D6
Cuervos Mex. 129 F5
Cugir Romania 59 J2
Cuiabá Amazonas Brazil 143 G5
Cuiabá Mato Grosso Brazil 143 G7
Cuiabá r. Brazil 143 G7
Cuihua China see Daguan
Cuijiang China see Ninghua
Cuijk Neth. 52 F3
Cuilcagh hill Ireland/U.K. 51 E3
Cuillin Hills U.K. 50 C3
Cuillin Sound sea chan. U.K. 50 C3
Cuilo Angola 99 B4
Cuiluan China 74 C3
Cuité r. Brazil 145 C2
Cuito r. Angola 99 C5
Cuito Cuanavale Angola 99 B5
Cukai Malaysia 71 C6
Çukurca Turkey 88 A2
Çukurova plat. Turkey 85 B1
Culcairn Australia 112 C5
Culebra, Sierra de la mts Spain 57 C3
Culfa Azer. 91 G3
Culgoa r. Australia 112 C2
Culiacán Mex. 136 C4
Culiacán Rosales Mex. see Culiacán
Culion Phil. 69 F4
Culion i. Phil. 68 F4
Cullen U.K. 50 G3
Cullen Point Australia 110 C1
Cullera Spain 57 F4
Cullivoe U.K. 50 [inset]
Cullman U.S.A. 133 C5
Cullybackey U.K. 51 F3
Cul Mòr hill U.K. 50 D2
Culpeper U.S.A. 135 G4
Cultural Landscape of the Serra de Tramuntana tourist site Spain 57 H4
Cultural Sites of Al Ain tourist site U.A.E. 87 I5
Culuene r. Brazil 143 H6
Culver, Point Australia 109 D8
Culverden N.Z. 113 D6
Cumaná Venez. 142 F1
Cumari Brazil 145 A2
Cumbal, Nevado de vol. Col. 142 C3
Cumberland KY U.S.A. 134 D5
Cumberland MD U.S.A. 135 F4
Cumberland VA U.S.A. 135 F5
Cumberland r. U.S.A. 132 C4
Cumberland, Lake U.S.A. 134 C5
Cumberland Lake Canada 121 K4
Cumberland Mountains U.S.A. 134 D5
Cumberland Peninsula Canada 119 L3
Cumberland Plateau U.S.A. 132 C5
Cumberland Point U.S.A. 130 F2
Cumberland Sound sea chan. Canada 119 L3
Cumbernauld U.K. 50 F5
Cumbres de Majalca, Parque Nacional nat. park Mex. 127 G7
Cumbres de Monterey, Parque Nacional nat. park Mex. 131 C7
Cumbum India 84 C3
Cumlosen Germany 53 L1
Cummings U.S.A. 128 B2
Cummins Australia 111 A7
Cummins Range hills Australia 108 D4
Cumnock Australia 112 D4
Cumnock U.K. 50 E5
Çumra Turkey 90 D3
Cumuruxatiba Brazil 145 D2
Cunagua Cuba see Bolivia
Cunderdin Australia 109 B7
Cunene r. Angola 99 B5
also known as Kunene
Cuneo Italy 58 B2
Cung Sơn Vietnam 71 E4
Cunnamulla Australia 112 B2
Cunningsburgh U.K. 50 [inset]
Cupar U.K. 50 F4
Cupica, Golfo de b. Col. 142 C2
Curaçá Brazil 143 K5
Curaçá r. Brazil 142 D4

▶Curaçao terr. West Indies 137 K6
Self-governing Netherlands territory.

Curaray r. Ecuador 142 D4
Curdlawidny Lagoon salt flat Australia 111 B6
Curia Switz. see Chur
Curicó Chile 144 B4
Curitiba Brazil 145 A4
Curitibanos Brazil 145 A4
Curlewis Australia 112 E3
Curnamona Australia 111 B6
Currabubula Australia 112 E3
Currais Novos Brazil 143 K5
Curran U.S.A. 134 D1
Currane, Lough l. Ireland 51 B6
Currant U.S.A. 129 F2
Curranyalpa Australia 112 B3
Currawilla Australia 110 C5
Currawinya National Park Australia 112 B2
Currie Australia 106 E5
Currie U.S.A. 129 F1
Currituck U.S.A. 135 G5

Currockbilly, Mount Australia 112 E5
Curtis Channel Australia 110 F5
Curtis Island Australia 110 E4
Curtis Island N.Z. 107 I5
Curuá r. Brazil 143 H5
Curup Indon. 68 C7
Curupira, Serra mts Brazil/Venez. 142 F3
Cururupu Brazil 143 J4
Curvelo Brazil 145 B2
Curwood, Mount hill U.S.A. 130 F2
Cusco Peru 142 D6
Cushendall U.K. 51 F2
Cushendun U.K. 51 F2
Cushing U.S.A. 131 D4
Cusseta U.S.A. 133 C5
Custer MT U.S.A. 126 G3
Custer SD U.S.A. 130 C3
Cut Bank U.S.A. 126 E2
Cuthbert U.S.A. 133 C6
Cuthbertson Falls Australia 108 F3
Cut Knife Canada 121 I4
Cutler Ridge U.S.A. 133 D7
Cuttaburra Creek r. Australia 112 B2
Cuttack India 84 E1
Cuvelai Angola 99 B5
Cuxhaven Germany 47 L4
Cuya Chile 142 D7
Cuyahoga Falls U.S.A. 134 E3
Cuyama U.S.A. 128 D4
Cuyama r. U.S.A. 128 C4
Cuyo Islands Phil. 69 G4
Cuyuni r. Guyana 143 G2
Cuzco Peru see Cusco
Cwmbrân U.K. 49 D7
Cyangugu Rwanda 98 C4
Cyclades is Greece 59 K6
Cydonia Greece see Chania
Cygnet U.S.A. 134 D3
Cymru admin. div. U.K. see Wales
Cynthiana U.S.A. 134 C4
Cypress Hills Canada 121 I5
Cyprus country Asia 85 A2
Cyrenaica hist. area Libya 97 F2
Cythera i. Greece see Kythira
Czar Canada 121 I4
Czechia country Europe 47 O6

▶Czechoslovakia
Divided in 1993 into the Czech Republic and Slovakia.

Czech Republic country see Czechia
Czernowitz Ukr. see Chernivtsi
Czersk Poland 47 P4
Częstochowa Poland 47 Q5

D

Đa, Sông r. Vietnam see Black
Da'an China 74 B3
Ḑabāb, Jabal aḑ mt. Jordan 85 B4
Dabakala Côte d'Ivoire 96 C4
Daban China 73 L4
Dabao China 76 D2
Daba Shan mts China 77 F1
Dabba China see Daocheng
Dabein Myanmar 70 B3
Dabhoi India 82 C5
Ḑab'ī, Wādī aḑ watercourse Jordan 85 C4
Dabie Shan mts China 77 G2
Dablana India 82 C4
Dabola Guinea 96 B3
Dabqig China 73 J5
Dąbrowa Górnicza Poland 47 Q5
Dabs Nur l. China 74 A3
Dabu Guangdong China 77 H3
Dabu Guangxi China see Liucheng
Dabusu Pao l. China see Dabs Nur
Dacca Bangl. see Dhaka
Dachau Germany 47 M6
Dachuan China see Dazhou
Dacre Canada 135 G1
Dadaab Kenya 98 E3
Daday Turkey 90 D2
Dade City U.S.A. 133 D6
Dadeville U.S.A. 133 C5
Dādkān Iran 89 F5
Dadohae Haesang National Park S. Korea 75 B6
Dadong China see Donggang
Dadra India see Achalpur
Dadu Pak. 89 G5
Daecheong-do i. S. Korea 75 B5
Daegu S. Korea 75 C6
Daeheuksan-gundo is S. Korea 75 B6
Daejeon S. Korea 75 B5
Daejeong S. Korea 75 B6
Daet Phil. 69 G4
Dafang China 76 E3
Dafeng China 77 I1
Dafla Hills India 83 H4
Dafoe Canada 121 J5
Dafoe r. Canada 121 M4
Dagana Senegal 96 B3
Dagcagoin China see Zoigê
Dagcanglhamo China see Langmusi
Daghmar Oman 88 E6
Dağlıq Qarabağ disp. terr. Azer. see Nagorno-Karabakh
Daglung China 83 G3
Dagö i. Estonia see Hiiumaa
Dagon Myanmar see Rangoon
Daguan China 76 D3
Daguokui Shan hill China 74 C3
Dagupan Phil. 69 G3
Dagxoi Sichuan China see Sowa
Dagxoi Sichuan China see Yidun
Dagzê China 83 G3
Dagzê Co salt l. China 83 F3
Dahadinni r. Canada 120 E2
Dahalach, Isole is Eritrea see Dahlak Archipelago
Dahana des. Saudi Arabia see Ad Dahnā'
Dahe Guangxi China see Ziyuan
Dahe Heilong. China 74 D3
Daheiding Shan mt. China 74 C3
Dahei Shan mts China 74 B4
Dahej India 82 C5

Da Hinggan Ling mts China 74 A2
Daḩl, Nafūd ad des. Saudi Arabia 88 B6
Dahlak Archipelago is Eritrea 86 F6
Dahlak Marine National Park Eritrea 86 F6
Daḩl al Furayy well Saudi Arabia 88 B5
Dahlem Germany 52 G4
Dahlenburg Germany 53 K1
Dahm, Ramlat des. Saudi Arabia/Yemen 86 G6
Dahmani Tunisia 58 C7
Dahme/Mark Germany 53 N3
Dahn Germany 53 H5
Dahnā' plain Saudi Arabia 88 B5
Dahod India 82 C5
Dahomey country Africa see Benin
Dahongliutan China 82 D2
Dahra Senegal see Dara
Dähre Germany 53 K2
Dahūk/Dihok Iraq 91 F3
Dai i. Indon. 108 E1
Daik Indon. 68 C7
Daik-U Myanmar 70 B3
Đai Lanh, Mui pt Vietnam 71 E4
Dailekh Nepal 83 E3
Dailly U.K. 50 E5
Daimiel Spain 57 E4
Daingean Uí Chúis Ireland 51 B5
Dainkognubma China 76 C1
Daintree National Park Australia 110 D3
Dair, Jebel ed mt. Sudan 86 D7
Dairen China see Dalian
Dai-sen vol. Japan 75 D6
Daisetsu-zan Kokuritsu-kōen nat. park Japan 74 F4
Daishan China 77 I2
Daiyun Shan mts China 77 H3
Dajarra Australia 110 B4
Dajin Chuan r. China 76 D2
Da Juh China 83 H1

▶Dakar Senegal 96 B3
Capital of Senegal.

Dākhilah, Wāḩāt ad oasis Egypt 86 C4
Dakhla W. Sahara 96 B2
Dakhla Oasis oasis Egypt see Dākhilah, Wāḩāt ad
Đắk Lăk, Cao Nguyên plat. Vietnam 71 E4
Dakoank India 71 A6
Dakol'ka r. Belarus 43 F5
Dakor India 82 C5
Dakoro Niger 96 D3
Dakota City IA U.S.A. 130 E3
Dakota City NE U.S.A. 130 D3
Đakovica Kosovo see Gjakovë
Đakovo Croatia 58 H2
Daktuy Russia 74 B1
Dala Angola 99 C5
Dalaba Guinea 96 B3
Dalai China see Da'an
Dalain Hob China 80 J3
Dālakī Iran 88 C4
Dalälven r. Sweden 45 J6
Dalaman Turkey 59 M6
Dalandzadgad Mongolia 72 I4
Dalap-Uliga-Darrit Marshall Is see Delap-Uliga-Djarrit
Đa Lat Vietnam 71 E5
Dalatando Angola see N'dalatando
Dalaud India 82 C5
Dalauda India 82 C5
Dalbandin Pak. 89 G4
Dalbeattie U.K. 50 F6
Dalbeg Australia 110 D4
Dalby Australia 112 E1
Dalby Isle of Man 48 C4
Dale Hordaland Norway 45 D6
Dale Sogn og Fjordane Norway 45 D6
Dale City U.S.A. 135 G4
Dale Hollow Lake U.S.A. 134 C5
Dalen Neth. 52 G2
Dalet Myanmar 70 A3
Daletme Myanmar 70 A2
Dalfors Sweden 45 I6
Dalgān Iran 88 E5
Dalgety Australia 112 D6
Dalgety r. Australia 109 A6
Dalhart U.S.A. 131 C4
Dalhousie Canada 123 I4
Dalhousie, Cape Canada 118 F2
Dali Shaanxi China 77 F1
Dali Yunnan China 76 D3
Dalian China 73 M5
Daliang China see Shunde
Daliang Shan mts China 76 D2
Dalin China 74 A4
Dalizi China 74 B4
Dalkeith U.K. 50 F5
Dallas OR U.S.A. 126 C3
Dallas TX U.S.A. 131 D5
Dalles City U.S.A. see The Dalles
Dall Island U.S.A. 120 C4
Dalmā i. U.A.E. 88 D5
Dalmacija reg. Bos. & Herz./Croatia see Dalmatia
Dalmas, Lac l. Canada 123 H3
Dalmatia reg. Bos. & Herz./Croatia 78 A2
Dalmau India 82 E4
Dalmellington U.K. 50 E5
Dalmeny Canada 121 J4
Dalmi India 83 F5
Dal'negorsk Russia 74 D3
Dal'nerechensk Russia 74 D3
Dal'niye Zelentsy Russia 42 H1
Dalny China see Dalian
Daloa Côte d'Ivoire 96 C4

▶Dalol (abandoned) Eth. 86 F7
Highest recorded annual mean temperature in the world.

Daloloia Group is P.N.G. 110 E1
Dalou Shan mts China 76 E3
Dalqān well Saudi Arabia 88 B5
Dalry U.K. 50 E5
Dalrymple U.K. 50 E5
Dalrymple, Lake Australia 110 D4
Daltenganj India see Daltonganj
Dalton Canada 122 D4
Dalton S. Africa 101 J5

Dalton GA U.S.A. 133 C5
Dalton MA U.S.A. 135 I2
Dalton PA U.S.A. 135 H3
Daltonganj India 83 F4
Dalton-in-Furness U.K. 48 D4
Daludalu Indon. 71 C7
Daluo China 76 D4
Daly r. Australia 108 E3
Daly City U.S.A. 128 B3
Daly River Australia 108 E3
Daly Waters Australia 108 F4
Damagaram Takaya Niger 96 D3
Daman India 84 B1
Daman and Diu union terr. India 84 A1
Damanhūr Egypt 90 C5
Damanhûr Egypt see Damanhūr
Damant Lake Canada 121 J2
Damão India see Daman
Damar i. Indon. 108 E1
Damara Cent. Afr. Rep. 98 B3
Damaraland reg. Namibia 99 B6
Damas Syria see Damascus

▶Damascus Syria 85 C3
Capital of Syria.

Damascus U.S.A. 134 E5
Damaturu Nigeria 96 E3
Damāvand Iran 88 D3
Damāvand, Qolleh-ye mt. Iran 88 D3
Dambulla Sri Lanka 84 D5
Damdy Kazakh. 80 B1
Dāmghān Iran 88 D2
Damianópolis Brazil 145 B1
Damietta Egypt see Dumyāţ
Daming Shan mts China 77 F4
Dāmiyā Jordan 85 B3
Damjong China 76 B1
Damlasu Turkey 85 D1
Dammam Saudi Arabia 86 H4
Damme Belgium 52 D3
Damme Germany 53 I2
Damoh India 82 D5
Damour Lebanon 85 B3
Dampar, Tasik l. Malaysia 71 C7
Dampier Archipelago is Australia 108 B5
Dampier Island P.N.G. see Karkar Island
Dampier Land reg. Australia 108 C4
Dampier Strait P.N.G. 69 L8
Dampir, Selat sea chan. Indon. 69 I7
Damqoq Zangbo r. China 83 F3
Dam Qu r. China 76 B1
Dâmrei, Chuŏr Phnum mts Cambodia 71 D5
Damroh India 76 B2
Damwâld Neth. 52 G1
Damwoude Neth. see Damwâld
Damxoi China see Comai
Damxung China see Gongtang
Ḑānā Jordan 85 B4
Dana Nepal 83 E3
Danakil reg. Africa 98 E2
Danané Côte d'Ivoire 96 C4
Đa Năng Vietnam 70 E3
Đa Năng, Vung b. Vietnam 70 E3
Danao Phil. 69 G4
Danata Turkm. 88 D2
Danba China 76 D2
Danbury CT U.S.A. 135 I3
Danbury NC U.S.A. 132 D4
Danby U.S.A. 135 I2
Danby Lake U.S.A. 129 F4
Dandaragan Australia 109 A7
Dande Eth. 98 D3
Dandeldhura Nepal 82 E3
Dandeli India 84 B3
Dandong China 75 B4
Dandot Pak. 89 I3
Dandridge U.S.A. 132 D4
Dane r. U.K. 48 E5
Daneborg Greenland 153 I2
Danese U.S.A. 134 E5
Danfeng China see Shizong
Dangan Liedao i. China 77 G4
Dangara Tajik. see Danghara
Dangbi China 74 C3
Dangchang China 76 E1
Dangchengwan China see Subei
Danger Islands atoll Cook Is see Pukapuka
Danger Point S. Africa 100 D8
Danghara Tajik. 89 H2
Danghe Nanshan mts China 80 H4
Dang La pass China see Tanggula Shankou
Dangla Shan mts China see Tanggula Shan
Dangqên China 83 G3
Dângrêk, Chuŏr Phnum mts Cambodia/Thai. see Phanom Dong Rak, Thiu Khao
Dangriga Belize 136 G5
Dangshan China 77 H1
Dangtu China 77 H2
Daniel's Harbour Canada 123 K4
Daniëlskuil S. Africa 100 F5
Danilov Russia 42 I4
Danilovka Russia 43 J6
Danilovskaya Vozvyshennost' hills Russia 42 H4
Danjiang China see Leishan
Danjiangkou China 77 F1
Danjiangkou Shuiku resr China 77 F1
Danjo-guntō is Japan 75 C6
Ḑank Oman 88 E6
Dankhar India 82 D2
Dankov Russia 43 H5
Danlí Hond. 137 G6
Danmark country Europe see Denmark
Dannebrog Ø i. Greenland see Qillak
Dannenberg (Elbe) Germany 53 L1
Dannenwalde Germany 53 N1
Dannevirke N.Z. 113 F5
Dannhauser S. Africa 101 J5
Dano Burkina Faso 96 C3
Danshui Taiwan 77 I3
Dansville U.S.A. 135 G2
Danta India 82 C4
Dantan India 83 F5
Dantevada India see Dantewada
Dantewada India 84 D2
Dantewara India see Dantewada
Dantu China see Zhenjiang

▶Danube r. Europe 47 P6
2nd longest river in Europe. Also spelt Donau (Austria/Germany) or Duna (Hungary) or Dunaj (Slovakia) or Dunărea (Romania) or Dunav (Bulgaria/Croatia/Yugoslavia) or Dunay (Ukraine).

Danube Delta Romania/Ukr. 59 M2
Danubyu Myanmar 70 A3
Danville IL U.S.A. 134 B3
Danville IN U.S.A. 134 B4
Danville KY U.S.A. 134 C5
Danville OH U.S.A. 134 D3
Danville PA U.S.A. 135 G3
Danville VA U.S.A. 134 F5
Danville VT U.S.A. 135 I1
Danxian China see Danzhou
Danzhai China 76 E3
Danzhou Guangxi China 77 F3
Danzhou Hainan China 77 F5
Danzig Poland see Gdańsk
Danzig, Gulf of Poland/Russia see Gdańsk, Gulf of
Daocheng China 76 D2
Daokou China see Huaxian
Dao Tay Sa is S. China Sea see Paracel Islands
Daoud Alg. see Aïn Beïda
Daoukro Côte d'Ivoire 96 C4
Daozhen China 76 E2
Dapaong Togo 96 D3
Dapha Bum mt. India 83 I4
Dapitan Phil. 69 G5
Daporijo India 83 H4
Đắp Sơn La resr Vietnam 70 C2
Dapu China see Liucheng
Da Qaidam China 80 I4
Daqiao China 76 D3
Daqing China 74 B3
Daqiu China 77 H3
Dāq Mashī Iran 88 E3
Daqu Shan i. China 77 I2
Dara Senegal 96 B3
Dar'ā Syria 85 C3
Dâra, Gebel mt. Egypt see Dārah, Jabal
Dārāb Iran 88 D4
Dārāgāh Iran 88 D4
Dārah, Jabal mt. Egypt 90 D6
Dārakūyeh Iran 88 D4
Dārān Iran 88 C3
Daraut-Korgon Kyrg. 89 I2
Darazo Nigeria 96 E3
Darband Tajik. 89 H2
Darband, Kūh-e mt. Iran 88 E4
Darband-e Ḩajjī Boland Turkm. 89 F2
Darbhanga India 83 F4
Darcang China 76 C1
Dardanelle U.S.A. 131 E5
Dardanelles strait Turkey 59 L4
Dardania prov. Europe see Kosovo
Dardesheim Germany 53 K3
Dardo China see Kangding
Dar el Beida Morocco see Casablanca
Darende Turkey 90 E3

▶Dar es Salaam Tanz. 99 D4
Former capital of Tanzania.

Dāreyn, Kūh-e mt. Iran 88 E3
Darfo Boario Terme Italy 58 D2
Dargai Pak. 89 H3
Dargaville N.Z. 113 D2
Dargo Australia 112 C6
Dargo Zangbo r. China 83 F3
Darhan Mongolia 72 J3
Darien U.S.A. 133 D6
Darién, Golfo del g. Col. 142 C2
Darién, Parque Nacional de nat. park Panama 137 I7
Dariga Pak. 89 G5
Darīganga Mongolia 73 K3
Darjeeling India see Darjiling
Darjiling India 83 G4
Darkhazīneh Iran 88 C4

▶Darling r. Australia 112 B3
2nd longest river in Oceania, and a major part of the longest (Murray-Darling).

Darling Downs hills Australia 112 D1
Darling Range hills Australia 109 A8
Darlington U.K. 48 F4
Darlington U.S.A. 130 F3
Darlington Point Australia 112 C5
Darlot, Lake salt flat Australia 109 C6
Darłowo Poland 47 P3
Darma Pass China/India 82 E3
Darmstadt Germany 53 I5
Darnah Libya 90 A4
Darnall S. Africa 101 J5
Darnick Australia 112 A4
Darnley, Cape Antarctica 152 E2
Daroca Spain 57 F3
Darong China 77 H3
Daroot-Korgon Kyrg. see Daraut-Korgon
Darovskoy Russia 42 J4
Darr watercourse Australia 110 C4
Darreh Bīd Iran 88 E3
Darreh-ye Shahr Iran 88 B3
Darsi India 84 C3
Dart r. U.K. 49 D8
Dartford U.K. 49 H7
Dartmoor Australia 111 C8
Dartmoor hills U.K. 49 C8
Dartmoor National Park U.K. 49 D8
Dartmouth Canada 123 J5
Dartmouth U.K. 49 D8
Dartmouth, Lake salt flat Australia 111 D5
Dartmouth Reservoir Australia 112 C6
Darton U.K. 48 F5
Daru P.N.G. 69 K8
Daru Sierra Leone 96 B4
Daruba Indon. 69 H6
Darvaza Turkm. see Içoguz
Darvoz, Qatorkŭhi mts Tajik. 89 H2
Darwāzagêy Afgh. 89 G4
Darwen U.K. 48 E5

▶**Darwin** Australia **108** E3
Capital of Northern Territory.

Darwin, Monte *mt.* Chile **144** C8
Daryācheh-ye Orūmīyeh *salt l.* Iran *see* **Urmia, Lake**
Dar'yalyktakyr, Ravnina *plain* Kazakh. **80** B2
Dar"yoi Amu *r.* Asia *see* **Amudar'ya**
Darzāb Afgh. **89** G3
Dārzīn Iran **88** E4
Dās *i.* U.A.E. **88** D5
Dasada India **82** B5
Dashhowuz Turkm. *see* **Daşoguz**
Dashkesan Azer. *see* **Daşkäsän**
Dashkhovuz Turkm. *see* **Daşoguz**
Dashköpri Turkm. *see* **Daşköpri**
Dashoguz Turkm. *see* **Daşoguz**
Dasht Iran **88** E2
Dashtiari Iran **89** F5
Daska Pak. **89** I3
Daşkäsän Azer. **91** G2
Daşköpri Turkm. **89** F2
Daşoguz Turkm. **87** I1
Daspar *mt.* Pak. **89** I2
Dassel Germany **53** J3
Dastgerdān Iran **88** E3
Datadian Indon. **68** F6
Datça Turkey **59** L6
Date Japan **74** F4
Date Creek *watercourse* U.S.A. **129** G4
Dateland U.S.A. **129** G5
Datha India **82** C5
Datia India **82** D4
Datian China **77** H3
Datian Ding *mt.* China **77** F4
Datil U.S.A. **129** J4
Datong *Anhui* China **77** H2
Datong *Heilong.* China **74** B3
Datong *Shanxi* China **73** K4
Datong He *r.* China **72** I5
Dattapur India **84** C1
Datu, Tanjung *c.* Indon./Malaysia **71** E7
Daudkandi Bangl. **83** G5
Daugava *r.* Latvia **45** N8
Daugavpils Latvia **45** O9
Daulatabad India **84** B2
Daulatabad Iran *see* **Malāyer**
Daulatpur Bangl. **83** G5
Daun Germany **52** G4
Daungyu *r.* Myanmar **70** A2
Dauphin Canada **121** K5
Dauphiné *reg.* France **56** G4
Dauphiné, Alpes du *mts* France **56** G4
Dauphin Lake Canada **121** L5
Daurie Creek *r.* Australia **109** A6
Dausa India **82** D4
Dâu Tiêng, Hô *resr* Vietnam **71** D5
Dava U.K. **50** F3
Davanagere India *see* **Davangere**
Davangere India **84** B3
Davao Phil. **69** H5
Davao Gulf Phil. **69** H5
Dāvarī Iran **88** E5
Dāvarzan Iran **88** E2
Davel S. Africa **101** I4
Davenport *IA* U.S.A. **130** F3
Davenport *WA* U.S.A. **126** D3
Davenport Downs Australia **110** C5
Davenport Range *hills* Australia **108** F5
Daventry U.K. **49** F6
Daveyton S. Africa **101** I4
David Panama **137** H7
David City U.S.A. **130** D3
David Glacier Antarctica **152** H1
Davidson Canada **121** J5
Davidson, Mount *hill* Australia **108** E5
Davis *research station* Antarctica **152** E2
Davis *r.* Australia **108** C5
Davis *CA* U.S.A. **128** C2
Davis *WV* U.S.A. **134** F4
Davis, Mount *hill* U.S.A. **134** F4
Davis Bay Antarctica **152** G2
Davis Dam U.S.A. **129** F4
Davis Inlet (abandoned) Canada **123** J3
Davis Island *i.* Myanmar *see* **Than Kyun**
Davis Sea Antarctica **152** F2
Davis Strait Canada/Greenland **119** M3
Davlekanovo Russia **41** Q5
Davos Switz. **56** I3
Davy Lake Canada **121** I3
Dawa Co *l.* China **83** F3
Dawa Wenz *r.* Eth. **98** E3
Dawaxung China **83** F3
Dawê China **76** D2
Dawei Myanmar **71** B4
Dawei *r. mouth* Myanmar *see* **Tavoy**
Dawera *i.* Indon. **108** E1
Dawmat al Jandal Saudi Arabia **91** E5
Dawna Range *mts* Myanmar/Thai. **70** B3
Dawna Taungdan *mts* Myanmar/Thai. *see* **Dawna Range**
Dawo China *see* **Maqên**
Dawqah Oman **87** H6
Dawson *r.* Australia **110** E4
Dawson Canada **120** B1
Dawson *GA* U.S.A. **133** C6
Dawson *ND* U.S.A. **130** D2
Dawson, Mount Canada **120** G5
Dawson Bay Canada **121** K4
Dawson Creek Canada **120** F4
Dawson Inlet Canada **121** M2
Dawson Range *mts* Canada **120** A2
Dawsons Landing Canada **120** E5
Dawu *Hubei* China **77** G2
Dawu *Qinghai* China *see* **Maqên**
Dawu Taiwan **77** I4
Dawukou China *see* **Shizuishan**
Dawu Shan *hill* China **77** G2
Dax France **56** D5
Daxian China *see* **Dazhou**
Daxiang Ling *mts* China **76** D2
Daxin China **76** E4
Daxing *Yunnan* China *see* **Ninglang**
Daxing *Yunnan* China *see* **Lüchun**
Daxing'an Ling *mts* China *see* **Da Hinggan Ling**
Da Xueshan *mts* China **76** D2
Dayan China *see* **Lijiang**
Dayangshu China **74** B2
Dayao China **76** D3
Dayao Shan *mts* China **77** F4
Daye China **77** G2
Daying China **76** E2
Daying Jiang *r.* China **76** C3
Dayishan China *see* **Guanyun**
Daylesford Australia **112** B6
Daylight Pass U.S.A. **128** E3
Dayong China *see* **Zhangjiajie**
Dayr Abū Sa'īd Jordan **85** B3
Dayr az Zawr Syria **91** F4
Dayr Ḥāfir Syria **85** C1
Dayrī', Wādī *watercourse* Saudi Arabia **91** F6
Daysland Canada **121** H4
Dayton *OH* U.S.A. **134** C4
Dayton *TN* U.S.A. **132** C5
Dayton *VA* U.S.A. **135** F4
Dayton *WA* U.S.A. **126** D3
Daytona Beach U.S.A. **133** D6
Dayu Ling *mts* China **77** G3
Da Yunhe *canal* China **77** H1
Dayyīna *i.* U.A.E. **88** D5
Dazhongji China *see* **Dafeng**
Dazhou China **76** E2
Dazhou Dao *i.* China **77** F5
Dazhu China **76** E2
Dazu China **76** E2
Dazu Rock Carvings *tourist site* China **76** E2
De Aar S. Africa **100** G6
Dead *r.* Ireland **51** D5
Deadman Lake U.S.A. **128** E4
Deadman's Cay Bahamas **133** F8
Dead Mountains U.S.A. **129** F4

▶**Dead Sea** *salt l.* Asia **85** B4
Lowest point in Asia and the world.

Deadwood U.S.A. **130** C2
Deakin Australia **109** E7
Deal U.K. **49** I7
Dealesville S. Africa **101** G5
De'an China **77** G2
Dean, Forest of U.K. **49** E7
Deán Funes Arg. **144** D4
Deanuvuotna *inlet* Norway *see* **Tanafjorden**
Dearborn U.S.A. **134** D2
Dearne *r.* U.K. **48** F5
Deary U.S.A. **126** D3
Dease *r.* Canada **120** D3
Dease Lake Canada **120** D3
Dease Lake Canada **120** D3
Dease Strait Canada **118** H3

▶**Death Valley** *depr.* U.S.A. **128** E3
Lowest point in the Americas.

Death Valley Junction U.S.A. **128** E3
Death Valley National Park U.S.A. **128** E3
Deauville France **56** E2
Deaver U.S.A. **126** F3
De Baai S. Africa *see* **Port Elizabeth**
Debao China **76** E4
Debar Macedonia **59** I4
Debden Canada **121** J4
Debenham U.K. **49** I6
De Beque U.S.A. **129** I2
De Biesbosch, Nationaal Park *nat. park* Neth. **52** E3
Débo, Lac *l.* Mali **96** C3
Deborah East, Lake *salt flat* Australia **109** B7
Deborah West, Lake *salt flat* Australia **109** B7
Debrecen Hungary **59** I1
Debre Markos Eth. **86** E7
Debre Tabor Eth. **86** E7
Debre Zeyit Eth. **98** D3
Decatur *AL* U.S.A. **133** C5
Decatur *GA* U.S.A. **133** C5
Decatur *IL* U.S.A. **130** F4
Decatur *IN* U.S.A. **134** C3
Decatur *MI* U.S.A. **134** C2
Decatur *MS* U.S.A. **131** F5
Decatur *TX* U.S.A. **131** D5

▶**Deccan** *plat.* India **84** C2
Plateau making up most of southern and central India.

Deception Bay Australia **112** F1
Dechang China **76** D3
Děčín Czechia **47** O5
Decker U.S.A. **126** G3
Decorah U.S.A. **130** F3
Dedap *i.* Indon. *see* **Penasi, Pulau**
Dedaye Myanmar **70** A3
Deddington U.K. **49** F7
Dedegöl Dağları *mts* Turkey **59** N6
Dedeleben Germany **53** K2
Dedelstorf Germany **53** K2
Dedemsvaart Neth. **52** G2
Dedo de Deus *mt.* Brazil **145** B4
Dédougou Burkina Faso **96** C3
Dedovichi Russia **42** F4
Dedu China *see* **Wudalianchi**
Dee *r.* Ireland **51** F4
Dee *est.* U.K. **48** D5
Dee *r. England/Wales* U.K. **49** D5
Dee *r. Scotland* U.K. **50** G3
Deel *r. Cork/Limerick* Ireland **51** D5
Deel *r. Meath/Westmeath* Ireland **51** F4
Deep Bay H.K. China **77** [inset]
Deep Creek Lake U.S.A. **134** F4
Deep Creek Range *mts* U.S.A. **129** G2
Deep River Canada **122** F5
Deepwater Australia **112** E2
Deeri Somalia **98** E3
Deering U.S.A. **118** B3
Deering, Mount Australia **109** E6
Deer Island U.S.A. **118** B4
Deer Lake Canada **121** M4
Deer Lake *l.* Canada **121** M4
Deer Lodge U.S.A. **126** E3
Deesa India *see* **Disa**
Deeth U.S.A. **126** E4
Defeng China *see* **Liping**
Defensores del Chaco, Parque Nacional *nat. park* Para. **144** D2
Defiance U.S.A. **134** C3
Defiance Plateau U.S.A. **129** I4
Degana India **82** C4
Degeh Bur Eth. **98** E3
Degema Nigeria **96** D4
Deggendorf Germany **53** M6
Degh *r.* Pak. **89** I4
De Goorn Neth. **52** E2
De Grey *r.* Australia **108** B5
De Groote Peel, Nationaal Park *nat. park* Neth. **52** F3
Degtevo Russia **43** I6
De Haan Belgium **52** D3
Dê Hadē Ghar Afgh. **89** G4
Dehak Seydābād Iran **89** F4
Dehaq Iran **88** C3
Dehdasht Iran **88** C4
Deh-e Shū Afgh. **89** F4
Dehestān-e Bālā Iran **88** D4
Dehgolān Iran **88** B3
Dehgon Afgh. **89** F3
Dehī Afgh. **89** G3
Dehkūyeh Iran **88** D5
Dehlorān Iran **88** B3
De Hoge Veluwe, Nationaal Park *nat. park* Neth. **52** F2
De Hoop Nature Reserve S. Africa **100** E8
Dehqonobod Uzbek. **89** G2
Dehradun India *see* **Dehra Dun**
Dehra Dun India **82** D3
Dehram Iran **88** D4
Dehri India **83** F4
Deim Zubeir South Sudan **97** F4
Deinze Belgium **52** D4
Deir-ez-Zor Syria *see* **Dayr az Zawr**
Dej Romania **59** J1
Deji China *see* **Rinbung**
Dejiang China **77** F2
De Jouwer Neth. *see* **Joure**
DeKalb U.S.A. **130** F3
De Kalb *MS* U.S.A. **131** F5
De Kalb *TX* U.S.A. **131** E5
De Kalb Junction U.S.A. **135** H1
De-Kastri Russia **74** F2
Dekemhare Eritrea **86** E6
Dekhkanabad Uzbek. *see* **Dehqonobod**
Dekina Nigeria **96** D4
Dékoa Cent. Afr. Rep. **98** B3
De Koog Neth. **52** E1
De Kooy Neth. **52** E2
Delaki Indon. **108** D2
Delamar Lake U.S.A. **129** F3
DeLand U.S.A. **133** D6
Delano U.S.A. **128** D4
Delano Peak U.S.A. **129** G2

▶**Delap-Uliga-Djarrit** Marshall Is **150** H5
Capital of the Marshall Islands, on Majuro atoll.

Delareyville S. Africa **101** G4
Delaronde Lake Canada **121** J4
Delavan U.S.A. **122** C6
Delaware U.S.A. **134** D3
Delaware *r.* U.S.A. **135** H4
Delaware *state* U.S.A. **135** H4
Delaware, East Branch *r.* U.S.A. **135** H3
Delaware Bay U.S.A. **135** H4
Delaware Lake U.S.A. **134** D3
Delaware Water Gap National Recreational Area *park* U.S.A. **135** H3
Delay *r.* Canada **123** H2
Delbarton U.S.A. **134** D5
Delbrück Germany **53** I3
Delburne Canada **120** H4
Delegate Australia **112** D6
De Lemmer Neth. *see* **Lemmer**
Delémont Switz. **56** H3
Delevan *CA* U.S.A. **128** B2
Delevan *NY* U.S.A. **135** F2
Delfinópolis Brazil **145** B3
Delft Neth. **52** E2
Delfzijl Neth. **52** G1
Delgada, Point U.S.A. **128** A1
Delgado, Cabo *c.* Moz. **99** E5
Delgerhaan Mongolia **72** I3
Delhi Canada **134** E2
Delhi China *see* **Delingha**

▶**Delhi** India **82** D3
2nd most populous city in Asia and the world.

Delhi *CO* U.S.A. **127** G5
Delhi *LA* U.S.A. **131** F5
Delhi *NY* U.S.A. **135** H2
Delice Turkey **90** D3
Delice *r.* Turkey **90** D2
Delījān Iran **88** C3
Délįne Canada **120** F1
Delingha China **80** I4
Delisle Canada **121** J5
Delitzsch Germany **53** M3
Delligsen Germany **53** J3
Dell Rapids U.S.A. **130** D3
Dellys Alg. **57** H5
Del Mar U.S.A. **128** E5
Delmenhorst Germany **53** I1
Delnice Croatia **58** F2
Del Norte U.S.A. **127** G5
De-Longa, Ostrova *is* Russia **65** Q2
De Long Islands Russia *see* **De-Longa, Ostrova**
De Long Mountains U.S.A. **118** B3
De Long Strait Russia *see* **Longa, Proliv**
Deloraine Canada **121** K5
Delphi U.S.A. **134** B3
Delphos U.S.A. **134** C3
Delportshoop S. Africa **100** G5
Delray Beach U.S.A. **133** D7
Delrey U.S.A. **134** A3
Del Río Mex. **127** F7
Del Rio U.S.A. **131** C6
Delsbo Sweden **45** J6
Delta *CO* U.S.A. **129** I2
Delta *OH* U.S.A. **134** C3
Delta *UT* U.S.A. **129** G2
Delta Downs Australia **110** C3
Delta Junction U.S.A. **118** D3
Deltona U.S.A. **133** D6
Delungra Australia **112** E2
Delvin Ireland **51** E4
Delvinë Albania **59** I5
Delwara India **82** C4
De Maasduinen, Nationaal Park *nat. park* Neth. **52** G3
Demanda, Sierra de la *mts* Spain **57** E2
Demavend *mt.* Iran *see* **Damāvand, Qolleh-ye**
Demba Dem. Rep. Congo **99** C4
Dembī Dolo Eth. **86** D8
Demerara Guyana *see* **Georgetown**
Demerara Abyssal Plain *sea feature* S. Atlantic Ocean **148** E5
Demidov Russia **43** F5
Deming U.S.A. **127** G6
Demirci Turkey **59** M5
Demirköy Turkey **59** L4
Demirtaş Turkey **85** A1
Demmin Germany **47** N4
Demopolis U.S.A. **133** C5
DeMotte U.S.A. **134** B3
Dempo, Gunung *vol.* Indon. **68** C7
Dêmqog China **82** D2
Demta Indon. **69** K7
Dê Mūsá Qal'ah Rōd *r.* Afgh. **89** G3
Dem'yanovo Russia **42** J3
De Naawte S. Africa **100** E6
Denakil *reg.* Africa *see* **Danakil**

▶**Denali** U.S.A. **118** C3
Highest mountain in North America.

Denali National Park and Preserve U.S.A. **118** C3
Denan Eth. **98** E3
Denbigh Canada **135** G1
Denbigh U.K. **48** D5
Den Bosch Neth. *see* **'s-Hertogenbosch**
Den Burg Neth. **52** E1
Den Chai Thai. **70** C3
Dendâra Mauritania **96** C3
Dendermonde Belgium **52** E3
Dendi *mt.* Eth. **98** D3
Dendre *r.* Belgium **52** E3
Dendron S. Africa *see* **Mogwadi**
Denezhkin Kamen', Gora *mt.* Russia **41** R3
Dêngka China *see* **Têwo**
Dêngkagoin China *see* **Têwo**
Dengkou China **72** J4
Dêngqên China **76** B2
Dengta China **77** G4
Dengxian China *see* **Dengzhou**
Dengzhou China **77** G1
Den Haag Neth. *see* **The Hague**
Denham Australia **109** A6
Denham *r.* Australia **108** E3
Den Ham Neth. **52** G2
Denham Range *mts* Australia **110** E4
Den Helder Neth. **52** E2
Denholm Canada **121** I4
Dénia Spain **57** G4
Denial Bay Australia **111** A7
Deniliquin Australia **112** B5
Denio U.S.A. **126** D4
Denison *IA* U.S.A. **130** E3
Denison *TX* U.S.A. **131** D5
Denison, Cape Antarctica **152** G2
Denison Plains Australia **108** E4
Deniyaya Sri Lanka **84** D5
Denizli Turkey **59** M6
Denman Australia **112** E4
Denman Glacier Antarctica **152** F2
Denmark Australia **106** B5
Denmark *country* Europe **45** G8
Denmark U.S.A. **134** B1
Denmark Strait Greenland/Iceland **40** A2
Dennis, Lake *salt flat* Australia **108** E5
Dennison *IL* U.S.A. **134** B4
Dennison *OH* U.S.A. **134** E3
Denny U.K. **50** F4
Denov Uzbek. **89** G2
Denow Uzbek. *see* **Denov**
Denpasar Indon. **108** A2
Denton *MD* U.S.A. **135** H4
Denton *TX* U.S.A. **131** D5
D'Entrecasteaux, Point Australia **109** A8
D'Entrecasteaux, Récifs *reef* New Caledonia **107** G3
D'Entrecasteaux Islands P.N.G. **106** F2
D'Entrecasteaux National Park Australia **109** A8

▶**Denver** *CO* U.S.A. **126** G5
Capital of Colorado.

Denver *PA* U.S.A. **135** G3
Denys *r.* Canada **122** F3
Deo India **83** F4
Deoband India **82** D3
Deogarh *Jharkhand* India *see* **Deoghar**
Deogarh *Odisha* India **83** F5
Deogarh *Rajasthan* India **82** C4
Deogarh *Uttar Prad.* India **82** D4
Deogarh *mt.* India **83** E5
Deoghar India **83** F4
Deolali India **84** B2
Deoli India **83** F5
Deomali *mt.* India **84** D2
Deori India **82** D5
Deoria India **83** E4
Deosai, Plains of Pak. **82** C2
Deosil India **83** E5
Deothang Bhutan **83** G4
De Panne Belgium **52** C3
De Pere U.S.A. **134** A1
Deposit U.S.A. **135** H2
Deputatskiy Russia **65** O3
Dêqên *Xizang* China **83** G3
Dêqên *Xizang* China *see* **Dagzê**
Dêqên *Xizang* China **83** G3
De Queen U.S.A. **131** E5
Dera Ghazi Khan Pak. **89** H4
Dera Ismail Khan Pak. **89** H4
Derajat *reg.* Pak. **89** H4
Derawar Fort Pak. **89** H4
Derbent Russia **91** H2
Derbesiye Turkey *see* **Şenyurt**
Derbur China **74** A2
Derby Australia **108** C4
Derby U.K. **49** F6
Derby *CT* U.S.A. **135** I3
Derby *KS* U.S.A. **131** D4
Derby *NY* U.S.A. **135** F2
Đerdap, Nacionalni Park *nat. park* Serbia **59** J2
Dereham U.K. **49** H6
Derg *r.* Ireland/U.K. **51** E3
Derg, Lough *l.* Ireland **51** D5
Dergachi Russia **43** K6
Dergachi Ukr. *see* **Derhachi**
Derhachi Ukr. **43** H6
DeRidder U.S.A. **131** E6
Derik Turkey **91** F3
Derm Namibia **100** D2
Derna Libya *see* **Darnah**
Dernberg, Cape Namibia **100** B4
Derom, Mount Antarctica **152** D2
Dêrong China **76** C2
Déroute, Passage de la *strait* Channel Is/France **49** E9
Derravaragh, Lough *l.* Ireland **51** E4
Derry U.K. *see* **Londonderry**
Derry U.S.A. **135** J2
Derryveagh Mountains *hills* Ireland **51** D3
Dêrub China **82** D2
Derudeb Sudan **86** E6
De Rust S. Africa **100** F7
Derventa Bos. & Herz. **58** G2
Derwent *r. England* U.K. **48** F6
Derwent *r. England* U.K. **48** G5
Derwent Water *l.* U.K. **48** D4
Derzhavinsk Kazakh. **80** C1
Derzhavinskiy Kazakh. *see* **Derzhavinsk**
Desaguadero *r.* Arg. **144** C4
Désappointement, Îles du *is* Fr. Polynesia **151** K6
Desatoya Mountains U.S.A. **128** E2
Deschambault Lake Canada **121** K4
Deschutes *r.* U.S.A. **126** C3
Desē Eth. **98** D2
Deseado *r.* Arg. **144** C7
Desengaño, Punta *pt* Arg. **144** C7
Deseret U.S.A. **129** G2
Deseret Peak U.S.A. **129** G1
Deseronto Canada **135** G1
Desert Canal Pak. **89** H4
Desert Center U.S.A. **129** F5
Desert Lake U.S.A. **129** F3
Desert View U.S.A. **129** H3
Deshler U.S.A. **134** D3
De Smet U.S.A. **130** D2

▶**Des Moines** *IA* U.S.A. **130** E3
Capital of Iowa.

Des Moines *NM* U.S.A. **131** C4
Des Moines *r.* U.S.A. **130** F3
Desna *r.* Russia/Ukr. **43** F6
Desnogorsk Russia **43** G5
Desolación, Isla *i.* Chile **144** B8
Des Plaines U.S.A. **134** B2
Dessau-Roßlau Germany **53** M3
Dessye Eth. *see* **Desē**
Destelbergen Belgium **52** D3
Destruction Bay Canada **153** A2
Desventuradas, Islas *is* S. Pacific Ocean **151** O7
Desvres France **52** B4
Detah Canada **120** H2
Dete Zimbabwe **99** C5
Detmold Germany **53** I3
Detrital Wash *watercourse* U.S.A. **129** F3
Detroit U.S.A. **134** D2
Detroit Lakes U.S.A. **130** E2
Dett Zimbabwe *see* **Dete**
Deua National Park Australia **112** D5
Deuben Germany **53** M3
Deurne Neth. **52** F3
Deutschland *country* Europe *see* **Germany**
Deutschlandsberg Austria **47** O7
Deutzen Germany **53** M3
Deva Romania **59** J2
Deva U.K. *see* **Chester**
Devana U.K. *see* **Aberdeen**
Devangere India *see* **Davangere**
Devanhalli India **84** C3
Deve Bair *pass* Bulg./Macedonia *see* **Velbŭzhdki Prokhod**
Develi Turkey **90** D3
Deventer Neth. **52** G2
Deveron *r.* U.K. **50** G3
Devét skal *hill* Czechia **47** P6
Devgarh India **84** B2
Devghar India *see* **Deoghar**
Devikot India **82** B4
Devil's Bridge U.K. **49** D6
Devils Gate *pass* U.S.A. **128** D2
Devils Lake U.S.A. **130** D1
Devils Paw *mt.* U.S.A. **120** C3
Devils Peak U.S.A. **128** D3
Devil's Point Bahamas **133** F7
Devine U.S.A. **131** D6
Devizes U.K. **49** F7
Devli India **82** C4
Devnya Bulg. **59** L3
Devon *r.* U.K. **50** F4
Devon Island Canada **119** I2
Devonport Australia **111** [inset]
Devrek Turkey **59** N4
Devrukh India **84** B2
Dewa, Tanjung *pt* Indon. **71** A7
Dewas India **82** D5
De Weerribben-Wieden, Nationaal Park *nat. park* Neth. **52** G2
Dewetsdorp S. Africa **101** H5
De Witt *AR* U.S.A. **131** F5
De Witt *IA* U.S.A. **130** F3
Dewsbury U.K. **48** F5
Dexing China **77** H2
Dexter *ME* U.S.A. **135** K1
Dexter *MI* U.S.A. **134** D2
Dexter *MO* U.S.A. **131** F4
Dexter *NM* U.S.A. **127** G6
Dexter *NY* U.S.A. **135** G1
Deyang China **76** E2
Dey-Dey Lake *salt flat* Australia **109** E7
Deyhūk Iran **88** E3
Deyong, Tanjung *pt* Indon. **69** J8
Dez *r.* Iran **86** G3
Dezadeash Lake Canada **120** B2
Dezfūl Iran **88** C3

▶**Dezhneva, Mys** *c.* Russia **65** T3
Most easterly point of Asia.

Dezhou *Shandong* China **73** L5
Dezhou *Sichuan* China *see* **Dechang**
Dezh Shāhpūr Iran *see* **Marīvān**
Dhabarau India **83** E4
Dhahab, Wādī adh *r.* Syria **85** B3
Dhahran Saudi Arabia **88** C5

▶**Dhaka** Bangl. **83** G5
Capital of Bangladesh. 9th most populous city in the world.

Dhalbhum *reg.* India **83** F5
Dhalgaon India **84** B2
Dhamār Yemen **86** F7
Dhamoni India **82** D4
Dhamtari India **84** D1
Dhana Pak. **89** H5
Dhana Sar Pak. **89** H4
Dhanbad India **83** F5
Dhanera India **82** C4
Dhang Range *mts* Nepal **83** E3
Dhankuta Nepal **83** F4
Dhansia India **82** C3
Dhar India **82** C5
Dharampur India **84** B1
Dharamsala India **82** D2
Dharan Nepal **83** F4
Dharashiv India *see* **Osmanabad**
Dhari India **82** B5
Dharmapuri India **84** C3
Dharmavaram India **84** C3
Dharmsala *Hima. Prad.* India *see* **Dharamsala**
Dharmsala *Odisha* India **83** F5
Dharnaoda India **82** D4
Dharug National Park Australia **112** E4
Dharur India **84** C2
Dharwad India **84** B3
Dharwar India *see* **Dharwad**
Dharwas India **82** D2
Dhasan *r.* India **82** D4
Dhāt al Ḥājj Saudi Arabia **90** E5

▶**Dhaulagiri I** *mt.* Nepal **83** E3
7th highest mountain in Asia and the world.

Dhaulpur India *see* **Dholpur**
Dhaura India **82** D4
Dhaurahra India **82** E4
Dhawlagiri *mt.* Nepal *see* **Dhaulagiri I**
Dhebar Lake India *see* **Jaisamand Lake**
Dhekelia Sovereign Base Area *military base* Cyprus **85** A2
Dhemaji India **83** H4
Dhenkanal India **84** E1
Dhībān Jordan **85** B4
Dhidhimótikhon Greece *see* **Didymoteicho**
Dhing India **83** H4
Dhirwah, Wādī adh *watercourse* Jordan **85** C4
Dhodhekánisos *is* Greece *see* **Dodecanese**
Dhola India **82** B5
Dholera India **82** C5
Dholpur India **82** D4
Dhomokós Greece *see* **Domokos**
Dhone India **84** C3
Dhoraji India **82** B5
Dhori India **82** B5
Dhrangadhra India **82** B5
Dhubāb Yemen **86** F7
Dhubri India **83** G4
Dhuburi India *see* **Dhubri**
Dhudial Pak. **89** I3
Dhule India **84** B1
Dhulia India *see* **Dhule**
Dhulian India **83** F4
Dhulian Pak. **89** I3
Dhuma India **82** D5
Dhund *r.* India **82** D4
Dhupgarh *mt.* India **82** D5
Dhurwai India **82** D4
Dhuusa Marreeb Somalia **98** E3
Dia *i.* Greece **59** K7
Diablo, Mount U.S.A. **128** C3
Diablo, Picacho del *mt.* Mex. **127** E7
Diablo Range *mts* U.S.A. **128** C3
Diagbe Dem. Rep. Congo **98** C3
Diamante Arg. **144** D4
Diamantina *watercourse* Australia **110** B5
Diamantina Brazil **145** C2
Diamantina, Chapada *plat.* Brazil **145** C1
Diamantina Deep *sea feature* Indian Ocean **149** O8
Diamantina Gates National Park Australia **110** C4
Diamantino Brazil **143** G6
Diamond Islets Australia **110** E3
Diamond Peak U.S.A. **129** F2
Dianbai China **77** F4
Diancang Shan *mt.* China **76** D3
Dian Chi *l.* China **76** D3
Diandioumé Mali **96** C3
Diane Bank *sea feature* Australia **110** E2
Dianjiang China **76** E2
Dianópolis Brazil **143** I6
Dianyang China *see* **Shidian**
Diaobingshan China **74** A4
Diaoling China **74** C3
Diapaga Burkina Faso **96** D3
Diarizos *r.* Cyprus **85** A2
Diavolo, Mount *hill* India **71** A4
Diaz Point Namibia **100** B4
Dibaya Dem. Rep. Congo **99** C4
Dibella *well* Niger **96** E3
Dibeng S. Africa **100** F4
Dibete Botswana **101** H2
Dibrugarh India **83** H4
Dibse Syria *see* **Dibsī**
Dibsī Syria **85** D2
Dickens U.S.A. **131** C5
Dickinson U.S.A. **130** C2
Dicle *r.* Asia *see* **Tigris**
Dīdēsa Wenz *r.* Eth. **98** D3
Didiéni Mali **96** C3
Didsbury Canada **120** H5
Didwana India **82** C4
Didymoteicho Greece **59** L4

Die France 56 G4
Dieblich Germany 53 H4
Diébougou Burkina Faso 96 C3
Dieburg Germany 53 I5
Diedenhofen France see Thionville
Diefenbaker, Lake Canada 121 I5
Diego de Almagro, Isla i. Chile 144 A8
Diégo Suarez Madag. see Antsirañana
Diekirch Lux. 52 G5
Diéma Mali 96 C3
Diemel r. Germany 53 J3
Điện Biên Vietnam see Điện Biên Phu
Điện Biên Phu Vietnam 70 C2
Diên Châu Vietnam 70 D3
Diên Khanh Vietnam 71 E4
Diepholz Germany 53 I2
Dieppe France 52 B5
Dierks U.S.A. 131 E5
Di'er Songhua Jiang r. China see Songhua Jiang
Diessen Neth. 52 F3
Diest Belgium 52 F4
Dietikon Switz. 56 I3
Diez Germany 53 I4
Diffa Niger 96 E3
Digby Canada 123 I5
Diggi India 82 C4
Diglur India 84 C2
Digne France see Digne-les-Bains
Digne-les-Bains France 56 H4
Digoin France 56 F3
Digos Phil. 69 H5
Digras India 84 C1
Digri Pak. 89 H5
Digul r. Indon. 69 K8
Digya National Park Ghana 96 C4
Dihang r. India see Brahmaputra
Dihok Iraq see Dahūk/Dihok
Dihourse, Lac l. Canada 123 I2
Diinsoor Somalia 98 E3
Dijon France 56 G3
Dik Chad 97 E4
Diken India 82 C4
Dikhil Djibouti 86 F7
Dikili Turkey 59 L5
Dik'losmta mt. Russia 43 J8
Diksmuide Belgium 52 C3
Dikson Russia 64 J2
Dīla Eth. 98 D3
Dilārām Afgh. 89 F3
Dilaram Iran 88 E4

▶Dili East Timor 108 D2
Capital of East Timor (Timor-Leste).

Di Linh Vietnam 71 E5
Dillenburg Germany 53 I4
Dilley U.S.A. 131 D6
Dillingen an der Donau Germany 47 M6
Dillingen/Saar Germany 52 G5
Dillingham U.S.A. 118 C4
Dillon r. Canada 121 I4
Dillon MT U.S.A. 126 E3
Dillon SC U.S.A. 133 E5
Dillwyn U.S.A. 135 F5
Dilolo Dem. Rep. Congo 99 C5
Dilsen Belgium 52 F3
Dimapur India 83 H4
Dimashq Syria see Damascus
Dimbokro Côte d'Ivoire 96 C4
Dimboola Australia 111 C8
Dimitrov Ukr. see Dymytrov
Dimitrovgrad Bulg. 59 K3
Dimitrovgrad Russia 43 K5
Dimitrovo Bulg. see Pernik
Dimmitt U.S.A. 131 C5
Dimona Israel 85 B4
Dimpho Pan salt pan Botswana 100 E3
Dinagat i. Phil. 69 H4
Dinajpur Bangl. 83 G4
Dinan France 56 C2
Dinant Belgium 52 E4
Dinapur India 83 F4
Dinar Turkey 59 N5
Dīnār, Kūh-e mt. Iran 88 C4
Dinara Planina mts Bos. & Herz./Croatia see Dinaric Alps
Dinaric Alps mts Bos. & Herz./Croatia 58 G2
Dinbych U.K. see Denbigh
Dinbych-y-pysgod U.K. see Tenby
Dinder National Park Sudan 97 G3
Dindi r. India 84 C2
Dindigul India 84 C4
Dindima Nigeria 96 E3
Dindiza Moz. 101 K2
Dindori India 82 E5
Dingcheng China see Dingyuan
Dingelstädt Germany 53 K3
Dinggyê China 83 F3
Dingla Nepal 83 F4
Dingle Ireland see Daingean Uí Chúis
Dingle Bay Ireland 51 B5
Dingnan China 77 G3
Dingo Australia 110 E4
Dingolfing Germany 53 M6
Dingping China see Linshui
Dingtao China 77 G1
Dinguiraye Guinea 96 B3
Dingwall U.K. 50 E3
Dingxi China 76 E1
Dingyuan China 77 H1
Dinh Lâp Vietnam 70 D2
Dinkelsbühl Germany 53 K5
Dinokwe Botswana 101 H2
Dinosaur U.S.A. 129 I1
Dinosaur National Monument nat. park U.S.A. 129 I1
Dinslaken Germany 52 G3
Dinwiddie U.S.A. 135 G5
Dioïla Mali 96 C3
Dionísio Cerqueira Brazil 144 F3
Diorama Brazil 145 A2
Dioscurias Georgia see Sokhumi
Diouloulou Senegal 96 B3
Diourbel Senegal 96 B3
Dipayal Nepal 82 E3
Diphu India 83 H4
Dipkarpaz Cyprus see Rizokarpason
Diplo Pak. 89 H5
Dipperu National Park Australia 110 E4
Dipu China see Anji
Dir reg. Pak. 89 I3
Dirang India 83 H4
Diré Mali 96 C3
Direction, Cape Australia 110 C2
Dirē Dawa Eth. 98 E3
Dirico Angola 99 C5
Dirj Libya 96 E1
Dirk Hartog Island Australia 109 A6
Dirranbandi Australia 112 D2
Ḑirs Saudi Arabia 98 E2
Dirschau Poland see Tczew
Dirty Devil r. U.S.A. 129 H3
Disa India 82 C4
Disang r. India 83 H4
Disappointment, Cape S. Georgia 144 I8
Disappointment, Cape U.S.A. 126 B3
Disappointment, Lake salt flat Australia 109 C5
Disappointment Islands Fr. Polynesia see Désappointement, Îles du
Disappointment Lake Canada 123 J3
Disaster Bay Australia 112 D6
Discovery Bay Australia 111 C8
Disko i. Greenland see Qeqertarsuaq
Disko Bugt b. Greenland see Qeqertarsuup Tunua
Dismal Swamp U.S.A. 132 E4
Dispur India 83 G4
Disputanta U.S.A. 135 G5
Disraeli Canada 123 H5
Diss U.K. 49 I6
Distrito Federal admin. dist. Brazil 145 B1
Disūq Egypt 90 C5
Ditloung S. Africa 100 F5
Dittaino r. Sicily Italy 58 F6
Diu India 84 A1
Dīvāndarreh Iran 88 B3
Divehi country Indian Ocean see Maldives
Divi, Point India 84 D3
Divichi Azer. see Şabran
Divide Mountain U.S.A. 120 A2
Divinópolis Brazil 145 B3
Divnoye Russia 43 I7
Divo Côte d'Ivoire 96 C4
Divriği Turkey 90 E3
Diwana Pak. 89 G5
Diwaniyah Iraq see Ad Dīwānīyah
Dixfield U.S.A. 135 J1
Dixon CA U.S.A. 128 C2
Dixon IL U.S.A. 130 F3
Dixon KY U.S.A. 134 B5
Dixon MT U.S.A. 126 E3
Dixon Entrance sea chan. Canada/U.S.A. 120 C4
Dixonville Canada 120 G3
Dixville Canada 135 J1
Diyadin Turkey 91 F3
Diyarbakır Turkey 91 F3
Diz Pak. 89 F5
Diz Chah Iran 88 D3
Dize Turkey see Yüksekova
Dizney U.S.A. 134 D5
Djado Niger 96 E2
Djado, Plateau du Niger 96 E2
Djaja, Puntjak mt. Indon. see Jaya, Puncak
Djakarta Indon. see Jakarta
Djakovica Kosovo see Gjakovë
Djakovo Croatia see Đakovo
Djambala Congo 98 B4
Djanet Alg. 96 D2
Djarrit-Uliga-Dalap Marshall Is see Delap-Uliga-Djarrit
Djelfa Alg. 57 H6
Djéma Cent. Afr. Rep. 98 C3
Djenné Mali 96 C3
Djenoun, Garet el mt. Alg. 96 D2
Djibloho Equat. Guinea 96 E4
Djibo Burkina Faso 96 C3
Djibouti country Africa 86 F7

▶Djibouti Djibouti 86 F7
Capital of Djibouti.

Djidjelli Alg. see Jijel
Djizak Uzbek. see Jizzax
Djougou Benin 96 D4
Djoum Cameroon 96 E4
Djourab, Erg du des. Chad 97 E3
Djúpivogur Iceland 44 [inset 1]
Djurås Sweden 45 I6
Djurdjura, Parc National du nat. park Alg. 57 I5
Dmitriya Lapteva, Proliv sea chan. Russia 65 P2
Dmitriyev-L'govskiy Russia 43 G5
Dmitriyevsk Ukr. see Makiyivka
Dmitrov Russia 42 H4
Dmytriyevs'k Ukr. see Makiyivka
Dnepr r. Europe see Dnieper
Dneprodzerzhinsk Ukr. see Dniprodzerzhyns'k
Dnepropetrovsk Ukr. see Dnipropetrovs'k

▶Dnieper r. Europe 43 G7
3rd longest river in Europe.
Also spelt Dnepr (Russia) or Dnipro (Ukraine) or Dnyapro (Belarus).

Dniester r. Ukr. 43 F6
also spelt Dnister (Ukraine) or Nistru (Moldova)
Dnipro r. Europe see Dnieper
Dniprodzerzhyns'k Ukr. 43 G6
Dnipropetrovs'k Ukr. 43 G6
Dnister r. Ukr. see Dniester
Dno Russia 42 F4
Dnyapro r. Europe see Dnieper
Doaba Pak. 89 H3
Đoan Hung Vietnam 70 D2
Doba Chad 97 E4
Doba China see Toiba
Dobele Latvia 45 M8
Döbeln Germany 53 N3
Doberai, Jazirah pen. Indon. 69 I7
Doberai Peninsula Indon. see Doberai, Jazirah
Dobo Indon. 69 I8
Doboj Bos. & Herz. 58 H2
Doborjī Iran 88 D4
Döbraberg hill Germany 53 L4
Dobrich Bulg. 59 L3
Dobrinka Russia 43 I5
Dobroye Russia 43 H5
Dobrudja reg. Romania see Dobruja
Dobruja reg. Romania 59 L3
Dobrush Belarus 43 F5
Dobryanka Russia 41 R4
Dobzha China 83 G3
Đốc, Mui pt Vietnam 70 D3
Doce r. Brazil 145 D2
Dochart r. U.K. 50 E4
Docking U.K. 49 H6
Doctor Hicks Range hills Australia 109 D7
Doctor Pedro P. Peña Para. 144 D2
Doda India 82 C2
Doda Betta mt. India 84 C4
Dod Ballapur India 84 C3
Dodecanese is Greece 59 L7
Dodekanisa is Greece see Dodecanese
Dodekanisos is Greece see Dodecanese
Dodge City U.S.A. 130 C4
Dodgeville U.S.A. 130 F3
Dodman Point U.K. 49 C8

▶Dodoma Tanz. 99 D4
Capital of Tanzania.

Dodsonville U.S.A. 134 D4
Doetinchem Neth. 52 G3
Dog r. Canada 122 C4
Dogai Coring salt l. China 83 G2
Dogaicoring Qangco salt l. China 83 G2
Doğanşehir Turkey 90 E3
Dogên Co l. China 83 G3
Doghārūn Iran 89 F3
Dog Island Canada 123 J2
Dog Lake Man. Canada 121 L5
Dog Lake Ont. Canada 122 C4
Dog Lake Ont. Canada 122 D4
Dōgo i. Japan 75 D5
Dogondoutchi Niger 96 D3
Dog Rocks is Bahamas 133 E7
Doğubeyazıt Turkey 91 G3
Doğu Menteşe Dağları mts Turkey 59 M6
Dogxung Zangbo r. China 83 F3
Do'gyaling China 83 G3

▶Doha Qatar 88 C5
Capital of Qatar.

Dohad India see Dahod
Dohazari Bangl. 83 H5
Dohrighat India 83 E4
Doi i. Fiji 107 I4
Doi Inthanon National Park Thai. 70 B3
Doi Luang National Park Thai. 70 B3
Doire U.K. see Londonderry
Doi Saket Thai. 70 B3
Dois Irmãos, Serra dos hills Brazil 143 J5
Dokan, Sadd Iraq 91 G4
Dok-do i. N. Pacific Ocean see Liancourt Rocks
Dokhara, Dunes de des. Alg. 54 F5
Dokka Norway 45 G6
Dokkum Neth. 52 F1
Dokog He r. China 76 D2
Dokri Pak. 89 H5
Dokshukino Russia see Nartkala
Dokshytsy Belarus 45 O9
Dokuchayeva, Mys c. Russia 74 G3
Dokuchayevka Kazakh. see Karamendy
Dokuchayevs'k Ukr. 43 H7
Dolbenmaen U.K. 49 C6
Dol-de-Bretagne France 56 D2
Dole France 56 G3
Dolgellau U.K. 49 D6
Dolgen Germany 53 N1
Dolgiy, Ostrov i. Russia 42 L1
Dolgorukovo Russia 43 H5
Dolina Ukr. see Dolyna
Dolinsk Russia 74 F3
Dolisie Congo 99 B4
Dolleman Island Antarctica 152 L2
Dollnstein Germany 53 L6
Dolok, Pulau i. Indon. 69 J8
Dolomites mts Italy 58 D2
Dolomiti mts Italy see Dolomites
Dolomiti Bellunesi, Parco Nazionale delle nat. park Italy 58 D1
Dolomitiche, Alpi mts Italy see Dolomites
Dolonnur China see Duolun
Dolo Odo Eth. 98 E3
Dolores Arg. 144 E5
Dolores Uruguay 144 E4
Dolores U.S.A. 129 I3
Dolphin and Union Strait Canada 118 G3
Dolphin Head hd Namibia 100 B3
Đô Lương Vietnam 70 D3
Dolyna Ukr. 43 D6
Domaila India 82 D3
Domaniç Turkey 59 M5
Domar China 80 F5
Domartang China 76 B2
Domažlice Czechia 53 M5
Domba China 76 B1
Dom Bākh Iran 88 B3
Dombås Norway 44 F5
Dombóvár Hungary 58 H1
Dombrau Poland see Dąbrowa Górnicza
Dombrovitsa Ukr. see Dubrovytsya
Dombrowa Poland see Dąbrowa Górnicza
Domda China see Qingshuihe
Dome Creek Canada 120 F4
Dome Rock Mountains U.S.A. 129 F5
Domeyko Chile 144 B3
Domfront France 56 D2
Dominica country West Indies 137 L5
Dominicana, República country West Indies see Dominican Republic
Dominican Republic country West Indies 137 J5
Dominion, Cape Canada 119 K3
Dominique i. Fr. Polynesia see Hiva Oa
Dömitz Germany 53 L1
Dom Joaquim Brazil 145 C2
Dommel r. Neth. 52 F3
Domo Eth. 98 E3
Domokos Greece 59 J5
Dompu Indon. 108 B2
Domula China see Duomula
Domuyo, Volcán vol. Arg. 144 B5
Domville, Mount hill Australia 112 E2
Don Mex. 127 F8

▶Don r. Russia 43 H7
5th longest river in Europe.

Don r. U.K. 50 G3
Don, Xé r. Laos 70 D4
Donaghadee U.K. 51 G3
Donaghmore U.K. 51 F3
Donald Australia 112 A6
Donaldsonville U.S.A. 131 F6
Donalsonville U.S.A. 133 C6
Doñana, Parque Nacional de nat. park Spain 57 C5
Donau r. Europe see Danube
Donauwörth Germany 53 K6
Don Benito Spain 57 D4
Doncaster U.K. 48 F5
Dondo Angola 99 B4
Dondo Moz. 99 D5
Dondra Head hd Sri Lanka 84 D5
Donegal Ireland 51 D3
Donegal Bay Ireland 51 D3
Donets'k Ukr. 43 H7
Donetsko-Amrovsiyevka Ukr. see Amvrosiyivka
Donets'kyy Kryazh hills Russia/Ukr. 43 H6
Donga r. Cameroon/Nigeria 96 D4
Dong'an China 77 F3
Dongane, Lagoa lag. Moz. 101 L3
Dongara Australia 109 A7
Dongbo China see Mêdog
Dongchuan Yunnan China see Yao'an
Dongchuan Yunnan China see Tangdan
Dongchuan Yunnan China 76 D3
Dongco China 83 F2
Dong Co l. China 83 F2
Dong Dabsan Hu salt l. China 83 H1
Dongducheon S. Korea 75 B5
Dongfang China 77 F5
Dongfanghong China 74 D3
Donggang Liaoning China 75 B5
Donggang Shandong China 77 H1
Donggi Conag l. China 76 C1
Donggou China see Donggang
Donggu China 77 G3
Dongguan China 77 G4
Donghae S. Korea 75 C5
Dong Hai sea N. Pacific Ocean see East China Sea
Dong Haxat China 74 B3
Đồng Hới Vietnam 70 D3
Donghuang China see Xishui
Dongjiang Shuiku resr China 77 G3
Dongjug China 76 B2
Dongkou China 77 F3
Donglan China 76 E3
Dongliao He r. China 74 A4
Dongmen China see Luocheng
Dongminzhutun China 74 A3
Dongning China 74 C3
Dongo Angola 99 B5
Dongo Dem. Rep. Congo 98 B3
Dongola Sudan 86 D6
Dongou Congo 98 B3
Dong Phraya Yen esc. Thai. 70 C4
Dongping Guangdong China 77 G4
Dongping Hunan China see Anhua
Dongpo China see Meishan
Dongqiao China 83 G3
Dongshan Fujian China 77 H4
Dongshan Jiangsu China 77 I2
Dongshan Jiangxi China see Shangyou
Dongshao China 77 G3
Dongsheng Nei Mongol China 73 K5
Dongsheng Sichuan China see Shuangliu
Dongtai China 77 I1
Dongting Hu l. China 77 G2
Dongtou China 77 I3
Đông Triêu Vietnam 70 D2
Dong Ujimqin Qi China see Uliastai
Đông Văn Vietnam 70 D2
Dongxiang China 77 H2
Dongxi Liandao i. China 77 H1
Dongxing Guangxi China 76 E4
Dongxing Heilong. China 74 B3
Dongyang China 77 I2
Dongying China 73 L5
Dongzhi China 77 H2
Donkerbroek Neth. 52 G1
Don Kêv Cambodia 71 D5
Donnacona Canada 123 H5
Donnellys Crossing N.Z. 113 D2
Donner Pass U.S.A. 128 C2
Donnersberg hill Germany 53 H5
Donostia Spain see San Sebastián
Donousa i. Greece 59 K6
Donoussa i. Greece see Donousa
Donskoye Russia 43 I7
Donyztau, Sor dry lake Kazakh. 80 A2
Dooagh Ireland 51 B4
Doomadgee Australia 110 B3
Doon r. U.K. 50 E5
Doon, Loch l. U.K. 50 E5
Doonbeg r. Ireland 51 C5
Doorn Neth. 52 F2
Door Peninsula U.S.A. 134 B1
Doorwerth Neth. 52 F3
Doqêmo China 76 B2
Doqên Co l. China 83 G3
Dor Israel 85 B3
Dora U.S.A. 131 C5
Dora, Lake salt flat Australia 108 C5
Dorado Mex. 131 B7
Dorah Pass Pak. 89 H2
Doran Lake Canada 121 I2
Dorbiljin China see Emin
Dorbod China 74 B3
Dorbod Qi China see Ulan Hua
Dorchester U.K. 49 E8
Dordabis Namibia 100 C2
Dordogne r. France 56 D4
Dordrecht Neth. 52 E3
Dordrecht S. Africa 101 H6
Doreenville Namibia 100 D2
Doré Lake Canada 121 J4
Doré Lake l. Canada 121 J4
Dores do Indaiá Brazil 145 B2
Dorgê Co l. China 83 H2
Dörgön Nuur salt l. Mongolia 80 H2
Dori Burkina Faso 96 C3
Doring r. S. Africa 100 D6
Dorisvale Australia 108 E3
Dorking U.K. 49 G7
Dormagen Germany 52 G3
Dormans France 52 D5
Dormidontovka Russia 74 D3
Dornoch U.K. 50 E3
Dornoch Firth est. U.K. 50 E3
Dornum Germany 53 H1
Doro Mali 96 C3
Dorob National Park Namibia 100 B2
Dorogobuzh Russia 43 G5
Dorogorskoye Russia 42 J2
Doroḩ Iran 89 F3
Dorohoi Romania 43 E7
Dorostol Bulg. see Silistra
Dorotea Sweden 44 J4
Dorpat Estonia see Tartu
Dorre Island Australia 109 A6
Dorrigo Australia 112 F3
Dorris U.S.A. 126 C4
Dorset Canada 135 F1
Dorsoidong Co l. China 83 G2
Dortmund Germany 53 H3
Dörtyol Turkey 85 C1
Dorūd Iran 88 C3
Dorum Germany 53 I1
Doruma Dem. Rep. Congo 98 C3
Dorūneh, Kūh-e mts Iran 88 E3
Dörverden Germany 53 J2
Dorylaeum Turkey see Eskişehir
Dos Bahías, Cabo c. Arg. 144 C6
Dos de Mayo Peru 142 C5
Doshakh, Koh-i- mt. Afgh. see Dū Shākh, Kōh-e
Đỗ Sơn Vietnam 70 D2
Dos Palos U.S.A. 128 C3
Dosse r. Germany 53 M2
Dosso Niger 96 D3
Dothan U.S.A. 133 C6
Dotsero U.S.A. 129 J2
Douai France 52 D4
Douala Cameroon 96 D4
Douarnenez France 56 B2
Double Headed Shot Cays is Bahamas 133 D8
Double Island H.K. China 77 [inset]
Double Island Point Australia 111 F5
Double Mountain Fork r. U.S.A. 131 C5
Double Peak U.S.A. 128 D4
Double Point Australia 110 D3
Double Springs U.S.A. 133 C5
Doubs r. France/Switz. 56 G3
Doubtful Sound inlet N.Z. 113 A7
Doubtless Bay N.Z. 113 D2
Douentza Mali 96 C3
Dougga tourist site Tunisia 58 C6

▶Douglas Isle of Man 48 C4
Capital of the Isle of Man.

Douglas S. Africa 100 F5
Douglas U.K. 50 F5
Douglas AZ U.S.A. 127 F7
Douglas GA U.S.A. 133 D6
Douglas WY U.S.A. 126 G4
Douglas Reef i. Japan see Okino-Tori-shima
Douglasville U.S.A. 133 C5
Douhudi China see Gong'an
Doulatpur Bangl. see Daulatpur
Douliu Taiwan 77 I4
Doullens France 52 C4
Douna Mali 96 C3
Doune U.K. 50 E4
Doupovské hory mts Czechia 53 N4
Dourada, Serra hills Brazil 145 A2
Dourada, Serra mts Brazil 145 A1
Dourados Brazil 144 F2
Douro r. Port. 57 B3
also known as Duero (Spain)
Doushi China see Gong'an
Doushui Shuiku resr China 77 G3
Douve r. France 49 F9
Douzy France 52 F5
Dove r. U.K. 49 F6
Dove Brook Canada 123 K3
Dove Creek U.S.A. 129 I3
Dover U.K. 49 I7

▶Dover DE U.S.A. 135 H4
Capital of Delaware.

Dover NH U.S.A. 135 J2
Dover NJ U.S.A. 135 H3
Dover OH U.S.A. 134 E3
Dover TN U.S.A. 132 C4
Dover, Strait of France/U.K. 56 E1
Dover-Foxcroft U.S.A. 135 K1
Dovey r. U.K. 49 D6
Dovrefjell Nasjonalpark nat. park Norway 44 F5
Dowagiac U.S.A. 134 B3
Dowi, Tanjung pt Indon. 71 B7
Dowlaiswaram India 84 D2
Dowlatābād Afgh. 89 F3
Dowlatābād Fārs Iran 88 C4
Dowlatābād Fārs Iran 88 D4
Dowlatābād Khorāsān-e Raẕavī Iran 88 E2
Dowlatābād Khorāsān-e Raẕavī Iran 89 F2
Dowlat Khān Afgh. 89 H3
Dowlatyār Afgh. 89 G3
Downieville U.S.A. 128 C2
Downpatrick U.K. 51 G3
Downsville U.S.A. 135 H2
Doyle U.S.A. 128 C1
Doylestown U.S.A. 135 H3
Dozdān r. Iran 88 E5
Dōzen is Japan 75 D5
Dozois, Réservoir resr Canada 122 F5
Dozulé France 49 G9
Drâa, Hamada du plat. Alg. 54 C6
Dracena Brazil 145 A3
Drachten Neth. 52 G1
Drăgănești-Olt Romania 59 K2
Drăgășani Romania 59 K2
Dragonera, Isla i. Spain see Sa Dragonera
Dragoon U.S.A. 129 H5
Dragsfjärd Fin. 45 M6
Draguignan France 56 H5
Drahichyn Belarus 45 N10
Drake Australia 112 F2
Drake U.S.A. 130 C2
Drakensberg mts S. Africa 101 I3
Drake Passage S. Atlantic Ocean 148 D9
Drakes Bay U.S.A. 128 B3
Drama Greece 59 K4
Drammen Norway 45 G7
Drang, Ia r. Cambodia 71 D4
Drangedal Norway 45 F7
Dransfeld Germany 53 J3
Draper, Mount U.S.A. 120 B3
Draperstown U.K. 51 F3
Drapsaca Afgh. see Kunduz
Dras India 82 C2
Drasan Pak. 89 I2
Drau r. Europe see Drava
Dráva r. Europe see Drava
Drava r. Europe 58 H2
also known as Drau (Austria), Drave or Drava (Slovenia and Croatia), Dráva (Hungary)
Drave r. Europe see Drava
Drayton Valley Canada 120 H4
Drazinda Pak. 89 H4
Dréan Alg. 58 B6
Dreistelzberge hill Germany 53 J4
Drentse Hoofdvaart canal Neth. 52 G2
Drepano, Akra pt Greece see Laimos, Akrotirio
Dresden Canada 134 D2
Dresden Germany 47 N5
Dreux France 52 B6
Drevsjø Norway 45 H6
Drewryville U.S.A. 135 G5
Dri China 76 C2
Driffield U.K. 48 G4
Driftwood U.S.A. 135 F3
Driggs U.S.A. 126 F4
Drillham Australia 112 E1
Drimoleague Ireland 51 C6
Drina r. Bos. & Herz./Serbia 59 H2
Driscoll Island Antarctica 152 J1
Drissa Belarus see Vyerkhnyadzvinsk
Drniš Croatia 58 G3
Drobeta-Turnu Severin Romania 59 J2
Drochtersen Germany 53 J1
Drogheda Ireland 51 F4
Drogichin Belarus see Drahichyn
Drogobych Ukr. see Drohobych
Drohobych Ukr. 43 D6
Droichead Átha Ireland see Drogheda
Droichead Nua Ireland see Newbridge
Droitwich U.K. see Droitwich Spa
Droitwich Spa U.K. 49 E6
Dromedary, Cape Australia 112 E6
Dromod Ireland 51 E4
Dromore Northern Ireland U.K. 51 E3
Dromore Northern Ireland U.K. 51 F3
Dronfield U.K. 48 F5
Dronning Louise Land reg. Greenland 153 I1
Dronning Maud Land reg. Antarctica see Queen Maud Land
Dronten Neth. 52 F2
Druk-Yul country Asia see Bhutan
Drumheller Canada 121 H5
Drummond atoll Kiribati see Tabiteuea
Drummond U.S.A. 126 E3
Drummond, Lake U.S.A. 135 G5
Drummond Island Kiribati see McKean
Drummond Range hills Australia 110 D5
Drummondville Canada 123 G5
Drummore U.K. 50 E6
Drury Lake Canada 120 C2
Druskieniki Lith. see Druskininkai
Druskininkai Lith. 45 N10
Druzhina Russia 65 P3
Druzhnaya Gorka Russia 45 Q7
Dry r. Australia 108 F3
Dryanovo Bulg. 59 K3
Dryberry Lake Canada 121 M5
Dryden Canada 121 M5
Dryden U.S.A. 135 G2
Dry Fork r. U.S.A. 126 G4
Drygalski Ice Tongue Antarctica 152 H1
Drygalski Island Antarctica 152 F2
Dry Lake U.S.A. 129 F3
Dry Lake l. U.S.A. 130 D1
Drymen U.K. 50 E4
Dry Ridge U.S.A. 134 C4
Drysdale r. Australia 108 D3
Drysdale River National Park Australia 108 D3
Dry Tortugas is U.S.A. 133 D7
Du'an China 77 F4
Duaringa Australia 110 E4
Duarte, Pico mt. Dom. Rep. 137 J5
Duartina Brazil 145 A3
Ḑubā Saudi Arabia 86 E4
Dubai U.A.E. 88 D5
Dubakella Mountain U.S.A. 128 B1
Dubawnt r. Canada 121 L2
Dubawnt Lake Canada 121 K2
Dubayy U.A.E. see Dubai
Dubbo Australia 112 D4

▶Dublin Ireland 51 F4
Capital of Ireland.

Dublin U.S.A. 133 D5
Dubna Russia 42 H4
Dubno Ukr. 43 E6
Dubois ID U.S.A. 126 E3
Dubois IN U.S.A. 134 B4
Du Bois U.S.A. 135 F3
Dubovka Russia 43 J6
Dubovskoye Russia 43 I7
Dubréka Guinea 96 B4
Dubris U.K. see Dover
Dubrovnik Croatia 58 H3
Dubrovytsya Ukr. 43 E6
Dubuque U.S.A. 130 F3
Dubysa r. Lith. 45 M9
Đức Bôn Vietnam 71 D5
Duc de Gloucester, Îles du is Fr. Polynesia 151 K7
Duchang China 77 H2
Ducheng China see Yunan
Duchesne U.S.A. 129 H1
Duchesne r. U.S.A. 129 I1

Duchess Canada 121 I5
Duchess (abandoned) Australia 110 B4
Ducie Island *atoll* Pitcairn Is 151 L7
Duck Bay Canada 121 K4
Duck Creek *r.* Australia 108 B5
Duck Lake Canada 121 J4
Duckwater Peak U.S.A. 129 F2
Duc Tho Vietnam 70 D3
Dudelange Lux. 52 G5
Duderstadt Germany 53 K3
Dudhi India 83 E4
Dudhwa India 82 E3
Dudinka Russia 64 J3
Dudley U.K. 49 E6
Dudleyville U.S.A. 129 H5
Dudna *r.* India 84 C2
Dudu India 82 C4
Duékoué Côte d'Ivoire 96 C4
Duen, Bukit *vol.* Indon. 68 C7
Duero *r.* Spain 57 C3
also known as Douro (Portugal)
Duffel Belgium 52 E3
Dufferin, Cape Canada 122 F2
Duffer Peak U.S.A. 126 D4
Duff Islands Solomon Is 107 G2
Duffreboy, Lac *l.* Canada 123 H2
Dufftown U.K. 50 F3
Dufourspitze *mt.* Italy/Switz. 56 H4
Dufrost, Pointe *pt* Canada 122 F1
Dugi Otok *i.* Croatia 58 F2
Dugi Rat Croatia 58 G3
Du He *r.* China 77 F1
Dúiche Sheigheach *reg.* Ireland *see* **Joyce Country**
Duida-Marahuaca, Parque Nacional *nat. park* Venez. 142 E3
Duisburg Germany 52 G3
Dujiangyan China 76 D2
Dukathole S. Africa 101 H6
Duke Island U.S.A. 120 D4
Duke of Clarence *atoll* Tokelau *see* **Nukunonu**
Duke of Gloucester Islands Fr. Polynesia *see* **Duc de Gloucester, Îles du**
Duke of York *atoll* Tokelau *see* **Atafu**
Duk Fadiat South Sudan 97 G4
Dukhovnitskoye Russia 43 K5
Duki Pak. 89 H4
Duki Russia 74 D2
Duki *r.* Russia 74 D2
Dukou China *see* **Panzhihua**
Dūkštas Lith. 45 O9
Dulac U.S.A. 131 F6
Dulan China 80 I4
Dulce *r.* Arg. 144 D4
Dulce U.S.A. 127 G5
Dul'durga Russia 73 K2
Dulhunty *r.* Australia 110 C1
Dulishi Hu *salt l.* China 83 E2
Duliu Jiang *r.* China 77 F3
Dullewala Pak. 89 H4
Dullstroom S. Africa 101 J3
Dülmen Germany 53 H3
Dulmera India 82 C3
Dulovo Bulg. 59 L3
Duluth U.S.A. 130 E2
Dulverton U.K. 49 D7
Dūmā Syria 85 C3
Dumaguete Phil. 69 G5
Dumai Indon. 71 C7
Dumaran *i.* Phil. 68 G4
Dumaresq *r.* Australia 112 E2
Dumas U.S.A. 131 C5
Ḑumayr Syria 85 C3
Ḑumayr, Jabal *mts* Syria 85 C3
Dumbakh Iran *see* **Dom Bākh**
Dumbarton U.K. 50 E5
Dumbe S. Africa 101 J4
Ďumbier *mt.* Slovakia 47 Q6
Dumchele India 82 D2
Dumdum *i.* Indon. 71 D7
Dum Duma India 83 H4
Dumfries U.K. 50 F5
Dumka India 83 F4
Dumont d'Urville *research station* Antarctica 152 G2
Dumont d'Urville Sea Antarctica 152 G2
Dümpelfeld Germany 52 G4
Dumyāṭ Egypt *see* **Dumyāṭ**
Dumyāṭ Egypt 90 C5
Duna *r.* Europe *see* **Danube**
Dünaburg Latvia *see* **Daugavpils**
Dunaj *r.* Europe *see* **Danube**
Dunajská Streda Slovakia 47 P7
Dunakeszi Hungary 59 H1
Dunany Point Ireland 51 F4
Dunărea *r.* Europe *see* **Danube**
Dunării, Delta Romania/Ukr. *see* **Danube Delta**
Dunaújváros Hungary 58 H1
Dunav *r.* Europe *see* **Danube**
Dunay *r.* Europe *see* **Danube**
Dunayivtsi Ukr. 43 E6
Dunbar Australia 110 C3
Dunbar U.K. 50 G4
Dunblane U.K. 50 F4
Dunboyne Ireland 51 F4
Duncan Canada 120 F5
Duncan *AZ* U.S.A. 129 I5
Duncan *OK* U.S.A. 131 D5
Duncan, Cape Canada 122 E3
Duncan, Lac *l.* Canada 122 F3
Duncan Lake Canada 120 H2
Duncan Passage India 71 A5
Duncansby Head *hd* U.K. 50 F2
Duncan Town Bahamas 133 F8
Duncormick Ireland 51 F5
Dundaga Latvia 45 M8
Dundalk Ireland 51 F3
Dundalk U.S.A. 135 G4
Dundalk Bay Ireland 51 F4
Dundas Canada 134 F2
Dundas, Lake *salt flat* Australia 109 C8
Dundas Island Canada 120 D4
Dundas Strait Australia 108 E2
Dún Dealgan Ireland *see* **Dundalk**
Dundee S. Africa 101 J5
Dundee U.K. 50 G4
Dundee *MI* U.S.A. 134 D3
Dundee *NY* U.S.A. 135 G2
Dundonald U.K. 51 G3
Dundoo Australia 112 B1
Dundrennan U.K. 50 F6
Dundrum U.K. 51 G3
Dundrum Bay U.K. 51 G3
Dundwa Range *mts* India/Nepal 83 E4
Dune, Lac *l.* Canada 122 G2
Dunedin N.Z. 113 C7
Dunedin U.S.A. 133 D6
Dunfermline U.K. 50 F4
Dungannon U.K. 51 F3
Dún Garbhán Ireland *see* **Dungarvan**
Dungarpur India 82 C5
Dungarvan Ireland 51 E5
Dung Co *l.* China 83 G3
Dungeness *hd* U.K. 49 H8
Dungeness, Punta *pt* Arg. 144 C8
Düngenheim Germany 53 H4
Dungiven U.K. 51 F3
Dungog Australia 112 E4
Dungu Dem. Rep. Congo 98 C3
Dungun Malaysia 71 C6
Dungunab Sudan 86 E5
Dunhua China 74 C4
Dunhuang China 80 H3
Dunkeld Australia 112 D1
Dunkeld U.K. 50 F4
Dunkellin *r.* Ireland 51 D4
Dunkerque France *see* **Dunkirk**
Dunkery Hill *hill* U.K. 49 D7
Dunkirk France 52 C3
Dunkirk U.S.A. 134 F2
Dún Laoghaire Ireland 51 F4
Dunlap *IA* U.S.A. 130 E3
Dunlap *TN* U.S.A. 132 C5
Dunlavin Ireland 51 F4
Dunleer Ireland 51 F4
Dunloy U.K. 51 F2
Dunmanway Ireland 51 C6
Dunmarra Australia 108 F4
Dunmor U.S.A. 134 B5
Dunmore Ireland 51 D4
Dunmore U.S.A. 135 H3
Dunmore Town Bahamas 133 E7
Dunmurry U.K. 51 G3
Dunnet Head *hd* U.K. 50 F2
Dunnigan U.S.A. 128 C2
Dunning U.S.A. 130 C3
Dunnville Canada 134 F2
Dunnville U.S.A. 134 C5
Dunolly Australia 112 A6
Dunoon U.K. 50 E5
Dunphy U.S.A. 128 E1
Duns U.K. 50 G5
Dunseith U.S.A. 130 C1
Dunstable U.K. 49 G7
Dunstan Mountains N.Z. 113 B7
Dun-sur-Meuse France 52 F5
Duntroon N.Z. 113 C7
Dunvegan Lake Canada 121 J2
Dunyapur Pak. 89 H4
Duolun China 73 L4
Duomula China 83 E2
Dupang Ling *mts* China 77 F3
Duperré Alg. *see* **Aïn Defla**
Dupnitsa Bulg. 59 J3
Dupree U.S.A. 130 C2
Duque de Bragança Angola *see* **Calandula**
Dūrā West Bank 85 B4
Durack *r.* Australia 108 D3
Durack Range *hills* Australia 108 D4
Dura Europos Syria *see* **Aş Şālihīyah**
Durağan Turkey 90 D2
Durance *r.* France 56 G5
Durand U.S.A. 130 F2
Durango Mex. 131 B7
Durango *state* Mex. 131 B7
Durango Spain 57 E2
Durango U.S.A. 129 J3
Durānī *reg.* Afgh. 89 G4
Durant U.S.A. 131 D5
Durazno Uruguay 144 E4
Durazzo Albania *see* **Durrës**
Durban S. Africa 101 J5
Durban-Corbières France 56 F5
Durbanville S. Africa 100 D7
Durbin U.S.A. 134 F4
Durbun Pak. 89 G4
Durbuy Belgium 52 F4
Düren Germany 52 G4
Düren Iran 88 E3
Durg India 82 E5
Durgapur Bangl. 83 G4
Durgapur India 83 F5
Durham Canada 134 E1
Durham U.K. 48 F4
Durham U.S.A. 132 E5
Durham Downs Australia 111 C5
Duri Indon. 71 C7
Dūrī Rōd *r.* Afgh. 89 G4
Durlas Ireland *see* **Thurles**
Durleşti Moldova 59 M1
Durmersheim Germany 53 I6
Durmitor *mt.* Montenegro 59 H3
Durmitor, Nacionalni Park *nat. park* Montenegro 58 H3
Durness U.K. 50 E2
Durocortorum France *see* **Reims**
Durong South Australia 111 E5
Durostorum Bulg. *see* **Silistra**
Durour Island P.N.G. *see* **Aua Island**
Durovernum U.K. *see* **Canterbury**
Durrës Albania 59 H4
Durrie Australia 110 C5
Durrington U.K. 49 F7
Dursey Island Ireland 51 B6
Dursunbey Turkey 59 M5
Duru China *see* **Wuchuan**
Durukhsi Somalia 98 E3
Durusu Gölü *l.* Turkey 59 M4
Durūz, Jabal ad *mt.* Syria 85 C3
D'Urville, Tanjung *pt* Indon. 69 J7
D'Urville Island N.Z. 113 D5
Duşak Turkm. 89 E2
Dushai Pak. 89 G4
Dū Shākh, Kōh-e *mt.* Afgh. 89 F3
Dushan China 76 E3
▶Dushanbe Tajik. 89 H2
Capital of Tajikistan.
Dusheti Georgia 91 G2
Dushore U.S.A. 135 G3
Dusse-Alin', Khrebet *mts* Russia 74 D2
Düsseldorf Germany 52 G3
Dusty *NM* U.S.A. 129 J5
Dusty *WA* U.S.A. 126 D3
Dutch East Indies *country* Asia *see* **Indonesia**
Dutch Guiana *country* S. America *see* **Suriname**
Dutch Mountain U.S.A. 129 G1
Dutlwe Botswana 100 F2
Dutse Nigeria 96 D3
Dutsin-Ma Nigeria 96 D3
Dutton *r.* Australia 110 C4
Dutton Canada 134 E2
Dutton U.S.A. 126 F3
Dutton, Lake *salt flat* Australia 111 B6
Dutton, Mount U.S.A. 129 G2
Dutywa S. Africa 101 I7
Duudka, Taagga *reg.* Somalia 98 E3
Duval Canada 121 J5
Duvert, Lac *l.* Canada 123 H2
Duvno Bos. & Herz. *see* **Tomislavgrad**
Duyun China 76 E3
Duzab Pak. 89 F5
Düzce Turkey 59 N4
Duzdab Iran *see* **Zāhedān**
Dvina *r.* Europe *see* **Zapadnaya Dvina**
Dvina *r.* Russia *see* **Severnaya Dvina**
Dvinsk Latvia *see* **Daugavpils**
Dvinskaya Guba *g.* Russia 42 H2
Dwarka India 82 B5
Dwarsberg S. Africa 101 H3
Dwên Iraq 91 G3
Dwingelderveld, Nationaal Park *nat. park* Neth. 52 G2
Dworshak Reservoir U.S.A. 126 E3
Dwyka S. Africa 100 E7
Dyat'kovo Russia 43 G5
Dyce U.K. 50 G3
Dyer, Cape Canada 119 L3
Dyer Bay Canada 134 E1
Dyersburg U.S.A. 131 F4
Dyfi *r.* U.K. *see* **Dovey**
Dyfrdwy *r.* U.K. *see* **Dee**
Dyje *r.* Austria/Czechia 47 P6
Dyke U.K. 50 F3
▶Dykh-Tau, Gora *mt.* Russia 91 F2
2nd highest mountain in Europe.
Dyle *r.* Belgium 52 E4
Dyleň *hill* Czechia 53 M5
Dylewska Góra *hill* Poland 47 Q4
Dymytrov Ukr. 43 H6
Dynevor Downs Australia 112 B2
Dyoki S. Africa 101 I6
Dyrrhachium Albania *see* **Durrës**
Dysart Australia 110 E4
Dysselsdorp S. Africa 100 F7
Dyurtyuli Russia 41 Q4
Dzadrān *reg.* Afgh. 89 H3
Dzamīn Üüd Mongolia 73 K4
Dzanga-Ndoki, Parc National de *nat. park* Cent. Afr. Rep. 98 B3
▶Dzaoudzi Mayotte 99 E5
Capital of Mayotte.
Dzaudzhikau Russia *see* **Vladikavkaz**
Dzavhan Mongolia 80 H2
Dzerzhinsk Belarus *see* **Dzyarzhynsk**
Dzerzhinsk Russia 42 I4
Dzhagdy, Khrebet *mts* Russia 74 C1
Dzhaki-Unakhta Yakbyyana, Khrebet *mts* Russia 74 D2
Dzhalal-Abad Kyrg. *see* **Jalal-Abad**
Dzhalil' Russia 41 Q4
Dzhalilabad Azer. *see* **Cälilabad**
Dzhalinda Russia 74 A1
Dzhaltyr Kazakh. *see* **Zhaltyr**
Dzhambeyty Kazakh. *see* **Zhympity**
Dzhambul Kazakh. *see* **Taraz**
Dzhankoy Crimea 43 G7
Dzhanybek Kazakh. *see* **Zhanibek**
Dzharkent Kazakh. *see* **Zharkent**
Dzhava Georgia *see* **Java**
Dzhetygara Kazakh. *see* **Zhitikara**
Dzhezkazgan Kazakh. *see* **Zhezkazgan**
Dzhidinskiy Khrebet *mts* Mongolia/Russia 80 J1
Dzhirgatal' Tajik. *see* **Jirghatol**
Dzhizak Uzbek. *see* **Jizzax**
Dzhokhar Ghala Russia *see* **Groznyy**
Dzhubga Russia 90 E1
Dzhugdzhur, Khrebet *mts* Russia 65 O4
Dzhul'fa Azer. *see* **Culfa**
Dzhuma Uzbek. *see* **Juma**
Dzhusaly Kazakh. *see* **Zhosaly**
Działdowo Poland 47 R4
Dzūkijos nacionalinis parkas *nat. park* Lith. 45 N9
Dzungarian Basin China *see* **Junggar Pendi**
Dzungarian Gate *pass* China/Kazakh. 80 F2
Dzüünharaa Mongolia 72 J3
Dzuunmod Mongolia 72 J3
Dzyaniskavichy Belarus 45 O10
Dzyarzhynsk Belarus 45 O10
Dzyatlavichy Belarus 45 O10

E

Eabamet Lake Canada 122 D4
Eads U.S.A. 130 C4
Eagar U.S.A. 129 I4
Eagle *r.* Canada 123 K3
Eagle *AK* U.S.A. 118 D3
Eagle *CO* U.S.A. 126 G5
Eagle Cap *mt.* U.S.A. 126 D3
Eagle Crags *mt.* U.S.A. 128 E4
Eagle Creek *r.* Canada 121 J4
Eagle Lake Canada 121 M5
Eagle Lake *CA* U.S.A. 128 C1
Eagle Lake *ME* U.S.A. 132 G2
Eagle Mountain U.S.A. 129 F5
Eagle Mountain *hill* U.S.A. 130 F2
Eagle Pass U.S.A. 131 C6
Eagle Peak U.S.A. 127 G7
Eagle Plain Canada 118 E3
Eagle River U.S.A. 130 F2
Eagle Rock U.S.A. 134 F5
Eaglesham Canada 120 G4
Eap *i.* Micronesia *see* **Yap**
Ear Falls Canada 121 M5
Earlimart U.S.A. 128 D4
Earl's Seat *hill* U.K. 50 E4
Earlston U.K. 50 G5
Earn *r.* U.K. 50 F4
Earn, Loch *l.* U.K. 50 E4
Earp U.S.A. 129 F4
Earth U.S.A. 131 C5
Easington U.K. 48 H5
Easley U.S.A. 133 D5
East Alligator *r.* Australia 108 F3
East Antarctica *reg.* Antarctica 152 F1
East Ararat U.S.A. 135 H3
East Aurora U.S.A. 135 F2
East Bay *inlet* U.S.A. 133 C6
East Bengal *country* Asia *see* **Bangladesh**
Eastbourne U.K. 49 H8
East Branch Clarion River Reservoir U.S.A. 135 F3
East Caicos *i.* Turks and Caicos Is 133 G8
East Cape N.Z. 113 G3
East Cape Russia *see* **Dezhneva, Mys**
East Carbon City U.S.A. 129 H2
East Caroline Basin *sea feature* N. Pacific Ocean 150 F5
East China Sea N. Pacific Ocean 73 N6
East Coast Bays N.Z. 113 E3
East Dereham U.K. *see* **Dereham**
Eastend Canada 121 I5
▶Easter Island S. Pacific Ocean 151 M7
Part of Chile.
Eastern Cape *prov.* S. Africa 101 H6
Eastern Desert Egypt 86 D4
Eastern Fields *reef* Australia 110 D1
Eastern Ghats *mts* India 84 C4
▶Eastern Island U.S.A. 150 I4
Most northerly point of Oceania.
Eastern Nara *canal* Pak. 89 H5
Eastern Samoa *terr.* S. Pacific Ocean *see* **American Samoa**
Eastern Sayan Mountains Russia *see* **Vostochnyy Sayan**
Eastern Taurus *plat.* Turkey *see* **Güneydoğu Toroslar**
Eastern Transvaal *prov.* S. Africa *see* **Mpumalanga**
Easterville Canada 121 L4
Easterwâlde Neth. *see* **Oosterwolde**
East Falkland *i.* Falkland Is 144 E8
East Falmouth U.S.A. 135 J3
East Frisian Islands Germany 47 K4
Eastgate U.S.A. 128 E2
East Greenwich U.S.A. 135 J3
East Grinstead U.K. 49 G7
Easthampton U.S.A. 135 I2
East Hampton U.S.A. 135 I3
East Hartford U.S.A. 135 I3
East Indiaman Ridge *sea feature* Indian Ocean 149 O7
East Jordan U.S.A. 134 C1
East Kilbride U.K. 50 E5
Eastlake U.S.A. 134 E3
East Lamma Channel H.K. China 77 [inset]
Eastland U.S.A. 131 D5
East Lansing U.S.A. 134 C2
Eastleigh U.K. 49 F8
East Liverpool U.S.A. 134 E3
East London S. Africa 101 H7
East Lynn Lake U.S.A. 134 D4
Eastmain Canada 122 F3
Eastmain *r.* Canada 122 F3
Eastman U.S.A. 133 D5
East Mariana Basin *sea feature* N. Pacific Ocean 150 G5
Eastmere Australia 110 D4
East Naples U.S.A. 133 D7
Easton *MD* U.S.A. 135 G4
Easton *PA* U.S.A. 135 H3
East Orange U.S.A. 135 H3
East Pacific Rise *sea feature* N. Pacific Ocean 151 M4
East Pakistan *country* Asia *see* **Bangladesh**
East Palestine U.S.A. 134 E3
East Park Reservoir U.S.A. 128 B2
East Point Canada 123 J5
Eastport U.S.A. 132 H2
East Providence U.S.A. 135 J3
East Range *mts* U.S.A. 128 E1
East Retford U.K. *see* **Retford**
East St Louis U.S.A. 130 F4
East Sea N. Pacific Ocean *see* **Japan, Sea of**
East Shoal Lake Canada 121 L5
East Siberian Sea Russia 65 P2
East Side Canal *r.* U.S.A. 128 D4
East Stroudsburg U.S.A. 135 H3
East Tavaputs Plateau U.S.A. 129 I2
▶East Timor *country* Asia 108 D2
Former Portuguese territory. Gained independence from Indonesia in 2002.
East Toorale Australia 112 B3
East Troy U.S.A. 134 A2
East Verde *r.* U.S.A. 129 H4
Eastville U.S.A. 135 H5
East-Vlylân Neth. *see* **Oost-Vlieland**
East York Canada 134 F2
Eaton U.S.A. 134 C4
Eatonia Canada 121 I5
Eaton Rapids U.S.A. 134 C2
Eatonton U.S.A. 133 D5
Eau Claire U.S.A. 130 F2
Eau Claire, Lac à l' *l.* Canada 122 G2
Eau Claire, Rivière à l' *r.* Canada 122 G2
Eauripik *atoll* Micronesia 69 K5
Eauripik Rise-New Guinea Rise *sea feature* N. Pacific Ocean 150 F5
Eaurypyg *atoll* Micronesia *see* **Eauripik**
Ebbw Vale U.K. 49 D7
Ebebiyin Equat. Guinea 96 E4
Ebenerde Namibia 100 C3
Ebensburg U.S.A. 135 F3
Eber Gölü *l.* Turkey 59 N5
Ebergötzen Germany 53 K3
Eberswalde Germany 47 N4
Ebetsu Japan 74 F4
Ebian China 76 D2
Ebi Nor *salt l.* China *see* **Ebinur Hu**
Ebinur Hu *salt l.* China 80 F3
Eboli Italy 58 F4
Ebolowa Cameroon 96 E4
Ebony Namibia 100 B2
Ebre *r.* Spain *see* **Ebro**
Ebro *r.* Spain 57 G3
Ebstorf Germany 53 K1
Eburacum U.K. *see* **York**
Ebusus *i.* Spain *see* **Ibiza**
Ecbatana Iran *see* **Hamadān**
Eceabat Turkey 59 L4
Ech Chélif Alg. *see* **Chlef**
Echegárate, Puerto *pass* Spain 57 E2
Echeng China *see* **Ezhou**
Echeverria, Pico *mt.* Mex. 127 E7
Echizen Japan 75 E6
Echmiadzin Armenia *see* **Vagharshapat**
Echo U.S.A. 126 D3
Echo Bay *N.W.T.* Canada 120 G1
Echo Bay *Ont.* Canada 122 D5
Echo Cliffs U.S.A. 129 H3
Echoing *r.* Canada 121 M4
Echt Neth. 52 F3
Echternach Lux. 52 G5
Echuca Australia 112 B6
Echzell Germany 53 I4
Écija Spain 57 D5
Eckental Germany 53 L5
Eckernförde Germany 47 L3
Eclipse Sound *sea chan.* Canada 119 J2
Écrins, Parc National des *nat. park* France 56 H4
Ecuador *country* S. America 142 C4
Écueils, Pointe aux *pt* Canada 122 F2
Ed Eritrea 86 F7
Ed Sweden 45 G7
Edam Neth. 52 F2
Eday *i.* U.K. 50 G1
Ed Da'ein Sudan 97 F3
Ed Damazin Sudan 86 D7
Ed Damer Sudan 86 D6
Ed Debba Sudan 86 D6
Eddies Cove Canada 123 K4
Ed Dueim Sudan 86 D7
Eddystone Point Australia 111 [inset]
Eddyville U.S.A. 131 F4
Ede Neth. 52 F2
Edéa Cameroon 96 E4
Edehon Lake Canada 121 L2
Edéia Brazil 145 A2
Eden Australia 112 D6
Eden *r.* U.K. 48 D4
Eden *NC* U.S.A. 134 F5
Eden *TX* U.S.A. 131 D6
Edenburg S. Africa 101 G5
Edendale N.Z. 113 B8
Edenderry Ireland 51 E4
Edenton U.S.A. 132 E4
Edenville S. Africa 101 H4
Eder *r.* Germany 53 J3
Eder-Stausee *resr* Germany 53 I3
Edessa Greece 59 J4
Edessa Turkey *see* **Şanlıurfa**
Edewecht Germany 53 H1
Edfu Egypt *see* **Idfū**
Edgar Ranges *hills* Australia 108 C4
Edgartown U.S.A. 135 J3
Edgecumbe Island Solomon Is *see* **Utupua**
Edgefield U.S.A. 133 D5
Edge Island Svalbard *see* **Edgeøya**
Edgemont U.S.A. 130 C3
Edgeøya *i.* Svalbard 64 D2
Edgerton Canada 121 I4
Edgerton U.S.A. 134 C3
Edgeworthstown Ireland 51 E4
Édhessa Greece *see* **Edessa**
Edina U.S.A. 130 E3
Edinboro U.S.A. 134 E3
Edinburg *TX* U.S.A. 131 D7
Edinburg *VA* U.S.A. 135 F4
▶Edinburgh U.K. 50 F5
Capital of Scotland.
Edirne Turkey 59 L4
Edith, Mount U.S.A. 126 F3
Edith Cavell, Mount Canada 120 G4
Edith Ronne Land *ice feature* Antarctica *see* **Ronne Ice Shelf**
Edjeleh Libya 96 D2
Edjudina Australia 109 C7
Edku Egypt *see* **Idkū**
Edmond U.S.A. 131 D5
Edmonds U.S.A. 126 C3
▶Edmonton Canada 120 H4
Capital of Alberta.
Edmonton U.S.A. 134 C5
Edmore *MI* U.S.A. 134 C2
Edmore *ND* U.S.A. 130 D1
Edmund Lake Canada 121 M4
Edmundston Canada 123 H5
Edna U.S.A. 131 D6
Edna Bay U.S.A. 120 C4
Edo Japan *see* **Tōkyō**
Edom *hist. area* Israel/Jordan 85 B4
Édouard, Lac *l.* Dem. Rep. Congo/Uganda *see* **Edward, Lake**
Edremit Turkey 59 L5
Edremit Körfezi *b.* Turkey 59 L5
Edrengiyn Nuruu *mts* Mongolia 80 I3
Edsbyn Sweden 45 I6
Edson Canada 120 G4
Eduni, Mount Canada 120 D1
Edward *r. N.S.W.* Australia 112 B5
Edward *r. Qld* Australia 110 C2
Edward, Lake Dem. Rep. Congo/Uganda 98 C4
Edward, Mount Antarctica 152 L1
Edwardesabad Pak. *see* **Bannu**
Edwards U.S.A. 135 H1
Edward's Creek Australia 111 A6
Edwards Plateau U.S.A. 131 C6
Edwardsville U.S.A. 130 F4
Edward VII Peninsula Antarctica 152 I1
Edziza, Mount Canada 120 D3
Eeklo Belgium 52 D3
Eel *r.* U.S.A. 128 A1
Eel, South Fork *r.* U.S.A. 128 B1
Eem *r.* Neth. 52 F2
Eemshaven *pt* Neth. 52 G1
Eenrum Neth. 52 G1
Eenzamheid Pan *salt pan* S. Africa 100 E4
Eesti *country* Europe *see* **Estonia**
Éfaté *i.* Vanuatu 107 G3
Effingham U.S.A. 130 F4
Efsus Turkey *see* **Afşin**
Egadi, Isole *is Sicily* Italy 58 D5
Egan Range *mts* U.S.A. 129 F2
Eganville Canada 135 G1
Egedesminde Greenland *see* **Aasiaat**
Eger *r.* Germany 53 M4
Eger Hungary 47 R7
Egersund Norway 45 E7
Egerton, Mount *hill* Australia 109 B6
Eggegebirge *hills* Germany 53 I3
Egg Lake Canada 121 J4
Eggolsheim Germany 53 L5
Eghezée Belgium 52 E4
Egilsstaðir Iceland 44 [inset 1]
Eğin Turkey *see* **Kemaliye**
Eğirdir Turkey 59 N6
Eğirdir Gölü *l.* Turkey 59 N6
Eglinton U.K. 51 E2
Egmond aan Zee Neth. 52 E2
Egmont, Cape N.Z. 113 D4
Egmont, Mount *vol.* N.Z. *see* **Taranaki, Mount**
Egmont National Park N.Z. 113 E4
eGoli S. Africa *see* **Johannesburg**
Eğrigöz Dağı *mts* Turkey 59 M5
Egton U.K. 48 G4
Éguas *r.* Brazil 145 B1
Egvekinot Russia 65 T3
▶Egypt *country* Africa 86 C4
3rd most populous country in Africa.
Ehden Lebanon 85 B2
Ehen Hudag China 72 I5
Ehingen (Donau) Germany 47 L6
Ehle *r.* Germany 53 L2
Ehra-Lessien Germany 53 K2
Ehrenberg U.S.A. 129 F5
Ehrenberg Range *hills* Australia 109 E5
Eibelstadt Germany 53 K5
Eibergen Neth. 52 G2
Eichenzell Germany 53 J4
Eichstätt Germany 53 L6
Eidfjord Norway 45 E6
Eidsvold Australia 110 E5
Eidsvoll Norway 45 G6
Eifel *hills* Germany 52 G4
Eigg *i.* U.K. 50 C4
Eight Degree Channel India/Maldives 84 B5
Eights Coast Antarctica 152 K2
Eighty Mile Beach Australia 108 C4
Eilat Israel 85 B5
Eildon Australia 112 B6
Eildon, Lake Australia 112 C6
Eileen Lake Canada 121 J2
Eilenburg Germany 53 M3
Eil Malk *i.* Palau 69 I5
Eimke Germany 53 K2
Einasleigh Australia 110 D3
Einasleigh *r.* Australia 110 C3
Einbeck Germany 53 J3
Eindhoven Neth. 52 F3
Einme Myanmar 70 A3
Einsiedeln Switz. 56 I3
Éire *country* Europe *see* **Ireland**
Eirik Ridge *sea feature* N. Atlantic Ocean 148 F2
Eiriosgaigh *i.* U.K. *see* **Eriskay**
Eirunepé Brazil 142 E5
Eisberg *hill* Germany 53 J3
Eiseb *watercourse* Namibia 99 C5
Eisenach Germany 53 K4
Eisenberg Germany 53 L4
Eisenhower, Mount Canada *see* **Castle Mountain**
Eisenhüttenstadt Germany 47 O4
Eisenstadt Austria 47 P7
Eisfeld Germany 53 K4
Eisleben, Lutherstadt Germany 53 L3
Eite, Loch *inlet* U.K. *see* **Etive, Loch**
Eiterfeld Germany 53 J4
Eivissa Spain *see* **Ibiza**
Eivissa *i.* Spain *see* **Ibiza**
Ejea de los Caballeros Spain 57 F2
Ejeda Madag. 99 E6
Ejin Horo Qi China *see* **Altan Xiret**
Ejin Qi China *see* **Dalain Hob**
Ejmiadzin Armenia *see* **Vagharshapat**
Ekalaka U.S.A. 126 G3
Ekenäs Fin. 45 M7
Ekerem Turkm. 88 D2
Ekeren Belgium 52 E3
Eketahuna N.Z. 113 E5
Ekimchan Russia 74 D1
Ekinyazı Turkey 85 D1
Ekonda Russia 65 L3
Ekostrovskaya Imandra, Ozero *l.* Russia 44 R3
Ekshärad Sweden 45 H6
Eksjö Sweden 45 I8
Eksteenfontein S. Africa 100 C5
Ekström Ice Shelf Antarctica 152 B2
Ekwan *r.* Canada 122 E3
Ekwan Point Canada 122 E3
Ela Myanmar 70 B3
El Aaiún W. Sahara *see* **Laâyoune**
Elafonisou, Steno *sea chan.* Greece 59 J6
El 'Agrûd *well* Egypt *see* **Al 'Ajrūd**
Elaia, Cape Cyprus 85 B2
El 'Alamein Egypt *see* **Al 'Alamayn**
El 'Âmirîya Egypt *see* **Al 'Āmirīyah**
Elands *r.* S. Africa 101 I3
Elandsdoorn S. Africa 101 I3
El Aouinet Alg. 58 B7
Elar Armenia *see* **Abovyan**
El Araïche Morocco *see* **Larache**

El Arba, Tizi hill Alg. 57 H5
El Arco Mex. 127 E7
El Ariana Tunisia see L'Ariana
El Aricha Alg. 54 D5
El 'Arîsh Egypt see Al 'Arīsh
El Arrouch Alg. 58 B6
El Ashmûnein Egypt see Al Ashmūnayn
El Asnam Alg. see Chlef
Elassona Greece 59 J5
Elat Israel see Eilat
Elato atoll Micronesia 69 L5
Elazığ Turkey 91 E3
Elba U.S.A. 133 C6
Elba, Isola d' i. Italy 58 D3
El'ban Russia 74 E2
El Barco de Valdeorras Spain see O Barco
El Barreal salt l. Mex. 127 G7
Elbasan Albania 59 I4
El Batroun Lebanon see Batroûn
El Baúl Venez. 142 E2
El Bawîti Egypt see Al Bawīṭī
El Bayadh Alg. 54 E5
Elbe r. Germany 53 J1
also known as Labe (Czech Republic)
Elbe-Havel-Kanal canal Germany 53 L2
El Béqaa valley Lebanon 85 C2
Elbert, Mount U.S.A. 126 G5
Elberta U.S.A. 129 H2
Elberton U.S.A. 133 D5
Elbeuf France 56 E2
Elbeyli Turkey 85 C1
Elbing Poland see Elbląg
Elbistan Turkey 90 E3
Elbląg Poland 47 Q3
El Boulaïda Alg. see Blida
Elbow Canada 121 J5
Elbow Lake U.S.A. 130 D2
El Bozal Mex. 131 C8
El Brasil Mex. 131 C7

El'brus mt. Russia 91 F2
Highest mountain in Europe.

Elburg Neth. 52 F2
El Burgo de Osma Spain 57 E3
Elburz Mountains Iran 88 C2
El Cajon U.S.A. 128 E5
El Callao Venez. 142 F2
El Campo U.S.A. 131 D6
El Capitan Mountain U.S.A. 127 G6
El Capulín r. Mex. 131 C7
El Casco Mex. 131 B7
El Centro U.S.A. 129 F5
El Cerro Bol. 142 F7
Elche Spain see Elche-Elx
Elche-Elx Spain 57 F4
El Chilicote Mex. 131 B6
Elcho Island Australia 110 A1
El Coca Ecuador see Coca
El Cocuy, Parque Nacional nat. park Col. 142 D2
El Cuyo Mex. 133 C8
Elda Spain 57 F4
El Dátil Mex. 127 E7
El Desemboque Mex. 127 E7
El Diamante Mex. 131 C6
El'dikan Russia 65 O3
El Djezair country Africa see Algeria
El Djezair Alg. see Algiers
El Doctor Mex. 129 F6
Eldon U.S.A. 130 E4
Eldorado Arg. 144 F3
Eldorado Brazil 145 A4
El Dorado Col. 142 D3
El Dorado Mex. 124 F7
El Dorado AR U.S.A. 131 E5
El Dorado KS U.S.A. 130 D4
Eldorado U.S.A. 131 C6
El Dorado Venez. 142 F2
Eldorado Mountains U.S.A. 129 F4
Eldoret Kenya 98 D3
Elea, Cape Cyprus see Elaia, Cape
Eleanor U.S.A. 134 E4
Electric Peak U.S.A. 126 F3
Elefantes r. Moz./S. Africa see Olifants
El Eglab plat. Alg. 96 C2
El Ejido Spain 57 E5
El Encanto Col. 142 D4
Elend Germany 53 K3
Elephanta Caves tourist site India 84 B2
Elephant Butte Reservoir U.S.A. 127 G6
Elephant Island Antarctica 152 A2
Elephant Pass Sri Lanka 84 D4
Elephant Point Bangl. 83 H5
Eleşkirt Turkey 91 F3
El Eulma Alg. 54 F4
Eleuthera i. Bahamas 133 E7
Eleven Point r. U.S.A. 131 F4
El Fahs Tunisia 58 C6
El Faiyûm Egypt see Al Fayyūm
El Fasher Sudan 97 F3
El Ferrol Spain see Ferrol
El Ferrol del Caudillo Spain see Ferrol
Elfershausen Germany 53 J4
El Fud Eth. 98 E3
El Fuerte Mex. 127 F8
El Fula Sudan 98 C2
El Gara Egypt see Qārah
El Geneina Sudan 97 F3
El Geteina Sudan 86 D7
El Ghardaqa Egypt see Hurghada
El Ghor plain Jordan/West Bank see Al Ghawr
Elgin U.K. 50 F3
Elgin IL U.S.A. 130 F3
Elgin ND U.S.A. 130 C2
Elgin NV U.S.A. 129 F3
Elgin TX U.S.A. 131 D6
El'ginskiy Russia 65 P3
El Gîza Egypt see Giza
El Goléa Alg. 54 E5
El Golfo de Santa Clara Mex. 127 E7
Elgon, Mount Kenya/Uganda 78 C6
El Hadjar Alg. 58 B6
El-Hagounia W. Sahara 96 B2
El Ḥammâm Egypt see Al Ḥammām
El Ḥammâmi reg. Mauritania 96 B2
El Ḥank esc. Mali/Mauritania 96 C2
El Ḥarra Egypt see Al Ḥarrah
El Hazim Jordan see Al Ḥazīm
El Ḥeiz Egypt see Al Ḥayz
El Hierro i. Canary Is 96 B2
El Homr Alg. 54 E6
El Homra Sudan 86 D7
Elhovo Bulg. 59 L3
Eliase Indon. 108 E2
Elías Piña Dom. Rep. 137 J5
Elichpur India see Achalpur
Elida U.S.A. 134 C3
Elie U.K. 50 G4
Elila r. Dem. Rep. Congo 98 C4
Elim U.S.A. 118 B3
Elimberrum France see Auch
Eling China see Yinjiang
Elingampangu Dem. Rep. Congo 98 C4
Eliot, Mount Canada 123 J2
Élisabethville Dem. Rep. Congo see Lubumbashi
Eliseu Martins Brazil 143 J5
El Iskandarîya Egypt see Alexandria
Elista Russia 43 J7
Elizabeth NJ U.S.A. 135 H3
Elizabeth WV U.S.A. 134 E4
Elizabeth, Mount hill Australia 108 D4
Elizabeth Bay Namibia 100 B4
Elizabeth City U.S.A. 132 E4
Elizabeth Island Pitcairn Is see Henderson Island
Elizabeth Point Namibia 100 B4
Elizabethton U.S.A. 132 D4
Elizabethtown IL U.S.A. 130 F4
Elizabethtown KY U.S.A. 134 C5
Elizabethtown NC U.S.A. 133 E5
Elizabethtown NY U.S.A. 135 I1
El Jadida Morocco 54 C5
El Jaralito Mex. 131 B7
El Jem Tunisia 58 D7
Elk r. Canada 120 H5
Ełk Poland 47 S4
Elk r. U.S.A. 135 H4
El Kaa Lebanon see Qaa
El Kab Sudan 86 D6
Elkader U.S.A. 130 F3
El Kala Alg. 58 C6
Elk City U.S.A. 131 D5
Elkedra Australia 110 A4
Elkedra watercourse Australia 110 B4
El Kef Tunisia see Le Kef
El Kelaâ des Srarhna Morocco 54 C5
Elkford Canada 120 H5
Elk Grove U.S.A. 128 C2
El Khalil West Bank see Hebron
El Khandaq Sudan 86 D6
El Khârga Egypt see Al Khārijah
El Kharrûba Egypt see Al Kharrūbah
Elkhart IN U.S.A. 134 C3
Elkhart KS U.S.A. 131 C4
El Khartûm Sudan see Khartoum
El Khenachich esc. Mali see El Khnâchîch
El Khnâchîch esc. Mali 96 C2
Elkhorn U.S.A. 130 F3
Elkhorn City U.S.A. 134 D5
Elki Turkey see Beytüşşebap
Elkin U.S.A. 132 D4
Elkins U.S.A. 134 F4
Elk Island National Park Canada 121 H4
Elk Lake Canada 122 E5
Elk Lake l. U.S.A. 134 C1
Elkland U.S.A. 135 G3
Elk Mountain U.S.A. 126 G4
Elk Mountains U.S.A. 129 J2
Elko Canada 120 H5
Elko U.S.A. 129 F1
Elk Point Canada 121 I4
Elk Point U.S.A. 130 D3
Elk Springs U.S.A. 129 I1
Elkton MD U.S.A. 135 H4
Elkton VA U.S.A. 135 F4
El Kûbri Egypt see Al Kūbrī
El Kuntilla Egypt see Al Kuntillah
Elkview U.S.A. 134 E4
Ellas country Europe see Greece
Ellaville U.S.A. 133 C5
Ell Bay Canada 121 O1
Ellef Ringnes Island Canada 119 H2
Ellen, Mount U.S.A. 129 H2
Ellenburg Depot U.S.A. 135 I1
Ellendale U.S.A. 130 D2
Ellensburg U.S.A. 126 C3
Ellenville U.S.A. 135 H3
El León, Cerro mt. Mex. 131 B7
Ellesmere, Lake N.Z. 113 D6

Ellesmere Island Canada 119 J2
4th largest island in North America and 10th in the world.

Ellesmere Island National Park Reserve Canada see Quttinirpaaq National Park
Ellesmere Port U.K. 48 E5
Ellettsville U.S.A. 134 B4
Ellice r. Canada 121 K1
Ellice Island atoll Tuvalu see Funafuti
Ellice Islands country S. Pacific Ocean see Tuvalu
Ellicott City U.S.A. 135 G4
Ellijay U.S.A. 133 C5
Ellingen Germany 53 K5
Elliot S. Africa 101 H6
Elliot, Mount Australia 110 D3
Elliotdale S. Africa 101 I6
Elliot Knob mt. U.S.A. 134 F4
Elliot Lake Canada 122 E5
Elliott Australia 108 F4
Elliston U.S.A. 134 E5
Ellon U.K. 50 G3
Ellora Caves tourist site India 84 B1
Ellsworth KS U.S.A. 130 D4
Ellsworth ME U.S.A. 132 G2
Ellsworth NE U.S.A. 130 C3
Ellsworth WI U.S.A. 130 E2
Ellsworth Land reg. Antarctica 152 K1
Ellsworth Mountains Antarctica 152 L1
Ellwangen (Jagst) Germany 53 K6
El Maghreb country Africa see Morocco
Elmakuz Dağı mt. Turkey 85 A1
Elmalı Turkey 59 M6
El Malpais National Monument nat. park U.S.A. 129 J4
El Manṣûra Egypt see Al Manṣūrah
El Maṭarîya Egypt see Al Maṭarīyah
El Mazâr Egypt see Al Mazār
El Meghaïer Alg. 54 F5
El Milia Alg. 54 F4
El Minya Egypt see Al Minyā
Elmira Ont. Canada 134 E2
Elmira P.E.I. Canada 123 J5
Elmira MI U.S.A. 134 C1
Elmira NY U.S.A. 135 G2
El Mirage U.S.A. 129 G5
El Moral Spain 57 E5
Elmore Australia 112 B6
El Mreyyé reg. Mauritania 96 C3
Elmshorn Germany 53 J1
El Muglad Sudan 86 C7
Elmvale Canada 134 F1
Elnesvågen Norway 44 E5
El Nevado, Cerro mt. Col. 142 D3
El Oasis Mex. 129 F5
El Obeid Sudan 86 D7
El Odaiya Sudan 86 C7
El Oro Mex. 131 C7
Elorza Venez. 142 E2
El Oued Alg. 54 F5
Eloy U.S.A. 129 H5
El Palmito Mex. 131 B7
El Paso IL U.S.A. 130 F3
El Paso KS U.S.A. see Derby
El Paso TX U.S.A. 127 G7
Elphin U.K. 50 D2
Elphinstone Island i. Myanmar see Thayawthadangyi Kyun
El Portal U.S.A. 128 D3
El Porvenir Mex. 131 B6
El Porvenir Panama 137 I7
El Prat de Llobregat Spain 57 H3
El Progreso Hond. 136 G5
El Puerto de Santa María Spain 57 C5
El Qâhira Egypt see Cairo
El Qasimiye r. Lebanon 85 B3
El Quds Israel/West Bank see Jerusalem
El Quṣeima Egypt see Al Quṣaymah
El Quṣeir Egypt see Al Quṣayr
El Qûṣîya Egypt see Al Qūṣīyah
El Regocijo Mex. 131 B8
El Reno U.S.A. 131 D5
Elrose Canada 121 I5
Elsa Canada 120 C2
El Ṣaff Egypt see Aṣ Ṣaff
El Sahuaro Mex. 127 E7
El Salado Mex. 131 C7
El Salto Mex. 131 B8
El Salvador country Central America 136 G6
El Salvador Chile 144 C3
El Salvador Mex. 131 C7
Elsass reg. France see Alsace
El Sauz Mex. 127 G7
Else r. Germany 53 I2
El Sellûm Egypt see As Sallūm
Elsey Australia 108 F3
El Shallûfa Egypt see Ash Shallūfah
El Sharana Australia 108 F3
El Shaṭṭ Egypt see Ash Shaṭṭ
Elsie U.S.A. 134 C2
Elsinore Denmark see Helsingør
Elsinore U.S.A. 129 G2
Elsinore Lake U.S.A. 128 E5
El Sueco Mex. 127 G7
El Suweis Egypt see Suez
El Suweis governorate Egypt see As Suways
El Tama, Parque Nacional nat. park Venez. 142 D2
El Tarf Alg. 58 C6
El Teleno mt. Spain 57 C2
El Temascal Mex. 131 D7
El Thamad Egypt see Ath Thamad
El Tigre Venez. 142 F2
Eltmann Germany 53 K5
El'ton Russia 43 J6
El'ton, Ozero l. Russia 43 J6
El Tren Mex. 127 E7
El Tuparro, Parque Nacional nat. park Col. 142 E2
El Ṭûr Egypt see Aṭ Ṭūr
El Turbio Arg. 144 B8
El Uqṣur Egypt see Luxor
Eluru India 84 D2
Elva Estonia 45 O7
Elvanfoot U.K. 50 F5
Elvas Port. 57 C4
Elverum Norway 45 G6
Elvira Brazil 142 D5
El Wak Kenya 98 E3
El Wâṭya well Egypt see Al Wāṭiyah
Elwood IN U.S.A. 134 C3
Elwood NE U.S.A. 130 D3
El Wuz Sudan 86 D7
Elx Spain see Elche-Elx
Elxleben Germany 53 K3
Ely U.K. 49 H6
Ely MN U.S.A. 130 F2
Ely NV U.S.A. 129 F2
Elyria U.S.A. 134 D3
Elz Germany 53 I4
El Zagâzîg Egypt see Az Zaqāzīq
Elze Germany 53 J2
Émaé i. Vanuatu 107 G3
eMakhazeni S. Africa 101 J3
eMalahleni S. Africa 101 I3
Emām Taqī Iran 88 E2
Emån r. Sweden 45 J8
eManzimtoti S. Africa 101 J6
Emas, Parque Nacional das nat. park Brazil 143 H7
Emba Kazakh. 80 A2
Embalenhle S. Africa 101 I4
Embarcación Arg. 144 D2
Embarras Portage Canada 121 I3
Embi Kazakh. see Emba
Embira r. Brazil see Envira
Emborcação, Represa de resr Brazil 145 B2
Embrun Canada 135 H1
Embu Kenya 98 D4
Emden Germany 53 H1
Emden Deep sea feature N. Pacific Ocean see Cape Johnson Depth
Emei China see Emeishan
Emeishan China 76 D2
Emei Shan mt. China 76 D2
Emerald Australia 110 E4
Emeril Canada 123 I3
Emerita Augusta Spain see Mérida
Emerson Canada 121 L5
Emerson U.S.A. 134 D4
Emery U.S.A. 129 H2
Emesa Syria see Homs
Emet Turkey 59 M5
Emgwenya S. Africa 101 J3
eMgwenya S. Africa 101 J3
Emigrant Pass U.S.A. 128 E1
Emigrant Valley U.S.A. 129 F3
Emi Koussi mt. Chad 97 E3
Emile r. Canada 120 G2
Emiliano Zapata Mex. 136 F5
Emin China 80 F2
Emine, Nos pt Bulg. 59 L3
Eminence U.S.A. 134 C4
Eminska Planina hills Bulg. 59 L3
Emirdağ Turkey 59 N5
Emir Dağı mt. Turkey 59 N5
Emir Dağları mts Turkey 59 N5
Emissi, Tarso mt. Chad 97 E2
eMjindini S. Africa 101 J3
eMkhondo S. Africa 101 J4
Emmaboda Sweden 45 I8
Emmaste Estonia 45 M7
Emmaville Australia 112 E2
Emmeloord Neth. 52 F2
Emmelshausen Germany 53 H4
Emmen Neth. 52 G2
Emmen Switz. 56 I3
Emmerich am Rhein Germany 52 G3
Emmet Australia 110 D5
Emmetsburg U.S.A. 130 E3
Emmett U.S.A. 126 D4
Emmiganuru India 84 C3
Emo Canada 121 M5
Emona Slovenia see Ljubljana
eMondlo S. Africa 101 J4
Emory Peak U.S.A. 131 C6
Empalme Mex. 127 F8
Empangeni S. Africa 101 J5
Emperor Seamount Chain sea feature N. Pacific Ocean 150 H2
Emperor Trough sea feature N. Pacific Ocean 150 H2
Empingham Reservoir U.K. see Rutland Water
Emplawas Indon. 108 E2
Empoli Italy 58 D3
Emporia KS U.S.A. 130 D4
Emporia VA U.S.A. 135 G5
Emporium U.S.A. 135 F3
Empress Canada 121 I5
Empty Quarter des. Saudi Arabia see Rub' al Khālī
Ems r. Germany 53 H1
Emsdale Canada 134 F1
Emsdetten Germany 53 H2
Ems-Jade-Kanal canal Germany 53 H1
eMzinoni S. Africa 101 I4
Enafors Sweden 44 H5
Encantadas, Serra das hills Brazil 144 F4
Encarnación Para. 144 E3
Enchi Ghana 96 C4
Encinal U.S.A. 131 D6
Encinitas U.S.A. 128 E5
Encino U.S.A. 127 G6
Encruzilhada Brazil 145 C1
Endako Canada 120 E4
Endau-Rompin National Park nat. park Malaysia 71 C7
Ende Indon. 108 C2
Endeavour Strait Australia 110 C1
Endeh Indon. see Ende
Enderby Canada 120 G5
Enderby atoll Micronesia see Puluwat
Enderby Land reg. Antarctica 152 D2
Endicott U.S.A. 135 G2
Endicott Mountains U.S.A. 118 C3
EnenKio terr. N. Pacific Ocean see Wake Island
Energodar Ukr. see Enerhodar
Enerhodar Ukr. 43 G7
Enewetak atoll Marshall Is 150 G5
Enez Turkey 59 L4
Enfe Lebanon 85 B2
Enfião, Ponta do pt Angola 99 B5
Enfidaville Tunisia 58 D6
Enfield U.S.A. 132 E4
Engan Norway 44 F5
Engaru Japan 74 F3
En Gedi Israel 85 B4
Engelhard U.S.A. 132 F5
Engel's Russia 43 J6
Engelschmangat sea chan. Neth. 52 E1
Enggano i. Indon. 68 C8
Enghien Belgium 52 E4
England admin. div. U.K. 49 E6
Englee Canada 123 L4
Englehart Canada 122 F5
Englewood FL U.S.A. 133 D7
Englewood OH U.S.A. 134 C4
English r. Canada 121 M5
English U.S.A. 134 B4
English Bazar India see Ingraj Bazar
English Channel France/U.K. 49 F9
English Coast Antarctica 152 L2
Engozero Russia 42 G2
Enhlalakahle S. Africa 101 J5
Enid U.S.A. 131 D4
Eniwa Japan 74 F4
Eniwetok atoll Marshall Is see Enewetak
Enjiang China see Yongfeng
Enkeldoorn Zimbabwe see Chivhu
Enkhuizen Neth. 52 F2
Enköping Sweden 45 J7
Enna Sicily Italy 58 F6
Ennadai Lake Canada 121 K2
En Nahud Sudan 86 C7
Ennedi, Massif mts Chad 97 F3
Ennell, Lough l. Ireland 51 E4
Enngonia Australia 112 B2
Enning U.S.A. 130 C2
Ennis Ireland 51 D5
Ennis MT U.S.A. 126 F3
Ennis TX U.S.A. 131 D5
Enniscorthy Ireland 51 F5
Enniskillen U.K. 51 E3
Ennistymon Ireland 51 C5
Enn Nâqoûra Lebanon 85 B3
Enns r. Austria 47 O6
Eno Fin. 44 Q5
Enoch U.S.A. 129 G3
Enontekiö Fin. 44 M2
Enosburg Falls U.S.A. 135 I1
Enos Corner U.S.A. 134 B4
Enping China 77 G4
Ens Neth. 52 F2
Ensay Australia 112 C6
Enschede Neth. 52 G2
Ense Germany 53 I3
Ensenada Mex. 127 D7
Enshi China 77 F2
Ensley U.S.A. 133 C6
Entebbe Uganda 98 D3
Enterprise Canada 120 G2
Enterprise AL U.S.A. 133 C6
Enterprise OR U.S.A. 126 D3
Enterprise UT U.S.A. 129 G3
Entre Ríos Bol. 142 F8
Entre Rios Brazil 143 H5
Entre Rios de Minas Brazil 145 B3
Entroncamento Port. 57 B4
Enugu Nigeria 96 D4
Enurmino Russia 65 T3
Envira Brazil 142 D5
Envira r. Brazil 142 D5
'En Yahav Israel 85 B4
Enyamba Dem. Rep. Congo 98 C4
Eochaill Ireland see Youghal
Epe Neth. 52 F2
Epéna Congo 98 B3
Épernay France 52 D5
Ephraim U.S.A. 129 H2
Ephrata U.S.A. 135 G3
Épi i. Vanuatu 107 G3
Epidamnus Albania see Durrës
Épinal France 56 H2
Episkopi Bay Cyprus 85 A2
Episkopis, Kolpos b. Cyprus see Episkopi Bay
ePitoli S. Africa see Pretoria
Epomeo, Monte hill Italy 58 E4
Epping U.K. 49 H7
Epping Forest National Park Australia 110 D4
Eppstein Germany 53 I4
Eppynt, Mynydd hills U.K. 49 D6
Epsom U.K. 49 G7
Epte r. France 52 B5
Eqlīd Iran 88 D4
Equatorial Guinea country Africa 96 D4
Équeurdreville-Hainneville France 49 F9
Erac Creek watercourse Australia 112 B1
Erandol India 84 B1
Erawadi r. Myanmar see Irrawaddy
Erawan National Park Thai. 71 B4
Erbaa Turkey 90 E2
Erbendorf Germany 53 M5
Erbeskopf hill Germany 52 H5
Erbet Iraq 91 G4
Ercan airport Cyprus 85 A2
Erciş Turkey 91 F3
Erciyes Dağı mt. Turkey 90 D3
Érd Hungary 58 H1
Erdaobaihe China see Baihe
Erdaogou Bingzhan China 76 B1
Erdao Jiang r. China 74 B4
Erdek Turkey 59 L4
Erdemli Turkey 85 B1
Erdenedalay Mongolia 72 I3
Erdenet Mongolia 80 J2
Erdenetsagaan Mongolia 73 L3
Erdi reg. Chad 97 F3
Erdniyevskiy Russia 43 J7

Erebus, Mount vol. Antarctica 152 H1
Highest active volcano in Antarctica.

Erechim Brazil 144 F3
Ereentsav Mongolia 73 L3
Ereğli Konya Turkey 90 D3
Ereğli Zonguldak Turkey 59 N4
Erego Moz. see Errego
Erei, Monti mts Sicily Italy 58 F6
Erementaū Kazakh. see Yereymentau
Erenhot China 73 K4
Erepucu, Lago de l. Brazil 143 G4
Erevan Armenia see Yerevan
Erfurt Germany 53 L4
Erfurt airport Germany 53 K4
Ergani Turkey 91 E3
'Erg Chech des. Alg./Mali 96 C2
Ergene r. Turkey 59 L4
Ērgļi Latvia 45 N8
Ergu China 74 C3
Ergun China 73 M2
Ergun He r. China/Russia see Argun'
Ergun Youqi China see Ergun
Ergun Zuoqi China see Gegen Gol
Er Hai l. China 76 D3
Erhulai China 74 B4
Eriboll, Loch inlet U.K. 50 E2
Ericht r. U.K. 50 F4
Ericht, Loch l. U.K. 50 E4
Erickson Canada 121 L5
Erie KS U.S.A. 131 E4
Erie PA U.S.A. 134 E2
Erie, Lake Canada/U.S.A. 134 E2
'Erîgât des. Mali 96 C3
Erik Eriksenstretet sea chan. Svalbard 64 D2
Eriksdale Canada 121 L5
Erimo-misaki c. Japan 74 F4
Erin Canada 134 E2
Erinpura Road India 82 C4
Eriskay i. U.K. 50 B3
Eritrea country Africa 86 E6
Erlangen Germany 53 L5
Erlangping China 77 F1
Erldunda Australia 109 F6
Erlistoun watercourse Australia 109 C6
Erlong Shan mt. China 74 C4
Erlongshan Shuiku resr China 74 B4
Ermak Kazakh. see Aksu
Ermelo Neth. 52 F2
Ermelo S. Africa 101 I4
Ermenek Turkey 85 A1
Ermenek r. Turkey 85 A1
Ermont Egypt see Armant
Ermoupoli Greece 59 K6
Ernakulam India 84 C4
Erne r. Ireland/U.K. 51 D3
Ernest Giles Range hills Australia 109 C6
Erode India 84 C4
Eromanga Australia 111 C5
Erongo admin. reg. Namibia 100 B1
Erp Neth. 52 F3
Erqu China see Zhouzhi
Errabiddy Hills Australia 109 A6
Er Rachidia Morocco 54 D5
Errego Moz. 99 D5
Er Remla Tunisia 58 D7
Er Renk South Sudan 86 D7
Errigal hill Ireland 51 D2
Errinundra National Park Australia 112 D6
Erris Head hd Ireland 51 B3
Errol U.S.A. 135 J1
Erromango i. Vanuatu 107 G3
Erronan i. Vanuatu see Futuna
Erseka Albania see Ersekë
Ersekë Albania 59 I4
Erskine U.S.A. 130 D2
Ersmark Sweden 44 L5
Ertai China 80 H2
Ertil' Russia 43 I6
Ertis r. Kazakh./Russia see Irtysh
Ertix He r. China/Kazakh. 80 G2
Ērtra country Africa see Eritrea
Eruh Turkey 91 F3
Erwin U.S.A. 132 D4
Erwitte Germany 53 I3
Erxleben Sachsen-Anhalt Germany 53 L2
Erxleben Sachsen-Anhalt Germany 53 L2
Eryuan China 76 C3
Erzerum Turkey see Erzurum
Erzgebirge mts Czechia/Germany 53 N4
Erzhan China 74 B2
Erzin Turkey 85 C1
Erzincan Turkey 91 E3
Erzurum Turkey 91 F3
Esa-ala P.N.G. 110 E1
Esan-misaki pt Japan 74 F4
Esashi Japan 74 F3
Esbjerg Denmark 45 F9
Esbo Fin. see Espoo
Escalante U.S.A. 129 H3
Escalante r. U.S.A. 129 H3
Escalante Desert U.S.A. 129 G3
Escalón Mex. 131 B7
Escambia r. U.S.A. 133 C6
Escanaba U.S.A. 132 C2
Escárcega Mex. 136 F5
Escatrón Spain 57 F3
Escaut r. Belgium 52 D4
Esch Neth. 52 F3
Eschede Germany 53 K2
Eschscholtz atoll Marshall Is see Bikini
Esch-sur-Alzette Lux. 52 F5
Eschwege Germany 53 K3
Eschweiler Germany 52 G4
Escondido r. Mex. 131 C6
Escondido U.S.A. 128 E5
Escudilla mt. U.S.A. 129 I5
Escuinapa Mex. 136 C4
Escuintla Guat. 136 F6
Eséka Cameroon 96 E4
Eşen Turkey 59 M6
Esenguly Turkm. 88 D2
Esenguly Döwlet Gorugy nature res. Turkm. 88 D2
Esens Germany 53 H1
Eşfahān Iran 88 C3
Esfarayen, Reshteh-ye mts Iran 88 E2
Esfedān Iran 89 E3
Eshan China 76 D3
Eshkanān Iran 88 D5
Eshowe S. Africa 101 J5
'Eshqābād Iran 88 E3
eSikhaleni S. Africa 101 J5
Esil Kazakh. see Yesil'
Esil r. Kazakh./Russia see Yesil'
Esk Australia 112 F1
Esk r. Australia 111 [inset]
Esk r. U.K. 48 D4
Eskdalemuir U.K. 50 F5
Esker Canada 123 I3
Eskifjörður Iceland 44 [inset 1]
Eski Gediz Turkey 59 M5
Eskilstuna Sweden 45 J7
Eskimo Lakes Canada 118 E3
Eskimo Point Canada see Arviat
Eskipazar Turkey 90 D2
Eskişehir Turkey 59 N5
Eski-Yakkabog' Uzbek. 89 G2
Esla r. Spain 57 C3
Eslāmābād-e Gharb Iran 88 B3
Esler Dağı mt. Turkey 59 M6
Eslohe (Sauerland) Germany 53 I3
Eslöv Sweden 45 H9
Esmā'īlī-ye Pā'īn Iran 88 E4
Eşme Turkey 59 M5
Esmeraldas Ecuador 142 C3
Esmont U.S.A. 135 F5
Esnagami Lake Canada 122 D4
Esnes France 52 D4
Espakeh Iran 89 F5
Espalion France 56 F4
España country Europe see Spain
Espanola Canada 122 E5
Espanola U.S.A. 131 B4
Espelkamp Germany 53 I2
Esperance Australia 109 C8
Esperance Bay Australia 109 C8
Esperanza research station Antarctica 152 A2
Esperanza Arg. 144 B8
Esperanza Mex. 127 F8
Espichel, Cabo c. Port. 57 B4
Espigão, Serra do mts Brazil 145 A4
Espigüete mt. Spain 57 D2
Espinazo Mex. 131 C7
Espinhaço, Serra do mts Brazil 145 C2
Espinosa Brazil 145 C1
Espírito Santo Brazil see Vila Velha
Espírito Santo state Brazil 145 C2
Espírito Santo do Pinhal Brazil 145 B3
Espiritu Santo i. Vanuatu 107 G3
Espíritu Santo, Isla i. Mex. 124 E7
Espoo Fin. 45 N6
Espuña mt. Spain 57 F5
Esqueda Mex. 127 F7
Esquel Arg. 144 B6

Esquimalt Canada 120 F5
Essaouira Morocco 96 C1
Essen Belgium 52 E3
Essen Germany 52 H3
Essen (Oldenburg) Germany 53 H2
Essequibo r. Guyana 143 G2
Essex Canada 134 D2
Essex *CA* U.S.A. 129 F4
Essex *MD* U.S.A. 135 G4
Essex *NY* U.S.A. 135 I1
Essexville U.S.A. 134 D2
Esslingen am Neckar Germany 53 J6
Es-Smara W. Sahara 96 B2
Esso Russia 65 Q4
Essoyla Russia 42 G3
Est, Canal de l' France 52 G6
Est, Île de l' *i.* Canada 123 J5
Est, Pointe de l' *pt* Canada 123 J4
Estación Marítima Antárctica *research station* Chile 152 A2
Estados, Isla de los *i.* Arg. 144 D8
Estahbān Iran 88 D4
Estância Brazil 143 K6
Estancia U.S.A. 127 G6
Estand, Kūh-e *mt.* Iran 89 F4
Estats, Pic d' *mt.* France/Spain 56 E5
Estcourt S. Africa 101 I5
Este *r.* Germany 53 J1
Estelí Nicaragua 137 G6
Estella Spain 57 E2
Estepa Spain 57 D5
Estepona Spain 57 D5
Esteras de Medinaceli Spain 57 E3
Esterhazy Canada 121 K5
Estero Bay U.S.A. 128 C4
Esteros Para. 144 D2
Estevan Canada 121 K5
Estevan Group *is* Canada 120 D4
Estherville U.S.A. 130 E3
Estill U.S.A. 133 D5
Eston Canada 121 I5
Estonia *country* Europe 45 N7
Estonskaya S.S.R. *country* Europe *see* Estonia
Estrées-St-Denis France 52 C5
Estrela Brazil 145 A5
Estrela, Serra da *mts* Port. 57 C3
Estrela do Sul Brazil 145 B2
Estrella *mt.* Spain 57 E4
Estrella, Punta *pt* Mex. 127 E7
Estremoz Port. 57 C4
Estrondo, Serra *hills* Brazil 143 I5
Etadunna Australia 111 B6
Etah India 82 D4
Étain France 52 F5
Étamamiou Canada 123 K4
Étampes France 56 F2
Étaples France 52 B4
Etawah *Rajasthan* India 82 D4
Etawah *Uttar Prad.* India 82 D4
Ethandakukhanya S. Africa 101 J4
Ethelbert Canada 121 K5
Ethel Creek Australia 109 C5
E'Thembini S. Africa 100 F5

▶Ethiopia *country* Africa 98 D3
2nd most populous country in Africa.

Etimesgut Turkey 90 D3
Etive, Loch *inlet* U.K. 50 D4

▶Etna, Mount *vol. Sicily* Italy 58 F6
Highest active volcano in Europe.

Etne Norway 45 D7
Etobicoke Canada 134 F2
Etolin Strait U.S.A. 118 B3
Etorofu-tō *i.* Russia *see* Iturup, Ostrov
Etosha National Park Namibia 99 B5
Etosha Pan *salt pan* Namibia 99 B5
Etoumbi Congo 98 B3
Etrek *r.* Iran/Turkm. *see* Atrek
Etrek Turkm. 88 D2
Étrépagny France 52 B5
Étretat France 49 H9
Ettelbruck Lux. 52 G5
Etten-Leur Neth. 52 E3
Ettlingen Germany 53 I6
Ettrick Water *r.* U.K. 50 F5
Euabalong Australia 112 C4
Euboea *i.* Greece *see* Evvoia
Eucla Australia 109 E7
Euclid U.S.A. 134 E3
Euclides da Cunha Brazil 143 K6
Eucumbene, Lake Australia 112 D6
Eudistes, Lac des *l.* Canada 123 I4
Eudora U.S.A. 131 F5
Eudunda Australia 111 B7
Eufaula *AL* U.S.A. 133 C6
Eufaula *OK* U.S.A. 131 E5
Eufaula Lake *resr* U.S.A. 131 E5
Eugene U.S.A. 126 C3
Eugenia, Punta *pt* Mex. 127 E8
Eugowra Australia 112 D4
Eulo Australia 112 B2
Eumungerie Australia 112 D3
Eungella Australia 110 E4
Eungella National Park Australia 110 E4
Eunice *LA* U.S.A. 131 E6
Eunice *NM* U.S.A. 131 C5
Eupen Belgium 52 G4

▶Euphrates *r.* Asia 91 G5
Longest river in western Asia. Also known as Al Furāt (Iraq/Syria) or Fırat (Turkey).

Eura Fin. 45 M6
Eure *r.* France 52 B5
Eureka *CA* U.S.A. 126 B4
Eureka *KS* U.S.A. 130 D4
Eureka *MT* U.S.A. 126 E2
Eureka *NV* U.S.A. 129 F2
Eureka *OH* U.S.A. 134 D4
Eureka *SD* U.S.A. 130 D2
Eureka *UT* U.S.A. 129 G2
Eureka Sound *sea chan.* Canada 119 J2
Eureka Springs U.S.A. 131 E4
Eureka Valley U.S.A. 128 E3
Euriowie Australia 111 C6
Euroa Australia 112 B6
Eurombah Australia 111 E5
Eurombah Creek *r.* Australia 111 E5
Europa, Île *i.* Indian Ocean 99 E6
Europa, Punta de *pt* Gibraltar *see* Europa Point
Europa Point Gibraltar 57 D5
Euskirchen Germany 52 G4
Eutaw U.S.A. 133 C5
Eutsuk Lake Canada 120 E4
Eutzsch Germany 53 M3
Eva Downs Australia 108 F4
Evans, Lac *l.* Canada 122 F4
Evans, Mount U.S.A. 126 G5
Evansburg Canada 120 H4
Evans City U.S.A. 134 E3
Evans Head Australia 112 F2
Evans Head *hd* Australia 112 F2
Evans Ice Stream Antarctica 152 L1
Evans Strait Canada 121 P2
Evanston *IL* U.S.A. 134 B2
Evanston *WY* U.S.A. 126 F4
Evansville Canada 122 E5
Evansville *IN* U.S.A. 134 B5
Evansville *WY* U.S.A. 126 G4
Evant U.S.A. 131 D6
Eva Perón Arg. *see* La Plata
Evart U.S.A. 134 C2
Evaton S. Africa 101 H4
Evaz Iran 88 D5
Evening Shade U.S.A. 131 F4
Evensk Russia 65 Q3
Everard, Lake *salt flat* Australia 111 A6
Everard, Mount Australia 109 F5
Everard Range *hills* Australia 109 F6
Everdingen Neth. 52 F3
Everek Turkey *see* Develi

▶Everest, Mount China/Nepal 83 F4
Highest mountain in Asia and the world.

Everett *PA* U.S.A. 135 F3
Everett *WA* U.S.A. 126 C3
Evergem Belgium 52 D3
Everglades *swamp* U.S.A. 133 D7
Everglades National Park U.S.A. 133 D7
Evergreen U.S.A. 133 C6
Evesham Australia 110 C4
Evesham U.K. 49 F6
Evesham, Vale of *valley* U.K. 49 F6
Evijärvi Fin. 44 M5
Evje Norway 45 E7
Évora Port. 57 C4
Evoron, Ozero *l.* Russia 74 E2
Évreux France 52 B5
Evros *r.* Bulg. *see* Maritsa
Evros *r.* Turkey *see* Meriç
Evrotas *r.* Greece 59 J6
Évry France 52 C6
Evrychou Cyprus 85 A2
Evrykhou Cyprus *see* Evrychou
Evvoia *i.* Greece 59 K5
Ewan Australia 110 D3
Ewaso Ngiro *r.* Kenya 98 E3
Ewe, Loch *b.* U.K. 50 D3
Ewing U.S.A. 134 D5
Ewo Congo 98 B4
Exaltación Bol. 142 E6
Excelsior S. Africa 101 H5
Excelsior Mountain U.S.A. 128 D2
Excelsior Mountains U.S.A. 128 D2
Exe *r.* U.K. 49 D8
Exeter Australia 112 E5
Exeter Canada 134 E2
Exeter U.K. 49 D8
Exeter *CA* U.S.A. 128 D3
Exeter *NH* U.S.A. 135 J2
Exeter Lake Canada 121 I1
Exloo Neth. 52 G2
Exminster U.K. 49 D8
Exmoor *hills* U.K. 49 D7
Exmoor National Park U.K. 49 D7
Exmore U.S.A. 135 H5
Exmouth Australia 108 A5
Exmouth U.K. 49 D8
Exmouth, Mount Australia 112 D3
Exmouth Gulf Australia 108 A5
Exmouth Lake Canada 120 H1
Exmouth Plateau *sea feature* Indian Ocean 149 P7
Expedition National Park Australia 110 E5
Expedition Range *mts* Australia 110 E5
Exploits *r.* Canada 123 L4
Exton U.S.A. 135 H3
Extremadura *aut. comm.* Spain 57 D4
Exuma Cays *is* Bahamas 133 E7
Exuma Sound *sea chan.* Bahamas 133 F7
Eyasi, Lake *salt l.* Tanz. 98 D4
Eyawadi *r.* Myanmar *see* Irrawaddy
Eye U.K. 49 I6
Eyeberry Lake Canada 121 J2
Eyelenoborsk Russia 41 S3
Eyemouth U.K. 50 G5
Eyjafjörður *inlet* Iceland 44 [inset 1]
Eyl Somalia 98 E3
Eylau Russia *see* Bagrationovsk
Eynsham U.K. 49 F7
Eyre Creek *watercourse* Australia 110 B5
Eyre Mountains N.Z. 113 B7
Eyre Peninsula Australia 111 A7
Eystrup Germany 53 J2
Eysturoy *i.* Faroe Is 44 [inset 2]
Ezakheni S. Africa 101 J5
Ezel U.S.A. 134 D5
Ezenzeleni S. Africa 101 I4
Ezequiel Ramos Mexía, Embalse *resr* Arg. 144 C5
Ezhou China 77 G2
Ezhva Russia 42 K3
Ezine Turkey 59 L5
Ezo *i.* Japan *see* Hokkaidō
Ezousa *r.* Cyprus 85 A2

F

Faaborg Denmark 45 G9
Faadhippolhu Maldives 84 B5
Faafxadhuun Somalia 98 E3
Fabens U.S.A. 127 G7
Faber, Mount *hill* Sing. 71 [inset]
Faber Lake Canada 120 G2
Fåborg Denmark *see* Faaborg
Fabriano Italy 58 E3
Faches-Thumesnil France 52 D4
Fachi Niger 96 E3
Fada Chad 97 F3
Fada-N'Gourma Burkina Faso 96 D3
Fadghāmī Syria 91 F4
Fadiffolu Atoll Maldives *see* Faadhippolhu
Fadippolu Atoll Maldives *see* Faadhippolhu
Faenza Italy 58 D2
Færoerne *terr.* N. Atlantic Ocean *see* Faroe Islands
Faeroes *terr.* N. Atlantic Ocean *see* Faroe Islands
Făgăraş Romania 59 K2

▶Fagatogo American Samoa 107 I3
Capital of American Samoa.

Fagersta Sweden 45 I7
Fagne *reg.* Belgium 52 E4
Fagurhólsmýri Iceland 44 [inset 1]
Fagwir South Sudan 86 D8
Fahraj Iran 88 D4
Fā'id Egypt 90 D5
Fairbanks U.S.A. 118 D3
Fairborn U.S.A. 134 C4
Fairbury U.S.A. 130 D3
Fairchance U.S.A. 134 F4
Fairfax U.S.A. 135 G4
Fairfield *CA* U.S.A. 128 B2
Fairfield *IA* U.S.A. 130 F3
Fairfield *ID* U.S.A. 126 E4
Fairfield *IL* U.S.A. 130 F4
Fairfield *OH* U.S.A. 134 C4
Fairfield *TX* U.S.A. 131 D6
Fair Haven U.S.A. 135 I2
Fair Head *hd* U.K. 51 F2
Fair Isle *i.* U.K. 50 H1
Fairlee U.S.A. 135 I2
Fairlie N.Z. 113 C7
Fairmont *MN* U.S.A. 130 E3
Fairmont *WV* U.S.A. 134 E4
Fair Oaks U.S.A. 134 B3
Fairview Australia 110 D2
Fairview Canada 120 G3
Fairview *MI* U.S.A. 134 C1
Fairview *OK* U.S.A. 131 D4
Fairview *PA* U.S.A. 134 E2
Fairview *UT* U.S.A. 129 H2
Fairview Park *H.K.* China 77 [inset]
Fairweather, Cape U.S.A. 120 B3
Fairweather, Mount Canada/U.S.A. 120 B3
Fais *i.* Micronesia 69 K5
Faisalabad Pak. 89 I4
Faissault France 52 E5
Faith U.S.A. 130 C2
Faīzābād Afgh. 89 H2
Faizabad Afgh. *see* Faīzābād
Faizabad India 83 E4
Fakaofo *atoll* Tokelau 107 I2
Fakaofu *atoll* Tokelau *see* Fakaofo
Fakenham U.K. 49 H6
Fåker Sweden 44 I5
Fakfak Indon. 69 I7
Fakhrābād Iran 88 D4
Fakiragram India 83 G4
Fako *vol.* Cameroon *see* Cameroun, Mont
Fal *r.* U.K. 49 C8
Falaba Sierra Leone 96 B4
Falaise Lake Canada 120 G2
Falam Myanmar 70 A2
Falāvarjān Iran 88 C3
Falcon Lake Canada 121 M5
Falcon Lake *l.* Mex./U.S.A. 131 D7
Falenki Russia 42 K4
Falfurrias U.S.A. 131 D7
Falher Canada 120 G4
Falkenberg Sweden 45 H8
Falkenberg/Elster Germany 53 N3
Falkenhagen Germany 53 M1
Falkenhain Germany 53 M3
Falkensee Germany 53 N2
Falkenstein Germany 53 M5
Falkirk U.K. 50 F5
Falkland U.K. 50 F4
Falkland Escarpment *sea feature* S. Atlantic Ocean 148 E9

▶Falkland Islands *terr.* S. Atlantic Ocean 144 E8
United Kingdom Overseas Territory.

Falkland Plateau *sea feature* S. Atlantic Ocean 148 E9
Falkland Sound *sea chan.* Falkland Is 144 D8
Falköping Sweden 45 H7
Fallbrook U.S.A. 128 E5
Fallieres Coast Antarctica 152 L2
Falling Spring U.S.A. 134 E5
Fallon U.S.A. 128 D2
Fall River U.S.A. 135 J3
Fall River Pass U.S.A. 126 G4
Falls City U.S.A. 130 E3
Falmouth U.K. 49 B8
Falmouth *KY* U.S.A. 134 C4
Falmouth *VA* U.S.A. 135 G4
False *r.* Canada 123 H2
False Bay S. Africa 100 D8
False Point India 83 F5
Falster *i.* Denmark 45 G9
Fălticeni Romania 43 E7
Falun Sweden 45 I6
Famagusta Cyprus 85 A2
Famagusta Bay Cyprus *see* Ammochostos Bay
Fameck France 52 G5
Fāmenīn Iran 88 C3
Fame Range *hills* Australia 109 C6
Family Lake Canada 121 M5
Family Well Australia 108 D5
Fāmūr, Daryācheh-ye *l.* Iran 88 C4
Fana Mali 96 C3
Fanad Head *hd* Ireland 51 E2
Fandriana Madag. 99 E6
Fane *r.* Ireland 51 F4
Fang Thai. 70 B3
Fangcheng *Guangxi* China 77 F4
Fangcheng *Henan* China 77 G1
Fangchenggang China *see* Fangcheng
Fangdou Shan *mts* China 77 F2
Fangliao Taiwan 77 I4
Fangshan Taiwan 77 I4
Fangxian China 77 F1
Fangzheng China 74 C3
Fankuai China 77 F2
Fankuaidian China *see* Fankuai
Fanling *H.K.* China 77 [inset]
Fannich, Loch *l.* U.K. 50 D3
Fannūj Iran 89 E5
Fano Italy 58 E3
Fanshan *Anhui* China 77 H2
Fanshan *Zhejiang* China 77 I3
Fanum Fortunae Italy *see* Fano
Faqīh Aḥmadān Iran 88 C4
Farab Turkm. *see* Farap
Faraba Mali 96 B3
Faradofay Madag. *see* Tôlañaro
Farafangana Madag. 99 E6
Farāfirah, Wāḥāt al *oasis* Egypt 86 C4
Farafra Oasis *oasis* Egypt *see* Farāfirah, Wāḥāt al
Farāh Afgh. 89 F3
Faraḥābād Iran *see* Khezerābād
Farallon de Medinilla *i.* N. Mariana Is 69 L3
Farallon de Pajaros *vol.* N. Mariana Is 69 K2
Farallones de Cali, Parque Nacional *nat. park* Col. 142 C3
Faranah Guinea 96 B3
Farap Turkm. 89 F2
Fararah Oman 87 I6
Farasān, Jazā'ir *is* Saudi Arabia 86 F6
Faraulep *atoll* Micronesia 69 K5
Fareham U.K. 49 F8
Farewell, Cape Greenland 119 N3
Farewell, Cape N.Z. 113 D5
Farewell Spit N.Z. 113 D5
Färgelanda Sweden 45 H7
Farghona Uzbek. *see* Farg'ona
Fargo U.S.A. 130 D2
Farg'ona Uzbek. 87 L1
Faribault U.S.A. 130 E2
Faribault, Lac *l.* Canada 123 H2
Faridabad India 82 D3
Faridkot India 82 C3
Faridpur Bangl. 83 G5
Farīmān Iran 89 E3
Farkhār Afgh. 89 H2
Farkhor Tajik. 89 H2
Farmahīn Iran 88 C3
Farmer Island Canada 122 E2
Farmerville U.S.A. 131 E5
Farmington Canada 120 F4
Farmington *ME* U.S.A. 135 J1
Farmington *MO* U.S.A. 130 F4
Farmington *NH* U.S.A. 135 J2
Farmington *NM* U.S.A. 129 I3
Farmington Hills U.S.A. 134 D2
Far Mountain Canada 120 E4
Farmville U.S.A. 135 F5
Farnborough U.K. 49 G7
Farne Islands U.K. 48 F3
Farnham U.K. 49 G7
Farnham, Lake *salt flat* Australia 109 D6
Farnham, Mount Canada 120 G5
Faro Brazil 143 G4
Faro Canada 120 C2
Faro Port. 57 C5
Fårö *i.* Sweden 45 K8
Faroe-Iceland Ridge *sea feature* Arctic Ocean 153 I2

▶Faroe Islands *terr.* N. Atlantic Ocean 44 [inset 2]
Self-governing Danish territory.

Fårösund Sweden 45 K8
Farquhar, Atoll de *is* Seychelles 99 F5
Farquharson Tableland *hills* Australia 109 C6
Farrāshband Iran 88 D4
Farr Bay Antarctica 152 F2
Farristown U.S.A. 134 C5
Farsund Norway 45 E7
Fārūj Iran 88 E2
Farwell *MI* U.S.A. 134 C2
Farwell *TX* U.S.A. 131 C5
Fasā Iran 88 D4
Fasano Italy 58 G4
Faşikan Geçidi *pass* Turkey 85 A1
Faßberg Germany 53 K2
Fastiv Ukr. 43 F6
Fastov Ukr. *see* Fastiv
Fatehabad India 82 C3
Fatehgarh India 82 D4
Fatehpur *Rajasthan* India 82 C4
Fatehpur *Uttar Prad.* India 82 E4
Fatick Senegal 96 B3
Fattoilep *atoll* Micronesia *see* Faraulep
Faughan *r.* U.K. 51 E2
Faulkton U.S.A. 130 D2
Faulquemont France 52 G5
Fauresmith S. Africa 101 G5
Fauske Norway 44 I3
Faust Canada 120 H4
Fawcett Canada 120 H4
Fawley U.K. 49 F8
Fawn *r.* Canada 121 N4
Faxaflói *b.* Iceland 44 [inset 1]
Faxälven *r.* Sweden 44 J5
Faya Chad 97 E3
Fayette *AL* U.S.A. 133 C5
Fayette *MO* U.S.A. 130 E4
Fayette *MS* U.S.A. 131 F6
Fayette *OH* U.S.A. 134 C3
Fayetteville *AR* U.S.A. 131 E4
Fayetteville *NC* U.S.A. 133 E5
Fayetteville *TN* U.S.A. 133 C5
Fayetteville *WV* U.S.A. 134 E4
Fâyid Egypt *see* Fā'id
Faylakah *i.* Kuwait 88 C4
Fazao Malfakassa, Parc National de *nat. park* Togo 96 D4
Fazilka India 82 C3
Fazrān, Jabal *hill* Saudi Arabia 88 C5
Fdérik Mauritania 96 B2
Fead Group *is* P.N.G. *see* Nuguria Islands
Feale *r.* Ireland 51 C5
Fear, Cape U.S.A. 133 E5
Featherston N.Z. 113 E5
Feathertop, Mount Australia 112 C6
Fécamp France 56 E2
Federal District *admin. dist.* Brazil *see* Distrito Federal
Federalsburg U.S.A. 135 H4
Federated Malay States *country* Asia *see* Malaysia
Fedusar India 82 C4
Fehet Lake Canada 121 M1
Fehmarn *i.* Germany 47 M3
Fehrbellin Germany 53 M2
Feia, Lagoa *lag.* Brazil 145 C3
Feicheng China *see* Feixian
Feijó Brazil 142 D5
Feilding N.Z. 113 E5
Feio *r.* Brazil *see* Aguapeí
Feira de Santana Brazil 145 D1
Feixi China 77 H2
Feixian China 77 H1
Fejd el Abiod *pass* Alg. 58 B6
Feke Turkey 90 D3
Felanitx Spain 57 H4
Feldberg Germany 53 N1
Feldberg *mt.* Germany 47 L7
Feldkirch Austria 47 L7
Feldkirchen in Kärnten Austria 47 O7
Felidhe Atholhu Maldives 81 D11
Felidu Atoll Maldives *see* Felidhe Atholhu
Felipe C. Puerto Mex. 136 G5
Felixlândia Brazil 145 B2
Felixstowe U.K. 49 I7
Felixton S. Africa 101 J5
Fellowsville U.S.A. 134 F4
Felsina Italy *see* Bologna
Felton U.S.A. 135 H4
Feltre Italy 58 D1
Femunden *l.* Norway 44 G5
Femundsmarka Nasjonalpark *nat. park* Norway 44 H5
Fenaio, Punta del *pt* Italy 58 D3
Fence Lake U.S.A. 129 I4
Fener Burnu *hd* Turkey 85 B1
Fénérive Madag. *see* Fenoarivo Atsinanana
Fengari *mt.* Greece 59 K4
Fengcheng *Fujian* China *see* Yongding
Fengcheng *Fujian* China *see* Anxi
Fengcheng *Fujian* China *see* Lianjiang
Fengcheng *Guangdong* China *see* Xinfeng
Fengcheng *Guangxi* China *see* Fengshan
Fengcheng *Guizhou* China *see* Tianzhu
Fengcheng *Jiangxi* China 77 G2
Fenggang *Fujian* China *see* Shaxian
Fenggang *Guizhou* China 76 E3
Fenggang *Jiangxi* China *see* Yihuang
Fengguang China 74 B3
Fenghuang China 77 F3
Fengjiaba China *see* Wangcang
Fengjie China 77 F2
Fengkai China 77 F4
Fenglin Taiwan 77 I4
Fengman China 74 B4
Fengming *Shaanxi* China *see* Qishan
Fengming *Sichuan* China *see* Pengshan
Fengqing China 76 C3
Fengshan *Fujian* China *see* Luoyuan
Fengshan *Guangxi* China 76 E3
Fengshan *Hubei* China *see* Luotian
Fengshan *Yunnan* China *see* Fengqing
Fengshuba Shuiku *resr* China 77 G3
Fengtongzhai Nature Reserve *nature res.* China 76 D2
Fengxian China 76 E1
Fengxiang *Heilong.* China *see* Luobei
Fengxiang *Yunnan* China *see* Lincang
Fengyang China 77 H1
Fengyuan Taiwan 77 I3
Fengzhen China 73 K4
Feni Bangl. 83 G5
Feni Islands P.N.G. 106 F2
Fennville U.S.A. 134 B2
Feno, Capo di *c. Corsica* France 56 I6
Fenoarivo Atsinanana Madag. 99 E5
Fenshui Guan *pass* China 77 H3
Fenton U.S.A. 134 D2
Fenua Ura *atoll* Fr. Polynesia *see* Manuae
Fenyi China 77 G3
Feodosiya Crimea 90 D1
Fer, Cap de *c.* Alg. 58 B6
Férai Greece *see* Feres
Ferdows Iran 88 E3
Fère-Champenoise France 52 D6
Feres Greece 59 L4
Fergus Canada 134 E2
Fergus Falls U.S.A. 130 D2
Ferguson Lake Canada 121 L2
Fergusson Island P.N.G. 106 F2
Fériana Tunisia 58 C7
Ferizaj Kosovo 59 I3
Ferkessédougou Côte d'Ivoire 96 C4
Fermo Italy 58 E3
Fermont Canada 123 I3
Fermoselle Spain 57 C3
Fermoy Ireland 51 D5
Fernandina, Isla *i. Galápagos* Ecuador 142 [inset]
Fernandina Beach U.S.A. 133 D6
Fernando de Magallanes, Parque Nacional *nat. park* Chile 144 B8
Fernando de Noronha *i.* Brazil 148 F6
Fernandópolis Brazil 145 A3
Fernando Poó *i.* Equat. Guinea *see* Bioko
Fernão Dias Brazil 145 B2
Ferndale U.S.A. 128 A1
Ferndown U.K. 49 F8
Fernlee Australia 112 C2
Fernley U.S.A. 128 D2
Ferns Ireland 51 F5
Ferozepore India *see* Firozpur
Ferrara Italy 58 D2
Ferreira Gomes Brazil 143 H3
Ferro, Capo *c. Sardinia* Italy 58 C4
Ferrol Spain 57 B2
Ferron U.S.A. 129 H2
Ferros Brazil 145 C2
Ferryland Canada 123 L5
Ferryville Tunisia *see* Menzel Bourguiba
Fertő-tavi *nat. park* Hungary 58 G1
Ferwerd Neth. 52 F1
Ferwert Neth. *see* Ferwerd
Fès Morocco 54 D5
Feshi Dem. Rep. Congo 99 B4
Fessenden U.S.A. 130 D2
Festus U.S.A. 130 F4
Fété Bowé Senegal 96 B3
Fethard Ireland 51 E5
Fethiye *Malatya* Turkey *see* Yazıhan
Fethiye *Muğla* Turkey 59 M6
Fethiye Körfezi *b.* Turkey 59 M6
Fetisovo Kazakh. 91 I2
Fetlar *i.* U.K. 50 [inset]
Fettercairn U.K. 50 G4
Feucht Germany 53 L5
Feuchtwangen Germany 53 K5
Feuilles, Rivière aux *r.* Canada 123 H2
Fevral'sk Russia 74 C1
Fevzipaşa Turkey 90 E3
Feyẓābād *Kermān* Iran 88 D4
Feyẓābād *Khorāsān-e Raẓavī* Iran 88 E3
Fez Morocco *see* Fès
Fezzan *hist. area* Libya 96 E2
Ffestiniog U.K. 49 D6
Fianarantsoa Madag. 99 E6
Fichē Eth. 98 D3
Fichtelgebirge *hills* Germany 53 M4
Field U.S.A. 134 D5
Fier Albania 59 H4
Fiery Creek *r.* Australia 110 B3
Fiery Cross Reef S. China Sea 68 E5
Fife Lake U.S.A. 134 C1
Fife Ness *pt* U.K. 50 G4
Fifield Australia 112 C4
Fifth Meridian Canada 120 H3
Figeac France 56 F4
Figueira da Foz Port. 57 B3
Figueras Spain *see* Figueres
Figueres Spain 57 H2
Figuig Morocco 54 D5
Figuil Cameroon 97 E4

▶Fiji *country* S. Pacific Ocean 107 H3
4th most populous and 5th largest country in Oceania.

Fīk' Eth. 98 E3
Filadelfia Para. 144 D2
Filchner Ice Shelf Antarctica 152 A1
Filey U.K. 48 G4
Filibe Bulg. *see* Plovdiv
Filingué Niger 96 D3
Filipinas *country* Asia *see* Philippines
Filippiada Greece 59 I5
Filipstad Sweden 45 I7
Fillan Norway 44 F5
Fillmore *CA* U.S.A. 128 D4
Fillmore *UT* U.S.A. 129 G2
Fils *r.* Germany 53 J6
Fītu Eth. 98 E3
Fimbul Ice Shelf Antarctica 152 C2
Finch Canada 135 H1
Findhorn *r.* U.K. 50 F3
Fındık Turkey 88 A2
Findlay U.S.A. 134 D3
Fine U.S.A. 135 H1
Fīn-e 'Olyā Iran 88 C3
Finger Lake Canada 121 M4
Finger Lakes U.S.A. 135 G2
Finike Turkey 59 N6
Finike Körfezi *b.* Turkey 59 N6
Finisterre Spain *see* Fisterra
Finisterre, Cabo *c.* Spain *see* Finisterre, Cape
Finisterre, Cape Spain 57 B2
Finke *watercourse* Australia 110 A5
Finke, Mount *hill* Australia 109 F7
Finke Bay Australia 108 E3
Finke Gorge National Park Australia 109 F6
Finland *country* Europe 44 O5
Finland, Gulf of Europe 45 M7

▶Finlay *r.* Canada 120 E3
Part of the Mackenzie-Peace-Finlay, the 2nd longest river in North America.

Finlay, Mount Canada 120 E3
Finlay Forks Canada 120 F4
Finley U.S.A. 130 D2
Finn *r.* Ireland 51 E3
Finne *ridge* Germany 53 L3
Finnigan, Mount Australia 110 D2
Finniss, Cape Australia 109 F8
Finnmarksvidda *reg.* Norway 44 H2
Finnsnes Norway 44 J2
Fins Oman 88 E6
Finschhafen P.N.G. 69 L8
Finspång Sweden 45 I7
Fintona U.K. 51 E3
Finucane Range *hills* Australia 110 C4
Fionn Loch *l.* U.K. 50 D3
Fionnphort U.K. 50 C4
Fiordland National Park N.Z. 113 A7
Fir *reg.* Saudi Arabia 88 B4
Fırat *r.* Asia *see* Euphrates
Firebaugh U.S.A. 128 C3
Firedrake Lake Canada 121 J2
Firenze Italy *see* Florence
Fireside Canada 120 E3
Firk, Sha'īb *watercourse* Iraq 91 G5
Firmat Arg. 144 D4
Firminy France 56 G4
Firmum Italy *see* Fermo
Firmum Picenum Italy *see* Fermo
Firovo Russia 42 G4
Firozabad India 82 D4
Firozkoh *reg.* Afgh. 89 G3
Firozpur India 82 C3
First State National Historical Site *nat. park* U.S.A. 135 H4
Fīrūzābād Iran 88 D4
Fīrūzkūh Iran 88 D3
Firyuza Turkm. *see* Pōwrize
Fischbach Germany 53 H5
Fischersbrunn Namibia 100 B3
Fish *watercourse* Namibia 100 C5
Fisher (abandoned) Australia 109 E7
Fisher Bay Antarctica 152 G2
Fisher Glacier Antarctica 152 E2
Fisher River Canada 121 L5
Fishers U.S.A. 134 B4
Fishers Island U.S.A. 135 J3

Fisher Strait Canada 119 J3
Fishguard U.K. 49 C7
Fishing Creek U.S.A. 135 G4
Fishing Lake Canada 121 M4
Fish Lake Canada 120 F2
Fish Point U.S.A. 134 D2
Fish Ponds *H.K.* China 77 [inset]
Fiske, Cape Antarctica 152 L2
Fiskenæsset Greenland *see* Qeqertarsuatsiaat
Fismes France 52 D5
Fisterra Spain 57 B2
Fisterra, Cabo *c.* Spain *see* Finisterre, Cape
Fitchburg U.S.A. 130 F3
Fitri, Lac *l.* Chad 97 E3
Fitzgerald Canada 121 I3
Fitzgerald U.S.A. 133 D6
Fitzgerald River National Park Australia 109 B8
Fitz Hugh Sound *sea chan.* Canada 120 D5
Fitz Roy Arg. 144 C7
Fitzroy *r.* Australia 108 C4
Fitz Roy, Cerro *mt.* Arg. 144 B7
Fitzroy Crossing Australia 108 D4
Fitzwilliam Island Canada 134 E1
Fiume Croatia *see* Rijeka
Fivemiletown U.K. 51 E3
Five Points U.S.A. 128 C3
Fizi Dem. Rep. Congo 99 C4
Fizuli Azer. *see* Füzuli
Flå Norway 45 F6
Flagstaff S. Africa 101 I6
Flagstaff U.S.A. 129 H4
Flagstaff Lake U.S.A. 132 G2
Flaherty Island Canada 122 F2
Flambeau *r.* U.S.A. 130 F2
Flamborough Head *hd* U.K. 48 G4
Fläming *hills* Germany 53 M2
Flaming Gorge Reservoir U.S.A. 126 F4
Flaminksvlei *salt pan* S. Africa 100 E6
Flanagan *r.* Canada 121 M4
Flandre *reg.* France 52 C4
Flannagan Lake U.S.A. 134 D5
Flannan Isles U.K. 50 B2
Flåsjön *l.* Sweden 44 I4
Flat *r.* Canada 120 E2
Flat *r.* U.S.A. 134 C2
Flat Creek Canada 120 B2
Flathead *r.* U.S.A. 124 E2
Flathead Lake U.S.A. 126 E3
Flatiron *mt.* U.S.A. 126 E3
Flat Island S. China Sea 68 F4
Flat Lick U.S.A. 134 D5
Flattery, Cape Australia 110 D2
Flattery, Cape U.S.A. 126 B2
Flat Top *mt.* Canada 120 B2
Flatwillow Creek *r.* U.S.A. 126 G3
Flatwoods U.S.A. 134 E4
Fleetmark Germany 53 L2
Fleetwood Australia 110 D4
Fleetwood U.K. 48 D5
Fleetwood U.S.A. 135 H3
Flekkefjord Norway 45 E7
Flemingsburg U.S.A. 134 D4
Flemington U.S.A. 135 H3
Flen Sweden 45 J7
Flensburg Germany 47 L3
Flers France 56 D2
Flesherton Canada 134 E1
Fletcher Lake Canada 121 I2
Fletcher Peninsula Antarctica 152 L2
Fleur de Lys Canada 123 K4
Fleur-de-May, Lac *l.* Canada 123 I4
Flinders *r.* Australia 110 C3
Flinders Chase National Park Australia 111 B7
Flinders Group National Park Australia 110 D2
Flinders Island Australia 111 [inset]
Flinders Passage Australia 110 E3
Flinders Ranges *mts* Australia 111 B7
Flinders Ranges National Park Australia 111 B6
Flinders Reefs Australia 110 E3
Flin Flon Canada 121 K4
Flint U.K. 48 D5
Flint U.S.A. 134 D2
Flint *r.* U.S.A. 133 C6
Flint Island Kiribati 151 J6
Flinton Australia 112 D1
Flisa Norway 45 H6

▶Flissingskiy, Mys *c.* Russia 64 H2
Most easterly point of Europe.

Flixecourt France 52 C4
Flodden U.K. 48 E3
Flöha Germany 53 N4
Flood Range *mts* Antarctica 152 J1
Flora *r.* Australia 108 E3
Flora U.S.A. 134 B3
Florac France 56 F4
Florala U.S.A. 133 C6
Florange France 52 G5
Flora Reef Australia 110 D3
Floreana, Isla *i.* *Galápagos* Ecuador 142 [inset]
Florence Italy 58 D3
Florence *AL* U.S.A. 133 C5
Florence *AZ* U.S.A. 129 H5
Florence *CO* U.S.A. 127 G5
Florence *OR* U.S.A. 126 B4
Florence *SC* U.S.A. 133 E5
Florence *WI* U.S.A. 130 F2
Florence Junction U.S.A. 129 H5
Florencia Col. 142 C3
Florennes Belgium 52 E4
Florentia Italy *see* Florence
Florentino Ameghino, Embalse *resr* Arg. 144 C6
Flores *r.* Arg. 144 E5
Flores Guat. 136 G5
Flores *i.* Indon. 108 C2
Flores, Laut *sea* Indon. 108 B1
Flores Island Canada 120 E5
Flores Sea Indon. *see* Flores, Laut
Floresta Brazil 143 K5
Floresville U.S.A. 131 D6
Floriano Brazil 143 J5
Florianópolis Brazil 145 A4
Florida Uruguay 144 E4
Florida *state* U.S.A. 133 D6
Florida, Straits of Bahamas/U.S.A. 133 D8
Florida Bay U.S.A. 133 D7
Florida City U.S.A. 133 D7
Florida Islands Solomon Is 107 G2
Florida Keys *is* U.S.A. 133 D7
Florin U.S.A. 128 C2
Florina Greece 59 I4
Florissant U.S.A. 130 F4
Florø Norway 45 D6
Flour Lake Canada 123 I3
Floyd U.S.A. 134 E5
Floyd, Mount U.S.A. 129 G4
Floydada U.S.A. 131 C5
Fluessen *l.* Neth. 52 F2
Flushing Neth. *see* Vlissingen
Fly *r.* P.N.G. 69 K8
Flying Fish, Cape Antarctica 152 K2
Flying Mountain U.S.A. 129 I6
Flylân *i.* Neth. *see* Vlieland
Foam Lake Canada 121 K5
Foča Bos. & Herz. 58 H3
Foça Turkey 59 L5
Fochabers U.K. 50 F3
Focşani Romania 59 L2
Fogang China 77 G4
Foggia Italy 58 F4
Fogi Indon. 69 H7
Fogo *i.* Cape Verde 96 [inset]
Fogo Island Canada 123 L4
Foinaven *hill* U.K. 50 E2
Foix France 56 E5
Folda *sea chan.* Norway 44 I3
Foldereid Norway 44 H4
Foldfjorden *sea chan.* Norway 44 G4
Folegandros *i.* Greece 59 K6
Foleyet Canada 122 E4
Foley Island Canada 119 K3
Foligno Italy 58 E3
Folkestone U.K. 49 I7
Folkingham U.K. 49 G6
Folkston U.S.A. 133 D6
Folldal Norway 44 G5
Follonica Italy 58 D3
Folsom Lake U.S.A. 128 C2
Fomboni Comoros 99 E5
Fomento Cuba 133 E8
Fomin Russia 43 I7
Fominskaya Russia 42 K2
Fominskoye Russia 42 I4
Fonda U.S.A. 135 H2
Fond-du-Lac Canada 121 J3
Fond du Lac *r.* Canada 121 J3
Fond du Lac U.S.A. 134 A2
Fondevila Spain 57 B3
Fondi Italy 58 E4
Fonni *Sardinia* Italy 58 C4
Fonsagrada Spain *see* A Fonsagrada
Fonseca, Golfo do *b.* Central America 136 G6
Fontaine Lake Canada 121 J3
Fontanges Canada 123 H3
Fontas Canada 120 F3
Fontas *r.* Canada 120 F3
Fonte Boa Brazil 142 E4
Fonteneau, Lac *l.* Canada 123 J4
Fontur *pt* Iceland 44 [inset 1]
Foochow China *see* Fuzhou
Foot's Bay Canada 134 F1
Foping China 77 F1
Foraker, Mount U.S.A. 118 C3
Foraulep *atoll* Micronesia *see* Faraulep
Forbes Australia 112 D4
Forbes, Mount Canada 120 G4
Forchheim Germany 53 L5
Ford *r.* U.S.A. 132 C2
Ford City U.S.A. 128 D4
Førde Norway 45 D6
Forde Lake Canada 121 L2
Fordham U.K. 49 H6
Fordingbridge U.K. 49 F8
Ford Range *mts* Antarctica 152 J1
Fords Bridge Australia 112 B2
Fordsville U.S.A. 134 B5
Fordyce U.S.A. 131 E5
Forécariah Guinea 96 B4
Forel, Mont *mt.* Greenland 119 O3
Foreland *hd* U.K. 49 F8
Foreland Point U.K. 49 D7
Foremost Canada 126 F2
Foresight Mountain Canada 120 E4
Forest Canada 134 E2
Forest *MS* U.S.A. 131 F5
Forest *OH* U.S.A. 134 D3
Forestburg Canada 121 H4
Forest Creek *r.* Australia 110 C3
Foreste Casentinesi, Monte Falterona e Campigna, Parco Nazionale delle *nat. park* Italy 58 D3
Forest Hill Australia 112 C5
Forest Ranch U.S.A. 128 C2
Forestville Canada 123 H4
Forestville *CA* U.S.A. 128 B2
Forestville *MI* U.S.A. 134 D2
Forfar U.K. 50 G4
Forgan U.S.A. 131 C4
Forges-les-Eaux France 52 B5
Forillon, Parc National de *nat. park* Canada 123 I4
Forked River U.S.A. 135 H4
Forks U.S.A. 126 B3
Fork Union U.S.A. 135 F5
Forlì Italy 58 E2
Forman U.S.A. 130 D2
Formby U.K. 48 D5
Formentera *i.* Spain 57 G4
Formentor, Cap de *c.* Spain 57 H4
Formerie France 52 B5
Former Yugoslav Republic of Macedonia *country* Europe *see* Macedonia
Formiga Brazil 145 B3
Formosa Arg. 144 E3
Formosa *country* Asia *see* Taiwan
Formosa Brazil 145 B1
Formosa, Serra *hills* Brazil 143 G6
Formosa Bay Kenya *see* Ungwana Bay
Formosa Strait China/Taiwan *see* Taiwan Strait
Formoso *r.* *Bahia* Brazil 145 B1
Formoso *r.* *Tocantins* Brazil 145 A1
Fornos Moz. 101 L2
Forres U.K. 50 F3
Forrest *Vic.* Australia 112 A7
Forrest *W.A.* Australia 109 E7
Forrestal Range *mts* Antarctica 152 A1
Forrest City U.S.A. 131 F5
Forrest Lake Canada 121 I3
Forrest Lakes *salt flat* Australia 109 E7
Fors Sweden 44 J5
Forsayth Australia 110 C3
Forsnäs Sweden 44 M3
Forssa Fin. 45 M6
Forster Australia 112 F4
Forsyth *GA* U.S.A. 133 D5
Forsyth *MT* U.S.A. 126 G3
Forsyth Range *hills* Australia 110 C4
Fort Abbas Pak. 89 I4
Fort Albany Canada 122 E3
Fortaleza Brazil 143 K4
Fort Amsterdam U.S.A. *see* New York
Fort Archambault Chad *see* Sarh
Fort Ashby U.S.A. 135 F4
Fort Assiniboine Canada 120 H4
Fort Augustus U.K. 50 E3
Fort Beaufort S. Africa 101 H7
Fort Benton U.S.A. 126 F3
Fort Brabant Canada *see* Tuktoyaktuk
Fort Bragg U.S.A. 128 B2
Fort Branch U.S.A. 134 B4
Fort Carillon U.S.A. *see* Ticonderoga
Fort Charlet Alg. *see* Djanet
Fort Chimo Canada *see* Kuujjuaq
Fort Chipewyan Canada 121 I3
Fort Collins U.S.A. 126 G4
Fort-Coulonge Canada 122 F5
Fort Crampel Cent. Afr. Rep. *see* Kaga Bandoro
Fort-Dauphin Madag. *see* Tôlañaro
Fort Davis U.S.A. 131 C6

▶Fort-de-France Martinique 137 L6
Capital of Martinique.

Fort de Kock Indon. *see* Bukittinggi
Fort de Polignac Alg. *see* Illizi
Fort Dodge U.S.A. 130 E3
Fort Duchesne U.S.A. 129 I1
Fort Edward U.S.A. 135 I2
Fortescue *r.* Australia 108 B5
Forte Veneza Brazil 143 H5
Fort Flatters Alg. *see* Bordj Omer Driss
Fort Foureau Cameroon *see* Kousséri
Fort Franklin Canada *see* Déline
Fort Gardel Alg. *see* Zaouatallaz
Fort Gay U.S.A. 134 D4
Fort George Canada *see* Chisasibi
Fort Good Hope Canada 118 F3
Fort Gouraud Mauritania *see* Fdérik
Forth *r.* U.K. 50 F4
Forth, Firth of *est.* U.K. 50 F4
Fort Hertz Myanmar *see* Putao
Fortification Range *mts* U.S.A. 129 F2
Fortín General Mendoza Para. 144 D2
Fortín Leonida Escobar Para. 144 D2
Fortín Madrejón Para. 144 E2
Fortín Pilcomayo Arg. 144 D2
Fortín Ravelo Bol. 142 F7
Fortín Sargento Primero Leyes Arg. 144 E2
Fortín Suárez Arana Bol. 142 F7
Fortín Teniente Juan Echauri López Para. 144 D2
Fort Jameson Zambia *see* Chipata
Fort Johnston Malawi *see* Mangochi
Fort Kent U.S.A. 132 G2
Fort Lamy Chad *see* Ndjamena
Fort Laperrine Alg. *see* Tamanrasset
Fort Laramie U.S.A. 126 G4
Fort Lauderdale U.S.A. 133 D7
Fort Liard Canada 120 F2
Fort Mackay Canada 121 I3
Fort Macleod Canada 120 H5
Fort Madison U.S.A. 130 F3
Fort Manning Malawi *see* Mchinji
Fort McMurray Canada 121 I3
Fort McPherson Canada 118 E3
Fort Monroe National Monument *nat. park* U.S.A. 135 G5
Fort Morgan U.S.A. 130 C3
Fort Munro Pak. 89 H4
Fort Myers U.S.A. 133 D7
Fort Myers Beach U.S.A. 133 D7
Fort Nelson Canada 120 F3
Fort Nelson *r.* Canada 120 F3
Fort Norman Canada *see* Tulita
Fort Orange U.S.A. *see* Albany
Fort Payne U.S.A. 133 C5
Fort Peck U.S.A. 126 G2
Fort Peck Reservoir U.S.A. 126 G3
Fort Pierce U.S.A. 133 D7
Fort Portal Uganda 98 D3
Fort Providence Canada 120 G2
Fort Randall U.S.A. *see* Cold Bay
Fort Resolution Canada 120 H2
Fortrose N.Z. 113 B8
Fortrose U.K. 50 E3
Fort Rosebery Zambia *see* Mansa
Fort Rousset Congo *see* Owando
Fort Rupert Canada *see* Waskaganish
Fort St James Canada 120 E4
Fort St John Canada 120 F3
Fort Sandeman Pak. *see* Zhob
Fort Saskatchewan Canada 120 H4
Fort Scott U.S.A. 130 E4
Fort Severn Canada 122 D2
Fort-Shevchenko Kazakh. 78 E2
Fort Simpson Canada 120 F2
Fort Smith Canada 121 H2
Fort Smith U.S.A. 131 E5
Fort Stockton U.S.A. 131 C6
Fort Sumeshwar *mt.* India 83 F4
Fort Sumner U.S.A. 127 G6
Fort Supply U.S.A. 131 D4
Fort Thomas U.S.A. 129 I5
Fort Trinquet Mauritania *see* Bîr Mogreïn
Fortuna U.S.A. 130 C1
Fortune Bay Canada 123 L5
Fort Valley U.S.A. 133 D5
Fort Vermilion Canada 120 G3
Fort Victoria Zimbabwe *see* Masvingo
Fort Ware Canada *see* Ware
Fort Wayne U.S.A. 134 C3
Fort William U.K. 50 D4
Fort Worth U.S.A. 131 D5
Fort Yates U.S.A. 130 C2
Fort Yukon U.S.A. 118 D3
Forum Iulii France *see* Fréjus
Forūr-e Bozorg, Jazīreh-ye *i.* Iran 88 D5
Forūr-e Kūchek, Jazīreh-ye *i.* Iran 88 D5
Forvik Norway 44 H4
Foshan China 77 G4
Fossano Italy 58 B2
Fossil U.S.A. 126 C3
Fossil Downs Australia 108 D4
Foster Australia 112 C7
Foster U.S.A. 134 C4
Foster, Mount Canada/U.S.A. 120 C3
Foster Lakes Canada 121 J3
Fostoria U.S.A. 134 D3
Fotadrevo Madag. 99 E6
Fotherby U.K. 48 G5
Fotokol Cameroon 97 E3
Fotuna *i.* Vanuatu *see* Futuna
Fougères France 56 D2
Foula *i.* U.K. 50 [inset]
Foul Island Myanmar 70 A3
Foulness Point U.K. 49 H7
Foul Point Sri Lanka 84 D4
Foumban Cameroon 96 E4
Foundation Ice Stream *glacier* Antarctica 152 L1
Fount U.S.A. 134 D5
Fountains Abbey and Studley Royal Water Garden (NT) *tourist site* U.K. 48 F4
Fourches, Mont des *hill* France 56 G2
Four Corners U.S.A. 128 E4
Fouriesburg S. Africa 101 I5
Fourmies France 52 E4
Fournier, Lac *l.* Canada 123 I4
Fournoi *i.* Greece 59 L6
Fourpeaked Mountain U.S.A. 118 C4
Fouta Djallon *reg.* Guinea 96 B3
Foveaux Strait N.Z. 113 A8
Fowey *r.* U.K. 49 C8
Fowler *CO* U.S.A. 127 G5
Fowler *IN* U.S.A. 134 B3
Fowler Ice Rise Antarctica 152 L1
Fowlers Bay S.A. Australia 109 F7
Fowlers Bay *b.* Australia 109 F8
Fowlerville U.S.A. 134 C2
Fox *r.* *B.C.* Canada 120 E3
Fox *r.* *Man.* Canada 121 M3
Fox *r.* U.S.A. 130 F3
Fox Creek Canada 120 G4
Fox Creek U.S.A. 134 C5
Foxdale Isle of Man 48 C4
Foxe Basin *g.* Canada 119 K3
Foxe Channel Canada 119 J3
Foxe Peninsula Canada 119 K3
Fox Glacier N.Z. 113 C6
Fox Islands U.S.A. 118 B4
Fox Lake Canada 120 H3
Fox Mountain Canada 120 C2
Fox Valley Canada 121 I5
Foyers U.K. 50 E3
Foyle *r.* Ireland/U.K. 51 E3
Foyle, Lough *b.* Ireland/U.K. 51 E2
Foynes Ireland 51 C5
Foz de Areia, Represa de *resr* Brazil 145 A4
Foz do Cunene Angola 99 B5
Foz do Iguaçu Brazil 144 F3
Fraga Spain 57 G3
Frakes, Mount Antarctica 152 K1
Framingham U.S.A. 135 J2
Framnes Mountains Antarctica 152 E2
Franca Brazil 145 B3
Français, Récif des *reef* New Caledonia 107 G3
Francavilla Fontana Italy 58 G4

▶France *country* Europe 56 F3
3rd largest and 4th most populous country in Europe.

Frances Australia 111 C8
Frances Lake Canada 120 D2
Frances Lake Canada 120 D2
Franceville Gabon 98 B4
Francis Canada 121 K5
Francis *atoll* Kiribati *see* Beru
Francis, Lake U.S.A. 135 J1
Francisco de Orellana Ecuador *see* Coca
Francisco I. Madero *Coahuila* Mex. 131 C7
Francisco I. Madero *Durango* Mex. 131 B7
Francisco Zarco Mex. 128 E5
Francistown Botswana 99 C6
Francois Canada 123 K5
François Lake Canada 120 E4
Francois Peron National Park Australia 109 A6
Francs Peak U.S.A. 126 F4
Franeker Neth. 52 F1
Frankenberg (Eder) Germany 53 I3
Frankenberg/Sachsen Germany 53 N4
Frankenhöhe *hills* Germany 47 M6
Frankenmuth U.S.A. 134 D2
Frankenthal (Pfalz) Germany 53 I5
Frankenwald *mts* Germany 53 L4
Frankford Canada 135 G1
Frankfort *IN* U.S.A. 134 B3

▶Frankfort *KY* U.S.A. 134 C4
Capital of Kentucky.

Frankfort *MI* U.S.A. 134 B1
Frankfort *OH* U.S.A. 134 D4
Frankfurt Germany *see* Frankfurt am Main
Frankfurt (Oder) Germany 47 O4
Frankfurt am Main Germany 53 I4
Frank Hann National Park Australia 109 C8
Frankin Lake U.S.A. 129 F1
Fränkische Alb *hills* Germany 53 K6
Fränkische Schweiz *reg.* Germany 53 L5
Frankland, Cape Australia 111 [inset]
Franklin *AZ* U.S.A. 129 I5
Franklin *GA* U.S.A. 133 C5
Franklin *IN* U.S.A. 134 B4
Franklin *KY* U.S.A. 134 B5
Franklin *LA* U.S.A. 131 F6
Franklin *MA* U.S.A. 135 J2
Franklin *NC* U.S.A. 133 D5
Franklin *NE* U.S.A. 130 D3
Franklin *NH* U.S.A. 135 J2
Franklin *PA* U.S.A. 134 F3
Franklin *TN* U.S.A. 132 C5
Franklin *TX* U.S.A. 131 D6
Franklin *VA* U.S.A. 135 G5
Franklin *WV* U.S.A. 134 F4
Franklin Bay Canada 153 A2
Franklin D. Roosevelt Lake *resr* U.S.A. 126 D2
Franklin Furnace U.S.A. 134 D4
Franklin-Gordon National Park Australia 111 [inset]
Franklin Island Antarctica 152 H1
Franklin Mountains Canada 120 F2
Franklin Strait Canada 119 I2
Franklinton U.S.A. 131 F6
Franklinville U.S.A. 135 F2
Frankston Australia 112 B7
Fränsta Sweden 44 J5
Frantsa-Iosifa, Zemlya *is* Russia 64 G2
Franz Canada 122 D4
Franz Josef Glacier N.Z. 113 C6
Frasca, Capo della *c.* *Sardinia* Italy 58 C5
Frascati Italy 58 E4
Fraser *r.* Australia 108 C4
Fraser *r.* *B.C.* Canada 120 F5
Fraser *r.* *Nfld. and Lab.* Canada 123 J2
Fraser, Mount *hill* Australia 109 B6
Fraserburg S. Africa 100 E6
Fraserburgh U.K. 50 G3
Fraserdale Canada 122 E4
Fraser Island Australia 110 F5
Fraser Lake Canada 120 E4
Fraser Plateau Canada 120 E4
Fraser Range *hills* Australia 109 C8
Frauenfeld Switz. 56 I3
Fray Bentos Uruguay 144 E4
Frazeysburg U.S.A. 134 D3
Frechen Germany 52 G4
Freckleton U.K. 48 E5
Frederic U.S.A. 134 C1
Frederica U.S.A. 135 H4
Fredericia Denmark 45 F9
Frederick *MD* U.S.A. 135 G4
Frederick *OK* U.S.A. 131 D5
Frederick Reef Australia 110 F4
Fredericksburg *TX* U.S.A. 131 D6
Fredericksburg *VA* U.S.A. 135 G4
Fredericktown U.S.A. 130 F4

▶Fredericton Canada 123 I5
Capital of New Brunswick.

Frederikshåb Greenland *see* Paamiut
Frederikshavn Denmark 45 G8
Frederiksværk Denmark 45 H9
Fredonia *AZ* U.S.A. 129 G3
Fredonia *KS* U.S.A. 131 E4
Fredonia *NY* U.S.A. 134 F2
Fredonia *WI* U.S.A. 134 B2
Fredrika Sweden 44 K4
Fredrikshamn Fin. *see* Hamina
Fredrikstad Norway 45 G7
Freedonyer Peak U.S.A. 128 C1
Freehold U.S.A. 135 H3
Freeland U.S.A. 135 H3
Freeling Heights *hill* Australia 111 B6
Freel Peak U.S.A. 128 D2
Freels, Cape Canada 123 L4
Freeman U.S.A. 130 D3
Freeman, Lake U.S.A. 134 B3
Freeport Bahamas 133 E7
Freeport *FL* U.S.A. 133 C6
Freeport *IL* U.S.A. 130 F3
Freeport *TX* U.S.A. 131 E6
Freer U.S.A. 131 D7
Free Soil U.S.A. 134 B1
Free State *prov.* S. Africa 101 H5

▶Freetown Sierra Leone 96 B4
Capital of Sierra Leone.

Frégate, Lac de la *l.* Canada 122 G3
Fregenal de la Sierra Spain 57 C4
Fregon Australia 109 F6
Fréhel, Cap *c.* France 56 C2
Frei (Chile) *research station* Antarctica 152 A2
Freiberg Germany 53 N4
Freiburg Switz. *see* Fribourg
Freiburg im Breisgau Germany 47 K6
Freisen Germany 53 H5
Freising Germany 47 M6
Freistadt Austria 47 O6
Fréjus France 56 H5
Fremantle Australia 109 A8
Fremont *CA* U.S.A. 128 C3
Fremont *IN* U.S.A. 134 C3
Fremont *MI* U.S.A. 134 C2
Fremont *NE* U.S.A. 130 D3
Fremont *OH* U.S.A. 134 D3
Fremont *r.* U.S.A. 129 H2
Fremont Junction U.S.A. 129 H2
Frenchburg U.S.A. 134 D5
French Cay *i.* Turks and Caicos Is 133 F8
French Congo *country* Africa *see* Congo

▶French Guiana *terr.* S. America 143 H3
French Overseas Department.

French Guinea *country* Africa *see* Guinea
French Island Australia 112 B7
French Lick U.S.A. 134 B4
Frenchman *r.* U.S.A. 126 G2
Frenchman Lake *CA* U.S.A. 128 C2
Frenchman Lake *NV* U.S.A. 129 F3
Frenchpark Ireland 51 D4
French Pass N.Z. 113 D5

▶French Polynesia *terr.* S. Pacific Ocean 151 K7
French Overseas Country.

French Somaliland *country* Africa *see* Djibouti

▶French Southern and Antarctic Lands *terr.* Indian Ocean 149 M8
French Overseas Territory.

French Sudan *country* Africa *see* Mali
French Territory of the Afars and Issas *country* Africa *see* Djibouti
Frenda Alg. 57 G6
Frentsjer Neth. *see* Franeker
Freren Germany 53 H2
Fresco *r.* Brazil 143 H5
Freshford Ireland 51 E5
Fresnillo Mex. 136 D4
Fresno U.S.A. 128 D3
Fresno *r.* U.S.A. 128 C3
Fresno Reservoir U.S.A. 126 F2
Fressel, Lac *l.* Canada 122 G3
Freu, Cap des *c.* Spain 57 H4
Freudenberg Germany 53 H4
Freudenstadt Germany 47 L6
Frévent France 52 C4
Frew *watercourse* Australia 110 A4
Frewena Australia 110 A3
Freycinet Estuary *inlet* Australia 109 A6
Freycinet Peninsula Australia 111 [inset]
Freyenstein Germany 53 M1
Freyming-Merlebach France 52 G5
Fria Guinea 96 B3
Fria, Cape Namibia 99 B5
Friant U.S.A. 128 D3
Frías Arg. 144 C3
Fribourg Switz. 56 H3
Friday Harbor U.S.A. 126 C2
Friedeburg Germany 53 H1
Friedens U.S.A. 135 F3
Friedland Russia *see* Pravdinsk
Friedrichshafen Germany 47 L7
Friedrichskanal *canal* Germany 53 L2
Friend U.S.A. 130 D3
Friendly Islands *country* S. Pacific Ocean *see* Tonga
Friendship U.S.A. 130 F3
Friesack Germany 53 M2
Friese Wad *tidal flat* Neth. 52 F1
Friesoythe Germany 53 H1
Frinton-on-Sea U.K. 49 I7
Frio *r.* U.S.A. 131 D6
Frio *watercourse* U.S.A. 131 C5
Frisco Mountain U.S.A. 129 G2
Frissell, Mount *hill* U.S.A. 135 I2
Fritzlar Germany 53 J3
Frjentsjer Neth. *see* Franeker
Frobisher Bay Canada *see* Iqaluit
Frobisher Bay *b.* Canada 119 L3
Frobisher Lake Canada 121 I3
Frohavet *b.* Norway 44 F5
Frohburg Germany 53 M3
Froissy France 52 C5
Frolovo Russia 43 I6
Frome *watercourse* Australia 111 B6
Frome U.K. 49 E7
Frome *r.* U.K. 49 E8
Frome, Lake *salt flat* Australia 111 B6
Frome Downs Australia 111 B6
Fröndenberg/Ruhr Germany 53 H3
Frontera *Coahuila* Mex. 131 C7
Frontera *Tabasco* Mex. 136 F5
Fronteras Mex. 127 F7
Front Royal U.S.A. 135 F4
Frosinone Italy 58 E4
Frostburg U.S.A. 135 F4
Frøya *i.* Norway 44 F5
Fruges France 52 C4
Fruita U.S.A. 129 I2
Fruitland U.S.A. 129 H1
Fruitvale U.S.A. 129 I2
Frunze Kyrg. *see* Bishkek
Frusino Italy *see* Frosinone
Fruška Gora, Nacionalni Park *nat. park* Serbia 59 H2
Frýdek-Místek Czechia 47 Q6
Fu'an China 77 H3
Fucheng *Anhui* China *see* Fengyang
Fucheng *Shaanxi* China *see* Fuxian
Fuchuan China 77 F3
Fuchun Jiang *r.* China 77 I2
Fude China 77 H3
Fuding China 77 I3
Fudul *reg.* Saudi Arabia 88 B6
Fuenlabrada Spain 57 E3
Fuerte *r.* Mex. 127 F8
Fuerte Olimpo Para. 144 E2
Fuerteventura *i.* Canary Is 96 B2
Fufeng China 76 E1
Fuga *i.* Phil. 69 G3
Fugong China 76 C3
Fugou China 77 G1
Fuhai China 80 G2
Fuḩaymī Iraq 91 F4
Fujairah U.A.E. 88 E5
Fujeira U.A.E. *see* Fujairah
Fuji Japan 75 E6
Fujian *prov.* China 77 H3
Fuji-Hakone-Izu Kokuritsu-kōen *nat. park* Japan 75 E6
Fujin China 74 C3
Fujinomiya Japan 75 E6
Fuji-san *vol.* Japan 75 E6
Fujiyoshida Japan 75 E6
Fûka Egypt *see* Fūkah
Fūkah Egypt 90 B5
Fukien *prov.* China *see* Fujian
Fukuchiyama Japan 75 D6
Fukue-jima *i.* Japan 75 C6
Fukui Japan 75 E5
Fukuoka Japan 75 C6
Fukushima Japan 75 F5
Fukuyama Japan 75 C7
Fûl, Gebel *hill* Egypt *see* Fūl, Jabal
Fūl, Jabal *hill* Egypt 85 A5
Fulchhari Bangl. 83 G4
Fulda Germany 53 J4
Fulda *r.* Germany 53 J3
Fulham U.K. 49 G7
Fuli *Anhui* China 77 H1
Fuli *Heilong.* China *see* Jixian
Fuling China 76 E2
Fulitun China *see* Jixian
Fullerton *CA* U.S.A. 128 E5
Fullerton *NE* U.S.A. 130 D3
Fullerton, Cape Canada 121 N2
Fulton *IN* U.S.A. 134 B3
Fulton *MO* U.S.A. 130 F4
Fulton *MS* U.S.A. 131 F5
Fulton *NY* U.S.A. 135 G2
Fumane Moz. 101 K3
Fumay France 52 E5
Fumin China 76 D3

Funabashi Japan **75** E6
Funafuti *atoll* Tuvalu **107** H2
Funan China **77** G1

▶**Funchal** Madeira **96** B1
Capital of Madeira.

Fundão Brazil **145** C2
Fundão Port. **57** C3
Fundi Italy *see* **Fondi**
Fundición Mex. **127** F8
Fundy, Bay of *g.* Canada **123** I5
Fundy National Park Canada **123** I5
Fünen *i.* Denmark *see* **Fyn**
Funeral Peak U.S.A. **128** E3
Fünfkirchen Hungary *see* **Pécs**
Funhalouro Moz. **101** L2
Funing *Jiangsu* China **77** H1
Funing *Yunnan* China **76** E4
Funiu Shan *mts* China **77** F1
Funtua Nigeria **96** D3
Funzie U.K. **50** [inset]
Fuqing China **77** H3
Fürgun, Küh-e *mt.* Iran **88** E5
Furmanov Russia **42** I4
Furmanovka Kazakh. *see* **Moyynkum**
Furmanovo Kazakh. *see* **Zhalpaktal**
Furnás *hill* Spain **57** G4
Furnas, Represa *resr* Brazil **145** B3
Furneaux Group *is* Australia **111** [inset]
Furnes Belgium *see* **Veurne**
Furong China *see* **Wan'an**
Fürstenau Germany **53** H2
Fürstenberg/Havel Germany **53** N1
Fürstenwalde/Spree Germany **47** O4
Fürth Germany **53** K5
Furth im Wald Germany **53** M5
Fury and Hecla Strait Canada **119** J3
Fusan S. Korea *see* **Busan**
Fushun China **74** A4
Fushuncheng China *see* **Shuncheng**
Fusong China **74** B4
Fu Tau Pun Chau *i. H.K.* China **77** [inset]
Futuna *i.* Vanuatu **107** H3
Futuna Islands Wallis and Futuna *see* **Horn, Îles de**
Fuxian *Liaoning* China *see* **Wafangdian**
Fuxian *Shaanxi* China **73** J5
Fuxian Hu *l.* China **76** D3
Fuxin China **73** M4
Fuxing China *see* **Wangmo**
Fuxinzhen China *see* **Fuxin**
Fuyang *Anhui* China **77** G1
Fuyang *Guangxi* China *see* **Fuchuan**
Fuyang *Zhejiang* China **77** H2
Fuying Dao *i.* China **77** I3
Fuyu *Anhui* China *see* **Susong**
Fuyu *Heilong.* China **74** B3
Fuyu *Jilin* China *see* **Songyuan**
Fuyu *Jilin* China **74** B3
Fuyuan *Heilong.* China **74** D2
Fuyuan *Yunnan* China **76** E3
Fuyun China **80** G2
Fuzhou *Fujian* China **77** H3
Fuzhou *Jiangxi* China **77** H3
Füzuli Azer. **91** G3
Fyn *i.* Denmark **45** G9
Fyne, Loch *inlet* U.K. **50** D5
F.Y.R.O.M *country* Europe *see* **Macedonia**

G

Gaâfour Tunisia **58** C6
Gaafu Atoll Maldives *see* **Huvadhu Atholhu**
Gaalkacyo Somalia **98** E3
Gabakly Turkm. **89** F2
Gabasumdo China *see* **Tongde**
Gabbs U.S.A. **128** E2
Gabbs Valley Range *mts* U.S.A. **128** D2
Gabd Pak. **89** F5
Gabela Angola **99** B5
Gaberones Botswana *see* **Gaborone**
Gabès Tunisia **54** G5
Gabès, Golfe de *g.* Tunisia **54** G5
Gabo Island Australia **112** D6
Gabon *country* Africa **98** B4

▶**Gaborone** Botswana **101** G3
Capital of Botswana.

Gābrīk Iran **88** E5
Gabrovo Bulg. **59** K3
Gabú Guinea-Bissau **96** B3
Gadag-Betigeri India **84** B3
Gadaisu P.N.G. **110** E1
Gadap Pak. **89** G5
Gadchiroli India **84** D1
Gäddede Sweden **44** I4
Gadê China **76** C1
Gades Spain *see* **Cádiz**
Gadhda India **82** B5
Gadhka India **89** H6
Gadra Pak. **89** H5
Gadsden U.S.A. **133** C5
Gadwal India **84** C2
Gadyach Ukr. *see* **Hadyach**
Gaer U.K. **49** D7
Găeşti Romania **59** K2
Gaeta Italy **58** E4
Gaeta, Golfo di *g.* Italy **58** E4
Gaferut *i.* Micronesia **69** L5
Gaffney U.S.A. **133** D5
Gafsa Tunisia **58** C7
Gagarin Russia **43** G5
Gagnoa Côte d'Ivoire **96** C4
Gagnon Canada **123** H4
Gago Coutinho Angola *see* **Lumbala N'guimbo**
Gagra Georgia **43** I8
Gaiab *watercourse* Namibia **100** D5
Gaibanda Bangl. *see* **Gaibandha**
Gaibandha Bangl. **83** G4
Gaïdouronisi *i.* Greece **59** K7
Gaifi, Wâdi el *watercourse* Egypt *see* **Jayfī, Wādī al**
Gail U.S.A. **131** C5
Gaildorf Germany **53** J6
Gaillac France **56** E5
Gaillimh Ireland *see* **Galway**
Gaillon France **52** B5
Gainesboro U.S.A. **134** C5
Gainesville *FL* U.S.A. **133** D6
Gainesville *GA* U.S.A. **133** D5
Gainesville *MO* U.S.A. **131** E4
Gainesville *TX* U.S.A. **131** D5
Gainsborough U.K. **48** G5
Gairdner, Lake *salt flat* Australia **111** A6
Gairloch U.K. **50** D3
Gair Loch *b.* U.K. **50** D3
Gajah Hutan, Bukit *hill* Malaysia **71** C6
Gajipur India *see* **Ghazipur**
Gajol India **83** G4
Gakarosa *mt.* S. Africa **100** F4
Gala China **83** G3
Galaasiya Uzbek. *see* **Galaosiyo**
Gala Co *l.* China **83** G3
Galâla el Baḥarîya, Gebel el *plat.* Egypt *see* **Jalālah al Baḥrīyah, Jabal**
Galana *r.* Kenya **98** E4
Galanta Slovakia **47** P6
Galaosiyo Uzbek. **89** G2
Galápagos, Parque Nacional *nat. park* Ecuador **142** [inset]

▶**Galapagos Islands** *is* Ecuador **151** O6
Part of Ecuador. Most westerly point of South America.

Galapagos Rise *sea feature* Pacific Ocean **151** N6
Galashiels U.K. **50** G5
Galaţi Romania **59** M2
Galatina Italy **58** H4
Gala Water *r.* U.K. **50** G5
Galax U.S.A. **134** E5
Galaýmor Turkm. **89** F3
Galbally Ireland **51** D5
Galdhøpiggen *mt.* Norway **45** F6
Galeana *Chihuahua* Mex. **127** G7
Galeana *Nuevo León* Mex. **131** C7
Galena *AK* U.S.A. **118** C3
Galena *IL* U.S.A. **130** F3
Galena *MD* U.S.A. **135** H4
Galena *MO* U.S.A. **131** E4
Galera, Punta *pt* Chile **144** B6
Galesburg *IL* U.S.A. **130** F3
Galesburg *MI* U.S.A. **134** C2
Galeshewe S. Africa **100** G5
Galeton U.S.A. **135** G3
Galey *r.* Ireland **51** C5
Galheirão *r.* Brazil **145** B1
Galiano Island Canada **120** F5
Galich Russia **42** I4
Galichskaya Vozvyshennost' *hills* Russia **42** I4
Galicia *aut. comm.* Spain **57** C2
Galičica *nat. park* Macedonia **59** I4
Galilee, Lake *salt flat* Australia **110** D4
Galilee, Sea of *l.* Israel **85** B3
Galion U.S.A. **134** D3
Galite, Canal de la *sea chan.* Tunisia **58** C6
Galiuro Mountains U.S.A. **129** H5
Galizia *aut. comm.* Spain *see* **Galicia**
Gallabat Sudan **86** E7
G'allaorol Uzbek. **89** G1
Gallatin *MO* U.S.A. **130** E4
Gallatin *TN* U.S.A. **134** B5
Galle Sri Lanka **84** D5
Gallego Rise *sea feature* Pacific Ocean **151** M6
Gallegos *r.* Arg. **144** C8
Gallia *country* Europe *see* **France**

▶**Gallinas, Punta** *pt* Col. **142** D1
Most northerly point of South America.

Gallipoli Italy **58** H4
Gallipoli Turkey **59** L4
Gallipolis U.S.A. **134** D4
Gällivare Sweden **44** L3
Gällö Sweden **44** I5
Gallo Island U.S.A. **135** G2
Gallo Mountains U.S.A. **129** I4
Gallup U.S.A. **129** I4
Galmisdale U.K. **50** C4
Galmudug *reg.* Somalia **98** E3
Galong Australia **112** D5
Galoya Sri Lanka **84** D4
Gal Oya National Park Sri Lanka **84** D5
Galston U.K. **50** E5
Galt U.S.A. **128** C2
Galtat-Zemmour W. Sahara **96** B2
Galtee Mountains *hills* Ireland **51** D5
Galtymore *hill* Ireland **46** C4
Galūgāh, Kūh-e *mts* Iran **88** D4
Galveston *IN* U.S.A. **134** B3
Galveston *TX* U.S.A. **131** E6
Galveston Bay U.S.A. **131** E6
Galwa Nepal **83** E3
Galway Ireland **51** C4
Galway Bay Ireland **51** C4
Gâm, Sông *r.* Vietnam **70** D2
Gamalakhe S. Africa **101** J6
Gamba China **83** G3
Gamba Gabon **98** A4
Gambēla Eth. **98** D3
Gambēla National Park Eth. **98** D3
Gambell U.S.A. **118** A3
Gambella Eth. *see* **Gambēla**
Gambia, The *country* Africa **96** B3
Gambier, Îles *is* Fr. Polynesia **151** L7
Gambier Islands Australia **111** B7
Gambier Islands Fr. Polynesia *see* **Gambier, Îles**
Gambo Canada **123** L4
Gamboma Congo **98** B4
Gamboula Cent. Afr. Rep. **98** B3
Gamda China *see* **Zamtang**
Gamêtî Canada **120** G1
Gamlakarleby Fin. *see* **Kokkola**
Gamleby Sweden **45** J8
Gammelstaden Sweden **44** M4
Gamova, Mys *pt* Russia **74** C4
Gamshadzai Kūh *mts* Iran **89** F4
Gamtog China **76** C2
Gamud *mt.* Eth. **98** D3
Gana China **76** D1
Ganado U.S.A. **129** I4
Ga-Nala S. Africa **101** I4
Gananoque Canada **135** G1
Gäncä Azer. **91** G2
Gancheng China **77** F5
Ganda Angola **99** B5
Gandaingoin China **83** G3
Gandajika Dem. Rep. Congo **99** C4
Gandak Barrage Nepal **83** E4
Gandari Mountain Pak. **89** H4
Gandava Pak. **89** G4
Gander Canada **123** L4
Ganderkesee Germany **53** I1
Gandesa Spain **57** G3
Gandhidham India **82** B5
Gandhinagar India **82** C5
Gandhi Sagar *resr* India **82** C4
Gandia Spain **57** F4
Gandzha Azer. *see* **Gäncä**
Ganga *r.* Bangl./India *see* **Ganges**
Ganga Cone *sea feature* Indian Ocean *see* **Ganges Cone**
Gangán Arg. **144** C6
Ganganagar India **82** C3
Gangapur India **82** D4
Ganga Sera India **82** B4
Gangaw Myanmar **70** A2
Gangawati India **84** C3
Gangaw Range *mts* Myanmar **70** B2
Gangca China **80** J4
Gangdisê Shan *mts* China **83** E3
Ganges *r.* Bangl./India **83** G5
also known as Ganga
Ganges France **56** F5
Ganges, Mouths of the Bangl./India **83** G5
Ganges Cone *sea feature* Indian Ocean **149** N4
Ganghwa S. Korea **75** B5
Gangneung S. Korea **75** C5
Gangouyi China **72** J5
Gangra Turkey *see* **Çankırı**
Gangtok India **83** G4
Gangu China **76** E1
Gani Indon. **69** H7
Gan Jiang *r.* China **77** H2
Ganjig China **73** M4
Ganluo China **76** D2
Ganmain Australia **112** C5
Gannan China **74** A3
Gannat France **56** F3
Gannett Peak U.S.A. **126** F4
Ganq China **80** H4
Ganshui China **76** E2
Gansu *prov.* China **76** D1
Gantheaume Point Australia **108** C4
Gantsevichi Belarus *see* **Hantsavichy**
Ganxian China **77** G3
Ganye Nigeria **96** E4
Ganyu China **77** H1
Ganyushkino Kazakh. **41** P6
Ganzhou China **77** G3
Ganzi South Sudan **97** G4
Gao Mali **96** C3
Gaocheng China *see* **Litang**
Gaocun China *see* **Mayang**
Gaohe China *see* **Huaining**
Gaohebu China *see* **Huaining**
Gaoleshan China *see* **Xianfeng**
Gaoliangjian China *see* **Hongze**
Gaomudang China **77** F3
Gaoping China **77** G1
Gaotai China **80** I4
Gaoth Dobhair Ireland **51** D2
Gaoting China *see* **Daishan**
Gaotingzhen China *see* **Daishan**
Gaoua Burkina Faso **96** C3
Gaoual Guinea **96** B3
Gaoxiong Taiwan *see* **Kaohsiung**
Gaoyao China *see* **Zhaoqing**
Gaoyou China **77** H1
Gaoyou Hu *l.* China **77** H1
Gap France **56** H4
Gapuwiyak Australia **110** A2
Gaqoi China **83** E3
Gar China **82** E2
Gar Pak. **89** F5
Gar' *r.* Russia **74** C1
Gara, Lough *l.* Ireland **51** D4
Garabekevyul Turkm. *see* **Garabekewül**
Garabekewül Turkm. **89** G2
Garabil Belentligi *hills* Turkm. **89** F2
Garabogaz Turkm. **91** I2
Garabogaz Aylagy *b.* Turkm. *see* **Garabogazköl Aýlagy**
Garabogazköl Aylagy *b.* Turkm. *see* **Garabogazköl Aýlagy**
Garabogazköl Aýlagy *b.* Turkm. **91** I2
Garabogazköl Bogazy *sea chan.* Turkm. **91** I2
Garägheh Iran **89** F4
Garagum *des.* Turkm. *see* **Karakum Desert**
Garagum Kanaly *canal* Turkm. **89** F2
Garah Australia **112** D2
Garalo Mali **96** C3
Garamätnyýaz Turkm. **89** G2
Garamba *r.* Dem. Rep. Congo **98** C3
Garamba, Parc National de la *nat. park* Dem. Rep. Congo **98** C3
Garanhuns Brazil **143** K5
Ga-Rankuwa S. Africa **101** H3
Garapuava Brazil **145** B2
Gárasavvon Sweden *see* **Karesuando**
Garautha India **82** D4
Garba China *see* **Jiulong**
Garbahaarrey Somalia **98** E3
Garba Tula Kenya **98** D3
Garberville U.S.A. **128** B1
Garbo China *see* **Lhozhag**
Garbsen Germany **53** J2
Garça Brazil **145** A3
Garco China **83** G2
Garda, Lago di Italy *see* **Garda, Lake**
Garda, Lake Italy **58** D2
Garde, Cap de *c.* Alg. **58** B6
Gardelegen Germany **53** L2
Garden City U.S.A. **130** C4
Garden Hill Canada **121** M4
Garden Mountain U.S.A. **134** E5
Garden Route National Park *nat. park* S. Africa **100** F7
Gardeyz Afgh. *see* **Gardēz**
Gardēz Afgh. **89** H3
Gardinas Belarus *see* **Hrodna**
Gardiner U.S.A. **135** K1
Gardiner, Mount Australia **108** F5
Gardiner Range *hills* Australia **108** E4
Gardiners Island U.S.A. **135** I3
Gardīz Afgh. *see* **Gardēz**
Gardner *atoll* Micronesia *see* **Faraulep**
Gardner U.S.A. **135** J2
Gardner Inlet Antarctica **152** L1
Gardner Island *atoll* Kiribati *see* **Nikumaroro**
Gardner Pinnacles *is* U.S.A. **150** I4
Gáregasnjárga Fin. *see* **Karigasniemi**
Garelochhead U.K. **50** E4
Gargano, Parco Nazionale del *nat. park* Italy **58** F4
Gargantua, Cape Canada **122** D5
Gargünsa China *see* **Gar**
Gargždai Lith. **45** L9
Garhchiroli India *see* **Gadchiroli**
Garhi *Madh. Prad.* India **84** C1
Garhi *Rajasthan* India **82** C5
Garhi Khairo Pak. **89** G4
Garhwa India **83** E4
Gari Russia **41** S4
Gariau Indon. **69** I7
Garibaldi, Mount Canada **120** F5
Gariep Dam *resr* S. Africa **101** G6
Garies S. Africa **100** C6
Garig Gunak Barlu National Park Australia **108** F2
Garigliano *r.* Italy **58** E4
Garissa Kenya **98** D4
Garkalne Latvia **45** N8
Garkung Caka *l.* China **83** F2
Garland U.S.A. **131** D5
Garm Tajik. *see* **Gharm**
Garmāb *Khorāsān-e Jonūbī* Iran **89** E3
Garmāb *Semnān* Iran **88** E3
Garm Āb, Chashmeh-ye *spring* Iran **88** E3
Garmsār Iran **88** D3
Garm Sēr *reg.* Afgh. **89** F4
Garner *IA* U.S.A. **130** E3
Garner *KY* U.S.A. **134** D5
Garnett U.S.A. **130** E4
Garnpung Lake *imp. l.* Australia **112** A4
Garo Hills India **83** G4
Garonne *r.* France **56** D4
Garoowe Somalia **98** E3
Garopaba Brazil **145** A5
Garoua Cameroon **96** E4
Garoua Boulai Cameroon **97** E4
Garqêntang China *see* **Sog**
Garré Arg. **144** D5
Garrett U.S.A. **134** C3
Garrison U.S.A. **130** E2
Garruk Pak. **89** G4
Garry *r.* U.K. **50** E3
Garrychyrla Turkm. *see* **Garryçyrla**
Garryçyrla Turkm. **89** F2
Garry Lake Canada **121** K1
Garrynahine U.K. **50** C2
Garsen Kenya **98** E4
Garshy Turkm. *see* **Garşy**
Garsila Sudan **97** F3
Garşy Turkm. **91** I2
Gartar China *see* **Pamai**
Garth U.K. **49** D6
Gartog China *see* **Markam**
Gartok China *see* **Garyarsa**
Gartow Germany **53** L1
Garub Namibia **100** C4
Garvagh U.K. **51** F3
Garve U.K. **50** E3
Garwa India *see* **Garhwa**
Garwha India *see* **Garhwa**
Gar Xincun China **82** E2
Gary *IN* U.S.A. **134** B3
Gary *WV* U.S.A. **134** E5
Garyarsa China **82** E3
Garyi China **76** C2
Garyū-zan *mt.* Japan **75** D6
Garza García Mex. **131** C7
Garzê China **76** C2
Gasan-Kuli Turkm. *see* **Esenguly**
Gas City U.S.A. **134** C3
Gascogne *reg.* France *see* **Gascony**
Gascogne, Golfe de *g.* France *see* **Gascony, Gulf of**
Gascony *reg.* France **56** D5
Gascony, Gulf of France **56** C5
Gascoyne *r.* Australia **109** A6
Gascoyne Junction Australia **109** A6
Gasherbrum I *mt.* China/Pak. **82** D2
Gashua Nigeria **96** E3
Gask Iran **89** E3
Gaspar Cuba **133** E8
Gaspar, Selat *sea chan.* Indon. **68** D7
Gaspé Canada **123** I4
Gaspé, Cap *c.* Canada **123** I4
Gaspésie, Péninsule de la *pen.* Canada **123** I4
Gassan *vol.* Japan **75** F5
Gassaway U.S.A. **134** E4
Gasselte Neth. **52** G2
Gasteiz Spain *see* **Vitoria-Gasteiz**
Gastello Russia **74** F2
Gaston U.S.A. **135** G5
Gaston, Lake U.S.A. **135** G5
Gastonia U.S.A. **133** D5
Gata, Cabo de *c.* Spain **57** E5
Gata, Cape Cyprus **85** A2
Gata, Sierra de *mts* Spain **57** C3
Gataga *r.* Canada **120** E3
Gatas, Akra *c.* Cyprus *see* **Gata, Cape**
Gatchina Russia **45** Q7
Gate City U.S.A. **134** D5
Gatehouse of Fleet U.K. **50** E6
Gatentiri Indon. **69** K8
Gateshead U.K. **48** F4
Gates of the Arctic National Park and Preserve U.S.A. **118** C3
Gatesville U.S.A. **131** D6
Gateway U.S.A. **129** I2
Gatīj Iran **88** E5
Gatineau Canada **135** H1
Gatineau *r.* Canada **122** G5
Gatong China *see* **Jomda**
Gatooma Zimbabwe *see* **Kadoma**
Gatton Australia **112** F1
Gatvand Iran **88** C3
Gatyana S. Africa *see* **Willowvale**
Gau *i.* Fiji **107** H3
Gauer Lake Canada **121** L3
Gauhati India *see* **Guwahati**
Gaujas nacionālais parks *nat. park* Latvia **45** N8
Gaul *country* Europe *see* **France**
Gaula *r.* Norway **44** G5
Gaume *reg.* Belgium **52** F5
Gaurama Brazil **145** A4
Gauribidanur India **84** C3
Gauteng *prov.* S. Africa **101** I4
Gavarr Armenia **91** G2
Gāvbūs, Kūh-e *mts* Iran **88** D5

▶**Gavdos** *i.* Greece **59** K7
Most southerly point of Europe.

Gaven Reefs Spratly Is **68** E4
Gavião *r.* Brazil **145** C1
Gavīleh Iran **88** B3
Gav Khūnī Iran **88** D3
Gävle Sweden **45** J6
Gavrilovka Vtoraya Russia **43** I5
Gavrilov-Yam Russia **42** H4
Gawachab Namibia **100** C4
Gawai Myanmar **76** C3
Gawan India **83** F4
Gawilgarh Hills India **82** D5
Gawler Australia **111** B7
Gawler Ranges *hills* Australia **111** A7
Gaxun Nur *salt l.* China **80** J3
Gaya India **83** F4
Gaya Niger **96** D3
Gaya He *r.* China **74** C4
Gayéri Burkina Faso **96** D3
Gaylord U.S.A. **134** C1
Gayndah Australia **111** E5
Gayny Russia **42** L3
Gaysin Ukr. *see* **Haysyn**
Gayutino Russia **42** H4
Gaza *disp. terr.* Asia **85** B4

▶**Gaza** Gaza **85** B4
Capital of Gaza.

Gaza *prov.* Moz. **101** K2
Gazan Pak. **89** G4
Gazandzhyk Turkm. *see* **Bereket**
Gazanjyk Turkm. *see* **Bereket**
Gaza Strip *disp. terr.* Asia *see* **Gaza**
Gaz-e Barkhūār Iran **88** C3
Gaziantep Turkey **90** E3
Gaziantep *prov.* Turkey **85** C1
Gazibenli Turkey *see* **Yahyalı**
Gazīk Iran **89** F3
Gazimağusa Cyprus *see* **Famagusta**
Gazimurskiy Khrebet *mts* Russia **73** L2
Gazimurskiy Zavod Russia **73** L2
Gazipaşa Turkey **85** A1
Gazli Uzbek. **89** F1
Gaz Māhū Iran **88** E5
Gbarnga Liberia **96** C4
Gboko Nigeria **96** D4
Gcuwa S. Africa **101** I7
Gdańsk Poland **47** Q3
Gdańsk, Gulf of Poland/Russia **47** Q3
Gdańska, Zatoka *g.* Poland/Russia *see* **Gdańsk, Gulf of**
Gdingen Poland *see* **Gdynia**
Gdov Russia **45** O7
Gdynia Poland **47** Q3
Geaidnovuohppi Norway **44** M2
Gearhart Mountain U.S.A. **126** C4
Gearraidh na h-Aibhne U.K. *see* **Garrynahine**
Gebe *i.* Indon. **69** H6
Gebesee Germany **53** K3
Geçitkale Cyprus *see* **Lefkonikon**
Gedaref Sudan **86** E7
Gedern Germany **53** J4
Gedinne Belgium **52** E5
Gediz *r.* Turkey **59** L5
Gedney Drove End U.K. **49** H6
Gedong, Tanjong *pt* Sing. **71** [inset]
Gedser Denmark **45** G9
Geel Belgium **52** F3
Geelong Australia **112** B7
Geelvink Channel Australia **109** A7
Geel Vloer *salt pan* S. Africa **100** E5
Gees Gwardafuy *c.* Somalia *see* **Gwardafuy, Gees**
Geeste Germany **53** H2
Geesthacht Germany **53** K1
Gegen Gol China **74** A2
Ge Hu *l.* China **77** H2
Geidam Nigeria **96** E3
Geiersberg *hill* Germany **53** J5
Geikie *r.* Canada **121** K3
Geilenkirchen Germany **52** G4
Geilo Norway **45** F6
Geiranger Norway **44** E5
Geislingen an der Steige Germany **53** J6
Geisûm, Gezâ'ir *is* Egypt *see* **Qaysūm, Juzur**
Geita Tanz. **98** D4
Geithain Germany **53** M3
Gejiu China **76** D4
Gëkdepe Turkm. **88** E2
Gela *Sicily* Italy **58** F6
Gêladaindong *mt.* China **83** G2
Geladī Eth. **98** E3
Gelang, Tanjung *pt* Malaysia **71** C7
Geldern Germany **52** G3
Gelendzhik Russia **90** E1
Gelibolu Turkey *see* **Gallipoli**
Gelidonya Burnu *pt* Turkey *see* **Yardımcı Burnu**
Gelincik Dağı *mt.* Turkey **59** N5
Gelnhausen Germany **53** J4
Gelsenkirchen Germany **52** H3
Gemas Malaysia **71** C7
Gemena Dem. Rep. Congo **98** B3
Geminokağı Cyprus *see* **Karavostasi**
Gemlik Turkey **59** M4
Gemona del Friuli Italy **58** E1
Gemsa Egypt *see* **Jamsah**
Gemsbok National Park Botswana **100** E3
Gemsbokplein *well* S. Africa **100** E4
Genalē Wenz *r.* Eth. **98** E3
Genappe Belgium **52** E4
General Acha Arg. **144** D5
General Alvear Arg. **144** C5
General Belgrano II *research station* Antarctica *see* **Belgrano II**
General Bravo Mex. **131** D7

▶**General Carrera, Lago** *l.* Arg./Chile **144** B7
Deepest lake in South America.

General Conesa Arg. **144** D6
General Freire Angola *see* **Muxaluando**
General Juan Madariaga Arg. **144** E5
General La Madrid Arg. **144** D5
General Machado Angola *see* **Camacupa**
General Pico Arg. **144** D5
General Pinedo Arg. **144** D3
General Roca Arg. **144** C5
General Salgado Brazil **145** A3
General San Martín *research station* Antarctica *see* **San Martín**
General Santos Phil. **69** H5
General Simón Bolívar Mex. **131** C7
General Trías Mex. **127** G7
General Villegas Arg. **144** D5
Genesee U.S.A. **135** G3
Geneseo U.S.A. **135** G2
Geneva S. Africa **101** H4
Geneva Switz. **56** H3
Geneva *AL* U.S.A. **133** C6
Geneva *IL* U.S.A. **134** A3
Geneva *NE* U.S.A. **130** D3
Geneva *NY* U.S.A. **135** G2
Geneva *OH* U.S.A. **134** E3
Geneva, Lake France/Switz. **56** H3
Genève Switz. *see* **Geneva**
Genf Switz. *see* **Geneva**
Gengda China *see* **Gana**
Genglou China **77** H2
Gengma China **76** C4
Gengxuan China *see* **Gengma**
Genhe China *see* **Gegen Gol**
Genichesk Ukr. *see* **Heniches'k**
Genji India **82** C5
Genk Belgium **52** F4
Gennargentu, Parco Nazionale del *nat. park Sardinia* Italy **58** C4
Gennep Neth. **52** F3
Genoa Australia **112** D6
Genoa Italy **58** C2
Genoa, Gulf of Italy **58** C2
Genova Italy *see* **Genoa**
Genova, Golfo di Italy *see* **Genoa, Gulf of**
Gent Belgium *see* **Ghent**
Genthin Germany **53** M2
Gentioux, Plateau de France **56** F4
Genua Italy *see* **Genoa**
Geographe Bay Australia **109** A8
Geographical Society Ø *i.* Greenland **119** P2
Geoje-do *i.* S. Korea **75** C6
Geok-Tepe Turkm. *see* **Gëkdepe**
Geongju S. Korea **75** C6
Georga, Zemlya *i.* Russia **64** F1
George *r.* Canada **123** I2
George S. Africa **100** F7
George, Lake Australia **112** D5
George, Lake *FL* U.S.A. **133** D6
George, Lake *NY* U.S.A. **135** I2
George Land *i.* Russia *see* **Georga, Zemlya**
Georges Mills U.S.A. **135** I2
George Sound *inlet* N.Z. **113** A7
Georgetown Australia **110** C3

▶**George Town** Cayman Is **137** H5
Capital of the Cayman Islands.

▶**Georgetown** Guyana **143** G2
Capital of Guyana.

George Town Malaysia **71** C6
Georgetown *DE* U.S.A. **135** H4
Georgetown *GA* U.S.A. **133** C6
Georgetown *IL* U.S.A. **134** B4
Georgetown *KY* U.S.A. **134** C4
Georgetown *OH* U.S.A. **134** D4
Georgetown *SC* U.S.A. **133** E5
Georgetown *TX* U.S.A. **131** D6
George VI Sound *sea chan.* Antarctica **152** L2
George V Land *reg.* Antarctica **152** G2
George West U.S.A. **131** D6
Georgia *country* Asia **91** F2
Georgia *state* U.S.A. **133** D5
Georgia, Strait of Canada **120** E5
Georgiana U.S.A. **131** G6
Georgian Bay Canada **134** E1
Georgian Bay Islands National Park Canada **134** F1
Georgienne, Baie *b.* Canada *see* **Georgian Bay**
Georgina *watercourse* Australia **110** B5
Georgiu-Dezh Russia *see* **Liski**
Georgiyevka *Vostochnyy Kazakhstan* Kazakh. **80** F2
Georgiyevka *Zhambylskaya Oblast'* Kazakh. *see* **Korday**
Georgiyevsk Russia **91** F1
Georgiyevskoye Russia **42** J4
Georg von Neumayer *research station* Antarctica *see* **Neumayer III**
Gera Germany **53** M4
Geraardsbergen Belgium **52** D4
Geral, Serra *mts* Brazil **145** A4
Geral de Goiás, Serra *hills* Brazil **145** B1
Geraldine N.Z. **113** C7
Geral do Paraná, Serra *hills* Brazil **145** B1
Geraldton Australia **109** A7
Gerar, Naḥal *watercourse* Israel **85** B4
Gerber U.S.A. **128** B1
Gercüş Turkey **91** F3
Gerede Turkey **90** D2
Gerik Malaysia **71** C6
Gerlach U.S.A. **128** D1
Germain, Grand Lac *l.* Canada **123** I4
Germaine, Lac *l.* Canada **123** I3
Germania *country* Europe *see* **Germany**
Germanicea Turkey *see* **Kahramanmaraş**
Germansen Landing Canada **120** E4

German South-West Africa country Africa see Namibia
Germantown OH U.S.A. 134 C4
Germantown WI U.S.A. 134 A2

▶Germany country Europe 47 L5
2nd most populous country in Europe.

Germersheim Germany 53 I5
Germī Iran 88 C2
Gernsheim Germany 53 I5
Gerolstein Germany 52 G4
Gerolzhofen Germany 53 K5
Gerona Spain see Girona
Gerrit Denys is P.N.G. see Lihir Group
Gers r. France 56 E4
Gersfeld (Rhön) Germany 53 J4
Gersoppa India 84 B3
Gerstungen Germany 53 K4
Gerwisch Germany 53 L2
Géryville Alg. see El Bayadh
Gêrzê China 83 F2
Gerze Turkey 90 D2
Gescher Germany 52 H3
Gesoriacum France see Boulogne-sur-Mer
Gessie U.S.A. 134 B3
Gestro Wenz, Wabē r. Eth. 78 D6
Gete r. Belgium 52 F4
Gettysburg PA U.S.A. 135 G4
Gettysburg SD U.S.A. 130 D2
Gettysburg National Military Park nat. park U.S.A. 135 G4
Getz Ice Shelf Antarctica 152 J2
Geumeo-do i. S. Korea 75 B6
Geumpang Indon. 71 B6
Geureudong, Gunung vol. Indon. 71 B6
Geurie Australia 112 D4
Gevaş Turkey 91 F3
Gevgelija Macedonia 59 J4
Gêwārām Band Afgh. 89 G4
Gexto Spain see Algorta
Gey Iran see Nīkshahr
Geyikli Turkey 59 L5
Geylegphug Bhutan 83 G4
Geysdorp S. Africa 101 G4
Geyserville U.S.A. 128 B2
Geyve Turkey 59 N4
Gezīr Iran 88 D5
Ghaap Plateau S. Africa 100 F4
Ghāb, Wādī al r. Syria 85 C2
Ghabāghib Syria 85 C3
Ghabeish Sudan 86 C7
Ghadaf, Wādī al watercourse Jordan 85 C4
Ghadamés Libya see Ghadāmis
Ghadāmis Libya 96 D1
Ghaghara r. India 83 F4
Ghaibi Dero Pak. 89 G5
Ghalend Iran 89 F4
Ghallaorol Uzbek. see G'allaorol
Ghana country Africa 96 C4
Ghanādah, Rās pt U.A.E. 88 D5
Ghantila India 82 B5
Ghanwā Saudi Arabia 86 G4
Ghanzi Botswana 99 C6
Ghanzi admin. dist. Botswana 100 F2
Ghap'an Armenia see Kapan
Ghār, Ras al pt Saudi Arabia 88 C5
Ghardaïa Alg. 54 E5
Gharghoda India 84 D1
Ghârib, Gebel mt. Egypt see Ghārib, Jabal
Ghārib, Jabal mt. Egypt 90 D5
Gharm Tajik. 89 H2
Gharqābād Iran 88 C3
Gharwa India see Garhwa
Gharyān Libya 97 E1
Ghāt Libya 96 E2
Ghatgaon India 83 F5
Ghatol India 82 C5
Ghawdex i. Malta see Gozo
Ghazal, Bahr el watercourse Chad 97 E3
Ghazaouet Alg. 57 F6
Ghaziabad India 82 D3
Ghazi Ghat Pak. 89 H4
Ghazipur India 83 E4
Ghazna Afgh. see Ghaznī
Ghaznī Afgh. 89 H3
Ghaznī Rōd r. Afgh. 89 G3
Ghazzah Gaza see Gaza
Ghebar Gumbad Iran 88 E3
Ghent Belgium 52 D3
Gheorghe Gheorghiu-Dej Romania see Onești
Gheorgheni Romania 59 K1
Gherla Romania 59 J1
Ghijduwon Uzbek. see G'ijduvon
Ghilzai reg. Afgh. 89 G4
Ghīnah, Wādī al watercourse Saudi Arabia 85 D4
Ghisonaccia Corsica France 56 I5
Ghōrak Afgh. 89 G3
Ghōriyān Afgh. 89 F3
Ghost Lake Canada 120 H2
Ghotaru India 82 B4
Ghotki Pak. 89 H5
Ghudamis Libya see Ghadāmis
Ghugri r. India 83 F4
Ghurayfah hill Saudi Arabia 85 C4
Ghūrī Iran 88 D4
Ghurrab, Jabal hill Saudi Arabia 88 B5
Ghuwayṭah, Nafūd al des. Saudi Arabia 85 D5
Ghuzor Uzbek. see G'uzor
Ghyvelde France 52 C3
Giaginskaya Russia 91 F1
Gialias r. Cyprus 85 A2
Gia Nghia Vietnam 71 D4
Gianisada i. Greece 59 L7
Giannitsa Greece 59 J4
Giant's Castle mt. S. Africa 101 I5
Giant's Causeway lava field U.K. 51 F2
Gianysada i. Greece see Gianisada
Gia Rai Vietnam 71 D5
Giarre Sicily Italy 58 F6
Gibb r. Australia 108 D3
Gibbonsville U.S.A. 126 E3
Gibeon Namibia 100 C3
Gibraltar terr. Europe 57 D5

▶Gibraltar Gibraltar 148 H3
United Kingdom Overseas Territory.

Gibraltar, Strait of Morocco/Spain 57 C6
Gibraltar Range National Park Australia 112 F2
Gibson Australia 109 C8
Gibson City U.S.A. 134 A3
Gibson Desert Australia 109 C6
Gichgeniyn Nuruu mts Mongolia 80 H2
Gidar Pak. 89 G4
Giddalur India 84 C3
Giddi, Gebel el hill Egypt see Jiddī, Jabal al
Giddings U.S.A. 131 D6
Gīdolē Eth. 97 G4
Gien France 56 F3
Gießen Germany 53 I4
Gīfān-e 'Olyā Iran 88 E2
Gifford r. Canada 119 J2
Gifhorn Germany 53 K2
Gift Lake Canada 120 H4
Gifu Japan 75 E6
Giganta, Cerro mt. Mex. 127 F8
Gigha i. U.K. 50 D5
Gīgiga Eth. see Jijiga
G'ijduvon Uzbek. 89 G1
Gijón Spain see Gijón/Xixón
Gijón/Xixón Spain 57 D2
Gila r. U.S.A. 129 F5
Gila Bend U.S.A. 129 G5
Gila Bend Mountains U.S.A. 129 G5
Gīlān-e Gharb Iran 88 B3
Gilbert r. Australia 110 C3
Gilbert AZ U.S.A. 129 H5
Gilbert WV U.S.A. 134 E5
Gilbert Islands Kiribati 150 H5
Gilbert Islands country Pacific Ocean see Kiribati
Gilbert Peak U.S.A. 129 H1
Gilbert Ridge sea feature Pacific Ocean 150 H6
Gilbert River Australia 110 C3
Gilbués Brazil 143 I5
Gil Chashmeh Iran 88 E3
Gilé Moz. 99 D5
Gilead hist. area Jordan 85 B3
Giles Creek r. Australia 108 E4
Gilford Island Canada 120 E5
Gilgai Australia 112 E2
Gilgandra Australia 112 D3
Gil Gil Creek r. Australia 112 D2
Gilgit Pak. 82 C2
Gilgit r. Pak. 87 L2
Gilgit-Baltistan admin. div. Pak. 89 I2
Gilgunnia Australia 112 C4
Gılındire Turkey see Aydıncık
Gillam Canada 121 M3
Gillen, Lake salt flat Australia 109 D6
Gilles, Lake salt flat Australia 111 B7
Gillett U.S.A. 135 G3
Gillette U.S.A. 126 G3
Gilliat Australia 110 C4
Gillingham England U.K. 49 E7
Gillingham England U.K. 49 H7
Gilling West U.K. 48 F4
Gilman U.S.A. 134 B3
Gilmer U.S.A. 131 E5
Gilmour Island Canada 122 F2
Gilroy U.S.A. 128 C3
Gīmbī Eth. 98 D3
Gimcheon S. Korea 75 C5
Gimhae S. Korea 75 C6
Gimhwa S. Korea 75 B5
Gimli Canada 121 L5
Gimol'skoye, Ozero l. Russia 42 G3
Ginebra, Laguna l. Bol. 142 E6
Gineifa Egypt see Junayfah
Gin Gin Australia 110 E5
Gingin Australia 109 A7
Gingolx Canada 120 D4
Gīnīr Eth. 98 E3
Ginosa Italy 58 G4
Ginzo de Limia Spain see Xinzo de Limia
Gioia del Colle Italy 58 G4
Gipouloux r. Canada 122 G3
Gippsland reg. Australia 112 B7
Girâ, Wâdi watercourse Egypt see Jirā', Wādī
Girān Rīg mt. Iran 88 E4
Girard U.S.A. 134 E2
Girardin, Lac l. Canada 123 I2
Girdab Iran 88 E3
Giresun Turkey 90 E2
Girgenti Sicily Italy see Agrigento
Giridh India see Giridih
Giridih India 83 F4
Girilambone Australia 112 C3
Girishk Afgh. 89 G4
Girna r. India 82 C5
Gir National Park India 82 B5
Girne Cyprus see Kyrenia
Girón Ecuador 142 C4
Giron Sweden see Kiruna
Girona Spain 57 H3
Gironde est. France 56 D4
Girot Pak. 89 I3
Girral Australia 112 C4
Girraween National Park Australia 112 E2
Girvan U.K. 50 E5
Girvas Russia 42 G3
Gisborne N.Z. 113 G4
Giscome Canada 120 F4
Gislaved Sweden 45 H8
Gisors France 52 B5
Gissar Tajik. see Hisor
Gissar Range mts Tajik./Uzbek. 89 G2
Gissarskiy Khrebet mts Tajik./Uzbek. see Gissar Range
Gitarama Rwanda 98 C4
Gitega Burundi 98 C4
Giuba r. Somalia see Jubba
Giulianova Italy 58 E3
Giurgiu Romania 59 K3
Giuvala, Pasul pass Romania 59 K2
Gīvar Iran 88 E2
Givet France 52 E4
Givors France 56 G4
Givry-en-Argonne France 52 E6
Giyani S. Africa 101 J2
Giza Egypt 90 C5
Gizhiga Russia 65 R3
Gjakovë Kosovo 59 I3
Gjilan Kosovo 59 I3
Gjirokastër Albania 59 I4
Gjirokastra Albania see Gjirokastër
Gjoa Haven Canada 119 I3
Gjøra Norway 44 F5
Gjøvik Norway 45 G6
Gkinas, Akrotirio pt Greece 59 M6
Glace Bay Canada 123 K5
Glacier Bay National Park and Preserve U.S.A. 120 B3
Glacier National Park Canada 120 G5
Glacier National Park U.S.A. 126 E2
Glacier Peak vol. U.S.A. 126 C2
Gladstad Norway 44 G4
Gladstone Australia 110 E4
Gladstone Canada 121 L5
Gladwin U.S.A. 134 C2
Gladys U.S.A. 134 F5
Gladys Lake Canada 120 C3
Glamis U.K. 50 F4
Glamis U.S.A. 129 F5
Glamoč Bos. & Herz. 58 G2
Glan r. Germany 53 H5
Glandorf Germany 53 I2
Glanton U.K. 48 F3
Glasgow U.K. 50 E5
Glasgow KY U.S.A. 134 C5
Glasgow MT U.S.A. 126 G2
Glasgow VA U.S.A. 134 F5
Glaslyn Canada 121 I4
Glass, Loch l. U.K. 50 E3
Glass Mountain U.S.A. 128 D3
Glastonbury U.K. 49 E7
Glauchau Germany 53 M4
Glazov Russia 42 L4
Gleiwitz Poland see Gliwice
Glen U.S.A. 135 J1
Glen Allen U.S.A. 135 G5
Glen Alpine Dam S. Africa 101 I2
Glenamaddy Ireland 51 D4
Glenamoy r. Ireland 51 C3
Glen Arbor U.S.A. 134 C1
Glenbawn, Lake Australia 112 E4
Glenboro Canada 121 L5
Glen Canyon gorge U.S.A. 129 H3
Glen Canyon Dam U.S.A. 129 H3
Glencoe Canada 134 E2
Glencoe S. Africa 101 J5
Glencoe U.S.A. 130 E2
Glendale AZ U.S.A. 129 G5
Glendale CA U.S.A. 128 D4
Glendale UT U.S.A. 129 G3
Glendale Lake U.S.A. 135 F3
Glen Davis Australia 112 E4
Glenden Australia 110 E4
Glendive U.S.A. 126 G3
Glendon Canada 121 I4
Glendo Reservoir U.S.A. 126 G4
Glenfield U.S.A. 135 H2
Glengavlen Ireland 51 E3
Glengyle Australia 110 B5
Glen Innes Australia 112 E2
Glenluce U.K. 50 E6
Glen Lyon U.S.A. 135 G3
Glenlyon Peak Canada 120 C2
Glen More valley U.K. 50 E3
Glenmorgan Australia 112 D1
Glenn U.S.A. 128 B2
Glennallen U.S.A. 118 D3
Glennie U.S.A. 134 D1
Glenns Ferry U.S.A. 126 E4
Glenora Canada 120 D3
Glenore Australia 110 C3
Glenormiston Australia 110 B4
Glenreagh Australia 112 F3
Glen Rose U.S.A. 131 D5
Glenrothes U.K. 50 F4
Glens Falls U.S.A. 135 I2
Glen Shee valley U.K. 50 F4
Glenties Ireland 51 D3
Glenveagh National Park Ireland 51 E2
Glenville U.S.A. 134 E4
Glenwood AR U.S.A. 131 E5
Glenwood IA U.S.A. 130 E3
Glenwood MN U.S.A. 130 E2
Glenwood NM U.S.A. 129 I5
Glenwood Springs U.S.A. 129 J2
Glevum U.K. see Gloucester
Glinde Germany 53 K1
Glittertinden mt. Norway 45 F6
Gliwice Poland 47 Q5
Globe U.S.A. 129 H5
Glogau Poland see Głogów
Głogów Poland 47 P5
Glomfjord Norway 44 H3
Glomma r. Norway 44 G7
Glommersträsk Sweden 44 K4
Glorieuses, Îles is Indian Ocean 99 E5
Glorioso Islands Indian Ocean see Glorieuses, Îles
Gloster U.S.A. 131 F6
Gloucester Australia 112 E3
Gloucester U.K. 49 E7
Gloucester MA U.S.A. 135 J2
Gloucester VA U.S.A. 135 G5
Gloversville U.S.A. 135 H2
Glovertown Canada 123 L4
Glöwen Germany 53 M2
Glubinnoye Russia 74 D3
Glubokiy Krasnoyarskiy Kray Russia 72 H2
Glubokiy Rostovskaya Oblast' Russia 43 I6
Glubokoye Belarus see Hlybokaye
Glubokoye Kazakh. 80 F1
Gluggarnir hill Faroe Is 44 [inset 2]
Glukhov Ukr. see Hlukhiv
Glusburn U.K. 48 F5
Glynebwy U.K. see Ebbw Vale
Gmelinka Russia 43 J6
Gmünd Austria 47 O6
Gmunden Austria 47 N7
Gnarp Sweden 45 J5
Gnarrenburg Germany 53 J1
Gnesen Poland see Gniezno
Gniezno Poland 47 P4
Gnjilane Kosovo see Gjilan
Gnowangerup Australia 109 B8
Gnows Nest Range hills Australia 109 B7
Goa India 84 B3
Goa state India 84 B3
Goageb Namibia 100 C4
Goalen Head hd Australia 112 E6
Goalpara India 83 G4
Goat Fell hill U.K. 50 D5
Goba Eth. 98 E3
Gobabis Namibia 100 D2
Gobannium U.K. see Abergavenny
Gobas Namibia 100 D4
Gobernador (abandoned) U.S.A. 129 J3
Gobi Desert des. China/Mongolia 72 J4
Gobindpur India 83 F5
Gobles U.S.A. 134 C2
Gobō Japan 75 D6
Goch Germany 52 G3
Gochas Namibia 100 D3
Go Công Vietnam 71 D5
Godalming U.K. 49 G7
Godavari r. India 84 D2
Godavari, Cape India 84 D2
Godda India 83 F4
Godē Eth. 98 E3
Godere Eth. 98 E3
Goderich Canada 134 E2
Goderville France 49 H9
Godhavn Greenland see Qeqertarsuaq
Godhra India 82 C5
Godia Creek b. India 89 H6
Gods r. Canada 121 M3
Gods Lake Canada 121 M4
God's Mercy, Bay of Canada 121 O2
Godthåb Greenland see Nuuk
Godwin-Austen, Mount China/Pak. see K2
Goedereede Neth. 52 D3
Goedgegun Swaziland see Nhlangano
Goegap Nature Reserve S. Africa 100 D5
Goélands, Lac aux l. Canada 123 J3
Goes Neth. 52 D3
Gogama Canada 122 E5
Gogebic Range hills U.S.A. 130 F2
Gogra r. India see Ghaghara
Goheung S. Korea 75 B6
Goiana Brazil 143 L5
Goiandira Brazil 145 A2
Goianésia Brazil 145 A1
Goiânia Brazil 145 A2
Goiás Brazil 145 A1
Goiás state Brazil 145 A2
Goidhoo Maldives 84 B5
Goifulha Fehendhu Atoll Maldives see Goidhoo
Goinsargoin China 76 C2
Goioerê Brazil 144 F2
Gojra Pak. 89 I4
Gokak India 84 B2
Gokarn India 84 B3
Gök Çay r. Turkey 85 A1
Gökçeada i. Turkey 59 K4
Gökdepe Turkm. see Gëkdepe
Gökdere r. Turkey 85 A1
Goklenkuy, Solonchak salt l. Turkm. 88 E1
Gökova Körfezi b. Turkey 59 L6
Gokprosh Hills Pak. 89 F5
Göksun Turkey 90 E3
Göksu Parkı Turkey 85 A1
Gokteik Myanmar 70 B2
Gokwe Zimbabwe 99 C5
Gol Norway 45 F6
Golaghat India 83 H4
Golbāf Iran 88 E4
Gölbaşı Turkey 90 E3
Golconda U.S.A. 128 E1
Gölcük Turkey 59 M4
Gold U.S.A. 135 G3
Goldap Poland 47 S3
Gold Beach U.S.A. 126 B4
Goldberg Germany 53 M1
Gold Coast country Africa see Ghana
Gold Coast Australia 112 F2
Golden U.S.A. 126 G5
Golden Bay N.Z. 113 D5
Goldendale U.S.A. 126 C3
Goldene Aue reg. Germany 53 K3
Golden Gate Highlands National Park S. Africa 101 I5
Golden Hinde mt. Canada 120 E5
Golden Lake Canada 135 G1
Golden Prairie Canada 121 I5
Goldenstedt Germany 53 I2
Goldfield U.S.A. 128 E3
Goldsand Lake Canada 121 K3
Goldsboro U.S.A. 133 E5
Goldstone Lake U.S.A. 128 E4
Goldsworthy (abandoned) Australia 108 B5
Goldthwaite U.S.A. 131 D6
Goldvein U.S.A. 135 G4
Göle Turkey 91 F2
Goleta U.S.A. 128 D4
Golets-Davydov, Gora mt. Russia 73 J2
Gölgeli Dağları mts Turkey 59 M6
Goliad U.S.A. 131 D6
Golingka China see Gongbo'gyamda
Gölköy Turkey 90 E2
Gollel Swaziland see Lavumisa
Golm Germany 53 M2
Golmberg hill Germany 53 N2
Golmud China 80 H4
Golovnino Russia 74 G4
Golpāyegān Iran 88 C3
Gölpazarı Turkey 59 N4
Golspie U.K. 50 F3
Gol Vardeh Iran 89 F3
Golyama Syutkya mt. Bulg. 59 K4
Golyam Persenk mt. Bulg. 59 K4
Golyshi Russia see Vetluzhskiy
Golzow Germany 53 M2
Goma Dem. Rep. Congo 98 C4
Gōmal Kēlay Afgh. 89 H3
Gomang Co salt l. China 83 G3
Gomati r. India 87 N4
Gombak, Bukit hill Sing. 71 [inset]
Gombe Nigeria 96 E3
Gombe r. Tanz. 99 D4
Gombi Nigeria 96 E3
Gombroon Iran see Bandar-e 'Abbās
Gomel' Belarus see Homyel'
Gómez Palacio Mex. 131 C7
Gomīsh Tappeh Iran 88 D2
Gommern Germany 53 L2
Gomo Co salt l. China 83 F2
Gonābād Iran 88 E2
Gonaïves Haiti 137 J5
Gonarezhou National Park Zimbabwe 99 D6
Gonâve, Île de la i. Haiti 137 J5
Gonbad, Chāh-e well Iran 88 D3
Gonbad-e Kāvūs Iran 88 D2
Gonda India 83 E4
Gondal India 82 B5
Gondar Eth. see Gonder
Gonder Eth. 98 D2
Gondia India see Gondiya
Gondiya India 82 E5
Gönen Turkey 59 L4
Gonfreville-l'Orcher France 49 H9
Gong'an China 77 G2
Gongbalou China see Gamba
Gongbo'gyamda China 76 B2
Gongchang China see Longxi
Gongcheng China 77 F3
Gongga Shan mt. China 76 D2
Gonghe Qinghai China 80 J4
Gonghe Yunnan China see Mouding
Gongjiang China see Yudu
Gongogi r. Brazil 145 D1
Gongolgon Australia 112 C3
Gongquan China 76 E2
Gongtang China 83 G3
Gongwang Shan mts China 76 D3
Gongxian China see Gongquan
Gonjo China see Kasha
Gonjog China see Coqên
Gonzales CA U.S.A. 128 C3
Gonzales TX U.S.A. 131 D6
Gonzha Russia 74 B1
Goochland U.S.A. 135 G5
Goodenough, Cape Antarctica 152 G2
Goodenough Island P.N.G. 106 F2
Gooderham Canada 135 F1
Good Hope, Cape of S. Africa 100 D8
Good Hope Mountain Canada 126 B2
Gooding U.S.A. 126 E4
Goodland IN U.S.A. 134 B3
Goodland KS U.S.A. 130 C4
Goodlettsville U.S.A. 134 B5
Goodooga Australia 112 C2
Goodspeed Nunataks Antarctica 152 E2
Goole U.K. 48 G5
Goolgowi Australia 112 B5
Goolma Australia 112 D4
Gooloogong Australia 112 D4
Goomalling Australia 109 B7
Goombalie Australia 112 B2
Goondiwindi Australia 112 E2
Goongarrie, Lake salt flat Australia 109 C7
Goongarrie National Park Australia 109 C7
Goonyella Australia 110 D4
Goorly, Lake salt flat Australia 109 B7
Goose Bay Canada see Happy Valley-Goose Bay
Goose Creek U.S.A. 133 D5
Goose Lake U.S.A. 126 C4
Gooty India 84 C3
Gopalganj Bangl. 83 G5
Gopalganj India 83 F4
Gopeshwar India 82 D3
Göppingen Germany 53 J6
Gorakhnath mt. India 82 B5
Gorakhpur India 83 E4
Goražde Bos. & Herz. 58 H3
Gorczański Park Narodowy nat. park Poland 47 R6
Gorda, Punta pt U.S.A. 128 A1
Gördes Turkey 59 M5
Gordil Cent. Afr. Rep. 98 C3
Gordon r. Canada 121 O1
Gordon U.K. 50 G5
Gordon U.S.A. 130 C3
Gordon, Lake Australia 111 [inset]
Gordon Downs Australia 108 E4
Gordon Lake Canada 121 I3
Gordon Lake U.S.A. 135 F4
Gordonsville U.S.A. 135 F4
Goré Chad 97 E4
Gorē Eth. 98 D3
Gore N.Z. 113 B8
Gore U.S.A. 135 F4
Gorebridge U.K. 50 F5
Gore Point pt U.S.A. 118 C4
Gorey Ireland 51 F5
Gorg Iran 89 E4
Gorgān Iran 88 D2
Gorgān, Khalīj-e Iran 88 D2
Gorge Range hills Australia 108 B5
Gorgona, Isla i. Col. 142 C3
Gorham U.S.A. 135 J1
Gori Georgia 86 F1
Gorinchem Neth. 52 E3
Goris Armenia 91 G3
Gorizia Italy 58 E2
Gorki Belarus see Horki
Gor'kiy Russia see Nizhniy Novgorod
Gor'kovskoye Vodokhranilishche resr Russia 42 I4
Gorlice Poland 43 D6
Görlitz Germany 47 O5
Gorlovka Ukr. see Horlivka
Gorna Dzhumaya Bulg. see Blagoevgrad
Gorna Oryahovitsa Bulg. 59 K3
Gornji Milanovac Serbia 59 I2
Gornji Vakuf Bos. & Herz. 58 G3
Gorno-Altaysk Russia 80 G1
Gornotrakiyska Nizina lowland Bulg. 59 K3
Gornozavodsk Permskiy Kray Russia 41 R4
Gornozavodsk Sakhalinskaya Oblast' Russia 74 F3
Gornyak Russia 80 F1
Gornyy Russia 43 K6
Gornyye Klyuchi Russia 74 D3
Goro i. Fiji see Koro
Gorodenka Ukr. see Horodenka
Gorodets Russia 42 I4
Gorodishche Penzenskaya Oblast' Russia 43 J5
Gorodishche Volgogradskaya Oblast' Russia 43 J6
Gorodok Belarus see Haradok
Gorodok Russia see Zakamensk
Gorodok Khmel'nyts'ka Oblast' Ukr. see Horodok
Gorodok L'vivs'ka Oblast' Ukr. see Horodok
Gorodovikovsk Russia 43 I7
Goroka P.N.G. 69 L8
Gorokhovets Russia 42 I4
Gorom Gorom Burkina Faso 96 C3
Gorong, Kepulauan is Indon. 69 I7
Gorongosa mt. Moz. 99 D5
Gorongosa, Parque Nacional da nat. park Moz. 99 D5
Gorontalo Indon. 69 G6
Gorshechnoye Russia 43 H6
Gort Ireland 51 D4
Gort an Choirce Ireland 51 D2
Gorūh Iran 88 E4
Gorutuba r. Brazil 145 C1
Goryachiy Klyuch Russia 91 E1
Goryeong S. Korea 75 C6
Görzke Germany 53 M2
Gorzów Wielkopolski Poland 47 O4
Gosainthan mt. China see Xixabangma Feng
Gosforth U.K. 48 F3
Goshen CA U.S.A. 128 D3
Goshen IN U.S.A. 134 C3
Goshen NH U.S.A. 135 I2
Goshen NY U.S.A. 135 H3
Goshen VA U.S.A. 134 F5
Goshoba Turkm. see Goşoba
Goslar Germany 53 K3
Goşoba Turkm. 91 I2
Gospić Croatia 58 F2
Gosport U.K. 49 F8
Gossi Mali 96 C3
Gostivar Macedonia 59 I4
Gosu China 76 C1
Göteborg Sweden see Gothenburg
Götene Sweden 45 H7
Gotenhafen Poland see Gdynia
Gotha Germany 53 K4
Gothenburg Sweden 45 G8
Gothenburg U.S.A. 130 C3
Gotland i. Sweden 45 K8
Gotō-rettō is Japan 75 C6
Gotse Delchev Bulg. 59 J4
Gotska Sandön i. Sweden 45 K7
Gōtsu Japan 75 D6
Göttingen Germany 53 J3
Gott Peak Canada 120 F5
Gottwaldow Czechia see Zlín
Gouda Neth. 52 E2
Goudiri Senegal 96 B3
Goudoumaria Niger 96 E3
Goûgaram Niger 96 D3

▶Gough Island S. Atlantic Ocean 148 H8
Dependency of Tristan da Cunha.

Gouin, Réservoir resr Canada 122 G4
Goulburn Australia 112 D5
Goulburn r. N.S.W. Australia 112 E4
Goulburn r. Vic. Australia 112 B6
Goulburn Islands Australia 108 F2
Goulburn River National Park Australia 112 E4
Gould Coast Antarctica 152 J1
Goulou atoll Micronesia see Ngulu
Goundam Mali 96 C3
Goundi Chad 97 E4
Goupil, Lac l. Canada 123 H3
Gouraya Alg. 57 G5
Gourcy Burkina Faso 96 C3
Gourdon France 56 E4
Gouré Niger 96 E3
Gouripur Bangl. 83 G4
Gourits r. S. Africa 100 E8
Gourma-Rharous Mali 96 C3
Gournay-en-Bray France 52 B5
Goussainville France 52 C5
Gouverneur U.S.A. 135 H1
Governador Valadares Brazil 145 C2
Governor's Harbour Bahamas 133 E7
Govĭ Altayn Nuruu mts Mongolia 80 I3
Govind Ballash Pant Sagar resr India 83 E4
Gowanda U.S.A. 135 F2
Gowan Range hills Australia 110 D5
Gowna, Lough l. Ireland 51 E4
Goya Arg. 144 E3
Göyçay Azer. 91 G2
Goyder watercourse Australia 109 F6
Göygöl Azer. 91 G2
Goymatdag hills Turkm. 88 D1
Göynük Turkey 59 N4
Goyoum Cameroon 96 E4
Goz-Beïda Chad 97 F3
Gozha Co salt l. China 82 E2
Gözkaya Turkey 85 C1
Gozo i. Malta 58 F6
Graaff-Reinet S. Africa 100 G7
Grabfeld plain Germany 53 K4
Grabo Côte d'Ivoire 96 C4
Grabouw S. Africa 100 D8
Grabow Germany 53 L1
Gračac Croatia 58 F2
Gracefield Canada 122 F5
Gracey U.S.A. 134 B5
Gradaús, Serra dos hills Brazil 143 H5
Gradiška Bos. & Herz. see Bosanska Gradiška
Grady U.S.A. 131 C5
Gräfenhainichen Germany 53 M3
Grafenwöhr Germany 53 L5
Grafton Australia 112 F2
Grafton ND U.S.A. 130 D1
Grafton WI U.S.A. 134 B2
Grafton WV U.S.A. 134 E4
Grafton, Cape Australia 110 D3
Grafton, Mount U.S.A. 129 F2
Grafton Passage Australia 110 D3
Graham NC U.S.A. 132 E4
Graham TX U.S.A. 131 D5
Graham, Mount U.S.A. 129 I5
Graham Bell Island Russia see Greem-Bell, Ostrov
Graham Island B.C. Canada 120 C4
Graham Island Nunavut Canada 119 I2
Graham Land reg. Antarctica 152 L2
Grahamstown S. Africa 101 H7
Grahovo Bos. & Herz. see Bosansko Grahovo
Graigue Ireland 51 F5
Grajaú Brazil 143 I5
Grajaú r. Brazil 143 J4
Grammont Belgium see Geraardsbergen
Grammos mt. Greece 59 I4
Grampian Mountains U.K. 50 E4
Grampians National Park Australia 111 C8
Granada Nicaragua 137 G6
Granada Spain 57 E5

Granada U.S.A. **130** C4
Granard Ireland **51** E4
Granbury U.S.A. **131** D5
Granby Canada **123** G5
Gran Canaria *i.* Canary Is **96** B2
Gran Chaco *reg.* Arg./Para. **144** D3
Grand *r. MO* U.S.A. **134** B2
Grand *r. SD* U.S.A. **130** C2
Grand Atlas *mts* Morocco *see* **Haut Atlas**
Grand Bahama *i.* Bahamas **133** E7
Grand Ballon *mt.* France **47** K7
Grand Bank Canada **123** L5
Grand Banks of Newfoundland *sea feature* N. Atlantic Ocean **148** E3
Grand-Bassam Côte d'Ivoire **96** C4
Grand Bay-Westfield Canada **123** I5
Grand Bend Canada **134** E2
Grand Blanc U.S.A. **134** D2
Grand Canal Ireland **51** E4
Grand Canary *i.* Canary Is *see* **Gran Canaria**
Grand Canyon U.S.A. **129** G3
Grand Canyon *gorge* U.S.A. **129** G3
Grand Canyon National Park U.S.A. **129** G3
Grand Canyon-Parashant National Monument *nat. park* U.S.A. **129** G3
Grand Cayman *i.* Cayman Is **137** H5
Grand Drumont *mt.* France **47** K7
Grande *r. Bahia* Brazil **145** B1
Grande *r. São Paulo* Brazil **145** A3
Grande, Bahía *b.* Arg. **144** C8
Grande, Ilha *i.* Brazil **145** B3
Grande Cache Canada **120** G4
Grande Comore *i.* Comoros *see* **Ngazidja**
Grande de Matagalpa *r.* Nicaragua **137** H6
Grande Prairie Canada **120** G4
Grand Erg Occidental *des.* Alg. **54** D5
Grand Erg Oriental *des.* Alg. **54** F6
Grande-Rivière Canada **123** I4
Gran Desierto de Altar, Reserva de la Biosfera *tourist site* Mex. **127** E7
Gran Desierto del Pinacate, Parque Natural del *tourist site* Mex. **127** E7
Grandes, Salinas *salt marsh* Arg. **144** C4
Grande-Vallée Canada **123** I4
Grand Falls Canada **123** I5
Grand Falls-Windsor Canada **123** L4
Grand Forks Canada **120** G5
Grand Forks U.S.A. **130** D2
Grand Gorge U.S.A. **135** H2
Grand Haven U.S.A. **134** B2
Grandin, Lac *l.* Canada **120** G1
Grandioznyy, Pik *mt.* Russia **72** H2
Grand Island U.S.A. **130** D3
Grand Isle U.S.A. **131** F6
Grand Junction U.S.A. **129** I2
Grand-Lahou Côte d'Ivoire **96** C4
Grand Lake *N.B.* Canada **123** I5
Grand Lake *Nfld. and Lab.* Canada **123** J3
Grand Lake *Nfld. and Lab.* Canada **123** K4
Grand Lake *LA* U.S.A. **131** E6
Grand Lake *MI* U.S.A. **134** D1
Grand Lake St Marys U.S.A. **134** C3
Grand Ledge U.S.A. **134** C2
Grand Manan Island Canada **123** I5
Grand Marais *MI* U.S.A. **132** C2
Grand Marais *MN* U.S.A. **130** F2
Grand-Mère Canada **123** G5
Grand Mesa U.S.A. **129** J2
Grândola Port. **57** B4
Grand Passage New Caledonia **107** G3
Grand Pré, Landscape of *tourist site* Canada **123** I5
Grand Rapids Canada **121** L4
Grand Rapids *MI* U.S.A. **134** C2
Grand Rapids *MN* U.S.A. **130** E2
Grand-Sault Canada *see* **Grand Falls**
Grand St-Bernard, Col du *pass* Italy/Switz. *see* **Great St Bernard Pass**
Grand Teton *mt.* U.S.A. **126** F4
Grand Teton National Park U.S.A. **126** F4
Grand Traverse Bay U.S.A. **134** C1

▶**Grand Turk** Turks and Caicos Is **137** J4
Capital of the Turks and Caicos Islands.

Grandville U.S.A. **134** C2
Grandvilliers France **52** B5
Grand Wash Cliffs *mts* U.S.A. **129** F4
Grange Ireland **51** E6
Grängesberg Sweden **45** I6
Grangeville U.S.A. **126** D3
Granisle Canada **120** E4
Granite Falls U.S.A. **130** E2
Granite Mountain U.S.A. **128** E1
Granite Mountains *CA* U.S.A. **129** F4
Granite Mountains *CA* U.S.A. **129** F5
Granite Peak *MT* U.S.A. **126** F3
Granite Peak *UT* U.S.A. **129** G1
Granite Range *mts AK* U.S.A. **120** A3
Granite Range *mts NV* U.S.A. **128** D1
Granitola, Capo *c. Sicily* Italy **58** E6
Granja Brazil **143** J4
Gran Laguna Salada *l.* Arg. **144** C6
Gränna Sweden **45** I7
Gran Paradiso *mt.* Italy **58** B2
Gran Paradiso, Parco Nazionale del *nat. park* Italy **58** B2
Gran Pilastro *mt.* Austria/Italy **47** M7
Gran San Bernardo, Colle del *pass* Italy/Switz. *see* **Great St Bernard Pass**
Gran Sasso e Monti della Laga, Parco Nazionale del *nat. park* Italy **58** E3
Granschütz Germany **53** M3
Gransee Germany **53** N1
Grant U.S.A. **130** C3
Grant, Mount U.S.A. **128** E2
Grantham U.K. **49** G6
Grant Island Antarctica **152** J2
Grant Lake Canada **120** G1
Grantown-on-Spey U.K. **50** F3
Grant Range *mts* U.S.A. **129** F2
Grants U.S.A. **129** J4
Grants Pass U.S.A. **126** C4
Grantsville *UT* U.S.A. **129** G1
Grantsville *WV* U.S.A. **134** E4
Granville France **56** D2
Granville *AZ* U.S.A. **129** I5
Granville *NY* U.S.A. **135** I2
Granville *TN* U.S.A. **134** C5
Granville (abandoned) Canada **120** B2
Granville Lake Canada **121** K3
Grão Mogol Brazil **145** C2
Grapevine Mountains U.S.A. **128** E3
Gras, Lac de *l.* Canada **121** I1
Graskop S. Africa **101** J3
Grasplatz Namibia **100** B4
Grass *r.* Canada **121** L3
Grass *r.* U.S.A. **135** H1
Grasse France **56** H5
Grassflat U.S.A. **135** F3
Grassington U.K. **48** F4
Grasslands National Park Canada **121** J5
Grass Range U.S.A. **126** F3
Grass Valley U.S.A. **128** C2
Grassy Butte U.S.A. **130** C2
Grästorp Sweden **45** H7
Gratz U.S.A. **134** C4
Graudenz Poland *see* **Grudziądz**
Graus Spain **57** G2
Gravataí Brazil **145** A5
Grave, Pointe de *pt* France **56** D4
Gravelbourg Canada **121** J5
Gravel Hill Lake Canada **121** K2
Gravelines France **52** C4
Gravelotte S. Africa **101** J2
Gravenhurst Canada **134** F1
Grave Peak U.S.A. **126** E3
Gravesend Australia **112** E2
Gravesend U.K. **49** H7
Gravina in Puglia Italy **58** G4
Grawn U.S.A. **134** C1
Gray France **56** G3
Gray *GA* U.S.A. **133** D5
Gray *KY* U.S.A. **134** C5
Gray *ME* U.S.A. **135** J2
Grayback Mountain U.S.A. **126** C4
Gray Lake Canada **121** I2
Grayling *r.* Canada **120** E3
Grayling U.S.A. **134** C1
Grays U.K. **49** H7
Grays Harbor *inlet* U.S.A. **126** B3
Grays Lake U.S.A. **126** F4
Grayson U.S.A. **134** D4
Graz Austria **47** O7
Greasy Lake Canada **120** F2
Great Abaco *i.* Bahamas **133** E7
Great Australian Bight *g.* Australia **109** E8
Great Baddow U.K. **49** H7
Great Bahama Bank *sea feature* Bahamas **133** E7
Great Barrier Island N.Z. **113** E3
Great Barrier Reef Australia **110** D1
Great Barrier Reef Marine Park (Cairns Section) Australia **110** D3
Great Barrier Reef Marine Park (Capricorn Section) Australia **110** E4
Great Barrier Reef Marine Park (Central Section) Australia **110** E3
Great Barrier Reef Marine Park (Far North Section) Australia **110** D2
Great Barrington U.S.A. **135** I2
Great Basalt Wall National Park Australia **110** D3
Great Basin U.S.A. **128** E2
Great Basin National Park U.S.A. **129** F2
Great Bear *r.* Canada **120** E1

▶**Great Bear Lake** Canada **120** G1
4th largest lake in North America and 7th in the world.

Great Belt *sea chan.* Denmark **45** G9
Great Bend U.S.A. **130** D4
Great Bitter Lake Egypt **85** A4
Great Blasket Island Ireland **51** B5

▶**Great Britain** *i.* U.K. **46** G4
Largest island in Europe and 8th in the world.

Great Clifton U.K. **48** D4
Great Coco Island Cocos Is **68** A4
Great Cumbrae *i.* U.K. **50** E5
Great Dismal Swamp National Wildlife Refuge *nature res.* U.S.A. **135** G5
Great Dividing Range *mts* Australia **112** B6
Great Eastern Erg *des.* Alg. *see* **Grand Erg Oriental**
Greater Antarctica *reg.* Antarctica *see* **East Antarctica**
Greater Antilles *is* Caribbean Sea **137** H4
Greater Khingan Mountains China *see* **Da Hinggan Ling**
Greater Tunb *i.* The Gulf *see* **Tonb-e Bozorg, Jazīreh-ye**
Great Exuma *i.* Bahamas **133** F8
Great Falls U.S.A. **126** F3
Great Fish *r.* S. Africa **101** H7
Great Fish Point S. Africa **101** H7
Great Fish River Reserve Complex *nature res.* S. Africa **101** H7
Great Gandak *r.* India **83** F4
Great Ganges *atoll* Cook Is *see* **Manihiki**
Great Guana Cay *i.* Bahamas **133** E7
Great Himalayan National Park India **82** D3
Great Inagua *i.* Bahamas **137** J4
Great Karoo *plat.* S. Africa **100** F7
Great Kei *r.* S. Africa **101** I7
Great Lake Australia **111** [inset]
Great Limpopo Transfrontier Park Africa **101** J2
Great Malvern U.K. **49** E6
Great Meteor Tablemount *sea feature* N. Atlantic Ocean **148** G4
Great Namaqualand *reg.* Namibia **100** C4
Great Nicobar *i.* India **71** A6
Great Ormes Head *hd* U.K. **48** D5
Great Ouse *r.* U.K. **49** H6
Great Oyster Bay Australia **111** [inset]
Great Palm Islands Australia **110** D3
Great Plains U.S.A. **130** C3
Great Point U.S.A. **135** J3
Great Rift Valley Africa **98** D4
Great Ruaha *r.* Tanz. **99** D4
Great Sacandaga Lake U.S.A. **135** H2
Great St Bernard Pass Italy/Switz. **58** B2
Great Salt Lake U.S.A. **129** G1
Great Salt Lake Desert U.S.A. **129** G1
Great Sand Hills Canada **121** I5
Great Sand Sea *des.* Egypt/Libya **90** B5
Great Sandy Desert Australia **108** C5
Great Sandy Island Australia *see* **Fraser Island**
Great Sandy National Park Austr. **111** F5
Great Sea Reef Fiji **107** H3

▶**Great Slave Lake** Canada **120** H2
Deepest and 5th largest lake in North America and 10th largest in the world.

Great Smoky Mountains U.S.A. **133** C5
Great Smoky Mountains National Park U.S.A. **132** D5
Great Snow Mountain Canada **120** E3
Greatstone-on-Sea U.K. **49** H8
Great Stour *r.* U.K. **49** I7
Great Torrington U.K. **49** C8
Great Victoria Desert Australia **109** E7
Great Wall *research station* Antarctica **152** A2
Great Wall *tourist site* China **73** L4
Great Waltham U.K. **49** H7
Great Western Erg *des.* Alg. *see* **Grand Erg Occidental**
Great Western Torres Islands Myanmar **71** B5
Great Whernside *hill* U.K. **48** F4
Great Yarmouth U.K. **49** I6
Grebenkovskiy Ukr. *see* **Hrebinka**
Grebyonka Ukr. *see* **Hrebinka**
Greco, Cape Cyprus *see* **Greko, Cape**
Gredos, Sierra de *mts* Spain **57** D3
Greece *country* Europe **59** I5
Greece U.S.A. **135** G2
Greeley *CO* U.S.A. **126** G4
Greeley *NE* U.S.A. **130** D3
Greem-Bell, Ostrov *i.* Russia **64** H1
Green *r. KY* U.S.A. **134** B5
Green *r. WY* U.S.A. **129** I2
Green Bay U.S.A. **134** A1
Green Bay *b.* U.S.A. **134** B1
Greenbrier U.S.A. **134** B5
Greenbrier *r.* U.S.A. **134** E5
Green Cape Australia **112** E6
Greencastle Bahamas **133** E7
Greencastle U.K. **51** F3
Greencastle U.S.A. **134** B4
Green Cove Springs U.S.A. **133** D6
Greene *ME* U.S.A. **135** J1
Greene *NY* U.S.A. **135** H2
Greeneville U.S.A. **132** D4
Greenfield *CA* U.S.A. **128** C3
Greenfield *IN* U.S.A. **134** C4
Greenfield *MA* U.S.A. **135** I2
Greenfield *OH* U.S.A. **134** D4
Green Head *hd* Australia **109** A7
Greenhill Island Australia **108** F2
Green Island Taiwan *see* **Lü Dao**
Green Lake Canada **121** J4

▶**Greenland** *terr.* N. America **119** N3
Self-governing Danish territory. Largest island in North America and the world, and 3rd largest political entity in North America.

Greenland Basin *sea feature* Arctic Ocean **153** I2
Greenland Fracture Zone *sea feature* Arctic Ocean **153** I1
Greenland Sea Greenland/Svalbard **64** A2
Greenlaw U.K. **50** G5
Green Mountains U.S.A. **135** I1
Greenock U.K. **50** E5
Greenore Ireland **51** F3
Greenport U.S.A. **135** I3
Green River P.N.G. **69** K7
Green River *UT* U.S.A. **129** H2
Green River *WY* U.S.A. **126** F4
Green River Lake U.S.A. **134** C5
Greensboro U.S.A. **133** D5
Greensburg *IN* U.S.A. **134** C4
Greensburg *KS* U.S.A. **130** D4
Greensburg *KY* U.S.A. **134** C5
Greensburg *LA* U.S.A. **131** F6
Greensburg *PA* U.S.A. **134** F3
Greens Peak U.S.A. **129** I4
Greenstone Point U.K. **50** D3
Green Swamp U.S.A. **133** E5
Greentown U.S.A. **134** C3
Greenup *IL* U.S.A. **130** F4
Greenup *KY* U.S.A. **134** D4
Green Valley Canada **135** H1
Greenville Liberia **96** C4
Greenville *AL* U.S.A. **133** C6
Greenville *IL* U.S.A. **130** F4
Greenville *KY* U.S.A. **134** B5
Greenville *ME* U.S.A. **132** G2
Greenville *MI* U.S.A. **134** C2
Greenville *MS* U.S.A. **131** F5
Greenville *NC* U.S.A. **132** E5
Greenville *NH* U.S.A. **135** J2
Greenville *OH* U.S.A. **134** C3
Greenville *PA* U.S.A. **134** E3
Greenville *SC* U.S.A. **133** D5
Greenville *TX* U.S.A. **131** D5
Greenwich *atoll* Micronesia *see* **Kapingamarangi**
Greenwich *CT* U.S.A. **135** I3
Greenwich *OH* U.S.A. **134** D3
Greenwood *AR* U.S.A. **131** E5
Greenwood *IN* U.S.A. **134** B4
Greenwood *MS* U.S.A. **131** F5
Greenwood *SC* U.S.A. **133** D5
Gregory *r.* Australia **110** B3
Gregory, Lake *salt flat S.A.* Australia **111** B6
Gregory, Lake *salt flat W.A.* Australia **108** D5
Gregory, Lake *salt flat W.A.* Australia **109** B6
Gregory Downs Australia **110** B3
Gregory National Park Australia **108** E4
Gregory Range *hills Qld* Australia **110** C3
Gregory Range *hills W.A.* Australia **108** C5
Greifswald Germany **47** N3
Greiz Germany **53** M4
Greko, Cape Cyprus **85** B2
Gremyachinsk Russia **41** R4
Grenå Denmark *see* **Grenaa**
Grenaa Denmark **45** G8
Grenada U.S.A. **131** F5
Grenada *country* West Indies **137** L6
Grenade France **56** E5
Grenen *spit* Denmark **45** G8
Grenfell Australia **112** D4
Grenfell Canada **121** K5
Grenoble France **56** G4
Grense-Jakobselv Norway **44** Q2
Grenville, Cape Australia **110** C1
Grenville Island Fiji *see* **Rotuma**
Greshak Pak. **89** G5
Gresham U.S.A. **126** C3
Gressåmoen Nasjonalpark *nat. park* Norway **44** H4
Greta *r.* U.K. **48** E4
Gretna U.K. **50** F6
Gretna *LA* U.S.A. **131** F6
Gretna *VA* U.S.A. **134** F5
Greußen Germany **53** K3
Grevelingen *sea chan.* Neth. **52** D3
Greven Germany **53** H2
Grevena Greece **59** I4
Grevenbicht Neth. **52** F3
Grevenbroich Germany **52** G3
Grevenmacher Lux. **52** G5
Grevesmühlen Germany **47** M4
Grey, Cape Australia **110** B2
Greybull U.S.A. **126** F3
Greybull *r.* U.S.A. **126** F3
Grey Hunter Peak Canada **120** C2
Grey Islands Canada **123** L4
Greylock, Mount U.S.A. **135** I2
Greymouth N.Z. **113** C6
Grey Range *hills* Australia **112** A2
Grey's Plains Australia **109** A6
Greytown S. Africa **101** J5
Grez-Doiceau Belgium **52** E4
Gribanovskiy Russia **43** I6
Gridley U.S.A. **128** C2
Griffin U.S.A. **133** C5
Griffith Australia **112** C5
Grigan *i.* N. Mariana Is *see* **Agrihan**
Grik Malaysia *see* **Gerik**
Grim, Cape Australia **111** [inset]
Grimari Cent. Afr. Rep. **98** C3
Grimma Germany **53** M3
Grimmen Germany **47** N3
Grimnitzsee *l.* Germany **53** N2
Grimsby U.K. **48** G5
Grímsey *i.* Iceland **44** [inset 1]
Grimshaw Canada **120** G3
Grímsstaðir Iceland **44** [inset 1]
Grimstad Norway **45** F7
Grindavík Iceland **44** [inset 1]
Grindsted Denmark **45** F9
Grind Stone City U.S.A. **134** D1
Grindul Chituc *spit* Romania **59** M2
Grinnell Peninsula Canada **119** I2
Griqualand East *reg.* S. Africa **101** I6
Griqualand West *reg.* S. Africa **100** F5
Griquatown S. Africa **100** F5
Grise Fiord Canada **119** J2
Grishino Ukr. *see* **Krasnoarmiys'k**
Gris Nez, Cap *c.* France **52** B4
Gritley U.K. **50** G2
Grizzly Bear Mountain *hill* Canada **120** F1
Grmeč *mts* Bos. & Herz. **58** G2
Grobbendonk Belgium **52** E3
Groblersdal S. Africa **101** I3
Groblershoop S. Africa **100** F5
Grodno Belarus *see* **Hrodna**
Groen *watercourse* N. Cape S. Africa **100** F6
Groen *watercourse Northern Cape/Western Cape* S. Africa **100** C6
Groix, Île de *i.* France **56** C3
Grombalia Tunisia **58** D6
Gronau (Westfalen) Germany **52** H2
Grong Norway **44** H4
Groningen Neth. **52** G1
Groninger Wad *tidal flat* Neth. **52** G1
Grønland *terr.* N. America *see* **Greenland**
Groom Lake U.S.A. **129** F3
Groot-Aar Pan *salt pan* S. Africa **100** E4
Groot Berg *r.* S. Africa **100** D7
Groot Brakrivier S. Africa **100** F8
Grootdraaidam *dam* S. Africa **101** I4
Grootdrink S. Africa **100** E5
Groote Eylandt *i.* Australia **110** B2
Grootfontein Namibia **99** B5
Groot Karas Berg *plat.* Namibia **100** D4
Groot Letaba *r.* S. Africa **101** J2
Groot Marico S. Africa **101** H3
Groot Swartberge *mts* S. Africa **100** E7
Grootvloer *salt pan* S. Africa **100** E5
Groot Winterberg *mt.* S. Africa **101** H7
Gros Morne National Park Canada **123** K4
Gross Barmen Namibia **100** C2
Große Aue *r.* Germany **53** J2
Große Laaber *r.* Germany **53** M6
Großengottern Germany **53** K3
Großenkneten Germany **53** I2
Großenlüder Germany **53** J4
Großer Arber *mt.* Germany **53** N5
Großer Beerberg *hill* Germany **53** K4
Großer Eyberg *hill* Germany **53** H5
Großer Gleichberg *hill* Germany **53** K4
Großer Kornberg *hill* Germany **53** M4
Großer Osser *mt.* Czechia/Germany **53** N5
Großer Rachel *mt.* Germany **47** N6
Grosser Speikkogel *mt.* Austria **47** O7
Grosseto Italy **58** D3
Grossevichi Russia **74** E3
Groß-Gerau Germany **53** I5
Großglockner *mt.* Austria **47** N7
Groß Oesingen Germany **53** K2
Großrudestedt Germany **53** L3
Groß Schönebeck Germany **53** N2
Gross Ums Namibia **100** D2
Großvenediger *mt.* Austria **47** N7
Gros Ventre Range *mts* U.S.A. **126** F4
Groswater Bay Canada **123** K3
Groton U.S.A. **130** D2
Grottoes U.S.A. **135** F4
Grou Neth. **52** F1
Groundhog *r.* Canada **122** E4
Grouw Neth. *see* **Grou**
Grove U.S.A. **131** E4
Grove City U.S.A. **134** D4
Grove Hill U.S.A. **133** C6
Grove Mountains Antarctica **152** E2
Grover Beach U.S.A. **128** C4
Grovertown U.S.A. **134** B3
Groveton *NH* U.S.A. **135** J1
Groveton *TX* U.S.A. **131** E6
Growler Mountains U.S.A. **129** G5
Groznyy Russia **91** G2
Grubišno Polje Croatia **58** G2
Grudovo Bulg. *see* **Sredets**
Grudziądz Poland **47** Q4
Grünau Namibia **100** D4
Grünberg Poland *see* **Zielona Góra**
Grundarfjörður Iceland **44** [inset 1]
Grundy U.S.A. **134** D5
Gruñidora Mex. **131** C7
Grünstadt Germany **53** I5
Gruver U.S.A. **131** C4
Gruzinskaya S.S.R. *country* Asia *see* **Georgia**
Gryazi Russia **43** H5
Gryazovets Russia **42** I4
Gryfice Poland **47** O4
Gryfino Poland **47** O4
Gryfów Śląski Poland **47** O5
Gryllefjord Norway **44** J2
Grytviken S. Georgia **144** I8
Gua India **83** F5
Guacanayabo, Golfo de *b.* Cuba **137** I4
Guachochi Mex. **127** G8
Guadajoz *r.* Spain **57** D5
Guadalajara Mex. **136** D4
Guadalajara Spain **57** E3
Guadalcanal *i.* Solomon Is **107** G2
Guadalete *r.* Spain **57** C5
Guadalope *r.* Spain **57** F3
Guadalquivir *r.* Spain **57** C5
Guadalupe Mex. **131** C7
Guadalupe *i.* Mex. **127** D7
Guadalupe *watercourse* Mex. **128** E5
Guadalupe U.S.A. **128** C4
Guadalupe, Sierra de *mts* Spain **57** D4
Guadalupe Aguilera Mex. **131** B7
Guadalupe Bravos Mex. **127** G7
Guadalupe Mountains National Park U.S.A. **127** G7
Guadalupe Peak U.S.A. **127** G7
Guadalupe Victoria *Baja California* Mex. **129** F5
Guadalupe Victoria *Durango* Mex. **131** B7
Guadarrama, Sierra de *mts* Spain **57** D3

▶**Guadeloupe** *terr.* West Indies **137** L5
French Overseas Department.

Guadeloupe Passage Caribbean Sea **137** L5
Guadiana *r.* Port./Spain **57** C5
Guadix Spain **57** E5
Guafo, Isla *i.* Chile **144** B6
Guaíba Brazil **145** A5
Guaiçuí Brazil **145** B2
Guaíra Brazil **144** F2
Guajaba, Cayo *i.* Cuba **133** E8
Guaje, Llano de *plain* Mex. **131** C7
Guajira, Península de la *pen.* Col. **142** D1
Gualala U.S.A. **128** B2
Gualeguay Arg. **144** E4
Gualeguaychu Arg. **144** E4
Gualicho, Salina *salt flat* Arg. **144** C6

▶**Guam** *terr.* N. Pacific Ocean **69** K4
United States Unincorporated Territory.

Guamblin, Isla *i.* Chile **144** A6
Guampí, Sierra de *mts* Venez. **142** E2
Guamúchil Mex. **127** F8
Guanabacoa Cuba **133** D8
Guanacevi Mex. **131** B7
Guanahacabibes, Península de *pen.* Cuba **133** C8
Guanajay Cuba **133** D8
Guanajuato Mex. **136** D4
Guanambi Brazil **145** C1
Guanare Venez. **142** E2
Guandu China **77** G3
Guane Cuba **137** H4
Guang'an China **76** E2
Guangchang China **77** H3
Guangdong *prov.* China **77** [inset]
Guanghai China **77** G4
Guanghan China **76** E2
Guanghua China *see* **Laohekou**
Guangming China *see* **Xide**
Guangming Ding *mt.* China **77** H2
Guangnan China **76** E3
Guangshan China **77** G2
Guangxi *aut. reg.* China *see* **Guangxi Zhuangzu Zizhiqu**
Guangxi Zhuangzu Zizhiqu *aut. reg.* China **76** F4
Guangyuan China **76** E1
Guangze China **77** H3
Guangzhou China **77** G4
Guanhães Brazil **145** C2
Guanhe Kou *r. mouth* China **77** H1
Guanipa *r.* Venez. **142** F2
Guanling China **76** E3
Guanmian Shan *mts* China **77** F2
Guannan China **77** H1
Guanpo China **77** F1
Guanshui China **74** B4
Guansuo China *see* **Guanling**
Guantánamo Cuba **137** I4
Guanxian China *see* **Dujiangyan**
Guanyang China **77** F3
Guanyinqiao China **76** D2
Guanyun China **77** H1
Guapé Brazil **145** B3
Guapí Col. **142** C3
Guaporé *r.* Bol./Brazil **142** E6
Guaporé Brazil **145** A5
Guaqui Bol. **142** E7
Guará *r.* Brazil **145** B1
Guarabira Brazil **143** K5
Guaranda Ecuador **142** C4
Guarapari Brazil **145** C3
Guarapuava Brazil **145** A4
Guararapes Brazil **145** A3
Guaratinguetá Brazil **145** B3
Guaratuba Brazil **145** A4
Guaratuba, Baía de *b.* Brazil **145** A4
Guarda Port. **57** C3
Guardafui, Cape Somalia *see* **Gwardafuy, Gees**
Guardiagrele Italy **58** F3
Guardo Spain **57** D2
Guárico, del Embalse *resr* Venez. **142** E2
Guarujá Brazil **145** B3
Guasave Mex. **127** F8
Guasdualito Venez. **142** D2

▶**Guatemala** *country* Central America **136** F5
4th most populous country in North America.

▶**Guatemala City** Guat. **136** F6
Capital of Guatemala.

Guaviare *r.* Col. **142** E3
Guaxupé Brazil **145** B3
Guayaquil Ecuador **142** C4
Guayaquil, Golfo de *g.* Ecuador **142** B4
Guaymas Mex. **127** F8
Guazhou China **80** I3
Guba Eth. **98** D2
Gubakha Russia **41** R4
Gubbi India **84** C3
Gubio Nigeria **96** E3
Gubkin Russia **43** H6
Gucheng *Hubei* China **77** F1
Gucheng *Yunnan* China **76** D3
Gudari India **84** D2
Gudbrandsdalen *valley* Norway **45** F6
Gudermes Russia **91** G2
Gudivada India **84** D2
Gudiyattam India **84** C3
Gudur *Andhra Prad.* India **84** C3
Gudur *Andhra Prad.* India **84** C3
Gudvangen Norway **45** E6
Gudzhal *r.* Russia **74** D2
Gué, Rivière du *r.* Canada **123** H2
Guecho Spain *see* **Algorta**
Guéckédou Guinea **96** B4
Guelma Alg. **58** B6
Guelmim Morocco **96** B2
Guelph Canada **134** E2
Guémez Mex. **131** D8
Guénange France **52** G5
Guerara Alg. **54** E5
Guérard, Lac *l.* Canada **123** I2
Guercif Morocco **54** D5
Guéret France **56** E3

▶**Guernsey** *terr.* Channel Is **49** E9
United Kingdom Crown Dependency.

Guernsey U.S.A. **126** G4
Guérou Mauritania **96** B3
Guerrah Et-Tarf *salt pan* Alg. **58** B7
Guerrero Negro Mex. **127** E8
Guers, Lac *l.* Canada **123** I2
Gueugnon France **56** G3
Gufeng China *see* **Pingnan**
Gufu China *see* **Xingshan**
Gugē *mt.* Eth. **98** D3
Gügerd, Küh-e *mts* Iran **88** D3
Guguan *i.* N. Mariana Is **69** L3
Guhakolak, Tanjung *pt* Indon. **68** D8
Guhe China **77** H2
Güh Küh *mt.* Iran **88** E5
Gührän Iran **88** E5
Guhuai China *see* **Pingyu**
Guiana Basin *sea feature* N. Atlantic Ocean **148** E5
Guiana Highlands *mts* S. America **142** E2
Guichi China *see* **Chizhou**
Guidan-Roumji Niger **96** D3
Guider Cameroon **97** E4
Guiding China **76** E3
Guidong China **77** G3
Guidonia Montecelio Italy **58** E4
Guigang China **77** F4
Guiglo Côte d'Ivoire **96** C4
Guignicourt France **52** D5
Guija Moz. **101** K3
Guiji Shan *mts* China **77** I2
Guildford U.K. **49** G7
Guilford U.S.A. **132** G2
Guilherme Capelo Angola *see* **Cacongo**
Guilin China **77** F3
Guillaume-Delisle, Lac *l.* Canada **122** F2
Guimarães Brazil **143** J4
Guimarães Port. **57** B3
Guinan China *see* **Mangra**
Guinea *country* Africa **96** B3
Guinea, Gulf of Africa **96** D4
Guinea Basin *sea feature* N. Atlantic Ocean **148** H5
Guinea-Bissau *country* Africa **96** B3
Guinea-Conakry *country* Africa *see* **Guinea**
Guinea Ecuatorial *country* Africa *see* **Equatorial Guinea**
Guiné-Bissau *country* Africa *see* **Guinea-Bissau**
Guinée *country* Africa *see* **Guinea**
Güines Cuba **137** H4
Guînes France **52** B4
Guines, Lac *l.* Canada **123** J3
Guingamp France **56** C2
Guipavas France **56** B2
Guiping China **77** F4
Güira de Melena Cuba **133** D8
Guiratinga Brazil **143** H7
Guiscard France **52** D5
Guise France **52** D5
Guishan China *see* **Xinping**
Guishan Dao *i.* Taiwan **77** I3
Guishun China **76** E3
Guixi *Chongqing* China *see* **Dianjiang**
Guixi *Jiangxi* China **77** H2
Guiyang *Guizhou* China **76** E3
Guiyang *Hunan* China **77** G3
Guizhou *prov.* China **76** E3
Guizi China **77** F4
Gujarat *state* India **82** C5
Gujar Khan Pak. **89** I3
Gujerat *state* India *see* **Gujarat**
Gujranwala Pak. **89** I3
Gujrat Pak. **89** I3
Gukovo Russia **43** H6
Gulabgarh India **82** D2
Gulbarga India *see* **Kalaburagi**
Gulbene Latvia **45** O8
Gul'cha Kyrg. *see* **Gülchö**
Gülchö Kyrg. **80** D3
Gülcihan Turkey **85** B1

Gülek Boğazı pass Turkey 90 D3
Gulfport U.S.A. 131 F6
Gulgong Australia 112 D4
Gulian China 74 A1
Gulin China 76 E3
Gulistan Uzbek. see Guliston
Guliston Uzbek. 80 C3
Gülitz Germany 53 L1
Guliya Shan mt. China 74 A2
Gulja China see Yining
Gul Kach Pak. 89 H4
Gul'kevichi Russia 91 F1
Gull Lake Canada 121 I5
Gullrock Lake Canada 121 M5
Gullträsk Sweden 44 L3
Güllük Körfezi b. Turkey 59 L6
Gülnar Turkey 85 A1
Gulü China see Xincai
Gulu Uganda 98 D3
Guluwuru Island Australia 110 B1
Gulyayevskiye Koshki, Ostrova is Russia 42 L1
Guma China see Pishan
Gumal r. Pak. 89 H4
Gumare Botswana 99 C5
Gumbaz Pak. 89 H4
Gumbinnen Russia see Gusev
Gumdag Turkm. 88 D2
Gumel Nigeria 96 D3
Gümgüm Turkey see Varto
Gumi S. Korea 75 C5
Gumla India 83 F5
Gummersbach Germany 53 H3
Gümüşhacıköy Turkey 90 D2
Gümüşhane Turkey 91 E2
Guna India 82 D4
Gunan China see Qijiang
Guna Terara mt. Eth. 86 E7
Gunbar Australia 112 B5
Gunbower Australia 112 B5
Güncang China 76 B2
Gund r. Tajik. see Gunt
Gundabooka National Park nat. park Australia 111 D6
Gundagai Australia 112 D5
Gundelsheim Germany 53 J5
Güney Turkey 59 M5
Güneydoğu Toroslar plat. Turkey 90 F3
Gunglilap Myanmar 70 B1
Gungu Dem. Rep. Congo 99 B4
Gunib Russia 91 G2
Gunisao r. Canada 121 L4
Gunisao Lake Canada 121 L4
Gunnaur India 82 D3
Gunnbjørn Fjeld nunatak Greenland 119 P3
Gunnedah Australia 112 E3
Gunning Australia 112 D5
Gunnison U.S.A. 127 G5
Gunnison r. U.S.A. 129 I2
Güns Hungary see Kőszeg
Gunsan S. Korea 75 B6
Gunt r. Tajik. 89 H2
Guntakal India 84 C3
Güntersberge Germany 53 K3
Guntur India 84 D2
Gunung Gading National Park Malaysia 71 E7
Gunung Leuser, Taman Nasional nat. park Indon. 71 B7
Gunung Niyut, Suaka Margasatwa nature res. Indon. 71 E7
Gunung Palung, Taman Nasional nat. park Indon. 68 E7
Gunungsitoli Indon. 71 B7
Günyüzü Turkey 90 C3
Gunza Angola see Porto Amboim
Günzburg Germany 47 M6
Gunzenhausen Germany 53 K5
Guo He r. China 77 H1
Guovdageaidnu Norway see Kautokeino
Guozhen China see Chencang
Gupis Pak. 82 C1
Gurbantünggüt Shamo des. China 80 G3
Gurdaspur India 82 C2
Gurdon U.S.A. 131 E5
Gurdzhaani Georgia see Gurjaani
Güre Turkey 59 M5
Gurgan Iran see Gorgān
Gurgaon India 82 D3
Gurgei, Jebel mt. Sudan 97 F3
Gurha India 82 B4
Guri, Embalse de resr Venez. 142 F2
Gurinhatã Brazil 145 A2
Gurjaani Georgia 91 G2
Gur Khar Iran 89 E4
Guro Moz. 99 D5
Gurşunmagdan Kärhanasy Turkm. 89 G2
Guru China 83 G3
Gürün Turkey 90 E3
Gurupá Brazil 143 H4
Gurupi Brazil 143 I6
Gurupi r. Brazil 143 I4
Gurupi, Serra do hills Brazil 143 I4
Guru Sikhar mt. India 82 C4
Guruzala India 84 C2
Gur'yev Kazakh. see Atyrau
Gur'yevsk Russia 45 L9
Gur'yevskaya Oblast' admin. div. Kazakh. see Atyrauskaya Oblast'
Gusau Nigeria 96 D3
Güsen Germany 53 L2
Gusev Russia 45 M9
Gushan China 75 A5
Gushgy Turkm. see Serhetabat
Gushi China 77 G1
Gusino Russia 43 F5
Gusinoozersk Russia 72 J2
Gus'-Khrustal'nyy Russia 42 I5
Guspini Sardinia Italy 58 C5
Gustav Holm, Kap c. Greenland see Tasiilap Karra
Gustavo Sotelo Mex. 127 E7
Güsten Germany 53 L3
Gustine U.S.A. 128 C3
Güstrow Germany 47 N4
Gütenfelde Germany 53 N2
Gütersloh Germany 53 I3
Guthrie AZ U.S.A. 129 I5
Guthrie KY U.S.A. 134 B5
Guthrie OK U.S.A. 131 D5
Guthrie TX U.S.A. 131 C5
Gutian Fujian China 77 H3
Gutian Fujian China 77 H3
Gutian Shuiku resr China 77 H3
Guting China see Yutai
Gutsuo China 83 F3
Guwahati India 83 G4
Guwlumaýak Turkm. 88 D1
Guxhagen Germany 53 J3
Guxian China 77 G3
Guyana country S. America 143 G2
Guyane Française terr. S. America see French Guiana
Guyang Hunan China see Guzhang
Guyang Nei Mongol China 73 K4
Guyenne reg. France 56 D4
Guy Fawkes River National Park Australia 112 F3
Guyi China see Sanjiang
Guymon U.S.A. 131 C4
Guyra Australia 112 E3
Guysborough Canada 123 J5
Guyuan Hebei China 73 L4
Guyuan Ningxia China 72 J5
Guzarah Afgh. 89 F3
Güzelolük Turkey 85 B1
Güzelyurt Cyprus see Morfou
Guzhang China 77 F2
Guzhen China 77 H1
Guzhou China see Rongjiang
Guzmán Mex. 127 G7
Guzmán, Lago de l. Mex. 127 G7
G'uzor Uzbek. 89 G2
Gvardeysk Russia 45 L9
Gvasyugi Russia 74 E3
Gwa Myanmar 70 A3
Gwabegar Australia 112 D3
Gwadar West Bay Pak. 89 F5
Gwaii Haanas Canada 120 C4
Gwaii Haanas National Park Reserve and Haida Heritage Site Canada 120 D4
Gwal Haidarzai Pak. 89 H4
Gwalior India 82 D4
Gwanda Zimbabwe 99 C6
Gwane Dem. Rep. Congo 98 C3
Gwangcheon S. Korea 75 B5
Gwangju S. Korea 75 B6
Gwardafuy, Gees c. Somalia 98 F2
Gwash Pak. 89 G4
Gwatar Bay Pak. 89 F5
Gwedaukkon Myanmar 70 A1
Gweebarra Bay Ireland 51 D3
Gwelo Zimbabwe see Gweru
Gwêr Iraq 91 F3
Gweru Zimbabwe 99 C5
Gweta Botswana 99 C6
Gwinner U.S.A. 130 D2
Gwoza Nigeria 96 E3
Gwydir r. Australia 112 D2
Gyablung China 76 B2
Gyaca China 76 B2
Gyagartang China 76 D1
Gya'gya China see Saga
Gyaijêpozhanggê China see Zhidoi
Gyai Qu r. China 76 B2
Gyaisi China see Jiulong
Gyali i. Greece 59 L6
Gyamotang China see Dêngqên
Gyamug China 82 E2
Gyandzha Azer. see Gäncä
Gyangkar China see Dinggyê
Gyangnyi Caka salt l. China 83 F2
Gyangrang China 83 F3
Gyangtse China see Gyangzê
Gyangzê China 83 G3
Gyaring China 76 C1
Gyaring Co l. China 83 G3
Gyaring Hu l. China 76 C1
Gyarishing India 76 B3
Gyaros i. Greece 59 K6
Gyarubtang China 76 B2
Gydan, Khrebet mts Russia see Kolymskoye Nagor'ye
Gydan Peninsula Russia 64 I2
Gydanskiy Poluostrov pen. Russia see Gydan Peninsula
Gyêgu China see Yushu
Gyêmdong China 76 B2
Gyimda China 76 B2
Gyirong Xizang China 83 F3
Gyirong Xizang China 83 F3
Gyiza China 76 B1
Gyldenløve Fjord inlet Greenland see Umiiviip Kangertiva
Gympie Australia 111 F5
Gyobingauk Myanmar 70 A3
Gyöngyös Hungary 47 Q7
Győr Hungary 58 G1
Gypsum Point Canada 120 H2
Gypsumville Canada 121 L5
Gyrfalcon Islands Canada 123 H2
Gytheio Greece 59 J6
Gyula Hungary 59 I1
Gyulafehérvár Romania see Alba Iulia
Gyümai China see Tarlag
Gyumri Armenia 91 F2
Gyzylarbat Turkm. see Serdar
Gyzylbaýdak Turkm. 89 F2
Gzhatsk Russia see Gagarin

H

Haa Bhutan 83 G4
Haa-Alif Atoll Maldives see Ihavandhippolhu
Ha'apai Group is Tonga 107 I3
Haapajärvi Fin. 44 N5
Haapavesi Fin. 44 N4
Haapsalu Estonia 45 M7
Ha 'Arava watercourse Israel/Jordan see 'Arabah, Wādī al
Ha'Arava, Naḥal watercourse Israel/Jordan see Jayb, Wādī al
Haarlem Neth. 52 E2
Haarlem S. Africa 100 F7
Haarstrang ridge Germany 53 H3
Hab r. Pak. 89 G5
Habahe China 80 G2
Habana Cuba see Havana
Habarane Sri Lanka 84 D4
Habarōn well Saudi Arabia 88 C6
Habaswein Kenya 98 D3
Habay Canada 120 G3
Ḥabbān Yemen 86 G7
Ḥabbānīyah, Hawr al l. Iraq 91 F4
Hab Chauki Pak. 89 G5
Habiganj Bangl. 83 G4
Habra India 83 G5
Hachijō-jima i. Japan 75 E6
Hachinohe Japan 74 F4
Hachita U.S.A. 129 I6
Hacıköy Turkey see Çekerek
Hacıqabul Azer. 91 H2
Hack, Mount Australia 111 B6
Hackberry U.S.A. 129 G4
Hackensack U.S.A. 135 H3
Hacufera Moz. 99 D6
Ḥadabat al Jilf al Kabīr plat. Egypt see Jilf al Kabīr, Haḍabat al
Hadagalli India 84 B3
Hadapu China 76 E1
Hadayang China 74 B2
Ḥadd, Ra's al pt Oman 89 E6
Haddington U.K. 50 G5
Haddumati Atoll Maldives see Hahdhunmathi
Haddunmahti Atoll Maldives see Hahdhunmathi
Hadejia Nigeria 96 E3
Ḥadera Israel 85 B3
Ḥadera, Naḥal r. Israel 85 B3
Haderslev Denmark 45 F9
Hadhramaut reg. Yemen see Ḥaḍramawt
Hādī, Jabal al mts Jordan 85 C4
Hadım Turkey 90 D3
Hadjer Hadid Chad 97 F3
Hadleigh U.K. 49 H6
Hadong S. Korea 75 B6
Ḥadraj, Wādī watercourse Saudi Arabia 85 C4
Ḥaḍramawt reg. Yemen 98 E2
Hadranum Sicily Italy see Adrano
Hadrian's Wall tourist site U.K. 48 E3
Hadrumetum Tunisia see Sousse
Hadsund Denmark 45 G8
Hadyach Ukr. 43 G6
Haeju N. Korea 75 B5
Haeju-man b. N. Korea 75 B5
Haenam S. Korea 75 B6
Haenertsburg S. Africa 101 I2
Ha'erbin China see Harbin
Ḥafar al 'Atk well Saudi Arabia 88 B5
Ḥafar al Bāṭin Saudi Arabia 86 G4
Hafford Canada 121 J4
Hafik Turkey 90 E3
Ḥafīrah, Qā' al salt pan Jordan 85 C4
Hafirat Nasah Saudi Arabia 88 B5
Hafizabad Pak. 89 I3
Haflong India 83 H4
Hafnarfjörður Iceland 44 [inset 1]
Hafren r. U.K. see Severn
Haftgel Iran 88 C4
Hafursfjörður b. Iceland 44 [inset 1]
Haga Myanmar see Hakha
Hagar Nish Plateau Eritrea 86 E6

▶Hagåtña Guam 69 K4
Capital of Guam.

Hagelberg hill Germany 53 M2
Hagen Germany 53 H3
Hagenow Germany 53 L1
Hagerhill U.S.A. 134 D5
Hagerstown U.S.A. 135 G4
Hagfors Sweden 45 H6
Haggin, Mount U.S.A. 126 E3
Hagi Japan 75 C6
Ha Giang Vietnam 70 D2
Hagley U.K. 49 E6
Hag's Head hd Ireland 51 C5
Hague U.S.A. 135 I2
Hague, Cap de la c. France 56 D2
Haguenau France 53 H6
Hahajima-rettō is Japan 75 F8
Hahdhunmathi Maldives 81 D11
Hahoe tourist site S. Korea 75 C5
Hai Tanz. 97 G5
Hai'an China 77 F4
Haib watercourse Namibia 100 C5
Haibowan China see Wuhai
Haicheng Guangdong China see Haifeng
Haicheng Liaoning China 73 M4
Haida Gwaii Canada 120 C4
Hai Dương Vietnam 70 D2
Haifa Israel 85 B3
Haifa, Bay of Israel 85 B3
Haifeng China 77 G4
Haig Australia 109 D7
Haiger Germany 53 I4
Haikakan country Asia see Armenia
Haikang China see Leizhou
Haikou China 77 F4
Ḥā'il Saudi Arabia 91 F6
Hailey U.S.A. 126 E4
Haileybury Canada 122 F5
Hailin China 74 C3
Hailong China see Meihekou
Hailsham U.K. 49 H8
Hailun China 74 B3
Hailuoto Fin. 44 N4
Hainan prov. China 77 F5
Hainan Dao i. China 77 F5
Hai-nang Myanmar 70 B2
Hainan Strait China 77 F5
Hainaut reg. France 52 D4
Haines U.S.A. 120 C3
Haines Junction Canada 120 B2
Haines Road Canada/U.S.A. 120 B2
Hainichen Germany 53 N4
Hainleite ridge Germany 53 K3
Hai Phong Vietnam 70 D2
Haiphong Vietnam see Hai Phong
Haiqing China 74 D3
Haitan Dao i. China 77 H3
Haitangwan China 77 F5
Haiti country West Indies 137 J5
Haitou China 77 F5
Hai Triêu Vietnam 71 E4
Haiwee Reservoir U.S.A. 128 E3
Haiya Sudan 86 E6
Haiyan Qinghai China 72 I5
Haiyan Zhejiang China 77 I2
Haiyang China see Xiuning
Haiyang Dao i. China 75 A5
Haiyou China see Sanmen
Haizhou Wan b. China 77 H1
Hajdúböszörmény Hungary 59 I1
Hajeb El Ayoun Tunisia 58 C7
Hajhir mt. Yemen 87 H7
Haji Mahesar Pak. 89 G4
Hajipur India 83 F4
Hajir reg. Saudi Arabia 88 C5
Ḥajjah Yemen 86 F6
Ḥājj 'Alī Qolī, Kavīr-e salt l. Iran 88 D3
Ḥājjīābād Fārs Iran 88 D4
Ḥājjīābād Hormozgān Iran 88 D4
Ḥājjīābād Yazd Iran 88 D3
Haka Myanmar see Hakha
Hakha Myanmar 70 A2
Hakkâri Turkey 91 F3
Hakkas Sweden 44 L3
Hakken-zan mt. Japan 75 D6
Hako-dake mt. Japan 74 F3
Hakodate Japan 74 F4
Hakos Mountains Namibia 100 C2
Hakseen Pan salt pan S. Africa 100 E4
Hakui Japan 75 E5
Haku-san vol. Japan 75 E5
Hal Belgium see Halle
Hala Pak. 89 H5
Ḥalab Syria see Aleppo
Ḥalabjah/Helebce Iraq 91 G4
Halaç Turkm. 89 G2
Halahai China 74 B3
Ḥalā'ib Sudan 86 E5
Halaib Triangle terr. Egypt 86 E5
Halâl, Gebel hill Egypt see Hilāl, Jabal
Ha Lam Vietnam 70 E4
Ḥalāniyāt, Juzur al is Oman 87 I6
Hālawa U.S.A. 127 [inset]
Halba Lebanon 85 C2
Halberstadt Germany 53 L3
Halcon, Mount Phil. 69 G4
Halden Norway 45 G7
Haldensleben Germany 53 L2
Haldwani India 82 D3
Hale watercourse Australia 110 A5
Hale U.S.A. 134 D1
Hāleh Iran 88 D5
Haleparki Deresi r. Syria/Turkey see Quwayq, Nahr
Halesowen U.K. 49 E6
Halesworth U.K. 49 I6
Half Assini Ghana 96 C4
Halfmoon Bay N.Z. 113 B8
Halfway r. Canada 120 F3
Halfway Ireland 51 D6
Halfweg Neth. 52 E2
Halhgol Mongolia 73 L3
Halia India 83 E4
Ḥalībīyah Syria 91 E4
Haliburton Canada 135 F1
Haliburton Highlands hills Canada 135 F1
Halicarnassus Turkey see Bodrum

▶Halifax Canada 123 J5
Capital of Nova Scotia.

Halifax U.K. 48 F5
Halifax NC U.S.A. 132 E4
Halifax VA U.S.A. 135 F5
Halifax, Mount Australia 110 D3
Ḥalīmah mt. Lebanon/Syria 85 C2
Halkirk U.K. 50 F2
Hall U.S.A. 134 C5
Hälla Sweden 44 J5
Halladale r. U.K. 50 F2
Halla-san National Park S. Korea 75 B6
Hall Beach Canada 119 J3
Halle Belgium 52 E4
Halle Neth. 52 G3
Halle (Saale) Germany 53 L3
Halleck U.S.A. 129 F1
Hällefors Sweden 45 I7
Hallein Austria 47 N7
Halle-Neustadt Germany 53 L3
Hallett, Cape Antarctica 152 H2
Hallettsville U.S.A. 131 D6
Halley research station Antarctica 152 B1
Hallgreen, Mount Antarctica 152 B2
Halliday U.S.A. 130 C2
Halliday Lake Canada 121 I2
Hall Islands Micronesia 150 G5
Hällnäs Sweden 44 K4
Hallock U.S.A. 130 D1
Hall Peninsula Canada 119 L3
Hallsberg Sweden 45 I7
Halls Creek Australia 108 D4
Halls Gap U.S.A. 134 C5
Halls Lake Canada 135 F1
Hallstead U.S.A. 135 H3
Halluin Belgium 52 D4
Hallviken Sweden 44 I5
Halmahera i. Indon. 69 H6
Halmahera, Laut sea Indon. 69 H7
Halmahera Sea sea Indon. see Halmahera, Laut
Halmstad Sweden 45 H8
Ha Long Vietnam 70 D2
Hals Denmark 45 G8
Hälsingborg Sweden see Helsingborg
Halsua Fin. 44 N5
Haltern am See Germany 53 H3
Haltwhistle U.K. 48 E4
Ḥālūl i. Qatar 88 D5
Ḥalvān Iran 88 E3
Halver Germany 53 H3
Haly, Mount hill Australia 112 E1
Ham France 52 D5
Hamada Japan 75 D6
Hamadān Iran 88 C3
Ḥamāh Syria 85 C2
Hamam Turkey 85 C1
Hamamatsu Japan 75 E6
Hamar Norway 45 G6
Ḥamâṭa, Gebel mt. Egypt see Ḥamāṭah, Jabal
Ḥamāṭah, Jabal mt. Egypt 86 D5
Hamatonbetsu Japan 74 F3
Hambantota Sri Lanka 84 D5
Hambergen Germany 53 I1
Hambleton Hills U.K. 48 F4
Hamburg Germany 53 J1
Hamburg land Germany 53 J1
Hamburg S. Africa 101 H7
Hamburg AR U.S.A. 131 F5
Hamburg NY U.S.A. 135 F2
Hamburgisches Wattenmeer, Nationalpark nat. park Germany 47 L4
Ḥamḍ, Wādī al watercourse Saudi Arabia 86 E4
Hamden U.S.A. 135 I3
Hämeenlinna Fin. 45 N6
HaMelaḥ, Yam salt l. Asia see Dead Sea
Hamelin Australia 109 A6
Hameln Germany 53 J2
Hamersley Lakes salt flat Australia 109 B7
Hamersley Range mts Australia 108 B5
Hamhŭng N. Korea 75 B5
Hami China 80 H3
Hamid Sudan 86 D5
Hamilton Qld Australia 110 C4
Hamilton S.A. Australia 111 A5
Hamilton Vic. Australia 111 C8
Hamilton watercourse Qld Australia 110 B4
Hamilton watercourse S.A. Australia 111 A5

▶Hamilton Bermuda 137 L2
Capital of Bermuda.

Hamilton Canada 134 F2
Hamilton r. Canada see Churchill
Hamilton N.Z. 113 E3
Hamilton U.K. 50 E5
Hamilton AL U.S.A. 133 C5
Hamilton CO U.S.A. 129 J1
Hamilton MI U.S.A. 134 B2
Hamilton MT U.S.A. 126 E3
Hamilton NY U.S.A. 135 H2
Hamilton OH U.S.A. 134 C4
Hamilton TX U.S.A. 131 D6
Hamilton, Mount CA U.S.A. 128 C3
Hamilton, Mount NV U.S.A. 129 F2
Hamilton City U.S.A. 128 B2
Hamilton Inlet Canada 123 K3
Hamilton Mountain hill U.S.A. 135 H2
Ḥamīm, Wādī al watercourse Libya 55 I5
Hamina Fin. 45 O6
Hamirpur Hima. Prad. India 82 D3
Hamirpur Uttar Prad. India 82 E4
Hamitabat Turkey see Isparta
Hamju N. Korea 75 B5
Hamlet U.S.A. 133 E5
Hamlin TX U.S.A. 131 C5
Hamlin WV U.S.A. 134 D4
Hamm Germany 53 H3
Ḥammām al 'Alīl Iraq 91 F3
Hammam Boughrara Alg. 57 F6
Hammamet Tunisia 58 D6
Hammamet, Golfe de g. Tunisia 58 D6
Ḥammār, Hawr al imp. l. Iraq 91 G5
Hammarstrand Sweden 44 J5
Hammelburg Germany 53 J4
Hammerdal Sweden 44 I5
Hammerfest Norway 44 M1
Hamminkeln Germany 52 G3
Hammond U.S.A. 134 B3
Hammone, Lac l. Canada 123 K4
Hammonton U.S.A. 135 H4
Ham Ninh Vietnam 71 D5
Hamoir Belgium 52 F4
Hampden Sydney U.S.A. 135 F5
Hampshire Downs hills U.K. 49 F7
Hampton AR U.S.A. 131 E5
Hampton IA U.S.A. 130 E3
Hampton NH U.S.A. 135 J2
Hampton SC U.S.A. 133 D5
Hampton VA U.S.A. 135 G5
Hampton Tableland reg. Australia 109 D8
Ḥamrā', Al Ḥamādah al plat. Libya 96 E2
Ḥamrā, Birkat al well Saudi Arabia 91 F5
Hamra, Vâdii watercourse Syria/Turkey see Ḥimār, Wādī al
Hamrā Jūdah plat. Saudi Arabia 88 C5
Hamrat esh Sheikh Sudan 86 C7
Ham Tân Vietnam 71 D5
Hamta Pass India 82 D2
Hāmūn Ṣāberī, Daryācheh-ye marsh Afgh./Iran 89 F4
Hamunt Kūh hill Iran 89 F5
Hamur Turkey 91 F3
Hamwic U.K. see Southampton
Hāna U.S.A. 127 [inset]
Hanábana r. Cuba 133 D8
Hanahai watercourse Botswana/Namibia 100 F2
Ḥanak Saudi Arabia 86 E4
Hanakpınar Turkey see Çınar
Hanalei U.S.A. 127 [inset]
Hanamaki Japan 75 F5
Hanang mt. Tanz. 99 D4
Hanau Germany 53 I4
Hanbin China see Ankang
Hanchang China see Pingjiang
Hancheng China 77 F1
Hanchuan China 77 G2
Hancock MD U.S.A. 135 F4
Hancock NY U.S.A. 135 H3
Handa Island U.K. 50 D2
Handan China 73 K5
Handeni Tanz. 99 D4
HaNegev des. Israel see Negev
HaNeqarot, Naḥal watercourse Israel 85 B4
Hanfeng China see Kaixian
Hanford U.S.A. 128 D3
Hangan Myanmar 70 B4
Hangayn Nuruu mts Mongolia 80 I2
Hangchow China see Hangzhou
Hangchuan China see Guangze
Hangö Fin. see Hanko
Hangu China see Qianshangjie
Hanguang China 77 G3
Hangya China 80 I4
Hangzhou China 77 I2
Hangzhou Wan b. China 77 I2
Hani Turkey 91 F3
Hanish Kabir i. Yemen see Suyūl Ḥanīsh
Hanjia China see Pengshui
Hankensbüttel Germany 53 K2
Hankey S. Africa 100 G7
Hanko Fin. 45 M7
Hanksville U.S.A. 129 H2
Hanle India 82 D2
Hanley Canada 121 J5
Hann, Mount hill Australia 108 D3
Hanna Canada 121 I5
Hannagan Meadow U.S.A. 129 I5
Hannah Bay Canada 122 E4
Hannibal MO U.S.A. 130 F4
Hannibal NY U.S.A. 135 G2
Hannover Germany 53 J2
Hannoversch Münden Germany 53 J3
Hann Range mts Australia 109 F5
Hannut Belgium 52 F4
Hanöbukten b. Sweden 45 I9
Hanoi Vietnam see Ha Nôi

▶Ha Nôi Vietnam 70 D2
Capital of Vietnam.

Hanover Canada 134 E1
Hanover Germany see Hannover
Hanover S. Africa 100 G6
Hanover NH U.S.A. 135 I2
Hanover PA U.S.A. 135 G4
Hanover VA U.S.A. 135 G5
Hansen Mountains Antarctica 152 D2
Hanshou China 77 F2
Han Shui r. China 77 G2
Hansi India 82 D3
Hansnes Norway 44 K2
Hanstholm Denmark 45 F8
Han-sur-Nied France 52 G6
Hantsavichy Belarus 45 O10
Hanumangarh India 82 C3
Hanwood Australia 112 C5
Hanyang China see Caidian
Hanyang Feng mt. China 77 G2
Hanyin China 77 F1
Hanzhong China 76 E1
Hao atoll Fr. Polynesia 151 K7
Haora India 83 G5
Haparanda Sweden 44 N4
Happy Jack U.S.A. 129 H4
Happy Valley-Goose Bay Canada 123 J3
Ḥaql Saudi Arabia 85 B5
Haqshah well Saudi Arabia 88 C6
Ḥaraḍ well Saudi Arabia 88 C5
Ḥarad, Jabal al mt. Jordan 85 B5
Ḥaraḍh Saudi Arabia 86 G5
Haradok Belarus 43 F5
Haramachi Japan 75 F5
Haramukh mt. India 82 C2
Haran Turkey see Harran
Harappa Road Pak. 89 I4
Harar Eth. see Hārer

▶Harare Zimbabwe 99 D5
Capital of Zimbabwe.

Ḥarāsīs, Jiddat al des. Oman 87 I6
Harāt Iran 88 D4
Haraze-Mangueigne Chad 97 F3
Harb, Jabal mt. Saudi Arabia 90 D6
Harbin China 74 B3
Harboi Hills Pak. 89 G4
Harbor Beach U.S.A. 134 D2
Harchoka India 83 E5
Harda India 82 D5
Harda Khas India see Harda
Hardangerfjorden sea chan. Norway 45 D7
Hardangervidda plat. Norway 45 E6
Hardangervidda Nasjonalpark nat. park Norway 45 E6
Hardap admin. reg. Namibia 100 C3
Hardap Dam Namibia 100 C3
Hardap Recreation Resort nature res. Namibia 100 C3
Hardenberg Neth. 52 G2
Harderwijk Neth. 52 F2
Hardeveld mts S. Africa 100 D6
Hardheim Germany 53 J5
Hardin U.S.A. 126 G3
Harding S. Africa 101 I6
Harding Range hills Australia 109 B6
Hardinsburg IN U.S.A. 134 B4
Hardinsburg KY U.S.A. 134 B5
Hardoi India 82 E4
Hardwar India see Haridwar
Hardwick U.S.A. 135 I1
Hardy U.S.A. 131 F4
Hardy Reservoir U.S.A. 134 C2
Hare Bay Canada 123 L4
Ḥareiḍīn, Wâdi watercourse Egypt see Ḥurayḍin, Wādī
Harelbeke Belgium 52 D4
Haren Neth. 52 G1
Haren (Ems) Germany 53 H2
Hārer Eth. 98 E3
Harf el Mreffi mt. Lebanon 85 B3
Hargeisa Somalia see Hargeysa
Hargele Eth. 98 E3

▶Hargeysa Somalia 98 E3
Capital of Somaliland.

Harghita-Mădăraş, Vârful mt. Romania 59 K1
Harhorin Mongolia 80 J2
Har Hu l. China 80 I4
Ḥaricha, Ḥamâda El des. Mali 96 C2
Haridwar India 82 D3
Ḥarif, Har mt. Israel 85 B4
Harihar India 84 B3
Harihari N.Z. 113 C6
Hariharpur India 84 B3
Ḥārim Syria 85 C1
Ḥarīm, Jabal al mt. Oman 88 E5
Harima-nada b. Japan 75 D6
Haringhat r. Bangl. 83 G5
Haringvliet est. Neth. 52 E3
Ḥarīr, Wādī al r. Syria 85 C3
Hari Rōd r. Afgh./Iran 89 F2
Harjavalta Fin. 45 M6
Harlan IA U.S.A. 130 E3
Harlan KY U.S.A. 134 D5
Harlan County Lake U.S.A. 130 D3
Harlech U.K. 49 C6
Harleston U.K. 49 I6
Harlingen Neth. 52 F1
Harlingen U.S.A. 131 D7

Harlow U.K. 49 H7
Harlowton U.S.A. 126 F3
Harly France 52 D5
Harman U.S.A. 134 F4
Harmancık Turkey 59 M5
Harmanli Bulg. 59 K4
Harmony U.S.A. 135 K1
Harmsdorf Germany 53 K1
Harnai India 84 B2
Harnai Pak. 89 G4
Harnes France 52 C4
Harney Basin U.S.A. 126 D4
Harney Lake U.S.A. 126 D4
Härnösand Sweden 44 J5
Harns Neth. see Harlingen
Har Nuur l. Mongolia 80 H2
Haroldswick U.K. 50 [inset]
Harper Liberia 96 C4
Harper U.S.A. 131 D4
Harper, Mount U.S.A. 118 D3
Harper Creek r. Canada 120 H3
Harper Lake U.S.A. 128 E4
Harp Lake Canada 123 J3
Harpstedt Germany 53 I2
Harquahala Mountains U.S.A. 127 E6
Harrai India 82 D5
Harran Turkey 85 D1
Harrand Pak. 89 H4
Harricana, Rivière d' r. Canada 122 F4
Harriet Tubman Underground Railroad National Monument nat. park U.S.A. 135 H4
Harrington Australia 112 F3
Harrington U.S.A. 135 H4
Harris, Lake salt flat Australia 111 A6
Harris, Mount Australia 109 E6
Harris, Sound of sea chan. U.K. 50 B3
Harrisburg AR U.S.A. 131 F5
Harrisburg IL U.S.A. 130 F4
Harrisburg NE U.S.A. 130 C3

▶Harrisburg PA U.S.A. 135 G3
Capital of Pennsylvania.

Harrismith Australia 109 B8
Harrison AR U.S.A. 131 E4
Harrison MI U.S.A. 134 C1
Harrison NE U.S.A. 130 C3
Harrison OH U.S.A. 134 C4
Harrison, Cape Canada 123 K3
Harrison Bay U.S.A. 118 C2
Harrisonburg LA U.S.A. 131 F6
Harrisonburg VA U.S.A. 135 F4
Harrisonville U.S.A. 130 E4
Harriston Canada 134 E2
Harrisville MI U.S.A. 134 D1
Harrisville NY U.S.A. 135 H1
Harrisville PA U.S.A. 134 E3
Harrisville WV U.S.A. 134 E4
Harrodsburg IN U.S.A. 134 B4
Harrodsburg KY U.S.A. 134 C5
Harrodsville N.Z. see Otorohanga
Harrogate U.K. 48 F5
Harrowsmith Canada 135 G1
Harry S. Truman Reservoir U.S.A. 130 E4
Har Sai Shan mt. China 76 C1
Harsefeld Germany 53 J1
Harsīn Iran 88 B3
Harşit r. Turkey 90 E2
Hârşova Romania 59 L2
Harstad Norway 44 J2
Harsud India 82 D5
Harsum Germany 53 J2
Hart r. Canada 118 E3
Hart U.S.A. 134 B2
Hartbees watercourse S. Africa 100 E5
Hartberg Austria 47 O7
Harteigan mt. Norway 45 E6
Harter Fell hill U.K. 48 E4

▶Hartford CT U.S.A. 135 I3
Capital of Connecticut.

Hartford KY U.S.A. 134 B5
Hartford MI U.S.A. 134 B2
Hartford City U.S.A. 134 C3
Hartland U.K. 49 C8
Hartland U.S.A. 135 K1
Hartland Point U.K. 49 C7
Hartlepool U.K. 48 F4
Hartley U.S.A. 131 C5
Hartley Zimbabwe see Chegutu
Hartley Bay Canada 120 D4
Hartola Fin. 45 O6
Harts r. S. Africa 101 G5
Härtsfeld hills Germany 53 K6
Harts Range mts Australia 109 F5
Hartsville U.S.A. 134 B5
Hartswater S. Africa 100 G4
Hartville U.S.A. 131 E4
Hartwell U.S.A. 133 D5
Ḩarūrī, 'Irq al des. Saudi Arabia 88 B5
Har Us Nuur l. Mongolia 80 H2
Hārūt r. Afgh. 89 F3
Harūz Iran 88 E4
Harvard, Mount U.S.A. 126 G5
Harvey Australia 109 A8
Harvey U.S.A. 130 C2
Harvey Mountain U.S.A. 128 C1
Harwich U.K. 49 I7
Haryana state India 82 D3
Harz hills Germany 47 M5
Har Zin Israel 85 B4
Ḩaşāh, Wādī al watercourse Jordan 85 B4
Ḩaşāh, Wādī al watercourse Jordan/Saudi Arabia 85 C4
Hasalbag China 89 J2
Häsänabad Azer. 91 H3
Ḩasanah, Wādī watercourse Egypt 85 A4
Hasan Dağı mts Turkey 90 D3
Hasan Guli Turkm. see Esenguly
Hasankeyf Turkey 91 F3
Ḩasan Kūlah Afgh. 89 F3
Hasanur India 84 C4
Hasardag mt. Turkm. 88 E2
Hasbaïya Lebanon 85 B3
Hasbaya Lebanon see Hasbaïya
Hase r. Germany 53 H2
Haselünne Germany 53 H2
HaSharon plain Israel 85 B3
Hashtgerd Iran 88 C3
Hashtpar Iran see Tālesh
Hashtrūd Iran 88 B2
Haskell U.S.A. 131 D5
Haskovo Bulg. 59 K4
Haslemere U.K. 49 G7
Hăşmaşul Mare mt. Romania 59 K1
Ḩaşş, Jabal al hills Syria 85 C1
Hassan India 84 C3
Hassayampa watercourse U.S.A. 129 G5
Haßberge hills Germany 53 K4
Hasselt Belgium 52 F4
Hasselt Neth. 52 G2
Hassi Bel Guebbour Alg. 96 D2
Hassi Messaoud Alg. 54 F5
Hässleholm Sweden 45 H8
Hastings Australia 112 B7
Hastings r. Australia 112 F3
Hastings Canada 135 G1
Hastings N.Z. 113 F4
Hastings U.K. 49 H8
Hastings MI U.S.A. 134 C2
Hastings MN U.S.A. 130 E2
Hastings NE U.S.A. 130 D3
Hata India 83 E4
Hatanbulag Mongolia 73 J4
Hatay Turkey see Antakya
Hatay prov. Turkey 85 C1
Hatch U.S.A. 129 G3
Hatches Creek (abandoned) Australia 110 A4
Hatchet Lake Canada 121 K3
Hatfield Australia 112 A4
Hatfield U.K. 48 G5
Hatgal Mongolia 80 J1
Hath India 84 D1
Hat Head National Park Australia 112 F3
Hathras India 82 D4
Ha Tiên Vietnam 71 D5
Ha Tinh Vietnam 70 D3
Hatisar Bhutan see Geylegphug
Hatod India 82 C5
Hato Hud East Timor see Hatudo
Hatra Iraq 91 F4
Hattah Australia 111 C7
Hattah Kulkyne National Park Australia 111 C7
Hatteras, Cape U.S.A. 133 F5
Hatteras Abyssal Plain sea feature S. Atlantic Ocean 148 D4
Hattfjelldal Norway 44 H4
Hattiesburg U.S.A. 131 F6
Hattingen Germany 53 H3
Hattras Passage Myanmar 71 B4
Hatudo East Timor 108 D2
Hat Yai Thai. 71 C6
Hau Bon Vietnam see A Yun Pa
Haubstadt U.S.A. 134 B4
Haud reg. Eth. 98 E3
Hauge Norway 45 E7
Haugesund Norway 45 D7
Haukeligrend Norway 45 E7
Haukipudas Fin. 44 N4
Haukivesi l. Fin. 44 P5
Haultain r. Canada 121 J4
Hauraki Gulf N.Z. 113 E3
Haut Atlas mts Morocco 54 C5
Haute-Normandie admin. reg. France see Normandie
Haute-Volta country Africa see Burkina Faso
Haut-Folin hill France 56 G3
Hauts Plateaux Alg. 54 D5

▶Havana Cuba 137 H4
Capital of Cuba.

Havana U.S.A. 130 F3
Havant U.K. 49 G8
Havasu, Lake U.S.A. 129 F4
Havel r. Germany 53 L2
Havelange Belgium 52 F4
Havelberg Germany 53 M2
Havelock Canada 135 G1
Havelock N.Z. 113 D5
Havelock Swaziland see Bulembu
Havelock U.S.A. 133 E5
Havelock Falls Australia 108 F3
Havelock Island India 71 A5
Havelock North N.Z. 113 F4
Haverfordwest U.K. 49 C7
Haverhill U.S.A. 135 J2
Haveri India 84 B3
Haversin Belgium 52 F4
Havixbeck Germany 53 H3
Havlíčkův Brod Czechia 47 O6
Havøysund Norway 44 N1
Havran Turkey 59 L5
Havre U.S.A. 126 F2
Havre Aubert, Île du i. Canada 123 J5
Havre Rock i. Kermadec Is 107 I5
Havre-St-Pierre Canada 123 J4
Havza Turkey 90 D2
Hawai'i i. U.S.A. 127 [inset]
Hawai'ian Islands N. Pacific Ocean 150 I4
Hawaiian Ridge sea feature N. Pacific Ocean 150 I4
Hawai'i Volcanoes National Park U.S.A. 127 [inset]
Ḩawallī Kuwait 88 C4
Hawar i. Bahrain see Ḩuwār
Hawarden U.K. 48 D5
Hawea, Lake N.Z. 113 B7
Hawera N.Z. 113 E4
Hawes U.K. 48 E4
Hawesville U.S.A. 134 B5
Hāwī U.S.A. 127 [inset]
Hawick U.K. 50 G5
Ḩawīzah, Hawr al imp. l. Iraq 91 G5
Hawkdun Range mts N.Z. 113 B7
Hawke Bay N.Z. 113 F4
Hawkes Bay Canada 123 K4
Hawkins Peak U.S.A. 129 G3
Hawlēr Iraq see Arbīl/Hewlêr
Hawley U.S.A. 135 H3
Hawng Luk Myanmar 70 B2
Ḩawrān, Wādī watercourse Iraq 91 F4
Ḩawshah, Jibāl al mts Saudi Arabia 88 B6
Hawston S. Africa 100 D8
Hawthorne U.S.A. 128 D2
Haxby U.K. 48 F4
Hay Australia 112 B5
Hay watercourse Australia 110 B5
Hay r. Canada 120 H2
Hayachine-san mt. Japan 75 F5
Hayastan country Asia see Armenia
Haydān, Wādī al r. Jordan 85 B4
Hayden AZ U.S.A. 129 H5
Hayden CO U.S.A. 129 J1
Hayden IN U.S.A. 134 C4
Hayes r. Man. Canada 121 M3
Hayes r. Nunavut Canada 119 I3
Hayes Halvø pen. Greenland 119 L2
Hayfield Reservoir U.S.A. 129 F5
Hayfork U.S.A. 128 B1
Hayl, Wādī watercourse Syria 85 C3
Hayl, Wādī al watercourse Syria 85 D2
Hayle U.K. 49 B8
Haymā' Oman 87 I6
Haymana Turkey 90 D3
Haymarket U.S.A. 135 G4
Hay-on-Wye U.K. 49 D6
Hayrabolu Turkey 59 L4
Hay River Canada 118 G3
Hay River Reserve Canada 120 H2
Hays KS U.S.A. 130 D4
Hays MT U.S.A. 126 F2
Ḩays Yemen 86 F7
Haysville U.S.A. 131 D4
Haysyn Ukr. 43 F6
Ḩayṭān, Jabal hill Egypt 85 A4
Hayward CA U.S.A. 128 B3
Hayward WI U.S.A. 130 F2
Haywards Heath U.K. 49 G8
Hazar Turkm. 88 D2
Hazārah Jāt reg. Afgh. 89 G3
Hazard U.S.A. 134 D5
Hazaribag India see Hazaribagh
Hazaribagh India 83 F5
Hazaribagh Range mts India 83 E5
Hazār Masjed, Kūh-e mts Iran 88 E2
Hazebrouck France 52 C4
Hazelton Canada 120 E4
Hazen Strait Canada 119 G2
Hazerswoude-Rijndijk Neth. 52 E2
Hazhdanahr reg. Afgh. 89 G2
Hazira India 82 C5
Hazleton IN U.S.A. 134 B4
Hazleton PA U.S.A. 135 H3
Hazlett, Lake salt flat Australia 108 E5
Ḩazm al Jawf Yemen 86 F6
Ḩazrat-e Sulţān Afgh. 89 G2
H. Bouchard Arg. 144 D4
Headford Ireland 51 C4
Headingly Australia 110 B4
Head of Bight b. Australia 109 E7
Healdsburg U.S.A. 128 B2
Healesville Australia 112 B6
Healy U.S.A. 118 D3
Heanor U.K. 49 F5
Hearadh, Ceann a Deas na pen. U.K. see South Harris
Heard Island Indian Ocean 149 M9

▶Heard Island and McDonald Islands terr. Indian Ocean 149 M9
Australian External Territory.

Hearne U.S.A. 131 D6
Hearne Lake Canada 121 H2
Hearrenfean Neth. see Heerenveen
Hearst Canada 122 E4
Hearst Island Antarctica 152 L2
Heart r. U.S.A. 130 C2
Heart of Neolithic Orkney tourist site U.K. 50 F1
Heathcote Australia 112 B6
Heathfield U.K. 49 H8
Heathsville U.S.A. 135 G5
Hebbardsville U.S.A. 134 B5
Hebbronville U.S.A. 131 D7
Hebei prov. China 73 L5
Hebel Australia 112 C2
Heber U.S.A. 129 H4
Heber City U.S.A. 129 H1
Heber Springs U.S.A. 131 E5
Hebi China see Shancheng
Hebron Canada 123 J2
Hebron U.S.A. 130 D3
Hebron West Bank 85 B4
Hecate Strait Canada 120 D4
Hecheng Jiangxi China see Zixi
Hecheng Zhejiang China see Qingtian
Hechi China 77 F3
Hechuan Chongqing China 76 E2
Hechuan Jiangxi China see Yongxin
Hecla Island Canada 121 L5
Hede China see Sheyang
Hede Sweden 44 H5
Hedemora Sweden 45 I6
He Devil Mountain U.S.A. 126 D3
Hedi Shuiku resr China 77 F4
Heech Neth. see Heeg
Heeg Neth. 52 F2
Heek Germany 52 H2
Heer Belgium 52 E4
Heerde Neth. 52 G2
Heerenveen Neth. 52 F2
Heerhugowaard Neth. 52 E2
Heerlen Neth. 52 F4
Ḩefa Israel see Haifa
Ḩefa, Mifraz Israel see Haifa, Bay of
Hefei China 77 H2
Hefeng China 77 F2
Heflin U.S.A. 133 C5
Hegang China 74 C3
Heho Myanmar 70 B2
Heidan r. Jordan see Haydān, Wādī al
Heidberg hill Germany 53 L3
Heide Germany 47 L3
Heide Namibia 100 C2
Heidelberg Germany 53 I5
Heidelberg S. Africa 101 I4
Heidenheim an der Brenz Germany 53 K6
Heihe China 74 B2
Heilbron S. Africa 101 H4
Heilbronn Germany 53 J5
Heiligenhafen Germany 47 M3
Hei Ling Chau i. H.K. China 77 [inset]
Heilongjiang prov. China 74 C3
Heilong Jiang r. China/Russia 74 D2
also known as Amur (Russia)
Heilsbronn Germany 53 K5
Heilungkiang prov. China see Heilongjiang
Heinola Fin. 45 O6
Heinze Islands Myanmar 71 B4
Heirnkut Myanmar 70 A1
Heishi Beihu l. China 83 E2
Heishui China 76 D1
Heisker Islands U.K. see Monach Islands
Heist-op-den-Berg Belgium 52 E3
Ḩeiṭân, Gebel hill Egypt see Ḩayṭān, Jabal
Hejaz reg. Saudi Arabia see Hijaz
Hejiang China 76 E2
He Jiang r. China 77 F4
Hejing China 80 G3
Hekimhan Turkey 90 E3
Hekla vol. Iceland 44 [inset 1]
Hekou Gansu China 72 I5
Hekou Hubei China 77 G2
Hekou Jiangxi China see Yanshan
Hekou Sichuan China see Yajiang
Hekou Yunnan China 76 D4
Helagsfjället mt. Sweden 44 H5
Helam India 76 B3
Helan Shan mts China 72 J5
Helbra Germany 53 L3
Helen atoll Palau 69 I6
Helena AR U.S.A. 131 F5

▶Helena MT U.S.A. 126 E3
Capital of Montana.

Helen Reef Palau 69 I6
Helensburgh U.K. 50 E4
Helen Springs Australia 108 F4
Ḩelez Israel 85 B4
Helgoland i. Germany 47 K3
Helgoländer Bucht g. Germany 47 L3
Heligoland i. Germany see Helgoland
Heligoland Bight g. Germany see Helgoländer Bucht
Heliopolis Lebanon see Ba'albek
Helixi China see Ningguo
Hella Iceland 44 [inset 1]
Helland Norway 44 J2
Hellas country Europe see Greece
Helleh r. Iran 88 C4
Hellespont strait Turkey see Dardanelles
Hellevoetsluis Neth. 52 E3
Hellhole Gorge National Park Australia 110 D5
Hellín Spain 57 F4
Hellinikon tourist site Greece 90 A3
Hells Canyon gorge U.S.A. 126 D3
Hell-Ville Madag. see Andoany
Helmand r. Afgh. 89 F4
Helmand, Hāmūn salt flat Afgh./Iran 89 F4
Helmantica Spain see Salamanca
Helmbrechts Germany 53 L4
Helme r. Germany 53 L3
Helmeringhausen Namibia 100 C3
Helmond Neth. 52 F3
Helmsdale U.K. 50 F2
Helmsdale r. U.K. 50 F2
Helmstedt Germany 53 L2
Helong China 74 C4
Helper U.S.A. 129 H2
Helpter Berge hills Germany 53 N1
Helsingborg Sweden 45 H8
Helsingfors Fin. see Helsinki
Helsingør Denmark 45 H8

▶Helsinki Fin. 45 N6
Capital of Finland.

Helston U.K. 49 B8
Helvécia Brazil 145 D2
Helvetic Republic country Europe see Switzerland
Ḩelwân Egypt see Ḩulwān
Hemel Hempstead U.K. 49 G7
Hemet U.S.A. 128 E5
Hemingford U.S.A. 130 C3
Hemlock Lake U.S.A. 135 G2
Hemmingen Germany 53 J2
Hemmingford Canada 135 I1
Hemmoor Germany 53 J1
Hempstead U.S.A. 131 D6
Hemsby U.K. 49 I6
Hemse Sweden 45 K8
Henan China 76 D1
Henan prov. China 77 G1
Henares r. Spain 57 E3
Henashi-zaki pt Japan 75 E4
Henbury Australia 109 F6
Hendek Turkey 59 N4
Henderson KY U.S.A. 134 B5
Henderson NC U.S.A. 132 E4
Henderson NV U.S.A. 129 F3
Henderson NY U.S.A. 135 G2
Henderson TN U.S.A. 131 F5
Henderson TX U.S.A. 131 E5
Henderson Island Pitcairn Is 151 L7
Hendersonville NC U.S.A. 133 D5
Hendersonville TN U.S.A. 134 B5
Henderville atoll Kiribati see Aranuka
Hendon U.K. 49 G7
Hendorābī, Jazīreh-ye i. Iran 88 D5
Hendy-Gwyn U.K. see Whitland
Hengām Iran 89 E5
Hengduan Shan mts China 76 C2
Hengelo Neth. 52 G2
Hengfeng China 77 H2
Hengnan China see Hengyang
Hengshan China 74 C3
Heng Shan mt. China 77 G3
Hengshui Hebei China 73 L5
Hengshui Jiangxi China see Chongyi
Hengxian China 77 F4
Hengyang Hunan China 77 G3
Hengyang Hunan China 77 G3
Hengzhou China see Hengxian
Heniches'k Ukr. 43 G7
Henley N.Z. 113 C7
Henley-on-Thames U.K. 49 G7
Henlopen, Cape U.S.A. 135 H4
Hennef (Sieg) Germany 53 H4
Hennenman S. Africa 101 H4
Hennepin U.S.A. 130 F3
Hennessey U.S.A. 131 D4
Hennigsdorf Germany 53 N2
Henniker U.S.A. 135 J2
Henning U.S.A. 134 B3
Henrietta U.S.A. 131 D5
Henrietta Maria, Cape Canada 122 E3
Henrieville U.S.A. 129 H3
Henrique de Carvalho Angola see Saurimo
Henry, Cape U.S.A. 135 G5
Henry Ice Rise Antarctica 152 A1
Henryk Arctowski research station Antarctica see Arctowski
Henry Kater, Cape Canada 119 L3
Henry Mountains U.S.A. 129 H2
Hensall Canada 134 E2
Henshaw, Lake U.S.A. 128 E5
Henteyn Nuruu mts Mongolia 73 J3
Hentiesbaai Namibia 100 B2
Henty Australia 112 C5
Henzada Myanmar see Hinthada
Heping Guangdong China 77 G3
Heping Guizhou China see Huishui
Heping Guizhou China see Yanhe
Hepo China see Jiexi
Heppner U.S.A. 126 D3
Heptanesus is Greece see Ionian Islands
Hepu China 77 F4
Heqing China 76 D3
Heraclea Turkey see Ereğli
Heraclea Pontica Turkey see Ereğli
Heraklion Greece see Iraklion
Herald Cays atolls Australia 110 E3
Herāt Afgh. 89 F3
Hérault r. France 56 F5
Herbertabad India 71 A5
Herbert Downs Australia 110 B4
Herbert River Falls National Park Australia 110 D3
Herbert Wash salt flat Australia 109 D6
Herborn Germany 53 I4
Herbstein Germany 53 J4
Hercules Dome ice feature Antarctica 152 K1
Herdecke Germany 53 H3
Herdorf Germany 53 H4
Hereford U.K. 49 E6
Hereford U.S.A. 131 C5
Hereheretue atoll Fr. Polynesia 151 K7
Herent Belgium 52 E4
Herford Germany 53 I2
Heringen (Werra) Germany 53 K4
Herington U.S.A. 130 D4
Herīs Iran 88 B2
Herisau Switz. 56 I3
Herkimer U.S.A. 135 H2
Herlen Gol r. China/Mongolia 73 L3
Herlen He r. China/Mongolia see Herlen Gol
Herleshausen Germany 53 K3
Herlong U.S.A. 128 C1
Herm i. Channel Is 49 E9
Hermanas Mex. 131 C7
Herma Ness hd U.K. 50 [inset]
Hermann U.S.A. 130 F4
Hermannsburg Germany 53 K2
Hermanus S. Africa 100 D8
Hermel Lebanon 85 C2
Hermes, Cape S. Africa 101 I6
Hermidale Australia 112 C3
Hermiston U.S.A. 126 D3
Hermitage MO U.S.A. 130 E4
Hermitage PA U.S.A. 134 E3
Hermitage Bay Canada 123 K5
Hermite, Islas is Chile 144 C9
Hermit Islands P.N.G. 69 L7
Hermon, Mount Lebanon/Syria 85 B3
Hermonthis Egypt see Armant
Hermopolis Magna Egypt see Al Ashmūnayn
Hermosa U.S.A. 129 J3
Hermosillo Mex. 127 F7
Hernandarias Para. 144 F3
Hernando U.S.A. 131 F5
Herndon CA U.S.A. 128 D3
Herndon PA U.S.A. 135 G3
Herndon WV U.S.A. 134 E5
Herne Germany 53 H3
Herne Bay U.K. 49 I7
Herning Denmark 45 F8
Heroica Nogales Mex. see Nogales
Heroica Puebla de Zaragoza Mex. see Puebla
Hérouville-St-Clair France 49 G9
Herowābād Iran see Khalkhāl
Herrera del Duque Spain 57 D4
Herrieden Germany 53 K5
Hershey U.S.A. 135 G3
Hertford U.K. 49 G7
Hertzogville S. Africa 101 G5
Herve Belgium 52 F4
Hervé, Lac l. Canada 123 H3
Hervey Islands Cook Is 151 J7
Herzberg Germany 53 M2
Herzberg (Elster) Germany 53 N3
Herzlake Germany 53 H2
Herzliyya Israel 85 B3
Herzogenaurach Germany 53 K5
Herzsprung Germany 53 M1
Ḩeşār Būshehr Iran 88 C4
Ḩeşār Hormozgān Iran 88 E5
Ḩeşār Zanjān Iran 88 C2
Hesdin France 52 C4
Hesel Germany 53 H1
Heshan China 77 F4
Heshengqiao China 77 G2
Hesperia U.S.A. 128 E4
Hesperus U.S.A. 129 I3
Hesperus Peak U.S.A. 129 I3
Hesquiat Canada 120 E5
Hess r. Canada 120 C2
Heßdorf Germany 53 K5
Hesse land Germany see Hessen
Hesselberg hill Germany 53 K5
Hessen land Germany 53 J4
Hessisch Lichtenau Germany 53 J3
Hess Mountains Canada 120 C2
Het r. Laos 70 D2
Hetauda Nepal 83 F4
Heteren Neth. 52 F3
Hetou China 77 F4
Hettinger U.S.A. 130 C2
Hetton U.K. 48 E4
Hettstedt Germany 53 L3
Hève, Cap de la c. France 49 H9
Hevron West Bank see Hebron
Hexham U.K. 48 E4
Hexian Anhui China 77 H2
Hexian Guangxi China see Hezhou
Heyang China 77 F1
Ḩeydarābād Iran 89 F4
Heydebreck Poland see Kędzierzyn-Koźle
Heysham U.K. 48 E4
Heyshope Dam S. Africa 101 J4
Heyuan China 77 G4
Heywood U.K. 48 E5
Heze China 77 G1
Hezhang China 76 E3
Hezheng China 76 D1
Hezhou China 77 F3
Hezuo China 76 D1
Hezuozhen China see Hezuo
Hialeah U.S.A. 133 D7
Hiawassee U.S.A. 133 D5
Hiawatha U.S.A. 130 E4
Hibbing U.S.A. 130 E2
Hibbs, Point Australia 111 [inset]
Hibernia Reef Australia 108 C3
Hīchān Iran 89 F5
Hicks, Point Australia 112 D6
Hicks Bay N.Z. 113 G3
Hicks Lake Canada 121 K2
Hicksville U.S.A. 134 C3
Hico U.S.A. 131 D5
Hidaka Japan 74 F4
Hidaka-sanmyaku mts Japan 74 F4
Hidalgo Mex. 131 D7
Hidalgo del Parral Mex. 131 B7
Hidrolândia Brazil 145 A2
Hierosolyma Israel/West Bank see Jerusalem
Higashi-suidō sea chan. Japan 75 C6
Higgins U.S.A. 131 C4
Higgins Bay U.S.A. 135 H2
Higgins Lake U.S.A. 134 C1
High Atlas mts Morocco see Haut Atlas
High Desert U.S.A. 126 C4
High Island i. H.K. China 77 [inset]
High Island U.S.A. 131 E6
High Island Reservoir H.K. China 77 [inset]
Highland Peak CA U.S.A. 128 D2
Highland Peak NV U.S.A. 129 F3
Highlands U.S.A. 135 I3
Highland Springs U.S.A. 135 G5
High Level Canada 120 G3
Highmore U.S.A. 130 D2
High Point U.S.A. 132 E5
High Point hill U.S.A. 135 H3
High Prairie Canada 120 G4
High River Canada 120 H5
Highrock Lake Man. Canada 121 K4
Highrock Lake Sask. Canada 121 J3
High Springs U.S.A. 133 D6
High Tatras mts Poland/Slovakia see Tatra Mountains
High Wycombe U.K. 49 G7
Higuera de Zaragoza Mex. 127 F8
Higüey Dom. Rep. 137 K5
Hiiumaa i. Estonia 45 M7
Hījānah, Buḩayrat al imp. l. Syria 85 C3
Hijaz reg. Saudi Arabia 86 E4
Ḩikmah, Ra's al pt Egypt 90 B5
Hiko U.S.A. 129 F3
Hikone Japan 75 E6
Hikurangi mt. N.Z. 113 G3
Hila Indon. 108 D1
Hilāl, Jabal hill Egypt 85 A4
Hilāl, Ra's al pt Libya 86 B3
Hilary Coast Antarctica 152 H1
Hildale U.S.A. 129 G3
Hildburghausen Germany 53 K4
Hilders Germany 53 K4
Hildesheim Germany 53 J2
Hillah Iraq 91 G4
Hill City U.S.A. 130 D4
Hillegom Neth. 52 E2
Hill End Australia 112 D4
Hillerød Denmark 45 H9
Hillgrove Australia 110 D3
Hill Island Lake Canada 121 I2
Hillman U.S.A. 134 D1
Hillsboro ND U.S.A. 130 D2
Hillsboro NM U.S.A. 127 G6
Hillsboro OH U.S.A. 134 D4
Hillsboro OR U.S.A. 126 C3
Hillsboro TX U.S.A. 131 D5
Hillsdale IN U.S.A. 134 B4
Hillsdale MI U.S.A. 134 C3
Hillside Australia 108 B5
Hillston Australia 112 B4
Hillsville U.S.A. 134 E5
Hilo U.S.A. 127 [inset]
Hilton Australia 110 B4
Hilton S. Africa 101 J5
Hilton U.S.A. 135 G2
Hilton Head Island U.S.A. 133 D5
Hilvan Turkey 90 E3
Hilversum Neth. 52 F2
Himachal Pradesh state India 82 D3
Himalaya mts Asia 82 D2
Himalchul mt. Nepal 83 F3
Himanka Fin. 44 M4
Ḩimār, Wādī al watercourse Syria/Turkey 85 D1
Himarë Albania 59 H4
Himatnagar India 82 C5
Himeji Japan 75 D6
Ḩimş Syria see Homs
Ḩimş, Baḩrat resr Syria see Qaţţīnah, Buḩayrat
Hinchinbrook Island Australia 110 D3
Hinckley U.K. 49 F6
Hinckley MN U.S.A. 130 E2
Hinckley UT U.S.A. 129 G2
Hinckley Reservoir U.S.A. 135 H2
Hindaun India 82 D4
Hinderwell U.K. 48 G4
Hindley U.K. 48 E5
Hindman U.S.A. 134 D5
Hindmarsh, Lake dry lake Australia 111 C8
Hindu Kush mts Afgh./Pak. 89 G3
Hindupur India 84 C3

Hines Creek Canada 120 G3
Hinesville U.S.A. 133 D6
Hinganghat India 84 C1
Hingoli India 84 C2
Hınıs Turkey 91 F3
Hinnøya *i.* Norway 44 I2
Hinojosa del Duque Spain 57 D4
Hinsdale U.S.A. 135 I2
Hinte Germany 53 H1
Hinthada Myanmar 70 A3
Hinton Canada 120 G4
Hinton U.S.A. 134 E5
Hiort *i.* U.K. *see* **St Kilda**
Hippolytushoef Neth. 52 E2
Hipponium Italy *see* **Vibo Valentia**
Hippo Regius Alg. *see* **Annaba**
Hippo Zarytus Tunisia *see* **Bizerte**
Hirabit Dağ *mt.* Turkey 91 G3
Hiraizumi *tourist site* Japan 75 F5
Hirakud Dam India 83 E5
Hirakud Reservoir India 83 E5
Hirapur India 82 D4
Hiriyur India 84 C3
Hirosaki Japan 74 F4
Hiroshima Japan 75 D6
Hirschaid Germany 53 L5
Hirschberg Germany 53 L4
Hirschberg *mt.* Germany 47 M7
Hirschberg Poland *see* **Jelenia Góra**
Hirschenstein *mt.* Germany 53 M6
Hirson France 52 E5
Hîrşova Romania *see* **Hârşova**
Hirtshals Denmark 45 F8
Hisar India 82 C3
Hisarköy Turkey *see* **Domaniç**
Hisarönü Turkey 59 O4
Ḥisb, Sha'īb *watercourse* Iraq 91 G5
Ḥisbān Jordan 85 B4
Hisiu P.N.G. 69 L8
Hisor Tajik. 89 H2
Hisor tizmasi *mts* Tajik./Uzbek. *see* **Gissar Range**
Hispalis Spain *see* **Seville**
Hispania *country* Europe *see* **Spain**

▶**Hispaniola** *i.* Caribbean Sea 137 J4
Consists of the Dominican Republic and Haiti.

Hispur Glacier Pak. 82 C1
Hissar India *see* **Hisar**
Hisua India 83 F4
Ḥisyah Syria 85 C2
Hīt Iraq 91 F4
Hitachi Japan 75 F5
Hitachinaka Japan 75 F5
Hitra *i.* Norway 44 F5
Hitzacker (Elbe) Germany 53 L1
Hiva Oa *i.* Fr. Polynesia 151 K6
Hixon Canada 120 F4
Hixson Cay *reef* Australia 110 F4
Hiyyon, Naḥal *watercourse* Israel 85 B4
Hizan Turkey 91 F3
Hjälmaren *l.* Sweden 45 I7
Hjerkinn Norway 44 F5
Hjo Sweden 45 I7
Hjørring Denmark 45 G8
Hkakabo Razi *mt.* China/Myanmar 76 C2
Hlaingdet Myanmar 70 B2
Hlane Royal National Park Swaziland 101 J4
Hlatikulu Swaziland 101 J4
Hlegu Myanmar 70 B3
Hlohlowane S. Africa 101 H5
Hlotse Lesotho 101 I5
Hluhluwe-Umfolozi Park *nature res.* S. Africa 101 J5
Hlukhiv Ukr. 43 G6
Hlung-Tan Myanmar 70 B2
Hlusha Belarus 43 F5
Hlybokaye Belarus 45 O9
Ho Ghana 96 D4
Hoa Binh *Hoa Binh* Vietnam 70 D2
Hoa Binh *Nghê An* Vietnam 70 D3
Hoachanas Namibia 100 D2
Hoagland U.S.A. 134 C3
Hoang Liên Sơn *mts* Vietnam 70 C2
Hoang Sa *is* S. China Sea *see* **Paracel Islands**

▶**Hobart** Australia 111 [inset]
Capital of Tasmania.

Hobart U.S.A. 131 D5
Hobbs U.S.A. 131 C5
Hobbs Coast Antarctica 152 J1
Hobe Sound U.S.A. 133 D7
Hobiganj Bangl. *see* **Habiganj**
Hobro Denmark 45 F8
Hobyo Somalia 98 E3
Höchberg Germany 53 J5
Hochfeiler *mt.* Austria/Italy *see* **Gran Pilastro**
Hochfeld Namibia 99 B6
Hochharz, Nationalpark *nat. park* Germany 53 K3
Hô Chi Minh Vietnam *see* **Ho Chi Minh City**
Ho Chi Minh City Vietnam 71 D5
Hochschwab *mt.* Austria 47 O7
Hochschwab *mts* Austria 47 O7
Hockenheim Germany 53 I5
Ḥôḍ *reg.* Mauritania 96 C3
Hoddesdon U.K. 49 G7
Hodeidah Yemen 86 F7
Hodgenville U.S.A. 134 C5
Hodgson Downs Australia 108 F3
Hódmezővásárhely Hungary 59 I1
Hodna, Chott el *salt l.* Alg. 57 I6
Hodo-dan *pt* N. Korea 75 B5
Ho Dynasty Citadel *tourist site* Vietnam 76 E4
Ho Dynasty Citadel *tourist site* Vietnam 70 D2
Hoek van Holland Neth. *see* **Hook of Holland**
Hoensbroek Neth. 52 F4
Hoeryŏng N. Korea 74 C4
Hof Germany 53 L4
Hoffman Mountain U.S.A. 135 I2
Hofheim in Unterfranken Germany 53 K4
Hofmeyr S. Africa 101 G6
Höfn Iceland 44 [inset 1]
Hofors Sweden 45 J6
Hofsjökull *ice cap* Iceland 44 [inset 1]
Hofsós Iceland 44 [inset 1]
Hōfu Japan 75 C6
Höganäs Sweden 45 H8
Hogan Group *is* Australia 112 C7
Hogansburg U.S.A. 135 H1
Hogback Mountain U.S.A. 130 C3
Hoge Vaart *canal* Neth. 52 F2
Hogg, Mount Canada 120 C2
Hoggar *plat.* Alg. *see* **Ahaggar**
Hog Island U.S.A. 135 H5
Högsby Sweden 45 J8
Hohenloher Ebene *plain* Germany 53 J5
Hohenmölsen Germany 53 M3
Hohennauen Germany 53 M2
Hohensalza Poland *see* **Inowrocław**
Hohenwald U.S.A. 132 C5
Hohenwartetalsperre *resr* Germany 53 L4
Hoher Dachstein *mt.* Austria 47 N7
Hohe Rhön *mts* Germany 53 J4
Hohe Tauern *mts* Austria 47 N7
Hohhot China 73 K4
Höhmorït Mongolia 80 H2
Hohneck *mt.* France 56 H2
Hoh Sai Hu *l.* China 83 H2
Hoh Xil Hu *salt l.* China 83 G2
Hoh Xil Shan *mts* China 83 G2
Hôi An Vietnam 70 E4
Hoima Uganda 98 D3
Hojagala Turkm. 88 E2
Hojai India 83 H4
Hojambaz Turkm. 89 G2
Højryggen *mts* Greenland 119 M2
Hokitika N.Z. 113 C6
Hokkaidō *i.* Japan 74 F4
Hokksund Norway 45 F7
Hol Norway 45 F6
Holbæk Denmark 45 G9
Holbeach U.K. 49 H6
Holbrook Australia 112 C5
Holbrook U.S.A. 129 H4
Holden U.S.A. 129 G2
Holdenville U.S.A. 131 D5
Holdrege U.S.A. 130 D3
Holgate U.S.A. 134 C3
Holguín Cuba 137 I4
Holin He *r.* China 74 B3
Höljes Sweden 45 H6
Holland *country* Europe *see* **Netherlands**
Holland *MI* U.S.A. 134 B2
Holland *NY* U.S.A. 135 F2
Hollandia Indon. *see* **Jayapura**
Hollick-Kenyon Peninsula Antarctica 152 L2
Hollick-Kenyon Plateau Antarctica 152 K1
Hollidaysburg U.S.A. 135 F3
Hollis *AK* U.S.A. 120 C4
Hollis *OK* U.S.A. 131 D5
Hollister U.S.A. 128 C3
Holly U.S.A. 134 D2
Hollyhill U.S.A. 134 C5
Holly Springs U.S.A. 131 F5
Hollywood *CA* U.S.A. 129 D4
Hollywood *FL* U.S.A. 133 D7
Holm Norway 44 H4
Holmes Reef Australia 110 D3
Holmes Summit Antarctica 152 B1
Holmestrand Norway 45 G7
Holmgard Russia *see* **Velikiy Novgorod**
Holm Ø *i.* Greenland *see* **Kiatassuaq**
Holmön *i.* Sweden 44 L5
Holmsund Sweden 44 L5
Ḥolon Israel 85 B3
Holoog Namibia 100 C4
Holothuria Banks *reef* Australia 108 D3
Holroyd *r.* Australia 110 C2
Holstebro Denmark 45 F8
Holstein U.S.A. 130 E3
Holsteinsborg Greenland *see* **Sisimiut**
Holston *r.* U.S.A. 132 D4
Holsworthy U.K. 49 C8
Holt U.K. 49 I6
Holt U.S.A. 134 C2
Holton U.S.A. 134 B2
Holwerd Neth. 52 F1
Holwert Neth. *see* **Holwerd**
Holycross Ireland 51 E5
Holy Cross U.S.A. 118 C3
Holy Cross, Mount of the U.S.A. 126 G5
Holyhead U.K. 48 C5
Holyhead Bay U.K. 48 C5
Holy Island *England* U.K. 48 F3
Holy Island *Wales* U.K. 48 C5
Holyoke U.S.A. 130 C3
Holy See Europe *see* **Vatican City**
Holywell U.K. 48 D5
Holzhausen Germany 53 M3
Holzkirchen Germany 47 M7
Holzminden Germany 53 J3
Homand Iran 89 E3
Homāyūnshahr Iran *see* **Khomeynīshahr**
Homberg (Efze) Germany 53 J3
Hombori Mali 96 C3
Homburg Germany 53 H5
Home Bay Canada 119 L3
Homécourt France 52 F5
Homer *GA* U.S.A. 133 D5
Homer *LA* U.S.A. 131 E5
Homer *MI* U.S.A. 134 C2
Homer *NY* U.S.A. 135 G2
Homerville U.S.A. 133 D6
Homestead Australia 110 D4
Homnabad India 84 C2
Homoine Moz. 101 L2
Homs Libya *see* **Al Khums**
Homs Syria 85 C2
Homyel' Belarus 43 F5
Honan *prov.* China *see* **Henan**
Honavar India 84 B3
Honawad India 84 B2
Honaz Turkey 59 M6
Hon Chông Vietnam 71 D5
Hondeklipbaai S. Africa 100 C6
Hondo U.S.A. 131 D6
Hondsrug *reg.* Neth. 52 G1

▶**Honduras** *country* Central America 137 G6
5th largest country in North America.

Hønefoss Norway 45 G6
Honesdale U.S.A. 135 H3
Honey Lake *salt l.* U.S.A. 128 C1
Honeyoye Lake U.S.A. 135 G2
Honfleur France 56 E2
Hong, Mouths of the Vietnam *see* **Red River, Mouths of the**
Hông, Sông *r.* Vietnam *see* **Red**
Hongchuan China *see* **Hongya**
Hongguo China *see* **Panxian**
Honghai Wan *b.* China 77 G4
Honghe China 76 D4
Hong He *r.* China 77 G1
Honghe Hani Rice Terraces *tourist site* China 76 D4
Honghu China 77 G2
Hongjiang *Hunan* China 77 F3
Hongjiang *Sichuan* China *see* **Wangcang**
Hong Kong *H.K.* China 77 [inset]
Hong Kong *aut. reg.* China 77 [inset]
Hong Kong Harbour *sea chan.* H.K. China 77 [inset]
Hong Kong Island *H.K.* China 77 [inset]
Hongliuwan China *see* **Aksay**
Hongliuyuan China 80 I3
Hongqiao China *see* **Qidong**
Hongqizhen China *see* **Wuzhishan**
Hongshan China 77 G2
Hongshilazi China 74 B4
Hongshui He *r.* China 76 F4
Hongueo, Détroit d' *sea chan.* Canada 123 I4
Hongwŏn N. Korea 75 B4
Hongxing China 74 A3
Hongya China 76 D2
Hongyuan China 76 D1
Hongze China 77 H1
Hongze Hu *l.* China 77 H1

▶**Honiara** Solomon Is 107 F2
Capital of the Solomon Islands.

Honiton U.K. 49 D8
Honkajoki Fin. 45 M6
Honningsvåg Norway 44 N1
Honoka'a U.S.A. 127 [inset]

▶**Honolulu** U.S.A. 127 [inset]
Capital of Hawaii.

▶**Honshū** *i.* Japan 75 D6
Largest island in Japan, 3rd largest in Asia and 7th in the world.

Hood, Mount *vol.* U.S.A. 126 C3
Hood Point Australia 109 B8
Hood Point P.N.G. 110 D1
Hood River U.S.A. 126 C3
Hoogeveen Neth. 52 G2
Hoogezand-Sappemeer Neth. 52 G1
Hooghly *r. mouth* India *see* **Hugli**
Hooker U.S.A. 131 C4
Hook Head *hd* Ireland 51 F5
Hook of Holland Neth. 52 E3
Hook Reef Australia 110 E3
Hoonah U.S.A. 120 C3
Hooper Bay U.S.A. 153 B2
Hooper Island U.S.A. 135 G4
Hoopeston U.S.A. 134 B3
Hoopstad S. Africa 101 G4
Höör Sweden 45 H9
Hoorn Neth. 52 F2
Hoosick U.S.A. 135 I2
Hoover Dam U.S.A. 129 F3
Hoover Memorial Reservoir U.S.A. 134 D3
Hopa Turkey 91 F2
Hope Canada 120 F5
Hope *r.* N.Z. 113 D6
Hope *AR* U.S.A. 131 E5
Hope *IN* U.S.A. 134 C4
Hope, Lake *salt flat* Australia 109 C8
Hope, Point *pt* U.S.A. 118 B3
Hopedale Canada 123 J3
Hopefield S. Africa 100 D7
Hopei *prov.* China *see* **Hebei**
Hope Mountains Canada 123 J3
Hope Saddle *pass* N.Z. 113 D5
Hopes Advance, Baie *b.* Canada 123 H2
Hopes Advance, Cap *c.* Canada 119 L3
Hopes Advance Bay Canada *see* **Aupaluk**
Hopetoun Australia 111 C7
Hopetown S. Africa 100 G5
Hopewell U.S.A. 135 G5
Hopewell Islands Canada 122 F2
Hopin Myanmar 70 B1
Hopkins *r.* Australia 111 C8
Hopkins, Lake *salt flat* Australia 109 E6
Hopkinsville U.S.A. 134 B5
Hopland U.S.A. 128 B2
Hoquiam U.S.A. 126 C3
Hor China 76 D1
Horasan Turkey 91 F2
Hörby Sweden 45 H9

▶**Horizon Deep** *sea feature* S. Pacific Ocean 150 I7
Deepest point in the Tonga Trench, and 2nd in the world.

Horki Belarus 43 F5
Horlick Mountains Antarctica 152 K1
Horlivka Ukr. 43 H6
Hormoz, Jazīreh-ye *i.* Iran 88 E5
Hormoz, Kūh-e *mt.* Iran 88 D5
Hormuz, Strait of Iran/Oman 88 E5
Horn Austria 47 O6
Horn *r.* Canada 120 G2
Horn *c.* Iceland 44 [inset 1]

▶**Horn, Cape** Chile 144 C9
Most southerly point of South America.

Horn, Îles de *is* Wallis and Futuna 107 I3
Hornavan *l.* Sweden 44 J3
Hornbrook U.S.A. 126 C4
Hornburg Germany 53 K2
Horncastle U.K. 48 G5
Horndal Sweden 45 J6
Horne, Îles de *is* Wallis and Futuna Is *see* **Horn, Îles de**
Horneburg Germany 53 J1
Hörnefors Sweden 44 K5
Hornell U.S.A. 135 G2
Hornepayne Canada 122 D4
Hornillos Mex. 127 F8
Hornisgrinde *mt.* Germany 47 L6
Hornkranz Namibia 100 C2
Horn Mountains Canada 120 F2
Hornos, Cabo de Chile *see* **Horn, Cape**
Hornoy-le-Bourg France 52 B5
Horn Peak Canada 120 D2
Hornsby Australia 112 E4
Hornsea U.K. 48 G5
Hornslandet *pen.* Sweden 45 J6
Horodenka Ukr. 43 E6
Horodnya Ukr. 43 F6
Horodok *Khmel'nyts'ka Oblast'* Ukr. 43 E6
Horodok *L'vivs'ka Oblast'* Ukr. 43 D6
Horokanai Japan 74 F3
Horoshiri-dake *mt.* Japan 74 F4
Horqin Youyi Qianqi China *see* **Ulanhot**
Horqin Zuoyi Houqi China *see* **Ganjig**
Horqin Zuoyi Zhongqi China *see* **Baokang**
Horrabridge U.K. 49 C8
Horrocks Australia 109 A7
Horru China 83 G3
Horse Cave U.S.A. 134 C5
Horsefly Canada 120 F4
Horseheads U.S.A. 135 G2
Horse Islands Canada 123 L4
Horseleap Ireland 51 D4
Horsens Denmark 45 F9
Horseshoe Bend Australia 109 F6
Horseshoe Reservoir U.S.A. 129 H4
Horseshoe Seamounts *sea feature* N. Atlantic Ocean 148 G3
Horsham Australia 111 C8
Horsham U.K. 49 G7
Horšovský Týn Czechia 53 M5
Horst *hill* Germany 53 J4
Hörstel Germany 53 H2
Horten Norway 45 G7
Hortobágyi *nat. park* Hungary 59 I1
Horton *r.* Canada 118 F3
Horwood Lake Canada 122 E4
Hosapete India 84 C3
Hösbach Germany 53 J4
Hose, Pegunungan *mts* Malaysia 68 E6
Ḥoseynābād Iran 88 B3
Ḥoseynīyeh Iran 88 C4
Hoshab Pak. 89 F5
Hoshangabad India 82 D5
Hoshiarpur India 82 C3
Hospital Ireland 51 D5
Hosta Butte *mt.* U.S.A. 129 I4
Hotagen *r.* Sweden 44 I5
Hotahudo East Timor *see* **Hatudo**
Hotan China 82 E1
Hotazel S. Africa 100 F4
Hot Creek Range *mts* U.S.A. 128 E2
Hotgi India 84 C2
Hotham *r.* Australia 109 B8
Hoting Sweden 44 J4
Hot Springs *AR* U.S.A. 131 E5
Hot Springs *NM* U.S.A. *see* **Truth or Consequences**
Hot Springs *SD* U.S.A. 130 C3
Hot Sulphur Springs U.S.A. 126 G4
Hottah Lake Canada 120 G1
Hottentots Bay Namibia 100 B4
Hottentots Point Namibia 100 B4
Houayxay Laos 70 C2
Houdan France 52 B6
Houffalize Belgium 52 F4
Hougang Sing. 71 [inset]
Houghton *MI* U.S.A. 130 F2
Houghton *NY* U.S.A. 135 F2
Houghton Lake U.S.A. 134 C1
Houghton Lake *l.* U.S.A. 134 C1
Houghton le Spring U.K. 48 F4
Houie Moc, Phou *mt.* Laos 70 C2
Houlton U.S.A. 132 H2
Houma China 77 F1
Houma U.S.A. 131 F6
Houmen China 77 G4
House Range *mts* U.S.A. 129 G2
Houston Canada 120 E4
Houston *MO* U.S.A. 131 F4
Houston *MS* U.S.A. 131 F5
Houston *TX* U.S.A. 131 E6
Houtman Abrolhos *is* Australia 109 A7
Houton U.K. 50 F2
Houwater S. Africa 100 F6
Hovd Mongolia 80 H2
Hove U.K. 49 G8
Hoveton U.K. 49 I6
Hovmantorp Sweden 45 I8
Hövsgöl Nuur *l.* Mongolia 80 J1
Howar, Wadi *watercourse* Sudan 86 C6
Howard Australia 110 F5
Howard *PA* U.S.A. 135 G3
Howard *SD* U.S.A. 130 D2
Howard *WI* U.S.A. 134 A1
Howard City U.S.A. 134 C2
Howard Lake Canada 121 J2
Howden U.K. 48 G5
Howe, Cape Australia 112 D6
Howe, Mount Antarctica 152 J1
Howell U.S.A. 134 D2
Howick Canada 135 I1
Howick S. Africa 101 J5
Howland U.S.A. 132 G2

▶**Howland Island** *terr.* N. Pacific Ocean 107 I1
United States Unincorporated Territory.

Howlong Australia 112 C5
Howrah India *see* **Haora**
Howth Ireland 51 F4
Ḥowz *well* Iran 88 E3
Ḥowz-e Khān *well* Iran 88 E3
Ḥowz-e Panj Iran 88 E4
Ḥowz-e Panj *waterhole* Iran 88 D3
Howz i-Mian i-Tak Iran 88 D3
Hô Xa Vietnam 70 D3
Höxter Germany 53 J3
Hoy *i.* U.K. 50 F2
Hoya Germany 53 J2
Høyanger Norway 45 E6
Hoyerswerda Germany 47 O5
Høylandet Norway 44 H4
Hoym Germany 53 L3
Höytiäinen *l.* Fin. 44 P5
Hoyt Peak U.S.A. 129 H1
Hpa-an Myanmar 70 B3
Hpapun Myanmar 70 B3
Hpungan Pass India/Myanmar 70 B1
Hradec Králové Czechia 47 O5
Hradiště *hill* Czechia 53 N4
Hrasnica Bos. & Herz. 58 H3
Hrazdan Armenia 91 G2
Hrebinka Ukr. 43 G6
Hrodna Belarus 45 M10
Hrvatska *country* Europe *see* **Croatia**
Hrvatsko Grahovo Bos. & Herz. *see* **Bosansko Grahovo**
Hsenwi Myanmar 70 B2
Hsiang Kang *H.K.* China *see* **Hong Kong**
Hsi-hseng Myanmar 70 B2
Hsin-chia-p'o *country* Asia *see* **Singapore**
Hsin-chia-p'o Sing. *see* **Singapore**
Hsinchu Taiwan 77 I3
Hsinking China *see* **Changchun**
Hsinying Taiwan *see* **Xinying**
Hsipaw Myanmar 70 B2
Hsi-sha Ch'ün-tao *is* S. China Sea *see* **Paracel Islands**
Hsü-chou China *see* **Xuzhou**
Huab *watercourse* Namibia 99 B6
Huachinera Mex. 127 F7
Huacho Peru 142 C6
Huachuan China 74 C3
Huade China 73 K4
Huadian China 74 B4
Huadu China 77 G4
Hua Hin Thai. 71 B4
Huai'an *Jiangsu* China *see* **Chuzhou**
Huai'an *Jiangsu* China 77 H1
Huaibei China 77 H1
Huaibin China 77 G1
Huaicheng *Guangdong* China *see* **Huaiji**
Huaicheng *Jiangsu* China *see* **Chuzhou**
Huaide China 74 B4
Huaidian China *see* **Shenqiu**
Huai Had National Park Thai. 70 D3
Huaihua China 77 F3
Huaiji China 77 G4
Huai Kha Khaeng Wildlife Reserve *nature res.* Thai. 70 B4
Huailillas *mt.* Peru 142 C5
Huainan China 77 H1
Huaining *Anhui* China 77 H2
Huaining *Anhui* China *see* **Shipai**
Huaiyang China 77 G1
Huaiyin *Jiangsu* China *see* **Huai'an**
Huaiyin *Jiangsu* China 77 H1
Huaiyuan China 77 H1
Huajialing China 76 E1
Huajuápan de León Mex. 136 E5
Hualapai Peak U.S.A. 129 G4
Hualian Taiwan *see* **Hualien**
Hualien Taiwan 77 I3
Huallaga *r.* Peru 142 C5
Huambo Angola 99 B5
Huanan China 74 C3
Huancane Peru 142 E7
Huancavelica Peru 142 C6
Huancayo Peru 142 C6
Huangbei China 77 G3
Huangcaoba China *see* **Xingyi**
Huang-chou China *see* **Huanggang**
Huangchuan China 77 G1
Huanggang China 77 G2
Huang Hai *sea* N. Pacific Ocean *see* **Yellow Sea**
Huang He *r.* China *see* **Yellow River**
Huangjian China 77 I1
Huang-kang China *see* **Huanggang**
Huangling China 77 F1
Huangliu China 77 F5
Huanglongsi China *see* **Kaifeng**
Huangmao Jian *mt.* China 77 H3
Huangmei China 77 G2
Huangpu China 77 G4
Huangqi China 77 H3
Huangshan China 77 H2
Huangshi China 77 G2
Huangtu Gaoyuan *plat.* China 73 J5
Huangyan China 77 I2
Huangzhou China *see* **Huanggang**
Huaning China 76 D3
Huanjiang China 77 F3
Huanren China 74 B4
Huanshan China *see* **Yuhuan**
Huánuco Peru 142 C5
Huaping China 76 D3
Huaping Yu *i.* Taiwan 77 I3
Huaqiao China 76 E2
Huaqiaozhen China *see* **Huaqiao**
Huaraz Peru 142 C5
Huarmey Peru 142 C6
Huarong China 77 G2
Huascarán, Nevado de *mt.* Peru 142 C5
Huasco Chile 144 B3
Hua Shan *mt.* China 77 F1
Huashixia China 76 C1
Huashulinzi China 74 B4
Huatabampo Mex. 127 F8
Huaxian *Guangdong* China *see* **Huadu**
Huaxian *Henan* China 77 G1
Huayang China *see* **Jixi**
Huayin China 77 F1
Huayuan China 77 F2
Huazangsi China *see* **Tianzhu**
Hubballi India 84 B3
Hubbard, Mount Canada/U.S.A. 120 B2
Hubbard, Pointe *pt* Canada 123 I2
Hubbard Lake U.S.A. 134 D1
Hubbart Point Canada 121 M3
Hubei *prov.* China 77 G2
Hubli India *see* **Hubballi**
Hückelhoven Germany 52 G3
Hucknall U.K. 49 F5
Huddersfield U.K. 48 F5
Huder China 74 A2
Hudiksvall Sweden 45 J6
Hudson *MA* U.S.A. 135 J2
Hudson *MD* U.S.A. 135 G4
Hudson *MI* U.S.A. 134 C3
Hudson *NH* U.S.A. 135 J2
Hudson *NY* U.S.A. 135 I2
Hudson *r.* U.S.A. 135 I3
Hudson, Baie d' *sea* Canada *see* **Hudson Bay**
Hudson, Détroit d' *strait* Canada *see* **Hudson Strait**
Hudson Bay Canada 121 K4
Hudson Bay *sea* Canada 119 J4
Hudson Falls U.S.A. 135 I2
Hudson Island Tuvalu *see* **Nanumanga**
Hudson Mountains Antarctica 152 K2
Hudson's Hope Canada 120 F3
Hudson Strait Canada 119 K3
Huê Vietnam 70 D3
Huehuetenango Guat. 136 F5
Huehueto, Cerro *mt.* Mex. 131 B7
Huelva Spain 57 C5
Huentelauquén Chile 144 B4
Huépac Mex. 127 F7
Huércal-Overa Spain 57 F5
Huertecillas Mex. 131 C7
Huesca Spain 57 F2
Huéscar Spain 57 E5
Hughenden Australia 110 D4
Hughes *r.* Canada 121 K3
Hughes (abandoned) Australia 109 E7
Hughson U.S.A. 128 C3
Hugli *r. mouth* India 83 F5
Hugli-Chinsurah India 83 G5
Hugo *CO* U.S.A. 130 C4
Hugo *OK* U.S.A. 131 E5
Hugo Lake U.S.A. 131 E5
Hugoton U.S.A. 131 C4
Huhehot China *see* **Hohhot**
Huhhot China *see* **Hohhot**
Huhudi S. Africa 100 G4
Hui'an China 77 H3
Hui'anpu China 72 J5
Huiarau Range *mts* N.Z. 113 F4
Huib-Hoch Plateau Namibia 100 C4
Huichang China 77 G3
Huicheng *Anhui* China *see* **Shexian**
Huicheng *Guangdong* China *see* **Huilai**
Huidong China 76 D3
Huijbergen Neth. 52 E3
Huila, Nevado de *vol.* Col. 142 C3
Huíla, Planalto da Angola 99 B5
Huilai China 77 H4
Huili China 76 D3
Huimanguillo Mex. 136 F5
Huinan China *see* **Nanhui**
Huining China 76 E1
Huishi China *see* **Huining**
Huishui China 76 E3
Huiten Nur *l.* China 83 G2
Huitong China 77 F3
Huittinen Fin. 45 M6
Huixian *Gansu* China 76 E1
Huixian *Henan* China 77 G1
Huiyang China *see* **Huizhou**
Huize China 76 D3
Huizhou China 77 G4
Hujr Saudi Arabia 86 F4
Hukawng Valley Myanmar 70 B1
Hukuntsi Botswana 100 E2
Hulan China 74 B3
Hulan Ergi China 74 A3
Ḥulayfah Saudi Arabia 86 F4
Ḥulayḥilah *well* Syria 85 D2
Huliao China *see* **Dabu**
Hulilan Iran 88 B3
Hulin China 74 D3
Hull Canada 135 H1
Hull U.K. *see* **Kingston upon Hull**
Hull Island *atoll* Kiribati *see* **Orona**
Hultsfred Sweden 45 I8
Hulun China *see* **Hulun Buir**
Hulun Buir China 73 L3
Hulun Nur *l.* China 73 L3
Ḥulwān Egypt 90 C5
Huma China 74 B2
Humahuaca Arg. 144 C2
Humaitá Brazil 142 F5
Humaya *r.* Mex. 127 G8
Humaym *well* U.A.E. 88 D6
Humayyān, Jabal *hill* Saudi Arabia 88 B5
Humber, Mouth of the U.K. 48 H5
Humboldt Canada 121 J4
Humboldt *AZ* U.S.A. 129 G4
Humboldt *NE* U.S.A. 130 E3
Humboldt *NV* U.S.A. 128 D1
Humboldt *r.* U.S.A. 128 D1
Humboldt Bay U.S.A. 126 B4
Humboldt Range *mts* U.S.A. 128 D1
Humbolt Salt Marsh U.S.A. 128 E2
Hume *r.* Canada 120 D1
Humeburn Australia 112 B1
Hu Men *sea chan.* China 77 G4
Hume Reservoir Australia 112 C5
Humphrey Island *atoll* Cook Is *see* **Manihiki**
Humphreys, Mount U.S.A. 128 D3
Humphreys Peak U.S.A. 129 H4
Hūn Libya 97 E2
Húnaflói *b.* Iceland 44 [inset 1]
Hunan *prov.* China 77 F3
Hundeluft Germany 53 M3
Hunedoara Romania 59 J2
Hünfeld Germany 53 J4
Hungary *country* Europe 55 H2
Hungerford Australia 112 B2
Hŭngnam N. Korea 75 B5
Hung Shui Kiu *H.K.* China 77 [inset]
Hưng Yên Vietnam 70 D2
Hunjiang China *see* **Baishan**
Huns Mountains Namibia 100 C4
Hunstanton U.K. 49 H6
Hunte *r.* Germany 53 I1
Hunter *r.* Australia 112 E4
Hunter Island Australia 111 [inset]
Hunter Island Canada 120 D5
Hunter Island S. Pacific Ocean 107 H4
Hunter Islands Australia 111 [inset]
Huntingburg U.S.A. 134 B4
Huntingdon Canada 135 H1
Huntingdon U.K. 49 G6

Huntingdon PA U.S.A. 135 G3
Huntingdon TN U.S.A. 131 F4
Huntington IN U.S.A. 134 C3
Huntington OR U.S.A. 126 D3
Huntington WV U.S.A. 134 D4
Huntington Beach U.S.A. 128 D5
Huntington Creek r. U.S.A. 129 F1
Huntly N.Z. 113 E3
Huntly U.K. 50 G3
Hunt Mountain U.S.A. 126 G3
Huntsville Canada 134 F1
Huntsville AL U.S.A. 133 C5
Huntsville AR U.S.A. 131 E4
Huntsville TN U.S.A. 134 C5
Huntsville TX U.S.A. 131 E6
Hunza reg. Pak. 82 C1
Huolin He r. China see Holin He
Huolongmen China 74 B2
Hương Khê Vietnam 70 D3
Huonville Australia 111 [inset]
Huoqiu China 77 H1
Huoshan China 77 H2
Huoshao Tao i. Taiwan see Lü Dao
Hupeh prov. China see Hubei
Hupnik r. Turkey 85 C1
Hupu India 76 B2
Ḩūr Iran 88 E4
Hurault, Lac l. Canada 123 H3
Ḩuraydīn, Wādī watercourse Egypt 85 A4
Huraysān reg. Saudi Arabia 88 B6
Hurd, Cape Canada 134 E1
Hurd Island Kiribati see Arorae
Hüren Tovon Uul mt. Mongolia 80 I3
Hurghada Egypt 86 D4
Hurler's Cross Ireland 51 D5
Hurley NM U.S.A. 129 I5
Hurley WI U.S.A. 130 F2
Hurmagai Pak. 89 G4
Huron CA U.S.A. 128 C3
Huron SD U.S.A. 130 D2

▶Huron, Lake Canada/U.S.A. 134 D1
2nd largest lake in North America and 4th in the world.

Hurricane U.S.A. 129 G3
Hursley U.K. 49 F7
Hurst Green U.K. 49 H7
Husain Nika Pak. 89 H4
Húsavík Norðurland eystra Iceland 44 [inset 1]
Húsavík Vestfirðir Iceland 44 [inset 1]
Huseyinabat Turkey see Alaca
Huseyinli Turkey see Kızılırmak
Hūshak Iran 89 F5
Hushan Zhejiang China see Wuyi
Hushan Zhejiang China 77 H2
Hushan Zhejiang China see Cixi
Huși Romania 59 M1
Huskvarna Sweden 45 I8
Husn Jordan see Al Ḩişn
Ḩusn Āl 'Abr Yemen 86 G6
Husnes Norway 45 D7
Husum Germany 47 L3
Husum Sweden 44 K5
Hutag-Öndör Mongolia 80 J2
Hutchinson KS U.S.A. 130 D4
Hutchinson MN U.S.A. 130 E2
Hutch Mountain U.S.A. 129 H4
Hutou China 74 D3
Hutsonville U.S.A. 134 B4
Hutton, Mount hill Australia 111 E5
Hutton Range hills Australia 109 C6
Huvadhu Atholhu Maldives 81 D11
Hüvek Turkey see Bozova
Hūvīān, Kūh-e mts Iran 89 E5
Ḩuwār i. Bahrain 88 C5
Huwaytat reg. Saudi Arabia 85 C5
Huxi China 77 G3
Huzhong China 74 A2
Huzhou China 77 I2
Hvannadalshnúkur vol. Iceland 44 [inset 1]
Hvar i. Croatia 58 G3
Hvide Sande Denmark 45 F8
Hvíta r. Iceland 44 [inset 1]
Hwange Zimbabwe 99 C5
Hwange National Park Zimbabwe 99 C5
Hwang Ho r. China see Yellow River
Hwedza Zimbabwe 99 D5
Hwlffordd U.K. see Haverfordwest
Hyannis MA U.S.A. 135 J3
Hyannis NE U.S.A. 130 C3
Hyargas Nuur salt l. Mongolia 80 H2
Hyco Lake U.S.A. 134 F5
Hyde N.Z. 113 C7
Hyden Australia 109 B8
Hyden U.S.A. 134 D5
Hyde Park U.S.A. 135 I1
Hyderabad India 84 C2
Hyderabad Pak. 89 H5
Hydra i. Greece see Ydra
Hyères France 56 H5
Hyères, Îles d' is France 56 H5
Hyesan N. Korea 74 C4
Hyland, Mount Australia 112 F3
Hyland Post Canada 120 D3
Hyllestad Norway 45 D6
Hyltebruk Sweden 45 H8
Hyndman Peak U.S.A. 126 E4
Hyōno-sen mt. Japan 75 D6
Hyrynsalmi Fin. 44 P4
Hysham U.S.A. 126 G3
Hythe Canada 120 G4
Hythe U.K. 49 I7
Hyūga Japan 75 C6
Hyvinkää Fin. 45 N6

I

Iaciara Brazil 145 B1
Iaco r. Brazil 142 E5
Iaçu Brazil 145 C1
Iadera Croatia see Zadar
Iaeger U.S.A. 134 E5
Iakora Madag. 99 E6
Ialomița r. Romania 59 L2
Ianca Romania 59 L2
Iași Romania 59 L1
Iba Phil. 69 F3
Ibadan Nigeria 96 D4
Ibagué Col. 142 C3
Ibaiti Brazil 145 A3
Ibapah U.S.A. 129 G1
Ibarra Ecuador 142 C3
Ibb Yemen 86 F7
Ibbenbüren Germany 53 H2
Iberá, Esteros del marsh Arg. 144 E3
Iberia Peru 142 E6

▶Iberian Peninsula Europe 57
Consists of Portugal, Spain and Gibraltar.

Iberville, Lac d' l. Canada 123 G3
Ibeto Nigeria 96 D3
iBhayi S. Africa see Port Elizabeth
Ibi Indon. 71 B6
Ibi Nigeria 96 D4
Ibiá Brazil 145 B2
Ibiaí Brazil 145 B2
Ibiapaba, Serra da hills Brazil 143 J4
Ibiassucê Brazil 145 C1
Ibicaraí Brazil 145 D1
Ibiquera Brazil 145 C1
Ibirama Brazil 145 A4
Ibiranhém Brazil 145 C2
Ibitinga Brazil 145 A3
Ibiza Spain 57 G4
Ibiza i. Spain 57 G4
Iblei, Monti mts Sicily Italy 58 F6
Ibn Buşayyiş well Saudi Arabia 88 B5
Ibotirama Brazil 143 J6
Iboundji, Mont hill Gabon 98 B4
Ibrā' Oman 88 E6
İbradı Turkey 90 C3
Ibrī Oman 88 E6
Ica r. Col. see Putumayo
Ica Peru 142 C6
Içana Brazil 142 E3
Içana r. Brazil 142 E3
Icaria i. Greece see Ikaria
Icatu Brazil 143 J4
Iceberg Canyon gorge U.S.A. 129 F3
İçel Turkey see Mersin

▶Iceland country Europe 44 [inset 1]
2nd largest island in Europe.

Iceland Basin sea feature N. Atlantic Ocean 148 G2
Icelandic Plateau sea feature N. Atlantic Ocean 153 I2
Ichalkaranji India 84 B2
Ichifusa-yama mt. Japan 75 C6
Ichinomiya Japan 75 E6
Ichinoseki Japan 75 F5
Ichinskaya Sopka, Vulkan vol. Russia 65 Q4
Ichkeul, Parc National de l' nat. park Tunisia 58 C6
Ichnya Ukr. 43 G6
Ichtegem Belgium 52 D3
Ichtershausen Germany 53 K4
Icó Brazil 143 K5
Iconha Brazil 145 C3
Iconium Turkey see Konya
Icosium Alg. see Algiers
Iculisma France see Angoulême
Icy Cape U.S.A. 118 B2
Id Turkey see Narman
Idabel U.S.A. 131 E5
Ida Grove U.S.A. 130 E3
Idah Nigeria 96 D4
Idaho state U.S.A. 126 E3
Idaho City U.S.A. 126 E4
Idaho Falls U.S.A. 126 E4
Idalia National Park Australia 110 D5
Idar India 82 C5
Idar-Oberstein Germany 53 H5
Ideriyn Gol r. Mongolia 80 J2
Idfū Egypt 86 D5
Idhra i. Greece see Ydra
Idi Amin Dada, Lake Dem. Rep. Congo/Uganda see Edward, Lake
Idiofa Dem. Rep. Congo 99 B4
Idivuoma Sweden 44 M2
Idkū Egypt 90 C5
Idle r. U.K. 48 G5
Idlewild airport U.S.A. see John F. Kennedy
Idlib Syria 85 C2
Idra i. Greece see Ydra
Idre Sweden 45 H6
Idrija Slovenia 58 E1
Idstein Germany 53 I4
Idutywa S. Africa see Dutywa
Idzhevan Armenia see Ijevan
Iecava Latvia 45 N8
Iepê Brazil 145 A3
Ieper Belgium 52 C4
Ierapetra Greece 59 K7
Ierissou, Kolpos b. Greece 59 J4
Iešjávri l. Norway 44 N2
Ifakara Tanz. 99 D4
Ifalik atoll Micronesia 69 K5
Ifaluk atoll Micronesia see Ifalik
Ifanadiana Madag. 99 E6
Ife Nigeria 96 D4
Ifenat Chad 97 E3
Iferouâne Niger 96 D3
Iffley Australia 110 C3
Ifjord Norway 44 O1
Ifôghas, Adrar des hills Mali 96 D3
Iforas, Adrar des hills Mali see Ifôghas, Adrar des
Igan Sarawak Malaysia 68 E6
Iganga Uganda 97 G4
Igarapava Brazil 145 B3
Igarka Russia 64 J3
Igatpuri India 84 B2
Igbeti Nigeria see Igbetti
Igbetti Nigeria 96 D4
Igdir Iran 88 B2
Iğdır Turkey 91 G3
Iggesund Sweden 45 J6
Igikpak, Mount U.S.A. 118 C3
Igizyar China 89 J2
Iglesias Sardinia Italy 58 C5
Iglesiente reg. Sardinia Italy 58 C5
Igloolik Canada 119 J3
Igluligaarjuk Canada see Chesterfield Inlet
Ignace Canada 121 N5
Ignacio Zaragoza Chihuahua Mex. 127 G7
Ignacio Zaragoza Zacatecas Mex. 131 C8
Ignalina Lith. 45 O9
İğneada Turkey 59 L4
İğneada Burnu pt Turkey 59 M4
Ignoitijala India 71 A5
iGoli S. Africa see Johannesburg
Igoumenitsa Greece 59 I5
Igra Russia 41 Q4
Igrim Russia 41 S3
Iguaçu r. Brazil 145 A4
Iguaçu, Saltos do waterfall Arg./Brazil see Iguaçu Falls
Iguaçu Falls Arg./Brazil 144 F3
Iguaí Brazil 145 C1
Iguala Mex. 136 E5
Igualada Spain 57 G3
Iguape Brazil 145 B4
Iguaraçu Brazil 145 A3
Iguatama Brazil 145 B3
Iguatemi Brazil 144 F2
Iguatu Brazil 143 K5
Iguazú, Cataratas do waterfall Arg./Brazil see Iguaçu Falls
Iguéla Gabon 98 A4
Iguidi, Erg des. Alg./Mauritania 96 C2
Igunga Tanz. 99 D4
Iharaña Madag. 99 E5
Ihavandhippolhu Maldives 84 B5
Ihavandiffulu Atoll Maldives see Ihavandhippolhu
Ihosy Madag. 99 E6
Ihtiman Bulg. 59 J3
Ih Tol Gol China 74 A2
Iide-san mt. Japan 75 E5
Iijärvi l. Fin. 44 O2
Iijoki r. Fin. 44 N4
Iisalmi Fin. 44 O5
Iizuka Japan 75 C6
Ijebu-Ode Nigeria 96 D4
Ijevan Armenia 91 G2
IJmuiden Neth. 52 E2
IJssel r. Neth. 52 F2
IJsselmeer l. Neth. 52 F2
Ijzer r. France see Yser
Ikaahuk Canada see Sachs Harbour
Ikaalinen Fin. 45 M6
Ikageleng S. Africa 101 H3
Ikageng S. Africa 101 H4
iKapa S. Africa see Cape Town
Ikare Nigeria 96 D4
Ikaria i. Greece 59 L6
Ikast Denmark 45 F8
Ikeda Japan 74 F4
Ikela Dem. Rep. Congo 98 C4
Ikhutseng S. Africa 100 G5
Iki-Burul Russia 43 J7
Ikom Nigeria 96 D4
Iksan S. Korea 75 B6
Ikungu Tanz. 99 D4
Ilagan Phil. 69 G3
Ilaisamis Kenya 98 D3
Īlām Iran 88 B3
Ilam Nepal 83 F4
Ilan Taiwan see Yilan
Ilave Peru 142 E7
Iława Poland 47 Q4
Ilazārān, Kūh-e mt. Iran 88 E4
Île-à-la-Crosse Canada 121 J4
Île-à-la-Crosse, Lac l. Canada 121 J4
Ilebo Dem. Rep. Congo 99 C4
Île-de-France admin. reg. France 52 C6
Île Europa i. Indian Ocean see Europa, Île
Ilek Kazakh. 41 Q5
Ilemi Triangle terr. Africa 98 D3
Ilen r. Ireland 51 C6
Ileret Kenya 98 D3
Ileza Russia 42 I3
Ilfeld Germany 53 K3
Ilford Canada 121 M3
Ilford U.K. 49 H7
Ilfracombe Australia 110 D4
Ilfracombe U.K. 49 C7
Ilgaz Turkey 90 D2
Ilgın Turkey 90 C3
Ilha Grande resr Brazil 144 F2
Ilha Solteíra, Represa resr Brazil 145 A3
Ílhavo Port. 57 B3
Ilhéus Brazil 145 D1
Ili Kazakh. see Kapshagay
Iliamna Lake U.S.A. 118 C4
İliç Turkey 90 E3
Il'ichevsk Azer. see Şärur
Il'ichevsk Ukr. see Chornomors'k
Ilici Spain see Elche-Elx
Iligan Phil. 69 G5
Ilimananngip Nunaa i. Greenland 119 P2
Il'inka Russia 43 J7
Il'inskiy Permskiy Kray Russia 41 R4
Il'inskiy Sakhalinskaya Oblast' Russia 74 F3
Il'insko-Podomskoye Russia 42 J3
Ilion U.S.A. 135 H2
Ilium tourist site Turkey see Troy
Iliysk Kazakh. see Kapshagay
Ilkal India 84 C3
Ilkeston U.K. 49 F6
Ilkley U.K. 48 F5
Illapel Chile 144 B4
Illéla Niger 96 D3
Iller r. Germany 47 L6
Illichivs'k Ukr. see Chornomors'k
Illimani, Nevado de mt. Bol. 142 E7
Illinois r. U.S.A. 130 F4
Illinois state U.S.A. 134 A3
Illizi Alg. 96 D2
Illogwa watercourse Australia 110 A5
Ilm r. Germany 53 L3
Ilmajoki Fin. 44 M5
Il'men', Ozero l. Russia 42 F4
Ilmenau Germany 53 K4
Ilmenau r. Germany 53 K1
Ilminster U.K. 49 E8
Ilo Peru 142 D7
Iloilo Phil. 69 G4
Ilomantsi Fin. 44 Q5
Ilong India 76 B3
Ilorin Nigeria 96 D4
Ilovlya Russia 43 I6
Ilsede Germany 53 K2
Iluka Australia 112 F2
Ilulissat Greenland 119 M3
Iluppur India 84 C4
Ilva i. Italy see Elba, Isola d'
Imabari Japan 75 D6
Imaichi Japan see Nikkō
Imala Moz. 99 D5
Imam-baba Turkm. 89 F2
İmamoğlu Turkey 90 D3
Imām Şāḩib Afgh. 89 H2
Iman Russia see Dal'nerechensk
Iman r. Russia 74 D3
Imari Japan 75 C6
Imaruí Brazil 145 A5
Imataca, Serranía de mts Venez. 142 F2
Imatra Fin. 45 P6
Imbituva Brazil 145 A4
imeni 26 Bakinskikh Komissarov Azer. see Häsänabad
imeni Petra Stuchki Latvia see Aizkraukle
Īmī Eth. 98 E3
Imishli Azer. see İmişli
İmişli Azer. 91 H3
Imit Pak. 82 C1
Imja-do i. S. Korea 75 B6
Imlay U.S.A. 128 D1
Imlay City U.S.A. 134 D2
Imola Italy 58 D2
iMonti S. Africa see East London
Impendle S. Africa 101 I5
Imperatriz Brazil 143 I5
Imperia Italy 58 C3
Imperial CA U.S.A. 129 F5
Imperial NE U.S.A. 130 C3
Imperial Beach U.S.A. 128 E5
Imperial Dam U.S.A. 129 F5
Imperial Valley plain U.S.A. 129 F5
Imperieuse Reef Australia 108 B4
Impfondo Congo 98 B3
Imphal India 83 H4
İmralı Adası i. Turkey 59 M4
İmroz Turkey 59 K4
İmroz i. Turkey see Gökçeada
Imtān Syria 85 C3
Imuris Mex. 127 F7
In r. Russia 74 D2
Ina Japan 75 E6
Inambari r. Peru 142 E6
Inari Fin. 44 O2
Inarijärvi l. Fin. 44 O2
Inarijoki r. Fin./Norway 44 N2
Inca Spain 57 H4
İnce Burnu pt Turkey 59 L4
İnce Burun pt Turkey 90 D2
Inch Ireland 51 F5
Inchard, Loch b. U.K. 50 D2
Incheon S. Korea 75 B5
Inchicronan Lough l. Ireland 51 D5
Inch'ŏn S. Korea see Incheon
Incirli Turkey see Karasu
Indaal, Loch b. U.K. 50 C5
Indalsälven r. Sweden 44 J5
Indalstø Norway 45 D6
Inda Silasē Eth. 98 D2
Indaw Myanmar 70 A2
Indawgyi Lake Myanmar 76 C3
Indé Mex. 131 B7
Independence CA U.S.A. 128 D3
Independence IA U.S.A. 130 F3
Independence KS U.S.A. 131 E4
Independence KY U.S.A. 134 C4
Independence MO U.S.A. 130 E4
Independence VA U.S.A. 134 E5
Independence Mountains U.S.A. 126 D4
Inder China 74 A3
Inderbor Kazakh. 78 E2
Indi India 84 C2

▶India country Asia 81 E7
2nd most populous country in Asia and the world. 3rd largest country in Asia and 7th in the world.

Indian r. Canada 120 B2
Indiana U.S.A. 134 F3
Indiana state U.S.A. 134 B3
Indian-Antarctic Ridge sea feature Southern Ocean 150 D9

▶Indianapolis U.S.A. 134 B4
Capital of Indiana.

Indian Cabins Canada 120 G3
Indian Desert India/Pak. see Thar Desert
Indian Harbour Canada 123 K3
Indian Head Canada 121 K5
Indian Lake U.S.A. 135 H2
Indian Lake l. NY U.S.A. 135 H2
Indian Lake l. OH U.S.A. 134 D3
Indian Lake l. PA U.S.A. 135 F3

▶Indian Ocean 149
3rd largest ocean in the world.

Indianola IA U.S.A. 130 E3
Indianola MS U.S.A. 131 F5
Indian Peak U.S.A. 129 G2
Indian Springs IN U.S.A. 134 B4
Indian Springs NV U.S.A. 129 F3
Indian Wells U.S.A. 129 H4
Indiga Russia 42 K2
Indigirka r. Russia 65 P2
Indigskaya Guba b. Russia 42 K2
Inđija Serbia 59 I2
Indin Lake Canada 120 H1
Indio U.S.A. 128 E5
Indira Point India 71 A6
Indira Priyadarshini Pench National Park India 82 D5
Indispensable Reefs Solomon Is 107 G3
Indjija Serbia see Inđija
Indo-China reg. Asia 70 D3

▶Indonesia country Asia 68 E7
3rd most populous country in Asia and 4th in the world.

Indore India 82 C5
Indrapura, Gunung vol. Indon. see Kerinci, Gunung
Indravati r. India 84 D2
Indre r. France 56 E3
Indulkana Australia 109 F6
Indur India see Nizamabad
Indus r. China/Pak. 89 G6
also known as Sênggê Zangbo or Shiquan He
Indus, Mouths of the Pak. 89 G5
Indus Cone sea feature Indian Ocean 149 M4
Indwe S. Africa 101 H6
İnebolu Turkey 90 D2
İnegöl Turkey 59 M4
Inevi Turkey see Cihanbeyli
Inez U.S.A. 134 D5
Infantes Spain see Villanueva de los Infantes
Infiernillo, Presa resr Mex. 136 D5
Ing, Nam Mae r. Thai. 70 C2
Inga Russia 44 S3
Ingalls, Mount U.S.A. 128 C2
Ingelmunster Belgium 52 D4
Ingenika r. Canada 120 E3
Ingersoll Canada 134 E2
Ingham Australia 110 D3
Ingichka Uzbek. 89 G2
Ingleborough hill U.K. 48 E4
Inglefield Land reg. Greenland 119 K2
Ingleton U.K. 48 E4
Inglewood Qld Australia 112 E2
Inglewood Vic. Australia 112 A6
Inglewood U.S.A. 128 D5
Ingoka Pum mt. Myanmar 70 B1
Ingoldmells U.K. 48 H5
Ingolstadt Germany 53 L6
Ingomar Australia 109 F7
Ingomar U.S.A. 126 G3
Ingonish Canada 123 J5
Ingraj Bazar India 83 G4
Ingram U.S.A. 134 F5
Ingray Lake Canada 120 G1
Ingrid Christensen Coast Antarctica 152 E2
Ingwavuma S. Africa 101 K4
Ingwavuma r. S. Africa/Swaziland see Ngwavuma
Ingwiller France 53 H6
Inhaca Moz. 101 K3
Inhaca, Península pen. Moz. 101 K4
Inhambane Moz. 101 L2
Inhambane prov. Moz. 101 L2
Inhaminga Moz. 99 D5
Inharrime Moz. 101 L3
Inhassoro Moz. 99 D6
Inhaúmas Brazil 145 B1
Inhobim Brazil 145 C1
Inhumas Brazil 145 A2
Inírida Col. 142 E3
Inis Ireland see Ennis
Inis Córthaidh Ireland see Enniscorthy
Inishark i. Ireland 51 B4
Inishbofin i. Ireland 51 B4
Inisheer i. Ireland 51 C4
Inishkea North i. Ireland 51 B3
Inishkea South i. Ireland 51 B3
Inishmaan i. Ireland 51 C4
Inishmore i. Ireland 51 C4
Inishmurray i. Ireland 51 D3
Inishowen pen. Ireland 51 E2
Inishowen Head hd Ireland 51 F2
Inishtrahull i. Ireland 51 E2
Inishturk i. Ireland 51 B4
Injune Australia 111 E5
Inkerman Australia 110 C3
Inkeroinen Fin. 45 O6
Inklin Canada 120 C3
Inklin r. Canada 120 C3
Inkylap Turkm. 89 F2
Inland Kaikoura Range mts N.Z. 113 D6
Inland Sea Japan see Seto-naikai
Inlet U.S.A. 135 H2
Inn r. Europe 47 M7
Innaanganeq c. Greenland 119 L2
Innamincka Australia 111 C5
Innamincka Regional Reserve nature res. Australia 111 C5
Inndyr Norway 44 I3
Inner Sound sea chan. U.K. 50 D3
Innes National Park Australia 111 B7
Innisfail Australia 110 D3
Innisfail Canada 120 H4
Innokent'yevka Russia 74 C2
Innoko r. U.S.A. 118 C3
Innsbruck Austria 47 M7
Innuksuak r. Canada 122 F2
Inny r. Ireland 51 E4
Inocência Brazil 145 A2
Inongo Dem. Rep. Congo 98 B4
İnönü Turkey 59 N5
Inoucdjouac Canada see Inukjuak
Inowrocław Poland 47 Q4
In Salah Alg. 96 D2
Insch U.K. 50 G3

▶Inscription, Cape Australia 110 B3
Most westerly point of Oceania.

Insein Myanmar 70 B3
Insterburg Russia see Chernyakhovsk
Inta Russia 41 S2
Interamna Italy see Teramo
Interlaken Switz. 56 H3
International Falls U.S.A. 130 E1
Interview Island India 71 A4
Intracoastal Waterway canal U.S.A. 131 E6
Intutu Peru 142 D4
Inubō-zaki pt Japan 75 F6
Inukjuak Canada 122 F2
Inuvialuit area Canada 118 E3
Inuvik Canada 118 E3
Inveraray U.K. 50 D4
Inverbervie U.K. 50 G4
Invercargill N.Z. 113 B8
Inverell Australia 112 E2
Invergordon U.K. 50 E3
Inverkeithing U.K. 50 F4
Inverleigh Australia 110 C3
Invermay Canada 121 K5
Inverness Canada 123 J5
Inverness U.K. 50 E3
Inverness CA U.S.A. 128 B2
Inverness FL U.S.A. 133 D6
Inverurie U.K. 50 G3
Investigator Channel Myanmar 71 B4
Investigator Group is Australia 109 F8
Investigator Ridge sea feature Indian Ocean 149 O6
Investigator Strait Australia 111 B7
Inwood U.S.A. 135 F4
Inya Russia 80 G1
Inyanga Zimbabwe see Nyanga
Inyokern U.S.A. 128 E4
Inyo Mountains U.S.A. 128 D3
Inyonga Tanz. 99 D4
Inza Russia 43 J5
Inzhavino Russia 43 I5
Ioannina Greece 59 I5
Iokan'ga r. Russia 42 H2
Iola U.S.A. 130 E4
Iolgo, Khrebet mts Russia 80 G1
Iolotan' Turkm. see Ýolöten
Iona Canada 123 J5
Iona i. U.K. 50 C4
Iona, Parque Nacional do nat. park Angola 99 B5
Ione U.S.A. 128 E2
Iongo Angola 99 B4
Ionia U.S.A. 134 C2
Ionian Islands Greece 59 H5
Ionian Sea Greece/Italy 58 H5
Ionioi Nisoi is Greece see Ionian Islands
Ios i. Greece 59 K6
Iowa state U.S.A. 130 E3
Iowa City U.S.A. 130 F3
Iowa Falls U.S.A. 130 E3
Ipameri Brazil 145 A2
Ipanema Brazil 145 C2
Ipáría Peru 142 D5
Ipatinga Brazil 145 C2
Ipatovo Russia 43 I7
Ipelegeng S. Africa 101 G4
Ipiales Col. 142 C3
Ipiaú Brazil 145 D1
Ipirá Brazil 145 D1
Ipiranga Brazil 145 A4
iPitoli S. Africa see Pretoria
Ipixuna r. Brazil 142 F5
Ipoh Malaysia 71 C6
Iporá Brazil 145 A2
Ippy Cent. Afr. Rep. 98 C3
İpsala Turkey 59 L4
Ipswich Australia 112 F1
Ipswich U.K. 49 I6
Ipswich U.S.A. 130 D2
Ipu Brazil 143 J4

▶Iqaluit Canada 119 L3
Capital of Nunavut.

Iquique Chile 144 B2
Iquiri r. Brazil see Ituxi
Iquitos Peru 142 D4
Īrafshān reg. Iran 89 F5
Iraí Brazil 144 F3
Irakleio Greece see Iraklion
Iraklion Greece 59 K7
Iramaia Brazil 145 C1
Iran country Asia 88 D3
Iran, Pegunungan mts Indon. 68 E6
Īrānshahr Iran 89 F5
Irapuato Mex. 136 D4
Iraq country Asia 91 F4
Irará Brazil 145 D1
Irati Brazil 145 A4
Irayel' Russia 42 L2
Irazú, Volcán vol. Costa Rica 137 H7
Irbid Jordan 85 B3
Irbil Iraq see Arbīl/Hewlêr
Irbit Russia 64 H4
Irecê Brazil 143 J6
Ireland country Europe 51 E4

▶Ireland i. Ireland/U.K. 51
3rd largest island in Europe.

Irema Dem. Rep. Congo 98 C4
Iri S. Korea see Iksan
Irian, Teluk b. Indon. see Cenderawasih, Teluk
Iriba Chad 97 F3
Īrī Dāgh mt. Iran 88 B2
Iriga Phil. 69 G4
Irîgui reg. Mali/Mauritania 96 C3
Iringa Tanz. 99 D4
Iriri r. Brazil 143 H4
Irish Free State country Europe see Ireland
Irish Sea Ireland/U.K. 51 G4
Irituia Brazil 143 I4
'Irj well Saudi Arabia 88 C5
Irkutsk Russia 72 I2
Irma Canada 121 I4
Irmak Turkey 90 D3
Irminger Basin sea feature N. Atlantic Ocean 148 F2
Iron Baron Australia 111 B7
Irondequoit U.S.A. 135 G2
Iron Mountain U.S.A. 130 F2
Iron Mountain mt. U.S.A. 129 G3
Iron Range National Park Australia 110 C2
Iron River U.S.A. 130 F2
Ironton MO U.S.A. 130 F4
Ironton OH U.S.A. 134 D4
Ironwood Forest National Monument nat. park U.S.A. 129 H5
Iroquois r. U.S.A. 134 B3
Iroquois Falls Canada 122 E4
Irosin Phil. 69 G4
Irpen' Ukr. see Irpin'
Irpin' Ukr. 43 F6
Irrawaddy r. Myanmar 70 A4
Irrawaddy, Mouths of the Myanmar 70 A4
Irshad Pass Afgh./Pak. 89 I2
Irta Russia 42 K3
Irthing r. U.K. 48 E4

▶Irtysh r. Kazakh./Russia 80 E1
5th longest river in Asia and 10th in the world, and a major part of the 2nd longest in Asia (Ob'-Irtysh).

Irun Spain 57 F2
Iruña Spain see Pamplona
Iruñea Spain see Pamplona
Irvine U.K. 50 E5

Irvine CA U.S.A. 128 E5
Irvine KY U.S.A. 134 D5
Irvine Glacier Antarctica 152 L2
Irving U.S.A. 131 D5
Irvington U.S.A. 134 B5
Irwin r. Australia 109 A7
Irwinton U.S.A. 133 D5
Isa Nigeria 96 D3
Isaac r. Australia 110 E4
Isabel U.S.A. 130 C2
Isabela Phil. 69 G5
Isabela, Isla i. Galápagos Ecuador 142 [inset]
Isabelia, Cordillera mts Nicaragua 137 G6
Isabella Lake U.S.A. 128 D4
Isachsen, Cape Canada 119 H2
Ísafjarðardjúp est. Iceland 44 [inset 1]
Ísafjörður Iceland 44 [inset 1]
Isa Khel Pak. 89 H3
Isalo, Massif de l' mts Madag. 99 E6
Isalo, Parc National de l' nat. park Madag. 99 E6
Isar r. Germany 53 M6
Isbister U.K. 50 [inset]
Ischia, Isola d' i. Italy 58 E4
Ise Japan 75 E6
Isère r. France 56 G4
Isère, Pointe pt Fr. Guiana 143 H2
Iserlohn Germany 53 H3
Isernhagen Germany 53 J2
Isernia Italy 58 F4
Ise-shima Kokuritsu-kōen nat. park Japan 75 E6
Ise-wan b. Japan 75 E6
Iseyin Nigeria 96 D4
Isfahan Iran see Eşfahān
Isfana Kyrg. 89 H2
Isheyevka Russia 43 K5
Ishigaki Japan 73 M8
Ishikari-wan b. Japan 74 F4
Ishinomaki Japan 75 F5
Ishinomaki-wan b. Japan 73 Q5
Ishioka Japan 75 F5
Īshkamish Afgh. 89 H2
Ishpeming U.S.A. 132 C2
Ishqoshim Tajik. 89 H2
Ishtikhon Uzbek. see Ishtixon
Ishtixon Uzbek. 89 G2
Ishurdi Bangl. 83 G4
Ishwardi Bangl. see Ishurdi
Isiboro Sécure, Parque Nacional nat. park Bol. 142 E7
Isigny-sur-Mer France 49 F9
Işıklar Dağı mts Turkey 59 L4
Işıklı Turkey 59 M5
Isil'kul' Russia 64 I4
iSimangaliso Wetland Park nature res. S. Africa 101 K4
Isipingo S. Africa 101 J5
Isiro Dem. Rep. Congo 98 C3
Isisford Australia 110 D5
Iskar r. Bulg. 59 K3
Iskateley Russia 42 L2
İskenderun Turkey 85 C1
İskenderun Körfezi b. Turkey 85 B1
İskilip Turkey 90 D2
Iskitim Russia 64 J4
Iskushuban Somalia 98 F2
Isla r. Scotland U.K. 50 F4
Isla r. Scotland U.K. 50 G3
Isla Gorge National Park Australia 110 E5
İslahiye Turkey 90 E3
Islamabad India see Anantnag
▶Islamabad Pak. 89 I3
Capital of Pakistan.
Islamgarh Pak. 89 H5
Islamkot Pak. 89 H5
Island r. Canada 120 F2
Ísland country Europe see Iceland
Island U.S.A. 134 B5
Island Falls U.S.A. 132 G2
Island Lagoon salt flat Australia 111 B6
Island Lake Canada 121 M4
Island Lake l. Canada 121 M4
Island of Meroe, Archaeological Sites of tourist site Sudan 97 G3
Island Pond U.S.A. 135 J1
Islands, Bay of N.Z. 113 E2
Islay i. U.K. 50 C5
▶Isle of Man terr. Irish Sea 48 C4
United Kingdom Crown Dependency.
Isle of Wight U.S.A. 135 G5
Isle Royale National Park U.S.A. 130 F2
Ismail Ukr. see Izmayil
Ismâ'ilîya Egypt see Al Ismā'īlīyah
Ismâ'ilîya governorate Egypt see Al Ismā'īlīyah
Ismailly Azer. see İsmayıllı
İsmayıllı Azer. 91 H2
Isojoki Fin. 44 L5
Isoka Zambia 99 D5
Isokylä Fin. 44 O3
Isokyrö Fin. 44 M5
Isola di Capo Rizzuto Italy 58 G5
Ispahan Iran see Eşfahān
Isparta Turkey 59 N6
Isperih Bulg. 59 L3
Ispikan Pak. 89 F5
İspir Turkey 91 F2
Ispisar Tajik. see Khŭjand
Isplinji Pak. 89 G4
Israel country Asia 85 B4
Israelite Bay Australia 109 C8
Isra'īl country Asia see Israel
Isselburg Germany 52 G3
Issia Côte d'Ivoire 96 C4
Issoire France 56 F4
Issyk-Kul' Kyrg. see Balykchy
Issyk-Kul', Ozero salt l. Kyrg. see Ysyk-Köl
Istālif Afgh. 89 H3
▶İstanbul Turkey 59 M4
Most populous city in Europe.
İstanbul Boğazı strait Turkey see Bosporus
Istaravshan Tajik. 89 H2
Īstgāh-e Eznā Iran 88 C3
Istiaia Greece 59 J5
Istik r. Tajik. 89 I2
Istočni Drvar Bos. & Herz. 58 G2
Istra pen. Croatia see Istria
Istres France 56 G5
Istria pen. Croatia 58 E2
Iswardi Bangl. see Ishurdi
Itabapoana r. Brazil 145 C3
Itaberá Brazil 145 A3
Itaberaba Brazil 145 C1
Itaberaí Brazil 145 A2
Itabira Brazil 145 C2
Itabirito Brazil 145 C3
Itabuna Brazil 145 D1
Itacajá Brazil 143 I5
Itacarambi Brazil 145 B1
Itacoatiara Brazil 143 G4
Itaeté Brazil 145 C1
Itagmatana Iran see Hamadān
Itaguaçu Brazil 145 C2
Itaí Brazil 145 A3
Itaiópolis Brazil 145 A4
Itäisen Suomenlahden kansallispuisto nat. park Fin. 45 O6
Itaituba Brazil 143 G4
Itajaí Brazil 145 A4
Itajubá Brazil 145 B3
Itajuípe Brazil 145 D1
Italia country Europe see Italy
Italia, Laguna l. Bol. 142 F6
▶Italy country Europe 58 E3
5th most populous country in Europe.
Itamarandiba Brazil 145 C2
Itambé Brazil 145 C1
Itambé, Pico de mt. Brazil 145 C2
It Amelân i. Neth. see Ameland
Itampolo Madag. 99 E6
Itanagar India 83 H4
Itanguari r. Brazil 145 B1
Itanhaém Brazil 145 B4
Itanhém Brazil 145 C2
Itanhém r. Brazil 145 D2
Itaobim Brazil 145 C2
Itapaci Brazil 145 A1
Itapajipe Brazil 145 A2
Itapebi Brazil 145 D1
Itapecerica Brazil 145 B3
Itapecuru Mirim Brazil 143 J4
Itapemirim Brazil 145 C3
Itaperuna Brazil 145 C3
Itapetinga Brazil 145 C1
Itapetininga Brazil 145 A3
Itapeva Brazil 145 A3
Itapeva, Lago l. Brazil 145 A5
Itapicuru Brazil 143 J6
Itapicuru, Serra de hills Brazil 143 I5
Itapipoca Brazil 143 K4
Itapira Brazil 145 B3
Itaporanga Brazil 145 A3
Itapuã Brazil 145 A5
Itaqui Brazil 144 E3
Itararé Brazil 145 A4
Itarsi India 82 D5
Itarumã Brazil 145 A2
Itatiba Brazil 145 B3
Itatuba Brazil 142 F5
Itaúna Brazil 145 B3
Itaúnas Brazil 145 D2
Itbayat i. Phil. 69 G2
Itchen Lake Canada 121 H1
Itea Greece 59 J5
Ithaca MI U.S.A. 134 C2
Ithaca NY U.S.A. 135 G2
It Hearrenfean Neth. see Heerenveen
iThekweni S. Africa see Durban
Ith Hils ridge Germany 53 J2
Ithrah Saudi Arabia 85 C4
Itilleq Greenland 119 M3
Itimbiri r. Dem. Rep. Congo 98 C3
Itinga Brazil 145 C2
Itiquira Brazil 143 H7
Itiruçu Brazil 145 C1
Itiúba, Serra de hills Brazil 143 K6
Itō Japan 75 E6
iTswane S. Africa see Pretoria
Ittiri Sardinia Italy 58 C4
Ittoqqortoormiit Greenland 119 P2
Itu Brazil 145 B3
Itu Aba Island Spratly Is 68 E4
Ituaçu Brazil 145 C1
Ituberá Brazil 145 D1
Ituí r. Brazil 142 D4
Ituiutaba Brazil 145 A2
Itumbiara Brazil 145 A2
Itumbiara, Barragem resr Brazil 145 A2
Ituni Guyana 143 G2
Itupiranga Brazil 143 I5
Ituporanga Brazil 145 A4
Iturama Brazil 145 A2
Iturbide Mex. 131 D7
Ituri r. Dem. Rep. Congo 98 C3
Iturup, Ostrov i. Russia 74 G3
Itutinga Brazil 145 B3
Ituxi r. Brazil 142 F5
Ītyop'ia country Africa see Ethiopia
Itz r. Germany 53 K5
Itzehoe Germany 47 L4
Iuka U.S.A. 131 F5
Iul'tin Russia 65 T3
Ivalo Fin. 44 O2
Ivalojoki r. Fin. 44 O2
Ivanava Belarus 45 N10
Ivanhoe Australia 112 B4
Ivanhoe U.S.A. 130 D2
Ivanhoe Lake Canada 121 J2
Ivankiv Ukr. 43 F6
Ivankovtsy Russia 74 D2
Ivano-Frankivs'k Ukr. 43 E6
Ivano-Frankovsk Ukr. see Ivano-Frankivs'k
Ivanovka Russia 74 B2
Ivanovo Belarus see Ivanava
Ivanovo tourist site Bulg. 59 K3
Ivanovo Russia 42 I4
Ivanteyevka Russia 43 K5
Ivantsevichi Belarus see Ivatsevichy
Ivatsevichy Belarus 45 N10
Ivaylovgrad Bulg. 59 L4
Ivdel' Russia 41 S3
Ivittuut Greenland 119 N3
Iviza i. Spain see Ibiza
Ivory Coast country Africa see Côte d'Ivoire
Ivrea Italy 58 B2
İvrindi Turkey 59 L5
Ivris Ughelt'ekhili pass Georgia 91 G2
Ivry-la-Bataille France 52 B6
Ivugivik Canada see Ivujivik
Ivujivik Canada 119 K3
Ivyanyets Belarus 45 O10
Ivydale U.S.A. 134 E4
Iwaki Japan 75 F5
Iwaki-san vol. Japan 74 F4
Iwakuni Japan 75 D6
Iwamizawa Japan 74 F4
Iwo Nigeria 96 D4
Iwye Belarus 45 N10
Ixelles Belgium 52 E4
Ixiamas Bol. 142 E6
Ixmiquilpán Mex. 136 E4
Ixopo S. Africa 101 J6
Ixtlán Mex. 136 D4
Ixworth U.K. 49 H6
İyirmi Altı Bakı Komissarı Azer. see Hăsănabad
Izabal, Lago de l. Guat. 136 G5
Īzadkhāst Iran see Shāhīn Dezh
Īzad Khvāst Iran 88 D4
Izberbash Russia 91 G2
Izegem Belgium 52 D4
Īzeh Iran 88 C4
Izgal Pak. 89 I3
Izhevsk Russia 41 Q4
Izhma Respublika Komi Russia 42 L2
Izhma Respublika Komi Russia see Sosnogorsk
Izhma r. Russia 42 L2
Izmail Ukr. see Izmayil
Izmayil Ukr. 59 M2
İzmir Turkey 59 L5
İzmir Körfezi g. Turkey 59 L5
İzmit Turkey 59 M4
İzmit Körfezi b. Turkey 59 M4
Izozog Bol. 142 F7
Izozog, Bañados del swamp Bol. 142 F7
Izra' Syria 85 C3
Iztochni Rodopi mts Bulg. 59 K4
Izu-hantō pen. Japan 75 E6
Izumo Japan 75 D6
▶Izu-Ogasawara Trench sea feature N. Pacific Ocean 150 F3
5th deepest trench in the world.
Izu-shotō is Japan 75 E6
Izyaslav Ukr. 43 E6
Iz"yayu Russia 42 M2
Izyum Ukr. 43 H6

J

Jabal Dab Saudi Arabia 88 C6
Jabalón r. Spain 57 D4
Jabalpur India 82 D5
Jabbūl, Sabkhat al salt flat Syria 85 C2
Jabir reg. Oman 88 E6
Jabiru Australia 108 F3
Jablah Syria 85 B2
Jablanica Bos. & Herz. 58 G3
Jaboatão dos Guararapes Brazil 143 L5
Jaboticabal Brazil 145 A3
Jabung, Tanjung pt Indon. 68 C7
Jacaraci Brazil 145 C1
Jacareacanga Brazil 143 G5
Jacareí Brazil 145 B3
Jacarezinho Brazil 145 A3
Jáchymov Czechia 53 M4
Jacinto Brazil 145 C2
Jack r. Australia 110 D2
Jack Lake Canada 135 F1
Jackman U.S.A. 132 G2
Jacksboro U.S.A. 131 D5
Jackson Australia 112 D1
Jackson AL U.S.A. 133 C6
Jackson CA U.S.A. 128 C2
Jackson GA U.S.A. 133 D5
Jackson KY U.S.A. 134 D5
Jackson MI U.S.A. 134 C2
Jackson MN U.S.A. 130 E3
▶Jackson MS U.S.A. 131 F5
Capital of Mississippi.
Jackson NC U.S.A. 132 E4
Jackson OH U.S.A. 134 D4
Jackson TN U.S.A. 131 F5
Jackson WY U.S.A. 126 F4
Jackson, Mount Antarctica 152 L2
Jackson Head hd N.Z. 113 B6
Jacksonville AR U.S.A. 131 E5
Jacksonville FL U.S.A. 133 D6
Jacksonville IL U.S.A. 130 F4
Jacksonville NC U.S.A. 133 E5
Jacksonville OH U.S.A. 134 D4
Jacksonville TX U.S.A. 131 E6
Jacksonville Beach U.S.A. 133 D6
Jack Wade U.S.A. 118 D3
Jacmel Haiti 137 J5
Jacobabad Pak. 89 H4
Jacobina Brazil 143 J6
Jacob Lake U.S.A. 129 G3
Jacobsdal S. Africa 100 G5
Jacques-Cartier, Détroit de sea chan. Canada 123 I4
Jacques-Cartier, Mont mt. Canada 123 I4
Jacques Cartier Passage Canada see Jacques-Cartier, Détroit de
Jacuí Brazil 145 B3
Jacuípe r. Brazil 143 K6
Jacundá Brazil 143 I4
Jaddangi India 84 D2
Jaddi, Ras pt Pak. 89 F5
Jadebusen b. Germany 53 I1
J. A. D. Jensen Nunatakker nunataks Greenland 119 N3
Jadotville Dem. Rep. Congo see Likasi
Jādū Libya 96 E1
Jaén Spain 57 E5
Ja'farābād Iran 88 E2
Jaffa, Cape Australia 111 B8
Jaffna Sri Lanka 84 C4
Jafr, Qā' al imp. l. Jordan 85 C4
Jagadhri India 82 D3
Jagalur India 84 C3
Jagatsinghapur India see Jagatsinghpur
Jagatsinghpur India 83 F5
Jagdalpur India 84 D2
Jagdaqi China 74 B2
Jagersfontein S. Africa 101 G5
Jaggang China 82 D2
Jaggayyapeta India 84 D2
Jagsamka China see Luding
Jagst r. Germany 53 J5
Jagtial India 84 C2
Jaguariaíva Brazil 145 A4
Jaguaripe Brazil 145 D1
Jagüey Grande Cuba 133 D8
Jahām, 'Irq des. Saudi Arabia 88 B5
Jahanabad India see Jehanabad
Jahmah well Iraq 91 G5
Jahrom Iran 88 D4
Jaicós Brazil 143 J5
Jaigarh India 84 B2
Jailolo Gilolo i. Indon. see Halmahera
Jainpur India 83 E4
Jaintapur Bangl. see Jaintiapur
Jaintiapur Bangl. 83 H4
Jaipur India 82 C4
Jaipurhat Bangl. see Joypurhat
Jais India 83 E4
Jaisalmer India 82 B4
Jaisamand Lake India 82 C4
Jaitaran India 82 C4
Jaitgarh hill India 84 C1
Jajapur India see Jajpur
Jajarkot Nepal 87 N4
Jajce Bos. & Herz. 58 G2
Jajnagar state India see Odisha
Jajpur India 83 F5
Jakān mt. Afgh. 89 G4
Jakar Bhutan 83 G4
▶Jakarta Indon. 68 D8
Capital of Indonesia.
Jakes Corner Canada 120 C2
Jakhau India 82 B5
Jäkkvik Sweden 44 J3
Jakliat India 82 C3
Jakobshavn Greenland see Ilulissat
Jakobstad Fin. 44 M5
Jal U.S.A. 131 C5
Jalaid China see Inder
Jalājil Saudi Arabia 88 B5
Jalālābād Afgh. 89 H3
Jalal-Abad Kyrg. 80 D3
Jalālah al Baḩrīyah, Jabal plat. Egypt 90 C5
Jalalpur Pirwala Pak. 89 H4
Jalāmīd, Ḩazm al ridge Saudi Arabia 91 E5
Jalandhar India 82 C3
Jalapa Mex. see Xalapa
Jalapa Enríquez Mex. see Xalapa
Jālaq Iran 89 F5
Jalasjärvi Fin. 44 M5
Jalaun India 82 D4
Jalawlā' Iraq 91 G4
Jaldrug India 84 C2
Jales Brazil 145 A3
Jalesar India 82 D4
Jalgaon India 82 C5
Jalībah Iraq 91 G5
Jalingo Nigeria 96 E4
Jallābī Iran 88 E5
Jalna India 84 B2
Jalón r. Spain 57 F3
Jalor India see Jalore
Jalore India 82 C4
Jalpa Mex. 136 D4
Jalpaiguri India 83 G4
Jālū Libya 97 F2
Jalūlā Iraq see Jalawlā'
Jām reg. Iran 89 F3
Jam, Minaret of tourist site Afgh. 89 G3
Jamaica country West Indies 137 I5
Jamaica Channel Haiti/Jamaica 137 I5
Jamalpur Bangl. 83 G4
Jamalpur India 83 F4
Jamanxim r. Brazil 143 G4
Jambi Indon. 68 C7
Jambin Australia 110 E5
Jambo India 82 C4
Jambuair, Tanjung pt Indon. 71 B6
Jamda India 83 F5
Jamekunte India 84 C2
James r. N. Dakota/S. Dakota U.S.A. 130 D3
James r. VA U.S.A. 135 G5
James, Baie b. Canada see James Bay
Jamesabad Pak. 89 H5
James Bay Canada 122 E3
Jamesburg U.S.A. 135 H3
Jameson Land reg. Greenland 119 P2
James Peak N.Z. 113 B7
James Ranges mts Australia 109 F6
James Ross Island Antarctica 152 A2
James Ross Strait Canada 119 I3
Jamestown Australia 111 B7
Jamestown Canada see Wawa
Jamestown S. Africa 101 H6
▶Jamestown St Helena 148 H7
Capital of St Helena.
Jamestown ND U.S.A. 130 D2
Jamestown NY U.S.A. 134 F2
Jamestown TN U.S.A. 134 C5
Jamkhed India 84 B2
Jammu India 82 C2
Jammu and Kashmir hist. area Asia see Kashmir
Jammu and Kashmir admin. dist. India 82 D2
Jamnagar India 82 B5
Jampur Pak. 89 H4
Jamrud Pak. 89 H3
Jämsä Fin. 45 N6
Jamsah Egypt 90 D6
Jämsänkoski Fin. 44 N6
Jamshedpur India 83 F5
Jamtari Nigeria 96 E4
Jamui India 83 F4
Jamuna r. Bangl. see Raimangal
Jamuna r. Bangl. see Brahmaputra
Jamuna r. India see Yamuna
Janā i. Saudi Arabia 88 C5
Janāb, Wādī al watercourse Jordan 85 C4
Janakpur India 83 E5
Janaúba Brazil 145 C1
Jand Pak. 89 I3
Jandaia Brazil 145 A2
Jandaq Iran 88 D3
Jandola Pak. 89 H3
Jandowae Australia 112 E1
Janesville CA U.S.A. 128 C1
Janesville WI U.S.A. 130 F3
Jangada do Sul Brazil 145 A4
Jangal Iran 88 E3
Jangamo Moz. 101 L3
Jangaon India 84 C2
Jang Bogo research station Antarctica 152 H2
Janggi-gap pt S. Korea 75 C5
Jangheung S. Korea 75 B6
Jangipur India 83 G4
Jangnga Turkm. see Jaňňa
Jangngai Ri mts China 83 F2
Jangpyeong S. Korea 75 C5
Jänickendorf Germany 53 N2
Jani Khel Pak. 89 H3
Janīn West Bank 85 B3
Janjanbureh Gambia 96 B3
▶Jan Mayen terr. Arctic Ocean 153 I2
Part of Norway.
Jan Mayen Fracture Zone sea feature Arctic Ocean 153 I2
Jaňňa Turkm. 88 D1
Janos Mex. 127 F7
Jans Bay Canada 121 I4
Jansenville S. Africa 100 G7
Januária Brazil 145 B1
Janūb Sīnā' governorate Egypt 85 A5
Janûb Sînâ' governorate Egypt see Janūb Sīnā'
Janzar mt. Pak. 89 F5
Jaodar Pak. 89 F5
Japan country Asia 75 D5
Japan, Sea of N. Pacific Ocean 75 D5
Japan Alps National Park Japan see Chūbu-Sangaku Kokuritsu-kōen
Japan Trench sea feature N. Pacific Ocean 150 F3
Japiim Brazil 142 D5
Japurá r. Brazil 142 F4
Jarābulus Syria 85 D1
Jaraguá Brazil 145 A1
Jaraguá, Serra mts Brazil 145 A4
Jaraguá do Sul Brazil 145 A4
Jarash Jordan 85 B3
Jarboesville U.S.A. see Lexington Park
Jardine River National Park Australia 110 C1
Jardines de la Reina, Archipiélago de los is Cuba 137 I4
Jardinésia Brazil 145 A2
Jardinópolis Brazil 145 B3
Jargalang China 74 A4
Jargalant Bayanhongor Mongolia 80 I2
Jargalant Hovd Mongolia see Hovd
Jari r. Brazil 143 H4
Järna Sweden 45 J7
Jarocin Poland 47 P5
Jarosław Poland 43 D6
Järpen Sweden 44 H5
Jarqo'rg'on Uzbek. 89 G2
Jarqŭrghon Uzbek. see Jarqo'rg'on
Jarrettsville U.S.A. 135 G4
Jaru Brazil 142 F6
Jarud China see Lubei
Järvakandi Estonia 45 N7
Järvenpää Fin. 45 N6
▶Jarvis Island terr. S. Pacific Ocean 150 J6
United States Unincorporated Territory.
Jarwa India 83 E4
Jashpur India 83 F5
Jāsk-e Kohneh Iran 88 E5
Jasliq Uzbek. 91 J2
Jasło Poland 43 D6
Jasol India 82 C4
Jason Islands Falkland Is 144 D8
Jason Peninsula Antarctica 152 L2
Jasonville U.S.A. 134 B4
Jasper Canada 120 G4
Jasper AL U.S.A. 133 C5
Jasper FL U.S.A. 133 D6
Jasper GA U.S.A. 133 C5
Jasper IN U.S.A. 134 B4
Jasper NY U.S.A. 135 G2
Jasper TN U.S.A. 133 C5
Jasper TX U.S.A. 131 E6
Jasper National Park Canada 120 G4
Jasrasar India 82 C4
Jaşşān Iraq 91 G4
Jassy Romania see Iaşi
Jastrzębie-Zdrój Poland 47 Q6
Jaswantpura India 82 C4
Jászberény Hungary 59 H1
Jataí Brazil 145 A2
Jatapu r. Brazil 143 G4
Jath India 84 B2
Jati Pak. 89 H5
Jatibonico Cuba 133 E8
Játiva Spain see Xàtiva
Jatoi Janubi Pak. 89 H4
Jaú Brazil 145 A3
Jaú r. Brazil 142 F4
Jaú, Parque Nacional do nat. park Brazil 142 F4
Jaua-Sarisariñama, Parque Nacional nat. park Venez. 142 F3
Jauja Peru 142 C6
Jaunlutriņi Latvia 45 M8
Jaunpiebalga Latvia 45 O8
Jaunpur India 83 E4
Jauri Iran 89 F4
Java Georgia 91 F2
▶Java i. Indon. 108 A1
5th largest island in Asia.
Javaés r. Brazil see Formoso
Javari r. Brazil/Peru see Yavarí
Java Ridge sea feature Indian Ocean 149 P6
Java Sea Indon. see Jawa, Laut
▶Java Trench sea feature Indian Ocean 149 P6
Deepest point in the Indian Ocean.
Jävenitz Germany 53 L2
Jävre Sweden 44 L4
Jawa i. Indon. see Java
Jawa, Laut sea Indon. 68 E7
Jawhar India 84 B2
Jawhar Somalia 98 E3
Jawor Poland 47 P5
Jay U.S.A. 131 E4
▶Jaya, Puncak mt. Indon. 69 J7
Highest mountain in Oceania.
Jayakusumu mt. Indon. see Jaya, Puncak
Jayakwadi Sagar l. India 84 B2
Jayantiapur Bangl. see Jaintiapur
Jayapura Indon. 69 K7
Jayawijaya, Pegunungan mts Indon. 69 J7
Jayb, Wādī al watercourse Israel/Jordan 85 B4
Jayfi, Wādī al watercourse Egypt 85 B4
Jaypur India 84 D2
Jayrūd Syria 85 C3
Jayton U.S.A. 131 C5
Jāzān Saudi Arabia 86 F6
Jazminal Mex. 131 C7
Jaz Mūrīān, Hāmūn-e salt marsh Iran 88 E5
Jbail Lebanon 85 B2
J. C. Murphey Lake U.S.A. 134 B3
Jean U.S.A. 129 F4
Jean Marie River Canada 120 F2
Jeannin, Lac l. Canada 123 I2
Jebāl Bārez, Kūh-e mts Iran 88 E4
Jebel, Bahr el r. Africa see White Nile
Jebel Abyad Plateau Sudan 86 C6
Jech Doab lowland Pak. 89 I4
Jecheon S. Korea 75 C5
Jedburgh U.K. 50 G5
Jeddah Saudi Arabia 86 E5
Jedeida Tunisia 58 C6
Jeetze r. Germany 53 L1
Jefferson IA U.S.A. 130 E3
Jefferson NC U.S.A. 132 D4
Jefferson OH U.S.A. 134 E3
Jefferson TX U.S.A. 131 E5
Jefferson, Mount U.S.A. 128 E2
Jefferson, Mount vol. U.S.A. 126 C3
▶Jefferson City U.S.A. 130 E4
Capital of Missouri.
Jeffersonville GA U.S.A. 133 D5
Jeffersonville IN U.S.A. 134 C4
Jeffersonville OH U.S.A. 134 D4
Jeffreys Bay S. Africa 100 G8
Jehanabad India 83 F4
Jeju S. Korea 75 B6
Jeju-haehyeop sea chan. S. Korea 75 B6
Jejuí Guazú r. Para. 144 E2
Jēkabpils Latvia 45 N8
Jekegūr Iran 89 F5
Jelbart Ice Shelf Antarctica 152 B2
Jelenia Góra Poland 47 O5
Jelep La pass China/India 83 G4
Jelgava Latvia 45 M8
Jellico U.S.A. 134 C5
Jellicoe Canada 122 D4
Jelloway U.S.A. 134 D3
Jemaja i. Indon. 71 D7
Jember Indon. 68 E8
Jempang, Danau l. Indon. 68 F7
Jena Germany 53 L4
Jena U.S.A. 131 E6
Jendouba Tunisia 58 C6
Jengish Chokusu mt. China/Kyrg. see Pobeda Peak
Jenkins U.S.A. 134 D5
Jenne Mali see Djenné
Jenner Canada 121 I5
Jennings r. Canada 120 C3
Jennings U.S.A. 131 E6
Jenolan Caves Australia 112 E4
Jenpeg Canada 121 L4
Jensen U.S.A. 129 I1
Jens Munk Island Canada 119 K3
Jeongeup S. Korea 75 B6
Jeonju S. Korea 75 B6
Jeparit Australia 111 C8
Jequié Brazil 145 C1
Jequitaí r. Brazil 145 B2
Jequitinhonha Brazil 145 C2
Jequitinhonha r. Brazil 145 D1
Jerba, Île de i. Tunisia 54 G5
Jerbar South Sudan 97 G4
Jereh Iran 88 C4
Jérémie Haiti 137 J5
Jerez Mex. 136 D4
Jerez de la Frontera Spain 57 C5
Jergol Norway 44 N2
Jergucat Albania 59 I5
Jericho Australia 110 D4
Jericho West Bank 85 B4
Jerichow Germany 53 M2
Jerid, Chott el salt l. Tunisia 54 F5
Jerilderie Australia 112 B5
Jerimoth Hill U.S.A. 135 J3
Jeroaquara Brazil 145 A1
Jerome U.S.A. 126 E4
Jerruck Pak. 89 H5
▶Jersey terr. Channel Is 49 E9
United Kingdom Crown Dependency.
Jersey City U.S.A. 135 H3
Jersey Shore U.S.A. 135 G3
Jerseyville U.S.A. 130 F4
Jerumenha Brazil 143 J5
▶Jerusalem Israel/West Bank 85 B4
De facto capital of Israel, disputed.

Jervis Bay Australia **112** E5
Jervis Bay *b.* Australia **112** E5
Jervis Bay Territory *admin. div.* Australia **112** E5
Jesenice Slovenia **58** F1
Jesenice, Vodní nádrž *resr* Czechia **53** M4
Jesi Italy **58** E3
Jesselton *Sabah* Malaysia *see* **Kota Kinabalu**
Jessen (Elster) Germany **53** M3
Jessheim Norway **45** G6
Jessore Bangl. **83** G5
Jesteburg Germany **53** J1
Jesu Maria Island P.N.G. *see* **Rambutyo Island**
Jesup U.S.A. **133** D6
Jesús María, Barra *spit* Mex. **131** D7
Jetmore U.S.A. **130** D4
Jetpur India **82** B5
Jever Germany **53** H1
Jewell Ridge U.S.A. **134** E5
Jewish Autonomous Oblast *admin. div.* Russia *see* **Yevreyskaya Avtonomnaya Oblast'**
Jeypur India *see* **Jaypur**
Jezercë, Maja *mt.* Albania **59** H3
Jezzine Lebanon **85** B3
Jhabua India **82** C5
Jhajhar India *see* **Jhajjar**
Jhajjar India **82** D3
Jhal Pak. **89** G4
Jhalawar India **82** D4
Jhal Jhao Pak. **89** G5
Jhang Pak. **89** I4
Jhansi India **82** D4
Jhanzi *r.* India **70** A1
Jhapa Nepal **83** F4
Jharia India **83** F5
Jharkhand *state* India **83** F5
Jharsuguda India **83** F5
Jhawani Nepal **83** F4
Jhelum *r.* India/Pak. **89** I4
Jhelum Pak. **89** I3
Jhenaidah Bangl. **83** G5
Jhenaidaha Bangl. *see* **Jhenaidah**
Jhenida Bangl. *see* **Jhenaidah**
Jhimpir Pak. **89** H5
Jhingtubum *mt.* India **76** B3
Jhudo Pak. **89** H5
Jhumritilaiya India **83** F4
Jhund India **82** B5
Jhunjhunun India **82** C3
Jiachuan China **76** E1
Jiachuanzhen China *see* **Jiachuan**
Jiading *Jiangxi* China *see* **Xinfeng**
Jiading *Shanghai* China **77** I2
Jiahe China **77** G3
Jiajiang China **76** D2
Jiamusi China **74** C3
Ji'an *Jiangxi* China **77** G3
Ji'an *Jilin* China **74** B4
Jianchuan China **76** C3
Jiande China **77** H2
Jiangbei China *see* **Yubei**
Jiangbiancun China **77** G3
Jiangcheng China **76** D4
Jiangcun China **77** F3
Jiangdu China **77** H1
Jiange China *see* **Pu'an**
Jianghong China **77** F4
Jiangjin China **76** E2
Jiangjunmiao China **80** G3
Jiangkou *Guangdong* China *see* **Fengkai**
Jiangkou *Guizhou* China **77** F3
Jiangkou *Shaanxi* China **76** E1
Jiangling China *see* **Jingzhou**
Jiangluo China **76** E1
Jiangmen China **77** G4
Jiangna China *see* **Yanshan**
Jiangshan China **77** H2
Jiangsi China *see* **Dejiang**
Jiangsu *prov.* China **77** H1
Jiangxi *prov.* China **77** G3
Jiangxia China **77** G2
Jiangyan China **77** I1
Jiangyin China **77** I2
Jiangyou China **76** E2
Jiangzhesongrong China **83** F3
Jianjun China *see* **Yongshou**
Jiankang China **76** D3
Jianli China **77** G2
Jian'ou China **77** H3
Jianping China *see* **Langxi**
Jianshe China *see* **Baiyü**
Jianshi China **77** F2
Jianshui China **76** D4
Jianshui Hu *l.* China **83** E2
Jianxing China **76** E2
Jianyang *Fujian* China **77** H3
Jianyang *Sichuan* China **76** E2
Jiaochang China **76** D1
Jiaochangba China *see* **Jiaochang**
Jiaocheng China *see* **Jiaoling**
Jiaohe China **74** B4
Jiaojiang China *see* **Taizhou**
Jiaokui China *see* **Yiliang**
Jiaoling China **77** H3
Jiaopingdu China **76** D3
Jiaowei China **77** H3
Jiaozuo China **77** G1
Jiasa China **76** D3
Jiashan China *see* **Mingguang**
Jia Tsuo La *pass* China **83** F3
Jiawang China **77** H1
Jiaxian China **77** G1
Jiaxing China **77** I2
Jiayi Taiwan **77** I4
Jiayin China **74** C2
Jiayuguan China **80** I4
Jiazi China **77** H4
Jībūtī *country* Africa *see* **Djibouti**
Jibuti Djibouti *see* **Djibouti**
Jiddah Saudi Arabia *see* **Jeddah**
Jiddī, Jabal al *hill* Egypt **85** A4
Jido S. Korea **75** B6
Jidong China **74** C3
Jiehkkevárri *mt.* Norway **44** K2
Jieshi China **77** G4
Jieshipu China **76** E1
Jieshi Wan *b.* China **77** G4
Jiexi China **77** G4
Jiexiu China **73** K5
Jieyang China **77** H4
Jieznas Lith. **45** N9
Jigzhi China **76** D1
Jiḥār, Wādī al *watercourse* Syria **85** C2
Jihlava Czechia **47** O6
Jījah Afgh. **89** F3
Jijel Alg. **54** F4
Jijiga Eth. **98** E3
Jījīrud Iran **88** C3
Jijü China **76** D2
Jil'ād *reg.* Jordan *see* **Gilead**
Jilf al Kabīr, Haḍabat al *plat.* Egypt **86** C5
Jilh al 'Ishār *plain* Saudi Arabia **88** B5
Jilib Somalia **98** E3
Jilin China **74** B4
Jilin *prov.* China **74** B4
Jilin Hada Ling *mts* China **74** B4
Jiliu He *r.* China **74** A2
Jilo India **82** C4
Jilong Taiwan *see* **Keelung**
Jīma Eth. **98** D3
Jiménez *Chihuahua* Mex. **131** B7
Jiménez *Coahuila* Mex. **131** C6
Jiménez *Tamaulipas* Mex. **131** D7
Jimía, Cerro *mt.* Hond. **136** G5
Jimsar China **80** G3
Jim Thorpe U.S.A. **135** H3
Jinan China **73** L5
Jin'an China *see* **Songpan**
Jinbi China *see* **Dayao**
Jinchang China **72** I5
Jincheng *Shanxi* China **77** G1
Jincheng *Sichuan* China **76** E2
Jincheng *Yunnan* China *see* **Wuding**
Jinchengjiang China *see* **Hechi**
Jinchuan *Gansu* China *see* **Jinchang**
Jinchuan *Jiangxi* China *see* **Xingan**
Jind India **82** D3
Jinding China *see* **Lanping**
Jindo S. Korea **75** B6
Jin-do *i.* S. Korea **75** B6
Jindřichův Hradec Czechia **47** O6
Jin'e China *see* **Longchang**
Jingbian China **73** J5
Jingchuan China **76** E1
Jingde China **77** H2
Jingdezhen China **77** H2
Jingellic Australia **112** C5
Jinggangshan China *see* **Ciping**
Jinggang Shan *hill* China **77** G3
Jinggongqiao China **77** H2
Jinggu China **76** D4
Jing He *r.* China **77** F1
Jinghong China **76** D4
Jingle China **73** K5
Jingmen China **77** G2
Jingpo China **74** C4
Jingpo Hu *resr* China **74** C4
Jingsha China *see* **Jingzhou**
Jingtai China **72** I5
Jingxi China **76** E4
Jingxian *Anhui* China **77** H2
Jingxian *Hunan* China *see* **Jingzhou**
Jingyang China *see* **Jingde**
Jingyu China **74** B4
Jingyuan China **72** I5
Jingzhou *Hubei* China **77** G2
Jingzhou *Hubei* China **77** G2
Jingzhou *Hunan* China **77** F3
Jinhae S. Korea **75** C6
Jinhe *Nei Mongol* China **74** A2
Jinhe *Yunnan* China *see* **Jinping**
Jinhu China **77** H1
Jinhua *Yunnan* China *see* **Jianchuan**
Jinhua *Zhejiang* China **77** H2
Jining *Nei Mongol* China *see* **Ulan Qab**
Jining *Shandong* China **77** H1
Jinja Uganda **98** D3
Jinjiang *Hainan* China *see* **Chengmai**
Jinjiang *Yunnan* China **76** D3
Jin Jiang *r.* China **77** G2
Jinka Eth. **98** D3
Jinmen Taiwan **77** H3
Jinmen Dao *i.* Taiwan **77** H3
Jinmu Jiao *pt* China **77** F5
Jinning China **76** D3
Jinotepe Nicaragua **137** G6
Jinping *Guizhou* China **77** F3
Jinping *Yunnan* China **76** D4
Jinping *Yunnan* China *see* **Qiubei**
Jinping Shan *mts* China **76** D3
Jinsen S. Korea *see* **Incheon**
Jinsha China **76** E3
Jinsha Jiang *r.* China *see* **Yangtze**
Jinshan *Nei Mongol* China *see* **Guyang**
Jinshan *Shanghai* China *see* **Zhujing**
Jinshan *Yunnan* China *see* **Lufeng**
Jinshi *Hunan* China **77** F2
Jinshi *Hunan* China *see* **Xinning**
Jintur India **84** C2
Jinxi *Anhui* China *see* **Taihu**
Jinxi *Jiangxi* China **77** H3
Jinxi *Liaoning* China *see* **Lianshan**
Jin Xi *r.* China **77** H3
Jinxian China **77** H2
Jinxiang China **77** H1
Jinyun China **77** I2
Jinz, Qā' al *salt flat* Jordan **85** C4
Jinzhai China **77** G2
Jinzhong China **73** K5
Jinzhou China **73** M4
Jinzhu China *see* **Daocheng**
Ji-Paraná Brazil **142** F6
Jipijapa Ecuador **142** B4
Ji Qu *r.* China **76** C2
Jiquiriçá Brazil **145** D1
Jiquitaia Brazil **145** D2
Jirā', Wādī *watercourse* Egypt **85** A5
Jirānīyāt, Shi'bān al *watercourse* Saudi Arabia **85** D4
Jirghatol Tajik. **89** H2
Jiri *r.* India **70** A1
Jiri-san *mt.* S. Korea **75** B6
Jīroft Iran **88** E4
Jirriiban Somalia **98** E3
Jirwān Saudi Arabia **88** C6
Jirwan *well* Saudi Arabia **88** C6
Jishou China **77** F2
Jisr ash Shughūr Syria **85** C2
Jitian China *see* **Lianshan**
Jitra Malaysia **71** C6
Jiu *r.* Romania **59** J3
Jiuding Shan *mt.* China **76** D2
Jiuhe China **76** C3
Jiujiang *Jiangxi* China **77** G2
Jiujiang *Jiangxi* China **77** H2
Jiulian China *see* **Mojiang**
Jiuling Shan *mts* China **77** G2
Jiulong China **76** D2
Jiuqian China **77** F3
Jiuquan China **80** I4
Jiuxu China **76** E3
Jiuzhou Jiang *r.* China **77** F4
Jiwani Pak. **89** F5
Jiwen China **74** A2
Jixi *Anhui* China **77** H2
Jixi *Heilong.* China **74** C3
Jixian China **74** C3
Jiyuan China **77** G1
Jīzah, Ahrāmāt al *tourist site* Egypt *see* **Pyramids of Giza**
Jizzakh Uzbek. *see* **Jizzax**
Jizzax Uzbek. **89** G1
Joaçaba Brazil **145** A4
Joaíma Brazil **145** C2
João Belo Moz. *see* **Xai-Xai**
João de Almeida Angola *see* **Chibia**
João Maria, Albardão do *coastal area* Brazil **144** F4
João Pessoa Brazil **143** L5
João Pinheiro Brazil **145** B2
Joaquín V. González Arg. **144** D3
Job Peak U.S.A. **128** D2
Jocketa Germany **53** M4
Joda India **83** F5
Jodhpur India **82** C4
Jodiya India **82** B5
Joensuu Fin. **44** P5
Jōetsu Japan **75** E5
Jofane Moz. **99** D6
Joffre, Mount Canada **120** H5
Jogbura Nepal **82** E3
Jõgeva Estonia **45** O7
Jogjakarta Indon. *see* **Yogyakarta**
Johannesburg S. Africa **101** H4
Johannesburg U.S.A. **128** E4
Johan Peninsula Canada **119** K2
Johi Pak. **89** G5
John Day U.S.A. **126** D3
John Day *r.* U.S.A. **126** C3
John D'Or Prairie Canada **120** H3
John F. Kennedy *airport* U.S.A. **135** I3
John H. Kerr Reservoir U.S.A. **135** F5
John Jay, Mount Canada/U.S.A. **120** D3
John o' Groats U.K. **50** F2
Johnson U.S.A. **130** C4
Johnsonburg U.S.A. **135** F3
Johnson City *NY* U.S.A. **135** H2
Johnson City *TN* U.S.A. **132** D4
Johnson City *TX* U.S.A. **131** D6
Johnsondale U.S.A. **128** D4
Johnson Draw *watercourse* U.S.A. **131** C6
Johnson's Crossing Canada **120** C2
Johnston, Lake *salt flat* Australia **109** C8
Johnston and Sand Islands *terr.* N. Pacific Ocean *see* **Johnston Atoll**

▶**Johnston Atoll** *terr.* N. Pacific Ocean **150** I4
United States Unincorporated Territory.

Johnstone U.K. **50** E5
Johnstone Lake Canada *see* **Old Wives Lake**
Johnston Range *hills* Australia **109** B7
Johnstown Ireland **51** E5
Johnstown *NY* U.S.A. **135** H2
Johnstown *PA* U.S.A. **135** F3
Johor, Selat *strait* Malaysia/Sing. **71** [inset]
Johor, Sungai *r.* Malaysia **71** [inset]
Johor Bahru Malaysia **71** [inset]
Johore Bahru Malaysia *see* **Johor Bahru**
Jõhvi Estonia **45** O7
Joinville Brazil **145** A4
Joinville France **56** G2
Joinville Island Antarctica **152** A2
Jokkmokk Sweden **44** K3
Jökulsá *r.* Iceland **44** [inset 1]
Jökulsá á Fjöllum *r.* Iceland **44** [inset 1]
Jökulsá í Fljótsdal *r.* Iceland **44** [inset 1]
Jolfā Iran **88** B2
Joliet U.S.A. **134** A3
Joliet, Lac *l.* Canada **122** F4
Joliette Canada **123** G5
Jolly Lake Canada **121** H1
Jolo Phil. **69** G5
Jolo *i.* Phil. **69** G5
Jomda China **76** C2
Jonancy U.S.A. **134** D5
Jonava Lith. **45** N9
Jonê China **76** D1
Jonesboro *AR* U.S.A. **131** F5
Jonesboro *LA* U.S.A. **131** E5
Jones Sound *sea chan.* Canada **119** J2
Jonesville *MI* U.S.A. **134** C3
Jonesville *VA* U.S.A. **134** D5
Jonglei Canal South Sudan **86** D8
Jönköping Sweden **45** I8
Jonquière Canada **123** H4
Joplin U.S.A. **131** E4
Joppa Israel *see* **Tel Aviv-Yafo**
Jora India **82** D4
Jordan *country* Asia **85** C4
Jordan *r.* Asia **85** B4
Jordan U.S.A. **126** G3
Jordan *r.* U.S.A. **126** D4
Jordânia Brazil **145** C1
Jordet Norway **45** H6
Jorhat India **83** H4
Jork Germany **53** J1
Jörn Sweden **44** L4
Joroinen Fin. **44** O5
Jørpeland Norway **45** E7
Jos Nigeria **96** D4
José de San Martín Arg. **144** B6
Joseph, Lac *l.* Canada **123** I3
Joseph Bonaparte Gulf Australia **108** E3
Joseph City U.S.A. **129** H4
Joshimath India **82** D3
Joshipur India **84** E1
Joshua Tree National Park U.S.A. **129** F5
Jos Plateau Nigeria **96** D4
Jostedalsbreen Nasjonalpark *nat. park* Norway **45** E6
Jotunheimen Nasjonalpark *nat. park* Norway **45** F6
Jouaiya Lebanon **85** B3
Joubertina S. Africa **100** F7
Jouberton S. Africa **101** H4
Jõuga Estonia **45** O7
Joûnié Lebanon **85** B3
Joure Neth. **52** F2
Joutsa Fin. **45** O6
Joutseno Fin. **45** P6
Jouy-aux-Arches France **52** G5
Jovellanos Cuba **133** D8
Jowai India **83** H4
Jowand Afgh. **89** G3
Jowr Deh Iran **88** C2
Joy, Mount Canada **120** C2
Joyce Country *reg.* Ireland **51** C4
Joypurhat Bangl. **83** G4
Juan Aldama Mex. **131** C7
Juancheng China **77** G1
Juan de Fuca Strait Canada/U.S.A. **124** C2
Juan Fernández, Archipiélago *is* S. Pacific Ocean **151** O8
Juan Fernández Islands S. Pacific Ocean *see* **Juan Fernández, Archipiélago**
Juanjuí Peru **142** C5
Juankoski Fin. **44** P5
Juan Mata Ortíz Mex. **127** F7
Juárez Mex. **131** C7
Juárez, Sierra de *mts* Mex. **127** D6
Juazeiro Brazil **143** J5
Juazeiro do Norte Brazil **143** K5
Juba *r.* Somalia *see* **Jubba**

▶**Juba** South Sudan **97** G4
Capital of South Sudan.

Jubba *r.* Somalia **98** E4
Jubbah Saudi Arabia **91** F5
Jubbulpore India *see* **Jabalpur**
Jubilee Lake *salt flat* Australia **109** D7
Juby, Cap *c.* Morocco **96** B2
Juchitán Mex. **136** E5
Jucuruçu Brazil **145** D2
Jucuruçu *r.* Brazil **145** D2
Judaberg Norway **45** D7
Judaidat al Hamir Iraq **91** F5
Judayyidat 'Ar'ar *well* Iraq **91** F5
Judenburg Austria **47** O7
Judian China **76** C3
Judith Gap U.S.A. **126** F3
Juegang China *see* **Rudong**
Juelsminde Denmark **45** G9
Juerana Brazil **145** D2
Jugar China *see* **Sêrxü**
Juigalpa Nicaragua **137** G6
Juillet, Lac *l.* Canada **123** J3
Juína Brazil **143** G6
Juist *i.* Germany **52** H1
Juiz de Fora Brazil **145** C3
Ju Ju Klu Turkm. **89** F2
Julaca Bol. **142** E8
Julesburg U.S.A. **130** C3
Julia Brazil **142** E4
Juliaca Peru **142** D7
Julia Creek Australia **110** C4
Julian U.S.A. **128** E5
Julian, Lac *l.* Canada **122** F3
Julianadorp Neth. **52** E2
Julian Alps *mts* Slovenia *see* **Julijske Alpe**
Julianatop *mt.* Indon. *see* **Mandala, Puncak**
Juliana Top *mt.* Suriname **143** G3
Julianehåb Greenland *see* **Qaqortoq**
Jülich Germany **52** G4
Julijske Alpe *mts* Slovenia **58** E1
Julimes Mex. **131** B6
Juliomagus France *see* **Angers**
Julius, Lake Australia **110** B4
Jullundur India *see* **Jalandhar**
Juma Uzbek. **89** G2
Jumbilla Peru **142** C5
Jumilla Spain **57** F4
Jumla Nepal **83** E3
Jümme *r.* Germany **53** H1
Jumna *r.* India *see* **Yamuna**
Jump *r.* U.S.A. **130** F2
Junagadh India **82** B5
Junagarh India **84** D2
Junan China **77** H1
Junayfah Egypt **85** A4
Junction *TX* U.S.A. **131** D6
Junction *UT* U.S.A. **129** G2
Junction City *KS* U.S.A. **130** D4
Junction City *KY* U.S.A. **134** C5
Junction City *OR* U.S.A. **126** C3
Jundiaí Brazil **145** B3
Jundian China **77** F1

▶**Juneau** *AK* U.S.A. **120** C3
Capital of Alaska.

Juneau *WI* U.S.A. **130** F3
Juneau Icefield Canada **120** C3
Junee Australia **112** C5
Jûn el Khudr *b.* Lebanon **85** B3
Jungar Qi China *see* **Shagedu**
Jungfrau *mt.* Switz. **56** H3
Junggar Pendi *basin* China **80** G2
Juniata *r.* U.S.A. **135** G3
Junín Arg. **144** D4
Junín Peru **142** C6
Junior U.S.A. **134** F4
Juniper Mountain U.S.A. **129** I1
Juniper Mountains U.S.A. **129** G4
Junipero Serro Peak U.S.A. **128** C3
Junlian China **76** E2
Junmenling China **77** G3
Juno U.S.A. **131** C6
Junsele Sweden **44** J5
Junshan Hu *l.* China **77** H2
Junxi China *see* **Datian**
Junxian China *see* **Danjiangkou**
Ju'nyung China **76** C1
Ju'nyunggoin China *see* **Ju'nyung**
Juodupė Lith. **45** N8
Jupiá Brazil **145** A3
Jupía, Represa *resr* Brazil **145** A3
Jupiter U.S.A. **133** D7
Juquiá *r.* Brazil **145** B4
Jur *r.* South Sudan **86** C8
Jura *mts* France/Switz. **56** G4
Jura *i.* U.K. **50** D4
Jur'ā, Nafūd al *des.* Saudi Arabia **88** B5
Jura, Sound of *sea chan.* U.K. **50** D5
Jurací Brazil **145** C1
Jurbarkas Lith. **45** M9
Jurf ad Darāwīsh Jordan **85** B4
Jürgenstorf Germany **53** M1
Jurhen Ul *mts* China **83** G2
Jurm Afgh. **89** H2
Jūrmala Latvia **45** M8
Jurmu Fin. **44** O4
Jurong Sing. **71** [inset]
Jurong, Sungai *r.* Sing. **71** [inset]
Jurong Island *reg.* Sing. **71** [inset]
Juruá *r.* Brazil **142** E4
Juruena *r.* Brazil **143** G5
Juruti Brazil **143** G4
Jurva Fin. **44** L5
Jūshqān Iran **88** E2
Jūsīyah Syria **85** C2
Jussara Brazil **145** A1
Justice U.S.A. **134** E5
Jutaí Brazil **142** E5
Jutaí *r.* Brazil **142** E4
Jüterbog Germany **53** N3
Jutiapa Guat. **136** G6
Juticalpa Hond. **137** G6
Jutis Sweden **44** J3
Jutland *pen.* Denmark **45** F8
Juuka Fin. **44** P5
Juva Fin. **44** O6
Juventud, Isla de la *i.* Cuba **137** H4
Juye China **77** H1
Jūyom Iran **88** D4
Jūzak Iran **89** F4
Južnoukrajinsk Ukr. *see* **Yuzhnoukrayins'k**
Jwaneng Botswana **100** G3
Jylland *pen.* Denmark *see* **Jutland**
Jyväskylä Fin. **44** N5

K

▶**K2** *mt.* China/Pak. **82** D2
2nd highest mountain in Asia and the world.

Ka *r.* Nigeria **96** D3
Kaa-Iya del Gran Chaco, Parque Nacional *nat. park* Bol. **142** F7
Kaakhka Turkm. *see* **Kaka**
Ka'ala *mt.* U.S.A. **127** [inset]
Kaapstad S. Africa *see* **Cape Town**
Kaarina Fin. **45** M6
Kaarßen Germany **53** L1
Kaarst Germany **52** G3
Kaavi Fin. **44** P5
Kaba China *see* **Habahe**
Kabakly Turkm. *see* **Gabakly**
Kabala Sierra Leone **96** B4
Kabale Uganda **98** C4
Kabalega Falls National Park Uganda *see* **Murchison Falls National Park**
Kabalo Dem. Rep. Congo **99** C4
Kabambare Dem. Rep. Congo **99** C4
Kabanbay Kazakh. **80** F2
Kabangu Dem. Rep. Congo **99** C5
Kabanjahe Indon. **71** B7
Kabara *i.* Fiji **107** I3
Kabarega National Park Uganda *see* **Murchison Falls National Park**
Kabaw Valley Myanmar **70** A2
Kabbani *r.* India **84** C3
Kåbdalis Sweden **44** L3
Kabid, Mushāsh al *well* Jordan **85** C5
Kabinakagami *r.* Canada **122** D4
Kabinakagami Lake Canada **122** D4
Kabinda Dem. Rep. Congo **99** C4
Kabīr, Nahr al *r.* Syria **85** B2
Kabīrkūh *mts* Iran **88** B3
Kabo Cent. Afr. Rep. **98** B3
Kābol Afgh. *see* **Kābul**
Kabompo *r.* Zambia **99** C5
Kabongo Dem. Rep. Congo **99** C4
Kaboré Tambi, Parc National de *nat. park* Burkina Faso **96** C3
Kabūdar Āhang Iran **88** C3
Kabūd Gonbad Iran *see* **Kalāt**

▶**Kābul** Afgh. **89** H3
Capital of Afghanistan.

Kābul *r.* Afgh. **89** I3
Kabuli P.N.G. **69** L7
Kabunda Dem. Rep. Congo **99** C5
Kabunduk Indon. **108** B2
Kaburuang *i.* Indon. **69** H6
Kabūtar Khān Iran **88** E4
Kabwe Zambia **99** C5
Kāchā Kūh *mts* Iran/Pak. **89** F4
Kachalinskaya Russia **43** J6
Kachchh, Great Rann of *marsh* India *see* **Kachchh, Rann of**
Kachchh, Gulf of India **82** B5
Kachchh, Little Rann of *marsh* India **82** B5
Kachchh, Rann of *marsh* India **82** B4
Kachia Nigeria **96** D4
Kachkanar Russia **41** R4
K'ach'reti Georgia **91** G2
Kachug Russia **72** J2
Kaçkar Dağı *mt.* Turkey **91** F2
Kadaingti Myanmar **70** B3
Kadaiyanallur India **84** C4
Kadanai *r.* Afgh./Pak. **89** G4
Kadan Kyun *i.* Myanmar **71** B4
Kadapa India **84** C3
Kadavu *i.* Fiji **107** H3
Kadavu Passage Fiji **107** H3
Kaddam *l.* India **84** C2
Kade Ghana **96** C4
Kadi India **82** C5
Kadıköy Turkey **59** M4
Kadınhanı Turkey **90** D3
Kadiolo Mali **96** C3
Kadiri India **84** C3
Kadirli Turkey **90** E3
Kadiyevka Ukr. *see* **Stakhanov**
Kadmat *atoll* India **84** B4
Ka-do *i.* N. Korea **75** B5
Kadok Malaysia **71** C6
Kadoka U.S.A. **130** C3
Kadoma Zimbabwe **99** C5
Kadonkani Myanmar **70** A4
Kadu Myanmar **70** B1
Kadugli Sudan **86** C7
Kaduna Nigeria **96** D3
Kaduna *r.* Nigeria **96** D4
Kadusam *mt.* China/India **83** I3
Kaduy Russia **42** H4
Kadyy Russia **42** I4
Kadzherom Russia **42** L2
Kaédi Mauritania **96** B3
Kaélé Cameroon **97** E3
Kaeng Krachan National Park Thai. **71** B4
Kaesŏng N. Korea **75** B5
Kāf Saudi Arabia **85** C4
Kafa Crimea *see* **Feodosiya**
Kafakumba Dem. Rep. Congo **99** C4
Kafan Armenia *see* **Kapan**
Kafanchan Nigeria **96** D4

▶**Kaffeklubben Ø** *i.* Greenland **153** I1
Most northerly point of North America.

Kaffrine Senegal **96** B3
Kafireas, Akra *pt* Greece *see* **Ntoro, Kavo**
Kafiristan *reg.* Pak. **89** H3
Kafr ash Shaykh Egypt **90** C5
Kafr el Sheikh Egypt *see* **Kafr ash Shaykh**
Kafue Zambia **99** C5
Kafue *r.* Zambia **99** C5
Kafue National Park Zambia **99** C5
Kaga Japan **75** E5
Kaga Bandoro Cent. Afr. Rep. **98** B3
Kagan Pak. **89** I3
Kagan Uzbek. *see* **Kogon**
Kagang China **76** D1
Kaganovichabad Tajik. *see* **Kolkhozobod**
Kaganovichi Pervyye Ukr. *see* **Polis'ke (abandoned)**
Kagarlyk Ukr. *see* **Kaharlyk**
Kåge Sweden **44** L4
Kağızman Turkey **91** F2
Kagmar Sudan **86** D7
Kagoshima Japan **75** C7
Kagoshima *pref.* Japan **75** C7
Kagul Moldova *see* **Cahul**
Kahama Tanz. **98** D4
Kaharlyk Ukr. **43** F6
Kaherekoau Mountains N.Z. **113** A7
Kahīrī Iran **89** F5
Kahla Germany **53** L4
Kahmard *reg.* Afgh. **89** G3
Kahnūj-e Pā'īn Iran **88** E4
Kahoka U.S.A. **130** F3
Kaho'olawe *i.* U.S.A. **127** [inset]
Kahperusvaarat *mts* Fin. **44** L2
Kahramanmaraş Turkey **90** E3
Kahror Pakka Pak. **89** H4
Kahta Turkey **90** E3
Kahuku U.S.A. **127** [inset]
Kahuku Point U.S.A. **127** [inset]
Kahurangi National Park N.Z. **113** D5
Kahurangi Point N.Z. **113** D5
Kahuta Pak. **89** I3
Kahuzi-Biega, Parc National du *nat. park* Dem. Rep. Congo **98** C4
Kai, Kepulauan *is* Indon. **69** I8
Kaiapoi N.Z. **113** D6
Kaibab U.S.A. **129** G3
Kaibab Plateau U.S.A. **129** G3
Kai Besar *i.* Indon. **69** I8
Kaibito Plateau U.S.A. **129** H3
Kaifeng *Henan* China **77** G1
Kaifeng *Henan* China **77** G1
Kaihua *Yunnan* China *see* **Wenshan**
Kaihua *Zhejiang* China **77** H2
Kaiingveld *reg.* S. Africa **100** E5
Kaijiang China **76** E2
Kai Kecil *i.* Indon. **69** I8
Kai Keung Leng *H.K.* China **77** [inset]
Kaikoura N.Z. **113** D6
Kailas *mt.* China *see* **Kangrinboqê Feng**
Kailasahar India *see* **Kailashahar**
Kailashahar India **83** H4
Kailas Range *mts* China *see* **Gangdisê Shan**
Kaili China **76** E3
Kailu China **73** M4
Kailua U.S.A. **127** [inset]
Kailua-Kona U.S.A. **127** [inset]
Kaimana Indon. **69** I7
Kaimanawa Mountains N.Z. **113** E4
Kaimar China **76** B1
Kaimur Range *hills* India **82** E4
Käina Estonia **45** M7
Kainan Japan **75** D6
Kainda Kyrg. *see* **Kayyngdy**
Kaindy Kyrg. *see* **Kayyngdy**
Kainji Lake National Park Nigeria **96** D4
Kaipara Harbour N.Z. **113** E3
Kaiparowits Plateau U.S.A. **129** H3
Kaiping China **77** G4
Kaipokok Bay Canada **123** K3
Kairana India **82** D3
Kairiru Island P.N.G. **69** K7
Kaironi Indon. **69** I7
Kairouan Tunisia **58** D7
Kaiserslautern Germany **53** H5
Kaiser Wilhelm II Land *reg.* Antarctica **152** E2
Kaitaia N.Z. **113** D2
Kaitangata N.Z. **113** B8
Kaitawa N.Z. **113** F4
Kaithal India **82** D3
Kaitum Sweden **44** L3
Kaiwatu Indon. **108** D2
Kaiwi Channel U.S.A. **127** [inset]
Kaixian China **77** F2
Kaiyang China **76** E3
Kaiyuan *Liaoning* China **74** B4
Kaiyuan *Yunnan* China **76** D4
Kajaani Fin. **44** O4
Kajabbi Australia **110** C4
Kajakī Suflá Afgh. **89** G3
Kajarabie, Lake Australia **112** D1
Kajīrān Afgh. **89** G3
Kaka Turkm. **89** E2
Kakabeka Falls Canada **122** C4

Kakadu National Park Australia 108 F3
Kakagi Lake Canada 121 M5
Kakamas S. Africa 100 E5
Kakamega Kenya 98 D3
Kakana India 71 A5
Kakar Pak. 89 G5
Kakata Liberia 96 B4
Kake U.S.A. 120 C3
Kakenge Dem. Rep. Congo 99 C4
Kakerbeck Germany 53 L2
Kakhi Azer. see Qax
Kakhovka Ukr. 59 O1
Kakhovs'ke Vodoskhovyshche resr Ukr. 43 G7
Kakhul Moldova see Cahul
Kākī Iran 88 C4
Kakinada India 84 D2
Kakisa Canada 120 G2
Kakisa r. Canada 120 G2
Kakisa Lake Canada 120 G2
Kakogawa Japan 75 D6
Kakori India 82 E4
Kakshaal-Too mts China/Kyrg. 80 E3
Kaktovik U.S.A. 118 D2
Kakul Pak. 89 I3
Kakwa r. Canada 120 G4
Kala Pak. 89 H4
Kala Tanz. 99 D4
Kalaâ Kebira Tunisia 58 D7
Kalaallit Nunaat terr. N. America see Greenland
Kalabahi Indon. 108 D2
Kalabáka Greece see Kalampaka
Kalabgur India 84 C2
Kalabo Zambia 99 C5
Kalaburagi India 84 C2
Kalābust Afgh. 89 G4
Kalach Russia 43 I6
Kalacha Dida Kenya 98 D3
Kalach-na-Donu Russia 43 I6
Kaladan r. India/Myanmar 70 A2
Kaladar Canada 135 G1
Ka Lae pt U.S.A. 127 [inset]
Kalagwe Myanmar 70 B2
Kalahari Desert Africa 100 F2
Kalahari Gemsbok National Park S. Africa 100 E3
Kalaikhum Tajik. see Qalaikhumb
Kalai-Khumb Tajik. see Qalaikhumb
Kalajoki Fin. 44 M4
Kalam India 84 C1
Kalam Pak. 89 I3
Kalámai Greece see Kalamata
Kalamare Botswana 101 H2
Kalamaria Greece 59 J4
Kalamata Greece 59 J6
Kalamazoo U.S.A. 134 C2
Kalampaka Greece 59 I5
Kalanchak Ukr. 59 O1
Kalandi Pak. 89 F4
Kalandula Angola see Calandula
Kalannie Australia 109 B7
Kalanshiyū ar Ramlī al Kabīr, Sarīr des. Libya 86 B3
Kālān Zīād Iran 89 E5
Kalapana (abandoned) U.S.A. 127 [inset]
Kalār, Kūh-e mt. Iran 88 C4
Kalār/Kelar Iraq 91 G4
Kalasin Thai. 70 C3
Kalāt Afgh. see Qalāt
Kalāt Khorāsān-e Razavī Iran 89 E2
Kalāt Sīstān va Balūchestān Iran 89 E5
Kalat Balochistan Pak. 89 G4
Kalat Balochistan Pak. 89 G5
Kalāt, Kūh-e mt. Iran 88 E3
Kalāteh Kabūdeh Iran 89 F3
Kalaupapa U.S.A. 127 [inset]
Kalaus r. Russia 43 J7
Kalaw Myanmar 70 B2
Kälbäcär Azer. 91 G2
Kalbarri Australia 109 A6
Kalbarri National Park Australia 109 A6
Kalbe (Milde) Germany 53 L2
Kale Turkey 59 M6
Kalecik Turkey 90 D2
Kalefeld Germany 53 K3
Kaleindaung inlet Myanmar 70 A3
Kalélé Benin 96 D3
Kalemie Dem. Rep. Congo 99 C4
Kalemyo Myanmar 70 A2
Kāl-e Namak Iran 88 D3
Kalevala Russia 44 Q4
Kalewa Myanmar 70 A2
Kaleybar Iran 88 B2
Kalgan China see Zhangjiakou
Kalghatgi India 84 B3
Kalgoorlie Australia 109 C7
Kāl Gūsheh Iran 88 E4
Kali Croatia 58 F2
Kali r. India/Nepal 82 E3
Kaliakra, Nos pt Bulg. 59 M3
Kali Gandaki r. Nepal 83 F4
Kaligiri India 84 C3
Kalikata India see Kolkata
Kalima Dem. Rep. Congo 98 C4
Kalimantan reg. Indon. 68 E7
Kálimnos i. Greece see Kalymnos
Kalinin Russia see Tver'
Kalinina, imeni Tajik. see Cheshtebe
Kalinin Adyndaky Tajik. see Cheshtebe
Kaliningrad Russia 45 L9
Kalinino Armenia see Tashir
Kalinino Russia 42 I4
Kalininsk Russia 43 J6
Kalininskaya Russia 43 H7
Kalinjara India 82 C5
Kalinkavichy Belarus 43 F5
Kalinkovichi Belarus see Kalinkavichy
Kalisch Poland see Kalisz
Kalispell U.S.A. 126 E2
Kalisz Poland 47 Q5
Kalitva r. Russia 43 I6
Kaliua Tanz. 99 D4
Kaliujar India 82 E4
Kalix Sweden 44 M4
Kalkalighat India 83 H4
Kalkalpen, Nationalpark nat. park Austria 47 O7
Kalkan Turkey 59 M6
Kalkaska U.S.A. 134 C1
Kalkfeld Namibia 99 B6
Kalkfonteindam dam S. Africa 101 G5
Kalkhochalpen, Nationalpark nat. park Austria 47 N7
Kalkudah Sri Lanka 84 D5
Kall Germany 52 G4
Kallang r. Sing. 71 [inset]
Kallaste Estonia 45 O7
Kallavesi l. Fin. 44 O5
Kallsedet Sweden 44 H5
Kallsjön l. Sweden 44 H5
Kallur India 84 C2
Kalmar Sweden 45 J8
Kalmard Iran 88 E3
Kalmarsund sea chan. Sweden 45 J8
Kalmit hill Germany 53 I5
Kalmūkh Qal'eh Iran 88 E2
Kalmunai Sri Lanka 84 D5
Kalmykia aut. rep. Russia see Kalmykiya-Khalm'g-Tangch, Respublika
Kalmykiya-Khalm'g-Tangch, Respublika aut. rep. Russia 91 G1
Kalmykovo Kazakh. see Taypak
Kalmytskaya Avtonomnaya Oblast' aut. rep. Russia see Kalmykiya-Khalm'g-Tangch, Respublika
Kalnai India 83 E5
Kalodnaye Belarus 45 O11
Kalol India 82 C5
Kalomo Zambia 99 C5
Kalone Peak Canada 120 E4
Kalpa India 82 D3
Kalpeni atoll India 84 B4
Kalpetta India 84 C4
Kalpi India 82 D4
Kalsubai mt. India 82 C6
Kaltag U.S.A. 118 C3
Kaltensundheim Germany 53 K4
Kaltukatjara Australia 109 E6
Kalu India 89 I4
Kaluga Russia 43 H5
Kalukalukuang i. Indon. 68 F8
Kalundborg Denmark 45 G9
Kalush Ukr. 43 E6
Kalvakol India 84 C2
Kälviä Fin. 44 M5
Kal'ya Russia 41 R3
Kalyan India 84 B2
Kalyandurg India 87 M7
Kalyansingapuram India 84 D2
Kalyazin Russia 42 H4
Kalymnos i. Greece 59 L6
Kama Dem. Rep. Congo 98 C4
Kama Myanmar 70 A3

▶Kama r. Russia 42 L4
4th longest river in Europe.

Kamaishi Japan 75 F5
Kamalamai Nepal 83 F4
Kamalia Pak. 89 I4
Kaman Turkey 90 D3
Kamaniskeg Lake Canada 135 G1
Kamanjab Namibia 99 B5
Kamarān i. Yemen 86 F6
Kamaran Island Yemen see Kamarān
Kamarod Pak. 89 F5
Kamaron Sierra Leone 96 B4
Kamashi Uzbek. see Qamashi
Kamasin India 82 E4
Kambaiti Myanmar 70 B1
Kambalda Australia 109 C7
Kambam India 84 C4
Kambara i. Fiji see Kabara
Kambia Sierra Leone 96 B4
Kambing, Pulau i. East Timor see Ataúro, Ilha de
Kambo-san mt. N. Korea see Kwanmo-bong
Kambove Dem. Rep. Congo 99 C5
Kambūt Libya 90 B5
Kamchatka, Poluostrov pen. Russia see Kamchatka Peninsula
Kamchatka Basin sea feature Bering Sea 150 H2
Kamchatka Peninsula Russia 65 Q4
Kamchia r. Bulg. 59 L3
Kameia, Parque Nacional de nat. park Angola see Cameia, Parque Nacional da
Kamelik r. Russia 43 K5
Kamen Germany 53 H3
Kamen', Gory mt. Russia 64 K3
Kamenets-Podol'skiy Ukr. see Kam"yanets'-Podil's'kyy
Kamenitsa mt. Bulg. 59 J4
Kamenjak, Rt pt Croatia 58 E2
Kamenka Arkhangel'skaya Oblast' Russia 42 J2
Kamenka Penzenskaya Oblast' Russia 43 J5
Kamenka Primorskiy Kray Russia 74 E3
Kamenka-Bugskaya Ukr. see Kam"yanka-Buz'ka
Kamenka-Strumilovskaya Ukr. see Kam"yanka-Buz'ka
Kamen'-na-Obi Russia 72 E2
Kamennogorsk Russia 45 P6
Kamennomostskiy Russia 91 F1
Kamenolomni Russia 43 I7
Kamenongue Angola see Camanongue
Kamen'-Rybolov Russia 74 D3
Kamenskoye Russia 65 R3
Kamenskoye Ukr. see Dniprodzerzhyns'k
Kamensk-Shakhtinskiy Russia 43 I6
Kamensk-Ural'skiy Russia 64 H4
Kamet mt. China 82 D3
Kamiesberge mts S. Africa 100 D6
Kamieskroon S. Africa 100 C6
Kamileroi Australia 110 C3
Kamilukuak Lake Canada 121 K2
Kamina Dem. Rep. Congo 99 C4
Kaminak Lake Canada 121 M2
Kaminuriak Lake Canada see Qamanirjuaq Lake
Kamishihoro Japan 74 F4
Kamloops Canada 120 F5
Kamlung China 76 C1
Kamo Armenia see Gavarr
Kamoke Pak. 89 I4
Kamonia Dem. Rep. Congo 99 C4

▶Kampala Uganda 98 D3
Capital of Uganda.

Kampar r. Indon. 68 C6
Kampar Malaysia 71 C6
Kampara India 84 D1
Kampen Neth. 52 F2
Kampene Dem. Rep. Congo 98 C4
Kamphaeng Phet Thai. 70 B3
Kampinoski Park Narodowy nat. park Poland 47 R4
Kâmpóng Cham Cambodia 71 D5
Kâmpóng Chhnăng Cambodia 71 D4
Kâmpóng Khleăng Cambodia 71 D4
Kâmpóng Saôm Cambodia see Sihanoukville
Kâmpóng Spœ Cambodia 71 D5
Kâmpóng Thum Cambodia 71 D4
Kâmpóng Trâbêk Cambodia 71 D5
Kâmpôt Cambodia 71 D5
Kampuchea country Asia see Cambodia
Kamrau, Teluk b. Indon. 69 I7
Kamsack Canada 121 K5
Kamskoye Vodokhranilishche resr Russia 41 R4
Kamsuuma Somalia 98 E3
Kamuchawie Lake Canada 121 K3
Kamuli Uganda 98 D3
Kam"yanets'-Podil's'kyy Ukr. 43 E6
Kam"yanka-Buz'ka Ukr. 43 E6
Kamyanyets Belarus 45 M10
Kāmyārān Iran 88 B3
Kamyshin Russia 43 J6
Kamystybas, Ozero l. Kazakh. 80 B2
Kamyzyak Russia 43 K7
Kamzar Oman 88 E5
Kanaaupscow r. Canada 122 F3
Kanab U.S.A. 129 G3
Kanab Creek r. U.S.A. 129 G3
Kanairiktok r. Canada 123 K3
Kanak Pak. 89 G4
Kananga Dem. Rep. Congo 99 C4
Kanangio, Mount vol. P.N.G. 69 L7
Kanangra-Boyd National Park Australia 112 E4
Kanarak India see Konarka
Kanarraville U.S.A. 129 G3
Kanas watercourse Namibia 100 C4
Kanash Russia 42 J5
Kanauj India see Kannauj
Kanazawa Japan 75 E5
Kanbalu Myanmar 70 A2
Kanchanaburi Thai. 71 B4
Kanchanjanga mt. India/Nepal see Kangchenjunga
Kanchipuram India 84 C3
Kand mt. Pak. 89 G4
Kanda Pak. 89 G4
Kandahār Afgh. 89 G4
Kandalaksha Russia 44 R3
Kandalakshskiy Zaliv g. Russia 44 R3
Kandang Indon. 71 B7
Kandar Indon. 108 E2
Kandavu i. Fiji see Kadavu
Kandavu Passage Fiji see Kadavu Passage
Kandé Togo 96 D4
Kandenmarai mt. India 84 C2
Kandh Kot Pak. 89 H4
Kandi Benin 96 D3
Kandi India 84 C2
Kandiaro Pak. 89 H5
Kandıra Turkey 59 N4
Kandos Australia 112 D4
Kandreho Madag. 99 E5
Kandrian P.N.G. 69 L8
Kandukur India 84 C3
Kandy Sri Lanka 84 D5
Kandyagash Kazakh. 80 A2
Kane U.S.A. 135 F3
Kane Bassin b. Greenland 153 K1
Kaneh watercourse Iran 88 D5
Kāne'ohe U.S.A. 127 [inset]
Kaneti Pak. 89 G4
Kanevskaya Russia 43 H7
Kang Botswana 100 F2
Kang (abandoned) Afgh. 89 F4
Kangaamiut Greenland 119 M3
Kangaarsussuaq c. Greenland 119 K2
Kangaba Mali 96 C3
Kangal Turkey 90 E3
Kangān Iran 88 E5
Kangandala, Parque Nacional de nat. park Angola see Cangandala, Parque Nacional de
Kangar Malaysia 71 C6
Kangaroo Island Australia 111 B7
Kangaroo Point Australia 110 B3
Kangaslampi Fin. 44 P5
Kangasniemi Fin. 44 O6
Kangāvar Iran 88 B3

▶Kangchenjunga mt. India/Nepal 83 G4
3rd highest mountain in Asia and the world.

Kangding China 76 D2
Kangean, Kepulauan is Indon. 68 F8
Kangen r. South Sudan 97 G4
Kangerlussuaq Greenland 119 M3
Kangerlussuaq inlet Greenland 119 M3
Kangerlussuaq inlet Greenland 153 J2
Kangersuatsiaq Greenland 119 M2
Kangertittivaq sea chan. Greenland 119 P2
Kanggye N. Korea 74 B4
Kangikajik c. Greenland 119 P2
Kangiqsualujjuaq Canada 123 I2
Kangirsuk Canada 123 H1
Kang Krung National Park Thai. 71 B5
Kangle Gansu China 76 D1
Kangle Jiangxi China see Wanzai
Kangmar China 83 F3
Kango Gabon 98 B3
Kangping China 74 A4
Kangri Karpo La China/India 83 I3
Kangrinboqê Feng mt. China 82 E3
Kangsangdobdê China see Xainza
Kangto mt. China/India 83 H4
Kangtog China 83 F2
Kangxian China 76 E1
Kanibongan Sabah Malaysia 68 F5
Kanigiri India 84 C3
Kanin, Poluostrov pen. Russia 42 J2
Kanin Nos Russia 153 G2
Kanin Nos, Mys c. Russia 42 I1
Kaninskiy Bereg coastal area Russia 42 I2
Kanjiroba mt. Nepal 83 E3
Kankaanpää Fin. 45 M6
Kankakee U.S.A. 134 B3
Kankan Guinea 96 C3
Kanker India 84 D1
Kankesanturai Sri Lanka 84 D4
Kankossa Mauritania 96 B3
Kanmaw Kyun i. Myanmar 71 B5
Kannauj India 82 D4
Kanniya Kumari c. India see Comorin, Cape
Kannonkoski Fin. 44 N5
Kannur India 84 B4
Kannus Fin. 44 M5
Kano Nigeria 96 D3
Kanonpunt pt S. Africa 100 E8
Kanosh U.S.A. 129 G2
Kanovlei Namibia 99 B5
Kanoya Japan 75 C7
Kanpur Odisha India 84 E1
Kanpur Uttar Prad. India 82 E4
Kanrach reg. Pak. 89 G5
Kansai airport Japan 75 D6
Kansas U.S.A. 134 B4
Kansas r. U.S.A. 130 E4
Kansas state U.S.A. 130 D4
Kansas City KS U.S.A. 130 E4
Kansas City MO U.S.A. 130 E4
Kansk Russia 65 K4
Kansu prov. China see Gansu
Kantang Thai. 71 B6
Kantara hill Cyprus 85 A2
Kantaralak Thai. 71 D4
Kantavu i. Fiji see Kadavu
Kantchari Burkina Faso 96 D3
Kantemirovka Russia 43 H6
Kanthi India 83 F5
Kantishna r. U.S.A. 118 C3
Kanton atoll Kiribati 107 I2
Kantulong Myanmar 70 B3
Kanturk Ireland 51 D5
Kanuku Mountains Guyana 143 G3
Kanur India 84 C3
Kanus Namibia 100 D4
Kanyakubja India see Kannauj
Kanyamazane S. Africa 101 J3
Kanye Botswana 101 G3
Kaôh Kŏng Cambodia 71 C5
Kaôh Kŏng Cambodia 71 C5
Kaohsiung Taiwan 77 I4
Kaokoveld plat. Namibia 99 B5
Kaolack Senegal 96 B3
Kaoma Zambia 99 C5
Kaouadja Cent. Afr. Rep. 98 C3
Kapa S. Africa see Cape Town
Kapa'a U.S.A. 127 [inset]
Kapa'au U.S.A. 127 [inset]
Kapan Armenia 91 G3
Kapanga Dem. Rep. Congo 99 C4
Kaparhā Iran 88 C4
Kapatu Zambia 99 D4
Kap Dan Greenland see Kulusuk
Kapellen Belgium 52 E3
Kapello, Akra pt Greece see Kapello, Akrotirio
Kapello, Akrotirio pt Greece 59 J6
Kapellskär Sweden 45 K7
Kapelskär Sweden see Kapellskär
Kapingamarangi atoll Micronesia 150 G5
Kapingamarangi Rise sea feature N. Pacific Ocean 150 G5
Kapıorman Dağları mts Turkey 59 N4
Kapip Pak. 89 H4
Kapiri Mposhi Zambia 99 C5
Kapisillit Greenland 119 M3
Kapiskau r. Canada 122 E3
Kapit Sarawak Malaysia 68 E6
Kapiti Island N.Z. 113 E5
Kaplankyr, Chink hills Asia 91 I2
Kaplankyr Döwlet Gorugy nature res. Turkm. 88 E1
Kapoeta South Sudan 97 G4
Kapondai, Tanjung pt Indon. 69 G8
Kaposvár Hungary 58 G1
Kappel Germany 53 H5
Kappeln Germany 47 L3
Kapshagay Kazakh. 80 E3
Kapshagay, Vodokhranilishche resr Kazakh. 80 E3
Kapsukas Lith. see Marijampol
Kaptai Bangl. 83 H5
Kapuas r. Indon. 68 D7
Kapuriya India 82 C4
Kapurthala India 82 C3
Kapuskasing Canada 122 E4
Kapustin Yar Russia 43 J6
Kaputar mt. Australia 112 E3
Kaputir Kenya 98 D3
Kapuvár Hungary 58 G1
Kapydzhik, Gora mt. Armenia/Azer. see Qazangöldağ
Kapyl' Belarus 45 O10
Kaqung China 89 J2
Kara India 82 E4
Kara Togo 96 D4
Kara r. Turkey 91 F3
Kara Art Pass China 89 I2
Kara-Balta Kyrg. 80 D3
Karabalyk Kazakh. 78 F1
Karabaur, Uval hills Kazakh./Uzbek. 91 I2
Karabekaul' Turkm. see Garabekewül
Karabiga Turkey 59 L4
Karabil', Vozvyshennost' hills Turkm. see Garabil Belentligi
Kara-Bogaz-Gol, Proliv sea chan. Turkm. see Garabogazköl Bogazy
Kara-Bogaz-Gol'skiy Zaliv b. Turkm. see Garabogazköl Aýlagy
Karabük Turkey 90 D2
Karaburun Turkey 59 L5
Karabutak Kazakh. 80 B2
Karacabey Turkey 59 M4
Karacaköy Turkey 59 M4
Karacalı Dağ mt. Turkey 91 E3
Karaçal Tepe mt. Turkey 85 A1
Karacasu Turkey 59 M6
Karaca Yarımadası pen. Turkey 59 N6
Karachayevsk Russia 91 F2
Karachev Russia 43 G5

▶Karachi Pak. 89 G5
10th most populous city in the world.

Karacurun Turkey see Hilvan
Karad India 84 B2
Kara Dağ hill Turkey 85 D1
Kara Dağ mt. Turkey 90 D3
Kara-Dar'ya Uzbek. see Payshanba
Kara Deniz sea Asia/Europe see Black Sea
Karagan Russia 74 A1
Karagandy Kazakh. 80 D2
Karagayly Kazakh. 80 E2
Karaginskiy Zaliv b. Russia 65 R4
Karagiye, Vpadina depr. Kazakh. 91 H2
Karagola India 83 F4
Karahallı Turkey 59 M5
Karahasanlı Turkey 90 D3
Karaikal India 84 C4
Karaikkudi India 84 C4
Karaisalı Turkey 90 D3
Karaitivu i. Sri Lanka 84 C4
Karaj Iran 88 C3
Karak Jordan see Al Karak
Karakalli Turkey see Özalp
Kara Kara National Park Australia 112 A6
Karakax China see Moyu
Karakax He r. China 82 E1
Karakelong i. Indon. 69 H6
Karaklis Armenia see Vanadzor
Karakoçan Turkey 91 F3
Kara-Köl Kyrg. 79 G2
Karakol Kyrg. 80 E3
Karakoram Pass China/India 82 D2
Karakoram Range mts Asia 79 G3
Kara K'orē Eth. 98 D2
Karakorum Range mts Asia see Karakoram Range
Karaköse Turkey see Ağrı
Kara Kul' Kyrg. see Kara-Köl
Karakul', Ozero l. Tajik. see Qarokŭl
Kara Kum des. Turkm. see Karakum Desert
Karakum, Peski Kazakh. see Karakum Desert
Karakum Desert Kazakh. 78 E2
Karakum Desert Turkm. 88 F2
Karakumskiy Kanal canal Turkm. see Garagum Kanaly
Karakurt Turkey 91 F2
Karakuş Dağı ridge Turkey 59 N5
Karal Chad 97 E3
Karala Estonia 45 L7
Karalundi Australia 109 B6
Karama, Bone r. Indon. 68 F7
Karaman Turkey 90 D3
Karaman prov. Turkey 85 A1
Karamanlı Turkey 59 M6
Karamay China 80 F2
Karambar Pass Afgh./Pak. 89 I2
Karamea N.Z. 113 D5
Karamea Bight b. N.Z. 113 C5
Karamendy Kazakh. 80 B1
Karamiran China 83 F1
Karamiran Shankou pass China 83 F1
Karamürsel Turkey 59 M4
Karamyshevo Russia 45 P8
Karān i. Saudi Arabia 88 C5
Karangasem Indon. 108 A2
Karanja India 84 C1
Karanjia India 82 E5
Karapınar Gaziantep Turkey 85 C1
Karapınar Konya Turkey 90 D3
!Karas admin. reg. Namibia 100 C4
Karasay China 83 E1
Karasburg Namibia 100 D5
Kara Sea Russia 64 I2
Kárášjohka Norway see Karasjok
Karasjok Norway 44 N2
Kara Strait Russia see Karskiye Vorota, Proliv
Karasu r. Syria/Turkey 85 C1
Karasu Bitlis Turkey see Hizan
Karasu Sakarya Turkey 59 N4
Karasu r. Turkey 91 F3
Karasubazar Crimea see Bilohirs'k
Karasuk Russia 64 I4
Karāt Iran 89 F3
Karataş Turkey 85 B1
Karataş Burnu hd Turkey see Fener Burnu
Karatau Kazakh. 80 D3
Karatau, Khrebet mts Kazakh. 80 C3
Karatax Shan mts China 82 E2
Karatepe Turkey 85 A1
Karathuri Myanmar 71 B5
Karatsu Japan 75 C6
Karaudanawa Guyana 143 G3
Karauli India 82 D4
Karavan Kyrg. see Kerben
Karavostasi Cyprus 85 A2
Karawang Indon. 68 D8
Karayılan Turkey 85 C1
Karayulgun China 80 F3
Karazhal Kazakh. 80 D2
Karbalā' Iraq 91 G4
Karben Germany 53 I4
Karcag Hungary 59 I1
Karden Germany 53 H4
Kardhítsa Greece see Karditsa
Karditsa Greece 59 I5
Kärdla Estonia 45 M7
Kardzhali Bulg. 59 K4
Karee S. Africa 101 H5
Kareeberge mts S. Africa 100 E6
Kareima Sudan 86 D6
Kareli India 82 D5
Karelia aut. rep. Russia see Kareliya, Respublika
Kareliya, Respublika aut. rep. Russia 44 R5
Karel'skaya A.S.S.R. aut. rep. Russia see Kareliya, Respublika
Karel'skiy Bereg coastal area Russia 44 R3
Karema Tanz. 99 D4
Karera India 82 D4
Karesuando Sweden 44 M2
Kārevāndar Iran 89 F5
Kārēz Afgh. 89 F3
Kārēz Ilyās Afgh. 89 F3
Kargalinskaya Russia 91 G2
Kargalinski Russia see Kargalinskaya
Kargapazarı Dağları mts Turkey 91 F3
Karghalik China see Yecheng
Kargı Turkey 90 D2
Kargil India 82 D2
Kargilik China see Yecheng
Kargıpınarı Turkey 85 B1
Kargopol' Russia 42 H3
Kari Nigeria 96 E3
Karīān Iran 88 E5
Kariba Zimbabwe 99 C5
Kariba, Lake resr Zambia/Zimbabwe 99 C5
Kariba Dam Zambia/Zimbabwe 99 C5
Kariba-yama vol. Japan 74 E4
Karibib Namibia 100 B1
Karigasniemi Fin. 44 N2
Karijini National Park Australia 109 B5
Karijoki Fin. 44 L5
Karikachi-tōge pass Japan 74 F4
Karikari, Cape N.Z. 113 D2
Karimata, Pulau-pulau is Indon. 68 D7
Karimata, Selat str. Indon. 68 D7
Karimganj India 83 H4
Karimnagar India 84 C2
Karimun Besar i. Indon. 71 C7
Karimunjawa, Pulau-pulau is Indon. 68 E8
Káristos Greece see Karystos
Karjat Mahar. India 84 B2
Karjat Mahar. India 84 B2
Karkaraly Kazakh. 80 E2
Karkar Island P.N.G. 69 L7
Karkh Pak. 89 G5
Karkinits'ka Zatoka g. Crimea 59 O2
Kärkölä Fin. 45 N6
Karkonoski Park Narodowy nat. park Czechia/Poland see Krkonošský národní park
Karksi-Nuia Estonia 45 N7
Karkūk Iraq see Kirkūk
Karlachi Pak. 89 H3
Karlholmsbruk Sweden 45 J6
Karlik Shan mts China 80 H3
Karlıova Turkey 91 F3
Karlivka Ukr. 43 G6
Karl Marks, Qullai mt. Tajik. 89 I2
Karl-Marx-Stadt Germany see Chemnitz
Karlovac Croatia 58 F2
Karlovka Ukr. see Karlivka
Karlovo Bulg. 59 K3
Karlovy Vary Czechia 53 M4
Karlsbad Germany 53 I6
Karlsborg Sweden 45 I7
Karlsburg Romania see Alba Iulia
Karlshamn Sweden 45 I8
Karlskoga Sweden 45 I7
Karlskrona Sweden 45 I8
Karlsruhe Germany 53 I5
Karlstad Sweden 45 H7
Karlstad U.S.A. 130 D1
Karlstadt Germany 53 J5
Karluk U.S.A. 118 C4
Karlyk Turkm. 89 G2
Karmala India 84 B2
Karmel, Har hill Israel see Carmel, Mount
Karmona Spain see Córdoba
Karmøy i. Norway 45 D7
Karmpur Pak. 89 I4
Karnal India 82 D3
Karnaphuli Reservoir Bangl. 83 H5
Karnataka state India 84 B3
Karnavati India see Ahmadabad
Karnes City U.S.A. 131 D6
Karnobat Bulg. 59 L3
Karodi Pak. 89 G5
Karoi Zimbabwe 99 C5
Karokpi Myanmar 70 B4
Karo La pass China 83 G3
Karong India 83 H4
Karonga Malawi 99 D4
Karonie Australia 109 C7
Karoo National Park S. Africa 100 F7
Karoonda Australia 111 B7
Karora Eritrea 86 E6
Káros i. Greece see Keross
Karossa Indon. 68 F7
Karossa, Tanjung pt Indon. 108 B2
Karow Germany 53 M1
Karpasia pen. Cyprus 85 B2
Karpas Peninsula Cyprus see Karpasia
Karpathos i. Greece 59 L7
Karpathou, Steno sea chan. Greece 59 L6
Karpaty mts Europe see Carpathian Mountains
Karpenisi Greece 59 I5
Karpilovka Belarus see Aktsyabrski
Karpinsk Russia 41 S4
Karpogory Russia 42 J2
Karpuz r. Turkey 85 A1
Karratha Australia 108 B5
Karroo plat. S. Africa see Great Karoo
Karrychirla Turkm. see Garryçyrla
Kars Turkey 91 F2
Kärsämäki Fin. 44 N5
Kārsava Latvia 45 O8
Karshi Uzbek. see Qarshi
Karskiye Vorota, Proliv strait Russia 64 G3
Karskoye More sea Russia see Kara Sea
Karstädt Germany 53 L1
Karstula Fin. 44 N5
Karsu Turkey 85 C1
Karsun Russia 43 J5
Kartal Turkey 59 M4
Kartaly Russia 64 H4
Kartayel' Russia 42 L2
Karttula Fin. 44 O5
Karumba Australia 110 C3
Karumbhar Island India 82 B5
Kārūn, Kūh-e hill Iran 88 C4
Kārūn, Rūd-e r. Iran 88 C4
Karuni Indon. 108 B2
Karur India 84 C4
Karvia Fin. 44 M5
Karviná Czechia 47 Q6
Karwar India 84 B3
Karyagino Azer. see Füzuli
Karymskoye Russia 73 K2
Karynzharyk, Peski des. Kazakh. 91 I2
Karystos Greece 59 K5
Kaş Turkey 59 M6
Kasa India 84 B2
Kasaba Turkey see Turgutlu
Kasabonika Canada 122 C3
Kasabonika Lake Canada 122 C3

Kāsah Murgh mts Afgh. 89 F3
Kasaï r. Dem. Rep. Congo 98 B4
also known as Kwa
Kasaï, Plateau du Dem. Rep. Congo 99 C4
Kasaji Dem. Rep. Congo 99 C5
Kasama Zambia 99 D5
Kasan Uzbek. see Koson
Kasane Botswana 99 C5
Kasaragod India 84 B3
Kasargod India see Kasaragod
Kasargode India see Kasaragod
Kasatkino Russia 74 C2
Kasba Lake Canada 121 K2
Kasba Tadla Morocco 54 C5
Kasenga Dem. Rep. Congo 99 C5
Kasengu Dem. Rep. Congo 99 C4
Kasese Dem. Rep. Congo 98 C4
Kasese Uganda 98 D3
Kasevo Russia see Neftekamsk
Kasganj India 82 D4
Kasha China 76 C2
Kashabowie Canada 122 C4
Kāshān Iran 88 C3
Kashary Russia 43 I6
Kashechewan Canada 122 E3
Kashgar China see Kashi
Kashi China 80 E4
Kashihara Japan 75 D6
Kashima-nada b. Japan 75 F5
Kashin Russia 42 H4
Kashipur India 82 D3
Kashira Russia 43 H5
Kashiwazaki Japan 75 E5
Kashkarantsy Russia 42 H2
Kashkū'iyeh Iran 88 D4
Kāshmar Iran 88 E3
Kashmir hist. area Asia 82 D2
Kashmir, Vale of reg. India 82 C2
Kashyr Kazakh. 72 D2
Kashyukulu Dem. Rep. Congo 99 C4
Kasi India see Varanasi
Kāsigar Afgh. 89 H3
Kasimov Russia 43 I5
Kaskattama r. Canada 121 N3
Kaskinen Fin. 44 L5
Kas Klong i. Cambodia see Kŏng, Kaôh
Kaskö Fin. see Kaskinen
Kaslo Canada 120 G5
Kasmere Lake Canada 121 K3
Kasongo Dem. Rep. Congo 99 C4
Kasongo-Lunda Dem. Rep. Congo 99 B4
Kasos i. Greece 59 L7
Kaspīy Mangy Oypaty lowland Kazakh./Russia see Caspian Lowland
Kaspiysk Russia 91 G2
Kaspiyskiy Russia see Lagan'
Kaspiyskoye More l. Asia/Europe see Caspian Sea
Kassa Slovakia see Košice
Kassala Sudan 86 E6
Kassandras, Akra pt Greece see Kassandras, Akrotirio
Kassandras, Akrotirio pt Greece 59 J5
Kassandras, Kolpos b. Greece 59 J4
Kassel Germany 53 J3
Kasserine Tunisia 58 C7
Kastag Pak. 89 F5
Kastamonu Turkey 90 D2
Kastellaun Germany 53 H4
Kastelli Greece see Kissamos
Kastéllion Greece see Kissamos
Kastellorizon i. Greece see Megisti
Kasterlee Belgium 52 E3
Kastoria Greece 59 I4
Kastornoye Russia 43 H6
Kastsyukovichy Belarus 43 G5
Kasulu Tanz. 99 D4
Kasumkent Russia 91 H2
Kasungu Malawi 99 D5
Kasungu National Park Malawi 99 D5
Kasur Pak. 89 I4
Katâdtlit Nunât terr. N. America see Greenland
Katahdin, Mount U.S.A. 132 G2
Katah Sang Srah Afgh. 89 G3
Kataklik India 82 D2
Katako-Kombe Dem. Rep. Congo 98 C4
Katakwi Uganda 98 D3
Katana India 82 C5
Katangi India 82 D5
Katanning Australia 109 B8
Katavi National Park Tanz. 99 D4
Katāwāz reg. Afgh. 89 G3
Katchall i. India 71 A6
Katea Dem. Rep. Congo 99 C4
Katerini Greece 59 J4
Katesh Tanz. 99 D4
Kate's Needle mt. Canada/U.S.A. 120 C3
Katete Zambia 99 D5
Katherîna, Gebel mt. Egypt see Kātrīnā, Jabal
Katherine Australia 108 F3
Katherine Gorge National Park Australia see Nitmiluk National Park
Kathi India 89 I6
Kathiawar pen. India 82 B5
Kathihar India see Katihar
Kathiraveli Sri Lanka 84 D4
Kathiwara India 82 C5
Kathleen Falls Australia 108 E3

▶Kathmandu Nepal 83 F4
Capital of Nepal.

Kathu S. Africa 100 F4
Kathua India 82 C2
Kati Mali 96 C3
Katihar India 83 F4
Katikati S. Africa 101 H7
Katima Mulilo Namibia 99 C5
Katimik Lake Canada 121 L4
Katiola Côte d'Ivoire 96 C4
Kā Tiritiri o te Moana mts N.Z. see Southern Alps

▶Kati Thanda-Lake Eyre Australia 111 B6
Largest lake in Oceania and lowest point.

Kati Thanda-Lake Eyre (North) Australia 111 B6
Kati Thanda-Lake Eyre (South) Australia 111 B6
Kati Thanda-Lake Eyre National Park Australia 111 B6
Katkop Hills S. Africa 100 E6
Katlehong S. Africa 101 I4
Katmai National Park and Preserve U.S.A. 118 C4
Katmandu Nepal see Kathmandu
Katni India 82 E5
Kato Achaïa Greece 59 I5
Katoomba Australia 112 E4
Katowice Poland 47 Q5
Katoya India 83 G5
Katrancık Dağı mts Turkey 59 M6
Kātrīnā, Jabal mt. Egypt 90 D5
Katrine, Loch l. U.K. 50 E4
Katrineholm Sweden 45 J7
Katse Dam Lesotho 101 I5
Katsina Nigeria 96 D3
Katsina-Ala Nigeria 96 D4
Katsuura Japan 75 F6
Kattaktoc, Cap c. Canada 123 I2
Kattamudda Well Australia 108 D5
Kattaqo'rg'on Uzbek. 89 G2
Kattaqŭrghon Uzbek. see Kattaqo'rg'on
Kattegat strait Denmark/Sweden 45 G8
Kattowitz Poland see Katowice
Katumbar India 82 D4
Katunino Russia 42 J4
Katuri Pak. 89 H4
Katwa India see Katoya
Katwijk aan Zee Neth. 52 E2
Katzenbuckel hill Germany 53 J5
Kaua'i i. U.S.A. 127 [inset]
Kaua'i Channel U.S.A. 127 [inset]
Kaub Germany 53 H4
Kaufungen Germany 53 J3
Kauhajoki Fin. 44 M5
Kauhava Fin. 44 M5
Kaukauna U.S.A. 134 A1
Kaukkwe Hills Myanmar 70 B1
Kaukonen Fin. 44 N3
Ka'ula i. U.S.A. 127 [inset]
Kaulakahi Channel U.S.A. 127 [inset]
Kaumajet Mountains Canada 123 J2
Kaunakakai U.S.A. 127 [inset]
Kaunas Lith. 45 M9
Kaunata Latvia 45 O8
Kaundy, Vpadina depr. Kazakh. 91 I2
Kaunia Bangl. 83 G4
Kaura-Namoda Nigeria 96 D3
Kau Sai Chau i. H.K. China 77 [inset]
Kaustinen Fin. 44 M5
Kautokeino Norway 44 M2
Kau-ye Kyun i. Myanmar 71 B5
Kavadarci Macedonia 59 J4
Kavak Turkey 90 E2
Kavaklıdere Turkey 59 M6
Kavala Greece 59 K4
Kavalas, Kolpos b. Greece 59 K4
Kavalerovo Russia 74 D3
Kavali India 84 D3
Kavango Zambezi Transfrontier Conservation Area res. Africa 99 C5
Kavār Iran 88 D4
Kavaratti India 84 B4
Kavaratti atoll India 84 B4
Kavarna Bulg. 59 M3
Kavendou, Mont mt. Guinea 96 B3
Kaveri r. India 84 C4
Kavīr Iran 88 C3
Kavīr, Chāh-e well Iran 88 E3
Kavīr, Dasht-e des. Iran 88 D3
Kavīr Kūshk well Iran 88 E3
Kavkasioni mts Asia/Europe see Caucasus
Kawa Myanmar 70 B3
Kawagama Lake Canada 135 F1
Kawagoe Japan 75 E6
Kawaguchi Japan 75 E6
Kawaihae U.S.A. 127 [inset]
Kawaikini U.S.A. 127 [inset]
Kawakawa N.Z. 113 E2
Kawambwa Zambia 99 C4
Kawana Zambia 99 C5
Kawardha India 82 E5
Kawartha Highlands Signature Site park Canada 135 F1
Kawartha Lakes Canada 135 F1
Kawasaki Japan 75 E6
Kawau Island N.Z. 113 E3
Kawawachikamach Canada 123 I3
Kawdut Myanmar 70 B4
Kawerau N.Z. 113 F4
Kawhia N.Z. 113 E4
Kawhia Harbour N.Z. 113 E4
Kawich Peak U.S.A. 128 E3
Kawich Range mts U.S.A. 128 E3
Kawinaw Lake Canada 121 L4
Kaw Lake U.S.A. 131 D4
Kawlin Myanmar 70 A2
Kawm Umbū Egypt 86 D5
Kawngmeum Myanmar 70 B2
Kawthaung Myanmar 71 B5
Kaxgar China see Kashi
Kaxgar He r. China 80 E4
Kax He r. China 80 F3
Kaxtexi Shan mts China 83 E1
Kaya Burkina Faso 96 C3
Kayadibi Turkey 90 E3
Kayan r. Indon. 68 F6
Kayankulam India 84 C4
Kayar India 84 C2
Kaycee U.S.A. 126 G4
Kaydak, Sor dry lake Kazakh. 91 I1
Kaydanovo Belarus see Dzyarzhynsk
Kayembe-Mukulu Dem. Rep. Congo 99 C4
Kayenta U.S.A. 129 H3
Kayes Mali 96 B3
Kaylahgay (abandoned) Afgh. 89 H3
Kaymaz Turkey 59 N5
Kaynar Kazakh. 80 E2
Kaynar Turkey 90 E3
Kayseri Turkey 90 D3
Kayuyu Dem. Rep. Congo 98 C4
Kayyngdy Kyrg. 80 D3
Kazach'ye Russia 65 O2
Kazakh Azer. see Qazax
Kazakhskaya S.S.R. country Asia see Kazakhstan
Kazakhskiy Zaliv b. Kazakh. 91 I2

▶Kazakhstan country Asia 78 F2
4th largest country in Asia and 9th in the world.

Kazakhstan Kazakh. see Aksay
Kazakh Steppe plain Kazakh. see Saryarka
Kazakstan country Asia see Kazakhstan
Kazan r. Canada 121 M2
Kazan' Russia 42 K5
Kazandzhik Turkm. see Bereket
Kazanka r. Russia 42 K5
Kazanlak Bulg. 59 K3
Kazanlı Turkey 85 B1
Kazan-rettō is Japan see Volcano Islands
Kazatin Ukr. see Kozyatyn

▶Kazbek mt. Georgia/Russia 43 J8
4th highest mountain in Europe.

Kaz Dağı mts Turkey 59 L5
Kāzerūn Iran 88 C4
Kazhym Russia 42 K3
Kazidi Tajik. see Qozide
Kazi Magomed Azer. see Hacıqabul
Kazincbarcika Hungary 43 D6
Kaziranga National Park India 83 H4
K'azreti Georgia 91 G2
Kaztalovka Kazakh. 41 P6
Kazy Turkm. 88 E2
Kazym r. Russia 41 T3
Kazym-Mys Russia 41 T3
Kea i. Greece see Tzia
Keady U.K. 51 F3
Keams Canyon U.S.A. 129 H4
Kéamu i. Vanuatu see Anatom
Kearney U.S.A. 130 D3
Kearny U.S.A. 129 H5
Keban Turkey 90 E3
Keban Barajı resr Turkey 90 E3
Kébémèr Senegal 96 B3
Kebili Tunisia 54 F5
Kebīr, Nahr al r. Lebanon/Syria 85 B2
Kebkabiya Sudan 97 F3
Kebnekaise mt. Sweden 44 K3
Kebock Head hd U.K. 50 C2
K'ebrī Dehar Eth. 98 E3
Kech reg. Pak. 89 F5
Kechika r. Canada 120 E3
Keçiborlu Turkey 59 N6
Kecskemét Hungary 59 H1
Keda Georgia 91 F2
Kėdainiai Lith. 45 M9
Kedairu Passage Fiji see Kadavu Passage
Kedgwick Canada 123 I5
Kedian China 77 G2
Kedong China 74 B3
Kédougou Senegal 96 B3
Kedva r. Russia 42 L2
Kędzierzyn-Koźle Poland 47 Q5
Keele r. Canada 120 E1
Keele Peak Canada 120 D2
Keeler U.S.A. 128 E3
Keeley Lake Canada 121 I4
Keeling Islands terr. Indian Ocean see Cocos (Keeling) Islands
Keelung Taiwan 77 I3
Keen, Mount hill U.K. 50 G4
Keene CA U.S.A. 128 D4
Keene KY U.S.A. 134 C5
Keene NH U.S.A. 135 I2
Keene OH U.S.A. 134 E3
Keeper Hill hill Ireland 51 D5
Keepit, Lake resr Australia 112 E3
Keep River National Park Australia 108 E3
Keerbergen Belgium 52 E3
Keer-weer, Cape Australia 110 C2
Keetmanshoop Namibia 100 D4
Keewatin Canada 121 M5
Kefallinía i. Greece see Cephalonia
Kefallonia i. Greece see Cephalonia
Kefamenanu Indon. 108 D2
Kefe Crimea see Feodosiya
Keffi Nigeria 96 D4
Keflavík Iceland 44 [inset 1]
Kê Ga, Mui pt Vietnam 71 E5
Kegalla Sri Lanka 84 D5
Kegen Kazakh. 80 E3
Keglo, Baie de b. Canada 123 I2
Keg River Canada 120 G3
Kegul'ta Russia 43 J7
Kehra Estonia 45 N7
Kehsi Mansam Myanmar 70 B2
Keighley U.K. 48 F5
Keila Estonia 45 N7
Keimoes S. Africa 100 E5
Keitele Fin. 44 O5
Keitele l. Fin. 44 O5
Keith Australia 111 C8
Keith U.K. 50 G3
Keith Arm b. Canada 120 F1
Kejimkujik National Park Canada 123 I5
Kekaha U.S.A. 127 [inset]
Kékes mt. Hungary 47 R7
Kekri India 82 C4
Kelaa i. Maldives 84 B5
K'elafo Eth. 98 E3
Kelberg Germany 52 G4
Kelheim Germany 53 L6
Kelibia Tunisia 58 D6
Kelif Uzboýy marsh Turkm. 89 F2
Kelīrī Iran 88 E5
Kelkheim (Taunus) Germany 53 I4
Kelkit Turkey 91 E2
Kelkit r. Turkey 90 E2
Kéllé Congo 98 B4
Keller Lake Canada 120 F2
Kellett, Cape Canada 118 F2
Kelleys Island U.S.A. 134 D3
Kelliher Canada 121 K5
Kelloselkä Fin. 44 P3
Kells Ireland 51 F4
Kells r. U.K. 51 F3
Kelly U.S.A. 134 B5
Kelly Lake Canada 120 E1
Kelly Range hills Australia 109 C6
Kelmė Lith. 45 M9
Kelmis Belgium 52 G4
Kélo Chad 97 E4
Kelowna Canada 120 G5
Kelp Head hd Canada 120 E5
Kelseyville U.S.A. 128 B2
Kelso U.K. 50 G5
Kelso U.S.A. 126 C3
Kelso (abandoned) U.S.A. 129 F4
Keluang Malaysia 71 C7
Kelvington Canada 121 K4
Kem' Russia 42 G2
Kem' r. Russia 42 G2
Ke Macina Mali see Macina
Kemah Turkey 90 E3
Kemaliye Turkey 90 E3
Kemalpaşa Turkey 59 L5
Kemano (abandoned) Canada 120 E4
Kembé Cent. Afr. Rep. 98 C3
Kemeneshát hills Hungary 58 G1
Kemer Antalya Turkey 59 N6
Kemer Muğla Turkey 59 M6
Kemer Barajı resr Turkey 59 M6
Kemerovo Russia 64 J4
Kemi Fin. 44 N4
Kemijärvi Fin. 44 O3
Kemijärvi l. Fin. 44 O3
Kemijoki r. Fin. 44 N4
Kemiö Fin. see Kimito
Kemir Turkm. see Keymir
Kemmerer U.S.A. 126 F4
Kemnath Germany 53 L5
Kemnay U.K. 50 G3
Kemp Coast reg. Antarctica see Kemp Land
Kempele Fin. 44 N4
Kempen Germany 52 G3
Kempisch Kanaal canal Belgium 52 F3
Kemp Land reg. Antarctica 152 D2
Kemp Peninsula Antarctica 152 A2
Kemp's Bay Bahamas 133 E7
Kempsey Australia 112 F3
Kempt, Lac l. Canada 122 G5
Kempten (Allgäu) Germany 47 M7
Kempton U.S.A. 134 B3
Kempton Park S. Africa 101 I4
Kemptville Canada 135 H1
Kemujan i. Indon. 68 E8
Ken r. India 82 E4
Kenai U.S.A. 118 C3
Kenai Fiords National Park U.S.A. 118 C4
Kenai Mountains U.S.A. 118 C4
Kenamu r. Canada 123 K3
Kenansville U.S.A. 133 E5
Kenâyis, Râs el pt Egypt see Ḥikmah, Ra's al
Kenbridge U.S.A. 135 F5
Kendal U.K. 48 E4
Kendall Australia 112 F3
Kendall, Cape Canada 119 J3
Kendallville U.S.A. 134 C3
Kendari Indon. 69 G7
Kendawangan Indon. 68 E7
Kendégué Chad 97 E3
Kendirli-Kiyasan, Plato plat. Kazakh. 91 I2
Kendrapara India 83 F5
Kendraparha India see Kendrapara
Kendrick Peak U.S.A. 129 H4
Kendujhar India see Kendujhargarh
Kendujhargarh India 83 F5
Kendyrlisor, Solonchak salt l. Kazakh. 91 I2
Kenebri Australia 112 D3
Kenedy U.S.A. 131 D6
Kenema Sierra Leone 96 B4
Kenge Dem. Rep. Congo 99 B4
Keng Lap Myanmar 70 C2
Kengtung Myanmar 70 B2
Kenhardt S. Africa 100 E5
Kéniéba Mali 96 B3
Kenitra Morocco 54 C5
Kenmare Ireland 51 C6
Kenmare U.S.A. 130 C1
Kenmare River inlet Ireland 51 B6
Kenmore U.S.A. 135 F2
Kenn Germany 52 G5
Kenna U.S.A. 131 C5
Kennebec U.S.A. 130 D3
Kennebec r. U.S.A. 132 G2
Kennebunkport U.S.A. 135 J2
Kennedy, Cape U.S.A. see Canaveral, Cape
Kennedy Range National Park Australia 109 A6
Kennedy Town H.K. China 77 [inset]
Kenner U.S.A. 131 F6
Kennet r. U.K. 49 G7
Kenneth Range hills Australia 109 B5
Kennett U.S.A. 131 F4
Kennewick U.S.A. 126 D3
Kenn Reef Australia 110 F4
Kenogami r. Canada 122 D4
Keno Hill Canada 120 C2
Kenora Canada 121 M5
Kenosha U.S.A. 134 B2
Kenozero, Ozero l. Russia 42 H3
Kent r. U.K. 48 E4
Kent OH U.S.A. 134 E3
Kent TX U.S.A. 131 B6
Kent VA U.S.A. 134 E5
Kent WA U.S.A. 126 C3
Kentani S. Africa see Centane
Kent Group is Australia 111 [inset]
Kentland U.S.A. 134 B3
Kenton U.S.A. 134 D3
Kent Peninsula Canada 118 H3
Kentucky state U.S.A. 134 C5
Kentucky Lake U.S.A. 131 F4
Kenya country Africa 98 D3

▶Kenya, Mount Kenya 98 D4
2nd highest mountain in Africa.

Kenyir, Tasik resr Malaysia 71 C6
Keokuk U.S.A. 130 F3
Keoladeo National Park India 82 D4
Keonjhar India see Kendujhargarh
Keonjhargarh India see Kendujhargarh
Keosauqua U.S.A. 130 F3
Keowee, Lake resr U.S.A. 133 D5
Kepina r. Russia 42 I2
Keppel Bay Australia 110 E4
Kepsut Turkey 59 M5
Kera India 83 F5
Kerāh Iran 88 E4
Kerala state India 84 B4
Kerang Australia 112 A5
Kerava Fin. 45 N6
Kerba Alg. 57 G5
Kerbela Iraq see Karbalā'
Kerben Kyrg. 80 D3
Kerbi r. Russia 74 E1
Kerbodot, Lac l. Canada 123 I3
Kerch Crimea 90 E1
Kerchem"ya Russia 42 L3
Kerema P.N.G. 69 L8
Keremeos Canada 120 G5
Kerempe Burun pt Turkey 90 D2
Keren Eritrea 86 E6
Kerepakupai Merú waterfall Venez. see Angel Falls
Kerewan Gambia 96 B3
Kergeli Turkm. 88 E2
Kerguélen, Îles is Indian Ocean 149 M9
Kerguelen Islands Indian Ocean see Kerguélen, Îles
Kerguelen Plateau sea feature Indian Ocean 149 M9
Kericho Kenya 98 D4
Kerikeri N.Z. 113 D2
Kerimäki Fin. 44 P6
Kerinci, Gunung vol. Indon. 68 C7
Kerinci Seblat, Taman Nasional nat. park Indon. 68 C7
Kerintji vol. Indon. see Kerinci, Gunung
Keriya He watercourse China 72 E5
Keriya Shankou pass China 83 E2
Kerken Germany 52 G3
Kerkennah, Îles is Tunisia 58 D7
Kerkiçi Turkm. 89 G2
Kerkini, Limni l. Greece 59 J4
Kerkinitis, Limni l. Greece see Kerkini, Limni
Kérkira i. Greece see Corfu
Kerkouane tourist site Tunisia 58 D6
Kerkyra Greece 59 H5
Kerkyra i. Greece see Corfu
Kerma Sudan 86 D6
Kermadec Islands S. Pacific Ocean 107 I5

▶Kermadec Trench sea feature S. Pacific Ocean 150 I8
4th deepest trench in the world.

Kermān Iran 88 E4
Kerman U.S.A. 128 C3
Kermān, Bīābān-e Iran 88 E4
Kermānshāh Kermānshāh Iran 88 B3
Kermānshāh Yazd Iran 88 D4
Kermine Uzbek. see Navoiy
Kermit U.S.A. 131 C6
Kern r. U.S.A. 128 D4
Kernertut, Cap c. Canada 123 I2
Keros Russia 42 L3
Keross i. Greece 59 K6
Kérouané Guinea 96 C4
Kerpen Germany 52 G4
Kerr, Cape Antarctica 152 H1
Kerrobert Canada 121 I5
Kerrville U.S.A. 131 D6
Kerry Head hd Ireland 51 C5
Kerteminde Denmark 45 G9
Kerulen r. China/Mongolia see Herlen Gol
Kerur India 84 B2
Keryneia Cyprus see Kyrenia
Kerzaz Alg. 96 C2
Kerzhenets r. Russia 42 J4
Kesagami Lake Canada 122 E4
Kesälahti Fin. 44 P6
Keşan Turkey 59 L4
Keşap Turkey 43 H8
Kesariya India 83 F4
Kesennuma Japan 75 F5
Keshan China 74 B2
Keshena U.S.A. 134 A1
Keshod India 82 B5
Keshvar Iran 88 C3
Keskin Turkey 90 D3
Keskozero Russia 42 G3
Kesova Gora Russia 42 H4
Kessel Neth. 52 G3
Kestell S. Africa 101 I5
Kesten'ga Russia 44 Q4
Kestilä Fin. 44 O4
Keswick Canada 134 F1
Keswick U.K. 48 D4
Keszthely Hungary 58 G1
Ketapang Indon. 68 E7
Ketchikan U.S.A. 120 D4
Keti Bandar Pak. 89 G5
Ketmen', Khrebet mts China/Kazakh. 80 F3
Kettering U.K. 49 G6
Kettering U.S.A. 134 C4
Kettle r. Canada 120 G5
Kettle Creek r. U.S.A. 135 G3
Kettle Falls U.S.A. 126 D2
Kettleman City U.S.A. 128 D3
Kettle River Range mts U.S.A. 126 D2
Keuka U.S.A. 135 G2
Keuka Lake U.S.A. 135 G2
Keumgang, Mount N. Korea see Kumgang-san
Keumsang, Mount N. Korea see Kumgang-san
Keuruu Fin. 44 N5
Kew Turks and Caicos Is 133 F8
Kewanee U.S.A. 130 F3
Kewaunee U.S.A. 134 B1
Keweenaw Bay U.S.A. 130 F2
Keweenaw Peninsula U.S.A. 130 F2
Keweenaw Point U.S.A. 132 C2
Key, Lough l. Ireland 51 D3
Keyala South Sudan 97 G4
Keyano Canada 123 G3
Keya Paha r. U.S.A. 130 D3
Key Harbour Canada 122 E5
Keyihe China 74 A2
Key Largo U.S.A. 133 D7
Keymir Turkm. 88 D2
Keynsham U.K. 49 E7
Keyser U.S.A. 135 F4
Keystone Lake U.S.A. 131 D4
Keystone Peak U.S.A. 129 H6
Keysville U.S.A. 135 F5
Keytesville U.S.A. 130 E4
Keyvy, Vozvyshennost' hills Russia 42 H2
Key West U.S.A. 133 D7
Kez Russia 41 Q4
Kezi Zimbabwe 99 C6
Kgalagadi admin. dist. Botswana 100 E3
Kgalagadi Transfrontier Park Botswana/S. Africa 101 D2
Kgalazadi admin. dist. Botswana see Kgalagadi
Kgatlen admin. dist. Botswana see Kgatleng
Kgatleng admin. dist. Botswana 101 H3
Kgomofatshe Pan salt pan Botswana 100 E2
Kgoro Pan salt pan Botswana 100 G3
Kgotsong S. Africa 101 H4
Khabab Syria 85 C3
Khabar Iran 88 D4
Khabarikha Russia 42 L2
Khabarovsk Russia 74 D2
Khabarovskiy Kray admin. div. Russia 74 D2
Khabarovsk Kray admin. div. Russia see Khabarovskiy Kray
Khabary Russia 72 D2
Khabis Iran see Shahdād
Khachmas Azer. see Xaçmaz
Khadar, Jabal mt. Oman 88 E6
Khadīr Afgh. 89 G3
Khadro Pak. 89 H5
Khadzhiolen Turkm. 88 E2
Khafs Banbān well Saudi Arabia 88 B5
Khagaria India 83 F4
Khagrachari Bangl. 83 G5
Khagrachhari Bangl. see Khagrachari
Khairgarh Pak. 89 H4
Khairpur Punjab Pak. 89 I4
Khairpur Sindh Pak. 89 H5
Khāīz, Kūh-e mt. Iran 88 C4
Khajuha India 82 E4
Khāk-e Jabār-e Bālā Afgh. 89 H3
Khakhea Botswana 100 F3
Khākrēz Afgh. 89 G4
Khākrēz reg. Afgh. 89 G4
Khalajestan reg. Iran 88 C3
Khalatse India 82 D2
Khalifat mt. Pak. 89 G4
Khalīj Surt g. Libya see Sirte, Gulf of
Khalilabad India 83 E4
Khalīlī Iran 88 D5
Khalkabad Turkm. 89 F1
Khalkhāl Iran 88 C2
Khálki i. Greece see Chalki
Khalkís Greece see Chalkida
Khallikot India 84 E2
Khalturin Russia see Orlov
Khamar-Daban, Khrebet mts Russia 72 I2
Khamaria India 84 D1
Khambhat India 82 C5
Khambhat, Gulf of India 84 A2
Khamgaon India 84 C1
Khamis Mushayţ Saudi Arabia 86 F6
Khamkeut Laos 70 D3
Khamma well Saudi Arabia 88 B5
Khammam India 84 D2
Khammouan Laos see Thakhèk
Khamr Yemen 86 F6
Khamra Russia 65 M3
Khamseh reg. Iran 88 C3
Khan, Nâm r. Laos 70 C3
Khānābād Afgh. 89 H2
Khān al Baghdādī Iraq 91 F4
Khān al Mashāhidah Iraq 91 G4
Khān al Muşallá Iraq 91 G4
Khanapur India 84 B2
Khān ar Raḩbah Iraq 91 G5
Khanasur Pass Iran/Turkey 91 G3
Khanbalik China see Beijing
Khānch Iran 88 B2
Khandu India 89 I6
Khandwa India 82 D5
Khandyga Russia 65 O3
Khanewal Pak. 89 H4
Khanh Hung Vietnam see Soc Trăng
Khaniá Greece see Chania
Khānī Yek Iran 88 D4
Khanka, Lake China/Russia 74 D3
Khanka, Ozero l. China/Russia see Khanka, Lake
Khankendi Azer. see Xankändi
Khanna India 82 D3
Khannā, Qā' salt pan Jordan 85 C3
Khanpur Balochistan Pak. 89 H4
Khanpur Punjab Pak. 89 H4
Khān Ruḩābah Iraq see Khān ar Raḩbah
Khansar Pak. 89 H4
Khān Shaykhūn Syria 85 C2
Khantayskoye, Ozero l. Russia 64 K3
Khanthabouli Laos see Savannakhét
Khanty-Mansiysk Russia 64 H3
Khān Yūnus Gaza 85 B4
Khanzi admin. dist. Botswana see Ghanzi
Khao Ang Rua Nai Wildlife Reserve nature res. Thai. 71 C4
Khao Banthat Wildlife Reserve nature res. Thai. 71 B6
Khao Chum Thong Thai. 71 B5
Khaoen Si Nakarin National Park Thai. 71 B4
Khao Laem, Ang Kep Nam Thai. 70 B4
Khao Laem National Park Thai. 70 B4
Khao Luang National Park Thai. 71 B5
Khao Pu-Khao Ya National Park Thai. 71 B6
Khao Soi Dao Wildlife Reserve nature res. Thai. 71 C4
Khao Sok National Park Thai. 71 B5
Khao Yai National Park Thai. 71 C4
Khaplu Pak. 80 E4
Khaptad National Park Nepal 82 E3
Kharabali Russia 43 J7
Kharagpur Bihar India 83 F4
Kharagpur W. Bengal India 83 F5
Kharāmeh Iran 88 D4
Khārān r. Iran 87 I4
Kharānaq, Kūh-e mt. Iran 88 D3
Kharari India see Abu Road
Kharda India 84 B2
Khardi India 82 C6
Khardong La pass India see Khardung La
Khardung La pass India 82 D2
Kharfiyah Iraq 91 G5
Kharga Egypt see Al Khārijah
Kharga r. Russia 74 D1
Khârga, El Wâhât el oasis Egypt see Khārijah, Wāḩāt al

Kharga Oasis Egypt see Khārijah, Wāḥāt al
Kharg Islands Iran 88 C4
Khargone India 82 C5
Khari r. Rajasthan India 82 C4
Khari r. Rajasthan India 82 C4
Kharian Pak. 89 I3
Khariar India 84 D1
Khārijah, Wāḥāt al oasis Egypt 86 D5
Kharīm, Gebel hill Egypt see Kharīm, Jabal
Kharīm, Jabal hill Egypt 85 A4
Kharkhara r. India 82 E5
Kharkiv Ukr. 43 H6
Khar'kov Ukr. see Kharkiv
Kharlovka Russia 42 H1
Kharlu Russia 44 Q6
Kharōṭī reg. Afgh. 89 H3
Kharovsk Russia 42 I4
Kharsia India 83 E5

▶Khartoum Sudan 86 D6
Capital of Sudan. 5th most populous city in Africa.

Kharwār reg. Afgh. 89 H3
Khasavyurt Russia 91 G2
Khāsh Iran 89 F4
Khāsh, Dasht-e Afgh. 89 F4
Khashm el Girba Sudan 86 E7
Khashm Ṣana' Saudi Arabia 90 E6
Khāsh Rōd Afgh. 89 F4
Khāsh Rōd r. Afgh. 89 F4
Khashuri Georgia 91 F2
Khasi Hills India 83 G4
Khatanga Russia 65 L2
Khatanga, Gulf of Russia see Khatangskiy Zaliv
Khatangskiy Zaliv b. Russia 65 L2
Khatayakha Russia 42 M2
Khatinza Pass Pak. 89 H2
Khatmat al Malāha Oman 88 E5
Khatyrka Russia 65 S3
Khaur Pak. 89 I3
Khavda India 82 B5
Khāwāk, Kōtal-e Afgh. 89 H3
Khayamnandi S. Africa 101 G6
Khayang mt. India 83 H4
Khaybar Saudi Arabia 86 E4
Khayelitsha S. Africa 100 D8
Khayrān, Ra's al pt Oman 88 E6
Khefa Israel see Haifa
Khehuene, Ponta pt Moz. 101 L2
Khemis Miliana Alg. 57 H5
Khemmarat Thai. 70 D3
Khenchela Alg. 58 B7
Khenifra Morocco 54 C5
Kherrata Alg. 57 I5
Kherreh Iran 88 D5
Khersan r. Iran 88 C4
Kherson Ukr. 59 O1
Kheta r. Russia 65 L2
Kheyrābād Iran 88 D4
Khezerābād Iran 88 D2
Khezrī Dasht-e Bayāz Iran 88 E3
Khiching India 83 F5
Khilok Russia 73 K2
Khilok r. Russia 73 J2
Khinganskiy Zapovednik nature res. Russia 74 C2
Khinsar Pak. 89 H5
Khíos i. Greece see Chios
Khipro Pak. 89 H5
Khisrow Afgh. 89 G3
Khitai Dawan pass China 82 D2
Khīyāv Iran 88 B2
Khiytola Russia 45 P6
Khlevnoye Russia 43 H5
Khlong, Mae r. Thai. 71 C4
Khlong Saeng Wildlife Reserve nature res. Thai. 71 B5
Khlong Wang Chao National Park Thai. 70 B3
Khlung Thai. 71 C4
Khmel'nik Ukr. see Khmil'nyk
Khmel'nitskiy Ukr. see Khmel'nyts'kyy
Khmel'nyts'kyy Ukr. 43 E6
Khmer Republic country Asia see Cambodia
Khmil'nyk Ukr. 43 E6
Khoai, Hon i. Vietnam 71 D5
Khobi Georgia 91 F2
Khodā Āfarīd spring Iran 88 E3
Khodzha-Kala Turkm. see Hojagala
Khodzhambaz Turkm. see Hojambaz
Khodzhent Tajik. see Khŭjand
Khodzheyli Uzbek. see Xo'jayli
Khojand Tajik. see Khŭjand
Khokhowe Pan salt pan Botswana 100 E3
Khokhropar Pak. 89 H5
Khoksar India 82 D2
Kholm Poland see Chełm
Kholm Russia 42 F4
Kholmsk Russia 74 F3
Kholon Israel see Ḥolon
Khomas admin. reg. Namibia 100 C2
Khomas Highland hills Namibia 100 B2
Khomeyn Iran 88 C3
Khomeynīshahr Iran 88 C3
Khong, Mae Nam r. Asia see Mekong
Khonj Iran 88 D5
Khonj, Kūh-e mts Iran 88 D5
Khon Kaen Thai. 70 C3
Khon Kriel Cambodia see Kon Kriel
Khonsa India 83 H4
Khonuu Russia 65 P3
Khoper r. Russia 43 I6
Khor Russia 74 D3
Khor r. Russia 74 D3
Khorāsān, Chāh-e well Iran 88 D3
Khorat Plateau Thai. 70 C3
Khorda India see Khordha
Khordha India 84 E1
Khorey-Ver Russia 42 M2
Khorinsk Russia 73 J2
Khorixas Namibia 99 B6
Khormūj, Kūh-e mt. Iran 88 C4
Khorog Tajik. see Khorugh
Khorol Russia 74 D3
Khorol Ukr. 43 G6
Khoroslū Dāgh hills Iran 88 B2
Khorramābād Iran 88 C3
Khorramshahr Iran 88 C4
Khorugh Tajik. 89 H2
Khosheutovo Russia 43 J7
Khoshgort Russia 41 T2
Khōst Afgh. 89 H3
Khōst reg. Afgh./Pak. 89 H3
Khosūyeh Iran 88 D4
Khotan China see Hotan
Khouribga Morocco 54 C5
Khovaling Tajik. 89 H2
Khowrjān Iran 88 D4
Khreum Myanmar 70 A2
Khroma r. Russia 65 P2
Khromtau Kazakh. 80 A1
Khrushchev Ukr. see Svitlovods'k
Khrysokhou Bay Cyprus see Chrysochou Bay
Khrystynivka Ukr. 43 F6
Khudumelapye Botswana 100 G2
Khudzhand Tajik. see Khŭjand
Khufaysah, Khashm al hill Saudi Arabia 88 B6
Khugiana Afgh. see Pīr Zādah
Khuis Botswana 100 E4
Khŭjand Tajik. 80 C3
Khŭjayli Uzbek. see Xo'jayli
Khu Khan Thai. 71 D4
Khulays Saudi Arabia 86 E5
Khulkhuta Russia 43 J7
Khulm Afgh. 89 G2
Khulm, Daryā-ye r. Afgh. 89 G2
Khulna Bangl. 83 G5
Khulo Georgia 91 F2
Khuma S. Africa 101 H4
Khunayzīr, Jabal al mts Syria 85 C2
Khūnīk Iran 88 E3
Khūnīnshahr Iran see Khorramshahr
Khunjerab Pass China/Pak. 82 C1
Khun Yuam Thai. 70 B3
Khūr Iran 88 E3
Khūran sea chan. Iran 88 D5
Khurays Saudi Arabia 86 G4
Khurda India see Khordha
Khurdha India see Khordha
Khurja India 82 D3
Khurmāliq Afgh. 89 F3
Khurmuli Russia 74 E2
Khushab Pak. 89 I3
Khushalgarh Pak. 89 H3
Khushshah, Wādī al watercourse Jordan/Saudi Arabia 85 C5
Khust Ukr. 43 D6
Khutse Game Reserve nature res. Botswana 100 G2
Khutsong S. Africa 101 H4
Khutu r. Russia 74 E2
Khuzdar Pak. 89 G5
Khvāf Iran 89 F3
Khvāf reg. Iran 89 F3
Khvājeh Iran 88 B2
Khvalynsk Russia 43 K5
Khvānsār Iran 88 C3
Khvodrān Iran 88 D4
Khvormūj Iran 88 C4
Khvors Iran 88 D3
Khvoy Iran 88 B2
Khvoynaya Russia 42 G4
Khwaja Amran mt. Pak. 89 G4
Khwājah Dū Kōh hill Afgh. 89 G2
Khwājah Muḥammad, Kōh-e mts Afgh. 89 H2
Khyber Pakhtunkhwa prov. Pak. 89 H3
Khyber Pass Afgh./Pak. 89 H3
Kiama Australia 112 E5
Kiamichi r. U.S.A. 131 E5
Kiangsi prov. China see Jiangxi
Kiangsu prov. China see Jiangsu
Kiantajärvi l. Fin. 44 P4
Kīāsar Iran 88 D2
Kiatassuaq i. Greenland 119 M2
Kibaha Tanz. 99 D4
Kibali r. Dem. Rep. Congo 98 C3
Kibangou Congo 98 B4
Kibaya Tanz. 99 D4
Kiboga Uganda 98 D3
Kibombo Dem. Rep. Congo 98 C4
Kibondo Tanz. 98 D4
Kibre Mengist Eth. 97 G4
Kibris country Asia see Cyprus
Kibungo Rwanda 98 D4
Kičevo Macedonia 59 I4
Kichmengskiy Gorodok Russia 42 J4
Kiçik Qafqaz mts Asia see Lesser Caucasus
Kicking Horse Pass Canada 120 G5
Kidal Mali 96 D3
Kidderminster U.K. 49 E6
Kidepo Valley National Park Uganda 98 D3
Kidira Senegal 96 B3
Kidmang India 82 D2
Kidnappers, Cape N.Z. 113 F4
Kidsgrove U.K. 49 E5
Kiel Germany 47 M3
Kiel U.S.A. 134 A2
Kiel Canal Germany 47 L3
Kielce Poland 47 R5
Kielder Water resr U.K. 48 E3
Kieler Bucht b. Germany 47 M3
Kienge Dem. Rep. Congo 99 C5
Kierspe Germany 53 H3

▶Kiev Ukr. 43 F6
Capital of Ukraine.

Kiffa Mauritania 96 B3
Kifisia Greece 59 J5
Kifrī Iraq 91 G4

▶Kigali Rwanda 98 D4
Capital of Rwanda.

Kiğı Turkey 91 F3
Kiglapait Mountains Canada 123 J2
Kigoma Tanz. 99 C4
Kihlanki Fin. 44 M3
Kihniö Fin. 44 M5
Kīholo U.S.A. 127 [inset]
Kiiminki Fin. 44 N4
Kii-sanchi mts Japan 75 D6
Kii-suidō sea chan. Japan 75 D6
Kikerino Russia 45 P7
Kikinda Serbia 59 I2
Kikki Pak. 89 F5
Kikládhes is Greece see Cyclades
Kiknur Russia 42 J4
Kikonai Japan 74 F4
Kikori P.N.G. 69 K8
Kikori r. P.N.G. 69 K8
Kikwit Dem. Rep. Congo 99 B4
Kilafors Sweden 45 J6
Kilar India 82 D2
Kīlauea U.S.A. 127 [inset]
Kīlauea Volcano U.S.A. 127 [inset]
Kilchu N. Korea 74 C4
Kilcoole Ireland 51 F4
Kilcormac Ireland 51 E4
Kilcoy Australia 112 F1
Kildare Ireland 51 F4
Kil'dinstroy Russia 44 R2
Kilemary Russia 42 J4
Kilembe Dem. Rep. Congo 99 B4
Kilfinan U.K. 50 D5
Kilgore U.S.A. 131 E5
Kilham U.K. 48 E3
Kilia Ukr. see Kiliya
Kılıç Dağı mt. Syria/Turkey see Aqra', Jabal al
Kilifi Kenya 98 D4
Kilik Pass China 82 C1

▶Kilimanjaro vol. Tanz. 98 D4
Highest mountain in Africa.

Kilimanjaro National Park Tanz. 98 D4
Kilinailau Islands P.N.G. 106 F2
Kilindoni Tanz. 99 D4
Kilingi-Nõmme Estonia 45 N7
Kilis Turkey 85 C1
Kilis prov. Turkey 85 C1
Kiliya Ukr. 59 M2
Kilkee Ireland 51 C5
Kilkeel U.K. 51 G3
Kilkenny Ireland 51 E5
Kilkhampton U.K. 49 C8
Kilkis Greece 59 J4
Killala Ireland 51 C3
Killala Bay Ireland 51 C3
Killaloe Ireland 51 D5
Killam Canada 121 I4
Killarney N.T. Australia 108 E4
Killarney Qld Australia 112 F2
Killarney Canada 122 E5
Killarney Ireland 51 C5
Killarney National Park Ireland 51 C6
Killary Harbour b. Ireland 51 C4
Killbuck U.S.A. 134 E3
Killeen U.S.A. 131 D6
Killenaule Ireland 51 E5
Killimor Ireland 51 D4
Killin U.K. 50 E4
Killinchy U.K. 51 G3
Killíni mt. Greece see Kyllini
Killinick Ireland 51 F5
Killorglin Ireland 51 C5
Killurin Ireland 51 F5
Killybegs Ireland 51 D3
Kilmacrenan Ireland 51 E2
Kilmaine Ireland 51 C4
Kilmallock Ireland 51 D5
Kilmaluag U.K. 50 C3
Kilmarnock U.K. 50 E5
Kilmelford U.K. 50 D4
Kil'mez' Russia 42 K4
Kil'mez' r. Russia 42 K4
Kilmona Ireland 51 D6
Kilmore Australia 112 B6
Kilmore Quay Ireland 51 F5
Kilosa Tanz. 99 D4
Kilpisjärvi Fin. 44 L2
Kilrea U.K. 51 F3
Kilrush Ireland 51 C5
Kilsyth U.K. 50 E5
Kiltan atoll India 84 B4
Kiltullagh Ireland 51 D4
Kilwa Masoko Tanz. 99 D4
Kilwinning U.K. 50 E5
Kim U.S.A. 131 C4
Kimba Australia 109 G8
Kimba Congo 98 B4
Kimball U.S.A. 130 C3
Kimball, Mount U.S.A. 118 D3
Kimbe P.N.G. 106 F2
Kimberley S. Africa 100 G5
Kimberley Plateau Australia 108 D4
Kimberley Range hills Australia 109 B6
Kimch'aek N. Korea 75 C4
Kimhae S. Korea see Gimhae
Kimhandu mt. Tanz. 99 D4
Kími Greece see Kymi
Kimito Fin. 45 M6
Kimjŏngsuk N. Korea 74 B4
Kimmirut Canada 119 L3
Kimolos i. Greece 59 K6
Kimovsk Russia 43 H5
Kimpese Dem. Rep. Congo 99 B4
Kimpoku-san mt. Japan see Kinpoku-san
Kimry Russia 42 H4
Kimsquit Canada 120 E4
Kimvula Dem. Rep. Congo 99 B4
Kinabalu, Gunung mt. Sabah Malaysia 68 F5
Kinango Kenya 99 D4
Kinaskan Lake Canada 120 D3
Kinbasket Lake Canada 120 G4
Kinbrace U.K. 50 F2
Kincaid Canada 121 J5
Kincardine Canada 134 E1
Kincardine U.K. 50 F4
Kinchega National Park Australia 111 C7
Kincolith Canada see Gingolx
Kinda Dem. Rep. Congo 99 C4
Kindat Myanmar 70 A2
Kinde U.S.A. 134 D2
Kinder Scout hill U.K. 48 F5
Kindersley Canada 121 I5
Kindia Guinea 96 B3
Kindu Dem. Rep. Congo 98 C4
Kinel' Russia 43 K5
Kineshma Russia 42 I4
King Abdullah Economic City Saudi Arabia 78 C4
Kingaroy Australia 112 E1
King Christian Island Canada 119 H2
King City U.S.A. 128 C3
King Edward VII Land pen. Antarctica see Edward VII Peninsula
Kingfield U.S.A. 135 J1
Kingfisher U.S.A. 131 D5
King George U.S.A. 135 G4
King George, Mount Canada 126 E2
King George Island Antarctica 152 A2
King George Islands Canada 122 F2
King George Islands Fr. Polynesia see Roi Georges, Îles du
King Hill hill Australia 108 C5
Kingisepp Russia 45 P7
King Island Australia 111 [inset]
King Island Canada 120 E4
King Island Myanmar see Kadan Kyun
Kingisseppa Estonia see Kuressaare
Kinglake National Park Australia 112 B6
King Leopold and Queen Astrid Coast Antarctica 152 E2
King Leopold Range National Park Australia 108 D4
King Leopold Ranges hills Australia 108 D4
Kingman U.S.A. 129 F4

▶Kingman Reef terr. N. Pacific Ocean 150 J5
United States Unincorporated Territory.

King Mountain Canada 120 D3
King Mountain hill U.S.A. 131 C6
Kingoonya Australia 111 A6
King Peak Antarctica 152 L1
King Peninsula Antarctica 152 K2
Kingri Pak. 89 H4
Kings r. Ireland 51 E5
Kings r. CA U.S.A. 128 C3
Kings r. NV U.S.A. 126 D4
King Salmon U.S.A. 118 C4
Kingsbridge U.K. 49 D8
Kingsburg U.S.A. 128 D3
Kings Canyon National Park U.S.A. 128 D3
Kingscliff Australia 112 F2
Kingscote Australia 111 B7
Kingscourt Ireland 51 F4
King Sejong research station Antarctica 152 A2
King's Lynn U.K. 49 H6
Kingsmill Group is Kiribati 107 H2
Kingsnorth U.K. 49 H7
King Sound b. Australia 108 C4
Kings Peak U.S.A. 129 H1
Kingsport U.S.A. 132 D4
Kingston Australia 111 [inset]
Kingston Canada 135 G1

▶Kingston Jamaica 137 I5
Capital of Jamaica.

▶Kingston Norfolk I. 107 G4
Capital of Norfolk Island.

Kingston MO U.S.A. 130 E4
Kingston NY U.S.A. 135 H3
Kingston OH U.S.A. 134 D4
Kingston PA U.S.A. 135 H3
Kingston Peak U.S.A. 129 F4
Kingston South East Australia 111 B8
Kingston upon Hull U.K. 48 G5

▶Kingstown St Vincent 137 L6
Capital of St Vincent.

Kingstree U.S.A. 133 E5
Kingsville U.S.A. 131 D7
Kingswood U.K. 49 E7
Kington U.K. 49 D6
Kingungi Dem. Rep. Congo 99 B4
Kingurutik r. Canada 123 J2
Kingussie U.K. 50 E3
King William U.S.A. 135 G5
King William Island Canada 119 I3
King William's Town S. Africa 101 H7
Kingwood TX U.S.A. 131 E6
Kingwood WV U.S.A. 134 F4
Kinloch N.Z. 113 B7
Kinloss U.K. 50 F3
Kinmen Taiwan see Jinmen
Kinmen i. Taiwan see Jinmen Dao
Kinmount Canada 135 F1
Kinna Sweden 45 H8
Kinnegad Ireland 51 E4
Kinneret, Yam l. Israel see Galilee, Sea of
Kinniyai Sri Lanka 84 D4
Kinnula Fin. 44 N5
Kinoje r. Canada 122 E3
Kinoosao Canada 121 K3
Kinpoku-san mt. Japan 75 E5
Kinross U.K. 50 F4
Kinsale Ireland 51 D6
Kinsale U.S.A. 135 G4

▶Kinshasa Dem. Rep. Congo 99 B4
Capital of the Democratic Republic of the Congo. 3rd most populous city in Africa.

Kinsley U.S.A. 130 D4
Kinsman U.S.A. 134 E3
Kinston U.S.A. 133 E5
Kintore U.K. 50 G3
Kintyre pen. U.K. 50 D5
Kin-U Myanmar 70 A2
Kinushseo r. Canada 122 E3
Kinyeti mt. South Sudan 97 G4
Kinzig r. Germany 53 I4
Kiowa CO U.S.A. 126 G5
Kiowa KS U.S.A. 131 D4
Kipahigan Lake Canada 121 K4
Kiparissía Greece see Kyparissia
Kipawa, Lac l. Canada 122 F5
Kipling Canada 121 K5
Kipling Station Canada see Kipling
Kipnuk U.S.A. 118 B4
Kiptopeke U.S.A. 135 H5
Kipungo Angola see Quipungo
Kipushi Dem. Rep. Congo 99 C5
Kirakira Solomon Is 107 G3
Kirandul India 84 D2
Kirchdorf Germany 53 I2
Kirchheimbolanden Germany 53 I5
Kirchheim unter Teck Germany 53 J6
Kircubbin U.K. 51 G3
Kirdimi Chad 97 E3
Kirenga r. Russia 73 J1
Kirensk Russia 65 L4
Kireyevsk Russia 43 H5
Kirghizia country Asia see Kyrgyzstan
Kirghiz Range mts Kazakh./Kyrg. 80 D3
Kirgizskaya S.S.R. country Asia see Kyrgyzstan
Kirgizskiy Khrebet mts Kazakh./Kyrg. see Kirghiz Range
Kirgizstan country Asia see Kyrgyzstan
Kiri Dem. Rep. Congo 98 B4
Kiribati country Pacific Ocean 150 I6
Kırıkhan Turkey 85 C1
Kırıkkale Turkey 90 D3
Kirillov Russia 42 H4
Kirillovo (abandoned) Russia 74 F3
Kirin China see Jilin
Kirin prov. China see Jilin
Kirinda Sri Lanka 84 D5
Kirinyaga mt. Kenya see Kenya, Mount
Kirishi Russia 42 G4
Kirishima-Yaku Kokuritsu-kōen nat. park Japan 75 C7
Kirishima-yama vol. Japan 75 C7
Kiritimati atoll Kiribati 151 J5
Kiriwina Islands P.N.G. see Trobriand Islands
Kırkağaç Turkey 59 L5
Kirk Bulāg Dāgi mt. Iran 88 B2
Kirkby U.K. 48 E5
Kirkby in Ashfield U.K. 49 F5
Kirkby Lonsdale U.K. 48 E4
Kirkby Stephen U.K. 48 E4
Kirkcaldy U.K. 50 F4
Kirkcolm U.K. 50 D6
Kirkcudbright U.K. 50 E6
Kirkenær Norway 45 H6
Kirkenes Norway 44 Q2
Kirkfield Canada 135 F1
Kirkintilloch U.K. 50 E5
Kirkkonummi Fin. 45 N6
Kirkland U.S.A. 129 G4
Kirkland Lake Canada 122 E4
Kırklareli Turkey 59 L4
Kirklin U.S.A. 134 B3
Kirk Michael Isle of Man 48 C4
Kirkoswald U.K. 48 E4
Kirkpatrick, Mount Antarctica 152 H1
Kirksville U.S.A. 130 E3
Kirkūk Iraq 91 G4
Kirkwall U.K. 50 G2
Kirkwood S. Africa 101 G7
Kirman Iran see Kermān
Kirn Germany 53 H5
Kirov Kaluzhskaya Oblast' Russia 43 G5
Kirov Kirovskaya Oblast' Russia 42 K4
Kirova, imeni Kazakh. see Kopbirlik
Kirova, Zaliv b. Azer. see Qızılağac Körfäzi
Kirovabad Azer. see Gäncä
Kirovabad Tajik. see Panj
Kirovakan Armenia see Vanadzor
Kirovo Ukr. see Kirovohrad
Kirovo-Chepetsk Russia 42 K4
Kirovo-Chepetskiy Russia see Kirovo-Chepetsk
Kirovograd Ukr. see Kirovohrad
Kirovohrad Ukr. 43 G6
Kirovsk Leningradskaya Oblast' Russia 42 F4
Kirovsk Murmanskaya Oblast' Russia 44 R3
Kirovsk Turkm. see Badabaýhan
Kirovs'ke Crimea 90 D1
Kirovskiy Amurskaya Oblast' Russia 74 B1
Kirovskiy Primorskiy Kray Russia 74 D3
Kirovskoye Crimea see Kirovs'ke
Kırpaşa pen. Cyprus see Karpasia
Kirpili Turkm. 88 E2
Kirriemuir U.K. 50 F4
Kirs Russia 42 L4
Kirsanov Russia 43 I5
Kırşehir Turkey 90 D3
Kirthar National Park Pak. 89 G5
Kirthar Range mts Pak. 89 G5
Kirtland U.S.A. 129 I3
Kirtorf Germany 53 J4
Kiruna Sweden 44 L3
Kirundu Dem. Rep. Congo 98 C4
Kirwan Escarpment Antarctica 152 B2
Kiryū Japan 75 E5
Kisa Sweden 45 I8
Kisama, Parque Nacional de nat. park Angola see Quiçama, Parque Nacional do
Kisandji Dem. Rep. Congo 99 B4
Kisangani Dem. Rep. Congo 98 C3
Kisantu Dem. Rep. Congo 99 B4
Kisar i. Indon. 108 D2
Kisaran Indon. 71 B7
Kiselevka Russia 74 E2
Kiselevsk Russia 72 F2
Kīsh, Jazīreh-ye i. Iran 88 D5
Kishanganj India 83 F4
Kishangarh Madh. Prad. India 82 D4
Kishangarh Rajasthan India 82 B4
Kishangarh Rajasthan India 82 C4
Kishangarh Rajasthan India 82 D4
Kishi Nigeria 96 D4
Kishim Afgh. 89 H2
Kishindih-ye Bālā Afgh. 89 G2
Kishinev Moldova see Chişinău
Kishkenekol' Kazakh. 79 G1
Kishoreganj Bangl. 83 G4
Kishorganj Bangl. see Kishoreganj
Kisi Nigeria see Kishi
Kisii Kenya 98 D4
Kiska Island U.S.A. 65 S4
Kiskittogisu Lake Canada 121 L4
Kiskitto Lake Canada 121 L4
Kiskunfélegyháza Hungary 59 H1
Kiskunhalas Hungary 59 H1
Kiskunsági nat. park Hungary 59 H1
Kislovodsk Russia 91 F2
Kismaayo Somalia 98 E4
Kismayu Somalia see Kismaayo
Kisoro Uganda 97 F5
Kispiox Canada 120 E4
Kispiox r. Canada 120 E4
Kissamos Greece 59 J7
Kisseraing Island Myanmar see Kanmaw Kyun
Kissidougou Guinea 96 B4
Kissimmee U.S.A. 133 D6
Kissimmee, Lake U.S.A. 133 D7
Kississing Lake Canada 121 K4
Kistendey Russia 43 I5
Kistigan Lake Canada 121 M4
Kistna r. India see Krishna
Kisumu Kenya 98 D4
Kisykkamys Kazakh. see Zhanakala
Kita Mali 96 C3
Kitab Uzbek. see Kitob
Kita-Daitō-jima i. Japan 73 O7
Kitaibaraki Japan 75 F5
Kita-Iō-jima vol. Japan 69 K1
Kitakami Japan 75 F5
Kita-Kyūshū Japan 75 C6
Kitale Kenya 98 D3
Kitami Japan 74 F4
Kit Carson U.S.A. 130 C4
Kitchener Canada 134 E2
Kitchigama r. Canada 122 F4
Kitee Fin. 44 Q5
Kitgum Uganda 98 D3
Kíthira i. Greece see Kythira
Kíthnos i. Greece see Kythnos
Kiti, Cape Cyprus see Kition, Cape
Kitimat Canada 120 D4
Kitinen r. Fin. 44 O3
Kition, Cape Cyprus 85 A2
Kitiou, Akra c. Cyprus see Kition, Cape
Kitkatla Canada 120 D4
Kitob Uzbek. 89 G2
Kitsault Canada 120 D4
Kittanning U.S.A. 134 F3
Kittatinny Mountains hills U.S.A. 135 H3
Kittery U.S.A. 135 J2
Kittilä Fin. 44 N3
Kittur India 84 B3
Kitty Hawk U.S.A. 132 F4
Kitui Kenya 98 D4
Kitwanga Canada 120 D4
Kitwe Zambia 99 C5
Kitzbüheler Alpen mts Austria 47 N7
Kitzingen Germany 53 K5
Kitzscher Germany 53 M3
Kiu Lom, Ang Kep Nam Thai. 70 B3
Kiunga P.N.G. 69 K8
Kiuruvesi Fin. 44 O5
Kivalina U.S.A. 118 B3
Kivijärvi Fin. 44 N5
Kiviõli Estonia 45 O7
Kivu, Lac Dem. Rep. Congo/Rwanda 98 C4
Kiwaba N'zogi Angola 99 B4
Kiwai Island P.N.G. 69 K8
Kiyev Ukr. see Kiev
Kiyevskoye Vodokhranilishche resr Ukr. see Kyivs'ke Vodoskhovyshche
Kıyıköy Turkey 59 M4
Kizel Russia 41 R4
Kizema Russia 42 J3
Kızılcadağ Turkey 59 M6
Kızılca Dağ mt. Turkey 90 C3
Kızılcahamam Turkey 90 D2
Kızıldağ mt. Turkey 85 A1
Kızıldağ mt. Turkey 85 B1
Kızıl Dağı mt. Turkey 90 E3
Kızılırmak Turkey 90 D2
Kızılırmak r. Turkey 90 D2
Kızıltepe Turkey 91 F3
Kizilyurt Russia 91 G2
Kızkalesi Turkey 85 B1
Kizlyar Russia 91 G2
Kizlyarskiy Zaliv b. Russia 91 G1
Kizner Russia 42 K4
Kizyl-Arbat Turkm. see Serdar
Kizyl-Atrek Turkm. see Etrek
Kjøllefjord Norway 44 O1
Kjøpsvik Norway 44 J2
Kladno Czechia 47 O5
Klagenfurt am Wörthersee Austria 47 O7
Klagetoh U.S.A. 129 I4
Klaipėda Lith. 45 L9
Klaksvík Faroe Is 44 [inset 2]
Klamath U.S.A. 126 B4
Klamath r. U.S.A. 118 F5
Klamath Falls U.S.A. 126 C4
Klamath Mountains U.S.A. 126 C4
Klang Malaysia 71 C7
Klarälven r. Sweden 45 H7
Klatovy Czechia 47 N6
Klawer S. Africa 100 D6
Klazienaveen Neth. 52 G2
Kleides Islands Cyprus 85 B2
Kleinbegin S. Africa 100 E5
Klein Karas Namibia 100 D4
Klein Nama Land reg. S. Africa see Namaqualand
Klein Roggeveldberge mts S. Africa 100 E7
Kleinsee S. Africa 100 C5
Klemtu Canada 120 D4
Klerksdorp S. Africa 101 H4
Kletnya Russia 43 G5
Kletsk Belarus see Klyetsk
Kletskaya Russia 43 I6
Kletskiy Russia see Kletskaya
Kleve Germany 52 G3
Klidhes Islands Cyprus see Kleides Islands
Klimkovka Russia 42 K4
Klimovo Russia 43 G5
Klin Russia 42 H4
Klingenberg am Main Germany 53 J5
Klingenthal Germany 53 M4
Klingkang, Banjaran mts Indon./Malaysia 68 E6
Klink Germany 53 M1
Klínovec mt. Czechia 53 N4
Klintehamn Sweden 45 K8
Klintsy Russia 43 G5
Ključ Bos. & Herz. 58 G2
Kłodzko Poland 47 P5
Klondike r. Canada 120 B1
Klondike Gold Rush National Historical Park nat. park U.S.A. 120 C3
Kloosterhaar Neth. 52 G2
Klosterneuburg Austria 47 P6
Klötze (Altmark) Germany 53 L2
Kluane Lake Canada 120 B2
Kluane National Park Canada 120 B2
Kluang Malaysia see Keluang

Kluczbork Poland 47 Q5
Klukhori Russia see Karachayevsk
Klukhorskiy, Pereval Georgia/Russia 91 F2
Klukwan U.S.A. 120 C3
Klyetsk Belarus 45 O10
Klyuchevskaya Sopka, Vulkan vol. Russia 65 R4
Klyuchi Russia 74 B2
Knåda Sweden 45 I6
Knaresborough U.K. 48 F4
Knee Lake Man. Canada 121 M4
Knee Lake Sask. Canada 121 J4
Knetzgau Germany 53 K5
Knife r. U.S.A. 130 C2
Knight Inlet Canada 120 E5
Knighton U.K. 49 D6
Knights Landing U.S.A. 128 C2
Knightstown U.S.A. 134 C4
Knin Croatia 58 G2
Knittelfeld Austria 47 O7
Knjaževac Serbia 59 J3
Knob Lake Canada see Schefferville
Knob Lick U.S.A. 134 C5
Knob Peak hill Australia 108 E3
Knock Ireland 51 D4
Knockalongy hill Ireland 51 D3
Knockalough Ireland 51 C5
Knockanaffrin hill Ireland 51 E5
Knockboy hill Ireland 51 C6
Knock Hill hill U.K. 50 G3
Knockmealdown Mountains hills Ireland 51 D5
Knocknaskagh hill Ireland 51 D5
Knokke-Heist Belgium 52 D3
Knorrendorf Germany 53 N1
Knowle U.K. 49 F6
Knowlton Canada 135 I1
Knox IN U.S.A. 134 B3
Knox PA U.S.A. 134 F3
Knox, Cape Canada 120 C4
Knox Coast Antarctica 152 F2
Knoxville GA U.S.A. 133 D5
Knoxville TN U.S.A. 132 D5
Knud Rasmussen Land reg. Greenland 119 L2
Knysna S. Africa 100 F8
Ko, Gora mt. Russia 74 E3
Koartac Canada see Quaqtaq
Koba Indon. 68 D7
Kobanê Syria see 'Ayn al 'Arab
Kobbfoss Norway 44 P2
Kobda Kazakh. 80 A1
Kōbe Japan 75 D6
København Denmark see Copenhagen
Kobenni Mauritania 96 C3
Koblenz Germany 53 H4
Koboldo Russia 74 D1
Kobrin Belarus see Kobryn
Kobroör i. Indon. 69 I8
Kobryn Belarus 45 N10
Kobuk Valley National Park U.S.A. 118 C3
Kobuleti Georgia 91 F2
Kocaeli Turkey see İzmit
Kocaeli Yarımadası pen. Turkey 59 M4
Kočani Macedonia 59 J4
Kocasu r. Turkey 59 M4
Kočevje Slovenia 58 F2
Koch Bihar India 83 G4
Kocher r. Germany 53 J5
Kochevo Russia 41 Q4
Kochi India 84 C4
Kōchi Japan 75 D6
Koçhisar Turkey see Kızıltepe
Koch Island Canada 119 K3
Kochkor Kyrg. 80 E3
Kochkorka Kyrg. see Kochkor
Kochkurovo Russia 43 J5
Kochubeyevskoye Russia 91 F1
Kod India 84 B3
Kodala India 84 E2
Kodarma India 83 F4
Koderma India see Kodarma
Kodiak U.S.A. 118 C4
Kodiak Island U.S.A. 118 C4
Kodibeleng Botswana 101 H2
Kodino Russia 42 H3
Kodiyakkarai India 84 C4
Kodok South Sudan 86 D8
Kodyma Ukr. 43 F6
Kodzhaele mt. Bulg./Greece 59 K4
Koedoesberg mts S. Africa 100 E7
Koegrabie S. Africa 100 E5
Koekenaap S. Africa 100 D6
Koersel Belgium 52 F3
Koës Namibia 100 D3
Kofa Mountains U.S.A. 129 G5
Koffiefontein S. Africa 100 G5
Koforidua Ghana 96 C4
Kōfu Japan 75 E6
Kogaluc r. Canada 122 F2
Kogaluc, Baie de b. Canada 122 F2
Kogaluk r. Canada 123 J2
Kogan Australia 112 E1
Køge Denmark 45 H9
Kogon r. Guinea 96 B3
Kogon Uzbek. 89 G2
Kohan Pak. 89 G5
Kohat Pak. 89 H3
Koh-e Şayyād Afgh. 89 G2
Kōhestān reg. Afgh. 89 H3
Kohila Estonia 45 N7
Kohima India 83 H4
Kohistan reg. Pak. 89 I3
Kōhistānāt Afgh. 89 G3
Kohler Range mts Antarctica 152 K2
Kohlu Pak. 89 H4
Kohtla-Järve Estonia 45 O7
Koidern Mountain Canada 120 A2
Koidu Sierra Leone see Koidu-Sefadu
Koidu-Sefadu Sierra Leone 96 B4
Koihoa India 71 A5
Koilkonda India 84 C2
Koin N. Korea 75 B4
Koin r. Russia 42 K3
Kojonup Australia 109 B8
Kokand Uzbek. see Qo'qon
Kōkar Fin. 45 L7
Kokchetav Kazakh. see Kokshetau
Kokemäenjoki r. Fin. 45 L6
Kokerboom Namibia 100 D5
Ko Kha Thai. 70 B3
Kokkilai Sri Lanka 84 D4
Kokkola Fin. 44 M5
Koko Nigeria 96 D3
Kokomo U.S.A. 134 B3
Kokong Botswana 100 F3
Kokos i. Indon. 71 A7
Kokosi S. Africa 101 H4
Kokpekty Kazakh. 80 F2
Koksan N. Korea 75 B5
Kokshaal-Tau, Khrebet mts China/Kyrg. see Kakshaal-Too
Koksharka Russia 42 J4
Kokshetau Kazakh. 79 F1
Koksoak r. Canada 123 H2
Kokstad S. Africa 101 I6
Koktal Kazakh. 80 E3
Kokterek Kazakh. 43 K6
Kola i. Indon. 69 I8
Kola Russia 44 R2
Kolachi r. Pak. 89 G5
Kolahoi mt. India 82 C2
Kolaka Indon. 69 G7
Ko Lanta Thai. 71 B6
Kola Peninsula Russia 42 H2
Kolar Chhattisgarh India 84 D2
Kolar Karnataka India 84 C3
Kolār, Kūh-e hill Iran 88 C4
Kolaras India 82 D4
Kolar Gold Fields India 84 C3
Kolari Fin. 44 M3
Kolarovgrad Bulg. see Shumen
Kolasib India 83 H4
Kolayat India 82 C4
Kolberg Poland see Kołobrzeg
Kol'chugino Russia 42 H4
Kolda Senegal 96 B3
Kolding Denmark 45 F9
Kole Kasaï-Oriental Dem. Rep. Congo 98 C4
Kole Orientale Dem. Rep. Congo 98 C3
Koléa Alg. 57 H5
Koler Sweden 44 L4
Kolguyev, Ostrov i. Russia 42 K1
Kolhan reg. India 83 F5
Kolhapur India 84 B2
Kolhumadulu Maldives 81 D11
Kolikata India see Kolkata
Kõljala Estonia 45 M7
Kolkasrags pt Latvia 45 M8
Kolkata India 83 G5
Kolkhozabad Khatlon Tajik. see Vose'
Kolkhozabad Khatlon Tajik. see Kolkhozobod
Kolkhozobod Tajik. 89 H2
Kollam India 84 C4
Kolleru Lake India 84 D2
Kollum Neth. 52 G1
Kolmanskop (abandoned) Namibia 100 B4
Köln Germany see Cologne
Köln-Bonn airport Germany 53 H4
Kołobrzeg Poland 47 O3
Kologriv Russia 42 J4
Kolokani Mali 96 C3
Kolombangara i. Solomon Is 107 F2
Kolomea Ukr. see Kolomyya
Kolomna Russia 43 H5
Kołomyja Ukr. see Kolomyya
Kolomyya Ukr. 43 E6
Kolondiéba Mali 96 C3
Kolonedale Indon. 69 G7
Koloni Cyprus 85 A2
Kolonkwaneng Botswana 100 E4
Kolozsvár Romania see Cluj-Napoca
Kolpashevo Russia 64 J4
Kol'skiy Poluostrov pen. Russia see Kola Peninsula
Kölük Turkey see Kahta
Koluli Eritrea 86 F7
Kolumadulu Atoll Maldives see Kolhumadulu
Kolva r. Russia 42 M2
Kolvan India 84 B2
Kolvereid Norway 44 G4
Kolvik Norway 44 N1
Kolvitskoye, Ozero l. Russia 44 R3
Kolwa reg. Pak. 89 G5
Kolwezi Dem. Rep. Congo 99 C5
Kolyma r. Russia 65 R3
Kolyma Lowland Russia see Kolymskaya Nizmennost'
Kolyma Range mts Russia see Kolymskoye Nagor'ye
Kolymskaya Nizmennost' lowland Russia 65 Q3
Kolymskoye Nagor'ye mts Russia 65 R3
Kolyshley Russia 43 J5
Kom mt. Bulg. 59 J3
Komadugu-Gana watercourse Nigeria 96 E3
Komaggas S. Africa 100 C5
Komaio P.N.G. 69 K8
Komaki Japan 75 E6
Komandnaya, Gora mt. Russia 74 E2
Komandorskiye Ostrova is Russia 65 R4
Komárno Slovakia 47 Q7
Komati r. Swaziland 101 J3
Komatipoort S. Africa 101 J3
Komatsu Japan 75 E5
Komba i. Indon. 108 C1
Komga S. Africa 101 H7
Komintern Ukr. see Marhanets'
Kominternivs'ke Ukr. 59 N1
Komiža Croatia 58 G3
Komló Hungary 58 H1
Kommunarsk Ukr. see Alchevs'k
Komodo, Taman Nasional nat. park Indon. 108 B2
Kôm Ombo Egypt see Kawm Umbū
Komono Congo 98 B4
Komoran i. Indon. 69 J8
Komotini Greece 59 K4
Kompong Cham Cambodia see Kâmpóng Cham
Kompong Chhnang Cambodia see Kâmpóng Chhnăng
Kompong Kleang Cambodia see Kâmpóng Khleăng
Kompong Som Cambodia see Sihanoukville
Kompong Speu Cambodia see Kâmpóng Spœ
Kompong Thom Cambodia see Kâmpóng Thum
Komrat Moldova see Comrat
Komsberg mts S. Africa 100 E7
Komsomol Kazakh. see Karabalyk
Komsomolabad Tajik. see Darband
Komsomolets Kazakh. see Karabalyk
Komsomolets, Ostrov i. Russia 64 K1
Komsomol's'k Ukr. 43 G6
Komsomol'skiy Chukotskiy Avtonomnyy Okrug Russia 153 C2
Komsomol'skiy Khanty-Mansiyskiy Avtonomnyy Okrug-Yugra Russia see Yugorsk
Komsomol'skiy Respublika Kalmykiya-Khalm'g-Tangch Russia 43 J7
Komsomol'sk-na-Amure Russia 74 E2
Komsomol'skoye Kazakh. 80 B1
Komsomol'skoye Russia 43 J6
Kömürlü Turkey 91 F2
Kon India 83 E4
Konacık Turkey 85 B1
Konada India 84 D2
Konarak India see Konarka
Konarka India 83 F6
Konch India 82 D4
Kondagaon India 84 D2
Kondinin Australia 109 B8
Kondinskoye Russia see Oktyabr'skoye
Kondoa Tanz. 99 D4
Kondol' Russia 43 J5
Kondopoga Russia 42 G3
Kondoz Afgh. see Kunduz
Kondrovo Russia 43 G5
Köneürgenç Turkm. 87 I1
Kong Cameroon 96 E4
Kông, Kaôh i. Cambodia 71 C5
Kông, Tônlé r. Cambodia 71 D4
Kong, Xé r. Laos 70 D4
Kong Christian IX Land reg. Greenland 119 O3
Kong Christian X Land reg. Greenland 119 P2
Kongelab atoll Marshall Is see Rongelap
Kong Frederik IX Land reg. Greenland 119 M3
Kong Frederik VI Kyst coastal area Greenland 119 N3
Kongolo Dem. Rep. Congo 99 C4
Kongor South Sudan 97 G4
Kong Oscars Fjord inlet Greenland 119 P2
Kongoussi Burkina Faso 96 C3
Kongsberg Norway 45 F7
Kongsvinger Norway 45 H6
Kongur Shan mt. China 80 E4
Königsberg Russia see Kaliningrad
Königsee Germany 53 L4
Königswinter Germany 53 H4
Königs Wusterhausen Germany 53 N2
Konimekh Uzbek. see Konimex
Konimex Uzbek. 89 G1
Konin Poland 47 Q4
Konjic Bos. & Herz. 58 G3
Konkiep watercourse Namibia 100 C5
Kon Kriel Cambodia 71 C4
Könnern Germany 53 L3
Konnevesi Fin. 44 O5
Konosha Russia 42 I3
Konotop Ukr. 43 G6
Konpara India 83 E5
Kon Plông Vietnam 71 E4
Konqi He r. China 80 G3
Konso Eth. 98 D3
Konso Cultural Landscape tourist site Eth. 97 G4
Konstantinograd Ukr. see Krasnohrad
Konstantinovka Russia 74 B2
Konstantinovka Ukr. see Kostyantynivka
Konstantinovy Lázně Czechia 53 M5
Konstanz Germany 47 L7
Kontha Myanmar 70 B2
Kontiolahti Fin. 44 P5
Konttila Fin. 44 O4
Kon Tum Vietnam 71 D4
Kon Tum, Cao Nguyên Vietnam 71 E4
Könugard Ukr. see Kiev
Konushin, Mys pt Russia 42 I2
Konya Turkey 90 D3
Konz Germany 52 G5
Konzhakovskiy Kamen', Gora mt. Russia 41 R4
Koocanusa, Lake resr Canada/U.S.A. 120 H5
Kooch Bihar India see Koch Bihar
Kookynie Australia 109 C7
Koolyanobbing Australia 109 B7
Koondrook Australia 112 B5
Koorawatha Australia 112 D5
Koordarrie Australia 108 A5
Kootenay r. Canada 120 G5
Kootenay Lake Canada 120 G5
Kootenay National Park Canada 120 G5
Kootjieskolk S. Africa 100 E6
Kópasker Iceland 44 [inset 1]
Kopbirlik Kazakh. 80 E2
Koper Slovenia 58 E2
Kopet Dag mts Iran/Turkm. 88 E2
Kopet-Dag, Khrebet mts Iran/Turkm. see Kopet Dag
Köpetdag Gershi mts Iran/Turkm. see Kopet Dag
Kopili r. India 83 G4
Köping Sweden 45 J7
Köpmanholmen Sweden 44 K5
Kopong Botswana 101 G3
Koppal India 84 C3
Koppang Norway 45 G6
Kopparberg Sweden 45 I7
Koppeh Dāgh mts Iran/Turkm. see Kopet Dag
Köppel hill Germany 53 H4
Koppi r. Russia 74 F2
Koppies S. Africa 101 H4
Koppieskraal Pan salt pan S. Africa 100 E4
Koprivnica Croatia 58 G1
Köprülü Turkey 85 A1
Köprülü Kanyon Milli Parkı nat. park Turkey 59 N6
Kopyl' Belarus see Kapyl'
Kora India 82 E4
Korablino Russia 43 I5
K'orahē Eth. 98 E3
Korak Pak. 89 G5
Koramlik China 83 F1
Korangal India 84 C2
Korangi Pak. 89 G5
Koraput India 84 D2
Korat Thai. see Nakhon Ratchasima
Koratla India 84 C2
Korba India 83 E5
Korbach Germany 53 I3
Korçë Albania 59 I4
Korčula Croatia 58 G3
Korčula i. Croatia 58 G3
Korčulanski Kanal sea chan. Croatia 58 G3
Korday Kazakh. 80 D3
Kord Küy Iran 88 D2
Kords reg. Iran 89 F5
Korea, North country Asia 75 B5
Korea, South country Asia 75 B5
Korea Bay g. China/N. Korea 75 B5
Korea Strait Japan/S. Korea 75 C6
Koregaon India 84 B2
Korenovsk Russia 91 E1
Korenovskaya Russia see Korenovsk
Korepino Russia 41 R3
Korets' Ukr. 43 E6
Körfez Turkey 59 M4
Korff Ice Rise Antarctica 152 L1
Korfovskiy Russia 74 D2
Korgalzhyn Kazakh. 80 D1
Korgen Norway 44 H3
Korhogo Côte d'Ivoire 96 C4
Koribundu Sierra Leone 96 B4
Kori Creek inlet India 82 B5
Korinthiakos Kolpos sea chan. Greece see Corinth, Gulf of
Korinthos Greece see Corinth
Kőris-hegy hill Hungary 58 G1
Koritnik mt. Albania 59 I3
Koritsa Albania see Korçë
Kōriyama Japan 75 F5
Korkuteli Turkey 59 N6
Korla China 80 G3
Kormakitis, Cape Cyprus 85 A2
Körmend Hungary 58 G1
Kornati, Nacionalni Park nat. park Croatia 58 F3
Korneyevka Russia 43 K6
Koro Côte d'Ivoire 96 C4
Koro i. Fiji 107 H3
Koro Mali 96 C3
Koroc r. Canada 123 I2
Köroğlu Dağları mts Turkey 59 O4
Köroğlu Tepesi mt. Turkey 90 D2
Korogwe Tanz. 99 D4
Koroneia, Limni l. Greece 59 J4
Korong Vale Australia 112 A6
Koronia, Limni l. Greece see Koroneia, Limni

▶Koror Palau 69 I5
Former capital of Palau.

Koro Sea b. Fiji 107 H3
Korosten' Ukr. 43 F6
Korostyshiv Ukr. 43 F6
Koro Toro Chad 97 E3
Korpilahti Fin. 44 N5
Korpo Fin. 45 L6
Korppoo Fin. see Korpo
Korsakov Russia 74 F3
Korsnäs Fin. 44 L5
Korsør Denmark 45 G9
Korsun'-Shevchenkivs'kyy Ukr. 43 F6
Korsun'-Shevchenkovskiy Ukr. see Korsun'-Shevchenkivs'kyy
Korsze Poland 47 R3
Kortesjärvi Fin. 44 M5
Korti Sudan 86 D6
Kortkeros Russia 42 K3
Kortrijk Belgium 52 D4
Korvala Fin. 44 O3
Koryakskaya Sopka, Vulkan vol. Russia 65 Q4
Koryakskoye Nagor'ye mts Russia 65 S3
Koryazhma Russia 42 J3
Kos i. Greece 59 L6
Kosa Russia 41 Q4
Kosam India 82 E4
Kosan N. Korea 75 B5
Kościan Poland 47 P4
Kosciusko, Mount Australia see Kosciuszko, Mount
Kosciuszko, Mount Australia 112 D6
Kosciuszko National Park Australia 112 D6
Köse Turkey 91 E2
Köseçobanlı Turkey 85 A1
Kosgi India 84 C2
Kosh-Agach Russia 80 G2
Koshikijima-rettō is Japan 75 C7
Koshk Afgh. 89 F3
Koshki Russia 43 K5
Kosi Bay S. Africa 101 K4
Košice Slovakia 43 D6
Kosigi India 84 C3
Koskullskulle Sweden 44 L3
Köslin Poland see Koszalin
Kosma r. Russia 42 K2
Koson Uzbek. 89 G2
Kosŏng N. Korea 75 C5
Kosova prov. Europe see Kosovo

▶Kosovo country Europe 59 I3
Gained independence from Serbia in February 2008.

Kosovo-Metohija prov. Europe see Kosovo
Kosovska Mitrovica Kosovo see Mitrovicë
Kosrae atoll Micronesia 150 G5
Kösseine hill Germany 53 L5
Kosta-Khetagurovo Russia see Nazran'
Kostanay Kazakh. 78 F1
Kostenets Bulg. 59 J3
Kosti Sudan 86 D7
Kostinbrod Bulg. 59 J3
Kostino Russia 64 J3
Kostomuksha Russia 44 Q4
Kostopil' Ukr. 43 E6
Kostopol' Ukr. see Kostopil'
Kostroma Russia 42 I4
Kostrzyn nad Odrą Poland 47 O4
Kostyantynivka Ukr. 43 H6
Kostyukovichi Belarus see Kastsyukovichy
Kos'yu Russia 41 R2
Koszalin Poland 47 P3
Kőszeg Hungary 58 G1
Kota Andhra Prad. India 84 D3
Kota Chhattisgarh India 83 E5
Kota Rajasthan India 82 C4
Kota Baharu Malaysia see Kota Bharu
Kotabaru Kalimantan Indon. 68 F7
Kotabaru Sumatra Indon. 71 B7
Kota Bharu Malaysia 71 C6
Kotabumi Indon. 68 C7
Kot Addu Pak. 89 H4
Kota Kinabalu Sabah Malaysia 68 F5
Kotamobagu Indon. 69 G6
Kotaneelee Range mts Canada 120 E2
Kotaparh India 84 D2
Kotapinang Indon. 71 C7
Kotatengah Indon. 71 C7
Kota Tinggi Malaysia 71 C7
Kotcho r. Canada 120 F3
Kotcho Lake Canada 120 F3
Kot Diji Pak. 89 H5
Kotel'nich Russia 42 K4
Kotel'nikovo Russia 43 I7
Kotel'nyy, Ostrov i. Russia 65 O2
Kotgar India 84 D2
Kotgarh India 82 D3
Kothagudem India see Kottagudem
Köthen (Anhalt) Germany 53 L3
Kotido Uganda 97 G4
Kotikovo Russia 74 D3
Kot Imamgarh Pak. 89 H5
Kotka Fin. 45 O6
Kot Kapura India 82 C3
Kotkino Russia 42 K2
Kotlas Russia 42 J3
Kotli Pak. 89 I3
Kotlik U.S.A. 118 B3
Kötlutangi pt Iceland 44 [inset 1]
Kotly Russia 45 P7
Kotovo Russia 43 J6
Kotovsk Russia 43 I5
Kotra India 82 C4
Kotra Pak. 89 G4
Kotri r. India 84 D2
Kot Sarae Pak. 89 G6
Kottagudem India 84 D2
Kottarakara India 84 C4
Kottayam India 84 C4
Kotte Sri Lanka see Sri Jayewardenepura Kotte
Kotto r. Cent. Afr. Rep. 98 C3
Kotturu India 84 C3
Kotuy r. Russia 65 L2
Kotzebue U.S.A. 118 B3
Kotzebue Sound sea chan. U.S.A. 118 B3
Kouango Cent. Afr. Rep. 98 C3
Koubia Guinea 96 B3
Kouchibouguac National Park Canada 123 I5
Koudougou Burkina Faso 96 C3
Kouebokkeveld mts S. Africa 100 D7
Koufey Niger 96 E3
Koufonisi i. Greece 59 L7
Kougaberge mts S. Africa 100 F7
Koukdjuak, Great Plain of the Canada 119 K3
Koukourou r. Cent. Afr. Rep. 98 B3
Koulen Cambodia see Kulên
Koulikoro Mali 96 C3
Koumac New Caledonia 107 G4
Koumpentoum Senegal 96 B3
Koumra Chad 97 E4
Koundâra Guinea 96 B3
Kountze U.S.A. 131 E6
Koupéla Burkina Faso 96 C3
Kourou Fr. Guiana 143 H2
Kouroussa Guinea 96 C3
Kousséri Cameroon 97 E3
Koutiala Mali 96 C3
Kouvola Fin. 45 O6
Kovallberget Sweden 44 J4
Kovdor Russia 44 Q3
Kovel' Ukr. 43 E6
Kovernino Russia 42 I4
Kovilpatti India 84 C4
Kovno Lith. see Kaunas
Kovrov Russia 42 I4
Kovylkino Russia 43 I5
Kovzhskoye, Ozero l. Russia 42 H3
Kowanyama Australia 110 C2
Kowloon H.K. China 77 [inset]
Kowloon Peak hill H.K. China 77 [inset]
Kowloon Peninsula H.K. China 77 [inset]
Kowŏn N. Korea 75 B5
Koxrap China 89 J2
Kōyama-misaki pt Japan 75 C6
Koyamutthoor India see Coimbatore
Köyceğiz Turkey 59 M6
Koygorodok Russia 42 K3
Koyna Reservoir India 84 B2
Köýtendag Turkm. 89 G2
Koyuk U.S.A. 118 B3
Koyukuk r. U.S.A. 118 C3
Koyulhisar Turkey 90 E2
Kozağacı Turkey see Günyüzü
Kō-zaki pt Japan 75 C6
Kozan Turkey 90 D3
Kozani Greece 59 I4
Kozara mts Bos. & Herz. 58 G2
Kozara, Nacionalni Park nat. park Bos. & Herz. 58 G2
Kozarska Dubica Bos. & Herz. see Bosanska Dubica
Kozelets' Ukr. 43 F6
Kozel'sk Russia 43 G5
Kozhikode India 84 B4
Kozhva Russia 42 M2
Kozlu Turkey 59 N4
Kozly Russia 43 H5
Koz'modem'yansk Russia 42 J4
Kožuf mts Greece/Macedonia 59 J4
Kōzu-shima i. Japan 75 E6
Kozyatyn Ukr. 43 F6
Kpandae Ghana 96 C4
Kra, Isthmus of Thai. 71 B5
Krabi Thai. 71 B5
Kra Buri Thai. 71 B5
Krâchéh Cambodia 71 D4
Kraddsele Sweden 44 J4
Kragerø Norway 45 F7
Kraggenburg Neth. 52 F2
Kragujevac Serbia 59 I2

▶Krakatau vol. Indon. 68 D8
2nd deadliest recorded volcanic eruption (1883).

Krakau Poland see Kraków
Kraków Poland 47 Q5
Krakower See l. Germany 53 M1
Krâlănh Cambodia 71 C4
Kralendijk Bonaire 137 K6
Kramators'k Ukr. 43 H6
Kramfors Sweden 44 J5
Krammer est. Neth. 52 E3
Kranidi Greece 59 J6
Kranj Slovenia 58 F1
Kranji Reservoir Sing. 71 [inset]
Kranskop S. Africa 101 J5
Krasavino Russia 42 J3
Krasilov Ukr. see Krasyliv
Krasino Russia 64 G2
Kraskino Russia 74 C4
Krāslava Latvia 45 O9
Kraslice Czechia 53 M4
Krasnaya Gorbatka Russia 42 I5
Krasnoarmeysk Russia 43 J6
Krasnoarmeysk Ukr. see Krasnoarmiys'k
Krasnoarmiys'k Ukr. 43 H6
Krasnoborsk Russia 42 J3
Krasnodar Russia 90 E1
Krasnodar Kray admin. div. Russia see Krasnodarskiy Kray
Krasnodarskiy Kray admin. div. Russia 90 E1
Krasnodon Ukr. 43 H6
Krasnogorodsk Russia 45 P8
Krasnogorsk Russia 74 F2
Krasnogorskoye Russia 42 L4
Krasnograd Ukr. see Krasnohrad
Krasnogvardeysk Uzbek. see Bulung'ur
Krasnogvardeyskoye Russia 43 I7
Krasnohrad Ukr. 43 G6
Krasnohvardiys'ke Crimea 43 G7
Krasnokamsk Russia 41 R4
Krasnoperekops'k Crimea 43 G7
Krasnopol'ye Russia 74 F2
Krasnorechenskiy Russia 74 D3
Krasnoslobodsk Russia 43 I5
Krasnotur'insk Russia 41 S4
Krasnoufimsk Russia 41 R4
Krasnovishersk Russia 41 R3
Krasnovodsk Turkm. see Türkmenbaşy
Krasnovodsk, Mys pt Turkm. 88 D2
Krasnovodskoye Plato plat. Turkm. 91 I2
Krasnowodsk Aylagy b. Turkm. see Türkmenbaşy Aýlagy
Krasnoyarovo Russia 74 C2
Krasnoyarsk Russia 64 K4
Krasnoyarskoye Vodokhranilishche resr Russia 72 G2
Krasnoye Lipetskaya Oblast' Russia 43 H5
Krasnoye Respublika Kalmykiya-Khalm'g-Tangch Russia see Ulan Erge
Krasnoznamenskiy Kazakh. see Yegindykol'
Krasnoznamenskoye Kazakh. see Yegindykol'
Krasnyy Russia 43 F5
Krasnyy Chikoy Russia 73 J2
Krasnyye Baki Russia 42 J4
Krasnyy Kamyshanik Russia see Komsomol'skiy
Krasnyy Kholm Russia 42 H4
Krasnyy Kut Russia 43 J6
Krasnyy Luch Ukr. 43 H6
Krasnyy Lyman Ukr. see Lyman
Krasnyy Yar Russia 43 K7
Krasyliv Ukr. 43 E6
Kratie Cambodia see Krâchéh
Kratke Range mts P.N.G. 69 L8
Kraulshavn Greenland see Nuussuaq
Krâvanh, Chuŏr Phnum mts Cambodia/Thai. see Cardamom Range
Kraynovka Russia 91 G2
Krefeld Germany 52 G3
Kremenchug Ukr. see Kremenchuk
Kremenchugskoye Vodokhranilishche resr Ukr. see Kremenchuts'ke Vodoskhovyshche
Kremenchuk Ukr. 43 G6
Kremenchuts'ke Vodoskhovyshche resr Ukr. 43 G6
Křemešník hill Czechia 47 O6
Kremges Ukr. see Svitlovods'k
Kremmidi, Akra pt Greece see Kremmydi, Akrotirio
Kremmydi, Akrotirio pt Greece 59 J6
Krems Austria see Krems an der Donau
Krems an der Donau Austria 47 O6
Kresta, Zaliv g. Russia 65 T3
Kresttsy Russia 42 G4
Kretinga Lith. 45 L9
Kreuzau Germany 52 G4
Kreuztal Germany 53 H4
Kreva Belarus 45 O9
Kribi Cameroon 96 D4
Krichev Belarus see Krychaw
Kriel S. Africa see Ga-Nala
Krikellos Greece 59 I5
Kril'on, Mys c. Russia 74 F3
Krishna India 84 C2
Krishna r. India 84 D2
Krishnanagar India 83 G5
Krishnarajanagara India 84 C3
Krishnaraja Sagara l. India 84 C3
Kristiania Norway see Oslo
Kristiansand Norway 45 E7
Kristianstad Sweden 45 I8
Kristiansund Norway 44 E5
Kristiinankaupunki Fin. see Kristinestad
Kristinehamn Sweden 45 I7
Kristinestad Fin. 44 L5
Kristinopol' Ukr. see Chervonohrad
Kriti i. Greece see Crete
Kritiko Pelagos sea Greece 59 K6
Krivoy Rog Ukr. see Kryvyy Rih
Križevci Croatia 58 G1
Krk i. Croatia 58 F2

Krka, Nacionalni Park nat. park Croatia 58 F3
Krkonošský národní park nat. park Czechia/Poland 47 O5
Krokom Sweden 44 I5
Krokstadøra Norway 44 F5
Krokstranda Norway 44 I3
Krolevets' Ukr. 43 G6
Kronach Germany 53 L4
Kronoby Fin. 44 M5
Kronprins Christian Land reg. Greenland 153 I1
Kronprins Frederik Bjerge nunataks Greenland 119 O3
Kronshtadt Russia 45 P7
Kronstadt Romania see Braşov
Kronstadt Russia see Kronshtadt
Kronwa Myanmar 70 B4
Kroonstad S. Africa 101 H4
Kropotkin Russia 91 F1
Kropstädt Germany 53 M3
Krosno Poland 43 D6
Krotoszyn Poland 47 P5
Kruger National Park S. Africa 101 J2
Kruglikovo Russia 74 D2
Kruglyakov Russia see Oktyabr'skiy
Krui Indon. 68 C8
Kruisfontein S. Africa 100 G8
Kruja Albania see Krujë
Krujë Albania 59 H4
Krumovgrad Bulg. 59 K4
Krungkao Thai. see Ayutthaya
Krung Thep Thai. see Bangkok
Krupa Bos. & Herz. see Bosanska Krupa
Krupa na Uni Bos. & Herz. see Bosanska Krupa
Krupki Belarus 43 F5
Krusenstern, Cape U.S.A. 118 B3
Kruševac Serbia 59 I3
Krušné hory mts Czechia 53 M4
Kruzof Island U.S.A. 120 C3
Krychaw Belarus 43 F5
Krylov Seamount sea feature N. Atlantic Ocean 148 G4
Krymsk Russia 90 E1
Krymskaya Russia see Krymsk
Krystynopol Ukr. see Chervonohrad
Krytiko Pelagos sea Greece see Kritiko Pelagos
Kryvyy Rih Ukr. 43 G7
Ksabi Alg. 54 D6
Ksar Chellala Alg. 57 H6
Ksar el Boukhari Alg. 57 H6
Ksar el Kebir Morocco 57 D6
Ksar-es-Souk Morocco see Er Rachidia
Ksenofontova Russia 41 R3
Kshirpai India 83 F5
Ksour Essaf Tunisia 58 D7
Kstovo Russia 42 J4
Kū', Jabal al hill Saudi Arabia 86 G4
Kuah Malaysia 71 B6
Kuaidamao China see Tonghua
Kuala Belait Brunei 68 E6
Kuala Dungun Malaysia see Dungun
Kuala Kangsar Malaysia 71 C6
Kualakapuas Indon. 68 E7
Kuala Kerai Malaysia 71 C6
Kuala Lipis Malaysia 71 C6

▶Kuala Lumpur Malaysia 71 C7
Joint capital (with Putrajaya) of Malaysia.

Kuala Nerang Malaysia 71 C6
Kuala Pilah Malaysia 71 C7
Kuala Rompin Malaysia 71 C7
Kuala Selangor Malaysia 71 C7
Kualasimpang Indon. 71 B6
Kuala Terengganu Malaysia 71 C6
Kualatungal Indon. 68 C7
Kuamut Sabah Malaysia 68 F5
Kuandian China 74 B4
Kuantan Malaysia 71 C7
Kuba Azer. see Quba
Kuban' r. Russia 43 H7
Kubār Syria 91 E4
Kubaybāt Syria 85 C2
Kubaysah Iraq 91 F4
Kubenskoye, Ozero l. Russia 42 H4
Kubrat Bulg. 59 L3
Kubuang Indon. 68 F6
Kuchaman Road India 89 I5
Kuchema Russia 42 I2
Kuching Sarawak Malaysia 68 E6
Küchnay Darwēshān Afgh. 89 G4
Kucing Sarawak Malaysia see Kuching
Kuçovë Albania 59 H4
Kuda India 82 B5
Kudal India 84 B3
Kudap Indon. 71 C7
Kudat Sabah Malaysia 68 F5
Kudligi India 84 C3
Kudremukh mt. India 84 B3
Kudus Indon. 68 E8
Kudymkar Russia 41 Q4
Ku'erqisi China see Fuyun
Kufstein Austria 47 N7
Kugaaruk Canada 119 J3
Kugesi Russia 42 J4
Kugka Lhai China 83 G3
Kugluktuk Canada 118 G3
Kugmallit Bay Canada 153 A2
Kūh, Khār mt. Iran 88 D4
Kūh, Ra's-al- pt Iran 88 E5
Kūh, Shīr mt. Iran 88 D4
Kūhak Iran 89 F5
Kuhanbokano mt. China 83 E3
Kuhbier Germany 53 M1
Kūhdasht Iran 88 B3
Kūhīn Iran 88 C2
Kuhmo Fin. 44 P4
Kuhmoinen Fin. 45 N6
Kūhpāyeh mt. Iran 88 E4
Kūhrān, Kūh-e mt. Iran 88 E5
Kühren Germany 53 M3
Kuhsān Afgh. 89 F3
Kui Buri Thai. 71 B4
Kuis Namibia 100 C3
Kuiseb watercourse Namibia 100 B2
Kuitan China 77 G4
Kuito Angola 99 B5
Kuitun China see Kuytun
Kuiu Island U.S.A. 120 C3
Kuivaniemi Fin. 44 N4
Kujang N. Korea 75 B5
Kuji Japan 75 F4
Kujū-san vol. Japan 75 C6
Kukan Russia 74 D2
Kukës Albania 59 I3
Kukesi Albania see Kukës
Kukmor Russia 42 K4
Kukshi India 82 C5
Kukunuru India 84 D2
Kükürtli Turkm. 88 E2
Kūl r. Iran 88 D5
Kula Turkey 59 M5
Kulaisila India 83 F5
Kula Kangri mt. Bhutan/China 83 G3
Kulanch reg. Pak. 89 F5
Kulandy Kazakh. 80 A2
Kular Russia 65 O2
Kuldīga Latvia 45 L8
Kuldja China see Yining
Kul'dur Russia 74 C2
Kule Botswana 100 E2
Kulebaki Russia 43 I5
Kulên Cambodia 71 D4
Kulgera Australia 109 F6
Kulikovo Russia 42 J3
Kulim Malaysia 71 C6
Kulin Australia 109 B8
Kulja Australia 109 B7
Kulkyne watercourse Australia 112 B3
Kullu India 82 D3
Kulmbach Germany 53 L4
Kŭlob Tajik. 89 H2
Kuloy Russia 42 I3
Kuloy r. Russia 42 I2
Kulp Turkey 91 F3
Kul'sary Kazakh. 78 E2
Külsheim Germany 53 J5
Kulu India see Kullu
Kulu Turkey 90 D3
Kulunda Russia 72 D2
Kulundinskaya Ravnina plain Kazakh./Russia 72 D2
Kulundinskoye, Ozero salt l. Russia 72 D2
Kulusuk Greenland 119 O3
Kulwin Australia 111 C7
Kulyab Tajik. see Kŭlob
Kuma r. Russia 43 J7
Kumagaya Japan 75 E5
Kumai, Teluk b. Indon. 68 E7
Kumalar Dağı mts Turkey 59 N5
Kumamoto Japan 75 C6
Kumano Japan 75 E6
Kumanovo Macedonia 59 I3
Kumara Russia 74 B2
Kumasi Ghana 96 C4
Kumayri Armenia see Gyumri
Kumba Cameroon 96 D4
Kumbakonam India 84 C4
Kumbe Indon. 69 K8
Kümbet Turkey 59 N5
Kumbharli Ghat mt. India 84 B2
Kumbla India 84 B3
Kumchuru Botswana 100 F2
Kum-Dag Turkm. see Gumdag
Kumdah Saudi Arabia 86 G5
Kumel well Iran 88 D3
Kumeny Russia 42 K4
Kumertau Russia 64 G4
Kumgang-san mt. N. Korea 75 C5
Kumguri India 83 G4
Kumi Uganda 97 G4
Kumla Sweden 45 I7
Kumlu Turkey 85 C1
Kummersdorf-Alexanderdorf Germany 53 N2
Kumo Nigeria 96 E3
Kumon Range mts Myanmar 70 B1
Kumphawapi Thai. 70 C3
Kums Namibia 100 D5
Kumta India 84 B3
Kumu Dem. Rep. Congo 98 C3
Kumukh Russia 91 G2
Kumul China see Hami
Kumund India 84 D1
Kumylzhenskaya Russia see Kumylzhenskiy
Kumylzhenskiy Russia 43 I6
Kun r. Myanmar 70 B3
Kunar Sīnd r. Afgh. 89 H3
Kunashir, Ostrov i. Russia 74 G3
Kunashirskiy Proliv sea chan. Japan/Russia see Nemuro-kaikyō
Kunchaung Myanmar 70 B2
Kunchuk Tso salt l. China 83 E2
Kunda Estonia 45 O7
Kunda India 83 E4
Kundapura India 84 B3
Kundelungu, Parc National de nat. park Dem. Rep. Congo 99 C5
Kundelungu Ouest, Parc National de nat. park Dem. Rep. Congo 99 C5
Kundia India 82 C4
Kundur i. Indon. 68 C6
Kunduz Afgh. 89 H2
Kunene r. Angola see Cunene
Kuneneng admin. dist. Botswana see Kweneng
Künes China see Xinyuan
Kungälv Sweden 45 G8
Kunghit Island Canada 120 D4
Kungsbacka Sweden 45 H8
Kungshamn Sweden 45 G7
Kungu Dem. Rep. Congo 98 B3
Kungur mt. China see Kongur Shan
Kungur Russia 41 R4
Kunhing Myanmar 70 B2
Kuni r. India 84 C2
Kunié i. New Caledonia see Pins, Île des
Kunigal India 84 C3
Kunimi-dake mt. Japan 75 C6
Kunkavav India 82 B5
Kunlong Myanmar 70 B2

▶Kunlun Shan mts China 82 D1
Location of highest active volcano in Asia.

Kunlun Shankou pass China 83 H2
Kunming China 76 D3
Kunshan China 77 I2
Kununurra Australia 108 E3
Kunwak r. Canada 121 L2
Kun'ya Russia 42 F4
Kunyang Yunnan China see Jinning
Kunyang Zhejiang China see Pingyang
Kunya-Urgench Turkm. see Köneürgenç
Künzelsau Germany 53 J5
Künzels-Berg hill Germany 53 L3
Kuocang Shan mts China 77 I2
Kuohijärvi l. Fin. 45 N6
Kuoloyarvi Russia 44 P3
Kuopio Fin. 44 O5
Kuortane Fin. 44 M5
Kupa r. Croatia/Slovenia 58 G2
Kupang Indon. 108 C2
Kupari India 83 F5
Kupiškis Lith. 45 N9
Kupreanof Island U.S.A. 120 C3
Kupwara India 82 C2
Kup''yans'k Ukr. 43 H6
Kuqa China 80 F3
Kur r. Russia 74 D2
Kura r. Asia 91 G2
also known as Kur (Armenia), Kür (Azerbaijan), Mt'k'vari (Georgia)
Kuragino Russia 72 G2
Kurakh Russia 43 J8
Kurama Range mts Asia 87 K1
Kuraminskiy Khrebet mts Asia see Kurama Range
Kūrān Dap Iran 89 E5
Kurashiki Japan 75 D6
Kurasia India 83 E5
Kurayn i. Saudi Arabia 88 C5
Kurayoshi Japan 75 D6
Kurchatov Russia 43 G6
Kürd, Köh-e mt. Afgh. 89 G3
Kürdämir Azer. 91 H2
Kurdistan hist. area Asia 91 F3
Kure Japan 75 D6
Küre Turkey 90 D2
Kure Atoll U.S.A. 150 I4
Kuressaare Estonia 45 M7
Kurgal'dzhino Kazakh. see Korgalzhyn
Kurgal'dzhinskiy Kazakh. see Korgalzhyn
Kurgan Russia 64 H4
Kurganinsk Russia 91 F1
Kurgannaya Russia see Kurganinsk
Kurgantyube Tajik. see Qŭrghonteppa
Kūrī Afgh. 89 H2
Kuri India 82 B4
Kuria Muria Islands Oman see Ḥalāniyāt, Juzur al
Kuridala (abandoned) Australia 110 C4
Kurigram Bangl. 83 G4
Kurikka Fin. 44 M5
Kuril Basin sea feature Sea of Okhotsk 150 F2
Kuril Islands Russia 74 H3
Kurilovka Russia 43 K6
Kuril'sk Russia 74 G3
Kuril'skiye Ostrova is Russia see Kuril Islands
Kuril Trench sea feature N. Pacific Ocean 150 F3
Kurkino Russia 43 H5
Kurmashkino Kazakh. see Kurshim
Kurmuk Sudan 86 D7
Kurnool India 84 C3
Kurow N.Z. 113 C7
Kurram Pak. 89 H3
Kurri Kurri Australia 112 E4
Kursavka Russia 91 F1
Kürshim Kazakh. see Kurshim
Kurshim Kazakh. 80 F2
Kurshskiy Zaliv b. Lith./Russia see Courland Lagoon
Kuršių marios b. Lith./Russia see Courland Lagoon
Kursk Russia 43 H6
Kurskaya Russia 91 G1
Kurskiy Zaliv b. Lith./Russia see Courland Lagoon
Kurşunlu Turkey 90 D2
Kurtalan Turkey 91 F3
Kurtoğlu Burnu pt Turkey 59 M6
Kurtpınar Turkey 85 B1
Kurucaşile Turkey 90 D2
Kuruçay Turkey 90 E3
Kurukshetra India 82 D3
Kuruk Tag mts China 80 G3
Kuruman S. Africa 100 F4
Kuruman watercourse S. Africa 100 E4
Kurume Japan 75 C6
Kurumkan Russia 73 K2
Kurunegala Sri Lanka 84 D5
Kurupam India 84 D2
Kurush, Jebel hills Sudan 86 D5
Kur'ya Russia 41 R3
Kuryk Kazakh. 91 H2
Kuşadası Turkey 59 L6
Kuşadası, Gulf of b. Turkey 59 L6
Kusaie atoll Micronesia see Kosrae
Kusary Azer. see Qusar
Kuşcenneti nature res. Turkey 85 B1
Kuschke Nature Reserve S. Africa 101 I3
Kusel Germany 53 H5
Kuş Gölü l. Turkey 59 L4
Kushalgarh India 82 C5
Kushchëvskaya Russia 43 H7
Kushimoto Japan 75 D6
Kushiro Japan 74 G4
Kushka Turkm. see Serhetabat
Kushk-e Kuhnah Afgh. 89 F3
Kushkopala Russia 42 J3
Kushtagi India 84 C3
Kushtia Bangl. 83 G5
Kushtih Iran 89 E4
Kuskan Turkey 85 A1
Kuskokwim r. U.S.A. 118 B3
Kuskokwim Bay U.S.A. 118 B4
Kuskokwim Mountains U.S.A. 118 C3
Kuşluyan Turkey see Gölköy
Kusmuryn Kazakh. 78 F1
Kusŏng N. Korea 75 B5
Kustanay Kazakh. see Kostanay
Küstence Romania see Constanța
Küstenkanal canal Germany 53 H1
Kustia Bangl. see Kushtia
Kut, Ko i. Thai. 71 C5
Kuta Indon. 68 F8
Kūt 'Abdollāh Iran 88 C4
Kutacane Indon. 71 B7
Kütahya Turkey 59 M5
Kutaisi Georgia 91 F2
Kut-al-Imara Iraq see Al Kūt
Kutan Russia 91 G1
Kutanibong Indon. 71 B7
Kutaraja Indon. see Banda Aceh
Kutch, Gulf of India see Kachchh, Gulf of
Kutch, Rann of marsh India see Kachchh, Rann of
Kutchan Japan 74 F4
Kutina Croatia 58 G2
Kutjevo Croatia 58 G2
Kutkai Myanmar 70 B2
Kutno Poland 47 Q4
Kutru India 84 D2
Kūt Seyyed Na'īm Iran 88 C4
Kutu Dem. Rep. Congo 98 B4
Kutubdia Island Bangl. 83 G5
Kutum Sudan 97 F3
Kutztown U.S.A. 135 H3
Kuujjua r. Canada 118 G2
Kuujjuaq Canada 123 H2
Kuujjuarapik Canada 122 F3
Kuusamo Fin. 44 P4
Kuusankoski Fin. 45 O6
Kuvango Angola 99 B5
Kuvshinovo Russia 42 G4
Kuwait country Asia 88 B4

▶Kuwait Kuwait 88 B4
Capital of Kuwait.

Kuwajleen atoll Marshall Is see Kwajalein
Kūyah/Koye Iraq 91 G3
Kuybyshev Novosibirskaya Oblast' Russia 64 I4
Kuybyshev Respublika Tatarstan Russia see Bolgar
Kuybyshev Samarskaya Oblast' Russia see Samara
Kuybysheve Ukr. 43 H7
Kuybyshevka-Vostochnaya Russia see Belogorsk
Kuybyshevskoye Vodokhranilishche resr Russia 43 K5
Kuyeda Russia 41 R4
Kuygan Kazakh. 80 D2
Kuytun China 80 F3
Kuytun Russia 72 I2
Kuyucak Turkey 59 M6
Kuzino Russia 41 R4
Kuznechnoye Russia 45 P6
Kuznetsk Russia 43 J5
Kuznetsovo Russia 74 E3
Kuznetsovs'k Ukr. 43 E6
Kuzovatovo Russia 43 J5
Kvænangen sea chan. Norway 44 L1
Kvaløya i. Norway 44 K2
Kvalsund Norway 44 M1
Kvarnerić sea chan. Croatia 58 F2
Kvitøya ice feature Svalbard 64 E2
Kwa r. Dem. Rep. Congo see Kasaï
Kwabhaca S. Africa see Mount Frere
Kwadelen atoll Marshall Is see Kwajalein
KwaDukuza S. Africa 101 J5
Kwajalein atoll Marshall Is 150 H5
Kwajok South Sudan 97 F4
Kwale Nigeria 96 D4
KwaMashu S. Africa 101 J5
KwaMhlanga S. Africa 101 I3
Kwa Mtoro Tanz. 99 D4
Kwangchow China see Guangzhou
Kwangju S. Korea see Gwangju
Kwangsi Chuang Autonomous Region aut. reg. China see Guangxi Zhuangzu Zizhiqu
Kwangtung prov. China see Guangdong
Kwanmo-bong mt. N. Korea 74 C4
KwaNobuhle S. Africa 101 G7
KwaNojoli S. Africa 101 G7
Kwanonqubela S. Africa 101 H7
KwaNonzame S. Africa 100 G6
Kwanza r. Angola see Cuanza
Kwatarkwashi Nigeria 96 D3
Kwatinidubu S. Africa 101 H7
KwaZamokuhle S. Africa 101 I4
KwaZamukucinga S. Africa 100 G7
Kwazamuxolo S. Africa 100 G6
KwaZanele S. Africa 101 I4
KwaZulu-Natal prov. S. Africa 101 J5
Kweichow prov. China see Guizhou
Kweiyang China see Guiyang
Kwekwe Zimbabwe 99 C5
Kweneng admin. dist. Botswana 100 G2
Kwenge r. Dem. Rep. Congo 99 B4
Kwetabohigan r. Canada 122 E4
Kwezi-Naledi S. Africa 101 H6
Kwidzyn Poland 47 Q4
Kwikila P.N.G. 69 L8
Kwilu r. Angola/Dem. Rep. Congo 99 B4
Kwoka mt. Indon. 69 I7
Kyabra Australia 111 C5
Kyabram Australia 112 B6
Kyadet Myanmar 70 A2
Kyaikkami Myanmar 70 B3
Kyaiklat Myanmar 70 A3
Kyaikto Myanmar 70 B3
Kyakhta Russia 72 J2
Kyalite Australia 112 A5
Kyancutta Australia 109 F8
Kyangin Myanmar 70 B3
Kyangngoin China 76 B2
Kyaukhnyat Myanmar 70 B3
Kyaukkyi Myanmar 70 B3
Kyaukme Myanmar 70 B2
Kyaukpadaung Myanmar 70 A2
Kyaukpyu Myanmar 70 A3
Kyaukse Myanmar 70 B2
Kyauktaw Myanmar 70 A2
Kyaunggon Myanmar 70 A3
Kybartai Lith. 45 M9
Kyebogyi Myanmar 70 B3
Kyêbxang Co l. China 83 G2
Kyeikdon Myanmar 70 B3
Kyeikywa Myanmar 70 B3
Kyeintali Myanmar 70 A3
Kyela Tanz. 99 D4
Kyelang India 82 D2
Kyidaunggan Myanmar 70 B3
Kyiv Ukr. see Kiev
Kyivs'ke Vodoskhovyshche resr Ukr. 43 F6
Kyklades is Greece see Cyclades
Kyle Canada 121 I5
Kyle of Lochalsh U.K. 50 D3
Kyll r. Germany 52 G5
Kyllini mt. Greece 59 J6
Kymi Greece 59 K5
Kymis, Akra pt Greece see Kymis, Akrotirio
Kymis, Akrotirio pt Greece 59 K5
Kynazhegubskoye Vodokhranilishche l. Russia 44 R3
Kyneton Australia 112 B6
Kynuna Australia 110 C4
Kyoga, Lake Uganda 98 D3
Kyōga-misaki pt Japan 75 D6
Kyogle Australia 112 F2
Kyong Myanmar 70 B2
Kyonpyaw Myanmar 70 A3
Kyōto Japan 75 D6
Kyparissia Greece 59 I6
Kypros country Asia see Cyprus
Kyra Russia 73 K3
Kyra Panagia i. Greece 59 K5
Kyrenia Cyprus 85 A2
Kyrenia Mountains Cyprus see Pentadaktylos Range
Kyrgyz Ala-Too mts Kazakh./Kyrg. see Kirghiz Range
Kyrgyzstan country Asia 80 D3
Kyritz Germany 53 M2
Kyrksæterøra Norway 44 F5
Kyrta Russia 41 R3
Kyssa Russia 42 J2
Kytalyktakh Russia 65 O3
Kythira i. Greece 59 J6
Kythnos i. Greece 59 K6
Kyunglung China 82 E3
Kyunhla Myanmar 70 A2
Kyuquot Canada 120 E5
Kyurdamir Azer. see Kürdämir
Kyūshū i. Japan 75 C7
Kyushu-Palau Ridge sea feature N. Pacific Ocean 150 F4
Kyustendil Bulg. 59 J3
Kywebwe Myanmar 70 B3
Kywong Australia 112 C5
Kyyev Ukr. see Kiev
Kyyiv Ukr. see Kiev
Kyyjärvi Fin. 44 N5
Kyzyl Russia 80 H1
Kyzyl-Art, Pereval pass Kyrg./Tajik. see Kyzylart Pass
Kyzylart Pass Kyrg./Tajik. 89 I2
Kyzyl-Burun Azer. see Siyäzän
Kyzyl-Kiya Kyrg. see Kyzyl-Kyya
Kyzylkum, Peski des. Kazakh./Uzbek. see Kyzylkum Desert
Kyzylkum Desert Kazakh./Uzbek. 80 B3
Kyzyl-Kyya Kyrg. 80 D3
Kyzyl-Mazhalyk Russia 80 H1
Kyzylorda Kazakh. 80 C3
Kyzylrabot Tajik. see Qizilrabot
Kyzylsay Kazakh. 91 I2
Kyzylysor Kazakh. 91 H1
Kyzylzhar Kazakh. 80 C2
Kzyl-Dzhar Kazakh. see Kyzylzhar
Kzyl-Orda Kazakh. see Kyzylorda
Kzyltu Kazakh. see Kishkenekol'

L

Laagri Estonia 45 N7
Laamu Atoll Maldives see Hahdhunmathi
La Angostura, Presa de resr Mex. 136 F5
Laanila Fin. 44 O2
Laascaanood Somalia 98 E3
Laasqoray Somalia 98 E2

▶Laâyoune W. Sahara 96 B2
Capital of Western Sahara.

La Babia Mex. 131 C6
La Baie Canada 123 H4
La Banda Arg. 144 D3
La Barge U.S.A. 126 F4
Labasa Fiji 107 H3
La Baule-Escoublac France 56 C3
Labe r. Germany see Elbe
Labé Guinea 96 B3
La Belle U.S.A. 133 D7
Laberge, Lake Canada 120 C2
Labian, Tanjung pt Malaysia 68 F5
La Biche, Lac l. Canada 121 H4
Labinsk Russia 91 F1
Labis Malaysia 71 C7
La Boquilla Mex. 131 B7
Labouheyre France 56 D4
Laboulaye Arg. 144 D4
Labozhskoye Russia 42 L2
Labrador reg. Canada 123 J3
Labrador City Canada 123 I3
Labrador Sea Canada/Greenland 119 M3
Labrang China see Xiahe
Lábrea Brazil 142 F5
Labuan Malaysia 68 F5
Labudalin China see Ergun
Labuhanbilik Indon. 71 C7
Labuhanruku Indon. 71 B7
Labuna Indon. 69 H7
Labutta Myanmar 70 A3
Labyrinth, Lake salt flat Australia 111 A6
Labytnangi Russia 64 H3
Laç Albania 59 H4
La Cadena Mex. 131 B7
Lac-Allard Canada 123 J4
La Calle Alg. see El Kala
La Cañiza Spain see A Cañiza
La Capelle France 52 D5
La Carlota Arg. 144 D4
La Carolina Spain 57 E4
Lăcăuţi, Vârful mt. Romania 59 L2
Laccadive, Minicoy and Amindivi Islands union terr. India see Lakshadweep
Laccadive Islands is India see Lakshadweep
Laccadive Sea Indian Ocean 81 D9
Lac du Bonnet Canada 121 L5
Lacedaemon Greece see Sparti
La Ceiba Hond. 137 G5
Lacepede Bay Australia 111 B8
Lacepede Islands Australia 108 C4
Lacha, Ozero l. Russia 42 H3
La Chaux-de-Fonds Switz. 56 H3
Lachendorf Germany 53 K2
Lachine U.S.A. 134 D1

▶Lachlan r. Australia 112 A5
5th longest river in Oceania.

La Chorrera Panama 137 I7
Lachute Canada 122 G5
Laçın Azer. 91 G3
La Ciotat France 56 G5
Lac La Biche Canada 121 I4
Lac la Martre Canada see Whatî
Lacolle Canada 135 I1
La Colorada Sonora Mex. 127 F7
La Colorada Zacatecas Mex. 131 C8
Lacombe Canada 120 H4
Laconi Sardinia Italy 58 C5
Laconia U.S.A. 135 J2
La Corey Canada 121 I4
La Coruña Spain see A Coruña
La Crete Canada 120 G3
La Crosse KS U.S.A. 130 D4
La Crosse VA U.S.A. 135 F5
La Crosse WI U.S.A. 130 F3
La Cruz Mex. 136 C4
La Cuesta Mex. 131 C6
La Cygne U.S.A. 130 E4
Ladainha Brazil 145 C2
Ladakh reg. India/Pak. 82 D2
Ladakh Range mts India 82 D2
Ladang, Ko i. Thai. 71 B6
La Demajagua Cuba 133 D8
Ladik Turkey 90 D2
Lādīz Iran 89 F4
Ladnun India 82 C4

▶Ladoga, Lake Russia 42 F3
2nd largest lake in Europe.

Ladong China 77 F3
Ladozhskoye Ozero l. Russia see Ladoga, Lake
Ladrone Islands China see Wanshan Qundao
Ladrones terr. N. Pacific Ocean see Northern Mariana Islands
Ladu mt. India 83 H4
Ladue r. Canada/U.S.A. 120 A2
Ladva-Vetka Russia 42 G3
Ladybank U.K. 50 F4
Ladybrand S. Africa 101 H5
Lady Frere S. Africa 101 H6
Lady Grey S. Africa 101 H6
Ladysmith S. Africa 101 I5
Ladysmith U.S.A. 130 F2
Ladzhanurges Georgia see Lajanurp'ekhi
Lae P.N.G. 69 L8
Laem Ngop Thai. 71 C4
Lærdalsøyri Norway 45 E6
La Esmeralda Bol. 142 F8
Læsø i. Denmark 45 G8
Lafayette Alg. see Bougaa
La Fayette U.S.A. 133 C5
Lafayette IN U.S.A. 134 B3
Lafayette LA U.S.A. 131 E6
Lafayette TN U.S.A. 134 B5
Lafé Cuba 133 C8
La Fère France 52 D5
Laferte r. Canada 120 G2
La Ferté-Gaucher France 52 D6
La Ferté-Milon France 52 D5
La Ferté-sous-Jouarre France 52 D6
Lafia Nigeria 96 D4
Lafiagi Nigeria 96 D4
Laflamme r. Canada 122 F4
Lafleche Canada 121 J5
La Flèche France 56 D3
LaFollette U.S.A. 134 C5
La Forest, Lac l. Canada 123 H3
Laforge Canada 123 G3
Laforge r. Canada 123 G3
Lāft Iran 88 D5
Laful India 71 A6
La Galissonnière, Lac l. Canada 123 J4

▶La Galite i. Tunisia 58 C6
Most northerly point of Africa.

La Gallega Mex. 131 B7
Lagan' Russia 43 J7
Lagan r. U.K. 51 G3
Lagarto Brazil 143 K6
Lage Germany 53 I3
Lågen r. Norway 45 G7
Lages Brazil 145 A4
Lage Vaart canal Neth. 52 F2
Lagg U.K. 50 D5
Laggan U.K. 50 E3
Laghouat Alg. 54 E5
Lagkor Co salt l. China 83 F2
La Gloria Mex. 131 D7
Lago Agrio Ecuador see Nueva Loja
Lagoa Santa Brazil 145 C2
Lagoa Vermelha Brazil 145 A5
Lagodekhi Georgia 91 G2
Lagolândia Brazil 145 A1
La Gomera i. Canary Is 96 B2
Lagong i. Indon. 71 E7

▶Lagos Nigeria 96 D4
Former capital of Nigeria. Most populous city in Africa.

Lagos Port. 57 B5
Lagosa Tanz. 99 C4
La Grande r. Canada 122 F3
La Grande U.S.A. 126 D3
La Grande 3, Réservoir resr Canada 122 G3
La Grande 4, Réservoir resr Canada 122 G3
La Grange Australia 108 C4
La Grange CA U.S.A. 128 C3
La Grange GA U.S.A. 133 C5
Lagrange U.S.A. 134 C3
La Grange KY U.S.A. 132 C4
La Grange TX U.S.A. 131 D6
La Gran Sabana plat. Venez. 142 F2

La Grita Venez. 142 D2
Laguna Brazil 145 A5
Laguna, Picacho de la mt. Mex. 136 B4
Laguna Dam U.S.A. 129 F5
Laguna Mountains U.S.A. 128 E5
Lagunas Chile 144 C2
Laguna San Rafael, Parque Nacional nat. park Chile 144 B7
Laha China 74 B2
La Habana Cuba see Havana
La Habra U.S.A. 128 E5
Lahad Datu Sabah Malaysia 68 F5
Laharpur India 82 E4
Lahat Indon. 68 C7
Lahe Myanmar 70 A1
Lahemaa rahvuspark nat. park Estonia 45 N7
Lahewa Indon. 71 B7
Laḩij Yemen 86 F7
Lāhījān Iran 88 C2
Lahn r. Germany 53 H4
Lahnstein Germany 53 H4
Laholm Sweden 45 H8
Lahontan Reservoir U.S.A. 128 D2
Lahore Pak. 89 I4
Lahri Pak. 89 H4
Lāhrūd Iran 88 B2
Lahti Fin. 45 N6
Laï Chad 97 E4
Lai'an China 77 H1
Laibach Slovenia see Ljubljana
Laibin China 77 F4
Laidley Australia 112 F1
Laifeng China 77 F2
L'Aigle France 56 E2
Laihia Fin. 44 M5
Lai-hka Myanmar 70 B2
Lai-Hsak Myanmar 70 B2
Laimakuri India 83 H4
Laimos, Akrotirio pt Greece 59 J5
Laingsburg S. Africa 100 E7
Laingsburg U.S.A. 134 C2
Lainioälven r. Sweden 44 M3
Lair U.S.A. 134 C4
Lairg U.K. 50 E2
La Isabela Cuba 133 D8
Laishevo Russia 42 K5
Laitila Fin. 45 L6
Laives Italy 58 D1
Laiwu China 73 L5
Laiwui Indon. 69 H7
Laiyang China 73 M5
Laizhou China 73 L5
Laizhou Wan b. China 73 L5
Lajamanu Australia 108 E4
Lajanurp'ekhi Georgia 91 F2
Lajeado Brazil 145 A5
Lajes Brazil 143 K5
La Junta Mex. 127 G7
La Junta U.S.A. 130 C4
Lakadiya India 82 B5
L'Akagera, Parc National de nat. park Rwanda see Akagera National Park
La Kagera, Parc National de nat. park Rwanda see Akagera National Park
Lake U.S.A. 134 D5
Lake Andes U.S.A. 130 D3
Lakeba i. Fiji 107 I3
Lake Bardawil Reserve nature res. Egypt 85 A4
Lake Bolac Australia 112 A6
Lake Butler U.S.A. 133 D6
Lake Cargelligo Australia 112 C4
Lake Cathie Australia 112 F3
Lake Charles U.S.A. 131 E6
Lake City CO U.S.A. 129 J3
Lake City FL U.S.A. 133 D6
Lake City MI U.S.A. 134 C1
Lake Clark National Park and Preserve U.S.A. 118 C3
Lake Clear U.S.A. 135 H1
Lake District National Park U.K. 48 D4
Lake Eildon National Park Australia 112 B6
Lake Elsinore U.S.A. 128 E5
Lakefield Australia 110 D2
Lakefield Canada 135 F1
Lake Forest U.S.A. 134 B2
Lake Gairdner National Park Australia 111 B7
Lake Geneva U.S.A. 130 F3
Lake George MI U.S.A. 134 C2
Lake George NY U.S.A. 135 I2
Lake Grace Australia 109 B8
Lake Harbour Canada see Kimmirut
Lake Havasu City U.S.A. 129 F4
Lakehurst U.S.A. 135 H3
Lake Isabella U.S.A. 128 D4
Lake Jackson U.S.A. 131 E6
Lake King Australia 109 B8
Lake Kopiago P.N.G. 69 K8
Lakeland FL U.S.A. 133 D7
Lakeland GA U.S.A. 133 D6
Lake Louise Canada 120 G5
Lakemba i. Fiji see Lakeba
Lake Mills U.S.A. 130 E3
Lake Nash Australia 110 B4
Lake Odessa U.S.A. 134 C2
Lake Paringa N.Z. 113 B6
Lake Placid FL U.S.A. 133 D7
Lake Placid NY U.S.A. 135 I1
Lake Pleasant U.S.A. 135 H2
Lakeport CA U.S.A. 128 B2
Lakeport MI U.S.A. 134 D2
Lake Providence U.S.A. 131 F5
Lake Range mts U.S.A. 128 D1
Lake River Canada 122 E3
Lakes Entrance Australia 112 D6
Lakeside AZ U.S.A. 129 I4
Lakeside VA U.S.A. 135 G5
Lakes of Ounianga tourist site Chad 97 F3
Lake Superior National Marine Conservation Area park Canada 122 D4
Lake Tabourie Australia 112 E5
Lake Tekapo N.Z. 113 C7
Lake Torrens National Park Australia 111 B6
Lakeview MI U.S.A. 134 C2
Lakeview OH U.S.A. 134 D3
Lakeview OR U.S.A. 126 C4
Lake Village U.S.A. 131 F5
Lake Wales U.S.A. 133 D7
Lakewood CO U.S.A. 126 G5
Lakewood NJ U.S.A. 135 H3
Lakewood NY U.S.A. 134 F2
Lakewood OH U.S.A. 134 E3
Lake Worth U.S.A. 133 D7
Lakha India 82 B4
Lakhdenpokh'ya Russia 44 Q6
Lakhimpur Assam India see North Lakhimpur
Lakhimpur Uttar Prad. India 82 E4
Lakhisarai India 83 F4
Lakhish, Naḩal r. Israel 85 B4
Lakhnadon India 82 D5
Lakhpat India 82 B5
Lakhtar India 82 B5
Lakin U.S.A. 130 C4
Lakitusaki r. Canada 122 E3
Lakki Marwat Pak. 89 H3
Lakonikos Kolpos b. Greece 59 J6
Lakor i. Indon. 108 E2
Lakota Côte d'Ivoire 96 C4
Lakota U.S.A. 130 D1
Laksefjorden sea chan. Norway 44 O1
Lakselv Norway 44 N1
Lakshadweep India 84 B4
Lakshadweep union terr. India 84 B4
Lakshettipet India 84 C2
Lakshmipur Bangl. 83 G5
Laksmipur Bangl. see Lakshmipur
Lalaghat India 83 H4
Lalbara India 84 D1
L'Alcora Spain 57 F3
Lāleh Zār, Kūh-e mt. Iran 88 E4
Lalganj India 83 F4
Lālī Iran 88 C3
La Ligua Chile 144 B4
Laliki Indon. 108 D1
Lalin China 74 B3
Lalín Spain 57 B2
La Línea de la Concepción Spain 57 D5
Lalin He r. China 74 B3
Lalitpur India 82 D4
Lalitpur Nepal see Patan
Lalmanirhat Bangl. see Lalmonirhat
Lalmonirhat Bangl. 83 G4
La Loche Canada 121 I3
La Loche, Lac l. Canada 121 I3
La Louvière Belgium 52 E4
Lal'sk Russia 42 J3
Lalung La pass China 83 F3
Lama Bangl. 83 H5
La Macarena, Parque Nacional nat. park Col. 142 D3
La Maddalena Sardinia Italy 58 C4
Lamadian China 74 B3
Lamadianzi China see Lamadian
La Malbaie Canada 123 H5
La Mancha Mex. 131 C7
La Mancha reg. Spain 57 E4
La Manche strait France/U.K. see English Channel
La Máquina Mex. 131 B6
Lamar CO U.S.A. 130 C4
Lamar MO U.S.A. 131 E4
La Marmora, Punta mt. Sardinia Italy 58 C5
La Marque U.S.A. 131 E6
La Martre, Lac l. Canada 120 G2
Lamas r. Turkey 85 B1
La Mauricie, Parc National de nat. park Canada 123 G5
Lambaréné Gabon 98 B4
Lambasa Fiji see Labasa
Lambayeque Peru 142 C5
Lambay Island Ireland 51 G4
Lambert atoll Marshall Is see Ailinglaplap

▶Lambert Glacier Antarctica 152 E2
Largest glacier in the world.

Lambert's Bay S. Africa 100 D7
Lambeth Canada 134 E2
Lambi India 82 C3
Lambourn Downs hills U.K. 49 F7
Lame Indon. 71 B7
Lamego Port. 57 C3
Lamèque, Île i. Canada 123 I5
La Merced Arg. 144 C3
La Merced Peru 142 C6
Lāmerd Iran 88 D5
Lameroo Australia 111 C7
La Mesa U.S.A. 128 E5
Lamesa U.S.A. 131 C5
Lamia Greece 59 J5
Lamington National Park Australia 112 F2
La Misión Mex. 128 E5
Lamma Island H.K. China 77 [inset]
Lammerlaw Range mts N.Z. 113 B7
Lammermuir Hills U.K. 50 G5
Lammhult Sweden 45 I8
Lammi Fin. 45 N6
Lamont CA U.S.A. 128 D4
Lamont WY U.S.A. 126 G4
La Montaña de Covadonga, Parque Nacional de nat. park Spain see Picos de Europa, Parque Nacional de los
La Mora Mex. 131 C7
La Morita Chihuahua Mex. 131 B6
La Morita Coahuila Mex. 131 C6
Lamotrek atoll Micronesia 69 L5
LaMoure U.S.A. 130 D2
Lampang Thai. 70 B3
Lam Pao, Ang Kep Nam Thai. 70 C3
Lampasas U.S.A. 131 D6
Lampazos Mex. 131 C7
Lampedusa, Isola di i. Sicily Italy 58 E7
Lampeter U.K. 49 C6
Lamphun Thai. 70 B3
Lampsacus Turkey see Lâpseki
Lam Tin H.K. China 77 [inset]
Lamu Kenya 98 E4
Lamu Myanmar 70 A3
Lan, Loi mt. Myanmar/Thai. 70 B3
Lāna'i i. U.S.A. 127 [inset]
Lāna'i City U.S.A. 127 [inset]
Lanao, Lake Phil. 69 G5
Lanark Canada 135 G1
Lanark U.K. 50 F5
Lanbi Kyun i. Myanmar 71 B5
Lancang China 76 C4
Lancang Jiang r. Asia see Mekong
Lancaster Canada 135 H1
Lancaster U.K. 48 E4
Lancaster CA U.S.A. 128 D4
Lancaster KY U.S.A. 134 C5
Lancaster MO U.S.A. 130 E3
Lancaster NH U.S.A. 135 J1
Lancaster OH U.S.A. 134 D4
Lancaster PA U.S.A. 135 G3
Lancaster SC U.S.A. 133 D5
Lancaster VA U.S.A. 135 G5
Lancaster WI U.S.A. 130 F3
Lancaster Canal U.K. 48 E5
Lancaster Sound strait Canada 119 J2
Lanchow China see Lanzhou
Landana Angola see Cacongo
Landau an der Isar Germany 53 M6
Landau in der Pfalz Germany 53 I5
Landeck Austria 47 M7
Landeh Iran 88 C4
Lander watercourse Australia 108 E5
Lander U.S.A. 126 F4
Landesbergen Germany 53 J2
Landfall Island India 71 A4
Landhi Pak. 89 G5
Landis Canada 121 I4
Landor Australia 109 B6
Landsberg Poland see Gorzów Wielkopolski
Landsberg am Lech Germany 47 M6
Land's End pt U.K. 49 B8
Landshut Germany 53 M6
Landskrona Sweden 45 H9
Landstuhl Germany 53 H5
Land Wursten reg. Germany 53 I1
Lanesborough Ireland 51 E4
Lang, Nam r. Myanmar 70 B2
La'nga Co l. China 82 E3
Langao China 77 F1
Langar Afgh. 89 H3
Langberg mts S. Africa 100 F5
Langdon U.S.A. 130 D1
Langeac France 56 F4
Langeberg mts S. Africa 100 D7
Langeland i. Denmark 45 G9
Längelmäki Fin. 45 N6
Langelsheim Germany 53 K3
Langen Germany 53 I1
Langenburg Canada 121 K5
Langenhagen Germany 53 J2
Langenhahn Germany 53 H4
Langenlonsheim Germany 53 H5
Langenthal Switz. 56 H3
Langenweddingen Germany 53 L2
Langeoog Germany 53 H1
Langesund Norway 45 F7
Langfang China 73 L5
Langgapayung Indon. 71 B7
Langgar China 76 B2
Langgöns Germany 53 I4
Langholm U.K. 48 E3
Langjan Nature Reserve S. Africa 101 I2
Langjökull ice cap Iceland 44 [inset 1]
Langka Indon. 71 B6
Langkawi i. Malaysia 71 B6
Lang Kha Toek, Khao mt. Thai. 71 B5
Langklip S. Africa 100 E5
Langley Canada 120 F5
Langley U.S.A. 134 D5
Langlo Crossing Australia 111 D5
Langmusi China 76 D1
Langong, Xé r. Laos 70 D3
Langøya i. Norway 44 I2
Langphu mt. China 83 F3
Langport U.K. 49 E7
Langqên Zangbo r. China 82 D3
Langqi China 77 H3
Langres France 56 G3
Langres, Plateau de France 56 G3
Langru China 82 D1
Langsa Indon. 71 B6
Langsa, Teluk b. Indon. 71 B6
Långsele Sweden 44 J5
Lang Sơn Vietnam 70 D2
Langtang National Park Nepal 83 F3
Langtao Myanmar 70 B1
Langting India 83 H4
Langtoft U.K. 48 G4
Langtry U.S.A. 131 C6
Languan China see Lantian
Languedoc reg. France 56 E5
Långvattnet Sweden 44 L4
Langwedel Germany 53 J2
Langxi China 77 H2
Langzhong China 76 E2
Lanigan Canada 121 J5
Lanín, Parque Nacional nat. park Arg. 144 B5
Lanín, Volcán vol. Arg./Chile 144 B5
Lanji India 82 E5
Lanka country Asia see Sri Lanka
Länkäran Azer. 91 H3
Lannion France 56 C2
Lanping China 76 C3
Lansån Sweden 44 M3
L'Anse U.S.A. 130 F2
Lanshan China 77 G3

▶Lansing U.S.A. 134 C2
Capital of Michigan.

Lanta, Ko i. Thai. 71 B6
Lantau Island H.K. China 77 [inset]
Lantau Peak hill H.K. China 77 [inset]
Lantian China 77 F1
Lantoto National Park South Sudan 98 D3
Lanxi Heilong. China 74 B3
Lanxi Zhejiang China 77 H2
Lan Yu i. Taiwan 77 I4
Lanzarote i. Canary Is 96 B2
Lanzhou China 72 I5
Lanzi China 74 A3
Laoag City Phil. 69 G3
Laoang Phil. 69 H4
Laobie Shan mts China 76 C4
Laobu China 77 F3
Lao Cai Vietnam 70 C2
Laodicea Syria see Latakia
Laodicea Turkey see Denizli
Laodicea ad Lycum Turkey see Denizli
Laodicea ad Mare Syria see Latakia
Laohekou China 77 F1
Laohupo China see Logpung
Laojie China see Yongping
Laojunmiao China 80 I4
Lao Ling mts China 74 B4
Lao Mangnai China 80 H4
Laon France 52 D5
La Oroya Peru 142 C6
Laos country Asia 70 C3
Laotougou China 74 C4
Laotu Dingzi hill China 74 B4
Laowohi pass India see Khardung La
Laoye Ling mts Heilongjiang/Jilin China 74 C4
Laoye Ling mts Jilin China 74 B3
Lapa Brazil 145 A4
La Palma i. Canary Is 96 B2
La Palma Panama 137 I7
La Palma U.S.A. 129 H5
La Palma del Condado Spain 57 C5
La Panza Range mts U.S.A. 128 C4
La Paragua Venez. 142 F2
La Parilla Mex. 131 B8
La Paya, Parque Nacional nat. park Col. 142 D3
La Paz Arg. 144 E4

▶La Paz Bol. 142 E7
Joint capital (with Sucre) of Bolivia.

La Paz Hond. 136 G6
La Paz Mex. 136 B4
La Pedrera Col. 142 E4
Lapeer U.S.A. 134 D2
La Perla Mex. 131 B6
La Pérouse Strait Japan/Russia 74 F3
La Pesca Mex. 131 D8
Lapinlahti Fin. 44 O5
Lapithos Cyprus 85 A2
Lap Lae Thai. 70 C3
La Plant U.S.A. 130 C2
La Plata Arg. 144 E4
La Plata MD U.S.A. 135 G4
La Plata MO U.S.A. 130 E3
La Plata, Isla i. Ecuador 142 B4

▶La Plata, Río de sea chan. Arg./Uruguay 144 E4
Part of the Río de la Plata - Paraná, 2nd longest river in South America and 9th in the world.

La Plonge, Lac l. Canada 121 J4
Lapmežciems Latvia 45 M8
La Pola Spain 57 D2
La Pola Siero Spain 57 D2
Lapominka Russia 42 I2
La Porte U.S.A. 134 B3
Laporte U.S.A. 135 G3
Laporte, Mount Canada 120 E2
La Potherie, Lac l. Canada 123 G2
La Poza Grande Mex. 127 E8
Lappajärvi Fin. 44 M5
Lappajärvi l. Fin. 44 M5
Lappeenranta Fin. 45 P6
Lappersdorf Germany 53 M5
Lappi Fin. 45 L6
Lappland reg. Europe 44 K3
La Pryor U.S.A. 131 D6
Lâpseki Turkey 59 L4
Laptevo Russia see Yasnogorsk
Laptev Sea Russia 65 N2
Lapua Fin. 44 M5
Lapurdum France see Bayonne
La Purísima Mex. 127 E8
Laqiya Arbain well Sudan 86 C5
La Quiaca Arg. 144 C2
L'Aquila Italy 58 E3
La Quinta U.S.A. 128 E5
Lār Iran 88 D5
Larache Morocco 57 C6
Lārak, Jazīreh-ye i. Iran 88 E5
Laramie U.S.A. 126 G4
Laramie r. U.S.A. 126 G4
Laramie Mountains U.S.A. 126 G4
Laranda Turkey see Karaman
Laranjal Paulista Brazil 145 B3
Laranjeiras do Sul Brazil 144 F3
Laranjinha r. Brazil 145 A3
Larantuka Indon. 108 C2
Larat Indon. 108 E1
Larat i. Indon. 108 E1
Larba Alg. 57 H5
Lärbro Sweden 45 K8
L'Ardenne, Plateau de plat. Belgium see Ardennes
Laredo Spain 57 E2
Laredo U.S.A. 131 D7
La Reina Adelaida, Archipiélago de is Chile 144 B8
Largeau Chad see Faya
Largo U.S.A. 133 D7
Largs U.K. 50 E5
L'Ariana Tunisia 58 D6
Larimore U.S.A. 130 D2
La Rioja Arg. 144 C3
La Rioja aut. comm. Spain 57 E2
Larisa Greece 59 J5
Larissa Greece see Larisa
Laristan reg. Iran 88 E5
Larkana Pak. 89 H5
Lark Harbour Canada 123 K4
Lark Passage Australia 110 D2
Larnaca Cyprus 85 A2
Larnaka Cyprus see Larnaca
Larnaka Bay Cyprus 85 A2
Larnakos, Kolpos b. Cyprus see Larnaka Bay
Larne U.K. 51 G3
Larned U.S.A. 130 D4
La Robla Spain 57 D2
La Roche-en-Ardenne Belgium 52 F4
La Rochelle France 56 D3
La Roche-sur-Yon France 56 D3
La Roda Spain 57 E4
La Romana Dom. Rep. 137 K5
La Ronge Canada 121 J4
La Ronge, Lac l. Canada 121 J4
La Rosa Mex. 131 C7
La Rosita Mex. 131 C6
Larrey Point Australia 108 B4
Larrimah Australia 108 F3
Lars Christensen Coast Antarctica 152 E2
Larsen Ice Shelf Antarctica 152 L2
Larsmo Fin. 44 M5
Larvik Norway 45 G7
La Sal U.S.A. 129 I2
LaSalle Canada 135 I1
La Salle U.S.A. 122 C6
Las Animas U.S.A. 130 C4
Las Anod Somalia see Laascaanood
La Sarre Canada 122 F4
Las Avispas Mex. 127 F7
La Savonnière, Lac l. Canada 123 G3
Lascano Uruguay 144 F4
La Scie Canada 123 L4
Las Cruces CA U.S.A. 128 C4
Las Cruces NM U.S.A. 127 G6
La Selle, Pic mt. Haiti 137 J5
La Serena Chile 144 B3
Las Esperanças Mex. 131 C7
La Seu d'Urgell Spain 57 G2
Las Flores Arg. 144 E5
Las Guacamatas, Cerro mt. Mex. 127 F7
Lāshār, Rūd-e r. Iran 89 F5
Lashburn Canada 121 I4
Lāsh-e Juwayn Afgh. 89 F4
Las Heras Mendoza Arg. 144 C4
Las Heras Santa Cruz Arg. 144 C7
Lashio Myanmar 70 B2
Lashkar India 82 D4
Lashkar Gāh Afgh. 89 G4
Las Juntas Chile 144 C3
Las Lomitas Arg. 144 D2
Las Marismas marsh Spain 57 C5
Las Martinetas Arg. 144 C7
Las Mesteñas Mex. 131 B6
Las Minas, Cerro de mt. Hond. 136 G6
Las Nopaleras, Cerro mt. Mex. 131 C7
La Société, Archipel de is Fr. Polynesia see Society Islands
Las Palmas watercourse Mex. 128 E5

▶Las Palmas de Gran Canaria Canary Is 96 B2
Joint capital (with Santa Cruz de Tenerife) of the Canary Islands.

Las Petas Bol. 143 G7
La Spezia Italy 58 C2
Las Plumas Arg. 144 C6
Laspur Pak. 89 I2
Lassance Brazil 145 B2
Lassen Peak vol. U.S.A. 128 C1
Lassen Volcanic National Park U.S.A. 128 C1
Las Tablas Panama 137 H7
Last Chance U.S.A. 130 C4
Last Mountain Lake Canada 121 J5
Las Tórtolas, Cerro mt. Chile 144 C3
Lastoursville Gabon 98 B4
Lastovo i. Croatia 58 G3
Las Tres Vírgenes, Volcán vol. Mex. 127 E8
Lastrup Germany 53 H2
Las Tunas Cuba 137 I4
Las Varas Chihuahua Mex. 127 G7
Las Varas Nayarit Mex. 136 C4
Las Varillas Arg. 144 D4
Las Vegas NM U.S.A. 127 G6
Las Vegas NV U.S.A. 129 F3
Las Villuercas mt. Spain 57 D4
La Tabatière Canada 123 K4
Latacunga Ecuador 142 C4
Latady Island Antarctica 152 L2
Latakia Syria 85 B2
La Teste-de-Buch France 56 D4
Latham Australia 109 B7
Lathen Germany 53 H2
Latheron U.K. 50 F2
Lathi India 82 B4
Latho India 82 D2
Lathrop U.S.A. 128 C3
Latina Italy 58 E4
La Tortuga, Isla i. Venez. 142 E1
Latrobe U.S.A. 134 F3
Laṭrūn West Bank 85 B4
Lattaquié Syria see Latakia
Lattrop Neth. 52 G2
La Tuque Canada 123 G5
Latur India 84 C2
Latvia country Europe 45 N8
Latvija country Europe see Latvia
Latviyskaya S.S.R. country Europe see Latvia
Lauca, Parque Nacional nat. park Chile 142 E7
Lauchhammer Germany 47 N5
Lauder U.K. 50 G5
Laudio Spain 57 E2
Lauenbrück Germany 53 J1
Lauenburg (Elbe) Germany 53 K1
Lauf an der Pegnitz Germany 53 L5
Laufen Switz. 56 H3
Lauge Koch Kyst reg. Greenland 119 L2
Laughlen, Mount Australia 109 F5
Laughlin Peak U.S.A. 127 G5
Lauka Estonia 45 M7
Launceston Australia 111 [inset]
Launceston U.K. 49 C8
Laune r. Ireland 51 C5
Launggyaung Myanmar 70 B1
Launglon Myanmar 71 B4
Launglon Bok Islands Myanmar 71 B4
La Unión Bol. 142 F7
Laura Australia 110 D2
Laurel DE U.S.A. 135 H4
Laurel MS U.S.A. 131 F6
Laurel MT U.S.A. 126 F3
Laureldale U.S.A. 135 H3
Laurel Hill hills U.S.A. 134 F4
Laurencekirk U.K. 50 G4
Laurieton Australia 112 F3
Laurinburg U.S.A. 133 E5
Lauru i. Solomon Is see Choiseul
Lausanne Switz. 56 H3
Laut i. Indon. 68 F7
Laut i. Indon. 71 E6
Lautem East Timor 108 D2
Lauterbach (Hessen) Germany 53 J4
Laut Kecil, Kepulauan is Indon. 68 F8
Lautoka Fiji 107 H3
Lauvuskylä Fin. 44 P5
Lauwersmeer l. Neth. 52 G1
Lava Beds National Monument nat. park U.S.A. 126 C4
Laval Canada 122 G5
Laval France 56 D2
La Vall d'Uixó Spain 57 F4
Lāvān, Jazīreh-ye i. Iran 88 D5
Lavapié, Punta pt Chile 144 B5
Lāvar Iran 88 C4
Laveaga Peak U.S.A. 128 C3
La Vega Dom. Rep. 137 J5
Laverne U.S.A. 131 D4
Laverton Australia 109 C7
La Víbora Mex. 131 C7
La Vila Joíosa Spain see Villajoyosa-La Vila Joiosa
La Viña Peru 142 C5
Lavongai i. P.N.G. see New Hanover
Lavras Brazil 145 B3
Lavumisa Swaziland 101 J4
Lavushi-Manda National Park Zambia 99 D5
Lawa India 82 C4
Lawa Myanmar 70 B1
Lawa Pak. 89 H3
Lawashi r. Canada 122 E3
Law Dome ice feature Antarctica 152 F2
Lawit, Gunung mt. Malaysia 71 C6
Lawksawk Myanmar 70 B2
Lawn Hill National Park Australia 110 B3
Lawra Ghana 96 C3
Lawrence IN U.S.A. 134 B4
Lawrence KS U.S.A. 130 E4
Lawrence MA U.S.A. 135 J2
Lawrenceburg IN U.S.A. 134 C4
Lawrenceburg KY U.S.A. 134 C4
Lawrenceburg TN U.S.A. 132 C5
Lawrenceville GA U.S.A. 133 D5
Lawrenceville IL U.S.A. 134 B4
Lawrenceville VA U.S.A. 135 G5
Lawrence Wells, Mount hill Australia 109 C6
Lawton U.S.A. 131 D5
Lawz, Jabal al mt. Saudi Arabia 90 D5
Laxå Sweden 45 I7
Laxey Isle of Man 48 C4
Laxgalts'ap Canada 120 D4
Lax Kw'alaams Canada 120 D4
Laxo U.K. 50 [inset]
Laya r. Russia 42 M2
Laydennyy, Mys c. Russia 42 J1
Laylá Saudi Arabia 86 G5
Laylá salt pan Saudi Arabia 85 D4
Laysan Island U.S.A. 150 I4
Laytonville U.S.A. 128 B2
Layyah Pak. 89 H4
Laza Myanmar 70 B1
Lazarev Russia 74 F1
Lazarevac Serbia 59 I2
Lázaro Cárdenas Mex. 136 D5
Lazdijai Lith. 45 M9
Lazikou China 76 D1
Lazo Primorskiy Kray Russia 74 D4
Lazo Respublika Sakha (Yakutiya) Russia 65 O3
Lead U.S.A. 130 C2
Leader Water r. U.K. 50 G5
Leadville Australia 112 D4
Leaf r. U.S.A. 131 F6
Leaf Bay Canada see Tasiujaq
Leaf Rapids Canada 121 K3
Leakey U.S.A. 131 D6
Leaksville U.S.A. see Eden
Leamington Canada 134 D2
Leane, Lough l. Ireland 51 C5
Leap Ireland 51 C6
Leatherhead U.K. 49 G7
L'Eau d'Heure l. Belgium 52 E4
Leavenworth IN U.S.A. 134 B4
Leavenworth KS U.S.A. 130 E4
Leavenworth WA U.S.A. 126 C3
Leavitt Peak U.S.A. 128 D2
Lebach Germany 52 G5
Lebanon country Asia 85 B2
Lebanon IN U.S.A. 134 B3
Lebanon KY U.S.A. 134 C5
Lebanon MO U.S.A. 130 E4
Lebanon NH U.S.A. 135 I2
Lebanon OH U.S.A. 134 C4
Lebanon OR U.S.A. 126 C3
Lebanon PA U.S.A. 135 G3
Lebanon TN U.S.A. 132 C4
Lebanon VA U.S.A. 134 D5
Lebanon Junction U.S.A. 134 C5
Lebanon Mountains Lebanon see Liban, Jebel
Lebbeke Belgium 52 E3
Lebec U.S.A. 128 D4
Lebedyan' Russia 43 H5
Lebel-sur-Quévillon Canada 122 F4
Le Blanc France 56 E3
Lębork Poland 47 P3
Lebowakgomo S. Africa 101 I3
Lebrija Spain 57 C5
Łebsko, Jezioro lag. Poland 47 P3
Lebu Chile 144 B5
Lebyazh'ye Kazakh. see Akku
Lebyazh'ye Russia 42 K4
Le Caire Egypt see Cairo
Le Cateau-Cambrésis France 52 D4
Le Catelet France 52 D4
Lecce Italy 58 H4
Lecco Italy 58 C2
Lech r. Austria/Germany 47 M7
Lechaina Greece 59 I6
Lechang China 77 G3
Le Chasseron mt. Switz. 56 H3
Le Chesne France 52 E5
Lechtaler Alpen mts Austria 47 M7
Leck Germany 47 L3
Lecompte U.S.A. 131 E6
Le Creusot France 56 G3
Le Crotoy France 52 B4
Lectoure France 56 E5
Ledang, Gunung mt. Malaysia 71 C7
Ledbury U.K. 49 E6
Ledesma Spain 57 D3
Ledmore U.K. 50 E2
Ledmozero Russia 44 R4
Ledong Hainan China 70 E3
Ledong Hainan China 77 F5
Le Dorat France 56 E3
Leduc Canada 120 H4
Lee r. Ireland 51 D6
Lee IN U.S.A. 134 B3

Lee MA U.S.A. 135 I2
Leech Lake U.S.A. 130 E2
Leeds U.K. 48 F5
Leedstown U.K. 49 B8
Leek Neth. 52 G1
Leek U.K. 49 E5
Leende Neth. 52 F3
Leer (Ostfriesland) Germany 53 H1
Leesburg FL U.S.A. 133 D6
Leesburg GA U.S.A. 133 C6
Leesburg OH U.S.A. 134 D4
Leesburg VA U.S.A. 135 G4
Leese Germany 53 J2
Lee Steere Range hills Australia 109 C6
Leesville U.S.A. 131 E6
Leesville Lake OH U.S.A. 134 E3
Leesville Lake VA U.S.A. 134 F5
Leeton Australia 112 C5
Leeu-Gamka S. Africa 100 E7
Leeuwarden Neth. 52 F1
Leeuwin, Cape Australia 109 A8
Leeuwin-Naturaliste National Park Australia 109 A8
Lee Vining U.S.A. 128 D3
Leeward Islands Caribbean Sea 137 L5
Lefka Cyprus 85 A2
Lefkada Greece 59 I5
Lefkada i. Greece 59 I5
Lefkás Greece see Lefkada
Lefke Cyprus see Lefka
Lefkimmi Greece 59 I5
Lefkoniko Cyprus see Lefkonikon
Lefkonikon Cyprus 85 A2
Lefkoşa Cyprus see Nicosia
Lefkosia Cyprus see Nicosia
Lefroy r. Canada 123 H2
Lefroy, Lake salt flat Australia 109 C7
Legarde r. Canada 122 D4
Legazpi Phil. 69 G4
Legden Germany 52 H2
Legges Tor mt. Australia 111 [inset]
Leghorn Italy see Livorno
Legnago Italy 58 D2
Legnica Poland 47 P5
Le Grand U.S.A. 128 C3
Legune Australia 108 E3
Leh India 82 D2
Le Havre France 56 E2
Lehi U.S.A. 129 H1
Lehighton U.S.A. 135 H3
Lehmo Fin. 44 P5
Lehre Germany 53 K2
Lehrte Germany 53 J2
Lehtimäki Fin. 44 M5
Lehututu Botswana 100 E2
Leibnitz Austria 47 O7
Leicester U.K. 49 F6
Leichhardt r. Australia 106 B3
Leichhardt Falls Australia 110 B3
Leichhardt Range mts Australia 110 D4
Leiden Neth. 52 E2
Leie r. Belgium 52 D3
Leigh N.Z. 113 E3
Leigh U.K. 48 E5
Leighton Buzzard U.K. 49 G7
Leiktho Myanmar 70 B3
Leimen Germany 53 I5
Leine r. Germany 53 J2
Leinefelde Germany 53 K3
Leinster Australia 109 C6
Leinster reg. Ireland 51 F4
Leinster, Mount hill Ireland 51 F5
Leipsic U.S.A. 134 D3
Leipsoi i. Greece 59 L6
Leipzig Germany 53 M3
Leipzig-Halle airport Germany 53 M3
Leiranger Norway 44 I3
Leiria Port. 57 B4
Leirvik Norway 45 D7
Leishan China 77 F3
Leisler, Mount hill Australia 109 E5
Leisnig Germany 53 M3
Leitchfield U.S.A. 134 B5
Leith Hill hill U.K. 49 G7
Leiva, Cerro mt. Col. 142 D3
Leixlip Ireland 51 F4
Leiyang China 77 G3
Leizhou China 77 F4
Leizhou Bandao pen. China 77 F4
Leizhou Wan b. China 77 F4
Lek r. Neth. 52 E3
Leka Norway 44 G4
Lékana Congo 98 B4
Le Kef Tunisia 58 C6
Lekhainá Greece see Lechaina
Lekitobi Indon. 69 G7
Lekkersing S. Africa 100 C5
Lékoni Gabon 98 B4
Leksand Sweden 45 I6
Leksozero, Ozero l. Russia 44 Q5
Lelai, Tanjung pt Indon. 69 H6
Leland U.S.A. 134 C1
Leli China see Tianlin
Lélouma Guinea 96 B3
Lelystad Neth. 52 F2
Le Maire, Estrecho de sea chan. Arg. 144 C9
Léman, Lac l. France/Switz. see Geneva, Lake
Le Mans France 56 E2
Le Mars U.S.A. 130 D3
Lemberg France 53 H5
Lemberg Ukr. see L'viv
Lembruch Germany 53 I2
Lemdiyya Alg. see Médéa
Leme Brazil 145 B3
Lemele Neth. 52 G2
Lemesos Cyprus see Limassol
Lemgo Germany 53 I2
Lemhi Range mts U.S.A. 126 E3
Lemi Fin. 45 O6
Lemieux Islands Canada 119 L3
Lemmenjoen kansallispuisto nat. park Fin. 44 N2
Lemmer Neth. 52 F2
Lemmon U.S.A. 130 C2
Lemmon, Mount U.S.A. 129 H5
Lemnos i. Greece see Limnos
Lemoncove U.S.A. 128 D3
Lemoore U.S.A. 128 D3
Le Moyne, Lac l. Canada 123 H2
Lemro r. Myanmar 70 A2
Lemtybozh Russia 41 R3
Le Murge hills Italy 58 G4
Lemvig Denmark 45 F8
Lem"yu r. Russia 42 M3
Lena r. Russia 72 J1
Lena U.S.A. 134 A1
Lena, Mount U.S.A. 129 I1
Lenadoon Point Ireland 51 C3
Lena Pillars Nature Park tourist site Russia 65 N3
Lenchung Tso salt l. China 83 E2
Lençóis Brazil 145 C1
Lençóis Maranhenses, Parque Nacional dos nat. park Brazil 143 J4
Lendery Russia 44 Q5
Le Neubourg France 49 H9
Lengerich Germany 53 H2
Lenglong Ling mts China 72 I5
Lengshuijiang China 77 F3
Lenham U.K. 49 H7
Lenhovda Sweden 45 I8
Lenin, Qullai mt. Kyrg./Tajik. see Lenin Peak
Lenina, Pik mt. Kyrg./Tajik. see Lenin Peak
Leninabad Tajik. see Khŭjand
Leninakan Armenia see Gyumri
Lenin Atyndagy Choku mt. Kyrg./Tajik. see Lenin Peak
Lenine Crimea 90 D1
Leningrad Russia see St Petersburg
Leningrad Tajik. 89 H2
Leningrad Oblast admin. div. Russia see Leningradskaya Oblast'
Leningradskaya Russia 43 H7
Leningradskaya Oblast' admin. div. Russia 45 R7
Leningradskiy Russia 65 S3
Leningradskiy Tajik. see Leningrad
Lenino Crimea see Lenine
Leninobod Tajik. see Khŭjand
Lenin Peak Kyrg./Tajik. 89 I2
Leninsk Kazakh. see Baykonyr
Leninsk Russia 43 J6
Leninskiy Russia 43 H5
Leninsk-Kuznetskiy Russia 64 J4
Leninskoye Kirovskaya Oblast' Russia 42 J4
Leninskoye Yevreyskaya Avtonomnaya Oblast' Russia 74 D3
Lenkoran' Azer. see Länkäran
Lenne r. Germany 53 H3
Lennoxville Canada 135 J1
Lenoir U.S.A. 132 D5
Lenore U.S.A. 134 D5
Lenore Lake Canada 121 J4
Lenox U.S.A. 135 I2
Lens France 52 C4
Lensk Russia 65 M3
Lenti Hungary 58 G1
Lentini Sicily Italy 58 F6
Lenya Myanmar 71 B5
Lenzen (Elbe) Germany 53 L1
Léo Burkina Faso 96 C3
Leoben Austria 47 O7
Leodhais, Eilean i. U.K. see Lewis, Isle of
Leominster U.K. 49 E6
Leominster U.S.A. 135 J2
León Mex. 136 D4
León Nicaragua 137 G6
León Spain 57 D2
Leon r. U.S.A. 131 D6
Leonardtown U.S.A. 135 G4
Leonardville Namibia 100 D2
Leongatha Australia 112 B7
Leonidi Greece see Leonidio
Leonidio Greece 59 J6
Leonidovo Russia 74 F2
Leonora Australia 109 C7
Leopold U.S.A. 134 E4
Leopold and Astrid Coast Antarctica see King Leopold and Queen Astrid Coast
Léopold II, Lac l. Dem. Rep. Congo see Mai-Ndombe, Lac
Leopoldina Brazil 145 C3
Leopoldo de Bulhões Brazil 145 A2
Léopoldville Dem. Rep. Congo see Kinshasa
Leoti U.S.A. 130 C4
Leoville Canada 121 J4
Lepalale S. Africa see Lephalale
Lepaya Latvia see Liepāja
Lepel' Belarus see Lyepyel'
Lepellé r. Canada 123 H1
Lephalala r. S. Africa 101 H2
Lephalale S. Africa 101 H2
Lephepe Botswana 101 G2
Lephoi S. Africa 101 G6
Leping China 77 H2
Lepontine Alps mts Italy/Switz. 58 C1
Leppävirta Fin. 44 O5
Lepreau, Point Canada 123 I5
Lepsa Kazakh. see Lepsi
Lepsi Kazakh. 80 E2
Le Puy France see Le Puy-en-Velay
Le Puy-en-Velay France 56 F4
Le Quesnoy France 52 D4
Lerala Botswana 101 H2
Leratswana S. Africa 101 H5
Léré Mali 96 C3
Lereh Indon. 69 J7
Leribe Lesotho see Hlotse
Lérida Col. 142 D4
Lérida Spain see Lleida
Lerik Azer. 91 H3
Lerma Spain 57 E2
Lermontov Russia 91 F1
Lermontovka Russia 74 D3
Lermontovskiy Russia see Lermontov
Leros i. Greece 59 L6
Le Roy U.S.A. 135 G2
Le Roy, Lac l. Canada 122 G2
Lerum Sweden 45 H8
Lerwick U.K. 50 [inset]
Les Amirantes is Seychelles see Amirante Islands
Lesbos i. Greece 59 K5
Les Cayes Haiti 137 J5
Leshan China 76 D2
Leshukonskoye Russia 42 J2
Lesi watercourse South Sudan 97 F4
Leskhimstroy Ukr. see Syeverodonets'k
Leskovac Serbia 59 I3
Leslie U.S.A. 134 C2
Lesneven France 56 B2
Lesnoy Kirovskaya Oblast' Russia 42 L4
Lesnoy Murmanskaya Oblast' Russia see Umba
Lesnoye Russia 42 G4
Lesogorskoye Russia 74 F2
Lesopil'noye Russia 74 D3
Lesosibirsk Russia 64 K4
Lesotho country Africa 101 I5
Lesozavodsk Russia 74 D3
L'Espérance Rock i. Kermadec Is 107 I5
Les Pieux France 49 F9
Les Sables-d'Olonne France 56 D3
Lesse r. Belgium 52 E4
Lesser Antarctica reg. Antarctica see West Antarctica
Lesser Antilles is Caribbean Sea 137 K6
Lesser Caucasus mts Asia 91 F2
Lesser Himalaya mts India/Nepal 82 D3
Lesser Khingan Mountains China see Xiao Hinggan Ling
Lesser Slave Lake Canada 120 H4
Lesser Tunb i. The Gulf see Tonb-e Küchek, Jazīreh-ye
Lessines Belgium 52 D4
Lester U.S.A. 134 E5
Lestijärvi Fin. 44 N5
Les Vans France 56 G4
Lesvos i. Greece see Lesbos
Leszno Poland 47 P5
Letaba S. Africa 101 J2
Letchworth Garden City U.K. 49 G7
Le Télégraphe hill France 56 G3
Leteri India 82 D4
Letha Range mts Myanmar 70 A2
Lethbridge Alta Canada 121 H5
Lethbridge Nfld. and Lab. Canada 123 L4
Leti i. Indon. 108 D2
Leti, Kepulauan is Indon. 108 D2
Leticia Col. 142 E4
Letlhakeng Botswana 101 G3
Letnerechenskiy Russia 42 G2
Letniy Navolok Russia 42 H2
Le Touquet-Paris-Plage France 52 B4
Letpadan Myanmar 70 A3
Le Tréport France 52 B4
Letsitele S. Africa 101 J2
Letsopa S. Africa 101 G4
Letterkenny Ireland 51 E3
Letung Indon. 71 D7
Lëtzebuerg country Europe see Luxembourg
Letzlingen Germany 53 L2
Léua Angola 99 C5
Leucas Greece see Lefkada
Leucate, Étang de l. France 56 F5
Leuchars U.K. 50 G4
Leukas Greece see Lefkada
Leunovo Russia 42 I2
Leupp U.S.A. 129 H4
Leupung Indon. 71 A6
Leura Australia 110 E4
Leusden Neth. 52 F2
Leuser, Gunung mt. Indon. 71 B7
Leutershausen Germany 53 K5
Leuven Belgium 52 E4
Levadeia Greece see Livadeia
Levan U.S.A. 129 H2
Levanger Norway 44 G5
Levante, Riviera di coastal area Italy 58 C2
Levanto Italy 58 C2
Levashi Russia 91 G2
Levelland U.S.A. 131 C5
Leven England U.K. 48 G5
Leven Scotland U.K. 50 G4
Leven, Loch l. U.K. 50 F4
Lévêque, Cape Australia 108 C4
Leverkusen Germany 52 G3
Lévézou mts France 56 F4
Levice Slovakia 47 Q6
Levin N.Z. 113 E5
Lévis Canada 123 H5
Levitha i. Greece 59 L6
Levittown NY U.S.A. 135 I3
Levittown PA U.S.A. 135 H3
Levkás i. Greece see Lefkada
Levkímmi Greece see Lefkimmi
Levskigrad Bulg. see Karlovo
Lev Tolstoy Russia 43 H5
Levuka Fiji 107 H3
Lévy, Cap c. France 49 F9
Lewe Myanmar 70 B3
Lewerberg mt. S. Africa 100 C5
Lewes U.K. 49 H8
Lewes U.S.A. 135 H4
Lewis CO U.S.A. 129 I3
Lewis IN U.S.A. 134 B4
Lewis KS U.S.A. 130 D4
Lewis, Isle of i. U.K. 50 C2
Lewis, Lake salt flat Australia 108 F5
Lewisburg KY U.S.A. 134 B5
Lewisburg PA U.S.A. 135 G3
Lewisburg WV U.S.A. 134 E5
Lewis Cass, Mount Canada/U.S.A. 120 D3
Lewis Hills hill Canada 123 K4
Lewis Pass N.Z. 113 D6
Lewis Range hills Australia 108 E5
Lewis Range mts U.S.A. 126 E2
Lewis Smith, Lake U.S.A. 133 C5
Lewiston ID U.S.A. 126 D3
Lewiston ME U.S.A. 135 J1
Lewistown IL U.S.A. 130 F3
Lewistown MT U.S.A. 126 F3
Lewistown PA U.S.A. 135 G3
Lewisville U.S.A. 131 E5
Lexington KY U.S.A. 134 C4
Lexington MI U.S.A. 134 D2
Lexington NC U.S.A. 132 D5
Lexington NE U.S.A. 130 D3
Lexington TN U.S.A. 131 F5
Lexington VA U.S.A. 134 F5
Lexington Park U.S.A. 135 G4
Leyden Neth. see Leiden
Leye China 76 E3
Leyla Dāgh mt. Iran 88 B2
Leyte i. Phil. 69 G4
Lezha Albania see Lezhë
Lezhë Albania 59 H4
Lezhi China 76 E2
Lezhu China 77 G4
L'gov Russia 43 G6
Lharigarbo China 83 G2
Lhasa China 83 G3
Lhasoi China 76 B2
Lhatog China 76 C2
Lhaviyani Atoll Maldives see Faadhippolhu
Lhazê Xizang China 76 B2
Lhazê Xizang China 83 F3
Lhazhong China 83 F3
Lhokkruet Indon. 71 A6
Lhokseumawe Indon. 71 B6
Lhoksukon Indon. 71 B6
Lhoma China 83 G3
Lhorong China 76 B2
▶Lhotse mt. China/Nepal 83 F4
4th highest mountain in Asia and the world.
Lhozhag China 83 G3
Lhuentse Bhutan 83 G4
Lhünzê China 76 B2
Lhünzhub China see Poindo
Liakoura mt. Greece 59 J5
Liancheng China see Guangnan
Liancourt France 52 C5
Liancourt Rocks i. N. Pacific Ocean 75 C5
Liandu China see Lishui
Liangdang China 76 E1
Liangdaohe China see Zaring
Lianghe Chongqing China 77 F2
Lianghe Sichuan China 76 D2
Lianghe Yunnan China 76 C3
Lianghekou Chongqing China see Lianghe
Lianghekou Gansu China 76 E1
Liangping China 76 E2
Liangshan China see Liangping
Liang Shan mt. Myanmar 70 B1
Liangshi China see Shaodong
Liangtian China 77 F4
Liangyuan China see Shangqiu
Liangzhou China see Wuwei
Liangzi Hu l. China 77 G2
Lianhe China see Qianjiang
Lianhua China 77 G3
Lianhua Shan mts China 77 G4
Lianjiang Fujian China 77 H3
Lianjiang Jiangxi China see Xingguo
Liannan China 77 G3
Lianping China 77 G3
Lianran China see Anning
Lianshan Guangdong China 77 G3
Lianshan Liaoning China 73 M4
Lianshui China 77 H1
Liant, Cape i. Thai. see Samae San, Ko
Liantang China see Nanchang
Lianxian China see Lianzhou
Lianyin China 74 A1
Lianyungang China 77 H1
Lianzhou Guangdong China 77 G3
Lianzhou Guangxi China see Hepu
Liaocheng China 73 L5
Liaodong Bandao pen. China 73 M4
Liaodong Wan b. China 73 M4
Liaogao China see Songtao
Liao He r. China 74 A4
Liaoning prov. China 74 A4
Liaoyang China 74 A4
Liaoyuan China 74 B4
Liaozhong China 74 A4
Liapades Greece 59 H5
Liard r. Canada 120 F2
Liard Highway Canada 120 F2
Liard Plateau Canada 120 E2
Liard River Canada 120 E3
Liari Pak. 89 G5
Liathach mt. U.K. 50 D3
Liban country Asia see Lebanon
Liban, Jebel mts Lebanon 85 C2
Libau Latvia see Liepāja
Libby U.S.A. 126 E2
Libenge Dem. Rep. Congo 98 B3
Liberal U.S.A. 131 C4
Liberdade Brazil 145 B3
Liberec Czechia 47 O5
Liberia country Africa 96 C4
Liberia Costa Rica 137 G6
Liberty IN U.S.A. 134 C4
Liberty KY U.S.A. 134 C5
Liberty ME U.S.A. 135 K1
Liberty MO U.S.A. 130 E4
Liberty MS U.S.A. 131 F6
Liberty NY U.S.A. 135 H3
Liberty TX U.S.A. 131 E6
Liberty Lake U.S.A. 135 G4
Libin Belgium 52 F5
Libnī, Gebel hill Egypt see Libnī, Jabal
Libnī, Jabal hill Egypt 85 A4
Libo China 76 E3
Libobo, Tanjung pt Indon. 69 H7
Libode S. Africa 101 I6
Libong, Ko i. Thai. 71 B6
Libourne France 56 D4
Libral Well Australia 108 D5
Libre, Sierra mts Mex. 127 F7
▶Libreville Gabon 98 A3
Capital of Gabon.
▶Libya country Africa 97 E2
4th largest country in Africa.
Libyan Desert Egypt/Libya 86 C5
Libyan Plateau Egypt 90 B5
Licantén Chile 144 B4
Licata Sicily Italy 58 E6
Lice Turkey 91 F3
Lich Germany 53 I4
Lichas pen. Greece 59 J5
Licheng Guangxi China see Lipu
Licheng Jiangsu China see Jinhu
Lichfield U.K. 49 F6
Lichinga Moz. 99 D5
Lichte Germany 53 L4
Lichtenau Germany 53 I3
Lichtenburg S. Africa 101 H4
Lichtenfels Germany 53 L4
Lichtenvoorde Neth. 52 G3
Lichuan Hubei China 77 F2
Lichuan Jiangxi China 77 H3
Lida Belarus 45 N10
Liddel Water r. U.K. 50 G5
Lidfontein Namibia 100 D3
Lidköping Sweden 45 H7
Lidsjöberg Sweden 44 I4
Liebenau Germany 53 J2
Liebenburg Germany 53 K2
Liebenwalde Germany 53 N2
Liebig, Mount Australia 109 E5
Liechtenstein country Europe 56 I3
Liège Belgium 52 F4
Liegnitz Poland see Legnica
Lieksa Fin. 44 Q5
Lielupe r. Latvia 45 N8
Lielvārde Latvia 45 N8
Lienart Dem. Rep. Congo 98 C3
Lienchung i. Taiwan see Mazu Dao
Liên Nghia Vietnam 71 E5
Liên Sơn Vietnam 71 E4
Lienz Austria 47 N7
Liepāja Latvia 45 L8
Liepaya Latvia see Liepāja
Lier Belgium 52 E3
Lierre Belgium see Lier
Lieshout Neth. 52 F3
Lietuva country Europe see Lithuania
Liévin France 52 C4
Lièvre, Rivière du r. Canada 122 G5
Liezen Austria 47 O7
Liffey r. Ireland 51 F4
Lifford Ireland 51 E3
Lifi Mahuida mt. Arg. 144 C6
Lifou i. New Caledonia 107 G4
Lifu i. New Caledonia see Lifou
Līgatne Latvia 45 N8
Lightning Ridge Australia 112 C2
Ligny-en-Barrois France 52 F6
Ligonha r. Moz. 99 D5
Ligonier U.S.A. 134 C3
Ligui Mex. 127 F8
Ligure, Mar sea France/Italy see Ligurian Sea
Ligurian Sea France/Italy 58 C3
Ligurienne, Mer sea France/Italy see Ligurian Sea
Ligurta U.S.A. 129 F5
Lihir Group is P.N.G. 106 F2
Lihou Reef and Cays Australia 110 E3
Lihua China 77 F3
Liivi laht b. Estonia/Latvia see Riga, Gulf of
Liji China 77 H1
Lijiang Yunnan China 76 D3
Lijiang Yunnan China see Yuanjiang
Lijiazhai China 77 G2
Lika reg. Croatia 58 F2
Likasi Dem. Rep. Congo 99 C5
Likati Dem. Rep. Congo 98 C3
Likely Canada 120 F4
Likhachevo Ukr. see Pervomays'kyy
Likhachyovo Ukr. see Pervomays'kyy
Likhapani India 83 H4
Likhás pen. Greece see Lichas
Likhoslavl' Russia 42 G4
Liku Indon. 68 D6
Likurga Russia 42 I4
L'Île-Rousse Corsica France 56 I5
Lilienthal Germany 53 I1
Liling China 77 G3
Lilla Pak. 89 I3
Lilla Edet Sweden 45 H7
Lille Belgium 52 E3
Lille France 52 D4
Lille (Lesquin) airport France 52 D4
Lille Bælt sea chan. Denmark see Little Belt
Lillebonne France 49 H9
Lillehammer Norway 45 G6
Lillers France 52 C4
Lillesand Norway 45 F7
Lillestrøm Norway 45 G7
Lilley U.S.A. 134 C2
Lillholmsjö Sweden 44 I5
Lillian, Point hill Australia 109 D6
Lillington U.S.A. 133 E5
Lillooet Canada 120 F5
Lillooet r. Canada 120 F5
Lillooet Range mts Canada 120 F5
▶Lilongwe Malawi 99 D5
Capital of Malawi.
Lilydale Australia 111 B7
▶Lima Peru 142 C6
Capital of Peru. 4th most populous city in South America.
Lima MT U.S.A. 126 E3
Lima NY U.S.A. 135 G2
Lima OH U.S.A. 134 C3
Lima Duarte Brazil 145 C3
Liman Russia 43 J7
Limar Indon. 108 D1
Limassol Cyprus 85 A2
Limavady U.K. 51 F2
Limay r. Arg. 144 C5
Limbaži Latvia 45 N8
Limbunya Australia 108 E4
Limburg an der Lahn Germany 53 I4
Lim Chu Kang hill Sing. 71 [inset]
Lime Acres S. Africa 100 F5
Limeira Brazil 145 B3
Limerick Ireland 51 D5
Limestone Point Canada 121 L4
Limingen Norway 44 H4
Limingen l. Norway 44 H4
Limington U.S.A. 135 J2
Liminka Fin. 44 N4
Limmen Bight b. Australia 110 B2
Limmen National Park Australia 108 F3
Limnos i. Greece 59 K5
Limoeiro Brazil 143 K5
Limoges Canada 135 H1
Limoges France 56 E4
Limón Costa Rica see Puerto Limón
Limon U.S.A. 130 C4
Limonlu Turkey 85 B1
Limonum France see Poitiers
Limousin reg. France 56 E4
Limoux France 56 F5
Limpopo, Parque Nacional do nat. park S. Africa 101 J2
Limpopo prov. S. Africa 101 I2
Limpopo r. S. Africa/Zimbabwe 101 K3
Limu China 77 F3
Līnah well Saudi Arabia 91 F5
Linakhamari Russia 44 Q2
Lin'an China see Jianshui
Linares Chile 144 B5
Linares Mex. 131 D7
Linares Spain 57 E4
Lincang China 76 D4
Lincheng Hainan China see Lingao
Lincheng Hunan China see Huitong
Linchuan China see Fuzhou
Linck Nunataks nunataks Antarctica 152 K1
Lincoln Arg. 144 D4
Lincoln U.K. 48 G5
Lincoln CA U.S.A. 128 C2
Lincoln IL U.S.A. 130 F3
Lincoln MI U.S.A. 134 D1
▶Lincoln NE U.S.A. 130 D3
Capital of Nebraska.
Lincoln City IN U.S.A. 134 B4
Lincoln City OR U.S.A. 126 B3
Lincoln Island Paracel Is 68 E3
Lincoln National Park Australia 111 A7
Lincoln Sea Canada/Greenland 153 J1
Lincolnshire Wolds hills U.K. 48 G5
Lincolnton U.S.A. 133 D5
Linda, Serra hills Brazil 145 C1
Linda Creek watercourse Australia 110 B4
Lindau Germany 53 M2
Lindau (Bodensee) Germany 47 L7
Lindeman Group is Australia 110 E4
Linden Canada 120 H5
Linden Germany 53 I4
Linden Guyana 143 G2
Linden AL U.S.A. 133 C5
Linden MI U.S.A. 134 D2
Linden TN U.S.A. 132 C5
Linden TX U.S.A. 131 E5
Linden Grove U.S.A. 130 E2
Lindern (Oldenburg) Germany 53 H2
Lindesnes c. Norway 45 E7
Líndhos Greece see Lindos
Lindi r. Dem. Rep. Congo 98 C3
Lindi Tanz. 99 D4
Lindian China 74 B3
Lindisfarne i. U.K. see Holy Island
Lindley S. Africa 101 H4
Lindos Greece 55 J4
Lindos, Akra pt Greece see Gkinas, Akrotirio
Lindsay Canada 135 F1
Lindsay CA U.S.A. 128 D3
Lindsay MT U.S.A. 126 G3
Lindsborg U.S.A. 130 D4
Lindside U.S.A. 134 E5
Lindum U.K. see Lincoln
Line Islands Kiribati 151 J5
Linesville U.S.A. 134 E3
Linfen China 73 K5
Lingampet India 84 C2
Linganamakki Reservoir India 84 B3
Lingao China 77 F5
Lingayen Phil. 69 G3
Lingbi China 77 H1
Lingcheng Anhui China see Lingbi
Lingcheng Guangxi China see Lingshan
Lingcheng Hainan China see Lingshui
Lingchuan Guangxi China 77 F3
Lingchuan Shanxi China 77 G1
Lingelethu S. Africa 101 H7
Lingen (Ems) Germany 53 H2
Lingga, Kepulauan is Indon. 68 D7
Lingle U.S.A. 126 G4
Lingling China 77 F3
Lingomo Dem. Rep. Congo 98 C3
Lingshan China 77 F4
Lingshui China 77 F5
Lingshui Wan b. China 77 F5
Lingsugur India 84 C2
Lingtai China 76 E1
Linguère Senegal 96 B3
Lingui China 77 F3
Lingxi China see Yongshun
Lingxia China 74 A3
Lingxian China see Yanling
Lingxiang China 77 G2
Lingyang China see Cili
Lingyun China 76 E3
Lingzi Tang reg. China 82 D2
Linh, Ngok mt. Vietnam 70 D4
Linhai China 77 I2
Linhares Brazil 145 C2
Linhe China see Bayannur
Linhpa Myanmar 70 A1
Linjiang China 74 B4
Linjin China 77 F1
Linköping Sweden 45 I7
Linkou China 74 C3
Linli China 77 F2
Linlithgow U.K. 50 F5
Linn MO U.S.A. 130 F4
Linn TX U.S.A. 131 D7
Linn, Mount U.S.A. 128 B1
Linnansaaren kansallispuisto nat. park Fin. 44 P5
Linnhe, Loch inlet U.K. 50 D4
Linnich Germany 52 G4
Linosa, Isola di i. Sicily Italy 58 E7
Linquan China 77 G1
Linru Henan China see Ruzhou
Linru Henan China 77 G1
Lins Brazil 145 A3
Linshu China 77 H1
Linshui China 76 E2
Lintan China 76 D1
Lintao China 76 D1
Linton IN U.S.A. 134 B4
Linton ND U.S.A. 130 C2
Linwu China 77 G3
Linxi China 73 L4
Linxia China 76 D1
Linxiang China 77 G2
Linyi Shandong China 73 L5
Linyi Shandong China 77 H1
Linying China 77 G1
Linz Austria 47 O6
Lion, Golfe du g. France 56 F5

Lions, Gulf of France see Lion, Golfe du
Lions Bay Canada 120 F5
Lioua Chad 97 E3
Lipari Sicily Italy 58 F5
Lipari, Isole is Italy 58 F5
Lipetsk Russia 43 H5
Lipin Bor Russia 42 H3
Liping China 77 F3
Lipova Romania 59 I1
Lipovtsy Russia 74 C3
Lippe r. Germany 53 G3
Lippstadt Germany 53 I3
Lipsoí i. Greece see Leipsoi
Lipti Lekh pass Nepal 82 E3
Liptrap, Cape Australia 112 B7
Lipu China 77 F3
Lira Uganda 98 D3
Liranga Congo 98 B4
Lircay Peru 142 D6
Lisala Dem. Rep. Congo 98 C3
Lisbellaw U.K. 51 E3
Lisboa Port. see Lisbon

▶Lisbon Port. 57 B4
Capital of Portugal.

Lisbon ME U.S.A. 135 J1
Lisbon NH U.S.A. 135 J1
Lisbon OH U.S.A. 134 E3
Lisburn U.K. 51 F3
Liscannor Bay Ireland 51 C5
Lisdoonvarna Ireland 51 C4
Lishan Taiwan 77 I3
Lishe Jiang r. China 76 D3
Lishi China see Dingnan
Lishu China 74 B4
Lishui China 77 H2
Li Shui r. China 77 F2
Lisichansk Ukr. see Lysychans'k
Lisieux France 56 E2
Liskeard U.K. 49 C8
Liski Russia 43 H6
L'Isle-Adam France 52 C5
Lismore Australia 112 F2
Lismore Ireland 51 E5
Lisnarrick U.K. 51 E3
Lisnaskea U.K. 51 E3
Liss mt. Saudi Arabia 85 D4
Lissa Poland see Leszno
Lister, Mount Antarctica 152 H1
Listowel Canada 134 E2
Listowel Ireland 51 C5
Lit Sweden 44 I5
Litang Guangxi China 77 F4
Litang Sichuan China 76 D2
Lītāni, Nahr el r. Lebanon 85 B3
Litchfield CA U.S.A. 128 C1
Litchfield CT U.S.A. 135 I3
Litchfield IL U.S.A. 130 F4
Litchfield MI U.S.A. 134 C2
Litchfield MN U.S.A. 130 E2
Lit-et-Mixe France 56 D4
Lithgow Australia 112 E4
Lithino, Akra pt Greece see Lithino, Akrotirio
Lithino, Akrotirio pt Greece 59 K7
Lithuania country Europe 45 M9
Lititz U.S.A. 135 G3
Litoměřice Czechia 47 O5
Litovko Russia 74 D2
Litovskaya S.S.R. country Europe see Lithuania
Little r. U.S.A. 131 E6
Little Abaco i. Bahamas 133 E7
Little Abitibi r. Canada 122 E4
Little Abitibi Lake Canada 122 E4
Little Andaman i. India 71 A5
Little Bahama Bank sea feature Bahamas 133 E7
Little Barrier Island i. N.Z. 113 E3
Little Belt sea chan. Denmark 45 F9
Little Belt Mountains U.S.A. 126 F3
Little Bitter Lake Egypt 85 A4
Little Cayman i. Cayman Is 137 H5
Little Churchill r. Canada 121 M3
Little Chute U.S.A. 134 A1
Little Coco Island Cocos Is 71 A4
Little Colorado r. U.S.A. 129 H3
Little Creek Peak U.S.A. 129 G3
Little Current Canada 122 E5
Little Current r. Canada 122 D4
Little Desert National Park Australia 111 C8
Little Egg Harbor inlet U.S.A. 135 H4
Little Exuma i. Bahamas 133 F8
Little Falls U.S.A. 130 E2
Littlefield AZ U.S.A. 129 G3
Littlefield TX U.S.A. 131 C5
Little Fork r. U.S.A. 130 E1
Little Grand Rapids Canada 121 M4
Littlehampton U.K. 49 G8
Little Inagua Island Bahamas 133 F8
Little Karas Berg plat. Namibia 100 D4
Little Karoo plat. S. Africa 100 E7
Little Lake U.S.A. 128 E4
Little Mecatina r. Canada see Petit Mécatina
Little Mecatina Island Canada see Petit Mécatina, Île du
Little Minch sea chan. U.K. 50 B3
Little Missouri r. U.S.A. 130 C2
Little Namaqualand reg. S. Africa see Namaqualand
Little Nicobar i. India 71 A6
Little Ouse r. U.K. 49 H6
Little Pamir mts Asia 89 I2
Little Rancheria r. Canada 120 D2
Little Red River Canada 120 H3

▶Little Rock U.S.A. 131 E5
Capital of Arkansas.

Littlerock U.S.A. 128 E4
Little Sable Point U.S.A. 134 B2
Little Salmon Lake Canada 120 C2
Little Salt Lake U.S.A. 129 G3
Little Sandy Desert Australia 109 B5
Little San Salvador i. Bahamas 133 F7
Little Smoky Canada 120 G4
Little Tibet reg. India/Pak. see Ladakh
Littleton U.S.A. 126 G5
Little Valley U.S.A. 135 F2
Little Wind r. U.S.A. 126 F4
Litunde Moz. 99 D5
Liu'an China see Lu'an
Liuba China 76 E1
Liucheng China 77 F3
Liuchong He r. China 76 E3
Liuchow China see Liuzhou
Liuhe China 74 B4
Liuheng Dao i. China 77 I2
Liujiachang China 77 F2
Liujiaxia Shuiku resr China 76 D1
Liukesong China 74 B3
Liulin China see Jonê
Liupan Shan mts China 76 E1
Liupanshui China 76 E3
Liuqiu Yu i. Taiwan 77 I4
Liuquan China 77 H1
Liuwa Plain National Park Zambia 99 C5
Liuyang China 77 G2
Liuzhan China 74 B2
Liuzhi China 76 E3
Liuzhou China 77 F3
Livadeia Greece 59 J5
Līvāni Latvia 45 O8
Live Oak U.S.A. 133 D6
Liveringa Australia 106 C3
Livermore CA U.S.A. 128 C3
Livermore KY U.S.A. 134 B5
Livermore, Mount U.S.A. 131 B6
Livermore Falls U.S.A. 135 J1
Liverpool Australia 112 E4
Liverpool Canada 123 I5
Liverpool U.K. 48 E5
Liverpool Bay Canada 118 E3
Liverpool Plains Australia 112 E3
Liverpool Range mts Australia 112 D3
Livia U.S.A. 134 B5
Livingston U.K. 50 F5
Livingston AL U.S.A. 131 F5
Livingston KY U.S.A. 134 C5
Livingston MT U.S.A. 126 F3
Livingston TN U.S.A. 134 C5
Livingston TX U.S.A. 131 E6
Livingston, Lake U.S.A. 131 E6
Livingstone Zambia 99 C5
Livingston Island Antarctica 152 L2
Livingston Manor U.S.A. 135 H3
Livno Bos. & Herz. 58 G3
Livny Russia 43 H5
Livojoki r. Fin. 44 O4
Livonia MI U.S.A. 134 D2
Livonia NY U.S.A. 135 G2
Livorno Italy 58 D3
Livramento do Nossa Senhora Brazil 145 C1
Liwā Oman 88 E5
Liwā', Wādī al watercourse Syria 85 C3
Liwale Tanz. 99 D4
Lixian Gansu China 76 E1
Lixian Sichuan China 76 D2
Lixiang Jiang r. China 76 D4
Lixus Morocco see Larache
Liyang China see Hexian
Liyuan China see Sangzhi
Lizard U.K. 49 B9
Lizarda Brazil 143 I5
Lizard Point U.K. 49 B9
Lizarra Spain see Estella
Lizemores U.S.A. 134 E4
Liziping China 76 D2
Lizy-sur-Ourcq France 52 D5
Ljouwert Neth. see Leeuwarden

▶Ljubljana Slovenia 58 F1
Capital of Slovenia.

Ljugarn Sweden 45 K8
Ljungan r. Sweden 44 J5
Ljungaverk Sweden 44 J5
Ljungby Sweden 45 H8
Ljusdal Sweden 45 J6
Ljusnan r. Sweden 45 J6
Ljusne Sweden 45 J6
Llaima, Volcán vol. Chile 144 B5
Llandissilio U.K. see Presteigne
Llanbadarn Fawr U.K. 49 C6
Llanbedr Pont Steffan U.K. see Lampeter
Llanbister U.K. 49 D6
Llandeilo U.K. 49 D7
Llandissilio U.K. 49 C7
Llandovery U.K. 49 D7
Llandrindod Wells U.K. 49 D6
Llandudno U.K. 48 D5
Llandysul U.K. 49 C6
Llanegwad U.K. 49 C7
Llanelli U.K. 49 C7
Llanfair Caereinion U.K. 49 D6
Llanfair-ym-Muallt U.K. see Builth Wells
Llangefni U.K. 48 C5
Llangollen U.K. 49 D6
Llangurig U.K. 49 D6
Llanllyfni U.K. 49 C5
Llannerch-y-medd U.K. 48 C5
Llannor U.K. 49 C6
Llano Mex. 127 F7
Llano U.S.A. 131 D6
Llano r. U.S.A. 131 D6
Llano Estacado plain U.S.A. 131 C5
Llanos plain Col./Venez. 142 E2
Llanquihue, Lago l. Chile 144 B6
Llanrhystud U.K. 49 C6
Llantrisant U.K. 49 D7
Llanuwchllyn U.K. 49 D6
Llanwnog U.K. 49 D6
Llanymddyfri U.K. see Llandovery
Llay U.K. 49 D5
Lleida Spain 57 G3
Llerena Spain 57 C4
Llíria Spain 57 F4
Llodio Spain see Laudio
Lloyd George, Mount Canada 120 E3
Lloyd Lake Canada 121 I3
Lloydminster Canada 121 I4
Lluchmayor Spain see Llucmajor
Llucmajor Spain 57 H4

▶Llullaillaco, Volcán vol. Chile 144 C2
Highest active volcano in South America and the world.

Lô, Sông r. China/Vietnam 70 D2
Loa r. Chile 144 B2
Loa U.S.A. 129 H2
Loango Congo 99 B4
Loban' r. Russia 42 K4
Lobatejo mt. Spain 57 D5
Lobatse Botswana 101 G3
Lobaye r. Cent. Afr. Rep. 98 B3
Löbejün Germany 53 L3
Lobéké, Parc National de nat. park Cameroon 97 E4
Löbenberg hill Germany 53 M3
Loberia Arg. 144 E5
Lobito Angola 99 B5
Lobos Arg. 144 E5
Lobos, Cabo c. Mex. 127 E7
Lobos, Isla i. Mex. 127 F8
Lobos de Tierra, Isla i. Peru 142 B5
Loburg Germany 53 M2
Lôc Binh Vietnam 70 D2
Lochaline U.K. 50 D4
Loch Baghasdail U.K. see Lochboisdale
Lochboisdale U.K. 50 B3
Lochcarron U.K. 50 D3
Lochearnhead U.K. 50 E4
Lochem Neth. 52 G2
Lochern National Park Australia 110 C5
Loches France 56 E3
Loch Garman Ireland see Wexford
Lochgelly U.K. 50 F4
Lochgilphead U.K. 50 D4
Lochinver U.K. 50 D2
Loch Lomond and the Trossachs National Park U.K. 50 E4
Lochmaddy U.K. 50 B3
Lochnagar mt. U.K. 50 F4
Loch na Madadh U.K. see Lochmaddy
Loch Raven Reservoir U.S.A. 135 G4
Lochy, Loch l. U.K. 50 E4
Lock Australia 111 A7
Lockerbie U.K. 50 F5
Lockhart Australia 112 C5
Lockhart U.S.A. 131 D6
Lock Haven U.S.A. 135 G3
Löcknitz r. Germany 53 L1
Lockport U.S.A. 135 F2
Lôc Ninh Vietnam 71 D5
Lod Israel 85 B4
Loddon r. Australia 112 A5
Lodève France 56 F5
Lodeynoye Pole Russia 42 G3
Lodge, Mount Canada/U.S.A. 120 B3
Lodhikheda India 82 D5
Lodhran Pak. 89 H4
Lodi Italy 58 C2
Lodi CA U.S.A. 128 C2
Lodi OH U.S.A. 134 D3
Lødingen Norway 44 I2
Lodja Dem. Rep. Congo 98 C4
Lodomeria Russia see Vladimir
Lodrani India 82 B5
Lodwar Kenya 98 D3
Łódź Poland 47 Q5
Loei Thai. 70 C3
Loeriesfontein S. Africa 100 D6
Lofoten is Norway 44 H2
Lofusa South Sudan 97 G4
Log Russia 43 I6
Loga Niger 96 D3
Logan IA U.S.A. 130 E3
Logan OH U.S.A. 134 D4
Logan UT U.S.A. 126 F4
Logan WV U.S.A. 134 E5

▶Logan, Mount Canada 120 A2
2nd highest mountain in North America.

Logan, Mount U.S.A. 126 C2
Logan Creek r. Australia 110 D4
Logan Lake Canada 120 F5
Logan Mountains Canada 120 D2
Logansport IN U.S.A. 134 B3
Logansport LA U.S.A. 131 E6
Logatec Slovenia 58 F2
Logpung China 76 D1
Logroño Spain 57 E2
Lohardaga India 83 F5
Loharu India 82 C3
Lohatlha S. Africa 100 F5
Lohawat India 82 C4
Lohfelden Germany 53 J3
Lohil r. China/India see Zayü Qu
Lohiniva Fin. 44 N3
Lohit r. India 83 H4
Lohjanjärvi l. Fin. 45 M6
Löhne Germany 53 I2
Lohne (Oldenburg) Germany 53 I2
Lohtaja Fin. 44 M4
Loi, Nam r. Myanmar 70 C2
Loikaw Myanmar 70 B3
Loi-lem Myanmar 70 B2
Loi Lun Myanmar 70 B2
Loimaa Fin. 45 M6
Loipyet Hills Myanmar 70 B1
Loire r. France 56 C3
Loja Ecuador 142 C4
Loja Spain 57 D5
Lokan tekojärvi l. Fin. 44 O3
Lokchim r. Russia 42 K3
Lokeren Belgium 52 E3
Lokgwabe Botswana 100 E3
Lokichar Kenya 78 C6
Lokichokio Kenya 98 D3
Lokilalaki, Gunung mt. Indon. 69 G7
Løkken Denmark 45 F8
Løkken Norway 44 F5
Loknya Russia 42 F4
Lokoja Nigeria 96 D4
Lokolama Dem. Rep. Congo 98 B4
Lokossa Benin 96 D4
Lokot' Russia 43 G5
Loktak Lake India 83 H4
Lol South Sudan 97 F4
Lola Guinea 96 C4
Lola, Mount U.S.A. 128 C2
Loleta U.S.A. 128 A1
Loliondo Tanz. 98 D4
Lolland i. Denmark 45 G9
Lolo U.S.A. 126 E3
Loloda Indon. 69 H6
Lolo Pass U.S.A. 126 E3
Lolowau Indon. 71 B7
Lolwane S. Africa 100 F4
Lom Bulg. 59 J3
Lom Norway 45 F6
Loma U.S.A. 129 I2
Lomami r. Dem. Rep. Congo 98 C3
Lomar Pass Afgh. 89 G3
Lomas, Bahía de b. Chile 144 C8
Lomas de Zamora Arg. 144 E4
Lombarda, Serra hills Brazil 143 H3
Lomblen i. Indon. 108 C2
Lombok Indon. 108 B2
Lombok i. Indon. 108 B2
Lombok, Selat sea chan. Indon. 108 A2

▶Lomé Togo 96 D4
Capital of Togo.

Lomela Dem. Rep. Congo 98 C4
Lomela r. Dem. Rep. Congo 97 F5
Lomira U.S.A. 134 A2
Lomme France 52 C4
Lommel Belgium 52 F3
Lomond Canada 123 K4
Lomond, Loch l. U.K. 50 E4
Lomonosov Russia 45 P7
Lomonosov Ridge sea feature Arctic Ocean 153 B1
Lomovoye Russia 42 I2
Lomphat Cambodia see Lumphăt
Lompoc U.S.A. 128 C4
Lom Sak Thai. 70 C3
Łomża Poland 47 S4
Lơn, Hon i. Vietnam 71 E4
Lonar India 84 C2
Londa Bangl. 83 G5
Londa India 84 B3
Londinières France 52 B5
Londinium U.K. see London
Londoko Russia 74 D2
London Canada 134 E2

▶London U.K. 49 G7
Capital of the United Kingdom and of England. 4th most populous city in Europe.

London KY U.S.A. 134 C5
London OH U.S.A. 134 D4
Londonderry U.K. 51 E3
Londonderry OH U.S.A. 134 D4
Londonderry VT U.S.A. 135 I2
Londonderry, Cape Australia 108 D3
Londrina Brazil 145 A3
Lone Pine U.S.A. 128 D3
Long Thai. 70 B3
Longa Angola 99 B5
Longa, Proliv sea chan. Russia 65 S2
Long'an China 76 E4
Long Ashton U.K. 49 E7
Longbao China 76 C1
Long Bay U.S.A. 133 E5
Longbeach N.Z. 113 C7
Long Beach U.S.A. 128 D5
Longbo China see Shuangpai
Long Branch U.S.A. 135 I3
Longchang China 76 E2
Longcheng Anhui China see Xiaoxian
Longcheng Guangdong China see Longmen
Longcheng Yunnan China see Chenggong
Longchuan China see Nanhua
Longchuan Jiang r. China 76 C4
Long Creek r. Canada 121 K5
Long Creek U.S.A. 126 D3
Long Eaton U.K. 49 F6
Longford Ireland 51 E4
Longgang Chongqing China see Dazu
Longgang Guangdong China 77 G4
Longhoughton U.K. 48 F3
Longhui China 77 F3
Longhurst, Mount Antarctica 152 H1
Long Island Bahamas 133 F8
Long Island N.S. Canada 123 I5
Long Island Nunavut Canada 122 F3
Long Island India 71 A4
Long Island P.N.G. 69 L8
Long Island U.S.A. 135 I3
Long Island Sound sea chan. U.S.A. 135 I3
Longjiang China 74 A3
Longjin China see Qingliu
Longju China 76 B2
Longlac Canada 122 D4
Long Lake l. Canada 122 D4
Long Lake U.S.A. 135 H2
Long Lake l. ME U.S.A. 132 G2
Long Lake l. MI U.S.A. 134 D1
Long Lake l. ND U.S.A. 130 C2
Long Lake l. NY U.S.A. 135 H1
Longli China 76 E3
Longlin China 76 E3
Longling China 76 C3
Longmeadow U.S.A. 135 I2
Long Melford U.K. 49 H6
Longmen Guangdong China 77 G4
Longmen Heilong. China 74 B2
Longmen Shan hill China 77 F1
Longmen Shan mts China 76 E1
Longming China 76 E4
Longmont U.S.A. 126 G4
Longnan Gansu China 76 E1
Longnan Jiangxi China 77 G3
Long Phu Vietnam 71 D5
Longping China see Luodian
Long Point Canada 134 E2
Long Point Man. Canada 121 L4
Long Point Ont. Canada 134 E2
Long Point N.Z. 113 B8
Long Point Bay Canada 134 E2
Long Prairie U.S.A. 130 E2
Long Preston U.K. 48 E4
Longquan Guizhou China see Danzhai
Longquan Guizhou China see Fenggang
Longquan Hunan China see Xintian
Longquan Xi r. China 77 I2
Long Range Mountains Nfld. and Lab. Canada 123 K4
Long Range Mountains Nfld. and Lab. Canada 123 K5
Longreach Australia 110 D4
Longriba China 76 D1
Longshan Guizhou China see Longli
Longshan Hunan China 77 F2
Longshan Yunnan China see Longling
Long Shan mts China 76 E1
Longshanlu China see Shizhong
Longsheng China 77 F3
Longs Peak U.S.A. 126 G4
Long Stratton U.K. 49 I6
Longtom Lake Canada 120 G1
Longtown U.K. 48 E3
Longue-Pointe-de-Mingan Canada 123 I4
Longueuil Canada 122 G5
Longuyon France 52 F5
Longvale U.S.A. 128 B2
Longview TX U.S.A. 131 E5
Longview WA U.S.A. 126 C3
Longwangmiao China 74 D3
Longwei Co l. China 83 G2
Longxi China 76 E1
Longxian Guangdong China see Wengyuan
Longxian Shaanxi China 76 E1
Longxingchang China see Wuyuan
Longxi Shan mt. China 77 H3
Longxu China see Cangwu
Long Xuyên Vietnam 71 D5
Longyan China 77 H3

▶Longyearbyen Svalbard 64 C2
Capital of Svalbard.

Longzhen China 74 B2
Longzhou China 76 E4
Longzhouping China see Changyang
Löningen Germany 53 H2
Lonoke U.S.A. 131 F5
Lonpo Myanmar 70 B2
Lönsboda Sweden 45 I8
Lons-le-Saunier France 56 G3
Lonton Myanmar 70 B1
Looc Phil. 69 G4
Loochoo Islands Japan see Ryukyu Islands
Loogootee U.S.A. 134 B4
Lookout, Cape Canada 122 E3
Lookout, Cape U.S.A. 133 E5
Lookout, Point Australia 112 F1
Lookout, Point U.S.A. 134 D1
Lookout Mountain U.S.A. 129 I4
Lookout Point Australia 109 B8
Loolmalasin vol. crater Tanz. 98 D4
Loon Canada 122 C4
Loon r. Canada 120 H3
Loongana Australia 109 D7
Loon Lake Canada 121 I4
Loop Head hd Ireland 51 C5
Lop China 82 E1
Lopasnya Russia see Chekhov
Lopatina, Gora mt. Russia 74 F2
Lop Buri Thai. 70 C4
Lopez Phil. 69 G4
Lopez, Cap c. Gabon 98 A4
Lop Nur salt flat China 80 H3
Lopphavet b. Norway 44 L1
Loptyuga Russia 42 K3
Loqung China 76 C1
Lora Pak. 89 G5
Lora r. Venez. 142 D2
Lora, Hāmūn-i- dry lake Afgh./Pak. 89 G4
Lora del Río Spain 57 D5
Lorain U.S.A. 134 D3
Loralai Pak. 89 H4
Loralai r. Pak. 89 H4
Loramie, Lake U.S.A. 134 C3
Lorca Spain 57 F5
Lorch Germany 53 H4
Lordegān Iran 88 C4
Lord Howe Atoll Solomon Is see Ontong Java Atoll
Lord Howe Island Australia 107 F5
Lord Howe Rise sea feature S. Pacific Ocean 150 G7
Lord Loughborough Island Myanmar 71 B5
Lordsburg U.S.A. 129 I5
Lore East Timor 108 D2
Lore Lindu, Taman Nasional nat. park Indon. 68 G7
Lorena Brazil 145 B3
Lorengau P.N.G. 69 L7
Lorentz, Taman Nasional nat. park Indon. 69 J7
Loreto Arg. 144 D3
Loreto Brazil 143 I5
Loreto Mex. 127 F8
Lorient France 56 C3
Lorillard r. Canada 121 N1
Loring U.S.A. 126 G2
Lorn, Firth of est. U.K. 50 D4
Lorne Australia 110 D5
Lorne watercourse Australia 110 B3
Loropéni Burkina Faso 96 C3
Lorrain, Plateau France 53 G6
Lorraine Australia 110 B3
Lorraine admin. reg. France see Alsace, Champagne-Ardenne et Lorraine
Lorraine reg. France 52 F5
Lorsch Germany 53 I5
Lorup Germany 53 H2
Losal India 82 C4
Los Alamos CA U.S.A. 128 C4
Los Alamos NM U.S.A. 127 G6
Los Alerces, Parque Nacional nat. park Arg. 144 B6
Los Ángeles Chile 144 B5

▶Los Angeles U.S.A. 128 D4
3rd most populous city in North America.

Los Angeles Aqueduct canal U.S.A. 128 D4
Los Arabos Cuba 133 D8
Los Banos U.S.A. 128 C3
Los Blancos Arg. 144 D2
Los Cerritos watercourse Mex. 127 F8
Los Coronados, Islas is Mex. 128 E5
Los Gigantes, Llanos de plain Mex. 131 B6
Los Glaciares, Parque Nacional nat. park Arg. 144 B8
Losheim am See Germany 52 G5
Los Hoyos Mex. 127 F7
Lošinj i. Croatia 58 F2
Los Juríes Arg. 144 D3
Los Katios, Parque Nacional nat. park Col. 137 I7
Loskop Dam S. Africa 101 I3
Los Lunas U.S.A. 127 G6
Los Menucos Arg. 144 C6
Los Mochis Mex. 127 F8
Los Molinos U.S.A. 128 B1
Losombo Dem. Rep. Congo 98 B3
Los Palacios Cuba 133 D8
Los Remedios r. Mex. 131 B7
Los Roques, Islas is Venez. 142 E1
Losser Neth. 52 G2
Lossie r. U.K. 50 F3
Lossiemouth U.K. 50 F3
Lößnitz Germany 53 M4
Lost Creek KY U.S.A. 134 D5
Lost Creek WV U.S.A. 134 E4
Los Teques Venez. 142 E1
Los Testigos is Venez. 142 F1
Lost Hills U.S.A. 128 D4
Lost Trail Pass U.S.A. 126 E3
Lostwithiel U.K. 49 C8
Los Vidrios Mex. 129 G6
Los Vilos Chile 144 B4
Lot r. France 56 E4
Lota Chile 144 B5
Loṭfābād Turkm. 88 E2
Lothringen reg. France see Lorraine
Lotikipi Plain Kenya/South Sudan 98 D3
Loto Dem. Rep. Congo 98 C4
Lotsane r. Botswana 101 I2
Lot's Wife i. Japan see Sōfu-gan
Lotta r. Fin./Russia 44 Q2
also known as Lutto
Lotte Germany 53 H2
Louangnamtha Laos 70 C2
Louangphabang Laos 70 C3
Loubomo Congo see Dolisie
Loudéac France 56 C2
Loudi China 77 F3
Louga Senegal 96 B3
Loughborough U.K. 49 F6
Lougheed Island Canada 119 H2
Loughor r. U.K. 49 C7
Loughrea Ireland 51 D4
Loughton U.K. 49 H7
Louhans France 56 G3
Louisa KY U.S.A. 134 D4
Louisa VA U.S.A. 135 G4
Louisbourg Canada 123 K5
Louisburg Canada see Louisbourg
Louisburgh Ireland 51 C4
Louise Falls Canada 120 G2
Louis-Gentil Morocco see Youssoufia
Louisiade Archipelago is P.N.G. 110 F1
Louisiana U.S.A. 130 F4
Louisiana state U.S.A. 131 F6
Louis Trichardt S. Africa see Makhado
Louisville GA U.S.A. 133 D5
Louisville IL U.S.A. 130 F4
Louisville KY U.S.A. 134 C4
Louisville MS U.S.A. 131 F5
Louisville Ridge sea feature S. Pacific Ocean 150 I8
Louis-XIV, Pointe pt Canada 122 F3
Loukhi Russia 44 R3
Loukoléla Congo 98 B4
Loukouo Congo 97 E5
Loulé Port. 57 B5
Loum Cameroon 96 D4
Louny Czechia 47 N5
Loup r. U.S.A. 130 D3
Loups Marins, Lacs des lakes Canada 122 G2
Loups Marins, Petit lac des l. Canada 123 G2
Lourdes Canada 123 K4
Lourdes France 56 D5
Lourenço Marques Moz. see Maputo
Lousã Port. 57 B3
Loushan China 74 C3
Loushanguan China see Tongzi
Louth Australia 112 B3
Louth U.K. 48 G5
Loutra Aidipsou Greece 59 J5
Louvain Belgium see Leuven
Louviers France 52 B5
Louwater-Suid Namibia 100 C2
Louwsburg S. Africa 101 J4
Lövånger Sweden 44 L4
Lovat' r. Russia 42 F4
Lovech Bulg. 59 K3
Lovell U.S.A. 135 J1
Lovelock U.S.A. 128 D1
Lovendegem Belgium 52 D3
Lovers Leap mt. U.S.A. 134 E5
Loviisa Fin. 45 O6
Lovington U.S.A. 131 C5
Lovozero Russia 42 G1
Lóvua Lunda Norte Angola 99 C4
Lóvua Moxico Angola 99 C5
Low, Cape Canada 119 J3
Lowa Dem. Rep. Congo 98 C4
Lowa r. Dem. Rep. Congo 98 C4
Lowarai Pass Pak. 89 H3
Lowell IN U.S.A. 134 B3
Lowell MA U.S.A. 135 J2
Lower Arrow Lake Canada 120 G5
Lower California pen. Mex. see Baja California
Lower Glenelg National Park Australia 111 C8
Lower Granite Gorge U.S.A. 129 G4
Lower Hutt N.Z. 113 E5
Lower Laberge Canada 120 C2
Lower Lake U.S.A. 128 B2
Lower Lough Erne l. U.K. 51 E3
Lower Post Canada 120 D3
Lower Red Lake U.S.A. 130 E2
Lower Saxony land Germany see Niedersachsen
Lower Tunguska r. Russia see Nizhnyaya Tunguska
Lower Zambezi National Park Zambia 99 C5
Lowestoft U.K. 49 I6
Łowicz Poland 47 Q4
Low Island Kiribati see Starbuck Island
Lowrah, Hāmūn-e dry lake Afgh./Pak. see Lora, Hāmūn-i-
Lowther Hills U.K. 50 F5
Lowville U.S.A. 135 H2
Loxstedt Germany 53 I1

Loxton Australia 111 C7
Loyal, Loch *l.* U.K. 50 E2
Loyalsock Creek *r.* U.S.A. 135 G3
Loyalton U.S.A. 128 C2
Loyalty Islands New Caledonia *see* Loyauté, Îles
Loyang China *see* Luoyang
Loyauté, Îles *is* New Caledonia 107 G4
Loyev Belarus *see* Loyew
Loyew Belarus 43 F6
Lozère, Mont *mt.* France 56 F4
Loznica Serbia 59 H2
Lozova Ukr. 43 H6
Lozovaya Ukr. *see* Lozova
Lua *r.* Dem. Rep. Congo 98 B3
Luacano Angola 99 C5
Lu'an China 77 H2
Luân Châu Vietnam 70 C2
Luanchuan China 77 F1

▶Luanda Angola 99 B4
Capital of Angola. 4th most populous city in Africa.

Luang, Khao *mt.* Thai. 71 B5
Luang, Thale *lag.* Thai. 71 C6
Luang Namtha Laos *see* Louangnamtha
Luang Phrabang, Thiu Khao *mts* Laos/Thai. 70 C3
Luang Prabang Laos *see* Louangphabang
Luanhaizi China 76 B1
Luanshya Zambia 99 C5
Luanza Dem. Rep. Congo 99 C4
Luao Angola *see* Luau
Luarca Spain 57 C2
Luashi Dem. Rep. Congo 99 C5
Luau Angola 99 C5
Luba Equat. Guinea 96 D4
Lubaczów Poland 43 D6
Lubalo Angola 99 B4
Lubānas ezers *l.* Latvia 45 O8
Lubang Islands Phil. 68 F4
Lubango Angola 99 B5
Lubao Dem. Rep. Congo 99 C4
Lubartów Poland 43 D6
Lübbecke Germany 53 I2
Lubbeskolk *salt pan* S. Africa 100 D5
Lubbock U.S.A. 131 C5
Lübbow Germany 53 L2
Lübeck Germany 47 M4
Lubeck U.S.A. 134 E4
Lubefu Dem. Rep. Congo 99 C4
Lubei China 73 M4
Lüben Poland *see* Lubin
Lubersac France 56 E4
Lubin Poland 47 P5
Lublin Poland 43 D6
Lubnān *country* Asia *see* Lebanon
Lubnān, Jabal *mts* Lebanon *see* Liban, Jebel
Lubny Ukr. 43 G6
Lubok Antu *Sarawak* Malaysia 68 E6
Lübtheen Germany 53 L1
Lubudi Dem. Rep. Congo 99 C4
Lubuklinggau Indon. 68 C7
Lubukpakam Indon. 71 B7
Lubuksikaping Indon. 68 C6
Lubumbashi Dem. Rep. Congo 99 C5
Lubutu Dem. Rep. Congo 98 C4
Lübz Germany 53 M1
Lucala Angola 99 B4
Lucan Canada 134 E2
Lucan Ireland 51 F4
Lucania, Mount Canada 120 A2
Lucapa Angola 99 C4
Lucas U.S.A. 134 B5
Lucasville U.S.A. 134 D4
Lucca Italy 58 D3
Luce Bay U.K. 50 E6
Lucedale U.S.A. 131 F6
Lucélia Brazil 145 A3
Lucena Phil. 69 G4
Lucena Spain 57 D5
Lučenec Slovakia 47 Q6
Lucera Italy 58 F4
Lucerne Switz. 56 I3
Lucerne Valley U.S.A. 128 E4
Lucero Mex. 127 G7
Luchegorsk Russia 74 D3
Lucheng *Guangxi* China *see* Luchuan
Lucheng *Sichuan* China *see* Kangding
Luchuan China 77 F4
Lüchun China 76 D4
Lucipara, Kepulauan *is* Indon. 69 H8
Łuck Ukr. *see* Luts'k
Luckeesarai India *see* Lakhisarai
Luckenwalde Germany 53 N2
Luckhoff S. Africa 100 G5
Lucknow Canada 134 E2
Lucknow India 82 E4
Lücongpo China 77 F2
Lucrecia, Cabo *c.* Cuba 137 I4
Lucusse Angola 99 C5
Lucy Creek Australia 110 B4
Lüda China *see* Dalian
Lü Dao *i.* Taiwan 77 I4
Lüdenscheid Germany 53 H3
Lüderitz Namibia 100 B4
Ludewa Tanz. 99 D5
Ludhiana India 82 C3
Ludian China 76 D3
Luding China 76 D2
Ludington U.S.A. 134 B2
Ludlow U.K. 49 E6
Ludlow U.S.A. 128 E4
Ludogorie *reg.* Bulg. 59 L3
Ludowici U.S.A. 133 D6
Ludvika Sweden 45 I6
Ludwigsburg Germany 53 J6
Ludwigsfelde Germany 53 N2
Ludwigshafen am Rhein Germany 53 I5
Ludwigslust Germany 53 L1
Ludza Latvia 45 O8
Luebo Dem. Rep. Congo 99 C4
Luena Angola 99 B5
Luena Flats *plain* Zambia 99 C5
Lüeyang China 76 E1
Lufeng *Guangdong* China 77 G4
Lufeng *Yunnan* China 76 D3
Lufkin U.S.A. 131 E6
Lufu China *see* Shilin
Luga Russia 45 P7
Luga *r.* Russia 45 P7
Lugano Switz. 56 I3
Lugansk Ukr. *see* Luhans'k
Lugau/Erzgebirge Germany 53 M4
Lügde Germany 53 J3
Lugdunum France *see* Lyon
Lugg *r.* U.K. 49 E6
Lugnaquilla *hill* Ireland 51 F5
Lugo Italy 58 D2
Lugo Spain 57 C2
Lugoj Romania 59 I2
Luhans'k Ukr. 43 H6
Luhe China 77 H1
Luhe *r.* Germany 53 K1
Luḩfī, Wādī *watercourse* Jordan 85 C3
Luhit *r.* China/India *see* Zayü Qu
Luhua China *see* Heishui
Luhuo China 76 D2
Luhyny Ukr. 43 F6
Luia Angola 99 C4
Luiana Angola 99 C5
Luichow Peninsula China *see* Leizhou Bandao
Luik Belgium *see* Liège
Luimneach Ireland *see* Limerick
Luiro *r.* Fin. 44 O3
Luis Echeverría Álvarez Mex. 128 E5
Luitpold Coast Antarctica 152 A1
Luiza Dem. Rep. Congo 99 C4
Lujiang China 77 H2
Lüjing China 76 E1
Lukachek Russia 74 D1
Lukapa Angola *see* Lucapa
Lukavac Bos. & Herz. 58 H2
Lukenga, Lac *l.* Dem. Rep. Congo 99 C4
Lukenie *r.* Dem. Rep. Congo 98 B4
Lukh *r.* Russia 42 I4
Lukhī Afgh. 89 F4
Lukhovitsy Russia 43 H5
Luk Keng *H.K.* China 77 [inset]
Lukou China *see* Zhuzhou
Lukovit Bulg. 59 K3
Łuków Poland 43 D6
Lukoyanov Russia 43 J5
Lukusuzi National Park Zambia 99 D5
Luleå Sweden 44 M4
Luleälven *r.* Sweden 44 M4
Lüleburgaz Turkey 59 L4
Lüliang China 73 K5
Luliang China 76 D3
Lüliang Shan *mts* China 73 K5
Lulimba Dem. Rep. Congo 99 C4
Luling U.S.A. 131 D6
Lulonga *r.* Dem. Rep. Congo 98 B3
Luluabourg Dem. Rep. Congo *see* Kananga
Lumachomo China 83 F3
Lumajang Indon. 68 E8
Lumajangdong Co *salt l.* China 82 E2
Lumbala *Moxico* Angola *see* Lumbala Kaquengue
Lumbala *Moxico* Angola *see* Lumbala N'guimbo
Lumbala Kaquengue Angola 99 C5
Lumbala N'guimbo Angola 99 C5
Lumberton U.S.A. 133 E5
Lumbini Nepal 83 E4
Lumbis Indon. 68 F6
Lumbrales Spain 57 C3
Lumezzane Italy 58 D2
Lumi P.N.G. 69 K7
Lumphăt Cambodia 71 D4
Lumpkin U.S.A. 133 C5
Lumsden Canada 121 J5
Lumsden N.Z. 113 B7
Lumut Malaysia 71 C6
Lumut, Tanjung *pt* Indon. 68 D7
Luna U.S.A. 129 I5
Lunan China *see* Shilin
Lunan Bay U.K. 50 G4
Lunan Lake Canada 121 M1
Lunan Shan *mts* China 76 D3
Luna Pier U.S.A. 134 D3
Lund Pak. 89 H5
Lund Sweden 45 H9
Lund *NV* U.S.A. 129 F2
Lund *UT* U.S.A. 129 G2
Lundar Canada 121 L5
Lundy U.K. 49 C7
Lune *r.* Germany 53 I1
Lune *r.* U.K. 48 E4
Lüneburg Germany 53 K1
Lüneburger Heide *reg.* Germany 53 K1
Lünen Germany 53 H3
Lunenburg U.S.A. 135 F5
Lunéville France 56 H2
Lunga *r.* Zambia 99 C5
Lungdo China 83 E2
Lunggar China 83 E3
Lung Kwu Chau *i. H.K.* China 77 [inset]
Lungleh India *see* Lunglei
Lunglei India 83 H5
Lungmari *mt.* China 83 F3
Lungmu Co *salt l.* China 82 E2
Lungwebungu *r.* Zambia 99 C5
Lunh Nepal 83 E3
Luni India 82 C4
Luni *r.* India 82 B4
Luni *r.* Pak. 89 H4
Luninets Belarus *see* Luninyets
Luning U.S.A. 128 D2
Luninyets Belarus 45 O10
Lunkaransar India 82 C3
Lunkha India 82 C3
Lünne Germany 53 H2
Lunsar Sierra Leone 96 B4
Lunsklip S. Africa 101 I3
Luntai China 80 F3
Luobei China 74 C3
Luobuzhuang China 80 G4
Luocheng *Fujian* China *see* Hui'an
Luocheng *Guangxi* China 77 F3
Luodian China 76 E3
Luoding China 77 F4
Luodou Sha *i.* China 77 F4
Luohe China 77 G1
Luo He *r.* China 77 G1
Luonan China 77 F1
Luoning China 77 F1
Luoping China 76 E3
Luotian China 77 G2
Luoto Fin. *see* Larsmo
Luoxiao Shan *mts* China 77 G3
Luoxiong China *see* Luoping
Luoyang *Guangdong* China *see* Boluo
Luoyang *Henan* China 77 G1
Luoyang *Zhejiang* China *see* Taishun
Luoyuan China 77 H3
Luozigou China 74 C4
Lupane Zimbabwe 99 C5
Lupanshui China *see* Liupanshui
Lupeni Romania 59 J2
Lupilichi Moz. 99 D5
Lupton U.S.A. 129 I4
Luqiao China *see* Luding
Luqu China 76 D1
Lu Qu *r.* China *see* Tao He
Luquan China 70 C1
Luray U.S.A. 135 F4
Luremo Angola 99 B4
Lurgan U.K. 51 F3
Luring China *see* Oma
Lúrio Moz. 99 E5
Lurio *r.* Moz. 99 E5
Lūr Kōh *mt.* Afgh. 89 F3

▶Lusaka Zambia 99 C5
Capital of Zambia.

Lusambo Dem. Rep. Congo 99 C4
Lusancay Islands and Reefs P.N.G. 106 F2
Lusangi Dem. Rep. Congo 99 C4
Luseland Canada 121 I4
Lush, Mount *hill* Australia 108 D4
Lushi China 77 F1
Lushnja Albania *see* Lushnjë
Lushnjë Albania 59 H4
Lushui China *see* Luzhang
Lushuihe China 74 B4
Lüsigang China 77 I1
Lusikisiki S. Africa 101 I6
Lusk U.S.A. 126 G4
Luso Angola *see* Luena
Lussvale Australia 112 C1
Lut, Bahrat *salt l.* Asia *see* Dead Sea
Lūt, Dasht-e *des.* Iran *see* Lūt, Kavīr-e
Lūt, Kavīr-e *des.* Iran 88 E4
Lutetia France *see* Paris
Lūt-e Zangī Aḩmad *des.* Iran 88 E4
Luther U.S.A. 134 C1
Luther Lake Canada 134 E2
Luton U.K. 49 G7
Łutselk'e Canada 121 I2
Luts'k Ukr. 43 E6
Luttelgeest Neth. 52 F2
Luttenberg Neth. 52 G2
Lutto *r.* Fin./Russia *see* Lotta
Lutz U.S.A. 133 D6
Lützelbach Germany 53 J5
Lützow-Holm Bay Antarctica 152 D2
Lutzputs S. Africa 100 E5
Lutzville S. Africa 100 D6
Luumäki Fin. 45 O6
Luuq Somalia 98 E3
Luverne *AL* U.S.A. 133 C6
Luverne *MN* U.S.A. 130 D3
Luvuei Angola 99 C5
Luvuvhu *r.* S. Africa 101 J2
Luwero Uganda 98 D3
Luwingu Zambia 99 C5
Luwuk Indon. 69 G7
Luxembourg *country* Europe 52 G5

▶Luxembourg Lux. 52 G5
Capital of Luxembourg.

Luxemburg *country* Europe *see* Luxembourg
Luxeuil-les-Bains France 56 H3
Luxi *Hunan* China *see* Wuxi
Luxi *Yunnan* China *see* Mangshi
Luxi *Yunnan* China 76 D3
Luxolweni S. Africa 101 G6
Luxor Egypt 86 D4
Luyi China 77 G1
Luyksgestel Neth. 52 F3
Luza Russia 42 J3
Luza *r.* Russia 42 J3
Luza *r.* Russia 42 M2
Luzern Switz. *see* Lucerne
Luzhai China 77 F3
Luzhang China 76 C3
Luzhou China 76 E2
Luzhskaya Russia 45 P7
Luziânia Brazil 145 B2
Luzon *i.* Phil. 69 G3
Luzon Strait Phil. 69 G2
Luzy France 56 F3
L'viv Ukr. 43 E6
L'vov Ukr. *see* L'viv
Lwów Ukr. *see* L'viv
Lyady Russia 45 P7
Lyakhavichy Belarus 45 O10
Lyakhovichi Belarus *see* Lyakhavichy
Lyallpur Pak. *see* Faisalabad
Lyamtsa Russia 42 H2
Lycia *hist. area* Turkey 59 M6
Lyck Poland *see* Ełk
Lycksele Sweden 44 K4
Lycopolis Egypt *see* Asyūţ
Lydd U.K. 49 H8
Lydda Israel *see* Lod
Lyddan Ice Rise Antarctica 152 B2
Lydia *hist. area* Turkey 59 L5
Lydney U.K. 49 E7
Lyel'chytsy Belarus 43 F6
Lyell, Mount U.S.A. 128 D3
Lyell Brown, Mount *hill* Australia 109 E5
Lyell Island Canada 120 D4
Lyepyel' Belarus 45 P9
Lykens U.S.A. 135 G3
Lyman Ukr. 43 H6
Lyman U.S.A. 126 F4
Lyme Bay U.K. 49 E8
Lyme Regis U.K. 49 E8
Lymington U.K. 49 F8
Lynchburg *OH* U.S.A. 134 D4
Lynchburg *TN* U.S.A. 132 C5
Lynchburg *VA* U.S.A. 134 F5
Lynchville U.S.A. 135 J1
Lyndhurst *N.S.W.* Australia 112 D4
Lyndhurst *Qld* Australia 110 D3
Lyndhurst *S.A.* Australia 111 B6
Lyndon Australia 109 A5
Lyndon *r.* Australia 109 A5
Lyndonville U.S.A. 135 I1
Lyne *r.* U.K. 48 D4
Lyness U.K. 50 F2
Lyngdal Norway 45 E7
Lynn U.K. *see* King's Lynn
Lynn *IN* U.S.A. 134 C3
Lynn *MA* U.S.A. 135 J2
Lynndyl U.S.A. 129 G2
Lynn Lake Canada 121 K3
Lynton U.K. 49 D7
Lynx Lake Canada 121 J2
Lyon France 56 G4
Lyon *r.* U.K. 50 F4
Lyon Mountain U.S.A. 135 I1
Lyons Australia 109 F7
Lyons France *see* Lyon
Lyons *GA* U.S.A. 133 D5
Lyons *NY* U.S.A. 135 G2
Lyons Falls U.S.A. 135 H2
Lyozna Belarus 43 F5
Lyra Reef P.N.G. 106 F2
Lys *r.* France 52 D4
Lysekil Sweden 45 G7
Lyskovo Russia 42 J4
Ly Sơn, Đao *i.* Vietnam 70 E4
Lys'va Russia 41 R4
Lysychans'k Ukr. 43 H6
Lysyye Gory Russia 43 J6
Lytham St Anne's U.K. 48 D5
Lytton Canada 120 F5
Lyuban' Belarus 45 P10
Lyubertsy Russia 41 N4
Lyubeshiv Ukr. 43 E6
Lyubim Russia 42 I4
Lyubytino Russia 42 G4
Lyudinovo Russia 43 G5
Lyunda *r.* Russia 42 J4
Lyzha *r.* Russia 42 M2

M

Ma, Nâm *r.* Laos 70 C2
Ma, Nam *r.* Myanmar 70 B2
Ma'agan Israel 85 B3
Maale Maldives *see* Male
Maale Atholhu *atoll* Maldives *see* Male Atholhu
Maalhosmadulu Atholhu Uthuruburi *atoll* Maldives *see* Maalhosmadulu Uthuruburi
Maalhosmadulu Uthuruburi Maldives 84 B5
Ma'ān Jordan 85 B4
Maan Turkey *see* Nusratiye
Maaninka Fin. 44 O5
Maaninkavaara Fin. 44 P3
Ma'anshan China 77 H2
Maardu Estonia 45 N7
Maarianhamina Fin. *see* Mariehamn
Ma'arrat an Nu'mān Syria 85 C2
Maarssen Neth. 52 F2
Maas *r.* Neth. 52 E3
also known as Meuse (Belgium/France)
Maaseik Belgium 52 F3
Maasin Phil. 69 G4
Maasmechelen Belgium 52 F4
Maas-Schwalm-Nette, Naturpark *nat. park* Germany/Neth. 52 F3
Maastricht Neth. 52 F4
Maaza Plateau Egypt 90 C6
Maba *Guangdong* China *see* Qujiang
Maba *Jiangsu* China 77 H1
Mabai China *see* Maguan
Mabalane Moz. 101 K2
Mabana Dem. Rep. Congo 98 C3
Mabaruma Guyana 142 G2
Mabein Myanmar 70 B2
Mabel Creek Australia 109 F7
Mabel Downs Australia 108 D4
Mabella Canada 122 C4
Mabel Lake Canada 120 G5
Maberly Canada 135 G1
Mabian China 76 D2
Mablethorpe U.K. 48 H5
Mabopane S. Africa 101 I3
Mabote Moz. 101 L2
Mabou Canada 123 J5
Mabrak, Jabal *mt.* Jordan 85 B4
Mabuasehube Game Reserve *nature res.* Botswana 100 F3
Mabule Botswana 100 G3
Mabutsane Botswana 100 F3
Macá, Monte *mt.* Chile 144 B7
Macadam Plains Australia 109 B6
Macaé Brazil 145 C3
Macajuba Brazil 145 C1
Macaloge Moz. 99 D5
MacAlpine Lake Canada 119 H3
Macamic Canada 122 F4
Macandze Moz. 101 K2
Macao China 77 G4
Macao *aut. reg.* China 77 G4
Macapá Brazil 143 H3
Macará Ecuador 142 C4
Macarani Brazil 145 C1
Macarretane Moz. 101 K3
Macas Ecuador 142 C4
Macassar Indon. *see* Makassar
Macau Brazil 143 K5
Macau China *see* Macao
Macaúba Brazil 143 H6
Macauley Island N.Z. 107 I5
Macclenny U.S.A. 133 D6
Macclesfield U.K. 48 E5
Macdiarmid Canada 122 C4
Macdonald, Lake *salt flat* Australia 109 E5
Macdonald Range *hills* Australia 108 D3
MacDonnell Ranges *mts* Australia 109 E5
MacDowell Lake Canada 121 M4
Macduff U.K. 50 G3
Macedo de Cavaleiros Port. 57 C3
Macedon *mt.* Australia 112 B6
Macedon *country* Europe *see* Macedonia
Macedonia *country* Europe 59 I4
Maceió Brazil 143 K5
Macenta Guinea 96 C4
Macerata Italy 58 E3
Macfarlane, Lake *salt flat* Australia 111 B7
Macgillycuddy's Reeks *mts* Ireland 51 C6
Machachi Ecuador 142 C4
Machaila Moz. 101 K2
Machakos Kenya 98 D4
Machala Ecuador 142 C4
Machali China 76 C1
Machanga Moz. 99 D6
Machar Marshes South Sudan 86 D8
Machattie, Lake *salt flat* Australia 110 B5
Machatuine Moz. 101 K3
Machault France 52 E5
Machaze Moz. *see* Chitobe
Macheng China 77 G2
Macherla India 84 C2
Machhagan India 83 F5
Machias *ME* U.S.A. 132 H2
Machias *NY* U.S.A. 135 F2
Machilipatnam India 84 D2
Machiques Venez. 142 D1
Māch Kowr Iran 89 F5
Machrihanish U.K. 50 D5
Machu Picchu *tourist site* Peru 142 D6
Machynlleth U.K. 49 D6
Macia Moz. 101 K3
Macias Nguema *i.* Equat. Guinea *see* Bioko
Măcin Romania 59 M2
Macina Mali 96 C3
Macintyre *r.* Australia 112 E2
Macintyre Brook *r.* Australia 112 E2
Mack U.S.A. 129 I2
Maçka Turkey 91 E2
Mackay Australia 110 E4
MacKay *r.* Canada 121 I3
Mackay U.S.A. 126 E3
Mackay, Lake *salt flat* Australia 108 E5
MacKay Lake Canada 121 I2
Mackenzie *r.* Australia 110 E4
Mackenzie Canada 120 F4

▶Mackenzie *r.* Canada 120 F2
Part of the Mackenzie-Peace-Finlay, the 2nd longest river in North America.

Mackenzie Guyana *see* Linden
Mackenzie *atoll* Micronesia *see* Ulithi
Mackenzie Bay Antarctica 152 E2
Mackenzie Bay Canada 118 E3
Mackenzie Highway Canada 120 G2
Mackenzie King Island Canada 119 G2
Mackenzie Mountains Canada 120 C1

▶Mackenzie-Peace-Finlay *r.* Canada 118 E3
2nd longest river in North America.

Mackillop, Lake *salt flat* Australia *see* Yamma Yamma, Lake
Mackintosh Range *hills* Australia 109 D6
Macklin Canada 121 I4
Macksville Australia 112 F3
Maclean Australia 112 F2
Maclear S. Africa 101 I6
MacLeod Canada *see* Fort Macleod
MacLeod, Lake *imp. l.* Australia 109 A6
Macmillan *r.* Canada 120 C2
Macmillan Pass Canada 120 D2
Macomb U.S.A. 130 F3
Macomer *Sardinia* Italy 58 C4
Mâcon France 56 G3
Macon *GA* U.S.A. 133 D5
Macon *MO* U.S.A. 130 E4
Macon *MS* U.S.A. 131 F5
Macon *OH* U.S.A. 134 D4
Macondo Angola 99 C5
Macoun Lake Canada 121 K3
Macpherson Robertson Land *reg.* Antarctica *see* Mac. Robertson Land
Macpherson's Strait India 71 A5
Macquarie *r.* Australia 112 C3
Macquarie, Lake *b.* Australia 112 E4

▶Macquarie Island S. Pacific Ocean 150 G9
Part of Australia. Most southerly point of Oceania.

Macquarie Marshes Australia 112 C3
Macquarie Mountain Australia 112 D4
Macquarie Ridge *sea feature* S. Pacific Ocean 150 G9
MacRitchie Reservoir Sing. 71 [inset]
Mac. Robertson Land *reg.* Antarctica 152 E2
Macroom Ireland 51 D6
Macumba Australia 111 A5
Macumba *watercourse* Australia 111 B5
Macuzari, Presa *resr* Mex. 127 F8
Mādabā Jordan 85 B4
Madadeni S. Africa 101 J4

▶Madagascar *country* Africa 99 E6
Largest island in Africa and 4th in the world.

Madagascar Basin *sea feature* Indian Ocean 149 L7
Madagascar Ridge *sea feature* Indian Ocean 149 K8
Madagasikara *country* Africa *see* Madagascar
Madakasira India 84 C3
Madama Niger 97 E2
Madan Bulg. 59 K4
Madanapalle India 84 C3
Madang P.N.G. 69 L8
Madaoua Niger 96 D3
Madaripur Bangl. 83 G5
Madau Turkm. *see* Madaw
Madaw Turkm. 88 D2
Madawaska Canada 135 G1
Madawaska *r.* Canada 135 G1
Madaya Myanmar 70 B2
Madded India 84 D2

▶Madeira *r.* Brazil 142 G4
4th longest river in South America.

▶Madeira *terr.* N. Atlantic Ocean 96 B1
Autonomous Region of Portugal.

Madeira, Arquipélago da *terr.* N. Atlantic Ocean *see* Madeira
Madeleine, Îles de la *is* Canada 123 J5
Madeleine, Monts de la *mts* France 56 F3
Maden Turkey 91 E3
Madera Mex. 127 F7
Madera U.S.A. 128 C3
Madgaon India *see* Margao
Madha India 84 B2
Madhavpur India 82 B5
Madhepura India 83 F4
Madhipura India *see* Madhepura
Madhubani India 83 F4
Madhya Pradesh *state* India 82 D5
Madibogo S. Africa 101 G4
Madidi *r.* Bol. 142 E6
Madikeri India 84 B3
Madikwe Game Reserve *nature res.* S. Africa 101 H3
Madill U.S.A. 131 D5
Madīnat ash Shamāl Qatar 88 C5
Madingo-Kayes Congo 99 B4
Madingou Congo 99 B4
Madison *FL* U.S.A. 133 D6
Madison *GA* U.S.A. 133 D5
Madison *IN* U.S.A. 134 C4
Madison *ME* U.S.A. 135 K1
Madison *NE* U.S.A. 130 D3
Madison *SD* U.S.A. 130 D2
Madison *VA* U.S.A. 135 F4

▶Madison *WI* U.S.A. 130 F3
Capital of Wisconsin.

Madison *WV* U.S.A. 134 E4
Madison *r.* U.S.A. 126 F3
Madison Heights U.S.A. 134 F5
Madisonville *KY* U.S.A. 134 B5
Madisonville *TX* U.S.A. 131 E6
Madiun Indon. 68 E8
Madley, Mount *hill* Australia 109 C6
Madoc Canada 135 G1
Mado Gashi Kenya 98 D3
Madoi China *see* Machali
Madona Latvia 45 O8
Madpura India 82 B4
Madra Dağı *mts* Turkey 59 L5
Madrakah Saudi Arabia 86 E5
Madrakah, Ra's *c.* Oman 87 I6
Madras India *see* Chennai
Madras *state* India *see* Tamil Nadu
Madras U.S.A. 126 C3
Madre, Laguna *lag.* Mex. 131 D7
Madre, Laguna *lag.* U.S.A. 131 D7
Madre de Dios *r.* Peru 142 E6
Madre de Dios, Isla *i.* Chile 144 A8
Madre del Sur, Sierra *mts* Mex. 136 D5
Madre Mountain U.S.A. 129 J4
Madre Occidental, Sierra *mts* Mex. 127 F7
Madre Oriental, Sierra *mts* Mex. 131 C7

▶Madrid Spain 57 E3
Capital of Spain. 5th most populous city in Europe.

Madridejos Spain 57 E4
Madruga Cuba 133 D8
Madugula India 84 D2
Madura *i.* Indon. 68 E8
Madura, Selat *sea chan.* Indon. 68 E8
Madurai India 84 C4
Madurantakam India 84 C3
Madvār, Kūh-e *mt.* Iran 88 D4
Madwas India 83 E4
Maé *i.* Vanuatu *see* Émaé
Maebashi Japan 75 E5
Mae Hong Son Thai. 70 B3
Mae Ping National Park Thai. 70 B3
Mae Ramat Thai. 70 B3
Mae Sai Thai. 70 B2
Mae Sariang Thai. 70 B3
Mae Sot Thai. 70 B3
Mae Suai Thai. 70 B3
Mae Tuen Wildlife Reserve *nature res.* Thai. 70 B3
Maevatanana Madag. 99 E5
Maéwo *i.* Vanuatu 107 G3
Mae Wong National Park Thai. 70 B4
Mae Yom National Park Thai. 70 C3
Mafadi *mt.* S. Africa 101 I5
Mafeking Canada 121 K4
Mafeteng Lesotho 101 H5
Maffra Australia 112 C6
Mafia Island Tanz. 99 D4
Mafikeng S. Africa *see* Mahikeng
Mafinga Tanz. 99 D4
Mafra Brazil 145 A4
Mafraq Jordan *see* Al Mafraq
Magabeni S. Africa 101 J6
Magadan Russia 65 Q4
Magadi Kenya 98 D4
Magaiza Moz. 101 K2
Magallanes Chile *see* Punta Arenas
Magallanes, Estrecho de Chile *see* Magellan, Strait of
Magangué Col. 142 D2
Mağara Dağı *mt.* Turkey 85 A1
Magaramkent Russia 91 H2
Magaria Niger 96 D3
Magarida P.N.G. 110 E1
Magas Russia 91 G2
Magazine Mountain *hill* U.S.A. 131 E5
Magdagachi Russia 74 B1
Magdalena Bol. 142 F6
Magdalena *r.* Col. 142 D1
Magdalena *Baja California Sur* Mex. 127 E8
Magdalena *Sonora* Mex. 127 F7
Magdalena *r.* Mex. 127 F7
Magdalena, Bahía *b.* Mex. 136 B4
Magdalena, Isla *i.* Chile 144 B6
Magdeburg Germany 53 L2
Magdelaine Cays *atoll* Australia 110 E3
Magee, Island *pen.* U.K. 51 G3
Magellan, Strait of Chile 144 B8
Magellan Seamounts *sea feature* N. Pacific Ocean 150 F4
Magenta, Lake *salt flat* Australia 109 B8
Magerøya *i.* Norway 44 N1
Maggiorasca, Monte *mt.* Italy 58 C2
Maggiore, Lago Italy *see* Maggiore, Lake
Maggiore, Lake Italy 58 C2

Maghâgha Egypt see Maghāghah
Maghāghah Egypt 90 C5
Maghama Mauritania 96 B3
Maghâra, Gebel hill Egypt see Maghārah, Jabal
Maghārah, Jabal hill Egypt 85 A4
Maghera U.K. 51 F3
Magherafelt U.K. 51 F3
Maghnia Alg. 57 F6
Maghull U.K. 48 E5
Magilligan Point U.K. 51 F2
Magma U.S.A. 129 H5
Magna Grande mt. Sicily Italy 58 F6
Magnetic Island Australia 110 D3
Magnetic Passage Australia 110 D3
Magnetity Russia 44 R2
Magnitogorsk Russia 64 G4
Magnolia AR U.S.A. 131 E5
Magnolia MS U.S.A. 131 F6
Magny-en-Vexin France 52 B5
Mago Russia 74 F1
Màgoé Moz. 99 D5
Magog Canada 135 I1
Mago National Park Eth. 98 D3
Magosa Cyprus see Famagusta
Magpie r. Canada 123 I4
Magpie, Lac l. Canada 123 I4
Magṭa' Laḥjar Mauritania 96 B3
Magu, Chashmeh-ye well Iran 88 E3
Magu, Khrebet mts Russia 74 E1
Maguan China 76 E4
Magude Moz. 101 K3
Magueyal Mex. 131 C7
Magura Bangl. 83 G5
Maguse Lake Canada 121 M2
Magway Myanmar see Magwe
Magwe Myanmar 70 A2
Magyar Köztársaság country Europe see Hungary
Magyichaung Myanmar 70 A2
Mahābād Iran 88 B2
Mahabharat Range mts Nepal 83 F4
Mahaboobnagar India see Mahbubnagar
Mahad India 84 B2
Mahadeo Hills India 82 D5
Mahaffey U.S.A. 135 F3
Mahajan India 82 C3
Mahajanga Madag. 99 E5
Mahakam r. Indon. 68 F7
Mahalapye Botswana 101 H2
Mahale Mountains National Park Tanz. 99 C4
Mahalevona Madag. 99 E5
Maḥallāt Iran 88 C3
Māhān Iran 88 E4
Mahanadi r. India 84 E1
Mahanoro Madag. 99 E5
Maha Oya Sri Lanka 84 D5
Maharashtra state India 84 B2
Maha Sarakham Thai. 70 C3
Mahasham, Wâdi el watercourse Egypt see Muhashsham, Wādī al
Mahaxai Laos 70 D3
Mahbubabad India 84 D2
Mahbubnagar India 84 C2
Mahd adh Dhahab Saudi Arabia 86 F5
Mahdia Alg. 57 G6
Mahdia Guyana 143 G2
Mahdia Tunisia 58 D7
Mahdūm Syria 85 C1
Mahe China 76 E1
Mahé i. Seychelles 149 L6
Mahendragiri mt. India 84 E2
Mahendranagar Nepal 82 E3
Mahenge Tanz. 99 D4
Mahesana India 82 C5
Mahi r. India 82 C5
Mahia Peninsula N.Z. 113 F4
Mahikeng S. Africa 101 G3
Mahilyow Belarus 43 F5
Mahim India 84 B2
Māhīrūd Iran 89 F3
Mahjān Iran 88 D4
Mahlabatini S. Africa 101 J5
Mahlsdorf Germany 53 L2
Maḥmūdābād Iran 88 D2
Maḥmūd-e 'Erāqī Afgh. see Maḥmūd-e Rāqī
Maḥmūd-e Rāqī Afgh. 89 H3
Mahnomen U.S.A. 130 D2
Maho Sri Lanka 84 D5
Mahoba India 82 D4
Maholi India 82 E4
Mahón Spain see Maó
Mahony Lake Canada 120 E1
Mahrauni India 82 D4
Mahrès Tunisia 58 D7
Mahsana India see Mahesana
Mahudaung mts Myanmar 70 A2
Māhukona U.S.A. 127 [inset]
Mahur India 84 C2
Mahuva India 82 B5
Mahwa India 82 D4
Mahya Dağı mt. Turkey 59 L4
Mai i. Vanuatu see Émaé
Maiaia Moz. see Nacala
Maibong India 70 A1
Maicao Col. 142 D1
Maicasagi r. Canada 122 F4
Maicasagi, Lac l. Canada 122 F4
Maichen China 77 F4
Maīdān Shahr Afgh. 89 H3
Maidenhead U.K. 49 G7
Maidstone Canada 121 I4
Maidstone U.K. 49 H7
Maiduguri Nigeria 96 E3
Mai Gudo mt. Eth. 98 D3
Maigue r. Ireland 51 D5
Maihar India 82 E4
Maiji Shan mt. China 76 E1
Maikala Range hills India 82 E5
Maiko r. Dem. Rep. Congo 98 C3
Maiko, Parc National de la nat. park Dem. Rep. Congo 98 C4
Mailan Hill mt. India 83 E5
Mailly-le-Camp France 52 E6
Mailsi Pak. 89 I4
Maīmanah Afgh. 89 G3
Main r. Germany 53 I4
Main r. U.K. 51 F3
Main Brook Canada 123 L4
Mainburg Germany 53 L6
Main Channel lake channel Canada 134 E1
Maindargi India 84 C2
Mai-Ndombe, Lac l. Dem. Rep. Congo 98 B4
Main-Donau-Kanal canal Germany 53 K5
Maindong China see Coqên
Main Duck Island Canada 135 G2
Maine state U.S.A. 135 K1
Maine, Gulf of Canada/U.S.A. 135 K2
Maine Hanari, Cerro hill Col. 142 D4
Maïné-Soroa Niger 96 E3
Maingkaing Myanmar 70 A1
Maingkwan Myanmar 70 B1
Maingy Island Myanmar 71 B4
Mainhardt Germany 53 J5
Mainkung China 76 C2
Mainland i. Scotland U.K. 50 F1
Mainland i. Scotland U.K. 50 [inset]
Mainleus Germany 53 L4
Mainoru Australia 108 F3
Mainpat reg. India 83 E5
Mainpuri India 82 D4
Main Range National Park Australia 112 F2
Maintenon France 52 B6
Maintirano Madag. 99 E5
Mainz Germany 53 I4
Maio i. Cape Verde 96 [inset]
Maipú Arg. 144 E5
Maish Vaya U.S.A. 129 G5
Maiskhal Island Bangl. 83 G5
Maisons-Laffitte France 52 C6
Maitengwe Botswana 99 C6
Maitland N.S.W. Australia 112 E4
Maitland S.A. Australia 111 B7
Maitland r. Australia 108 B5
Maitri research station Antarctica 152 C2
Maiwo i. Vanuatu see Maéwo
Maiyu, Mount hill Australia 108 E4
Maíz, Islas del is Nicaragua 137 H6
Maizar Pak. 89 H3
Maizuru Japan 75 D6
Majdel Aanjar tourist site Lebanon 85 B3
Majella, Parco Nazionale della nat. park Italy 58 F3
Majene Indon. 68 F7
Majestic U.S.A. 134 D5
Majhūd well Saudi Arabia 88 C6
Majī Eth. 98 D3
Majiang Guangxi China 77 F4
Majiang Guizhou China 76 E3
Majiazi China 74 B2
Majnābād Iran 89 F3
Majöl country N. Pacific Ocean see Marshall Islands
Major, Puig mt. Spain 57 H4
Majorca i. Spain 57 H4
Mājro atoll Marshall Is see Majuro
Majunga Madag. see Mahajanga
Majuro atoll Marshall Is 150 H5
Majwemasweu S. Africa 101 H5
Makabana Congo 98 B4
Makale Indon. 69 F7

▶Makalu mt. China/Nepal 83 F4
5th highest mountain in Asia and the world.

Makalu Barun National Park Nepal 83 F4
Makanpur India 82 E4
Makanshy Kazakh. 80 F2
Makari Mountain National Park Tanz. see Mahale Mountains National Park
Makarov Russia 74 F2
Makarov Basin sea feature Arctic Ocean 153 B1
Makarska Croatia 58 G3
Makarwal Pak. 89 H3
Makar'ye Russia 42 K4
Makar'yev Russia 42 I4
Makasar, Selat strait Indon. see Makassar, Selat
Makassar Indon. 68 F8
Makassar, Selat str. Indon. 68 F7
Makassar Strait Indon. see Makassar, Selat
Makat Kazakh. 78 E2
Makatini Flats lowland S. Africa 101 K4
Makedonija country Europe see Macedonia
Makeni Sierra Leone 96 B4
Makete Tanz. 99 D4
Makeyevka Ukr. see Makiyivka
Makgadikgadi depr. Botswana 99 C6
Makgadikgadi Pans National Park Botswana 99 C6
Makhachkala Russia 91 G2
Makhad Pak. 89 H3
Makhado S. Africa 101 I2
Makhāzin, Kathīb al des. Egypt 85 A4
Makhâzin, Kathîb el des. Egypt see Makhāzin, Kathīb al
Makhazine, Barrage El dam Morocco 57 D6
Makhmūr/Mexmûr Iraq 91 F4
Makhtal India 84 C2
Makin atoll Kiribati see Butaritari
Makindu Kenya 98 D4
Makinsk Kazakh. 79 G1
Makira i. Solomon Is 107 G3
Makiyivka Ukr. 43 H6
Makkah Saudi Arabia see Mecca
Makkovik Canada 123 K3
Makkovik, Cape Canada 123 K3
Makkum Neth. 52 F1
Makó Hungary 59 I1
Makokou Gabon 98 B3
Makopong Botswana 100 F3
Makotipoko Congo 97 E5
Makran reg. Iran/Pak. 89 F5
Makrana India 82 C4
Makran Coast Range mts Pak. 89 F5
Makri India 84 D2
Maksatikha Russia 42 G4
Maksi India 82 D5
Maksimovka Russia 74 E3
Maksotag Iran 89 F4
Maksudangarh India 82 D5
Mākū Iran 88 B2
Makunguwiro Tanz. 99 D5
Makurdi Nigeria 96 D4
Makwassie S. Africa 101 G4
Mal India 83 G4
Mala Ireland see Mallow
Mala i. Solomon Is see Malaita
Malå Sweden 44 K4
Mala, Punta pt Panama 137 H7
Malabar Coast India 84 B3

▶Malabo Equat. Guinea 96 D4
Capital of Equatorial Guinea.

Malaca Spain see Málaga
Malacca Malaysia see Melaka
Malacca, Strait of Indon./Malaysia 71 B6
Malad City U.S.A. 126 E4
Maladzyechna Belarus 45 O9
Malá Fatra, Národný park nat. park Slovakia 47 Q6
Málaga Spain 57 D5
Malaga U.S.A. 131 B5
Malagasy Republic country Africa see Madagascar
Málainn Mhóir Ireland 51 D3
Malaita i. Solomon Is 107 G2
Malakal South Sudan 86 D8
Malakanagiri India see Malkangiri
Malakheti Nepal 82 E3
Malakula i. Vanuatu 107 G3
Malan, Ras pt Pak. 89 G5
Malang Indon. 68 E8
Malangana Nepal see Malangwa
Malange Angola see Malanje
Malangwa Nepal 83 F4
Malanje Angola 99 B4
Malappuram India 84 C4
Mälaren l. Sweden 45 J7
Malargüe Arg. 144 C5
Malartic Canada 122 F4
Malaspina Glacier U.S.A. 120 A3
Malatya Turkey 90 E3
Malavalli India 84 C3
Malawi country Africa 99 D5
Malawi, Lake Africa see Nyasa, Lake
Malawi National Park Zambia see Nyika National Park
Malaya pen. Malaysia see Peninsular Malaysia
Malaya Pera Russia 42 L2
Malaya Vishera Russia 42 G4
Malaybalay Phil. 69 H5
Malāyer Iran 88 C3
Malay Peninsula Asia 71 B4
Malay Reef Australia 110 E3
Malaysia country Asia 68 D5
Malaysia, Semenanjung pen. Malaysia see Peninsular Malaysia
Malazgirt Turkey 91 F3
Malbon Australia 110 C4
Malbork Poland 47 Q3
Malborn Germany 52 G5
Malchin Germany 47 N4
Malcolm (abandoned) Australia 109 C7
Malcolm, Point Australia 109 C8
Malcolm Island Myanmar 71 B5
Maldegem Belgium 52 D3
Malden U.S.A. 131 F4
Malden Island Kiribati 151 J6
Maldives country Indian Ocean 81 D10
Maldon Australia 112 B6
Maldon U.K. 49 H7
Maldonado Uruguay 144 F4

▶Male Maldives 81 D11
Capital of the Maldives.

Maleas, Akra pt Greece see Maleas, Akrotirio
Maleas, Akrotirio pt Greece 59 J6
Male Atholhu Maldives 81 D11
Male Atoll Maldives see Male Atholhu
Malebogo S. Africa 101 G5
Malegaon Mahar. India 84 B1
Malegaon Mahar. India 84 C2
Malek, Chāh-e well Iran 88 D3
Malé Karpaty hills Slovakia 47 P6
Malek Mīrzā, Chāh-e well Iran 88 D4
Malek Sīāh Kōh mt. Afgh. 89 F4
Malele Dem. Rep. Congo 99 B4
Maleševski Planini mts Bulg./Macedonia 59 J4
Malgobek Russia 91 G2
Malgomaj l. Sweden 44 J4
Malḥa, Naqb mt. Egypt see Māliḥah, Naqb
Malhada Brazil 145 C1
Malheur r. U.S.A. 126 D3
Malheur Lake U.S.A. 126 D4
Mali country Africa 96 C3
Mali Dem. Rep. Congo 98 C4
Mali Guinea 96 B3
Maliana East Timor 108 D2
Malianjing China 80 I3
Māliḥah, Naqb mt. Egypt 85 A5
Malik Naro mt. Pak. 89 F4
Mali Kyun i. Myanmar 71 B4
Malili Indon. 69 G7
Malin Ukr. see Malyn
Malindi Kenya 98 E4
Malines Belgium see Mechelen
Malin Head hd Ireland 51 E2
Malipo China 76 E4
Mali Raginac mt. Croatia 58 F2
Malita Phil. 69 H5
Malka r. Russia 91 G2
Malkangiri India 84 D2
Malkapur India 84 B2
Malkara Turkey 59 L4
Mal'kavichy Belarus 45 O10
Malko Tarnovo Bulg. 59 L4
Mallacoota Australia 112 D6
Mallacoota Inlet b. Australia 112 D6
Mallaig U.K. 50 D4
Mallani reg. India 89 H5
Mallawī Egypt 90 C6
Mallee Cliffs National Park Australia 111 C7
Mallery Lake Canada 121 L1
Mallet Brazil 145 A4
Mallorca i. Spain see Majorca
Mallow Ireland 51 D5
Mallowa Well Australia 108 D5
Mallwyd U.K. 49 D6
Malm Norway 44 G4
Malmberget Sweden 44 L3
Malmedy Belgium 52 G4
Malmesbury S. Africa 100 D7
Malmesbury U.K. 49 E7
Malmö Sweden 45 H9
Malmyzh Russia 42 K4
Maloca Brazil 143 G3
Malone U.S.A. 135 H1
Malonje mt. Tanz. 99 D4
Maloshuyka Russia 42 H3
Måløy Norway 44 D6
Maloyaroslavets Russia 43 H5
Malozemel'skaya Tundra lowland Russia 42 K2
Malpelo, Isla de i. N. Pacific Ocean 137 H8
Malprabha r. India 84 C2
Malta country Europe 58 F7
Malta Latvia 45 O8
Malta ID U.S.A. 126 E4
Malta MT U.S.A. 126 G2
Malta Channel Italy/Malta 58 F6
Maltahöhe Namibia 100 C3
Maltby U.K. 48 F5
Maltby le Marsh U.K. 48 H5
Malton U.K. 48 G4
Maluku is Indon. see Moluccas
Maluku, Laut sea Indon. 69 H6
Ma'lūlā, Jabal mts Syria 85 C3
Malung Sweden 45 H6
Maluti Mountains Lesotho 101 I5
Malu'u Solomon Is 107 G2
Malvan India 84 B2
Malvasia Greece see Monemvasia
Malvern U.K. see Great Malvern
Malvern U.S.A. 131 E5
Malvérnia Moz. see Chicualacuala
Malvinas, Islas terr. S. Atlantic Ocean see Falkland Islands
Malyn Ukr. 43 F6
Malyy Anyuy r. Russia 65 R3
Malyye Derbety Russia 43 J7
Malyy Kavkaz mts Asia see Lesser Caucasus
Malyy Lyakhovskiy, Ostrov i. Russia 65 P2
Mamadysh Russia 42 K5
Mamafubedu S. Africa 101 I4
Mamatān Nāwēr l. Afgh. 89 G4
Mamba China 76 B2
Mambaí Brazil 145 B1
Mambasa Dem. Rep. Congo 98 C3
Mamburao Phil. 69 G4
Mamelodi S. Africa 101 I3
Mamfe Cameroon 96 D4
Mamit India 83 H5
Mammoth U.S.A. 129 H5
Mammoth Cave National Park U.S.A. 134 B5
Mammoth Reservoir U.S.A. 128 D3
Mamonas Brazil 145 C1
Mamoré r. Bol./Brazil 142 E6
Mamou Guinea 96 B3
Mampikony Madag. 99 E5
Mampong Ghana 96 C4
Mamuju Indon. 68 F7
Mamuno Botswana 100 E2
Man Côte d'Ivoire 96 C4
Man India 84 B2
Man r. India 84 B2
Man U.S.A. 134 E5

▶Man, Isle of terr. Irish Sea 48 C4
United Kingdom Crown Dependency.

Manacapuru Brazil 142 F4
Manacor Spain 57 H4
Manado Indon. 69 G6

▶Managua Nicaragua 137 G6
Capital of Nicaragua.

Manakara Madag. 99 E6
Manakau mt. N.Z. 113 D6
Manākhah Yemen 86 F6

▶Manama Bahrain 88 C5
Capital of Bahrain.

Manamadurai India 84 C4
Mana Maroka National Park S. Africa 101 H5
Manamelkudi India 84 C4
Manam Island P.N.G. 69 L7
Mananara Avaratra Madag. 99 E5
Manangoora Australia 110 B3
Mananjary Madag. 99 E6
Manantali, Lac de l. Mali 96 B3
Manantenina Madag. 99 E6
Mana Pass China/India 82 D3
Mana Pools National Park Zimbabwe 99 C5

▶Manapouri, Lake N.Z. 113 A7
Deepest lake in Oceania.

Manasa India 82 C4
Manas He r. China 80 G2
Manas Hu l. China 80 G2
Manāṣīr reg. U.A.E. 88 D6

▶Manaslu mt. Nepal 83 F3
8th highest mountain in Asia and the world.

Manas National Park nature res. Bhutan 83 G4
Manassas U.S.A. 135 G4
Manastir Macedonia see Bitola
Man-aung Myanmar 70 A3
Man-aung Kyun Myanmar 70 A3
Manaus Brazil 142 F4
Manavgat Turkey 90 C3
Manbazar India 83 F5
Manbij Syria 85 C1
Manby U.K. 48 H5
Mancelona U.S.A. 134 C1
Manchar India 84 B2
Manchester U.K. 48 E5
Manchester CT U.S.A. 135 I3
Manchester IA U.S.A. 130 F3
Manchester KY U.S.A. 134 D5
Manchester MD U.S.A. 135 G4
Manchester MI U.S.A. 134 C2
Manchester NH U.S.A. 135 J2
Manchester OH U.S.A. 134 D4
Manchester TN U.S.A. 132 C5
Manchester VT U.S.A. 135 I2
Mancılık Turkey 90 E3
Mand Pak. 89 F5
Mand, Rūd-e r. Iran 88 C4
Manda Tanz. 99 D4
Manda, Jabal mt. South Sudan 97 F4
Manda, Parc National de nat. park Chad 97 E4
Mandabe Madag. 99 E6
Mandai Sing. 71 [inset]
Mandal Norway 45 E7

▶Mandala, Puncak mt. Indon. 69 K7
3rd highest mountain in Oceania.

Mandalay Myanmar 70 B2
Mandale Myanmar see Mandalay
Mandalgovĭ Mongolia 72 J3
Mandalī Iraq 91 G4
Mandal-Ovoo Mongolia 72 I4
Mandalt China 73 K4
Mandan U.S.A. 130 C2
Mandas Sardinia Italy 58 C5
Mandasa India 84 E2
Mandasor India see Mandsaur
Mandav Hills India 82 B5
Mandera Kenya 98 E3
Manderfield U.S.A. 129 G2
Manderscheid Germany 52 G4
Mandeville Jamaica 137 I5
Mandeville N.Z. 113 B7
Mandha India 82 B4
Mandhoúdhion Greece see Mantoudi
Mandi India 82 D3
Mandiana Guinea 96 C3
Mandié Moz. 99 D5
Mandini S. Africa 101 J5
Mandira Dam India 83 F5
Mandla India 82 E5
Mandleshwar India 82 C5
Mandrael India 82 D4
Mandritsara Madag. 99 E5
Mandsaur India 82 C4
Mandurah Australia 109 A8
Manduria Italy 58 G4
Mandvi India 82 B5
Mandya India 84 C3
Manerbio Italy 58 D2
Manevychi Ukr. 43 E6
Manfalūṭ Egypt 90 C6
Manfredonia Italy 58 F4
Manfredonia, Golfo di g. Italy 58 G4
Manga Brazil 145 C1
Manga Burkina Faso 96 C3
Mangabeiras, Serra das hills Brazil 143 I6
Mangai Dem. Rep. Congo 98 B4
Mangaia i. Cook Is 151 J7
Mangakino N.Z. 113 E4
Mangalagiri India 84 D2
Mangaldai India see Mangaldoi
Mangaldoi India 70 A1
Mangalia Romania 59 M3
Mangalmé Chad 97 E3
Mangalore India see Mangaluru
Mangaluru India 84 B3
Mangaon India 84 B2
Mangareva Islands Fr. Polynesia see Gambier, Îles
Mangaung Free State S. Africa 101 H5
Mangaung Free State S. Africa see Bloemfontein
Mangawan India 83 E4
Ma'ngê China see Luqu
Mangea i. Cook Is see Mangaia
Mangghyshlaq Kazakh. see Mangistau
Mangghystaū Kazakh. see Mangistau
Mangghystaū admin. div. Kazakh. see Mangystauskaya Oblast'
Mangghyt Uzbek. see Mang'it
Manghāl Afgh. 89 F3
Manghit Uzbek. see Mang'it
Mangin Range mts Myanmar see Mingin Range
Mangistau Kazakh. 91 H2
Mang'it Uzbek. 80 B3
Mangla Bangl. see Mongla
Mangla China see Mangra
Mangla Pak. 89 I3
Mangnai China 80 H4
Mangochi Malawi 99 D5
Mangoky r. Madag. 99 E6
Mangole i. Indon. 69 H7
Mangoli India 84 B2
Mangotsfield U.K. 49 E7
Mangqystaū Shyghanaghy b. Kazakh. see Mangystau, Zaliv
Mangra China 76 D1
Mangrol India 82 B5
Mangrul India 84 C1
Mangshi China 76 C3
Mangualde Port. 57 C3
Manguéni, Plateau du Niger 96 E2
Mangui China 74 A2
Mangula Zimbabwe see Mhangura
Mangum U.S.A. 131 D5
Manguri Australia 109 F7
Mangyshlak Kazakh. see Mangistau
Mangyshlak Oblast admin. div. Kazakh. see Mangystauskaya Oblast'
Mangyshlakskaya Oblast' admin. div. Kazakh. see Mangystauskaya Oblast'
Mangystau Kazakh. see Mangistau
Mangystau, Poluostrov pen. Kazakh. 91 H1
Mangystau, Zaliv b. Kazakh. 91 H1
Mangystauskaya Oblast' admin. div. Kazakh. 91 I2
Manhā Brazil 145 B1
Manhattan U.S.A. 130 D4
Manhica Moz. 101 K3
Manhoca Moz. 101 K4
Manhuaçu Brazil 145 C3
Manhuaçu r. Brazil 145 C2
Mani China 83 F2
Mania r. Madag. 99 E5
Maniago Italy 58 E1
Manicouagan Canada 123 H4
Manicouagan r. Canada 123 H4
Manicouagan, Petit Lac l. Canada 123 I3
Manicouagan, Réservoir resr Canada 123 H4
Manic Trois, Réservoir resr Canada 123 H4
Manīfah Saudi Arabia 88 C5
Maniganggo China 76 C2
Manigotagan Canada 121 L5
Manihiki atoll Cook Is 150 J6
Maniitsoq Greenland 119 M3
Manikchhari Bangl. 83 H5
Manikgarh India see Rajura

▶Manila Phil. 69 G4
Capital of the Philippines.

Manila U.S.A. 126 F4
Manildra Australia 112 D4
Manilla Australia 112 E3
Maningrida Australia 108 F3
Manipur India see Imphal
Manipur state India 83 H4
Manisa Turkey 59 L5
Manistee U.S.A. 134 B1
Manistee r. U.S.A. 134 B1
Manistique U.S.A. 132 C2
Manitoba prov. Canada 121 L4
Manitoba, Lake Canada 121 L5
Manito Lake Canada 121 I4
Manitou Canada 121 L5
Manitou, Lake U.S.A. 134 B3
Manitou Beach U.S.A. 135 G2
Manitou Falls Canada 121 M5
Manitou Islands U.S.A. 134 B1
Manitoulin Island Canada 122 E5
Manitouwadge Canada 122 D4
Manitowoc U.S.A. 134 B1
Maniwaki Canada 122 G5
Manizales Col. 142 C2
Manja Madag. 99 E6
Manjarabad India 84 B3
Manjeri India 84 C4
Manjhand Pak. 89 H5
Manjhi India 83 F4
Manjra r. India 84 C2
Man Kabat Myanmar 70 B1
Mankaiana Swaziland see Mankayane
Mankato KS U.S.A. 130 D4
Mankato MN U.S.A. 130 E2
Mankayane Swaziland 101 J4
Mankera Pak. 89 H4
Mankono Côte d'Ivoire 96 C4
Mankota Canada 121 J5
Manlay Mongolia 72 J4
Manley Hot Springs U.S.A. 118 C3
Manmad India 84 B1
Mann r. Australia 108 F3
Mann, Mount Australia 109 E6
Manna Indon. 68 C7
Man Na Myanmar 70 B2
Mannahill Australia 111 B7
Mannar Sri Lanka 84 C4
Mannar, Gulf of India/Sri Lanka 84 C4
Manneru r. India 84 D3
Mannessier, Lac l. Canada 123 H3
Mannheim Germany 53 I5
Mannicolo Islands Solomon Is see Vanikoro Islands
Manning r. Australia 112 F3
Manning Canada 120 G3
Manning U.S.A. 133 D5
Mannington U.S.A. 134 E4
Manningtree U.K. 49 I7
Mann Ranges mts Australia 109 E6
Mannsville KY U.S.A. 134 C5
Mannsville NY U.S.A. 135 G2
Mannu, Capo c. Sardinia Italy 58 C4
Mannville Canada 121 I4
Manoel Ribas Brazil 145 A4
Manoel Vitorino Brazil 145 C1
Man-of-War Rocks is U.S.A. see Gardner Pinnacles
Manoharpur India 82 D4
Manohar Thana India 82 D4
Manokotak U.S.A. 118 C4
Manokwari Indon. 69 I7
Manoron Myanmar 71 B5
Manosque France 56 G5
Manouane r. Canada 123 H4
Manouane, Lac l. Canada 123 H4
Manouba Tunisia 58 D6
Manovo-Gounda Saint Floris, Parc National du nat. park Cent. Afr. Rep. 98 C3
Man Pan Myanmar 70 B2
Manp'o N. Korea 74 B4
Manra i. Kiribati 107 I2
Manresa Spain 57 G3
Mansa Gujarat India 82 C5
Mansa Punjab India 82 C3
Mansa Zambia 99 C5
Mansakonko Gambia 96 B3
Man Sam Myanmar 70 B2
Mansehra Pak. 87 L3
Mansel Island Canada 119 K3
Mansfield Australia 112 C6
Mansfield U.K. 49 F5
Mansfield LA U.S.A. 131 E5
Mansfield OH U.S.A. 134 D3
Mansfield PA U.S.A. 135 G3
Mansfield, Mount U.S.A. 135 I1
Man Si Myanmar 70 B1
Mansi Myanmar 70 A1
Manso r. Brazil see Mortes, Rio das
Manta Ecuador 142 B4
Mantaro r. Peru 142 D6
Manteca U.S.A. 128 C3
Mantena Brazil 145 C2
Manteo U.S.A. 132 F5
Mantes-la-Jolie France 52 B6
Mantiqueira, Serra da mts Brazil 145 B3
Manton U.S.A. 134 C1
Mantoudi Greece 59 J5
Mantova Italy see Mantua
Mäntsälä Fin. 45 N6
Mänttä Fin. 44 N5
Mantua Cuba 133 C8
Mantua Italy 58 D2
Mantuan Downs Australia 110 D5
Manturovo Russia 42 J4
Mäntyharju Fin. 45 O6
Mäntyjärvi Fin. 44 O3
Manú Peru 142 D6
Manu, Parque Nacional del nat. park Peru 142 D6

Manuae atoll Fr. Polynesia 151 J7
Manu'a Islands American Samoa 107 I3
Manuelzinho Brazil 143 H5
Manui i. Indon. 69 G7
Manukau N.Z. 113 E3
Manukau Harbour N.Z. 113 E3
Manunda watercourse Australia 111 B7
Manusela, Taman Nasional nat. park Indon. 69 H7
Manus Island P.N.G. 69 L7
Manvi India 84 C3
Many U.S.A. 131 E6
Manyakatana S. Africa 101 J3
Manyana Botswana 101 G3
Manyas Turkey 59 L4
Manyas Gölü l. Turkey see Kuş Gölü
Many Island Lake Canada 121 I5
Manyoni Tanz. 99 D4
Manzai Pak. 89 H3
Manzanares Spain 57 E4
Manzanillo Cuba 137 I4
Manzanillo Mex. 136 D5
Manzhouli China 73 L3
Manzini Swaziland 101 J4
Mao Chad 97 E3
Maó Spain 57 I4
Maoba Guizhou China 76 E3
Maoba Hubei China 77 F2
Maobi Tou c. Taiwan 77 I4
Mao'ergai China 76 D1
Maoke, Pegunungan mts Indon. 69 J7
Maokeng S. Africa 101 H4
Maokui Shan mt. China 74 A4
Maolin China 74 A4
Maoming China 77 F4
Ma On Shan hill H.K. China 77 [inset]
Maopi T'ou c. Taiwan see Maobi Tou
Maopora i. Indon. 108 D1
Maotou Shan mt. China 76 D3
Mapai Moz. 101 J2
Mapam Yumco l. China 83 E3
Mapanza Zambia 99 C5
Maphodi S. Africa 101 G6
Mapimí Mex. 131 C7
Mapimí, Bolsón de des. Mex. 131 B7
Mapinhane Moz. 101 L2
Mapiri Bol. 142 E7
Maple r. MI U.S.A. 134 C2
Maple r. ND U.S.A. 130 D2
Maple Creek Canada 121 I5
Maple Heights U.S.A. 134 E3
Maple Peak U.S.A. 129 I5
Mapmaker Seamounts sea feature N. Pacific Ocean 150 H4
Mapoon Australia 110 C1
Mapor i. Indon. 71 D7
Mapoteng Lesotho 101 H5
Maprik P.N.G. 69 K7
Mapuera r. Brazil 143 G4
Mapulanguene Moz. 101 K3
Mapungubwe National Park S. Africa 101 I2

▶Maputo Moz. 101 K3
Capital of Mozambique.

Maputo prov. Moz. 101 K3
Maputo r. Moz./S. Africa 101 K4
Maputo, Baía de b. Moz. 101 K4
Maputsoe Lesotho 101 H5
Maqanshy Kazakh. see Makanshy
Maqar an Na'am well Iraq 91 F5
Maqat Kazakh. see Makat
Maqên China 76 D1
Maqên Kangri mt. China 76 C1
Maqnā Saudi Arabia 90 D5
Maqteïr reg. Mauritania 96 B2
Maqu China 76 D1
Ma Qu r. China see Yellow River
Maquan He r. China see Damqoq Zangbo
Maquela do Zombo Angola 99 B4
Maquinchao Arg. 144 C6
Mar r. Pak. 89 G5
Mar, Serra do mts Rio de Janeiro/São Paulo Brazil 145 B3
Mar, Serra do mts Rio Grande do Sul/Santa Catarina Brazil 145 A5
Mara r. Canada 121 I1
Mara India 83 E5
Mara S. Africa 101 I2
Maraã Brazil 142 E4
Marabá Brazil 143 I5
Maraboon, Lake resr Australia 110 E4
Maracá, Ilha de i. Brazil 143 H3
Maracaibo Venez. 142 D1
Maracaibo, Lago de Venez. see Maracaibo, Lake
Maracaibo, Lake Venez. 142 D2
Maracaju Brazil 144 E2
Maracaju, Serra de hills Brazil 144 E2
Maracanda Uzbek. see Samarqand
Maracás Brazil 145 C1
Maracás, Chapada de hills Brazil 145 C1
Maracay Venez. 142 E1
Marādah Libya 97 E2
Maradi Niger 96 D3
Marāgheh Iran 88 B2
Marahuaca, Cerro mt. Venez. 142 E3
Marajó, Baía de est. Brazil 143 I4
Marajó, Ilha de i. Brazil 143 H4
Marakele National Park S. Africa 101 H3
Maralal Kenya 98 D3
Maralbashi China see Bachu
Maralinga Australia 109 E7
Maralwexi China see Bachu
Maramasike i. Solomon Is 107 G2
Maramba Zambia see Livingstone
Marambio research station Antarctica 152 A2
Maran Malaysia 71 C7
Marana U.S.A. 129 H5
Marand Iran 88 B2
Marandellas Zimbabwe see Marondera
Marang Malaysia 71 C6
Marang Myanmar 71 B5
Maranhão r. Brazil 145 A1
Maranoa r. Australia 112 D1
Marañón r. Peru 142 D4
Marão Moz. 101 L3
Marão mt. Port. 57 C3
Mara Rosa Brazil 145 A1

Maraş Turkey see Kahramanmaraş
Marathon Canada 122 D4
Marathon FL U.S.A. 133 D7
Marathon NY U.S.A. 135 G2
Marathon TX U.S.A. 131 C6
Maratua i. Indon. 68 F6
Maraú Brazil 145 D1
Maravillas Creek watercourse U.S.A. 131 C6
Marbella Spain 57 D5
Marble Bar Australia 108 B5
Marble Canyon U.S.A. 129 H3
Marble Canyon gorge U.S.A. 129 H3
Marble Hall S. Africa 101 I3
Marble Hill U.S.A. 131 F4
Marble Island Canada 121 N2
Marbul Pass India 82 C2
Marburg Germany 53 I4
Marburg S. Africa 101 J6
Marburg Slovenia see Maribor
Marca, Ponta do pt Angola 99 B5
Marcali Hungary 58 G1
Marcelino Ramos Brazil 145 A4
March U.K. 49 H6
Marche reg. France 56 E3
Marche-en-Famenne Belgium 52 F4
Marchena Spain 57 D5
Marchinbar Island Australia 110 B1
Mar Chiquita, Laguna l. Arg. 144 D4
Marchtrenk Austria 47 O6
Marco U.S.A. 133 D7
Marcoing France 52 D4
Marcona Peru 142 C7
Marcopeet Islands Canada 122 F2
Marcus Baker, Mount U.S.A. 118 D3
Marcy, Mount U.S.A. 135 I1
Mardan Pak. 89 I3
Mar del Plata Arg. 144 E5
Mardīan Afgh. 89 G2
Mardin Turkey 91 F3
Maré i. New Caledonia 107 G4
Maree, Loch l. U.K. 50 D3
Mareh Ḥoseynābād Iran 89 E5
Marengo IA U.S.A. 130 E3
Marengo IN U.S.A. 134 B4
Marengo OH U.S.A. 134 D3
Marevo Russia 42 G4
Marfa U.S.A. 131 B6
Marganets Ukr. see Marhanets'
Margao India 84 B3
Margaret r. Australia 108 D4
Margaret watercourse Australia 111 B6
Margaret, Mount hill Australia 108 B5
Margaret Lake Alta Canada 120 H3
Margaret Lake N.W.T. Canada 120 G1
Margaret River Australia 109 A8
Margaretville U.S.A. 135 H2
Margarita, Isla de i. Venez. 142 F1
Margaritovo Russia 74 D4
Margate U.K. 49 I7
Margeride, Monts de la mts France 56 F4
Margherita, Lake Eth. see Abaya, Lake

▶Margherita Peak Dem. Rep. Congo/Uganda 98 C3
3rd highest mountain in Africa.

Marghilon Uzbek. see Marg'ilon
Marg'ilon Uzbek. 80 D3
Mārgō, Dasht-e des. Afgh. 89 F4
Mārgo, Dasht-i- des. Afgh. see Mārgō, Dasht-e
Margog Caka l. China 83 F2
Margraten Neth. 52 F4
Marguerite Canada 120 F4
Marguerite, Pic mt. Dem. Rep. Congo/Uganda see Margherita Peak
Marguerite Bay Antarctica 152 L2
Margyang China 83 G3
Marhaj Khalīl Iraq 91 G4
Marhanets' Ukr. 43 G7
Marhoum Alg. 54 D5
Mari Myanmar 70 B1
Maria atoll Fr. Polynesia 151 J7
María Elena Chile 144 C2
Maria Island Australia 110 A2
Maria Island Myanmar 71 B5
Maria Island National Park Australia 111 [inset]
Mariala National Park Australia 111 D5
Mariana Brazil 145 C3
Marianao Cuba 133 D8
Mariana Ridge sea feature N. Pacific Ocean 150 F4

▶Mariana Trench sea feature N. Pacific Ocean 150 F5
Deepest trench in the world.

Mariani India 83 H4
Mariánica, Cordillera mts Spain see Morena, Sierra
Marian Lake Canada 120 G2
Marianna AR U.S.A. 131 F5
Marianna FL U.S.A. 133 C6
Mariano Machado Angola see Ganda
Mariánské Lázně Czechia 53 M5
Marias r. U.S.A. 126 F3
Marías, Islas is Mex. 136 C4

▶Mariato, Punta pt Panama 137 H7
Most southerly point of North America.

Maria van Diemen, Cape N.Z. 113 D2
Ma'rib Yemen 86 G6
Maribor Slovenia 58 F1
Marica r. Bulg. see Maritsa
Maricopa AZ U.S.A. 129 G5
Maricopa CA U.S.A. 128 D4
Maricopa Mountains U.S.A. 129 G5
Maridi South Sudan 97 F4
Marie Byrd Land reg. Antarctica 152 J1
Marie-Galante i. Guadeloupe 137 L5
Mariehamn Fin. 45 K6
Mariembero r. Brazil 145 A1
Marienbad Czechia see Mariánské Lázně
Marienberg Germany 53 N4
Marienburg Poland see Malbork
Marienhafe Germany 53 H1
Mariental Namibia 100 C3
Marienwerder Poland see Kwidzyn
Mariestad Sweden 45 H7

Mariet r. Canada 122 F2
Marietta GA U.S.A. 133 C5
Marietta OH U.S.A. 134 E4
Marietta OK U.S.A. 131 D5
Marignane France 56 G5
Marii, Mys pt Russia 66 G2
Mariinsk Russia 64 J4
Mariinskiy Posad Russia 42 J4
Marijampolė Lith. 45 M9
Marília Brazil 145 A3
Marillana Australia 108 B5
Marimba Angola 99 B4
Marin mt. Pak. 89 G4
Marín Spain 57 B2
Marina U.S.A. 128 C3
Marina di Gioiosa Ionica Italy 58 G5
Mar'ina Gorka Belarus see Mar''ina Horka
Mar''ina Horka Belarus 45 P10
Marinduque i. Phil. 69 G4
Marinette U.S.A. 134 B1
Maringá Brazil 145 A3
Maringa r. Dem. Rep. Congo 98 B3
Marinha Grande Port. 57 B4
Marion AL U.S.A. 133 C5
Marion AR U.S.A. 131 F5
Marion IL U.S.A. 130 F4
Marion IN U.S.A. 134 C3
Marion KS U.S.A. 130 D4
Marion MI U.S.A. 134 C1
Marion NY U.S.A. 135 G2
Marion OH U.S.A. 134 D3
Marion SC U.S.A. 133 E5
Marion VA U.S.A. 134 E5
Marion, Lake U.S.A. 133 D5
Marion Reef Australia 110 F3
Maripa Venez. 142 E2
Mariposa U.S.A. 128 D3
Marisa Indon. 69 G6
Mariscal José Félix Estigarribia Para. 144 D2
Maritime Alps mts France/Italy 56 H4
Maritime Kray admin. div. Russia see Primorskiy Kray
Maritimes, Alpes mts France/Italy see Maritime Alps
Maritsa r. Bulg. 59 L4
also known as Euros (Greece), Marica (Bulgaria), Meriç (Turkey)
Marittime, Alpi mts France/Italy see Maritime Alps
Mariupol' Ukr. 43 H7
Mariusa, Parque Nacional nat. park Venez. 142 F2
Marīvān Iran 88 B3
Marjan Afgh. see Mashōrêy
Marjayoûn Lebanon 85 B3
Marka Somalia 98 E3
Markala Mali 96 C3
Markam China 76 C2
Markaryd Sweden 45 H8
Markaz-e Sayyidābād Afgh. 89 H3
Markdale Canada 134 E1
Marken S. Africa 101 I2
Markermeer l. Neth. 52 F2
Market Deeping U.K. 49 G6
Market Drayton U.K. 49 E6
Market Harborough U.K. 49 G6
Markethill U.K. 51 F3
Market Weighton U.K. 48 G5
Markha r. Russia 65 M3
Markham Canada 134 F2
Markit China 80 E4
Markkleeberg Germany 53 M3
Markleeville U.S.A. 128 D2
Marklohe Germany 53 J2
Markog Qu r. China 76 D1
Markounda Cent. Afr. Rep. 98 B3
Markovo Russia 65 S3
Markranstädt Germany 53 M3
Marks Russia 43 J6
Marks U.S.A. 131 F5
Marksville U.S.A. 131 E6
Marktheidenfeld Germany 53 J5
Marktredwitz Germany 53 M4
Marl Germany 52 H3
Marla Australia 109 F6
Marlborough Downs hills U.K. 49 F7
Marle France 52 D5
Marlette U.S.A. 134 D2
Marlin U.S.A. 131 D6
Marlinton U.S.A. 134 E4
Marlo Australia 112 D6
Marmagao India 84 B3
Marmande France 56 E4
Marmara, Sea of g. Turkey 59 M4
Marmara Denizi g. Turkey see Marmara, Sea of
Marmara Gölü l. Turkey 59 M5
Marmarica reg. Libya 90 B5
Marmaris Turkey 59 M6
Marmarth U.S.A. 130 C2
Marmet U.S.A. 134 E4
Marmion, Lake salt l. Australia 109 C7
Marmion Lake Canada 121 N5
Marmolada mt. Italy 58 D1
Marne r. France 52 C6
Marne au Rhin, Canal de la France 52 G6
Marne-la-Vallée France 52 C6
Marnitz Germany 53 L1
Maroantsetra Madag. 99 E5
Maroc country Africa see Morocco
Marol Pak. 82 D2
Maroldsweisach Germany 53 K4
Maromokotro mt. Madag. 99 E5
Marondera Zimbabwe 99 D5
Maroochydore Australia 112 F1
Maroonah Australia 109 A5
Maroon Peak U.S.A. 126 G5
Marosvásárhely Romania see Târgu Mureş
Marotiri is Fr. Polynesia 151 K6
Maroua Cameroon 97 E3
Marovoay Madag. 99 E5
Marqadah Syria 91 F4
Mar Qu r. China see Markog Qu
Marquard S. Africa 101 H5
Marquesas Islands Fr. Polynesia 151 K6
Marquesas Keys is U.S.A. 133 D7
Marquette U.S.A. 132 C2
Marquez U.S.A. 131 D6
Marquion France 52 D4
Marquise France 52 B4

Marquises, Îles is Fr. Polynesia see Marquesas Islands
Marra Australia 112 A3
Marra r. Australia 112 C3
Marra, Jebel mt. Sudan 97 F3
Marra, Jebel plat. Sudan 97 F3
Marracuene Moz. 101 K3
Marrakech Morocco 54 C5
Marrakesh Morocco see Marrakech
Marrangua, Lagoa l. Moz. 101 L3
Marrar Australia 112 C5
Marrawah Australia 111 [inset]
Marree Australia 111 B6
Marrowbone U.S.A. 134 C5
Marruecos country Africa see Morocco
Marrupa Moz. 99 D5
Marryat Australia 109 F6
Marsá al 'Alam Egypt 86 D4
Marsa 'Alam Egypt see Marsá al 'Alam
Marsá al Burayqah Libya 97 E1
Marsabit Kenya 98 D3
Marsala Sicily Italy 58 E6
Marsá Maṭrūḥ Egypt 90 B5
Marsberg Germany 53 I3
Marsciano Italy 58 E3
Marsden Australia 112 C4
Marsden Canada 121 I4
Marsdiep sea chan. Neth. 52 E2
Marseille France 56 G5
Marseilles France see Marseille
Marsfjället mt. Sweden 44 I4
Marshall watercourse Australia 110 B4
Marshall AR U.S.A. 131 E5
Marshall IL U.S.A. 134 B4
Marshall MI U.S.A. 134 C2
Marshall MN U.S.A. 130 E2
Marshall MO U.S.A. 130 E4
Marshall TX U.S.A. 131 E5
Marshall Islands country N. Pacific Ocean 150 H5
Marshalltown U.S.A. 130 E3
Marshfield MO U.S.A. 131 E4
Marshfield WI U.S.A. 130 F2
Marsh Harbour Bahamas 133 E7
Mars Hill U.S.A. 132 H2
Marsh Island U.S.A. 131 F6
Marsh Peak U.S.A. 129 I1
Marsh Point Canada 121 M3
Marsing U.S.A. 126 D4
Märsta Sweden 45 J7
Marsyaty Russia 41 S3
Martaban, Gulf of Myanmar see Mottama, Gulf of
Martapura Indon. 68 E7
Marten River Canada 122 F5
Marte R. Gómez, Presa resr Mex. 131 D7
Martha's Vineyard i. U.S.A. 135 J3
Martigny Switz. 56 H3
Martim Vaz, Ilhas is S. Atlantic Ocean see Martin Vas, Ilhas
Martin r. Canada 120 F2
Martin Slovakia 47 Q6
Martin MI U.S.A. 134 C2
Martin SD U.S.A. 130 C3
Martinez Lake U.S.A. 129 F5
Martinho Campos Brazil 145 B2

▶Martinique terr. West Indies 137 L6
French Overseas Department.

Martinique Passage Dominica/Martinique 137 L5
Martin Peninsula Antarctica 152 K2
Martinsburg U.S.A. 135 G4
Martins Ferry U.S.A. 134 E3
Martinsville IL U.S.A. 134 B4
Martinsville IN U.S.A. 134 B4
Martinsville VA U.S.A. 134 F5

▶Martin Vas, Ilhas is S. Atlantic Ocean 148 G7
Most easterly point of South America.

Martin Vaz Islands S. Atlantic Ocean see Martin Vas, Ilhas
Martök Kazakh. see Martok
Martok Kazakh. 78 E1
Marton N.Z. 113 E5
Martorell Spain 57 G3
Martos Spain 57 E5
Martuni Armenia 91 G2
Ma'rūf Afgh. 89 G4
Maruim Brazil 143 K6
Marukhis Ughelt'ekhili pass Georgia/Russia 91 F2
Marulan Australia 112 D5
Marusthali reg. India 89 H5
Marvast Iran 88 D4
Marvdasht Iran 88 D4
Marvejols France 56 F4
Marvine, Mount U.S.A. 129 H2
Marwayne Canada 121 I4
Mary r. Australia 108 E3
Mary Turkm. 89 F2
Maryborough Qld Australia 111 F5
Maryborough Vic. Australia 112 A6
Marydale S. Africa 100 F5
Mary Frances Lake Canada 121 J2
Mary Lake Canada 121 K2
Maryland state U.S.A. 135 G4
Maryport U.K. 48 D4
Mary's Harbour Canada 123 L3
Marysvale U.S.A. 129 G2
Marysville CA U.S.A. 128 C2
Marysville KS U.S.A. 130 D4
Marysville OH U.S.A. 134 D3
Maryvale N.T. Australia 109 F6
Maryvale Qld Australia 110 D3
Maryville MO U.S.A. 130 E3
Maryville TN U.S.A. 132 D5
Marzagão Brazil 145 A2
Marzahna Germany 53 M2
Masada tourist site Israel 85 B4
Masāhūn, Kūh-e mt. Iran 88 D4
Masai Steppe plain Tanz. 99 D4
Masaka Uganda 98 D4
Masakhane S. Africa 101 H6
Masalembu Besar i. Indon. 68 E8
Masallı Azer. 91 H3
Masan S. Korea 75 C6
Masasi Tanz. 99 D5

Masavi Bol. 142 F7
Masbate Phil. 69 G4
Masbate i. Phil. 69 G4
Mascara Alg. 57 G6
Mascarene Basin sea feature Indian Ocean 149 L7
Mascarene Plain sea feature Indian Ocean 149 L7
Mascarene Ridge sea feature Indian Ocean 149 L6
Mascote Brazil 145 D1
Masein Myanmar 70 A2
Masela Indon. 108 E2
Masela i. Indon. 108 E2

▶Maseru Lesotho 101 H5
Capital of Lesotho.

Mashai Lesotho 101 I5
Mashan China 77 F4
Masherbrum mt. Pak. 82 D2
Mashhad Iran 89 E2
Mashishing S. Africa 101 J3
Mashkel, Hamun-i- salt flat Pak. 89 F4
Mashkel, Rudi-i r. Pak. 89 F5
Mashki Chah Pak. 89 F4
Mashōrêy Afgh. 89 H3
Masi Norway 44 M2
Masiáca Mex. 127 F8
Masibambane S. Africa 101 H6
Masīlah, Wādī al watercourse Yemen 86 H6
Masilo S. Africa 101 H5
Masi-Manimba Dem. Rep. Congo 99 B4
Masindi Uganda 98 D3
Masinyusane S. Africa 100 F6
Masira, Gulf of Oman see Maşīrah, Khalīj
Maşīrah, Jazīrat i. Oman 87 I5
Maşīrah, Khalīj b. Oman 87 I6
Masira Island Oman see Maşīrah, Jazīrat
Masjed Soleymān Iran 88 C4
Mask, Lough l. Ireland 51 C4
Maskūtān Iran 89 E5
Maslovo Russia 41 S3
Masoala, Tanjona c. Madag. 99 F5
Mason MI U.S.A. 134 C2
Mason OH U.S.A. 134 C4
Mason TX U.S.A. 131 D6
Mason, Lake salt flat Australia 109 B6
Mason Bay N.Z. 113 A8
Mason City U.S.A. 130 E3
Masontown U.S.A. 134 F4
Masqaţ Oman see Muscat
Masqaţ reg. Oman see Muscat
'Masrūg well Oman 88 D6
Massa Italy 58 D2
Massachusetts state U.S.A. 135 I2
Massachusetts Bay U.S.A. 135 J2
Massadona U.S.A. 129 I1
Massafra Italy 58 G4
Massakory Chad 97 E3
Massa Marittima Italy 58 D3
Massangena Moz. 99 D6
Massango Angola 99 B4
Massawa Eritrea 86 E6
Massawippi, Lac l. Canada 135 I1
Massena U.S.A. 135 H1
Massenya Chad 97 E3
Masset Canada 120 C4
Massieville U.S.A. 134 D4
Massif Central mts France 56 F4
Massilia France see Marseille
Massillon U.S.A. 134 E3
Massinga Moz. 101 L2
Massingir Moz. 101 K2
Massingir, Barragem de resr Moz. 101 K2
Masson Island Antarctica 152 F2
Mastchoh Tajik. 89 H2
Masteksay Kazakh. 43 K6
Masterton N.Z. 113 E5
Masticho, Akra pt Greece see Oura, Akrotirio
Mastung Pak. 78 F4
Mastūrah Saudi Arabia 86 E5
Masty Belarus 45 N10
Masuda Japan 75 C6
Masuku Gabon see Franceville
Masulipatam India see Machilipatnam
Masulipatnam India see Machilipatnam
Masuna i. American Samoa see Tutuila
Masvingo Zimbabwe 99 D6
Masvingo prov. Zimbabwe 101 J1
Maswa Tanz. 98 D4
Maswaar i. Indon. 69 I7
Maşyāf Syria 85 C2
Mat, Nam r. Laos 70 D3
Mata Myanmar 70 B1
Matabeleland South prov. Zimbabwe 101 I1
Matachewan Canada 122 E5
Matad Mongolia 73 L3
Matadi Dem. Rep. Congo 99 B4
Matador U.S.A. 131 C5
Matagalpa Nicaragua 137 G6
Matagami Canada 122 F4
Matagami, Lac l. Canada 122 F4
Matagorda Island U.S.A. 131 D6
Matak i. Indon. 71 D7
Matakana Island N.Z. 113 F3
Matala Angola 99 B5
Maţāli', Jabal hill Saudi Arabia 91 F6
Matam Senegal 96 B3
Matamey Niger 96 D3
Matamoras U.S.A. 135 H3
Matamoros Coahuila Mex. 131 C7
Matamoros Tamaulipas Mex. 131 D7
Matandu r. Tanz. 99 D4
Matane Canada 123 I4
Matanzas Cuba 137 H4
Matapan, Cape pt Greece see Tainaro, Akrotirio
Matapédia, Lac l. Canada 123 I4
Maţār well Saudi Arabia 88 B5
Matara Sri Lanka 84 D5
Mataram Indon. 108 B2
Matarani Peru 142 D7
Mataranka Australia 108 F3
Mataripe Brazil 145 D1
Mataró Spain 57 H3
Matasiri i. Indon. 68 F7
Matatiele S. Africa 101 I6

Matatila Reservoir India 82 D4
Mataura N.Z. 113 B8
Mata-Utu Wallis and Futuna see Matā'utu

▶Matā'utu Wallis and Futuna 107 I3
Capital of Wallis and Futuna.

Matawai N.Z. 113 F4
Matay Kazakh. 80 E2
Matcha Tajik. see Mastchoh
Mat Con, Hon i. Vietnam 70 D3
Mategua Bol. 142 F6
Matehuala Mex. 131 C8
Matemanga Tanz. 99 D5
Matera Italy 58 G4
Mateur Tunisia 58 C6
Mathaji India 82 B4
Matheson Canada 122 E4
Mathews U.S.A. 135 G5
Mathis U.S.A. 131 D6
Mathoura Australia 112 B5
Mathura India 82 D4
Mati Phil. 69 H5
Matiali India 83 G4
Matias Cardoso Brazil 145 C1
Matías Romero Mex. 136 E5
Matimekosh Canada 123 I3
Matin India 83 E5
Matinenda Lake Canada 122 E5
Matizi China 76 D1
Matla r. India 83 G5
Matlabas r. S. Africa 101 H2
Matli Pak. 89 H5
Matlock U.K. 49 F5
Mato, Cerro mt. Venez. 142 E2
Matobo Hills Zimbabwe 99 C6
Mato Grosso state Brazil 145 A1
Mato Grosso, Planalto do plat. Brazil 143 H7
Matola Moz. 101 K3
Matopo Hills Zimbabwe see Matobo Hills
Matos Costa Brazil 145 A4
Matosinhos Port. 57 B3
Mato Verde Brazil 145 C1
Maţraḩ Oman 88 E6
Matroosberg mt. S. Africa 100 D7
Matsue Japan 75 D6
Matsumoto Japan 75 E5
Matsu Tao i. Taiwan see Mazu Dao
Matsuyama Japan 75 D6
Mattagami r. Canada 122 E4
Mattamuskeet, Lake U.S.A. 132 E5
Mattawa Canada 122 F5
Matterhorn mt. Italy/Switz. 58 B2
Matterhorn mt. U.S.A. 126 E4
Matthew Town Bahamas 137 J4
Maţţī, Sabkhat salt pan Saudi Arabia 88 D6
Mattoon U.S.A. 130 F4
Matturai Sri Lanka see Matara
Matuku i. Fiji 107 H3
Matumbo Angola 99 B5
Maturín Venez. 142 F2
Matusadona National Park Zimbabwe 99 C5
Matwabeng S. Africa 101 H5
Maty Island P.N.G. see Wuvulu Island
Mau India see Maunath Bhanjan
Maúa Moz. 99 D5
Maubeuge France 52 D4
Maubin Myanmar 70 A3
Ma-ubin Myanmar 70 B1
Maubourguet France 56 E5
Mauchline U.K. 50 E5
Maudaha India 82 E4
Maude Australia 111 D7
Maud Seamount sea feature S. Atlantic Ocean 148 I10
Mau-é-ele Moz. see Marão
Maués Brazil 143 G4
Maughold Head hd Isle of Man 48 C4
Maug Islands N. Mariana Is 69 L2
Maui i. U.S.A. 127 [inset]
Maukkadaw Myanmar 70 A2
Maulbronn Germany 53 I6
Maule r. Chile 144 B5
Maulvi Bazar Bangl. see Moulvibazar
Maumee U.S.A. 134 D3
Maumee Bay U.S.A. 134 D3
Maumere Indon. 108 C2
Maumturk Mountains hills Ireland 51 C4
Maun Botswana 99 C5
Mauna Kea vol. U.S.A. 127 [inset]
Mauna Loa vol. U.S.A. 127 [inset]
Maunath Bhanjan India 83 E4
Maunatlala Botswana 101 H2
Maungaturoto N.Z. 113 E3
Maungdaw Myanmar 70 A2
Maungmagan Islands Myanmar 71 B4
Maurepas, Lake U.S.A. 131 F6
Mauriac France 56 F4
Maurice country Indian Ocean see Mauritius
Maurice, Lake salt flat Australia 109 E7
Maurik Neth. 52 F3
Mauritania country Africa 96 B3
Mauritanie country Africa see Mauritania
Mauritius country Indian Ocean 149 L7
Maurs France 56 F4
Mauston U.S.A. 130 F3
Mava Dem. Rep. Congo 98 C3
Mavago Moz. 99 D5
Mavan, Kūh-e hill Iran 88 E3
Mavanza Moz. 101 L2
Mavinga Angola 99 C5
Mavrovo nat. park Macedonia 59 I4
Mavume Moz. 101 L2
Mavuya S. Africa 101 H6
Ma Wan i. H.K. China 77 [inset]
Māwān, Khashm hill Saudi Arabia 88 B6
Mawana India 82 D3
Mawanga Dem. Rep. Congo 99 B4
Ma Wang Dui tourist site China 77 G2
Mawei China 77 H3
Mawjib, Wādī al r. Jordan 85 B4
Mawkmai Myanmar 70 B2
Mawlaik Myanmar 70 A2
Mawlamyaing Myanmar see Moulmein
Mawlamyine Myanmar see Moulmein
Mawqaq Saudi Arabia 91 F6

Mawson research station Antarctica 152 E2
Mawson Coast Antarctica 152 E2
Mawson Escarpment Antarctica 152 E2
Mawson Peninsula Antarctica 152 H2
Maw Taung mt. Myanmar 71 B5
Mawza' Yemen 86 F7
Maxán Arg. 144 C3
Maxhamish Lake Canada 120 F3
Maxia, Punta mt. Sardinia Italy 58 C5
Maxixe Moz. 101 L2
Maxmo Fin. 44 M5
May, Isle of i. U.K. 50 G4
Maya r. Russia 65 O3
Mayaguana i. Bahamas 133 F8
Mayaguana Passage Bahamas 133 F8
Mayagüez Puerto Rico 137 K5
Mayahi Niger 96 D3
Mayak Russia 74 E2
Mayakovskiy, Qullai mt. Tajik. 89 H2
Mayakovskogo, Pik mt. Tajik. see Mayakovskiy, Qullai
Mayama Congo 98 B4
Maya Mountains Belize/Guat. 136 G5
Mayan China see Mayanhe
Mayang China 77 F3
Mayanhe China 76 E1
Mayar hill U.K. 50 F4
Maybeury U.S.A. 134 E5
Maybole U.K. 50 E5
Maych'ew Eth. 98 D2
Maydān Shahr Afgh. see Maīdān Shahr
Maydh Somalia 86 G7
Maydos Turkey see Eceabat
Mayen Germany 53 H4
Mayenne France 56 D2
Mayenne r. France 56 D3
Mayer U.S.A. 129 G4
Mayêr Kangri mt. China 83 F2
Mayersville U.S.A. 131 F5
Mayerthorpe Canada 120 H4
Mayfield N.Z. 113 C6
Mayi He r. China 74 C3
Maykop Russia 91 F1
Mayna Respublika Khakasiya Russia 64 K4
Mayna Ul'yanovskaya Oblast' Russia 43 J5
Mayni India 84 B2
Maynooth Canada 135 G1
Mayo Canada 120 C2
Mayo U.S.A. 133 D6
Mayo Alim Cameroon 96 E4
Mayoko Congo 98 B4
Mayo Lake Canada 120 C2
Mayo Landing Canada see Mayo
Mayor, Puig mt. Spain see Major, Puig
Mayor Island N.Z. 113 F3
Mayor Pablo Lagerenza Para. 144 D1

▶Mayotte terr. Africa 99 E5
French Overseas Department.

Mayskiy Amurskaya Oblast' Russia 74 C1
Mayskiy Kabardino-Balkarskaya Respublika Russia 91 G2
Mays Landing U.S.A. 135 H4
Mayson Lake Canada 121 J3
Maysville U.S.A. 134 D4
Mayumba Gabon 98 B4
Mayum La pass China 83 E3
Mayuram India 84 C4
Mayville MI U.S.A. 134 D2
Mayville ND U.S.A. 130 D2
Mayville NY U.S.A. 134 F2
Mayville WI U.S.A. 134 A2
Mazabuka Zambia 99 C5
Mazaca Turkey see Kayseri
Mazagan Morocco see El Jadida
Mazar China 82 D1
Mazār, Kōh-e mt. Afgh. 89 G3
Mazara, Val di valley Sicily Italy 58 E6
Mazara del Vallo Sicily Italy 58 E6
Mazār-e Sharīf Afgh. 89 G2
Mazāri' reg. U.A.E. 88 D6
Mazatán Mex. 127 F7
Mazatlán Mex. 136 C4
Mazatzal Peak U.S.A. 129 H4
Mazdaj Iran 91 H4
Mazdāvand Iran 89 F2
Mažeikiai Lith. 45 M8
Maẓhūr, 'Irq al des. Saudi Arabia 88 A5
Mazīm Oman 88 E6
Mazocahui Mex. 127 F7
Mazocruz Peru 142 E7
Mazomora Tanz. 99 D4
Mazongshan China 80 I3
Mazowiecka, Nizina reg. Poland 47 R4
Mazu Dao i. Taiwan 77 I3
Mazunga Zimbabwe 99 C6
Mazyr Belarus 43 F5
Mazzouna Tunisia 58 C7

▶Mbabane Swaziland 101 J4
Capital of Swaziland.

Mbabo, Tchabal mt. Cameroon 96 E4
Mbahiakro Côte d'Ivoire 96 C4
Mbaïki Cent. Afr. Rep. 98 B3
Mbakaou, Lac de l. Cameroon 96 E4
Mbala Zambia 99 D4
Mbale Uganda 98 D3
Mbalmayo Cameroon 96 E4
Mbam r. Cameroon 96 E4
Mbandaka Dem. Rep. Congo 98 B4
M'banza Congo Angola 99 B4
Mbarara Uganda 97 G5
Mbari r. Cent. Afr. Rep. 98 C3
Mbaswana S. Africa 101 K4
Mbemkuru r. Tanz. 99 D4
Mbeya Tanz. 99 D4
Mbhashe r. S. Africa 101 I7
Mbinga Tanz. 99 D5
Mbini Equat. Guinea 96 D4
Mbizi Zimbabwe 99 D6
Mboki Cent. Afr. Rep. 98 C3
Mbombela S. Africa 101 J3
Mbomo Congo 98 B3
Mbouda Cameroon 96 E4
Mbour Senegal 96 B3
Mbout Mauritania 96 B3
Mbozi Tanz. 99 D4
Mbrès Cent. Afr. Rep. 98 B3
Mbuji-Mayi Dem. Rep. Congo 99 C4
Mbulu Tanz. 98 D4
Mburucuyá Arg. 144 E3
McAdam Canada 123 I5
McAlester U.S.A. 131 E5
McAlister mt. Australia 112 D5
McAllen U.S.A. 131 D7
McArthur r. Australia 110 B2
McArthur U.S.A. 134 D4
McArthur Mills Canada 135 G1
McBain U.S.A. 134 C1
McBride Canada 120 F4
McCall U.S.A. 126 D3
McCamey U.S.A. 131 C6
McCammon U.S.A. 126 E4
McCauley Island Canada 120 D4
McClintock, Mount Antarctica 152 H1
McClintock Channel Canada 119 H2
McClintock Range hills Australia 108 D4
McClure, Lake U.S.A. 128 C3
McClure Strait Canada 118 G2
McClusky U.S.A. 130 C2
McComb U.S.A. 131 F6
McConaughy, Lake U.S.A. 130 C3
McConnellsburg U.S.A. 135 G4
McConnelsville U.S.A. 134 E4
McCook U.S.A. 130 C3
McCormick U.S.A. 133 D5
McCrea r. Canada 120 H2
McCreary Canada 121 L5
McDame (abandoned) Canada 120 D3
McDermitt U.S.A. 126 D4
McDonald Islands Indian Ocean 149 M9
McDonald Peak U.S.A. 126 E3
McDonough U.S.A. 133 C5
McDougall's Bay S. Africa 100 C5
McDowell Peak U.S.A. 129 H5
McFarland U.S.A. 128 D4
McGill U.S.A. 129 F2
McGivney Canada 123 I5
McGrath AK U.S.A. 118 C3
McGrath MN U.S.A. 130 E2
McGraw U.S.A. 135 G2
McGregor r. Canada 120 F4
McGregor S. Africa 100 D7
McGregor, Lake Canada 120 H5
McGregor Range hills Australia 111 C5
McGuire, Mount U.S.A. 126 E3
Mchinga Tanz. 99 D4
Mchinji Malawi 99 D5
McIlwraith Range hills Australia 110 C2
McInnes Lake Canada 121 M4
McIntosh U.S.A. 130 C2
McKay Range hills Australia 108 C5
McKean i. Kiribati 107 I2
McKee U.S.A. 134 C5
McKenzie r. U.S.A. 126 C3
McKinlay r. Australia 110 C4
McKinley, Mount mt. U.S.A. see Denali
McKinney U.S.A. 131 D5
McKittrick U.S.A. 128 D4
McLaughlin U.S.A. 130 C2
McLeansboro U.S.A. 130 F4
McLennan Canada 120 G4
McLeod r. Canada 120 H4
McLeod Bay Canada 121 I2
McLeod Lake Canada 120 F4
McLoughlin, Mount U.S.A. 126 C4
McMillan, Lake U.S.A. 131 B5
McMinnville OR U.S.A. 126 C3
McMinnville TN U.S.A. 132 C5
McMurdo research station Antarctica 152 H1
McMurdo Sound b. Antarctica 152 H1
McNary U.S.A. 129 I4
McNaughton Lake Canada see Kinbasket Lake
McPherson U.S.A. 130 D4
McQuesten r. Canada 120 B2
McRae U.S.A. 133 D5
McTavish Arm b. Canada 120 G1
McVeytown U.S.A. 135 G3
McVicar Arm b. Canada 120 F1
Mdantsane S. Africa 101 H7
M'Daourouch Alg. 58 B6
M'Đrăk Vietnam 71 E4
Mê, Hon i. Vietnam 70 D3
Mead, Lake resr U.S.A. 129 F3
Meade U.S.A. 131 C4
Meade r. U.S.A. 118 C2
Meadow Australia 109 A6
Meadow SD U.S.A. 130 C2
Meadow UT U.S.A. 129 G2
Meadow Lake Canada 121 I4
Meadville MS U.S.A. 131 F6
Meadville PA U.S.A. 134 E3
Meaford Canada 134 E1
Meaken-dake vol. Japan 74 G4
Mealhada Port. 57 B3
Mealy Mountains Canada 123 K3
Meandarra Australia 112 D1
Meander River Canada 120 G3
Meaux France 52 C6
Mecca Saudi Arabia 86 E5
Mecca CA U.S.A. 128 E5
Mecca OH U.S.A. 134 E3
Mechanic Falls U.S.A. 135 J1
Mechanicsville U.S.A. 135 G5
Mechelen Belgium 52 E3
Mechelen Neth. 52 F4
Mecherchar i. Palau see Eil Malk
Mecheria Alg. 54 D5
Mechernich Germany 52 G4
Mecitözü Turkey 90 D2
Meckenheim Germany 52 H4
Mecklenburger Bucht b. Germany 47 M3
Mecklenburg-Vorpommern land Germany 53 M1
Mecklenburg-West Pomerania land Germany see Mecklenburg-Vorpommern
Meda r. Australia 108 C4
Meda Port. 57 C3
Medak India 84 C2
Medan Indon. 71 B7
Medanosa, Punta pt Arg. 144 C7
Médanos de Coro, Parque Nacional nat. park Venez. 142 E1
Medawachchiya Sri Lanka 84 D4
Médéa Alg. 57 H5
Medebach Germany 53 I3
Medellín Col. 142 C2
Meden r. U.K. 48 G5
Medenine Tunisia 54 G5
Mederdra Mauritania 96 B3
Medford NY U.S.A. 135 I3
Medford OK U.S.A. 131 D4
Medford OR U.S.A. 126 C4
Medford WI U.S.A. 130 F2
Medgidia Romania 59 M2
Media U.S.A. 135 H4
Mediaş Romania 59 K1
Medicine Bow r. U.S.A. 126 G4
Medicine Bow Mountains U.S.A. 126 G4
Medicine Bow Peak U.S.A. 126 G4
Medicine Hat Canada 121 I5
Medicine Lake U.S.A. 126 G2
Medicine Lodge U.S.A. 131 D4
Medina Brazil 145 C2
Medina Saudi Arabia 86 E5
Medina ND U.S.A. 130 D2
Medina NY U.S.A. 135 F2
Medina OH U.S.A. 134 E3
Medinaceli Spain 57 E3
Medina del Campo Spain 57 D3
Medina de Rioseco Spain 57 D3
Medina Lake U.S.A. 131 D6
Medinipur India 83 F5
Mediolanum Italy see Milan
Mediterranean Sea 54 K5
Medjerda, Monts de la mts Alg. 58 B6
Mednyy, Ostrov i. Russia 150 H2
Médoc reg. France 56 D4
Mêdog China 76 B2
Medora U.S.A. 130 C2
Medstead Canada 121 I4
Meduro atoll Marshall Is see Majuro
Medvedevo Russia 42 J4
Medveditsa r. Russia 43 I6
Medvednica mts Croatia 58 F2
Medvezh'i, Ostrova is Russia 65 R2
Medvezh'ya, Gora mt. Russia 74 E3
Medvezh'ya. Gora vol. Russia 74 H3
Medvezh'yegorsk Russia 42 G3
Medway r. U.K. 49 H7
Meekatharra Australia 109 B6
Meeker CO U.S.A. 129 J1
Meeker OH U.S.A. 134 D3
Meelpaeg Reservoir Canada 123 K4
Meemu Atoll Maldives see Mulakatholhu
Meerane Germany 53 M4
Meerlo Neth. 52 G3
Meerut India 82 D3
Mega Escarpment Eth./Kenya 98 D3
Megalopoli Greece 59 J6
Megamo Indon. 69 I7
Mégantic, Lac l. Canada 123 H5
Megara Greece 59 J5
Megezez mt. Eth. 98 D3

▶Meghalaya state India 83 G4
Highest mean annual rainfall in the world.

Meghasani mt. India 83 F5
Meghri Armenia 91 G3
Megin Turkm. 88 E2
Megisti i. Greece 59 M6
Megri Armenia see Meghri
Mehamn Norway 44 O1
Mehar Pak. 89 G5
Meharry, Mount Australia 109 B5
Mehbubnagar India see Mahbubnagar
Mehdia Tunisia see Mahdia
Meherpur Bangl. 83 G5
Meherrin U.S.A. 135 F5
Meherrin r. U.S.A. 135 G5
Mehlville U.S.A. 130 F4
Mehrakān salt marsh Iran 88 D5
Mehrān Hormozgān Iran 88 D5
Mehrān Īlām Iran 88 B3
Mehren Germany 52 G4
Mehrestān Iran 89 F4
Mehrīz Iran 88 D4
Mehsana India see Mahesana
Mehtar Lām Afgh. 89 H3
Meia Ponte r. Brazil 145 A2
Meicheng China see Minqing
Meiganga Cameroon 97 E4
Meighen Island Canada 119 I2
Meigu China 76 D2
Meihekou China 74 B4
Meikeng China 77 G3
Meikle r. Canada 120 G3
Meikle Says Law hill U.K. 50 G5
Meiktila Myanmar 70 A2
Meilin China see Ganxian
Meilleur r. Canada 120 E2
Meilü China see Wuchuan
Meine Germany 53 K2
Meinersen Germany 53 K2
Meiningen Germany 53 K4
Meishan Anhui China see Jinzhai
Meishan Sichuan China 76 D2
Meishan Shuiku resr China 77 G2
Meißen Germany 47 N5
Meister r. Canada 120 D2
Meitan China 76 E3
Meixi China 74 C3
Meixian China see Meizhou
Meixing China see Xiaojin
Meizhou China 77 H3
Mej r. India 82 D4
Mejicana mt. Arg. 144 C3
Mejillones Chile 144 B2
Mékambo Gabon 98 B3
Mek'elē Eth. 98 D2
Mekelle Eth. see Mek'elē
Mékhé Senegal 96 B3
Mekhtar Pak. 89 H4
Meknassy Tunisia 58 C7
Meknès Morocco 54 C5
Mekong r. Asia 70 D4
also known as Mae Nam Khong (Laos/Thailand)
Mekong, Mouths of the Vietnam 71 D5
Mekoryuk U.S.A. 118 B3
Melaka Malaysia 71 C7
Melanau, Gunung hill Indon. 71 E7
Melanesia is Pacific Ocean 150 G6
Melanesian Basin sea feature Pacific Ocean 150 G5

▶Melbourne Australia 112 B6
Capital of Victoria. 2nd most populous city in Oceania.

Melbourne U.S.A. 133 D6
Melby U.K. 50 [inset]
Meldorf Germany 47 L3

▶Melekeok Palau 69 I5
Capital of Palau.

Melekess Russia see Dimitrovgrad
Melenki Russia 43 I5
Melet Turkey see Mesudiye
Mélèzes, Rivière aux r. Canada 123 H2
Melfa U.S.A. 135 H5
Melfi Chad 97 E3
Melfi Italy 58 F4
Melfort Canada 121 J4
Melhus Norway 44 G5
Meliadine Lake Canada 121 M2
Melide Spain 57 C2

▶Melilla N. Africa 57 E6
Autonomous Community of Spain.

Melimoyu, Monte mt. Chile 144 B6
Meliskerke Neth. 52 D3
Melita Canada 121 K5
Melitene Turkey see Malatya
Melitopol' Ukr. 43 G7
Melk Austria 47 O6
Melka Guba Eth. 98 D3
Melksham U.K. 49 E7
Mellakoski Fin. 44 N3
Mellansel Sweden 44 K5
Melle Germany 53 I2
Mellerud Sweden 45 H7
Mellette U.S.A. 130 D2
Mellid Spain see Melide
Mellilia N. Africa see Melilla
Mellrichstadt Germany 53 K4
Mellum i. Germany 53 I1
Melmoth S. Africa 101 J5
Mel'nichoye Russia 74 D3
Melo Uruguay 144 F4
Meloco Moz. 99 D5
Melolo Indon. 108 C2
Melozitna r. U.S.A. 118 C3
Melrhir, Chott salt l. Alg. 54 F5
Melrose Australia 109 C6
Melrose U.K. 50 G5
Melrose U.S.A. 130 E2
Melsungen Germany 53 J3
Melton Australia 112 B6
Melton Mowbray U.K. 49 G6
Melun France 56 F2
Melville Canada 121 K5
Melville, Cape Australia 110 D2
Melville, Lake Canada 123 K3
Melville Bugt b. Greenland see Qimusseriarsuaq
Melville Island Australia 108 E2
Melville Island Canada 119 H2
Melville Peninsula Canada 119 J3
Melvin U.S.A. 134 A3
Melvin, Lough l. Ireland/U.K. 51 D3
Mêmar Co salt l. China 83 E2
Memba Moz. 99 E5
Memberamo r. Indon. 69 J7
Memel Lith. see Klaipėda
Memel S. Africa 101 I4
Memmelsdorf Germany 53 K5
Memmingen Germany 47 M7
Mempawah Indon. 68 D6
Memphis tourist site Egypt 90 C5
Memphis MI U.S.A. 134 D2
Memphis TN U.S.A. 131 F5
Memphis TX U.S.A. 131 C5
Memphrémagog, Lac l. Canada 135 I1
Mena Ukr. 43 G6
Mena U.S.A. 131 E5
Menado Indon. see Manado
Ménaka Mali 96 D3
Menard U.S.A. 131 D6
Menasha U.S.A. 134 A1
Mendanha Brazil 145 C2
Mendarik i. Indon. 71 D7
Mende France 56 F4
Mendefera Eritrea 86 E7
Mendeleyev Ridge sea feature Arctic Ocean 153 B1
Mendeleyevsk Russia 42 L5
Mendenhall U.S.A. 131 F6
Mendenhall, Cape U.S.A. 118 B4
Mendenhall Glacier U.S.A. 120 C3
Méndez Mex. 131 D7
Mendī Eth. 98 D3
Mendi P.N.G. 69 K8
Mendip Hills U.K. 49 E7
Mendocino U.S.A. 128 B2
Mendocino, Cape U.S.A. 128 A1
Mendocino, Lake U.S.A. 128 B2
Mendooran Australia 112 D3
Mendota CA U.S.A. 128 C3
Mendota IL U.S.A. 130 F3
Mendoza Arg. 144 C4
Menemen Turkey 59 L5
Ménerville Alg. see Thenia
Mengban China 76 D4
Mengcheng China 77 H1
Menghai China 76 D4
Mengjin China 77 G1
Mengla China 76 D4
Menglang China see Lancang
Menglie China see Jiangcheng
Mengyang China see Mingshan
Mengzi China 76 D4
Menihek Canada 123 I3
Menihek Lakes Canada 123 I3
Menindee Australia 111 C7
Menindee, Lake Australia 111 C7
Ménistouc, Lac l. Canada 123 I3
Menkere Russia 65 N3
Mennecy France 52 C6
Menominee U.S.A. 134 B1
Menomonee Falls U.S.A. 134 A2
Menomonie U.S.A. 130 F2
Menongue Angola 99 B5
Menorca i. Spain see Minorca
Mentawai, Kepulauan is Indon. 68 B7
Mentawai, Selat sea chan. Indon. 68 C7
Menteroda Germany 53 K3
Mentmore U.S.A. 129 I4
Menton France 56 H5
Mentone U.S.A. 131 C6
Menuf Egypt see Minūf
Menzel Bourguiba Tunisia 58 C6
Menzelet Barajı resr Turkey 90 E3
Menzelinsk Russia 41 Q4
Menzel Temime Tunisia 58 D6
Menzies Australia 109 C7
Menzies, Mount Antarctica 152 E2
Meobbaai b. Namibia 100 B3
Meoqui Mex. 131 B6
Meppel Neth. 52 G2
Meppen Germany 53 H2
Mepuze Moz. 101 K2
Meqheleng S. Africa 101 H5
Mequon U.S.A. 134 B2
Merak Indon. 68 D8
Meråker Norway 44 G5
Merano Italy 58 D1
Meratswe r. Botswana 100 G2
Merauke Indon. 69 K8
Merca Somalia see Marka
Mercantour, Parc National du nat. park France 56 H4
Merced U.S.A. 128 C3
Merced r. U.S.A. 128 C3
Mercedes Arg. 144 E3
Mercedes Uruguay 144 E4
Mercer ME U.S.A. 135 K1
Mercer PA U.S.A. 134 E3
Mercer WI U.S.A. 130 F2
Mercês Brazil 145 C3
Mercury Islands N.Z. 113 E3
Mercy, Cape Canada 119 L3
Merdenik Turkey see Göle
Mere Belgium 52 D4
Mere U.K. 49 E7
Meredith U.S.A. 135 J2
Meredith, Lake U.S.A. 131 C5
Merefa Ukr. 43 H6
Merga Oasis Sudan 86 C6
Mergui Myanmar see Myeik
Mergui Archipelago is Myanmar 71 B5
Meriç r. Turkey 59 L4
also known as Evros (Greece), Marica, Maritsa (Bulgaria)
Mérida Mex. 136 G4
Mérida Spain 57 C4
Mérida Venez. 142 D2
Mérida, Cordillera de mts Venez. 142 D2
Meriden U.S.A. 135 I3
Meridian MS U.S.A. 131 F5
Meridian TX U.S.A. 131 D6
Mérignac France 56 D4
Merijärvi Fin. 44 N4
Merikarvia Fin. 45 L6
Merimbula Australia 112 D6
Merín, Laguna l. Brazil/Uruguay see Mirim, Lagoa
Meringur Australia 111 C7
Merir i. Palau 69 I6
Merjayoun Lebanon see Marjayoûn
Merkel U.S.A. 131 C5
Merluna Australia 110 C2
Mermaid Reef Australia 108 B4
Meron, Har mt. Israel 85 B3
Merowe Sudan 86 D6
Merowe Dam Sudan 86 D6
Mêrqung Co l. China 83 F3
Merredin Australia 109 B7
Merrick hill U.K. 50 E5
Merrickville Canada 135 H1
Merrill MI U.S.A. 134 C2
Merrill WI U.S.A. 130 F2
Merrill, Mount Canada 120 E2
Merrillville U.S.A. 134 B3
Merriman U.S.A. 130 C3
Merritt Canada 120 F5
Merritt Island U.S.A. 133 D6
Merriwa Australia 112 E4
Merrygoen Australia 112 D3
Mersa Fatma Eritrea 86 F7
Mersa Maṭrûḥ Egypt see Marsá Maṭrūḥ
Mersch Lux. 52 G5
Merseburg Germany 53 L3
Mersey est. U.K. 48 E5
Mersin Turkey 85 B1
Mersin prov. Turkey 85 A1
Mersing Malaysia 71 C7
Mērsrags Latvia 45 M8
Merta India 82 C4
Merthyr Tydfil U.K. 49 D7
Mértola Port. 57 C5
Mertz Glacier Antarctica 152 G2
Mertz Glacier Tongue Antarctica 152 G2
Mertzon U.S.A. 131 C6
Méru France 52 C5

▶Meru vol. Tanz. 98 D4
4th highest mountain, and highest active volcano in Africa.

Merui Pak. 89 F4
Merv Turkm. see Mary
Merweville S. Africa 100 E7
Merzifon Turkey 90 D2
Merzig Germany 52 G5
Merz Peninsula Antarctica 152 L2
Mesa AZ U.S.A. 129 H5
Mesa NM U.S.A. 127 G6
Mesabi Range hills U.S.A. 130 E2
Mesagne Italy 58 G4
Mesa Negra mt. U.S.A. 129 J4
Mesara, Ormos b. Greece see Messaras, Kolpos
Mesa Verde National Park U.S.A. 129 I3
Meschede Germany 53 I3
Mese Myanmar 70 B3
Meselefors Sweden 44 J4
Mesgouez, Lac Canada 122 G4
Meshed Iran see Mashhad
Meshkān Iran 88 E2
Meshra' Er Req South Sudan 86 C8
Mesick U.S.A. 134 C1
Mesimeri Greece 59 J4
Mesolongi Greece 59 I5
Mesolóngion Greece see Mesolongi
Mesopotamia hist. area Iraq 91 F4
Mesopotamia Marshlands National Park Iraq 91 G5
Mesquita Brazil 145 C2
Mesquite NV U.S.A. 129 F3
Mesquite TX U.S.A. 131 D5
Mesquite Lake U.S.A. 129 F4
Messaad Alg. 54 E5
Messana Sicily Italy see Messina
Messaras, Kolpos b. Greece 59 K7
Messina Sicily Italy 58 F5
Messina, Strait of Italy 58 F5
Messina, Stretta di Italy see Messina, Strait of
Messini Greece 59 J6
Messiniakos Kolpos b. Greece 59 J6
Mesta r. Bulg. 59 K4
Mesta r. Greece see Nestos
Mesta, Akrotirio pt Greece 59 K5
Mestghanem Alg. see Mostaganem
Mestlin Germany 53 L1
Meston, Akra pt Greece see Mesta, Akrotirio
Mestre Italy 58 E2
Mesudiye Turkey 90 E2
Meta r. Col./Venez. 142 E2
Métabetchouan Canada 123 H4
Meta Incognita Peninsula Canada 119 L3
Metairie U.S.A. 131 F6
Metallifere, Colline mts Italy 58 D3
Metán Arg. 144 C3
Meteghan Canada 123 I5
Meteor Depth sea feature S. Atlantic Ocean 148 G9
Methoni Greece 59 I6
Methuen U.S.A. 135 J2
Methven U.K. 50 F4
Metionga Lake Canada 122 C4
Metković Croatia 58 G3
Metlaoui Tunisia 54 F5
Metoro Moz. 99 D5
Metro Indon. 68 D8
Metropolis U.S.A. 131 F4
Metsada tourist site Israel see Masada
Metter U.S.A. 133 D5
Mettet Belgium 52 E4
Mettingen Germany 53 H2
Mettler U.S.A. 128 D4
Mettur India 84 C4
Metu Eth. 98 D3
Metz France 52 G5
Metz U.S.A. 134 C3
Meulaboh Indon. 71 B6
Meureudu Indon. 71 B6
Meuse r. Belgium/France 52 F3
also known as Maas (Netherlands)
Meuse, Côtes de ridge France 52 E5
Meuselwitz Germany 53 M3
Mevagissey U.K. 49 C8
Mêwa China 76 D1
Mexia U.S.A. 131 D6
Mexiana, Ilha i. Brazil 143 I3
Mexicali Mex. 129 F5
Mexican Hat U.S.A. 129 I3
Mexicanos, Lago de los l. Mex. 127 G7
Mexican Water U.S.A. 129 I3

▶Mexico country Central America 136 D4
2nd most populous and 3rd largest country in North America, and 10th most populous country in the world.

México Mex. see Mexico City
Mexico ME U.S.A. 135 J1
Mexico MO U.S.A. 130 F4
Mexico NY U.S.A. 135 G2
Mexico, Gulf of Mex./U.S.A. 125 H6

▶Mexico City Mex. 136 E5
Capital of Mexico. Most populous city in North America and 4th in the world.

Meybod Iran 88 D3
Meydanī, Ra's-e pt Iran 88 E5
Meyenburg Germany 53 M1
Meyersdale U.S.A. 134 F4
Meymeh Iran 88 C3
Meynypil'gyno Russia 153 C2
Mezada tourist site Israel see Masada
Mezdra Bulg. 59 J3
Mezen' Russia 42 J2
Mezen' r. Russia 42 J2
Mézenc, Mont mt. France 56 G4
Mezenskaya Guba b. Russia 42 I2
Mezhdurechensk Kemerovskaya Oblast' Russia 72 F2
Mezhdurechensk Respublika Komi Russia 42 K3
Mezhdurech'ye Russia see Shali
Mezhdusharskiy, Ostrov i. Russia 64 G2
Mezitli Turkey 85 B1
Mezőtúr Hungary 59 I1
Mežvidi Latvia 45 O8
Mfolozi r. S. Africa 101 K5
Mhàil, Rubh' a' pt U.K. 50 C5
Mhangura Zimbabwe 99 D5
Mhlume Swaziland 101 J4
Mhow India 82 C5
Mi r. Myanmar 83 H5
Miahuatlán Mex. 136 E5
Miajadas Spain 57 D4
Miaméré Cent. Afr. Rep. 98 B3
Miami AZ U.S.A. 129 H5

▶Miami FL U.S.A. 133 D7
5th most populous city in North America.

Miami OK U.S.A. 131 E4
Miami Beach U.S.A. 133 D7
Miancaowan China 76 C1
Miāndehī Iran 88 E3
Miāndoāb Iran 88 B2
Miandrivazo Madag. 99 E5
Mīāneh Iran 88 B2
Miang, Phu mt. Thai. 70 C3
Mianhua Yu i. Taiwan 77 I3
Miani India 89 I4
Miani Hor b. Pak. 89 G5
Miān Jōy Afgh. 89 G3
Mianning China 76 D2
Mianwali Pak. 89 H3

Mianxian China 76 E1
Mianyang Hubei China see Xiantao
Mianyang Shaanxi China see Mianxian
Mianyang Sichuan China 76 E2
Mianzhu China 76 E2
Miaoli Taiwan 77 I3
Miarinarivo Madag. 99 E5
Miarritze France see Biarritz
Miass Russia 64 H4
Mica Creek Canada 120 G4
Mica Mountain U.S.A. 129 H5
Micang Shan mts China 76 E1
Michalovce Slovakia 43 D6
Michel Canada 121 I4
Michelau in Oberfranken Germany 53 L4
Michelson, Mount U.S.A. 118 D3
Michelstadt Germany 53 J5
Michendorf Germany 53 N2
Micheng China see Midu
Michigan state U.S.A. 134 C2

▶Michigan, Lake U.S.A. 134 B2
3rd largest lake in North America and 5th in the world.

Michigan City U.S.A. 134 B3
Michinberi India 84 D2
Michipicoten Bay Canada 122 D5
Michipicoten Island Canada 122 D5
Michipicoten River Canada 122 D5
Michurin Bulg. see Tsarevo
Michurinsk Russia 43 I5
Micronesia country N. Pacific Ocean see Micronesia, Federated States of
Micronesia is Pacific Ocean 150 F5
Micronesia, Federated States of country N. Pacific Ocean 150 G5
Midai i. Indon. 71 D7
Mid-Atlantic Ridge sea feature Atlantic Ocean 148 E4
Mid-Atlantic Ridge sea feature Atlantic Ocean 148 G7
Middelburg Neth. 52 D3
Middelburg E. Cape S. Africa 101 G6
Middelburg Mpumalanga S. Africa 101 I3
Middelfart Denmark 45 F9
Middelharnis Neth. 52 E3
Middelwit S. Africa 101 H3
Middle Alkali Lake U.S.A. 126 C4
Middle America Trench sea feature N. Pacific Ocean 151 N5
Middle Andaman i. India 71 A4
Middle Atlas mts Morocco see Moyen Atlas
Middle Bay Canada 123 K4
Middlebourne U.S.A. 134 E4
Middleburg U.S.A. 135 G3
Middleburgh U.S.A. 135 H2
Middlebury IN U.S.A. 134 C3
Middlebury VT U.S.A. 135 I1
Middle Caicos i. Turks and Caicos Is 133 G8
Middle Concho r. U.S.A. 131 C6
Middle Congo country Africa see Congo
Middle Island Thai. see Tasai, Ko
Middle Loup r. U.S.A. 130 D3
Middlemarch N.Z. 113 C7
Middlemount Australia 110 E4
Middle River U.S.A. 135 G4
Middlesbrough U.K. 48 F4
Middle Strait India see Andaman Strait
Middleton Australia 110 C4
Middleton Canada 123 I5
Middleton Island atoll American Samoa see Rose Island
Middletown CA U.S.A. 128 B2
Middletown CT U.S.A. 135 I3
Middletown NY U.S.A. 135 H3
Middletown VA U.S.A. 135 F4
Midelt Morocco 54 D5
Midhurst U.K. 49 G8
Midi, Canal du France 56 F5
Mid-Indian Basin sea feature Indian Ocean 149 N6
Mid-Indian Ridge sea feature Indian Ocean 149 M7
Midland Canada 135 F1
Midland IN U.S.A. 134 B4
Midland MI U.S.A. 134 C2
Midland SD U.S.A. 130 C2
Midland TX U.S.A. 131 C5
Midland (abandoned) U.S.A. 129 F5
Midleton Ireland 51 D6
Midnapore India see Medinipur
Midnapur India see Medinipur
Midongy Atsimo Madag. 99 E6
Mid-Pacific Mountains sea feature N. Pacific Ocean 150 G4
Midu China 76 D3
Miðvágur Faroe Is 44 [inset 2]
Midway Oman see Thamarīt

▶Midway Islands terr. N. Pacific Ocean 150 I4
United States Unincorporated Territory.

Midway Well Australia 109 C5
Midwest U.S.A. 126 G4
Midwest City U.S.A. 131 D5
Midwoud Neth. 52 F2
Midyat Turkey 91 F3
Midye Turkey see Kıyıköy
Mid Yell U.K. 50 [inset]
Midzhur mt. Bulg./Serbia 90 A2
Miehikkälä Fin. 45 O6
Miekojärvi l. Fin. 44 N3
Mielec Poland 43 D6
Mieraslompola Fin. 44 O2
Mierašluoppal Fin. see Mieraslompola
Miercurea Ciuc Romania 59 K1
Mieres Spain see Mieres del Camín
Mieres del Camín Spain 57 D2
Mī'ēso Eth. 98 E3
Mieste Germany 53 L2
Mifflinburg U.S.A. 135 G3
Mifflintown U.S.A. 135 G3
Migang Shan mt. China 76 E1
Migdol S. Africa 101 G4
Miging India 76 B2
Miguel Auza Mex. 131 C7
Miguel Hidalgo, Presa resr Mex. 127 F8
Mihalıççık Turkey 59 N5
Mihara Japan 75 D6
Mihintale Sri Lanka 84 D4
Mihmandar Turkey 85 B1
Mijares r. Spain see Millárs
Mijdrecht Neth. 52 E2
Mikhaylov Russia 43 H5
Mikhaylovgrad Bulg. see Montana
Mikhaylov Island Antarctica 152 E2
Mikhaylovka Amurskaya Oblast' Russia 74 C2
Mikhaylovka Primorskiy Kray Russia 74 D4
Mikhaylovka Tul'skaya Oblast' Russia see Kimovsk
Mikhaylovka Volgogradskaya Oblast' Russia 43 I6
Mikhaylovsk Russia 91 F1
Mikhaylovskoye Altayskiy Kray Russia 80 E1
Mikhaylovskoye Stavropol'skiy Kray Russia see Mikhaylovsk
Mikhrot Timna Israel 85 B5
Mikir Hills India 83 H4
Mikkeli Fin. 45 O6
Mikkelin mlk Fin. 45 O6
Mikkwa r. Canada 120 H3
Míkonos i. Greece see Mykonos
Mikoyan Armenia see Yeghegnadzor
Mikulkin, Mys c. Russia 42 J2
Mikumi National Park Tanz. 99 D4
Mikun' Russia 42 K3
Mikuni-sanmyaku mts Japan 75 E5
Mikura-jima i. Japan 75 E6
Milaca U.S.A. 130 E2
Miladhunmadulu Maldives 84 B5
Miladummadulu Atoll Maldives see Miladhunmadulu
Milan Italy 58 C2
Milan MI U.S.A. 134 D2
Milan MO U.S.A. 130 E3
Milan OH U.S.A. 134 D3
Milange Moz. 99 D5
Milano Italy see Milan
Milas Turkey 59 L6
Milazzo Sicily Italy 58 F5
Milazzo, Capo di c. Sicily Italy 58 F5
Milbank U.S.A. 130 D2
Milbridge U.S.A. 132 H2
Milde r. Germany 53 L2
Mildenhall U.K. 49 H6
Mildura Australia 111 C7
Mile China 76 D3
Mileiz, Wâdi el watercourse Egypt see Mulayz, Wādī al
Miles Australia 112 E1
Miles City U.S.A. 126 G3
Milestone Ireland 51 D5
Miletto, Monte mt. Italy 58 F4
Mileura Australia 109 B6
Milford Ireland 51 E2
Milford DE U.S.A. 135 H4
Milford IL U.S.A. 134 B3
Milford MA U.S.A. 135 J2
Milford MI U.S.A. 134 D2
Milford NE U.S.A. 130 D3
Milford NH U.S.A. 135 J2
Milford PA U.S.A. 135 H3
Milford UT U.S.A. 129 G2
Milford VA U.S.A. 135 G4
Milford Haven U.K. 49 B7
Milford Sound N.Z. 113 A7
Milford Sound inlet N.Z. 113 A7
Milgarra Australia 110 C3
Milh, Bahr al l. Iraq see Razāzah, Buhayrat ar
Milh, Qurayyāt al l. Jordan 85 C4
Miliana Alg. 57 H5
Milid Turkey see Malatya
Milikapiti Australia 108 E2
Miling Australia 109 B7
Milk r. U.S.A. 126 G2
Milk, Wadi el watercourse Sudan 86 D6
Mil'kovo Russia 65 Q4
Millaa Millaa Australia 110 D3
Millárs r. Spain 57 F4
Millau France 56 F4
Millbrook Canada 135 F1
Mill Creek r. U.S.A. 128 B1
Milledgeville U.S.A. 133 D5
Mille Lacs lakes U.S.A. 130 E2
Mille Lacs, Lac des l. Canada 119 I5
Millen U.S.A. 133 D5
Millennium Island atoll Kiribati see Caroline Island
Miller U.S.A. 130 D2
Miller Lake Canada 134 E1
Millerovo Russia 43 I6
Millersburg OH U.S.A. 134 E3
Millersburg PA U.S.A. 135 G3
Millers Creek U.S.A. 134 D5
Millersville U.S.A. 135 G4
Millerton Lake U.S.A. 128 D3
Millet Canada 120 H4
Milleur Point U.K. 50 D5
Mill Hall U.S.A. 135 G3
Millicent Australia 111 C8
Millington MI U.S.A. 134 D2
Millington TN U.S.A. 131 F5
Millinocket U.S.A. 132 G2
Mill Island Canada 119 K3
Millmerran Australia 112 E1
Millom U.K. 48 D4
Millport U.K. 50 E5
Millsboro U.S.A. 135 H4
Mills Creek watercourse Australia 110 C4
Mills Lake Canada 120 G2
Millstone KY U.S.A. 134 D5
Millstone WV U.S.A. 134 E4
Millstream-Chichester National Park Australia 108 B5
Millthorpe Australia 112 D4
Milltown Canada 123 I5
Milltown U.S.A. 126 E3
Millungera Australia 110 C3
Millville U.S.A. 135 H4
Millwood U.S.A. 134 B5
Millwood Lake U.S.A. 131 E5
Milly Milly Australia 109 B6
Milne Land i. Greenland see Ilimanangip Nunaa
Milner U.S.A. 129 I1
Milo r. Guinea 96 C3
Milogradovo Russia 74 D4
Miloli'i U.S.A. 127 [inset]
Milos i. Greece 59 K6
Milparinka Australia 111 C6
Milpitas U.S.A. 128 C3
Milroy U.S.A. 135 G3
Milton N.Z. 113 B8
Milton DE U.S.A. 135 H4
Milton NH U.S.A. 135 J2
Milton WV U.S.A. 134 D4
Milton Keynes U.K. 49 G6
Miltown Malbay Ireland 51 C5
Miluo China 77 G2
Milverton Canada 134 E2
Milwaukee U.S.A. 134 B2

▶Milwaukee Deep sea feature Caribbean Sea 148 D4
Deepest point in the Puerto Rico Trench (deepest in the Atlantic).

Mimbres watercourse U.S.A. 129 J5
Mimili Australia 109 F6
Mimisal India 84 C4
Mimizan France 56 D4
Mimongo Gabon 98 B4
Mimosa Rocks National Park Australia 112 E6
Mina Mex. 131 C7
Mina U.S.A. 128 D2
Mīnāb Iran 88 E5
Minaçu Brazil 145 A1
Minahasa, Semenanjung pen. Indon. 69 G6
Minahassa Peninsula Indon. see Minahasa, Semenanjung
Minaker Canada see Prophet River
Mīnakh Syria 85 C1
Minaki Canada 121 M5
Minamia Australia 108 F3
Minami-Daitō-jima i. Japan 73 O7
Minami-Iō-jima vol. Japan 69 K2
Min'an China see Longshan
Minas Indon. 71 C7
Minas Uruguay 144 E4
Minas de Matahambre Cuba 133 D8
Minas Gerais state Brazil 145 B2
Minas Novas Brazil 145 C2
Minatitlán Mex. 136 F5
Minbu Myanmar 70 A2
Minbya Myanmar 70 A2
Minchinmávida vol. Chile 144 B6
Mindanao i. Phil. 69 H5
Mindanao Trench sea feature N. Pacific Ocean see Philippine Trench
Mindelo Cape Verde 96 [inset]
Minden Canada 135 F1
Minden Germany 53 I2
Minden LA U.S.A. 131 E5
Minden NE U.S.A. 124 H3
Minden NV U.S.A. 128 D2
Mindon Myanmar 70 A3
Mindoro i. Phil. 69 G4
Mindoro Strait Phil. 69 F4
Mindouli Congo 98 B4
Mine Head hd Ireland 51 E6
Minehead U.K. 49 D7
Mineola U.S.A. 135 I3
Mineral U.S.A. 135 G4
Mineral'nyye Vody Russia 91 F1
Mineral Wells TX U.S.A. 131 D5
Mineral Wells WV U.S.A. 134 E4
Minersville PA U.S.A. 135 G3
Minersville UT U.S.A. 129 G2
Minerva U.S.A. 134 E3
Minerva Reefs Fiji 107 I4
Minfeng China 83 E1
Minga Dem. Rep. Congo 99 C5
Mingäçevir Azer. 91 G2
Mingäçevir Su Anbarı resr Azer. 91 G2
Mingala Cent. Afr. Rep. 98 C3
Mingan, Îles de is Canada 123 J4
Mingan Archipelago National Park Reserve Canada see Archipel-de-Mingan, Réserve du Parc National de l'
Mingbuloq Uzbek. 80 B3
Mingechaur Azer. see Mingäçevir
Mingechaurskoye Vodokhranilishche resr Azer. see Mingäçevir Su Anbarı
Mingenew Australia 109 A7
Mingfeng China see Yuan'an
Minggang China 77 G1
Mingguang China 77 H1
Mingin Range mts Myanmar 70 A2
Minglanilla Spain 57 F4
Mingoyo Tanz. 99 D5
Mingshan China 76 D2
Mingshui Gansu China 80 I3
Mingshui Heilong. China 74 B3
Mingulay i. U.K. 50 B4
Mingxi China 77 H3
Mingzhou China see Suide
Minhe China see Jinxian
Minhla Bago Myanmar 70 A3
Minhla Magway Myanmar 70 A3
Minho r. Port./Spain see Miño
Minicoy atoll India 84 B4
Minigwal, Lake salt flat Australia 109 C7
Minilya Australia 109 A5
Minilya r. Australia 109 A5
Minipi Lake Canada 123 J3
Miniss Lake Canada 121 N5
Minitonas Canada 121 K4
Minjian China see Mabian
Min Jiang r. Fujian China 77 H3
Min Jiang r. Sichuan China 76 E2
Minna Nigeria 96 D4
Minna Bluff pt Antarctica 152 H1
Minne Sweden 44 I5
Minneapolis KS U.S.A. 130 D4
Minneapolis MN U.S.A. 130 E2
Minnedosa Canada 121 L5
Minnehaha Springs U.S.A. 134 F4
Minneola U.S.A. 131 C4
Minnesota r. U.S.A. 130 E2
Minnesota state U.S.A. 130 E2
Minnewaukan U.S.A. 130 D1
Minnitaki Lake Canada 121 N5
Miño r. Port./Spain 57 B3 also known as Minho
Minorca i. Spain 57 H3
Minot U.S.A. 130 C1
Minqing China 77 H3
Minquan China 77 G1
Min Shan mts China 76 D1
Minsin Myanmar 70 A1

▶Minsk Belarus 45 O10
Capital of Belarus.

Mińsk Mazowiecki Poland 47 R4
Minsterley U.K. 49 E6
Mintaka Pass China/Pak. 82 C1
Minto, Lac l. Canada 122 G2
Minto, Mount Antarctica 152 H2
Minto Inlet Canada 118 G2
Minton Canada 121 J5
Mīnūdasht Iran 88 D2
Minūf Egypt 90 C5
Minusinsk Russia 72 G2
Minvoul Gabon 98 B3
Minxian China 76 E1
Minya Konka mt. China see Gongga Shan
Minywa Myanmar 70 A2
Minzong India 83 I4
Mio U.S.A. 134 C1
Miquelon Canada 122 F4
Miquelon i. St Pierre and Miquelon 123 K5
Mīrābād Afgh. 89 F4
Mirabela Brazil 145 B2
Mirador, Parque Nacional de nat. park Brazil 143 I5
Mīrah, Wādī al watercourse Iraq/Saudi Arabia 91 F4
Miraí Brazil 145 C3
Miraj India 84 B2
Miramar Arg. 144 E5
Miramichi Canada 123 I5
Miramichi Bay Canada 123 I5
Mirampellou, Kolpos b. Greece 59 K7
Mirampelou, Kolpos b. Greece see Mirampellou, Kolpos
Miranda Brazil 144 E2
Miranda Moz. see Macaloge
Miranda U.S.A. 128 B1
Miranda, Lake salt flat Australia 109 C6
Miranda de Ebro Spain 57 E2
Mirandela Port. 57 C3
Mirandola Italy 58 D2
Mirante Brazil 145 C1
Mirante, Serra do hills Brazil 145 A3
Mirassol Brazil 145 A3
Mir-Bashir Azer. see Tärtär
Mirbāṭ Oman 87 H6
Mirboo North Australia 112 C7
Mirepoix France 56 E5
Mirgarh Pak. 89 I4
Mirgorod Ukr. see Myrhorod
Miri Sarawak Malaysia 68 E6
Miri mt. Pak. 89 F4
Mirialguda India 84 C2
Miri Hills India 83 H4
Mirim, Lagoa l. Brazil/Uruguay 144 F4
Mirim, Lagoa do l. Brazil 145 A5
Mirintu watercourse Australia 112 A2
Mirjan India 84 B3
Mirny research station Antarctica 152 F2
Mirnyy Arkhangel'skaya Oblast' Russia 42 I3
Mirnyy Respublika Sakha (Yakutiya) Russia 65 M3
Mirond Lake Canada 121 K4
Mironovka Ukr. see Myronivka
Mirow Germany 53 M1
Mirpur Khas Pak. 89 H5
Mirpur Sakro Pak. 89 G5
Mirs Bay H.K. China 77 [inset]
Mirtoan Sea Greece see Myrtoo Pelagos
Miryalaguda India see Mirialguda
Miryang S. Korea 75 C6
Mirzachirla Turkm. see Murzechirla
Mirzachul Uzbek. see Guliston
Mirzapur India 83 E4
Mirzawal India 82 C3
Misaw Lake Canada 121 K3
Miscou Island Canada 123 I5
Misehkow r. Canada 122 C4
Mīsh, Kūh-e hill Iran 88 E3
Misha India 71 A6
Mishawaka U.S.A. 134 B3
Mishicot U.S.A. 134 B1
Mi-shima i. Japan 75 C6
Mishmi Hills India 83 H3
Mishvan' Russia 42 L2
Misima Island P.N.G. 110 F1
Misis Dağ hills Turkey 85 B1
Miskin Oman 88 E6
Miskitos, Cayos is Nicaragua 137 H6
Miskolc Hungary 43 D6
Mismā, Tall al hill Jordan 85 C3
Misoöl i. Indon. 69 I7
Misquah Hills U.S.A. 130 F2
Misr country Africa see Egypt
Misraç Turkey see Kurtalan
Miṣrātah Libya 97 E1
Missinaibi r. Canada 122 E4
Mission Beach Australia 110 D3
Mission Viejo U.S.A. 128 E5
Missisa r. Canada 122 D3
Missisa Lake Canada 122 D3
Missisicabi r. Canada 122 F4
Mississauga Canada 134 F2
Mississinewa Lake U.S.A. 134 C3

▶Mississippi r. U.S.A. 131 F6
4th longest river in North America, and a major part of the longest (Mississippi-Missouri).

Mississippi state U.S.A. 131 F5
Mississippi Delta U.S.A. 131 F6
Mississippi Lake Canada 135 G1

▶Mississippi-Missouri r. U.S.A. 125 I4
Longest river in North America and 4th in the world.

Mississippi Sound sea chan. U.S.A. 131 F6
Missolonghi Greece see Mesolongi
Missoula U.S.A. 126 E3

▶Missouri r. U.S.A. 130 F4
3rd longest river in North America, and a major part of the longest (Mississippi-Missouri).

Missouri state U.S.A. 130 E4
Mistanipisipou r. Canada 123 J4
Mistassibi r. Canada 119 K5
Mistassini Canada 123 G4
Mistassini r. Canada 123 G4
Mistassini, Lac l. Canada 122 G4
Mistastin Lake Canada 123 J3
Mistelbach Austria 47 P6
Mistinibi, Lac l. Canada 123 J2
Mistissini Canada 122 G4
Misty Fiords National Monument Wilderness nat. park U.S.A. 120 D4
Misumba Dem. Rep. Congo 99 C4
Misurata Libya see Miṣrātah
Mitchell Australia 111 D5
Mitchell r. N.S.W. Australia 112 F2
Mitchell r. Qld Australia 110 C2
Mitchell r. Vic. Australia 112 C6
Mitchell Canada 134 E2
Mitchell IN U.S.A. 134 B4
Mitchell OR U.S.A. 126 C3
Mitchell SD U.S.A. 130 D3
Mitchell, Lake Australia 110 D3
Mitchell, Mount U.S.A. 132 D5
Mitchell and Alice Rivers National Park Australia 110 C2
Mitchell Island Cook Is see Nassau
Mitchell Island atoll Tuvalu see Nukulaelae
Mitchell Point Australia 108 E2
Mitchelstown Ireland 51 D5
Mīt Ghamr Egypt 90 C5
Mīt Ghamr Egypt see Mīt Ghamr
Mithi Pak. 89 H5
Mithrau Pak. 89 H5
Mithri Pak. 89 G4
Mitilini Greece see Mytilini
Mitkof Island U.S.A. 120 C3
Mito Japan 75 F5
Mitole Tanz. 99 D4
Mitre mt. N.Z. 113 E5
Mitre Island Solomon Is 107 H3
Mitrofanovka Russia 43 H6
Mitrovica Kosovo see Mitrovicë
Mitrovicë Kosovo 59 I3
Mitsinjo Madag. 99 E5
Mits'iwa Eritrea see Massawa
Mitta Mitta Australia 112 C6
Mittellandkanal canal Germany 53 I2
Mitterteich Germany 53 M5
Mittimatalik Canada see Pond Inlet
Mittweida Germany 53 M4
Mitú Col. 142 D3
Mitumba, Chaîne des mts Dem. Rep. Congo 99 C5
Mitzic Gabon 98 B3
Miughalaigh i. U.K. see Mingulay
Miura Japan 75 E6
Mixian China see Xinmi
Miyake-jima i. Japan 75 E6
Miyako Japan 75 F5
Miyakonojō Japan 75 C7
Miyang China see Mile
Miyani India 82 B5
Miyazaki Japan 75 C7
Miyazu Japan 75 D6
Miyi China 76 D3
Miyoshi Japan 75 D6
Mīzān 'Alāqahdārī Afgh. 89 G3
Mīzan Teferī Eth. 98 D3
Mizdah Libya 97 E1
Mizen Head hd Ireland 51 C6
Mizhhir"ya Ukr. 43 D6
Mizo Hills state India see Mizoram
Mizoram state India 83 H5
Mizpé Ramon Israel 85 B4
Mjölby Sweden 45 I7
Mkata Tanz. 99 D4
Mkushi Zambia 99 C5
Mladá Boleslav Czechia 47 O5
Mladenovac Serbia 59 I2
Mława Poland 47 R4
Mlilwane Nature Reserve Swaziland 101 J4
Mljet i. Croatia 58 G3
Mlungisi S. Africa 101 H6
Mlu Prey Cambodia 71 D4
Mmabatho S. Africa 101 G3
Mmamabula Botswana 101 H2
Mmathethe Botswana 101 G3
Mo Norway 45 D6
Moa i. Indon. 108 E2
Moab hist. area Jordan 85 B4
Moab U.S.A. 129 I2
Moa Island Australia 110 C1
Moala i. Fiji 107 H3
Mo'allā Iran 88 D3
Moamba Moz. 101 K3
Moanda Gabon 98 B4
Moapa U.S.A. 129 F3
Moate Ireland 51 E4
Mobārakeh Iran 88 C3
Mobayembongo Dem. Rep. Congo see Mobayi-Mbongo
Mobayi-Mbongo Dem. Rep. Congo 98 C3
Moberly U.S.A. 130 E4
Moberly Lake Canada 120 F4
Mobha India 82 C5
Mobile AL U.S.A. 131 F6
Mobile AZ U.S.A. 129 G5
Mobile Bay U.S.A. 131 F6
Moble watercourse Australia 112 B1
Mobridge U.S.A. 130 C2
Mobutu, Lake Dem. Rep. Congo/Uganda see Albert, Lake
Mobutu Sese Seko, Lake Dem. Rep. Congo/Uganda see Albert, Lake
Moca Geçidi pass Turkey 85 A1
Moçambique country Africa see Mozambique
Moçambique Moz. 99 E5
Moçâmedes Angola see Namibe
Môc Châu Vietnam 70 D2
Mocha Yemen 86 F7
Mocha, Isla i. Chile 144 B5
Mochirma, Parque Nacional nat. park Venez. 142 F1
Mochudi Botswana 101 H3
Mochudi admin. dist. Botswana see Kgatleng
Mocimboa da Praia Moz. 99 E5
Möckern Germany 53 L2
Möckmühl Germany 53 J5
Mockträsk Sweden 44 L4
Mocoa Col. 142 C3
Mococa Brazil 145 B3
Mocoduene Moz. 101 L2
Mocorito Mex. 127 G8
Moctezuma Chihuahua Mex. 127 G7
Moctezuma San Luis Potosí Mex. 136 D4
Moctezuma Sonora Mex. 127 F7
Mocuba Moz. 99 D5
Mocun China 77 G4
Modan Indon. 69 I7
Modane France 56 H4
Modder r. S. Africa 101 G5
Modena Italy 58 D2
Modena U.S.A. 129 G3
Modesto U.S.A. 128 C3
Modesto Lake U.S.A. 128 C3
Modimolle S. Africa 101 I3
Modjadjiskloof S. Africa 101 J2
Modung China 76 C2
Moe Australia 112 C7
Moel Sych hill U.K. 49 D6
Moelv Norway 45 G6
Moen Norway 44 K2
Moenkopi U.S.A. 129 H3
Moenkopi Wash r. U.S.A. 129 H4
Moeraki Point N.Z. 113 C7
Moero, Lake Dem. Rep. Congo/Zambia see Mweru, Lake
Moers Germany 52 G3
Moffat U.K. 50 F5
Moga India 82 C3

▶Mogadishu Somalia 98 E3
Capital of Somalia.

Mogador Morocco see Essaouira
Mogadore Reservoir U.S.A. 134 E3
Moganyaka S. Africa 101 I3
Mogaung Myanmar 70 B1
Mogdy Russia 74 D2
Mögelin Germany 53 M2
Mogi das Cruzes Brazil 145 B3
Mogilev Belarus see Mahilyow
Mogilev Podol'skiy Ukr. see Mohyliv-Podil's'kyy
Mogi Mirim Brazil 145 B3
Mogiquiçaba Brazil 145 D2
Mogocha Russia 73 L2
Mogod mts Tunisia 58 C6
Mogoditshane Botswana 101 G3
Mogollon Mountains U.S.A. 129 I5
Mogollon Plateau U.S.A. 129 H4
Mogontiacum Germany see Mainz
Mogroum Chad 97 E3
Moguqi China 74 A3
Mogwadi S. Africa 101 I2
Mogwadi r. S. Africa 101 I2
Mogwase S. Africa 101 H3
Mogzon Russia 73 K2
Mohács Hungary 58 H2
Mohaka r. N.Z. 113 F4
Mohala India 84 D1
Mohale Dam Lesotho 101 I5
Mohale's Hoek Lesotho 101 H6
Mohali India 82 D3
Mohall U.S.A. 130 C1
Moḥammad Iran 88 E3
Moḥammadābād Iran 88 E4
Mohammadia Alg. 57 G6
Mohan r. India/Nepal 82 E3
Mohana India 82 D4
Mohave, Lake U.S.A. 129 F4
Mohawk r. U.S.A. 135 I2
Mohawk Mountains U.S.A. 129 G5
Mohenjo Daro tourist site Pak. 89 H5
Moher, Cliffs of Ireland 51 C5
Mohill Ireland 51 E4
Möhne r. Germany 53 H3
Möhnetalsperre resr Germany 53 I3
Mohon Peak U.S.A. 129 G4
Mohoro Tanz. 99 D4
Mohyliv-Podil's'kyy Ukr. 43 E6
Moi Norway 45 E7
Moijabana Botswana 101 H2
Moincêr China 82 E3
Moine Moz. 101 K3
Moinești Romania 59 L1
Mointy Kazakh. see Moyynty
Mo i Rana Norway 44 I3
Moirang India 76 B3
Mõisaküla Estonia 45 N7
Moisie Canada 123 I4
Moisie r. Canada 123 I4
Moissac France 56 E4
Mojave U.S.A. 128 D4
Mojave r. U.S.A. 128 E4
Mojave Desert U.S.A. 128 E4
Mojiang China 76 D4
Mojos, Llanos de plain Bol. 142 E6
Moju r. Brazil 143 I4
Mokala National Park S. Africa 100 G5
Mokama India 83 F4
Mokau N.Z. 113 E4
Mokau r. N.Z. 113 E4
Mokelumne r. U.S.A. 128 C2
Mokelumne Aqueduct canal U.S.A. 128 C2
Mokh, Gowd-e l. Iran 88 D4
Mokhoabong Pass Lesotho 101 I5
Mokhotlong Lesotho 101 I5
Mokhtārān Iran 88 E3
Moknine Tunisia 58 D7
Mokohinau Islands N.Z. 113 E2
Mokokchung India 83 H4
Mokolo Cameroon 97 E3
Mokolo r. S. Africa 101 H2
Mokopane S. Africa 101 I3
Mokpo S. Korea 75 B6
Mokrous Russia 43 J6
Moksha r. Russia 43 I5
Mokshan Russia 43 J5
Möksy Fin. 44 N5
Môktama Myanmar see Mottama
Môktama, Gulf of Myanmar see Mottama, Gulf of
Mokundurra India see Mukandwara
Mokwa Nigeria 96 D4
Molatón mt. Spain 57 F4
Moldavia country Europe see Moldova

Moldavskaya S.S.R. country Europe see Moldova
Molde Norway 44 E5
Moldjord Norway 44 I3
Moldova country Europe 43 F7
Moldoveanu, Vârful mt. Romania 59 K2
Moldovei de Sud, Câmpia plain Moldova 59 M1
Molega Lake Canada 123 I5
Molen r. S. Africa 101 I4
Mole National Park Ghana 96 C4
Molepolole Botswana 101 G3
Molėtai Lith. 45 N9
Molfetta Italy 58 G4
Molière Alg. see Bordj Bounaama
Molihong Shan mt. China see Morihong Shan
Molina de Aragón Spain 57 F3
Moline U.S.A. 131 D4
Moling mt. India 83 H3
Molkom Sweden 45 H7
Mollagara Turkm. 88 D2
Mollakara Turkm. see Mollagara
Mol Len mt. India 83 H4
Möllenbeck Germany 53 N1
Mollendo Peru 142 D7
Mölln Germany 53 K1
Mölnlycke Sweden 45 H8
Molochnyy Russia 44 R2
Molodechno Belarus see Maladzyechna
Moloka'i i. U.S.A. 127 [inset]
Moloma r. Russia 42 K4
Molong Australia 112 D4
Molopo watercourse Botswana/S. Africa 100 E5
Molotov Russia see Perm'
Molotovsk Kyrg. see Kayyngdy
Molotovsk Arkhangel'skaya Oblast' Russia see Severodvinsk
Molotovsk Kirovskaya Oblast' Russia see Nolinsk
Moloundou Cameroon 97 E4
Molson Lake Canada 121 L4
Molu i. Indon. 69 I8
Moluccas is Indon. 69 H7
Molucca Sea sea Indon. see Maluku, Laut
Molukken is Indon. see Moluccas
Moma Moz. 99 D5
Moma r. Russia 65 P3
Momba Australia 112 A3
Mombaça Brazil 143 K5
Mombasa Kenya 98 D4
Mombetsu Hokkaidō Japan see Monbetsu
Mombetsu Hokkaidō Japan see Hidaka
Mombi New India 83 H4
Mombum Indon. 69 J8
Momchilgrad Bulg. 59 K4
Momence U.S.A. 134 B3
Momī, Rhiy di- pt Yemen 87 H7
Mompós Col. 142 D2
Møn i. Denmark 45 H9
Mon India 83 H4
Mona U.S.A. 129 H2
Monaca U.S.A. 134 E3
Monach, Sound of sea chan. U.K. 50 B3
Monach Islands U.K. 50 B3
Monaco country Europe 56 H5
Monaco Basin sea feature N. Atlantic Ocean 148 G4
Monadhliath Mountains U.K. 50 E3
Monaghan Ireland 51 F3
Monahans U.S.A. 131 C6
Mona Passage Dom. Rep./Puerto Rico 137 K5
Monapo Moz. 99 E5
Monar, Loch l. U.K. 50 D3
Monarch Mountain Canada 120 E5
Monarch Pass U.S.A. 127 G5
Mona Reservoir U.S.A. 129 H2
Monashee Mountains Canada 120 G5
Monastir Macedonia see Bitola
Monastir Tunisia 58 D7
Monastyrishche Ukr. see Monastyryshche
Monastyryshche Ukr. 43 F6
Monbetsu Japan 74 F3
Moncalieri Italy 58 B2
Moncayo mt. Spain 57 F3
Monchegorsk Russia 44 R3
Mönchengladbach Germany 52 G3
Monchique Port. 57 B5
Moncks Corner U.S.A. 133 D5
Monclova Mex. 131 C7
Moncouche, Lac l. Canada 123 H4
Moncton Canada 123 I5
Mondego r. Port. 57 B3
Mondo Chad 97 E3
Mondovì Italy 58 B2
Mondragone Italy 58 E4
Mondy Russia 72 I2
Monemvasia Greece 59 J6
Monessen U.S.A. 134 F3
Moneta U.S.A. 126 G4
Moneygall Ireland 51 E5
Moneymore U.K. 51 F3
Monfalcone Italy 58 E2
Monfalut Egypt see Manfalūṭ
Monforte de Lemos Spain 57 C2
Monga Dem. Rep. Congo 98 C3
Mongala r. Dem. Rep. Congo 98 B3
Mongar Bhutan 83 G4
Mongbwalu Dem. Rep. Congo 98 D3
Mông Cai Vietnam 70 D2
Mongers Lake salt flat Australia 109 B7
Mong Hang Myanmar 70 B2
Mong Hkan Myanmar 70 C2
Mong Hpayak Myanmar 70 B2
Mong Hsat Myanmar 70 B2
Mong Hsawk Myanmar 70 B2
Mong Hsu Myanmar 70 B2
Monghyr India see Munger
Mong Kung Myanmar 70 B2
Mong Kyawt Myanmar 70 B3
Mongla Bangl. 83 G5
Mong Lin Myanmar 70 C2
Mong Loi Myanmar 70 C2
Mong Long Myanmar 70 B2
Mong Nai Myanmar 70 B2
Mong Nawng Myanmar 70 B2
Mongo Chad 97 E3
Mongolia country Asia 72 I3
Mongol Uls country Asia see Mongolia
Mongora Pak. 89 I3
Mongour hill U.K. 50 G4
Mong Pan Myanmar 70 B2
Mong Ping Myanmar 70 B2
Mong Pu Myanmar 70 B2
Mong Pu-awn Myanmar 70 B2
Mong Si Myanmar 70 B2
Mongu Zambia 99 C5
Mong Un Myanmar 70 C2
Monguno Nigeria 96 E3
Mong Yai Myanmar 70 B2
Mong Yang Myanmar 70 B2
Mong Yawn Myanmar 70 B2
Mong Yawng Myanmar 70 C2
Mönhhaan Mongolia 73 K3
Mönh Hayrhan Uul mt. Mongolia 80 H2
Moniaive U.K. 50 F5
Monitor Mountain U.S.A. 128 E2
Monitor Range mts U.S.A. 128 E2
Monivea Ireland 51 D4
Monkey Bay Malawi 99 D5
Monkira Australia 110 C5
Monkton Canada 134 E2
Monmouth U.K. 49 E7
Monmouth U.S.A. 130 F3
Monmouth Mountain Canada 120 F5
Monnow r. U.K. 49 E7
Mono, Punta pt Nicaragua 137 H6
Mono Lake U.S.A. 128 D2
Monolithos Greece 59 L6
Monomoy Point U.S.A. 135 J3
Monon U.S.A. 134 B3
Monopoli Italy 58 G4
Monreal del Campo Spain 57 F3
Monreale Sicily Italy 58 E5
Monroe IN U.S.A. 134 C3
Monroe LA U.S.A. 131 E5
Monroe MI U.S.A. 134 D3
Monroe NC U.S.A. 133 D5
Monroe WI U.S.A. 130 F3
Monroe Center U.S.A. 130 F2
Monroe Lake U.S.A. 134 B4
Monroeton U.S.A. 135 G3
▶Monrovia Liberia 96 B4
Capital of Liberia.
Mons Belgium 52 D4
Monschau Germany 52 G4
Monselice Italy 58 D2
Montabaur Germany 53 H4
Montagne d'Ambre, Parc National de nat. park Madag. 99 E5
Montagu S. Africa 100 E7
Montague Canada 123 J5
Montague MI U.S.A. 134 B2
Montague TX U.S.A. 131 D5
Montague Range hills Australia 109 B6
Montalto mt. Italy 58 F5
Montalto Uffugo Italy 58 G5
Montana Bulg. 59 J3
Montana state U.S.A. 126 F3
Montanhas do Tumucumaque, Parque Nacional nat. park Brazil 143 H3
Montargis France 56 F3
Montauban France 56 E4
Montauk U.S.A. 135 J3
Montauk Point U.S.A. 135 J3
Mont-aux-Sources mt. Lesotho 101 I5
Montbard France 56 G3
Montblanc Spain 57 G3
Montblanch Spain see Montblanc
Montbrison France 56 G4
Montceau-les-Mines France 56 G3
Montcornet France 52 E5
Mont-de-Marsan France 56 D5
Montdidier France 52 C5
Monte Alegre Brazil 143 H4
Monte Alegre de Goiás Brazil 145 B1
Monte Alegre de Minas Brazil 145 A2
Monte Azul Brazil 145 C1
Monte Azul Paulista Brazil 145 A3
Montebello Canada 122 G5
Montebello Islands Australia 108 A5
Montebelluna Italy 58 E2
Monte-Carlo Monaco 56 H5
Monte Cristi Dom. Rep. 137 J5
Monte Cristo S. Africa 101 H2
Monte Dourado Brazil 143 H4
Montego Bay Jamaica 137 I5
Montélimar France 56 G4
Monte Lindo r. Para. 144 E2
Montello U.S.A. 130 F3
Montemorelos Mex. 131 D7
Montemor-o-Novo Port. 57 B4
▶Montenegro country Europe 58 H3
Gained independence from Serbia in June 2006.
Montepulciano Italy 58 D3
Monte Quemado Arg. 144 D3
Montereau-Fault-Yonne France 56 F2
Monterey Mex. see Monterrey
Monterey CA U.S.A. 128 C3
Monterey VA U.S.A. 134 F4
Monterey Bay U.S.A. 128 B3
Montería Col. 142 C2
Monteros Arg. 144 C3
Monterrey Baja California Mex. 129 F5
Monterrey Nuevo León Mex. 131 C7
Montesano U.S.A. 126 C3
Montesano sulla Marcellana Italy 58 F4
Monte Santo Brazil 143 K6
Monte Santu, Capo di c. Sardinia Italy 58 C4
Montes Claros Brazil 145 C2
Montesilvano Italy 58 F3
Montevarchi Italy 58 D3
▶Montevideo Uruguay 144 E4
Capital of Uruguay.
Montevideo U.S.A. 130 E2
Montezuma U.S.A. 130 E3
Montezuma Creek U.S.A. 129 I3
Montezuma Peak U.S.A. 128 E3
Montfort Neth. 52 F3
Montgomery U.K. 49 D6
▶Montgomery AL U.S.A. 133 C5
Capital of Alabama.
Montgomery WV U.S.A. 134 E4
Montgomery Islands Australia 108 C3
Monthey Switz. 56 H3
Monticello AR U.S.A. 131 F5
Monticello FL U.S.A. 133 D6
Monticello IN U.S.A. 134 B3
Monticello KY U.S.A. 134 C5
Monticello MO U.S.A. 130 F3
Monticello NY U.S.A. 135 H3
Monticello UT U.S.A. 129 I3
Montieri, Poggio di mt. Italy 58 D3
Montignac France 56 E4
Montignies-le-Tilleul Belgium 52 E4
Montigny-lès-Metz France 52 G5
Montilla Spain 57 D5
Monti Sibillini, Parco Nazionale dei nat. park Italy 58 E3
Montividiu Brazil 145 A2
Montivilliers France 49 H9
Mont-Joli Canada 123 H4
Mont-Laurier Canada 122 G5
Montluçon France 56 F3
Montmagny Canada 123 H5
Montmédy France 52 F5
Montmirail France 52 D6
Montmorillon France 56 E3
Montmort-Lucy France 52 D6
Monto Australia 110 E5
Montour Falls U.S.A. 135 G2
Montoursville U.S.A. 135 G3
Montpelier ID U.S.A. 126 F4
▶Montpelier VT U.S.A. 135 I1
Capital of Vermont.
Montpellier France 56 F5
Montréal Canada 122 G5
Montreal r. Ont. Canada 122 D5
Montreal r. Ont. Canada 122 F5
Montreal Lake Canada 121 J4
Montreal Lake l. Canada 121 J4
Montréal-Mirabel airport Canada 122 G5
Montreal River Canada 122 D5
Montréal-Trudeau airport Canada 122 G5
Montreuil France 52 B4
Montreux Switz. 56 H3
Montrose well S. Africa 100 E4
Montrose U.K. 50 G4
Montrose CO U.S.A. 129 J2
Montrose PA U.S.A. 135 H3
Montross U.S.A. 135 G4
Monts, Pointe des pt Canada 123 I4
Mont-St-Aignan France 49 I9
▶Montserrat terr. West Indies 137 L5
United Kingdom Overseas Territory.
Montviel, Lac l. Canada 123 H3
Monument Valley reg. U.S.A. 129 H3
Monywa Myanmar 70 A2
Monza Italy 58 C2
Monze, Cape pt Pak. see Muari, Ras
Monzón Spain 57 G3
Mooi r. S. Africa 101 J5
Mooifontein Namibia 100 C4
Mookane Botswana 101 H2
Mookgophong S. Africa 101 I3
Mookgopong S. Africa see Mookgophong
Moolawatana Australia 111 B6
Moomba Australia 111 C6
Moomin Creek r. Australia 112 D2
Moonaree Australia 111 A6
Moonbi Range mts Australia 112 E3
Moonda Lake salt flat Australia 111 C5
Moonie Australia 112 E1
Moonie r. Australia 112 D2
Moora Australia 109 B7
Mooraberree Australia 110 C5
Moorcroft U.S.A. 126 G3
Moore r. Australia 109 A7
Moore U.S.A. 126 F3
Moore, Lake salt flat Australia 109 B7
Moore Embayment b. Antarctica 152 H1
Moorefield U.S.A. 135 F4
Moore Haven U.S.A. 133 D7
Moore Reef Australia 110 E3
Moore Reservoir U.S.A. 135 J1
Moore River National Park Australia 109 A7
Moores Island Bahamas 133 E7
Moorfoot Hills U.K. 50 F5
Moorhead U.S.A. 130 D2
Moorman U.S.A. 134 B5
Moornanyah Lake imp. l. Australia 112 A4
Mooroopna Australia 112 B6
Moorreesburg S. Africa 100 D7
Moorrinya National Park Australia 110 D4
Moose r. Canada 122 E4
Moose Factory Canada 122 E4
Moosehead Lake U.S.A. 132 G2
Moose Jaw Canada 121 J5
Moose Jaw r. Canada 121 J5
Moose Lake U.S.A. 130 E2
Mooselookmeguntic Lake U.S.A. 135 J1
Moose Mountain Creek r. Canada 121 K5
Moosilauke, Mount U.S.A. 135 J1
Moosomin Canada 121 K5
Moosonee Canada 122 E4
Mootwingee National Park Australia 111 C6
Mopane S. Africa 101 I2
Mopeia Moz. 99 D5
Mopipi Botswana 99 C6
Mopti Mali 96 C3
Moquegua Peru 142 D7
Mora Cameroon 97 E3
Mora Spain 57 E4
Mora Sweden 45 I6
Mora MN U.S.A. 130 E2
Mora NM U.S.A. 127 G6
Mora r. U.S.A. 127 G6
Moradabad India 82 D3
Morada Nova Brazil 143 K5
Moraine Lake Canada 121 J1
Moraleda, Canal sea chan. Chile 144 B6
Moram India 84 C2
Moramanga Madag. 99 E5
Moran U.S.A. 126 F4
Moranbah Australia 110 E4
Morang Nepal see Biratnagar
Morar, Loch l. U.K. 50 D4
Morari, Tso l. India 82 D2
Moratuwa Sri Lanka 84 C5
Morava reg. Czechia 47 P6
Moravia U.S.A. 135 G2
Morawa Australia 109 A7
Moray Firth b. U.K. 50 E3
Moray Range hills Australia 108 E3
Morbach Germany 52 H5
Morbeng S. Africa see Morebeng
Morbi India 82 B5
Morcenx France 56 D4
Morcillo Mex. 131 B7
Mordaga China 73 M2
Mor Dağı mt. Turkey 91 G3
Morden Canada 121 L5
Mordovo Russia 43 I5
Moreau r. U.S.A. 130 C2
Moreau, South Fork r. U.S.A. 130 C2
Morebeng S. Africa 101 I2
Morecambe U.K. 48 E4
Morecambe Bay U.K. 48 D4
Moree Australia 112 D2
Morehead P.N.G. 69 K8
Morehead U.S.A. 134 D4
Morehead City U.S.A. 137 I2
Moreland U.S.A. 134 C5
More Laptevykh sea Russia see Laptev Sea
Morelia Mex. 136 D5
Morella Australia 110 C4
Morella Spain 57 F3
Morelos Mex. 127 G8
Morena India 82 D4
Morena, Sierra mts Spain 57 C5
Morenci AZ U.S.A. 129 I5
Morenci MI U.S.A. 134 C3
Moreni Romania 59 K2
Moreno Mex. 127 F7
Moreno Valley U.S.A. 128 E5
Moresby, Mount Canada 120 C4
Moresby Island Canada see Gwaii Haanas
Moreswe Pan salt pan Botswana 100 G2
Moreton Bay Australia 112 F1
Moreton-in-Marsh U.K. 49 F7
Moreton Island Australia 112 F1
Moreton Island National Park Australia 112 F1
Moreuil France 52 C5
Morez France 56 H3
Morfou Cyprus 85 A2
Morfou Bay Cyprus 85 A2
Morgan U.S.A. 126 F4
Morgan City U.S.A. 131 F6
Morgan Hill U.S.A. 128 C3
Morganton U.S.A. 132 D5
Morgantown KY U.S.A. 134 B5
Morgantown WV U.S.A. 134 F4
Morgenzon S. Africa 101 I4
Morges Switz. 56 H3
Morghāb, Daryā-ye r. Afgh. 89 F3
Morhar r. India 83 F4
Mori China 80 H3
Mori Japan 74 F4
Moriah, Mount U.S.A. 129 F2
Moriarty's Range hills Australia 112 B2
Morice Lake Canada 120 E4
Morichal Col. 142 D3
Morihong Shan mt. China 74 B4
Morija Lesotho 101 H5
Morin Dawa China see Nirji
Moringen Germany 53 J3
Morioka Japan 75 F5
Moris Mex. 127 F7
Morisset Australia 112 E4
Moriyoshi-zan vol. Japan 75 F5
Morjärv Sweden 44 M3
Morjen r. Pak. 89 F4
Morki Russia 42 K4
Morlaix France 56 C2
Morley U.K. 48 F5
Mormam Flat Dam U.S.A. 129 H5
Mormant France 52 C6
Mormon Lake U.S.A. 129 H4
Mormugao India see Marmagao
Morne Diablotins vol. Dominica 137 L5
Morney watercourse Australia 110 C5
Mornington, Isla i. Chile 144 A7
Mornington Abyssal Plain sea feature S. Atlantic Ocean 148 C9
Mornington Island Australia 110 B3
Mornington Peninsula National Park Australia 112 B7
Moro Pak. 89 G5
Moro U.S.A. 126 C3
Morobe P.N.G. 69 L8
Morocco country Africa 96 C1
Morocco U.S.A. 134 B3
Morococala mt. Bol. 142 E7
Morogoro Tanz. 99 D4
Moro Gulf Phil. 69 G5
Morojaneng S. Africa 101 H5
Morokweng S. Africa 100 F4
Morombe Madag. 99 E6
Morón Cuba 133 E8
Mörön Mongolia 80 J2
Morondava Madag. 99 E6
Morón de la Frontera Spain 57 D5
▶Moroni Comoros 99 E5
Capital of the Comoros.
Moroni U.S.A. 129 H2
Moron Us He r. China see Tongtian He
Morotai i. Indon. 69 H6
Moroto Uganda 98 D3
Morozovsk Russia 43 I6
Morpeth Canada 134 E2
Morpeth U.K. 48 F3
Morphou Cyprus see Morfou
Morrill U.S.A. 134 C5
Morrilton U.S.A. 131 E5
Morrin Canada 121 H5
Morrinhos Brazil 145 A2
Morris Canada 121 L5
Morris IL U.S.A. 130 F3
Morris MN U.S.A. 130 E2
Morris PA U.S.A. 135 G3
Morrison U.S.A. 130 F3
Morristown AZ U.S.A. 129 G5
Morristown NJ U.S.A. 135 H3
Morristown NY U.S.A. 135 H1
Morristown TN U.S.A. 132 D4
Morrisville U.S.A. 135 H2
Morro Brazil 145 B2
Morro Bay U.S.A. 128 C4
Morro do Chapéu Brazil 143 J6
Morro Grande hill Brazil 143 H4
Morrosquillo, Golfo de b. Col. 142 C2
Morrumbene Moz. 101 L2
Morschen Germany 53 J3
Morse Canada 121 J5
Morse U.S.A. 131 C4
Morse, Cape Antarctica 152 G2
Morse Reservoir U.S.A. 134 B3
Morshanka Russia see Morshansk
Morshansk Russia 43 I5
Morsott Alg. 58 C7
Mort watercourse Australia 110 C4
Mortagne-au-Perche France 56 E2
Mortagne-sur-Sèvre France 56 D3
Mortara Italy 58 C2
Mortehoe U.K. 49 C7
Morteros Arg. 144 D4
Mortes, Rio das r. Brazil 145 A1
Mortimer's Bahamas 133 F8
Mortlake Australia 112 A7
Mortlock Islands Micronesia 150 G5
Mortlock Islands P.N.G. see Takuu Islands
Morton U.K. 49 G6
Morton TX U.S.A. 131 C5
Morton WA U.S.A. 126 C3
Morton National Park Australia 112 E5
Morundah Australia 112 C5
Morupule Botswana 101 H2
Moruroa atoll Fr. Polynesia see Mururoa
Moruya Australia 112 E5
Morven Australia 111 D5
Morven hill U.K. 50 F2
Morvern reg. U.K. 50 D4
Morvi India see Morbi
Morwell Australia 112 C7
Morzhovets, Ostrov i. Russia 42 I2
Mosbach Germany 53 J5
Mosborough U.K. 48 F5
Mosby U.S.A. 126 G3
▶Moscow Russia 42 H5
Capital of Russia. 2nd most populous city in Europe.
Moscow ID U.S.A. 126 D3
Moscow PA U.S.A. 135 H3
Moscow University Ice Shelf Antarctica 152 G2
Mosel r. Germany 53 H4
Moselebe watercourse Botswana 100 F3
Moselle r. France 52 G5
Möser Germany 53 L2
Moses, Mount U.S.A. 128 E1
Moses Lake U.S.A. 126 D3
Mosgiel N.Z. 113 C7
Moshaweng watercourse S. Africa 100 F4
Moshchnyy, Ostrov i. Russia 45 O7
Moshi Tanz. 98 D4
Mosh'yuga Russia 42 L2
Mosi-oa-Tunya waterfall Zambia/Zimbabwe see Victoria Falls
Mosjøen Norway 44 H4
Moskal'vo Russia 74 F1
Moskenesøy i. Norway 44 H3
Moskva Russia see Moscow
Moskva Tajik. 89 H2
Mosonmagyaróvár Hungary 47 P7
Mosquera Col. 142 C3
Mosquero U.S.A. 127 G6
Mosquito r. Brazil 145 C1
Mosquito Creek Lake U.S.A. 134 E3
Mosquito Lake Canada 121 K2
Mosquitos, Costa de coastal area Nicaragua 137 H6
Mosquitos, Golfo de los b. Panama 137 H7
Moss Norway 45 G7
Mossâmedes Angola see Namibe
Mossat U.K. 50 G3
Mossburn N.Z. 113 B7
Mosselbaai S. Africa see Mossel Bay
Mossel Bay S. Africa 100 F8
Mossel Bay b. S. Africa 100 F8
Mossgiel Australia 112 B4
Mossman Australia 110 D3
Mossoró Brazil 143 K5
Moss Vale Australia 112 E5
Mossy r. Canada 121 K4
Most Czechia 47 N5
Mostaganem Alg. 57 G6
Mostar Bos. & Her. 58 G3
Mostoos Hills Canada 121 I4
Mostovskoy Russia 91 F1
Mosty Belarus see Masty
Mosul Iraq 91 F3
Møsvatnet l. Norway 45 F7
Motala Sweden 45 I7
Motaze Moz. 101 K3
Motetema S. Africa 101 I3
Moth India 82 D4
Motherwell U.K. 50 F5
Motian Ling hill China 74 A4
Motihari India 83 F4
Motilla del Palancar Spain 57 F4
Motiti Island N.Z. 113 F3
Motokwe Botswana 100 F3
Motril Spain 57 E5
Motru Romania 59 J2
Mott U.S.A. 130 C2
Mottama Myanmar 70 B3
Mottama, Gulf of Myanmar 70 B3
Motu Ihupuku i. N.Z. see Campbell Island
Motul Mex. 136 G4
Mouaskar Alg. see Mascara
Mouding China 76 D3
Moudjéria Mauritania 96 B3
Moudros Greece 59 K5
Mouhijärvi Fin. 45 M6
Mouila Gabon 98 B4
Moulamein Australia 112 B5
Moulamein Creek r. Australia 112 A5
Moulavibazar Bangl. see Moulvibazar
Mould Bay (abandoned) Canada 118 G2
Moulèngui Binza Gabon 98 B4
Moulins France 56 F3
Moulmein Myanmar 70 B3
Moulouya r. Morocco 54 D4
Moultrie U.S.A. 133 D6
Moultrie, Lake U.S.A. 133 E5
Moulvibazar Bangl. 83 G4
Mound City KS U.S.A. 130 E4
Mound City SD U.S.A. 130 C2
Moundou Chad 97 E4
Moundsville U.S.A. 134 E4
Moŭng Cambodia 71 C4
Moŭng Rœssei Cambodia 71 C4
Mount Abu India 82 C4
Mountain r. Canada 120 D1
Mountainair U.S.A. 127 G6
Mountain Brook U.S.A. 133 C5
Mountain City U.S.A. 134 E5
Mountain Gate U.S.A. 126 C4
Mountain Home AR U.S.A. 131 E4
Mountain Home ID U.S.A. 126 E4
Mountain Home UT U.S.A. 129 H1
Mountain Lake Park U.S.A. 134 F4
Mountain View U.S.A. 131 E5
Mountain Zebra National Park S. Africa 101 G7
Mount Airy U.S.A. 134 E5
Mount Aspiring National Park N.Z. 113 B7
Mount Assiniboine Provincial Park Canada 120 H5
Mount Ayliff S. Africa 101 I6
Mount Ayr U.S.A. 130 E3
Mountbellew Ireland 51 D4
Mount Buffalo National Park Australia 112 C6
Mount Carmel U.S.A. 134 B4
Mount Carmel Junction U.S.A. 129 G3
Mount Coolon Australia 110 D4
Mount Darwin Zimbabwe 99 D5
Mount Denison Australia 108 F5
Mount Desert Island U.S.A. 132 G2
Mount Dutton Australia 111 A5
Mount Eba Australia 111 A6
Mount Elgon National Park Uganda 98 D3
Mount Fletcher S. Africa 101 I6
Mount Forest Canada 134 E2
Mount Frankland National Park Australia 109 B8
Mount Frere S. Africa 101 I6
Mount Gambier Australia 111 C8
Mount Gilead U.S.A. 134 D3
Mount Hagen P.N.G. 69 K8
Mount Holly U.S.A. 135 H4
Mount Hope Australia 112 B4
Mount Hope U.S.A. 134 E5
Mount Howitt Australia 111 C5
Mount Isa Australia 110 B4
Mount Jackson U.S.A. 135 F4
Mount Jewett U.S.A. 135 F3
Mount Joy U.S.A. 135 G3
Mount Kaputar National Park Australia 112 E3
Mount Keith Australia 109 C6
Mount Lofty Range mts Australia 111 B7
Mount Magnet Australia 109 B7
Mount Manara Australia 112 A4
Mount McKinley National Park U.S.A. see Denali National Park and Preserve
Mount Meadows Reservoir U.S.A. 128 C1
Mountmellick Ireland 51 E4
Mount Moorosi Lesotho 101 H6
Mount Morgan Australia 110 E4
Mount Morris MI U.S.A. 134 D2
Mount Morris NY U.S.A. 135 G2
Mount Murchison Australia 112 A3
Mount Nebo U.S.A. 134 E4
Mount Olivet U.S.A. 134 C4
Mount Pearl Canada 123 L5
Mount Pleasant Canada 123 I5
Mount Pleasant IA U.S.A. 130 F3
Mount Pleasant MI U.S.A. 134 C2
Mount Pleasant TX U.S.A. 131 E5
Mount Pleasant UT U.S.A. 129 H2
Mount Rainier National Park U.S.A. 126 C3
Mount Remarkable National Park Australia 111 B7
Mount Revelstoke National Park Canada 120 G5
Mount Robson Provincial Park Canada 120 G4
Mount Rogers National Recreation Area park U.S.A. 134 E5
Mount St Helens National Volcanic Monument nat. park U.S.A. 126 C3
Mount Sanford Australia 108 E4
Mount's Bay U.K. 49 B8
Mount Shasta U.S.A. 126 C4
Mountsorrel U.K. 49 F6
Mount Sterling U.S.A. 134 D4
Mount Swan Australia 110 A4
Mount Union U.S.A. 135 G3
Mount Vernon Australia 109 B6
Mount Vernon IL U.S.A. 130 F4
Mount Vernon IN U.S.A. 132 C4
Mount Vernon KY U.S.A. 134 C5
Mount Vernon MO U.S.A. 131 E4
Mount Vernon OH U.S.A. 134 D3
Mount Vernon TX U.S.A. 131 E5
Mount Vernon WA U.S.A. 126 C2
Mount William National Park Australia 111 [inset]
Mount Willoughby Australia 109 F6
Moura Australia 110 E5
Moura Brazil 142 F4
Moura Port. 57 C4
Mourdi, Dépression du depr. Chad 97 F3
Mourdiah Mali 96 C3
Mourne r. U.K. 51 E3
Mourne Mountains hills U.K. 51 F3
Mousa i. U.K. 50 [inset]
Mouscron Belgium 52 D4
Mousgougou Chad 98 B2
Moussafoyo Chad 97 E4
Moussoro Chad 97 E3
Moutamba Congo 98 B4
Mouth of the Yangtze China 77 I2
Moutong Indon. 69 G6
Mouy France 52 C5
Mouydir, Monts du plat. Alg. 96 D2
Mouzon France 52 F5

Movas Mex. 127 F7
Mowbullan, Mount Australia 112 E1
Moxey Town Bahamas 133 E7
Moy r. Ireland 51 C3
Moyale Eth. 98 D3
Moyen Atlas mts Morocco 54 C5
Moyen-Congo country Africa see Congo
Moyeni Lesotho 101 H6
Moynalyk Russia 80 I1
Moynaq Uzbek. see Mo'ynoq
Mo'ynoq Uzbek. 80 A3
Moyo i. Indon. 108 B2
Moyobamba Peru 142 C5
Moyock U.S.A. 135 G5
Moyola r. U.K. 51 F3
Moyu China 82 D1
Moyynkum Kazakh. 80 D3
Moyynkum, Peski des. Kazakh. 80 C3
Moyynty Kazakh. 80 D2
Mozambique country Africa 99 D6
Mozambique Channel Africa 99 E6
Mozambique Ridge sea feature Indian Ocean 149 K7
Mozdok Russia 91 G2
Mozhaysk Russia 43 H5
Mozhga Russia 42 L4
Mozo Myanmar 76 B4
Mozyr' Belarus see Mazyr
Mpaathutlwa Pan salt pan Botswana 100 E3
Mpanda Tanz. 99 D4
Mpen India 83 I4
Mpika Zambia 99 D5
Mpolweni S. Africa 101 J5
Mporokoso Zambia 99 D4
Mpulungu Zambia 99 D4
Mpumalanga prov. S. Africa 101 I4
Mpunde mt. Tanz. 99 D4
Mpwapwa Tanz. 99 D4
Mqanduli S. Africa 101 I6
Mqinvartsveri mt. Georgia/Russia see Kazbek
Mrauk-U Myanmar 70 A2
Mrewa Zimbabwe see Murehwa
Mrkonjić-Grad Bos. & Herz. 58 G2
M'Saken Tunisia 58 D7
Mshinskaya Russia 45 P7
M'Sila Alg. 57 I6
Msta r. Russia 42 F4
Mstislavl' Belarus see Mstsislaw
Mstsislaw Belarus 43 F5
Mtelo Kenya 98 D3
Mthatha S. Africa 101 I6
Mtoko Zimbabwe see Mutoko
Mtorwi Tanz. 99 D4
Mtsensk Russia 43 H5
Mts'ire Kavkasioni Asia see Lesser Caucasus
Mtubatuba S. Africa 101 K5
Mtunzini S. Africa 101 J5
Mtwara Tanz. 99 E5
Mu r. Myanmar 70 A2
Mu'āb, Jibāl reg. Jordan see Moab
Muanda Dem. Rep. Congo 99 B4
Muang Ham Laos 70 D2
Muang Hiam Laos 70 C2
Muang Hinboun Laos 70 D3
Muang Hôngsa Laos 70 C3
Muang Khi Laos 70 C3
Muang Không Laos 71 D4
Muang Khoua Laos 70 C2
Muang Lamam Laos see Xékong
Muang Mok Laos 70 D3
Muang Ngoy Laos 70 C2
Muang Ou Nua Laos 70 C2
Muang Pakbeng Laos 70 C3
Muang Paktha Laos 70 C2
Muang Pakxan Laos see Pakxan
Muang Phalan Laos 68 D3
Muang Phin Laos 70 D3
Muang Sam Sip Thai. 70 D4
Muang Sing Laos 70 C2
Muang Soum Laos 70 C3
Muang Souy Laos 70 C3
Muang Thadua Laos 70 C3
Muang Thai country Asia see Thailand
Muang Va Laos 70 C2
Muang Vangviang Laos 70 C3
Muang Xon Laos 70 C2
Muar Malaysia 71 C7
Muarabungo Indon. 68 C7
Muarateweh Indon. 68 E7
Murai, Ras pt Pak. 89 G5
Mu'ayqil, Khashm al hill Saudi Arabia 88 C5
Mubarek Uzbek. see Muborak
Mubarraz well Saudi Arabia 91 F5
Mubende Uganda 98 D3
Mubi Nigeria 96 E3
Muborak Uzbek. 89 G2
Mubur i. Indon. 71 D7
Mucajaí, Serra do mts Brazil 142 F3
Mucalic r. Canada 123 I2
Muccan Australia 108 C5
Much Germany 53 H4
Muchinga Escarpment Zambia 99 D5
Muchuan China 76 D2
Muck i. U.K. 50 C4
Mucojo Moz. 99 E5
Muconda Angola 99 C5
Mucubela Moz. 99 D5
Mucugê Brazil 145 C1
Mucur Turkey 90 D3
Mucuri Brazil 145 D2
Mucuri r. Brazil 145 D2
Mūd Iran 88 E3
Mudabidri India 84 B3
Mudan China see Heze
Mudanjiang China 74 C3
Mudan Jiang r. China 74 C3
Mudan Ling mts China 74 B4
Mudanya Turkey 59 M4
Mudaybī Oman 88 E6
Mudaysīsāt, Jabal al hill Jordan 85 C4
Muddus nationalpark nat. park Sweden 44 K3
Muddy r. U.S.A. 129 F3
Muddy Gap U.S.A. 126 G4
Muddy Peak U.S.A. 129 F3
Mudersbach Germany 53 H4
Mudgal India 84 C3
Mudgee Australia 112 D4
Mudhol India 84 B2
Mudigere India 84 B3
Mudjatik r. Canada 121 J3
Mud Lake U.S.A. 128 E3
Mudraya country Africa see Egypt
Mudurnu Turkey 59 N4
Mud'yuga Russia 42 H3
Mueda Moz. 99 D5
Mueller Range hills Australia 108 D4
Muertos Cays is Bahamas 133 D7
Muftyuga Russia 42 J2
Mufulira Zambia 99 C5
Mufumbwe Zambia 99 C5
Mufu Shan mts China 77 G2
Muğan Düzü lowland Azer. 91 H3
Mugarripug China 83 F2
Mughalbhin Pak. see Jati
Mughal Kot Pak. 89 H4
Mughal Sarai India 83 E4
Mūghār Iran 88 D3
Mughayrā' Saudi Arabia 85 C5
Mughayrā' well Saudi Arabia 88 B5
Muğla Turkey 59 M6
Mugodzhary, Gory mts Kazakh. 80 A2
Mugxung China 76 B1
Mūḩ, Sabkhat al imp. l. Syria 85 D2
Muhammad Ashraf Pak. 89 H5
Muhammad Qol Sudan 86 E5
Muhammarah Iran see Khorramshahr
Muhashsham, Wādī al watercourse Egypt 85 B4
Muḩaysh, Wādī al watercourse Jordan 85 C5
Muḩaysinīyah Syria 85 D1
Mühlanger Germany 53 M3
Mühlberg/Elbe Germany 53 N3
Mühlhausen/Thüringen Germany 53 K3
Mühlig-Hofmann Mountains Antarctica 152 C2
Muhos Fin. 44 N4
Muḩradah Syria 85 C2
Mui Bai Bung c. Vietnam see Ca Mau, Mui
Muié Angola 99 C5
Muineachán Ireland see Monaghan
Muir U.S.A. 134 C2
Muirkirk U.K. 50 E5
Muir of Ord U.K. 50 E3
Muite Moz. 99 D5
Mūjān, Chāh-e well Iran 88 D3
Muji China 82 D1
Muju S. Korea 75 B5
Mukacheve Ukr. 43 D6
Mukachevo Ukr. see Mukacheve
Mukah Sarawak Malaysia 68 E6
Mukalla Yemen 86 G7
Mukandwara India 82 D4
Mukdahan Thai. 70 D3
Mukden China see Shenyang
Muketei r. Canada 122 D3
Mukhen Russia 74 E2
Mukhino Russia 74 B1
Mukhtuya Russia see Lensk
Mūkīk, Chashmeh-ye spring Iran 88 E3
Mukinbudin Australia 109 B7
Mu Ko Chang Marine National Park Thai. 71 C5
Mukojima-rettō is Japan 75 F8
Mukry Turkm. 89 G2
Muktsar India 82 C3
Mukutawa r. Canada 121 L4
Mukwonago U.S.A. 134 A2
Mula r. India 84 B2
Mulainagiri mt. India 84 B3
Mulakatholhu Maldives 81 D11
Mulaku Atoll atoll Maldives see Mulakatholhu
Mulan China 74 C3
Mulanje, Mount Malawi 99 D5
Mulapula, Lake salt flat Australia 111 B6
Mulatos Mex. 127 F7
Mulayḩ Saudi Arabia 88 B5
Mulayḩah, Jabal hill U.A.E. 88 D5
Mulayz, Wādī al watercourse Egypt 85 A4
Mulchatna r. U.S.A. 118 C3
Mulde r. Germany 53 M3
Mule Creek NM U.S.A. 129 I5
Mule Creek WY U.S.A. 126 G4
Mulegé Mex. 127 E8
Mules i. Indon. 108 C2
Muleshoe U.S.A. 131 C5
Mulga Park Australia 109 E6
Mulgathing Australia 109 F7
Mulhacén mt. Spain 57 E5
Mülhausen France see Mulhouse
Mülheim an der Ruhr Germany 52 G3
Mulhouse France 56 H3
Muli China 76 D3
Muli Russia see Vysokogorniy
Mulia Indon. 69 J7
Muling Heilong. China 74 C3
Muling Heilong. China 74 C3
Muling He r. China 74 C3
Mull i. U.K. 50 D4
Mull, Sound of sea chan. U.K. 50 C4
Mullaghcleevaun hill Ireland 51 F4
Mullaittivu Sri Lanka 84 D4
Mullaley Australia 112 D3
Mullengudgery Australia 112 C3
Mullens U.S.A. 134 E5
Muller watercourse Australia 108 F5
Muller, Pegunungan mts Indon. 68 E6
Mullett Lake U.S.A. 134 C1
Mullewa Australia 109 A7
Mullica r. U.S.A. 135 H4
Mullingar Ireland 51 E4
Mullion Creek Australia 112 D4
Mull of Galloway c. U.K. 50 E6
Mull of Kintyre hd U.K. 50 D5
Mull of Oa hd U.K. 50 C5
Mullumbimby Australia 112 F2
Mulobezi Zambia 99 C5
Mulshi Lake India 84 B2
Multai India 82 D5
Multan Pak. 89 H4
Multia Fin. 44 N5
Multien reg. France 52 C6
Mulug India 84 C2

▶Mumbai India 84 B2
4th most populous city in Asia and 6th in the world.

Mumbil Australia 112 D4
Mumbwa Zambia 99 C5
Muminabad Tajik. see Leningrad
Mŭ'minobod Tajik. see Leningrad
Mun, Mae Nam r. Thai. 70 D4
Muna i. Indon. 69 G8
Muna Mex. 136 G4
Muna r. Russia 65 N3
Munabao Pak. 89 H5
Munaðarnes Iceland 44 [inset 1]
Münchberg Germany 53 L4
München Germany see Munich
München-Gladbach Germany see Mönchengladbach
Münchhausen Germany 53 I4
Muncho Lake Canada 120 E3
Muncie U.S.A. 134 C3
Muncoonie West, Lake salt flat Australia 110 B5
Muncy U.S.A. 135 G3
Munda Pak. 89 H4
Mundel Lake Sri Lanka 84 C5
Mundesley U.K. 49 I6
Mundford U.K. 49 H6
Mundiwindi (abandoned) Australia 109 C5
Mundra India 82 B5
Mundrabilla Australia 106 C5
Munds Park U.S.A. 129 H4
Mundubbera Australia 111 E5
Mundwa India 82 C4
Munfordville U.S.A. 134 C5
Mungallala Australia 111 D5
Mungana Australia 110 D3
Mungap-do i. S. Korea 75 B5
Mungári Moz. 99 D5
Mungbere Dem. Rep. Congo 98 C3
Mungeli India 83 E5
Munger India 83 F4
Mu Nggava i. Solomon Is see Rennell
Mungindi Australia 112 D2
Mungla Bangl. see Mongla
Mungo Angola 99 B5
Mungo, Lake Australia 112 A4
Mungo National Park Australia 112 A4
Munich Germany 47 M6
Munising U.S.A. 132 C2
Munjpur India 82 B5
Munkács Ukr. see Mukacheve
Munkebakken Norway 44 P2
Munkedal Sweden 45 G7
Munkfors Sweden 45 H7
Munkhafaḑ al Qaţţārah depr. Egypt see Qattara Depression
Munku-Sardyk, Gora mt. Mongolia/Russia 72 I2
Münnerstadt Germany 53 K4
Munnik S. Africa 101 I2
Munroe Lake Canada 121 L3
Munsan S. Korea 75 B5
Münster Hessen Germany 53 I5
Munster Germany 53 K2
Münster Nordrhein-Westfalen Germany 53 H3
Munster reg. Ireland 51 D5
Münsterland reg. Germany 53 H3
Muntadgin Australia 109 B7
Muntervary hd Ireland 51 C6
Munyal-Par sea feature India see Bassas de Pedro Padua Bank
Munzur Vadisi Milli Parkı nat. park Turkey 55 L4
Muojärvi l. Fin. 44 P4
Mương Nhe Vietnam 70 C2
Muong Sai Laos see Oudômxai
Muonio Fin. 44 M3
Muonioälven r. Fin./Sweden 44 M3
Muonionjoki r. Fin./Sweden see Muonioälven
Mupa, Parque Nacional da nat. park Angola 99 B5
Muping China see Baoxing
Muqaynimah well Saudi Arabia 88 C6
Muqdisho Somalia see Mogadishu
Muqêr Afgh. 89 G3
Muquém Brazil 145 A1
Muqui Brazil 145 C3
Muqur Afgh. 89 F3
Mur r. Austria 47 P7
also known as Mura (Croatia/Slovenia)
Mura r. Croatia/Slovenia see Mur
Murai, Tanjong pt Sing. 71 [inset]
Murai Reservoir Sing. 71 [inset]
Murakami Japan 75 E5
Murallón, Cerro mt. Chile 144 B7
Muramvya Burundi 98 C4
Murashi Russia 42 K4
Murat r. Turkey 91 E3
Muratlı Turkey 59 L4
Muraysah, Ra's al pt Libya 90 B5
Murchison watercourse Australia 109 A6
Murchison, Mount Antarctica 152 H2
Murchison, Mount hill Australia 109 B6
Murchison Falls National Park Uganda 98 D3
Murcia Spain 57 F5
Murcia aut. comm. Spain 57 F5
Murdo U.S.A. 130 C3
Murehwa Zimbabwe 99 D5
Mureşul r. Romania 59 I1
Muret France 56 E5
Murewa Zimbabwe see Murehwa
Murfreesboro AR U.S.A. 131 E5
Murfreesboro TN U.S.A. 132 C5
Murg r. Germany 53 I6
Murgab Tajik. see Murghob
Murgab Turkm. see Murgap
Murgab r. Turkm. see Murgap
Murgap Turkm. 89 F2
Murgap r. Turkm. 87 J2
Murgh, Kōtal-e Afgh. 89 H3
Murghāb reg. Afgh. 89 F3
Murgha Kibzai Pak. 89 H4
Murghob Tajik. 89 I2
Murgon Australia 111 E5
Murgoo Australia 109 B6
Muri India 83 F5
Muriaé Brazil 145 C3
Murid Pak. 89 G4
Muriege Angola 99 C4
Müritz l. Germany 53 M1
Müritz, Nationalpark nat. park Germany 53 N1
Murmansk Russia 44 R2
Murmanskaya Oblast' admin. div. Russia 44 S2
Murmanskiy Bereg coastal area Russia 42 G1
Murmansk Oblast admin. div. Russia see Murmanskaya Oblast'
Muro, Capo di c. Corsica France 56 I6
Murom Russia 42 I5
Muroran Japan 74 F4
Muros Spain 57 B2
Muroto Japan 75 D6
Muroto-zaki pt Japan 75 D6
Murphy ID U.S.A. 126 D4
Murphy NC U.S.A. 133 D5
Murphysboro U.S.A. 130 F4
Murrah reg. Saudi Arabia 88 C6
Murrah al Kubrá, Al Buḩayrah al l. Egypt see Great Bitter Lake
Murrah aş Şughrá, Al Buḩayrah al l. Egypt see Little Bitter Lake
Murramarang National Park nat. park Australia 112 I5
Murra Murra Australia 112 C2
Murrat el Kubra, Buheirat l. Egypt see Great Bitter Lake
Murrat el Sughra, Buheirat l. Egypt see Little Bitter Lake

▶Murray r. S.A. Australia 111 B7
3rd longest river in Oceania, and a major part of the longest (Murray-Darling).

Murray r. W.A. Australia 109 A8
Murray KY U.S.A. 131 F4
Murray UT U.S.A. 129 H1
Murray, Lake P.N.G. 69 K8
Murray, Lake U.S.A. 133 D5
Murray, Mount Canada 120 D2
Murray Bridge Australia 111 B7

▶Murray-Darling r. Australia 106 E5
Longest river in Oceania.

Murray Downs Australia 108 F5
Murray Range hills Australia 109 E6
Murraysburg S. Africa 100 F6
Murray Sunset National Park Australia 111 C7
Murrhardt Germany 53 J6
Murrieta U.S.A. 128 E5
Murringo Australia 112 D5
Murrisk reg. Ireland 51 C4
Murroogh Ireland 51 C4

▶Murrumbidgee r. Australia 112 A5
4th longest river in Oceania.

Murrumburrah Australia 112 D5
Murrurundi Australia 112 E3
Mursan India 82 D4
Murshidabad India 83 G4
Murska Sobota Slovenia 58 G1
Mürt Iran 89 F5
Murtoa Australia 111 C8
Murua i. P.N.G. see Woodlark Island
Murud India 84 B2
Murud, Gunung mt. Indon. 68 F6
Murujuga National Park Australia 108 B5
Murunkan Sri Lanka 84 D4
Murupara N.Z. 113 F4
Mururoa atoll Fr. Polynesia 151 K7
Murviedro Spain see Sagunto
Murwara India see Katni
Murwillumbah Australia 112 F2
Murzechirla Turkm. 89 F2
Murzūq Libya 97 E2
Murzuq, Ḩamādat plat. Libya 98 B1
Murzuq, Idhān des. Libya 96 E2
Mürzzuschlag Austria 47 O7
Muş Turkey 91 F3
Mūsā, Khowr-e b. Iran 88 C4
Mūsá, Ţal'at mt. Lebanon/Syria 85 C2
Musakhel Pak. 89 H4
Musala mt. Bulg. 59 J3
Musala i. Indon. 71 B7
Musan N. Korea 74 C4
Musandam Peninsula Oman/U.A.E. 88 E5
Musay'īd Qatar see Umm Sa'id

▶Muscat Oman 88 E6
Capital of Oman.

Muscat reg. Oman 88 E5
Muscat and Oman country Asia see Oman
Muscatine U.S.A. 130 F3
Musgrave Australia 110 C2
Musgrave Harbour Canada 123 L4
Musgrave Ranges mts Australia 109 E6
Mushayyish, Wādī al watercourse Jordan 85 C4
Mushie Dem. Rep. Congo 98 B4
Mushkaf Pak. 89 G4
Music Mountain U.S.A. 129 G4
Musina S. Africa 101 J2
Musinia Peak U.S.A. 129 H2
Muskeg r. Canada 120 F2
Muskeget Channel U.S.A. 135 J3
Muskegon U.S.A. 134 B2
Muskegon r. U.S.A. 134 B2
Muskegon Heights U.S.A. 134 B2
Muskeg River Canada 120 G4
Muskogee U.S.A. 131 E5
Muskoka, Lake Canada 134 F1
Muskrat Dam Lake Canada 121 N4
Musmar Sudan 86 E6
Musoma Tanz. 98 D4
Musquanousse, Lac l. Canada 123 J4
Musquaro, Lac l. Canada 123 J4
Mussau Island P.N.G. 69 L7
Musselburgh U.K. 50 F5
Musselkanaal Neth. 52 H2
Musselshell r. U.S.A. 126 G3
Mussende Angola 99 B5
Mustafakemalpaşa Turkey 59 M4
Mustjala Estonia 45 M7
Mustvee Estonia 45 O7
Musu-dan pt N. Korea 74 C4
Muswellbrook Australia 112 E4
Mūţ Egypt 86 C4
Mut Turkey 85 A1
Mutá, Ponta do pt Brazil 145 D1
Mutare Zimbabwe 99 D5
Mutayr reg. Saudi Arabia 88 B5
Mutina Italy see Modena
Muting Indon. 69 K8
Mutis Col. 142 C2
Mutnyy Materik Russia 42 L2
Mutoko Zimbabwe 99 D5
Mutsamudu Comoros 99 E5
Mutsu Japan 74 F4
Muttaburra Australia 110 D4
Mutton Island Ireland 51 C5
Muttukuru India 84 D3
Muttupet India 84 C4
Mutum Brazil 145 C2
Mutunópolis Brazil 145 A1
Mutur Sri Lanka 84 D4
Mutusjärvi r. Fin. 44 O2
Muurola Fin. 44 N3
Mu Us Shadi des. China 73 J5
Muxaluando Angola 99 B4
Muxi China see Muchuan
Muxima Angola 99 B4
Muyezerskiy Russia 44 R5
Muyinga Burundi 98 D4
Mŭynoq Uzbek. see Mo'ynoq
Muyu China 77 F2
Muyumba Dem. Rep. Congo 99 C4
Muyunkum, Peski des. Kazakh. see Moyynkum, Peski
Muzaffarabad Pak. 89 I3
Muzaffargarh Pak. 89 H4
Muzaffarnagar India 82 D3
Muzaffarpur India 83 F4
Muzamane Moz. 101 K2
Muzbel', Uval hills Kazakh. 91 I2
Muzhi Russia 41 S2
Mūzin Iran 89 F5
Muzon, Cape U.S.A. 120 C4
Múzquiz Mex. 131 C7
Muz Shan mt. China 82 E2
Muz Tag mt. China 83 F1
Muztagata mt. China 89 I2
Muztor Kyrg. see Toktogul
Mvadi Gabon 98 B3
Mvolo South Sudan 97 F4
Mvuma Zimbabwe 99 D5
Mwanza Malawi 99 D5
Mwanza Tanz. 98 D4
Mweelrea hill Ireland 51 C4
Mweka Dem. Rep. Congo 99 C4
Mwene-Ditu Dem. Rep. Congo 99 C4
Mwenezi Zimbabwe 99 D6
Mwenga Dem. Rep. Congo 98 C4
Mweru, Lake Dem. Rep. Congo/Zambia 99 C4
Mweru Wantipa National Park Zambia 99 C4
Mwimba Dem. Rep. Congo 99 C4
Mwinilunga Zambia 99 C5
Myadaung Myanmar 70 B2
Myadzyel Belarus 45 O9
Myajlar India 82 B4
Myall Lakes National Park Australia 112 F4
Myanaung Myanmar 70 A3
Myanmar country Asia 70 A2
Myauk-Oo Myanmar see Mrauk-U
Myaungmya Myanmar 70 A3
Myawadi Thai. 70 B3
Mybster U.K. 50 F2
Myebon Myanmar 70 A2
Myede Myanmar see Aunglan
Myeik Myanmar 71 B4
Myingyan Myanmar 70 A2
Myinkyado Myanmar 70 B2
Myinmoletkat mt. Myanmar 71 B4
Myitkyina Myanmar 70 B1
Myitson Myanmar 70 B2
Myitta Myanmar 71 B4
Myittha Myanmar 70 B2
Mykolayiv Ukr. 59 O1
Mykonos i. Greece 59 K6
Myla Russia 42 K2
Myla r. Russia 42 K2
Mylae Sicily Italy see Milazzo
Mylasa Turkey see Milas
Mymensing Bangl. see Mymensingh
Mymensingh Bangl. 83 G4
Mynämäki Fin. 45 M6
Myŏnggan N. Korea 74 C4
Myory Belarus 45 O9
My Phươc Vietnam 71 D5
Mýrdalsjökull ice cap Iceland 44 [inset 1]
Myre Norway 44 I2
Myrheden Sweden 44 L4
Myrhorod Ukr. 43 G6
Myrnam Canada 121 I4
Myronivka Ukr. 43 F6
Myrtle Beach U.S.A. 133 E5
Myrtleford Australia 112 C6
Myrtle Point U.S.A. 126 B4
Myrtoo Pelagos sea Greece 59 J6
Mys Chelyuskin Russia 153 E1
Mysia hist. area Turkey 59 L5
Mys Lazareva Russia see Lazarev
Myślibórz Poland 47 O4
My Sơn Sanctuary tourist site Vietnam 70 E4
Mysore India see Mysuru
Mysore state India see Karnataka
Mys Shmidta Russia 65 T3
Mysuru India 84 C3
Mysy Russia 42 L3
My Tho Vietnam 71 D5
Mytikas mt. Greece see Olympus, Mount
Mytilene i. Greece see Lesbos
Mytilini Greece 59 L5
Mytilini Strait Greece/Turkey 59 L5
Mytishchi Russia 42 H5
Myton U.S.A. 129 H1
Myyeldino Russia 42 L3
Mzamomhle S. Africa 101 H6
Mže r. Czechia 53 M5
Mzimba Malawi 99 D5
Mzuzu Malawi 99 D5

N

Naab r. Germany 53 M5
Nā'ālehu U.S.A. 127 [inset]
Naantali Fin. 45 M6
Naas Ireland 51 F4
Nááts'íhch'oh National Park Reserve nat. park Canada 120 D2
Naba Myanmar 70 B1
Nababeep S. Africa 100 C5
Nababganj Bangl. see Nawabganj
Nabadwip India see Navadwip
Nabarangapur India 84 D2
Nabarangpur India see Nabarangapur
Nabari Japan 75 E6
Nabatîyé et Tahta Lebanon 85 B3
Nabatiyet et Tahta Lebanon see Nabatîyé et Tahta
Nabberu, Lake salt flat Australia 109 C6
Nabburg Germany 53 M5
Naberera Tanz. 99 D4
Naberezhnyye Chelny Russia 41 Q4
Nabesna U.S.A. 120 A2
Nabeul Tunisia 58 D6
Nabha India 82 D3
Nabil'skiy Zaliv lag. Russia 74 F2
Nabire Indon. 69 J7
Nabi Younés, Ras en pt Lebanon 85 B3
Nāblus West Bank 85 B3
Nabq Protected Area nature res. Egypt 90 D5
Nābulus West Bank see Nāblus
Nacala Moz. 99 E5
Nachalovo Russia 43 K7
Nachicapau, Lac l. Canada 123 I2
Nachingwea Tanz. 99 D5
Nachna India 82 B4
Nachuge India 71 A5
Nacimiento Reservoir U.S.A. 128 C4
Naco U.S.A. 127 F7
Nacogdoches U.S.A. 131 E6
Nada China see Danzhou
Nadaleen r. Canada 120 C2
Nådendal Fin. see Naantali
Nadezhdinskoye Russia 74 D2
Nadiad India 82 C5
Nadol India 82 C4
Nador Morocco 57 E6
Nadqān, Qalamat well Saudi Arabia 88 C6
Nadūshan Iran 88 D3
Nadvirna Ukr. 43 E6
Nadvoitsy Russia 42 G3
Nadvornaya Ukr. see Nadvirna
Nadym Russia 64 I3
Næstved Denmark 45 G9
Nafarroa aut. comm. Spain see Navarra
Nafas, Ra's an mt. Egypt 85 B5
Nafḩa, Har hill Israel 85 B4
Nafpaktos Greece 59 I5
Nafplio Greece 59 J6
Naftalan Azer. 91 G2
Naft-e Safid Iran 88 C4
Naft-e Shāh Iran see Naft Shahr
Naft Shahr Iran 88 B3
Nafūsah, Jabal hills Libya 96 E1
Nafy Saudi Arabia 86 F4
Nag, Co l. China 83 G2
Naga Phil. 69 G4
Nagagami r. Canada 122 D4
Nagagami Lake Canada 122 D4
Nagahama Japan 75 D6
Naga Hills India 83 H4
Naga Hills state India see Nagaland
Nagaland state India 83 H4
Nagamangala India 84 C3
Nagambie Australia 112 B6
Nagano Japan 75 E5
Nagaoka Japan 75 E5
Nagaon India 83 H4
Nagapatam India see Nagapattinam
Nagapattinam India 84 C4
Nagar Hima. Prad. India 87 M3
Nagar Karnataka India 84 B3
Nagaram India 84 D2
Nagari Hills India 84 C3
Nagarjuna Sagar Reservoir India 84 C2
Nagar Parkar Pak. 89 H5
Nagar Untari India 83 E4
Nagasaki Japan 75 C6
Nagato Japan 75 C6
Nagaur India 82 C4
Nagbhir India 84 C1
Nagda India 82 C5
Nageezi U.S.A. 129 J3
Nagercoil India 84 C4
Nagha Kalat Pak. 89 G5
Nag' Ḩammâdî Egypt see Naj' Ḩammādī
Nagina India 82 D3
Nagold r. Germany 53 I6
Nagong Chu r. China see Parlung Zangbo
Nagorno-Karabakh disp. terr. Azer. 91 G3
Nagornyy Karabakh disp. terr. Azer. see Nagorno-Karabakh
Nagorsk Russia 42 K4
Nagoya Japan 75 E6
Nagpur India 82 D5
Nagqu China 76 B2
Nag Qu r. China 76 B2
Nagurskoye Russia 64 F1
Nagyatád Hungary 58 G1
Nagybecskerek Serbia see Zrenjanin
Nagyenyed Romania see Aiud
Nagykanizsa Hungary 58 G1
Nagyvárad Romania see Oradea
Naha Japan 73 N7
Nahan India 82 D3
Nahanni Butte Canada 120 F2
Nahanni National Park Reserve Canada 120 E2
Nahanni Range mts Canada 120 F2
Naharāyim Jordan 85 B3
Nahariyya Israel 85 B3
Nahāvand Iran 88 C3
Nahr Dijlah r. Asia see Tigris

Nahrīn Afgh. 89 H2
Nahrīn reg. Afgh. 89 H2
Nahuel Huapí, Parque Nacional nat. park Arg. 144 B6
Nahunta U.S.A. 133 D6
Naica Mex. 131 B7
Nai Ga Myanmar 76 C3
Naij Tal China 83 H2
Naikliu Indon. 108 C2
Nain Canada 123 J2
Nā'īn Iran 88 D3
Nainital India 82 D3
Naini Tal India see Nainital
Nairn U.K. 50 F3
Nairn r. U.K. 50 F3

▶Nairobi Kenya 98 D4
Capital of Kenya.

Naissus Serbia see Niš
Naivasha Kenya 98 D4
Najafābād Iran 88 C3
Na'jān Saudi Arabia 88 B5
Najd reg. Saudi Arabia 86 F4
Nájera Spain 57 E2
Naj' Ḥammādī Egypt 86 D4
Naji China 74 A2
Najibabad India 82 D3
Najin N. Korea 74 C4
Najitun China see Naji
Najrān Saudi Arabia 86 F6
Nakadōri-shima i. Japan 75 C6
Na Kae Thai. 70 D3
Nakambé r. Burkina Faso/Ghana see White Volta
Nakanbe r. Burkina Faso/Ghana see White Volta
Nakanno Russia 65 L3
Nakano-shima i. Japan 75 D5
Nakasongola Uganda 97 G4
Nakatsu Japan 75 C6
Nakatsugawa Japan 75 E6
Nakdong-gang r. S. Korea 75 C6
Nakfa Eritrea 86 E6
Nakhichevan' Azer. see Naxçıvan
Nakhl Egypt 85 A5
Nakhodka Russia 74 D4
Nakhola India 83 H4
Nakhon Nayok Thai. 71 C4
Nakhon Pathom Thai. 71 C4
Nakhon Phanom Thai. 70 D3
Nakhon Ratchasima Thai. 70 C4
Nakhon Sawan Thai. 70 C4
Nakhon Si Thammarat Thai. 71 B5
Nakhtarana India 82 B5
Nakina Canada 122 D4
Nakina r. Canada 120 C3
Naknek U.S.A. 118 C4
Nakonde Zambia 99 D4
Nakskov Denmark 45 G9
Nakuru Kenya 98 D4
Nakusp Canada 120 G5
Nal Pak. 89 G5
Nal r. Pak. 89 G5
Na-lang Myanmar 70 B2
Nalázi Moz. 101 K3
Nalbari India 83 G4
Nal'chik Russia 91 F2
Naldurg India 84 C2
Nalgonda India 84 C2
Naliya India 82 B5
Nallamala Hills India 84 C3
Nallıhan Turkey 59 N4
Nālūt Libya 96 E1
Namaacha Moz. 101 K3
Namacurra Moz. 99 D5
Namadgi National Park Australia 112 D5
Namahadi S. Africa 101 I4
Namak, Daryācheh-ye salt flat Iran 88 C3
Namak, Kavīr-e salt flat Iran 88 E3
Namakkal India 84 C4
Namakwaland reg. Namibia see Great Namaqualand
Namakzar-e Shadad salt flat Iran 88 E4
Namaland reg. Namibia see Great Namaqualand
Namangan Uzbek. 80 D3
Namaqualand reg. Namibia see Great Namaqualand
Namaqualand reg. S. Africa 100 C5
Namaqua National Park S. Africa 100 C6
Namas Indon. 69 K8
Namatanai P.N.G. 106 F2
Nambour Australia 112 F1
Nambucca Heads Australia 112 F3
Nambung National Park Australia 109 A7
Năm Căn Vietnam 71 D5
Namcha Barwa mt. China see Namjagbarwa Feng
Namche Bazar Nepal 83 F4
Nam Co salt l. China 83 G3
Namdalen valley Norway 44 H4
Namdalseid Norway 44 G4
Nam Đinh Vietnam 70 D2
Nam Du, Quân Đao i. Vietnam 71 D5
Namen Belgium see Namur
Nam-gang r. N. Korea 75 B5
Namhae-do i. S. Korea 75 B6
Namhsan Myanmar 70 B2
Namib Desert Namibia 100 B3
Namibe Angola 99 B5
Namibia country Africa 99 B6
Namibia Abyssal Plain sea feature N. Atlantic Ocean 148 I8
Namib-Naukluft Park nature res. Namibia 100 B3
Namie (abandoned) Japan 75 F5
Namīn Iran 91 H3
Namjagbarwa Feng mt. China 76 B2
Namlan Myanmar 70 B2
Nam Loi r. China see Nanlei He
Nam Nao National Park Thai. 70 C3
Namoi r. Australia 112 D3
Namonuito atoll Micronesia 69 L5
Nampa mt. Nepal 82 E3
Nampa U.S.A. 126 D4
Nampala Mali 96 C3
Nam Phong Thai. 70 C3
Namp'o N. Korea 75 B5
Nampula Moz. 99 D5
Namsai Myanmar 70 B1
Namsang Myanmar 70 B2
Namsen r. Norway 44 G4
Namsos Norway 44 G4
Nam Theun 2 resr Laos 70 D3
Namti Myanmar 70 B1
Namtok Myanmar 70 B3
Nam Tok Chattakan National Park Thai. 70 C3
Namton Myanmar 70 B2
Namtsy Russia 65 N3
Namtu Myanmar 70 B2
Namu Canada 120 E5
Namuli, Monte mt. Moz. 99 D5
Namuno Moz. 99 D5
Namur Belgium 52 E4
Namutoni Namibia 99 B5
Namwon S. Korea 75 B6
Namya Ra Myanmar 70 B1
Namyit Island S. China Sea 68 E4
Nan Thai. 70 C3
Nana Bakassa Cent. Afr. Rep. 98 B3
Nanaimo Canada 120 F5
Nanam N. Korea 74 C4
Nan'an China 77 H3
Nanango Australia 112 F1
Nananib Plateau Namibia 100 C3
Nanao Japan 75 E5
Nanatsu-shima i. Japan 75 E5
Nanbai China see Zunyi
Nanbin China see Shizhu
Nanbu China 76 E2
Nancha China 74 C3
Nanchang Jiangxi China 77 G2
Nanchang Jiangxi China 77 G2
Nanchong China 76 E2
Nanchuan China 76 E2
Nancowry i. India 71 A6
Nancun China 77 G1
Nancy France 52 G6
Nancy (Essey) airport France 52 G6
Nanda Devi mt. India 82 E3
Nanda Kot mt. India 82 E3
Nandan China 76 E3
Nandapur India 84 D2
Nanded India 84 C2
Nander India see Nanded
Nandewar Range mts Australia 112 E3
Nandod India 84 B1
Nandurbar India 82 C5
Nandyal India 84 C3
Nanfeng Guangdong China 77 F4
Nanfeng Jiangxi China 77 H3
Nang China 76 B2
Nanga Eboko Cameroon 96 E4

▶Nanga Parbat mt. Pak. 82 C2
9th highest mountain in Asia and the world.

Nangar National Park Australia 112 D4
Nangatayap Indon. 68 E7
Nangin Myanmar 71 B5
Nangnim-sanmaek mts N. Korea 75 B4
Nangqên China 76 C1
Nangulangwa Tanz. 99 D4
Nanguneri India 84 C4
Nanhua China 76 D3
Nanhui China 77 I2
Nanjian China 76 D3
Nanjiang China 76 E1
Nanjing China 77 H1
Nanji Shan i. China 77 I3
Nanka Jiang r. China 76 C4
Nankang China 77 G3
Nanking China see Nanjing
Nankova Angola 99 B5
Nanlei He r. China 76 C4
also known as Nam Loi (Myanmar)
Nanling China 77 H2
Nan Ling mts China 77 F3
Nanliu Jiang r. China 77 F4
Nanlong China see Nanbu
Nannilam India 84 C4
Nannine (abandoned) Australia 109 B6
Nanning China 77 F4
Nannup Australia 109 A8
Na Noi Thai. 70 C3
Nanortalik Greenland 119 N3
Nanouki atoll Kiribati see Nonouti
Nanouti atoll Kiribati see Nonouti
Nanpan Jiang r. China 76 E3
Nanping China 77 H3
Nanpu China see Pucheng
Nanri Dao i. China 77 H3
Nansei-shotō is Japan see Ryukyu Islands
Nansei-shotō Trench sea feature N. Pacific Ocean see Ryukyu Trench
Nansen Basin sea feature Arctic Ocean 153 H1
Nansen Sound sea chan. Canada 119 I1
Nan-sha Ch'ün-tao is S. China Sea see Spratly Islands
Nanshan China 77 [inset]
Nanshan Island S. China Sea 68 F4
Nansha Qundao is S. China Sea see Spratly Islands
Nansio Tanz. 98 D4
Nantes France 56 D3
Nantes à Brest, Canal de France 56 C3
Nanteuil-le-Haudouin France 52 C5
Nanthi Kadal Lagoon lag. Sri Lanka 84 D4
Nanticoke Canada 134 E2
Nanticoke U.S.A. 135 H4
Nantong China 77 I2
Nantou Taiwan 77 I4
Nantucket U.S.A. 135 J3
Nantucket Island U.S.A. 135 K3
Nantucket Sound g. U.S.A. 135 J3
Nantwich U.K. 49 E5
Nanumaga i. Tuvalu see Nanumanga
Nanumanga i. Tuvalu 107 H2
Nanumea atoll Tuvalu 107 H2
Nanuque Brazil 145 C2
Nanusa, Kepulauan is Indon. 69 H6
Nanxi China 76 E2
Nanxian China 77 G2
Nanxiong China 77 G3
Nanyang China 77 G1
Nanyuki Kenya 98 D4
Nanzhang China 77 F2
Nanzhao China see Zhao'an
Nanzhou China see Nanxian
Nao, Cabo de la c. Spain 57 G4
Naococane, Lac l. Canada 123 H3
Naoero country S. Pacific Ocean see Nauru
Naogaon Bangl. 83 G4
Naoli He r. China 74 D3
Nāomīd, Dasht-e des. Afgh./Iran 89 F3
Naoshera India 82 C2
Napa U.S.A. 128 B2
Napaktulik Lake Canada 121 H1
Napanee Canada 135 G1
Napasoq Greenland 119 M3
Naperville U.S.A. 134 A3
Napier N.Z. 113 F4
Napier Range hills Australia 108 D4
Napierville Canada 135 I1
Naples Italy 58 F4
Naples FL U.S.A. 133 D7
Naples ME U.S.A. 135 J2
Naples TX U.S.A. 131 E5
Naples UT U.S.A. 129 I1
Napo China 76 E4
Napoleon IN U.S.A. 134 C4
Napoleon ND U.S.A. 130 D2
Napoleon OH U.S.A. 134 C3
Napoli Italy see Naples
Naqadeh Iran 88 B2
Nara India 82 B5
Nara Japan 75 D6
Nara Mali 96 C3
Narach Belarus 45 O9
Naracoorte Australia 111 C8
Naradhan Australia 112 C4
Naralua India 83 F4
Naranjal Ecuador 142 C4
Naranjo Mex. 127 F8
Narasapur India 84 D2
Narasaraopet India 84 D2
Narasinghapur India 84 E1
Narathiwat Thai. 71 C6
Nara Visa U.S.A. 131 C5
Narayanganj Bangl. 83 G5
Narayanganj India 82 E5
Narayangarh India 82 C4
Narayanpur India 84 D2
Narbada r. India see Narmada
Narberth U.K. 49 C7
Narbo France see Narbonne
Narbonne France 56 F5
Narcea r. Spain 57 C2
Narcondam Island India 71 A4
Nardò Italy 58 H4
Narechi r. Pak. 89 H4
Narembeen Australia 109 B8
Nares Abyssal Plain sea feature S. Atlantic Ocean 148 D4
Nares Deep sea feature N. Atlantic Ocean 148 D4
Nares Strait Canada/Greenland 119 K2
Naretha Australia 109 D7
Narew r. Poland 47 R4
Narib Namibia 100 C3
Narikel Jinjira i. Bangl. see St Martin's Island
Narimanov Russia 43 J7
Narimskiy Khrebet mts Kazakh. see Naryn, Khrebet
Narince Turkey 90 E3
Narin Gol watercourse China 83 H1
Narizon, Punta pt Mex. 127 F8
Narkher India 82 D5
Narmada r. India 82 C5
Narman Turkey 91 F2
Narnaul India 82 D3
Narni Italy 58 E3
Narnia Italy see Narni
Narodnaya, Gora mt. Russia 41 S3
Naro-Fominsk Russia 43 H5
Narok Kenya 98 D4
Narooma Australia 112 E6
Narovchat Russia 43 I5
Narowlya Belarus 43 F6
Närpes Fin. 44 L5
Narrabri Australia 112 D3
Narragansett Bay U.S.A. 135 J3
Narran r. Australia 112 C2
Narrandera Australia 112 C5
Narran Lake Australia 112 C2
Narrogin Australia 109 B8
Narromine Australia 112 D4
Narrows U.S.A. 134 E5
Narrowsburg U.S.A. 135 H3
Narsapur India 84 C2
Narsaq Greenland 119 N3
Narshingdi Bangl. see Narsingdi
Narsimhapur India 82 D5
Narsingdi Bangl. 83 G5
Narsinghpur India see Narsimhapur
Narsipatnam India 84 D2
Nartkala Russia 91 F2
Naruto Japan 75 D6
Narva Estonia 45 P7
Narva Bay Estonia/Russia 45 O7
Narva laht b. Estonia/Russia see Narva Bay
Narva Reservoir resr Estonia/Russia 45 P7
Narva veehoidla resr Estonia/Russia see Narva Reservoir
Narvik Norway 44 J2
Narvskiy Zaliv b. Estonia/Russia see Narva Bay
Narvskoye Vodokhranilishche resr Estonia/Russia see Narva Reservoir
Narwana India 82 D3
Nar'yan-Mar Russia 42 L2
Naryn Kyrg. 80 E3
Naryn, Khrebet mts Kazakh. 80 F2
Näsåker Sweden 44 J5
Nashik India 84 B1
Nashua U.S.A. 135 J2
Nashville AR U.S.A. 131 E5
Nashville GA U.S.A. 133 D6
Nashville IN U.S.A. 134 B4
Nashville NC U.S.A. 132 E5
Nashville OH U.S.A. 134 D3

▶Nashville TN U.S.A. 132 C4
Capital of Tennessee.

Naṣīb Syria 85 C3
Näsijärvi l. Fin. 45 M6
Nasik India see Nashik
Nasinu Fiji 107 H3
Nasir Pak. 89 H4
Nasir South Sudan 86 D8
Nāṣir, Buḥayrat resr Egypt see Nasser, Lake
Nasirabad Bangl. see Mymensingh
Nasirabad India 82 C4
Naskaupi r. Canada 123 J3
Naṣr Egypt 90 C5
Naṣrānī, Jabal an mts Syria 85 C3
Naṣrīān Iran 88 B3
Nass r. Canada 120 D4
Nassau r. Australia 110 C2

▶Nassau Bahamas 133 E7
Capital of the Bahamas.

Nassau i. Cook Is 107 J3
Nassau U.S.A. 135 I2
Nassawadox U.S.A. 135 H5
Nasser, Lake resr Egypt 86 D5
Nässjö Sweden 45 I8
Nassuttooq inlet Greenland 119 M3
Nastapoca r. Canada 122 F2
Nastapoka Islands Canada 122 F2
Nasugbu Phil. 69 G4
Nasushiobara Japan 75 F5
Nasva Russia 42 F4
Nata Botswana 99 C6
Natal Brazil 143 K5
Natal Indon. 68 B6
Natal prov. S. Africa see KwaZulu-Natal
Natal Basin sea feature Indian Ocean 149 K8
Naṭanz Iran 88 C3
Natashquan Canada 123 J4
Natashquan r. Canada 123 J4
Natchez U.S.A. 131 F6
Natchitoches U.S.A. 131 E6
Nathalia Australia 112 B6
Nathia Gali Pak. 89 I3
Nati, Punta pt Spain 57 H3
Natillas Mex. 131 C7
National City U.S.A. 128 E5
Natitingou Benin 96 D3
Natividad, Isla i. Mex. 127 E8
Natividade Brazil 143 I6
Natkyizin Myanmar 70 B4
Natla r. Canada 120 D2
Natmauk Myanmar 70 A2
Nator Bangl. see Natore
Nátora Mex. 127 F7
Natore Bangl. 83 G4
Natori Japan 75 F5
Natron, Lake salt l. Tanz. 98 D4
Nattai National Park Australia 112 E5
Nattalin Myanmar 70 A3
Nattaung mt. Myanmar 70 B3
Na'tū Iran 89 F3
Natuashish Canada 123 J3
Natuna, Kepulauan is Indon. 71 D6
Natuna Besar i. Indon. 71 E6
Natural Bridges National Monument nat. park U.S.A. 129 H3
Naturaliste, Cape Australia 109 A8
Naturaliste Plateau sea feature Indian Ocean 149 P8
Naturita U.S.A. 129 I2
Nauchas Namibia 100 C2
Nau Co l. China 83 E2
Nauen Germany 53 M2
Naufragados, Ponta dos pt Brazil 145 A4
Naujoji Akmenė Lith. 45 M8
Naukh India 82 C4
Naukot Pak. 89 H5
Naumburg (Hessen) Germany 53 J3
Naumburg (Saale) Germany 53 L3
Naunglon Myanmar 70 B3
Naungpale Myanmar 70 B3
Naupada India 84 E2
Na'ūr Jordan 85 B4
Nauroz Kalat Pak. 89 G4
Naurskaya Russia 91 G2
Nauru i. Nauru 107 G2
Nauru country S. Pacific Ocean 107 G2
Naustdal Norway 45 D6
Nauta Peru 142 D4
Nautaca Uzbek. see Qarshi
Naute Dam Namibia 100 C4
Nava Mex. 131 C6
Navadwip India 83 G5
Navahrudak Belarus 45 N10
Navajo Lake U.S.A. 129 J3
Navajo Mountain U.S.A. 129 H3
Navalmoral de la Mata Spain 57 D4
Navalvillar de Pela Spain 57 D4
Navan Ireland 51 F4
Navangar India see Jamnagar
Navapolatsk Belarus 45 P9
Navarin, Mys c. Russia 65 S3
Navarra aut. comm. Spain 57 F2
Navarra, Comunidad Foral de aut. comm. Spain see Navarra
Navarre Australia 112 A6
Navarre aut. comm. Spain see Navarra
Navarro r. U.S.A. 128 B2
Navashino Russia 42 I5
Navasota U.S.A. 131 D6

▶Navassa Island terr. West Indies 137 I5
United States Unincorporated Territory.

Naver r. U.K. 50 E2
Näverede Sweden 44 I5
Navi Mumbai India 84 B2
Navlakhi India 82 B5
Navlya Russia 43 G5
Năvodari Romania 59 M2
Navoi Uzbek. see Navoiy
Navoiy Uzbek. 89 G1
Navojoa Mex. 127 F8
Navolato Mex. 136 C4
Návpaktos Greece see Nafpaktos
Návplion Greece see Nafplio
Navşar Turkey see Şemdinli
Navsari India 84 B1
Nawá Syria 85 C3
Nawabganj Bangl. 83 G4
Nawabshah Pak. 89 H5
Nawada India 83 F4
Nāwah Afgh. 89 G3
Nāwah-ye Gurz Afgh. 89 G3
Nawalgarh India 82 C4
Nawanshahr India 82 D3
Nawan Shehar India see Nawanshahr
Nawar, Dasht-i- depr. Afgh. see Nāwêr, Dasht-e
Nawarangpur India see Nabarangapur
Nāwêr, Dasht-e depr. Afgh. 89 G3
Nawngcho Myanmar see Nawnghkio
Nawnghkio Myanmar 70 B2
Nawng Hpa Myanmar 70 B2
Nawngleng Myanmar 70 B2
Nawoiy Uzbek. see Navoiy
Naxçıvan Azer. 91 G3
Naxos i. Greece 59 K6
Nayagarh India 84 E1
Nayak Afgh. 89 G3
Nayar Mex. 136 D4
Nāy Band, Kūh-e mt. Iran 88 E3
Nayong China 76 E3
Nayoro Japan 74 F3

▶Nay Pyi Taw Myanmar 70 B3
Capital of Myanmar.

Nazaré Brazil 145 D1
Nazareno Mex. 131 C7
Nazareth Israel see Naẓerat
Nazário Brazil 145 A2
Nazas Mex. 131 B7
Nazas r. Mex. 131 B7
Nazca Peru 142 D6
Nazca Ridge sea feature S. Pacific Ocean 151 O7
Naẓerat Israel 85 B3
Nāzīl Iran 89 F4
Nazilli Turkey 59 M6
Nazimabad Pak. 89 G5
Nazımiye Turkey 91 E3
Nazir Hat Bangl. 83 G5
Nazko Canada 120 F4
Nazran' Russia 91 G2
Nazrēt Eth. 98 D3
Nazwá Oman 88 E6
Ncojane Botswana 100 E2
N'dalatando Angola 99 B4
Ndélé Cent. Afr. Rep. 98 C3
Ndendé Gabon 98 B4
Ndende i. Solomon Is see Nendo
N'Djamena Chad see Ndjamena

▶Ndjamena Chad 97 E3
Capital of Chad.

Ndjouani i. Comoros see Ndzuani
Ndoi i. Fiji see Doi
Ndola Zambia 99 C5
Nduke i. Solomon Is see Kolombangara
Ndwedwe S. Africa 101 J5
Ndzuani i. Comoros 99 E5
Ne, Hon i. Vietnam 70 D3
Neabul Creek r. Australia 112 C1
Neagh, Lough l. U.K. 51 F3
Neah Bay U.S.A. 126 B2
Neale, Lake salt flat Australia 109 E6
Nea Liosia Greece 59 J5
Neapoli Greece 59 J6
Neapolis Italy see Naples
Nea Roda Greece 59 J4
Neath U.K. 49 D7
Neath r. U.K. 49 D7
Nebbi Uganda 98 D3
Nebine Creek r. Australia 112 C2
Neblina, Pico da mt. Brazil 142 E3
Nebo Australia 110 E4
Nebo, Mount U.S.A. 129 H2
Nebolchi Russia 42 G4
Nebraska state U.S.A. 130 C3
Nebraska City U.S.A. 130 E3
Nebrodi, Monti mts Sicily Italy 58 F6
Neches r. U.S.A. 131 E6
Nechisar National Park Eth. 98 D3
Nechranice, Vodní nádrž resr Czechia 53 N4
Neckar r. Germany 53 I5
Neckarsulm Germany 53 J5
Necker Island U.S.A. 150 J4
Necochea Arg. 144 E5
Nederland country Europe see Netherlands
Neder Rijn r. Neth. 52 F3
Nedlouc, Lac l. Canada 123 G2
Nedluk Lake Canada see Nedlouc, Lac
Nêdong China 83 G3
Nedre Soppero Sweden 44 L2
Nédroma Alg. 57 F6
Needle Mountain U.S.A. 126 F3
Needles U.S.A. 129 F4
Neemach India see Neemuch
Neemuch India 82 C4
Neenah U.S.A. 134 A1
Neepawa Canada 121 L5
Neergaard Lake Canada 119 J2
Neerijnen Neth. 52 F3
Neerpelt Belgium 52 F3
Neftçala Azer. 91 H3
Neftechala Azer. see Häsänabad
Neftechala Azer. see Neftçala
Neftegorsk Russia 43 K5
Neftegorsk (abandoned) Russia 74 F1
Neftekamsk Russia 41 Q4
Neftekumsk Russia 91 G1
Nefteyugansk Russia 64 I3
Neftezavodsk Turkm. see Seýdi
Neftezavodsk Turkm. see Seýdi
Nefyn U.K. 49 C6
Nefza Tunisia 58 C6
Negage Angola 99 B4
Negār Iran 88 E4
Negara Indon. 108 A2
Negēlē Eth. 98 D3
Negev des. Israel 85 B4
Negomane Moz. 99 D5
Negombo Sri Lanka 84 C5
Negotino Macedonia 59 J4
Negra, Cordillera mts Peru 142 C5
Negra, Punta pt Peru 142 B5
Negra, Serra mts Brazil 145 C2
Negrais, Cape Myanmar 70 A4
Négrine Alg. 58 B7
Negro r. Arg. 144 D6
Negro r. Mato Grosso do Sul Brazil 143 G7
Negro r. Paraná/Santa Catarina Brazil 145 A4
Negro r. S. America 142 G4
Negro, Cabo c. Morocco 57 D6
Negroponte i. Greece see Evvoia
Negros i. Phil. 69 G5
Negru Vodă, Podişul plat. Romania 59 M3
Nehbandān Iran 89 F4
Nehe China 74 B2
Neijiang China 76 E2
Neilburg Canada 121 I4
Neimenggu aut. reg. China see Nei Mongol Zizhiqu
Nei Mongol Zizhiqu aut. reg. China 74 A2
Neinstedt Germany 53 L3
Neiva Col. 142 C3
Neixiang China 77 F1
Nejanilini Lake Canada 121 L3
Nejd reg. Saudi Arabia see Najd
Nekā Iran 88 D2
Nek'emtē Eth. 98 D3
Nekrasovskoye Russia 42 I4
Nelang India 82 D3
Nelia Australia 110 C4
Nelidovo Russia 42 G4
Neligh U.S.A. 130 D3
Nel'kan Russia 65 P3
Nelligere India 84 C3
Nellore India 84 C3
Nelluz watercourse Turkey 85 D1
Nel'ma Russia 74 E3
Nelson Canada 120 G5
Nelson r. Canada 121 M3
Nelson N.Z. 113 D5
Nelson U.K. 48 E5
Nelson U.S.A. 129 G4
Nelson, Cape Australia 111 C8
Nelson, Cape P.N.G. 69 L8
Nelson, Estrecho strait Chile 144 A8
Nelson Bay Australia 112 F4
Nelson Forks Canada 120 F3
Nelsonia U.S.A. 135 H5
Nelson Lakes National Park N.Z. 113 D6
Nelson Reservoir U.S.A. 126 G2
Nelspruit S. Africa see Mbombela
Néma Mauritania 96 C3
Nema Russia 42 K4
Neman r. Belarus/Lith. see Nyoman
Neman Russia 45 M9
Nemausus France see Nîmes
Nemawar India 82 D5
Nemed Russia 42 L3
Nementcha, Monts des mts Alg. 58 B7
Nemetocenna France see Arras
Nemetskiy, Mys c. Russia 44 Q2
Nemirov Ukr. see Nemyriv
Nemiscau r. Canada 122 F4
Nemiscau, Lac l. Canada 122 F4
Nemor He r. China 74 B2
Nemours Alg. see Ghazaouet
Nemours France 56 F2
Nemrut Dağı mt. Turkey 91 F3
Nemunas r. Belarus/Lith. see Nyoman
Nemuro Japan 74 G4
Nemuro-kaikyō sea chan. Japan/Russia 74 G4
Nemyriv Ukr. 43 F6
Nenagh Ireland 51 D5
Nenana U.S.A. 118 D3
Nendo i. Solomon Is 107 G3
Nene r. U.K. 49 H6
Nenjiang China 74 B2
Nen Jiang r. China 74 B3
Neosho U.S.A. 131 E4
Nepal country Asia 83 E3
Nepalganj Nepal 83 E3
Nepean Canada 135 H1
Nepean, Point Australia 112 B7
Nephi U.S.A. 129 H2
Nephin hill Ireland 51 C3
Nephin Beg Range hills Ireland 51 C3
Nepisiguit r. Canada 123 I5
Nepoko r. Dem. Rep. Congo 98 C3
Nérac France 56 E4
Nerang Australia 112 F1
Nera Tso l. China 83 H3
Nerchinsk Russia 73 L2
Nerekhta Russia 42 I4
Néret, Lac l. Canada 123 H3
Neretva r. Bos. & Herz./Croatia 58 G3
Nêri Pünco l. China 83 G3
Neriquinha Angola 99 C5
Neris r. Lith. 45 M9
also known as Viliya (Belarus/Lithuania)
Nerl' r. Russia 42 H4
Nerópolis Brazil 145 A2
Neryungri Russia 65 N4
Nes Neth. 52 F1
Nes Norway 45 F6
Nes' Russia 42 J2
Nesbyen Norway 45 F6
Neskaupstaður Iceland 44 [inset 1]
Nesle France 52 C5
Nesna Norway 44 H3
Nesri India 84 B2
Ness r. U.K. 50 E3
Ness, Loch l. U.K. 50 E3
Ness City U.S.A. 130 D4
Nesse r. Germany 53 K4
Nesselrode, Mount Canada/U.S.A. 120 C3
Nestor Falls Canada 121 M5
Nestos r. Greece 59 K4
also known as Mesta
Nesvizh Belarus see Nyasvizh
Netanya Israel 85 B3
Netherlands country Europe 52 F2

▶Netherlands Antilles West Indies 137 K6
The Netherlands Antilles was dissolved into 5 contsituent dependencies of the Netherlands in Oct 2010.

Netphen Germany 53 I4
Netrakona Bangl. 83 G4
Netrokona Bangl. see Netrakona
Nettilling Lake Canada 119 K3
Neubrandenburg Germany 53 N1
Neuburg an der Donau Germany 53 L6
Neuchâtel Switz. 56 H3
Neuchâtel, Lac de l. Switz. 56 H3
Neuendettelsau Germany 53 K5
Neuenhaus Germany 52 G2

Neuenkirchen Germany 53 J1
Neuenkirchen (Oldenburg) Germany 53 I2
Neufchâteau Belgium 52 F5
Neufchâteau France 56 G2
Neufchâtel-en-Bray France 52 B5
Neufchâtel-Hardelot France 52 B4
Neuharlingersiel Germany 53 H1
Neuhausen Russia *see* Gur'yevsk
Neuhof Germany 53 J4
Neu Kaliß Germany 53 L1
Neukirchen Germany 53 J4
Neukirchen/Erzgebirge Germany 53 M4
Neukuhren Russia *see* Pionerskiy
Neum Bos. & Herz. 58 G3
Neumarkt in der Oberpfalz Germany 53 L5
Neumayer III *research station* Antarctica 152 B2
Neumünster Germany 47 L3
Neunburg vorm Wald Germany 53 M5
Neunkirchen Austria 47 P7
Neunkirchen Germany 53 H5
Neuquén Arg. 144 C5
Neuruppin Germany 53 M2
Neu Sandez Poland *see* Nowy Sącz
Neuse *r.* U.S.A. 133 E5
Neusiedler See *l.* Austria/Hungary 47 P7
Neusiedler See Seewinkel, Nationalpark *nat. park* Austria 47 P7
Neuss Germany 52 G3
Neustadt (Wied) Germany 53 H4
Neustadt am Rübenberge Germany 53 J2
Neustadt an der Aisch Germany 53 K5
Neustadt an der Hardt Germany *see* Neustadt an der Weinstraße
Neustadt an der Waldnaab Germany 53 M5
Neustadt an der Weinstraße Germany 53 I5
Neustadt bei Coburg Germany 53 L4
Neustadt-Glewe Germany 53 L1
Neustrelitz Germany 53 N1
Neutraubling Germany 53 M6
Neuville-lès-Dieppe France 52 B5
Neuwied Germany 53 H4
Neu Wulmstorf Germany 53 J1
Nevada *IA* U.S.A. 130 E3
Nevada *MO* U.S.A. 130 E4
Nevada *state* U.S.A. 126 D5
Nevada, Sierra *mts* Spain 57 E5
Nevada, Sierra *mts* U.S.A. 128 C1
Nevada City U.S.A. 128 C2
Nevado, Cerro *mt.* Arg. 144 C5
Nevado, Sierra del *mts* Arg. 144 C5
Nevasa India 84 B2
Nevatim Israel 85 B4
Nevdubstroy Russia *see* Kirovsk
Nevel' Russia 42 F4
Nevel'sk Russia 74 F3
Never Russia 74 B1
Nevers France 56 F3
Nevertire Australia 112 C3
Nevesinje Bos. & Herz. 58 H3
Nevinnomyssk Russia 91 F1
Nevşehir Turkey 90 D3
Nevskoye Russia 74 D3
New *r. CA* U.S.A. 129 F5
New *r. WV* U.S.A. 134 E5
Newala Tanz. 99 D5
New Albany *IN* U.S.A. 134 C4
New Albany *MS* U.S.A. 131 F5
New Amsterdam Guyana 143 G2
New Amsterdam U.S.A. *see* New York
Newark *DE* U.S.A. 135 H4
Newark *NJ* U.S.A. 135 H3
Newark *NY* U.S.A. 135 G2
Newark *OH* U.S.A. 134 D3
Newark Lake U.S.A. 129 F2
Newark Liberty *airport* U.S.A. 132 F3
Newark-on-Trent U.K. 49 G5
New Bedford U.S.A. 135 J3
Newberg U.S.A. 126 C3
New Berlin U.S.A. 135 H2
New Bern U.S.A. 133 E5
Newberry *IN* U.S.A. 134 B4
Newberry *MI* U.S.A. 132 C2
Newberry *SC* U.S.A. 133 D5
Newberry National Volcanic Monument *nat. park* U.S.A. 126 C4
Newberry Springs U.S.A. 128 E4
New Bethlehem U.S.A. 134 F3
Newbiggin-by-the-Sea U.K. 48 F3
New Bight Bahamas 133 F7
New Bloomfield U.S.A. 135 G3
Newboro Canada 135 G1
New Boston *OH* U.S.A. 134 D4
New Boston *TX* U.S.A. 131 E5
New Braunfels U.S.A. 131 D6
Newbridge Ireland 51 F4
New Britain *i.* P.N.G. 69 L8
New Britain U.S.A. 135 I3
New Britain Trench *sea feature* S. Pacific Ocean 150 G6
New Brunswick *prov.* Canada 123 I5
New Brunswick U.S.A. 135 H3
New Buffalo U.S.A. 134 B3
Newburgh Canada 135 G1
Newburgh U.K. 50 G3
Newburgh U.S.A. 135 H3
Newbury U.K. 49 F7
Newburyport U.S.A. 135 J2
Newby Bridge U.K. 48 E4

▶New Caledonia *terr.* S. Pacific Ocean 107 G4
French Overseas Collectivity.

New Caledonia Trough *sea feature* Tasman Sea 150 G7
New Carlisle Canada 123 I4
Newcastle Australia 112 E4
Newcastle Canada 135 F2
Newcastle Ireland 51 F4
Newcastle S. Africa 101 I4
Newcastle U.K. 51 G3
New Castle *CO* U.S.A. 129 J2
New Castle *IN* U.S.A. 134 C4
New Castle *KY* U.S.A. 134 C4
New Castle *PA* U.S.A. 134 E3
Newcastle *UT* U.S.A. 129 G3
New Castle *VA* U.S.A. 134 E5
Newcastle *WY* U.S.A. 126 G4
Newcastle Emlyn U.K. 49 C6
Newcastle-under-Lyme U.K. 49 E5
Newcastle upon Tyne U.K. 48 F4
Newcastle Waters Australia 108 F4
Newcastle West Ireland 51 C5
Newchwang China *see* Yingkou
New City U.S.A. 135 I3
Newcomb U.S.A. 129 I3
New Concord U.S.A. 134 E4
New Cumberland U.S.A. 134 E3
New Cumnock U.K. 50 E5
New Deer U.K. 50 G3

▶New Delhi India 82 D3
Capital of India.

New Don Pedro Reservoir U.S.A. 128 C3
Newell U.S.A. 130 C2
Newell, Lake *salt flat* Australia 109 D6
Newell, Lake Canada 121 I5
New England National Park Australia 112 F3
New England Range *mts* Australia 112 E3
New England Seamounts *sea feature* N. Atlantic Ocean 148 E3
Newenham, Cape U.S.A. 118 B4
Newent U.K. 49 E7
New Era U.S.A. 134 B2
Newfane *NY* U.S.A. 135 F2
Newfane *VT* U.S.A. 135 I2
New Forest National Park *nat. park* U.K. 49 F8
Newfoundland *i.* Canada 123 K4
Newfoundland *prov.* Canada *see* Newfoundland and Labrador
Newfoundland and Labrador *prov.* Canada 123 K3
Newfoundland Evaporation Basin *salt l.* U.S.A. 129 G1
New Galloway U.K. 50 E5
New Georgia *i.* Solomon Is 107 F2
New Georgia Islands Solomon Is 107 F2
New Georgia Sound *sea chan.* Solomon Is 107 F2
New Glasgow Canada 123 J5

▶New Guinea *i.* Indon./P.N.G. 69 K8
Largest island in Oceania and 2nd in the world.

New Halfa Sudan 86 E6
New Hampshire *state* U.S.A. 135 J1
New Hampton U.S.A. 130 E3
New Hanover *i.* P.N.G. 106 F2
Newhaven U.K. 49 H8
New Haven *CT* U.S.A. 135 I3
New Haven *IN* U.S.A. 134 C3
New Haven *WV* U.S.A. 134 E4
New Hebrides *country* S. Pacific Ocean *see* Vanuatu
New Hebrides Trench *sea feature* S. Pacific Ocean 150 H7
New Holland *country* Oceania *see* Australia
New Holstein U.S.A. 134 A2
New Iberia U.S.A. 131 F6
Newinn Ireland 51 E5
New Ireland *i.* P.N.G. 106 F2
New Jersey *state* U.S.A. 135 H4
New Kensington U.S.A. 134 F3
New Kent U.S.A. 135 G5
Newkirk U.S.A. 131 D4
New Lanark U.K. 50 F5
Newland Range *hills* Australia 109 C7
New Lexington U.S.A. 134 D4
New Liskeard Canada 122 F5
New London *CT* U.S.A. 135 I3
New London *MO* U.S.A. 130 F4
New Madrid U.S.A. 131 F4
Newman Australia 109 B5
Newman U.S.A. 128 C3
Newmarket Canada 134 F1
Newmarket Ireland 51 C5
Newmarket U.K. 49 H6
New Market U.S.A. 135 F4
Newmarket-on-Fergus Ireland 51 D5
New Martinsville U.S.A. 134 E4
New Meadows U.S.A. 126 D3
New Mexico *state* U.S.A. 127 G6
New Miami U.S.A. 134 C4
New Milford U.S.A. 135 H3
Newnan U.S.A. 133 C5
New Orleans U.S.A. 131 F6
New Paris *IN* U.S.A. 134 C3
New Paris *OH* U.S.A. 134 C4
New Philadelphia U.S.A. 134 E3
New Pitsligo U.K. 50 G3
New Plymouth N.Z. 113 E4
Newport *Mayo* Ireland 51 C4
Newport *Tipperary* Ireland 51 D5
Newport *England* U.K. 49 E6
Newport *England* U.K. 49 F8
Newport *Wales* U.K. 49 D7
Newport *AR* U.S.A. 131 F5
Newport *IN* U.S.A. 134 B4
Newport *KY* U.S.A. 134 C4
Newport *MI* U.S.A. 134 D3
Newport *NH* U.S.A. 135 I2
Newport *NJ* U.S.A. 135 H4
Newport *OR* U.S.A. 126 B3
Newport *RI* U.S.A. 135 J3
Newport *VT* U.S.A. 135 I1
Newport *WA* U.S.A. 126 D2
Newport Beach U.S.A. 128 E5
Newport News U.S.A. 135 G5
Newport Pagnell U.K. 49 G6
New Port Richey U.S.A. 133 D6
New Providence *i.* Bahamas 133 E7
Newquay U.K. 49 B8
New Roads U.S.A. 131 F6
New Rochelle U.S.A. 135 I3
New Rockford U.S.A. 130 D2
New Romney U.K. 49 H8
New Ross Ireland 51 F5
Newry Australia 108 E4
Newry U.K. 51 F3
New Siberia Islands Russia 65 P2
New Smyrna Beach U.S.A. 133 D6
New South Wales *state* Australia 112 C4
New Stanton U.S.A. 134 F3
Newton U.K. 48 E5
Newton *GA* U.S.A. 133 C6
Newton *IA* U.S.A. 130 E3
Newton *IL* U.S.A. 130 F4
Newton *KS* U.S.A. 130 D4
Newton *MA* U.S.A. 135 J2
Newton *MS* U.S.A. 131 F5
Newton *NC* U.S.A. 132 D5
Newton *NJ* U.S.A. 135 H3
Newton *TX* U.S.A. 131 E6
Newton Abbot U.K. 49 D8
Newton Mearns U.K. 50 E5
Newton Stewart U.K. 50 E6
Newtown Ireland 51 D5
Newtown *England* U.K. 49 E6
Newtown *Wales* U.K. 49 D6
Newtown U.S.A. 134 C4
New Town U.S.A. 130 C1
Newtownabbey U.K. 51 G3
Newtownards U.K. 51 G3
Newtownbarry Ireland *see* Bunclody
Newtownbutler U.K. 51 E3
Newtown Mount Kennedy Ireland 51 F4
Newtown St Boswells U.K. 50 G5
Newtownstewart U.K. 51 E3
New Ulm U.S.A. 130 E2
Newville U.S.A. 135 G3
New World Island Canada 123 L4

▶New York U.S.A. 135 I3
2nd most populous city in North America and 5th in the world.

New York *state* U.S.A. 135 H2

▶New Zealand *country* Oceania 113 D5
3rd largest and 3rd most populated country in Oceania.

Nexø Denmark 45 I9
Neya Russia 42 I4
Ney Bīd Iran 88 E4
Neyrīz Iran 88 D4
Neyshābūr Iran 88 E2
Nezhin Ukr. *see* Nizhyn
Nezperce U.S.A. 126 D3
Ngabé Congo 98 B4
Nga Chong, Khao *mt.* Myanmar/Thai. 70 B4
Ngagahtawng Myanmar 76 C3
Ngagau *mt.* Tanz. 99 D4
Ngalu Indon. 108 C2
Ngamring China 83 F3
Ngangla Ringco *salt l.* China 83 E3
Nganglong Kangri *mt.* China 82 E2
Nganglong Kangri *mts* China 82 E2
Ngangzê Co *salt l.* China 83 F3
Ngangzê Shan *mts* China 83 F3
Ngân Sơn Vietnam 70 D2
Ngaoundal Cameroon 96 E4
Ngaoundéré Cameroon 97 E4
Ngape Myanmar 70 A2
Ngaputaw Myanmar 70 A3
Ngarrab China *see* Gyaca
Ngathainggyaung Myanmar 70 A3
Ngau *i.* Fiji *see* Gau
Ngawa China *see* Aba
Ngazidja *i.* Comoros 99 E5
Ngcobo S. Africa 101 H6
Ngeaur *i.* Palau *see* Angaur
Ngeruangel *i.* Palau 69 I5
Ngga Pulu *mt.* Indon. *see* Jaya, Puncak
Ngiap *r.* Laos 70 C3
Ngilmina Indon. 108 D2
Ngiva Angola *see* Ondjiva
Ngo Congo 98 B4
Ngoako Ramalepe S. Africa *see* Modjadjiskloof
Ngoin, Co *salt l.* China 83 G3
Ngoko *r.* Cameroon/Congo 97 E4
Ngola Shankou *pass* China 76 C1
Ngom Qu *r.* China *see* Ji Qu
Ngoqumaima China 83 F2
Ngoring China 76 C1
Ngoring Hu *l.* China 76 C1
Ngourti Niger 96 E3
Ngqamakhwe S. Africa 101 H7
Nguigmi Niger 96 E3
Nguiu Australia 108 E2
Ngükang China 76 B2
Ngukurr Australia 108 F3
Ngulu *atoll* Micronesia 69 J5
Ngum, Ang Kep Nam Laos 70 C3
Ngunza Angola *see* Sumbe
Ngunza-Kabolu Angola *see* Sumbe
Nguru Nigeria 96 E3
Ngwaketse *admin. dist.* Botswana *see* Southern
Ngwane *country* Africa *see* Swaziland
Ngwathe S. Africa 101 H4
Ngwavuma *r.* S. Africa/Swaziland 101 K4
Ngwelezana S. Africa 101 J5
Nhachengue Moz. 101 L2
Nhamalabué Moz. 99 D5
Nha Trang Vietnam 71 E4
Nhecolândia Brazil 143 G7
Nhill Australia 111 C8
Nhlangano Swaziland 101 J4
Nho Quan Vietnam 70 D2
Nhow *i.* Fiji *see* Gau
Nhulunbuy Australia 110 B2
Niacam Canada 121 J4
Niafounké Mali 96 C3
Niagara U.S.A. 132 C2
Niagara Falls Canada 134 F2
Niagara Falls U.S.A. 134 F2
Niagara-on-the-Lake Canada 134 F2
Niagzu China 82 D2
Niah *Sarawak* Malaysia 68 E6
Niakaramandougou Côte d'Ivoire 96 C4

▶Niamey Niger 96 D3
Capital of Niger.

Nīām Kand Iran 88 E5
Niampak Indon. 69 H6
Niangara Dem. Rep. Congo 98 C3
Niangay, Lac *l.* Mali 96 C3
Nianzishan China 74 A3
Nias *i.* Indon. 71 B7
Niassa, Lago *l.* Africa *see* Nyasa, Lake
Niaur *i.* Palau *see* Angaur
Nīāzābād Iran 89 F3
Nibil Well Australia 108 D5
Nīca Latvia 45 L8

▶Nicaragua *country* Central America 137 G6
4th largest country in North America.

Nicaragua, Lake *l.* Nicaragua 137 G6
Nicastro Italy 58 G5
Nice France 56 H5
Nice U.S.A. 128 B2
Nicephorium Syria *see* Ar Raqqah
Niceville U.S.A. 133 C6
Nichicun, Lac *l.* Canada 123 H3
Nicholas Channel Bahamas/Cuba 133 D8
Nicholasville U.S.A. 134 C5
Nichols U.S.A. 134 A1
Nicholson *r.* Australia 110 B3
Nicholson Lake Canada 121 K2
Nicholson Range *hills* Australia 109 B6
Nicholville U.S.A. 135 H1
Nicobar Islands India 71 A5
Nicolaus U.S.A. 128 C2
Nicomedia Turkey *see* İzmit

▶Nicosia Cyprus 85 A2
Capital of Cyprus.

Nicoya, Península de *pen.* Costa Rica 137 G7
Nida Lith. 45 L9
Nidagunda India 84 C2
Nidd *r.* U.K. 48 F4
Nidda Germany 53 J4
Nidder *r.* Germany 53 I4
Nidzica Poland 47 R4
Niebüll Germany 47 L3
Nied *r.* France 52 G5
Niederanven Lux. 52 G5
Niederaula Germany 53 J4
Niedere Tauern *mts* Austria 47 N7
Niedersachsen *land* Germany 53 I2
Niedersächsisches Wattenmeer, Nationalpark *nat. park* Germany 52 G1
Niefang Equat. Guinea 96 E4
Niellé Côte d'Ivoire 96 C3
Nienburg (Weser) Germany 53 J2
Niers *r.* Germany 52 F3
Nierstein Germany 53 I5
Nieuwe Niedorp Neth. 52 E2
Nieuwerkerk aan den IJssel Neth. 52 E3
Nieuw Nickerie Suriname 143 G2
Nieuwolda Neth. 52 G1
Nieuwoudtville S. Africa 100 D6
Nieuwpoort Belgium 52 C3
Nieuw-Vossemeer Neth. 52 E3
Niğde Turkey 90 D3
Niger *country* Africa 96 D3

▶Niger *r.* Africa 96 D4
3rd longest river in Africa.

Niger, Mouths of the Nigeria 96 D4
Niger Cone *sea feature* S. Atlantic Ocean 148 I5

▶Nigeria *country* Africa 96 D4
Most populous country in Africa and 7th in the world.

Nighthawk Lake Canada 122 E4
Nigrita Greece 59 J4
Nihing Pak. 89 G4
Nihon *country* Asia *see* Japan
Niigata Japan 75 E5
Niihama Japan 75 D6
Ni'ihau *i.* U.S.A. 127 [inset]
Nii-jima *i.* Japan 75 E6
Niimi Japan 75 D6
Niitsu Japan 75 E5
Nijil, Wādī *watercourse* Jordan 85 B4
Nijkerk Neth. 52 F2
Nijmegen Neth. 52 F3
Nijverdal Neth. 52 G2
Nikel' Russia 44 Q2
Nikki Benin 96 D4
Nikkō Japan 75 E5
Nikkō Kokuritsu-kōen *nat. park* Japan 75 E5
Nikolayev Ukr. *see* Mykolayiv
Nikolayevka Russia 43 J5
Nikolayevsk Russia 43 J6
Nikolayevskiy Russia *see* Nikolayevsk
Nikolayevsk-na-Amure Russia 74 F1
Nikol'sk Russia 42 J4
Nikol'skiy Kazakh. *see* Satpayev
Nikol'skoye *Kamchatskiy Kray* Russia 65 R4
Nikol'skoye *Vologod. Obl.* Russia *see* Sheksna
Nikopol' Ukr. 43 G7
Niksar Turkey 90 E2
Nīkshahr Iran 89 F5
Nikšić Montenegro 58 H3
Nīkū Jahān Iran 89 F5
Nikumaroro *atoll* Kiribati 107 I2
Nikunau *i.* Kiribati 107 H2
Nīl, Bahr el *r.* Africa *see* Nile
Nilagiri India 83 F5
Niland U.S.A. 129 F5
Nilande Atoll Maldives *see* Nilandhe Atholhu
Nilandhe Atholhu Maldives 81 D11
Nilandhe Atoll Maldives *see* Nilandhe Atholhu
Nilang India *see* Nelang
Nilanga India 84 C2
Nilaveli Sri Lanka 84 D4

▶Nile *r.* Africa 90 C5
Longest river in Africa and the world.

Niles *MI* U.S.A. 134 B3
Niles *OH* U.S.A. 134 E3
Nilgiri Hills India 84 C4
Nīlī Afgh. 89 G3
Nīl Kōtal Afgh. 89 G3
Nilphamari Bangl. 83 G4
Nilsiä Fin. 44 P5
Nimach India *see* Neemuch
Niman *r.* Russia 74 D2
Nimba, Mont *mts* Africa *see* Richard-Molard, Mont
Nimbal India 84 B2
Nimberra Well Australia 109 C5
Nimelen *r.* Russia 74 E1
Nîmes France 56 G5
Nimmitabel Australia 111 E8
Nimrod Glacier Antarctica 152 H1
Nimu India 82 D2
Nimule South Sudan 97 G4
Nimwegen Neth. *see* Nijmegen
Nindigully Australia 112 D2
Nine Degree Channel India 84 B4
Nine Islands P.N.G. *see* Kilinailau Islands
Ninepin Group *is* H.K. China 77 [inset]
Ninetyeast Ridge *sea feature* Indian Ocean 149 N8
Ninety Mile Beach Australia 112 C7
Ninety Mile Beach N.Z. 113 D2
Nineveh U.S.A. 135 H2
Ningaloo Coast *tourist site* Australia 109 A5
Ning'an China 74 C3
Ningbo China 77 I2
Ningde China 77 H3
Ning'er China 76 D4
Ningguo China 77 H2
Ninghai China 77 I2
Ninghsia Hui Autonomous Region *aut. reg.* China *see* Ningxia Huizu Zizhiqu
Ninghua China 77 H3
Ningjiang China *see* Songyuan
Ningjing Shan *mts* China 76 C2
Ninglang China 76 D3
Ningming China 76 E4
Ningnan China 76 D3
Ningqiang China 76 E1
Ningwu China 73 K5
Ningxia *aut. reg.* China *see* Ningxia Huizu Zizhiqu
Ningxia Huizu Zizhiqu *aut. reg.* China 76 E1
Ningxian China 73 J5
Ningxiang China 77 G2
Ningzhou China *see* Huaning
Ninh Binh Vietnam 70 D2
Ninh Hoa Vietnam 71 E4
Ninigo Group *atolls* P.N.G. 69 K7
Ninnis Glacier Antarctica 152 G2
Ninnis Glacier Tongue Antarctica 152 H2
Ninohe Japan 75 F4
Niobrara *r.* U.S.A. 130 D3
Niokolo Koba, Parc National du *nat. park* Senegal 96 B3
Niono Mali 96 C3
Nioro Mali 96 C3
Niort France 56 D3
Nipani India 84 B2
Nipawin Canada 121 J4
Niphad India 84 B1
Nipigon Canada 119 J5
Nipigon, Lake Canada 119 J5
Nipishish Lake Canada 123 J3
Nipissing, Lake Canada 122 F5
Nippon *country* Asia *see* Japan
Nippon Hai *sea* N. Pacific Ocean *see* Japan, Sea of
Nipton U.S.A. 129 F4
Niquelândia Brazil 145 A1
Nīr Iran 88 B2
Nir Iran 88 D4
Nira *r.* India 84 B2
Nirji China 74 B2
Nirmal India 84 C2
Nirmali India 83 F4
Nirmal Range *hills* India 84 C2
Niš Serbia 59 I3
Nisa Port. 57 C4
Nisarpur India 84 B1
Niscemi *Sicily* Italy 58 F6
Nīshāpūr Iran *see* Neyshābūr
Nishino-shima *vol.* Japan 75 F8
Nishi-Sonogi-hantō *pen.* Japan 75 C6
Nisibis Turkey *see* Nusaybin
Nísiros *i.* Greece *see* Nisyros
Niskibi *r.* Canada 121 N3
Nisling *r.* Canada 120 B2
Nispen Neth. 52 E3
Nissan *r.* Sweden 45 H8
Nistru *r.* Ukr. *see* Dniester
Nisutlin *r.* Canada 120 C2
Nisyros *i.* Greece 59 L6
Niţā Saudi Arabia 88 C5
Nitchequon (abandoned) Canada 123 H3
Nitendi *i.* Solomon Is *see* Nendo
Niterói Brazil 145 C3
Nith *r.* U.K. 50 F5
Nitibe East Timor 108 D2
Niti Pass China/India 82 D3
Niti Shankou *pass* China/India *see* Niti Pass
Nitmiluk National Park Australia 108 F3
Nitra Slovakia 47 Q6
Nitro U.S.A. 134 E4
Niuafo'ou *i.* Tonga 107 I3
Niuatoputopu *i.* Tonga 107 I3

▶Niue *terr.* S. Pacific Ocean 107 J3
Self-governing New Zealand Overseas Territory.

Niujing China *see* Binchuan
Niulakita *i.* Tuvalu 107 H3
Niutao *i.* Tuvalu 107 H2
Niutoushan China 77 H2
Nivala Fin. 44 N5
Nive *watercourse* Australia 110 D5
Nivelles Belgium 52 E4
Niwai India 82 C4
Niwas India 82 E5
Nixia China *see* Sêrxü
Nixon U.S.A. 128 D2
Niya China *see* Minfeng
Niya He *r.* China 83 E1
Nizamabad India 84 C2
Nizam Sagar *l.* India 84 C2
Nizhnedevitsk Russia 43 H6
Nizhnekamsk Russia 42 K5
Nizhnekamskoye Vodokhranilishche *resr* Russia 41 Q4
Nizhnekolymsk Russia 65 R3
Nizhnetambovskoye Russia 74 E2
Nizhneudinsk Russia 72 H2
Nizhnevartovsk Russia 64 I3
Nizhnevolzhsk Russia *see* Narimanov
Nizhneyansk Russia 65 O2
Nizhniy Baskunchak Russia 43 J6
Nizhniye Kresty Russia *see* Cherskiy
Nizhniy Lomov Russia 43 I5
Nizhniy Novgorod Russia 42 I4
Nizhniy Odes Russia 42 L3
Nizhniy Pyandzh Tajik. *see* Panji Poyon
Nizhniy Tagil Russia 41 R4
Nizhnyaya Mola Russia 42 J2
Nizhnyaya Omra Russia 42 L3
Nizhnyaya Pirenga, Ozero *l.* Russia 44 R3
Nizhnyaya Tunguska *r.* Russia 64 J3
Nizhnyaya Tura Russia 41 R4
Nizhyn Ukr. 43 F6
Nizina *r.* U.S.A. 120 A2
Nizip Turkey 85 C1
Nízke Tatry, Národný park *nat. park* Slovakia 47 Q6
Nizwā Oman *see* Nazwá
Nizza France *see* Nice
Njallavarri *mt.* Norway 44 L2
Njavve Sweden 44 K3
Njombe Tanz. 99 D4
Njurundabommen Sweden 44 J5
Nkambe Cameroon 96 E4
Nkandla S. Africa 101 J5
Nkawkaw Ghana 96 C4
Nkhata Bay Malawi 99 D5
Nkhotakota Malawi 99 D5
Nkondwe Tanz. 99 D4
Nkongsamba Cameroon 96 D4
N'Kouilal, Tizi *pass* Alg. 57 I5
Nkululeko S. Africa 101 H6
Nkurenkuru Namibia 99 B5
Nkwenkwezi S. Africa 101 H7
Noakhali Bangl. 83 G5
Noatak *r.* U.S.A. 118 B3
Nobber Ireland 51 F4
Nobeoka Japan 75 C6
Noblesville U.S.A. 134 B3
Noboribetsu Japan 74 F4
Noccundra Australia 111 C5
Nockatunga Australia 111 C5
Nocona U.S.A. 131 D5
Noel Kempff Mercado, Parque Nacional *nat. park* Bol. 142 F6
Noelville Canada 122 E5
Nogales Mex. 127 F7
Nogales U.S.A. 127 F7
Nōgata Japan 75 C6
Nogent-le-Rotrou France 56 E2
Nogent-sur-Oise France 52 C5
Noginsk Russia 42 H5
Nogliki Russia 74 F2
Nogoa *r.* Australia 110 E4
Nohar India 82 C3
Noheji Japan 74 F4
Nohfelden Germany 52 H5
Noida India 82 D3
Noirmoutier, Île de *i.* France 56 C3
Noirmoutier-en-l'Île France 56 C3
Noisseville France 52 G5
Nokhowch, Kūh-e *mt.* Iran 89 F5
Nōkis Uzbek. *see* Nukus
Nok Kundi Pak. 89 F4
Nokomis Canada 121 J5
Nokomis Lake Canada 121 K3
Nokou Chad 97 E3
Nokrek Peak India 83 G4
Nola Cent. Afr. Rep. 98 B3
Nolin River Lake U.S.A. 134 B5
Nolinsk Russia 42 K4
No Mans Land *i.* U.S.A. 135 J3
Nome U.S.A. 118 B3
Nomgon Mongolia 72 J4
Nomhon China 80 I4
Nomoi Islands Micronesia *see* Mortlock Islands
Nomonde S. Africa 101 H6
Nomzha Russia 42 I4
Nonacho Lake Canada 121 I2
Nondweni S. Africa 101 J5
Nong'an China 74 B3
Nonghui China *see* Guang'an
Nong Khai Thai. 70 C3
Nongoma S. Africa 101 J4
Nongstoin India 83 G4
Nonidas Namibia 100 B2
Nonni *r.* China *see* Nen Jiang
Nonning Australia 111 B7
Nonnweiler Germany 52 G5
Nonoava Mex. 127 G8
Nonouti *atoll* Kiribati 107 H2
Nonthaburi Thai. 71 C4
Nonzwakazi S. Africa 100 G6
Noolyeanna Lake *salt flat* Australia 111 B5
Noondie, Lake *salt flat* Australia 109 B7
Noonkanbah Australia 108 D4
Noonthorangee Range *hills* Australia 111 C6
Noorama Creek *watercourse* Australia 112 B1
Noordbeveland *i.* Neth. 52 D3
Noorderhaaks *i.* Neth. 52 E2
Noordoost Polder Neth. 52 F2
Noordwijk Neth. 52 E2
Nootka Island Canada 120 E5
Nora *r.* Russia 74 C2
Norak Tajik. 89 H2
Norak, Obanbori *resr* Tajik. 89 H2
Norala Phil. 69 G5
Noranda Canada 122 F4
Nor-Bayazet Armenia *see* Gavarr
Norberg Sweden 45 I6
Nord Greenland *see* Station Nord
Nord, Canal du France 52 D4
Nordaustlandet *i.* Svalbard 64 D2
Nordegg Canada 120 G4
Norden Germany 53 H1
Nordenshel'da, Arkhipelag *is* Russia 64 K2
Nordenskjold Archipelago *is* Russia *see* Nordenshel'da, Arkhipelag
Norderney Germany 53 H1
Norderstedt Germany 53 K1
Nordfjordeid Norway 44 D6
Nordfold Norway 44 I3

Nordfriesische Inseln Germany see North Frisian Islands
Nordhausen Germany 53 K3
Nordholz Germany 53 I1
Nordhorn Germany 52 H2
Nord Kap c. Iceland see Horn
Nordkapp c. Norway see North Cape
Nordkinnhalvøya i. Norway 44 O1
Nordkjosbotn Norway 44 K2
Nordli Norway 44 H4
Nördlingen Germany 53 K6
Nordmaling Sweden 44 K5
Nord-og Østgrønland, Nationalparken i nat. park Greenland 119 O2
▶Nordostrundingen c. Greenland 153 I1
Most easterly point of North America.
Nord-Ostsee-Kanal Germany see Kiel Canal
Norðoyar i. Faroe Is 40 E3
Nord-Pas-de-Calais admin. reg. France see Nord-Pas-de-Calais et Picardie
Nord-Pas-de-Calais et Picardie admin. reg. France 52 C5
Nord-Pas de Calais Mining Basin tourist site France 52 D4
Nordpfälzer Bergland reg. Germany 53 H5
Nordre Strømfjord inlet Greenland see Nassuttooq
Nordrhein-Westfalen land Germany 53 H3
Nordvik Russia 65 M2
Nore r. Ireland 51 F5
Nore, Pic de mt. France 56 F5
Noreg country Europe see Norway
Norfolk NE U.S.A. 130 D3
Norfolk NY U.S.A. 135 H1
Norfolk VA U.S.A. 135 G5
▶Norfolk Island terr. S. Pacific Ocean 107 G4
Australian External Territory.
Norfolk Island Ridge sea feature Tasman Sea 150 H7
Norfork Lake U.S.A. 131 E4
Norg Neth. 52 G1
Norge country Europe see Norway
Norheimsund Norway 45 E6
Noril'sk Russia 64 J3
Norkyung China 83 G3
Norland Canada 135 F1
Norma Co l. China 83 G2
Norman U.S.A. 131 D5
Norman, Lake resr U.S.A. 132 D5
Normanby Island P.N.G. 110 E1
Normandes, Îles is English Chan. see Channel Islands
Normandia Brazil 143 G3
Normandie admin. reg. France 52 B5
Normandie reg. France see Normandy
Normandie, Collines de hills France 56 D2
Normandy reg. France 56 D2
Normanton Australia 110 C3
Norquay Canada 121 K5
Ñorquinco Arg. 144 B6
Norra Kvarken strait Fin./Sweden 44 L5
Norra Storfjället mts Sweden 44 I4
Norrent-Fontes France 52 C4
Norris Lake U.S.A. 134 D5
Norristown U.S.A. 135 H3
Norrköping Sweden 45 J7
Norrtälje Sweden 45 K7
Norseman Australia 109 C8
Norsjö Sweden 44 K4
Norsk Russia 74 C1
Norsup Vanuatu 107 G3
Norte, Punta pt Arg. 144 E5
Norte, Serra do hills Brazil 143 G6
Nortelândia Brazil 143 G6
Nörten-Hardenberg Germany 53 J3
North, Cape Antarctica 152 H2
North, Cape Canada 123 J5
Northallerton U.K. 48 F4
Northam Australia 109 B7
Northampton Australia 106 B4
Northampton U.K. 49 G6
Northampton MA U.S.A. 135 I2
Northampton PA U.S.A. 135 H3
North Andaman i. India 71 A4
North Anna r. U.S.A. 135 G5
North Arm b. Canada 120 H2
North Atlantic Ocean Atlantic Ocean 125 O4
North Augusta U.S.A. 133 D5
North Aulatsivik Island Canada 123 J2
North Australian Basin sea feature Indian Ocean 149 P6
North Baltimore U.S.A. 134 D3
North Battleford Canada 121 I4
North Bay Canada 122 F5
North Belcher Islands Canada 122 F2
North Berwick U.K. 50 G4
North Berwick U.S.A. 135 J2
North Bourke Australia 112 B3
North Branch U.S.A. 130 E2
North Caicos i. Turks and Caicos Is 133 G8
North Canton U.S.A. 134 E3
North Cape Canada 123 I5
North Cape Norway 44 N1
North Cape N.Z. 113 D2
North Cape U.S.A. 118 A4
North Caribou Lake Canada 121 N4
North Carolina state U.S.A. 132 E4
North Cascades National Park U.S.A. 126 C2
North Channel lake channel Canada 122 E5
North Channel U.K. 51 G2
North Charleston U.S.A. 133 E5
North Chicago U.S.A. 134 B2
Northcliffe Glacier Antarctica 152 F2
North Collins U.S.A. 135 F2
North Concho r. U.S.A. 131 C6
North Conway U.S.A. 135 J1
North Dakota state U.S.A. 130 C2
North Downs hills U.K. 49 G7
North East U.S.A. 134 F2
Northeast Foreland c. Greenland see Nordostrundingen
North-East Frontier Agency state India see Arunachal Pradesh
Northeast Pacific Basin sea feature N. Pacific Ocean 151 J4
Northeast Point Bahamas 133 F8
Northeast Providence Channel Bahamas 133 E7
North Edwards U.S.A. 128 E4
Northeim Germany 53 J3
Northern prov. S. Africa see Limpopo
Northern Areas admin. div. Pak. see Gilgit-Baltistan
Northern Cape prov. S. Africa 100 D5
Northern Cyprus disp. terr. Asia 85 A2
Northern Donets r. Russia/Ukr. 43 I7
also known as Severskiy Donets, Sivers'kyy Donets'
Northern Dvina r. Russia see Severnaya Dvina
Northern Indian Lake Canada 121 L3
Northern Ireland prov. U.K. 51 F3
Northern Lau Group is Fiji 107 I3
Northern Light Lake Canada 122 C4
▶Northern Mariana Islands terr. N. Pacific Ocean 69 K3
United States Commonwealth.
Northern Rhodesia country Africa see Zambia
Northern Sporades is Greece see Voreies Sporades
Northern Territory admin. div. Australia 106 D3
Northern Transvaal prov. S. Africa see Limpopo
North Esk r. U.K. 50 G4
Northfield MN U.S.A. 130 E2
Northfield VT U.S.A. 135 I1
North Foreland c. U.K. 49 I7
North Fork U.S.A. 128 D3
North Fork Pass Canada 118 E3
North French r. Canada 122 E4
North Frisian Islands Germany 47 L3
North Geomagnetic Pole Arctic Ocean 119 K2
North Grimston U.K. 48 G4
North Haven U.S.A. 135 I3
North Head hd N.Z. 113 E3
North Henik Lake Canada 121 L2
North Hero U.S.A. 135 I1
North Horr Kenya 98 D3
▶North Island N.Z. 113 D4
3rd largest island in Oceania.
North Jadito Canyon gorge U.S.A. 129 H4
North Judson U.S.A. 134 B3
North Kingsville U.S.A. 134 E3
North Knife r. Canada 121 M3
North Knife Lake Canada 121 L3
North Korea country Asia 75 B5
North Lakhimpur India 83 H4
North Las Vegas U.S.A. 129 F3
North Little Rock U.S.A. 131 E5
North Loup r. U.S.A. 130 D3
North Luangwa National Park Zambia 99 D5
North Magnetic Pole Canada 153 B1
North Malosmadulu Atoll Maldives see Maalhosmadulu Uthuruburi
North Mam Peak U.S.A. 129 J2
North Muskegon U.S.A. 134 B2
North Palisade mt. U.S.A. 128 D3
North Perry U.S.A. 134 E3
North Platte U.S.A. 130 C3
North Platte r. U.S.A. 130 C3
North Pole Arctic Ocean 153 I1
North Port U.S.A. 133 D7
North Reef Island India 71 A4
North Rhine-Westphalia land Germany see Nordrhein-Westfalen
North Rim U.S.A. 129 G3
North Rona i. U.K. see Rona
North Ronaldsay i. U.K. 50 G1
North Ronaldsay Firth sea chan. U.K. 50 G1
North Saskatchewan r. Canada 121 J4
North Schell Peak U.S.A. 129 F2
North Sea Europe 46 H2
North Seal r. Canada 121 L3
North Sentinel Island India 71 A5
North Shields U.K. 48 F3
North Shoal Lake Canada 121 L5
North Shoshone Peak U.S.A. 128 E2
North Siberian Lowland Russia 64 L2
North Sinai governorate Egypt see Shamāl Sīnā'
North Slope plain U.S.A. 118 D3
North Somercotes U.K. 48 H5
North Spirit Lake Canada 121 M4
North Stradbroke Island Australia 112 F1
North Sunderland U.K. 48 F3
North Syracuse U.S.A. 135 G2
North Taranaki Bight b. N.Z. 113 E4
North Terre Haute U.S.A. 134 B4
Northton U.K. 50 B3
North Tonawanda U.S.A. 135 F2
North Trap reef N.Z. 113 A8
North Troy U.S.A. 135 I1
North Tyne r. U.K. 48 E4
North Uist i. U.K. 50 B3
Northumberland National Park U.K. 48 E3
Northumberland Strait Canada 123 I5
North Vancouver Canada 120 F5
North Vernon U.S.A. 134 C4
Northville U.S.A. 135 H2
North Wabasca Lake Canada 120 H3
North Walsham U.K. 49 I6
Northway Junction U.S.A. 120 A2
North West prov. S. Africa 100 G4
Northwest Atlantic Mid-Ocean Channel N. Atlantic Ocean 148 E1
North West Cape Australia 108 A5
North West Frontier prov. Pak. see Khyber Pakhtunkhwa
North West Nelson Forest Park nat. park N.Z. see Kahurangi National Park
Northwest Pacific Basin sea feature N. Pacific Ocean 150 G3
Northwest Providence Channel Bahamas 133 E7
North West River Canada 123 K3
Northwest Territories admin. div. Canada 120 J2
Northwich U.K. 48 E5
North Wildwood U.S.A. 135 H4
North Windham U.S.A. 135 J2
Northwind Ridge sea feature Arctic Ocean 153 B1
Northwood U.S.A. 135 J2
North York Canada 134 F2
North York Moors moorland U.K. 48 G4
North York Moors National Park U.K. 48 G4
Norton U.K. 48 G4
Norton KS U.S.A. 130 D4
Norton VA U.S.A. 134 D5
Norton VT U.S.A. 135 J1
Norton de Matos Angola see Balombo
Norton Shores U.S.A. 134 B2
Norton Sound sea chan. U.S.A. 118 B3
Nortonville U.S.A. 134 B5
Norvegia, Cape Antarctica 152 B2
Norwalk CT U.S.A. 135 I3
Norwalk OH U.S.A. 134 D3
Norway country Europe 44 E6
Norway U.S.A. 135 J1
Norway House Canada 121 L4
Norwegian Basin sea feature N. Atlantic Ocean 148 H1
Norwegian Bay Canada 119 I2
Norwegian Sea N. Atlantic Ocean 153 H2
Norwich Canada 134 E2
Norwich U.K. 49 I6
Norwich CT U.S.A. 135 I3
Norwich NY U.S.A. 135 H2
Norwood CO U.S.A. 129 I2
Norwood NY U.S.A. 135 H1
Norwood OH U.S.A. 134 C4
Nose Lake Canada 121 I1
Noshiro Japan 75 F4
Nosovaya Russia 42 L1
Noşratābād Iran 89 E4
Noss, Isle of i. U.K. 50 [inset]
Nossebro Sweden 45 H7
Nossen Germany 53 N3
Nossob watercourse Africa 100 D2
also known as Nosop
Notakwanon r. Canada 123 J2
Notch Peak U.S.A. 129 G2
Noteć r. Poland 47 O4
Notikewin r. Canada 120 G3
Noto, Golfo di g. Sicily Italy 58 F6
Notodden Norway 45 F7
Noto-hantō pen. Japan 75 E5
Notre-Dame, Monts mts Canada 123 H5
Notre Dame Bay Canada 123 L4
Notre-Dame-de-Koartac Canada see Quaqtaq
Nottawasaga Bay Canada 134 E1
Nottaway r. Canada 122 F4
Nottingham U.K. 49 F6
Nottingham Island Canada 119 K3
Nottoway r. U.S.A. 135 G5
Nottuln Germany 53 H3
Notukeu Creek r. Canada 121 J5
Nouabalé-Ndoki, Parc National de nat. park Congo 98 B3
Nouâdhibou Mauritania 96 B2
Nouâdhibou, Râs c. Mauritania 96 B2
▶Nouakchott Mauritania 96 B3
Capital of Mauritania.
Nouâmghâr Mauritania 96 B3
Nouei Vietnam 70 D4
▶Nouméa New Caledonia 107 G4
Capital of New Caledonia.
Nouna Burkina Faso 96 C3
Noupoort S. Africa 100 G6
Nousu Fin. 44 P3
Nouveau-Brunswick prov. Canada see New Brunswick
Nouveau-Comptoir Canada see Wemindji
Nouvelle Calédonie i. S. Pacific Ocean 107 G4
Nouvelle Calédonie terr. S. Pacific Ocean see New Caledonia
Nouvelle-France, Cap de c. Canada 119 K3
Nouvelles Hébrides country S. Pacific Ocean see Vanuatu
Nova América Brazil 145 A1
Nova Chaves Angola see Muconda
Nova Freixa Moz. see Cuamba
Nova Friburgo Brazil 145 C3
Nova Gaia Angola see Cambundi-Catembo
Nova Goa India see Panaji
Nova Gradiška Croatia 58 G2
Nova Iguaçu Brazil 145 C3
Nova Kakhovka Ukr. 59 O1
Nova Lima Brazil 145 C2
Nova Lisboa Angola see Huambo
Novalukoml' Belarus 43 F5
Nova Mambone Moz. 99 D6
Nova Nabúri Moz. 99 D5
Nova Odesa Ukr. 43 F7
Nova Ponte Brazil 145 B2
Nova Ponte, Represa resr Brazil 145 B2
Novara Italy 58 C2
Nova Roma Brazil 145 B1
Nova Scotia prov. Canada 123 I6
Novato U.S.A. 128 B2
Nova Trento Brazil 145 A4
Nova Venécia Brazil 145 C2
Nova Xavantina Brazil 143 H6
Novaya Kakhovka Ukr. see Nova Kakhovka
Novaya Ladoga Russia 42 G3
Novaya Lyalya Russia 41 S4
Novaya Matsesta Russia 91 E2
Novaya Odessa Ukr. see Nova Odesa
Novaya Sibir', Ostrov i. Russia 65 P2
Novaya Zemlya is Russia 64 G2
Nova Zagora Bulg. 59 L3
Novelda Spain 57 F4
Nové Zámky Slovakia 47 Q7
Novgorod Russia see Velikiy Novgorod
Novgorod-Severskiy Ukr. see Novhorod-Sivers'kyy
Novgorod-Volynskiy Ukr. see Novohrad-Volyns'kyy
Novhorod-Sivers'kyy Ukr. 43 G6
Novi Grad Bos. & Herz. see Bosanski Novi
Novi Iskar Bulg. 59 J3
Novikovo Russia 74 F3
Novi Kritsim Bulg. see Stamboliyski
Novi Ligure Italy 58 C2
Novi Pazar Bulg. 59 L3
Novi Pazar Serbia 59 I3
Novi Sad Serbia 59 H2
Novo Acre Brazil 145 C1
Novoalekseyevka Kazakh. see Kobda
Novoaltaysk Russia 72 E2
Novoanninskiy Russia 43 I6
Novo Aripuanã Brazil 142 F5
Novoazovs'k Ukr. 43 H7
Novocheboksarsk Russia 42 J4
Novocherkassk Russia 43 I7
Novo Cruzeiro Brazil 145 C2
Novodugino Russia 42 G5
Novodvinsk Russia 42 I2
Novoekonomicheskoye Ukr. see Dymytrov
Novogeorgiyevka Russia 74 B2
Novogrudok Belarus see Navahrudak
Novo Hamburgo Brazil 145 A5
Novohradské hory mts Czechia 47 O6
Novohrad-Volyns'kyy Ukr. 43 E6
Novokhopersk Russia 43 I6
Novokiyevskiy Uval Russia 74 C2
Novokubansk Russia 91 F1
Novokubanskiy Russia see Novokubansk
Novokuybyshevsk Russia 43 K5
Novokuznetsk Russia 72 F2
Novolazarevskaya research station Antarctica 152 C2
Novolukoml' Belarus see Novalukoml'
Novo mesto Slovenia 58 F2
Novomikhaylovskiy Russia 90 E1
Novomoskovsk Russia 43 H5
Novomoskovs'k Ukr. 43 G6
Novonikolayevsk Russia see Novosibirsk
Novonikolayevskiy Russia 43 I6
Novooleksiyivka Ukr. 43 G7
Novo Paraíso Brazil 142 F3
Novopashiyskiy Russia see Gornozavodsk
Novopokrovka Russia 74 D3
Novopokrovskaya Russia 43 I7
Novopolotsk Belarus see Navapolatsk
Novopskov Ukr. 43 H6
Novo Redondo Angola see Sumbe
Novorossiyka Russia 74 C1
Novorossiysk Russia 90 E1
Novorybnaya Russia 65 L2
Novorzhev Russia 42 F4
Novoselovo Russia 72 G1
Novoselskoye Russia see Achkhoy-Martan
Novosel'ye Russia 45 P7
Novosergiyevka Russia 41 Q5
Novoshakhtinsk Russia 43 H7
Novosheshminsk Russia 42 K5
Novosibirsk Russia 64 J4
Novosibirskiye Ostrova is Russia see New Siberia Islands
Novosil' Russia 43 H5
Novosokol'niki Russia 42 F4
Novospasskoye Russia 43 J5
Novotroyits'ke Ukr. 43 G7
Novoukrainka Ukr. see Novoukrayinka
Novoukrayinka Ukr. 43 F6
Novoussuri (abandoned) Russia 74 E2
Novouzensk Russia 43 K6
Novovolyns'k Ukr. 43 E6
Novovoronezh Russia 43 H6
Novovoronezhskiy Russia see Novovoronezh
Novovoskresenovka Russia 74 B1
Novozybkov Russia 43 F5
Nový Jičín Czechia 47 P6
Novyy Afon Georgia see Akhali Atoni
Novyy Bor Russia 42 L2
Novyy Donbass Ukr. see Dymytrov
Novyye Petushki Russia see Petushki
Novyy Kholmogory Russia see Archangel
Novyy Margelan Uzbek. see Farg'ona
Novyy Nekouz Russia 42 H4
Novyy Oskol Russia 43 H6
Novyy Port Russia 64 I3
Novyy Urengoy Russia 64 I3
Novyy Urgal Russia 74 D2
Novyy Uzen' Kazakh. see Zhanaozen
Novyy Zay Russia see Zainsk
Now Iran 88 D4
Nowabganj Bangl. see Nawabganj
Nowata U.S.A. 131 E4
Nowdī Iran 88 C2
Nowgong India see Nagaon
Now Kharegan Iran 88 D2
Nowleye Lake Canada 121 K2
Nowogard Poland 47 O4
Noworadomsk Poland see Radomsko
Nowra Australia 112 E5
Nowrangapur India see Nabarangapur
Nowshera Pak. 89 I3
Nowyak Lake Canada 121 L2
Nowy Sącz Poland 47 R6
Nowy Targ Poland 47 R6
Now Zād Afgh. 89 G3
Noxen U.S.A. 135 G3
Noy, Xé r. Laos 70 D3
Noyabr'sk Russia 64 I3
Noyes Island U.S.A. 120 C4
Noyon France 52 C5
Noyon Mongolia 80 J3
Nozizwe S. Africa 101 G6
Nqutu S. Africa 101 J5
Nsanje Malawi 99 D5
Nsombo Zambia 99 C5
Nsukka Nigeria 96 D4
Nsumbu National Park Zambia see Sumbu National Park
Ntabankulu S. Africa 101 I6
Ntambu Zambia 99 C5
Ntha S. Africa 101 H4
Ntoro, Kavo pt Greece 59 K5
Ntoum Gabon 98 A3
Ntungamo Uganda 98 D4
Nuanetsi Zimbabwe see Mwenezi
Nu'aym reg. Oman 88 D6
Nuba Mountains Sudan 86 D7
Nubian Desert Sudan 86 D5
Nueces r. U.S.A. 131 D7
Nueltin Lake Canada 121 L2
Nueva Ciudad Guerrero Mex. 131 D7
Nueva Gerona Cuba 137 H4
Nueva Harberton Arg. 144 C8
Nueva Imperial Chile 144 B5
Nueva Loja Ecuador 142 C3
Nueva Rosita Mex. 131 C7
Nueva San Salvador El Salvador see Santa Tecla
Nueva Villa de Padilla Mex. 131 D7
Nueve de Julio Arg. see 9 de Julio
Nuevitas Cuba 137 I4
Nuevo, Golfo g. Arg. 144 D6
Nuevo Casas Grandes Mex. 127 G7
Nuevo Ideal Mex. 131 B7
Nuevo Laredo Mex. 131 D7
Nuevo León Mex. 129 F5
Nuevo León state Mex. 131 D7
Nuevo Rocatuerte Ecuador 142 C4
Nugaal watercourse Somalia 98 E3
Nugaaleed, Dooxo valley Somalia 98 E3
Nugget Point N.Z. 113 B8
Nugur India 84 D2
Nuguria Islands P.N.G. 106 F2
Nuh, Ras pt Pak. 89 F5
Nuhaka N.Z. 113 F4
Nui atoll Tuvalu 107 H2
Nui Con Voi r. Vietnam see Red
Nuiqsut U.S.A. 118 C2
Nui Thanh Vietnam 70 E4
Nujiang China 76 C2
Nu Jiang r. China/Myanmar see Salween
Nukey Bluff hill Australia 111 A7
Nukha Azer. see Şäki
▶Nuku'alofa Tonga 107 I4
Capital of Tonga.
Nukufetau atoll Tuvalu 107 H2
Nukuhiva i. Fr. Polynesia see Nuku Hiva
Nuku Hiva i. Fr. Polynesia 151 K6
Nukuhu P.N.G. 69 L8
Nukulaelae atoll Tuvalu 107 H2
Nukulailai atoll Tuvalu see Nukulaelae
Nukumanu Islands P.N.G. 107 F2
Nukunau i. Kiribati see Nikunau
Nukunono atoll Tokelau see Nukunonu
Nukunonu atoll Tokelau 107 I2
Nukus Uzbek. 80 A3
Nulato U.S.A. 118 C3
Nullagine Australia 108 C5
Nullarbor Australia 109 E7
Nullarbor National Park Australia 109 E7
Nullarbor Plain Australia 109 E7
Nullarbor Regional Reserve park Australia 109 E7
Nuluarniavik, Lac l. Canada 122 F2
Nulu'erhu Shan mts China 73 L4
Num i. Indon. 69 J7
Numalla, Lake salt flat Australia 112 B2
Numan Nigeria 98 B3
Numanuma P.N.G. 110 E1
Numazu Japan 75 E6
Numbulwar Australia 110 A2
Numedal valley Norway 45 F6
Numfoor i. Indon. 69 I7
Numin He r. China 74 B3
Numurkah Australia 112 B6
Nunaksaluk Island Canada 123 J3
Nunakuluut i. Greenland 119 N3
Nunap Isua c. Greenland see Farewell, Cape
Nunarsuit i. Greenland see Nunakuluut
Nunavik reg. Canada 122 G1
Nunavut admin. div. Canada 121 L2
Nunda U.S.A. 135 G2
Nundle Australia 112 E3
Nuneaton U.K. 49 F6
Nungba India 83 H4
Nungesser Lake Canada 121 M5
Nungnain Sum China 73 L4
Nunivak Island U.S.A. 118 B4
Nunkapasi India 84 E1
Nunkun mt. India 82 D2
Nunligran Russia 65 S3
Nuñomoral Spain 57 C3
Nunspeet Neth. 52 F2
Nuojiang China see Tongjiang
Nuoro Sardinia Italy 58 C4
Nupani i. Solomon Is 107 G3
Nuqrah Saudi Arabia 86 F4
Nūr Iran 88 C2
Nūrābād Iran 88 C4
Nurakita i. Tuvalu see Niulakita
Nurata Uzbek. see Nurota
Nur Dağları mts Turkey 85 B1
Nurek Tajik. see Norak
Nurek Reservoir Tajik. see Norak, Obanbori
Nurekskoye Vodokhranilishche resr Tajik. see Norak, Obanbori
Nuremberg Germany 53 L5
Nuri Mex. 127 F7
Nurla India 82 D2
Nurlat Russia 43 K5
Nurmes Fin. 44 P5
Nurmo Fin. 44 M5
Nürnberg Germany see Nuremberg
Nurota Uzbek. 80 C3
Nurri, Mount hill Australia 112 C3
Nūr Rūd r. Iran 88 D2
Nusawulan Indon. 69 I7
Nusaybin Turkey 91 F3
Nuşayrīyah, Jabal an mts Syria 85 C2
Nu Shan mts China 76 C3
Nushki Pak. 89 G4
Nusratiye Turkey 85 D1
Nutak Canada 123 J2
Nutarawit Lake Canada 121 L2
Nutrioso U.S.A. 129 I5
Nuttal Pak. 89 H4
Nutwood Downs Australia 108 F3
Nutzotin Mountains U.S.A. 120 A2
▶Nuuk Greenland 119 M3
Capital of Greenland.
Nuupas Fin. 44 O3
Nuussuaq Greenland 119 M2
Nuussuaq pen. Greenland 119 M2
Nuwaybi' al Muzayyinah Egypt 90 D5
Nuweiba el Muzeina Egypt see Nuwaybi' al Muzayyinah
Nuwerus S. Africa 100 D6
Nuweveldberge mts S. Africa 100 E7
Nuyts, Point Australia 109 B8
Nuyts Archipelago is Australia 109 F8
Nuzvid India 84 D2
Nwanedi Nature Reserve S. Africa 101 J2
Nxai Pan National Park Botswana 99 C5
Nyagan' Russia 41 T3
Nyagquka China see Yajiang
Nyagrong China see Xinlong
Nyahururu Kenya 98 D3
Nyah West Australia 112 A5
Nyainqêntanglha Feng mt. China 83 G3
Nyainqêntanglha Shan mts China 83 G3
Nyainrong China 76 B1
Nyainronglung China see Nyainrong
Nyåker Sweden 44 K5
Nyakh Russia see Nyagan'
Nyaksimvol' Russia 41 S3
Nyala Sudan 97 F3
Nyalam China see Congdü
Nyalikungu Tanz. see Maswa
Nyamandhlovu Zimbabwe 99 C5
Nyamtumbo Tanz. 99 D5
Nyande Zimbabwe see Masvingo
Nyandoma Russia 42 I3
Nyandomskaya Vozvyshennost' hills Russia 42 H3
Nyanga Congo 98 B4
Nyanga Zimbabwe 99 D5
Nyangani mt. Zimbabwe 99 D5
Nyangbo China 76 B2
Nyarling r. Canada 120 H2
▶Nyasa, Lake Africa 99 D4
3rd largest lake in Africa and 9th in the world.
Nyasaland country Africa see Malawi
Nyashabozh Russia 42 L2
Nyasvizh Belarus 45 O10
Nyaungdon Myanmar see Yandoon
Nyaunglebin Myanmar 70 B3
Nyborg Denmark 45 G9
Nyborg Norway 44 P1
Nybro Sweden 45 I8
Nyeboe Land reg. Greenland 119 M1
Nyêmo China 83 G3
Nyenchen Tanglha Range mts China see Nyainqêntanglha Shan
Nyeri Kenya 98 D4
Nyi, Co l. China 83 F2
Nyika National Park Zambia 99 D5
Nyimba Zambia 99 D5
Nyingchi Xizang China 76 B2
Nyingchi Xizang China 76 B2
Nyinma China see Maqu
Nyíregyháza Hungary 43 D7
Nyiru, Mount Kenya 98 D3
Nykarleby Fin. 44 M5
Nykøbing Falster Denmark 45 G9
Nykøbing Sjælland Denmark 45 G9
Nyköping Sweden 45 J7
Nyland Sweden 44 J5
Nylsvley nature res. S. Africa 101 I3
Nymagee Australia 112 C4
Nymboida National Park Australia 112 F2
Nynäshamn Sweden 45 J7
Nyngan Australia 112 C3
Nyogzê China 83 E3
Nyoman r. Belarus/Lith. 45 M10
also known as Neman or Nemunas
Nyon Switz. 56 H3
Nyons France 56 G4
Nýřany Czechia 53 N5
Nyrob Russia 41 R3
Nysa Poland 47 P5
Nysh Russia 74 F2
Nyssa U.S.A. 126 D4
Nystad Fin. see Uusikaupunki
Nytva Russia 41 R4
Nyuksenitsa Russia 42 J3
Nyunzu Dem. Rep. Congo 99 C4
Nyurba Russia 65 M3
Nyyskiy Zaliv lag. Russia 74 F1
Nzambi Congo 98 B4
Nzega Tanz. 99 D4
Nzérékoré Guinea 96 C4
N'zeto Angola 99 B4

O

Oahe, Lake U.S.A. 130 C2
O'ahu i. U.S.A. 127 [inset]
Oaitupu i. Tuvalu see Vaitupu
Oak Bluffs U.S.A. 135 J3
Oak City U.S.A. 129 G2
Oak Creek U.S.A. 129 J1
Oakdale U.S.A. 131 E6
Oakes U.S.A. 130 D2
Oakey Australia 112 E1
Oak Grove KY U.S.A. 134 B5
Oak Grove LA U.S.A. 131 F5
Oak Grove MI U.S.A. 134 C1
Oakham U.K. 49 G6
Oak Harbor U.S.A. 134 D3
Oak Hill OH U.S.A. 134 D4
Oak Hill WV U.S.A. 134 E5
Oakhurst U.S.A. 128 D3
Oak Lake Canada 121 K5
Oakland CA U.S.A. 128 B3
Oakland MD U.S.A. 134 F4
Oakland ME U.S.A. 135 K1
Oakland NE U.S.A. 130 D3
Oakland OR U.S.A. 126 C4
Oakland airport U.S.A. 128 B3
Oakland City U.S.A. 134 B4
Oaklands Australia 112 C5
Oak Lawn U.S.A. 134 B3
Oakley U.S.A. 130 C4
Oakover r. Australia 108 C5
Oak Park IL U.S.A. 134 B3
Oak Park MI U.S.A. 134 C2
Oak Park Reservoir U.S.A. 129 I1
Oakridge U.S.A. 126 C4
Oak Ridge U.S.A. 132 C4
Oakvale Australia 111 C7
Oak View U.S.A. 128 D4
Oakville Canada 134 F2

Oakwood *OH* U.S.A. **134** C3
Oakwood *TN* U.S.A. **134** B5
Oamaru N.Z. **113** C7
Oaro N.Z. **113** D6
Oasis *CA* U.S.A. **128** E3
Oasis *NV* U.S.A. **126** E4
Oates Coast *reg.* Antarctica *see* **Oates Land**
Oates Land *reg.* Antarctica **152** H2
Oaxaca Mex. **136** E5
Oaxaca de Juárez Mex. *see* **Oaxaca**

▶**Ob'** *r.* Russia **72** E2
Part of the Ob'-Irtysh, the 2nd longest river in Asia.

Ob, Gulf of *sea chan.* Russia *see* **Obskaya Guba**
Oba Canada **122** D4
Oba *i.* Vanuatu *see* **Aoba**
Obala Cameroon **96** E4
Obama Japan **75** D6
Oban U.K. **50** D4
O Barco Spain **57** C2
Obbia Somalia *see* **Hobyo**
Obdorsk Russia *see* **Salekhard**
Óbecse Serbia *see* **Bečej**
Obed Canada **120** G4
Ōbêh Afgh. **89** F3
Oberaula Germany **53** J4
Oberdorla Germany **53** K3
Oberhausen Germany **52** G3
Oberlin *KS* U.S.A. **130** C4
Oberlin *LA* U.S.A. **131** E6
Oberlin *OH* U.S.A. **134** D3
Obermoschel Germany **53** H5
Oberon Australia **112** D4
Oberpfälzer Wald *mts* Germany **53** M5
Obersinn Germany **53** J4
Oberthulba Germany **53** J4
Obertshausen Germany **53** I4
Oberwälder Land *reg.* Germany **53** J3
Obi *i.* Indon. **69** H7
Óbidos Brazil **143** G4
Obihiro Japan **74** F4
Obil'noye Russia **43** J7

▶**Ob'-Irtysh** *r.* Russia **64** H3
2nd longest river in Asia and 5th in the world.

Obluch'ye Russia **74** C2
Obninsk Russia **43** H5
Obo Cent. Afr. Rep. **98** C3
Obock Djibouti **86** F7
Ŏbŏk N. Korea **74** C4
Obokote Dem. Rep. Congo **98** C4
Obo Liang China **80** H4
Obouya Congo **98** B4
Oboyan' Russia **43** H6
Obozerskiy Russia **42** I3
Obregón, Presa *resr* Mex. **127** F8
Obrenovac Serbia **59** I2
Obruk Turkey **90** D3
Observatory Hill *hill* Australia **109** F7
Obshchiy Syrt *hills* Russia **41** Q5
Obskaya Guba *sea chan.* Russia **64** I3
Obuasi Ghana **96** C4
Ob''yachevo Russia **42** K3
Ocala U.S.A. **133** D6
Ocampo Mex. **131** C7
Ocaña Col. **142** D2
Ocaña Spain **57** E4
Occidental, Cordillera *mts* Chile **142** E7
Occidental, Cordillera *mts* Col. **142** C3
Occidental, Cordillera *mts* Peru **142** D7
Oceana U.S.A. **134** E5
Ocean Cay *i.* Bahamas **133** E7
Ocean City *MD* U.S.A. **135** H4
Ocean City *NJ* U.S.A. **135** H4
Ocean Falls Canada **120** E4
Ocean Island Kiribati *see* **Banaba**
Ocean Island *atoll* U.S.A. *see* **Kure Atoll**
Oceanside U.S.A. **128** E5
Ocean Springs U.S.A. **131** F6
Ochakiv Ukr. **59** N1
Och'amch'ire Georgia **91** F2
Ocher Russia **41** Q4
Ochiishi-misaki *pt* Japan **74** G4
Ochil Hills U.K. **50** F4
Ochito *r.* Pak. **89** G5
Ochrida, Lake Albania/Macedonia *see* **Ohrid, Lake**
Ochsenfurt Germany **53** K5
Ochtrup Germany **53** H2
Ocilla U.S.A. **133** D6
Ockelbo Sweden **45** J6
Ocolașul Mare, Vârful *mt.* Romania **59** K1
Oconomowoc U.S.A. **134** A2
Oconto U.S.A. **134** B1
Octeville-sur-Mer France **49** H9
October Revolution Island Russia *see* **Oktyabr'skoy Revolyutsii, Ostrov**
Ocussi *enclave* East Timor **108** D2
Ocussi-Ambeno *enclave* East Timor *see* **Ocussi**
Oda, Jebel *mt.* Sudan **86** E5
Ódáðahraun *lava field* Iceland **44** [inset 1]
Ŏdaejin N. Korea **74** C4
Odae-san National Park S. Korea **75** C5
Ōdate Japan **75** F4
Odawara Japan **75** E6
Odda Norway **45** E6
Odei *r.* Canada **121** L3
Odell U.S.A. **134** B3
Odem U.S.A. **131** D7
Odemira Port. **57** B5
Ödemiş Turkey **59** L5
Ödenburg Hungary *see* **Sopron**
Odense Denmark **45** G9
Odenwald *reg.* Germany **53** I5
Oder *r.* Germany **53** J3
also known as Odra (Poland)
Oderbucht *b.* Germany **47** O3
Oder-Havel-Kanal *canal* Germany **53** N2
Ödeshög Sweden **45** I7
Odessa Ukr. **59** N1
Odessa *TX* U.S.A. **131** C6
Odessa *WA* U.S.A. **126** D3
Odessus Bulg. *see* **Varna**
Odiel *r.* Spain **57** C5
Odienné Côte d'Ivoire **96** C4
Odintsovo Russia **42** H5
Odisha *state* India **84** E1
Ŏdŏngk Cambodia **71** D5
Odra *r.* Germany/Poland **47** Q6
also known as Oder (Germany)
Odzala-Kokoua, Parc National d' *nat. park* Congo **98** B3
Oea Libya *see* **Tripoli**
Oé-Cusse *enclave* East Timor *see* **Ocussi**
Oecussi *enclave* East Timor *see* **Ocussi**
Oeiras Brazil **143** J5
Oekussi *enclave* East Timor *see* **Ocussi**
Oelsnitz/Vogtland Germany **53** M4
Oenkerk Neth. **52** F1
Oenpelli Australia **108** F3
Oesel *i.* Estonia *see* **Hiiumaa**
Oeufs, Lac des *l.* Canada **123** G3
Of Turkey **91** F2
O'Fallon *r.* U.S.A. **126** G3
Ofanto *r.* Italy **58** G4
Ofaqim Israel **85** B4
Offa Nigeria **96** D4
Offenbach am Main Germany **53** I4
Offenburg Germany **47** K6
Oga Japan **75** E5
Ogadēn *reg.* Eth. **98** E3
Oga-hantō *pen.* Japan **75** E5
Ōgaki Japan **75** E6
Ogallala U.S.A. **130** C3
Ogasawara-shotō *is* Japan *see* **Bonin Islands**
Ogbomosho Nigeria *see* **Ogbomoso**
Ogbomoso Nigeria **96** D4
Ogden *IA* U.S.A. **130** E3
Ogden *UT* U.S.A. **126** F4
Ogden, Mount Canada **120** C3
Ogdensburg U.S.A. **135** H1
Ogidaki Canada **122** D5
Ogilvie *r.* Canada **118** E3
Ogilvie Mountains Canada **118** D3
Oglethorpe, Mount U.S.A. **133** C5
Oglio *r.* Italy **58** D2
Oglongi Russia **74** E1
Ogmore Australia **110** E4
Ogoamas, Gunung *mt.* Indon. **69** G6
Ogodzha Russia **74** D1
Ogoja Nigeria **96** D4
Ogoki *r.* Canada **122** D4
Ogoki Lake Canada **130** G1
Ogoki Reservoir Canada **122** C4
Ogoron Russia **74** C1
Ogosta *r.* Bulg. **59** J3
Ogre Latvia **45** N8
Ogulin Croatia **58** F2
Ogurchinskiy, Ostrov *i.* Turkm. *see* **Ogurjaly Adasy**
Ogurjaly Adasy *i.* Turkm. **88** D2
Oğuzeli Turkey **85** C1
Ohai N.Z. **113** A7
Ohakune N.Z. **113** E4
Ohanet Alg. **96** D2
Ōhata Japan **74** F4
Ohcejohka Fin. *see* **Utsjoki**
O'Higgins, Lago *l.* Chile **144** B7
Ohio *r.* U.S.A. **134** A5
Ohio *state* U.S.A. **134** D3
Ohm *r.* Germany **53** I4
Ohrdruf Germany **53** K4
Ohře *r.* Czechia **53** N4
Ohre *r.* Germany **53** L2
Ohrid Macedonia **59** I4
Ohrid, Lake Albania/Macedonia **59** I4
Ohridsko Ezero *l.* Albania/Macedonia *see* **Ohrid, Lake**
Ohrigstad S. Africa **101** J3
Öhringen Germany **53** J5
Ohrit, Liqeni i *l.* Albania/Macedonia *see* **Ohrid, Lake**
Ohura N.Z. **113** E4
Oich *r.* U.K. **50** E3
Oiga China **76** B2
Oignies France **52** C4
Oil City U.S.A. **134** F3
Oise *r.* France **52** C6
Oise à l'Aisne, Canal de l' France **52** D5
Ōita Japan **75** C6
Oiti *mt.* Greece **59** J5
Ojai U.S.A. **128** D4
Ojalava *i.* Samoa *see* **'Upolu**
Ojinaga Mex. **131** B6
Ojiya Japan **75** E5
Ojo Caliente U.S.A. **127** G5
Ojo de Laguna Mex. **127** G7

▶**Ojos del Salado, Nevado** *mt.* Arg./Chile **144** C3
2nd highest mountain in South America.

Oka *r.* Russia **43** I4
Oka *r.* Russia **72** I1
Okahandja Namibia **100** C1
Okahukura N.Z. **113** E4
Okakarara Namibia **99** B6
Okak Islands Canada **123** J2
Okanagan Lake Canada **120** G5
Okanda Sri Lanka **84** D5
Okano *r.* Gabon **98** B4
Okanogan U.S.A. **126** D2
Okanogan *r.* U.S.A. **126** D2
Okapi, Parc National de la *nat. park* Dem. Rep. Congo **98** C3
Okara Pak. **89** I4
Okarem Turkm. *see* **Ekerem**
Okataina *vol.* N.Z. *see* **Tarawera, Mount**
Okaukuejo Namibia **99** B5
Okavango *r.* Africa **99** C5

▶**Okavango Delta** *swamp* Botswana **99** C5
Largest oasis in the world.

Okavango Swamps Botswana *see* **Okavango Delta**
Okaya Japan **75** E5
Okayama Japan **75** D6
Okazaki Japan **75** E6
Okeechobee U.S.A. **133** D7
Okeechobee, Lake U.S.A. **133** D7
Okeene U.S.A. **131** D4
Okefenokee Swamp U.S.A. **133** D6
Okehampton U.K. **49** C8
Okemah U.S.A. **131** D5
Oker *r.* Germany **53** K2
Okha India **82** B5
Okha Russia **74** F1
Okha Rann *marsh* India **82** B5
Okhotsk Russia **65** P4
Okhotsk, Sea of Japan/Russia **74** G3
Okhotskoye More *sea* Japan/Russia *see* **Okhotsk, Sea of**
Okhtyrka Ukr. **43** G6
Okinawa *i.* Japan **75** B8
Okinawa-guntō *is* Japan *see* **Okinawa-shotō**
Okinawa-shotō *is* Japan **75** B8
Okino-Daitō-jima *i.* Japan **73** O8
Okino-Tori-shima *i.* Japan **73** P8
Oki-shotō *is* Japan **75** D5
Okkan Myanmar **70** A3
Oklahoma *state* U.S.A. **131** D5

▶**Oklahoma City** U.S.A. **131** D5
Capital of Oklahoma.

Okmulgee U.S.A. **131** D5
Okolona *KY* U.S.A. **134** C4
Okolona *MS* U.S.A. **131** F5
Okondja Gabon **98** B4
Okovskiy Les *for.* Russia **42** G5
Okoyo Congo **98** B4
Okpan, Gora *hill* Kazakh. **91** H1
Øksfjord Norway **44** M1
Oktemberyan Armenia *see* **Armavir**
Oktwin Myanmar **70** B3
Oktyabr' Kazakh. *see* **Kandyagash**
Oktyabr'sk Kazakh. *see* **Kandyagash**
Oktyabr'skiy Belarus *see* **Aktsyabrski**
Oktyabr'skiy *Amurskaya Oblast'* Russia **74** C1
Oktyabr'skiy *Arkhangel'skaya Oblast'* Russia **42** I3
Oktyabr'skiy *Kamchatskiy Kray* Russia **65** Q4
Oktyabr'skiy *Respublika Bashkortostan* Russia **41** Q5
Oktyabr'skiy *Volgogradskaya Oblast'* Russia **43** I7
Oktyabr'skoye Russia **41** T3
Oktyabr'skoy Revolyutsii, Ostrov *i.* Russia **65** K2
Okulovka Russia **42** G4
Okushiri-tō *i.* Japan **74** E4
Okusi *enclave* East Timor *see* **Ocussi**
Okuta Nigeria **96** D4
Okwa *watercourse* Botswana **100** G1
Ólafsvík Iceland **44** [inset 1]
Olakkur India **84** C3
Olancha U.S.A. **128** D3
Olancha Peak U.S.A. **128** D3
Öland *i.* Sweden **45** J8
Olary Australia **111** C7
Olathe *CO* U.S.A. **129** J2
Olathe *KS* U.S.A. **130** E4
Olavarría Arg. **144** D5
Oława Poland **47** P5
Olbernhau Germany **53** N4
Olbia *Sardinia* Italy **58** C4
Old Bahama Channel Bahamas/Cuba **133** E8
Old Bastar India **84** D2
Oldcastle Ireland **51** E4
Old Cork Australia **110** C4
Old Crow Canada **118** E3
Oldeboorn Neth. *see* **Aldeboarn**
Oldenburg Germany **53** I1
Oldenburg in Holstein Germany **47** M3
Oldenzaal Neth. **52** G2
Olderdalen Norway **44** L2
Old Forge U.S.A. **135** H2
Old Gidgee Australia **109** B6
Oldham U.K. **48** E5
Old Harbor U.S.A. **118** C4
Old Head of Kinsale *hd* Ireland **51** D6
Oldman *r.* Canada **120** I5
Oldmeldrum U.K. **50** G3
Old Perlican Canada **123** L5
Old River U.S.A. **128** D4
Olds Canada **120** H5
Old Speck Mountain U.S.A. **135** J1
Old Station U.S.A. **128** C1
Old Wives Lake Canada **121** J5
Olean U.S.A. **135** F2
Olecko Poland **47** S3
Olekma *r.* Russia **65** N3
Olekminsk Russia **65** N3
Olekminskiy Stanovik *mts* Russia **73** M2
Oleksandrivs'k Ukr. *see* **Zaporizhzhya**
Oleksandriya Ukr. **43** G6
Ølen Norway **45** D7
Olenegorsk Russia **44** R2
Olenek Russia **65** M3
Olenek *r.* Russia **65** M2
Olenek Bay Russia *see* **Olenekskiy Zaliv**
Olenekskiy Zaliv *b.* Russia **65** N2
Olenino Russia **42** G4
Olenitsa Russia **42** G2
Olenivs'ki Kar''yery Ukr. *see* **Dokuchayevs'k**
Olenya Russia *see* **Olenegorsk**
Oleshky Ukr. *see* **Tsyurupyns'k**
Olevs'k Ukr. **43** E6
Ol'ga Russia **74** D4
Olga, Lac *l.* Canada **122** F4
Olga, Mount Australia **109** E6
Ol'ginsk Russia **74** D1
Olginskoye Russia *see* **Kochubeyevskoye**
Ölgiy Mongolia **80** G2
Olhão Port. **57** C5
Olia Chain *mts* Australia **109** E6
Olifants *r.* Moz./S. Africa **101** J3
also known as Elefantes
Olifants *watercourse* Namibia **100** D3
Olifants S. Africa **101** J2
Olifants *r. W. Cape* S. Africa **100** D6
Olifants *r. W. Cape* S. Africa **100** E7
Olifantshoek S. Africa **100** F4
Olifantsrivierberge *mts* S. Africa **100** D7
Olimarao *atoll* Micronesia **69** L5
Olimbos *hill* Cyprus *see* **Olympos**
Olimbos *mt.* Greece *see* **Olympus, Mount**
Olimpos Beydağları Milli Parkı *nat. park* Turkey **59** N6
Olinda Brazil **143** L5
Olinga Moz. **99** D5
Olio Australia **110** C4
Oliphants Drift S. Africa **101** H3
Olisipo Port. *see* **Lisbon**
Oliva Spain **57** F4
Oliva, Cordillera de *mts* Arg./Chile **144** C3
Olivares, Cerro de *mt.* Arg./Chile **144** C4
Olive Hill U.S.A. **134** D4
Olivehurst U.S.A. **128** C2
Oliveira dos Brejinhos Brazil **145** C1
Olivença Moz. *see* **Lupilichi**
Olivenza Spain **57** C4
Oliver Lake Canada **121** K3
Olivet *MI* U.S.A. **134** C2
Olivet *SD* U.S.A. **130** D3
Olivia U.S.A. **130** E2
Olji China **72** I4
Ol'khovka Russia **43** J6
Ollagüe Chile **144** C2
Ollombo Congo **98** B4
Olmaliq Uzbek. **80** C3
Olmos Peru **142** C5
Olmütz Czechia *see* **Olomouc**
Olney U.K. **49** G6
Olney *IL* U.S.A. **130** F4
Olney *MD* U.S.A. **135** G4
Olney *TX* U.S.A. **131** D5
Olofström Sweden **45** I8
Olomane *r.* Canada **123** J4
Olomouc Czechia **47** P6
Olonets Russia **42** G3
Olongapo Phil. **69** G4
Oloron-Ste-Marie France **56** D5
Olosenga *atoll* American Samoa *see* **Swains Island**
Olot Spain **57** H2
Olot Uzbek. **89** F2
Olovyannaya Russia **73** L2
Oloy *r.* Russia **65** Q3
Oloy, Qatorkŭhi *mts* Asia *see* **Alai Range**
Olpe Germany **53** H3
Olsztyn Poland **47** R4
Olt *r.* Romania **59** K3
Olten Switz. **56** H3
Oltenița Romania **59** L2
Oltu Turkey **91** F2
Oluan Bi *c.* Taiwan **77** I4
Ol'viopol' Ukr. *see* **Pervomays'k**
Olymbos *hill* Cyprus *see* **Olympos**

▶**Olympia** U.S.A. **126** C3
Capital of Washington state.

Olympic National Park U.S.A. **126** C3
Olympos *hill* Cyprus **85** A2
Olympos Greece *see* **Olympus, Mount**
Olympos *nat. park* Greece *see* **Olympou, Ethnikos Drymos**
Olympou, Ethnikos Drymos *nat. park* Greece **59** J4
Olympus, Mount Cyprus **85** A2
Olympus, Mount Greece **59** J4
Olympus, Mount U.S.A. **126** C3
Olyutorskiy, Mys *c.* Russia **65** S4
Olyutorskiy Zaliv *b.* Russia **65** R4
Olzheras Russia *see* **Mezhdurechensk**
Oma China **83** E2
Oma *r.* Russia **42** J2
Omagh U.K. **51** E3
Omaha U.S.A. **130** E3
Omaheke *admin. reg.* Namibia **100** D2
Omal'skiy Khrebet *mts* Russia **74** E1
Oman *country* Asia **87** I6
Oman, Gulf of Asia **88** E5
Omaruru Namibia **99** B6
Omate Peru **142** D7
Omaweneno Botswana **100** F3
Omba *i.* Vanuatu *see* **Aoba**
Ombai, Selat *sea chan.* Indon. **108** D2
Ombalantu Namibia *see* **Outapi**
Omboué Gabon **98** A4
Ombu China **83** F3
Omdraaisvlei S. Africa **100** F6
Omdurman Sudan **86** D6
Omeo Australia **112** C6
Omer U.S.A. **134** D1
Ometepec Mex. **136** E5
Omgoy Wildlife Reserve *nature res.* Thai. **70** B3
Om Hajēr Eritrea **86** E7
Omīdīyeh Iran **88** C4
Omineca Mountains Canada **120** E3
Omirzak Kazakh. **91** H2
Omitara Namibia **100** C2
Ōmiya Japan **75** E6
Ommaney, Cape U.S.A. **120** C3
Ommen Neth. **52** G2
Omolon Russia **65** R3
Omo National Park Eth. **98** D3
Omsk Russia **64** I4
Omsukchan Russia **65** Q3
Ōmu Japan **74** F3
O-mu Myanmar **70** B2
Omu, Vârful *mt.* Romania **59** K2
Ōmura Japan **75** C6
Omutninsk Russia **42** L4
Onaman Lake Canada **122** D4
Onamia U.S.A. **130** E2
Onancock U.S.A. **135** H5
Onangué, Lac *l.* Gabon **98** B4
Onaping Lake Canada **122** E5
Onatchiway, Lac *l.* Canada **123** H4
Onavas Mex. **127** F7
Onawa U.S.A. **130** D3
Onaway U.S.A. **134** C1
Önay, Kōtal-e Afgh. **89** H3
Onbingwin Myanmar **71** B4
Oncativo Arg. **144** D4
Onchan Isle of Man **48** C4
Oncócua Angola **99** B5
Öncül Turkey **85** D1
Ondal India *see* **Andal**
Ondangwa Namibia **99** B5
Onderstedorings S. Africa **100** E6
Ondjiva Angola **99** B5
Ondo Nigeria **96** D4
Öndörhaan Mongolia **73** K3
Öndörshil Mongolia **73** J3
Ondozero Russia **42** G3
One Botswana **100** E2
One and a Half Degree Channel Maldives **81** D11
Onega Russia **42** H3
Onega *r.* Russia **42** H3

▶**Onega, Lake** Russia **42** G3
3rd largest lake in Europe.

Onega Bay *g.* Russia *see* **Onezhskaya Guba**
One Hundred and Fifty Mile House Canada *see* **150 Mile House**
One Hundred Mile House Canada *see* **100 Mile House**
Oneida *NY* U.S.A. **135** H2
Oneida *TN* U.S.A. **134** C5
Oneida Lake U.S.A. **135** H2
O'Neill U.S.A. **130** D3
Onekama U.S.A. **134** B1
Onekotan, Ostrov *i.* Russia **65** Q5
Oneonta *AL* U.S.A. **133** C5
Oneonta *NY* U.S.A. **135** H2
Onești Romania **59** L1
Onezhskaya Guba *g.* Russia **42** G2
Onezhskoye Ozero *l.* Russia *see* **Onega, Lake**
Ong *r.* India **84** D1
Onga Gabon **98** B4
Ongers *watercourse* S. Africa **100** F5
Ongiyn Gol *r.* Mongolia **80** J3
Ongjin N. Korea **75** B5
Ongole India **84** D3
Onida U.S.A. **130** C2
Onilahy *r.* Madag. **99** E6
Onistagane, Lac *l.* Canada **123** H4
Onitsha Nigeria **96** D4
Onjati Mountain Namibia **100** C2
Onjiva Angola *see* **Ondjiva**
Ono-i-Lau *i.* Fiji **107** I4
Onomichi Japan **75** D6
Onon *atoll* Micronesia *see* **Namonuito**
Onor, Gora *mt.* Russia **74** F2
Onotoa *atoll* Kiribati **107** H2
Onseepkans S. Africa **100** D5
Onslow Australia **108** A5
Onslow Bay U.S.A. **133** E5
Onstwedde Neth. **52** H1
Ontake-san *vol.* Japan **75** E6
Ontario *prov.* Canada **134** E1
Ontario U.S.A. **128** E4
Ontario, Lake Canada/U.S.A. **135** G2
Ontong Java Atoll Solomon Is **107** F2
Onutu *atoll* Kiribati *see* **Onotoa**
Onverwacht Suriname **143** G2
Onyx U.S.A. **128** D4
Oodnadatta Australia **111** A5
Oodweyne Somalia **98** E3
Ooolambeyan National Park Australia **111** D7
Ooldea Australia **109** E7
Ooldea Range *hills* Australia **109** E7
Oologah Lake *resr* U.S.A. **131** E4
Ooratippra *r.* Australia **110** B4
Oos-Londen S. Africa *see* **East London**
Oostburg Neth. **52** D3
Oostende Belgium *see* **Ostend**
Oostendorp Neth. **52** F2
Oosterhout Neth. **52** E3
Oosterschelde *est.* Neth. **52** D3
Oosterwolde Neth. **52** G2
Oostvleteren Belgium **52** C4
Oost-Vlieland Neth. **52** F1
Ootacamund India *see* **Udagamandalam**
Ootsa Lake Canada **120** E4
Ootsa Lake *l.* Canada **120** E4
Opal Mex. **131** C7
Opala Dem. Rep. Congo **98** C4
Oparino Russia **42** K4
Oparo *i.* Fr. Polynesia *see* **Rapa**
Opasatika *r.* Canada **122** E4
Opasatika Lake Canada **122** E4
Opasquia Canada **121** M4
Opataca, Lac *l.* Canada **122** G4
Opava Czechia **47** P6
Opel *hill* Germany **53** H5
Opelika U.S.A. **133** C5
Opelousas U.S.A. **131** E6
Opeongo Lake Canada **122** F5
Opheim U.S.A. **126** G2
Opienge Dem. Rep. Congo **98** C3
Opinaca *r.* Canada **122** F3
Opinaca, Réservoir *resr* Canada **122** F3
Opinnagau *r.* Canada **122** E3
Opiscotéo, Lac *l.* Canada **123** H3
Op Luang National Park Thai. **70** B3
Opmeer Neth. **52** E2
Opochka Russia **45** P8
Opocopa, Lac *l.* Canada **123** I3
Opodepe Mex. **136** B3
Opole Poland **47** P5
Oporto Port. **57** B3
Opotiki N.Z. **113** F4
Opp U.S.A. **133** C6
Oppdal Norway **44** F5
Oppeid Norway **44** I2
Oppeln Poland *see* **Opole**
Opportunity U.S.A. **126** D3
Opunake N.Z. **113** D4
Opuwo Namibia **99** B5
Oqsu *r.* Tajik. **89** I2
Oracle U.S.A. **129** H5
Oradea Romania **59** I1
Orahovac Kosovo *see* **Rahovec**
Orai India **82** D4
Oraibi U.S.A. **129** H4
Oraibi Wash *watercourse* U.S.A. **129** H4
Oral Kazakh. *see* **Ural'sk**
Oran Alg. **57** F6
Orán Arg. **144** D2
Orang India **83** H4
Ŏrang N. Korea **74** C4
Orange Australia **112** D4
Orange France **56** G4
Orange *r.* Namibia/S. Africa **100** C5
Orange *CA* U.S.A. **128** E5
Orange *MA* U.S.A. **135** I2
Orange *TX* U.S.A. **131** E6
Orange *VA* U.S.A. **135** F4
Orange, Cabo *c.* Brazil **143** H3
Orangeburg U.S.A. **133** D5
Orange City U.S.A. **130** D3
Orange Cone *sea feature* S. Atlantic Ocean **148** I8
Orange Free State *prov.* S. Africa *see* **Free State**
Orangeville Canada **134** E2
Orange Walk Belize **136** G5
Oranienburg Germany **53** N2
Oranje *r.* Namibia/S. Africa *see* **Orange**
Oranje Gebergte *hills* Suriname **143** G3
Oranjemund Namibia **100** C5

▶**Oranjestad** Aruba **137** J6
Capital of Aruba.

Oranmore Ireland **51** D4
Orapa Botswana **99** C6
Orăștie Romania **59** J2
Orașul Stalin Romania *see* **Brașov**
Oravais Fin. **44** M5
Orba Co *l.* China **82** E2
Orbetello Italy **58** D3
Orbost Australia **112** D6
Orcadas *research station* S. Atlantic Ocean **152** A2
Orchard City U.S.A. **129** J2
Orchha India **82** D4
Orchila, Isla *i.* Venez. **142** E1
Orchy *r.* U.K. **50** D4
Orcutt U.S.A. **128** C4
Ord *r.* Australia **108** E3
Ord U.S.A. **130** D3
Ord, Mount *hill* Australia **108** D4
Órdenes Spain *see* **Ordes**
Orderville U.S.A. **129** G3
Ordes Spain **57** B2
Ordesa y Monte Perdido, Parque Nacional de *nat. park* Spain **57** G2
Ord Mountain U.S.A. **128** E4
Ordos China *see* **Dongsheng**
Ord River Dam Australia **108** E4
Ordu *Hatay* Turkey *see* **Yayladağı**
Ordu *Ordu* Turkey **90** E2
Ordubad Azer. **91** G3
Ordway U.S.A. **130** C4
Ordzhonikidze Russia *see* **Vladikavkaz**
Ore Nigeria **96** D4
Oreana U.S.A. **128** D1
O Reăng Cambodia **71** D4
Örebro Sweden **45** I7
Oregon *IL* U.S.A. **130** F3
Oregon *OH* U.S.A. **134** D3
Oregon *state* U.S.A. **126** C4
Oregon City U.S.A. **126** C3
Orekhov Ukr. *see* **Orikhiv**
Orekhovo-Zuyevo Russia **42** H5
Orel' Kazakh. **80** G2
Orel Russia **43** H5
Orel, Gora *mt.* Russia **74** E1
Orel', Ozero *l.* Russia **74** E1
Orem U.S.A. **129** H1
Ore Mountains Czechia/Germany *see* **Erzgebirge**
Orenburg Russia **64** G4
Orense Spain *see* **Ourense**
Oreor Palau *see* **Koror**
Orepuki N.Z. **113** A8
Öresund *strait* Denmark/Sweden **45** H9
Oretana, Cordillera *mts* Spain *see* **Toledo, Montes de**
Orewa N.Z. **113** E3
Oreye Belgium **52** F4
Orfanou, Kolpos *b.* Greece **59** J4
Orford Australia **111** [inset]
Orford U.K. **49** I6
Orford Ness *hd* U.K. **49** I6
Organabo Fr. Guiana **143** H2
Organ Pipe Cactus National Monument *nat. park* U.S.A. **129** G5
Orge *r.* France **52** C6
Orhaneli Turkey **59** M5
Orhangazi Turkey **59** M4
Orhon Gol *r.* Mongolia **80** J2
Orichi Russia **42** K4
Oriental, Cordillera *mts* Bol. **142** E7
Oriental, Cordillera *mts* Col. **142** D2
Oriental, Cordillera *mts* Peru **142** E6
Orihuela Spain **57** F4
Orikhiv Ukr. **43** G7
Orillia Canada **134** F1
Orimattila Fin. **45** N6
Orin U.S.A. **126** G4
Orinoco *r.* Col./Venez. **142** F2
Orinoco, Delta del Venez. **142** F2
Orissa *state* India *see* **Odisha**
Orissaare Estonia **45** M7
Oristano *Sardinia* Italy **58** C5
Orivesi Fin. **45** N6
Orivesi *l.* Fin. **44** P5
Oriximiná Brazil **143** G4
Orizaba Mex. **136** E5

▶**Orizaba, Pico de** *vol.* Mex. **136** E5
Highest active volcano and 3rd highest mountain in North America.

Orizona Brazil **145** A2
Orkanger Norway **44** F5
Örkelljunga Sweden **45** H8
Orkla *r.* Norway **44** F5
Orkney S. Africa **101** H4
Orkney Islands *is* U.K. **50** F1
Orla U.S.A. **131** C6
Orland U.S.A. **128** B2
Orlândia Brazil **145** B3
Orlando U.S.A. **133** D6
Orland Park U.S.A. **134** B3
Orleans Brazil **145** A5
Orléans France **56** E3
Orleans *IN* U.S.A. **134** B4
Orleans *VT* U.S.A. **135** I1
Orléans, Île d' *i.* Canada **123** H5
Orléansville Alg. *see* **Chlef**
Orlik Russia **72** H2
Orlov Russia **42** K4
Orlov Gay Russia **43** K6
Orlovskiy Russia **43** I7
Ormara Pak. **89** G5
Ormara, Ras *hd* Pak. **89** G5
Ormiston Canada **121** J5
Ormoc Phil. **69** G4
Ormskirk U.K. **48** E5

Ormstown Canada 135 I1
Ornach Pak. 89 G5
Ornain r. France 52 E6
Orne r. France 56 D2
Ørnes Norway 44 H3
Örnsköldsvik Sweden 44 K5
Orobie, Alpi mts Italy 58 C1
Orobo, Serra do hills Brazil 145 C1
Orodara Burkina Faso 96 C3
Orofino U.S.A. 126 D3
Oro Grande U.S.A. 128 E4
Orogrande U.S.A. 127 G6
Orol Dengizi salt l. Kazakh./Uzbek. see Aral Sea
Oromocto Canada 123 I5
Oromocto Lake Canada 123 I5
Oron Israel 85 B4
Orona atoll Kiribati 107 I2
Orono U.S.A. 132 G2
Orontes r. Asia see 'Āṣī, Nahr al
Orontes r. Lebanon/Syria 85 C2
Oroqen Zizhiqi China see Alihe
Oroquieta Phil. 69 G5
Orós, Açude resr Brazil 143 K5
Orosei, Golfo di b. Sardinia Italy 58 C4
Orosháza Hungary 59 I1
Oroville U.S.A. 128 C2
Oroville, Lake U.S.A. 128 C2
Orqohan China 74 A2
Orr U.S.A. 130 E1
Orsa Sweden 45 I6
Orsha Belarus 43 F5
Orshanka Russia 42 J4
Orsk Russia 64 G4
Ørsta Norway 44 E5
Orta Toroslar plat. Turkey 85 A1
Ortegal, Cabo c. Spain 57 C2
Orthez France 56 D5
Ortigueira Spain 57 C2
Ortíz Mex. 127 F7
Ortles mt. Italy 58 D1
Orton U.K. 48 E4
Ortona Italy 58 F3
Ortonville U.S.A. 130 D2
Ortospana Afgh. see Kābul
Orulgan, Khrebet mts Russia 65 N3
Orumbo Namibia 100 C2
Orūmīyeh Iran see Urmia
Oruro Bol. 142 E7
Orvieto Italy 58 E3
Orville Coast Antarctica 152 L1
Orwell OH U.S.A. 134 E3
Orwell VT U.S.A. 135 I2
Oryol Russia see Orel
Os Norway 44 G5
Osa Russia 41 R4
Osa, Península de pen. Costa Rica 137 H7
Osage IA U.S.A. 130 E3
Osage WV U.S.A. 134 E4
Osage WY U.S.A. 126 G3
Ōsaka Japan 75 D6
Osakarovka Kazakh. 80 D1
Ōsaki Japan 75 F5
Osam r. Bulg. 59 K3
Osawatomie U.S.A. 130 E4
Osborne U.S.A. 130 D4
Osby Sweden 45 H8
Osceola IA U.S.A. 130 E3
Osceola MO U.S.A. 130 E4
Osceola NE U.S.A. 130 D3
Oschatz Germany 53 N3
Oschersleben (Bode) Germany 53 L2
Oschiri Sardinia Italy 58 C4
Ösel i. Estonia see Hiiumaa
Osetr r. Russia 43 H5
Ōse-zaki pt Japan 75 C6
Osgoode Canada 135 H1
Osgood Mountains U.S.A. 126 D4
Osh Kyrg. 80 D3
Oshakati Namibia 99 B5
Oshawa Canada 135 F2
Oshika-hantō pen. Japan 75 F5
Ō-shima i. Japan 74 E4
Ō-shima i. Japan 75 E6
Oshkosh NE U.S.A. 130 C3
Oshkosh WI U.S.A. 134 A1
Oshmyany Belarus see Ashmyany
Oshnavīyeh Iran 88 B2
Oshogbo Nigeria see Osogbo
Oshtorān Kūh mt. Iran 88 C3
Ōshū Japan 75 F5
Oshwe Dem. Rep. Congo 98 B4
Osijek Croatia 58 H2
Osilinka r. Canada 120 E3
Osimo Italy 58 E3
Osipenko Ukr. see Berdyans'k
Osipovichi Belarus see Asipovichy
Osiyan India 82 C4
oSizweni S. Africa 101 J4
Osječenica mts Bos. & Herz. 58 G2
Ösjön l. Sweden 44 I5
Oskaloosa U.S.A. 130 E3
Oskarshamn Sweden 45 J8
Öskemen Kazakh. see Ust'-Kamenogorsk

▶Oslo Norway 45 G7
Capital of Norway.

Oslofjorden sea chan. Norway 45 G7
Osmanabad India 84 C2
Osmancık Turkey 90 D2
Osmaneli Turkey 59 M4
Osmaniye Turkey 90 E3
Osmannagar India 84 C2
Os'mino Russia 45 P7
Osnabrück Germany 53 I2
Osnaburg atoll Fr. Polynesia see Mururoa
Osogbo Nigeria 96 D4
Osogovska Planina mts Bulg./Macedonia 59 J3
Osogovske Planine mts Bulg./Macedonia see Osogovska Planina
Osogovski Planini mts Bulg./Macedonia see Osogovska Planina
Osorno Chile 144 B6
Osorno Spain 57 D2
Osoyoos Canada 120 G5
Osøyro Norway 45 D6
Osprey Reef Australia 110 D2
Oss Neth. 52 F3
Ossa, Mount Australia 111 [inset]
Osseo U.S.A. 122 C5
Ossineke U.S.A. 134 D1
Ossining U.S.A. 135 I3
Ossipee U.S.A. 135 J2
Ossipee Lake U.S.A. 135 J2
Oßmannstedt Germany 53 L3
Ossokmanuan Lake Canada 123 I3
Ossora Russia 65 R4
Ostashkov Russia 42 G4
Ostbevern Germany 53 H2
Oste r. Germany 53 J1
Ostend Belgium 52 C3
Ostende Belgium see Ostend
Osterburg (Altmark) Germany 53 L2
Österbymo Sweden 45 I8
Österdalälven l. Sweden 45 H6
Østerdalen valley Norway 45 G5
Osterfeld Germany 53 L3
Osterholz-Scharmbeck Germany 53 I1
Osterode am Harz Germany 53 K3
Österreich country Europe see Austria
Östersund Sweden 44 I5
Osterwieck Germany 53 K3
Ostfriesische Inseln Germany see East Frisian Islands
Ostfriesland reg. Germany 53 H1
Östhammar Sweden 45 K6
Ostrava Czechia 47 Q6
Ostróda Poland 47 Q4
Ostrogozhsk Russia 43 H6
Ostrov Czechia 53 M4
Ostrov Russia 45 P8
Ostrovets Poland see Ostrowiec Świętokrzyski
Ostrovnoy Russia 153 G2
Ostrovskoye Russia 42 I4
Ostrov Vrangelya i. Russia see Wrangel Island
Ostrów Poland see Ostrów Wielkopolski
Ostrowiec Poland see Ostrowiec Świętokrzyski
Ostrowiec Świętokrzyski Poland 43 D6
Ostrów Mazowiecka Poland 47 R4
Ostrowo Poland see Ostrów Wielkopolski
Ostrów Wielkopolski Poland 47 P5
O'Sullivan Lake Canada 122 D4
Ōsumi-shotō is Japan 75 C7
Osuna Spain 57 D5
Oswego KS U.S.A. 131 E4
Oswego NY U.S.A. 135 G2
Oswestry U.K. 49 D6
Otago Peninsula N.Z. 113 C7
Otahiti i. Fr. Polynesia see Tahiti
Otaki N.Z. 113 E5
Otanmäki Fin. 44 O4
Otaru Japan 74 F4
Otavi Namibia 99 B5
Ōtawara Japan 75 F5
Otdia atoll Marshall Is see Wotje
Otelnuc, Lac l. Canada 123 H2
Otematata N.Z. 113 C7
Otepää Estonia 45 O7
Otgon Tenger Uul mt. Mongolia 80 I2
oThongathi S. Africa 101 J5
Otinapa Mex. 131 B7
Otira N.Z. 113 C6
Otis U.S.A. 130 C3
Otish, Monts hills Canada 123 H4
Otjinene Namibia 99 B6
Otjiwarongo Namibia 99 B6
Otjozondjupa admin. reg. Namibia 100 C1
Otley U.K. 48 F5
Otorohanga N.Z. 113 E4
Otoskwin r. Canada 121 N5
Otpor Russia see Zabaykal'sk
Otradnoye Russia see Otradnyy
Otradnyy Russia 43 K5
Otranto Italy 58 H4
Otranto, Strait of Albania/Italy 58 H4
Otrogovo Russia see Stepnoye
Otrozhnyy Russia 65 S3
Otsego Lake U.S.A. 135 H2
Ōtsu Japan 75 D6
Otta Norway 45 F6

▶Ottawa Canada 135 H1
Capital of Canada.

Ottawa r. Canada 122 G5
also known as Rivière des Outaouais
Ottawa IL U.S.A. 130 F3
Ottawa KS U.S.A. 130 E4
Ottawa OH U.S.A. 134 C3
Ottawa Islands Canada 122 E2
Otter r. U.K. 49 D8
Otterbein U.S.A. 134 B3
Otterburn U.K. 48 E3
Otter Rapids Canada 122 E4
Ottersberg Germany 53 J1
Ottignies Belgium 52 E4
Ottumwa U.S.A. 130 E3
Ottweiler Germany 53 H5
Otukpo Nigeria 96 D4
Oturkpo Nigeria see Otukpo
Otuzco Peru 142 C5
Otway, Cape Australia 112 A7
Otway National Park Australia 112 A7
Ouachita r. U.S.A. 131 F6
Ouachita, Lake U.S.A. 131 E5
Ouachita Mountains U.S.A. 131 E5
Ouadda Cent. Afr. Rep. 98 C3
Ouaddaï reg. Chad 97 F3

▶Ouagadougou Burkina Faso 96 C3
Capital of Burkina Faso.

Ouahigouya Burkina Faso 96 C3
Ouahran Alg. see Oran
Ouaka r. Cent. Afr. Rep. 98 B3
Oualâta Mauritania 96 C3
Oualâta, Dahr hills Mauritania 96 C3
Ouallam Niger 96 D3
Ouanda Djallé Cent. Afr. Rep. 98 C3
Ouando Cent. Afr. Rep. 98 C3
Ouango Cent. Afr. Rep. 98 C3
Ouara r. Cent. Afr. Rep. 98 C3
Ouarâne reg. Mauritania 96 C2
Ouargaye Burkina Faso 96 D3
Ouargla Alg. 54 F5
Ouarogou Burkina Faso see Ouargaye
Ouarzazate Morocco 54 C5
Ouasiemsca r. Canada 123 G4
Oubangui r. Cent. Afr. Rep./Dem. Rep. Congo see Ubangi
Oubergpas pass S. Africa 100 G7
Oudenaarde Belgium 52 D4
Oudômxai Laos 70 C2
Oudtshoorn S. Africa 100 F7
Oud-Turnhout Belgium 52 E3
Oued Tlélat Alg. 57 F6
Oued Zem Morocco 54 C5
Oued Zénati Alg. 58 B6
Ouessant, Île d' i. France 56 B2
Ouesso Congo 98 B3
Ouest, Pointe de l' pt Canada 123 I4
Ouezzane Morocco 57 D6
Oughter, Lough l. Ireland 51 E3
Ouguati Namibia 100 B1
Ouistreham France 49 G9
Oujda Morocco 57 F6
Oujeft Mauritania 96 B3
Oulainen Fin. 44 N4
Oulangan kansallispuisto nat. park Fin. 44 P3
Ouled Djellal Alg. 57 I6
Ouled Farès Alg. 57 G5
Ouled Naïl, Monts des mts Alg. 57 H6
Oulu Fin. 44 N4
Oulujärvi l. Fin. 44 O4
Oulujoki r. Fin. 44 N4
Oulunsalo Fin. 44 N4
Oulx Italy 58 B2
Oum-Chalouba Chad 97 F3
Oum el Bouaghi Alg. 58 B7
Oum-Hadjer Chad 97 E3
Ounasjoki r. Fin. 44 N3
Oundle U.K. 49 G6
Oungre Canada 121 K5
Ounianga Kébir Chad 97 F3
Oupeye Belgium 52 F4
Our r. Lux. 52 G5
Our, Vallée de l' valley Germany/Lux. 52 G5
Oura, Akrotirio pt Greece 59 L5
Ouray CO U.S.A. 129 J2
Ouray UT U.S.A. 129 I1
Ourcq r. France 52 D5
Ourense Spain 57 C2
Ouricuri Brazil 143 J5
Ourinhos Brazil 145 A3
Ouro r. Brazil 145 A1
Ouro Preto Brazil 145 C3
Ourthe r. Belgium 52 F4
Ous Russia 41 S3
Ouse r. England U.K. 48 G5
Ouse r. England U.K. 49 H8
Outaouais, Rivière des r. Canada see Ottawa
Outapi Namibia 99 B5
Outardes, Rivière aux r. Canada 123 H4
Outardes Quatre, Réservoir resr Canada 123 H4
Outer Hebrides is U.K. 50 B3
Outer Mongolia country Asia see Mongolia
Outer Santa Barbara Channel U.S.A. 128 D5
Outjo Namibia 99 B6
Outlook Canada 121 J5
Outokumpu Fin. 44 P5
Out Skerries is U.K. 50 [inset]
Ouvéa atoll New Caledonia 107 G4
Ouyanghai Shuiku resr China 77 G3
Ouyen Australia 111 C7
Ouzel r. U.K. 49 G6
Ovace, Punta d' mt. Corsica France 56 I6
Ovacık Turkey 85 A1
Ovada Italy 58 C2
Ovalle Chile 144 B4
Ovamboland reg. Namibia 99 B5
Ovan Gabon 98 B3
Ovar Port. 57 B3
Overath Germany 53 H4
Överkalix Sweden 44 M3
Overlander Roadhouse Australia 109 A6
Overland Park U.S.A. 130 E4
Overton U.S.A. 129 F3
Övertorneå Sweden 44 M3
Överum Sweden 45 J8
Overveen Neth. 52 E2
Ovid CO U.S.A. 130 C3
Ovid NY U.S.A. 135 G2
Oviedo Spain 57 D2
Øvre Anárjohka Nasjonalpark nat. park Norway 44 N2
Øvre Dividal Nasjonalpark nat. park Norway 44 K2
Øvre Rendal Norway 45 G6
Ovruch Ukr. 43 F6
Ovsyanka Russia 74 B1
Owando Congo 98 B4
Owa Rafa i. Solomon Is see Santa Ana
Owasco Lake U.S.A. 135 G2
Owase Japan 75 E6
Owatonna U.S.A. 130 E2
Owego U.S.A. 135 G2
Owel, Lough l. Ireland 51 E4
Owen Island Myanmar 71 B5
Owenmore r. Mayo Ireland 51 C3
Owenmore r. Sligo Ireland 51 D3
Owenreagh r. U.K. 51 E3
Owen River N.Z. 113 D5
Owens r. U.S.A. 128 E3
Owensboro U.S.A. 134 B5
Owen Sound Canada 134 E1
Owen Sound inlet Canada 134 E1
Owen Stanley Range mts P.N.G. 69 L8
Owenton U.S.A. 134 C4
Owerri Nigeria 96 D4
Owikeno Lake Canada 120 E5
Owingsville U.S.A. 134 D4
Owl r. Canada 121 M3
Owl Creek Mountains U.S.A. 126 F4
Owo Nigeria 96 D4
Owosso U.S.A. 134 C2
Owyhee U.S.A. 126 D4
Owyhee r. U.S.A. 126 D4
Owyhee Mountains U.S.A. 126 D4
Öxarfjörður b. Iceland 44 [inset 1]
Oxbow Canada 121 K5
Ox Creek r. U.S.A. 130 C1
Oxelösund Sweden 45 J7
Oxford N.Z. 113 D6
Oxford U.K. 49 F7
Oxford IN U.S.A. 134 B3
Oxford MA U.S.A. 135 J2
Oxford MD U.S.A. 135 G4
Oxford MS U.S.A. 131 F5
Oxford NC U.S.A. 132 E4
Oxford NY U.S.A. 135 H2
Oxford OH U.S.A. 134 C4
Oxford House Canada 121 M4
Oxford Lake Canada 121 M4
Oxley Australia 112 B5
Oxleys Peak Australia 112 E3
Oxley Wild Rivers National Park Australia 112 F3
Ox Mountains hills Ireland 51 C4
Oxnard U.S.A. 128 D4
Oxtongue Lake Canada 135 F1
Oxus r. Asia see Amudar'ya
Øya Norway 44 H3
Oyama Japan 75 E5
Oyapock r. Brazil/Fr. Guiana 143 H3
Oyem Gabon 98 B3
Oyen Canada 121 I5
Oykel r. U.K. 50 E3
Oyo Nigeria 96 D4
Oyonnax France 56 G3
Oyster Rocks is India 84 B3
Oyten Germany 53 J1
Oytograk China 83 E1
Oyukludağı mt. Turkey 85 A1
Oyyaylak China 83 F1
Özalp Turkey 91 G3
Ozamis Phil. 69 G5
Ozark AL U.S.A. 133 C6
Ozark AR U.S.A. 131 E5
Ozark MO U.S.A. 131 E4
Ozark Plateau U.S.A. 131 E4
Ozarks, Lake of the U.S.A. 130 E4
O'zbekiston country Asia see Uzbekistan
Özen Kazakh. see Kyzylsay
Ozernovskiy Russia 65 Q4
Ozernyy Russia 43 G5
Ozerpakh Russia 74 F1
Ozersk Russia 45 M9
Ozerskiy Russia 74 F3
Ozery Russia 43 H5
Ozeryane Russia 74 C2
Ozieri Sardinia Italy 58 C4
Ozinki Russia 43 K6
Oznachennoye Russia see Sayanogorsk
Ozona U.S.A. 131 C6
Ozuki Japan 75 C6

P

Paamiut Greenland 119 N3
Pa-an Myanmar see Hpa-an
Paanayarvi Natsional'nyy Park nat. park Russia 44 Q3
Paanopa i. Kiribati see Banaba
Paarl S. Africa 100 D7
Paatsjoki r. Europe see Patsoyoki
Paballelo S. Africa 100 E5
P'abal-li N. Korea 74 C4
Pabbay i. U.K. 50 B3
Pabianice Poland 47 Q5
Pabianitz Poland see Pabianice
Pabna Bangl. 83 G4
Pabradė Lith. 45 N9
Pab Range mts Pak. 89 G5
Pacaás Novos, Parque Nacional nat. park Brazil 142 F6
Pacaraimã, Serra mts S. America see Pakaraima Mountains
Pacasmayo Peru 142 C5
Pachagarh Bangl. see Panchagarh
Pachala South Sudan 97 G4
Pacheco Chihuahua Mex. 127 F7
Pacheco Zacatecas Mex. 131 C7
Pachikha Russia 42 J3
Pachino Sicily Italy 58 F6
Pachmarhi India 82 D5
Pachor India 82 D5
Pachora India 84 B1
Pachpadra India 82 C4
Pachuca Mex. 136 E4
Pachuca de Soto Mex. see Pachuca
Pacific-Antarctic Ridge sea feature S. Pacific Ocean 151 J9
Pacific Grove U.S.A. 128 C3

▶Pacific Ocean 150
Largest ocean in the world.

Pacific Rim National Park Canada 120 E5
Pacitan Indon. 68 E8
Packsaddle Australia 111 C6
Pacoval Brazil 143 H4
Pacuí r. Brazil 145 B2
Paczków Poland 47 P5
Padali Russia see Amursk
Padampur India 82 C3
Padang Indon. 68 C7
Padang i. Indon. 71 C7
Padang Endau Malaysia 71 C7
Padangpanjang Indon. 68 C7
Padangsidimpuan Indon. 71 B7
Padany Russia 42 G3
Padatha, Kūh-e mt. Iran 88 C3
Padaung Myanmar 70 A3
Padcaya Bol. 142 F8
Paddington Australia 112 B4
Paden City U.S.A. 134 E4
Paderborn Germany 53 I3
Paderborn/Lippstadt airport Germany 53 I3
Padeșu, Vârful mt. Romania 59 J2
Padibyu Myanmar 70 B2
Padilla Bol. 142 F7
Padjelanta nationalpark nat. park Sweden 44 J3
Padova Italy see Padua
Padrão, Ponta pt Angola 99 B4
Padrauna India 83 F4
Padre Island U.S.A. 131 D7
Padstow U.K. 49 C8
Padsvillye Belarus 45 O9
Padua India 84 D2
Padua Italy 58 D2
Paducah KY U.S.A. 131 F4
Paducah TX U.S.A. 131 C5
Padum India 82 D2
Paegam N. Korea 74 C4
Paektu-san mt. China/N. Korea see Baitou Shan
Pafos Cyprus see Paphos
Pafuri Moz. 101 J2
Pag Croatia 58 F2
Pag i. Croatia 58 F2
Paga Indon. 108 C2
Pagadian Phil. 69 G5
Pagai Selatan i. Indon. 68 C7
Pagalu i. Equat. Guinea see Annobón
Pagan i. N. Mariana Is 69 L3
Pagasitikos Kolpos b. Greece 59 J5
Pagatan Indon. 68 F7
Page U.S.A. 129 H3
Paget, Mount S. Georgia 144 I8
Paget Cay reef Australia 110 F3
Pagon i. N. Mariana Is see Pagan
Pagosa Springs U.S.A. 127 G5
Pagqên China see Gadê
Pagwa River Canada 122 D4
Pagwi P.N.G. 69 K7
Pāhala U.S.A. 127 [inset]
Pahang r. Malaysia 71 C7
Pahlgam India 82 C2
Pāhoa U.S.A. 127 [inset]
Pahokee U.S.A. 133 D7
Pahranagat Range mts U.S.A. 129 F3
Pahrump U.S.A. 129 F3
Pahuj r. India 82 D4
Pahute Mesa plat. U.S.A. 128 E3
Pai Thai. 70 B3
Paicines U.S.A. 128 C3
Paide Estonia 45 N7
Paignton U.K. 49 D8
Päijänne l. Fin. 45 N6
Paikü Co l. China 83 F3
Pailĭn Cambodia 71 C4
Pailolo Channel U.S.A. 127 [inset]
Paimio Fin. 45 M6
Painel Brazil 145 A4
Painesville U.S.A. 134 E3
Pains Brazil 145 B3
Painted Desert U.S.A. 129 H3
Painted Rock Dam U.S.A. 129 G5
Paint Hills Canada see Wemindji
Paint Rock U.S.A. 131 D6
Paintsville U.S.A. 134 D5
Paisley U.K. 50 E5
Paita Peru 142 B5
Paitou China 77 I2
Paiva Couceiro Angola see Quipungo
Paizhouwan China 77 G2
Pajala Sweden 44 M3
Paka Malaysia 71 C6
Pakala India 84 C3
Pakanbaru Indon. see Pekanbaru
Pakangyi Myanmar 70 A2
Pakaraima Mountains S. America 142 F3
Pakaur India see Pakur
Pakesley (abandoned) Canada 122 E5
Pakhachi Russia 65 R3
Pakhoi China see Beihai
Paki Nigeria 96 D3

▶Pakistan country Asia 89 H4
4th most populous country in Asia and 6th in the world.

Pakkat Indon. 71 B7
Paknampho Thai. see Nakhon Sawan
Pakokku Myanmar 70 A2
Pakowki Lake imp. l. Canada 121 I5
Pakpattan Pak. 89 I4
Pak Phanang Thai. 71 C5
Pak Phayun Thai. 71 C6
Pakruojis Lith. 45 M9
Paks Hungary 58 H1
Pakse Laos see Pakxé
Pak Tam Chung H.K. China 77 [inset]
Pak Thong Chai Thai. 70 C4
Pakur India 83 F4
Pakxan Laos 70 C3
Pakxé Laos 70 D4
Pakxeng Laos 70 C2
Pala Chad 97 E4
Pala Myanmar 71 B4
Palaestinia reg. Asia see Palestine
Palaiochora Greece 59 J7
Palaiseau France 52 C6
Palakkad India 84 C4
Palakkat India see Palakkad
Palamakoloi Botswana 100 F2
Palamau India see Palamu
Palamós Spain 57 H3
Palamu India 83 F5
Palana Russia 65 Q4
Palandur India 84 D1
Palangān, Kūh-e mts Iran 89 F4
Palangkaraya Indon. 68 E7
Palani India 84 C4
Palanpur India 82 C4
Palantak Pak. 89 G5
Palapye Botswana 101 H2
Palatka Russia 65 Q3
Palatka U.S.A. 133 D6
Palau country N. Pacific Ocean 69 I5
Palau Islands Palau 69 I5
Palauk Myanmar 71 B4
Palaw Myanmar 71 B4
Palawan i. Phil. 68 F5
Palawan Passage str. Phil. 68 F5
Palawan Trough sea feature N. Pacific Ocean 150 D5
Palayankottai India 84 C4
Palchal Lake India 84 D2
Paldiski Estonia 45 N7
Palekh Russia 42 I4
Palembang Indon. 68 C7
Palena Chile 144 B6
Palencia Spain 57 D2
Palermo Sicily Italy 58 E5
Palestine hist. area Asia 85 B3
Palestine U.S.A. 131 E6
Paletwa Myanmar 70 A2
Palezgir Chauki Pak. 89 H4
Palghat India see Palakkad
Palgrave, Mount hill Australia 109 A5
Palhoça Brazil 145 A4
Pali Chhattisgarh India 84 D1
Pali Mahar. India 84 B2
Pali Rajasthan India 82 C4

▶Palikir Micronesia 150 G5
Capital of Micronesia.

Palimé Togo 96 D4
Palinuro, Capo c. Italy 58 F4
Paliouri, Akra pt Greece see Paliouri, Akrotirio
Paliouri, Akrotirio pt Greece 59 J5
Palisade U.S.A. 129 I2
Paliseul Belgium 52 F5
Palitana India 82 B5
Palivere Estonia 45 M7
Palk Bay Sri Lanka 84 C4
Palkino Russia 45 P8
Palkonda Range mts India 84 C3
Palk Strait India/Sri Lanka 84 C4
Palla Bianca mt. Austria/Italy see Weißkugel
Pallamallawa Australia 112 E2
Pallas Green New Ireland 51 D5
Pallasovka Russia 43 J6
Pallas-Yllästunturin kansallispuisto nat. park Fin. 44 M2
Pallavaram India 84 D3
Palliser, Cape N.Z. 113 E5
Palliser, Îles is Fr. Polynesia 151 K7
Palliser Bay N.Z. 113 E5
Pallu India 82 C3
Palma r. Brazil 145 B1
Palma del Río Spain 57 D5
Palma de Mallorca Spain 57 H4
Palmaner India 84 C3
Palmares Brazil 143 K5
Palmares do Sul Brazil 145 A5
Palmas Paraná Brazil 145 A4
Palmas Tocantins Brazil 142 I6
Palmas, Cape Liberia 96 C4
Palm Bay U.S.A. 133 D7
Palmdale U.S.A. 128 D4
Palmeira Brazil 145 A4
Palmeira das Missões Brazil 144 F3
Palmeira dos Índios Brazil 143 K5
Palmeirais Brazil 143 J5
Palmeiras Brazil 145 C1
Palmeirinhas, Ponta das pt Angola 99 B4
Palmer research station Antarctica 152 L2
Palmer r. Australia 110 C3
Palmer watercourse Australia 109 F6
Palmer U.S.A. 118 D3
Palmer Land reg. Antarctica 152 L2
Palmerston N.T. Australia 108 E3
Palmerston N.T. Australia see Darwin
Palmerston Canada 134 E2
Palmerston atoll Cook Is 107 J3
Palmerston N.Z. 113 C7
Palmerston North N.Z. 113 E5
Palmerton U.S.A. 135 H3
Palmerville Australia 110 D2
Palmetto Point Bahamas 133 E7
Palmi Italy 58 F5
Palmira Col. 142 C3
Palmira Cuba 133 D8
Palm Springs U.S.A. 128 E5
Palmyra Syria see Tadmur
Palmyra MO U.S.A. 130 F4
Palmyra PA U.S.A. 135 G3
Palmyra VA U.S.A. 135 F5

▶Palmyra Atoll terr. N. Pacific Ocean 150 J5
United States Unincorporated Territory.

Palmyras Point India 83 F5
Palni Hills India 84 C4
Palo Alto U.S.A. 128 B3
Palo Blanco Mex. 131 C7
Palo Chino watercourse Mex. 127 E7
Palo Duro watercourse U.S.A. 131 C5
Paloich South Sudan 86 D7
Palojärvi Fin. 44 M2
Palojoensuu Fin. 44 M2
Palomaa Fin. 44 O2
Palomar Mountain U.S.A. 128 E5
Paloncha India 84 D2
Palo Pinto U.S.A. 131 D5
Palopo Indon. 69 G7
Palos, Cabo de c. Spain 57 F5
Palo Verde U.S.A. 129 F5
Paltamo Fin. 44 O4
Palu Indon. 68 F7
Palu i. Indon. 108 C2
Palu Turkey 91 E3
Pal'vart Turkm. 89 G2
Palwal India 82 D3
Palwancha India see Paloncha
Palyeskaya Nizina marsh Belarus/Ukr. see Pripet Marshes
Pamai China 76 D2

▶Pamana i. Indon. 108 C2
Most southerly point of Asia.

Pambarra Moz. 101 L1
Pambula Australia 112 D6
Pamidi India 84 C3
Pamiers France 56 E5
Pamir mts Asia 89 I2
Pamlico Sound sea chan. U.S.A. 133 E5
Pamouscachiou, Lac l. Canada 123 H4
Pampa U.S.A. 131 C5
Pampa de Infierno Arg. 144 D3
Pampas reg. Arg. 144 D5
Pampeluna Spain see Pamplona
Pamphylia hist. area Turkey 59 N6
Pamplin U.S.A. 135 F5
Pamplona Col. 142 D2
Pamplona Spain 57 F2
Pampow Germany 53 L1
Pamukova Turkey 59 N4
Pamzal India 82 D2
Pana U.S.A. 130 F4
Panaca U.S.A. 129 F3
Panache, Lake Canada 122 E5
Panagyurishte Bulg. 59 K3
Panaitan i. Indon. 68 D8

Panaji India 84 B3
Panama *country* Central America 137 H7
Panamá Panama *see* Panama City
Panamá, Canal de Panama 137 I7
Panama, Gulf of *g.* Panama 137 I7
Panama, Isthmus of Panama *see* Panamá, Istmo de
Panamá, Istmo de Panama 137 I7

▶Panama City Panama 137 I7
Capital of Panama.

Panama City U.S.A. 133 C6
Panamint Range *mts* U.S.A. 128 E3
Panamint Valley U.S.A. 128 E3
Panao Peru 142 C5
Panarea, Isola *i.* Italy 58 F5
Panarik Indon. 71 E7
Panay *i.* Phil. 69 G4
Pancake Range *mts* U.S.A. 129 F2
Pančevo Serbia 59 I2
Panchagarh Bangl. 83 G4
Pancsova Serbia *see* Pančevo
Panda Moz. 101 L3
Pandan, Selat *strait* Sing. 71 [inset]
Pandan Reservoir Sing. 71 [inset]
Pandeiros *r.* Brazil 145 B1
Pandharpur India 84 B2
Pandy U.K. 49 E7
Paneas Syria *see* Bāniyās
Panevėžys Lith. 45 N9
Panfilov Kazakh. *see* Zharkent
Pang, Nam *r.* Myanmar 70 B2
Panghsang Myanmar 70 B2
Pangi Range *mts* Pak. 89 I3
Pangkalanbuun Indon. 68 E7
Pangkalansusu Indon. 71 B6
Pangkalpinang Indon. 68 D7
Pangkalsiang, Tanjung *pt* Indon. 69 G7
Panglang Myanmar 70 B1
Pangman Canada 121 J5
Pangnirtung Canada 119 L3
Pangody Russia 64 I3
Pangong Tso *salt l.* China/India *see* Bangong Co
Pang Sida National Park Thai. 71 C4
Pang Sua, Sungai *r.* Sing. 71 [inset]
Pangtara Myanmar 76 C4
Pangu He *r.* China 74 B1
Panguitch U.S.A. 129 G3
Panhandle U.S.A. 131 C5
Panipat India 82 D3
Panir Pak. 89 G4
Panj Tajik. 89 H2
Panjāb Afgh. 89 G3
Panjakent Tajik. 89 G2
Panjang *i.* Indon. 71 E7
Panjang, Bukit Sing. 71 [inset]
Panjgur Pak. 89 G5
Panjim India *see* Panaji
Panji Poyon Tajik. 89 H2
Panjnad *r.* Pak. 89 H4
Panjshayr *reg.* Afgh. 89 H3
Pankakoski Fin. 44 Q5
Panlian China *see* Miyi
Panna India 82 E4
Panna *reg.* India 82 D4
Pannawonica Australia 108 B5
Pano Lefkara Cyprus 85 A2
Panorama Brazil 145 A3
Panormus *Sicily* Italy *see* Palermo
Panshi China 74 B4
Panshui China *see* Pu'an

▶Pantanal *marsh* Brazil 143 G7
Largest area of wetlands in the world.

Pantanal Matogrossense, Parque Nacional do *nat. park* Brazil 143 G7
Pantano U.S.A. 129 H6
Pantar *i.* Indon. 108 D2
Pantelaria *Sicily* Italy *see* Pantelleria
Pantelleria *Sicily* Italy 58 D6
Pantelleria, Isola di *i. Sicily* Italy 58 E6
Pantha Myanmar 70 A2
Panther *r.* U.S.A. 134 B5
Panth Piploda India 82 C5
Panticapaeum Crimea *see* Kerch
Pantonlabu Indon. 71 B6
Pánuco *Sinaloa* Mex. 131 B8
Pánuco *Veracruz* Mex. 136 E4
Panwari India 82 D4
Panxian China 76 E3
Panyu China 77 G4
Panzhihua China 76 D3
Panzi Dem. Rep. Congo 99 B4
Paola Italy 58 G5
Paola U.S.A. 130 E4
Paoli U.S.A. 134 B4
Paoua Cent. Afr. Rep. 98 B3
Paôy Pêt Cambodia 71 C4
Pápa Hungary 58 G1
Papa, Monte del *mt.* Italy 58 F4
Papagni *r.* India 84 C3
Papahānaumokuākea *tourist site* U.S.A. 150 I4
Pāpa'ikou U.S.A. 127 [inset]
Papakura N.Z. 113 E3
Papanasam India 84 C4
Papantla Mex. 136 E4
Paparoa National Park N.Z. 113 C6
Papa Stour *i.* U.K. 50 [inset]
Papa Westray *i.* U.K. 50 G1
Papay *i.* U.K. *see* Papa Westray

▶Papeete Fr. Polynesia 151 K7
Capital of French Polynesia.

Papenburg Germany 53 H1
Paphos Cyprus 85 A2
Paphus Cyprus *see* Paphos
Papillion U.S.A. 130 D3
Papoose Lake U.S.A. 129 F3
Pappenheim Germany 53 K6
Papua, Gulf of P.N.G. 69 K8

▶Papua New Guinea *country* Oceania 106 E2
2nd largest and 2nd most populous country in Oceania.

Pā Qal'eh Iran 88 D4
Par U.K. 49 C8
Pará *r.* Brazil 145 B2
Pará, Rio do *r.* Brazil 143 I4
Paraburdoo Australia 109 B5
Paracatu Brazil 145 B2
Paracatu *r.* Brazil 145 B2
Paracel Islands S. China Sea 68 E3
Parachilna Australia 111 B6
Parachute U.S.A. 129 I2
Paraćin Serbia 59 I3
Paracuru Brazil 143 K4
Pará de Minas Brazil 145 B2
Paradis Canada 122 F4
Paradise *r.* Canada 123 K3
Paradise U.S.A. 128 C2
Paradise Hill Canada 121 I4
Paradise Peak U.S.A. 128 E2
Paradise River Canada 123 K3
Paradwip India 83 F5
Paraetonium Egypt *see* Marsá Maṭrūḥ
Paragominas Brazil 143 I4
Paragould U.S.A. 131 F4
Paragua *i.* Phil. *see* Palawan
Paraguaçu Paulista Brazil 145 A3
Paraguay *r.* Arg./Para. 144 E3
Paraguay *country* S. America 144 E2
Paraíba do Sul *r.* Brazil 145 C3
Parainen Fin. *see* Pargas
Paraíso do Tocantins Brazil 143 I6
Paraisópolis Brazil 145 B3
Parak Iran 88 D5
Pārak Hūtān Iran 89 F5
Parakou Benin 96 D4
Paralakhemundi India 84 E2
Paralkot India 84 D2
Paramagudi India *see* Paramakkudi
Paramakkudi India 84 C4

▶Paramaribo Suriname 143 G2
Capital of Suriname.

Paramillo, Parque Nacional *nat. park* Col. 142 C2
Paramirim Brazil 145 C1
Paramo Frontino *mt.* Col. 142 C2
Paramus U.S.A. 135 H3
Paramushir, Ostrov *i.* Russia 65 Q4
Paran, Naḥal *watercourse* Israel 85 B4
Paraná Arg. 144 D4
Paranã Brazil 145 B1
Paraná *r.* Brazil 145 A1
Paraná *state* Brazil 145 A4

▶Paraná *r.* S. America 144 E4
Part of the Río de la Plata - Paraná, 2nd longest river in South America.

Paraná, Serra do *hills* Brazil 145 B1
Paranaguá Brazil 145 A4
Paranaíba Brazil 145 A2
Paranaíba *r.* Brazil 145 A3
Paranapiacaba, Serra *mts* Brazil 145 A4
Paranavaí Brazil 144 F2
Parangi Aru *r.* Sri Lanka 84 D4
Parang Pass India 82 D2
Parângul Mare, Vârful *mt.* Romania 59 J2
Parantan Sri Lanka 84 D4
Paraopeba Brazil 145 B2
Pārapāra Iraq 91 G4
Paraparaumu N.Z. 113 E5
Paras Mex. 131 D7
Paras Pak. 89 I3
Parasia India 82 D5
Parasnath *mt.* India 83 F5
Paraspori, Akra *pt* Greece *see* Paraspori, Akrotirio
Paraspori, Akrotirio *pt* Greece 59 L7
Parateca Brazil 145 C1
Paratinga Brazil 145 C1
Parāū, Kūh-e *mt.* Iraq 91 G4
Paraúna Brazil 145 A2
Parbhani India 84 C2
Parchim Germany 53 L1
Parding China 83 G2
Pardo *r. Bahia* Brazil 145 D1
Pardo *r. Mato Grosso do Sul* Brazil 144 F2
Pardo *r. São Paulo* Brazil 145 A3
Pardoo Australia 108 B5
Pardubice Czechia 47 O5
Parece Vela *i.* Japan *see* Okino-Tori-shima
Parecis, Serra dos *hills* Brazil 142 F6
Pareh Iran 88 B2
Parenda India 84 B2
Parent Canada 122 G5
Parent, Lac *l.* Canada 122 F4
Pareora N.Z. 113 C7
Parepare Indon. 68 F7
Parga Greece 59 I5
Pargas Fin. 45 M6
Parghelia Italy 58 F5
Pargi India 84 C2
Paria, Gulf of Trin. and Tob./Venez. 137 L6
Paria, Península de *pen.* Venez. 142 F1
Paria Plateau U.S.A. 129 G3
Parikkala Fin. 45 P6
Parikud Islands India 84 E2
Parima, Serra *mts* Brazil 142 F3
Parima-Tapirapecó, Parque Nacional *nat. park* Venez. 142 F3
Parintins Brazil 143 G4
Paris Canada 134 E2

▶Paris France 52 C6
Capital of France. 3rd most populous city in Europe.

Paris *IL* U.S.A. 134 B4
Paris *KY* U.S.A. 134 C4
Paris *MO* U.S.A. 130 E4
Paris *TN* U.S.A. 131 F4
Paris *TX* U.S.A. 131 E5
Paris (Charles de Gaulle) *airport* France 52 C5
Paris (Orly) *airport* France 52 C6
Paris Crossing U.S.A. 134 C4
Parit Buntar Malaysia 71 C6
Pārīz Iran 88 D4
Park U.K. 51 E3
Parkano Fin. 45 M5
Park City U.S.A. 134 B5
Parke Lake Canada 123 K3
Parker *AZ* U.S.A. 129 F4
Parker *CO* U.S.A. 126 G5
Parker Dam U.S.A. 129 F4
Parker Lake Canada 121 M2
Parker Range *hills* Australia 109 B8
Parkersburg U.S.A. 134 E4
Parkers Lake U.S.A. 134 C5
Parkes Australia 112 D4
Park Falls U.S.A. 130 F2
Park Forest U.S.A. 134 B3
Parkhar Tajik. *see* Farkhor
Parkhill Canada 134 E2
Park Rapids U.S.A. 130 E2
Parkutta Pak. 82 D2
Park Valley U.S.A. 126 E4
Parla Kimedi India *see* Paralakhemundi
Parlakimidi India *see* Paralakhemundi
Parli Vaijnath India 84 C2
Parlung Zangbo *r.* China 76 B2
Parma Italy 58 D2
Parma *ID* U.S.A. 126 D4
Parma *OH* U.S.A. 134 E3
Parnaíba Brazil 143 J4
Parnaíba *r.* Brazil 143 J4
Parnassos *mt.* Greece *see* Liakoura
Parnassus N.Z. 113 D6
Parner India 84 B2
Parnon *mts* Greece *see* Parnonas
Parnonas *mts* Greece 59 J6
Pärnu Estonia 45 N7
Pärnu-Jaagupi Estonia 45 N7
Paro Bhutan 83 G4
Paroikia Greece 59 K6
Parona Turkey *see* Fındık
Paroo *watercourse* Australia 112 A3
Paroo Channel *watercourse* Australia 112 A3
Paroo-Darling National Park Australia 111 C6
Paropamisus *mts* Afgh. *see* Safēd Kōh, Silsilah-ye
Paros Greece *see* Paroikia
Paros *i.* Greece 59 K6
Parowan U.S.A. 129 G3
Parral Chile 144 B5
Parramatta Australia 112 E4
Parramore Island U.S.A. 135 H5
Parras Mex. 131 C7
Parrett *r.* U.K. 49 D7
Parry, Cape Canada 153 A2
Parry, Kap *c.* Greenland *see* Kangaarsussuaq
Parry, Lac *l.* Canada 122 G2
Parry Bay Canada 119 J3
Parry Channel Canada 119 G2
Parry Islands Canada 119 G2
Parry Range *hills* Australia 108 A5
Parry Sound Canada 134 E1
Pārsīān Iran 88 D5
Parsnip Peak U.S.A. 129 F2
Parsons *KS* U.S.A. 131 E4
Parsons *WV* U.S.A. 134 F4
Parsons Range *hills* Australia 108 F3
Partabgarh India 84 B2
Partabpur India 83 E5
Partenstein Germany 53 J4
Parthenay France 56 D3
Partizansk Russia 74 D4
Partney U.K. 48 H5
Partridge *r.* Canada 122 E4
Partry Ireland 51 C4
Partry Mountains *hills* Ireland 51 C4
Paru *r.* Brazil 143 H4
Pārūd Iran 89 F5
Paryang China 83 E3
Parys S. Africa 101 H4
Pās, Chāh *well* Iran 88 D3
Pasa Dağı *mt.* Turkey 90 D3
Pasadena *CA* U.S.A. 128 D4
Pasadena *TX* U.S.A. 131 E6
Pasado, Cabo *c.* Ecuador 142 B4
Pa Sang Thai. 70 B3
Pasawng Myanmar 70 B3
Pascagama *r.* Canada 122 G4
Pascagoula U.S.A. 131 F6
Pascagoula *r.* U.S.A. 131 F6
Paşcani Romania 59 L1
Pasco U.S.A. 126 D3
Pascoal, Monte *hill* Brazil 145 D2
Pascua, Isla de *i.* S. Pacific Ocean *see* Easter Island
Pas de Calais *strait* France/U.K. *see* Dover, Strait of
Pasewalk Germany 47 O4
Pasfield Lake Canada 121 J3
Pasha Russia 42 G3
Pashih Haihsia *sea chan.* Phil./Taiwan *see* Bashi Channel
Pashkovo Russia 74 C2
Pashkovskiy Russia 43 H7
Pashū'īyeh Iran 88 E4
Pasi Ga Myanmar 70 B1
Pasighat India 83 H3
Pasinler Turkey 91 F3
Pasir Gudang Malaysia 71 [inset]
Pasir Mas Malaysia 71 C6
Pasir Putih Malaysia 71 C6
Paskūh Iran 89 F5
Pasni Pak. 149 M4
Paso de los Toros Uruguay 144 E4
Paso de San Antonio Mex. 131 C6
Pasok Myanmar 70 A2
Paso Robles U.S.A. 128 C4
Pasquia Hills Canada 121 K4
Passaic U.S.A. 135 H3
Passa Tempo Brazil 145 B3
Passau Germany 47 N6
Passo del San Gottardo Switz. *see* St Gotthard Pass
Passo Fundo Brazil 144 F3
Passos Brazil 145 B3
Passur *r.* Bangl. *see* Pusur
Passuri Nadi *r.* Bangl. *see* Pusur
Pastavy Belarus 45 O9
Pastaza *r.* Peru 142 C4
Pasto Col. 142 C3
Pastora Peak U.S.A. 129 I3
Pastos Bons Brazil 143 J5
Pasu Pak. 82 C1
Pasur Turkey *see* Kulp
Pasvalys Lith. 45 N8
Pasvikelva *r.* Europe *see* Patsoyoki
Patache, Punta *pt* Chile 144 B2
Patagonia *reg.* Arg. 144 B8
Pataliputra India *see* Patna
Patan *Gujarat* India *see* Somnath
Patan *Gujarat* India 82 C5
Patan *Mahar.* India 84 B2
Patan Nepal 83 F4
Patan Pak. 89 I3
Patandar, Koh-i- *mt.* Pak. 89 G5
Patargān, Daqq-e *salt flat* Iran 89 F3
Patavium Italy *see* Padua
Patea N.Z. 113 E4
Patea *inlet* N.Z. *see* Doubtful Sound
Pate Island Kenya 98 E4
Pateley Bridge U.K. 48 F4
Patensie S. Africa 100 G7
Patera India 82 D4
Paterson Australia 112 E4
Paterson *r.* Australia 112 C2
Paterson U.S.A. 135 H3
Paterson Range *hills* Australia 108 C5
Pathanamthitta India 84 C4
Pathankot India 82 C2
Pathari India 82 D5
Pathein Myanmar *see* Bassein
Pathfinder Reservoir U.S.A. 126 G4
Pathiu Thai. 71 B5
Pathum Thani Thai. 71 C4
Patía *r.* Col. 142 C3
Patiala India 82 D3
Patkai Bum *mts* India/Myanmar 83 H4
Patkaklik China 83 F1
Patmos *i.* Greece 59 L6
Patna *Bihar* India 83 F4
Patna *Odisha* India 83 F5
Patnagarh India 83 E5
Patnos Turkey 91 F3
Pato Branco Brazil 144 F3
Patoda India 84 B2
Patoka *r.* U.S.A. 134 B4
Patoka Lake U.S.A. 134 B4
Patos Albania 59 H4
Patos Brazil 143 K5
Patos, Lagoa dos *l.* Brazil 144 F4
Patos de Minas Brazil 145 B2
Patquía Arg. 144 C4
Patra Greece *see* Patras
Patrae Greece *see* Patras
Pátrai Greece *see* Patras
Patras Greece 59 I5
Patreksfjörður Iceland 44 [inset 1]
Patricio Lynch, Isla *i.* Chile 144 A7
Patrick Creek *watercourse* Australia 110 D4
Patrimônio Brazil 145 A2
Patrocínio Brazil 145 B2
Paṭrū Iran 89 E3
Patsoyoki *r.* Europe 44 Q2
Pattadakal *tourist site* India 84 B2
Pattani Thai. 71 C6
Pattaya Thai. 71 C4
Pattensen Germany 53 J2
Patterson *CA* U.S.A. 128 C3
Patterson *LA* U.S.A. 131 F6
Patterson, Mount Canada 120 C1
Patti India 83 E4
Pattijoki Fin. 44 N4
Pättikkä Fin. 44 L2
Patton U.S.A. 135 F3
Pattullo, Mount Canada 120 D3
Patu Brazil 143 K5
Patuakhali Bangl. 83 G5
Patuanak Canada 121 J4
Patuca, Punta *pt* Hond. 137 H5
Patur India 84 C1
Patuxent *r.* U.S.A. 135 G4
Patuxent Range *mts* Antarctica 152 L1
Patvinsuon kansallispuisto *nat. park* Fin. 44 Q5
Pau France 56 D5
Pauhunri *mt.* China/India 83 G4
Pauillac France 56 D4
Pauini Brazil 142 E5
Pauini *r.* Brazil 142 E5
Pauk Myanmar 70 A2
Paukkaung Myanmar 70 A3
Paulatuk Canada 153 A2
Paulden U.S.A. 129 G4
Paulding U.S.A. 134 C3
Paulicéia Brazil 145 A3
Paulis Dem. Rep. Congo *see* Isiro
Paul Island Canada 123 J2
Paulo Afonso Brazil 143 K5
Paulo de Faria Brazil 145 A3
Paulpietersburg S. Africa 101 J4
Paul Roux S. Africa 101 H5
Paulstown Ireland 51 E5
Pauls Valley U.S.A. 131 D5
Paumotu, Îles *is* Fr. Polynesia *see* Tuamotu Islands
Paung Myanmar 70 B3
Paungbyin Myanmar 70 A1
Paungde Myanmar 70 A3
Pauni India 84 C1
Pauri India 82 D3
Pavagada India 84 C3
Pavão Brazil 145 C2
Pāveh Iran 88 B3
Pavia Italy 58 C2
Pāvilosta Latvia 45 L8
Pavino Russia 42 J4
Pavlikeni Bulg. 59 K3
Pavlodar Kazakh. 80 E1
Pavlof Volcano U.S.A. 118 B4
Pavlograd Ukr. *see* Pavlohrad
Pavlohrad Ukr. 43 G6
Pavlovka Russia 43 J5
Pavlovo Russia 42 I5
Pavlovsk *Altayskiy Kray* Russia 72 E2
Pavlovsk *Voronezhskaya Oblast'* Russia 43 I6
Pavlovskaya Russia 43 H7
Pawahku Myanmar 70 B1
Pawai India 82 E4
Pawnee U.S.A. 131 D4
Pawnee *r.* U.S.A. 130 D4
Pawnee City U.S.A. 130 D3
Paw Paw *MI* U.S.A. 134 C2
Paw Paw *WV* U.S.A. 135 F4
Pawtucket U.S.A. 135 J3
Pawut Myanmar 71 B4
Paxson U.S.A. 118 D3
Paxton U.S.A. 134 A3
Payakumbuh Indon. 68 C7
Paya Lebar Sing. 71 [inset]
Pāy Böldak Ghar *mt.* Afgh. 89 G4
Payette U.S.A. 126 D3
Pay-Khoy, Khrebet *hills* Russia 64 H3
Payne Canada *see* Kangirsuk
Payne, Lac *l.* Canada 122 G2
Paynes Creek U.S.A. 128 C1
Paynes Find Australia 109 B7
Paynesville U.S.A. 130 E2
Paysandú Uruguay 144 E4
Payshanba Uzbek. 89 G1
Payson U.S.A. 129 H4
Pazar Turkey 91 F2
Pazarcık Turkey 90 E3
Pazardzhik Bulg. 59 K3
Pazin Croatia 58 E2
Pe Myanmar 71 B4
Peabody *KS* U.S.A. 130 D4
Peabody *MA* U.S.A. 135 J2

▶Peace *r.* Canada 120 I3
Part of the Mackenzie-Peace-Finlay, the 2nd longest river in North America.

Peace Point Canada 121 H3
Peace River Canada 120 G3
Peach Creek U.S.A. 134 E5
Peach Springs U.S.A. 129 G4
Peacock Hills Canada 121 I1
Peak Charles *hill* Australia 109 C8
Peak Charles National Park Australia 109 C8
Peak District National Park U.K. 48 F5
Peake *watercourse* Australia 111 B6
Peaked Mountain *hill* U.S.A. 132 G2
Peak Hill Australia 112 D4
Peak Hill (abandoned) Australia 109 B6
Peale, Mount U.S.A. 129 I2
Peanut U.S.A. 128 B1
Pearce (abandoned) U.S.A. 129 I6
Pearce Point Australia 108 E3
Pearisburg U.S.A. 134 E5
Pearl *r.* U.S.A. 131 F6
Pearl Harbor *inlet* U.S.A. 127 [inset]
Pearsall U.S.A. 131 D6
Pearson U.S.A. 133 D6
Pearston S. Africa 101 G7
Peary Channel Canada 119 I2
Peary Land *reg.* Greenland 153 J1
Pease *r.* U.S.A. 131 D5
Peawanuck Canada 122 D3
Pebane Moz. 99 D5
Pebas Peru 142 D4
Peć Kosovo *see* Pejë
Peçanha Brazil 145 C2
Peças, Ilha das *i.* Brazil 145 A4
Pechenga Russia 44 Q2
Pechora Russia 42 M2
Pechora *r.* Russia 42 L1
Pechora Sea Russia *see* Pechorskoye More
Pechorskaya Guba *b.* Russia 42 L1
Pechorskoye More *sea* Russia 153 G2
Pechory Russia 45 O8
Peck U.S.A. 134 D2
Pecos U.S.A. 131 C6
Pecos *r.* U.S.A. 131 C6
Pécs Hungary 58 H1
Pedda Vagu *r.* India 84 C2
Pedder, Lake Australia 111 [inset]
Peddie S. Africa 101 H7
Pedernales Dom. Rep. 137 J5
Pediaios *r.* Cyprus 85 A2
Pediva Angola 99 B5
Pedra Azul Brazil 145 C1
Pedra Preta, Serra da *mts* Brazil 145 A1
Pedras de Maria da Cruz Brazil 145 B1
Pedregulho Brazil 145 B3
Pedreiras Brazil 143 J4
Pedriceña Mex. 131 C7
Pedro, Point Sri Lanka 84 D4
Pedro Betancourt Cuba 133 D8
Pedro Canário Brazil 145 D2
Pedro II, Ilha *reg.* Brazil/Venez. 142 E3
Pedro Juan Caballero Para. 144 E2
Peebles U.K. 50 F5
Peebles U.S.A. 134 D4
Pee Dee *r.* U.S.A. 133 E5
Peekskill U.S.A. 135 I3
Peel *r.* Australia 112 E3
Peel *r.* Canada 118 E3
Peel Isle of Man 48 C4
Peer Belgium 52 F3
Peera Peera Poolanna Lake *salt flat* Australia 111 B5
Peerless Lake Canada 120 H3
Peerless Lake *l.* Canada 120 H3
Peers Canada 120 G4
Peery Lake *salt flat* Australia 112 A3
Pegasus Bay N.Z. 113 D6
Pegnitz Germany 53 L5
Pegu Myanmar 70 B3
Pegu Yoma *mts* Myanmar 70 A3
Pegysh Russia 42 K3
Pehuajó Arg. 144 D5
Peikang Taiwan *see* Beigang
Peine Chile 144 C2
Peine Germany 53 K2
Peint India 84 B1
Peipsi järv *l.* Estonia/Russia *see* Peipus, Lake
Peipus, Lake Estonia/Russia 45 O7
Peiraias Greece *see* Piraeus
Pei Shan *mts* China *see* Bei Shan
Peißen Germany 53 L3
Peixe Brazil 143 I6
Peixe *r.* Brazil 145 A1
Peixian *Jiangsu* China *see* Pizhou
Peixian *Jiangsu* China 77 H1
Peixoto de Azevedo Brazil 143 H6
Pejë Kosovo 59 I3
Pèk Laos *see* Phônsavan
Peka Lesotho 101 H5
Pekan Malaysia 71 C7
Pekanbaru Indon. 68 C6
Pekin U.S.A. 130 F3
Peking China *see* Beijing
Pekinga Benin 96 D3
Pelabohan Klang Malaysia *see* Pelabuhan Klang
Pelabuhan Klang Malaysia 71 C7
Pelagie, Isole *is Sicily* Italy 58 E7
Pelaihari Indon. 68 E7
Peleaga, Vârful *mt.* Romania 59 J2
Pelee Island Canada 134 D3
Pelee Point Canada 134 D3
Peles Russia 42 K3
Pélican, Lac du *l.* Canada 123 G2
Pelican Lake Canada 121 K4
Pelican Lake U.S.A. 130 E1
Pelican Narrows Canada 121 K4
Pelkosenniemi Fin. 44 O3
Pella S. Africa 100 D5
Pellatt Lake Canada 121 I1
Pelleluhu Islands P.N.G. 69 K7
Pello Fin. 44 M3
Pelly *r.* Canada 120 C2
Pelly Crossing Canada 120 B2
Pelly Lake Canada 121 K1
Pelly Mountains Canada 120 C2
Peloponnese *pen.* Greece 59 J6
Pelopónnesos *pen.* Greece *see* Peloponnese
Peloponnisos *pen.* Greece *see* Peloponnese
Pelotas Brazil 144 F4
Pelotas, Rio das *r.* Brazil 145 A4
Pelusium *tourist site* Egypt 85 A4
Pelusium, Bay of Egypt *see* Ṭīnah, Khalīj aṭ
Pemangkat Indon. 71 E7
Pematangsiantar Indon. 71 B7
Pemba Moz. 99 E5
Pemba Island Tanz. 99 D4
Pemberton Canada 120 F5
Pembina *r.* Canada 120 H4
Pembina *r.* U.S.A. 130 D1
Pembine U.S.A. 132 C2
Pembre Indon. 69 J8
Pembroke Canada 122 F5
Pembroke U.K. 49 C7
Pembroke U.S.A. 133 D5
Pembrokeshire Coast National Park U.K. 49 B7
Pen India 84 B2
Peña Cerredo *mt.* Spain *see* Torrecerredo
Peñalara *mt.* Spain 57 E3
Penamar Brazil 145 C1
Peña Nevada, Cerro *mt.* Mex. 136 E4
Penang Malaysia *see* George Town
Penang *i.* Malaysia *see* Pinang
Penápolis Brazil 145 A3
Peñaranda de Bracamonte Spain 57 D3
Penarie Australia 112 A5
Penarlâg U.K. *see* Hawarden
Peñarroya *mt.* Spain 57 F3
Peñarroya-Pueblonuevo Spain 57 D4
Penarth U.K. 49 D7
Peñas, Cabo de *c.* Spain 57 D2
Penas, Golfo de *g.* Chile 144 A7
Penasi, Pulau *i.* Indon. 71 A6
Pencoso, Alto de *hills* Arg. 144 C4
Pender U.S.A. 130 D3
Pendjari, Parc National de la *nat. park* Benin 96 D3
Pendle Hill *hill* U.K. 48 E5
Pendleton U.S.A. 126 D3
Pendleton Bay Canada 120 E4
Pend Oreille *r.* U.S.A. 126 D2
Pend Oreille Lake U.S.A. 126 D2
Pendra India 83 E5
Penduv India 84 B2
Pendzhikent Tajik. *see* Panjakent
Penebangan *i.* Indon. 68 D7
Peneda Gerês, Parque Nacional da *nat. park* Port. 57 B3
Penetanguishene Canada 134 F1
Penfro U.K. *see* Pembroke
Peng'an China 76 E2
Penganga *r.* India 84 C2
Peng Chau *i. H.K.* China 77 [inset]
Penge Dem. Rep. Congo 99 C4
Penge S. Africa 101 J3
Penghu Dao *i.* Taiwan 77 H4
P'enghu Lieh-tao *is* Taiwan *see* Penghu Qundao
Penghu Qundao *is* Taiwan 77 H4
Pengjia Yu *i.* Taiwan 77 I3
Peng Kang *hill* Sing. 71 [inset]
Penglaizhen China *see* Daying
Pengshan China 76 D2
Pengshui China 77 F2
Pengwa Myanmar 70 A2
Pengxi China 76 E2
Penha Brazil 145 A4
Penhoek Pass S. Africa 101 H6
Penhook U.S.A. 134 F5
Peniche Port. 57 B4
Penicuik U.K. 50 F5
Penig Germany 53 M4
Peninga Russia 44 R5
Peninsular Malaysia Malaysia 71 D6
Penitente, Serra do *hills* Brazil 143 I5
Penn U.S.A. *see* Penn Hills
Pennell Coast Antarctica 152 H2
Penn Hills U.S.A. 134 F3
Pennine, Alpi *mts* Italy/Switz. 58 B2
Pennine Alps *mts* Italy/Switz. *see* Pennine, Alpi
Pennines *hills* U.K. 48 E4
Pennington Gap U.S.A. 134 D5
Pennsburg U.S.A. 135 H3
Penns Grove U.S.A. 135 H4
Pennsville U.S.A. 135 H4
Pennsylvania *state* U.S.A. 134 F3
Pennville U.S.A. 134 C3
Penn Yan U.S.A. 135 G2
Penny Icecap Canada 119 L3
Penny Point Antarctica 152 H1
Penola Australia 111 C8
Peñón Blanco Mex. 131 B7
Penong Australia 109 F7
Penonomé Panama 137 H7
Penrhyn *atoll* Cook Is 151 J6
Penrhyn Basin *sea feature* S. Pacific Ocean 151 J6
Penrith Australia 112 E4
Penrith U.K. 48 E4
Pensacola U.S.A. 133 C6
Pensacola Mountains Antarctica 152 L1
Pensi La *pass* India 82 D2

Pentadaktylos Range *mts* Cyprus 85 A2
Pentakota India 84 D2
Pentecost Island Vanuatu 107 G3
Pentecôte, Île *i.* Vanuatu *see* Pentecost Island
Penticton Canada 120 G5
Pentire Point U.K. 49 B8
Pentland Australia 110 D4
Pentland Firth *sea chan.* U.K. 50 F2
Pentland Hills U.K. 50 F5
Pentwater U.S.A. 134 B2
Penwegon Myanmar 70 B3
Pen-y-bont ar Ogwr U.K. *see* Bridgend
Penygadair *hill* U.K. 49 D6
Penylan Lake Canada 121 J2
Penza Russia 43 J5
Penzance U.K. 49 B8
Penzhinskaya Guba *b.* Russia 65 R3
Peoria *AZ* U.S.A. 129 G5
Peoria *IL* U.S.A. 130 F3
Peotone U.S.A. 134 B3
Pequeña, Punta *pt* Mex. 127 E8
Pequop Mountains U.S.A. 129 F1
Peradeniya Sri Lanka 84 D5
Pera Head *hd* Australia 110 C2
Perak *i.* Malaysia 71 B6
Perales del Alfambra Spain 57 F3
Perambalur India 84 C4
Perämeren kansallispuisto *nat. park* Fin. 44 N4
Peräseinäjoki Fin. 44 M5
Percé Canada 123 I4
Percival Lakes *salt flat* Australia 108 D5
Percy U.S.A. 135 J1
Percy Isles Australia 110 E4
Percy Reach *l.* Canada 135 G1
Perdizes Brazil 145 B2
Perdu, Lac *l.* Canada 123 H4
Peregrebnoye Russia 41 T3
Pereira Col. 142 C3
Pereira Barreto Brazil 145 A3
Pereira de Eça Angola *see* Ondjiva
Pere Marquette *r.* U.S.A. 134 B2
Peremul Par *reef* India 84 B4
Peremyshlyany Ukr. 43 E6
Perenjori Australia 109 B7
Pereslavl'-Zalesskiy Russia 42 H4
Pereslavskiy Natsional'nyy Park *nat. park* Russia 42 H4
Pereyaslavka Russia 74 D3
Pereyaslav-Khmel'nitskiy Ukr. *see* Pereyaslav-Khmel'nyts'kyy
Pereyaslav-Khmel'nyts'kyy Ukr. 43 F6
Perforated Island Thai. *see* Bon, Ko
Pergamino Arg. 144 D4
Perhentian Besar, Pulau *i.* Malaysia 71 C6
Perho Fin. 44 N5
Péribonka, Lac *l.* Canada 123 H4
Perico Arg. 144 C2
Pericos Mex. 127 G8
Peridot U.S.A. 129 H5
Périgueux France 56 E4
Perijá, Parque Nacional *nat. park* Venez. 142 D2
Perijá, Sierra de *mts* Venez. 142 D2
Periyar India *see* Erode
Perkasie U.S.A. 135 H3
Perlas, Punta de *pt* Nicaragua 137 H6
Perleberg Germany 53 L1
Perm' Russia 41 R4
Permas Russia 42 J4
Pernambuco Brazil *see* Recife
Pernambuco Plain *sea feature* S. Atlantic Ocean 148 G6
Pernatty Lagoon *salt flat* Australia 111 B6
Pernem India 84 B3
Pernik Bulg. 59 J3
Pernov Estonia *see* Pärnu
Perojpur Bangl. *see* Pirojpur
Peron Islands Australia 108 E3
Péronne France 52 C5
Perpignan France 56 F5
Perranporth U.K. 49 B8
Perrégaux Alg. *see* Mohammadia
Perris U.S.A. 128 E5
Perros-Guirec France 56 C2
Perrot, Île *i.* Canada 135 I1
Perry *FL* U.S.A. 133 D6
Perry *GA* U.S.A. 133 D5
Perry *MI* U.S.A. 134 C2
Perry *OK* U.S.A. 131 D4
Perry Lake U.S.A. 130 E4
Perryton U.S.A. 131 C4
Perryville *AK* U.S.A. 118 C4
Perryville *MO* U.S.A. 130 F4
Perseverancia Bol. 142 F6
Pershore U.K. 49 E6
Persia *country* Asia *see* Iran
Persian Gulf Asia *see* The Gulf
Pertek Turkey 91 E3

▶Perth Australia 109 A7
Capital of Western Australia. 4th most populous city in Oceania.

Perth Canada 135 G1
Perth U.K. 50 F4
Perth Amboy U.S.A. 135 H3
Perth-Andover Canada 123 I5
Perth Basin *sea feature* Indian Ocean 149 P7
Pertominsk Russia 42 H2
Pertunmaa Fin. 45 O6
Pertusato, Capo *c. Corsica* France 56 I6
Peru *atoll* Kiribati *see* Beru

▶Peru *country* S. America 142 D6
3rd largest and 4th most populous country in South America.

Peru *IL* U.S.A. 130 F3
Peru *IN* U.S.A. 134 B3
Peru *NY* U.S.A. 135 I1
Peru-Chile Trench *sea feature* S. Pacific Ocean 151 O6
Perugia Italy 58 E3
Peruru India 84 C3
Perusia Italy *see* Perugia
Péruwelz Belgium 52 D4
Pervomaysk Russia 43 I5
Pervomays'k Ukr. 43 F6
Pervomayskiy Kazakh. 80 F1
Pervomayskiy *Arkhangel'skaya Oblast'* Russia *see* Novodvinsk
Pervomayskiy *Tambovskaya Oblast'* Russia 43 I5
Pervomays'kyy Ukr. 43 H6
Pervorechenskiy (abandoned) Russia 65 R3
Pervyy Brat, Gora *hill* Russia 74 F1
Pesaro Italy 58 E3
Pescadores *is* Taiwan *see* Penghu Qundao
Pescara Italy 58 F3
Pescara *r.* Italy 58 F3
Peschanokopskoye Russia 43 I7
Peschanoye Russia *see* Yashkul'
Peschanyy, Mys *pt* Kazakh. 91 H2
Pesha *r.* Russia 42 J2
Peshawar Pak. 89 H3
Peshkopi Albania 59 I4
Peshtera Bulg. 59 K3
Peski Turkm. 89 F2
Peskovka Russia 42 L4
Pesnica Slovenia 58 F1
Pessac France 56 D4
Pessin Germany 53 M2
Pestovo Russia 42 G4
Pestravka Russia 43 K5
Petaḥ Tiqwa Israel 85 B3
Petäjävesi Fin. 44 N5
Petaling Jaya Malaysia 71 C7
Petalion, Kolpos *sea chan.* Greece 59 K5
Petaluma U.S.A. 128 B2
Pétange Lux. 52 F5
Petatlán Mex. 136 D5
Petauke Zambia 99 D5
Petenwell Lake U.S.A. 130 F2
Peterbell Canada 122 E4
Peterborough Australia 111 B7
Peterborough Canada 135 F1
Peterborough U.K. 49 G6
Peterborough U.S.A. 135 J2
Peterculter U.K. 50 G3
Peterhead U.K. 50 H3
Peter I Island Antarctica 152 K2
Peter I Øy *i.* Antarctica *see* Peter I Island
Peter Lake Canada 121 M2
Peterlee U.K. 48 F4
Petermann Bjerg *nunatak* Greenland 119 P2
Petermann Ranges *mts* Australia 109 E6
Peter Pond Lake Canada 121 I4
Peters, Lac *l.* Canada 123 H2
Petersberg Germany 53 J4
Petersburg *AK* U.S.A. 120 C3
Petersburg *IL* U.S.A. 130 F4
Petersburg *IN* U.S.A. 134 B4
Petersburg *NY* U.S.A. 135 I2
Petersburg *VA* U.S.A. 135 G5
Petersburg *WV* U.S.A. 134 F4
Petersfield U.K. 49 G7
Petershagen Germany 53 I2
Petersville U.S.A. 118 C3
Peter the Great Bay Russia *see* Petra Velikogo, Zaliv
Peth India 84 B2
Petilia Policastro Italy 58 G5
Petit Atlas *mts* Morocco *see* Anti-Atlas
Petitcodiac Canada 123 I5
Petitjean Morocco *see* Sidi Kacem
Petit Mécatina *r.* Canada 123 K4
Petit Mécatina, Île du *i.* Canada 123 K4
Petit Morin *r.* France 52 D6
Petitot *r.* Canada 120 F2
Petit St-Bernard, Col du *pass* France 56 H4
Petit Saut, Barrage du *resr* Fr. Guiana 143 H3
Peto Mex. 136 G4
Petoskey U.S.A. 132 C2
Petra *tourist site* Jordan 85 B4
Petra Velikogo, Zaliv *b.* Russia 74 C4
Petre, Point Canada 135 G2
Petrich Bulg. 59 J4
Petrified Forest National Park U.S.A. 129 I4
Petrikau Poland *see* Piotrków Trybunalski
Petrikov Belarus *see* Pyetrykaw
Petrinja Croatia 58 G2
Petroaleksandrovsk Uzbek. *see* To'rtko'l
Petroglyphic Complexes of the Mongolian Altai *tourist site* Mongolia 72 F3
Petrograd Russia *see* St Petersburg
Petrohanski Prohod *pass* Bulg. 59 J3
Petrokov Poland *see* Piotrków Trybunalski
Petrolia Canada 134 D2
Petrolia U.S.A. 128 A1
Petrolina Brazil 143 J5
Petrolina de Goiás Brazil 145 A2
Petropavl Kazakh. *see* Petropavlovskoye
Petropavlovsk Russia *see* Petropavlovsk-Kamchatskiy
Petropavlovsk-Kamchatskiy Russia 65 Q4
Petropavlovskoye Kazakh. 79 F1
Petrópolis Brazil 145 C3
Petroșani Romania 59 J2
Petrovsk Russia 43 J5
Petrovskoye Russia *see* Svetlograd
Petrovsk-Zabaykal'skiy Russia 73 J2
Petrozavodsk Russia 42 G3
Petrus Steyn S. Africa 101 I4
Petrusville S. Africa 100 G6
Petsamo Russia *see* Pechenga
Pettau Slovenia *see* Ptuj
Petten Neth. 52 E2
Pettigo U.K. 51 E3
Petukhovo Russia 64 H4
Petushki Russia 42 H5
Petzeck *mt.* Austria 47 N7
Peuetsagu, Gunung *vol.* Indon. 71 B6
Peureula Indon. 71 B6
Pevek Russia 65 S3
Pêxung China 76 B1
Pey Ostān Iran 88 E3
Peza *r.* Russia 42 J2
Pezinok Slovakia 47 P6
Pezu Pak. 89 H3
Pfälzer Wald *hills* Germany 53 H5
Pforzheim Germany 53 I6
Pfungstadt Germany 53 I5
Phac Mo, Phu *mt.* Vietnam 70 C2
Phagameng S. Africa 101 I3
Phagwara India 82 C3
Phahameng S. Africa 101 H5
Phalaborwa S. Africa 101 J2
Phalodi India 82 C4
Phalsund India 82 B4
Phalta India 83 G5
Phaluai, Ko *i.* Thai. 71 B5
Phalut Peak India/Nepal 83 G4
Phan Thai. 70 B3
Phanat Nikhom Thai. 71 C4
Phangan, Ko *i.* Thai. 71 C5
Phang Hoei, San Khao *mts* Thai. 70 C3
Phangnga Thai. 71 B5
Phăng Xi Păng *mt.* Vietnam 70 C2
Phanom Dong Rak, Thiu Khao *mts* Cambodia/Thai. 71 D4
Phan Rang-Thap Cham Vietnam 71 E5
Phan Thiêt Vietnam 71 E5
Phapon Myanmar *see* Pyapon
Phat Diêm Vietnam 70 D2
Phatthalung Thai. 71 C6
Phawngpui India 83 H5
Phayam, Ko *i.* Thai. 71 B5
Phayao Thai. 70 B3
Phayuhakhiri Thai. 70 C4
Phek India 83 H4
Phelps Lake Canada 121 K3
Phen Thai. 70 C3
Phenix U.S.A. 135 F5
Phenix City U.S.A. 133 C5
Phet Buri Thai. 71 B4
Phetchabun Thai. 70 C3
Phiafai Laos 70 D4
Phichai Thai. 70 C3
Phichit Thai. 70 C3
Philadelphia Jordan *see* 'Ammān
Philadelphia Turkey *see* Alaşehir
Philadelphia *MS* U.S.A. 131 F5
Philadelphia *NY* U.S.A. 135 H1
Philadelphia *PA* U.S.A. 135 H4
Philip U.S.A. 130 C2
Philip Atoll Micronesia *see* Sorol
Philippeville Alg. *see* Skikda
Philippeville Belgium 52 E4
Philippi U.S.A. 134 E4
Philippi, Lake *salt flat* Australia 110 B5
Philippine Neth. 52 D3
Philippine Basin *sea feature* N. Pacific Ocean 150 E4
Philippines *country* Asia 69 G4
Philippine Sea N. Pacific Ocean 69 G3

▶Philippine Trench *sea feature* N. Pacific Ocean 150 E4
3rd deepest trench in the world.

Philippolis S. Africa 101 G6
Philippopolis Bulg. *see* Plovdiv
Philippsburg Germany 53 I5
Philipsburg *MT* U.S.A. 126 E3
Philipsburg *PA* U.S.A. 135 F3
Philip Smith Mountains U.S.A. 118 D3
Philipstown S. Africa 100 G6
Phillip Island Australia 112 B7
Phillips *ME* U.S.A. 135 J1
Phillips *WI* U.S.A. 130 F2
Phillipsburg U.S.A. 130 D4
Phillips Range *hills* Australia 108 D4
Philmont U.S.A. 135 I2
Philomelium Turkey *see* Akşehir
Phiritona S. Africa 101 H4
Phitsanulok Thai. 70 C3

▶Phnom Penh Cambodia 71 D5
Capital of Cambodia.

Phnum Pénh Cambodia *see* Phnom Penh
Pho, Laem *pt* Thai. 71 C6
Phoenicia U.S.A. 135 H2

▶Phoenix U.S.A. 127 E6
Capital of Arizona.

Phoenix Island Kiribati *see* Rawaki
Phoenix Islands Kiribati 107 I2
Phô Lu Vietnam 70 D2
Phon Thai. 70 C4
Phong Nha Vietnam 70 D3
Phôngsali Laos 70 C2
Phong Saly Laos *see* Phôngsali
Phong Thô Vietnam 70 C2
Phon Phisai Thai. 70 C3
Phônsavan Laos 70 C3
Phônsavan *mt.* Laos 70 C3
Phon Thong Thai. 70 C3
Phosphate Hill Australia 110 C4
Phrae Thai. 70 C3
Phra Nakhon Si Ayutthaya Thai. *see* Ayutthaya
Phrao Thai. 70 B3
Phra Saeng Thai. 71 B5
Phrom Phiram Thai. 70 C3
Phsar Réam Cambodia 71 C5
Phu Bai Vietnam 70 D3
Phuchong-Nayoi National Park Thai. 71 D4
Phu Cương Vietnam *see* Thu Dâu Môt
Phuket Thai. 71 B6
Phuket, Ko *i.* Thai. 71 B6
Phu Khieo Wildlife Reserve *nature res.* Thai. 70 C3
Phulabani India *see* Phulbani
Phulbani India 84 E1
Phulchhari Ghat Bangl. *see* Fulchhari
Phulji Pak. 89 G5
Phu Lôc *Soc Trăng* Vietnam 71 D5
Phu Lôc *Thưa Thiên-Huê* Vietnam 70 D3
Phu Luang National Park Thai. 70 C3
Phu Ly Vietnam 70 D2
Phumiphon, Khuan Thai. 70 B3
Phu My Vietnam 71 E4
Phung Hiêp Vietnam 71 D5
Phươc Bưu Vietnam 71 D5
Phươc Hai Vietnam 71 D5
Phu Phan National Park Thai. 70 C3
Phu Quôc, Đao *i.* Vietnam 71 C5
Phu Quôc, Quân *i.* Vietnam *see* Phu Quôc, Đao
Phu Quy, Đao *i.* Vietnam 71 E5
Phu Tho Vietnam 70 D2
Phu Vinh Vietnam *see* Tra Vinh
Phyu Myanmar 70 B3
Piaca Brazil 143 I5
Piacenza Italy 58 C2
Piacouadie, Lac *l.* Canada 123 H4
Piagochioui *r.* Canada 122 F3
Piai, Tanjung *pt* Malaysia 71 C7
Pian *r.* Australia 112 D3
Pianosa, Isola *i.* Italy 58 D3
Piatra Neamț Romania 59 L1
Piave *r.* Italy 58 E2
Pibor Post South Sudan 97 G4
Pic *r.* Canada 122 D4
Picacho U.S.A. 129 H5
Picachos, Cerro dos *mt.* Mex. 127 E7
Picardie *admin. reg.* France 52 C5
Picardie *reg.* France *see* Picardy
Picardy *admin. reg.* France *see* Picardie
Picardy *reg.* France 52 B5
Picauville France 49 F9
Picayune U.S.A. 131 F6
Piceance Creek *r.* U.S.A. 129 I1
Pichanal Arg. 144 D2
Pichhor India 82 D4
Pichilemu Chile 144 B4
Pichilingue Mex. 136 B4
Pickens U.S.A. 134 E4
Pickering Canada 134 F2
Pickering U.K. 48 G4
Pickering, Vale of *valley* U.K. 48 G4
Pickle Lake Canada 119 I4
Pico da Neblina, Parque Nacional do *nat. park* Brazil 142 E3
Picos Brazil 143 J5
Picos de Europa, Parque Nacional de los *nat. park* Spain 57 D2
Pico Truncado Arg. 144 C7
Picton Australia 112 E5
Picton Canada 135 G2
Picton N.Z. 113 E5
Pictou Canada 123 J5
Picture Butte Canada 121 H5
Pidarak Pak. 89 F5
Pidurutalagala *mt.* Sri Lanka 84 D5
Piedade Brazil 145 B3
Piedra de Águila Arg. 144 B6
Piedras, Punta *pt* Arg. 144 E5
Piedras, Río de las *r.* Peru 142 E6
Piedras Blancas Point U.S.A. 128 C4
Piedras Negras Mex. 131 C6
Pie Island Canada 122 C4
Pieksämäki Fin. 44 O5
Pielavesi Fin. 44 O5
Pielinen *l.* Fin. 44 P5
Pieljekaise nationalpark *nat. park* Sweden 44 J3
Pienaarsrivier S. Africa 101 I3
Pieniński Park Narodowy *nat. park* Poland 47 R6
Pieninský národný park *nat. park* Slovakia 47 R6
Pierce U.S.A. 130 D3
Pierce Lake Canada 121 M4
Pierceland Canada 121 I4
Pierceton U.S.A. 134 C3
Pieria *mts* Greece 59 J4
Pierowall U.K. 50 G1
Pierpont U.S.A. 134 E3

▶Pierre U.S.A. 130 C2
Capital of South Dakota.

Pierrelatte France 56 G4
Pietermaritzburg S. Africa 101 J5
Pietersaari Fin. *see* Jakobstad
Pietersburg S. Africa *see* Polokwane
Pie Town U.S.A. 129 I4
Pietra Spada, Passo di *pass* Italy 58 G5
Piet Retief S. Africa *see* eMkhondo
Pietrosa *mt.* Romania 59 K1
Pigeon U.S.A. 134 D2
Pigeon Bay Canada 134 D3
Pigeon Lake Canada 120 H4
Piggott U.S.A. 131 F4
Pigg's Peak Swaziland 101 J3
Pigs, Bay of Cuba 133 D8
Pihij India 82 C5
Pihkva järv *l.* Estonia/Russia *see* Pskov, Lake
Pihlajavesi *l.* Fin. 44 P6
Pihlava Fin. 45 L6
Pihtipudas Fin. 44 N5
Piippola Fin. 44 N4
Piispajärvi Fin. 44 P4
Pikalevo Russia 42 G4
Pike U.S.A. 134 E4
Pike Bay Canada 134 E1
Pikelot *i.* Micronesia 69 L5
Pikes Peak U.S.A. 126 G5
Piketon U.S.A. 134 D4
Pikeville *KY* U.S.A. 134 D5
Pikeville *TN* U.S.A. 132 C5
Pikinni *atoll* Marshall Is *see* Bikini
Piła Poland 47 P4
Pila, Kyun *i.* Myanmar 71 B5
Pilanesberg National Park S. Africa 101 H3
Pilão Arcado Brazil 143 J5
Pilar Arg. 144 E4
Pilar Para. 144 E3
Pilar de Goiás Brazil 145 A1
Pilaya *r.* Bol. 142 F8
Pilbara *reg.* Australia 108 B5
Pilcomayo *r.* Bol./Para. 142 F8
Piler India 84 C3
Pili, Cerro *mt.* Chile 144 C2
Pilibangan India 82 C3
Pilibhit India 82 D3
Pilipinas *country* Asia *see* Philippines
Pillau Russia *see* Baltiysk
Pillcopata Peru 142 D6
Pilliga Australia 112 D3
Pillsbury, Lake U.S.A. 128 B2
Pil'na Russia 42 J5
Pil'nya, Ozero *l.* Russia 42 M1
Pilões, Serra dos *mts* Brazil 145 B2
Pilos Greece *see* Pylos
Pilot Knob *mt.* U.S.A. 126 E3
Pilot Peak U.S.A. 128 E2
Pilot Station U.S.A. 118 B3
Pilsen Czechia *see* Plzeň
Piltene Latvia 45 L8
Pil'tun, Zaliv *lag.* Russia 74 F1
Pilu Pak. 89 H5
Pima U.S.A. 129 I5
Pimenta Bueno Brazil 142 F6
Pimento U.S.A. 134 B4
Pimpalner India 84 B1
Pin *r.* India 82 D2
Pin *r.* Myanmar 70 A2
Pinahat India 82 D4
Pinaleno Mountains U.S.A. 129 H5
Pinamar Arg. 144 E5
Pinang Malaysia *see* George Town
Pinang *i.* Malaysia 71 C6
Pınarbaşı Turkey 90 E3
Pinar del Río Cuba 137 H4
Pınarhisar Turkey 59 L4
Piñas Ecuador 142 C4
Pincher Creek Canada 120 H5
Pinckneyville U.S.A. 130 F4
Pinconning U.S.A. 134 D2
Pińczów Poland 47 R5
Pindaí Brazil 145 C1
Pindamonhangaba Brazil 145 B3
Pindar Australia 109 A7
Pindaré *r.* Brazil 143 J4
Píndhos Óros *mts* Greece *see* Pindus Mountains
Pindos *mts* Greece *see* Pindus Mountains
Pindrei India 82 E5
Pindus Mountains Greece 59 I5
Pine *watercourse* Australia 111 C7
Pine *r.* *MI* U.S.A. 134 C1
Pine *r.* *MI* U.S.A. 134 C2
Pine Bluff U.S.A. 131 E5
Pine Bluffs U.S.A. 126 G4
Pine Creek Australia 108 E3
Pine Creek *r.* U.S.A. 135 G3
Pinecrest U.S.A. 128 C2
Pinedale *NM* U.S.A. 129 I4
Pinedale *WY* U.S.A. 126 F4
Pine Dock Canada 121 L5
Pine Falls Canada 121 L5
Pine Flat Lake U.S.A. 128 D3
Pinega Russia 42 I2
Pinega *r.* Russia 42 I2
Pinegrove Australia 109 A6
Pine Grove U.S.A. 135 G3
Pine Hills U.S.A. 133 D6
Pinehouse Lake Canada 121 J4
Pinehouse Lake *l.* Canada 121 J4
Pineimuta *r.* Canada 121 N4
Pineios *r.* Greece 59 J5
Pine Island Bay Antarctica 151 N10
Pine Island Glacier Antarctica 152 K1
Pine Islands *FL* U.S.A. 133 D7
Pine Islands *FL* U.S.A. 133 D7
Pine Knot U.S.A. 134 C5
Pineland U.S.A. 131 E6
Pine Mountain U.S.A. 128 C4
Pine Peak U.S.A. 129 G4
Pine Point *pt* Canada 120 H2
Pine Point (abandoned) Canada 120 H2
Pineridge U.S.A. 128 D3
Pine Ridge U.S.A. 130 C3
Pinerolo Italy 58 B2
Pines, Akrotirio *pt* Greece 59 K4
Pines, Isle of *i.* Cuba *see* Juventud, Isla de la
Pines, Isle of *i.* New Caledonia *see* Pins, Île des
Pinetop U.S.A. 129 I4
Pinetown S. Africa 101 J5
Pine Valley U.S.A. 135 G2
Pineville *KY* U.S.A. 134 D5
Pineville *MO* U.S.A. 131 E4
Pineville *WV* U.S.A. 134 E5
Ping, Mae Nam *r.* Thai. 70 C4
Ping'an China 72 I5
Ping'anyi China *see* Ping'an
Pingba China 76 E3
Pingbian China 76 D4
Ping Dao *i.* China 77 H1
Pingdingbu China *see* Guyuan
Pingdingshan China 77 G1
Pingdong Taiwan *see* Pingtung
Pingdu *Jiangxi* China *see* Anfu
Pingdu *Shandong* China 73 L5
Pinggang China 74 B4
Pinghe China 77 H3
Pinghu China *see* Pingtang
Pingjiang China 77 G2
Pingjin China 76 E2
Pingle China 77 F3
Pingli China 77 F1
Pingliang China 76 E1
Pinglu China 77 F1
Pingma China *see* Tiandong
Pingnan China 77 H3
Pingqiao China 77 G1
Pingshan *Sichuan* China 76 E2
Pingshan *Yunnan* China *see* Luquan
Pingshi China 77 G3
Pingtan China 77 H3
Pingtan Dao *i.* China *see* Haitan Dao
Pingtang China 76 E3
Pingtung Taiwan 77 I4
Pingxi China *see* Yuping
Pingxiang *Guangxi* China 76 E4
Pingxiang *Jiangxi* China 77 G3
Pingyang *Heilong.* China 74 B2
Pingyang *Zhejiang* China 77 I3
Pingyi China 77 H1
Pingyu China 77 G1
Pingyuan China 76 D4
Pingzhai China *see* Liuzhi
Pinheiro Brazil 143 I4
Pinhoe U.K. 49 D8
Pini *i.* Indon. 68 B6
Piniós *r.* Greece *see* Pineios
Pinjin Australia 109 C7
Pink Mountain Canada 120 F3
Pinlaung Myanmar 70 B2
Pinlebu Myanmar 70 A1
Pinnacle *hill* U.S.A. 135 F4
Pinnacles National Park *nat. park* U.S.A. 128 C3
Pinnau *r.* Germany 53 J1
Pinneberg Germany 53 J1
Pinnes, Akra *pt* Greece *see* Pines, Akrotirio
Pinon Hills U.S.A. 128 E4
Pinos, Isla de *i.* Cuba *see* Juventud, Isla de la
Pinos, Mount U.S.A. 128 D4
Pinotepa Nacional Mex. 136 E5
Pins, Île des *i.* New Caledonia 107 G4
Pins, Pointe aux *pt* Canada 134 E2
Pinsk Belarus 45 O10
Pinta, Sierra *hill* U.S.A. 129 G5
Pintada Creek *watercourse* U.S.A. 127 G6
Pintados Chile 144 C2
Pintura U.S.A. 129 G3
Pioche U.S.A. 129 F3
Piodi Dem. Rep. Congo 99 C4
Pioneer Mountains U.S.A. 126 E3
Pioner, Ostrov *i.* Russia 64 K2
Pionerskiy *Kaliningradskaya Oblast'* Russia 45 L9
Pionerskiy *Khanty-Mansiyskiy Autonomnyy Okrug-Yugra* Russia 41 S3
Pionki Poland 47 R5
Piopio N.Z. 113 E4
Piopiotahi *inlet* N.Z. *see* Milford Sound
Piorini, Lago *l.* Brazil 142 F4
Piotrków Trybunalski Poland 47 Q5
Pipa Dingzi *mt.* China 74 C4
Pipar India 82 C4
Pipar Road India 82 C4
Piperi *i.* Greece 59 K5
Piper Peak U.S.A. 128 E3
Pipestone Canada 121 K5
Pipestone *r.* Canada 121 N4
Pipestone U.S.A. 130 D3
Pipli India 82 C3
Pipmuacan, Réservoir *resr* Canada 123 H4
Piqua U.S.A. 134 C3
Piquiri *r.* Brazil 145 A4
Pira Benin 96 D4
Piracanjuba Brazil 145 A2
Piracicaba Brazil 145 B3
Piracicaba *r.* Brazil 145 C2
Piracuruca Brazil 143 J4
Piraeus Greece 59 J6
Piraí do Sul Brazil 145 A4
Piráievs Greece *see* Piraeus
Piraju Brazil 145 A3
Pirajuí Brazil 145 A3
Pirallahı Adası Azer. 91 H2
Piranhas *Bahia* Brazil 145 C1
Piranhas *Goiás* Brazil 143 H7
Piranhas *r. Goiás* Brazil 145 A2
Piranhas *r. Rio Grande do Norte* Brazil 143 K5
Pirapora Brazil 145 B2
Pirassununga Brazil 145 B3
Piraube, Lac *l.* Canada 123 H4
Pirawa India 82 D4
Pirenópolis Brazil 145 A1
Pires do Rio Brazil 145 A2
Pírgos Greece *see* Pyrgos
Pirin, Natsionalen Park *nat. park* Bulg. 59 J4
Pirineos *mts* Europe *see* Pyrenees
Piripiri Brazil 143 J4
Pirlerkondu Turkey *see* Taşkent
Pirmasens Germany 53 H5
Pirojpur Bangl. 83 G5
Pir Panjal Pass India 82 C2
Pir Panjal Range *mts* India/Pak. 89 I3
Pīr Shūrān, Selseleh-ye *mts* Iran 89 F4
Piryatin Ukr. *see* Pyryatyn
Pīr Zādah Afgh. 89 G4
Pisa Italy 58 D3
Pisae Italy *see* Pisa
Pisagua Chile 142 D7
Pisang, Kepulauan *is* Indon. 69 I7
Pisaurum Italy *see* Pesaro
Pisco Peru 142 C6
Písek Czechia 47 O6
Pisha China *see* Ningnan
Pishan China 82 D1
Pīshīn Iran 80 B6
Pishin Pak. 89 G4
Pishīn Jān Afgh. 89 F3
Pishin Lora *r.* Pak. 89 G4
Pishpek Kyrg. *see* Bishkek
Pisidia *hist. area* Turkey 90 C3

▶Pissis, Cerro Arg. 144 C3
4th highest mountain in South America.

Pisté Mex. 136 G4
Pisticci Italy 58 G4
Pistoia Italy 58 D3
Pistoriae Italy *see* Pistoia
Pisuerga *r.* Spain 57 D3
Pita Guinea 96 B3
Pitaga Canada 123 I3
Pitanga Brazil 145 A4
Pitangui Brazil 145 B2
Pitar India 82 B5
Pitarpunga Lake *imp. l.* Australia 112 A5
Pitcairn, Henderson, Ducie and Oeno Islands *terr.* S. Pacific Ocean *see* Pitcairn Islands
Pitcairn Island Pitcairn Is 151 L7

▶Pitcairn Islands *terr.* S. Pacific Ocean 151 L7
United Kingdom Overseas Territory.

Piteå Sweden 44 L4
Piteälven *r.* Sweden 44 L4
Pitelino Russia 43 I5
Piterka Russia 43 J6
Pitești Romania 59 K2
Pithoragarh India 82 E3
Pitihra India 82 D5
Pitiquito Mex. 127 E7
Pitkyaranta Russia 42 F3
Pitlochry U.K. 50 F4
Pitong China *see* Pixian
Pitsane Siding Botswana 101 G3
Pitti *i.* India 84 B4
Pitt Island Canada 120 D4
Pitt Island N.Z. 107 I6
Pitt Islands Solomon Is *see* Vanikoro Islands
Pittsboro U.S.A. 131 F5
Pittsburg *KS* U.S.A. 131 E4
Pittsburg *TX* U.S.A. 131 E5
Pittsburgh U.S.A. 134 F3
Pittsfield *MA* U.S.A. 135 I2
Pittsfield *ME* U.S.A. 135 K1

Pittsfield VT U.S.A. 135 I2
Pittston U.S.A. 135 H3
Pittsworth Australia 112 E1
Pitz Lake Canada 121 L2
Piumhi Brazil 145 B3
Piura Peru 142 B5
Piute Mountains U.S.A. 129 F4
Piute Peak U.S.A. 128 D4
Piute Reservoir U.S.A. 129 G2
Piuthan Nepal 83 E3
Pivabiska r. Canada 122 E4
Pivka Slovenia 58 F2
Pixariá mt. Greece see Pyxaria
Pixian China 76 D2
Pixley U.S.A. 128 D4
Pizhanka Russia 42 K4
Pizhi Nigeria 96 D4
Pizhma Russia 42 J4
Pizhma r. Russia 42 K4
Pizhma r. Russia 42 L2
Pizhou China 77 H1
Placentia Canada 123 L5
Placentia Italy see Piacenza
Placentia Bay Canada 123 L5
Placerville CA U.S.A. 128 C2
Placerville CO U.S.A. 129 I2
Placetas Cuba 133 E8
Plácido de Castro Brazil 142 E6
Plain Dealing U.S.A. 131 E5
Plainfield CT U.S.A. 135 J3
Plainfield IN U.S.A. 134 B4
Plainfield VT U.S.A. 135 I1
Plains KS U.S.A. 131 C4
Plains TX U.S.A. 131 C5
Plainview U.S.A. 131 C5
Plainville IN U.S.A. 134 B4
Plainville KS U.S.A. 130 D4
Plainwell U.S.A. 134 C2
Plaka, Akra pt Greece see Plaka, Akrotirio
Plaka, Akrotirio pt Greece 59 L7
Plakoti, Cape Cyprus 85 B2
Plamondon Canada 121 H4
Planá Czechia 53 M5
Plana Cays is Bahamas 133 F8
Planada U.S.A. 128 C3
Planaltina Brazil 145 B1
Plane r. Germany 53 M2
Plankinton U.S.A. 130 D3
Plano U.S.A. 131 D5
Planura Brazil 145 A3
Plaquemine U.S.A. 131 F6
Plasencia Spain 57 C3
Plaster City U.S.A. 129 F5
Plaster Rock Canada 123 I5
Plastun Russia 74 E3
Platani r. Sicily Italy 58 E6
Platberg mt. S. Africa 101 I5
Plateau Antarctica
Platina U.S.A. 128 B1
Platinum U.S.A. 153 B3
Plato Col. 142 D2
Platte r. U.S.A. 130 E3
Platte City U.S.A. 130 E4
Plattling Germany 53 M6
Plattsburgh U.S.A. 135 I1
Plattsmouth U.S.A. 130 E3
Plau am See Germany 53 M1
Plauen Germany 53 M4
Plauer See l. Germany 53 M1
Plavsk Russia 43 H5
Playa Noriega, Lago l. Mex. 127 F7
Playas Ecuador 142 B4
Playas Lake U.S.A. 129 I6
Plây Ku Vietnam 71 E4
Pleasant, Lake U.S.A. 129 G5
Pleasant Bay U.S.A. 135 K3
Pleasant Grove U.S.A. 129 H1
Pleasant Hill Lake U.S.A. 134 D3
Pleasanton U.S.A. 131 D6
Pleasant Point N.Z. 113 C7
Pleasantville U.S.A. 135 H4
Pleasure Ridge Park U.S.A. 134 C4
Pleaux France 56 F4
Pledger Lake Canada 122 E4
Plei Doch Vietnam 71 D4
Plei Kân Vietnam 70 D4
Pleinfeld Germany 53 K5
Pleiße r. Germany 53 M3
Plenty watercourse Australia 110 B5
Plenty, Bay of g. N.Z. 113 F3
Plentywood U.S.A. 126 G2
Plesetsk Russia 42 I3
Pleshchentsy Belarus see Plyeshchanitsy
Plétipi, Lac l. Canada 123 H4
Plettenberg Germany 53 H3
Plettenberg Bay S. Africa 100 F8
Pleven Bulg. 59 K3
Plevna Bulg. see Pleven
Pljevlja Montenegro 59 H3
Płock Poland 47 Q4
Pločno mt. Bos. & Herz. 58 G3
Plodovoye Russia 42 F3
Ploemeur France 56 C3
Ploești Romania see Ploiești
Ploiești Romania 59 L2
Plomb du Cantal mt. France 56 F4
Ploskoye Russia see Stanovoye
Płoty Poland 47 O4
Ploudalmézeau France 56 B2
Plouzané France 56 B2
Plovdiv Bulg. 59 K3
Plover Cove Reservoir H.K. China 77 [inset]
Plozk Poland see Płock
Plum U.S.A. 134 F3
Plumridge Lakes salt flat Australia 109 D7
Plungė Lith. 45 L9
Plutarco Elías Calles, Presa resr Mex. 127 F7
Pluto, Lac l. Canada 123 H3
Plyeshchanitsy Belarus 45 O9
Ply Huey Wati, Khao mt. Myanmar/Thai. 70 B3
Plymouth U.K. 49 C8
Plymouth CA U.S.A. 128 C2
Plymouth IN U.S.A. 134 B3
Plymouth MA U.S.A. 135 J3
Plymouth NC U.S.A. 132 E5
Plymouth NH U.S.A. 135 J2
Plymouth WI U.S.A. 134 B2
▶Plymouth (abandoned) Montserrat 137 L5
Capital of Montserrat, abandoned in 1997 owing to volcanic activity. Temporary capital established at Brades.
Plymouth Bay U.S.A. 135 J3
Plynlimon hill U.K. 49 D6
Plyussa Russia 45 P7
Plzeň Czechia 47 N6
Pô Burkina Faso 96 C3
Po r. Italy 58 E2
Pobeda Peak China/Kyrg. 80 F3
Pobedy, Pik mt. China/Kyrg. see Pobeda Peak
Pocahontas U.S.A. 131 F4
Pocatello U.S.A. 126 E4
Pochayiv Ukr. 43 E6
Pochep Russia 43 G5
Pochinki Russia 43 J5
Pochinok Russia 43 G5
Pochutla Mex. 136 E5
Pocking Germany 47 N6
Pocklington U.K. 48 G5
Poções Brazil 145 C1
Pocomoke City U.S.A. 135 H4
Pocomoke Sound b. U.S.A. 135 H5
Poconé Brazil 143 G7
Pocono Mountains hills U.S.A. 135 H3
Pocono Summit U.S.A. 135 H3
Poços de Caldas Brazil 145 B3
Podanur India 84 C4
Poddor'ye Russia 42 F4
Podgorenskiy Russia 43 H6
▶Podgorica Montenegro 59 H3
Capital of Montenegro.
Podgornoye Russia 64 J4
Podile India 84 C3
Podișul Transilvaniei plat. Romania see Transylvanian Basin
Podkamennaya Tunguska r. Russia 65 K3
Podocarpus, Parque Nacional nat. park Ecuador 142 C4
Podol'sk Russia 43 H5
Podporozh'ye Russia 42 G3
Podujevë Kosovo 59 I3
Podujevo Kosovo see Podujevë
Podz' Russia 42 K3
Poelela, Lagoa l. Moz. 101 L3
Poeppel Corner salt flat Australia 111 B5
Poetovio Slovenia see Ptuj
Pofadder S. Africa 100 D5
Pogar Russia 43 G5
Poggibonsi Italy 58 D3
Pogradec Albania 59 I4
Pogranichnyy Russia 74 C3
Po Hai g. China see Bo Hai
Pohang S. Korea 75 C5
Pohnpei atoll Micronesia 150 G5
Pohri India 82 D4
Poi India 83 H4
Poiana Mare Romania 59 J3
Poindo China 83 G3
Poinsett, Cape Antarctica 152 F2
Point Arena U.S.A. 128 B2
Point au Fer Island U.S.A. 131 F6
Pointe à la Hache U.S.A. 131 F6
Pointe-à-Pitre Guadeloupe 137 L5
Pointe-Noire Congo 99 B4
Point Hope U.S.A. 118 B3
Point Lake Canada 120 H1
Point of Rocks U.S.A. 126 F4
Point Pelee National Park Canada 134 D3
Point Pleasant NJ U.S.A. 135 H3
Point Pleasant WV U.S.A. 134 D4
Poitiers France 56 E3
Poitou reg. France 56 E3
Poix-de-Picardie France 52 B5
Pojuca r. Brazil 145 D1
Pokaran India 82 B4
Pokataroo Australia 112 D2
Pokcha Russia 41 R3
Pokhara Nepal 83 E3
Pokhran Landi Pak. 89 G5
Pokhvistnevo Russia 41 Q5
Poko Dem. Rep. Congo 98 C3
Pokosnoye Russia 72 I1
P'ok'r Kovkas mts Asia see Lesser Caucasus
Pokrovka Primorskiy Kray Russia 74 C4
Pokrovka Zabaykal'skiy Kray Russia 74 A1
Pokrovsk Respublika Sakha (Yakutiya) Russia 65 N3
Pokrovsk Saratovskaya Oblast' Russia see Engel's
Pokrovskoye Russia 43 H7
Pokshen'ga r. Russia 42 J3
Pol India 82 C5
Pola Croatia see Pula
Polacca Wash watercourse U.S.A. 129 H4
Pola de Siero Spain see La Pola Siero
Poland country Europe 40 J5
Poland NY U.S.A. 135 H2
Poland OH U.S.A. 134 E3
Polar Plateau Antarctica 152 A1
Polatlı Turkey 90 D3
Polatsk Belarus 45 P9
Polavaram India 84 D2
Polcirkeln Sweden 44 L3
Pol-e Fasā Iran 88 D4
Pol-e Khātūn Iran 89 F2
Pol-e Sefīd Iran 88 D2
Polessk Russia 45 L9
Poles'ye marsh Belarus/Ukr. see Pripet Marshes
Polgahawela Sri Lanka 84 D5
Poli Cyprus see Polis
Políaigos i. Greece see Polyaigos
Police Poland 47 O4
Policoro Italy 58 G4
Poligny France 56 G3
Políkastron Greece see Polykastro
Polillo Islands Phil. 69 G3
Poliny Osipenko, imeni Russia 74 E1
Polis Cyprus 85 A2
Polis'ke (abandoned) Ukr. 43 F6
Polis'kyy Zapovidnyk nature res. Ukr. 43 F6
Politovo Russia 42 K2
Políyiros Greece see Polygyros
Polkowice Poland 47 P5
Pollachi India 84 C4
Pollard Islands U.S.A. see Gardner Pinnacles
Polle Germany 53 J3
Pollino, Monte mt. Italy 58 G5
Pollino, Parco Nazionale del nat. park Italy 58 G5
Pollock Pines U.S.A. 128 C2
Pollock Reef Australia 109 C8
Polmak Norway 44 O1
Polnovat Russia 41 T3
Polo Fin. 44 P4
Poloat atoll Micronesia see Puluwat
Pologi Ukr. see Polohy
Polohy Ukr. 43 H7
Polokwane S. Africa 101 I2
Polokwane r. S. Africa 101 J2
Polonne Ukr. 43 E6
Polonnoye Ukr. see Polonne
Polotsk Belarus see Polatsk
Polperro U.K. 49 C8
Polska country Europe see Poland
Polson U.S.A. 126 E3
Polta r. Russia 42 I2
Poltava Ukr. 43 G6
Poltoratsk Turkm. see Aşgabat
Põltsamaa Estonia 45 N7
Polunochnoye Russia 41 S3
Põlva Estonia 45 O7
Polvadera U.S.A. 127 G6
Polvijärvi Fin. 44 P5
Polyaigos i. Greece 59 K6
Polyanovgrad Bulg. see Karnobat
Polyarnyy Russia 44 R2
Polyarnyy (abandoned) Russia 65 S3
Polyarnyye Zori Russia 44 R3
Polyarnyy Ural mts Russia 41 S2
Polygyros Greece 59 J4
Polykastro Greece 59 J4
Polynesia is Pacific Ocean 150 I6
Polynésie Française terr. S. Pacific Ocean see French Polynesia
Pom Indon. 69 J7
Pomarkku Fin. 45 M6
Pombal Pará Brazil 143 H4
Pombal Paraíba Brazil 143 K5
Pombal Port. 57 B4
Pomene Moz. 101 L2
Pomeranian Bay Poland 47 O3
Pomeroy S. Africa 101 J5
Pomeroy U.K. 51 F3
Pomeroy OH U.S.A. 134 D4
Pomeroy WA U.S.A. 126 D3
Pomezia Italy 58 E4
Pomfret S. Africa 100 F3
Pomona Namibia 100 B4
Pomona U.S.A. 128 E4
Pomorie Bulg. 59 L3
Pomorskie, Pojezierze reg. Poland 47 O4
Pomorskiy Bereg coastal area Russia 42 G2
Pomorskiy Proliv sea chan. Russia 42 K1
Pomos Point Cyprus 85 A2
Pomo Tso l. China see Puma Yumco
Pomou, Akra pt Cyprus see Pomos Point
Pomozdino Russia 42 L3
Pompain China 76 B2
Pompano Beach U.S.A. 133 D7
Pompei Italy 58 F4
Pompéia Brazil 145 A3
Pompey France 52 G6
Pompeyevka Russia 74 C2
Ponape atoll Micronesia see Pohnpei
Ponask Lake Canada 121 M4
Ponazyrevo Russia 42 J4
Ponca City U.S.A. 131 D4
Ponce Puerto Rico 137 K5
Ponce de Leon Bay U.S.A. 133 D7
Poncheville, Lac l. Canada 122 F4
Pondichéry India see Puducherry
Pond Inlet Canada 153 K2
Ponds Bay Canada see Pond Inlet
Ponente, Riviera di coastal area Italy 58 B3
Poneto U.S.A. 134 C3
Ponferrada Spain 57 C2
Pongara, Pointe pt Gabon 98 A3
Pongaroa N.Z. 113 F5
Pongo watercourse South Sudan 97 F4
Pongola r. S. Africa 101 K4
Pongolapoort Dam l. S. Africa 101 J4
Ponnagyun Myanmar 70 A2
Ponnaiyar r. India 84 C4
Ponnampet India 84 B3
Ponnani India 84 B4
Ponnyadaung Range mts Myanmar 70 A2
Pono Indon. 69 I8
Ponoka Canada 120 H4
Ponoy r. Russia 42 I2
Pons r. Canada 123 H2
▶Ponta Delgada Arquipélago dos Açores 148 G3
Capital of the Azores.
Ponta Grossa Brazil 145 A4
Pontal Brazil 145 A3
Pontalina Brazil 145 A2
Pont-à-Mousson France 52 G6
Ponta Porã Brazil 144 E2
Pontarfynach U.K. see Devil's Bridge
Pont-Audemer France 49 H9
Pontault-Combault France 52 C6
Pontax r. Canada 122 F4
Pontchartrain, Lake U.S.A. 131 F6
Pontcysyllte Aqueduct tourist site U.K. 49 D6
Pont d'Arc tourist site France 56 G4
Pont-de-Loup Belgium 52 E4
Ponte Alta do Tocantins Brazil 143 I6
Ponte de Sor Port. 57 B4
Ponte Firme Brazil 145 B2
Pontefract U.K. 48 F5
Ponteix Canada 121 J5
Ponteland U.K. 48 F3
Ponte Nova Brazil 145 C3
Pontes e Lacerda Brazil 143 G7
Pontevedra Spain 57 B2
Ponthierville Dem. Rep. Congo see Ubundu
Pontiac IL U.S.A. 130 F3
Pontiac MI U.S.A. 134 D2
Pontiae is Italy see Ponziane, Isole
Pontianak Indon. 68 D7
Pontine Islands is Italy see Ponziane, Isole
Pont-l'Abbé France 56 B3
Ponto de Santa Cruz Brazil 145 C1
Pontoise France 52 C5
Ponton watercourse Australia 109 C7
Ponton Canada 121 L4
Pontotoc U.S.A. 131 F5
Pont-Ste-Maxence France 52 C5
Pontypool U.K. 49 D7
Pontypridd U.K. 49 D7
Ponza, Isola di i. Italy 58 E4
Ponziane, Isole is Italy 58 E4
Poochera Australia 109 F8
Poole U.K. 49 F8
Poole U.S.A. 134 B5
Poolowanna Lake salt flat Australia 111 B5
Poona India see Pune
Pooncarie Australia 111 C7
Poonch India see Punch
Poopelloe Lake salt l. Australia 112 B3
Poopó, Lago de l. Bol. 142 E7
Poor Knights Islands N.Z. 113 E2
Popayán Col. 142 C3
Poperinge Belgium 52 C4
Popigay r. Russia 65 L2
Popiltah Australia 111 C7
Popilta Lake imp. l. Australia 111 C7
Poplar r. Canada 121 L4
Poplar U.S.A. 126 G2
Poplar Bluff U.S.A. 131 F4
Poplar Camp U.S.A. 134 E5
Poplarville U.S.A. 131 F6
▶Popocatépetl, Volcán vol. Mex. 136 E5
5th highest mountain in North America.
Popokabaka Dem. Rep. Congo 99 B4
Popondetta P.N.G. 69 L8
Popovichskaya Russia see Kalininskaya
Popovo Bulg. 59 L3
Popovo Polje plain Bos. & Herz. 58 G3
Poppberg hill Germany 53 L5
Poppenberg hill Germany 53 K3
Poprad Slovakia 47 R6
Poquoson U.S.A. 135 G5
Porali r. Pak. 89 G5
Porangahau N.Z. 113 F5
Porangatu Brazil 145 A1
Porbandar India 82 B5
Porcher Island Canada 120 D4
Porcos r. Brazil 145 B1
Porcupine, Cape Canada 123 K3
Porcupine Abyssal Plain sea feature N. Atlantic Ocean 148 G2
Porcupine Gorge National Park Australia 110 D4
Porcupine Hills Canada 121 K4
Porcupine Mountains U.S.A. 130 F2
Poreč Croatia 58 E2
Porecatu Brazil 145 A3
Poretskoye Russia 43 J5
Pori Fin. 45 L6
Porirua N.Z. 113 E5
Porkhov Russia 45 P8
Porlamar Venez. 142 F1
Pormpuraaw Australia 110 C2
Pornic France 56 C3
Poronaysk Russia 74 F2
Porong China 83 G3
Poros Greece 59 J6
Porosozero Russia 42 G3
Porpoise Bay Antarctica 152 G2
Porsangerfjorden sea chan. Norway 44 N1
Porsangerhalvøya pen. Norway 44 N1
Porsgrunn Norway 45 F7
Porsuk r. Turkey 59 N5
Portadown U.K. 51 F3
Portaferry U.K. 51 G3
Portage MI U.S.A. 134 C2
Portage PA U.S.A. 135 F3
Portage WI U.S.A. 130 F3
Portage Lakes U.S.A. 134 E3
Portage la Prairie Canada 121 L5
Portal U.S.A. 130 C1
Port Alberni Canada 120 E5
Port Albert Australia 112 C7
Portalegre Port. 57 C4
Portales U.S.A. 131 C5
Port-Alfred Canada see La Baie
Port Alfred S. Africa 101 H7
Port Alice Canada 120 E5
Port Allegany U.S.A. 135 F3
Port Allen U.S.A. 131 F6
Port Alma Australia 110 E4
Port Angeles U.S.A. 126 C2
Port Antonio Jamaica 137 I5
Portarlington Ireland 51 E4
Port Arthur Australia 111 [inset]
Port Arthur U.S.A. 131 E6
Port Askaig U.K. 50 C5
Port Augusta Australia 111 B7
▶Port-au-Prince Haiti 137 J5
Capital of Haiti.
Port Austin U.S.A. 134 D1
Port aux Choix Canada 123 K4
Portavogie U.K. 51 G3
Port Beaufort S. Africa 100 E8
Port Blair India 71 A5
Port Bolster Canada 134 F1
Portbou Spain 57 H2
Port Burwell Canada 134 E2
Port Campbell Australia 112 A7
Port Campbell National Park Australia 112 A7
Port Carling Canada 134 F1
Port-Cartier Canada 123 I4
Port Chalmers N.Z. 113 C7
Port Charlotte U.S.A. 133 D7
Port Clements Canada 120 C4
Port Clinton U.S.A. 134 D3
Port Credit Canada 134 F2
Port-de-Paix Haiti 137 J5
Port Dickson Malaysia 71 C7
Port Douglas Australia 110 D3
Port Edward Canada 120 D4
Port Edward S. Africa 101 J6
Porteira Brazil 143 G4
Porteirinha Brazil 145 C1
Portel Brazil 143 H4
Port Elgin Canada 134 E1
Port Elizabeth S. Africa 101 G7
Port Ellen U.K. 50 C5
Port Erin Isle of Man 48 C4
Porter Lake N.W.T. Canada 121 J2
Porter Lake Sask. Canada 121 J3
Porter Landing Canada 120 D3
Porterville S. Africa 100 D7
Porterville U.S.A. 128 D3
Port Étienne Mauritania see Nouâdhibou
Port Everglades U.S.A. see Fort Lauderdale
Port Fitzroy N.Z. 113 E3
Port Francqui Dem. Rep. Congo see Ilebo
Port-Gentil Gabon 98 A4
Port Glasgow U.K. 50 E5
Port Harcourt Nigeria 96 D4
Port Harrison Canada see Inukjuak
Porthcawl U.K. 49 D7
Port Hedland Australia 108 B5
Port Henry U.S.A. 135 I1
Port Herald Malawi see Nsanje
Porthleven U.K. 49 B8
Porthmadog U.K. 49 C6
Port Hope Canada 135 F2
Port Hope Simpson Canada 123 L3
Port Hueneme U.S.A. 128 D4
Port Huron U.S.A. 134 D2
Portimão Port. 57 B5
Port Jackson Australia see Sydney
Port Jackson inlet Australia 112 E4
Port Keats Australia see Wadeye
Port Klang Malaysia see Pelabuhan Klang
Port Láirge Ireland see Waterford
Portland N.S.W. Australia 112 D4
Portland Vic. Australia 111 C8
Portland IN U.S.A. 134 C3
Portland ME U.S.A. 135 J2
Portland MI U.S.A. 134 C2
Portland OR U.S.A. 126 C3
Portland TN U.S.A. 134 B5
Portland, Isle of pen. U.K. 49 E8
Portland Bill hd U.K. see Bill of Portland
Portland Creek Pond l. Canada 123 K4
Portland Roads Australia 110 C2
Port-la-Nouvelle France 56 F5
Portlaoise Ireland 51 E4
Port Lavaca U.S.A. 131 D6
Portlaw Ireland 51 E5
Portlethen U.K. 50 G3
Port Lincoln Australia 111 A7
Port Loko Sierra Leone 96 B4
▶Port Louis Mauritius 149 L7
Capital of Mauritius.
Port-Lyautrey Morocco see Kenitra
Port Macquarie Australia 112 F3
Portmadoc U.K. see Porthmadog
Port McNeill Canada 120 E5
Port-Menier Canada 123 I4
▶Port Moresby P.N.G. 69 L8
Capital of Papua New Guinea.
Portnaguran U.K. 50 C2
Portnahaven U.K. 50 C5
Port nan Giúran U.K. see Portnaguran
Port Neill Australia 111 B7
Portneuf r. Canada 123 H4
Port Nis U.K. see Port of Ness
Port Noarlunga Australia 111 B7
Port Nolloth S. Africa 100 C5
Port Norris U.S.A. 135 H4
Port-Nouveau-Québec Canada see Kangiqsualujjuaq
Porto Port. see Oporto
Porto Acre Brazil 142 E5
Porto Alegre Brazil 145 A5
Porto Alexandre Angola see Tombua
Porto Amboim Angola 99 B5
Porto Amélia Moz. see Pemba
Porto Artur Brazil 143 G6
Porto Belo Brazil 145 A4
Porto de Moz Brazil 143 H4
Porto dos Gaúchos Óbidos Brazil 143 G6
Porto Esperança Brazil 143 G7
Porto Esperidião Brazil 143 G7
Portoferraio Italy 58 D3
Port of Ness U.K. 50 C2
Porto Franco Brazil 143 I5
▶Port of Spain Trin. and Tob. 137 L6
Capital of Trinidad and Tobago.
Porto Grande Brazil 143 H3
Portogruaro Italy 58 E2
Porto Jofre Brazil 143 G7
Portola U.S.A. 128 C2
Portomaggiore Italy 58 D2
Porto Mendes Brazil 144 F2
Porto Murtinho Brazil 144 E2
Porto Nacional Brazil 143 I6
▶Porto-Novo Benin 96 D4
Capital of Benin.
Porto Novo Cape Verde 96 [inset]
Porto Primavera, Represa resr Brazil 144 F2
Port Orchard U.S.A. 126 C3
Port Orford U.S.A. 126 B4
Porto Rico Angola 99 B4
Porto Santo, Ilha de i. Madeira 96 B1
Porto Seguro Brazil 145 D2
Porto Tolle Italy 58 E2
Porto Torres Sardinia Italy 58 C4
Porto União Brazil 145 A4
Porto-Vecchio Corsica France 56 I6
Porto Velho Brazil 142 F5
Portoviejo Ecuador 142 B4
Porto Walter Brazil 142 D5
Portpatrick U.K. 50 D6
Port Perry Canada 135 F1
Port Phillip Bay Australia 112 B7
Port Pirie Australia 111 B7
Port Radium Canada see Echo Bay
Portreath U.K. 49 B8
Portree U.K. 50 C3
Port Rexton Canada 123 L4
Port Royal U.S.A. 135 G4
Port Royal Sound inlet U.S.A. 133 D5
Portrush U.K. 51 F2
Port Safaga Egypt see Būr Safājah
Port Said Egypt 85 A4
Port St Joe U.S.A. 133 C6
Port St Mary Isle of Man 48 C4
Portsalon Ireland 51 E2
Port Sanilac U.S.A. 134 D2
Port Severn Canada 134 F1
Port Shepstone S. Africa 101 J6
Port Simpson Canada see Lax Kw'alaams
Portsmouth U.K. 49 F8
Portsmouth NH U.S.A. 135 J2
Portsmouth OH U.S.A. 134 D4
Portsmouth VA U.S.A. 135 G5
Portsoy U.K. 50 G3
Port Stanley Falkland Is see Stanley
Port Stephens b. Australia 112 F4
Portstewart U.K. 51 F2
Port St Lucie U.S.A. 133 D7
Port Sudan Sudan 86 E6
Port Swettenham Malaysia see Pelabuhan Klang
Port Talbot U.K. 49 D7
Porttipahdan tekojärvi l. Fin. 44 O2
Port Townsend U.S.A. 126 C2
Portugal country Europe 57 C4
Portugália Angola see Chitato
Portuguese East Africa country Africa see Mozambique
Portuguese Guinea country Africa see Guinea-Bissau
Portuguese Timor country Asia see East Timor
Portuguese West Africa country Africa see Angola
Portumna Ireland 51 D4
Portus Herculis Monoeci country Europe see Monaco
Port-Vendres France 56 F5
▶Port Vila Vanuatu 107 G3
Capital of Vanuatu.
Portville U.S.A. 135 F2
Port-Vladimir Russia 44 R2
Port Waikato N.Z. 113 E3
Port Washington U.S.A. 134 B2
Port William U.K. 50 E6
Porvenir Bol. 142 E6
Porvenir Chile 144 B8
Porvoo Fin. 45 N6
Posada Spain 57 D2
Posada de Llanera Spain see Posada
Posadas Arg. 144 E3
Posen Poland see Poznań
Posen U.S.A. 134 D1
Poseyville U.S.A. 134 B4
Poshekhon'ye Russia 42 H4
Poshekon'ye-Volodarsk Russia see Poshekhon'ye
Poshteh-ye Chaqvīr hill Iran 88 E4
Posht-e Kūh mts Iran 88 B3
Posht-e Rūd va Zamīndāvar reg. Afgh. see Zamīndāwar
Posht Kūh hill Iran 88 C2
Posio Fin. 44 P3
Poso Indon. 69 G7
Posof Turkey 91 F2
Possession Island Namibia 100 B4
Pößneck Germany 53 L4
Post U.S.A. 131 C5
Postavy Belarus see Pastavy
Poste-de-la-Baleine Canada see Kuujjuarapik
Poste Weygand Alg. 96 D2
Postmasburg S. Africa 100 F5
Poston U.S.A. 129 F4
Postville Canada 123 K3
Postville U.S.A. 122 C6
Postysheve Ukr. see Krasnoarmiys'k
Pota Indon. 108 C2
Pótam Mex. 127 F8
Poté Brazil 145 C2
Poteau U.S.A. 131 E5
Potegaon India 84 D2
Potentia Italy see Potenza
Potenza Italy 58 F4
Poth U.S.A. 131 D6
Poti Georgia 91 F2
Potikal India 84 D2
Potiraguá Brazil 145 D1
Potiskum Nigeria 96 E3
Potlatch U.S.A. 126 D3
Pot Mountain U.S.A. 126 E3
Po Toi i. H.K. China 77 [inset]
Potomac r. U.S.A. 135 G4
Potosí Bol. 142 E7
Potosi U.S.A. 130 F4
Potosi Mountain U.S.A. 129 F4
Potrerillos Chile 144 C3
Potrero del Llano Mex. 131 B6
Potsdam Germany 53 N2
Potsdam U.S.A. 135 H1
Potter U.S.A. 130 C3
Potterne U.K. 49 E7
Potters Bar U.K. 49 G7
Potter Valley U.S.A. 128 B2
Pottstown U.S.A. 135 H3
Pottsville U.S.A. 135 G3
Pottuvil Sri Lanka 84 D5
Potwar reg. Pak. 89 I3
Pouch Cove Canada 123 L5
Poughkeepsie U.S.A. 135 I3
Poulin de Courval, Lac l. Canada 123 H4
Poulton-le-Fylde U.K. 48 E5
Pouso Alegre Brazil 145 B3
Poŭthĭsăt Cambodia 71 C4
Poŭthĭsăt, Stœng r. Cambodia 71 D4
Považská Bystrica Slovakia 47 Q6
Povenets Russia 42 G3
Poverty Bay N.Z. 113 F4
Poverty Point tourist site U.S.A. 131 F5
Povlen mt. Serbia 59 H2
Póvoa de Varzim Port. 57 B3
Povorino Russia 43 I6
Povorotnyy, Mys hd Russia 74 D4
Poway U.S.A. 128 E5
Powder r. U.S.A. 126 G3
Powder, South Fork r. U.S.A. 126 G4

Powder River U.S.A. 126 G4
Powell r. U.S.A. 134 D5
Powell, Lake resr U.S.A. 129 H3
Powell Lake Canada 120 E5
Powell Mountain U.S.A. 128 D2
Powell Point Bahamas 133 E7
Powell River Canada 120 E5
Powhatan AR U.S.A. 131 F4
Powhatan VA U.S.A. 135 G5
Powo China 76 C1
Pöwrize Turkm. 88 E2
Poxoréo Brazil 143 H7
Poyang China 77 H2
Poyang Hu l. China 77 H2
Poyan Reservoir Sing. 71 [inset]
Poyarkovo Russia 74 C2
Pōzak, Jahīl-e marsh Afgh. 89 F4
Pozantı Turkey 90 D3
Požarevac Serbia 59 I2
Poza Rica Mex. 136 E4
Pozdeyevka Russia 74 C2
Požega Croatia 58 G2
Požega Serbia 59 I3
Pozharskoye Russia 74 D3
Poznań Poland 47 P4
Pozoblanco Spain 57 D4
Pozo Colorado Para. 144 E2
Pozsony Slovakia see Bratislava
Pozzuoli Italy 58 F4
Prabumulih Indon. 68 C7
Prachatice Czechia 47 O6
Prachi r. India 83 F6
Prachin Buri Thai. 71 C4
Prachuap Khiri Khan Thai. 71 B5
Prades France 56 F5
Prado Brazil 145 D2

▶Prague Czechia 47 O5
Capital of the Czech Republic.

Praha Czechia see Prague

▶Praia Cape Verde 96 [inset]
Capital of Cape Verde (Cabo Verde).

Praia do Bilene Moz. 101 K3
Prainha Brazil 143 H4
Prairie Australia 110 D4
Prairie r. U.S.A. 130 E2
Prairie Dog Town Fork r. U.S.A. 131 C5
Prairie du Chien U.S.A. 130 F3
Prairie River Canada 121 K4
Pram, Khao mt. Thai. 71 B5
Pran r. Thai. 71 C4
Pran Buri Thai. 71 B4
Prapat Indon. 71 B7
Prasonisi, Akra pt Greece see Prasonisi, Akrotirio
Prasonisi, Akrotirio pt Greece 59 L7
Prata Brazil 145 A2
Prata r. Brazil 145 A2
Pratas Islands is China 68 F2
Prat de Llobregat Spain see El Prat de Llobregat
Prathes Thai country Asia see Thailand
Prato Italy 58 D3
Pratt U.S.A. 130 D4
Prattville U.S.A. 133 C5
Pravdinsk Russia 45 L9
Praya Indon. 108 B2
Preăh, Prêk r. Cambodia 71 D4
Preăh Vihéar Cambodia 71 D4
Preble U.S.A. 135 G2
Prechistoye Smolenskaya Oblast' Russia 43 G5
Prechistoye Yaroslavskaya Oblast' Russia 42 I4
Precipice National Park Australia 110 E5
Preeceville Canada 121 K5
Pregolya r. Russia 45 L9
Preiļi Latvia 45 O8
Prêk Kák Cambodia 71 D4
Prelate Canada 121 I5
Premer Australia 112 D3
Prémery France 56 F3
Premnitz Germany 53 M2
Prentiss U.S.A. 131 F6
Prenzlau Germany 47 N4
Preparis Island Cocos Is 68 A4
Preparis North Channel Cocos Is 68 A4
Preparis South Channel Cocos Is 68 A4
Přerov Czechia 47 P6
Presa San Antonio Mex. 131 C7
Prescelly Mountains hills U.K. see Preseli, Mynydd
Prescott Canada 135 H1
Prescott AR U.S.A. 131 E5
Prescott AZ U.S.A. 129 G4
Prescott Valley U.S.A. 129 G4
Preseli, Mynydd hills U.K. 49 C7
Preševo Serbia 59 I3
Presidencia Roque Sáenz Peña Arg. 144 D3
Presidente Dutra Brazil 143 J5
Presidente Hermes Brazil 142 F6
Presidente Olegário Brazil 145 B2
Presidente Prudente Brazil 145 A3
Presidente Venceslau Brazil 145 A3
Presidio U.S.A. 131 B6
Preslav Bulg. see Veliki Preslav
Prešov Slovakia 43 D6
Prespa, Lake Europe 59 I4
Prespansko Ezero l. Europe see Prespa, Lake
Prespës, Liqeni i l. Europe see Prespa, Lake
Prespon, Ethnikos Drymos nat. park Greece 59 I4
Presque Isle ME U.S.A. 132 G2
Presque Isle MI U.S.A. 134 D1
Pressburg Slovakia see Bratislava
Presteigne U.K. 49 D6
Preston U.K. 48 E5
Preston ID U.S.A. 126 F4
Preston MN U.S.A. 130 E3
Preston MO U.S.A. 130 E4
Preston, Cape Australia 108 B5
Prestonpans U.K. 50 G5
Prestonsburg U.S.A. 134 D5
Prestwick U.K. 50 E5
Preto r. Bahia Brazil 143 J6
Preto r. Bahia Brazil 145 D1
Preto r. Minas Gerais Brazil 145 B2

▶Pretoria S. Africa 101 I3
Official capital of South Africa.

Pretoria-Witwatersrand-Vereeniging prov. S. Africa see Gauteng
Pretzsch Germany 53 M3
Preussisch-Eylau Russia see Bagrationovsk
Preußisch Stargard Poland see Starogard Gdański
Preveza Greece 59 I5
Prewitt U.S.A. 129 I4
Prey Vêng Cambodia 71 D5
Priaral'skiy Karakum des. Kazakh. 80 B2
Priargunsk Russia 73 L2
Pribilof Islands U.S.A. 118 A4
Priboj Serbia 59 H3
Price r. Australia 108 E3
Price NC U.S.A. 134 F5
Price UT U.S.A. 129 H2
Price r. U.S.A. 129 H2
Price Island Canada 120 D4
Prichard AL U.S.A. 131 F6
Prichard WV U.S.A. 134 D4
Pridorozhnoye Russia see Khulkhuta
Priekule Latvia 45 L8
Priekuļi Latvia 45 N8
Priel'brus'ye, Natsional'nyy Park nat. park Russia 43 I8
Prienai Lith. 45 M9
Prieska S. Africa 100 F5
Prievidza Slovakia 47 Q6
Prignitz reg. Germany 53 M1
Prijedor Bos. & Herz. 58 G2
Prijepolje Serbia 59 H3
Prikaspiyskaya Nizmennost' lowland Kazakh./Russia see Caspian Lowland
Prilep Macedonia 59 I4
Priluki Ukr. see Pryluky
Přimda Czechia 53 M5
Primero de Enero Cuba 133 E8
Primorsk Russia 45 P6
Primorsk Ukr. see Prymors'k
Primorskiy Kray admin. div. Russia 74 D3
Primorsko-Akhtarsk Russia 43 H7
Primo Tapia Mex. 128 E5
Primrose Lake Canada 121 I4
Prims r. Germany 52 G5
Prince Albert Canada 121 J4
Prince Albert S. Africa 100 F7
Prince Albert Mountains Antarctica 152 H1
Prince Albert National Park Canada 121 J4
Prince Albert Peninsula Canada 118 G2
Prince Albert Road S. Africa 100 E7
Prince Alfred, Cape Canada 118 F2
Prince Alfred Hamlet S. Africa 100 D7
Prince Charles Island Canada 119 K3
Prince Charles Mountains Antarctica 152 E2
Prince Edward Island prov. Canada 123 J5

▶Prince Edward Islands Indian Ocean 149 K9
Part of South Africa.

Prince Edward Point Canada 135 G2
Prince Frederick U.S.A. 135 G4
Prince George Canada 120 F4
Prince Harald Coast Antarctica 152 D2
Prince of Wales, Cape U.S.A. 118 B3
Prince of Wales Island Australia 110 C1
Prince of Wales Island Canada 119 I2
Prince of Wales Island U.S.A. 120 C4
Prince of Wales Strait Canada 118 G2
Prince Patrick Island Canada 118 G2
Prince Regent Inlet sea chan. Canada 119 I2
Prince Rupert Canada 120 D4
Princess Anne U.S.A. 135 H4
Princess Astrid Coast Antarctica 152 C2
Princess Charlotte Bay Australia 110 C2
Princess Elisabeth research station Antarctica 152 C2
Princess Elizabeth Land reg. Antarctica 152 E2
Princess Mary Lake Canada 121 L1
Princess Ragnhild Coast Antarctica 152 C2
Princess Royal Island Canada 120 D4
Princeton Canada 120 F5
Princeton CA U.S.A. 128 B2
Princeton IL U.S.A. 130 F3
Princeton IN U.S.A. 134 B4
Princeton MO U.S.A. 130 E3
Princeton NJ U.S.A. 135 H3
Princeton WV U.S.A. 134 E5
Prince William Sound b. U.S.A. 118 D3
Príncipe i. São Tomé and Príncipe 96 D4
Prineville U.S.A. 126 C3
Pring, Kaôh i. Cambodia 71 C5
Prins Harald Kyst coastal area Antarctica see Prince Harald Coast
Prinzapolka Nicaragua 137 H6
Priozersk Russia 45 Q6
Priozyorsk Russia see Priozersk
Pripet r. Belarus/Ukr. 43 F6
also spelt Pryp"yat' (Ukraine) or Prypyats' (Belarus)
Pripet Marshes Belarus/Ukr. 43 E6
Prirechnyy Russia 44 Q2

▶Prishtinë Kosovo 59 I3
Capital of Kosovo.

Priština Kosovo see Prishtinë
Pritzier Germany 53 L1
Pritzwalk Germany 53 M1
Privas France 56 G4
Privlaka Croatia 58 F2
Privolzhsk Russia 42 I4
Privolzhskaya Vozvyshennost' hills Russia 43 J6
Privolzhskiy Russia 43 J6
Privolzh'ye Russia 43 K5
Priyutnoye Russia 43 I7
Prizren Kosovo 59 I3
Probolinggo Indon. 68 E8
Probstzella Germany 53 L4
Probus U.K. 49 C8
Proddatur India 84 C3
Professor van Blommestein Meer resr Suriname 143 G3
Progreso Hond. see El Progreso
Progreso Mex. 131 C7
Progress research station Antarctica 152 E2
Progress Russia 74 C2
Prokhladnyy Russia 91 G2
Prokop'yevsk Russia 72 F2
Prokuplje Serbia 59 I3
Proletarsk Russia 43 I7
Proletarskaya Russia see Proletarsk
Proletarskoye Vodokhranilishche l. Russia 43 I7
Prome Myanmar see Pyè
Promissão Brazil 145 A3
Promissão, Represa resr Brazil 145 A3
Prophet r. Canada 120 F3
Prophet River Canada 120 F3
Propriá Brazil 143 K6
Proskurov Ukr. see Khmel'nyts'kyy
Prosser U.S.A. 126 D3
Protem S. Africa 100 E8
Provadia Bulg. 59 L3
Prøven Greenland see Kangersuatsiaq
Provence reg. France 56 G5
Providence KY U.S.A. 134 B5
Providence MD U.S.A. see Annapolis

▶Providence RI U.S.A. 135 J3
Capital of Rhode Island.

Providence, Cape N.Z. 113 A8
Providencia, Isla de i. Caribbean Sea 137 H6
Provideniya Russia 65 T3
Provincetown U.S.A. 135 J2
Provo U.S.A. 129 H1
Provost Canada 121 I4
Prudentópolis Brazil 145 A4
Prudhoe Bay U.S.A. 118 D2
Prüm Germany 52 G4
Prüm r. Germany 52 G5
Prunelli-di-Fiumorbo Corsica France 56 I5
Pruntytown U.S.A. 134 E4
Prusa Turkey see Bursa
Prushkov Poland see Pruszków
Pruszków Poland 47 R4
Prut r. Europe 43 F7
Prydz Bay Antarctica 152 E2
Pryluky Ukr. 43 G6
Prymors'k Ukr. 43 H7
Prymors'ke Ukr. see Sartana
Pryp"yat' r. Belarus/Ukr. see Pripet
Prypyats' r. Belarus/Ukr. see Pripet
Przemyśl Poland 43 D6
Przheval'sk Kyrg. see Karakol
Psara i. Greece 59 K5
Pskov Russia 45 P8
Pskov, Lake Estonia/Russia 45 O7
Pskov Oblast admin. div. Russia see Pskovskaya Oblast'
Pskovskaya Oblast' admin. div. Russia 45 P8
Pskovskoye Ozero l. Estonia/Russia see Pskov, Lake
Ptolemaïda Greece 59 I4
Ptolemais Israel see 'Akko
Ptuj Slovenia 58 F1
Pua Thai. 70 C3
Puaka hill Sing. 71 [inset]
Pu'an Guizhou China 76 E3
Pu'an Sichuan China 76 E2
Pucallpa Peru 142 D5
Pucheng Fujian China 77 H3
Pucheng Shaanxi China 77 F1
Puchezh Russia 42 I4
Puck Poland 47 Q3
Pūdah Tal, Shēlah-ye watercourse Afgh. 89 F4
Pudai watercourse Afgh. see Pūdah Tal, Shēlah-ye
Pūdanū Iran 88 D3
Pudasjärvi Fin. 44 O4
Pudimoe S. Africa 100 G4
Pudong China 66 E4
Pudozh Russia 42 H3
Pudsey U.K. 48 F5
Pudu China see Suizhou
Puduchcheri India see Puducherry
Puducherry India 84 C4
Puducherry union terr. India 84 C4
Pudukkottai India 84 C4
Puebla Baja California Mex. 129 F5
Puebla Puebla Mex. 136 E5
Puebla de Sanabria Spain 57 C2
Puebla de Zaragoza Mex. see Puebla
Pueblo U.S.A. 127 G5
Pueblo Yaqui Mex. 127 F8
Puelches Arg. 144 C5
Puelén Arg. 144 C5
Puente Genil Spain 57 D5
Pu'er China see Ning'er
Puerco watercourse U.S.A. 129 H4
Puerto Acosta Bol. 142 E7
Puerto Alegre Bol. 142 F6
Puerto Ángel Mex. 136 E5
Puerto Armuelles Panama 137 H7
Puerto Ayacucho Venez. 142 E2
Puerto Bahía Negra Para. see Bahía Negra
Puerto Baquerizo Moreno Galápagos Ecuador 142 [inset]
Puerto Barrios Guat. 136 G5
Puerto Cabello Venez. 142 E1
Puerto Cabezas Nicaragua 137 H6
Puerto Carreño Col. 142 E2
Puerto Casado Para. 144 E2
Puerto Cavinas Bol. 142 E6
Puerto Coig (abandoned) Arg. 144 C8
Puerto Cortés Mex. 136 B4
Puerto de Lobos Mex. 127 E7
Puerto Deseado Arg. 144 C7
Puerto Escondido Mex. 136 E5
Puerto Francisco de Orellana Ecuador see Coca
Puerto Frey Bol. 142 F6
Puerto Génova Bol. 142 E6
Puerto Guarani Para. 144 E2
Puerto Heath Bol. 142 E6
Puerto Huitoto Col. 142 D3
Puerto Isabel Bol. 143 G7
Puerto Leguízamo Col. 142 D4
Puerto Lempira Hond. 137 H5
Puerto Libertad Mex. 127 E7
Puerto Limón Costa Rica 137 H6
Puertollano Spain 57 D4
Puerto Lobos Arg. 144 C6
Puerto Madryn Arg. 144 C6
Puerto Maldonado Peru 142 E6
Puerto Máncora Peru 142 B4
Puerto México Mex. see Coatzacoalcos
Puerto Montt Chile 144 B6
Puerto Natales Chile 144 B8
Puerto Nuevo Col. 142 E2
Puerto Peñasco Mex. 127 E7
Puerto Pirámides Arg. 144 D6
Puerto Plata Dom. Rep. 137 J5
Puerto Portillo Peru 142 D5
Puerto Prado Peru 142 D6
Puerto Princesa Phil. 68 F5
Puerto Rico Arg. 144 E3
Puerto Rico Bol. 142 E6

▶Puerto Rico terr. West Indies 137 K5
United States Commonwealth.

▶Puerto Rico Trench sea feature Caribbean Sea 148 D4
Deepest trench in the Atlantic Ocean.

Puerto San Julián Arg. 144 C7
Puerto Santa Cruz Arg. 144 C8
Puerto Santander Col. 142 D4
Puerto Sastre Para. 144 E2
Puerto Saucedo Bol. 142 F6
Puerto Suárez Bol. 143 G7
Puerto Supe Peru 142 C6
Puerto Vallarta Mex. 136 C4
Puerto Victoria Peru 142 D5
Puerto Visser Arg. 144 C7
Puerto Yartou Chile 144 B8
Puerto Ybapobó Para. 144 E2
Pugachev Russia 43 K5
Pugal India 82 C3
Puge China 76 D3
Pūhāl-e Khamīr, Kūh-e mts Iran 88 D5
Puhiwaero c. N.Z. see South West Cape
Puigmal mt. France/Spain 56 F5
Pui O Wan b. H.K. China 77 [inset]
Puji China see Puge
Pukaki, Lake N.Z. 113 C7
Pukapuka atoll Cook Is 107 J3
Pukaskwa National Park Canada 122 D4
Pukatawagan Canada 121 K4
Pukchin N. Korea 75 B4
Pukch'ŏng N. Korea 75 C4
Pukekohe N.Z. 113 E3
Puketeraki Range mts N.Z. 113 D6
Pukeuri Junction N.Z. 113 C7
Puksubaek-san mt. N. Korea 74 B4
Pula China see Nyingchi
Pula Croatia 58 E2
Pula Sardinia Italy 58 C5
Pulap atoll Micronesia 69 L5
Pulaski NY U.S.A. 135 G2
Pulaski VA U.S.A. 134 E5
Pulaski WI U.S.A. 134 A1
Pulau Simeulue, Suaka Margasatwa nature res. Indon. 71 A7
Pul-e 'Alam Afgh. 89 H3
Pul-e Khumrī Afgh. 89 H3
Pulheim Germany 52 G3
Pulicat Lake inlet India 84 D3
Pulivendla India 84 C3
Pulkkila Fin. 44 N4
Pullman U.S.A. 126 D3
Pulozero Russia 44 R2
Púlpito, Punta pt Mex. 127 F8
Pulu China 82 E1
Pülümür Turkey 91 E3
Pulusuk atoll Micronesia 69 L5
Puluwat atoll Micronesia 69 L5
Pulwama India 89 I3
Pumasillo, Cerro mt. Peru 142 D6
Puma Yumco l. China 83 G3
Pumiao China see Yongning
Puná, Isla i. Ecuador 142 B4
Punakha Bhutan 83 G4
Punch India 82 C2
Punchaw Canada 120 F4
Punda Maria S. Africa 101 J2
Pundri India 82 D3
Pune India 84 B2
P'ungsan N. Korea 74 C4
Puning China 77 H4
Punjab state India 82 C3
Punjab prov. Pak. 89 H4
Punmah Glacier China/Pak. 82 D2
Puno Peru 142 D7
Punta, Cerro de mt. Puerto Rico 137 K5
Punta Abreojos Mex. 127 E8
Punta Alta Arg. 144 D5
Punta Arenas Chile 144 B8
Punta del Este Uruguay 144 F5
Punta Delgada Arg. 144 D6
Punta Gorda Belize 136 G5
Punta Gorda U.S.A. 133 D7
Punta Norte Arg. 144 D6
Punta Prieta Mex. 127 E7
Puntarenas Costa Rica 137 H6
Puntland area Somalia 98 E3
Punxsutawney U.S.A. 135 F3
Puokio Fin. 44 O4
Puolanka Fin. 44 O4
Puqi China see Chibi
Pur r. Russia 64 I3
Puracé, Volcán de vol. Col. 142 C3
Purcell U.S.A. 131 D5
Purcell Mountains Canada 120 G5
Purgatoire r. U.S.A. 130 C4
Puri India 84 E2
Purmerend Neth. 52 E2
Purna r. Mahar. India 82 D5
Purna r. Mahar. India 84 C2
Purnea India see Purnia
Purnia India 83 F4
Purnululu National Park Australia 108 E4
Pursat Cambodia see Poŭthĭsăt
Puruliya India 83 F5

▶Purus r. Peru 142 F4
3rd longest river in South America.

Puruvesi l. Fin. 44 P6
Purwodadi Indon. 68 E8
Puryŏng N. Korea 74 C4
Pusad India 84 C2
Pusan S. Korea see Busan
Pusatlı Dağı mt. Turkey 85 A1
Pushchino Russia 43 H5
Pushkin Russia 45 Q7
Pushkino Azer. see Biläsuvar
Pushkinskaya, Gora mt. Russia 74 F3
Pushkinskiye Gory Russia 45 P8
Pushma Russia 42 J3
Pusht-i-Rud reg. Afgh. see Zamīndāwar
Pūstīn Afgh. 89 F3
Pustoshka Russia 42 F4
Pusur r. Bangl. 83 G5
Putahow Lake Canada 121 K3
Putain Indon. 108 D2
Putao Myanmar 70 B1
Puteoli Italy see Pozzuoli
Puthein Myanmar see Bassein
Putian China 77 H3
Puting China see De'an
Puting, Tanjung pt Indon. 68 E7
Putlitz Germany 53 M1
Putna r. Romania 59 L2
Putney U.S.A. 135 I2
Putorana, Plato mts Russia 153 E2

▶Putrajaya Malaysia 71 C7
Joint capital (with Kuala Lumpur) of Malaysia.

Putre Chile 142 E7
Putsonderwater S. Africa 100 E5
Puttalam Sri Lanka 84 C4
Puttalam Lagoon Sri Lanka 84 C4
Puttelange-aux-Lacs France 52 G5
Putten Neth. 52 F2
Puttershoek Neth. 52 E3
Puttgarden Germany 47 M3
Putumayo r. Col. 142 D4
also known as Içá (Peru)
Putuo China 77 I2
Puumala Fin. 45 P6
Pu'u'ula'ula mt. U.S.A. 127 [inset]
Pu'uwai U.S.A. 127 [inset]
Puvirnituq Canada 122 F1
Puyallup U.S.A. 126 C3
Puyang China 77 G1
Puy de Sancy mt. France 56 F4
Puyehue, Parque Nacional nat. park Chile 144 B6
Puysegur Point N.Z. 113 A8
Puzla Russia 42 L3
Pweto Dem. Rep. Congo 99 C4
Pwinbyu Myanmar 70 A2
Pwllheli U.K. 49 C6
Pyal'ma Russia 42 G3
Pyalo Myanmar 70 A3
Pyamalaw r. Myanmar 70 A4
Pyandzh Tajik. see Panj
Pyaozero, Ozero l. Russia 44 Q3
Pyaozerskiy Russia 44 Q4
Pyapali India 84 C3
Pyapon Myanmar 70 A3
Pyasina r. Russia 64 J2
Pyatigorsk Russia 91 F1
Pyatikhatki Ukr. see P"yatykhatky
P"yatykhatky Ukr. 43 G6
Pyay Myanmar see Pyè
Pychas Russia 42 L4
Pyè Myanmar 70 A3
Pye, Mount hill N.Z. 113 B8
Pyeongchang S. Korea 75 C5
Pyeonghae S. Korea 75 C5
Pyeongtaek S. Korea 75 B5
Pyetrykaw Belarus 43 F5
Pygmalion Point India see Indira Point
Pyhäjoki Fin. 44 N4
Pyhäjoki r. Fin. 44 N4
Pyhäntä Fin. 44 O4
Pyhäsalmi Fin. 44 N5
Pyhäselkä l. Fin. 44 P5
Pyi Myanmar see Pyè
Pyin Myanmar see Pyè
Pyingaing Myanmar 70 A2
Pyinmana Myanmar 70 B3
Pyin-U-Lwin Myanmar 70 B2
Pyle U.K. 49 D7
Pyl'karamo Russia 64 J3
Pylos Greece 59 I6
Pymatuning Reservoir U.S.A. 134 E3
Pyŏktong N. Korea 74 B4
P'yŏnggang N. Korea 75 B5
P'yŏngsong N. Korea 75 B5

▶P'yŏngyang N. Korea 75 B5
Capital of North Korea.

Pyramid Hill Australia 112 B6
Pyramid Lake U.S.A. 128 D1
Pyramid Peak U.S.A. 129 J1
Pyramid Range mts U.S.A. 128 D2
Pyramids of Giza tourist site Egypt 90 C5
Pyrenees mts Europe 57 H2
Pyrénées mts Europe see Pyrenees
Pyrénées, Parc National des nat. park France/Spain 56 D5
Pyrgos Greece 59 I6
Pyryatyn Ukr. 43 G6
Pyrzyce Poland 47 O4
Pyshchug Russia 42 J4
Pytalovo Russia 45 O8
Pyxaria mt. Greece 59 J5

Q

Qaa Lebanon 85 C2
Qaanaaq Greenland 119 L2
Qabātīyah West Bank 85 B3
Qabnag China 76 B2
Qabqa China see Gonghe
Qacentina Alg. see Constantine
Qacha's Nek Lesotho 101 I6
Qāderābād Iran 88 D4
Qadirpur Pak. 89 I4
Qādis Afgh. 89 F3
Qādisīyah, Sadd dam Iraq 91 F4
Qadisiyah Dam Iraq see Qādisīyah, Sadd
Qā'emābād Iran 89 F4
Qā'emshahr Iran 88 D2
Qā'en Iran 88 E3
Qagan China 73 L3
Qagan Nur l. China 74 B3
Qagan Us Nei Mongol China 73 K4
Qagan Us Qinghai China see Dulan
Qagbasêrag China 76 B2
Qagca China 76 C1
Qagcaka China 83 E2
Qagchêng China see Xiangcheng
Qahremānshahr Iran see Kermānshāh
Qaidabad Pak. 89 H3
Qaidam He r. China 83 H1
Qaidam Pendi basin China 80 H4
Qainaqangma China 83 G2
Qaiṣār Afgh. 89 G3
Qaisar, Koh-i- mt. Afgh. see Qeyṣār, Kūh-e
Qakar China 82 E1
Qal'ah-ye Fārsī Afgh. 89 F3
Qal'ah-ye Now Afgh. 89 F3
Qal'ah-ye Rashīd Afgh. 89 G4
Qal'ah-ye Sang-e Takht Afgh. 89 G3
Qala-i-Kang Afgh. see Kang (abandoned)
Qalaikhumb Tajik. 89 H2
Qala Jamal Afgh. 89 F3
Qalāt Afgh. 89 G3
Qal'at al Ḥiṣn Syria 85 C2
Qal'at al Mu'aẓẓam Saudi Arabia 90 E6
Qal'at Bīshah Saudi Arabia 86 F5
Qal'at Dizah Iraq see Qeładize
Qal'at Muqaybirah, Jabal mt. Syria 85 D2
Qal'eh Dāgh mt. Iran 88 B2
Qal'eh-ye Shūrak well Iran 88 E3
Qalhāt Oman 88 E6
Qalīb Bāqūr well Iraq 91 G5
Qalluviartuuq, Lac l. Canada 122 G2
Qalyūb Egypt 90 C5
Qalyûb Egypt see Qalyūb
Qamalung China 76 C1
Qamanirjuaq Lake Canada 121 M2
Qamanittuaq Canada see Baker Lake
Qamashi Uzbek. 89 G2
Qamata S. Africa 101 H6
Qamdo China 76 C2
Qandahar Afgh. see Kandahār
Qandarānbāshī, Kūh-e mt. Iran 88 B2
Qandyaghash Kazakh. see Kandyagash
Qangzê China 82 D3
Qapān-e Pā'īn Iran 88 D2
Qapshaghay Kazakh. see Kapshagay
Qapshaghay Bögeni resr Kazakh. see Kapshagay, Vodokhranilishche
Qapugtang China see Zadoi
Qaqortoq Greenland 119 N3
Qara Āghach r. Iran see Mand, Rūd-e
Qarabutaq Kazakh. see Karabutak
Qaraçala Azer. 88 C2
Qara Ertis r. China/Kazakh. see Ertix He
Qaraghandy Kazakh. see Karagandy
Qaraghayly Kazakh. see Karagayly
Qārah Egypt 90 B5
Qārah Saudi Arabia 91 F5
Qarah Bāgh Afgh. 89 H3
Qarah Tīkān Iran 89 F2
Qarah-ye Taray mt. Afgh. 89 G3
Qarak China 89 J2
Qaraqum des. Turkm. see Karakum Desert
Qarasu Azer. 91 H2
Qara Şū Chāy r. Syria/Turkey see Karasu
Qarataū Kazakh. see Karatau
Qarataū Zhotasy mts Kazakh. see Karatau, Khrebet
Qara Tikan Iran 88 C2
Qarazhal Kazakh. see Karazhal
Qardho Somalia 98 E3
Qareh Chāy r. Iran 88 C3
Qareh Sū r. Iran 88 B2
Qarhan China 83 H1
Qarkilik China see Ruoqiang
Qarn al Kabsh, Jabal mt. Egypt 90 D5
Qarnayn i. U.A.E. 88 D5
Qarnein i. U.A.E. see Qarnayn
Qarn el Kabsh, Gebel mt. Egypt see Qarn al Kabsh, Jabal
Qarnobcho'l cho'li plain Uzbek. 89 G2
Qarokŭl l. Tajik. 89 I2
Qarqan China see Qiemo
Qarqan He r. China 80 G4
Qarqaraly Kazakh. see Karkaraly
Qarshi Uzbek. 89 G2
Qarshi cho'li plain Uzbek. 89 G2
Qarshi chŭli plain Uzbek. see Qarshi cho'li
Qartaba Lebanon 85 B2
Qārūh, Jazīrat i. Kuwait 88 C4
Qārūn, Birkat l. Egypt 90 C5
Qârûn, Birket l. Egypt see Qārūn, Birkat
Qaryat al Gharab Iraq 91 G5
Qaryat al Ulyā Saudi Arabia 88 B5
Qāsemābād Iran 88 E3
Qash Qā'ī reg. Iran 88 C4
Qasigiannguit Greenland 119 M3
Qaṣr al Farāfirah Egypt 90 B6
Qaṣr al Kharānah Jordan 85 C4
Qaṣr al Khubbāz Iraq 91 F4
Qaṣr-e Shīrīn Iran 88 B3
Qasr Farâfra Egypt see Qaṣr al Farāfirah
Qassimiut Greenland 119 N3
Qaṭanā Syria 85 C3
Qatar country Asia 88 C5
Qaṭmah Syria 85 C1
Qaṭrūyeh Iran 88 D4
Qaṭṭāfī, Wādī al watercourse Jordan 85 C4
Qaṭṭâra, Râs esc. Egypt see Qaṭṭārah, Ra's
Qattara Depression Egypt 90 B5
Qaṭṭārah, Ra's esc. Egypt 90 B5
Qaṭṭīnah, Buḥayrat resr Syria 85 C2
Qax Azer. 91 G2
Qaynar Kazakh. see Kaynar
Qaysīyah, Qā' al imp. l. Jordan 85 C4
Qaysūm, Juzur is Egypt 90 D6
Qayyārah Iraq 91 F4
Qazangödağ mt. Armenia/Azer. 91 G3
Qazaq Shyghanaghy b. Kazakh. see Kazakhskiy Zaliv

Qazaqstan country Asia see Kazakhstan
Qazax Azer. 86 G1
Qazi Ahmad Pak. 89 H5
Qāzī Deh Afgh. 89 H2
Qazvīn Iran 88 C2
Qeisûm, Gezâ'ir is Egypt see Qaysūm, Juzur
Qeisum Islands Egypt see Qaysūm, Juzur
Qeładize Iraq 91 G3
Qena Egypt see Qinā
Qeqertarsuaq Greenland 119 M3
Qeqertarsuaq i. Greenland 119 M3
Qeqertarsuatsiaat Greenland 119 M3
Qeqertarsuup Tunua b. Greenland 119 M3
Qeshm Iran 88 E5
Qeydār Iran 88 C2
Qeydū Iran 88 C3
Qeyşar, Chāh-e well Iran 88 D4
Qeyşār, Kūh-e mt. Afgh. 89 G3
Qezel Owzan, Rūdkhāneh-ye r. Iran 88 C2
Qeẓi'ot Israel 85 B4
Qian'an China 74 B3
Qiandao Hu resr China 77 H2
Qian Gorlos China 74 B3
Qianjiang Chongqing China 77 F2
Qianjiang Hubei China 77 G2
Qianjin Heilong. China 74 D3
Qianjin Jilin China 74 C3
Qianqihao China 74 A3
Qian Shan mts China 74 A4
Qianshangjie China 73 L5
Qianxi China 76 E3
Qiaocheng China see Bozhou
Qiaojia China 76 D3
Qiaoshan China see Huangling
Qiaowa China see Muli
Qiaowan China 80 I3
Qiaozhuang China see Qingchuan
Qibā' Saudi Arabia 91 G6
Qibing S. Africa 101 H5
Qichun China 77 G2
Qidong China 77 G3
Qidukou China 76 B1
Qiemo China 80 G4
Qijiang China 76 E2
Qijiaojing China 80 H3
Qikiqtarjuaq Canada 119 L3
Qila Ladgasht Pak. 89 F5
Qila Saifullah Pak. 89 H4
Qilian China 80 J4
Qilian Shan mts China 80 I4
Qillak i. Greenland 119 O3
Qiman Tag mts China 83 G1
Qimusseriarsuaq b. Greenland 119 L2
Qinā Egypt 86 D4
Qin'an China 76 E1
Qincheng China see Nanfeng
Qing'an China 74 B3
Qingchuan China 76 E1
Qingdao China 73 M5
Qinggang China 74 B3
Qinggil China see Qinghe
Qinghai prov. China 76 B1
Qinghai Hu salt l. China 80 J4
Qinghai Nanshan mts China 80 I4
Qinghe Heilong. China 74 C3
Qinghe Xinjiang China 80 H2
Qinghecheng China 74 B4
Qinghua China see Bo'ai
Qingjiang Jiangsu China see Huai'an
Qingjiang Jiangxi China see Zhangshu
Qing Jiang r. China 77 F2
Qingkou China see Ganyu
Qinglan China 77 F5
Qingliu China 77 H3
Qinglung China 76 G3
Qingpu China 77 I2
Qingquan China see Xishui
Qingshan China see Wudalianchi
Qingshui China 76 E1
Qingshuihe Nei Mongol China 73 K5
Qingshuihe Qinghai China 76 C1
Qingtian China 77 I2
Qingyang Anhui China 77 H2
Qingyang Gansu China 76 E1
Qingyang Jiangsu China see Sihong
Qingyuan Gansu China see Weiyuan
Qingyuan Guangdong China 77 G4
Qingyuan Guangxi China see Yizhou
Qingyuan Liaoning China 74 B4
Qingyuan Zhejiang China 77 H3
Qingzang Gaoyuan plat. China see Tibet, Plateau of
Qingzhen China 76 E3
Qinhuangdao China 73 L5
Qinjiang China see Shicheng
Qin Ling mts China 76 E1
Qinshui China 77 G1
Qinting China see Lianhua
Qinzhou China 77 F4
Qionghai China 77 F5
Qiongjiexue China see Qonggyai
Qionglai China 76 D2
Qionglai Shan mts China 76 D2
Qiongxi China see Hongyuan
Qiongzhong China 77 F5
Qiongzhou Haixia strait China see Hainan Strait
Qiqian China 74 A1
Qiqihar China 74 A3
Qīr Iran 88 D4
Qira China 82 E1
Qîraîya, Wâdi watercourse Egypt see Qurayyah, Wādī
Qiryat Shemona Israel 85 B3
Qishan China 76 E1
Qishon, Naḥal r. Israel 85 B3
Qitab ash Shāmah vol. crater Saudi Arabia 85 C4
Qitaihe China 74 C3
Qiubei China 76 E3
Qiujin China 77 G2
Qixing He r. China 74 D3
Qiyang China 77 F3
Qizhou Liedao i. China 77 F5
Qızılağac Körfäzi b. Azer. 88 C2
Qizil-Art, Aghbai pass Kyrg./Tajik. see Kyzylart Pass
Qizil Qal'ah Afgh. 89 H2
Qizilqum des. Kazakh./Uzbek. see Kyzylkum Desert
Qizilrabot Tajik. 89 I2
Qobād, Chāh-e well Iran 88 D3
Qobustan Azer. 91 H2
Qogir Feng mt. China/Pak. see K2
Qog Qi China see Sain Us
Qom Iran 88 C3
Qomdo China see Qumdo
Qomīsheh Iran see Shahreẓā
Qomolangma Feng mt. China/Nepal see Everest, Mount
Qomsheh Iran see Shahreẓā
Qonāq, Kūh-e hill Iran 88 C3
Qondūz Afgh. see Kunduz
Qonggyai China 83 G3
Qo'ng'irot Uzbek. 80 A3
Qong Muztag mt. China 83 E2
Qongrat Uzbek. see Qo'ng'irot
Qoornoq Greenland 119 M3
Qoqek China see Tacheng
Qo'qon Uzbek. 80 D3
Qorako'l Uzbek. 89 F2
Qorghalzhyn Kazakh. see Korgalzhyn
Qornet es Saouda mt. Lebanon 85 C2
Qorovulbozor Uzbek. 89 G2
Qorowulbozor Uzbek. see Qorovulbozor
Qorveh Iran 88 B3
Qo'shrabot Uzbek. 89 G1
Qostanay Kazakh. see Kostanay
Qoubaiyat Lebanon 85 C2
Qowowuyag mt. China/Nepal see Cho Oyu
Qozide Tajik. 89 H2
Quabbin Reservoir U.S.A. 135 I2
Quadra Island Canada 120 E5
Quadros, Lago dos l. Brazil 145 A5
Quail Mountains U.S.A. 128 E4
Quairading Australia 109 B8
Quakenbrück Germany 53 H2
Quakertown U.S.A. 135 H3
Quambatook Australia 112 A5
Quambone Australia 112 C3
Quamby Australia 110 C4
Quanah U.S.A. 131 D5
Quanbao Shan mt. China 77 F1
Quan Dao Hoang Sa is S. China Sea see Paracel Islands
Quan Dao Truong Sa is S. China Sea see Spratly Islands
Quang Ha Vietnam 70 D2
Quang Ngai Vietnam 70 E4
Quang Tri Vietnam 70 D3
Quan Hoa Vietnam 70 D2
Quan Long Vietnam see Ca Mau
Quannan China 77 G3
Quantock Hills U.K. 49 D7
Quanzhou Fujian China 77 H3
Quanzhou Guangxi China 77 F3
Qu'Appelle r. Canada 121 K5
Quaqtaq Canada 119 L3
Quarry Bay H.K. China 77 [inset]
Quartu Sant'Elena Sardinia Italy 58 C5
Quartzite Mountain U.S.A. 128 E3
Quartzsite U.S.A. 129 F5
Quba Azer. 91 H2
Qūchān Iran 88 E2
Qudaym Syria 85 D2
Queanbeyan Australia 112 D5

▶Québec Canada 123 H5
Capital of Québec.

Québec prov. Canada 135 I1
Quebra Anzol r. Brazil 145 B2
Quedlinburg Germany 53 L3
Queen Adelaide Islands Chile see La Reina Adelaida, Archipiélago de
Queen Anne U.S.A. 135 H4
Queen Bess, Mount Canada 126 B2
Queen Charlotte Canada 120 C4
Queen Charlotte Islands Canada see Haida Gwaii
Queen Charlotte Sound sea chan. Canada 120 D5
Queen Charlotte Strait Canada 120 E5
Queen Creek U.S.A. 129 H5
Queen Elizabeth Islands Canada 119 H2
Queen Elizabeth Land reg. Antarctica 152 L1
Queen Elizabeth National Park Uganda 98 C4
Queen Mary Land reg. Antarctica 152 F2
Queen Maud Gulf Canada 119 H3
Queen Maud Land reg. Antarctica 152 C2
Queen Maud Mountains Antarctica 152 J1
Queenscliff Australia 112 B7
Queensland state Australia 112 B1
Queenstown Australia 111 [inset]
Queenstown Ireland see Cobh
Queenstown N.Z. 113 B7
Queenstown S. Africa 101 H6
Queenstown Sing. 71 [inset]
Que'er Shan mts China 76 C1
Queets U.S.A. 126 B3
Queimada, Ilha i. Brazil 143 H4
Quelimane Moz. 99 D5
Quellón Chile 144 B6
Quelpart Island S. Korea see Cheju-do
Quemado U.S.A. 129 I4
Quemoy i. Taiwan see Jinmen Dao
Que Que Zimbabwe see Kwekwe
Querétaro Mex. 136 D4
Querétaro de Arteaga Mex. see Querétaro
Querfurt Germany 53 L3
Querobabi Mex. 127 F7
Quesnel Canada 120 F4
Quesnel Lake Canada 120 F4
Quetta Pak. 89 G4
Quetzaltenango Guat. 136 F6
Queuco Chile 144 B5
Quezaltenango Guat. see Quetzaltenango

▶Quezon City Phil. 69 G4
Former capital of the Philippines.

Qufu China 77 H1
Quibala Angola 99 B5
Quibaxe Angola 99 B4
Quibdó Col. 142 C2
Quiberon France 56 C3
Quiçama, Parque Nacional do nat. park Angola 99 B4
Quiet Lake Canada 120 C2
Quilengues Angola 99 B5
Quillabamba Peru 142 D6
Quillacollo Bol. 142 E7
Quillan France 56 F5
Quill Lakes Canada 121 J5
Quilmes Arg. 144 E4
Quilon India see Kollam
Quilpie Australia 112 B1
Quilpué Chile 144 B4
Quimbele Angola 99 B4
Quimilí Arg. 144 D3
Quimper France 56 B3
Quimperlé France 56 C3
Quinag hill U.K. 50 D2
Quincy CA U.S.A. 128 C2
Quincy FL U.S.A. 133 C6
Quincy IL U.S.A. 130 F4
Quincy IN U.S.A. 134 B4
Quincy MA U.S.A. 135 J2
Quincy MI U.S.A. 134 C3
Quincy OH U.S.A. 134 D3
Quines Arg. 144 C4
Quinga Moz. 99 E5
Quinn Canyon Range mts U.S.A. 129 F3
Quinto Spain 57 F3
Quionga Moz. 99 E5
Quipungo Angola 99 B5
Quirima Angola 99 B5
Quirimbas, Parque Nacional das nat. park Moz. 99 E5
Quirindi Australia 112 E3
Quirinópolis Brazil 145 A2
Quissanga Moz. 99 E5
Quitapa Angola 99 B5
Quitilipi Arg. 144 D3
Quitman GA U.S.A. 133 D6
Quitman MS U.S.A. 131 F5

▶Quito Ecuador 142 C4
Capital of Ecuador.

Quitovac Mex. 127 E7
Quixadá Brazil 143 K4
Quixeramobim Brazil 143 K5
Qujiang Guangdong China 77 G3
Qujiang Sichuan China see Quxian
Qujie China 77 F4
Qujing China 76 D3
Qulandy Kazakh. see Kulandy
Qulansiyah Yemen 87 H7
Qulbān Layyah well Iraq 88 B4
Qulsary Kazakh. see Kul'sary
Qulyndy Zhazyghy plain Kazakh./Russia see Kulundinskaya Ravnina
Qulzum, Baḥr al Egypt see Suez Bay
Qumar He r. China 72 G6
Qumarheyan China 80 H4
Qumarlêb China see Sêrwolungwa
Qumarrabdün China 76 B1
Qumbu S. Africa 101 I6
Qumdo China 76 B2
Qumqo'rgo'n Uzbek. 89 G2
Qumqūrghon Uzbek. see Qumqo'rgo'n
Qumrha S. Africa 101 H7
Qumulangma mt. China/Nepal see Everest, Mount
Qunayfidhah, Nafūd des. Saudi Arabia 88 B5
Qunayy well Saudi Arabia 88 B6
Qundüz Afgh. see Kunduz
Qŭnghirot Uzbek. see Qo'ng'irot
Quntamari China 83 G2
Qu'nyido China 76 C2
Quoich r. Canada 121 M1
Quoich, Loch l. U.K. 50 D3
Quoile r. U.K. 51 G3
Quoin Point S. Africa 100 D8
Quoxo r. Botswana 100 G2
Qŭqon Uzbek. see Qo'qon
Qurama, Qatorkŭhi mts Asia see Kurama Range
Qurama tizmasi mts Asia see Kurama Range
Qurayyah, Wādī watercourse Egypt 85 B4
Qŭrghonteppa Tajik. 89 H2
Qusainka China 76 C2
Qusar Azer. 91 H2
Qushan China 76 E2
Qŭshrabot Uzbek. see Qo'shrabot
Qushtepe Iraq 91 F3
Qusmuryn Kazakh. see Kusmuryn
Qusum China 82 D2
Quthing Lesotho see Moyeni
Quttinirpaaq National Park Canada 119 K1
Quwayq, Nahr r. Syria/Turkey 85 C2
Quxar China see Lhazê
Quxian Sichuan China 76 E2
Quxian Zhejiang China see Quzhou
Quyang China see Jingzhou
Quy Châu Vietnam 70 D3
Quyghan Kazakh. see Kuygan
Quy Nhơn Vietnam 71 E4
Quyon Canada 135 G1
Qūyūn Eshek i. Iran 88 B2
Quzhou China 77 H2
Qypshaq Köli salt l. Kazakh. see Azhibeksor, Ozero
Qyrghyz Zhotasy mts Kazakh./Kyrg. see Kirghiz Range
Qyteti Stalin Albania see Kuçovë
Qyzylorda Kazakh. see Kyzylorda
Qyzylqum des. Kazakh./Uzbek. see Kyzylkum Desert
Qyzyltū Kazakh. see Kishkenekol'
Qyzylzhar Kazakh. see Kyzylzhar

R

Raa Atoll Maldives see Maalhosmadulu Uthuruburi
Raab r. Austria 47 P7
Raab Hungary see Győr
Raahe Fin. 44 N4
Rääkkylä Fin. 44 P5
Raalte Neth. 52 G2
Raanujärvi Fin. 44 N3
Raasay i. U.K. 50 C3
Raasay, Sound of sea chan. U.K. 50 C3
Raba Indon. 108 B2
Rabang China 82 E2
Rabat Gozo Malta see Victoria
Rabat Malta 58 F7

▶Rabat Morocco 54 C5
Capital of Morocco.

Rabāṭak Afgh. 89 H2
Rabāṭ-e Jaldak Afgh. 89 G4
Rabaul P.N.G. 106 F2
Rabbath Ammon Jordan see 'Ammān
Rabbit r. Canada 120 E3
Rabbit Flat Australia 108 E5
Rabbitskin r. Canada 120 F2
Rābigh Saudi Arabia 86 E5
Rabnabad Islands Bangl. 83 G5
Râbniṭa Moldova see Rîbniṭa
Rabocheostrovsk Russia 42 G2
Racaka China 76 C2
Raccoon Cay i. Bahamas 133 F8
Race, Cape Canada 123 L5
Race Point U.S.A. 135 J2
Rachaïya Lebanon 85 B3
Rachal U.S.A. 131 D7
Rachaya Lebanon see Rachaïya
Rachel U.S.A. 129 F3
Rach Gia Vietnam 71 D5
Rach Gia, Vinh b. Vietnam 71 D5
Racibórz Poland 47 Q5
Racine WI U.S.A. 134 B2
Racine WV U.S.A. 134 E4
Rădăuți Romania 43 E7
Radcliff U.S.A. 134 C5
Radde Russia 74 C2
Radford U.S.A. 134 E5
Radisson Que. Canada 122 F3
Radisson Sask. Canada 121 J4
Radlinski, Mount Antarctica 152 K1
Radnevo Bulg. 59 K3
Radom Poland 47 R5
Radom Sudan 97 F4
Radomir Bulg. 59 J3
Radom National Park Sudan 97 F4
Radomsko Poland 47 Q5
Radoviš Macedonia 90 A2
Radstock U.K. 49 E7
Radstock, Cape Australia 109 F8
Radun' Belarus 45 N9
Radviliškis Lith. 45 M9
Radyvyliv Ukr. 43 E6
Rae Bareli India 82 E4
Rae-Edzo Canada see Behchokò
Raeside, Lake salt flat Australia 109 C7
Raetihi N.Z. 113 E4
Rāf hill Saudi Arabia 91 E5
Rafaela Arg. 144 D4
Rafaḥ Gaza 85 B4
Rafaï Cent. Afr. Rep. 98 C3
Rafḥā' Saudi Arabia 91 F5
Rafiah Gaza see Rafaḥ
Rafsanjān Iran 88 D4
Raft r. U.S.A. 126 E4
Raga South Sudan 97 F4
Rägelin Germany 53 M1
Ragged, Mount hill Australia 109 C8
Ragged Island Bahamas 133 F8
Rāgh Afgh. 89 H2
Rago Nasjonalpark nat. park Norway 44 J3
Ragösen Germany 53 M2
Ragueneau Canada 123 H4
Raguhn Germany 53 M3
Ragusa Croatia see Dubrovnik
Ragusa Sicily Italy 58 F6
Ra'gya China 76 D1
Raha Indon. 69 G7
Rahachow Belarus 43 F5
Rahad r. Sudan 86 D7
Rahaeng Thai. see Tak
Raḥbah, Manqa' imp. l. Syria 85 C3
Rahden Germany 53 I2
Rahimyar Khan Pak. 89 H4
Raḥmān, Chāh-e well Iran 89 E4
Rahovec Kosovo 59 I3
Rahuri India 84 B2
Rai, Hon i. Vietnam 71 D5
Raiatea i. Fr. Polynesia 151 J7
Raibu i. Indon. see Air
Raichur India 84 C2
Raiganj India 83 G4
Raigarh Chhattisgarh India 83 E5
Raigarh Odisha India 84 D2
Raijua i. Indon. 108 C2
Railroad Pass U.S.A. 128 E2
Railroad Valley U.S.A. 129 F2
Raimangal r. Bangl. 83 G5
Raimbault, Lac l. Canada 123 H3
Rainbow Lake Canada 120 G3
Raine Island Australia 110 D1
Rainelle U.S.A. 134 E5
Raini r. Pak. 89 H4
Rainier, Mount vol. U.S.A. 126 C3
Rainy r. Canada/U.S.A. 121 M5
Rainy Lake Canada/U.S.A. 125 I2
Rainy River Canada 121 M5
Raipur Chhattisgarh India 83 E5
Raipur W. Bengal India 83 F5
Raisen India 82 D5
Raisio Fin. 45 M6
Raismes France 52 D4
Raitalai India 82 D5
Raivavae i. Fr. Polynesia 151 K7
Raiwind Pak. 89 I4
Raja, Ujung pt Indon. 71 B7
Rajaampat, Kepulauan is Indon. 69 H7
Rajahmundry India 84 D2
Raja-Jooseppi Fin. 44 P2
Rajanpur Pak. 89 H4
Rajapalayam India 84 C4
Rajapur India 84 B2
Rajasthan state India 82 C4
Rajasthan Canal India 82 C3
Rajauri India see Rajouri
Rajbiraj Nepal 83 F4
Rajevadi India 84 B2
Rajgarh India 82 D4
Rájijovsset Fin. see Raja-Jooseppi
Rajkot India 82 B5
Raj Mahal India 82 C4
Rajmahal Hills India 83 F4
Rajnandgaon India 82 E5
Rajouri India 82 C2
Rajpipla India 82 C5
Rajpur India 82 C5
Rajpura India 82 D3
Rajputana Agency state India see Rajasthan
Rajsamand India 82 C4
Rajshahi Bangl. 83 G4
Rājū Syria 85 C1
Rajula India 84 A1
Rajur India 84 C1
Rajura India 84 C2
Raka China 83 F3
Rakan, Ra's pt Qatar 88 C5
Rakaposhi mt. Pak. 82 C1
Raka Zangbo r. China see Dogxung Zangbo
Rakhiv Ukr. 43 E6
Rakhni Pak. 89 H4
Rakhni r. Pak. 89 H4
Rakhshan r. Pak. 89 F5
Rakitnoye Belgorodskaya Oblast' Russia 43 G6
Rakitnoye Primorskiy Kray Russia 74 D3
Rakiura i. N.Z. see Stewart Island
Rakiura National Park nat. park N.Z. 113 A8
Rakke Estonia 45 O7
Rakkestad Norway 45 G7
Rakovski Bulg. 59 K3
Rakushechnyy, Mys pt Kazakh. 91 H2
Rakvere Estonia 45 O7

▶Raleigh U.S.A. 132 E5
Capital of North Carolina.

Ralston U.S.A. 135 G3
Ram r. Canada 120 F2
Ramagiri India 84 E2
Ramah U.S.A. 129 I4
Ramalho, Serra do hills Brazil 145 B1
Rāmallāh West Bank 85 B4
Ramanagaram India 84 C3
Ramanathapuram India 84 C4
Ramapo Deep sea feature N. Pacific Ocean 150 F3
Ramapur India 84 D1
Ramas, Cape India 84 B3
Ramatlabama S. Africa 101 G3
Rambhapur India 82 C5
Rambouillet France 52 B6
Rambutyo Island P.N.G. 69 L7
Ramciel South Sudan 97 G4
Rame Head hd Australia 112 D6
Rame Head hd U.K. 49 C8
Rameshki Russia 42 H4
Ramezān Kalak Iran 89 F5
Ramgarh Jharkhand India 83 F5
Ramgarh Rajasthan India 82 B4
Ramgarh Rajasthan India 82 C3
Ramgul reg. Afgh. 89 H3
Rāmhormoz Iran 88 C4
Ramingining Australia 108 F3
Ramitan Uzbek. see Romiton
Ramla Israel 85 B4
Ramlat Rabyānah des. Libya see Rebiana Sand Sea
Ramm, Jabal mts Jordan 85 B5
Ramnad India see Ramanathapuram
Râmnicu Sărat Romania 59 L2
Râmnicu Vâlcea Romania 59 K2
Ramon' Russia 43 H6
Ramona U.S.A. 128 E5
Ramos r. Mex. 131 B7
Ramotswa Botswana 101 G3
Rampur India 82 D3
Rampur Boalia Bangl. see Rajshahi
Ramree Myanmar 70 A3
Ramree Island Myanmar 70 A3
Rāmsar Iran 88 C2
Ramsele Sweden 44 J5
Ramsey Isle of Man 48 C4
Ramsey U.K. 49 G6
Ramsey U.S.A. 135 H3
Ramsey Bay Isle of Man 48 C4
Ramsey Island U.K. 49 B7
Ramsey Lake Canada 122 E5
Ramsgate U.K. 49 I7
Rāmshīr Iran 88 C4
Ramu Bangl. 83 H5
Ramusio, Lac l. Canada 123 J3
Ramygala Lith. 45 N9
Ranaghat India 83 G5
Rana Pratap Sagar resr India 82 C4
Ranapur India 82 C5
Ranasar India 82 B4
Rancagua Chile 144 B4
Rancharia Brazil 145 A3
Rancheria Canada 120 D2
Rancheria r. Canada 120 D2
Ranchi India 83 F5
Ranco, Lago l. Chile 144 B6
Rand Australia 112 C5
Randalstown U.K. 51 F3
Randers Denmark 45 G8
Randijaure l. Sweden 44 K3
Randolph ME U.S.A. 135 K1
Randolph UT U.S.A. 126 F4
Randolph VT U.S.A. 135 I2
Randsjö Sweden 44 H5
Råneå Sweden 44 M4
Ranérou Senegal 96 B3
Ranfurly N.Z. 113 C7
Rangae Thai. 71 C6
Rangamati Bangl. 83 H5
Rangapara India 83 H4
Rangeley Lake U.S.A. 135 J1
Rangely U.S.A. 129 I1
Ranger Lake Canada 122 E5
Rangiora N.Z. 113 D6
Rangitata r. N.Z. 113 C7
Rangitikei r. N.Z. 113 E5
Rangke China see Zamtang
Rangkŭl Tajik. 89 I2
Rangôn Myanmar see Rangoon

▶Rangoon Myanmar 70 B3
Former capital of Myanmar.

Rangoon r. Myanmar 70 B3
Rangpur Bangl. 83 G4
Rangsang i. Indon. 71 C7
Rangse Myanmar 70 A1
Ranibennur India 84 B3
Raniganj India 83 F5
Ranipur Pak. 89 H5
Raniwara India 82 C4
Rānīyah/Ranye Iraq 91 G3
Rankin U.S.A. 131 C6
Rankin Inlet Canada 121 M2
Rankins Springs Australia 112 C4
Ranna Estonia 45 O7
Rannes Australia 110 E5
Rannoch, Loch U.K. 50 E4
Ranong Thai. 71 B5
Ranot Thai. 71 C6
Ranpur India 82 B5
Rānsa Iran 88 C3
Ransby Sweden 45 H6
Rantasalmi Fin. 44 P5
Rantau i. Indon. 71 C7
Rantauprapat Indon. 71 B7
Rantoul U.S.A. 134 A3
Rantsila Fin. 44 N4
Ranua Fin. 44 O4
Ranyah, Wādī watercourse Saudi Arabia 86 F5
Rao Go mt. Laos/Vietnam 70 D3
Raohe China 74 D3
Raoui, Erg er des. Alg. 54 D6
Raoul Island Kermadec Is 107 I4
Rapa i. Fr. Polynesia 151 K7
Rapa-iti i. Fr. Polynesia see Rapa
Rapallo Italy 58 C2
Rapar India 82 B5
Raphoe Ireland 51 E3
Rapidan r. U.S.A. 135 G4
Rapid City U.S.A. 130 C2
Rapid River U.S.A. 132 C2
Rapla Estonia 45 N7
Rapur Andhra Prad. India 84 C3
Rapur Gujarat India 82 B5
Raqqa Syria see Ar Raqqah
Raquette Lake U.S.A. 135 H2
Rara National Park Nepal 83 E3
Raritan Bay U.S.A. 135 H3
Rarkan Pak. 89 H4
Raroia atoll Fr. Polynesia 151 K7
Rarotonga i. Cook Is 151 J7
Ras India 82 C4
Rasa, Punta pt Arg. 144 D6
Ra's al Ḥikmah Egypt 90 B5
Ras al Khaimah U.A.E. see Ra's al Khaymah
Ra's al Khaymah U.A.E. 88 D5
Ra's an Naqb Jordan 85 B4
Ras Dashen mt. Eth. see Ras Dejen

▶Ras Dejen mt. Eth. 98 D2
5th highest mountain in Africa.

Raseiniai Lith. 45 M9
Ras el Hikma Egypt see Ra's al Ḥikmah
Ra's Ghārib Egypt 90 D5
Rashad Sudan 86 D7
Rashīd Egypt see Rashīd
Rashīd Egypt 90 C5
Rasht Iran 88 C2
Ras Koh mt. Pak. 89 G4
Raskoh mts Pak. 89 G4
Raso, Cabo c. Arg. 144 C6
Rason Lake salt flat Australia 109 D7
Rasony Belarus 45 P9
Rasra India 83 E4
Rasshua, Ostrov i. Russia 73 S3
Rass Jebel Tunisia 58 D6
Rasskazovo Russia 43 I5
Rastatt Germany 53 I6
Rastede Germany 53 I1
Rastow Germany 53 L1
Rasūl watercourse Iran 88 D5
Rasul Pak. 89 I3
Ratae U.K. see Leicester
Rätan Sweden 44 I5
Ratanda S. Africa 101 I4
Ratangarh India 82 C3
Rätansbyn Sweden 44 I5
Rat Buri Thai. 71 B4
Rathangan Ireland 51 F4
Rathbun Lake U.S.A. 130 E3
Rathdowney Ireland 51 E5
Rathdrum Ireland 51 F5
Rathedaung Myanmar 70 A2
Rathenow Germany 53 M2
Rathfriland U.K. 51 F3
Rathkeale Ireland 51 D5
Rathlin Island U.K. 51 F2
Ratibor Poland see Racibórz
Ratingen Germany 52 G3
Ratisbon Germany see Regensburg
Ratiya India 82 C3
Rat Lake Canada 121 L3
Ratlam India 82 C5
Ratnagiri India 84 B2
Ratnapura Sri Lanka 84 D5
Ratne Ukr. 43 E6
Ratno Ukr. see Ratne
Raton U.S.A. 127 G5
Rattray Head hd U.K. 50 H3
Rättvik Sweden 45 I6
Ratz, Mount Canada 120 C3
Ratzeburg Germany 53 K1
Raub Malaysia 71 C7
Rauðamýri Iceland 44 [inset 1]
Raudhatain Kuwait 88 B4
Rauenstein Germany 53 L4
Raufarhöfn Iceland 44 [inset 1]
Raukumara Range mts N.Z. 113 F4
Raul Soares Brazil 145 C3
Rauma Fin. 45 L6
Raurkela India 83 F5
Rauschen Russia see Svetlogorsk
Rausu Japan 74 G3
Rautavaara Fin. 44 P5
Ravānsar Iran 88 B3
Rāvar Iran 88 E4
Ravat Kyrg. 89 H2
Ravels Belgium 52 E3
Ravena U.S.A. 135 I2
Ravenglass U.K. 48 D4
Ravenna Italy 58 E2
Ravenna NE U.S.A. 130 D3
Ravenna OH U.S.A. 134 E3

Ravensburg Germany 47 L7
Ravenshoe Australia 110 D3
Ravenswood Australia 110 D4
Ravi r. Pak. 89 H4
Ravnina Turkm. see Rawnina
Rāwah Iraq 91 F4
Rawaki i. Kiribati 107 I2
Rawalpindi Pak. 89 I3
Rawalpindi Lake Canada 120 H1
Rawāndūz/Rewanduz Iraq 91 G3
Rawi, Ko i. Thai. 71 B6
Rawicz Poland 47 P5
Rawlinna Australia 109 D7
Rawlins U.S.A. 126 G4
Rawlinson Range hills Australia 109 E6
Rawnina Mary Turkm. 89 F2
Rawnina Mary Turkm. 89 F2
Rawson Arg. 144 C6
Rawu China 76 C2
Raxón, Cerro mt. Guat. 136 G5
Ray, Cape Canada 123 K5
Raya, Bukit mt. Indon. 68 E7
Rayachoti India 84 C3
Rayadurg India 84 C3
Rayagada India 84 D2
Rayagarha India see Rayagada
Rayak Lebanon 85 C3
Raychikhinsk Russia 74 C2
Raydah Yemen 86 F6
Rayes Peak U.S.A. 128 D4
Rayevskiy Russia 41 Q5
Rayleigh U.K. 49 H7
Raymond U.S.A. 135 J2
Raymond Terrace Australia 112 E4
Raymondville U.S.A. 131 D7
Raymore Canada 121 J5
Rayner Glacier Antarctica 152 D2
Rayong Thai. 71 C4
Raystown Lake U.S.A. 135 F3
Raz, Pointe du pt France 56 B2
Razan Iran 88 C3
Rāzān Iran 88 C3
Razani Pak. 89 H3
Razāzah, Buḥayrat ar l. Iraq 91 F4
Razdan Armenia see Hrazdan
Razdel'naya Ukr. see Rozdil'na
Razdol'noye Russia 74 C4
Razeh Iran 88 C3
Razgrad Bulg. 59 L3
Razim, Lacul lag. Romania 59 M2
Razisi China 76 D1
Razlog Bulg. 59 J4
Razmak Pak. 89 H3
Ré, Île de i. France 56 D3
Reading U.K. 49 G7
Reading MI U.S.A. 134 C3
Reading OH U.S.A. 134 C4
Reading PA U.S.A. 135 H3
Reagile S. Africa 101 H3
Realicó Arg. 144 D5
Réalmont France 56 F5
Reăng Kései Cambodia 71 C4
Reasi India 82 C2
Reate Italy see Rieti
Rebais France 52 D6
Rebecca, Lake salt flat Australia 109 C7
Rebiana Sand Sea des. Libya 97 F2
Reboly Russia 44 Q5
Rebrikha Russia 72 E2
Rebun-tō i. Japan 74 F3
Recherche, Archipelago of the is Australia 109 C8
Rechitsa Belarus see Rechytsa
Rechna Doab lowland Pak. 89 I4
Rechytsa Belarus 43 F5
Recife Brazil 143 L5
Recife, Cape S. Africa 101 G8
Recklinghausen Germany 53 H3
Reconquista Arg. 144 E3
Recreo Arg. 144 C3
Rectorville U.S.A. 134 D4
Red r. Australia 110 C3
Red r. Canada 120 E3
Red r. Canada/U.S.A. 130 D1
Red r. LA U.S.A. 131 F6
Red r. TN U.S.A. 134 B5
Red r. Vietnam 70 D2
Redang i. Malaysia 71 C6
Red Bank NJ U.S.A. 135 H3
Red Bank TN U.S.A. 133 C5
Red Basin China see Sichuan Pendi
Red Bay Canada 123 K4
Red Bay Basque Whaling Station tourist site Canada 123 K4
Redberry Lake Canada 121 J4
Red Bluff U.S.A. 128 B1
Red Bluff Lake U.S.A. 131 C6
Red Butte mt. U.S.A. 129 G4
Redcar U.K. 48 F4
Redcliff Canada 126 F2
Redcliffe, Mount hill Australia 109 C7
Red Cliffs Australia 111 C7
Red Cloud U.S.A. 130 D3
Red Deer Canada 120 H4
Red Deer r. Alba/Sask. Canada 121 I5
Red Deer r. Man./Sask. Canada 121 K4
Red Deer Lake Canada 121 K4
Reddersburg S. Africa 101 H5
Redding U.S.A. 128 B1
Redditch U.K. 49 F6
Rede r. U.K. 48 E3
Redenção Brazil 143 H5
Redeyef Tunisia 58 C7
Redfield U.S.A. 130 D2
Red Granite Mountain Canada 120 B2
Red Hills U.S.A. 131 D4
Red Hook U.S.A. 135 I3
Red Indian Lake Canada 123 K4
Redkey U.S.A. 134 C3
Redkino Russia 42 H4
Redknife r. Canada 120 G2
Red Lake Canada 121 M5
Red Lake U.S.A. 129 G4
Red Lake r. U.S.A. 130 D2
Red Lake Falls U.S.A. 121 L6
Red Lakes U.S.A. 130 E1
Redlands U.S.A. 128 E4
Red Lion U.S.A. 135 G4
Red Lodge U.S.A. 126 F3
Redmesa U.S.A. 129 I3
Redmond OR U.S.A. 126 C3
Redmond UT U.S.A. 129 H2
Red Oak U.S.A. 130 E3
Redonda Island Canada 120 E5
Redondo Port. 57 C4
Redondo Beach U.S.A. 128 D5
Red Peak U.S.A. 126 E3
Red River, Mouths of the Vietnam 70 D2
Red Rock Canada 122 C4
Red Rock AZ U.S.A. 129 H5
Redrock U.S.A. 129 I5
Red Rock PA U.S.A. 135 G3
Redrock Lake Canada 120 H1
Red Sea Africa/Asia 86 D4
Redstone r. Canada 120 E1
Red Sucker Lake Canada 121 M4
Reduzum Neth. 52 F1
Redwater Canada 120 H4
Redway U.S.A. 128 B1
Red Wing U.S.A. 130 E2
Redwood City U.S.A. 128 B3
Redwood Falls U.S.A. 130 E2
Redwood National Park U.S.A. 126 B4
Redwood Valley U.S.A. 128 B2
Ree, Lough l. Ireland 51 E4
Reed U.S.A. 134 B5
Reed City U.S.A. 134 C2
Reedley U.S.A. 128 D3
Reedsport U.S.A. 126 B4
Reedsville U.S.A. 134 E4
Reedville U.S.A. 135 G5
Reedy U.S.A. 134 E4
Reedy Glacier Antarctica 152 J1
Reefton N.Z. 113 C6
Rees Germany 52 G3
Reese U.S.A. 134 D2
Reese r. U.S.A. 128 E1
Refahiye Turkey 90 E3
Refugio U.S.A. 131 D6
Rēgay Afgh. 89 G3
Regen Germany 53 N6
Regen r. Germany 53 M5
Regência Brazil 145 D2
Regensburg Germany 53 M5
Regenstauf Germany 53 M5
Reggane Alg. 96 D2
Reggio Calabria Italy see Reggio di Calabria
Reggio Emilia-Romagna Italy see Reggio nell'Emilia
Reggio di Calabria Italy 58 F5
Reggio Emilia Italy see Reggio nell'Emilia
Reggio nell'Emilia Italy 58 D2
Reghin Romania 59 K1

▶Regina Canada 121 J5
Capital of Saskatchewan.

Régina Fr. Guiana 143 H3
Rēgistān reg. Afgh. 89 G4
Registro Brazil 144 G2
Registro do Araguaia Brazil 145 A1
Regium Lepidum Italy see Reggio nell'Emilia
Regozero Russia 44 Q4
Rehau Germany 53 M4
Rehburg (Rehburg-Loccum) Germany 53 J2
Rehli India 82 D5
Rehoboth Namibia 100 C2
Rehoboth Bay U.S.A. 135 H4
Reḥovot Israel 85 B4
Reïbell Alg. see Ksar Chellala
Reibitz Germany 53 M3
Reichenbach im Vogtland Germany 53 M4
Reichshoffen France 53 H6
Reid Australia 109 E7
Reidh, Rubha pt U.K. 50 D3
Reidsville U.S.A. 132 E4
Reigate U.K. 49 G7
Reiley Peak U.S.A. 129 H5
Reims France 52 E5
Reinbek Germany 53 K1
Reindeer r. Canada 121 K4
Reindeer Island Canada 121 L4
Reindeer Lake Canada 121 K3
Reine Norway 44 H3
Reinosa Spain 57 D2
Reinsfeld Germany 52 G5
Reiphólsfjöll hill Iceland 44 [inset 1]
Reisaelva r. Norway 44 L2
Reisa Nasjonalpark nat. park Norway 44 M2
Reisjärvi Fin. 44 N5
Reitz S. Africa 101 I4
Rekapalle India 84 D2
Reken Germany 52 H3
Reliance Canada 121 I2
Relizane Alg. 57 G6
Rellano Mex. 131 B7
Rellingen Germany 53 J1
Remagen Germany 53 H4
Remarkable, Mount hill Australia 111 B7
Remedios Cuba 133 E8
Remeshk Iran 88 E5
Remhoogte Pass Namibia 100 C2
Remi France see Reims
Remmel Mountain U.S.A. 126 C2
Remscheid Germany 53 H3
Rena Norway 45 G6
Renaix Belgium see Ronse
Renam Myanmar 76 C3
Renapur India 84 C2
Rendsburg Germany 47 L3
René-Levasseur, Île i. Canada 123 H4
Renews Canada 123 L5
Renfrew Canada 135 G1
Renfrew U.K. 50 E5
Rengali Reservoir India 83 F5
Rengat Indon. 68 C7
Rengo Chile 144 B4
Renhe China 77 G2
Ren He r. China 77 F1
Renhua China 77 G3
Reni Ukr. 59 M2
Renland reg. Greenland see Tuttut Nunaat
Rennell i. Solomon Is 107 G3
Rennerod Germany 53 I4
Rennes France 56 D2
Rennick Glacier Antarctica 152 H2
Rennie Canada 121 M5
Reno r. Italy 58 E2
Reno U.S.A. 128 D2
Renovo U.S.A. 135 G3
Rensselaer U.S.A. 134 B3
Renswoude Neth. 52 F2
Renton U.S.A. 126 C3
Réo Burkina Faso 96 C3
Reo Indon. 108 C2
Repalle India 84 D2
Repetek Turkm. 89 F2
Repetek Döwlet Gorugy nature res. Turkm. 89 F2
Repolka Russia 45 P7
Repou, Tônle r. Laos 71 D4
Republic U.S.A. 126 D2
Republican r. U.S.A. 130 D4
Repulse Bay b. Australia 110 E4
Repulse Bay Canada 119 J3
Requena Peru 142 D5
Requena Spain 57 F4
Reşadiye Turkey 90 E2
Reserva Brazil 145 A4
Reserve U.S.A. 129 I5
Reshi China 77 F2
Reshm Iran 88 D3
Reshteh-ye Alborz mts Iran see Elburz Mountains
Resistencia Arg. 144 E3
Reşiţa Romania 59 I2
Resolute Canada 119 I2
Resolute Bay Canada see Resolute
Resolution Island Canada 119 L3
Resolution Island N.Z. 113 A7
Resplendor Brazil 145 C2
Restigouche r. Canada 123 I5
Resülayn Turkey see Ceylanpınar
Retalhuleu Guat. 136 F6
Retezat, Parcul Naţional nat. park Romania 59 J2
Retford U.K. 48 G5
Rethel France 52 E5
Rethem (Aller) Germany 53 J2
Réthimnon Greece see Rethymno
Rethymno Greece 59 K7
Retreat Australia 110 C5
Reuden Germany 53 M2

▶Réunion terr. Indian Ocean 149 L7
French Overseas Department.

Reus Spain 57 G3
Reusam, Pulau i. Indon. 71 B7
Reutlingen Germany 47 L6
Reval Estonia see Tallinn
Revda Russia 44 S3
Revel Estonia see Tallinn
Revel France 56 F5
Revelstoke Canada 120 G5
Revigny-sur-Ornain France 52 E6
Revillagigedo, Islas is Mex. 136 B5
Revillagigedo Island U.S.A. 120 D4
Revin France 52 E5
Revivim Israel 85 B4
Revolyutsii, Pik mt. Tajik. see Revolyutsiya, Qullai
Revolyutsiya, Qullai mt. Tajik. 89 I2
Rewa India 82 E4
Rewanduz Iraq see Rawāndūz/Rewanduz
Rewari India 82 D3
Rexburg U.S.A. 126 F4
Rexton Canada 123 I5
Rey Iran 88 C3
Reyābād Iran 88 D2
Reyes, Point U.S.A. 128 B2
Reyhanlı Turkey 85 C1
Reykir Iceland 44 [inset 1]
Reykjanes Ridge sea feature N. Atlantic Ocean 148 F2
Reykjanestá pt Iceland 44 [inset 1]

▶Reykjavík Iceland 44 [inset 1]
Capital of Iceland.

Reyneke, Ostrov i. Russia 74 E1
Reynoldsburg U.S.A. 134 D4
Reynolds Range mts Australia 108 F5
Reynosa Mex. 131 D7
Rezā Iran 88 D3
Reẓā'īyeh Iran see Urmia
Reẓā'īyeh, Daryācheh-ye salt l. Iran see Urmia, Lake
Rēzekne Latvia 45 O8
Rezvān Iran 89 F4
Rezvāndeh Iran see Rezvānshahr
Rezvānshahr Iran 88 C2
Rhaeadr Gwy U.K. see Rhayader
Rhayader U.K. 49 D6
Rheda-Wiedenbrück Germany 53 I3
Rhede Germany 52 G3
Rhegium Italy see Reggio di Calabria
Rheims France see Reims
Rhein r. Germany see Rhine
Rheine Germany 53 H2
Rheinland-Pfalz land Germany 53 H5
Rheinsberg Germany 53 M1
Rheinstetten Germany 53 I6
Rhemilès well Alg. 96 C2
Rhin r. France see Rhine
Rhine r. Germany 53 G3
also spelt Rhein (Germany) or Rhin (France)
Rhinebeck U.S.A. 135 I3
Rhinelander U.S.A. 130 F2
Rhineland-Palatinate land Germany see Rheinland-Pfalz
Rhinkanal canal Germany 53 M2
Rhinow Germany 53 M2
Rhiwabon U.K. see Ruabon
Rho Italy 58 C2
Rhode Island state U.S.A. 135 J3
Rhodes Greece 59 M6
Rhodes i. Greece 59 M6
Rhodesia country Africa see Zimbabwe
Rhodes Peak U.S.A. 126 E3
Rhodope Mountains Bulg./Greece 59 J4
Rhodus i. Greece see Rhodes
Rhône r. France/Switz. 56 G5
Rhum i. U.K. see Rum
Rhuthun U.K. see Ruthin
Rhydaman U.K. see Ammanford
Rhyl U.K. 48 D5
Riachão Brazil 143 I5
Riacho Brazil 145 C2
Riacho de Santana Brazil 145 C1
Riacho dos Machados Brazil 145 C1
Rialma Brazil 145 A1
Rialto U.S.A. 128 E4
Riau, Kepulauan is Indon. 68 C6
Ribadeo Spain 57 C2
Ribadesella/Ribeseya Spain 57 D2
Ribas do Rio Pardo Brazil 144 F2
Ribat-i-Shur waterhole Iran 88 E3
Ribáuè Moz. 99 D5
Ribble r. U.K. 48 E5
Ribblesdale valley U.K. 48 E4
Ribe Denmark 45 F9
Ribécourt-Dreslincourt France 52 C5
Ribeira r. Brazil 145 B4
Ribeirão Preto Brazil 145 B3
Ribemont France 52 D5
Ribérac France 56 E4
Riberalta Bol. 142 E6
Rîbniţa Moldova 43 F7
Ribnitz-Damgarten Germany 47 N3
Říčany Czechia 47 O6
Rice U.S.A. 135 F5
Rice Lake Canada 135 F1
Richard-Molard, Mont Africa 96 C4
Richards Bay S. Africa 101 K5
Richards Inlet Antarctica 152 H1
Richards Island Canada 118 E3
Richardson r. Canada 121 I3
Richardson U.S.A. 131 D5
Richardson Island Canada 120 G1
Richardson Lakes U.S.A. 135 J1
Richardson Mountains Canada 118 E3
Richardson Mountains N.Z. 113 B7
Richfield U.S.A. 129 G2
Richfield Springs U.S.A. 135 H2
Richford NY U.S.A. 135 G2
Richford VT U.S.A. 135 I1
Richgrove U.S.A. 128 D4
Richland U.S.A. 126 D3
Richland Center U.S.A. 130 F3
Richmond N.S.W. Australia 112 E4
Richmond Qld Australia 110 C4
Richmond Canada 135 H1
Richmond N.Z. 113 D5
Richmond KwaZulu-Natal S. Africa 101 J5
Richmond N. Cape S. Africa 100 F6
Richmond U.K. 48 F4
Richmond CA U.S.A. 128 B3
Richmond IN U.S.A. 134 C4
Richmond KY U.S.A. 134 C5
Richmond MI U.S.A. 134 D2
Richmond MO U.S.A. 130 E4
Richmond TX U.S.A. 131 E6

▶Richmond VA U.S.A. 135 G5
Capital of Virginia.

Richmond Dale U.S.A. 134 D4
Richmond Hill U.S.A. 133 D6
Richmond Range hills Australia 112 F2
Richvale U.S.A. 128 C2
Richwood U.S.A. 134 E4
Rico U.S.A. 129 I3
Ricomagus France see Riom
Riddell Nunataks Antarctica 152 E2
Rideau Lakes Canada 135 G1
Ridge r. Canada 122 D4
Ridgecrest U.S.A. 128 E4
Ridge Farm U.S.A. 134 B4
Ridgeland MS U.S.A. 131 F5
Ridgeland SC U.S.A. 133 D5
Ridgetop U.S.A. 134 B5
Ridgetown Canada 134 E2
Ridgeway OH U.S.A. 134 D3
Ridgeway VA U.S.A. 134 F5
Ridgway CO U.S.A. 129 J2
Ridgway PA U.S.A. 135 F3
Riding Mountain National Park Canada 121 K5
Riecito Venez. 142 E1
Riemst Belgium 52 F4
Riesa Germany 53 N3
Riesco, Isla i. Chile 144 B8
Riet watercourse S. Africa 100 E6
Rietavas Lith. 45 L9
Rietfontein S. Africa 100 E4
Rieti Italy 58 E3
Rifā'ī, Tall mt. Jordan/Syria 85 C3
Rifeng China see Lichuan
Rifle U.S.A. 129 J2
Rifstangi pt Iceland 44 [inset 1]
Rift Valley Lakes National Park Eth. see Abijatta-Shalla National Park

▶Rīga Latvia 45 N8
Capital of Latvia.

Riga, Gulf of Estonia/Latvia 45 M8
Rigain Pünco l. China 83 F2
Rigas jūras līcis b. Estonia/Latvia see Riga, Gulf of
Rigby U.S.A. 126 F4
Rīgestān reg. Afgh. see Rēgistān
Rigolet Canada 123 K3
Rigside U.K. 50 F5
Riia laht b. Estonia/Latvia see Riga, Gulf of
Riihimäki Fin. 45 N6
Riiser-Larsen Ice Shelf Antarctica 152 B2
Riito Mex. 129 F5
Rijau Nigeria 96 D3
Rijeka Croatia 58 F2
Rikā, Wādī ar watercourse Saudi Arabia 88 B6
Rikitgaib Indon. 71 B6
Rikor India 76 B2
Rikuchū-kaigan Kokuritsu-kōen nat. park Japan 75 F5
Rikuzen-takata Japan 75 F5
Rila mts Bulg. 59 J3
Rila China 83 F3
Riley U.S.A. 126 D4
Rileyville U.S.A. 135 F4
Rillieux-la-Pape France 56 G4
Rillito U.S.A. 129 H5
Rimah, Wādī ar watercourse Saudi Arabia 86 F4
Rimavská Sobota Slovakia 47 R6
Rimbey Canada 120 H4
Rimini Italy 58 E2
Rîmnicu Sărat Romania see Râmnicu Sărat
Rîmnicu Vîlcea Romania see Râmnicu Vâlcea
Rimouski Canada 123 H4
Rimpar Germany 53 J5
Rimsdale, Loch l. U.K. 50 E2
Rinbung China 83 G3
Rincão Brazil 145 A3
Rindal Norway 44 F5
Ringarooma Bay Australia 111 [inset]
Ringas India 82 C4
Ringe Germany 52 G2
Ringebu Norway 45 G6
Ringhkung Myanmar 70 B1
Ringkøbing Denmark 45 F8
Ringsend U.K. 51 F2
Ringsted Denmark 45 G9
Ringtor China 83 E3
Ringvassøya i. Norway 44 K2
Ringwood Australia 112 B6
Ringwood U.K. 49 F8
Rinjani, Gunung vol. Indon. 68 F8
Rinns Point U.K. 50 C5
Rinqênzê China 83 G3
Rinqin Xubco salt l. China 83 E3
Rinteln Germany 53 J2
Rinyirru (Lakefield) National Park Australia 110 D2
Río Abiseo, Parque Nacional nat. park Peru 142 C5
Rio Azul Brazil 145 A4
Riobamba Ecuador 142 C4
Rio Blanco U.S.A. 129 J2
Rio Bonito Brazil 145 C3
Rio Branco Brazil 142 E6
Río Branco, Parque Nacional do nat. park Brazil 142 F3
Río Bravo, Parque Internacional del nat. park Mex. 131 C6
Rio Brilhante Brazil 144 F2
Rio Casca Brazil 145 C3
Rio Claro Brazil 145 B3
Río Colorado Arg. 144 D5
Río Cuarto Arg. 144 D4
Rio das Ostras Brazil 145 C3
Rio das Pedras Moz. 101 L2
Rio de Contas Brazil 145 C1

▶Rio de Janeiro Brazil 145 C3
Former capital of Brazil. 3rd most populous city in South America.

Rio de Janeiro state Brazil 145 C3

▶Río de la Plata-Paraná r. S. America 144 E4
2nd longest river in South America and 9th in the world.

Rio Dell U.S.A. 128 A1
Rio do Sul Brazil 145 A4
Río Gallegos Arg. 144 C8
Río Grande Arg. 144 C8
Rio Grande Brazil 144 F4
Río Grande Mex. 131 C8
Rio Grande r. Mex./U.S.A. 127 G5
also known as Río Bravo del Norte
Rio Grande City U.S.A. 131 D7
Rio Grande del Norte National Monument nat. park U.S.A. 127 G6
Rio Grande do Sul state Brazil 145 A5
Rio Grande Rise sea feature S. Atlantic Ocean 148 F8
Riohacha Col. 142 D1
Río Hondo, Embalse resr Arg. 144 C3
Rioja Peru 142 C5
Río Lagartos Mex. 133 B8
Rio Largo Brazil 143 K5
Riom France 56 F4
Rio Manso, Represa do resr Brazil 143 G6
Río Mulatos Bol. 142 E7
Río Muni reg. Equat. Guinea 96 E4
Río Negro, Embalse del resr Uruguay 144 E4
Rioni r. Georgia 91 F2
Rio Novo Brazil 145 C3
Rio Pardo de Minas Brazil 145 C1
Rio Preto Brazil 145 C3
Rio Preto, Serra do hills Brazil 145 B2
Rio Rancho U.S.A. 127 G6
Río Tigre Ecuador 142 C4
Riou Lake Canada 121 J3
Rio Verde Brazil 145 A2
Rio Verde de Mato Grosso Brazil 143 H7
Rio Vista U.S.A. 128 C2
Ripky Ukr. 43 F6
Ripley England U.K. 48 F4
Ripley England U.K. 49 F5
Ripley NY U.S.A. 134 F2
Ripley OH U.S.A. 134 D4
Ripley WV U.S.A. 134 E4
Ripoll Spain 57 H2
Ripon U.K. 48 F4
Ripon U.S.A. 128 C3
Ripu India 83 G4
Risca U.K. 49 D7
Rishiri-tō i. Japan 74 F3
Rishon LeẔiyyon Israel 85 B4
Rish Pish Bālā Iran 89 F5
Rising Sun IN U.S.A. 134 C4
Rising Sun MD U.S.A. 135 G4
Risle r. France 49 H9
Risør Norway 45 F7
Rissa Norway 44 F5
Ristiina Fin. 45 O6
Ristijärvi Fin. 44 P4
Ristikent Russia 44 Q2
Risum China 82 D2
Ritchie S. Africa 100 G5
Ritchie's Archipelago is India 71 A4
Ritscher Upland mts Antarctica 152 B2
Ritsem Sweden 44 J3
Ritter, Mount U.S.A. 128 D3
Ritterhude Germany 53 I1
Ritzville U.S.A. 126 D3
Riu, Laem pt Thai. 71 B5
Riva del Garda Italy 58 D2
Rivas Nicaragua 137 G6
Rivera Arg. 144 D5
Rivera Uruguay 144 E4
Riverhead U.S.A. 135 I3
Riverhurst Canada 121 J5
Riverina Australia 109 C7
Riverina reg. Australia 112 B5
Riversdale S. Africa 100 E8
Riverside S. Africa 101 I6
Riverside U.S.A. 128 E5
Rivers Inlet Canada 120 E5
Riversleigh Australia 110 B3
Riverton N.Z. 113 B8
Riverton VA U.S.A. 135 F4
Riverton WY U.S.A. 126 F4
Riverview Canada 123 I5
Rivesaltes France 56 F5
Riviera Beach U.S.A. 133 D7
Rivière-du-Loup Canada 123 H5
Rivière-Pentecôte Canada 123 I4
Rivière-Pigou Canada 123 I4
Rivne Ukr. 43 E6
Rivungo Angola 99 C5
Riwaka N.Z. 113 D5
Riwoqê China see Racaka

▶Riyadh Saudi Arabia 86 G5
Capital of Saudi Arabia.

Riyan India 89 I5
Riza well Iran 88 D3
Rize Turkey 91 F2
Rizhao Shandong China see Donggang
Rizhao Shandong China 77 H1
Rizokarpaso Cyprus see Rizokarpason
Rizokarpason Cyprus 85 B2
Rīzū well Iran 88 E3
Rīzū'īyeh Iran 88 E4
Rjukan Norway 45 F7
Rjuvbrokkene mt. Norway 45 E7
Rkîz Mauritania 96 B3
Roa Norway 45 G6
Roachdale U.S.A. 134 B4
Roach Lake U.S.A. 129 F4
Roade U.K. 49 G6
Roads U.S.A. 134 D4

▶Road Town Virgin Is (U.K.) 137 L5
Capital of the British Virgin Islands.

Roan Norway 44 G4
Roan Fell hill U.K. 50 G5
Roan High Knob mt. U.S.A. 132 D4
Roanne France 56 G3
Roanoke IN U.S.A. 134 C3
Roanoke VA U.S.A. 134 F5
Roanoke r. U.S.A. 132 E4
Roanoke Rapids U.S.A. 132 E4
Roan Plateau U.S.A. 129 I2
Roaring Spring U.S.A. 135 F3
Roaringwater Bay Ireland 51 C6
Roatán Hond. 137 G5
Röbäck Sweden 44 L5
Robāţ-e Posht-e Bādām Iran 88 D3
Robāţ Karīm Iran 88 C3
Robāţ Sang Iran 88 E3
Robāţ Tork Iran 88 C3
Robb Canada 120 G4
Robbins Island Australia 111 [inset]
Robbinsville U.S.A. 133 D5
Robe Australia 111 B8
Robe r. Australia 108 A5
Robe r. Ireland 51 C4
Röbel/Müritz Germany 53 M1
Robe Noire, Lac de la l. Canada 123 J4
Robert-Bourassa, Réservoir resr Canada 122 F3
Robert Glacier Antarctica 152 D2
Robert Lee U.S.A. 131 C6
Roberts U.S.A. 126 E4
Roberts, Mount Australia 112 F2
Robertsburg U.S.A. 134 E4
Roberts Butte mt. Antarctica 152 H2
Roberts Creek Mountain U.S.A. 128 E2
Robertsfors Sweden 44 L4
Robertsganj India 83 E4
Robertson S. Africa 100 D7
Robertson, Lac l. Canada 123 K4
Robertson Bay Antarctica 152 H2
Robertson Island Antarctica 152 A2
Robertson Range hills Australia 109 C5
Robertsport Liberia 96 B4
Roberval Canada 123 G4
Robhanais, Rubha hd U.K. see Butt of Lewis
Robin Hood's Bay U.K. 48 G4
Robin's Nest hill H.K. China 77 [inset]
Robinson Canada 120 C2
Robinson U.S.A. 134 B4
Robinson Ranges hills Australia 109 B6
Robinson River Australia 110 B3
Robles Pass U.S.A. 129 H5
Roblin Canada 121 K5
Robsart Canada 121 I5
Robson, Mount Canada 120 G4
Robstown U.S.A. 131 D7
Roby U.S.A. 131 C5
Roçadas Angola see Xangongo
Rocha Uruguay 144 F4
Rochdale U.K. 48 E5
Rochechouart France 56 E4
Rochefort Belgium 52 F4
Rochefort France 56 D4
Rochefort, Lac l. Canada 123 G2
Rochegda Russia 42 I3
Rochester Australia 112 B6
Rochester U.K. 49 H7
Rochester IN U.S.A. 134 B3
Rochester MN U.S.A. 130 E2
Rochester NH U.S.A. 135 J2
Rochester NY U.S.A. 135 G2
Rochford U.K. 49 H7
Rochlitz Germany 53 M3
Roc'h Trévezel hill France 56 C2
Rock r. Canada 120 E2
Rockall i. N. Atlantic Ocean 40 D4
Rockall Bank sea feature N. Atlantic Ocean 148 G2
Rock Creek Canada 120 B1
Rock Creek U.S.A. 134 E3
Rock Creek r. U.S.A. 126 G2
Rockdale U.S.A. 131 D6

Rockefeller Plateau Antarctica 152 J1
Rockford AL U.S.A. 133 C5
Rockford IL U.S.A. 130 F3
Rockford MI U.S.A. 134 C2
Rockglen Canada 121 J5
Rockhampton Australia 110 E4
Rockhampton Downs Australia 108 F4
Rock Hill U.S.A. 133 D5
Rockingham Australia 109 A8
Rockingham U.S.A. 133 E5
Rockingham Bay Australia 110 D3
Rockinghorse Lake Canada 121 H1
Rock Island Canada 135 I1
Rock Island U.S.A. 130 F3
Rock Lake U.S.A. 130 D1
Rockland MA U.S.A. 135 J2
Rockland ME U.S.A. 132 G2
Rocknest Lake Canada 120 H1
Rockport IN U.S.A. 134 B5
Rockport TX U.S.A. 131 D7
Rock Rapids U.S.A. 130 D3
Rock River U.S.A. 126 G4
Rock Sound Bahamas 133 E7
Rock Springs MT U.S.A. 126 G3
Rocksprings U.S.A. 131 C6
Rock Springs WY U.S.A. 126 F4
Rockstone Guyana 143 G2
Rockville CT U.S.A. 135 I3
Rockville IN U.S.A. 134 B4
Rockville MD U.S.A. 135 G4
Rockwell City U.S.A. 130 E3
Rockwood MI U.S.A. 134 D2
Rockwood PA U.S.A. 134 F4
Rockyford Canada 120 H5
Rocky Harbour Canada 123 K4
Rocky Hill U.S.A. 134 D4
Rocky Island Lake Canada 122 E5
Rocky Lane Canada 120 G3
Rocky Mount U.S.A. 134 F5
Rocky Mountain House Canada 120 H4
Rocky Mountain National Park U.S.A. 126 G4
Rocky Mountains Canada/U.S.A. 124 F3
Rocourt-St-Martin France 52 D5
Rocroi France 52 E5
Rødberg Norway 45 F6
Rødbyhavn Denmark 45 G9
Roddickton Canada 123 L4
Rodeio Brazil 145 A4
Rodel U.K. 50 C3
Roden Neth. 52 G1
Rödental Germany 53 L4
Rodeo Arg. 144 C4
Rodeo Mex. 131 B7
Rodeo U.S.A. 127 F7
Rodez France 56 F4
Ródhos i. Greece see Rhodes
Rodi i. Greece see Rhodes
Roding Germany 53 M5
Rodney, Cape U.S.A. 118 B3
Rodniki Russia 42 I4
Rodolfo Sánchez Toboada Mex. 127 D7
Rodopi Planina mts Bulg./Greece see Rhodope Mountains
Rodos Greece see Rhodes
Rodos i. Greece see Rhodes
Rodosto Turkey see Tekirdağ
Rodrigues Island Mauritius 149 M7
Roe r. U.K. 51 F2
Roebourne Australia 108 B5
Roebuck Bay Australia 108 C4
Roedtan S. Africa 101 I3
Roe Plains Australia 109 D7
Roermond Neth. 52 F3
Roeselare Belgium 52 D4
Roes Welcome Sound sea chan. Canada 119 J3
Rogachev Belarus see Rahachow
Rogätz Germany 53 L2
Rogers U.S.A. 131 E4
Rogers, Mount U.S.A. 134 E5
Rogers City U.S.A. 134 D1
Rogers Lake U.S.A. 128 E4
Rogerson U.S.A. 126 E4
Rogersville U.S.A. 134 D5
Roggan r. Canada 122 F3
Roggan, Lac l. Canada 122 F3
Roggeveen Basin sea feature S. Pacific Ocean 151 O8
Roggeveld plat. S. Africa 100 E7
Roggeveldberge esc. S. Africa 100 E7
Roghadal U.K. see Rodel
Rognan Norway 44 I3
Rögnitz r. Germany 53 K1
Rogue r. U.S.A. 126 B4
Roha India 84 B2
Rohnert Park U.S.A. 128 B2
Rohrbach in Oberösterreich Austria 47 N6
Rohrbach-lès-Bitche France 53 H5
Rohri Sangar Pak. 89 H5
Rohtak India 82 D3
Roi Et Thai. 70 C3
Roi Georges, Îles du is Fr. Polynesia 151 K6
Rois-Bheinn hill U.K. 50 D4
Roisel France 52 D5
Roja Latvia 45 M8
Rojas Arg. 144 D4
Rokeby Australia 110 C2
Rokeby National Park Australia 110 C2
Rokiškis Lith. 45 N9
Roknäs Sweden 44 L4
Rokytne Ukr. 43 E6
Rolagang China 83 G2
Rola Kangri mt. China 83 G2
Rolândia Brazil 145 A3
Rolim de Moura Brazil 142 F6
Roll AZ U.S.A. 129 G5
Roll IN U.S.A. 134 C3
Rolla MO U.S.A. 130 F4
Rolla ND U.S.A. 130 D1
Rollag Norway 45 F6
Rolleston Australia 110 E5
Rolleville Bahamas 133 F8
Rolling Fork U.S.A. 131 F5
Rollins U.S.A. 126 E3
Roma Australia 111 E5
Roma Italy see Rome
Roma Lesotho 101 H5
Roma Sweden 45 K8
Romain, Cape U.S.A. 133 E5
Romaine r. Canada 123 J4
Roman Romania 59 L1
Romanâ, Câmpia plain Romania 59 J2
Romanche Gap sea feature S. Atlantic Ocean 148 G6
Romanet, Lac l. Canada 123 I2
Romang, Pulau i. Indon. 108 D1
Romania country Europe 59 K2
Roman-Kosh mt. Crimea 90 D1
Romano, Cape U.S.A. 133 D7
Romanovka Russia 73 K2
Romans-sur-Isère France 56 G4
Romanzof, Cape U.S.A. 118 B3
Rombas France 52 G5
Romblon Phil. 69 G4

▶Rome Italy 58 E4
Capital of Italy.

Rome GA U.S.A. 133 C5
Rome ME U.S.A. 135 K1
Rome NY U.S.A. 135 H2
Rome TN U.S.A. 134 B5
Rome City U.S.A. 134 C3
Romeo U.S.A. 134 D2
Romford U.K. 49 H7
Romilly-sur-Seine France 56 F2
Romiton Uzbek. 89 G2
Romney U.S.A. 135 F4
Romney Marsh reg. U.K. 49 H7
Romny Ukr. 43 G6
Rømø i. Denmark 45 F9
Romodanovo Russia 43 J5
Romorantin-Lanthenay France 56 E3
Rompin r. Malaysia 71 C7
Romsey U.K. 49 F8
Romulus U.S.A. 134 D2
Ron India 84 B3
Ron, Mui hd Vietnam 70 D3
Rona i. U.K. 50 D1
Ronas Hill hill U.K. 50 [inset]
Roncador, Serra do hills Brazil 143 H6
Roncador Reef Solomon Is 107 F2
Ronda Spain 57 D5
Ronda, Serranía de mts Spain 57 D5
Rondane Nasjonalpark nat. park Norway 45 F6
Rondon Brazil 144 F2
Rondonópolis Brazil 143 H7
Rondout Reservoir U.S.A. 135 H3
Rongcheng Anhui China see Qingyang
Rongcheng Guangxi China see Rongxian
Rongcheng Hubei China see Jianli
Rong Chu r. China 83 G3
Rongelap atoll Marshall Is 150 H5
Rongjiang Guizhou China 77 F3
Rongjiang Jiangxi China see Nankang
Rongjiawan China see Yueyang
Rongklang Range mts Myanmar 70 A2
Rongmei China see Hefeng
Rongshui China 77 F3
Rongwo China see Tongren
Rongxian China 77 F4
Rongyul China 76 C2
Rongzhag China see Danba
Rönlap atoll Marshall Is see Rongelap
Rønne Denmark 45 I9
Ronneby Sweden 45 I8
Ronne Entrance strait Antarctica 152 L2
Ronne Ice Shelf Antarctica 152 L1
Ronnenberg Germany 53 J2
Ronse Belgium 52 D4
Roodeschool Neth. 52 G1
Rooke Island P.N.G. see Umboi
Roordahuizum Neth. see Reduzum
Roorkee India 82 D3
Roosendaal Neth. 52 E3
Roosevelt AZ U.S.A. 129 H5
Roosevelt UT U.S.A. 129 I1
Roosevelt, Mount Canada 120 E3
Roosevelt Sub-glacial Island Antarctica 152 I1
Root r. Canada 120 F2
Root r. U.S.A. 130 F3
Ropar India see Rupnagar
Roper r. Australia 110 A2
Roper Bar Australia 108 F3
Roquefort France 56 D4
Roraima, Mount Guyana 142 F2
Rori India 82 C3
Rori Indon. 69 J7
Røros Norway 44 G5
Rørvik Norway 44 G4
Rosa, Punta pt Mex. 127 F8
Rosalia U.S.A. 126 D3
Rosamond U.S.A. 128 D4
Rosamond Lake U.S.A. 128 D4
Rosario Arg. 144 D4
Rosário Brazil 143 J4
Rosario Baja California Mex. 127 E7
Rosario Coahuila Mex. 131 C7
Rosario Sinaloa Mex. 136 C4
Rosario Sonora Mex. 124 F6
Rosario Zacatecas Mex. 131 C7
Rosario Venez. 142 D1
Rosário do Sul Brazil 144 F4
Rosário Oeste Brazil 143 G6
Rosarito Baja California Mex. 127 E7
Rosarito Baja California Mex. 128 E5
Rosarito Baja California Sur Mex. 127 F8
Rosarno Italy 58 F5
Roscoff France 56 C2
Roscommon Ireland 51 D4
Roscommon U.S.A. 134 C1
Roscrea Ireland 51 E5
Rose r. Australia 110 A2
Rose, Mount U.S.A. 128 D2
Rose Atoll American Samoa see Rose Island

▶Roseau Dominica 137 L5
Capital of Dominica.

Roseau U.S.A. 130 E1
Roseau r. U.S.A. 130 D1
Roseberth Australia 111 B5
Rose Blanche Canada 123 K5
Rosebud r. Canada 120 H5
Rosebud U.S.A. 126 G3
Roseburg U.S.A. 126 C4
Rose City U.S.A. 134 C1
Rosedale U.S.A. 131 F5
Rosedale Abbey U.K. 48 G4
Roseires Reservoir Sudan 86 D7
Rose Island atoll American Samoa 107 J3
Rosenberg U.S.A. 131 E6
Rosendal Norway 45 E7
Rosendal S. Africa 101 H5
Rosenheim Germany 47 N7
Rose Peak U.S.A. 129 I5
Rose Point pt Canada 120 D4
Roseto degli Abruzzi Italy 58 F3
Rosetown Canada 121 J5
Rosetta Egypt see Rashīd
Rose Valley Canada 121 K4
Roseville CA U.S.A. 128 C2
Roseville MI U.S.A. 134 D2
Roseville OH U.S.A. 134 D4
Rosewood Australia 112 F1
Roshchino Russia 45 P6
Rosh Pinah Namibia 100 C4
Roshtkala Tajik. see Roshtqal'a
Roshtqal'a Tajik. 89 H2
Rosignano Marittimo Italy 58 D3
Roșiori de Vede Romania 59 K2
Roskilde Denmark 45 H9
Roskruge Mountains U.S.A. 129 H5
Roslavl' Russia 43 G5
Roslyakovo Russia 44 R2
Roslyatino Russia 42 J4
Ross N.Z. 113 C6
Ross, Mount hill N.Z. 113 E5
Rossano Italy 58 G5
Rossan Point Ireland 51 D3
Ross Barnett Reservoir U.S.A. 131 F5
Ross Bay Junction Canada 123 I3
Rosscarbery Ireland 51 C6
Ross Dependency reg. Antarctica 152 I2
Rosseau, Lake Canada 134 F1
Rossel Island P.N.G. 110 F1
Ross Ice Shelf Antarctica 152 I1
Rossignol, Lac l. Canada 122 G3
Rössing Namibia 100 B2
Ross Island Antarctica 152 H1
Rossiyskaya Sovetskaya Federativnaya Sotsialisticheskaya Respublika country Asia/Europe see Russia
Rossland Canada 120 G5
Rosslare Ireland 51 F5
Rosslare Harbour Ireland 51 F5
Roßlau Germany 53 M3
Rosso Mauritania 96 B3
Ross-on-Wye U.K. 49 E7
Rossony Belarus see Rasony
Rossosh' Russia 43 H6
Ross River Canada 120 C2
Ross Sea Antarctica 152 H1
Roßtal Germany 53 K5
Røssvatnet l. Norway 44 I4
Rossville U.S.A. 134 B3
Roßwein Germany 53 N3
Rosswood Canada 120 D4
Rostāq Iran 88 D5
Rosthern Canada 121 J4
Rostock Germany 47 N3
Rostov Russia 42 H4
Rostov-na-Donu Russia 43 H7
Rostov-on-Don Russia see Rostov-na-Donu
Rosvik Sweden 44 L4
Roswell U.S.A. 127 G6
Rota i. N. Mariana Is 69 L4
Rot am See Germany 53 K5
Rotch Island Kiribati see Tamana
Rote i. Indon. 108 C2
Rotenburg (Wümme) Germany 53 J1
Roth Germany 53 L5
Rothaargebirge hills Germany 53 I4
Rothbury U.K. 48 F3
Rothenburg ob der Tauber Germany 53 K5
Rother r. U.K. 49 G8
Rothera research station Antarctica 152 L2
Rotherham U.K. 48 F5
Rothes U.K. 50 F3
Rothesay U.K. 50 D5
Rothwell U.K. 49 G6
Roti Indon. 108 C2
Roti i. Indon. see Rote
Roto Australia 112 B4
Rotomagus France see Rouen
Rotomanu N.Z. 113 C6
Rotondo, Monte mt. Corsica France 56 I5
Rotorua N.Z. 113 F4
Rotorua, Lake N.Z. 113 F4
Röttenbach Germany 53 L5
Rottendorf Germany 53 K5
Rottenmann Austria 47 O7
Rotterdam Neth. 52 E3
Rottleberode Germany 53 K3
Rottnest Island Australia 109 A8
Rottumeroog i. Neth. 52 G1
Rottweil Germany 47 L6
Rotuma i. Fiji 107 H3
Rotung India 76 B2
Rötviken Sweden 44 I5
Rötz Germany 53 M5
Roubaix France 52 D4
Rouen France 52 B5
Rough River Lake U.S.A. 134 B5
Roulers Belgium see Roeselare
Roumania country Europe see Romania
Roundeyed Lake Canada 123 H3
Round Hill hill U.K. 48 F4
Round Mountain Australia 112 F3
Round Rock AZ U.S.A. 129 I3
Round Rock TX U.S.A. 131 D6
Roundup U.S.A. 126 F3
Rousay i. U.K. 50 F1
Rouses Point U.S.A. 135 I1
Rouxville S. Africa 101 H6
Rouyn-Noranda Canada 122 F4
Rovaniemi Fin. 44 N3
Roven'ki Russia 43 H6
Rovereto Italy 58 D2
Rôviêng Cambodia 71 D4
Rovigo Italy 58 D2
Rovinj Croatia 58 E2
Rovno Ukr. see Rivne
Rovnoye Russia 43 J6
Rovuma r. Moz./Tanz. see Ruvuma
Rowena Australia 112 D2
Rowley Island Canada 119 K3
Rowley Shoals sea feature Australia 108 B4
Równe Ukr. see Rivne
Roxas Mindoro Phil. 69 G4
Roxas Palawan Phil. 68 F4
Roxas Panay Phil. 69 G4
Roxboro U.S.A. 132 E4
Roxburgh N.Z. 113 B7
Roxburgh Island Cook Is see Rarotonga
Roxby Downs Australia 111 B6
Roxo, Cabo c. Senegal 96 B3
Roy MT U.S.A. 126 F3
Roy NM U.S.A. 127 G5
Royal Canal Ireland 51 E4
Royal Chitwan National Park Nepal 83 F4
Royale, Île i. Canada see Cape Breton Island
Royale, Isle i. U.S.A. 130 F1
Royal Leamington Spa U.K. 49 F6
Royal Natal National Park S. Africa 101 I5
Royal National Park Australia 112 E5
Royal Oak U.S.A. 134 D2
Royal Sukla Phanta Wildlife Reserve Nepal 82 E3
Royal Tunbridge Wells U.K. 49 H7
Royal Wootton Bassett U.K. 49 F7
Royan France 56 D4
Roye France 52 C5
Roy Hill Australia 108 B5
Royston U.K. 49 G6
Rozdil'na Ukr. 59 N1
Rozivka Ukr. 43 H7
Rtishchevo Russia 43 I5
Ruabon U.K. 49 D6
Ruaha National Park Tanz. 99 D4
Ruahine Range mts N.Z. 113 F5
Ruanda country Africa see Rwanda

▶Ruapehu, Mount vol. N.Z. 113 E4
Highest active volcano in Oceania.

Ruapuke Island N.Z. 113 B8
Ruatoria N.Z. 113 G3
Ruba Belarus 43 F5

▶Rub' al Khālī des. Saudi Arabia 86 G6
Largest uninterrupted stretch of sand in the world.

Rubāṭ Māndêh r. Afgh. 89 F4
Rubaydā reg. Saudi Arabia 88 C5
Rubtsovsk Russia 80 F1
Ruby U.S.A. 118 C3
Ruby Dome mt. U.S.A. 129 F1
Ruby Mountains U.S.A. 129 F1
Rubys Inn U.S.A. 129 G3
Ruby Valley U.S.A. 129 F1
Rucheng China 77 G3
Ruckersville U.S.A. 135 F4
Rudall River National Park Australia 108 C5
Rudarpur India 83 E4
Ruda Śląska Poland 47 Q5
Rudauli India 83 E4
Rūdbār Iran 88 C2
Rudkøbing Denmark 45 G9
Rudnaya Pristan' Russia 74 D3
Rudnichnyy Russia 42 L4
Rudnik Ingichka Uzbek. see Ingichka
Rudnya Smolenskaya Oblast' Russia 43 F5
Rudnya Volgogradskaya Oblast' Russia 43 J6
Rudnyy Kazakh. 78 F1
Rudolf, Lake salt l. Eth./Kenya see Turkana, Lake

▶Rudol'fa, Ostrov i. Russia 64 G1
Most northerly point of Europe.

Rudolph Island Russia see Rudol'fa, Ostrov
Rudolstadt Germany 53 L4
Rudong China 77 I1
Rūdsar Iran 88 C2
Rue France 52 B4
Rufiji r. Tanz. 99 D4
Rufino Arg. 144 D4
Rufisque Senegal 96 B3
Rufrufua Indon. 69 I7
Rufunsa Zambia 99 C5
Rugao China 77 I1
Rugby U.K. 49 F6
Rugby U.S.A. 130 C1
Rugeley U.K. 49 F6
Rügen i. Germany 47 N3
Rugged Mountain Canada 120 E5
Rügland Germany 53 K5
Ruḥayyat al Ḥamr'ā' waterhole Saudi Arabia 88 B5
Ruhengeri Rwanda 98 C4
Ruhnu i. Estonia 45 M8
Ruhr r. Germany 53 G3
Ruhuna National Park Sri Lanka see Yala National Park
Rui'an China 77 I3
Ruicheng China 77 F1
Ruijin China 77 G3
Ruili China 76 C3
Ruin Point Canada 121 P2
Ruipa Tanz. 99 D4
Ruiz Mex. 136 C4
Ruiz, Nevado del vol. Col. 142 C3
Rujaylah, Ḥarrat ar lava field Jordan 85 C3
Rūjiena Latvia 45 N8
Ruk is Micronesia see Chuuk
Rukanpur Pak. 89 I4
Rukumkot Nepal 83 E3
Rukwa, Lake Tanz. 99 D4
Rulin China see Chengbu
Rulong China see Xinlong
Rum i. U.K. 50 C4
Rum, Jebel mts Jordan see Ramm, Jabal
Ruma Serbia 59 H2
Rumāh Saudi Arabia 86 G4
Rumania country Europe see Romania
Rumbek South Sudan 97 F4
Rumberpon i. Indon. 69 I7
Rum Cay i. Bahamas 133 F8
Rum Jungle (abandoned) Australia 108 E3
Rummānā hill Syria 85 D3
Rumphi Malawi 99 D5
Runan China 77 G1
Runaway, Cape N.Z. 113 F3
Runcorn U.K. 48 E5
Rundu Namibia 99 B5
Rundvik Sweden 44 K5
Rŭng, Kaôh i. Cambodia 71 C5
Rungwa Tanz. 99 D4
Rungwa r. Tanz. 99 D4
Runhe China 77 H1
Runing China see Runan
Runton Range hills Australia 109 C5
Ruokolahti Fin. 45 P6
Ruoqiang China 80 G4
Rupa India 83 H4
Rupat i. Indon. 71 C7
Rupert r. Canada 122 F4
Rupert ID U.S.A. 126 E4
Rupert WV U.S.A. 134 E5
Rupert Bay Canada 122 F4
Rupert Coast Antarctica 152 J1
Rupert House Canada see Waskaganish
Rupnagar India 82 D3
Rupshu reg. India 82 D2
Ruqqād, Wādī ar watercourse Israel 85 B3
Rural Retreat U.S.A. 134 E5
Rusaddir N. Africa see Melilla
Rusape Zimbabwe 99 D5
Ruschuk Bulg. see Ruse
Ruse Bulg. 59 K3
Rusera India 83 F4
Rush U.S.A. 134 D4
Rush Creek r. U.S.A. 130 C4
Rushden U.K. 49 G6
Rushinga Zimbabwe 99 D5
Rushville IL U.S.A. 130 F3
Rushville IN U.S.A. 134 C4
Rushville NE U.S.A. 130 C3
Rushworth Australia 112 B6
Rusk U.S.A. 131 E6
Russell Man. Canada 121 K5
Russell Ont. Canada 135 H1
Russell N.Z. 113 E2
Russell KS U.S.A. 130 D4
Russell PA U.S.A. 134 F3
Russell Bay Antarctica 152 J2
Russell Lake Man. Canada 121 K3
Russell Lake N.W.T. Canada 120 H2
Russell Lake Sask. Canada 121 J3
Russell Range hills Australia 109 C8
Russell Springs U.S.A. 134 C5
Russellville AL U.S.A. 131 G5
Russellville AR U.S.A. 131 E5
Russellville KY U.S.A. 134 B5
Rüsselsheim Germany 53 I4

▶Russia country Asia/Europe 64 I3
Largest country in Europe and Asia and the world. Most populous country in Europe and 9th in the world.

Russian r. U.S.A. 128 B2
Russian Federation country Asia/Europe see Russia
Russian Soviet Federal Socialist Republic country Asia/Europe see Russia
Russkiy, Ostrov i. Russia 74 C4
Russkiy Kameshkir Russia 43 J5
Rustāq Afgh. 89 H2
Rustavi Georgia 91 G2
Rustburg U.S.A. 134 F5
Rustenburg S. Africa 101 H3
Ruston U.S.A. 131 E5
Rutanzige, Lake Dem. Rep. Congo/Uganda see Edward, Lake
Ruteng Indon. 108 C2
Ruth U.S.A. 129 F2
Rüthen Germany 53 I3
Rutherglen Australia 112 C6
Ruther Glen U.S.A. 135 G5
Ruthin U.K. 49 D5
Ruthiyai India 82 D4
Ruth Reservoir U.S.A. 128 B1
Rutka r. Russia 42 J4
Rutland U.S.A. 135 I2
Rutland Water resr U.K. 49 G6
Rutledge Lake Canada 121 I2
Rutog Xizang China 76 B2
Rutög China see Dêrub
Rutog Xizang China 83 F3
Rutul Russia 91 G2
Ruukki Fin. 44 N4
Ruvuma r. Moz./Tanz. 99 E5
also known as Rovuma
Ruwayshid, Wādī watercourse Jordan 85 C3
Ruwayṭah, Wādī watercourse Jordan 85 C5
Ruweis U.A.E. 88 D5
Ruwenzori National Park Uganda see Queen Elizabeth National Park
Ruy Barbosa Brazil 145 C1
Rūy Dūāb Wuluswālī Afgh. 89 G3
Ruza Russia 42 H5
Ruzayevka Kazakh. 78 F1
Ruzayevka Russia 43 J5
Ruzhou China 77 G1
Ružomberok Slovakia 47 Q6
Rwanda country Africa 98 C4
Ryan, Loch b. U.K. 50 D5
Ryazan' Russia 43 H5
Ryazhsk Russia 43 I5
Rybachiy, Poluostrov pen. Russia 44 R2
Rybach'ye Kyrg. see Balykchy
Rybinsk Russia 42 H4

▶Rybinskoye Vodokhranilishche resr Russia 42 H4
5th largest lake in Europe.

Rybnik Poland 47 Q5
Rybnitsa Moldova see Rîbnița
Rybnoye Russia 43 H5
Rybreka Russia 42 G3
Ryd Sweden 45 I8
Rydberg Peninsula Antarctica 152 L2
Ryde U.K. 49 F8
Rye U.K. 49 H8
Rye r. U.K. 48 G4
Rye Bay U.K. 49 H8
Ryegate U.S.A. 126 F3
Rye Patch Reservoir U.S.A. 128 D1
Rykovo Ukr. see Yenakiyeve
Ryl'sk Russia 43 G6
Rylstone Australia 112 D4
Ryn-Peski des. Kazakh. 41 P6
Ryukyu Islands Japan 75 B8
Ryūkyū-rettō is Japan see Ryukyu Islands
Ryukyu Trench sea feature N. Pacific Ocean 150 E4
Rzeszów Poland 43 D6
Rzhaksa Russia 43 I5
Rzhev Russia 42 G4

S

Sa'ādah al Barṣā' pass Saudi Arabia 85 C5
Saal an der Donau Germany 53 L6
Saale r. Germany 53 L3
Saalfeld/Saale Germany 53 L4
Saanich Canada 120 F5
Saar land Germany see Saarland
Saar r. Germany 52 G5
Saarbrücken Germany 52 G5
Saaremaa i. Estonia 45 M7
Saarenkylä Fin. 44 N3
Saargau reg. Germany 52 G5
Saarijärvi Fin. 44 N5
Saari-Kämä Fin. 44 O3
Saarikoski Fin. 44 L2
Saaristomeren kansallispuisto nat. park Fin. see Skärgårdshavets nationalpark
Saarland land Germany 52 G5
Saarlouis Germany 52 G5
Saatlı Azer. 91 H3
Saatly Azer. see Saatlı
Sab'a Egypt see Saba'ah
Saba'ah Egypt 85 A4
Sab' Ābār Syria 85 C3
Šabac Serbia 59 H2
Sabadell Spain 57 H3
Sabae Japan 75 E6
Sabak Malaysia 71 C7
Sabalana i. Indon. 68 F8
Sabalana, Kepulauan is Indon. 68 F8
Sabana, Archipiélago de is Cuba 137 H4
Sabang Indon. 71 A6
Şabanözü Turkey 90 D2
Sabará Brazil 145 C2
Sabasṭīyah West Bank 85 B3
Sab'atayn, Ramlat as des. Yemen 86 G6
Sabaudia Italy 58 E4
Sabaya Bol. 142 E7
Sabelo S. Africa 100 F6
Ṣabḥā Jordan 85 C3
Sabhā Libya 97 E2
Ṣabḥā' Saudi Arabia 88 B6
Sabhrai India 82 B5
Sabi r. India 82 D3
Sabi r. Moz./Zimbabwe see Save
Sabie Moz. 101 K3
Sabie r. Moz./S. Africa 101 K3
Sabie S. Africa 101 J3
Sabina U.S.A. 134 D4
Sabinal Mex. 127 G7
Sabinal, Cayo i. Cuba 133 E8
Sabinas Mex. 131 C7
Sabinas r. Mex. 131 C7
Sabinas Hidalgo Mex. 131 C7
Sabine r. U.S.A. 131 E6
Sabine Lake U.S.A. 131 E6
Sabine Pass U.S.A. 131 E6
Sabini, Monti mts Italy 58 E3
Sabirabad Azer. 91 H2
Sabkhat al Bardawīl Reserve nature res. Egypt see Lake Bardawil Reserve
Sable, Cape Canada 123 I6
Sable, Cape U.S.A. 133 D7
Sable, Lac du l. Canada 123 I3
Sable Island Canada 123 K6
Sable Island National Park Reserve nat. park Canada 123 K6
Sabon Kafi Niger 96 D3
Şabran Azer. 91 H2
Sabrina Coast Antarctica 152 F2
Sabugal Port. 57 C3
Ṣabyā Saudi Arabia 86 F6
Sabzak, Kōtal-e Afgh. 89 F3
Sabzawar Afgh. see Shīndand
Sabzevār Iran 88 E2
Sabzvārān Iran see Jīroft
Sacalinul Mare, Insula i. Romania 59 M2
Sacaton U.S.A. 129 H5
Sac City U.S.A. 130 E3
Săcele Romania 59 K2
Sacheon S. Korea 75 C6
Sachigo r. Canada 121 N4
Sachigo Lake Canada 121 M4
Sachin India 82 C5
Sach Pass India 82 D2
Sachsen land Germany 53 N3
Sachsen-Anhalt land Germany 53 L2
Sachsenheim Germany 53 J6
Sachs Harbour Canada 118 F2
Sacirsuyu r. Syria/Turkey see Sājūr, Nahr
Sackpfeife hill Germany 53 I4
Sackville Canada 123 I5
Saco ME U.S.A. 135 J2
Saco MT U.S.A. 126 G2
Sacramento Brazil 145 B2

▶Sacramento U.S.A. 128 C2
Capital of California.

Sacramento r. U.S.A. 128 C2
Sacramento Mountains U.S.A. 127 G6
Sacramento Valley U.S.A. 128 B1
Sada S. Africa 101 H7
Sádaba Spain 57 F2
Sá da Bandeira Angola see Lubango
Ṣadad Syria 85 C2
Ṣa'dah Yemen 86 F6
Sadakphu mt. India/Nepal 83 G4
Sadao Thai. 71 C6
Saddat al Hindīyah Iraq 91 G4
Saddleback Mesa mt. U.S.A. 131 C5
Saddle Hill hill Australia 110 D2
Saddle Peak hill India 71 A4
Sadê China 76 D2
Sa Đec Vietnam 71 D5
Sadêng China 76 B2
Sadieville U.S.A. 134 C4
Sadīj watercourse Iran 88 E5
Sadiola Mali 96 B3

Sadiqabad Pak. 89 H4
Sad Ishtrāgh mt. Afgh./Pak. 89 I2
Sa'dīyah, Hawr as imp. l. Iraq 91 G4
Sa'dīyyat i. U.A.E. 88 D5
Sado r. Port. 57 B4
Sadoga-shima i. Japan 75 E5
Sadot Egypt see Sadūt (abandoned)
Sadovoye Russia 43 J7
Sa Dragonera i. Spain 57 H4
Sadras India 84 D3
Sadût Egypt see Sadūt (abandoned)
Sadūt (abandoned) Egypt 85 B4
Sæby Denmark 45 G8
Saena Julia Italy see Siena
Safad Israel see Ẕefat
Şafāshahr Iran 88 D4
Safayal Maqūf well Iraq 91 G5
Safēd Khir, Kōh-e mts Afgh. 89 H2
Sāfēd Kōh mts Afgh./Pak. 89 H3
Safēd Kōh, Silsilah-ye mts Afgh. 89 F3
Saffānīyah, Ra's as pt Saudi Arabia 88 C4
Säffle Sweden 45 H7
Safford U.S.A. 129 I5
Saffron Walden U.K. 49 H6
Safi Morocco 54 C5
Safid, Chashmeh-ye spring Iran 88 E3
Safīdār, Kūh-e mt. Iran 88 D4
Safiras, Serra das mts Brazil 145 C2
Şāfītā Syria 85 C2
Safonovo Arkhangel'skaya Oblast' Russia 42 K2
Safonovo Smolenskaya Oblast' Russia 43 G5
Safranbolu Turkey 90 D2
Saga China 83 F3
Saga Japan 75 C6
Saga Kazakh. 80 B1
Sagaing Myanmar 70 A2
Sagami-nada g. Japan 75 E6
Sagamore U.S.A. 134 F3
Saganthit Kyun i. Myanmar 71 B4
Sagar Karnataka India 84 B3
Sagar Karnataka India 84 C2
Sagar Madh. Prad. India 82 D5
Sagaredzho Georgia see Sagarejo
Sagarejo Georgia 91 G2
Sagar Island India 83 G5
Sagarmatha National Park Nepal 83 F4
Sagastyr Russia 65 N2
Sagavanirktok r. U.S.A. 118 D2
Sage U.S.A. 126 F4
Saggi, Har mt. Israel 85 B4
Saghand Iran 88 D3
Saginaw U.S.A. 134 D2
Saginaw Bay U.S.A. 134 D2
Saglek Bay Canada 123 J2
Sagloue Canada see Salluit
Sagone, Golfe de b. Corsica France 56 I5
Sagres Port. 57 B5
Sagthale India 82 C5
Saguache U.S.A. 127 G5
Sagua la Grande Cuba 137 H4
Saguaro Lake U.S.A. 129 H5
Saguaro National Park U.S.A. 129 H5
Saguenay r. Canada 123 H4
Sagunt Spain see Sagunto
Sagunto Spain 57 F4
Saguntum Spain see Sagunto
Sagzī Iran 88 D3
Sahagún Spain 57 D2
Sahand, Kūh-e mt. Iran 88 B2

▶ Sahara des. Africa 96 D3
Largest desert in the world.

Saharan Atlas mts Alg. see Atlas Saharien
Saharanpur India 82 D3
Sahara Well Australia 108 C5
Saharsa India 83 F4
Sahaswan India 82 D3
Sahat, Kūh-e hill Iran 88 D3
Sahatwar India 83 F4
Şahbuz Azer. 91 G3
Sahdol India see Shahdol
Sahebganj India see Sahibganj
Sahebgunj India see Sahibganj
Saheira, Wâdi el watercourse Egypt see Suhaymī, Wādī as
Sahel reg. Africa 96 C3
Sahibganj India 83 F4
Sahiwal Pak. 89 I4
Sahlābād Iran 89 E3
Şaḩm Oman 88 E5
Şaḩneh Iran 88 B3
Şaḩrā al Ḩijārah reg. Iraq 91 G5
Sahuaripa Mex. 127 F7
Sahuayo Mex. 136 D4
Sahuteng China see Zadoi
Sa Huynh Vietnam 71 E4
Sahyadri mts India see Western Ghats
Sahyadriparvat Range hills India 84 B1
Sai r. India 83 E4
Sai Buri Thai. 71 C6
Saïda Alg. 57 G6
Saïda Lebanon see Sidon
Sa'īdābād Iran 88 E5
Sai Dao Tai, Khao mt. Thai. 71 C4
Saïdia Morocco 57 E6
Sa'īdīyeh Iran see Solṭānīyeh
Saidpur Bangl. 83 G4
Saiha India 83 H5
Saihan Tal China 73 K4
Saijō Japan 75 D6
Saikai Kokuritsu-kōen nat. park Japan 75 C6
Saiki Japan 75 C6
Sai Kung H.K. China 77 [inset]
Sailana India 82 C5
Saimaa l. Fin. 45 P6
Saimbeyli Turkey 90 E3
Saindak Pak. 89 F4
St Abb's Head hd U.K. 50 G5
St Agnes U.K. 49 B8
St Agnes i. U.K. 49 A9
St Alban's Canada 123 L5
St Albans U.K. 49 G7
St Albans VT U.S.A. 135 I1
St Albans WV U.S.A. 134 E4
St Alban's Head hd U.K. see St Aldhelm's Head
St Albert Canada 120 H4
St Aldhelm's Head hd U.K. 49 E8
St-Amand-les-Eaux France 52 D4
St-Amand-Montrond France 56 F3
St-Amour France 56 G3
St-André, Cap pt Madag. see Vilanandro, Tanjona
St Andrews U.K. 50 G4
St Andrew Sound inlet U.S.A. 133 D6
St Anne U.S.A. 134 B3
St Ann's Bay Jamaica 137 I5
St Anthony Canada 123 L4
St Anthony U.S.A. 126 F4
St-Arnaud Alg. see El Eulma
St Arnaud Australia 112 A6
St Arnaud Range mts N.Z. 113 D6
St-Arnoult-en-Yvelines France 52 B6
St-Augustin Canada 123 K4
St Augustin r. Canada 123 K4
St Augustine U.S.A. 133 D6
St Austell U.K. 49 C8
St-Avertin France 56 E3
St-Avold France 52 G5
St Barbe Canada 123 K4

▶ St-Barthélemy i. West Indies 137 L5
French Overseas Collectivity.

St Bees U.K. 48 D4
St Bees Head hd U.K. 48 D4
St Bride's Bay U.K. 49 B7
St-Brieuc France 56 C2
St Catharines Canada 134 F2
St Catherines Island U.S.A. 133 D6
St Catherine's Point U.K. 49 F8
St-Céré France 56 E4
St-Chamond France 56 G4
St Charles ID U.S.A. 126 F4
St Charles MD U.S.A. 135 G4
St Charles MI U.S.A. 134 C2
St Charles MO U.S.A. 130 F4
St-Chély-d'Apcher France 56 F4
St Christopher and Nevis country West Indies see St Kitts and Nevis
St Clair r. Canada/U.S.A. 134 D2
St Clair, Lake Canada/U.S.A. 134 D2
St-Claude France 56 G3
St Clears U.K. 49 C7
St Cloud U.S.A. 130 E2
St Croix r. U.S.A. 122 B5
St Croix Falls U.S.A. 130 E2
St David U.S.A. 129 H6
St David's Head hd U.K. 49 B7
St-Denis France 52 C6

▶ St-Denis Réunion 149 L7
Capital of Réunion.

St-Denis-du-Sig Alg. see Sig
St-Dié-des-Vosges France 56 H2
St-Dizier France 52 E6
St-Domingue country West Ind es see Haiti
Sainte Anne Canada 121 L5
Ste-Anne, Lac l. Canada 123 I4
St Elias, Cape U.S.A. 118 D4

▶ St Elias, Mount U.S.A. 120 A2
4th highest mountain in North America.

St Elias Mountains Canada 120 A2
Ste-Marguerite r. Canada 123 I4
Ste-Marie, Cap c. Madag. see Vohimena, Tanjona
Sainte-Marie, Île i. Madag. see Boraha, Nosy
Ste-Maxime France 56 H5
Sainte Rose du Lac Canada 121 L5
Saintes France 56 D4
Sainte Thérèse, Lac l. Canada 120 F1
St-Étienne France 56 G4
St-Étienne-du-Rouvray France 52 B5
St-Fabien Canada 123 H4
St-Félicien Canada 123 G4
Saintfield U.K. 51 G3
St-Florent Corsica France 56 I5
St-Florent-sur-Cher France 56 F3
St-Flour France 56 F4
St Francis U.S.A. 130 C4
St Francis r. U.S.A. 131 F5
St Francis Isles Australia 109 F8
St Francisville U.S.A. 131 F6
St-François r. Canada 123 G5
St-François, Lac l. Canada 123 H5
St-Gaudens France 56 E5
St George Australia 112 D2
St George r. Australia 110 D3
St George AK U.S.A. 118 B4
St George SC U.S.A. 133 D5
St George UT U.S.A. 129 G3
St George, Point U.S.A. 126 B4
St George Island U.S.A. 118 B4
St George Range hills Australia 108 D4
St-Georges Canada 123 H5

▶ St George's Grenada 137 L6
Capital of Grenada.

St George's Bay Nfld. and Lab. Canada 123 K4
St George's Bay N.S. Canada 123 J5
St George's Channel Ireland/U.K. 51 F6
St George's Channel P.N.G. 106 F2
St George's Head hd Australia 112 E5
St Gotthard Hungary see Szentgotthárd
St Gotthard Pass Switz. 56 I3
St Govan's Head hd U.K. 49 C7
St Helen U.S.A. 134 C1
St Helena i. S. Atlantic Ocean 148 H7
St Helena U.S.A. 128 B2

▶ St Helena, Ascension and Tristan da Cunha terr. S. Atlantic Ocean 148 H7
United Kingdom Overseas Territory.

St Helena Bay S. Africa 100 D7
St Helens Australia 111 [inset]
St Helens U.K. 48 E5
St Helens U.S.A. 126 C3
St Helens, Mount vol. U.S.A. 126 C3
St Helens Point Australia 111 [inset]

▶ St Helier Channel Is 49 E9
Capital of Jersey.

Sainthiya India 83 F5
St-Hubert Belgium 52 F4
St-Hyacinthe Canada 123 G5
St Ignace U.S.A. 132 C2
St Ignace Island Canada 122 D4
St Ishmael U.K. 49 C7
St Ives England U.K. 49 B8
St Ives England U.K. 49 G6
St-Jacques, Cap Vietnam see Vung Tau
St-Jacques-de-Dupuy Canada 122 F4
St James MN U.S.A. 130 E3
St James MO U.S.A. 130 F4
St James, Cape Canada 120 D5
St-Jean r. Canada 123 I4
St-Jean, Lac l. Canada 123 G4
St-Jean-d'Acre Israel see 'Akko
St-Jean-d'Angély France 56 D4
St-Jean-de-Monts France 56 C3
St-Jean-sur-Richelieu Canada 135 I1
St-Jérôme Canada 122 G5
St Joe r. U.S.A. 126 D3
Saint John Canada 123 I5
St John U.S.A. 130 D4
St John r. U.S.A. 132 H2
St John, Cape Canada 123 L4
St John Bay Canada 123 K4
St John Island Canada 123 K4

▶ St John's Antigua and Barbuda 137 L5
Capital of Antigua and Barbuda.

▶ St John's Canada 123 L5
Capital of Newfoundland and Labrador.

St Johns AZ U.S.A. 129 I4
St Johns MI U.S.A. 134 C2
St Johns OH U.S.A. 134 C3
St Johns r. U.S.A. 133 D6
St Johnsbury U.S.A. 135 I1
St John's Chapel U.K. 48 E4
St Joseph IL U.S.A. 134 A3
St Joseph LA U.S.A. 131 F6
St Joseph MI U.S.A. 134 B2
St Joseph MO U.S.A. 130 E4
St Joseph r. U.S.A. 134 C3
St Joseph, Lake Canada 121 N5
St-Joseph-d'Alma Canada see Alma
St Joseph Island Canada 122 E5
St-Junien France 56 E4
St Just U.K. 49 B8
St-Just-en-Chaussée France 52 C5
St Keverne U.K. 49 B8
St Kilda i. U.K. 40 E4
St Kilda is U.K. 46 C2
St Kitts and Nevis country West Indies 137 L5
St-Laurent inlet Canada see St Lawrence
St-Laurent, Golfe du g. Canada see St Lawrence, Gulf of
St-Laurent-du-Maroni Fr. Guiana 143 H2
St Lawrence Canada 123 L5
St Lawrence inlet Canada 123 H4
St Lawrence, Cape Canada 123 J5
St Lawrence, Gulf of Canada 123 J4
St Lawrence Island U.S.A. 118 B3
St Lawrence Islands National Park Canada 135 H1
St Lawrence Seaway sea chan. Canada/U.S.A. 135 H1
St-Léonard Canada 123 G5
St Leonard U.S.A. 135 G4
St Lewis r. Canada 123 K3
St-Lô France 56 D2
St-Louis Senegal 96 B3
St Louis MI U.S.A. 134 C2
St Louis MO U.S.A. 130 F4
St Louis r. U.S.A. 122 B5
St Lucia country West Indies 137 L6
St Lucia, Lake S. Africa 101 K5
St Lucia Estuary S. Africa 101 K5
St Luke's Island Myanmar see Zadetkale Kyun
St Magnus Bay U.K. 50 [inset]
St-Maixent-l'École France 56 D3
St-Malo France 56 C2
St-Malo, Golfe de g. France 56 C2
St-Marc Haiti 137 J5
St Maries U.S.A. 126 D3
St Marks S. Africa 101 H7
St Mark's S. Africa see Cofimvaba

▶ St-Martin i. West Indies 137 L5
French Overseas Collectivity. The southern part of the island is the Dutch territory of Sint Maarten.

▶ St Maarten terr. West Indies 137 L5
Self-governing Netherlands Territory. The northern part of the island is the French Overseas Collectivity of St-Martin.

St Martin, Cape S. Africa 100 C7
St Martin, Lake Canada 121 L5
St Martin's i. U.K. 49 A9
St Martin's Island Bangl. 70 A2
St Mary Peak Australia 111 B6
St Mary Reservoir Canada 120 H5
St Mary's Canada 134 E2
St Mary's U.K. 50 G2
St Mary's i. U.K. 49 A9
St Marys PA U.S.A. 135 F3
St Marys WV U.S.A. 134 E4
St Marys r. U.S.A. 134 C3
St Mary's, Cape Canada 123 L5
St Mary's Bay Canada 123 L5
St Marys City U.S.A. 135 G4
St Matthew Island U.S.A. 118 A3
St Matthews U.S.A. 134 C4
St Matthew's Island Myanmar see Zadetkyi Kyun
St Matthias Group is P.N.G. 69 L7
St-Maurice r. Canada 123 G5
St Mawes U.K. 49 B8
St-Médard-en-Jalles France 56 D4
St Meinrad U.S.A. 134 B4
St Michaels U.S.A. 135 G4
St Michael's Bay Canada 123 L3
St-Mihiel France 52 F6
St-Nazaire France 56 C3
St Neots U.K. 49 G6
St-Nicolas Belgium see Sint-Niklaas
St-Nicolas, Mont hill Lux. 52 G5
St-Nicolas-de-Port France 56 H2
St-Omer France 52 C4
Saintonge reg. France 56 D4
St-Pacôme Canada 123 H5
St-Palais France 56 D5
St Paris U.S.A. 134 D3
St-Pascal Canada 123 H5
St Paul r. Canada 123 K4
St-Paul atoll Fr. Polynesia see Hereheretue
St Paul AK U.S.A. 118 A4

▶ St Paul MN U.S.A. 130 E2
Capital of Minnesota.

St Paul NE U.S.A. 130 D3
St-Paul, Île i. Indian Ocean 149 N8
St Paul Island U.S.A. 118 A4
St Peter and St Paul Rocks is N. Atlantic Ocean see São Pedro e São Paulo

▶ St Peter Port Channel Is 49 E9
Capital of Guernsey.

St Peter's Canada 123 J5
St Peters Canada 123 J5
St Petersburg Russia 45 Q7
St Petersburg U.S.A. 133 D7
St-Pierre mt. France 56 G5

▶ St-Pierre St Pierre and Miquelon 123 L5
Capital of St Pierre and Miquelon.

▶ St Pierre and Miquelon terr. N. America 123 K5
French Territorial Collectivity.

St-Pierre-d'Oléron France 56 D4
St-Pierre-le-Moûtier France 56 F3
St-Pol-sur-Ternoise France 52 C4
St-Pourçain-sur-Sioule France 56 F3
St-Quentin France 52 D5
St Regis U.S.A. 126 E3
St Regis Falls U.S.A. 135 H1
St-Rémi Canada 135 I1
St-Saëns France 52 B5
St Sebastian Bay S. Africa 100 E8
St-Siméon Canada 123 H5
St Simons Island U.S.A. 133 D6
St Theresa Point Canada 121 M4
St Thomas Canada 134 E2
St-Trond Belgium see Sint-Truiden
St-Tropez France 56 H5
St-Tropez, Cap de c. France 56 H5
St-Vaast-la-Hougue France 49 F9
St-Valery-en-Caux France 49 H9
St-Véran France 56 H4
St Vincent U.S.A. 130 D1
St Vincent country West Indies see St Vincent and the Grenadines
St Vincent, Cape Australia 111 [inset]
St Vincent, Cape Port. see São Vicente, Cabo de
St Vincent, Gulf Australia 111 B7
St Vincent and the Grenadines country West Indies 137 L6
St Vincent Passage St Lucia/St Vincent 137 L6
St-Vith Belgium 52 G4
St Walburg Canada 121 I4
St Williams Canada 134 E2
St-Yrieix-la-Perche France 56 E4
Sain Us China 72 J4
Saioa mt. Spain 57 F2
Saipal mt. Nepal 82 E3
Saipan i. N. Mariana Is 69 L3
Saiteli Turkey see Kadınhanı
Saittanulkki hill Fin. 44 N3
Sai Yok National Park Thai. 71 B4
Sajam Indon. 69 I7
Sajama, Nevado mt. Bol. 142 E7
Sājir Saudi Arabia 88 B5
Sājūr, Nahr r. Syria/Turkey 85 D1
Sak watercourse S. Africa 100 E5
Sakaide Japan 75 D6
Sakākā Saudi Arabia 91 F5
Sakakawea, Lake U.S.A. 130 C2
Sakami Canada 122 G3
Sakami r. Canada 122 F3
Sakami Lake Canada 122 F3
Sakar mts Bulg. 59 L4
Sakaraha Madag. 99 E6
Sak'art'velo country Asia see Georgia
Sakarya Turkey see Adapazarı
Sakarya r. Turkey 59 N4
Sakassou Côte d'Ivoire 96 C4
Sakata Japan 75 E5
Sakchu N. Korea 75 B4
Sakesar Pak. 89 I3
Sakhalin i. Russia 74 F2
Sakhalin Oblast admin. div. Russia see Sakhalinskaya Oblast'
Sakhalinskaya Oblast' admin. div. Russia 74 F2
Sakhalinskiy Zaliv b. Russia 74 F1
Sakhi India 82 C3
Sakhile S. Africa 101 I4
Şäki Azer. 91 G2
Saki Crimea see Saky
Saki Nigeria 96 D4
Šakiai Lith. 45 M9
Sakir mt. Pak. 89 G4
Sakishima-shotō is Japan 73 M8
Sakoli India 82 D5
Sakon Nakhon Thai. 70 D3
Sakrivier S. Africa 100 E6
Sakura Japan 75 F6
Saky Crimea 90 D1
Säkylä Fin. 45 M6
Säkzä'ī Afgh. 89 F3
Sal i. Cape Verde 96 [inset]
Sal r. Russia 43 I7
Sala Sweden 45 J7
Salaberry-de-Valleyfield Canada 135 H1
Salacgrīva Latvia 45 N8
Sala Consilina Italy 58 F4
Salada, Laguna salt l. Mex. 129 F5
Saladas Arg. 144 E3
Salado r. Buenos Aires Arg. 144 E5
Salado r. Santa Fe Arg. 144 D4
Salado r. Arg. 144 C5
Salado r. Mex. 131 D7
Salaga Ghana 96 C4
Salairskiy Kryazh ridge Russia 72 E2
Salajwe Botswana 100 G2
Şalālah Oman 87 H6
Salamanca Mex. 136 D4
Salamanca Spain 57 D3
Salamanca U.S.A. 135 F2
Salamanga Moz. 101 K4
Salamantica Spain see Salamanca
Salamat, Bahr r. Chad 97 E4
Salāmī Iran 89 E3
Salamina i. Greece 59 J6
Salamis tourist site Cyprus 85 A2
Salamis i. Greece see Salamina
Salamīyah Syria 85 C2
Salamonie r. U.S.A. 134 C3
Salamonie Lake U.S.A. 134 C3
Salang, Tōnal-e Afgh. 89 H3
Salantai Lith. 45 L8
Salar de Pocitos Arg. 144 C2
Salari Pak. 89 G5
Salas Spain 57 C2
Salaspils Latvia 45 N8
Salavan Laos 70 D4
Salawati i. Indon. 69 I7
Salawin, Mae Nam r. China/Myanmar see Salween
Salaya India 82 B5
Sala y Gómez, Isla i. S. Pacific Ocean 151 M7
Salazar Angola see N'dalatando
Salbris France 56 F3
Šalčininkai Lith. 45 N9
Salcombe U.K. 49 D8
Saldae Alg. see Bejaïa
Saldaña Spain 57 D2
Saldanha S. Africa 100 C7
Saldanha Bay S. Africa 100 C7
Saldus Latvia 45 M8
Sale Australia 112 C7
Saleh, Teluk b. Indon. 68 F8
Şāleḩābād Iran 88 C3
Salekhard Russia 64 H3
Salem India 84 C4
Salem AR U.S.A. 131 F4
Salem IL U.S.A. 130 F4
Salem IN U.S.A. 134 B4
Salem MA U.S.A. 135 J2
Salem MO U.S.A. 130 F4
Salem NJ U.S.A. 135 H4
Salem NY U.S.A. 135 I2
Salem OH U.S.A. 134 E3

▶ Salem OR U.S.A. 126 C3
Capital of Oregon.

Salem SD U.S.A. 130 D3
Salem VA U.S.A. 134 E5
Salen Scotland U.K. 50 D4
Salen Scotland U.K. 50 D4
Salerno Italy 58 F4
Salerno, Golfo di g. Italy 58 F4
Salernum Italy see Salerno
Salford U.K. 48 E5
Salgótarján Hungary 47 Q6
Salgueiro Brazil 143 K5
Salibabu i. Indon. 69 H6
Salida U.S.A. 127 G5
Salies-de-Béarn France 56 D5
Şalīḩān Afgh. 89 F4
Salihli Turkey 59 M5
Salihorsk Belarus 45 O10
Salima Malawi 99 D5
Salina KS U.S.A. 130 D4
Salina UT U.S.A. 129 H2
Salina, Isola i. Italy 58 F5
Salina Cruz Mex. 136 E5
Salinas Brazil 145 C2
Salinas Ecuador 142 B4
Salinas Mex. 136 D4
Salinas r. Mex. 131 D7
Salinas U.S.A. 128 C3
Salinas r. U.S.A. 128 C3
Salinas, Cabo de c. Spain see Salines, Cap de ses
Salinas, Ponta das pt Angola 99 B5
Salinas Peak U.S.A. 127 G6
Saline U.S.A. 134 D2
Saline r. U.S.A. 130 D4
Salines, Cap de ses c. Spain 57 H4
Saline Valley depr. U.S.A. 128 E3
Salinópolis Brazil 143 I4
Salinosó Lachay, Punta pt Peru 142 C6
Salisbury U.K. 49 F7
Salisbury MD U.S.A. 135 H4
Salisbury NC U.S.A. 132 D5
Salisbury Zimbabwe see Harare
Salisbury Plain U.K. 49 E7
Şalkhad Syria 85 C3
Salla Fin. 44 P3
Sallisaw U.S.A. 131 E5
Salluit Canada 153 K2
Sallum, Khalīj as b. Egypt 90 B5
Sallyana Nepal 83 E3
Salmās Iran 88 B2
Salmi Russia 42 F3
Salmo Canada 120 G5
Salmon U.S.A. 126 E3
Salmon r. U.S.A. 126 D3
Salmon Arm Canada 120 G5
Salmon Falls Creek r. U.S.A. 126 E4
Salmon Gums Australia 109 C8
Salmon Reservoir U.S.A. 135 H2
Salmon River Mountains U.S.A. 126 E3
Salmtal Germany 52 G5
Salo Fin. 45 M6
Salome U.S.A. 129 G5
Salon India 82 E4
Salon-de-Provence France 56 G5
Salonga Nord, Parc National de la nat. park Dem. Rep. Congo 98 C4
Salonica Greece see Thessaloniki
Salonika Greece see Thessaloniki
Saloum Delta tourist site Senegal 96 B3
Salpausselkä reg. Fin. 45 N6
Salqīn Syria 85 C1
Salses, Étang de l. France see Leucate, Étang de
Sal'sk Russia 43 I7
Salsomaggiore Terme Italy 58 C2
Salt Jordan see As Salṭ
Salt watercourse S. Africa 100 F7
Salt r. U.S.A. 129 G5
Salta Arg. 144 C2
Saltaire U.K. 48 F5
Saltash U.K. 49 C8
Saltcoats U.K. 50 E5
Saltee Islands Ireland 51 F5
Saltfjellet-Svartisen Nasjonalpark nat. park Norway 44 I3
Saltfjorden sea chan. Norway 44 H3
Salt Fork Arkansas r. U.S.A. 131 D4
Salt Fork Lake U.S.A. 134 E3
Saltillo Mex. 131 C7
Salt Lake India 89 I5

▶ Salt Lake City U.S.A. 129 H1
Capital of Utah.

Salt Lick U.S.A. 134 D4
Salto Brazil 145 B3
Salto Uruguay 144 E4
Salto da Divisa Brazil 145 D2
Salto Grande Brazil 145 A3
Salton Sea salt l. U.S.A. 129 F5
Salto Santiago, Represa de resr Brazil 144 F3
Salt Range hills Pak. 89 I3
Salt River Canada 121 H2
Saluda U.S.A. 135 G5
Sālūk, Kūh-e mt. Iran 88 E2
Salûm Egypt see As Sallūm
Salûm, Khalîg el b. Egypt see Sallum, Khalīj as
Salur India 84 D2
Saluzzo Italy 58 B2
Salvador Brazil 145 D1
Salvador country Central America see El Salvador
Salvador, Lake U.S.A. 131 F6
Salvaleón de Higüey Dom. Rep. see Higüey
Salvation Creek r. U.S.A. 129 H2
Salwah Saudi Arabia 98 F1
Salwah, Dawḩat b. Qatar/Saudi Arabia 88 C5
Salween r. China/Myanmar 76 C5
also known as Mae Nam Khong or Mae Nam Salawin or Nu Jiang (China) or Thanlwin (Myanmar)
Salyan Azer. 91 H3
Salyan Nepal see Sallyana
Sal'yany Azer. see Salyan
Salyersville U.S.A. 134 D5
Salzbrunn Namibia 100 C3
Salzburg Austria 47 N7
Salzgitter Germany 53 K2
Salzhausen Germany 53 K1
Salzkotten Germany 53 I3
Salzmünde Germany 53 L3
Salzwedel Germany 53 L2
Sam India 82 B4
Samae San, Ko i. Thai. 71 C4
Samagaltay Russia 80 H1
Samāh well Saudi Arabia 88 B4
Samaida Iran see Someydeh
Samaixung China 83 E2
Samakhixai Laos see Attapu
Samalanga Indon. 71 B6
Samalayuca Mex. 127 G7
Samalkot India 84 D2
Samālūṭ Egypt 90 C5
Samâlûţ Egypt see Samālūṭ
Samana Cay i. Bahamas 133 F8
Samanala mt. Sri Lanka see Adam's Peak
Samandağı Turkey 85 B1
Samangān Afgh. see Aībak
Samangān Iran 89 F3
Samani Japan 74 F4
Samanlı Dağları mts Turkey 59 M4
Samar Kazakh. see Samarskoye
Samar i. Phil. 69 H4
Samara Russia 43 K5
Samara r. Russia 41 Q5
Samarga Russia 74 E3
Samarinda Indon. 68 F7
Samarka Russia 74 D3
Samarkand Uzbek. see Samarqand
Samarkand, Pik mt. Tajik. see Samarqand, Qullai
Samarobriva France see Amiens
Samarqand Uzbek. 89 G2
Samarqand, Qullai mt. Tajik. 89 H2
Sāmarrā' Iraq 91 F4
Samarskoye Kazakh. 80 F2
Samasata Pak. 89 H4
Samastipur India 83 F4
Şamaxı Azer. 91 H2
Samba India 82 C2
Sambaliung mts Indon. 68 F6
Sambalpur India 83 E5
Sambar, Tanjung pt Indon. 68 E7
Sambas Indon. 71 E7
Sambat Ukr. see Kiev
Sambava Madag. 99 F5
Sambha India 83 G4
Sambhajinagar India see Aurangabad
Sambhal India 82 D3
Sambhar Lake India 82 C4
Sambir Ukr. 43 D6
Sambito r. Brazil 143 J5
Sâmbor Cambodia 71 D4
Sambor Ukr. see Sambir
Samborombón, Bahía b. Arg. 144 E5
Sambre r. Belgium/France 52 E4
Sambre à l'Oise, Canal de la France 52 D5
Samcheok S. Korea 75 C5
Samch'ŏnp'o S. Korea see Sacheon
Same Tanz. 98 D4
Samer France 52 B4
Sami India 82 B5
Samīrah Saudi Arabia 86 F4
Samīrum Iran see Īzad Khvāst

Samjiyŏn N. Korea 74 C4
Şämkir Azer. 91 G2
Sam Neua Laos see Xam Nua
Samoa country S. Pacific Ocean 107 I3
Samoa Basin sea feature S. Pacific Ocean 150 I7
Samoa i Sisifo country S. Pacific Ocean see Samoa
Samobor Croatia 58 F2
Samoded Russia 42 I3
Samokov Bulg. 59 J3
Šamorín Slovakia 47 P6
Samos i. Greece 59 L6
Samosir i. Indon. 71 B7
Samothrace i. Greece see Samothraki
Samothraki i. Greece 59 K4
Samoylovka Russia 43 I6
Sampit Indon. 68 E7
Sampit, Teluk b. Indon. 68 E7
Sâmraông Cambodia 71 C4
Sam Rayburn Reservoir U.S.A. 131 E6
Samrong Cambodia see Sâmraông
Samsang China 83 E3
Sam Sao, Phou mts Laos/Vietnam 70 C2
Samson U.S.A. 133 C6
Sâm Sơn Vietnam 70 D3
Samsun Turkey 90 E2
Samtī Afgh. 89 H2
Samuel, Represa de resr Brazil 142 F5
Samui, Ko i. Thai. 71 C5
Samut Prakan Thai. 71 C4
Samut Sakhon Thai. 71 C4
Samut Songkhram Thai. 71 C4
Samyai China 83 G3
San Mali 96 C3
San, Phou mt. Laos 70 C3
San, Tônlé r. Cambodia 71 D4

▶Şan'ā' Yemen 86 F6
Capital of Yemen.

Sanaa Yemen see Şan'ā'
SANAE IV research station Antarctica 152 B2
San Agostín U.S.A. see St Augustine
San Agustín, Cape Phil. 69 H5
San Agustin, Plains of U.S.A. 129 I5
San Agustín de Valle Fértil Arg. 144 C4
Sanak Island U.S.A. 118 B4
Sanandaj Iran 88 B3
San Andreas U.S.A. 128 C2
San Andrés, Isla de i. Caribbean Sea 137 H6
San Andres Mountains U.S.A. 127 G6
San Angelo U.S.A. 131 C6
San Antonio Chile 144 B4
San Antonio NM U.S.A. 127 G6
San Antonio TX U.S.A. 131 D6
San Antonio r. U.S.A. 131 D6
San Antonio, Cabo c. Cuba 137 H4
San Antonio del Mar Mex. 127 D7
San Antonio Oeste Arg. 144 D6
San Antonio Reservoir U.S.A. 128 C4
San Augustine U.S.A. 131 E6
San Benedetto del Tronto Italy 58 E3
San Benedicto, Isla i. Mex. 136 B5
San Benito U.S.A. 131 D7
San Benito r. U.S.A. 128 C3
San Benito Mountain U.S.A. 128 C3
San Bernardino U.S.A. 128 E4
San Bernardino Mountains U.S.A. 128 E4
San Bernardo Chile 144 B4
San Blas Mex. 127 F8
San Blas, Cape U.S.A. 133 C6
San Borja Bol. 142 E6
Sanbornville U.S.A. 135 J2
Sanbu China see Kaiping
San Buenaventura Mex. 131 C7
San Carlos Chile 144 B5
San Carlos Equat. Guinea see Luba
San Carlos Coahuila Mex. 131 C6
San Carlos Tamaulipas Mex. 131 D7
San Carlos U.S.A. 129 H5
San Carlos Venez. 142 E2
San Carlos de Bariloche Arg. 144 B6
San Carlos de Bolívar Arg. 144 D5
San Carlos Lake U.S.A. 129 H5
Sancha China 76 E1
Sanchahe China see Fuyu
Sancha He r. China 76 E3
Sanchakou China 80 I4
Sanchi India 82 D5
San Chien Pau mt. Laos 70 C2
Sanchor India 82 B4
San Clemente U.S.A. 128 E5
San Clemente Island U.S.A. 128 D5
Sanclêr U.K. see St Clears
San Cristóbal Arg. 144 D4
San Cristobal i. Solomon Is see Makira
San Cristóbal Venez. 142 D2
San Cristóbal, Isla i. Galápagos Ecuador 142 [inset]
San Cristóbal de las Casas Mex. 136 F5
Sancti Spíritus Cuba 137 I4
Sandagou Russia 74 D4
Sanda Island U.K. 50 D5
Sandakan Sabah Malaysia 68 F5
Sândăn Cambodia 71 D4
Sandane Norway 44 E6
Sandanski Bulg. 59 J4
Sandaré Mali 96 B3
Sandau (Elbe) Germany 53 M2
Sanday i. U.K. 50 G1
Sandbach U.K. 49 E5
Sandborn U.S.A. 134 B4
Sand Cay reef India 84 B4
Sandefjord Norway 45 G7
Sandercock Nunataks Antarctica 152 D2
Sanders U.S.A. 129 I4
Sandersleben Germany 53 L3
Sanderson U.S.A. 131 C6
Sandfire Australia 108 C4
Sand Fork U.S.A. 134 E4
Sandgate Australia 112 F1
Sandhead U.K. 50 E6
Sand Hill r. U.S.A. 130 D2
Sand Hills U.S.A. 130 C3
Sandia Peru 142 E6
San Diego Mex. 131 B6
San Diego CA U.S.A. 128 E5
San Diego TX U.S.A. 131 D7
San Diego, Sierra mts Mex. 127 F7
Sandıklı Turkey 59 N5
Sandila India 82 E4
Sand Lake Canada 122 D5
Sand Lake l. Canada 121 M5
Sandnes Norway 45 D7
Sandnessjøen Norway 44 H3
Sandoa Dem. Rep. Congo 99 C4
Sandomierz Poland 43 D6
San Donà di Piave Italy 58 E2
Sandover watercourse Australia 110 B4
Sandovo Russia 42 H4
Sandoway Myanmar see Thandwe
Sandown U.K. 49 F8
Sandoy i. Faroe Is 44 [inset 2]
Sand Point U.S.A. 118 B4
Sandpoint U.S.A. 126 D2
Sandray i. U.K. 50 B4
Sandringham Australia 110 B5
Şandrul Mare, Vârful mt. Romania 59 L1
Sandsjö Sweden 45 I6
Sandspit Canada 120 D4
Sand Springs U.S.A. 131 D4
Sand Springs Salt Flat U.S.A. 128 D2
Sandstone Australia 109 B6
Sandstone U.S.A. 130 E2
Sandu Guizhou China 76 E3
Sandu Hunan China 77 G3
Sandur Faroe Is 44 [inset 2]
Sandusky MI U.S.A. 134 D2
Sandusky OH U.S.A. 134 D3
Sandveld mts S. Africa 100 D6
Sandverhaar Namibia 100 C4
Sandvika Akershus Norway 45 G7
Sandvika Nord-Trøndelag Norway 44 H5
Sandviken Sweden 45 J6
Sandwich Bay Canada 123 K3
Sandwich Island Vanuatu see Éfaté
Sandwich Islands is N. Pacific Ocean see Hawai'ian Islands
Sandwick U.K. 50 [inset]
Sandwip Bangl. 83 G5
Sandy U.S.A. 129 H1
Sandy r. U.S.A. 135 K1
Sandy Bay Canada 121 K4
Sandy Cape Qld Australia 110 F5
Sandy Cape Tas. Australia 111 [inset]
Sandy Hook U.S.A. 134 D4
Sandy Hook pt U.S.A. 135 H3
Sandy Island Australia 108 C3
Sandykachi Turkm. see Sandykgaçy
Sandykgaçy Turkm. 89 F2
Sandykly Gumy des. Turkm. 89 F2
Sandy Lake Alta Canada 120 H4
Sandy Lake Ont. Canada 121 M4
Sandy Lake l. Canada 121 M4
Sandy Springs U.S.A. 133 C5
San Estanislao Para. 144 E2
San Esteban, Isla i. Mex. 127 E7
San Felipe Chile 144 B4
San Felipe Baja California Mex. 127 E7
San Felipe Chihuahua Mex. 127 G8
San Felipe Venez. 142 E1
San Felipe, Cayos de is Cuba 133 D8
San Felipe de Puerto Plata Dom. Rep. see Puerto Plata
San Fernando Chile 144 B4
San Fernando Mex. 131 D7
San Fernando watercourse Mex. 127 E7
San Fernando Phil. 69 G3
San Fernando Spain 57 C5
San Fernando Trin. and Tob. 137 L6
San Fernando U.S.A. 128 D4
San Fernando de Apure Venez. 142 E2
San Fernando de Atabapo Venez. 142 E3
San Fernando de Monte Cristi Dom. Rep. see Monte Cristi
Sanford FL U.S.A. 133 D6
Sanford ME U.S.A. 135 J2
Sanford MI U.S.A. 134 C2
Sanford NC U.S.A. 132 E5
Sanford, Mount U.S.A. 118 D3
Sanford Lake U.S.A. 134 C2
San Francisco Arg. 144 D4
San Francisco U.S.A. 128 B3
San Francisco, Cabo de c. Ecuador 142 B3
San Francisco, Passo de pass Arg./Chile 144 C3
San Francisco Bay inlet U.S.A. 128 B3
San Francisco del Oro Mex. 131 B7
San Francisco de Paula, Cabo c. Arg. 144 C7
Sang, Loi mt. Myanmar 70 B2
San Gabriel, Punta pt Mex. 127 E7
San Gabriel Mountains U.S.A. 128 D4
Sangachaly Azer. see Sanqaçal
Sangameshwar India 84 B2
Sangamon r. U.S.A. 130 F3
Sangān, Kōh-e mt. Afgh. 89 G3
Sangan, Koh-i- mt. Afgh. see Sangān, Kōh-e
Sangar Russia 65 N3
Sangareddi India see Sangareddy
Sangareddy India 84 C2
San Gavino Monreale Sardinia Italy 58 C5
Sangay, Parque Nacional nat. park Ecuador 142 C4
Sang Bar Afgh. 89 F3
Sangdankangsang Feng mt. China 83 G3
Sangeang i. Indon. 108 B2
Sanger U.S.A. 128 D3
Sangerfield U.S.A. 135 H2
Sangerhausen Germany 53 L3
Sang-e Surakh Iran 88 E2
Sanggarmai China 76 D1
Sanggau Indon. 68 E6
San Giovanni in Fiore Italy 58 G5
Sangir India 82 C5
Sangir i. Indon. 69 H6
Sangir, Kepulauan is Indon. 69 G6
Sangkapura Indon. 68 E8
Sangkulirang Indon. 68 F6
Sangli India 84 B2
Sangmai China see Dêrong
Sangmélima Cameroon 96 E4
Sangngagqoiling China 76 B2
Sango Zimbabwe 99 D6
Sangole India 84 B2
San Gorgonio Mountain U.S.A. 128 E4
Sangre de Cristo Range mts U.S.A. 127 G5
Sangrur India 82 C3
Sangu r. Bangl. 83 G5
Sanguem India 84 B3
Sangutane r. Moz. 101 K3
Sangzhi China 77 F2
Sanhe China see Sandu
San Hipólito, Punta pt Mex. 127 E8
Sanhūr Egypt 90 C5
Sanhûr Egypt see Sanhūr
San Ignacio Beni Bol. 142 E6
San Ignacio Santa Cruz Bol. 142 F7
San Ignacio Santa Cruz Bol. 142 F7
San Ignacio Baja California Mex. 127 E7
San Ignacio Durango Mex. 131 C7
San Ignacio Sonora Mex. 127 F7
San Ignacio Para. 144 E3
San Ignacio, Laguna l. Mex. 127 E8
Sanikiluaq Canada 122 F2
Sanin-kaigan Kokuritsu-kōen nat. park Japan 75 D6
San Jacinto U.S.A. 128 E5
San Jacinto Peak U.S.A. 128 E5
San Javier Bol. 142 F7
Sanjiang Guangdong China see Liannan
Sanjiang Guangxi China 77 F3
Sanjiang Guizhou China see Jinping
Sanjiangkou China 74 A4
Sanjiaocheng China see Haiyan
Sanjiaoping China 77 F2
Sanjō Japan 75 E5
San Joaquin r. U.S.A. 128 C2
San Joaquin Valley U.S.A. 128 C3
Sanjoli India 82 C5
San Jon U.S.A. 131 C5
San Jorge, Golfo de g. Arg. 144 C7
San Jorge, Golfo de g. Spain see Sant Jordi, Golf de

▶San José Costa Rica 137 H7
Capital of Costa Rica.

San Jose Phil. 69 G3
San Jose CA U.S.A. 128 C3
San Jose NM U.S.A. 127 G6
San Jose watercourse U.S.A. 129 J4
San José, Isla i. Mex. 136 B4
San José de Amacuro Venez. 142 F2
San José de Bavicora Mex. 127 G7
San Jose de Buenavista Phil. 69 G4
San José de Chiquitos Bol. 142 F7
San José de Comondú Mex. 127 F8
San José de Gracia Mex. 127 E8
San José de la Brecha Mex. 127 F8
San José de las Lajas Cuba 133 D8
San José del Cabo Mex. 136 C4
San José del Guaviare Col. 142 D3
San José de Mayo Uruguay 144 E4
San José de Raíces Mex. 131 C7
San Juan Arg. 144 C4
San Juan r. Costa Rica/Nicaragua 137 H6
San Juan mt. Cuba 133 D8
San Juan Mex. 127 G8
San Juan r. Mex. 131 D7

▶San Juan Puerto Rico 137 K5
Capital of Puerto Rico.

San Juan U.S.A. 129 J5
San Juan r. U.S.A. 129 H3
San Juan, Cabo c. Arg. 144 D8
San Juan, Cabo c. Equat. Guinea 96 D4
San Juan Bautista Para. 144 E3
San Juan Bautista de las Misiones Para. see San Juan Bautista
San Juan de Guadalupe Mex. 131 C7
San Juan de los Morros Venez. 142 E2
San Juan Mountains U.S.A. 129 J3
San Juan y Martínez Cuba 133 D8
San Justo Arg. 144 D4
Sankari Drug India 84 C4
Sankh r. India 81 F7
Sankhu India 82 C3
Sankra Chhattisgarh India 84 D1
Sankra Rajasthan India 82 B4
Sankt Augustin Germany 53 H4
Sankt Gallen Switz. 56 I3
Sankt-Peterburg Russia see St Petersburg
Sankt Pölten Austria 47 O6
Sankt Veit an der Glan Austria 47 O7
Sankt Vith Belgium see St-Vith
Sankt Wendel Germany 53 H5
Sanku India 82 D2
Şanlıurfa Turkey 90 E3
Şanlıurfa prov. Turkey 85 D1
San Lorenzo Arg. 144 D4
San Lorenzo Beni Bol. 142 E7
San Lorenzo Tarija Bol. 142 F8
San Lorenzo Ecuador 142 C3
San Lorenzo mt. Spain 57 E2
San Lorenzo, Isla i. Mex. 127 E7
San Lorenzo, Monte mt. Arg./Chile 144 B7
Sanlúcar de Barrameda Spain 57 C5
San Lucas Mex. 127 E8
San Lucas, Serranía de mts Col. 142 D2
San Luis Arg. 144 C4
San Luis AZ U.S.A. 129 F5
San Luis AZ U.S.A. 129 H5
San Luis CO U.S.A. 131 B4
San Luis, Isla i. Mex. 127 E7
San Luisito Mex. 127 E7
San Luis Obispo U.S.A. 128 C4
San Luis Obispo Bay U.S.A. 128 C4
San Luis Potosí Mex. 136 D4
San Luis Reservoir U.S.A. 128 C3
San Luis Río Colorado Mex. 129 F5
San Manuel U.S.A. 129 H5
San Marcial, Punta pt Mex. 127 F8
San Marcos U.S.A. 131 D6
San Marcos, Isla i. Mex. 127 E8
San Marino country Europe 58 E3

▶San Marino San Marino 58 E3
Capital of San Marino.

San Martín research station Antarctica 152 L2
San Martín Catamarca Arg. 144 C3
San Martín Mendoza Arg. 144 C4
San Martín, Lago l. Arg./Chile 144 B7
San Martín de los Andes Arg. 144 B6
San Mateo U.S.A. 128 B3
San Mateo Mountains U.S.A. 129 J4
San Matías Bol. 143 G7
San Matías, Golfo g. Arg. 144 D6
Sanmen China 77 I2
Sanmen Wan b. China 77 I2
Sanmenxia China 77 F1
San Miguel El Salvador 136 G6
San Miguel U.S.A. 128 C4
San Miguel r. U.S.A. 129 I2
San Miguel de Huachi Bol. 142 E7
San Miguel de Tucumán Arg. 144 C3
San Miguel Island U.S.A. 128 C4
Sanming China 77 H3
Sanndraigh i. U.K. see Sandray
Sannicandro Garganico Italy 58 F4
San Nicolás Durango Mex. 131 B7
San Nicolás Tamaulipas Mex. 131 D7
San Nicolas Island U.S.A. 128 D5
Sannieshof S. Africa 101 G4
Sanniquellie Liberia 96 C4
Sanok Poland 43 D6
San Pablo Bol. 142 E8
San Pablo Phil. 69 G4
San Pablo de Manta Ecuador see Manta
San Pedro Arg. 144 D2
San Pedro Bol. 142 F7
San Pedro Chile 144 C2
San-Pédro Côte d'Ivoire 96 C4
San Pedro Baja California Sur Mex. 124 E7
San Pedro Chihuahua Mex. 127 G7
San Pedro Para. see San Pedro de Ycuamandyyú
San Pedro watercourse U.S.A. 129 H5
San Pedro, Sierra de mts Spain 57 C4
San Pedro Channel U.S.A. 128 D5
San Pedro de Arimena Col. 142 D3
San Pedro de Atacama Chile 144 C2
San Pedro de las Colonias Mex. 131 C7
San Pedro de Macorís Dom. Rep. 137 K5
San Pedro de Ycuamandyyú Para. 144 E2
San Pedro Martir, Parque Nacional nat. park Mex. 127 E7
San Pedro Sula Hond. 136 G5
San Pierre U.S.A. 134 B3
San Pietro, Isola di i. Sardinia Italy 58 C5
San Pitch r. U.S.A. 129 H2
Sanqaçal Azer. 91 H2
Sanquhar U.K. 50 F5
Sanquianga, Parque Nacional nat. park Col. 142 C3
San Quintín, Cabo c. Mex. 127 D7
San Rafael Arg. 144 C4
San Rafael CA U.S.A. 128 B3
San Rafael NM U.S.A. 129 J4
San Rafael r. U.S.A. 129 H2
San Rafael Knob mt. U.S.A. 129 H2
San Rafael Mountains U.S.A. 128 C4
San Ramón Bol. 142 F6
Sanrao China 77 H3
Sanremo Italy 58 B3
San Roque Spain 57 B2
San Roque, Punta pt Mex. 127 E8
San Saba U.S.A. 131 D6
San Salvador i. Bahamas 133 F7

▶San Salvador El Salvador 136 G6
Capital of El Salvador.

San Salvador de Jujuy Arg. 144 C2
Sansanné-Mango Togo 96 D3
San Sebastián Arg. 144 C8
San Sebastián Spain 57 F2
San Sebastián de los Reyes Spain 57 E3
Sansepolcro Italy 58 E3
San Severo Italy 58 F4
San Simon U.S.A. 129 I5
Sanski Most Bos.-Herz. 58 G2
Sansoral Islands Palau see Sonsorol Islands
Sansui China 77 F3
Santa r. Peru 142 C5
Santa Ana Bol. 142 E7
Santa Ana El Salvador 136 G6
Santa Ana Mex. 127 F7
Santa Ana i. Solomon Is 107 G3
Santa Ana U.S.A. 128 E5
Santa Ana de Yacuma Bol. 142 E6
Santa Anna U.S.A. 131 D6
Santa Bárbara Brazil 145 C2
Santa Bárbara Cuba see La Demajagua
Santa Bárbara Mex. 131 B7
Santa Barbara U.S.A. 128 D4
Santa Bárbara, Ilha i. Brazil 145 D2
Santa Barbara Channel U.S.A. 128 C4
Santa Bárbara d'Oeste Brazil 145 B3
Santa Barbara Island U.S.A. 128 D5
Santa Catalina, Gulf of U.S.A. 128 E5
Santa Catalina, Isla i. Mex. 127 F8
Santa Catalina de Armada Spain 57 B2
Santa Catalina Island U.S.A. 128 D5
Santa Catarina state Brazil 145 A4
Santa Catarina Baja California Mex. 127 E7
Santa Catarina Nuevo León Mex. 131 C7
Santa Catarina, Ilha de i. Brazil 145 A4
Santa Clara Col. 142 E4
Santa Clara Cuba 137 I4
Santa Clara Mex. 131 B6
Santa Clara CA U.S.A. 128 C3
Santa Clara NM U.S.A. 129 I5
Santa Clara UT U.S.A. 129 G3
Santa Clarita U.S.A. 128 D4
Santa Clotilde Peru 142 D4
Santa Comba Angola see Waku-Kungo
Santa Croce, Capo c. Sicily Italy 58 F6
Santa Cruz Bol. 142 F7
Santa Cruz Brazil 143 K5
Santa Cruz Costa Rica 142 A1
Santa Cruz U.S.A. 128 B3
Santa Cruz watercourse U.S.A. 129 G5
Santa Cruz, Isla i. Galápagos Ecuador 142 [inset]
Santa Cruz, Isla i. Mex. 127 F8
Santa Cruz Cabrália Brazil 145 D2
Santa Cruz de Goiás Brazil 145 A2
Santa Cruz de la Palma Canary Is 96 B2
Santa Cruz del Sur Cuba 137 I4
Santa Cruz de Moya Spain 57 F4

▶Santa Cruz de Tenerife Canary Is 96 B2
Joint capital of the Canary Islands.

Santa Cruz do Sul Brazil 144 F3
Santa Cruz Island U.S.A. 128 D4
Santa Cruz Islands Solomon Is 107 G3
Santa Elena, Bahía de b. Ecuador 142 B4
Santa Elena, Cabo c. Costa Rica 137 G6
Santa Elena, Punta pt Ecuador 142 B4
Santa Eudóxia Brazil 145 B3
Santa Eufemia, Golfo di g. Italy 58 G5
Santa Fe Arg. 144 D4
Santa Fe Cuba 133 D8

▶Santa Fe U.S.A. 127 G6
Capital of New Mexico.

Santa Fé de Bogotá Col. see Bogotá
Santa Fé de Minas Brazil 145 B2
Santa Fé do Sul Brazil 145 A3
Santa Helena Brazil 143 I4
Santa Helena de Goiás Brazil 145 A2
Santai Sichuan China 76 E2
Santai Yunnan China 76 D3
Santa Inês Brazil 143 I4
Santa Inés, Isla i. Chile 152 L3
Santa Isabel Arg. 144 C5
Santa Isabel Equat. Guinea see Malabo
Santa Isabel i. Solomon Is 107 F2
Santa Juliana Brazil 145 B2
Santalpur India 82 B5
Santa Lucia Range mts U.S.A. 128 C3
Santa Margarita U.S.A. 128 C4
Santa Margarita, Isla i. Mex. 136 B4
Santa María Arg. 144 C3
Santa Maria Amazonas Brazil 143 G4
Santa Maria Distrito Federal Brazil 145 A1
Santa Maria Rio Grande do Sul Brazil 144 F3
Santa Maria Cape Verde 96 [inset]
Santa María r. Mex. 127 G7
Santa María Peru 142 D4
Santa Maria U.S.A. 128 C4
Santa Maria r. U.S.A. 129 G4
Santa Maria, Cabo de c. Moz. 101 K4
Santa Maria, Cabo de c. Port. 57 C5
Santa Maria, Chapadão de hills Brazil 145 B1
Santa Maria, Serra de hills Brazil 145 B1
Santa Maria da Vitória Brazil 145 B1
Santa María de Cuevas Mex. 131 B7
Santa Maria do Suaçuí Brazil 145 C2
Santa Maria Island Vanuatu 107 G3
Santa Maria Madalena Brazil 145 C3
Santa Maria Mountains U.S.A. 129 G4
Santa Marta Col. 142 D1
Santa Marta, Cabo de c. Angola 99 B5
Santa Marta Grande, Cabo de c. Brazil 145 A5
Santa Maura i. Greece see Lefkada
Santa Monica U.S.A. 128 D4
Santa Monica, Pico mt. Mex. 127 E8
Santa Monica Bay U.S.A. 128 D5
Santan Indon. 68 F7
Santana Brazil 145 C1
Santana r. Brazil 145 A2
Santana do Araguaia Brazil 143 H5
Santander Spain 57 E2
Santa Nella U.S.A. 128 C3
Santanilla, Islas is Caribbean Sea see Cisne, Islas del
Santan Mountain hill U.S.A. 129 H5
Sant'Antioco Sardinia Italy 58 C5
Sant'Antioco, Isola di i. Sardinia Italy 58 C5
Sant Antoni de Portmany Spain 57 G4
Santapilly India 84 D2
Santaquin U.S.A. 129 H2
Santa Quitéria Brazil 143 J4
Santarém Brazil 143 H4
Santarém Port. 57 B4
Santa Rita Mex. 131 C7
Santa Rosa Arg. 144 D5
Santa Rosa Brazil 144 F3
Santa Rosa Mex. 131 C7
Santa Rosa CA U.S.A. 128 B2
Santa Rosa NM U.S.A. 127 G6
Santa Rosa de Copán Hond. 136 G6
Santa Rosa de la Roca Bol. 142 F7
Santa Rosa dos Purus Brazil 142 D5
Santa Rosa Island U.S.A. 128 C5
Santa Rosalía Mex. 127 E8
Santa Rosa Range mts U.S.A. 126 D4
Santa Rosa Wash watercourse U.S.A. 129 G5
Santa Sylvina Arg. 144 D3
Santa Tecla El Salvador 136 G6
Santa Teresa Australia 109 F6
Santa Teresa r. Brazil 145 A1
Santa Teresa Mex. 131 D7
Santa Vitória Brazil 145 A2
Santa Ynez r. U.S.A. 128 C4
Santa Ysabel i. Solomon Is see Santa Isabel
Santee U.S.A. 128 E5
Santee r. U.S.A. 133 E5
Sant Francesc de Formentera Spain 57 G4
Santiago Brazil 144 F3
Santiago i. Cape Verde 96 [inset]

▶Santiago Chile 144 B4
Capital of Chile.

Santiago Dom. Rep. 137 J5
Santiago Panama 137 H7
Santiago Phil. 69 G3
Santiago, Isla i. Galápagos Ecuador 142 [inset]
Santiago de Compostela Spain 57 B2
Santiago de Cuba Cuba 137 I4
Santiago del Estero Arg. 144 D3
Santiago de los Caballeros Dom. Rep. see Santiago
Santiago de Veraguas Panama see Santiago
Santiaguillo, Laguna de l. Mex. 131 B7
Santianna Point Canada 121 P2
Santipur India see Shantipur
Sant Jordi, Golf de g. Spain 57 G3
Santo Amaro Brazil 145 D1
Santo Amaro de Campos Brazil 145 C3
Santo Anastácio Brazil 145 A3
Santo André Brazil 145 B3
Santo Ângelo Brazil 144 F3

▶Santo Antão i. Cape Verde 96 [inset]
Most westerly point of Africa.

Santo Antônio Brazil 142 F4
Santo Antônio r. Brazil 145 C2
Santo António São Tomé and Príncipe 96 D4
Santo Antônio, Cabo c. Brazil 145 D1
Santo Antônio da Platina Brazil 145 A3
Santo Antônio de Jesus Brazil 145 D1
Santo Antônio do Içá Brazil 142 E4
Santo Corazón Bol. 143 G7
Santo Domingo Cuba 133 D8

▶Santo Domingo Dom. Rep. 137 K5
Capital of the Dominican Republic.

Santo Domingo Baja California Mex. 127 E7
Santo Domingo Baja California Sur Mex. 127 F8
Santo Domingo country West Indies see Dominican Republic
Santo Domingo de Guzmán Dom. Rep. see Santo Domingo
Santo Hipólito Brazil 145 B2
Santorini i. Greece 59 K6
Santos Brazil 145 B3
Santos Dumont Brazil 145 C3
Santos Luzardo, Parque Nacional nat. park Venez. 142 E2
Santos Plateau sea feature S. Atlantic Ocean 148 E7
Santo Tomás Mex. 127 E7
Santo Tomás Peru 142 D6
Santo Tomé Arg. 144 E3
Sanup Plateau U.S.A. 129 G3
San Valentín, Cerro mt. Chile 144 B7
San Vicente El Salvador 136 G6
San Vicente Mex. 127 D7
San Vicente de Baracaldo Spain see Barakaldo
San Vicente de Cañete Peru 142 C6
San Vincenzo Italy 58 D3
San Vito, Capo c. Sicily Italy 58 E5
Sanwer India 82 C5
Sanya China 77 F5
Sanyuan China 77 F1
S. A. Nyýazow Adyndaky Turkm. 89 F2
Sanza Pombo Angola 99 B4
Sao, Phou mt. Laos 70 C3
São Bernardo do Campo Brazil 145 B3
São Borja Brazil 144 E3
São Carlos Brazil 145 B3
São Cristóvão Brazil 143 K6
São Domingos Brazil 145 B1
São Felipe, Serra de hills Brazil 145 B1
São Félix Brazil 145 D1
São Félix do Araguaia Brazil 143 H6
São Félix do Xingu Brazil 143 H5
São Fidélis Brazil 145 C3
São Francisco Brazil 145 B1

▶São Francisco r. Brazil 145 C1
5th longest river in South America.

São Francisco, Ilha de i. Brazil 145 A4
São Francisco de Paula Brazil 145 A5
São Francisco de Sales Brazil 145 A2
São Francisco do Sul Brazil 145 A4
São Gabriel Brazil 144 F4
São Gonçalo Brazil 145 C3
São Gonçalo do Abaeté Brazil 145 B2
São Gonçalo do Sapucaí Brazil 145 B3
São Gotardo Brazil 145 B2
São João, Ilhas de is Brazil 143 J4
São João da Barra Brazil 145 C3
São João da Boa Vista Brazil 145 B3
São João da Madeira Port. 57 B3
São João da Ponte Brazil 145 B1
São João del Rei Brazil 145 B3
São João do Paraíso Brazil 145 C1
São Joaquim Brazil 145 A5
São Joaquim da Barra Brazil 145 B3
São José Amazonas Brazil 142 E4
São José Santa Catarina Brazil 145 A4
São José do Rio Preto Brazil 145 A3
São José dos Campos Brazil 145 B3
São José dos Pinhais Brazil 145 A4
São Leopoldo Brazil 145 A5
São Lourenço Brazil 145 B3
São Lourenço r. Brazil 143 G7
São Luís Maranhão Brazil 143 J4
São Luís Pará Brazil 143 G4
São Luís de Montes Belos Brazil 145 A2
São Manuel Brazil 145 A3
São Marcos r. Brazil 145 B2
São Mateus Brazil 145 D2
São Mateus do Sul Brazil 145 A4
São Miguel i. Arquipélago dos Açores 148 G3
São Miguel r. Brazil 145 B2
São Miguel do Araguaia Brazil 145 A1
São Miguel do Tapuio Brazil 143 J5
Saône r. France 56 G4
Saoner India 82 D5
São Nicolau i. Cape Verde 96 [inset]

▶São Paulo Brazil 145 B3
Most populous city in South America and 7th in the world.

São Paulo state Brazil 145 A3
São Paulo de Olivença Brazil 142 E4
São Pedro da Aldeia Brazil 145 C3
São Pedro e São Paulo is N. Atlantic Ocean 148 G5
São Pires r. Brazil see Teles Pires
São Raimundo Nonato Brazil 143 J5
São Romão Amazonas Brazil 142 E5
São Romão Minas Gerais Brazil 145 B2
São Roque Brazil 145 B3
São Roque, Cabo de c. Brazil 143 K5
São Salvador Angola see M'banza Congo
São Salvador do Congo Angola see M'banza Congo
São Sebastião Brazil 145 B3
São Sebastião, Ilha do i. Brazil 145 B3
São Sebastião do Paraíso Brazil 145 B3
São Sebastião dos Poções Brazil 145 B1
São Simão Goiás Brazil 143 H7
São Simão São Paulo Brazil 145 B3
São Simão, Barragem de resr Brazil 145 A2

▶São Tomé São Tomé and Príncipe 96 D4
Capital of São Tomé and Príncipe.

São Tomé *i.* São Tomé and Príncipe 96 D4
São Tomé, Cabo de *c.* Brazil 145 C3
São Tomé, Pico de *mt.* São Tomé and Príncipe 96 D4
São Tomé and Príncipe *country* Africa 96 D4
Saoura, Oued *watercourse* Alg. 54 D6
São Vicente Brazil 145 B3
São Vicente *i.* Cape Verde 96 [inset]
São Vicente, Cabo de *c.* Port. 57 B5
Sapanca Turkey 59 N4
Sapaul India *see* Supaul
Şaphane Dağı *mt.* Turkey 59 N5
Sapo National Park Liberia 96 C4
Sapouy Burkina Faso 96 C3
Sapozhok Russia 43 I5
Sappa Creek *r.* U.S.A. 130 D3
Sapporo Japan 74 F4
Sapulpa U.S.A. 131 D4
Sapulut *Sabah* Malaysia 68 F6
Saputang China *see* Zadoi
Sāqī Iran 88 E3
Saqqez Iran 88 B2
Sarā Iran 88 B2
Sarāb Iran 88 B2
Sara Buri Thai. 71 C4
Saradiya India 82 B5
Saragossa Spain *see* Zaragoza
Saragt Turkm. 89 F2
Saraguro Ecuador 142 C4
Sarahs Turkm. *see* Saragt
Sarai Sidhu Pak. 89 I4

▶Sarajevo Bos. & Herz. 58 H3
Capital of Bosnia and Herzegovina.

Sarakhs Iran 89 F2
Saraktash Russia 64 G4
Saraland U.S.A. 131 F6
Saramati *mt.* India/Myanmar 70 A1
Saran' Kazakh. 80 D2
Saranac U.S.A. 134 C2
Saranac *r.* U.S.A. 135 I1
Saranac Lake U.S.A. 135 H1
Saranda Albania *see* Sarandë
Sarandë Albania 59 I5
Sarandib *country* Asia *see* Sri Lanka
Sarangani Islands Phil. 69 H5
Sarangpur India 82 D5
Saransk Russia 43 J5
Sara Peak Nigeria 96 D4
Saraphi Thai. 70 B3
Sarapul Russia 41 Q4
Sarāqib Syria 85 C2
Sarasota U.S.A. 133 D7
Saraswati *r.* India 89 H6
Sarata Ukr. 59 M1
Saratoga *CA* U.S.A. 128 B3
Saratoga *WY* U.S.A. 126 G4
Saratoga Springs U.S.A. 132 F3
Saratok *Sarawak* Malaysia 68 E6
Saratov Russia 43 J6
Saratovskoye Vodokhranilishche *resr* Russia 43 J5
Saratsina, Akrotirio *pt* Greece 59 K5
Sarāvān Iran 89 F5
Saray Turkey 59 L4
Sarayköy Turkey 59 M6
Sarayönü Turkey 90 D3
Sarazm *tourist site* Tajik. 80 C4
Sarbāz Iran 87 J4
Sarbāz *reg.* Iran 89 F5
Sarbhang Bhutan 83 G4
Sar Bīsheh Iran 87 I3
Sarda *r.* Nepal 83 E3
Sard Āb Afgh. 89 H2
Sardarshahr India 82 C3
Sardasht Iran 88 B2
Sardegna *i. Sardinia* Italy *see* Sardinia
Sardica Bulg. *see* Sofia
Sardinia *i. Sardinia* Italy 58 C4
Sardis *MS* U.S.A. 131 F5
Sardis *WV* U.S.A. 134 E4
Sardis Lake *resr* U.S.A. 131 F5
Sar-e Būm Afgh. 89 G3
Sareks nationalpark *nat. park* Sweden 44 J3
Sarektjåkkå *mt.* Sweden 44 J3
Sar-e Pol-e Žahāb Iran 88 B3
Sar-e Pul Afgh. 89 G2
Sar Eskandar Iran *see* Hashtrūd
Sargasso Sea N. Atlantic Ocean 151 P4
Sargodha Pak. 89 I3
Sarh Chad 97 E4
Sarhad *reg.* Iran 89 F4
Sārī Iran 88 D2
Saria *i.* Greece 59 L7
Sar-i-Bum Afgh. *see* Sar-e Būm
Sáric Mex. 127 F7
Sarigan *i.* N. Mariana Is 69 L3
Sarigh Jilganang Kol *salt l.* China 82 D2
Sarıgöl Turkey 59 M5
Sarıkamış Turkey 91 F2
Sarikei *Sarawak* Malaysia 68 E6
Sarikül, Qatorkŭhi *mts* China/Tajik. *see* Sarykol Range
Sarila India 82 D4
Sarina Australia 110 E4
Sarıoğlan *Kayseri* Turkey 90 D3
Sarıoğlan *Konya* Turkey *see* Belören
Sariqamish Kuli *salt l.* Turkm./Uzbek. *see* Sarykamyshskoye Ozero
Sarita U.S.A. 131 D7
Sarıveliler Turkey 85 A1
Sariwŏn N. Korea 75 B5
Sarıyar Barajı *resr* Turkey 59 N5
Sarıyer Turkey 59 M4
Sarız Turkey 90 E3
Sark *i.* Channel Is 49 E9
Sark, Safrā' as *esc.* Saudi Arabia 86 F4
Sarkand Kazakh. 80 E2
Şarkikaraağaç Turkey 59 N5
Şarkışla Turkey 90 E3
Şarköy Turkey 59 L4
Sarlath Range *mts* Afgh./Pak. 89 G4
Sarmi Indon. 69 J7
Särna Sweden 45 H6
Sarneh Iran 88 B3
Sarnen Switz. 56 I3
Sarni India *see* Amla
Sarnia Canada 134 D2
Sarny Ukr. 43 E6
Sarōbī Afgh. 89 H3
Sarolangun Indon. 68 C7
Saroma-ko *l.* Japan 74 F3
Saronikos Kolpos *g.* Greece 59 J6
Saros Körfezi *b.* Turkey 59 L4
Sarov Russia 43 I5
Sarpa, Ozero *l.* Russia 43 J6
Sarpan *i.* N. Mariana Is *see* Rota
Sarpsborg Norway 45 G7
Sarqant Kazakh. *see* Sarkand
Sarre *r.* France 52 H5
Sarrebourg France 52 H6
Sarreguemines France 52 H5
Sarria Spain 57 C2
Sarry France 52 E6
Sartana Ukr. 43 H7
Sartanahu Pak. 89 H5
Sartène *Corsica* France 56 I6
Sarthe *r.* France 56 D3
Sartu China *see* Daqing
Saruna Pak. 89 G5
Sarupsar India 82 C3
Şărur Azer. 91 G3
Sarvābād Iran 88 B3
Sárvár Hungary 58 G1
Sarv-e Bālā Iran 88 D3
Sarwar India 82 C4
Saryarka *plain* Kazakh. 80 D1
Sar Yazd Iran 88 D4
Sarygamysh Köli *salt l.* Turkm./Uzbek. *see* Sarykamyshskoye Ozero
Sary-Ishikotrau, Peski *des.* Kazakh. *see* Saryyesik-Atyrau, Peski
Sarykamyshskoye Ozero *salt l.* Turkm./Uzbek. 91 J2
Sarykol Range *mts* China/Tajik. 89 I2
Saryozek Kazakh. 80 E3
Saryozen *r.* Kazakh./Russia 43 K6
Saryshagan Kazakh. 80 D2
Sarysu *watercourse* Kazakh. 80 C2
Sarytash Kazakh. 91 H1
Sary-Tash Kyrg. 89 I2
Saryýazy Suw Howdany *resr* Turkm. 89 F2
Saryyesik-Atyrau, Peski *des.* Kazakh. 80 E2
Sarzha Kazakh. 91 H2
Sasar, Tanjung *pt* Indon. 108 B2
Sasaram India 83 F4
Sasebo Japan 75 C6
Saskatchewan *prov.* Canada 121 J4
Saskatchewan *r.* Canada 121 K4
Saskatoon Canada 121 J4
Saskylakh Russia 65 M2
Saslaya *mt.* Nicaragua 137 H6
Sasoi *r.* India 82 B5
Sasolburg S. Africa 101 H4
Sasovo Russia 43 I5
Sass *r.* Canada 120 H2
Sassandra Côte d'Ivoire 96 C4
Sassari *Sardinia* Italy 58 C4
Sassenberg Germany 53 I3
Sassnitz Germany 47 N3
Sass Town Liberia 96 C4
Sasykkol', Ozero *l.* Kazakh. 80 F2
Sasykoli Russia 43 J7
Sasyqköl *l.* Kazakh. *see* Sasykkol', Ozero
Satahual *i.* Micronesia *see* Satawal
Sata-misaki *c.* Japan 75 C7
Satana India 84 B1
Satan Pass U.S.A. 129 I4
Satara India 84 B2
Satara S. Africa 101 J3
Satawal *i.* Micronesia 69 L5
Sätbaev Kazakh. *see* Satpayev
Satevó Mex. 131 B7
Satevó *r.* Mex. 127 G8
Satırlar Turkey *see* Yeşilova
Satkania Bangl. 83 H5
Satkhira Bangl. 83 G5
Satluj *r.* India/Pak. 82 B3
Satmala Range *hills* India 84 C2
Satna India 82 E4
Satpayev Kazakh. 80 C2
Satpura Range *mts* India 82 C5
Satsuma-hantō *pen.* Japan 75 C7
Satsuma-Sendai Japan 75 C7
Sattahip Thai. 71 C4
Satteldorf Germany 53 K5
Satthwa Myanmar 70 A3
Satu Mare Romania 43 D7
Satun Thai. 71 C6
Satwas India 82 D5
Sauceda Mountains U.S.A. 129 G5
Saucillo Mex. 131 B6
Sauda Norway 45 E7
Sauðárkrókur Iceland 44 [inset 1]

▶Saudi Arabia *country* Asia 86 F4
5th largest country in Asia.

Sauer *r.* France 53 I6
Saugatuck U.S.A. 134 B2
Saugeen *r.* Canada 134 E1
Sāūjbolāgh Iran *see* Mahābād
Sauk Center U.S.A. 130 E2
Saulieu France 56 G3
Saulnois *reg.* France 52 G6
Sault Sainte Marie Canada 122 D5
Sault Sainte Marie U.S.A. 132 C2
Saumalkol' Kazakh. 78 F1
Saumarez Reef Australia 110 F4
Saumlakki Indon. 108 E2
Saumur France 56 D3
Saundatti India 84 B3
Saunders, Mount *hill* Australia 108 E3
Saunders Coast Antarctica 152 J1
Saurimo Angola 99 C4
Sautar Angola 99 B5
Sauvolles, Lac *l.* Canada 123 G3
Sava *r.* Europe 58 I2
Savage River Australia 111 [inset]
Savai'i *i.* Samoa 107 I3
Savala *r.* Russia 43 I6
Savalou Benin 96 D4
Savānāt Iran *see* Estahbān
Savane *r.* Canada 123 H4
Savanna U.S.A. 130 F3
Savannah *GA* U.S.A. 133 D5
Savannah *OH* U.S.A. 134 D3
Savannah *TN* U.S.A. 131 F5
Savannah *r.* U.S.A. 133 D5
Savannah Sound Bahamas 133 E7
Savannakhét Laos 70 D3
Savanna-la-Mar Jamaica 137 I5
Savant Lake Canada 122 C4
Savant Lake *l.* Canada 122 C4
Savanur India 84 B3
Sävar Sweden 44 L5
Savaştepe Turkey 59 L5
Savè Benin 96 D4
Save *r.* Moz./Zimbabwe 99 D6
Sāveh Iran 88 C3
Saverne France 53 H6
Saverne, Col de *pass* France 53 H6
Saviaho Fin. 44 P5
Savinskiy Russia 42 I3
Savitri *r.* India 84 B2
Savli India 82 C5
Savoie *reg.* France *see* Savoy
Savona Italy 58 C2
Savonlinna Fin. 44 P6
Savonranta Fin. 44 P5
Savoy *reg.* France 56 H3
Şavşat Turkey 91 F2
Sävsjö Sweden 45 I8
Savu *i.* Indon. 108 C2
Savukoski Fin. 44 P3
Savur Turkey 91 F3
Savu Sea Indon. *see* Sawu, Laut
Saw Myanmar 70 A2
Sawai Madhopur India 82 D4
Sawan Myanmar 70 B1
Sawar India 82 C4
Sawatch Range *mts* U.S.A. 126 G5
Sawel Mountain *hill* U.K. 51 E3
Sawi, Ao *b.* Thai. 71 B5
Sawn Myanmar 70 B2
Sawtell Australia 112 F3
Sawtooth Range *mts* U.S.A. 126 C2
Sawu Indon. 108 C2
Sawu *i.* Indon. *see* Savu
Sawu, Laut *sea* Indon. 108 C2
Sawye Myanmar 70 B2
Sawyer U.S.A. 134 B3
Saxilby U.K. 48 G5
Saxmundham U.K. 49 I6
Saxnäs Sweden 44 I4
Saxony *land* Germany *see* Sachsen
Saxony-Anhalt *land* Germany *see* Sachsen-Anhalt
Saxton U.S.A. 135 F3
Say Niger 96 D3
Sayabouri Laos *see* Xaignabouli
Sayak Kazakh. 80 E2
Sayanogorsk Russia 72 G2
Sayano-Shushenskoye Vodokhranilishche *resr* Russia 72 G2
Sayansk Russia 72 I2
Sayaq Kazakh. *see* Sayak
Saýat Turkm. 89 F2
Sayat Turkm. *see* Saýat
Şaydā Lebanon *see* Sidon
Sāyen Iran 88 D4
Sayer Island Thai. *see* Similan, Ko
Sayghān Afgh. 89 G3
Sayhan-Ovoo Mongolia 72 I3
Sayḥūt Yemen 86 H6
Sayingpan China 76 D3
Saykyn Kazakh. 41 P6
Saylac Somalia 97 H3
Saylan *country* Asia *see* Sri Lanka
Saynshand Mongolia 73 K4
Sayoa *mt.* Spain *see* Saioa
Sayot Turkm. *see* Saýat
Şayqal, Baḩr *imp. l.* Syria 85 C3
Sayqyn Kazakh. *see* Saykyn
Sayre *OK* U.S.A. 131 D5
Sayre *PA* U.S.A. 135 G3
Sayreville U.S.A. 135 H3
Sayula Mex. 136 F5
Sayyod Turkm. *see* Saýat
Sazdy Kazakh. 43 K7
Sazin Pak. 89 I3
Sbaa Alg. 54 D6
Sbeitla Tunisia 58 C7
Scaddan Australia 109 C8
Scafell Pike *hill* U.K. 48 D4
Scalasaig U.K. 50 C4
Scalea Italy 58 F5
Scalloway U.K. 50 [inset]
Scalpaigh, Eilean *i.* U.K. *see* Scalpay
Scalpay *i.* U.K. 50 C3
Scapa Flow *inlet* U.K. 50 F2
Scarba *i.* U.K. 50 D4
Scarborough Canada 134 F2
Scarborough Trin. and Tob. 137 L6
Scarborough U.K. 48 G4
Scarborough Reef *sea feature* S. China Sea 68 F3
Scariff Island Ireland 51 B6
Scarp *i.* U.K. 50 B2
Scarpanto *i.* Greece *see* Karpathos
Schaale *r.* Germany 53 K1
Schaalsee *l.* Germany 53 K1
Schaerbeek Belgium 52 E4
Schaffhausen Switz. 56 I3
Schafstädt Germany 53 L3
Schagen Neth. 52 E2
Schagerbrug Neth. 52 E2
Schakalskuppe Namibia 100 C4
Schärding Austria 47 N6
Scharendijke Neth. 52 D3
Scharteberg *hill* Germany 52 G4
Schaumburg U.S.A. 134 A2
Scheeßel Germany 53 J1
Schefferville Canada 123 I3
Scheibbs Austria 47 O6
Schelde *r.* Belgium *see* Scheldt
Scheldt *r.* Belgium 52 E3
Schell Creek Range *mts* U.S.A. 129 F2
Schellerten Germany 53 K2
Schellville U.S.A. 128 B2
Schenectady U.S.A. 135 I2
Schenefeld Germany 53 J1
Schermerhorn Neth. 52 E2
Schertz U.S.A. 131 D6
Schierling Germany 53 M6
Schiermonnikoog Neth. 52 G1
Schiermonnikoog *i.* Neth. 52 G1
Schiermonnikoog, Nationaal Park *nat. park* Neth. 52 G1
Schiffdorf Germany 53 I1
Schinnen Neth. 52 F4
Schio Italy 58 D2
Schkeuditz Germany 53 M3
Schleiden Germany 52 G4
Schleiz Germany 53 L4
Schleswig Germany 47 L3
Schleswig-Holstein *land* Germany 53 K1
Schleswig-Holsteinisches Wattenmeer, Nationalpark *nat. park* Germany 47 L3
Schleusingen Germany 53 K4
Schlitz Germany 53 J4
Schloß Holte-Stukenbrock Germany 53 I3
Schlüchtern Germany 53 J4
Schlüsselfeld Germany 53 K5
Schmalkalden Germany 53 K4
Schmallenberg Germany 53 I3
Schmidt Island Russia *see* Shmidta, Ostrov
Schmidt Peninsula Russia *see* Shmidta, Poluostrov
Schneeberg Germany 53 M4
Schneidemühl Poland *see* Piła
Schneidlingen Germany 53 L3
Schneverdingen Germany 53 J1
Schoharie U.S.A. 135 H2
Schönebeck Germany 53 M1
Schönebeck (Elbe) Germany 53 L2
Schönefeld *airport* Germany 53 N2
Schöningen Germany 53 K2
Schöntal Germany 53 J5
Schoolcraft U.S.A. 134 C2
Schoonhoven Neth. 52 E3
Schopfloch Germany 53 K5
Schöppenstedt Germany 53 K2
Schortens Germany 53 H1
Schouten Island Australia 111 [inset]
Schouten Islands P.N.G. 69 K7
Schrankogel *mt.* Austria 47 M7
Schreiber Canada 122 D4
Schroon Lake U.S.A. 135 I2
Schröttersburg Poland *see* Płock
Schulenburg U.S.A. 131 D6
Schuler Canada 121 I5
Schull Ireland 51 C6
Schultz Lake Canada 121 L1
Schüttorf Germany 53 H2
Schuyler U.S.A. 130 D3
Schuyler Lake U.S.A. 135 H2
Schuylkill Haven U.S.A. 135 G3
Schwabach Germany 53 L5
Schwäbische Alb *mts* Germany 47 L7
Schwäbisch Gmünd Germany 53 J6
Schwäbisch Hall Germany 53 J5
Schwaförden Germany 53 I2
Schwalm *r.* Germany 53 J3
Schwalmstadt-Ziegenhain Germany 53 J4
Schwandorf Germany 53 M5
Schwaner, Pegunungan *mts* Indon. 68 E7
Schwanewede Germany 53 I1
Schwarmstedt Germany 53 J2
Schwarze Elster *r.* Germany 53 M3
Schwarzenbek Germany 53 K1
Schwarzenberg/Erzgebirge Germany 53 M4
Schwarzer Mann *hill* Germany 52 G4
Schwarzrand *mts* Namibia 100 C3
Schwarzwald *mts* Germany *see* Black Forest
Schwatka Mountains U.S.A. 118 C3
Schwaz Austria 47 M7
Schwebheim Germany 53 K5
Schwedt/Oder Germany 47 O4
Schwegenheim Germany 53 I5
Schweich Germany 52 G5
Schweinfurt Germany 53 K4
Schweinitz Germany 53 N3
Schweinrich Germany 53 M1
Schweiz *country* Europe *see* Switzerland
Schweizer-Reneke S. Africa 101 G4
Schwelm Germany 53 H3
Schwerin Germany 53 L1
Schweriner See *l.* Germany 53 L1
Schwetzingen Germany 53 I5
Schwyz Switz. 56 I3
Sciacca *Sicily* Italy 58 E6
Scicli *Sicily* Italy 58 F6
Science Hill U.S.A. 134 C5
Scilly, Île *atoll* Fr. Polynesia *see* Manuae
Scilly, Isles of U.K. 49 A9
Scioto *r.* U.S.A. 134 D4
Scipio U.S.A. 129 G2
Scobey U.S.A. 126 G2
Scodra Albania *see* Shkodër
Scofield Reservoir U.S.A. 129 H2
Scole U.K. 49 I6
Scone Australia 112 E4
Scone U.K. 50 F4
Scoresby Land *reg.* Greenland 119 P2
Scoresbysund Greenland *see* Ittoqqortoormiit
Scoresby Sund *sea chan.* Greenland *see* Kangertittivaq
Scorno, Punta dello *pt Sardinia* Italy *see* Caprara, Punta
Scorpion Bight *b.* Australia 109 D8
Scotia Ridge *sea feature* S. Atlantic Ocean 152 A2
Scotia Sea S. Atlantic Ocean 148 F9
Scotland Canada 134 E2
Scotland *admin. div.* U.K. 50 F3
Scotland U.S.A. 135 G4
Scotstown Canada 123 H5
Scott U.S.A. 134 C3
Scott, Cape Australia 108 E3
Scott, Cape Canada 120 D5
Scott, Mount *hill* U.S.A. 131 D5
Scott Base *research station* Antarctica 152 H1
Scottburgh S. Africa 101 J6
Scott City U.S.A. 130 C4
Scott Coast Antarctica 152 H1
Scott Glacier Antarctica 152 I1
Scott Island Antarctica 152 H2
Scott Islands Canada 120 D5
Scott Lake Canada 121 J3
Scott Mountains Antarctica 152 D2
Scott Reef Australia 108 C3
Scottsbluff U.S.A. 130 C3
Scottsboro U.S.A. 133 C5
Scottsburg U.S.A. 134 C4
Scottsville *KY* U.S.A. 134 B5
Scottsville *VA* U.S.A. 135 F5
Scourie U.K. 50 D2
Scousburgh U.K. 50 [inset]
Scrabster U.K. 50 F2
Scranton U.S.A. 135 H3
Scunthorpe U.K. 48 G5
Scuol Switz. 56 J3
Scupi Macedonia *see* Skopje
Scutari Albania *see* Shkodër
Scutari, Lake Albania/Montenegro 59 H3
Seaboard U.S.A. 135 G5
Seabrook, Lake *salt flat* Australia 109 B7
Seaford U.K. 49 H8
Seaforth Canada 134 E2
Seal *r.* Canada 121 M3
Seal, Cape S. Africa 100 F8
Sea Lake Australia 111 C7
Seal Lake Canada 123 J3
Sealy U.S.A. 131 D6
Seaman U.S.A. 134 D4
Seaman Range *mts* U.S.A. 129 F3
Seamer U.K. 48 G4
Searchlight U.S.A. 129 F4
Searcy U.S.A. 131 F5
Searles Lake U.S.A. 128 E4
Seaside *CA* U.S.A. 127 C5
Seaside *OR* U.S.A. 126 C3
Seaside Park U.S.A. 135 H4
Seattle U.S.A. 126 C3
Seaview Range *mts* Australia 110 D3
Seba Indon. 108 C2
Sebago Lake U.S.A. 135 J2
Sebastea Turkey *see* Sivas
Sebastian U.S.A. 133 D7
Sebastián Vizcaíno, Bahía *b.* Mex. 127 E7
Sebasticook *r.* U.S.A. 135 K1
Sebasticook Lake U.S.A. 135 K1
Sebastopol Crimea *see* Sevastopol'
Sebastopol U.S.A. 128 B2
Sebatik *i.* Indon. 68 F6
Sebba Burkina Faso 96 D3
Seben Turkey 59 N4
Sebenico Croatia *see* Šibenik
Sebeş Romania 59 J2
Sebewaing U.S.A. 134 D2
Sebezh Russia 45 P8
Şebinkarahisar Turkey 90 E2
Sebree U.S.A. 134 B5
Sebring U.S.A. 133 D7
Sebrovo Russia 43 I6
Sebta N. Africa *see* Ceuta
Sebuku *i.* Indon. 68 F7
Sechelt Canada 120 F5
Sechenovo Russia 43 J5
Sechura Peru 142 B5
Sechura, Bahía de *b.* Peru 142 B5
Seckach Germany 53 J5
Second Mesa U.S.A. 129 H4
Secretary Island N.Z. 113 A7
Secunda S. Africa 101 I4
Secunderabad India 84 C2
Sedalia U.S.A. 130 E4
Sedam India 84 C2
Sedan France 52 E5
Sedan U.S.A. 131 D4
Sedan Dip Australia 110 C3
Seddon N.Z. 113 E5
Seddonville N.Z. 113 C5
Sederot Israel 85 B4
Sédhiou Gambia 96 B3
Sedlčany Czechia 47 O6
Sedlets Poland *see* Siedlce
Sedom Israel 85 B4
Sedona U.S.A. 129 H4
Sédrata Alg. 58 B6
Šeduva Lith. 45 M9
Seedorf Germany 53 K1
Seehausen Germany 53 L2
Seehausen (Altmark) Germany 53 L2
Seeheim Namibia 100 C4
Seeheim-Jugenheim Germany 53 I5
Seelig, Mount Antarctica 152 K1
Seelze Germany 53 J2
Seemandhra *state* India *see* Andhra Pradesh
Seenu Atoll Maldives *see* Addu Atholhu
Sées France 56 E2
Seesen Germany 53 K3
Seevetal Germany 53 K1
Sefare Botswana 101 H2
Seferihisar Turkey 59 L5
Sefīd, Kūh-e *mt.* Iran 88 C3
Sefid Kūh *mts* Afgh. 89 G3
Sefid Sang Iran 89 F3
Sefophe Botswana 101 H2
Segalstad Norway 45 G6
Segamat Malaysia 71 C7
Ségbana Benin 96 D3
Segeletz Germany 53 M2
Segezha Russia 42 G3
Segontia U.K. *see* Caernarfon
Segontium U.K. *see* Caernarfon
Segorbe Spain 57 F4
Ségou Mali 96 C3
Segovia *r.* Hond./Nicaragua *see* Coco
Segovia Spain 57 D3
Segozerskoye Vodokhranilishche *resr* Russia 42 G3
Seguam Island U.S.A. 118 A4
Séguédine Niger 96 E2
Séguéla Côte d'Ivoire 96 C4
Seguin U.S.A. 131 D6
Segura *r.* Spain 57 F4
Segura, Sierra de *mts* Spain 57 E5
Sehithwa Botswana 99 C6
Sehlabathebe National Park Lesotho 101 I5
Sehore India 82 D5
Sehwan Pak. 89 G5
Seibert U.S.A. 130 C4
Seignelay *r.* Canada 123 H4
Seikphyu Myanmar 70 A2
Seiland *i.* Norway 44 M1
Seille *r.* France 52 G5
Seinäjoki Fin. 44 M5
Seine *r.* Canada 121 N5
Seine *r.* France 52 A5
Seine, Baie de *b.* France 56 D2
Seine, Val de *valley* France 56 F2
Seistan *reg.* Iran *see* Sīstān
Sejny Poland 45 M9
Sekayu Indon. 68 C7
Seke China *see* Sêrtar
Sekoma Botswana 100 F3
Sekondi Ghana 96 C4
Sek'ot'a Eth. 98 D2
Sekura Indon. 71 E7
Şela Russia *see* Shali
Selama Malaysia 71 C6
Selaru *i.* Indon. 108 E2
Selassi Indon. 69 I7
Selatan, Tanjung *pt* Indon. 68 E7
Selat Makassar *strait* Indon. *see* Makassar, Selat
Selatpanjang Indon. 71 C7
Selawik U.S.A. 118 B3
Selayar, Pulau *i.* Indon. 69 G8
Selb Germany 53 M4
Selbekken Norway 44 F5
Selbu Norway 44 G5
Selby U.K. 48 F5
Selby U.S.A. 130 C2
Selbyville U.S.A. 135 H4
Selden U.S.A. 130 C4
Selebi-Phikwe Botswana 99 C6
Selebi-Pikwe Botswana *see* Selebi-Phikwe
Selemdzha *r.* Russia 74 C1
Selemdzhinsk Russia 74 C1
Selemdzhinskiy Khrebet *mts* Russia 74 D1
Selendi Turkey 59 M5

▶Selenga *r.* Mongolia/Russia 72 J2
Part of the Yenisey-Angara-Selenga, 3rd longest river in Asia.
Also known as Selenga Mörön.

Selenga Mörön *r.* Mongolia/Russia *see* Selenga
Seletar Sing. 71 [inset]
Seletar Reservoir Sing. 71 [inset]
Selety *r.* Kazakh. *see* Silety
Seletyteniz, Ozero *salt l.* Kazakh. *see* Siletyteniz, Ozero
Seleucia Turkey *see* Silifke
Seleucia Pieria Turkey *see* Samandağı
Selfridge U.S.A. 130 C2
Sel'gon Russia 74 D2
Sélibabi Mauritania 96 B3
Selibe-Phikwe Botswana *see* Selebi-Phikwe
Seligenstadt Germany 53 I4
Seliger, Ozero *l.* Russia 42 G4
Seligman U.S.A. 129 G4
Selikhino Russia 74 E2
Selîma Oasis Sudan 86 C5
Selimiye Turkey 59 L6
Selinsgrove U.S.A. 135 G3
Selizharovo Russia 42 G4
Seljord Norway 45 F7
Selkirk Canada 121 L5
Selkirk U.K. 50 G5
Selkirk Mountains Canada 120 G4
Sellafield U.K. 48 D4
Sellersburg U.S.A. 134 C4
Sellore Island Myanmar *see* Saganthit Kyun
Sells U.S.A. 129 H6
Selm Germany 53 H3
Selma *AL* U.S.A. 133 C5
Selma *CA* U.S.A. 128 D3
Selmer U.S.A. 131 F5
Selous, Mount Canada 120 C2
Selsey Bill *hd* U.K. 49 G8
Sel'tso Russia 43 G5
Selty Russia 42 L4
Selu *i.* Indon. 108 E1
Seluan *i.* Indon. 71 D6
Selvas *reg.* Brazil 142 D5
Selvin U.S.A. 134 B4
Selway *r.* U.S.A. 126 E3
Selwyn Lake Canada 121 J2
Selwyn Mountains Canada 120 D1
Selwyn Range *hills* Australia 110 B4
Sël'yb Russia 42 K3
Selz *r.* Germany 53 I5
Semarang Indon. 68 E8
Semau *i.* Indon. 108 C2
Sembawang Sing. 71 [inset]
Sembé Congo 98 B3
Şemdinli Turkey 91 G3
Semendire Serbia *see* Smederevo
Semenivka Ukr. 43 G5
Semenov Russia 42 J4
Semenovka Ukr. *see* Semenivka
Semey Kazakh. 80 F1
Semidi Islands U.S.A. 118 C4
Semikarakorsk Russia 43 I7
Semiluki Russia 43 H6
Seminoe Reservoir U.S.A. 126 G4
Seminole U.S.A. 131 C5
Semipalatinsk Kazakh. *see* Semey
Semirara Islands Phil. 69 G4
Semīrom Iran 88 C4
Sem Kolodezey Crimea *see* Lenine
Semnān Iran 88 D3
Semnān va Dāmghaān *reg.* Iran 88 D3
Semois *r.* Belgium/France 52 E5
Semois, Vallée de la *valley* Belgium/France 52 E5
Semyonovskoye *Arkhangel'skaya Oblast'* Russia *see* Bereznik
Semyonovskoye *Kostromskaya Oblast'* Russia *see* Ostrovskoye
Sena Bol. 142 E6
Sena Madureira Brazil 142 E5
Senanga Zambia 99 C5
Sendai Japan 75 F5
Sêndo China 76 B2
Senebui, Tanjung *pt* Indon. 71 C7
Seneca *KS* U.S.A. 130 D4
Seneca *OR* U.S.A. 126 D3
Seneca Lake U.S.A. 135 G2
Seneca Rocks U.S.A. 134 F4
Senecaville Lake U.S.A. 134 E4
Senegal *country* Africa 96 B3
Sénégal *r.* Mauritania/Senegal 96 B3
Seney U.S.A. 130 G2
Senftenberg Germany 47 O5
Senga Hill Zambia 99 D4
Sengerema Tanz. 98 D4
Sengeyskiy, Ostrov *i.* Russia 42 K1
Sênggê Zangbo *r.* China *see* Indus
Sengilen, Khrebet *mts* Russia 80 I1
Sengiley Russia 43 K5

Sengirli, Mys pt Kazakh. see Syngyrli, Mys
Senhor do Bonfim Brazil 143 J6
Senigallia Italy 58 E3
Senj Croatia 58 F2
Senja i. Norway 44 J2
Sen'kina Russia 42 K2
Şenköy Turkey 85 C1
Senlac S. Africa 100 F3
Senlin Shan mt. China 74 C4
Senlis France 52 C5
Sênmônoŭrôm Cambodia 71 D4
Sennar Sudan 86 D7
Sennen U.K. 49 B8
Senneterre Canada 122 F4
Senqu r. Lesotho 101 H6
Sens France 56 F2
Sensuntepeque El Salvador 136 G6
Senta Serbia 59 I2
Senthal India 82 D3
Sentinel U.S.A. 129 G5
Sentinel Peak Canada 120 F4
Sentosa i. Sing. 71 [inset]
Sento Sé Brazil 143 J5
Senwabarwana S. Africa 101 I2
Şenyurt Turkey 91 F3
Seocheon S. Korea 75 B5
Seo de Urgell Spain see La Seu d'Urgell
Seonath r. India 84 D1
Seongnam S. Korea 75 B5
Seoni India 82 D5
Seorak-san mt. S. Korea 75 C5
Seorak-san National Park S. Korea 75 C5
Seorinarayan India 83 E5
Seosan S. Korea 75 B5

▶Seoul S. Korea 75 B5
Capital of South Korea.

Separation Well Australia 108 C5
Sepik r. P.N.G. 69 K7
Sep'o N. Korea 75 B5
Sepon India 83 H4
Seppa India 83 H4
Sept-Îles Canada 123 I4
Sequoia National Park U.S.A. 128 D3
Serafimovich Russia 43 I6
Sêraitang China see Baima
Seram i. Indon. 69 H7
Seram, Laut sea Indon. 69 I7
Serang Indon. 68 D8
Serangoon Harbour b. Sing. 71 [inset]
Serapi, Gunung hill Indon. 71 E7
Serapong, Mount hill Sing. 71 [inset]
Serasan i. Indon. 71 E7
Serasan, Selat sea chan. Indon. 71 E7
Seraya i. Indon. 71 E7
Serbâl, Gebel mt. Egypt see Sirbāl, Jabal

▶Serbia country Europe 59 I3
Formerly known as Yugoslavia and as Serbia and Montenegro. Up to 1993 included Bosnia-Herzegovina, Croatia, Macedonia, Montenegro and Slovenia. Became independent from Montenegro in June 2006. Kosovo declared independence in February 2008.

Sêrbug Co l. China 83 G2
Sêrca China 76 B2
Serchhip India 83 H5
Serdar Turkm. 88 E2
Serdica Bulg. see Sofia
Serdo Eth. 98 E2
Serdoba r. Russia 43 J5
Serdobsk Russia 43 J5
Serebryansk Kazakh. 80 F2
Seredka Russia 45 P7
Şereflikoçhisar Turkey 90 D3
Serekunda Gambia 96 B3
Seremban Malaysia 71 C7
Serengeti National Park Tanz. 98 D4
Serenje Zambia 99 D5
Serezha r. Russia 42 I5
Sergach Russia 42 J5
Sergeyevka Russia 74 B2
Sergiyev Posad Russia 42 H4
Serh China 80 I4
Serhetabat Turkm. 89 F3
Serifos i. Greece 59 K6
Sérigny r. Canada 123 H3
Sérigny, Lac l. Canada 123 H3
Serik Turkey 90 C3
Seringapatam Reef Australia 108 C3
Sêrkang China see Nyainrong
Sermata i. Indon. 69 H8
Sermata, Kepulauan is Indon. 108 E2
Sermersuaq glacier Greenland 119 M2
Sermilik inlet Greenland 119 O3
Sernovodsk Russia 43 K5
Sernur Russia 42 K4
Sernyy Zavod Turkm. see Kükürtli
Seronga Botswana 99 C5
Serov Russia 41 S4
Serowe Botswana 101 H2
Serpa Port. 57 C5
Serpa Pinto Angola see Menongue
Serpentine Lakes salt flat Australia 109 E7
Serpukhov Russia 43 H5
Serra Brazil 145 C3
Serra Alta Brazil 145 A4
Serrachis r. Cyprus 85 A2
Serra da Bocaina, Parque Nacional da nat. park Brazil 145 B3
Serra da Canastra, Parque Nacional da nat. park Brazil 145 B3
Serra da Mesa, Represa resr Brazil 145 A1
Serra das Araras Brazil 145 B1
Serra do Divisor, Parque Nacional da nat. park Brazil 142 D5
Sérrai Greece see Serres
Serranía de la Neblina, Parque Nacional nat. park Venez. 142 E3
Serraria, Ilha i. Brazil see Queimada, Ilha
Serra Talhada Brazil 143 K5
Serre r. France 52 D5
Serres Greece 59 J4
Serrinha Brazil 143 K6
Serro Brazil 145 C2
Sers Tunisia 58 C6
Sertanópolis Brazil 145 A3
Sertãozinho Brazil 145 B3
Sêrtar China 76 D1
Sertavul Geçidi pass Turkey 85 A1
Sertolovo Russia 45 Q6
Seruai Indon. 71 B6
Serui Indon. 69 J7
Serule Botswana 99 C6
Seruna India 82 C3
Sêrwolungwa China 76 B1
Sêrxü China 76 C1
Seryshevo Russia 74 C2
Seseganaga Lake Canada 122 C4
Sese Islands Uganda 98 D4
Sesel country Indian Ocean see Seychelles
Sesfontein Namibia 99 B5
Seshachalam Hills India 84 C3
Sesheke Zambia 99 C5
Sesostris Bank sea feature India 84 A3
Sestri Levante Italy 58 C2
Sestroretsk Russia 45 P6
Set, Phou mt. Laos 70 D4
Sète France 56 F5
Sete Lagoas Brazil 145 B2
Setermoen Norway 44 K2
Setesdal valley Norway 45 E7
Seti r. Nepal 82 E3
Sétif Alg. 54 F4
Seto Japan 75 E6
Seto-naikai sea Japan 73 O6
Seto-naikai Kokuritsu-kōen nat. park Japan 75 D6
Setsan Myanmar 70 A3
Settat Morocco 54 C5
Settepani, Monte mt. Italy 58 C2
Settle U.K. 48 E4
Setúbal Port. 57 B4
Setúbal, Baía de b. Port. 57 B4
Seul, Lac l. Canada 121 M5
Sevan Armenia 91 G2
Sevan, Lake Armenia 91 G2
Sevan, Ozero l. Armenia see Sevan, Lake
Sevana Lich l. Armenia see Sevan, Lake
Sevastopol' Crimea 90 D1
Seven Islands Canada see Sept-Îles
Seven Islands Bay Canada 123 J2
Sevenoaks U.K. 49 H7
Seventy Mile House Canada see 70 Mile House
Sévérac-le-Château France 56 F4
Severn r. Australia 112 E2
Severn r. Canada 122 D3
Severn S. Africa 100 F4
Severn r. U.K. 49 E7
also known as Hafren
Severnaya Dvina r. Russia 42 I2
Severnaya Sos'va r. Russia 41 T3
Severnaya Zemlya is Russia 65 L1
Severn Lake Canada 121 N4
Severnoye Russia 41 Q5
Severnyy Nenetskiy Avtonomnyy Okrug Russia 42 K1
Severnyy Respublika Komi Russia 64 H3

▶Severnyy, Ostrov i. Russia 64 G2
4th largest island in Europe.

Severobaykal'sk Russia 73 J1
Severo-Baykal'skoye Nagor'ye mts Russia 65 M4
Severodonetsk Ukr. see Syeverodonets'k
Severodvinsk Russia 42 H2
Severo-Kuril'sk Russia 65 Q4
Severomorsk Russia 44 R2
Severoonezhsk Russia 42 H3
Severo-Sibirskaya Nizmennost' lowland Russia see North Siberian Lowland
Severoural'sk Russia 41 R3
Severo-Yeniseyskiy Russia 64 K3
Severskaya Russia 90 E1
Severskiy Donets r. Russia/Ukr. see Northern Donets
Sevier U.S.A. 129 G2
Sevier r. U.S.A. 129 G2
Sevier Desert U.S.A. 129 G2
Sevier Lake U.S.A. 129 G2
Sevierville U.S.A. 132 D5
Sevilla Col. 142 C3
Sevilla Spain see Seville
Seville Spain 57 D5
Sevlyush Ukr. see Vynohradiv
Sewani India 82 C3
Seward AK U.S.A. 118 D3
Seward NE U.S.A. 130 D3
Seward Mountains Antarctica 152 L2
Seward Peninsula U.S.A. 118 B3
Sexi Spain see Almuñécar
Sexsmith Canada 120 G4
Sextín Mex. 131 B7
Seyakha Russia 153 F2
Seychelles country Indian Ocean 149 L6
Seýdi Turkm. 89 F2
Seydişehir Turkey 90 C3
Seyðisfjörður Iceland 44 [inset 1]
Seyhan Turkey see Adana
Seyhan r. Turkey 85 B1
Seyitgazi Turkey 59 N5
Seym r. Russia/Ukr. 43 G6
Seymchan Russia 65 Q3
Seymour Australia 112 B6
Seymour S. Africa 101 H7
Seymour IN U.S.A. 134 C4
Seymour TX U.S.A. 131 D5
Seymour Inlet Canada 120 E5
Seymour Range mts Australia 109 F6
Seypan i. N. Mariana Is see Saipan
Sézanne France 52 D6
Sfakia Greece see Chora Sfakion
Sfântu Gheorghe Romania 59 K2
Sfax Tunisia 58 D7
Sfikia, Limni resr Greece see Sfikias, Limni
Sfikias, Limni resr Greece 59 J4
Sfîntu Gheorghe Romania see Sfântu Gheorghe
Sgiersch Poland see Zgierz
's-Graveland Neth. 52 F2
's-Gravenhage Neth. see The Hague
Sgurr Alasdair hill U.K. 50 C3
Sgurr Dhomhnuill hill U.K. 50 D4
Sgurr Mòr mt. U.K. 50 D3
Sgurr na Ciche mt. U.K. 50 D3
Shaanxi prov. China 76 F1
Shaartuz Tajik. see Shahritus
Shaban Pak. 89 G4
Shabani Zimbabwe see Zvishavane
Shabestar Iran 88 B2
Shabībī, Jabal ash mt. Jordan 85 B5
Shabla, Nos pt Bulg. 59 M3
Shabogamo Lake Canada 123 I3
Shabunda Dem. Rep. Congo 98 C4
Shache China 80 E4
Shackleton Coast Antarctica 152 H1
Shackleton Glacier Antarctica 152 I1
Shackleton Ice Shelf Antarctica 152 F2
Shackleton Range mts Antarctica 152 A1
Shadaogou China 77 F2
Shadaw Myanmar 70 B3
Shādegān Iran 88 C4
Shadihar Pak. 89 G4
Shady Cove U.S.A. 126 C4
Shady Spring U.S.A. 134 E5
Shadzud Tajik. 89 I2
Shafer, Lake U.S.A. 134 B3
Shafer Peak Antarctica 152 H2
Shafter U.S.A. 128 D4
Shaftesbury U.K. 49 E7
Shagamu r. Canada 122 D3
Shagedu China 73 K5
Shageluk U.S.A. 118 C3
Shaghyray Üstirti plat. Kazakh. see Shagyray, Plato
Shagonar Russia 80 H1
Shag Point N.Z. 113 C7
Shag Rocks is S. Georgia 144 H8
Shagyray, Plato plat. Kazakh. 80 A2
Shahabad Karnataka India 84 C2
Shahabad Rajasthan India 82 D4
Shahabad Uttar Prad. India 82 E4
Shāhābād Iran see Eslāmābād-e Gharb
Shah Alam Malaysia 71 C7
Shah Bandar Pak. 89 G5
Shahdād Iran 88 E4
Shahdol India 82 E5
Shahe China 77 F2
Shahejie China see Jiujiang
Shahezhen China see Jiujiang
Shāh Fōlād mt. Afgh. 89 G3
Shahid, Ras pt Pak. 89 F5
Shāhīn Dezh Iran 88 B2
Shāh Ismā'īl Afgh. 89 G4
Shāh Jahān, Kūh-e mts Iran 88 E2
Shahjahanpur India 82 D4
Shāh Kūh mt. Iran 88 E4
Shāhpūr Iran see Salmās
Shahrak Afgh. 89 G3
Shāhrakht Iran 89 F3
Shahr-e Bābak Iran 88 D4
Shahr-e Ghulghulah tourist site Afgh. 89 F4
Shahr-e Kord Iran 88 C3
Shahr-e Şafā Afgh. 89 G4
Shahreẓā Iran 88 C3
Shahrig Pak. 89 G4
Shahrisabz Uzbek. 89 G2
Shahr-i Sokhta tourist site Iran 89 F4
Shahriston Tajik. 89 H2
Shahritus Tajik. 89 H2
Shahr Sultan Pak. 89 H4
Shāhrūd Iran 88 D2
Shāhrūd, Rūdkhāneh-ye r. Iran 88 C2
Shāhrūd Bustām reg. Iran 88 D3
Shāh Savārān, Kūh-e mts Iran 88 E4
Shāh Taqī Iran see Emām Taqī
Shaighalu Pak. 89 H4
Shaikh Husain mt. Pak. 89 G4
Shaikhpura India see Sheikhpura
Shā'ir, Jabal mts Syria 85 C2
Sha'īra, Gebel mt. Egypt see Sha'īrah, Jabal
Sha'īrah, Jabal mt. Egypt 85 B5
Shaj'ah, Jabal hill Saudi Arabia 88 C5
Shajapur India 82 D5
Shajianzi China 74 B4
Shakaville S. Africa 101 J5
Shakh Tajik. see Shoh
Shākhbuz Azer. see Şahbuz
Shākhen Iran 89 E3
Shakhovskaya Russia 42 G4
Shakhrisabz Uzbek. see Shahrisabz
Shakhristan Tajik. see Shahriston
Shakhtinsk Kazakh. 80 D2
Shakhty Respublika Buryatiya Russia see Gusinoozersk
Shakhty Rostovskaya Oblast' Russia 43 I7
Shakhun'ya Russia 42 J4
Shaki Nigeria see Saki
Shakotan-hantō pen. Japan 74 F4
Shalakusha Russia 42 I3
Shalang China 77 F4
Shali Russia 91 G2
Shaliuhe China see Gangca
Shalkar India 82 D3
Shalkar Kazakh. 80 A2
Shalkarteniz, Solonchak salt marsh Kazakh. 80 B2
Shalqar Kazakh. see Shalkar
Shaluli Shan mts China 76 C2
Shaluni mt. India 83 I3
Shama r. Tanz. 99 D4
Shamāl Sīnā' governorate Egypt see Shamāl Sīnā'
Shamāl Sīnā' governorate Egypt 85 A4
Shāmat al Akbād des. Saudi Arabia 91 F5
Shamattawa Canada 121 N4
Shamattawa r. Canada 122 D3
Shambār Iran 88 C3
Shamgong Bhutan see Zhemgang
Shamil Iran 88 E5
Shāmīyah des. Iraq/Syria 85 D2
Shamkhor Azer. see Şämkir
Shamrock U.S.A. 131 C5
Shancheng Fujian China see Taining
Shancheng Henan China 73 K5
Shancheng Shandong China see Shanxian
Shand Afgh. 89 F4
Shandan China 80 J4
Shandong prov. China 77 H1
Shandong Bandao pen. China 73 M5
Shandur Pass Pak. 89 I2
Shangchao China 77 F3
Shangcheng China 77 G2
Shangchuan Dao i. China 77 G4
Shangdu China 73 K4
Shangganling China 74 C3

▶Shanghai China 77 I2
3rd most populous city in Asia and the world.

Shanghai mun. China 77 I2
Shangji China see Xichuan
Shangjie China see Yangbi
Shangjin China 77 F1
Shangluo China 77 F1
Shangmei China see Xinhua
Shangnan China 77 F1
Shangpa China see Fugong
Shangpai China see Feixi
Shangpaihe China see Feixi
Shangqiu Henan China see Suiyang
Shangqiu Henan China 77 G1
Shangrao China 77 H2
Shangshui China 77 G1
Shangyou China 77 G3
Shangyou Shuiku resr China 80 F3
Shangyu China 77 I2
Shangzhi China 74 B3
Shangzhou China see Shangluo
Shanhe Gansu China see Zhengning
Shanhe Heilong. China 74 B3
Shankou China 77 F4
Shanlaragh Ireland 51 C6
Shannon airport Ireland 51 D5
Shannon est. Ireland 51 D5
Shannon r. Ireland 51 D5
Shannon, Mouth of the Ireland 51 C5
Shannon National Park Australia 109 B8
Shannon Ø i. Greenland 153 I1
Shan Plateau Myanmar 70 B2
Shansi prov. China see Shanxi
Shantipur India 83 G5
Shantou China 77 H4
Shantung prov. China see Shandong
Shanwei China 77 G4
Shanxi prov. China 77 F1
Shanxian China 77 H1
Shanyang China 77 F1
Shaodong China 77 F3
Shaoguan China 77 G3
Shaowu China 77 H3
Shaoxing China 77 I2
Shaoyang China 77 F3
Shap U.K. 48 E4
Shapa China 77 F4
Shaping China see Ebian
Shapinsay i. U.K. 50 G1
Shapkina r. Russia 42 L2
Shapshal'skiy Khrebet mts Russia 80 G1
Shaqrā' Saudi Arabia 86 G4
Shār, Jabal mt. Saudi Arabia 90 D6
Sharaf well Iraq 91 F5
Sharan Jogizai Pak. 89 H4
Shardara Kazakh. 80 C3
Shardara, Step' plain Kazakh. 80 C3
Shari r. Cameroon/Chad see Chari
Shārī, Buḩayrat imp. l. Iraq 91 G4
Shari-dake vol. Japan 74 G4
Shārīmā Iran 88 E4
Sharjah U.A.E. 88 D5
Sharka-leb La pass China 83 G3
Sharkawshchyna Belarus 45 O9
Shark Bay Australia 109 A6
Shark Reef Australia 110 D2
Sharlyk Russia 41 Q5
Sharm ash Shaykh Egypt 90 D6
Sharm el Sheikh Egypt see Sharm ash Shaykh
Sharon U.S.A. 134 E3
Sharon Springs U.S.A. 130 C4
Sharpe Lake Canada 121 M4
Sharp Peak hill H.K. China 77 [inset]
Sharqat Iraq see Ash Sharqāţ
Sharqī, Jabal ash mts Lebanon/Syria 85 B3
Sharqiy Ustyurt Chink esc. Uzbek. 80 A3
Sharur Azer. see Şərur
Shar'ya Russia 42 J4
Shashe r. Botswana/Zimbabwe 99 C6
Shashemenē Eth. 98 D3
Shashi China see Jingzhou
Shasta U.S.A. 128 B1
Shasta, Mount vol. U.S.A. 126 C4
Shasta Lake U.S.A. 128 B1
Shatilki Belarus see Svyetlahorsk
Sha Tin H.K. China 77 [inset]
Shatki Russia 43 J5
Shaţnat as Salmās, Wādī watercourse Syria 85 D2
Shatoy Russia 91 G2
Shatsk Russia 43 I5
Shatsky Rise sea feature Pacific Ocean 150 G3
Shatt al Arab r. Iran/Iraq 91 H5
Shatura Russia 43 H5
Shaubak Jordan see Ash Shawbak
Shaunavon Canada 121 I5
Shaver Lake U.S.A. 128 D3
Shaw r. Australia 108 B5
Shawangunk Mountains hills U.S.A. 135 H3
Shawano U.S.A. 134 A1
Shawano Lake U.S.A. 134 A1
Shawinigan Canada 123 G5
Shawnee OK U.S.A. 131 D5
Shawnee WY U.S.A. 126 G4
Shawneetown U.S.A. 130 F4
Shaxian China 77 H3
Shay Gap (abandoned) Australia 108 C5
Shaykh, Jabal ash mt. Lebanon/Syria see Hermon, Mount
Shaykh Miskīn Syria 85 C3
Shāzand Iran 88 C3
Shchekino Russia 43 H5
Shchel'yayur Russia 42 L2
Shcherbakov Russia see Rybinsk
Shchigry Russia 43 H6
Shchors Ukr. 43 F6
Shchuchin Belarus see Shchuchyn
Shchuchyn Belarus 45 N10
Shebalino Russia 80 G1
Shebekino Russia 43 H6
Shebelē Wenz, Wabē r. Eth. 98 E3

▶Shebelē Wenz, Wabē r. Somalia 98 E3
5th longest river in Africa.

Sheboygan U.S.A. 134 B2
Shebshi Mountains Nigeria 96 E4
Shebunino Russia 74 F3
Shediac Canada 123 I5
Shedin Peak Canada 120 E4
Shedok Russia 91 F1
Sheelin, Lough l. Ireland 51 E4
Sheep Haven b. Ireland 51 E2
Sheepmoor S. Africa 101 J4
Sheep Mountain U.S.A. 129 J2
Sheep Peak U.S.A. 129 F3
Sheep's Head hd Ireland see Muntervary
Sheerness U.K. 49 H7
Sheet Harbour Canada 123 J5
Shefar'am Israel 85 B3
Sheffield N.Z. 113 D6
Sheffield U.K. 48 F5
Sheffield AL U.S.A. 133 C5
Sheffield PA U.S.A. 134 F3
Sheffield TX U.S.A. 131 C6
Sheffield Lake Canada 123 K4
Shēghē 'Ālāqahdārī Afgh. 89 G4
Sheghnān Afgh. 89 H2
Shegmas Russia 42 K2
Shehong China 76 E2
Sheikh, Jebel esh mt. Lebanon/Syria see Hermon, Mount
Sheikhpura India 83 F4
Sheikhupura Pak. 89 I4
Shējā' ul Mulk Kēlay Afgh. 89 H4
Shekak r. Canada 122 D4
Shekār Āb Iran 88 D3
Shekhawati reg. India 89 I5
Shekhem West Bank see Nāblus
Shekhpura India see Sheikhpura
Sheki Azer. see Şäki
Shek Kwu Chau i. H.K. China 77 [inset]
Shekou China 77 [inset]
Sheksna Russia 42 H4
Sheksninskoye Vodokhranilishche resr Russia 42 H4
Shek Uk Shan mt. H.K. China 77 [inset]
Shela China 76 B2
Shelagskiy, Mys pt Russia 65 S2
Shelbina U.S.A. 130 E4
Shelburn U.S.A. 134 B4
Shelburne N.S. Canada 123 I6
Shelburne Ont. Canada 134 E1
Shelburne Bay Australia 110 C1
Shelby MI U.S.A. 134 B2
Shelby MS U.S.A. 131 F5
Shelby MT U.S.A. 126 F2
Shelby NC U.S.A. 133 D5
Shelbyville IL U.S.A. 130 F4
Shelbyville IN U.S.A. 134 C4
Shelbyville KY U.S.A. 134 C4
Shelbyville TN U.S.A. 132 C5
Sheldon IA U.S.A. 130 E3
Sheldon IL U.S.A. 134 B3
Sheldrake Canada 123 I4
Shelek Kazakh. see Shilik
Shelikhova, Zaliv g. Russia 65 Q3
Shelikof Strait U.S.A. 118 C4
Shell U.S.A. 130 B2
Shellbrook Canada 121 J4
Shelley U.S.A. 126 E4
Shellharbour Australia 112 E5
Shell Lake Canada 121 J4
Shell Lake U.S.A. 130 F2
Shell Mountain U.S.A. 128 B1
Shelter Bay Canada see Port-Cartier
Shelter Island U.S.A. 135 I3
Shelter Point N.Z. 113 B8
Shelton U.S.A. 126 C3
Shemakha Azer. see Şamaxı
Shemordan Russia 42 K4
Shenandoah IA U.S.A. 130 E3
Shenandoah PA U.S.A. 135 G3
Shenandoah Mountains U.S.A. 134 F4
Shenandoah National Park U.S.A. 135 F4
Shendam Nigeria 96 D4
Shending Shan hill China 74 D3
Shengena mt. Tanz. 99 D4
Shengli China 77 G2
Shengli Feng mt. China/Kyrg. see Pobeda Peak
Shengping China 74 B3
Shengrenjian China see Pinglu
Sheng Shan i. China 77 I2
Shengsi China 77 I2
Shengsi Liedao is China 77 I2
Shenjiamen China see Putuo
Shenkursk Russia 42 I3
Shenmu China 73 K5
Shennong Ding mt. China 77 F2
Shennongjia China 77 F2
Shenqiu China 77 G1
Shenshu China 74 C3
Shensi prov. China see Shaanxi
Shentala Russia 43 K5
Shenton, Mount hill Australia 109 C7
Shenyang China 74 A4
Shenzhen China 77 G4
Sheopur India 82 D4
Shepetivka Ukr. 43 E6
Shepetovka Ukr. see Shepetivka
Shepherd Islands Vanuatu 107 G3
Shepherdsville U.S.A. 134 C5
Shepparton Australia 112 B6
Sheppey, Isle of i. U.K. 49 H7
Sheqi China 77 G1
Sherabad Uzbek. see Sherobod
Sherborne U.K. 49 E8
Sherbro Island Sierra Leone 96 B4
Sherbrooke Canada 123 H5
Sherburne U.S.A. 135 H2
Shercock Ireland 51 F4
Shereiq Sudan 86 D6
Shergaon India 83 H4
Shergarh India 82 C4
Sheridan AR U.S.A. 131 E5
Sheridan WY U.S.A. 126 G3
Sheringham U.K. 49 I6
Sherman U.S.A. 131 D5
Sherman Mountain U.S.A. 129 F1
Sherobod Uzbek. 89 G2
Sherpur Dhaka Bangl. 83 G4
Sherpur Rajshahi Bangl. 83 G4
Sherridon Canada 121 K4
's-Hertogenbosch Neth. 52 F3
Sherwood Forest reg. U.K. 49 F5
Sherwood Lake Canada 121 K2
Sheslay Canada 120 D3
Sheslay r. Canada 120 C3
Shethanei Lake Canada 121 L3
Shetland Islands is U.K. 50 [inset]
Shetpe Kazakh. 78 E2
Sheung Shui H.K. China 77 [inset]
Sheung Sze Mun sea chan. H.K. China 77 [inset]
Shevchenko Kazakh. see Aktau
Shevli r. Russia 74 D1
Shexian China 77 H2
Sheyang China 77 I1
Sheyenne r. U.S.A. 130 D2
Shey Phoksundo National Park Nepal 83 E3
Sheyţūr Iran 88 D4
Shezhin II Kazakh. 43 K6
Shiant Islands U.K. 50 C3
Shiashkotan, Ostrov i. Russia 65 Q5
Shibām Yemen 86 G6
Shibar, Kōtal-e Afgh. 89 H3
Shibata Japan 75 E5
Shibazhan China 74 B1
Shibh Jazīrat Sīnā' pen. Egypt see Sinai
Shibīn al Kawm Egypt 90 C5
Shibîn el Kôm Egypt see Shibīn al Kawm
Shibirghān Afgh. 89 G2
Shibogama Lake Canada 122 C3
Shibotsu-jima i. Russia see Zelenyy, Ostrov
Shicheng Fujian China see Zhouning
Shicheng Jiangxi China 77 H3
Shidād al Mismā' hill Saudi Arabia 85 D4
Shidao China 73 M5
Shidian China 76 C3
Shiel, Loch l. U.K. 50 D4
Shield, Cape Australia 110 B2
Shīeli Kazakh. see Shiyeli
Shīf Iran 88 C4
Shifa, Jabal ash mts Saudi Arabia 90 D5
Shifang China 76 E2
Shigatse China see Xigazê
Shiḩān mt. Jordan 85 B4
Shihezi China 80 G3
Shihkiachwang China see Shijiazhuang
Shijiao China see Fogang
Shijiazhuang China 73 K5
Shijiu Hu l. China 77 H2
Shijiusuo China see Rizhao
Shikag Lake Canada 122 C4
Shikar r. Pak. 89 F4
Shikarpur Pak. 89 H5
Shikengkong mt. China 77 G3
Shikhany Russia 43 J5
Shikohabad India 82 D4
Shikoku i. Japan 75 D6
Shikoku-sanchi mts Japan 75 D6
Shikotan, Ostrov i. Russia 74 G4
Shikotan-tō i. Russia see Shikotan, Ostrov
Shikotsu-Tōya Kokuritsu-kōen nat. park Japan 74 F4
Shildon U.K. 48 F4
Shilega Russia 42 J2
Shiliguri India 83 G4
Shilik Kazakh. 80 E3
Shilin China 76 D3
Shilipu China 77 G2
Shiliu China see Changjiang
Shilla mt. India 82 D2
Shillelagh Ireland 51 F5
Shillo, Naḥal r. Israel 85 B3
Shillong India 83 G4
Shillong Peak mt. India 83 G4
Shilovo Russia 43 I5
Shimada Japan 75 E6
Shimanovsk Russia 74 B1
Shimbiris mt. Somalia 98 E2
Shimen Gansu China 76 D1
Shimen Hunan China 77 F2
Shimen Yunnan China see Yunlong
Shimla India 82 D3
Shimoga India see Shivamogga
Shimokita-hantō pen. Japan 74 F4
Shimoni Kenya 99 D4
Shimonoseki Japan 75 C6
Shimsk Russia 42 F4
Shin, Loch l. U.K. 50 E2
Shināfīyah Iraq see Ash Shanāfīyah
Shinan China see Xingye
Shīndand Afgh. 89 F3
Shingbwiyang Myanmar 70 B1
Shing-gai Myanmar 70 B1
Shinghshal Pass Pak. 89 I2
Shingletown U.S.A. 128 C1
Shingū Japan 75 E6
Shingwedzi S. Africa 101 J2
Shingwedzi r. S. Africa 101 J2
Shīnkaī Afgh. 89 G4
Shīnkay Ghar Afgh. 89 H3
Shinnston U.S.A. 134 E4
Shinshār Syria 85 C2
Shinyanga Tanz. 98 D4
Shiocton U.S.A. 134 A1
Shiogama Japan 75 F5
Shiono-misaki c. Japan 75 D6
Shipai China 77 H2
Shiping China 76 D4
Shipki La China/India 82 D3
Shipman U.S.A. 135 F5
Shippegan Island Canada 123 I5
Shippensburg U.S.A. 135 G3
Shiprock U.S.A. 129 I3
Shiprock Peak U.S.A. 129 I3
Shipu China 77 I2
Shipunovo Russia 72 E2
Shiqi China see Zhongshan
Shiqian China 77 F3
Shiqiao China see Panyu
Shiquan China 77 F1
Shiquanhe Xizang China see Ali
Shiquanhe Xizang China see Gar
Shiquan He r. China see Indus
Shiquan Shuiku resr China 77 F1
Shira Russia 72 F2
Shīrābād Iran 88 C2
Shirakawa-go and Gokayama tourist site Japan 75 E5
Shirane-san vol. Japan 75 E5
Shirase Coast Antarctica 152 J1
Shirase Glacier Antarctica 152 D2
Shīrāz Iran 88 D4

Shire r. Malawi 99 D5
Shireza Pak. 89 G5
Shiriya-zaki c. Japan 74 F4
Shirkala reg. Kazakh. 80 A2
Shiroro Reservoir Nigeria 96 D3
Shirpur India 82 C5
Shirten Holoy Gobi des. China 80 I3
Shīrvān Iran 88 E2
Shisanzhan China 74 B2
Shishaldin Volcano U.S.A. 118 B4
Shisha Pangma mt. China see Xixabangma Feng
Shishou China 77 G2
Shitan China 77 G3
Shitang China 77 I2
Shithāthah Iraq 91 F4
Shīū' Iran 88 D5
Shiv India 82 B4
Shivamogga India 84 B3
Shiveegovĭ Mongolia 73 J3
Shiveluch, Vulkan vol. Russia 65 R4
Shivpuri India 82 D4
Shivwits U.S.A. 129 G3
Shivwits Plateau U.S.A. 129 G3
Shiwan Dashan mts China 76 E4
Shiwa N'gandu Zambia 99 D5
Shixing China 77 G3
Shiyan China 77 F1
Shiyeli Kazakh. 80 C3
Shizhong China 77 H1
Shizhu China 77 F2
Shizi China 77 H2
Shizilu China see Junan
Shizong China 76 D3
Shizuishan China 72 J5
Shizuoka Japan 75 E6

▶Shkhara mt. Georgia/Russia 91 F2
3rd highest mountain in Europe.

Shklov Belarus see Shklow
Shklow Belarus 43 F5
Shkodër Albania 59 H3
Shkodra Albania see Shkodër
Shkodrës, Liqeni i l. Albania/Montenegro see Scutari, Lake
Shmidta, Ostrov i. Russia 64 K1
Shmidta, Poluostrov pen. Russia 74 F1
Shoal Lake Canada 121 K5
Shoals U.S.A. 134 B4
Shōbara Japan 75 D6
Shoh Tajik. 89 H2
Shohi Pass Pak. see Tal Pass
Shokanbetsu-dake mt. Japan 74 F4
Sholakkorgan Kazakh. 80 C3
Sholapur India see Solapur
Sholaqqorghan Kazakh. see Sholakkorgan
Shomba r. Russia 44 R4
Shomvukovo Russia 42 K3
Shona Ridge sea feature S. Atlantic Ocean 148 I9
Shonzhy Kazakh. 80 E3
Shor India 82 D2
Shōrābak reg. Afgh. 89 G4
Shorap Pak. 89 G5
Shorapur India 84 C2
Sho'rchi Uzbek. 89 G2
Shorewood IL U.S.A. 134 A3
Shorewood WI U.S.A. 134 B2
Shorkot Pak. 89 I4
Shorkozakhly, Solonchak salt flat Turkm. 91 J2
Shoshone CA U.S.A. 128 E4
Shoshone ID U.S.A. 126 E4
Shoshone r. U.S.A. 126 F3
Shoshone Mountains U.S.A. 128 E2
Shoshone Peak U.S.A. 128 E3
Shoshong Botswana 101 H2
Shoshoni U.S.A. 126 F4
Shostka Ukr. 43 G6
Shotoran, Chashmeh-ye well Iran 88 D3
Shotor Khūn Afgh. 89 G3
Shouyang Shan mt. China 77 F1
Showak Sudan 86 E7
Show Low U.S.A. 129 H4
Shoyna Russia 42 J2
Shpola Ukr. 43 F6
Shqipëria country Europe see Albania
Shreve U.S.A. 134 D3
Shreveport U.S.A. 131 E5
Shrewsbury U.K. 49 E6
Shri Lanka country Asia see Sri Lanka
Shri Mohangarh India 82 B4
Shrirampur India 83 G5
Shu Kazakh. 80 D3
Shu r. Kazakh./Kyrg. 80 C3
Shū r. Kazakh./Kyrg. see Shu
Shu'ab, Ra's pt Yemen 87 H7
Shuajingsi China 76 D1
Shuangbai China 76 D3
Shuangcheng Fujian China see Zherong
Shuangcheng Heilong. China 74 B3
Shuanghe Hubei China 77 G2
Shuanghe Sichuan China 76 E2
Shuanghedagang China 74 C2
Shuangjiang Guizhou China see Jiangkou
Shuangjiang Hunan China see Tongdao
Shuangjiang Yunnan China see Eshan
Shuangliao China 74 A4
Shuangliu China 76 D2
Shuangpai China 77 F3
Shuangshipu China see Fengxian
Shuangxi China see Shunchang
Shuangyang China 74 B4
Shuangyashan China 74 C3
Shubarkudyk Kazakh. 80 A2
Shubayḩ well Saudi Arabia 85 D4
Shugozero Russia 42 G4
Shuidong China see Dianbai
Shuijing China 76 E1
Shuikou Guangxi China 76 E4
Shuikou Hunan China 77 F3
Shu-Ile, Gory mts Kazakh. 80 D3
Shuiluocheng China see Zhuanglang
Shuizhai China see Wuhua
Shulan China 74 B3
Shumagin Islands U.S.A. 118 B4
Shumba Zimbabwe 99 C5
Shumen Bulg. 59 L3
Shumerlya Russia 42 J5
Shumilina Belarus 43 F5
Shumyachi Russia 43 G5
Shūnan Japan 75 C6
Shunchang China 77 H3
Shuncheng China 74 A4
Shunde China 77 G4
Shuoxian China see Shuozhou
Shuozhou China 73 K5
Shuqrah Yemen 86 G7
Shūr r. Iran 88 D4
Shūr r. Iran 89 F3
Shūr watercourse Iran 88 D5
Shur watercourse Iran 88 E3
Shūr, Chāh-e well Iran 88 D3
Shūr, Rūd-e watercourse Iran 88 E4
Shūr Āb watercourse Iran 88 D4
Shūrjestān Iran 88 D4
Shūrū Iran 89 F4
Shuryshkarskiy Sor, Ozero l. Russia 41 T2
Shūsh Iran 88 C3
Shusha Azer. see Şuşa
Shūshtar Iran 88 C3
Shutfah, Qalamat well Saudi Arabia 88 D6
Shuwayḩān Syria 85 D2
Shuwaysh, Tall ash hill Jordan 85 C4
Shuya Ivanovskaya Oblast' Russia 42 I4
Shuya Respublika Kareliya Russia 42 G3
Shuyskoye Russia 42 I4
Shuẓāẓ, Jabal mt. Saudi Arabia 91 F6
Shwebo Myanmar 70 A2
Shwedwin Myanmar 70 A1
Shwegun Myanmar 70 B3
Shwegyin Myanmar 70 B3
Shweudaung mt. Myanmar 70 B2
Shyganak Kazakh. 80 D2
Shyghanaq Kazakh. see Shyganak
Shymkent Kazakh. 80 C3
Shyngystau, Khrebet mts Kazakh. 80 E2
Shyok India 82 D2
Shypuvate Ukr. 43 H6
Shyroke Ukr. 43 G7
Sia Indon. 69 I8
Siabu Indon. 71 B7
Siahan Range mts Pak. 89 F5
Sīah Cheshmeh Iran 88 B2
Sialkot Pak. 89 I3
Siam country Asia see Thailand
Sian China see Xi'an
Sian Russia 74 B1
Siang r. India see Brahmaputra
Siantan i. Indon. 71 D7
Siargao i. Phil. 69 H5
Siatlai Myanmar 70 A2
Siau i. Indon. 69 H6
Šiauliai Lith. 45 M9
Siazan' Azer. see Siyäzän
Si Bai, Lam r. Thai. 70 D4
Sibasa S. Africa 101 J2
Sibayi, Lake S. Africa 101 K4
Sibda China 76 C2
Šibenik Croatia 58 F3
Siberia reg. Russia 65 M3
Siberut i. Indon. 68 B7
Siberut, Selat sea chan. Indon. 68 B7
Sibi Pak. 89 G4
Sibidiri P.N.G. 69 K8
Sibigo Indon. 71 A7
Sibiloi National Park Kenya 98 D3
Sibir' reg. Russia see Siberia
Sibiti Congo 98 B4
Sibiu Romania 59 K2
Sibley U.S.A. 130 E3
Siboa Indon. 69 G6
Sibolga Indon. 71 B7
Siborongborong Indon. 71 B7
Sibu Sarawak Malaysia 68 E6
Sibut Cent. Afr. Rep. 98 B3
Sibuyan i. Phil. 69 G4
Sibuyan Sea Phil. 69 G4
Sicamous Canada 120 G5
Sicca Veneria Tunisia see Le Kef
Siccus watercourse Australia 111 B6
Sicheng Anhui China see Sixian
Sicheng Guangxi China see Lingyun
Sichon Thai. 71 B5
Sichuan prov. China 76 D2
Sichuan Pendi basin China 76 E2
Sicié, Cap c. France 56 G5
Sicilia i. Italy see Sicily
Sicilian Channel Italy/Tunisia 58 E6
Sicily i. Italy 58 F5
Sicuani Peru 142 D6
Siddhapur India see Sidhpur
Siddipet India 84 C2
Sideros, Akra pt Greece see Sideros, Akrotirio
Sideros, Akrotirio pt Greece 59 L7
Sidesaviwa S. Africa 100 F7
Sidhauli India 82 E4
Sidhi India 83 E4
Sidhpur India 82 C5
Sidi Aïssa Alg. 57 H6
Sidi Ali Alg. 57 G5
Sīdī Barrānī Egypt 90 B5
Sidi Bel Abbès Alg. 57 F6
Sidi Bennour Morocco 54 C5
Sidi Bou Sa'id Tunisia see Sidi Bouzid
Sidi Bouzid Tunisia 58 C7
Sidi el Barráni Egypt see Sīdī Barrānī
Sidi El Hani, Sebkhet de salt pan Tunisia 58 D7
Sidi Ifni Morocco 96 B2
Sidi Kacem Morocco 54 C5
Sidikalang Indon. 71 B7
Sidi Khaled Alg. 54 E5
Sid Lake Canada 121 J2
Sidlaw Hills U.K. 50 F4
Sidley, Mount Antarctica 152 J1
Sidli India 83 G4
Sidmouth U.K. 49 D8
Sidney IA U.S.A. 130 E3
Sidney MT U.S.A. 126 G3
Sidney NE U.S.A. 130 C3
Sidney OH U.S.A. 134 C3
Sidney Lanier, Lake U.S.A. 133 D5
Sidoktaya Myanmar 70 A2
Sidon Lebanon 85 B3
Sidr Egypt see Sudr
Siedlce Poland 43 D5
Sieg r. Germany 53 H4
Siegen Germany 53 I4
Siĕm Réab Cambodia 71 C4
Siem Reap Cambodia see Siĕm Réab
Si'en China see Huanjiang
Siena Italy 58 D3
Sieradz Poland 47 Q5
Si'erdingka China 76 B2
Sierra Blanca U.S.A. 127 G7
Sierra Colorada Arg. 144 C6
Sierra Grande Arg. 144 C6
Sierra Leone country Africa 96 B4
Sierra Leone Basin sea feature N. Atlantic Ocean 148 G5
Sierra Leone Rise sea feature N. Atlantic Ocean 148 G5
Sierra Madre Mountains U.S.A. 128 C4
Sierra Mojada Mex. 131 C7
Sierra Nevada, Parque Nacional nat. park Venez. 142 D2
Sierra Nevada de Santa Marta, Parque Nacional nat. park Col. 142 D1
Sierraville U.S.A. 128 C2
Sierra Vista U.S.A. 127 F7
Sierre Switz. 56 H3
Sievi Fin. 44 N5
Sifang Ling mts China 76 E4
Sifangtai China 74 B3
Sīfenī Eth. 98 E2
Sifnos i. Greece 59 K6
Sig Alg. 57 F6
Sigguup Nunaa pen. Greenland 119 M2
Sighetu Marmației Romania 43 D7
Sighișoara Romania 59 K1
Siglap Sing. 71 [inset]
Sigli Indon. 71 A6
Siglufjörður Iceland 44 [inset 1]
Signal de Botrange hill Belgium 52 G4
Signal de la Ste-Baume mt. France 56 G5
Signal Peak U.S.A. 129 F5
Signy research station Antarctica 152 A2
Signy-l'Abbaye France 52 E5
Sigourney U.S.A. 130 E3
Sigri, Akra pt Greece see Saratsina, Akrotirio
Sigsbee Deep sea feature G. of Mexico 151 N4
Sigüenza Spain 57 E3
Siguiri Guinea 96 C3
Sigulda Latvia 45 N8
Sigurd U.S.A. 129 H2
Sihanoukville Cambodia 71 C5
Sihaung Myauk Myanmar 70 A2
Sihawa India 84 D1
Sihong China 77 H1
Sihora India 82 E5
Sihui China 77 G4
Siikajoki Fin. 44 N4
Siilinjärvi Fin. 44 O5
Siirt Turkey 91 F3
Sijawal Pak. 82 B4
Sikaka Saudi Arabia see Sakākā
Sikandra Rao India 82 D4
Sikanni Chief Canada 120 F3
Sikanni Chief r. Canada 120 F3
Sikar India 82 C4
Sikaram mt. Afgh. 89 H3
Sikasso Mali 96 C3
Sikaw Myanmar 70 B2
Sikeston U.S.A. 131 F4
Sikhote-Alin' mts Russia 74 D4
Sikhote-Alinskiy Zapovednik nature res. Russia 74 E3
Sikinos i. Greece 59 K6
Sikka India 82 B5
Sikkim state India 83 G4
Siksjö Sweden 44 J4
Sil r. Spain 57 C2
Şila' i. Saudi Arabia 90 D6
Šilalė Lith. 45 M9
Si Lanna National Park Thai. 70 B3
Silas U.S.A. 131 F6
Silavatturai Sri Lanka 84 C4
Silawaih Agam vol. Indon. 71 A6
Silberberg hill Germany 53 J1
Silchar India 83 H4
Şile Turkey 59 M4
Sileru r. India 84 D2
Silesia reg. Czechia/Poland 47 P5
Silety r. Kazakh. 72 C2
Siletyteniz, Ozero salt l. Kazakh. 79 G1
Silghat India 83 H4
Siliana Tunisia 58 C6
Silifke Turkey 85 A1
Siliguri India see Shiliguri
Siling Co salt l. China 83 G3
Silipur India 82 D4
Silistra Bulg. 59 L2
Silistria Bulg. see Silistra
Silivri Turkey 59 M4
Siljan l. Sweden 45 I6
Silkeborg Denmark 45 F8
Sillajhuay mt. Chile 142 E7
Sillamäe Estonia 45 O7
Sille Turkey 90 D3
Silli India 83 F5
Sillod India 84 B1
Silobela S. Africa 101 J4
Silsby Lake Canada 121 M4
Silt U.S.A. 129 J2
Siltaharju Fin. 44 O3
Sīlūp r. Iran 89 F5
Šilutė Lith. 45 L9
Silvan Turkey 91 F3
Silvânia Brazil 145 A2
Silvassa India 84 B1
Silver Bank Passage Turks and Caicos Is 137 J4
Silver Bay U.S.A. 130 F2
Silver City NM U.S.A. 129 I5
Silver City NV U.S.A. 128 D2
Silver City (abandoned) Canada 120 B2
Silver Creek r. U.S.A. 129 H4
Silver Lake U.S.A. 126 C4
Silver Lake l. U.S.A. 128 E4
Silvermine Mountains hills Ireland 51 D5
Silver Peak Range mts U.S.A. 128 E3
Silver Spring U.S.A. 135 G4
Silver Springs U.S.A. 128 D2
Silverthrone Mountain Canada 120 E5
Silvertip Mountain Canada 120 F5
Silverton U.K. 49 D8
Silverton CO U.S.A. 129 J3
Silverton TX U.S.A. 131 C5
Sima China 83 G3
Simanggang Sarawak Malaysia see Sri Aman
Simao China 76 D4
Simard, Lac l. Canada 122 F5
Simaria India 83 F4
Simav Turkey 59 M5
Simav Dağları mts Turkey 59 M5
Simba Dem. Rep. Congo 98 C3
Simbirsk Russia see Ul'yanovsk
Simcoe Canada 134 E2
Simcoe, Lake Canada 134 F1
Simdega India 84 E1
Simēn mts Eth. 98 D2
Simēn Mountains Eth. see Simēn
Simeulue i. Indon. 71 B7

▶Simferopol' Crimea 90 D1
Capital of Crimea.

Sími i. Greece see Symi
Simikot Nepal 83 E3
Similan, Ko i. Thai. 71 B5
Simi Valley U.S.A. 128 D4
Simla India see Shimla
Simla U.S.A. 126 G5
Şimleu Silvaniei Romania 59 J1
Simlipal National Park India 83 F5
Simmerath Germany 52 G4
Simmern/Hunsrück Germany 53 H5
Simmesport U.S.A. 131 F6
Simms U.S.A. 126 F3
Simojärvi l. Fin. 44 O3
Simon Mex. 131 C7
Simonette r. Canada 120 G4
Simon Wash watercourse U.S.A. 129 I5
Simoom Sound Canada 120 E5
Simoon Sound Canada see Simoom Sound
Simpang Indon. 68 C7
Simpang Mangayau, Tanjung pt Malaysia 68 F5
Simpele Fin. 45 P6
Simplício Mendes Brazil 143 J5
Simplon Pass Switz. 56 I3
Simpson Canada 121 J5
Simpson U.S.A. 126 F2
Simpson Desert Australia 110 B5
Simpson Desert National Park Australia 110 B5
Simpson Desert Regional Reserve nature res. Australia 111 B5
Simpson Islands Canada 121 H2
Simpson Park Mountains U.S.A. 128 E2
Simpson Peninsula Canada 119 J3
Simrishamn Sweden 45 I9
Simushir, Ostrov i. Russia 73 S3
Sina r. India 84 B2
Sinabang Indon. 71 B7
Sinabung vol. Indon. 71 B7
Sinai pen. Egypt 85 A5
Sinai, Mont hill France 52 E5
Sinai al Janûbîya governorate Egypt see Janūb Sīnā'
Sinai ash Shamâlîya governorate Egypt see Shamāl Sīnā'
Si Nakarin, Ang Kep Nam Thai. 70 B4
Sinaloa state Mex. 127 F8
Sinalunga Italy 58 D3
Sinan China 77 F3
Sinancha Russia see Cheremshany
Sinbo Myanmar 70 B1
Sinbyubyin Myanmar 71 B4
Sinbyugyun Myanmar 70 A2
Sincan Turkey 90 E3
Sincelejo Col. 142 C2
Sinchu Taiwan see Taoyuan
Sinclair Mills Canada 120 F4
Sincora, Serra do hills Brazil 145 C1
Sind r. India 82 D4
Sind Pak. see Thul
Sind prov. Pak. see Sindh
Sinda Russia 74 E2
Sindari India 82 B4
Sindelfingen Germany 53 I6
Sindh prov. Pak. 89 H5
Sindhulimadi Nepal see Kamalamai
Sındırgı Turkey 59 M5
Sindor Russia 42 K3
Sindou Burkina Faso 96 C3
Sindri India 83 F5
Sind Sagar Doab lowland Pak. 89 H4
Sinel'nikovo Ukr. see Synel'nykove
Sines Port. 57 B5
Sines, Cabo de c. Port. 57 B5
Sinettä Fin. 44 N3
Sinfra Côte d'Ivoire 96 C4
Sing Myanmar 70 B2
Singa Sudan 86 D7
Singanallur India 84 C4
Singapore country Asia 71 [inset]

▶Singapore Sing. 71 [inset]
Capital of Singapore.

Singapore r. Sing. 71 [inset]
Singapore, Strait of Indon./Sing. 71 [inset]
Singapura country Asia see Singapore
Singapura Sing. see Singapore
Singapuru India 84 D2
Singaraja Indon. 108 A2
Sing Buri Thai. 70 C4
Singhampton Canada 134 E1
Singhana India 82 C3
Singida Tanz. 99 D4
Singidunum Serbia see Belgrade
Singkaling Hkamti Myanmar 70 A1
Singkawang Indon. 68 D6
Singkep i. Indon. 68 C7
Singkil Indon. 71 B7
Singkuang Indon. 71 B7
Singleton Australia 112 E4
Singleton, Mount hill N.T. Australia 108 E5
Singleton, Mount hill W.A. Australia 109 B7
Singora Thai. see Songkhla
Sin'gosan N. Korea see Kosan
Singra India 83 G4
Singri India 83 H4
Singu Myanmar 76 B4
Singwara India 84 D1
Sin'gye N. Korea 75 B5
Sinhala country Asia see Sri Lanka
Sinhkung Myanmar 70 B1
Sining China see Xining
Siniscola Sardinia Italy 58 C4
Sinj Croatia 58 G3
Sinjai Indon. 69 G8
Sinjār, Jabal mt. Iraq 91 F3
Sinkat Sudan 86 E6
Sinkiang aut. reg. China see Xinjiang Uygur Zizhiqu
Sinkiang Uighur Autonomous Region aut. reg. China see Xinjiang Uygur Zizhiqu
Sinmi-do i. N. Korea 75 B5
Sinn Germany 53 I4
Sinnamary Fr. Guiana 143 H2
Sinn Bishr, Gebel hill Egypt see Sinn Bishr, Jabal
Sinn Bishr, Jabal hill Egypt 85 A5
Sinneh Iran see Sanandaj
Sinoia Zimbabwe see Chinhoyi
Sinop Brazil 143 G6
Sinop Turkey 90 D2
Sinope Turkey see Sinop
Sinp'a N. Korea see Kimjŏngsuk
Sinp'o N. Korea 75 C4
Sinsang N. Korea 75 B5
Sinsheim Germany 53 I5
Sintang Indon. 68 E6
Sint Eustatius mun. West Indies 137 L5
Sint-Laureins Belgium 52 D3
Sint Martin terr. West Indies see St Maarten
Sint-Niklaas Belgium 52 E3
Sinton U.S.A. 131 D6
Sintra Port. 57 B4
Sint-Truiden Belgium 52 F4
Sinŭiju N. Korea 75 B4
Sinzig Germany 53 H4
Siófok Hungary 58 H1
Sioma Ngwezi National Park Zambia 99 C5
Sion Switz. 56 H3
Sion Mills U.K. 51 E3
Siorapaluk Greenland 119 K2
Sioux Center U.S.A. 125 H3
Sioux City U.S.A. 130 D3
Sioux Falls U.S.A. 130 D3
Sioux Lookout Canada 121 N5
Siphaqeni S. Africa see Flagstaff
Siping China 74 B4
Sipiwesk Canada 121 L4
Sipiwesk Lake Canada 121 L4
Siple, Mount Antarctica 152 J2
Siple Coast Antarctica 152 I1
Siple Dome ice feature Antarctica 152 J1
Siple Island Antarctica 152 J2
Siponj Tajik. see Bartang
Sipsey r. U.S.A. 131 F5
Sipura i. Indon. 68 B7
Sīq, Wādī as watercourse Egypt 85 A5
Sir r. Pak. 89 H6
Sir, Dar"yoi r. Asia see Syrdar'ya
Sira India 84 C3
Sira r. Norway 45 E7
Şīr Abū Nu'āyr i. U.A.E. 88 D5
Siracusa Sicily Italy see Syracuse
Siraha Nepal see Sirha
Sirajganj Bangl. 83 G4
Sir Alexander, Mount Canada 120 F4
Şiran Turkey 91 E2
Sirbāl, Jabal mt. Egypt 90 D5
Şīr Banī Yās i. U.A.E. 88 D5
Sircilla India see Sirsilla
Sirdaryo r. Asia see Syrdar'ya
Sirdaryo Uzbek. 80 C3
Sirdingka China see Si'erdingka
Sir Edward Pellew Group is Australia 110 B2
Sirha Nepal 83 F4
Sirḩān, Wādī as watercourse Jordan/Saudi Arabia 85 C4
Sirik, Tanjung pt Malaysia 68 E6
Siri Kit, Khuan Thai. 70 C3
Sirina i. Greece see Syrna
Sīrjā Iran 89 F5
Sir James MacBrien, Mount Canada 120 E2
Sīrjān Iran 88 D4
Sīrjān salt flat Iran 88 D4
Sirkazhi India 84 C4
Sirmilik National Park Canada 119 K2
Şırnak Turkey 91 F3
Sirohi India 82 C4
Sirombu Indon. 71 B7
Sironj India 82 D4
Síros i. Greece see Syros
Sirpur India 84 C2
Sirr, Nafūd as des. Saudi Arabia 88 B5
Sirretta Peak U.S.A. 128 D4
Sīrrī, Jazīreh-ye i. Iran 88 D5
Sirsa India 82 C3
Sir Sandford, Mount Canada 120 G5
Sirsi Karnataka India 84 B3
Sirsi Madh. Prad. India 82 D4
Sirsi Uttar Prad. India 82 D3
Sirsilla India 84 C2
Sirte Libya 97 E1
Sirte, Gulf of Libya 97 E1
Sir Thomas, Mount hill Australia 109 E6
Siruguppa India 84 C3
Sirur India 84 B2
Şirvan Azer. 91 H3
Şirvan Turkey 91 F3
Sirvel India 84 C3
Širvintai Lith. see Širvintos
Širvintos Lith. 45 N9
Sīrwān r. Iraq 91 G4
Sir Wilfrid Laurier, Mount Canada 120 G4
Sis Turkey see Kozan
Sisak Croatia 58 G2
Sisaket Thai. 70 D4
Siscia Croatia see Sisak
Sishen S. Africa 100 F4
Sishilipu China 76 E1
Sishuang Liedao is China 77 I3
Sisian Armenia 91 G3
Sisimiut Greenland 119 M3
Sisipuk Lake Canada 121 K4
Sisŏphŏn Cambodia 71 C4
Sissano P.N.G. 69 K7
Sisseton U.S.A. 130 D2
Sīstān reg. Iran 89 F4
Sisteron France 56 G4
Sisters is India 71 A5
Sīt Iran 88 E5
Sitamarhi India 83 F4
Sitang China see Sinan
Sitapur India 82 E4
Siteia Greece 59 L7
Siteki Swaziland 101 J4
Sithonia pen. Greece see Sithonias, Chersonisos
Sithonias, Chersonisos pen. Greece 59 J4
Sitía Greece see Siteia
Sitidgi Lake Canada 118 E3
Sitila Moz. 101 L2
Siting China 76 E3
Sítio do Mato Brazil 145 C1
Sitka U.S.A. 120 C3
Sitka National Historical Park nat. park U.S.A. 120 C3
Sitra oasis Egypt see Sitrah
Sitrah oasis Egypt 90 B5
Sittang r. Myanmar see Sittaung
Sittard Neth. 52 F4
Sittaung Myanmar 70 A1
Sittaung r. Myanmar 70 B3
Sittensen Germany 53 J1
Sittingbourne U.K. 49 H7
Sittoung r. Myanmar see Sittaung
Sittwe Myanmar see Akyab
Situbondo Indon. 68 E8
Siumpu i. Indon. 69 G8
Siuri India 83 F5
Sivaganga India 84 C4
Sivakasi India 84 C4
Sivaki Russia 74 B1
Sivan India see Siwan
Sivas Turkey 90 E3
Sivasagar India 83 H4
Sivaslı Turkey 59 M5
Siverek Turkey 91 E3
Siverskiy Russia 45 Q7
Sivers'kyy Donets' r. Russia/Ukr. see Northern Donets
Sivomaskinskiy Russia 41 S2
Sivrice Turkey 91 E3
Sivrihisar Turkey 59 N5
Sivukile S. Africa 101 I4
Sīwa Egypt see Sīwah
Sīwah Egypt 90 B5
Sīwah, Wāḩāt oasis Egypt 90 B5
Siwalik Range mts India/Nepal 82 D3
Siwan India 83 F4
Siwana India 82 C4
Siwa Oasis oasis Egypt see Sīwah, Wāḩāt
Sixian China 77 H1
Sixmilecross U.K. 51 E3
Siyabuswa S. Africa 101 I3
Siyāh Band, Kōh-e mts Afgh. 89 F3
Siyāh Gird Afgh. 89 G2
Siyāh Kōh mts Afgh. 89 G3
Siyäzän Azer. 91 H2
Sīyunī Iran 88 D3
Siziwang Qi China see Ulan Hua
Sjælland i. Denmark see Zealand
Sjenica Serbia 59 I3
Sjöbo Sweden 45 H9
Sjøvegan Norway 44 J2
Skadarsko Jezero, Nacionalni Park nat. park Montenegro 59 H3
Skadovs'k Ukr. 59 O1
Skaftárós r. mouth Iceland 44 [inset 1]
Skagafjörður inlet Iceland 44 [inset 1]
Skagen Denmark 45 G8
Skagerrak strait Denmark/Norway 45 F8
Skagit r. U.S.A. 126 C2
Skagway U.S.A. 153 A3
Skaidi Norway 44 N1
Skaland Norway 44 J2
Skalmodal Sweden 44 I4
Skanderborg Denmark 45 F8
Skaneateles Lake U.S.A. 135 G2
Skara Sweden 45 H7
Skardarsko Jezero l. Albania/Montenegro see Scutari, Lake
Skardu Pak. 82 C2
Skärgårdshavets nationalpark nat. park Fin. 45 L7
Skarnes Norway 45 G6
Skarżysko-Kamienna Poland 47 R5
Skaulo Sweden 44 L3
Skawina Poland 47 Q6
Skeena r. Canada 120 D4
Skeena Mountains Canada 120 D3
Skegness U.K. 48 H5
Skellefteå Sweden 44 L4
Skellefteälven r. Sweden 44 L4
Skelleftehamn Sweden 44 L4
Skelmersdale U.K. 48 E5
Skerries Ireland 51 F4
Ski Norway 45 G7
Skiathos i. Greece 59 J5
Skibbereen Ireland 51 C6
Skibotn Norway 44 L2
Skiddaw hill U.K. 48 D4
Skien Norway 45 F7
Skiermûntseach Neth. see Schiermonnikoog
Skiermûntseach i. Neth. see Schiermonnikoog
Skierniewice Poland 47 R5
Skikda Alg. 58 B6
Skipsea U.K. 48 G5
Skipton Australia 112 A6
Skipton U.K. 48 E5
Skirlaugh U.K. 48 G5
Skiros i. Greece see Skyros
Skive Denmark 45 F8
Skjern Denmark 45 F9
Skjolden Norway 45 E6
Skobelev Uzbek. see Farg'ona
Skobeleva, Pik mt. Kyrg. 89 I2
Skodje Norway 44 E5
Skoganvarri Norway 44 N2
Skokie U.S.A. 134 B2
Skomer Island U.K. 49 B7

Skopelos i. Greece 59 J5
Skopin Russia 43 H5

▶Skopje Macedonia 59 I4
Capital of Macedonia.

Skoplje Macedonia see Skopje
Skövde Sweden 45 H7
Skovorodino Russia 74 A1
Skowhegan U.S.A. 135 K1
Skrunda Latvia 45 M8
Skukum, Mount Canada 120 C2
Skukuza S. Africa 101 J3
Skull Valley U.S.A. 129 G4
Skuodas Lith. 45 L8
Skurup Sweden 45 H9
Skutskär Sweden 45 J6
Skvyra Ukr. 43 F6
Skye i. U.K. 50 C3
Skylge i. Neth. see Terschelling
Skyring, Seno b. Chile 144 B8
Skyros Greece 59 K5
Skyros i. Greece 59 K5
Skytrain Ice Rise Antarctica 152 L1
Slættaratindur hill Faroe Is 44 [inset 2]
Slagelse Denmark 45 G9
Slagnäs Sweden 44 K4
Slane Ireland 51 F4
Slaney r. Ireland 51 F5
Slantsy Russia 45 P7
Slashers Reefs Australia 110 D3
Slatina Croatia 58 G2
Slatina Romania 59 K2
Slaty Fork U.S.A. 134 E4
Slava Russia 74 C1
Slave r. Canada 121 H2
Slave Coast Africa 96 D4
Slave Lake Canada 120 H4
Slave Point Canada 120 H2
Slavgorod Belarus see Slawharad
Slavgorod Russia 72 D2
Slavkovichi Russia 45 P8
Slavonska Požega Croatia see Požega
Slavonski Brod Croatia 58 H2
Slavuta Ukr. 43 E6
Slavutych Ukr. 43 F6
Slavyanka Russia 74 C4
Slavyansk Ukr. see Slov"yans'k
Slavyanskaya Russia see Slavyansk-na-Kubani
Slavyansk-na-Kubani Russia 90 E1
Slawharad Belarus 43 F5
Sławno Poland 47 P3
Slayton U.S.A. 130 E3
Sleaford U.K. 49 G5
Slea Head hd Ireland 51 B5
Sleat Neth. see Sloten
Sleat, Sound of sea chan. U.K. 50 D3
Sled Lake Canada 121 J4
Sleeper Islands Canada 122 F2
Sleeping Bear Dunes Wilderness *nature res.* U.S.A. 134 B1
Slessor Glacier Antarctica 152 B1
Slick Rock U.S.A. 129 I2
Slide Mountain U.S.A. 135 H3
Slieve Bloom Mountains hills Ireland 51 E5
Slieve Car hill Ireland 51 C3
Slieve Donard hill U.K. 51 G3
Slieve Mish Mountains hills Ireland 51 B5
Slieve Snaght hill Ireland 51 E2
Sligachan U.K. 50 C3
Sligeach Ireland see Sligo
Sligo Ireland 51 D3
Sligo U.S.A. 134 F3
Sligo Bay Ireland 51 D3
Slinger U.S.A. 134 A2
Slippery Rock U.S.A. 134 E3
Slite Sweden 45 K8
Sliven Bulg. 59 L3
Sloan U.S.A. 129 F4
Sloat U.S.A. 128 C2
Sloboda Russia see Ezhva
Slobodchikovo Russia 42 K3
Slobodskoy Russia 42 K4
Slobozia Romania 59 L2
Slochteren Neth. 52 G1
Slonim Belarus 45 N10
Slootdorp Neth. 52 E2
Sloten Neth. 52 F2
Slough U.K. 49 G7
Slovakia country Europe 40 J6
Slovenia country Europe 58 F2
Slovenija country Europe see Slovenia
Slovenj Gradec Slovenia 58 F1
Slovensko country Europe see Slovakia
Slovenský raj, Národný park nat. park Slovakia 47 R6
Slov"yans'k Ukr. 43 H6
Słowiński Park Narodowy nat. park Poland 47 P3
Sluch r. Ukr. 43 E6
S'Lung, B'Nom mt. Vietnam 71 D5
Słupsk Poland 47 P3
Slussfors Sweden 44 J4
Slutsk Belarus 45 O10
Slyne Head hd Ireland 51 B4
Slyudyanka Russia 72 I2
Smăch, Kaôh i. Cambodia 71 C5
Small Point U.S.A. 135 K2
Smallwood Reservoir Canada 123 I3
Smalyavichy Belarus 45 P9
Smalyenskaya Wzwyshsha hills Belarus/Russia see Smolensko-Moskovskaya Vozvyshennost'
Smarhon' Belarus 45 O9
Smeaton Canada 121 J4
Smederevo Serbia 59 I2
Smederevska Palanka Serbia 59 I2
Smela Ukr. see Smila
Smethport U.S.A. 135 F3
Smidovich Russia 74 D2
Smila Ukr. 43 F6
Smilde Neth. 52 G2
Smiltene Latvia 45 N8
Smirnykh Russia 74 F2
Smith Canada 120 H4
Smith Center U.S.A. 130 D4
Smithers Canada 120 E4
Smithfield S. Africa 101 H6
Smithfield NC U.S.A. 132 E5
Smithfield UT U.S.A. 126 F4
Smith Glacier Antarctica 152 K1
Smith Island India 71 A4
Smith Island MD U.S.A. 135 G4
Smith Island VA U.S.A. 135 H5
Smith Mountain Lake U.S.A. 134 F5
Smith River Canada 120 E3
Smiths Falls Canada 135 G1
Smithton Australia 111 [inset]
Smithtown Australia 112 F3
Smithville OK U.S.A. 131 E5
Smithville WV U.S.A. 134 E4
Smoke Creek Desert U.S.A. 128 D1
Smoky Bay Australia 109 F8
Smoky Cape Australia 112 F3
Smoky Falls Canada 122 E4
Smoky Hill r. U.S.A. 130 C4
Smoky Hills KS U.S.A. 124 H4
Smoky Hills KS U.S.A. 130 D4
Smoky Lake Canada 121 H4
Smoky Mountains U.S.A. 126 E4
Smøla i. Norway 44 E5
Smolenka Russia 43 K6
Smolensk Russia 43 G5
Smolensk-Moscow Upland hills Belarus/Russia 43 G5
Smolensko-Moskovskaya Vozvyshennost' hills Belarus/Russia see Smolensk-Moscow Upland
Smolevichi Belarus see Smalyavichy
Smolyan Bulg. 59 K4
Smooth Rock Falls Canada 122 E4
Smoothrock Lake Canada 122 C4
Smoothstone Lake Canada 121 J4
Smørfjord Norway 44 N1
Smorgon' Belarus see Smarhon'
Smyley Island Antarctica 152 L2
Smyrna Turkey see İzmir
Smyrna U.S.A. 135 H4
Smyth Island atoll Marshall Is see Taongi
Snæfell mt. Iceland 44 [inset 1]
Snaefell hill Isle of Man 48 C4
Snag (abandoned) Canada 120 A2
Snake r. Canada 120 C1
Snake r. U.S.A. 126 D3
Snake Island Australia 112 C7
Snake Range mts U.S.A. 129 F2
Snake River Canada 120 F3
Snake River Plain U.S.A. 126 E4
Snare r. Canada 120 G2
Snare Lake Canada 121 J3
Snare Lakes Canada see Wekweètì
Snares Islands N.Z. 107 G6
Snåsa Norway 44 H4
Sneedville U.S.A. 134 D5
Sneek Neth. 52 F1
Sneem Ireland 51 C6
Sneeuberge mts S. Africa 100 G6
Snegamook Lake Canada 123 J3
Snegurovka Ukr. see Tetiyiv
Snelling U.S.A. 128 C3
Snettisham U.K. 49 H6
Snezhnogorsk Russia 64 J3
Snežnik mt. Slovenia 58 F2
Sniečkus Lith. see Visaginas
Snihurivka Ukr. 43 G7
Snits Neth. see Sneek
Snizort, Loch b. U.K. 50 C3
Snoqualmie Pass U.S.A. 126 C3
Snøtinden mt. Norway 44 H3
Snoul Cambodia see Snuŏl
Snover U.S.A. 134 D2
Snovsk Ukr. see Shchors
Snowbird Lake Canada 121 K2
Snowcrest Mountain Canada 120 G5
Snowdon mt. U.K. 49 C5
Snowdonia National Park U.K. 49 D6
Snowdrift Canada see Łutselk'e
Snowdrift r. Canada 121 I2
Snowflake U.S.A. 129 H4
Snow Hill U.S.A. 135 H4
Snow Lake Canada 121 K4
Snowville U.S.A. 126 E4
Snow Water Lake U.S.A. 129 F1
Snowy r. Australia 112 D6
Snowy Mountain U.S.A. 135 H2
Snowy Mountains Australia 112 C6
Snowy River National Park Australia 112 D6
Snug Corner Bahamas 133 F8
Snug Harbour Nfld. and Lab. Canada 123 L3
Snug Harbour Ont. Canada 134 E1
Snuŏl Cambodia 71 D4
Snyder U.S.A. 131 C5
Soalala Madag. 99 E5
Soalara Madag. 99 E6
Soan r. Pak. 89 H3
Soan-gundo is S. Korea 75 B6
Soanierana-Ivongo Madag. 99 E5
Soavinandriana Madag. 99 E5
Sobat r. South Sudan 86 D8
Sobger r. Indon. 69 K7
Sobinka Russia 42 I5
Sobradinho, Barragem de resr Brazil 143 J6
Sobral Brazil 143 J4
Sochi Russia 91 E2
Society Islands Fr. Polynesia 151 J7
Socorro Brazil 145 B3
Socorro Col. 142 D2
Socorro U.S.A. 127 G6
Socorro, Isla i. Mex. 136 B5
Socotra i. Yemen 87 H7
Soc Trăng Vietnam 71 D5
Socuéllamos Spain 57 E4
Soda Lake CA U.S.A. 128 D4
Soda Lake CA U.S.A. 128 E4
Sodankylä Fin. 44 O3
Soda Plains China 82 D2
Soda Springs U.S.A. 126 F4
Söderhamn Sweden 45 J6
Söderköping Sweden 45 J7
Södertälje Sweden 45 J7
Sodiri Sudan 86 C7
Sodo Eth. 98 D3
Södra Kvarken strait Fin./Sweden 45 K6
Sodus U.S.A. 135 G2
Soë Indon. 69 G8
Soekarno, Puntjak mt. Indon. see Jaya, Puncak
Soerabaia Indon. see Surabaya
Soerendonk Neth. 52 F3
Soest Germany 53 I3
Soest Neth. 52 F2
Sofala Australia 112 D4

▶Sofia Bulg. 59 J3
Capital of Bulgaria.

Sofiya Bulg. see Sofia
Sofiyevka Ukr. see Vil'nyans'k
Sofiysk Khabarovskiy Kray Russia 74 D1
Sofiysk Khabarovskiy Kray Russia 74 E2
Sofporog Russia 44 Q4
Sofrana i. Greece 59 L6
Softa Kalesi tourist site Turkey 85 A1
Sōfu-gan i. Japan 75 F7
Sog China 76 B2
Soğanlı Dağları mts Turkey 91 E2
Sogda Russia 74 D2
Sögel Germany 53 H2
Sogma China 82 E2
Søgne Norway 45 E7
Sognefjorden inlet Norway 45 D6
Sogruma China 76 D1
Söğüt Turkey 59 N4
Söğüt Dağı mts Turkey 59 M6
Soh Iran 88 C3
Sohâg Egypt see Sūhāj
Sohagpur India 82 D5
Soham U.K. 49 H6
Sohano P.N.G. 106 F2
Sohar Oman see Şuḩār
Sohawal India 82 E4
Sohela India 83 E5
Soheuksan-do i. S. Korea 75 B6
Sohng Gwe, Khao hill Myanmar/Thai. 71 B4
Sŏho-ri N. Korea 75 C4
Soignies Belgium 52 E4
Soila China 76 C2
Soini Fin. 44 N5
Soissons France 52 D5
Sojat India 82 C4
Sojat Road India 82 C4
Sok r. Russia 43 K5
Sokal' Ukr. 43 E6
Sokcho S. Korea 75 C5
Söke Turkey 59 L6
Sokhor, Gora mt. Russia 72 J2

▶Sokhumi Georgia 91 F2
Capital of Abkhazia.

Sokiryany Ukr. see Sokyryany
Sokodé Togo 96 D4
Soko Islands H.K. China 77 [inset]
Sokol Russia 42 I4
Sokolo Mali 96 C3
Sokolov Czechia 53 M4
Sokoto Nigeria 96 D3
Sokoto r. Nigeria 96 D3
Sokyryany Ukr. 43 E6
Sola Cuba 133 E8
Sola i. Tonga see Ata
Solan India 82 D3
Solana Beach U.S.A. 128 E5
Solander Island N.Z. 113 A8
Solapur India 84 B2
Soldotna U.S.A. 118 C3
Soledad U.S.A. 128 C3
Soledade Brazil 144 F3
Solenoye Russia 43 I7
Solfjellsjøen Norway 44 H3
Solginskiy Russia 42 I3
Solhan Turkey 91 F3
Soligalich Russia 42 I4
Soligorsk Belarus see Salihorsk
Solihull U.K. 49 F6
Solikamsk Russia 41 R4
Sol'-Iletsk Russia 64 G4
Solimões r. S. America see Amazon
Solingen Germany 52 H3
Solitaire Namibia 100 B2
Sol-Karmala Russia see Severnoye
Şollar Azer. 91 H2
Sollefteå Sweden 44 J5
Söllichau Germany 53 M3
Solling hills Germany 53 J3
Sollstedt Germany 53 K3
Sollum, Gulf of Egypt see Sallum, Khalīj as
Solms Germany 53 I4
Solnechnogorsk Russia 42 H4
Solnechnyy Amurskaya Oblast' Russia 74 A1
Solnechnyy Khabarovskiy Kray Russia 74 E2
Solok Indon. 68 C7
Solomon U.S.A. 129 I5
Solomon, North Fork r. U.S.A. 130 D4

▶Solomon Islands country S. Pacific Ocean 107 G2
4th largest and 5th most populous country in Oceania.

Solomon Sea S. Pacific Ocean 106 F2
Solon U.S.A. 135 K1
Solon Springs U.S.A. 130 F2
Solor i. Indon. 108 C2
Solor, Kepulauan is Indon. 108 C2
Solothurn Switz. 56 H3
Solovetskiye Ostrova is Russia 42 G2
Solov'yevsk Russia 74 B1
Šolta i. Croatia 58 G3
Solţānābād Kermān Iran 88 E4
Solţānābād Khorāsān-e Rażavī Iran 89 E3
Solţānābād Tehrān Iran 88 C3
Solţānīyeh Iran 88 C2
Soltau Germany 53 J2
Sol'tsy Russia 42 F4
Solvay U.S.A. 135 G2
Sölvesborg Sweden 45 I8
Solway Firth est. U.K. 50 F6
Solwezi Zambia 99 C5
Soma Turkey 59 L5
Somain France 52 D4
Somalia country Africa 98 E3
Somali Basin sea feature Indian Ocean 149 L6
Somaliland disp. terr. Somalia 98 E3
Somali Republic country Africa see Somalia
Sombo Angola 99 C4
Sombor Serbia 59 H2
Sombrero Channel India 71 A6
Sombrio, Lago do l. Brazil 145 A5
Somero Fin. 45 M6
Somerset KY U.S.A. 134 C5
Somerset MI U.S.A. 134 C2
Somerset OH U.S.A. 134 D4
Somerset PA U.S.A. 134 F4
Somerset, Lake Australia 112 F1
Somerset East S. Africa 101 G7
Somerset Island Canada 119 I2
Somerset Reservoir U.S.A. 135 I2
Somerset West S. Africa 100 D8
Somersworth U.S.A. 135 J2
Somerton U.S.A. 129 F5
Somerville NJ U.S.A. 135 H3
Somerville TN U.S.A. 131 F5
Someydeh Iran 88 B3
Somme r. France 52 B4
Somme, Canal de la France 52 C5
Sommen l. Sweden 45 I7
Sömmerda Germany 53 L3
Sommet, Lac du l. Canada 123 H3
Somnath India 82 B5
Somoniyon Tajik. 89 H2
Somutu Myanmar 70 B1
Son r. India 83 F4
Sonag China see Zêkog
Sonapur India see Subarnapur
Sonar r. India 82 D4
Sŏnbong N. Korea 74 C4
Sŏnch'ŏn N. Korea 75 B5
Sønderborg Denmark 45 F9
Sondershausen Germany 53 K3
Søndre Strømfjord Greenland see Kangerlussuaq
Søndre Strømfjord inlet Greenland see Kangerlussuaq
Sondrio Italy 58 C1
Sonepat India see Sonipat
Sonepur India see Subarnapur
Song, Loi mt. Myanmar 70 B2
Songbai Hubei China see Shennongjia
Songbai Hunan China 77 G3
Songbu China 77 G2
Sông Câu Vietnam 71 E4
Songcheng China see Xiapu
Sông Đa, Hồ resr Vietnam 70 D2
Songea Tanz. 99 D5
Songhua Hu resr China 74 B4
Songhua Jiang r. Heilongjiang/Jilin China 74 D3
Songhua Jiang r. Jilin China 74 B3
Songjiang China 77 I2
Songjianghe China 74 B4
Sŏngjin N. Korea see Kimch'aek
Songkan China 76 E2
Songkhla Thai. 71 C6
Songling China see Tarqi
Songlong Myanmar 70 B2
Songnim N. Korea 75 B5
Songo Angola 99 B4
Songo Moz. 99 D5
Songpan China 76 D1
Songshan China see Ziyun
Song Shan mt. China 77 G1
Songtao China 77 F2
Songxi China 77 H3
Songxian China 77 G1
Songyuan Fujian China see Songxi
Songyuan Jilin China 74 B3
Songzi China 77 F2
Sơn Hai Vietnam 71 E5
Sonid Youqi China see Saihan Tal
Sonid Zuoqi China see Mandalt
Sonipat India 82 D3
Sonkajärvi Fin. 44 O5
Sonkovo Russia 42 H4
Sơn La Vietnam 70 C2
Sonmiani Pak. 89 G5
Sonmiani Bay Pak. 89 G5
Sonneberg Germany 53 L4
Sono r. Minas Gerais Brazil 145 B2
Sono r. Tocantins Brazil 143 I5
Sonoma U.S.A. 128 B2
Sonoma Peak U.S.A. 128 E1
Sonora r. Mex. 127 F7
Sonora state Mex. 127 F7
Sonora CA U.S.A. 128 C3
Sonora KY U.S.A. 134 C5
Sonora TX U.S.A. 131 C6
Sonoran Desert U.S.A. 129 G5
Sonoran Desert National Monument nat. park U.S.A. 127 E6
Sonqor Iran 88 B3
Sonsogad mt. India 84 B3
Sonsonate El Salvador 136 G6
Sonsorol Islands Palau 69 I5
Sơn Tây Vietnam 70 D2
Sonwabile S. Africa 101 I6
Soochow China see Suzhou
Soomaaliya country Africa see Somalia
Sopi, Tanjung pt Indon. 69 H6
Sopo watercourse South Sudan 97 F4
Sopot Bulg. 59 K3
Sopot Poland 47 Q3
Sop Prap Thai. 70 B3
Sopron Hungary 58 G1
Sopur India 82 C2
Sora Italy 58 E4
Sorab India 84 B3
Sorada India 84 E2
Söråker Sweden 44 J5
Sorel Canada 123 G5
Soreq, Naḥal r. Israel 85 B4
Sorgun Turkey 90 D3
Sorgun r. Turkey 85 B1
Soria Spain 57 E3
Sorkh, Daqq-e salt flat Iran 88 D3
Sorkh, Kūh-e mts Iran 88 D3
Sorkhān Iran 88 E4
Sorkh Doz Afgh. 89 G4
Sorkheh Iran 88 D3
Sørli Norway 44 H4
Soro India 83 F5
Soroca Moldova 43 F6
Sorocaba Brazil 145 B3
Soroki Moldova see Soroca
Sorol atoll Micronesia 69 K5
Sorong Indon. 69 I7
Soroti Uganda 98 D3
Sørøya i. Norway 44 M1
Sorraia r. Port. 57 B4
Sørreisa Norway 44 K2
Sorrento Italy 58 F4
Sorsele Sweden 44 J4
Sorsogon Phil. 69 G4
Sortavala Russia 44 Q6
Sortland Norway 44 I2
Sortopolovskaya Russia 42 K3
Sorvizhi Russia 42 K4
Sosenskiy Russia 43 G5
Soshanguve S. Africa 101 I3
Sosna r. Russia 43 H5
Sosneado mt. Arg. 144 C4
Sosnogorsk Russia 42 L3
Sosnovka Arkhangel'skaya Oblast' Russia 42 J3
Sosnovka Kaliningradskaya Oblast' Russia 41 K5
Sosnovka Murmanskaya Oblast' Russia 42 I2
Sosnovka Tambovskaya Oblast' Russia 43 I5
Sosnovo Russia 45 Q6
Sosnovo-Ozerskoye Russia 73 K2
Sosnovyy Russia 44 R4
Sosnovyy Bor Russia 45 P7
Sosnowiec Poland 47 Q5
Sosnowitz Poland see Sosnowiec
Sos'va Khanty-Mansiyskiy Avtonomnyy Okrug-Yugra Russia 41 S3
Sos'va Sverdlovskaya Oblast' Russia 41 S4
Sotang China 76 B2
Sotara, Volcán vol. Col. 142 C3
Sotkamo Fin. 44 P4
Sotteville-lès-Rouen France 52 B5
Souanké Congo 98 B3
Soubré Côte d'Ivoire 96 C4
Souderton U.S.A. 135 H3
Soufflenheim France 53 H6
Soufli Greece 59 L4
Soufrière St Lucia 137 L6
Soufrière vol. St Vincent 137 L6
Sougueur Alg. 57 G6
Souillac France 56 E4
Souilly France 52 F5
Souk Ahras Alg. 58 B6
Souk el Arbaâ du Rharb Morocco 54 C5
Sŏul S. Korea see Seoul
Soulac-sur-Mer France 56 D4
Soulom France 56 D5
Sounding Creek r. Canada 121 I4
Souni Cyprus 85 A2
Soûr Lebanon see Tyre
Soure Brazil 143 I4
Sour el Ghozlane Alg. 57 H5
Souris Canada 121 K5
Souris r. Canada 121 L5
Souriya country Asia see Syria
Sousa Brazil 143 K5
Sousa Lara Angola see Bocoio
Sousse Tunisia 58 D7
Soustons France 56 D5

▶South Africa country Africa 100 F5
5th most populous country in Africa.

Southampton Canada 134 E1
Southampton U.K. 49 F8
Southampton U.S.A. 135 I3
Southampton, Cape Canada 119 J3
Southampton Island Canada 119 J3
South Andaman i. India 71 A5
South Anna r. U.S.A. 135 G5
South Anston U.K. 48 F5
South Aulatsivik Island Canada 123 J2
South Australia state Australia 106 D5
South Australian Basin sea feature Indian Ocean 149 P8
Southaven U.S.A. 131 F5
South Baldy mt. U.S.A. 127 G6
South Bank U.K. 48 F4
South Bass Island U.S.A. 134 D3
South Bend IN U.S.A. 134 B3
South Bend WA U.S.A. 126 C3
South Bluff pt Bahamas 133 F8
South Boston U.S.A. 135 F5
South Brook Canada 123 K4
South Carolina state U.S.A. 133 D5
South Charleston OH U.S.A. 134 D4
South Charleston WV U.S.A. 134 E4
South China Sea N. Pacific Ocean 68 F4
South Coast Town Australia see Gold Coast
South Dakota state U.S.A. 130 C2
South Downs hills U.K. 49 G8
South Downs National Park nat. park U.K. 49 G8
South East admin. dist. Botswana 101 G3
South East Cape Australia 111 [inset]
Southeast Cape U.S.A. 118 B3
Southeast Indian Ridge sea feature Indian Ocean 149 N8
South East Isles Australia 109 C8
Southeast Pacific Basin sea feature S. Pacific Ocean 151 M10
South East Point Australia 112 C7
Southend Canada 121 K3
Southend U.K. 50 D5
Southend-on-Sea U.K. 49 H7
Southern admin. dist. Botswana 100 G3
Southern Alps mts N.Z. 113 C6
Southern Cross Australia 109 B7
Southern Indian Lake Canada 121 L3
Southern Lau Group is Fiji 107 I3
Southern National Park South Sudan 97 F4
Southern Ocean 152 C2
Southern Pines U.S.A. 133 E5
Southern Rhodesia country Africa see Zimbabwe
Southern Uplands hills U.K. 50 E5
South Esk r. U.K. 50 F4
South Esk Tableland reg. Australia 108 D4
Southey Canada 121 J5
Southfield U.S.A. 134 D2
South Fiji Basin sea feature S. Pacific Ocean 150 H7
South Fork U.S.A. 128 B1
South Geomagnetic Pole Antarctica 152 F1
South Georgia i. S. Atlantic Ocean 144 I8

▶South Georgia and the South Sandwich Islands terr. S. Atlantic Ocean 144 I8
United Kingdom Overseas Territory

South Harris pen. U.K. 50 B3
South Haven U.S.A. 134 B2
South Henik Lake Canada 121 L2
South Hill U.S.A. 135 F5
South Honshu Ridge sea feature N. Pacific Ocean 150 F3
South Indian Lake Canada 121 L3

▶South Island N.Z. 113 D7
2nd largest island in Oceania.

South Junction Canada 121 M5
South Korea country Asia 75 B5
South Lake Tahoe U.S.A. 128 C2
South Luangwa National Park Zambia 99 D5
South Magnetic Pole Antarctica 152 G2
South Mills U.S.A. 135 G5
Southminster U.K. 49 H7
South Mountains hills U.S.A. 135 G4
South New Berlin U.S.A. 135 H2
South Orkney Islands S. Atlantic Ocean 148 F10
South Ossetia disp. terr. Georgia 91 G2
South Paris U.S.A. 135 J1
South Platte r. U.S.A. 130 C3
South Point Bahamas 133 F8
South Pole Antarctica 152 C1
Southport Qld Australia 112 F1
Southport Tas. Australia 111 [inset]
Southport U.K. 48 D5
Southport U.S.A. 135 G2
South Portland U.S.A. 135 J2
South Ronaldsay i. U.K. 50 G2
South Royalton U.S.A. 135 I2
South Salt Lake U.S.A. 129 H1
South Sand Bluff pt S. Africa 101 J6
South Sandwich Islands S. Atlantic Ocean 148 G9
South Sandwich Trench sea feature S. Atlantic Ocean 148 G9
South San Francisco U.S.A. 128 B3
South Saskatchewan r. Canada 121 J4
South Seal r. Canada 121 L3
South Shetland Islands Antarctica 152 A2
South Shetland Trough sea feature S. Atlantic Ocean 152 L2
South Shields U.K. 48 F3
South Sinai governorate Egypt see Janūb Sīnā'
South Solomon Trench sea feature S. Pacific Ocean 150 G6

▶South Sudan country Africa 97 G4
Gained independence from Sudan on 9 July 2011.

South Taranaki Bight b. N.Z. 113 E4
South Tasman Rise sea feature Southern Ocean 150 F9
South Tent mt. U.S.A. 129 H2
South Tons r. India 83 E4
South Twin Island Canada 122 F3
South Tyne r. U.K. 48 E4
South Uist i. U.K. 50 B3
South Wellesley Islands Australia 110 B3
South-West Africa country Africa see Namibia
South West Cape N.Z. 113 A8
South West Entrance sea chan. P.N.G. 110 E1
Southwest Indian Ridge sea feature Indian Ocean 149 K8
South West National Park Australia 111 [inset]
Southwest Pacific Basin sea feature S. Pacific Ocean 150 I8
South-West Peru Ridge sea feature S. Pacific Ocean see Nazca Ridge
South West Rocks Australia 112 F3
South Whitley U.S.A. 134 C3
South Wichita r. U.S.A. 131 D5
South Windham U.S.A. 135 J2
Southwold U.K. 49 I6
Southwood National Park Australia 112 E1
Soutpansberg mts S. Africa 101 I2
Souttouf, Adrar mts W. Sahara 96 B2
Soverato Italy 58 G5
Sovetsk Kaliningradskaya Oblast' Russia 45 L9
Sovetsk Kirovskaya Oblast' Russia 42 K4
Sovetskaya Gavan' Russia 74 F2
Sovetskiy Khanty-Mansiyskiy Avtonomnyy Okrug-Yugra Russia 41 S3
Sovetskiy Leningradskaya Oblast' Russia 45 P6
Sovetskiy Respublika Mariy El Russia 42 K4
Sovetskoye Chechenskaya Respublika Russia see Shatoy
Sovetskoye Stavropol'skiy Kray Russia see Zelenokumsk
Sovyets'kyy Crimea 90 D1
Sowa China 76 C2
Soweto S. Africa 101 H4
Şowma'eh Sarā Iran 88 C2
So'x Tajik. 89 H2
Sōya-kaikyō strait Japan/Russia see La Pérouse Strait
Sōya-misaki c. Japan 74 F3
Soyana r. Russia 42 I2
Soyma r. Russia 42 K2
Soyopa Mex. 127 F7
Sozh r. Europe 43 F6
Sozopol Bulg. 59 L3
Spa Belgium 52 F4

▶Spain country Europe 57 E3
4th largest country in Europe.

Spalato Croatia see Split
Spalatum Croatia see Split
Spalding U.K. 49 G6
Spanish Canada 122 E5
Spanish Fork U.S.A. 129 H1
Spanish Guinea country Africa see Equatorial Guinea
Spanish Netherlands country Europe see Belgium
Spanish Sahara disp. terr. Africa see Western Sahara

Spanish Town Jamaica 137 I5
Sparks U.S.A. 128 D2
Sparta Greece *see* **Sparti**
Sparta *GA* U.S.A. 133 D5
Sparta *KY* U.S.A. 134 C4
Sparta *MI* U.S.A. 134 C2
Sparta *NC* U.S.A. 134 E5
Sparta *TN* U.S.A. 132 C5
Spartanburg U.S.A. 133 D5
Sparti Greece 59 J6
Spartivento, Capo *c.* Italy 58 G6
Spas-Demensk Russia 43 G5
Spas-Klepiki Russia 43 I5
Spassk-Dal'niy Russia 74 D3
Spassk-Ryazanskiy Russia 43 I5
Spata (Eleftherios Venizelos) *airport* Greece 59 J6
Spatha, Akra *pt* Greece *see* **Spatha, Akrotirio**
Spatha, Akrotirio *pt* Greece 59 J7
Spearman U.S.A. 131 C4
Speedway U.S.A. 134 B4
Spence Bay Canada *see* **Taloyoak**
Spencer *IA* U.S.A. 130 E3
Spencer *ID* U.S.A. 126 E3
Spencer *IN* U.S.A. 134 B4
Spencer *NE* U.S.A. 130 D3
Spencer *WV* U.S.A. 134 E4
Spencer, Cape U.S.A. 120 B3
Spencer Bay Namibia 100 B3
Spencer Gulf *est.* Australia 111 B7
Spencer Range *hills* Australia 108 E3
Spennymoor U.K. 48 F4
Sperrgebiet National Park *nat. park* Namibia 100 B4
Sperrin Mountains *hills* U.K. 51 E3
Sperryville U.S.A. 135 F4
Spessart *reg.* Germany 53 J5
Spétsai *i.* Greece *see* **Spetses**
Spetses *i.* Greece 59 J6
Spey *r.* U.K. 50 F3
Speyer Germany 53 I5
Spezand Pak. 89 G4
Spice Islands Indon. *see* **Moluccas**
Spijk Neth. 52 G1
Spijkenisse Neth. 52 E3
Spilimbergo Italy 58 E1
Spilsby U.K. 48 H5
Spīn Bōldak Afgh. 89 G4
Spintangi Pak. 89 H4
Spirit Lake U.S.A. 130 E3
Spirit River Canada 120 G4
Spirovo Russia 42 G4
Spišská Nová Ves Slovakia 43 D6
Spiti *r.* India 82 D3

▶**Spitsbergen** *i.* Svalbard 64 C2
5th largest island in Europe.

Spittal an der Drau Austria 47 N7
Spitzbergen *i.* Svalbard *see* **Spitsbergen**
Split Croatia 58 G3
Split Lake Canada 121 L3
Split Lake *l.* Canada 121 L3
Spokane U.S.A. 126 D3
Spoletium Italy *see* **Spoleto**
Spoleto Italy 58 E3
Spŏng Cambodia 71 D4
Spoon *r.* U.S.A. 130 F3
Spooner U.S.A. 130 F2
Spornitz Germany 53 L1
Spotsylvania U.S.A. 135 G4
Spotted Horse U.S.A. 126 G3
Spranger, Mount Canada 120 F4
Spratly Islands S. China Sea 68 E4
Spray U.S.A. 126 D3
Spree *r.* Germany 47 N4
Sprimont Belgium 52 F4
Springbok S. Africa 100 C5
Springdale Canada 123 L4
Springdale U.S.A. 134 C4
Springe Germany 53 J2
Springer U.S.A. 127 G5
Springerville U.S.A. 129 I4
Springfield *CO* U.S.A. 130 C4

▶**Springfield** *IL* U.S.A. 130 F4
Capital of Illinois.

Springfield *KY* U.S.A. 134 C5
Springfield *MA* U.S.A. 135 I2
Springfield *MO* U.S.A. 131 E4
Springfield *OH* U.S.A. 134 D4
Springfield *OR* U.S.A. 126 C3
Springfield *TN* U.S.A. 134 B5
Springfield *VT* U.S.A. 135 I2
Springfield *WV* U.S.A. 135 F4
Springfontein S. Africa 101 G6
Spring Glen U.S.A. 129 H2
Spring Grove U.S.A. 134 A2
Springhill Canada 123 I5
Spring Hill U.S.A. 133 D6
Springhouse Canada 120 F5
Spring Mountains U.S.A. 129 F3
Springs Junction N.Z. 113 D6
Springsure Australia 110 E5
Spring Valley *MN* U.S.A. 130 E3
Spring Valley *NY* U.S.A. 135 H3
Springview U.S.A. 130 D3
Springville *CA* U.S.A. 128 D3
Springville *NY* U.S.A. 135 F2
Springville *PA* U.S.A. 135 H3
Springville *UT* U.S.A. 129 H1
Sprowston U.K. 49 I6
Spruce Grove Canada 120 H4
Spruce Knob *mt.* U.S.A. 132 E4
Spruce Mountain *CO* U.S.A. 129 I2
Spruce Mountain *NV* U.S.A. 129 F1
Spurn Head *hd* U.K. 48 H5
Spuzzum Canada 120 F5
Squam Lake U.S.A. 135 J2
Square Lake U.S.A. 123 H5
Squillace, Golfo di *g.* Italy 58 G5
Squires, Mount *hill* Australia 109 D6
Srbija *country* Europe *see* **Serbia**
Srbinje Bos. & Herz. *see* **Foča**
Srê Âmbĕl Cambodia 71 C5
Srebrenica Bos. & Herz. 59 H2
Sredets *Burgas* Bulg. 59 L3
Sredets *Sofia-Grad* Bulg. *see* **Sofia**
Sredinnyy Khrebet *mts* Russia 65 Q4
Sredna Gora *mts* Bulg. 59 J3
Srednekolymsk Russia 65 Q3
Sredne-Russkaya Vozvyshennost' *hills* Russia *see* **Central Russian Upland**
Sredne-Sibirskoye Ploskogor'ye *plat.* Russia *see* **Central Siberian Plateau**
Sredneye Kuyto, Ozero *l.* Russia 44 Q4
Sredniy Ural *mts* Russia 41 R4
Srednyaya Akhtuba Russia 43 J6
Sreepur Bangl. *see* **Sripur**
Srê Khtum Cambodia 71 D4
Srê Noy Cambodia 71 D4
Sretensk Russia 73 L2
Sri Aman *Sarawak* Malaysia 68 E6
Sriharikota Island India 84 D3

▶**Sri Jayewardenepura Kotte** Sri Lanka 84 C5
Capital of Sri Lanka.

Srikakulam India 84 E2
Sri Kalahasti India 84 C3
Sri Lanka *country* Asia 84 D5
Srinagar India 82 C2
Sri Pada *mt.* Sri Lanka *see* **Adam's Peak**
Sripur Bangl. 83 G4
Srirangam India 84 C4
Sri Thep *tourist site* Thai. 70 C3
Srivardhan India 84 B2
Staaten *r.* Australia 110 C3
Staaten River National Park Australia 110 C3
Stabroek Guyana *see* **Georgetown**
Stade Germany 53 J1
Staden Belgium 52 D4
Stadskanaal Neth. 52 G2
Stadtallendorf Germany 53 J4
Stadthagen Germany 53 J2
Stadtilm Germany 53 L4
Stadtlohn Germany 52 G3
Stadtoldendorf Germany 53 J3
Stadtroda Germany 53 L4
Staffa *i.* U.K. 50 C4
Staffelberg *hill* Germany 53 L4
Stafford U.K. 49 E6
Stafford U.S.A. 135 G4
Stafford Creek Bahamas 133 E7
Stafford Springs U.S.A. 135 I3
Stagg Lake Canada 120 H2
Staicele Latvia 45 N8
Staines-upon-Thames U.K. 49 G7
Stakhanov Ukr. 43 H6
Stakhanovo Russia *see* **Zhukovskiy**
Stalbridge U.K. 49 E8
Stalham U.K. 49 I6
Stalin Bulg. *see* **Varna**
Stalinabad Tajik. *see* **Dushanbe**
Stalingrad Russia *see* **Volgograd**
Staliniri Georgia *see* **Tskhinvali**
Stalino Ukr. *see* **Donets'k**
Stalinogorsk Russia *see* **Novomoskovsk**
Stalinogród Poland *see* **Katowice**
Stalinsk Russia *see* **Novokuznetsk**
Stalowa Wola Poland 43 D6
Stamboliyski Bulg. 59 K3
Stamford Australia 110 C4
Stamford U.K. 49 G6
Stamford *CT* U.S.A. 135 I3
Stamford *NY* U.S.A. 135 H2
Stampalia *i.* Greece *see* **Astypalaia**
Stampriet Namibia 100 D3
Stamsund Norway 44 H2
Stanardsville U.S.A. 135 F4
Stanberry U.S.A. 130 E3
Stancomb-Wills Glacier Antarctica 152 B1
Standard Canada 120 H5
Standdaarbuiten Neth. 52 E3
Standerton S. Africa 101 I4
Standish U.S.A. 134 D2
Stanfield U.S.A. 129 H5
Stanford *KY* U.S.A. 134 C5
Stanford *MT* U.S.A. 126 F3
Stanger S. Africa *see* **KwaDukuza**
Stanislaus *r.* U.S.A. 128 C3
Stanislav Ukr. *see* **Ivano-Frankivs'k**
Stanke Dimitrov Bulg. *see* **Dupnitsa**
Staňkov Czechia 53 N5
Stanley Australia 111 [inset]
Stanley *H.K.* China 77 [inset]

▶**Stanley** Falkland Is 144 E8
Capital of the Falkland Islands (Islas Malvinas).

Stanley U.K. 48 F4
Stanley *ID* U.S.A. 126 E3
Stanley *KY* U.S.A. 134 B5
Stanley *ND* U.S.A. 130 C1
Stanley *VA* U.S.A. 135 F4
Stanley, Mount *hill N.T.* Australia 108 E5
Stanley, Mount *hill Tas.* Australia 111 [inset]
Stanley, Mount Dem. Rep. Congo/Uganda *see* **Margherita Peak**
Stanleyville Dem. Rep. Congo *see* **Kisangani**
Stann Creek Belize *see* **Dangriga**
Stannington U.K. 48 F3
Stanovoye Russia 43 H5
Stanovoye Nagor'ye *mts* Russia 73 L1
Stanovoy Khrebet *mts* Russia 65 N4
Stansmore Range *hills* Australia 108 E5
Stanthorpe Australia 112 E2
Stanton U.K. 49 H6
Stanton *KY* U.S.A. 134 D5
Stanton *MI* U.S.A. 134 C2
Stanton *ND* U.S.A. 130 C2
Stanton *TX* U.S.A. 131 C5
Stapleton U.S.A. 130 C3
Starachowice Poland 47 R5
Stara Planina *mts* Bulg./Serbia *see* **Balkan Mountains**
Staraya Russa Russia 42 F4
Stara Zagora Bulg. 59 K3
Starbuck Island Kiribati 151 J6
Star City U.S.A. 134 B3
Starcke National Park Australia 110 D2
Stargard in Pommern Poland *see* **Stargard Szczeciński**
Stargard Szczeciński Poland 47 O4
Staritsa Russia 42 G4
Starke U.S.A. 133 D6
Starkville U.S.A. 131 F5
Star Lake U.S.A. 135 H1
Starnberger See *l.* Germany 47 M7
Starobel'sk Ukr. *see* **Starobil's'k**
Starobil's'k Ukr. 43 H6
Starogard Gdański Poland 47 Q4
Starokonstantinov Ukr. *see* **Starokostyantyniv**
Starokostyantyniv Ukr. 43 E6
Starominskaya Russia 43 H7
Staroshcherbinovskaya Russia 43 H7
Star Peak U.S.A. 128 D1
Start Point U.K. 49 D8
Starve Island Kiribati *see* **Starbuck Island**
Staryya Darohi Belarus 43 F5
Staryye Dorogi Belarus *see* **Staryya Darohi**
Staryy Kayak Russia 65 L2
Staryy Oskol Russia 43 H6
Staßfurt Germany 53 L3
State College U.S.A. 135 G3
State Line U.S.A. 131 F6
Staten Island Arg. *see* **Estados, Isla de los**
Statenville U.S.A. 133 D6
Statesboro U.S.A. 133 D5
Statesville U.S.A. 132 D5
Statia *mun.* West Indies *see* **Sint Eustatius**
Station U.S.A. 134 C4

▶**Station Nord** Greenland 153 I1
Most northerly point of North America.

Stauchitz Germany 53 N3
Staufenberg Germany 53 I4
Staunton U.S.A. 134 F4
Stavanger Norway 45 D7
Staveley U.K. 48 F5
Stavropol' Russia 91 F1
Stavropol Kray *admin. div.* Russia *see* **Stavropol'skiy Kray**
Stavropol'-na-Volge Russia *see* **Tol'yatti**
Stavropol'skaya Vozvyshennost' *hills* Russia 91 F1
Stavropol'skiy Kray *admin. div.* Russia 91 F1
Stayner Canada 134 E1
Stayton U.S.A. 126 C3
Steadville S. Africa 101 I5
Steamboat Springs U.S.A. 126 G4
Stearns U.S.A. 134 C5
Stebbins U.S.A. 118 B3
Steele Island Antarctica 152 L2
Steelville U.S.A. 130 F4
Steen *r.* Canada 120 G3
Steenderen Neth. 52 G2
Steenkampsberge *mts* S. Africa 101 J3
Steen River Canada 120 G3
Steens Mountain U.S.A. 126 D4
Steenstrup Gletscher *glacier* Greenland *see* **Sermersuaq**
Steenvoorde France 52 C4
Steenwijk Neth. 52 G2
Stefansson Island Canada 119 H2
Stegi Swaziland *see* **Siteki**
Steigerwald *mts* Germany 53 K5
Stein Germany 53 L5
Steinach Germany 53 L4
Steinaker Reservoir U.S.A. 129 I1
Steinbach Canada 121 L5
Steinfeld (Oldenburg) Germany 53 I2
Steinfurt Germany 53 H2
Steinhausen Namibia 99 B6
Steinheim Germany 53 J3
Steinkjer Norway 44 G4
Steinkopf S. Africa 100 C5
Steinsdalen Norway 44 G4
Stella S. Africa 100 G4
Stella Maris Bahamas 133 F8
Stellenbosch S. Africa 100 D7
Stello, Monte *mt. Corsica* France 56 I5
Stelvio, Parco Nazionale dello *nat. park* Italy 58 D1
Stenay France 52 F5
Stendal Germany 53 L2
Stenhousemuir U.K. 50 F4
Stenungsund Sweden 45 G7
Steornabhagh U.K. *see* **Stornoway**
Stepanakert Azer. *see* **Xankändi**
Stephens, Cape N.Z. 113 D5
Stephens City U.S.A. 135 F4
Stephens Lake Canada 121 M3
Stephenville U.S.A. 131 D5
Stepnoy Russia *see* **Elista**
Stepnoye Russia 43 J6
Sterkfontein Dam *resr* S. Africa 101 I5
Sterkstroom S. Africa 101 H6
Sterlet Lake Canada 121 I1
Sterlibashevo Russia 41 R5
Sterling S. Africa 100 E6
Sterling *CO* U.S.A. 130 C3
Sterling *IL* U.S.A. 130 F3
Sterling *MI* U.S.A. 134 C1
Sterling *UT* U.S.A. 129 H2
Sterling City U.S.A. 131 C6
Sterling Heights U.S.A. 134 D2
Sterlitamak Russia 64 G4
Stettin Poland *see* **Szczecin**
Stettler Canada 121 H4
Steubenville *KY* U.S.A. 134 C5
Steubenville *OH* U.S.A. 134 E3
Stevenage U.K. 49 G7
Stevenson U.S.A. 126 C3
Stevenson Lake Canada 121 L4
Stevens Point U.S.A. 130 F2
Stevens Village U.S.A. 118 D3
Stevensville *MI* U.S.A. 134 B2
Stevensville *PA* U.S.A. 135 G3
Stevns Klint *cliff* Denmark 45 H9
Stewart Canada 120 D4
Stewart *r.* Canada 120 B2
Stewart, Isla *i.* Chile 144 B8
Stewart Crossing Canada 120 B2
Stewart Island N.Z. 113 A8
Stewart Islands Solomon Is 107 G2
Stewart Lake Canada 119 J3
Stewarton U.K. 50 E5
Stewarts Point U.S.A. 128 B2
Stewiacke Canada 123 J5
Steynsburg S. Africa 101 G6
Steyr Austria 47 O6
Steytlerville S. Africa 100 G7
Stiens Neth. 52 F1
Stif Alg. *see* **Sétif**
Stigler U.S.A. 131 E5
Stikine *r.* Canada 120 C3
Stikine Plateau Canada 120 D3
Stikine Strait U.S.A. 120 C3
Stilbaai S. Africa 100 E8
Stiles U.S.A. 134 A1
Stillwater *MN* U.S.A. 130 E2
Stillwater *OK* U.S.A. 131 D4
Stillwater Range *mts* U.S.A. 128 D2
Stillwell U.S.A. 134 B3
Stilton U.K. 49 G6
Stilwell U.S.A. 131 E5
Stinnett U.S.A. 131 C5
Štip Macedonia 59 J4
Stirling Australia 108 F5
Stirling Canada 135 G1
Stirling U.K. 50 F4
Stirling Creek *r.* Australia 108 E4
Stirling Range National Park Australia 109 B8
Stittsville Canada 135 H1
Stjørdalshalsen Norway 44 G5
Stockbridge U.S.A. 134 C2
Stockerau Austria 47 P6
Stockheim Germany 53 L4

▶**Stockholm** Sweden 45 K7
Capital of Sweden.

Stockinbingal Australia 112 C5
Stockport U.K. 48 E5
Stockton *CA* U.S.A. 128 C3
Stockton *KS* U.S.A. 130 D4
Stockton *MO* U.S.A. 130 E4
Stockton *UT* U.S.A. 129 G1
Stockton Lake U.S.A. 130 E4
Stockton-on-Tees U.K. 48 F4
Stockville U.S.A. 130 C3
Stod Czechia 53 N5
Stœng Trêng Cambodia 71 D4
Stoer, Point of U.K. 50 D2
Stoke-on-Trent U.K. 49 E5
Stokesley U.K. 48 F4
Stokes Point Australia 111 [inset]
Stokes Range *hills* Australia 108 E4
Stokkseyri Iceland 44 [inset 1]
Stokkvågen Norway 44 H3
Stokmarknes Norway 44 I2
Stolac Bos. & Herz. 58 G3
Stolberg (Rheinland) Germany 52 G4
Stolbovoy Russia 153 G2
Stolbtsy Belarus *see* **Stowbtsy**
Stolin Belarus 45 O11
Stollberg Germany 53 M4
Stolp Poland *see* **Słupsk**
Stolzenau Germany 53 J2
Stone U.K. 49 E6
Stoneboro U.S.A. 134 E3
Stonecliffe Canada 122 F5
Stonecutters' Island *pen. H.K.* China 77 [inset]
Stonehaven U.K. 50 G4
Stonehenge Australia 110 C5
Stonehenge *tourist site* U.K. 49 F7
Stoner U.S.A. 129 I3
Stone Spheres of the Diquís *tourist site* Costa Rica 137 H7
Stonewall Canada 121 L5
Stonewall Jackson Lake U.S.A. 134 E4
Stony Creek U.S.A. 135 G5
Stony Lake Canada 121 L3
Stony Point U.S.A. 135 G2
Stony Rapids Canada 121 J3
Stony River U.S.A. 118 C3
Stooping *r.* Canada 122 E3
Stora Lulevatten *l.* Sweden 44 K3
Stora Sjöfallets nationalpark *nat. park* Sweden 44 J3
Storavan *l.* Sweden 44 K4
Store Bælt *sea chan.* Denmark *see* **Great Belt**
Støren Norway 44 G5
Storfjordbotn Norway 44 O1
Storforshei Norway 44 I3
Storjord Norway 44 I3
Storkerson Peninsula Canada 119 H2
Storm Bay Australia 111 [inset]
Stormberg S. Africa 101 H6
Storm Lake U.S.A. 130 E3
Stornosa *mt.* Norway 44 E6
Stornoway U.K. 50 C2
Storozhevsk Russia 42 L3
Storozhynets' Ukr. 43 E6
Storrs U.S.A. 135 I3
Storseleby Sweden 44 J4
Storsjön *l.* Sweden 44 I5
Storskrymten *mt.* Norway 44 F5
Storslett Norway 44 L2
Stortemelk *sea chan.* Neth. 52 F1
Storuman Sweden 44 J4
Storuman *l.* Sweden 44 J4
Storvik Sweden 45 J6
Storvorde Denmark 45 G8
Storvreta Sweden 45 J7
Story U.S.A. 126 G3
Stotfold U.K. 49 G6
Stoughton Canada 121 K5
Stour *r. England* U.K. 49 F6
Stour *r. England* U.K. 49 F8
Stour *r. England* U.K. 49 I7
Stour *r. England* U.K. 49 I7
Stourbridge U.K. 49 E6
Stourport-on-Severn U.K. 49 E6
Stout Lake Canada 121 M4
Stowbtsy Belarus 45 O10
Stowe U.S.A. 135 I1
Stowmarket U.K. 49 H6
Stoyba Russia 74 C1
Strabane U.K. 51 E3
Stradbally Ireland 51 E4
Stradbroke U.K. 49 I6
Stradella Italy 58 C2
Strakonice Czechia 47 N6
Stralsund Germany 47 N3
Strand S. Africa 100 D8
Stranda Norway 44 E5
Strangford U.K. 51 G3
Strangford Lough *inlet* U.K. 51 G3
Strangways *r.* Australia 108 F3
Stranraer U.K. 50 D6
Strasbourg France 56 H2
Strasburg U.S.A. 135 F4
Strasburg (Uckermark) Germany 53 N1
Strassburg France *see* **Strasbourg**
Stratford Australia 112 C6
Stratford Canada 134 E2
Stratford *CA* U.S.A. 128 D3
Stratford *TX* U.S.A. 131 C4
Stratford-upon-Avon U.K. 49 F6
Strathaven U.K. 50 E5
Strathmore Canada 120 H5
Strathmore *r.* U.K. 50 E2
Strathnaver Canada 120 F4
Strathroy Canada 134 E2
Strathspey *valley* U.K. 50 F3
Strathy U.K. 50 F2
Stratton U.K. 49 C8
Stratton U.S.A. 135 J1
Stratton Mountain U.S.A. 135 I2
Straubing Germany 53 M6
Straumnes *pt* Iceland 44 [inset 1]
Strawberry U.S.A. 129 H4
Strawberry Mountain U.S.A. 126 D3
Strawberry Reservoir U.S.A. 129 H1
Streaky Bay Australia 109 F8
Streaky Bay *b.* Australia 109 F8
Streator U.S.A. 130 F3
Street U.K. 49 E7
Streetsboro U.S.A. 134 E3
Strehaia Romania 59 J2
Strehla Germany 53 N3
Streich Mound *hill* Australia 109 C7
Strelka Russia 65 Q3
Strel'na *r.* Russia 42 H2
Strenči Latvia 45 N8
Streymoy *i.* Faroe Is 44 [inset 2]
Stříbro Czechia 53 M5
Strichen U.K. 50 G3
Strimonas *r.* Greece *see* **Strymonas**
Stroeder Arg. 144 D6
Strokestown Ireland 51 D4
Stroma, Island of U.K. 50 F2
Stromboli, Isola *i.* Italy 58 F5
Stromness S. Georgia 144 I8
Stromness U.K. 50 F2
Strömstad Sweden 45 G7
Strömsund Sweden 44 I5
Strongsville U.S.A. 134 E3
Stronsay *i.* U.K. 50 G1
Stroud Australia 112 E4
Stroud U.K. 49 E7
Stroud Road Australia 112 E4
Stroudsburg U.S.A. 135 H3
Struer Denmark 45 F8
Struga Macedonia 59 I4
Strugi-Krasnyye Russia 45 P7
Struis Bay S. Africa 100 E8
Strullendorf Germany 53 K5
Struma *r.* Bulg. 59 J4
also known as Strymonas (Greece)
Strumble Head *hd* U.K. 49 B6
Strumica Macedonia 59 J4
Struthers U.S.A. 134 E3
Stryama *r.* Bulg. 59 K3
Strydenburg S. Africa 100 F5
Strymonas *r.* Greece 59 J4
also known as Struma (Bulgaria)
Stryn Norway 44 E6
Stryy Ukr. 43 D6
Strzelecki, Mount *hill* Australia 108 F5
Strzelecki Regional Reserve *nature res.* Australia 111 B6
Stuart *FL* U.S.A. 133 D7
Stuart *NE* U.S.A. 130 D3
Stuart *VA* U.S.A. 134 E5
Stuart Lake Canada 120 E4
Stuart Range *hills* Australia 111 A6
Stuarts Draft U.S.A. 134 F4
Stuart Town Australia 112 D4
Stuchka Latvia *see* **Aizkraukle**
Stučka Latvia *see* **Aizkraukle**
Studholme Junction N.Z. 113 C7
Studsviken Sweden 44 K5
Stukely, Lac *l.* Canada 135 I1
Stung Treng Cambodia *see* **Stœng Trêng**
Stupart *r.* Canada 121 M4
Stupino Russia 43 H5
Sturge Island Antarctica 152 H2
Sturgeon *r. Ont.* Canada 122 F5
Sturgeon *r. Sask.* Canada 121 J4
Sturgeon Bay *b.* Canada 121 L4
Sturgeon Bay U.S.A. 134 B1
Sturgeon Bay Canal *lake channel* U.S.A. 134 B1
Sturgeon Falls Canada 122 F5
Sturgeon Lake *Ont.* Canada 121 N5
Sturgeon Lake *Ont.* Canada 135 F1
Sturgis *MI* U.S.A. 134 C3
Sturgis *SD* U.S.A. 130 C2
Sturt, Mount *hill* Australia 111 C6
Sturt Creek *watercourse* Australia 108 D4
Sturt National Park Australia 111 C6
Sturt Stony Desert Australia 111 C6
Stutterheim S. Africa 101 H7
Stuttgart Germany 53 J6
Stuttgart U.S.A. 131 F5
Stykkishólmur Iceland 44 [inset 1]
Styr *r.* Belarus/Ukr. 43 E5
Suaçuí Grande *r.* Brazil 145 C2
Suai East Timor 108 D2
Suakin Sudan 86 E6
Su'ao Taiwan 77 I3
Suaqui Grande Mex. 127 F7
Suau P.N.G. 110 E1
Subačius Lith. 45 N9
Subankhata India 83 G4
Subarnapur India 84 D1
Sūbāshī Iran 88 C3
Subay *reg.* Saudi Arabia 88 B5
Şubayḩah Saudi Arabia 85 D4
Subei China 80 H4
Subi Besar *i.* Indon. 71 E7
Subi Kecil *i.* Indon. 71 E7
Sublette U.S.A. 131 C4
Subotica Serbia 59 H1
Success, Lake U.S.A. 128 D3
Succiso, Alpe di *mts* Italy 58 D2
Suceava Romania 43 E7
Suchan Russia *see* **Partizansk**
Suck *r.* Ireland 51 D4
Suckling, Mount P.N.G. 110 E1
Suckow Germany 53 L1

▶**Sucre** Bol. 142 E7
Joint capital (with La Paz) of Bolivia.

Suczawa Romania *see* **Suceava**
Sud, Grand Récif du *reef* New Caledonia 107 G4
Suda Russia 42 H4
Sudak Crimea 90 D1

▶**Sudan** *country* Africa 97 F3
3rd largest country in Africa.

Suday Russia 42 I4
Sudayr *reg.* Saudi Arabia 88 B5
Sudbury Canada 122 E5
Sudbury U.K. 49 H6
Sudd *swamp* South Sudan 86 C8
Sude *r.* Germany 53 K1
Sudest Island P.N.G. *see* **Tagula Island**
Sudetenland *mts* Czechia/Poland *see* **Sudety**
Sudety *mts* Czechia/Poland 47 O5
Sudislavl' Russia 42 I4
Sudlersville U.S.A. 135 H4
Süd-Nord-Kanal *canal* Germany 52 H2
Sudogda Russia 42 I5
Sudr Egypt 85 A5
Suðuroy *i.* Faroe Is 44 [inset 2]
Sue *watercourse* South Sudan 97 F4
Sueca Spain 57 F4
Suez Egypt 85 A5
Suez, Gulf of Egypt 85 A5
Suez Bay Egypt 85 A5
Suez Canal Egypt 85 A4
Suffolk U.S.A. 135 G5
Sugarbush Hill *hill* U.S.A. 130 F2
Sugarloaf Mountain U.S.A. 135 J1
Sugarloaf Point Australia 112 F4
Sugun China 80 E4
Sūhāj Egypt 86 D4
Şuḩār Oman 88 E5
Suhaymī, Wādī as *watercourse* Egypt 85 A4
Sühbaatar Mongolia 72 J2
Suheli Par *i.* India 84 B4
Suhl Germany 53 K4
Suhlendorf Germany 53 K2
Suhul *reg.* Saudi Arabia 88 B6
Suhūl al Kidan *plain* Saudi Arabia 88 D6
Şuhut Turkey 59 N5
Sui Pak. 89 H4
Sui, Laem *pt* Thai. 71 B5
Suibin China 74 C3
Suid-Afrika *country* Africa *see* **South Africa**
Suide China 73 K5
Sui Dehar Pak. 89 H4
Suidzhikurmsy Turkm. *see* **Madaw**
Suifenhe China 74 C3
Suihua China 74 B3
Suileng China 74 B3
Suining *Hunan* China 77 F3
Suining *Jiangsu* China 77 H1
Suining *Sichuan* China 76 E2
Suippes France 52 E5
Suir *r.* Ireland 51 E5
Suisse *country* Europe *see* **Switzerland**
Suixi China 77 H1
Suixian *Henan* China 77 G1
Suixian *Hubei* China *see* **Suizhou**
Suiyang *Guizhou* China 76 E3
Suiyang *Henan* China 77 G1
Suiza *country* Europe *see* **Switzerland**
Suizhong China 73 M4
Suizhou China 77 G2
Sujangarh India 82 C4
Sujawal Pak. 89 H5
Suk *atoll* Micronesia *see* **Pulusuk**
Sukabumi Indon. 68 D8
Sukagawa Japan 75 F5
Sukarnapura Indon. *see* **Jayapura**
Sukarno, Puncak *mt.* Indon. *see* **Jaya, Puncak**
Sukchŏn N. Korea 75 B5
Sukhinichi Russia 43 G5
Sukhona *r.* Russia 42 J3
Sukhothai Thai. 70 B3
Sukhumi Georgia *see* **Sokhumi**
Sukhum-Kale Georgia *see* **Sokhumi**
Sukkertoppen Greenland *see* **Maniitsoq**
Sukkozero Russia 42 G3
Sukkur Pak. 89 H5
Sukma India 84 D2
Sukpay Russia 74 E3
Sukpay *r.* Russia 74 E3
Sukri *r. Rajasthan* India 82 C4
Sukri *r. Rajasthan* India 82 C4
Suktel *r.* India 84 D1
Sukun *i.* Indon. 108 C2
Sula *i.* Norway 45 D6
Sula *r.* Russia 42 K2
Sula, Kepulauan *is* Indon. 69 H7
Sulaiman Range *mts* Pak. 89 H4
Sulak Russia 91 G2
Sūlār Iran 88 C4
Sula Sgeir *i.* U.K. 50 C1
Sulawesi *i.* Indon. *see* **Celebes**
Sulaymān Beg Iraq 91 G4
Sulayyimah Saudi Arabia 88 B6
Sulci *Sardinia* Italy *see* **Sant'Antioco**
Sulcis *Sardinia* Italy *see* **Sant'Antioco**
Sule Skerry *i.* U.K. 50 E1
Sule Stack *i.* U.K. 50 E1
Sulingen Germany 53 I2
Sulitjelma Norway 44 J3
Sulkava Fin. 44 P6
Sullana Peru 142 B4
Sullivan *IL* U.S.A. 130 F4
Sullivan *IN* U.S.A. 134 B4
Sullivan Bay Canada 120 E5
Sullivan Island Myanmar *see* **Lanbi Kyun**
Sullivan Lake Canada 121 I5
Sulmo Italy *see* **Sulmona**
Sulmona Italy 58 E3
Sulphur *LA* U.S.A. 131 E6
Sulphur *OK* U.S.A. 131 D5
Sulphur *r.* U.S.A. 131 E5
Sulphur Springs U.S.A. 131 E5
Sultan Canada 122 E5

Sultan, Koh-i- mts Pak. 89 F4
Sultanabad India see Osmannagar
Sultānābād Iran see Ārāk
Sultan Dağları mts Turkey 59 N5
Sultanıye Turkey see Karapınar
Sultanpur India 83 E4
Sulu Archipelago is Phil. 69 G5
Sulu Basin sea feature N. Pacific Ocean 150 E5
Suluke China 82 C1
Sülüklü Turkey 90 D3
Sülüktü Kyrg. 89 H2
Sulusaray Turkey 90 E3
Sulu Sea N. Pacific Ocean 68 F5
Suluvvaulik, Lac l. Canada 123 G2
Sulyukta Kyrg. see Sülüktü
Sulzbach-Rosenberg Germany 53 L5
Sulzberger Bay Antarctica 152 I1
Sumāil Oman 88 E6
Sumampa Arg. 144 D3
Sumapaz, Parque Nacional nat. park Col. 142 D3
Sūmār Iran 88 B3
Sumatera i. Indon. see Sumatra

▶Sumatra i. Indon. 71 B7
2nd largest island in Asia and 6th in the world.

Šumava, Národní park nat. park Czechia 47 N6
Sumayl/Sêmêl Iraq 91 F3
Sumba i. Indon. 108 C2
Sumba, Selat sea chan. Indon. 108 B2
Sumbar r. Turkm. 88 D2
Sumbawa i. Indon. 108 B2
Sumbawabesar Indon. 108 B2
Sumbawanga Tanz. 99 D4
Sumbe Angola 99 B5
Sumbu National Park Zambia 99 D4
Sumburgh U.K. 50 [inset]
Sumburgh Head hd U.K. 50 [inset]
Sumdo China 76 D2
Sumdum, Mount U.S.A. 120 C3
Sumeih Sudan 86 C8
Sumenep Indon. 68 E8
Sumgait Azer. see Sumqayıt
Sumisu-jima i. Japan 73 Q6
Summer Beaver Canada 122 C3
Summerford Canada 123 L4
Summer Island U.S.A. 132 C2
Summer Isles U.K. 50 D2
Summerland Canada 120 G5
Summersville U.S.A. 134 E4
Summit Lake Canada 120 F4
Summit Mountain U.S.A. 128 E2
Summit Peak U.S.A. 127 G5
Sumnal China 82 D2
Sumner N.Z. 113 D6
Sumner, Lake N.Z. 113 D6
Sumon-dake mt. Japan 75 E5
Šumperk Czechia 47 P6
Sumpu Japan see Shizuoka
Sumqayıt Azer. 91 H2
Sumskiy Posad Russia 42 G2
Sumter U.S.A. 133 D5
Sumur India 82 D2
Sumy Ukr. 43 G6
Sumzom China 76 C2
Suna Russia 42 K4
Sunaj India 82 D4
Sunam India 82 C3
Sunamganj Bangl. 83 G4
Sunart, Loch inlet U.K. 50 D4
Şunaynah Oman 88 D6
Sunburst U.S.A. 126 F2
Sunbury Australia 112 B6
Sunbury OH U.S.A. 134 D3
Sunbury PA U.S.A. 135 G3
Suncheon S. Korea 75 B6
Sun City S. Africa 101 H3
Sun City AZ U.S.A. 129 G5
Sun City CA U.S.A. 128 E5
Sunda, Selat str. Indon. 68 C8
Sunda Kalapa Indon. see Jakarta
Sundance U.S.A. 126 G3
Sundarbans coastal area Bangl./India 83 G5
Sundarbans National Park Bangl./India 83 G5
Sundargarh India 83 F5
Sunda Shelf sea feature Indian Ocean 149 P5
Sunda Strait Indon. see Sunda, Selat
Sunda Trench sea feature Indian Ocean see Java Trench
Sunderland U.K. 48 F4
Sundern (Sauerland) Germany 53 I3
Sündiken Dağları mts Turkey 59 N5
Sundown National Park Australia 112 E2
Sundre Canada 120 H5
Sundridge Canada 122 F5
Sundsvall Sweden 44 J5
Sundukli, Peski des. Turkm. see Sandykly Gumy
Sundumbili S. Africa 101 J5
Sungaipenuh Indon. 68 C7
Sungai Petani Malaysia 71 C6
Sungari r. China see Songhua Jiang
Sungei Seletar Reservoir Sing. 71 [inset]
Sungkiang China see Songjiang
Sung Kong i. H.K. China 77 [inset]
Sungqu China see Songpan
Sungsang Indon. 68 C7
Sungurlu Turkey 90 D2
Sun Kosi r. Nepal 83 F4
Sunman U.S.A. 134 C4
Sunndal Norway 45 E6
Sunndalsøra Norway 44 F5
Sunne Sweden 45 H7
Sunnyside U.S.A. 126 D3
Sunnyvale U.S.A. 128 B3
Sun Prairie U.S.A. 130 F3
Sunset House Canada 120 G4
Sunset Peak hill H.K. China 77 [inset]
Suntar Russia 65 M3
Suntsar Pak. 89 F5
Sunwi-do i. N. Korea 75 B5
Sunwu China 74 B2
Sunyani Ghana 96 C4
Suolijärvet l. Fin. 44 P3
Suomi country Europe see Finland
Suomussalmi Fin. 44 P4
Suō-nada b. Japan 75 C6
Suonenjoki Fin. 44 O5
Suong r. Laos 70 C3
Suoyarvi Russia 42 G3
Supa India 84 B3
Supaul India 83 F4
Superior AZ U.S.A. 129 H5
Superior MT U.S.A. 126 E3
Superior NE U.S.A. 130 D3
Superior WI U.S.A. 130 E2

▶Superior, Lake Canada/U.S.A. 125 J2
Largest lake in North America and 2nd in the world.

Suphan Buri Thai. 71 C4
Süphan Dağı mt. Turkey 91 F3
Supiori i. Indon. 69 J7
Suponevo Russia 43 G5
Support Force Glacier Antarctica 152 A1
Sūq ash Shuyūkh Iraq 91 G5
Suqian China 77 H1
Suquṭrá i. Yemen see Socotra
Şūr Oman 89 E6
Sur, Point U.S.A. 128 C3
Sur, Punta pt Arg. 144 E5
Sura r. Russia 43 J4
Şuraabad Azer. 91 H2
Surabaya Indon. 68 E8
Sūrak Iran 88 E5
Surakarta Indon. 68 E8
Sūrān Iran 89 F5
Şūrān Syria 85 C2
Surat Australia 112 D1
Surat India 82 C5
Suratgarh India 82 C3
Surat Thani Thai. 71 B5
Surazh Russia 43 G5
Surbiton Australia 110 D4
Surdulica Serbia 59 J3
Sûre r. Lux. 52 G5
Surendranagar India 82 B5
Surf U.S.A. 128 C4
Surgut Russia 64 I3
Suri India see Siuri
Suriapet India 84 C2
Surigao Phil. 69 H5
Surin Thai. 70 C4
Surinam country S. America see Suriname
Suriname country S. America 143 G3
Surin Nua, Ko i. Thai. 71 B5
Surkhet Nepal 83 E3
Surkhon Uzbek. see Surxon
Sürmene Turkey 91 F2
Surovikino Russia 43 I6
Surpura India 82 C4
Surrah, Nafūd as des. Saudi Arabia 88 A6
Surrey Canada 120 F5
Surry U.S.A. 135 G5
Surskoye Russia 43 J5
Surt Libya see Sirte
Surtsey i. Iceland 44 [inset 1]
Sürü Hormozgān Iran 88 E5
Sürü Sīstān va Balūchestān Iran 88 E5
Suruç Turkey 85 D1
Surud, Raas pt Somalia 98 E2
Surud Ad mt. Somalia see Shimbiris
Suruga-wan b. Japan 75 E6
Surulangun Indon. 68 C7
Surwold Germany 53 H2
Surxon Uzbek. 89 G2
Suryapet India see Suriapet
Şuşa Azer. 91 G3
Susah Tunisia see Sousse
Susaki Japan 75 D6
Susan U.S.A. 135 G5
Sūsangerd Iran 88 C4
Susanino Russia 74 F1
Susanville U.S.A. 128 C1
Suşehri Turkey 90 E2
Suso Thai. 71 B6
Susong China 77 H2
Susquehanna U.S.A. 135 H3
Susquehanna r. U.S.A. 135 G4
Susquehanna, West Branch r. U.S.A. 135 G3
Susques Arg. 144 C2
Sussex U.S.A. 135 G5
Susuman Russia 65 P3
Susupu Indon. 69 H6
Susurluk Turkey 59 M5
Sutak India 82 D2
Sutherland Australia 112 E5
Sutherland S. Africa 100 E7
Sutherland U.S.A. 130 C3
Sutherland Range hills Australia 109 D6
Sutjeska, Nacionalni Park nat. park Bos. & Herz. 58 H3
Sutlej r. India/Pak. see Satluj
Sütlüce Turkey 85 A1
Sutter U.S.A. 128 C2
Sutterton U.K. 49 G6
Sutton Canada 135 I1
Sutton r. Canada 122 E3
Sutton U.K. 49 H6
Sutton NE U.S.A. 130 D3
Sutton WV U.S.A. 134 E4
Sutton Coldfield U.K. 49 F6
Sutton in Ashfield U.K. 49 F5
Sutton Lake Canada 122 D3
Sutton Lake U.S.A. 134 E4
Suttor r. Australia 110 D4
Suttsu Japan 74 F4
Sutwik Island U.S.A. 118 C4
Sutyr' r. Russia 74 D2

▶Suva Fiji 107 H3
Capital of Fiji.

Suvadiva Atoll Maldives see Huvadhu Atholhu
Suvalki Poland see Suwałki
Suvorov atoll Cook Is see Suwarrow
Suvorov Russia 43 H5
Suwa Japan 75 E5
Suwałki Poland 43 D5
Suwannaphum Thai. 70 C4
Suwannee r. U.S.A. 133 D6
Suwanose-jima i. Japan 75 C7
Suwarrow atoll Cook Is 107 J3
Suwayliḥ Jordan 85 B3
Suwayr well Saudi Arabia 91 F5
Suways, Khalīj as g. Egypt see Suez, Gulf of
Suways, Qanāt as canal Egypt see Suez Canal
Suweilih Jordan see Suwayliḥ
Suweis, Khalîg el g. Egypt see Suez, Gulf of
Suweis, Qanâ el canal Egypt see Suez Canal
Suwon S. Korea 75 B5
Suyūl Ḥanīsh i. Yemen 86 F7
Suz, Mys pt Kazakh. 91 I2
Suzaka Japan 75 E5
Suzdal' Russia 42 I4
Suzhou Anhui China 77 H1
Suzhou Gansu China see Jiuquan
Suzhou Jiangsu China 77 I2
Suzi He r. China 74 B4
Suzuka Japan 75 E6
Suzu-misaki pt Japan 75 E5
Sværholthalvøya pen. Norway 44 O1

▶Svalbard terr. Arctic Ocean 64 C2
Part of Norway.

Svappavaara Sweden 44 L3
Svartenhuk Halvø pen. Greenland see Sigguup Nunaa
Svatove Ukr. 43 H6
Svay Chék Cambodia 71 C4
Svay Riĕng Cambodia 71 D5
Svecha Russia 42 J4
Sveg Sweden 45 I5
Sveķi Latvia 45 O8
Svelgen Norway 44 D6
Svellingen Norway 44 F5
Švenčionėliai Lith. 45 N9
Švenčionys Lith. 45 O9
Svendborg Denmark 45 G9
Svensbu Norway 44 K2
Svenstavik Sweden 44 I5
Sverdlovsk Russia see Yekaterinburg
Sverdlovs'k Ukr. 43 H6
Sverdrup Islands Canada 119 I2
Sverige country Europe see Sweden
Sveti Nikole Macedonia 59 I4
Svetlaya Russia 74 E3
Svetlogorsk Belarus see Svyetlahorsk
Svetlogorsk Kaliningradskaya Oblast' Russia 45 L9
Svetlogorsk Krasnoyarskiy Kray Russia 64 J3
Svetlograd Russia 91 F1
Svetlovodsk Ukr. see Svitlovods'k
Svetlyy Kaliningradskaya Oblast' Russia 45 L9
Svetlyy Orenburgskaya Oblast' Russia 80 B1
Svetlyy Yar Russia 43 J6
Svetogorsk Russia 45 P6
Svíahnúkar vol. Iceland 44 [inset 1]
Svilaja mts Croatia 58 G3
Svilengrad Bulg. 59 L4
Svinecea Mare, Vârful mt. Romania 59 J2
Svir Belarus 45 O9
Svir' r. Russia 42 G3
Svishtov Bulg. 59 K3
Svitava r. Czechia 47 P6
Svitavy Czechia 47 P6
Svitlovods'k Ukr. 43 G6
Sviyaga r. Russia 42 K5
Svizzer, Parc Naziunal nat. park Switz. 58 D1
Svizzera country Europe see Switzerland
Svobodnyy Russia 74 C2
Svolvær Norway 44 I2
Svrljiške Planine mts Serbia 59 J3
Svyatoy Nos, Mys c. Russia 42 K2
Svyetlahorsk Belarus 43 F5
Swadlincote U.K. 49 F6
Swaffham U.K. 49 H6
Swain Reefs Australia 110 F4
Swainsboro U.S.A. 133 D5
Swains Island atoll American Samoa 107 I3
Swakop watercourse Namibia 100 B2
Swakopmund Namibia 100 B2
Swale r. U.K. 48 F4
Swallow Islands Solomon Is 107 G3
Swamihalli India 84 C3
Swampy r. Canada 123 H2
Swan r. Australia 109 A7
Swan r. Man./Sask. Canada 121 K4
Swan r. Ont. Canada 122 E3
Swanage U.K. 49 F8
Swandale U.S.A. 134 E4
Swan Hill Australia 112 A5
Swan Hills Canada 120 H4
Swan Lake B.C. Canada 120 D4
Swan Lake Man. Canada 121 K4
Swanley U.K. 49 H7
Swanquarter U.S.A. 133 E5
Swan Reach Australia 111 B7
Swan River Canada 121 K4
Swansea U.K. 49 D7
Swansea Bay U.K. 49 D7
Swanton CA U.S.A. 128 B3
Swanton VT U.S.A. 135 I1
Swartbergpas pass S. Africa 100 F7
Swart Nossob watercourse Namibia see Black Nossob
Swartruggens S. Africa 101 H3
Swartz Creek U.S.A. 134 D2
Swasey Peak U.S.A. 129 G2
Swat Kohistan reg. Pak. 89 I3
Swatow China see Shantou
Swayzee U.S.A. 134 C3
Swaziland country Africa 101 J4

▶Sweden country Europe 44 I5
5th largest country in Europe.

Sweet Home U.S.A. 126 C3
Sweet Springs U.S.A. 134 E5
Sweetwater U.S.A. 131 C5
Sweetwater r. U.S.A. 126 G4
Swellendam S. Africa 100 E8
Świdnica Poland 47 P5
Świdwin Poland 47 O4
Świebodzin Poland 47 O4
Świecie Poland 47 Q4
Swift Current Canada 121 J5
Swiftcurrent Creek r. Canada 121 J5
Swilly r. Ireland 51 E3
Swilly, Lough inlet Ireland 51 E2
Swindon U.K. 49 F7
Swinford Ireland 51 D4
Świnoujście Poland 47 O4
Swinton U.K. 50 G5
Swiss Confederation country Europe see Switzerland
Switzerland country Europe 56 I3
Swords Ireland 51 F4
Swords Range hills Australia 110 C4
Syamozero, Ozero l. Russia 42 G3
Syamzha Russia 42 I3
Syang Nepal 83 E3
Syas'stroy Russia 42 G3
Sychevka Russia 42 G5
Sydenham atoll Kiribati see Nonouti

▶Sydney Australia 112 E4
Capital of New South Wales. Most populous city in Oceania.

Sydney Canada 123 J5
Sydney Island Kiribati see Manra
Sydney Lake Canada 121 M5
Sydney Mines Canada 123 J5
Syedra tourist site Turkey 85 A1
Syeverodonets'k Ukr. 43 H6
Syke Germany 53 I2
Sykesville U.S.A. 135 F3
Syktyvkar Russia 42 K3
Sylarna mt. Norway/Sweden 44 H5
Sylhet Bangl. 83 G4
Syloga Russia 42 I3
Sylt i. Germany 47 L3
Sylva U.S.A. 133 D5
Sylvania GA U.S.A. 133 D5
Sylvania OH U.S.A. 134 D3
Sylvan Lake Canada 120 H4
Sylvester U.S.A. 133 D6
Sylvester, Lake salt flat Australia 110 A3
Sylvia, Mount Canada 120 E3
Symerton U.S.A. 134 A3
Symi i. Greece 59 L6
Synel'nykove Ukr. 43 G6
Syngyrli, Mys pt Kazakh. 91 I2
Synya Russia 41 R2
Syowa research station Antarctica 152 D2
Syracusae Sicily Italy see Syracuse
Syracuse Sicily Italy 58 F6
Syracuse KS U.S.A. 130 C4
Syracuse NY U.S.A. 135 G2
Syrdar'ya r. Asia 80 C3
Syrdar'ya Uzbek. see Sirdaryo
Syrdaryinskiy Uzbek. see Sirdaryo
Syria country Asia 90 E4
Syriam Myanmar see Thanlyin
Syrian Desert Asia 90 E4
Syrna i. Greece 59 L6
Syros i. Greece 59 K6
Syrskiy Russia 43 H5
Sysmä Fin. 45 N6
Sysola r. Russia 42 K3
Syumsi Russia 42 K4
Syurkum Russia 74 F2
Syurkum, Mys pt Russia 74 F2
Syzran' Russia 43 K5
Szabadka Serbia see Subotica
Szczecin Poland 47 O4
Szczecinek Poland 47 P4
Szczytno Poland 47 R4
Szechwan prov. China see Sichuan
Szeged Hungary 59 I1
Székesfehérvár Hungary 58 H1
Szekszárd Hungary 58 H1
Szentes Hungary 59 I1
Szentgotthárd Hungary 58 G1
Szigetvár Hungary 58 G1
Szolnok Hungary 59 I1
Szombathely Hungary 58 G1
Sztálinváros Hungary see Dunaújváros

T

Tābah Saudi Arabia 86 F4
Tabajara Brazil 142 F5
Tabakhmela Georgia see K'azreti
Tabalo P.N.G. 69 L7
Tabanan Indon. 108 A2
Ṭabaqah Ar Raqqah Syria see Ath Thawrah
Ṭabaqah Ar Raqqah Syria 85 D2
Tabar Islands P.N.G. 106 F2
Tabarka Tunisia 58 C6
Ṭabas-e Masīnā Iran 89 F3
Tabāsīn Iran 88 E4
Tābask, Kūh-e mt. Iran 88 C4
Tabatinga Amazonas Brazil 142 E4
Tabatinga São Paulo Brazil 145 A3
Tabatinga, Serra da hills Brazil 143 J6
T'abats'q'uri, T'ba l. Georgia 91 F2
Tabayin Myanmar 70 A2
Tabbita Australia 112 B5
Tabelbala Alg. 54 D6
Taber Canada 121 H5
Tabet, Nam r. Myanmar 70 B1
Tabiteuea atoll Kiribati 107 H2
Tabivere Estonia 45 O7
Tablas de Daimiel, Parque Nacional de las nat. park Spain 57 E4
Table Cape N.Z. 113 F4
Table Mountain National Park S. Africa 100 D8
Tabligbo Togo 96 D4
Tábor Czechia 47 O6
Tabora Tanz. 99 D4
Tabou Côte d'Ivoire 96 C4
Tabrīz Iran 88 B2
Tabuaeran atoll Kiribati 151 J5
Tabūk Saudi Arabia 90 E5
Tabulam Australia 112 F2
Tabuyung Indon. 71 B7
Tabwémasana, Mount Vanuatu 107 G3
Täby Sweden 45 K7
Tacalé Brazil 143 H3
Tacheng China 80 F2
Tachie Canada 120 E4
Tachov Czechia 53 M5
Tacloban Phil. 69 H4
Tacna Peru 142 D7
Tacoma U.S.A. 126 C3
Taco Pozo Arg. 144 D3
Tacuarembó Uruguay 144 E4
Tacupeto Mex. 127 F7
Tadcaster U.K. 48 F5
Tademaït, Plateau du Alg. 54 E6
Tadin New Caledonia 107 G4
Tadjikistan country Asia see Tajikistan
Tadjourah Djibouti 86 F7
Tadmur Syria 85 D2
Tadoule Lake Canada 121 L3
Tadoussac Canada 123 H4
Tadpatri India 84 C3
Tadwale India 84 C2
Tadzhikskaya S.S.R. country Asia see Tajikistan
Taean-haean National Park S. Korea 75 B5
Taebaek S. Korea 75 C5
Taedasa-do N. Korea 75 B5
Taedong-man b. N. Korea 75 B5
Taegu S. Korea see Daegu
Taehan-min'guk country Asia see South Korea
Taejŏn S. Korea see Daejeon
Taf r. U.K. 49 C7
Tafahi i. Tonga 107 I3
Tafalla Spain 57 F2
Tafeng China see Lanshan
Tafila Jordan see Aṭ Ṭafīlah
Tafí Viejo Arg. 144 C3
Tafresh Iran 88 C3
Taft Iran 88 D4
Taft U.S.A. 128 D4
Taftān, Kūh-e mt. Iran 89 F4
Taftanāz Syria 85 C2
Tafwap India 71 A6
Taganrog Russia 43 H7
Taganrog, Gulf of Russia/Ukr. 43 H7
Taganrogskiy Zaliv b. Russia/Ukr. see Taganrog, Gulf of
Tagarev, Gora mt. Iran/Turkm. 88 E2
Tagarkaty, Pereval pass Tajik. 89 I2
Tagaung Myanmar 70 B2
Tagchagpu Ri mt. China 83 E2
Tagdempt Alg. see Tiaret
Taghmon Ireland 51 F5
Tagish Canada 120 C2
Tagtabazar Turkm. 89 F3
Tagula P.N.G. 110 F1
Tagula Island P.N.G. 110 F1
Tagus r. Port. 57 B4
also known as Tajo (Portugal) or Tejo (Spain)
Taha China 74 B3
Tahaetkun Mountain Canada 120 G5
Tahan, Gunung mt. Malaysia 71 C6
Tahanroz'ka Zatoka b. Russia/Ukr. see Taganrog, Gulf of
Tahat, Mont mt. Alg. 96 D2
Tahe China 74 B1
Taheke N.Z. 113 D2
Tahiti i. Fr. Polynesia 151 K7
Tahlab, Dasht-i- plain Pak. 89 F4
Tahlequah U.S.A. 131 E5
Tahltan Canada 120 D3
Tahoe, Lake U.S.A. 128 C2
Tahoe Lake Canada 119 H3
Tahoe Vista U.S.A. 128 C2
Tahoka U.S.A. 131 C5
Tahoua Niger 96 D3
Tahrūd Iran 88 E4
Tahrūd r. Iran 88 E4
Tahtsa Peak Canada 120 E4
Tahulandang i. Indon. 69 H6
Tahuna Indon. 69 H6
Taï, Parc National de nat. park Côte d'Ivoire 96 C4
Tai'an China 73 L5
Taibai China 76 E1
Taibai Shan mt. China 76 E1
Taibei Taiwan see Taipei
Taibus Qi China see Baochang
T'aichung Taiwan see Taizhong
Taidong Taiwan see T'aitung
Taigong China see Taijiang
Taihang Shan mts China 73 K5
Taihang Shan mts China 73 K5
Taihape N.Z. 113 E4
Taihe Jiangxi China 77 G3
Taihe Sichuan China see Shehong
Taihezhen China see Shehong
Tai Ho Wan H.K. China 77 [inset]
Taihu China 77 H2
Tai Hu l. China 77 I2
Taijiang China 77 F3
Taikang China see Dorbod
Tailai China 74 A3
Tai Lam Chung Shui Tong resr H.K. China 77 [inset]
Tailem Bend Australia 111 B7
Tai Long Wan b. H.K. China 77 [inset]
Tai Mo Shan hill H.K. China 77 [inset]
Tain U.K. 50 F2
Tainan Taiwan 77 I4
T'ainan Taiwan see Tainan
Tainaro, Akra pt Greece see Tainaro, Akrotirio
Tainaro, Akrotirio pt Greece 59 J6
Taining China 77 H3
Tai O H.K. China 77 [inset]
Taiobeiras Brazil 145 C1

▶Taipei Taiwan 77 I3
Capital of Taiwan.

Taiping Guangdong China see Shixing
Taiping Guangxi China see Chongzuo
Taiping Guangxi China 77 F4
Taiping Malaysia 71 C6
Taipingchuan China 74 A3
Tai Po H.K. China 77 [inset]
Tai Poutini National Park N.Z. see Westland Tai Poutini National Park
Tairbeart U.K. see Tarbert
Tai Rom Yen National Park Thai. 71 B5
Tairuq Iran 88 B3
Tais P.N.G. 69 K8
Taishan China 77 G4
Tai Shek Mo hill H.K. China 77 [inset]
Taishun China 77 H3
Taissy France 52 E5
Taitao, Península de pen. Chile 144 B7
Tai Tapu N.Z. 113 D6
Tai To Yan mt. H.K. China 77 [inset]
T'aitung Taiwan 77 I4
Taivalkoski Fin. 44 P4
Taivaskero hill Fin. 44 N2
Taiwan country Asia 77 I4
T'aiwan Haihsia strait China/Taiwan see Taiwan Strait
Taiwan Haixia strait China/Taiwan see Taiwan Strait
Taiwan Shan mts Taiwan see Zhongyang Shanmo
Taiwan Strait China/Taiwan 77 H4
Taixian China see Jiangyan
Taixing China 77 I1
Taiyuan China 73 K5
Taizhao China 76 B2
Taizhong Taiwan see Fengyuan
Taizhong Taiwan 77 I3
Taizhou Jiangsu China 77 H1
Taizhou Zhejiang China 77 I2
Taizhou Liedao i. China 77 I2
Taizhou Wan b. China 77 I2
Taizi He r. China 74 B4
Ta'izz Yemen 86 F7
Tājābād Iran 88 E4
Tajerouine Tunisia 58 C7
Tajikistan country Asia 89 H2
Tajik National Park nat. park Tajik. 89 I2
Tajitos Mex. 127 E7
Tajjal Pak. 89 H5
Tajo r. Port. see Tagus
Tajrīsh Iran 88 C3
Tajumulco, Volcán de vol. Guat. 136 F5
Tak Thai. 70 B3
Takāb Iran 88 B2
Takabba Kenya 98 E3
Takahashi Japan 75 D6
Takamatsu Japan 75 D6
Takaoka Japan 75 E5
Takapuna N.Z. 113 E3
Ta karpo China 83 G4
Takatokwane Botswana 100 G3
Takatshwaane Botswana 100 E2
Takatsuki-yama mt. Japan 75 D6
Takayama Japan 75 E5
Tak Bai Thai. 71 C6
Takefu Japan see Echizen
Takengon Indon. 71 B6
Takeo Cambodia see Don Kêv
Take-shima i. N. Pacific Ocean see Liancourt Rocks
Tākestān Iran 88 C2
Takhemaret Alg. 57 G6
Takhini Hotspring Canada 120 C2
Ta Khli Thai. 70 C4
Ta Khmau Cambodia 71 D5
Takhta-Bazar Turkm. see Tagtabazar
Takhtah Pul Afgh. 89 G4
Takht Apān, Kūh-e mt. Iran 88 C3
Takhteh Iran 88 D4
Takht-e Soleymān mt. Iran 88 C2
Takht-e Soleymān tourist site Iran 88 B2
Takht-i-Bahi tourist site Pak. 89 H3
Takht-i-Sulaiman mt. Pak. 89 H4
Takijuq Lake Canada see Napaktulik Lake
Takingeun Indon. see Takengon
Takinoue Japan 74 F3
Takla Lake Canada 120 E4
Takla Landing Canada 120 E4
Takla Makan des. China see Taklimakan Desert
Taklimakan Desert China 82 E1
Taklimakan Shamo des. China see Taklimakan Desert
Takpa Shiri mt. China 76 B2
Taku Canada 120 C3
Takum Nigeria 96 D4
Takuu Islands P.N.G. 107 F2
Talab r. Iran/Pak. 89 F4
Talachyn Belarus 43 F5
Talaja India 82 C5
Talakan Amurskaya Oblast' Russia 74 C2
Talakan Khabarovskiy Kray Russia 74 D2
Talandzha Russia 74 C2
Talangbatu Indon. 68 D7
Talara Peru 142 B4
Talar-i-Band mts Pak. see Makran Coast Range
Talas Kyrg. 80 D3
Talas Ala-Too mts Kyrg. 80 D3
Talas Range mts Kyrg. see Talas Ala-Too
Talasskiy Alatau, Khrebet mts Kyrg. see Talas Ala-Too
Talaud, Kepulauan is Indon. 69 H6
Talavera de la Reina Spain 57 D4
Talawgyi Myanmar 70 B1
Talaya Russia 65 Q3
Talbehat India 82 D4
Talbīsah Syria 85 C2
Talbot, Mount hill Australia 109 D6
Talbotton U.S.A. 133 C5
Talbragar r. Australia 112 D4
Talca Chile 144 B5
Talcahuano Chile 144 B5
Taldan Russia 74 B1
Taldom Russia 42 H4
Taldykorgan Kazakh. 80 E3
Taldy-Kurgan Kazakh. see Taldykorgan
Taldyqorghan Kazakh. see Taldykorgan
Tālesh Iran 88 C2
Talgarth U.K. 49 D7
Talguppa India 84 B3
Talia Australia 111 A7
Taliabu i. Indon. 69 G7
Talikota India 84 C2
Talimardzhan Uzbek. see Tallimarjon
Talin Hiag China 74 B3
Taliparamba India 84 B3
Talisay Phil. 69 G4
Talış Dağları mts Azer./Iran 88 C2
Talitsa Russia 42 J4
Taliwang Indon. 108 B2
Talkeetna U.S.A. 118 C3
Talkeetna Mountains U.S.A. 118 D3
Talkh Āb Iran 88 E3
Tallacootra, Lake salt flat Australia 109 F7
Talladega U.S.A. 133 C5

▶Tallahassee U.S.A. 133 C6
Capital of Florida.

Tall al Aḥmar Syria 85 D1
Tall Baydar Syria 91 F3
Tall-e Ḥalāl Iran 88 D4
Tallimarjon Uzbek. 89 G2

▶Tallinn Estonia 45 N7
Capital of Estonia.

Tall Kalakh Syria 85 C2
Tall Kayf Iraq 91 F3
Tallow Ireland 51 D5
Tallulah U.S.A. 131 F5
Tall 'Uwaynāt Iraq 91 F3
Tallymerjen Uzbek. see Tallimarjon
Talmont-St-Hilaire France 56 D3
Tal'ne Ukr. 43 F6
Tal'noye Ukr. see Tal'ne
Taloda India 82 C5
Talodi Sudan 86 D7
Taloga U.S.A. 131 D4
Talon, Lac *l.* Canada 123 I3
Ta-long Myanmar 70 B2
Talos Dome *ice feature* Antarctica 152 H2
Ta Loung San *mt.* Laos 70 C2
Talovaya Russia 43 I6
Taloyoak Canada 119 I3
Tal Pass Pak. 89 I3
Talsi Latvia 45 M8
Tal Sīyāh Iran 89 F4
Taltal Chile 144 B3
Taltson *r.* Canada 121 H2
Talu China 76 B2
Tāluqān Afgh. 89 H2
Talvik Norway 44 M1
Talwood Australia 112 D2
Talyshskiye Gory *mts* Azer./Iran *see* Talış Dağları
Talyy Russia 42 L2
Tamala Australia 109 A6
Tamala Russia 43 I5
Tamale Ghana 96 C4
Tamana *i.* Kiribati 107 H2
Taman Negara National Park Malaysia 71 C6
Tamano Japan 75 D6
Tamanrasset Alg. 96 D2
Tamanthi Myanmar 70 A1
Tamaqua U.S.A. 135 H3
Tamar India 83 F5
Tamar Syria *see* Tadmur
Tamar *r.* U.K. 49 C8
Tamar Qareh Qūzī Iran 88 D2
Tamarugal, Pampa de *plain* Chile 142 E7
Tamasane Botswana 101 H2
Tamatave Madag. *see* Toamasina
Tamaulipas *state* Mex. 131 D7
Tambacounda Senegal 96 B3
Tambaqui Brazil 142 F5
Tambar Springs Australia 112 D3
Tambelan, Kepulauan *is* Indon. 71 D7
Tambelan Besar *i.* Indon. 71 D7
Tambo *r.* Australia 112 C6
Tambohorano Madag. 99 E5

▶Tambora, Gunung *vol.* Indon. 108 B2
Deadliest recorded volcanic eruption (1815).

Tamboritha *mt.* Australia 112 C6
Tambov Russia 43 I5
Tambovka Russia 74 C2
Tambura South Sudan 97 F4
Tamburi Brazil 145 C1
Tâmchekkeṭ Mauritania 96 B3
Tamdybulak Uzbek. *see* Tomdibuloq
Tâmega *r.* Port. 57 B3
Tamenghest Alg. *see* Tamanrasset
Tamenglong India 83 H4
Tamerza Tunisia 58 B7
Tamgak, Adrar *mt.* Niger 96 D3
Tamgué, Massif du *mt.* Guinea 96 B3
Tamiahua, Laguna de *lag.* Mex. 136 E4
Tamiang, Ujung *pt* Indon. 71 B6
Tamil Nadu *state* India 84 C4
Tamitsa Russia 42 H2
Ṭāmīya Egypt *see* Ṭāmīyah
Ṭāmīyah Egypt 90 C5
Tamkuhi India 83 F4
Tam Ky Vietnam 70 E4
Tammarvi *r.* Canada 121 K1
Tammerfors Fin. *see* Tampere
Tammisaari Fin. *see* Ekenäs
Tampa U.S.A. 133 D7
Tampa Bay U.S.A. 133 D7
Tampere Fin. 45 M6
Tampico Mex. 136 E4
Tampin Malaysia 71 C7
Tampines Sing. 71 [inset]
Tamsagbulag Mongolia 73 L3
Tamsweg Austria 47 N7
Tamu Myanmar 70 A1
Tamworth Australia 112 E3
Tamworth U.K. 49 F6
Tana *r.* Fin./Norway *see* Tenojoki
Tana *r.* Kenya 98 E4
Tana Madag. *see* Antananarivo
Tana *i.* Vanuatu *see* Tanna
Tana, Lake Eth. 98 D2
Tanabe Japan 75 D6
Tanabi Brazil 145 A3
Tana Bru Norway 44 P1
Tanada Lake U.S.A. 120 A2
Tanafjorden *inlet* Norway 44 P1
Tanah, Tanjung *pt* Indon. 68 D8
T'ana Hāyk' *l.* Eth. *see* Tana, Lake
Tanahgrogot Indon. 68 F7
Tanah Merah Malaysia 71 C6
Tanahputih Indon. 71 C7
Tanakeke *i.* Indon. 68 F8
Tanami Australia 108 E4
Tanami Desert Australia 108 E4
Tân An Vietnam 71 D5
Tanana *r.* U.S.A. 120 A2
Tananarive Madag. *see* Antananarivo
Tanandava Madag. 99 E6
Tancheng China *see* Pingtan
Tanch'ŏn N. Korea 75 C4
Tanda Côte d'Ivoire 96 C4
Tanda *Uttar Prad.* India 82 D3
Tanda *Uttar Prad.* India 83 E4
Tandag Phil. 69 H5
Ţăndărei Romania 59 L2
Tandaué Angola 99 B5
Tandi India 82 D2
Tandil Arg. 144 E5
Tando Adam Pak. 89 H5
Tando Allahyar Pak. 89 H5
Tando Bago Pak. 89 H5
Tandou Lake *imp. l.* Australia 111 C7
Tandragee U.K. 51 F3
Tandur India 84 C2
Tanduri Pak. 89 G4
Tanega-shima *i.* Japan 75 C7
Tanen Taunggyi *mts* Thai. 70 B3
Tanezrouft *reg.* Alg./Mali 96 C2
Ṭanf, Jabal aṭ *hill* Syria 85 D3
Tang, Kaôh *i.* Cambodia 71 C5
Tang, Ra's-e *pt* Iran 89 E5
Tanga Tanz. 99 D4
Tangail Bangl. 83 G4
Tanga Islands P.N.G. 106 F2
Tanganyika *country* Africa *see* Tanzania

▶Tanganyika, Lake Africa 99 C4
Deepest and 2nd largest lake in Africa, and 6th largest in the world.

Tangará Brazil 145 A4
Tangasseri India 84 C4
Tangdan China 76 D3
Tangeli Iran 88 D2
Tanger Morocco *see* Tangier
Tangerhütte Germany 53 L2
Tangermünde Germany 53 L2
Tang-e Sarkheh Iran 89 E5
Tanggor China 76 D1
Tanggulashan China 76 B1
Tanggula Shan *mt.* China 83 G2
Tanggula Shan *mts* China 83 G2
Tanggula Shankou *pass* China 83 G2
Tangguo China 83 F3
Tanghe China 77 G1
Tangier Morocco 57 D6
Tangiers Morocco *see* Tangier
Tang La *pass* China 83 G4
Tangla India 83 G4
Tanglag China 76 C1
Tanglin Sing. 71 [inset]
Tangmai China 76 B2
Tangnag China 76 D1
Tangorin Australia 110 D4
Tangra Yumco *salt l.* China 83 F3
Tangse Indon. 71 A6
Tangshan *Guizhou* China *see* Shiqian
Tangshan *Hebei* China 73 L5
Tangte *mt.* Myanmar 70 B2
Tangtse India *see* Tanktse
Tangwan China 77 F3
Tangwanghe China 74 C2
Tangyuan China 74 C3
Tangyung Tso *salt l.* China 83 F3
Tanhaçu Brazil 145 C1
Tanhua Fin. 44 O3
Tani Cambodia 71 D5
Taniantaweng Shan *mts* China 76 B2
Tanimbar, Kepulauan *is* Indon. 108 E1
Tanintharyi Myanmar *see* Tenasserim
Tanintharyi Myanmar *see* Tenasserim
Tanintharyi Myanmar *see* Tenasserim
Tanjah Morocco *see* Tangier
Tanjay Phil. 69 G5
Tanjore India *see* Thanjavur
Tanjung Indon. 68 F7
Tanjungbalai Indon. 71 B7
Tanjungkarang-Telukbetung Indon. *see* Bandar Lampung
Tanjungpandan Indon. 68 D7
Tanjungpinang Indon. 71 D7
Tanjungpura Indon. 71 B7
Tanjung Puting, Taman Nasional *nat. park* Indon. 68 E7
Tanjungredeb Indon. 68 F6
Tanjungselor Indon. 68 F6
Tankse India *see* Tanktse
Tanktse India 82 D2
Tankwa-Karoo National Park S. Africa 100 D7
Tanna *i.* Vanuatu 107 G3
Tannadice U.K. 50 G4
Tännäs Sweden 44 H5
Tanner, Mount Canada 120 G5
Tannu-Ola, Khrebet *mts* Russia 80 H1
Tanot India 82 B4
Tanout Niger 96 D3
Tansen Nepal 83 E4
Tanshui Taiwan *see* Danshui
Ṭanṭa Egypt *see* Ṭanṭā
Ṭanṭā Egypt 90 C5
Tan-Tan Morocco 96 B2
Tantu China 74 A3
Tanuku India 84 D2
Tanumbirini Australia 108 F4
Tanumshede Sweden 45 G7
Tanzania *country* Africa 99 D4
Tanzilla *r.* Canada 120 D3
Tao, Ko *i.* Thai. 71 B5
Tao'an China *see* Taonan
Taobh Tuath U.K. *see* Northton
Taocheng China *see* Daxin
Tao He *r.* China 76 D1
Taohong China *see* Longhui
Taohuajiang China *see* Taojiang
Taohuaping China *see* Longhui
Taojiang China 77 G2
Taolanaro Madag. *see* Tôlañaro
Taonan China 74 A3
Taongi *atoll* Marshall Is 150 H5
Taos U.S.A. 127 G5
Taounate Morocco 54 D5
Taourirt Morocco 54 D5
Taoxi China 77 H3
Taoyang China *see* Lintao
Taoyuan China 77 F2
Taoyuan Taiwan 77 I3
Tapa Estonia 45 N7
Tapachula Mex. 136 F6
Tapah Malaysia 71 C6
Tapajós *r.* Brazil 143 H4
Tapaktuan Indon. 71 B7
Tapauá Brazil 142 F5
Tapauá *r.* Brazil 142 F5
Taperoá Brazil 145 D1
Tapiau Russia *see* Gvardeysk
Tapis, Gunung *mt.* Malaysia 71 C6
Tapisuelas Mex. 127 F8
Taplejung Nepal 83 F4
Tap Mun Chau *i.* *H.K.* China 77 [inset]
Ta-pom Myanmar 70 B2
Tappahannock U.S.A. 135 G5
Tappeh, Kūh-e *hill* Iran 88 C3
Taprobane *country* Asia *see* Sri Lanka
Tapti *r.* India 82 C5
Tapuae-o-Uenuku *mt.* N.Z. 113 D5
Tapulonanjing *mt.* Indon. 71 B7
Tapurucuara Brazil 142 E4
Taputeouea *atoll* Kiribati *see* Tabiteuea
Taquara Brazil 145 A5
Taquari Brazil 145 A5
Taquari *r.* Brazil 143 G7
Taquaritinga Brazil 145 A3
Tar *r.* Ireland 51 E5
Tara Australia 112 E1
Ṭarābulus Lebanon *see* Tripoli
Ṭarābulus Libya *see* Tripoli
Tarahuwan India 82 E4
Tarai *reg.* India 83 G4
Tarakan Indon. 68 F6
Tarakan *i.* Indon. 68 F6
Tārakī *reg.* Afgh. 89 G3
Taraklı Turkey 59 N4
Taran, Mys *pt* Russia 45 K9
Tarana Australia 112 D4
Taranagar India 82 C3
Taranaki, Mount *vol.* N.Z. 113 E4
Tarancón Spain 57 E3
Tarangambadi India 84 C4
Tarangire National Park Tanz. 98 D4
Taranto Italy 58 G4
Taranto, Golfo di *g.* Italy 58 G4
Taranto, Gulf of Italy *see* Taranto, Golfo di
Tarapoto Peru 142 C5
Tarapur India 84 B2
Tararua Range *mts* N.Z. 113 E5
Tarascon-sur-Ariège France 56 E5
Tarasovskiy Russia 43 I6
Tarauacá Brazil 142 D5
Tarauacá *r.* Brazil 142 E5
Tarawera N.Z. 113 F4
Tarawera, Mount *vol.* N.Z. 113 F4
Taraz Kazakh. 80 D3
Tarazona Spain 57 F3
Tarazona de la Mancha Spain 57 F4
Tarbagatay, Khrebet *mts* Kazakh. 80 F2
Tarbat Ness *pt* U.K. 50 F3
Tarbert Ireland 51 C5
Tarbert *Scotland* U.K. 50 C3
Tarbert *Scotland* U.K. 50 D5
Tarbes France 56 E5
Tarboro U.S.A. 132 E5
Tarcoola Australia 109 F7
Tarcoon Australia 112 C3
Tarcoonyinna *watercourse* Australia 109 F6
Tarcutta Australia 112 C5
Tardoki-Yangi, Gora *mt.* Russia 74 E2
Taree Australia 112 F3
Tarella Australia 111 C6
Tarentum Italy *see* Taranto
Ṭarfā', Baṭn aṭ *depr.* Saudi Arabia 88 C6
Tarfaya Morocco 96 B2
Targa *well* Niger 96 D3
Targan China *see* Talin Hiag
Targhee Pass U.S.A. 126 F3
Targovishte Bulg. 59 L3
Târgovişte Romania 59 K2
Targuist Morocco 57 D6
Târgu Jiu Romania 59 J2
Târgu Mureş Romania 59 K1
Târgu Neamţ Romania 59 L1
Târgu Secuiesc Romania 59 L1
Targyailing China 83 F3
Tari P.N.G. 69 K8
Tariat Mongolia 80 I2
Tarif U.A.E. 88 D5
Tarifa Spain 57 D5
Tarifa, Punta de *pt* Spain 57 D5
Tarija Bol. 142 F8
Tarikere India 84 B3
Tariku *r.* Indon. 69 J7
Tarīm Yemen 86 G6
Tarim Basin China 80 F4
Tarime Tanz. 98 D4
Tarim He *r.* China 80 G3
Tarim Pendi *basin* China *see* Tarim Basin
Tarīn Kōṭ Afgh. 89 G3
Taritatu *r.* Indon. 69 J7
Tarka *r.* S. Africa 101 G7
Tarkastad S. Africa 101 H7
Tarkio U.S.A. 130 E3
Tarko-Sale Russia 64 I3
Tarkwa Ghana 96 C4
Tarlac Phil. 69 G3
Tarlag China 76 C1
Tarlo River National Park Australia 112 D5
Tarma Peru 142 C6
Tarmstedt Germany 53 J1
Tarn *r.* France 56 E4
Tärnaby Sweden 44 I4
Tarnak Rōd *r.* Afgh. 89 G4
Târnăveni Romania 59 K1
Tarnobrzeg Poland 43 D6
Tarnogskiy Gorodok Russia 42 I3
Tarnopol Ukr. *see* Ternopil'
Tarnów Poland 43 D6
Tarnowitz Poland *see* Tarnowskie Góry
Tarnowskie Góry Poland 47 Q5
Taro Co *salt l.* China 83 F3
Ṭārom Iran 88 D4
Taroom Australia 111 E5
Taroudannt Morocco 54 C5
Tarpaulin Swamp Australia 110 B3
Ṭarq Iran 88 C3
Tarqi China 73 M3
Tarquinia Italy 58 D3
Tarquinii Italy *see* Tarquinia
Tarrabool Lake *salt flat* Australia 110 A3
Tarraco Spain *see* Tarragona
Tarrafal Cape Verde 96 [inset]
Tarragona Spain 57 G3
Tårrajaur Sweden 44 K3
Tarran Hills *hill* Australia 112 C4
Tarrant Point Australia 110 B3
Tàrrega Spain 57 G3
Tarrong China *see* Nyêmo
Tarsus Turkey 85 B1
Tart China 83 H1
Tärtär Azer. 91 G2
Tartu Estonia 45 O7
Ṭarṭūs Syria 85 B2
Tarumovka Russia 91 G1
Tarung Hka *r.* Myanmar 70 B1
Tarutao, Ko *i.* Thai. 71 B6
Tarutao National Park Thai. 71 B6
Tarutung Indon. 71 B7
Tarvisium Italy *see* Treviso
Ṭarz Iran 88 E4
Tasai, Ko *i.* Thai. 71 B5
Taschereau Canada 122 F4
Taseko Mountain Canada 120 F5
Tashauz Turkm. *see* Daşoguz
Tashi Chho Bhutan *see* Thimphu
Tashigang Bhutan *see* Trashigang
Tashikuzuke Shan *mts* China 82 C1
Tashino Russia *see* Pervomaysk
Tashir Armenia 91 G2
Tashk, Daryācheh-ye *l.* Iran 88 D4
Tashkent Uzbek. *see* Toshkent
Tāshqurghān Afgh. *see* Khulm
Tashtagol Russia 72 F2
Tashtyp Russia 72 F2
Tasialujjuaq, Lac *l.* Canada 123 G2
Tasiat, Lac *l.* Canada 122 G2
Tasiilap Karra *c.* Greenland 119 O3
Tasiilaq Greenland 153 J2
Tasīl Syria 85 B3
Tasiujaq Canada 123 H2
Tasiusaq Greenland 119 M2
Taskala Kazakh. 41 Q5
Taşkent Turkey 85 A1
Tasker Niger 96 E3
Taskesken Kazakh. 80 F2
Taşköprü Turkey 90 D2
Tasman Abyssal Plain *sea feature* Tasman Sea 150 G8
Tasman Basin *sea feature* Tasman Sea 150 G8
Tasman Bay N.Z. 113 D5

▶Tasmania *state* Australia 111 [inset]
4th largest island in Oceania.

Tasman Islands P.N.G. *see* Nukumanu Islands
Tasman Mountains N.Z. 113 D5
Tasman Peninsula Australia 111 [inset]
Tasman Sea S. Pacific Ocean 106 H6
Taşova Turkey 90 E2
Tassara Niger 96 D3
Tassialouc, Lac *l.* Canada 122 G2
Tassili n'Ajjer, Parc National de *nat. park* Alg. 96 D2
Tasty Kazakh. 80 C3
Taşucu Turkey 85 A1
Tas-Yuryakh Russia 65 M3
Tata Morocco 54 C6
Tatabánya Hungary 58 H1
Tatamailau, Foho *mt.* East Timor 108 D2
Tataouine Tunisia 54 G5
Tatarbunary Ukr. 59 M2
Tatarsk Russia 64 I4
Tatarskiy Proliv *strait* Russia 74 F2
Tatar Strait Russia *see* Tatarskiy Proliv
Tate *r.* Australia 110 C3
Tateyama Japan 75 E6
Tathlina Lake Canada 120 G2
Tathlīth Saudi Arabia 86 F6
Tathlīth, Wādī *watercourse* Saudi Arabia 86 F5
Tathra Australia 112 D6
Tatinnai Lake Canada 121 L2
Tatishchevo Russia 43 J6
Tatkon Myanmar 70 B2
Tatla Lake Canada 120 E5
Tatla Lake *l.* Canada 120 E5
Tatlayoko Lake Canada 120 E5
Tatnam, Cape Canada 121 N3
Tatra Mountains Poland/Slovakia 47 Q6
Tatry *mts* Poland/Slovakia *see* Tatra Mountains
Tatrzański Park Narodowy *nat. park* Poland 47 Q6
Tatshenshini-Alsek Provincial Wilderness Park Canada 120 B3
Tatsinskaya Russia 43 I6
Tatuí Brazil 145 B3
Tatuk Mountain Canada 120 E4
Tatum U.S.A. 131 C5
Tatvan Turkey 91 F3
Tau Norway 45 D7
Tauá Brazil 143 J5
Tauapeçaçu Brazil 142 F4
Taubaté Brazil 145 B3
Tauber *r.* Germany 53 J5
Tauberbischofsheim Germany 53 J5
Taucha Germany 53 M3
Taufstein *hill* Germany 53 J4
Taukum, Peski *des.* Kazakh. 80 D3
Taumarunui N.Z. 113 E4
Taumaturgo Brazil 142 D5
Taung S. Africa 100 G4
Taungdwingyi Myanmar 70 A2
Taunggyi Myanmar 70 B2
Taung-ngu Myanmar 70 B3
Taungnyo Range *mts* Myanmar 70 B3
Taungtha Myanmar 70 A2
Taungup Myanmar 76 B5
Taunton U.K. 49 D7
Taunton U.S.A. 135 J3
Taunus *hills* Germany 53 H4
Taupo N.Z. 113 F4
Taupo, Lake N.Z. 113 E4
Tauragė Lith. 45 M9
Tauranga N.Z. 113 F3
Taurasia Italy *see* Turin
Taureau, Réservoir *resr* Canada 122 G5
Taurianova Italy 58 G5
Tauroa Point N.Z. 113 D2
Taurus Mountains Turkey 85 A1
Taute *r.* France 49 F9
Tauz Azer. *see* Tovuz
Tavas Turkey 59 M6
Tavastehus Fin. *see* Hämeenlinna
Taverham U.K. 49 I6
Taveuni *i.* Fiji 107 I3
Tavildara Tajik. 89 H2
Tavira Port. 57 C5
Tavistock Canada 134 E2
Tavistock U.K. 49 C8
Tavoy Myanmar *see* Dawei
Tavoy *r. mouth* Myanmar 71 B4
Tavoy Island Myanmar *see* Mali Kyun
Tavoy Point Myanmar 71 B4
Tavşanlı Turkey 59 M5
Taw *r.* U.K. 49 C7
Tawakkul China 82 E1
Tawang India 83 G4
Tawas City U.S.A. 134 D1
Tawau *Sabah* Malaysia 68 F6
Tawè Myanmar *see* Dawei
Tawe *r.* U.K. 49 D7
Ṭawī Ḥafīr *well* U.A.E. 88 D5
Ṭawī Murra *well* U.A.E. 88 D5
Tawmaw Myanmar 70 B1
Tawu Taiwan *see* Dawu
Taxkorgan China 80 E4
Tay *r.* Canada 120 C2
Tay *r.* U.K. 50 F4
Tay, Firth of *est.* U.K. 50 F4
Tay, Lake *salt flat* Australia 109 C8
Tay, Loch *l.* U.K. 50 E4
Tayandu, Kepulauan *is* Indon. 69 I8
Ṭaybād Iran 89 F3
Taybola Russia 44 R2
Taycheedah U.S.A. 134 A2
Tayinloan U.K. 50 D5
Taylor Canada 120 F3
Taylor *AK* U.S.A. 118 B3
Taylor *MI* U.S.A. 134 D2
Taylor *NE* U.S.A. 130 D3
Taylor *TX* U.S.A. 131 D6
Taylor, Mount U.S.A. 129 J4
Taylorsville U.S.A. 134 C4
Taylorville U.S.A. 130 F4
Taymā' Saudi Arabia 90 E6
Taymanī *reg.* Afgh. 89 F3
Taymura *r.* Russia 65 K3
Taymyr, Ozero *l.* Russia 65 L2
Taymyr, Poluostrov *pen.* Russia *see* Taymyr Peninsula
Taymyr Peninsula Russia 64 J2
Tây Ninh Vietnam 71 D5
Taypak Kazakh. 41 Q6
Taypaq Kazakh. *see* Taypak
Tayshet Russia 72 H1
Taytay Phil. 68 F4
Tayuan China 74 B2
Taz *r.* Russia 64 I3
Taza Morocco 54 D5
Tāza Khurmātū Iraq 91 G4
Taze Myanmar 70 A2
Tazewell *TN* U.S.A. 134 D5
Tazewell *VA* U.S.A. 134 E5
Tazin *r.* Canada 121 I2
Tazin Lake Canada 121 I3
Tāzirbū Libya 97 F2
Tazmalt Alg. 57 I5
Tazovskaya Guba *sea chan.* Russia 64 I3
Tbessa Alg. *see* Tébessa

▶Tbilisi Georgia 91 G2
Capital of Georgia.

Tbilisskaya Russia 43 I7
Tchad *country* Africa *see* Chad
Tchamba Togo 96 D4
Tchibanga Gabon 98 B4
Tchigaï, Plateau du Niger 97 E2
Tchin-Tabaradene Niger 96 D3
Tcholliré Cameroon 97 E4
Tchula U.S.A. 131 F5
Tczew Poland 47 Q3
Tê, Prêk *r.* Cambodia 71 D4
Teague, Lake *salt flat* Australia 109 C6
Te Anau N.Z. 113 A7
Te Anau, Lake N.Z. 113 A7
Teapa Mex. 136 F5
Te Araroa N.Z. 113 G3
Teate Italy *see* Chieti
Te Awamutu N.Z. 113 E4
Teba Indon. 69 J7
Tébarat Niger 96 D3
Tebas Indon. 71 E7
Tebay U.K. 48 E4
Tebesjuak Lake Canada 121 L2
Tébessa Alg. 58 C7
Tébessa, Monts de *mts* Alg. 58 C7
Tebingtinggi Indon. 71 B7
Tébourba Tunisia 58 C6
Téboursouk Tunisia 58 C6
T'ebulos Mta Georgia/Russia 91 G2
Tecate Mex. 128 E5
Tece Turkey 85 B1
Techiman Ghana 96 C4
Tecka Arg. 144 B6
Tecklenburger Land *reg.* Germany 53 H2
Tecoripa Mex. 127 F7
Técpan Mex. 136 D5
Tecuala Mex. 136 C4
Tecuci Romania 59 L2
Tecumseh *MI* U.S.A. 134 D3
Tecumseh *NE* U.S.A. 130 D3
Tedzhen Turkm. *see* Tejen
Teec Nos Pos U.S.A. 129 I3
Tees *r.* U.K. 48 F4
Teeswater Canada 134 E1
Tefé *r.* Brazil 142 F4
Tefenni Turkey 59 M6
Tegal Indon. 68 D8
Tegel *airport* Germany 53 N2
Tegid, Llyn *l.* U.K. *see* Bala Lake

▶Tegucigalpa Hond. 137 G6
Capital of Honduras.

Teguidda-n-Tessoumt Niger 96 D3
Tehachapi U.S.A. 128 D4
Tehachapi Mountains U.S.A. 128 D4
Tehachapi Pass U.S.A. 128 D4
Tehek Lake Canada 121 M1
Teheran Iran *see* Tehrān
Tehery Lake Canada 121 M1
Téhini Côte d'Ivoire 96 C4

▶Tehrān Iran 88 C3
Capital of Iran.

Tehri India *see* Tikamgarh
Tehuacán Mex. 136 E5
Tehuantepec, Gulf of *g.* Mex. 136 F5
Tehuantepec, Istmo de *isthmus* Mex. 136 F5
Teide, Pico del *vol.* Canary Is 96 B2
Teifi *r.* U.K. 49 C6
Teignmouth U.K. 49 D8
Teixeira de Freitas Brazil 145 D2
Teixeira de Sousa Angola *see* Luau
Teixeiras Brazil 145 C3
Teixeira Soares Brazil 145 A4
Tejakula Indon. 108 A2
Tejen Turkm. 89 F2
Tejo *r.* Port. *see* Tagus
Tejon Pass U.S.A. 128 D4
Tekapo, Lake N.Z. 113 C6
Tekax Mex. 136 G4
Tekeli Kazakh. 80 E3
Tekes China 80 F3
Tekeze *resr* Eth. 98 D2
Tekiliktag *mt.* China 82 E1
Tekin Russia 74 D2
Tekirdağ Turkey 59 L4
Tekka India 84 D2
Tekkali India 84 E2
Teknaf Bangl. 83 H5
Tekong Kechil, Pulau *i.* Sing. 71 [inset]
Te Kuiti N.Z. 113 E4
Tel *r.* India 84 D1
Télagh Alg. 57 F6
Telanaipura Indon. *see* Jambi
Telangana *state* India 84 C3
Tel Ashqelon *tourist site* Israel 85 B4
Télataï Mali 96 D3
Tel Aviv-Yafo Israel 85 B3
Telč Czechia 47 O6
Telchac Puerto Mex. 136 G4
Telekhany Belarus *see* Tsyelyakhany
Telêmaco Borba Brazil 145 A4
Teleorman *r.* Romania 59 K3
Telertheba, Djebel *mt.* Alg. 96 D2
Telescope Peak U.S.A. 128 E3
Teles Pires *r.* Brazil 143 G5
Telford U.K. 49 E6
Telgte Germany 53 H3
Télimélé Guinea 96 B3
Teljo, Jebel *mt.* Sudan 86 C7
Telkwa Canada 120 E4
Tell Atlas *mts* Alg. *see* Atlas Tellien
Tell City U.S.A. 134 B5
Teller U.S.A. 118 B3
Tell es Sultan West Bank *see* Jericho
Tellicherry India *see* Thalassery
Tellin Belgium 52 F4
Telloh Iraq 91 G5
Telluride U.S.A. 129 J3
Tel'mana, imeni Russia 74 D2
Tel'novskiy Russia 74 F2
Telok Anson Malaysia *see* Teluk Intan
Telo Martius France *see* Toulon
Telpoziz, Gora *mt.* Russia 41 R3
Telsen Arg. 144 C6
Telšiai Lith. 45 M9
Teltow Germany 53 N2
Teluk Anson Malaysia *see* Teluk Intan
Telukbetung Indon. *see* Bandar Lampung
Teluk Cenderawasih, Taman Nasional *nat. park* Indon. 69 I7
Teluk Intan Malaysia 71 C6
Temagami Lake Canada 122 F5
Temanggung Indon. 68 E8
Têmarxung China 83 G2
Temba S. Africa 101 I3
Tembagapura Indon. 69 J7
Tembenchi *r.* Russia 65 K3
Tembilahan Indon. 68 C7
Tembisa S. Africa 101 I4
Tembo Aluma Angola 99 B4
Teme *r.* U.K. 49 E6
Temecula U.S.A. 128 E5
Temerloh Malaysia *see* Temerluh
Temerluh Malaysia 71 C7
Teminabuan Indon. 69 I7
Temirtau Kazakh. 80 D1
Témiscamie *r.* Canada 123 G4
Témiscamie, Lac *l.* Canada 123 G4
Témiscaming Canada 122 F5
Témiscamingue, Lac *l.* Canada 122 F5
Témiscouata, Lac *l.* Canada 123 H5
Temmes Fin. 44 N4
Temnikov Russia 43 I5
Temora Australia 112 C5
Temósachic Mex. 127 G7
Tempe U.S.A. 129 H5
Tempe Downs Australia 109 F6
Temple *MI* U.S.A. 134 C1
Temple *TX* U.S.A. 131 D6
Temple Bar U.K. 49 C6
Temple Dera Pak. 89 H4
Templemore Ireland 51 E5
Temple Sowerby U.K. 48 E4
Templeton *watercourse* Australia 110 B4
Templin Germany 53 N1
Tempué Angola 99 B5
Temryuk Russia 90 E1
Temryukskiy Zaliv *b.* Russia 43 H7
Temuco Chile 144 B5
Temuka N.Z. 113 C7
Temuli China *see* Butuo
Tena Ecuador 142 C4
Tenabo Mex. 136 F4
Tenabo, Mount U.S.A. 128 E1
Tenali India 84 D2
Tenasserim Myanmar 71 B4
Tenasserim *r.* Myanmar 71 B4
Tenbury Wells U.K. 49 E6
Tenby U.K. 49 C7
Tendaho Eth. 98 E2
Tende, Col de *pass* France/Italy 56 H4
Ten Degree Channel India 71 A5
Tendō Japan 75 F5
Tenedos *i.* Turkey *see* Bozcaada
Ténenkou Mali 96 C3
Ténéré *reg.* Niger 96 D2
Ténéré du Tafassâsset *des.* Niger 96 E2
Tenerife *i.* Canary Is 96 B2
Ténès Alg. 57 G5
Teng, Nam *r.* Myanmar 70 B3
Tengah, Kepulauan *is* Indon. 68 F8

Tengah, Sungai r. Sing. 71 [inset]
Tengcheng China see Tengxian
Tengchong China 76 C3
Tengeh Reservoir Sing. 71 [inset]
Tengger Shamo des. China 72 I5
Tenggul i. Malaysia 71 C6
Tengiz, Ozero salt l. Kazakh. 80 C1
Tengréla Côte d'Ivoire 96 C3
Ten'gushevo Russia 43 I5
Tengxian China 77 F4
Teni India see Theni
Teniente Jubany research station Antarctica see Carlini
Tenke Dem. Rep. Congo 99 C5
Tenkeli Russia 65 P2
Tenkodogo Burkina Faso 96 C3
Ten Mile Lake salt flat Australia 109 C6
Ten Mile Lake Canada 123 K4
Tennant Creek Australia 108 F4
Tennessee r. U.S.A. 131 F4
Tennessee state U.S.A. 134 C5
Tennessee Pass U.S.A. 126 G5
Tennevoll Norway 44 J2
Tennille U.S.A. 133 D6
Tenojoki r. Fin./Norway 44 P1
Tenosique Mex. 136 F5
Tenteno Indon. 69 G7
Tenterden U.K. 49 H7
Tenterfield Australia 112 F2
Ten Thousand Islands U.S.A. 133 D7
Tentudia mt. Spain 57 C4
Tentulia Bangl. see Tetulia
Teodoro Sampaio Bahia Brazil 145 D1
Teodoro Sampaio São Paulo Brazil 144 F2
Teófilo Otoni Brazil 145 C2
Tepa Indon. 108 E1
Tepache Mex. 127 F7
Te Paki N.Z. 113 D2
Tepatitlán Mex. 136 D4
Tepehuanes Mex. 131 B7
Tepeköy Turkey see Karakoçan
Tepelenë Albania 59 I4
Tepelská vrchovina hills Czechia 53 M5
Tepequem, Serra mts Brazil 137 L8
Tepic Mex. 136 D4
Te Pirita N.Z. 113 C6
Teplá r. Czechia 53 M4
Teplice Czechia 47 N5
Teplogorka Russia 42 L3
Teploozersk Russia 74 C2
Teploye Russia 43 H5
Teploye Ozero Russia see Teploozersk
Tepoca, Cabo c. Mex. 127 E7
Tepopa, Punta pt Mex. 127 E7
Teq Teq Iraq 91 G4
Tequila Mex. 136 D4
Ter r. Spain 57 H2
Téra Niger 96 D3
Teramo Italy 58 E3
Terang Australia 112 A7
Ter Apel Neth. 52 H2
Tercan Turkey 91 F3
Terebovlya Ukr. 43 E6
Terekty Kazakh. 80 G2
Teresa Cristina Brazil 145 A4
Tereshka r. Russia 43 J6
Teresina Brazil 143 J5
Teresina de Goiás Brazil 145 B1
Teresita Col. 142 E3
Teresópolis Brazil 145 C3
Teressa Island India 71 A5
Terezinha Brazil 143 H3
Tergeste Italy see Trieste
Tergnier France 52 D5
Tergüün Bogd Uul mt. Mongolia 80 J3
Teriberka Russia 44 S2
Termas de Río Hondo Arg. 144 D3
Termez Uzbek. see Termiz
Termini Imerese Sicily Italy 58 E6
Términos, Laguna de lag. Mex. 136 F5
Termit and Tin Toumma National Nature and Cultural Reserve Niger 96 E3
Termit-Kaoboul Niger 96 E3
Termiz Uzbek. 89 G2
Termo U.S.A. 128 C1
Termoli Italy 58 F4
Termonde Belgium see Dendermonde
Tern r. U.K. 49 E6
Ternate Indon. 69 H6
Terneuzen Neth. 52 D3
Terney Russia 74 E3
Terni Italy 58 E3
Ternopil' Ukr. 43 E6
Ternopol' Ukr. see Ternopil'
Terpeniya, Mys c. Russia 74 G2
Terpeniya, Zaliv g. Russia 74 F2
Terra Alta U.S.A. 134 F4
Terra Bella U.S.A. 128 D4
Terrace Canada 120 D4
Terrace Bay Canada 122 D4
Terra Firma S. Africa 100 F3
Terråk Norway 44 H4
Terralba Sardinia Italy 58 C5
Terra Nova Bay Antarctica 152 H1
Terra Nova National Park Canada 123 L4
Terre Adélie reg. Antarctica see Adélie Land
Terrebonne Bay U.S.A. 131 F6
Terre Haute U.S.A. 134 B4
Terre-Neuve prov. Canada see Newfoundland and Labrador
Terre-Neuve-et-Labrador prov. Canada see Newfoundland and Labrador
Terres Australes et Antarctiques Françaises terr. Indian Ocean see French Southern and Antarctic Lands
Terry U.S.A. 126 G3
Terschelling i. Neth. 52 F1
Terskiy Bereg coastal area Russia 42 H2
Tertenia Sardinia Italy 58 C5
Terter Azer. see Tärtär
Teruel Spain 57 F3
Tervola Fin. 44 N3
Tes Mongolia 80 I2
Tešanj Bos. & Herz. 58 G2
Teseney Eritrea 86 E6
Tesha r. Russia 43 I5
Teshekpuk Lake U.S.A. 118 C2
Teshio Japan 74 F3
Teshio-gawa r. Japan 74 F3
Teslin Canada 120 C2
Teslin r. Canada 120 C2
Teslin Lake Canada 120 C2
Tesouras r. Brazil 145 A1
Tessalit Mali 96 D2
Tessaoua Niger 96 D3
Tessolo Moz. 101 L1
Test r. U.K. 49 F8
Testour Tunisia 58 C6
Tetachuck Lake Canada 120 E4
Tetas, Punta pt Chile 144 B2
Tete Moz. 99 D5
Te Teko N.Z. 113 F4
Teteriv r. Ukr. 43 F6
Teterow Germany 47 N4
Tetiyev Ukr. see Tetiyiv
Tetiyiv Ukr. 43 F6
Tetlin U.S.A. 120 A2
Tetlin Lake U.S.A. 120 A2
Tetney U.K. 48 G5
Teton r. U.S.A. 126 F3
Tétouan Morocco 57 D6
Tetovo Macedonia 59 I3
Tetuán Morocco see Tétouan
Tetulia Bangl. 83 G4
Tetulia sea chan. Bangl. 83 G5
Tetyukhe Russia see Dal'negorsk
Tetyukhe-Pristan' Russia see Rudnaya Pristan'
Tetyushi Russia 43 K5
Teuco r. Arg. 144 D2
Teufelsbach Namibia 100 C2
Teunom Indon. 71 A6
Teunom r. Indon. 71 A6
Te Urewera National Park N.Z. 113 F4
Teutoburger Wald hills Germany 53 I2
Teuva Fin. 44 L5
Tevere r. Italy see Tiber
Teverya Israel see Tiberias
Teviot r. U.K. 50 G5
Te Waewae Bay N.Z. 113 A8
Te Waipounamu i. N.Z. see South Island
Tewane Botswana 101 H2
Tewantin Australia 111 F5
Tewkesbury U.K. 49 E7
Têwo China 76 D1
Texarkana AR U.S.A. 131 E5
Texarkana TX U.S.A. 131 E5
Texas Australia 112 E2
Texas state U.S.A. 131 D6
Texel i. Neth. 52 E1
Texhoma U.S.A. 131 C4
Texoma, Lake U.S.A. 131 D5
Teyateyaneng Lesotho 101 H5
Teykovo Russia 42 I4
Teza r. Russia 42 I4
Tezpur India 83 H4
Tezu India 83 I4
Tha, Nâm r. Laos 70 C2
Thaa Atoll Maldives see Kolhumadulu
Tha-anne r. Canada 121 M2
Thabana-Ntlenyana mt. Lesotho 101 I5
Thaba Nchu S. Africa 101 H5
Thaba Putsoa mt. Lesotho 101 H5
Thaba-Tseka Lesotho 101 I5
Thabazimbi S. Africa 101 H3
Thab Lan National Park Thai. 71 C4
Tha Bo Laos 70 C3
Thabong S. Africa 101 H4
Thabyedaung Myanmar 76 C4
Thade r. Myanmar 70 A3
Thagyettaw Myanmar 71 B4
Tha Hin Thai. see Lop Buri
Thai Binh Vietnam 70 D2
Thailand country Asia 70 C4
Thailand, Gulf of Asia 71 C5
Thai Muang Thai. 71 B5
Thai Nguyên Vietnam 70 D2
Thaj Saudi Arabia 88 C5
Thakhèk Laos 70 D3
Thakurgaon Bangl. 83 G4
Thakurtola India 82 E5
Thal Germany 53 K4
Thala Tunisia 58 C7
Thalang Thai. 71 B5
Thalassery India 84 B4
Thal Desert Pak. 89 H4
Thale Germany 53 L3
Thaliparamba India see Taliparamba
Thallon Australia 112 D2
Thalo Pak. 89 G4
Thamaga Botswana 101 G3
Thamar, Jabal mt. Yemen 86 G7
Thamarīt Oman 87 H6
Thame r. U.K. 49 F7
Thames r. Ont. Canada 125 K3
Thames r. Ont. Canada 134 D2
Thames N.Z. 113 E3
Thames est. U.K. 49 H7
Thames r. U.K. 49 H7
Thamesford Canada 134 E2
Thana India see Thane
Thanatpin Myanmar 70 B3
Thandwe Myanmar 70 A3
Thane India 84 B2
Thanet, Isle of pen. U.K. 49 I7
Thangoo Australia 108 C4
Thangra India 82 D2
Thanh Hoa Vietnam 70 D3
Thanjavur India 84 C4
Than Kyun i. Myanmar 71 B5
Thanlwin r. China/Myanmar see Salween
Thanlyin Myanmar 70 B3
Thaolintoa Lake Canada 121 L2
Tha Pla Thai. 70 C3
Thap Put Thai. 71 B5
Thapsacus Syria see Dibsī
Thap Sakae Thai. 71 B5
Tharabwin Myanmar 71 B4
Tharad Gujarat India 82 B4
Tharad Gujarat India 82 B4
Thar Desert India/Pak. 89 H5
Thargomindah Australia 112 A1
Tharrawaw Myanmar 70 A3
Tharthār, Buḥayrat ath l. Iraq 91 F4
Tharwānīyyah U.A.E. 88 D6
Thasos i. Greece 59 K4
Thatcher U.S.A. 129 I5
Thât Khê Vietnam 70 D2
Thaton Myanmar 70 B3
Thatta Pak. 89 G5
Thaungdut Myanmar 70 A1
Tha Uthen Thai. 70 D3
Thayawthadangyi Kyun i. Myanmar 71 B4
Thayetmyo Myanmar 70 A3
Thazi Magway Myanmar 70 A3
Thazi Mandalay Myanmar 83 I5
The Aldermen Islands N.Z. 113 F3
Theba U.S.A. 129 G5
The Bahamas country West Indies 133 E7
Thebes Greece see Thiva
The Bluff Bahamas 133 E7
The Broads nat. park U.K. 49 I6
The Brothers is H.K. China 77 [inset]
The Cheviot hill U.K. 48 E3
The Dalles U.S.A. 126 C3
Thedford U.S.A. 130 C3
The Entrance Australia 112 E4
The Faither stack U.K. 50 [inset]
The Fens reg. U.K. 49 G6
The Gambia country Africa 96 B3
Thegon Myanmar 70 A3
The Grampians mts Australia 111 C8
The Great Oasis oasis Egypt see Khārijah, Wāḥāt al
The Grenadines is St Vincent 137 L6
The Gulf Asia 88 C4

▶The Hague Neth. 52 E2
Seat of government of the Netherlands.

The Hunters Hills N.Z. 113 C7
Thekulthili Lake Canada 121 I2
The Lakes National Park Australia 112 C6
Thelon r. Canada 121 L1
The Lynd Junction Australia 110 D3
Themar Germany 53 K4
Thembalihle S. Africa 101 I4
The Minch sea chan. U.K. 50 C2
The Naze c. Norway see Lindesnes
The Needles stack U.K. 49 F8
Theni India 84 C4
Thenia Alg. 57 H5
Theniet El Had Alg. 57 H6
The North Sound sea chan. U.K. 50 G1
Theodore Australia 110 E5
Theodore Canada 121 K5
Theodore Roosevelt Lake U.S.A. 129 H5
Theodore Roosevelt National Park U.S.A. 130 C2
Theodosia Crimea see Feodosiya
The Old Man of Coniston hill U.K. 48 D4
The Paps hill Ireland 51 C5
The Pas Canada 121 K4
The Pilot mt. Australia 112 D6
Thera i. Greece see Santorini
Thérain r. France 52 C5
Theresa U.S.A. 135 H1
Thermaïkos Kolpos g. Greece 59 J4
Thermopolis U.S.A. 126 F4
The Rock Australia 112 C5
Thérouanne France 52 C4
The Salt Lake salt flat Australia 111 C6

▶The Settlement Christmas I. 68 D9
Capital of Christmas Island.

The Skaw spit Denmark see Grenen
The Skelligs is Ireland 51 B6
The Slot sea chan. Solomon Is see New Georgia Sound
The Solent strait U.K. 49 F8
Thessalon Canada 122 E5
Thessalonica Greece see Thessaloniki
Thessaloniki Greece 59 J4
The Storr hill U.K. 50 C3
Thet r. U.K. 49 H6
The Terraces hills Australia 109 C7
Thetford U.K. 49 H6
Thetford Mines Canada 123 H5
Thetkethaung r. Myanmar 70 A4
The Triangle mts Myanmar 70 B1
The Trossachs hills U.K. 50 E4
The Twins Australia 111 A6
Theva-i-Ra reef Fiji see Ceva-i-Ra

▶The Valley Anguilla 137 L5
Capital of Anguilla.

Thevenard Island Australia 108 A5
Thévenet, Lac l. Canada 123 H2
Theveste Alg. see Tébessa
The Wash b. U.K. 49 H6
The Weald reg. U.K. 49 H7
The Woodlands U.S.A. 131 E6
Thibodaux U.S.A. 131 F6
Thicket Portage Canada 121 L4
Thief River Falls U.S.A. 130 D1
Thiel Neth. see Tiel
Thiel Mountains Antarctica 152 K1
Thielsen, Mount U.S.A. 126 C4
Thielt Belgium see Tielt
Thiérache reg. France 52 D5
Thiers France 56 F4
Thiès Senegal 96 B3
Thika Kenya 98 D4
Thiladhunmathi Maldives 84 B5
Thimbu Bhutan see Thimphu

▶Thimphu Bhutan 83 G4
Capital of Bhutan.

Thionville France 52 G5
Thira i. Greece see Santorini
Thirsk U.K. 48 F4
Thirty Mile Lake Canada 121 L2
Thiruvananthapuram India 84 C4
Thiruvannamalai India see Tiruvannamalai
Thiruvarur India 84 C4
Thiruvattiyur India see Tiruvottiyur
Thisted Denmark 45 F8
Thistle Creek Canada 120 B2
Thistle Lake Canada 121 I1
Thityabin Myanmar 70 A2
Thiu Khao Luang Phrabang mts Laos/Thai. see Luang Phrabang, Thiu Khao
Thiva Greece 59 J5
Thívai Greece see Thiva
Thlewiaza r. Canada 121 M2
Thoa r. Canada 121 I2
Thô Chu, Đao i. Vietnam 71 C5
Thoen Thai. 76 C5
Thoeng Thai. 70 C3
Thohoyandou S. Africa 101 J2
Tholen Neth. 52 E3
Tholen i. Neth. 52 E3
Tholey Germany 52 H5
Thomas Hill Reservoir U.S.A. 130 E4
Thomas Hubbard, Cape Canada 119 I1
Thomaston CT U.S.A. 135 I3
Thomaston GA U.S.A. 133 C5
Thomastown Ireland 51 E5
Thomasville AL U.S.A. 133 C6
Thomasville GA U.S.A. 133 D6
Thommen Belgium 52 G4
Thompson Canada 121 L4
Thompson r. Canada 120 F5
Thompson U.S.A. 129 I2
Thompson r. U.S.A. 124 I4
Thompson Falls U.S.A. 126 E3
Thompson Peak U.S.A. 127 G6
Thompson's Falls Kenya see Nyahururu
Thompson Sound Canada 120 E5
Thomson U.S.A. 133 D5
Thon Buri Thai. 71 C4
Thonokied Lake Canada 121 I1
Thoothukudi India see Tuticorin
Thoreau U.S.A. 129 I4
Thorn Neth. 52 F3
Thorn Poland see Toruń
Thornaby-on-Tees U.K. 48 F4
Thornapple r. U.S.A. 134 C2
Thornbury U.K. 49 E7
Thorne U.K. 48 G5
Thorne U.S.A. 128 D2
Thornton r. Australia 110 B3
Thorold Canada 134 F2
Thorshavn Faroe Is see Tórshavn
Thorshavnfjella reg. Antarctica see Thorshavnheiane
Thorshavnheiane reg. Antarctica 152 C2
Thota-ea-Moli Lesotho 101 H5
Thôt Nôt Vietnam 71 D5
Thouars France 56 D3
Thoubal India 83 H4
Thourout Belgium see Torhout
Thousand Islands Canada/U.S.A. 135 G1
Thousand Lake Mountain U.S.A. 129 H2
Thousand Oaks U.S.A. 128 D4
Thousandsticks U.S.A. 134 D5
Thrace hist. area Europe 59 L4
Thraki hist. area Europe see Thrace
Thrakiko Pelagos sea Greece 59 K4
Three Gorges Reservoir resr China 77 F2
Three Hills Canada 120 H5
Three Hummock Island Australia 111 [inset]
Three Kings Islands N.Z. 113 D2
Three Oaks U.S.A. 134 B3
Three Pagodas Pass Myanmar/Thai. 70 B4
Three Points, Cape Ghana 96 C4
Three Rivers U.S.A. 134 C3
Three Sisters mt. U.S.A. 126 C3
Three Springs Australia 109 A7
Thrissur India 84 C4
Throckmorton U.S.A. 131 D5
Throssell, Lake salt flat Australia 109 D6
Throssel Range hills Australia 108 C5
Thrushton National Park Australia 112 C1
Thư Ba Vietnam 71 D5
Thubun Lakes Canada 121 I2
Thu Dâu Môt Vietnam 71 D5
Thuddungra Australia 112 D5
Thu Đuc Vietnam 71 D5
Thuin Belgium 52 E4
Thul Pak. 89 H4
Thulaythāwāt Gharbī hill Syria 85 D2
Thule Greenland see Qaanaaq
Thule Air Base Greenland 119 L2
Thun Switz. 56 H3
Thunder Bay Canada 119 J5
Thunder Bay b. U.S.A. 134 D1
Thunder Creek r. Canada 121 J5
Thüngen Germany 53 J5
Thung Salaeng Luang National Park Thai. 70 C3
Thung Song Thai. 71 B5
Thung Yai Naresuan Wildlife Reserve nature res. Thai. 70 B4
Thüringen land Germany 53 K3
Thüringer Becken reg. Germany 53 L3
Thüringer Wald mts Germany 53 K4
Thuringia land Germany see Thüringen
Thuringian Forest mts Germany see Thüringer Wald
Thurles Ireland 51 E5
Thurn, Pass Austria 47 N7
Thursday Island Australia 110 C1
Thurso U.K. 50 F2
Thurso r. U.K. 50 F2
Thurston Island Antarctica 152 K2
Thurston Peninsula i. Antarctica see Thurston Island
Thüster Berg hill Germany 53 J2
Thuthukudi India see Tuticorin
Thwaite U.K. 48 E4
Thwaites Glacier Tongue Antarctica 152 K1
Thyatira Turkey see Akhisar
Thyborøn Denmark 45 F8
Thymerais reg. France 52 B6
Tianchang China 77 H1
Tiancheng China see Chongyang
Tianchi China see Lezhi
Tiandeng China 76 E4
Tiandong China 76 E4
Tianeti Georgia 91 G2
Tianfanjie China 77 H2
Tianjin China 73 L5
Tianjin mun. China 73 L5
Tianjun China 80 I4
Tianlin China 76 E3
Tianma China see Changshan
Tianmen China 77 G2
Tianqiaoling China 74 C4
Tianquan China 76 D2
Tianshan China 73 M4
Tian Shan mts China/Kyrg. see Tien Shan
Tianshui China 76 E1
Tianshuihai China 82 D2
Tiantai China 77 I2
Tiantang China see Yuexi
Tianyang China 76 E4
Tianzhou China see Tianyang
Tianzhu Gansu China 72 I5
Tianzhu Guizhou China 77 F3
Tiaret Alg. 57 G6
Tiassalé Côte d'Ivoire 96 C4
Tibagi Brazil 145 A4
Tibal, Wādī watercourse Iraq 91 F4
Tibati Cameroon 96 E4
Tibba Pak. 89 H4
Tibé, Pic de mt. Guinea 96 C4
Tiber r. Italy 58 E4
Tiberias Israel 85 B3
Tiberias, Lake Israel see Galilee, Sea of
Tiber Reservoir U.S.A. 126 F2
Tibesti mts Chad 97 E2
Tibet aut. reg. China see Xizang Zizhiqu
Tibet, Plateau of China 83 F2
Tibi India 89 I4
Tibistī, Sarīr des. Libya 97 E2
Tibooburra Australia 111 C6
Tibrikot Nepal 83 E3
Tibro Sweden 45 I7
Tibur Italy see Tivoli
Tiburón, Isla i. Mex. 127 E7
Ticehurst U.K. 49 H7
Tichborne Canada 135 G1
Tichégami r. Canada 123 G4
Tîchît Mauritania 96 C3
Tîchît, Dahr hills Mauritania 96 C3
Tichla W. Sahara 96 B2
Ticinum Italy see Pavia
Ticonderoga U.S.A. 135 I2
Ticul Mex. 136 G4
Tidaholm Sweden 45 H7
Tiddim Myanmar 70 A2
Tiden India 71 A6
Tidjikja Mauritania 96 B3
Tiefa China see Diaobingshan
Tiel Neth. 52 F3
Tieli China 74 B3
Tieling China 74 A4
Tielongtan China 82 D2
Tielt Belgium 52 D4
Tienen Belgium 52 E4
Tien Shan mts China/Kyrg. 72 D4
Tientsin China see Tianjin
Tientsin mun. China see Tianjin
Tiên Yên Vietnam 70 D2
Tierp Sweden 45 J6
Tierra Amarilla U.S.A. 127 G5

▶Tierra del Fuego, Isla Grande de i. Arg./Chile 144 C8
Largest island in South America.

Tierra del Fuego, Parque Nacional nat. park Arg. 144 C8
Tiétar r. Spain 57 D4
Tiétar, Valle del valley Spain 57 D3
Tietê r. Brazil 145 A3
Tieyon Australia 109 F6
Tiffin U.S.A. 134 D3
Tiflis Georgia see T'bilisi
Tifton U.S.A. 133 D6
Tiga Reservoir Nigeria 96 D3
Tigen Kazakh. 91 H1
Tigh Āb Iran 89 F5
Tigheciului, Dealurile hills Moldova 59 M2
Tighina Moldova see Bender
Tigiria India 84 E1
Tignère Cameroon 96 E4
Tignish Canada 123 I5
Tigranocerta Turkey see Siirt
Tigre r. Venez. 142 F2
Tigris r. Asia 91 G5
also known as Dicle (Turkey) or Nahr Dijlah (Iraq/Syria)
Tigrovaya Balka Zapovednik nature res. Tajik. 89 H2
Tiguidit, Falaise de esc. Niger 96 D3
Tīh, Gebel el plat. Egypt see Tīh, Jabal at
Tīh, Jabal at plat. Egypt 85 A5
Tijuana Mex. 128 E5
Tikamgarh India 82 D4
Tikanlik China 80 G3
Tikhoretsk Russia 43 I7
Tikhvin Russia 42 G4
Tikhvinskaya Gryada ridge Russia 42 G4
Tiki Basin sea feature S. Pacific Ocean 151 L7
Tikokino N.Z. 113 F4
Tikopia i. Solomon Is 107 G3
Tikrīt Iraq 91 F4
Tikse India 82 D2
Tikshozero, Ozero l. Russia 44 R3
Tiksi Russia 65 N2
Tiladummati Atoll Maldives see Thiladhunmathi
Tilaiya Reservoir India 83 F4
Tilbeşar Ovasi plain Turkey 85 C1
Tilbooroo Australia 112 B1
Tilburg Neth. 52 F3
Tilbury Canada 134 D2
Tilbury U.K. 49 H7
Tilcara Arg. 144 C2
Tilcha Creek watercourse Australia 111 C6
Tilden U.S.A. 131 D6
Tilemsès Niger 96 D3
Tilemsi, Vallée du watercourse Mali 96 D3
Tilhar India 82 D4
Tilimsen Alg. see Tlemcen
Tilin Myanmar 70 A2
Tillabéri Niger 96 D3
Tillamook U.S.A. 126 C3
Tillanchong Island India 71 A5
Tillia Niger 96 D3
Tillicoultry U.K. 50 F4
Tillsonburg Canada 134 E2
Tillyfourie U.K. 50 G3
Tilonia India 89 I5
Tilos i. Greece 59 L6
Tilothu India 83 F4
Tilpa Australia 112 B3
Tilsit Russia see Sovetsk
Tilt r. U.K. 50 F4
Tilton IL U.S.A. 134 B3
Tilton NH U.S.A. 135 J2
Tim Russia 43 H6
Ţimā Egypt 86 D4
Timah, Bukit Sing. 71 [inset]
Timah, Bukit hill Sing. 71 [inset]
Timakara i. India 84 B4
Timanskiy Kryazh ridge Russia 42 K2
Timar Turkey 91 F3
Timaru N.Z. 113 C7
Timashëvsk Russia 43 H7
Timashevskaya Russia see Timashëvsk
Timbedgha Mauritania 96 C3
Timber Creek Australia 106 D3
Timber Mountain U.S.A. 128 E3
Timberville U.S.A. 135 F4
Timbuktu Mali 96 C3
Timétrine reg. Mali 96 C3
Timiaouine Alg. 96 D2
Timimoun Alg. 54 E6
Timirist, Râs pt Mauritania 96 B3
Timiskaming, Lake Canada see Témiscamingue, Lac
Timişoara Romania 59 I2
Timmins Canada 122 E4
Timms Hill hill U.S.A. 130 F2
Timon Brazil 143 J5
Timor i. Indon. 108 D2
Timor-Leste country Asia see East Timor
Timor Loro Sae country Asia see East Timor
Timor Sea Australia/Indon. 106 C3
Timor Timur country Asia see East Timor
Timperley Range hills Australia 109 C6
Timrå Sweden 44 J5
Tin, Ra's at pt Libya 90 A4
Ţīna, Khalīg el b. Egypt see Ţīnah, Khalīj aţ
Tinah Syria 85 D1
Ţīnah, Khalīj aţ b. Egypt 85 A4
Tin Can Bay Australia 111 F5
Tindivanam India 84 C3
Tindouf Alg. 54 C6
Ti-n-Essako Mali 96 D3
Tinggi i. Malaysia 71 D7
Tingha Australia 112 E2
Tingis Morocco see Tangier
Tingo María Peru 142 C5
Tingréla Côte d'Ivoire see Tengréla
Tingsryd Sweden 45 I8
Tingvoll Norway 44 F5
Tingwall U.K. 50 F1
Tingzhou China see Changting
Tinharé, Ilha de i. Brazil 145 D1
Tinh Gia Vietnam 70 D3
Tinian i. N. Mariana Is 69 L4
Tini Heke is N.Z. see Snares Islands
Tinnelvelly India see Tirunelveli
Tinogasta Arg. 144 C3
Tinos Greece 59 K6
Tinos i. Greece 59 K6
Tinqueux France 52 D5
Tinrhert, Hamada de Alg. 96 D2
Tinsukia India 83 H4
Tintagel U.K. 49 C8
Tînţâne Mauritania 96 B3
Tintina Arg. 144 D3
Tintinara Australia 111 C7
Tioga U.S.A. 130 C1
Tioman i. Malaysia 71 D7
Ti On, Nui mt. Vietnam 70 D4
Tionesta U.S.A. 134 F3
Tionesta Lake U.S.A. 134 F3
Tipasa Alg. 57 H5
Tiphsah Syria see Dibsī
Tipperary Ireland 51 D5
Tipton CA U.S.A. 128 D3
Tipton IA U.S.A. 130 F3
Tipton IN U.S.A. 134 B3
Tipton MO U.S.A. 130 E4
Tipton, Mount U.S.A. 129 F4
Tiptop U.S.A. 134 E5
Tip Top Hill hill Canada 122 D4
Tiptree U.K. 49 H7
Tiptur India 84 C3
Tipturi India see Tiptur
Tiracambu, Serra do hills Brazil 143 I4
Tirah reg. Pak. 89 H3

▶Tirana Albania 59 H4
Capital of Albania.

Tiranë Albania see Tirana
Tirano Italy 58 D1
Tirari Desert Australia 111 B5

▶Tiraspol Moldova 59 M1
Capital of Transnistria.

Tiraz Mountains Namibia 100 C4
Tire Turkey 59 L5
Tirebolu Turkey 91 E2
Tiree i. U.K. 50 C4
Tîrgovişte Romania see Târgovişte
Tîrgu Jiu Romania see Târgu Jiu
Tîrgu Mureş Romania see Târgu Mureş
Tîrgu Neamţ Romania see Târgu Neamţ
Tîrgu Secuiesc Romania see Târgu Secuiesc
Tiri Pak. 89 G4
Tirich Mir mt. Pak. 89 H2
Tirlemont Belgium see Tienen
Tirna r. India 84 C2
Tîrnăveni Romania see Târnăveni
Tírnavos Greece see Tyrnavos
Tiros Brazil 145 B2
Tirourda, Col de pass Alg. 57 I5
Tīr Pul Afgh. 89 F3
Tirreno, Mare sea France/Italy see Tyrrhenian Sea
Tirso r. Sardinia Italy 58 C5
Tirthahalli India 84 B3
Tiruchchendur India 84 C4
Tiruchchirappalli India 84 C4
Tiruchengodu India 84 C4
Tirunelveli India 84 C4
Tirupati India 84 C3
Tiruppattur Tamil Nadu India 84 C3
Tiruppattur Tamil Nadu India 84 C4
Tiruppur India 84 C4
Tiruttani India 84 C3
Tiruttaraippundi India 84 C4
Tiruvallur India 84 C3
Tiruvannamalai India 84 C3
Tiruvottiyur India 84 D3
Tiru Well Australia 108 D5
Tisa r. Serbia 59 I2
also known as Tisza (Hungary), Tysa (Ukraine)
Tisdale Canada 121 J4
Tishomingo U.S.A. 131 D5
Ţīsīyah Syria 85 C3
Tissemsilt Alg. 57 G6

Tisza r. Serbia see Tisa
Titalya Bangl. see Tetulia
Titan Dome ice feature Antarctica 152 H1
Titao Burkina Faso 96 C3
Tit-Ary Russia 65 N2
Titawin Morocco see Tétouan
Titicaca, Lago Bol./Peru see Titicaca, Lake
▶Titicaca, Lake Bol./Peru 142 E7
Largest lake in South America.
Titi Islands N.Z. 113 A8
Titiea mt. N.Z. see Aspiring, Mount
Titlagarh India 84 D1
Titograd Montenegro see Podgorica
Titova Mitrovica Kosovo see Mitrovicë
Titovo Užice Serbia see Užice
Titovo Velenje Slovenia see Velenje
Titov Veles Macedonia see Veles
Titov Vrbas Serbia see Vrbas
Ti Tree Australia 108 F5
Titu Romania 59 K2
Titusville FL U.S.A. 133 D6
Titusville PA U.S.A. 134 F3
Tiu Chung Chau i. H.K. China 77 [inset]
Tiumpain, Rubha an hd U.K. see Tiumpan Head
Tiumpan Head hd U.K. 50 C2
Tiva watercourse Kenya 98 D4
Tivari India 82 C4
Tiverton Canada 134 E1
Tiverton U.K. 49 D8
Tivoli Italy 58 E4
Ṭīwī Oman 88 E6
Ti-ywa Myanmar 71 B4
Tizimín Mex. 136 G4
Tizi Ouzou Alg. 57 I5
Tiznap He r. China 82 D1
Tiznit Morocco 96 C2
Tiztoutine Morocco 57 E6
Tjaneni Swaziland 101 J3
Tjappsåive Sweden 44 K4
Tjeukemeer l. Neth. 52 F2
Tjirebon Indon. see Cirebon
Tjolotjo Zimbabwe see Tsholotsho
Tjorhom Norway 45 E7
Tkibuli Georgia see T'q'ibuli
Tlahualilo Mex. 131 C7
Tlaxcala Mex. 136 E5
Tl'ell Canada 120 D4
Tlemcen Alg. 57 F6
Tlhakalatlou S. Africa 100 F5
Tlholong S. Africa 101 I5
Tlokweng Botswana 101 G3
Tlyarata Russia 91 G2
To r. Myanmar 70 B3
Toad r. Canada 120 E3
Toad River Canada 120 E3
Toamasina Madag. 99 E5
Toana mts U.S.A. 129 F1
Toano U.S.A. 135 G5
Toa Payoh Sing. 71 [inset]
Toba China 76 C2
Toba, Danau l. Indon. 71 B7
Toba, Lake Indon. see Toba, Danau
Toba and Kakar Ranges mts Pak. 89 G4
Toba Gargaji Pak. 89 I4
Tobago i. Trin. and Tob. 137 L6
Tobelo Indon. 69 H6
Tobercurry Ireland 51 D3
Tobermorey Australia 110 B4
Tobermory Australia 112 A1
Tobermory Canada 134 E1
Tobermory U.K. 50 C4
Tobi i. Palau 69 I6
Tobin, Lake salt flat Australia 108 D5
Tobin, Mount U.S.A. 128 E1
Tobin Lake Canada 121 K4
Tobin Lake l. Canada 121 K4
Tobi-shima i. Japan 75 E5
Tobli Liberia 96 C4
Tobol r. Kazakh./Russia see Tobyl
Tobol'sk Russia 64 H4
Tobruk Libya see Tubruq
Tobseda Russia 42 L1
Tobyl r. Kazakh./Russia 78 F1
Tobysh r. Russia 42 K2
Tocache Nuevo Peru 142 C5
Tocantinópolis Brazil 143 I5
Tocantins r. Brazil 145 A1
Tocantins state Brazil 145 A1
Tocantinzinha r. Brazil 145 A1
Toccoa U.S.A. 133 D5
Tochi r. Pak. 89 H3
Töcksfors Sweden 45 G7
Tocopilla Chile 144 B2
Tocumwal Australia 112 B5
Tod, Mount Canada 120 G5
Todd watercourse Australia 110 A5
Todi Italy 58 E3
Todoga-saki pt Japan 75 F5
Todos Santos Mex. 136 B4
Toe Head hd U.K. 50 B3
Tofino Canada 120 E5
Toft U.K. 50 [inset]
Tofua i. Tonga 107 I3
Togatax China 82 E2
Togian i. Indon. 69 G7
Togian, Kepulauan is Indon. 69 G7
Togliatti Russia see Tol'yatti
Togo country Africa 96 D4
Togtoh China 73 K4
Togton He r. China 83 H2
Togton Heyan China see Tanggulashan
Tohatchi U.S.A. 129 I4
Toholampi Fin. 44 N5
Toiba China 83 G3
Toibalewe India 71 A5
Toijala Fin. 45 M6
Toili Indon. 69 G7
Toi-misaki pt Japan 75 C7
Toivakka Fin. 44 O5
Toiyabe Range mts U.S.A. 128 E2
Tojikiston country Asia see Tajikistan
Tok U.S.A. 120 A2
Tokar Sudan 86 E6
Tokara-rettō is Japan 75 C7
Tokarevka Russia 43 I6
Tokat Turkey 90 E2
Tok-do i. N. Pacific Ocean see Liancourt Rocks
▶Tokelau terr. S. Pacific Ocean 107 I2
New Zealand Overseas Territory.
Tokmak Kyrg. see Tokmok
Tokmak Ukr. 43 G7
Tokmok Kyrg. 80 E3
Tokomaru Bay N.Z. 113 G4
Tokoroa N.Z. 113 E4
Tokoza S. Africa 101 I4
Toksun China 80 G3
Tok-to i. N. Pacific Ocean see Liancourt Rocks
Toktogul Kyrg. 80 D3
Tokur Russia 74 D1
Tokushima Japan 75 D6
▶Tōkyō Japan 75 E6
Capital of Japan. Most populous city in Asia and the world.
Tolaga Bay N.Z. 113 G4
Tôlañaro Madag. 99 E6
Tolbo Mongolia 80 H2
Tolbukhin Bulg. see Dobrich
Tolbuzino Russia 74 B1
Toledo Brazil 144 F2
Toledo Spain 57 D4
Toledo IA U.S.A. 130 E3
Toledo OH U.S.A. 134 D3
Toledo OR U.S.A. 126 C3
Toledo, Montes de mts Spain 57 D4
Toledo Bend Reservoir U.S.A. 131 E6
Toletum Spain see Toledo
Toliara Madag. 99 E6
Tolitoli Indon. 69 G6
Tol'ka Russia 64 J3
Tolleson U.S.A. 129 G5
Tolmachevo Russia 45 P7
Tolo Dem. Rep. Congo 98 B4
Tolo Channel H.K. China 77 [inset]
Tolochin Belarus see Talachyn
Tolo Harbour b. H.K. China 77 [inset]
Tolosa France see Toulouse
Tolosa Spain 57 E2
Toluca Mex. 136 E5
Toluca de Lerdo Mex. see Toluca
To-lun China see Duolun
Tol'yatti Russia 43 K5
Tom' r. Russia 74 B2
Tomah U.S.A. 130 F3
Tomakomai Japan 74 F4
Tomales U.S.A. 128 B2
Tomali Indon. 69 G7
Tomamae Japan 74 F3
Tomanivi mt. Fiji 107 H3
Tomar Brazil 142 F4
Tomar Port. 57 B4
Tomari Russia 74 F3
Tomarza Turkey 90 D3
Tomaszów Lubelski Poland 43 D6
Tomaszów Mazowiecki Poland 47 R5
Tomatin U.K. 50 F3
Tomatlán Mex. 136 C5
Tomazina Brazil 145 A3
Tombador, Serra do hills Brazil 143 G6
Tombigbee r. U.S.A. 133 C6
Tomboco Angola 99 B4
Tombouctou Mali see Timbuktu
Tombstone U.S.A. 127 F7
Tombua Angola 99 B5
Tom Burke S. Africa 101 H2
Tomdibuloq Uzbek. 80 B3
Tome Moz. 101 L2
Tomelilla Sweden 45 H9
Tomelloso Spain 57 E4
Tomi Romania see Constanța
Tomingley Australia 112 D4
Tomini, Teluk g. Indon. 69 G7
Tominian Mali 96 C3
Tomintoul U.K. 50 F3
Tomislavgrad Bos. & Herz. 58 G3
Tomkinson Ranges mts Australia 109 E6
Tømmerneset Norway 44 I3
Tommot Russia 65 N4
Tomo r. Col. 142 E2
Tomóchic Mex. 127 G7
Tomortei China 73 K4
Tompkinsville U.S.A. 134 C5
Tom Price Australia 108 B5
Tomra China 83 F3
Tomsk Russia 64 J4
Toms River U.S.A. 135 H4
Tomtabacken hill Sweden 45 I8
Tomtor Russia 65 P3
Tomur Feng mt. China/Kyrg. see Pobeda Peak
Tomuzlovka r. Russia 43 J7
Tom White, Mount U.S.A. 118 D3
Tonalá Mex. 136 F5
Tonantins Brazil 142 E4
Tonb-e Bozorg, Jazīreh-ye i. The Gulf 88 D5
Tonb-e Kūchek, Jazīreh-ye i. The Gulf 88 D5
Tonbridge U.K. 49 H7
Tondano Indon. 69 G6
Tønder Denmark 45 F9
Tondi India 84 C4
Tone r. U.K. 49 E7
Tonekābon Iran 88 C2
Toney Mountain Antarctica 152 K1
Tonga country S. Pacific Ocean 107 I4
Tongariro National Park N.Z. 113 E4
Tongatapu Group is Tonga 107 I4
▶Tonga Trench sea feature S. Pacific Ocean 150 I7
2nd deepest trench in the world.
Tongbai Shan mts China 77 G1
Tongcheng China 77 H2
T'ongch'ŏn N. Korea 75 B5
Tongchuan Shaanxi China 77 F1
Tongchuan Sichuan China see Santai
Tongdao China 77 F3
Tongde China 76 D1
Tongeren Belgium 52 F4
Tongguan China 77 G2
Tonggu Zui pt China 77 F5
Tonghai China 76 D3
Tonghe China 74 C3
Tonghua Jilin China 74 B4
Tonghua Jilin China 74 B4
Tongi Bangl. see Tungi
Tongjiang Heilong. China 74 D3
Tongjiang Sichuan China 76 E2
Tongking, Gulf of China/Vietnam 70 E2
Tonglau Myanmar 70 B2
Tongle China see Leye
Tongliang China 76 E2
Tongliao China 73 M4
Tongling China 77 H2
Tonglu China 77 H2
Tongo Australia 112 A3
Tongo Lake salt flat Australia 112 A3
Tongren Guizhou China 77 F3
Tongren Qinghai China 76 D1
Tongres Belgium see Tongeren
Tongsa Bhutan see Trongsa
Tongshan China see Xuzhou
Tongta Myanmar 70 B2
Tongtian He r. Qinghai China see Yangtze
Tongue U.K. 50 E2
Tongue r. U.S.A. 126 G3
Tongue of the Ocean sea chan. Bahamas 133 E7
Tongxin China 72 J5
Tongyeong S. Korea 75 C6
Tongzi China 76 E2
Tónichi Mex. 127 F7
Tonk India 82 C4
Tonkin reg. Vietnam 70 D2
Tônlé Sab l. Cambodia see Tonle Sap
▶Tonle Sap l. Cambodia 71 C4
Largest lake in south-east Asia.
Tonopah AZ U.S.A. 129 G5
Tonopah NV U.S.A. 128 E2
Tønsberg Norway 45 G7
Tonstad Norway 45 E7
Tonto Creek watercourse U.S.A. 129 H5
Tonūrjeh Iran 88 E3
Tonzang Myanmar 70 A2
Tonzi Myanmar 70 A1
Toobeah Australia 112 D2
Tooele U.S.A. 129 G1
Toogoolawah Australia 112 F1
Tooma r. Australia 112 D6
Toompine Australia 112 B1
Toora Australia 112 C7
Tooraweenah Australia 112 D3
Toorberg mt. S. Africa 100 G7
Toowoomba Australia 112 E1
Tooxin Somalia 98 F2
Tōp Afgh. 89 H3
Top Boğazı Geçidi pass Turkey 85 C1
▶Topeka U.S.A. 130 E4
Capital of Kansas.
Topia Mex. 127 G8
Töplitz Germany 53 M2
Topoľčany Slovakia 47 Q6
Topolobampo Mex. 127 F8
Topolovgrad Bulg. 59 L3
Topozero, Ozero l. Russia 44 R4
Topsfield U.S.A. 132 H2
Torbalı Turkey 59 L5
Torbat-e Ḩeydarīyeh Iran 88 E3
Torbat-e Jām Iran 89 F3
Torbay Bay Australia 109 B8
Torbert, Mount U.S.A. 118 C3
Torbeyevo Russia 43 I5
Torch r. Canada 121 K4
Tordesillas Spain 57 D3
Tordesilos Spain 57 F3
Töre Sweden 44 M4
Torelló Spain 57 H2
Torenberg hill Neth. 52 F2
Toretam Kazakh. see Baykonyr
Torgau Germany 53 M3
Torgay Kazakh. 80 B2
Torghay Kazakh. see Torgay
Torgun r. Russia 43 J6
Torhout Belgium 52 D3
Torī Eth. 97 G4
Torino Italy see Turin
Tori-shima i. Japan 75 F7
Torit South Sudan 97 G4
Torkamānchāy Iran 88 B2
Tör Kham Afgh. 89 H3
Torkovichi Russia 42 F4
Tornado Mountain Canada 120 H5
Torneå Fin. see Tornio
Torneälven r. Sweden 44 N4
Torneträsk l. Sweden 44 K2
Torngat, Monts mts Canada see Torngat Mountains
Torngat Mountains Canada 123 I2
Tornio Fin. 44 N4
Toro Spain 57 D3
Toro, Pico del mt. Mex. 131 C7
Torom Russia 74 D1
▶Toronto Canada 134 F2
Capital of Ontario.
Toro Peak U.S.A. 128 E5
Toropets Russia 42 F4
Tororo Uganda 98 D3
Toros Dağları mts Turkey see Taurus Mountains
Torphins U.K. 50 G3
Torquay Australia 112 B7
Torquay U.K. 49 D8
Torrance U.S.A. 128 D5
Torrão Port. 57 B4
Torre mt. Port. 57 C3
Torreblanca Spain 57 G3
Torre Blanco, Cerro mt. Mex. 127 E6
Torrecerredo mt. Spain 57 D2
Torre del Greco Italy 58 F4
Torre de Moncorvo Port. 57 C3
Torrelavega Spain 57 D2
Torremolinos Spain 57 D5
▶Torrens, Lake imp. l. Australia 111 B6
2nd largest lake in Oceania.
Torrens Creek Australia 110 D4
Torrent Spain 57 F4
Torrente Spain see Torrent
Torreón Mex. 131 C7
Torres Brazil 145 A5
Torres Mex. 127 F7
Torres del Paine, Parque Nacional nat. park Chile 144 B8
Torres Islands Vanuatu 107 G3
Torres Novas Port. 57 B4
Torres Strait Australia 106 E2
Torres Vedras Port. 57 B4
Torrevieja Spain 57 F5
Torrey U.S.A. 129 H2
Torridge r. U.K. 49 C8
Torridon, Loch b. U.K. 50 D3
Torrijos Spain 57 D4
Torrington Australia 112 E2
Torrington CT U.S.A. 132 F3
Torrington WY U.S.A. 126 G4
Torsby Sweden 45 H6
▶Tórshavn Faroe Is 44 [inset 2]
Capital of the Faroe Islands.
Tortilla Flat U.S.A. 129 H5
To'rtko'l Uzbek. 80 B3
Törtköl Uzbek. see To'rtko'l
Tortolì Sardinia Italy 58 C5
Tortona Italy 58 C2
Tortosa Spain 57 G3
Tortum Turkey 91 F2
Ṭorūd Iran 88 D3
Torugart, Pereval pass China/Kyrg. see Turugart Pass
Torul Turkey 91 E2
Toruń Poland 47 Q4
Tory Island Ireland 51 D2
Tory Sound sea chan. Ireland 51 D2
Torzhok Russia 42 G4
Torzī Afgh. 89 G4
Tosa Japan 75 D6
Tosbotn Norway 44 H4
Tosca S. Africa 100 F3
Toscano, Arcipelago is Italy 58 C3
Tosham India 82 C3
Tōshima-yama mt. Japan 75 F4
▶Toshkent Uzbek. 80 C3
Capital of Uzbekistan.
Tosno Russia 42 F4
Toson Hu l. China 83 I1
Tostado Arg. 144 D3
Tostedt Germany 53 J1
Tosya Turkey 90 D2
Totapola mt. Sri Lanka 84 D5
Tôtes France 52 B5
Tot'ma Russia 42 I4
Totness Suriname 143 G2
Totten Glacier Antarctica 152 F2
Tottenham Australia 112 C4
Totton U.K. 49 F8
Tottori Japan 75 D6
Touba Côte d'Ivoire 96 C4
Touba Senegal 96 B3
Toubkal, Jebel mt. Morocco 54 C5
Toubkal, Parc National du nat. park Morocco 54 C5
Touboro Cameroon 97 E4
Tougan Burkina Faso 96 C3
Touggourt Alg. 54 F5
Tougué Guinea 96 B3
Touil Mauritania 96 B3
Toul France 52 F6
Touliu Taiwan see Douliu
Toulon France 56 G5
Toulon U.S.A. 130 F3
Toulouse France 56 E5
Toumodi Côte d'Ivoire 96 C4
Toupai China 77 F3
Tourane Vietnam see Đa Nẵng
Tourcoing France 52 D4
Tourgis Lake Canada 121 J1
Tourlaville France 49 F9
Tournai Belgium 52 D4
Tournon-sur-Rhône France 56 G4
Tournus France 58 A1
Touros Brazil 143 K5
Tours France 56 E3
Tousside, Pic mt. Chad 97 E2
Toussoro, Mont mt. Cent. Afr. Rep. 98 C3
Toutai China 74 B3
Touwsrivier S. Africa 100 E7
Toužim Czechia 53 M4
Tovarkovo Russia 43 G5
Tovil'-Dora Tajik. see Tavildara
Tovuz Azer. 91 G2
Towada Japan 74 F4
Towak Mountain hill U.S.A. 118 B3
Towanda U.S.A. 135 G3
Towaoc U.S.A. 129 I3
Towcester U.K. 49 G6
Tower Ireland 51 D6
Towner U.S.A. 130 C1
Townes Pass U.S.A. 128 E3
Townsend U.S.A. 126 F3
Townsend, Mount Australia 112 D6
Townshend Island Australia 110 E4
Townsville Australia 110 D3
Towot South Sudan 97 G4
Towson U.S.A. 135 G4
Towyn U.K. see Tywyn
Toy U.S.A. 128 D1
Toyah U.S.A. 131 C6
Toyama Japan 75 E5
Toyama-wan b. Japan 75 E5
Toyohashi Japan 75 E6
Toyokawa Japan 75 E6
Toyonaka Japan 75 D6
Toyooka Japan 75 D6
Toyota Japan 75 E6
Tozanlı Turkey see Almus
Tozê Kangri mt. China 83 E2
Tozeur Tunisia 54 F5
Tozi, Mount U.S.A. 118 C3
T'q'ibuli Georgia 91 F2
Traben Germany 52 H5
Trâblous Lebanon see Tripoli
Trabotivište Macedonia 59 J4
Trabzon Turkey 91 E2
Tracy CA U.S.A. 128 C3
Tracy MN U.S.A. 130 E2
Trading r. Canada 122 C4
Traer U.S.A. 130 E3
Trafalgar U.S.A. 134 B4
Trafalgar, Cabo c. Spain 57 C5
Traffic Mountain Canada 120 D2
Trail Canada 120 G5
Tràille, Rubha na pt U.K. 50 D5
Traill Island Greenland see Traill Ø
Traill Ø i. Greenland 119 P2
Trainor Lake Canada 120 F2
Trajectum Neth. see Utrecht
Trakai Lith. 45 N9
Tra Khuc, Sông r. Vietnam 70 E4
Trakiya reg. Europe see Thrace
Trakt Russia 42 K3
Trakya reg. Europe see Thrace
Tralee Ireland 51 C5
Tralee Bay Ireland 51 C5
Trá Li Ireland see Tralee
Tramandaí Brazil 145 A5
Tramán Tepuí mt. Venez. 142 F2
Trá Mhór Ireland see Tramore
Trâm Kák Cambodia 71 D5
Tramore Ireland 51 E5
Tranås Sweden 45 I7
Trancas Arg. 144 C3
Trancoso Brazil 145 D2
Tranemo Sweden 45 H8
Tranent U.K. 50 G5
Trang Thai. 71 B6
Trangan i. Indon. 108 F1
Trang An tourist site Vietnam 70 D2
Trangie Australia 112 C4
Trân Ninh, Cao Nguyên Laos 70 C3
Transantarctic Mountains Antarctica 152 H2
Trans Canada Highway Canada 121 H5
Transnistria disp. terr. Moldova 43 F7
Transylvanian Alps mts Romania 59 J2
Transylvanian Basin plat. Romania 59 K1
Trapani Sicily Italy 58 E5
Trapezus Turkey see Trabzon
Trapper Peak U.S.A. 126 E3
Trappes France 52 C6
Traralgon Australia 112 C7
Trashigang Bhutan 83 G4
Trasimeno, Lago l. Italy 58 E3
Trasvase, Canal de Spain 57 E4
Trat Thai. 71 C4
Tratani r. Pak. 89 H4
Traunsee l. Austria 47 N7
Traunstein Germany 47 N7
Travellers Lake imp. l. Australia 111 C7
Travers, Mount N.Z. 113 D6
Traverse City U.S.A. 134 C1
Tra Vinh Vietnam 71 D5
Travnik Bos. & Herz. 58 G2
Trbovlje Slovenia 58 F1
Tre, Hon i. Vietnam 71 E4
Treasury Islands Solomon Is 106 F2
Trebbin Germany 53 N2
Trebević, Nacionalni Park nat. park Bos. & Herz. 58 H3
Třebíč Czechia 47 O6
Trebinje Bos. & Herz. 58 H3
Trebišov Slovakia 43 D6
Trebizond Turkey see Trabzon
Trebnje Slovenia 58 F2
Trebur Germany 53 I5
Tree Island India 84 B4
Trefaldwyn U.K. see Montgomery
Treffurt Germany 53 K3
Treffynnon U.K. see Holywell
Tref-y-clawdd U.K. see Knighton
Trefynwy U.K. see Monmouth
Tregosse Islets and Reefs Australia 110 E3
Treinta y Tres Uruguay 144 F4
Trelew Arg. 144 C6
Trelleborg Sweden 45 H9
Trélon France 52 E4
Tremblant, Mont hill Canada 122 G5
Trembleur Lake Canada 120 E4
Tremiti, Isole is Italy 58 F3
Tremont U.S.A. 135 G3
Tremonton U.S.A. 126 E4
Tremp Spain 57 G2
Trenance U.K. 49 B8
Trenary U.S.A. 132 C2
Trenche r. Canada 123 G5
Trenčín Slovakia 47 Q6
Trendelburg Germany 53 J3
Trêng Cambodia 71 C4
Trenque Lauquén Arg. 144 D5
Trent Italy see Trento
Trent r. U.K. 49 G5
Trento Italy 58 D1
Trenton Canada 135 G1
Trenton FL U.S.A. 133 D6
Trenton GA U.S.A. 133 C5
Trenton KY U.S.A. 134 B5
Trenton MO U.S.A. 130 E3
Trenton NC U.S.A. 133 E5
Trenton NE U.S.A. 130 C3
▶Trenton NJ U.S.A. 135 H3
Capital of New Jersey.
Treorchy U.K. 49 D7
Trepassey Canada 123 L5
Tres Arroyos Arg. 144 D5
Tresco i. U.K. 49 A9
Três Corações Brazil 145 B3
Tres Esquinas Col. 142 C3
Tres Forcas, Cabo c. Morocco see Trois Fourches, Cap des
Três Lagoas Brazil 145 A3
Três Marias, Represa resr Brazil 145 B2
Tres Picachos, Sierra mts Mex. 127 G7
Tres Picos, Cerro mt. Arg. 144 D5
Três Pontas Brazil 145 B3
Tres Puntas, Cabo c. Arg. 144 C7
Três Rios Brazil 145 C3
Tretiy Severnyy Russia 41 S3
Tretten Norway 45 G6
Treuchtlingen Germany 53 K6
Treuenbrietzen Germany 53 M2
Treungen Norway 45 F7
Treves Germany see Trier
Treviglio Italy 58 C2
Treviso Italy 58 E2
Trevose Head hd U.K. 49 B8
Tri An, Hồ resr Vietnam 71 D5
Triánda Greece see Trianta
Triangle U.S.A. 135 G4
Trianta Greece 59 M6
Tribal Areas admin. div. Pak. 89 H3
Tribune U.S.A. 130 C4
Tricase Italy 58 H5
Trichinopoly India see Tiruchchirappalli
Trichur India see Thrissur
Tricot France 52 C5
Trida Australia 112 B4
Tridentum Italy see Trento
Trier Germany 52 G5
Trieste Italy 58 E2
Trieste, Golfo di g. Europe see Trieste, Gulf of
Trieste, Gulf of Europe 58 E2
Triglav mt. Slovenia 58 E1
Triglavski narodni park nat. park Slovenia 58 E1
Trikala Greece 59 I5
Tríkkala Greece see Trikala
▶Trikora, Puncak mt. Indon. 69 J7
2nd highest mountain in Oceania.
Trim Ireland 51 F4
Trincomalee Sri Lanka 84 D4
Trindade Brazil 145 A2
Trindade, Ilha da i. S. Atlantic Ocean 148 G7
Trinidad Bol. 142 F6
Trinidad Cuba 137 I4
Trinidad i. Trin. and Tob. 137 L6
Trinidad Uruguay 144 E4
Trinidad U.S.A. 127 G5
Trinidad country West Indies see Trinidad and Tobago
Trinidad and Tobago country West Indies 137 L6
Trinity U.S.A. 131 E6
Trinity r. CA U.S.A. 128 B1
Trinity r. TX U.S.A. 131 E6
Trinity Bay Canada 123 L5
Trinity Islands U.S.A. 118 C4
Trinity Range mts U.S.A. 128 D1
Trinkat Island India 71 A5
Trionto, Capo c. Italy 58 G5
Tripa r. Indon. 71 B7
Tripkau Germany 53 L1
Tripoli Greece 59 J6
Tripoli Lebanon 85 B2
▶Tripoli Libya 97 E1
Capital of Libya.
Trípolis Greece see Tripoli
Tripolis Lebanon see Tripoli
Tripolitania hist. area Libya 96 E1
Tripunittura India 84 C4
Tripura state India 83 G5
▶Tristan da Cunha i. S. Atlantic Ocean 148 H8
Part of St Helena, Ascension and Tristan da Cunha.
Trisul mt. India 82 D3
Triton Canada 123 L4
Triton Island atoll Paracel Is 68 E3
Trittau Germany 53 K1
Trittenheim Germany 52 G5
Trivandrum India see Thiruvananthapuram
Trivento Italy 58 F4
Trnava Slovakia 47 P6
Trobriand Islands P.N.G. 106 F2
Trochu Canada 120 H5
Trofors Norway 44 H4
Trogir Croatia 58 G3
Troia Italy 58 F4
Troisdorf Germany 53 H4
Trois Fourches, Cap des c. Morocco 57 E6
Trois-Ponts Belgium 52 F4
Trois-Rivières Canada 123 G5
Troitsko-Pechorsk Russia 41 R3
Troitskoye Altayskiy Kray Russia 72 E2
Troitskoye Khabarovskiy Kray Russia 74 E2
Troitskoye Respublika Kalmykiya-Khalm'g-Tangch Russia 43 J7
Troll research station Antarctica 152 C2
Trollhättan Sweden 45 H7
Trombetas r. Brazil 143 G4
Tromelin, Île i. Indian Ocean 149 L7
Tromelin Island Micronesia see Fais
Tromen, Volcán vol. Arg. 144 B5
Tromie r. U.K. 50 E3
Trompsburg S. Africa 101 G6
Tromsø Norway 44 K2
Trona U.S.A. 128 E4
Tronador, Monte mt. Arg. 144 B6
Trondheim Norway 44 G5
Trondheimsfjorden sea chan. Norway 44 F5
Trongsa Bhutan 83 G4
Troödos Mountains Cyprus 85 A2
Troon U.K. 50 E5
Tropeiros, Serra dos hills Brazil 145 B1
Tropic U.S.A. 129 G3
Tropic of Cancer 131 B8
Tropic of Capricorn 110 G4
Trosh Russia 42 L2
Trostan hill U.K. 51 F2
Trout r. B.C. Canada 120 E3
Trout r. N.W.T. Canada 120 G2
Trout Lake Alta Canada 120 H3
Trout Lake N.W.T. Canada 120 F2
Trout Lake l. N.W.T. Canada 120 F2
Trout Lake l. Ont. Canada 121 M5
Trout Peak U.S.A. 126 F3
Trout Run U.S.A. 135 G3
Trouville-sur-Mer France 49 H9
Trowbridge U.K. 49 E7
Troy tourist site Turkey 59 L5
Troy AL U.S.A. 133 C6
Troy KS U.S.A. 130 E4
Troy MI U.S.A. 134 D2

Troy MO U.S.A. 130 F4
Troy MT U.S.A. 126 E2
Troy NH U.S.A. 135 I2
Troy NY U.S.A. 135 I2
Troy OH U.S.A. 134 C3
Troy PA U.S.A. 135 G3
Troyan Bulg. 59 K3
Troyes France 56 G2
Troy Lake U.S.A. 128 E4
Troy Peak U.S.A. 129 F2
Trstenik Serbia 59 I3
Truc Giang Vietnam see Bên Tre
Trucial States country Asia see United Arab Emirates
Trud Russia 42 G4
Trufanova Russia 42 J2
Trujillo Hond. 137 G5
Trujillo Peru 142 C5
Trujillo Spain 57 D4
Trujillo Venez. 142 D2
Trujillo, Monte mt. Dom. Rep. see Duarte, Pico
Truk is Micronesia see Chuuk
Trulben Germany 53 H5
Trumbull, Mount U.S.A. 129 G3
Trumon Indon. 71 B7
Trundle Australia 112 C4
Trưng Hiệp Vietnam 70 D4
Trưng Khanh Vietnam 70 D2
Truong Sa is S. China Sea see Spratly Islands
Truro Canada 123 J5
Truro U.K. 49 B8
Truskmore hill Ireland 51 D3
Trutch Canada 120 F3
Truth or Consequences U.S.A. 127 G6
Trutnov Czechia 47 O5
Truuli Peak U.S.A. 118 C4
Truva tourist site Turkey see Troy
Trypiti, Akra pt Greece see Trypiti, Akrotirio
Trypiti, Akrotirio pt Greece 59 K7
Trysil Norway 45 H6
Trzebiatów Poland 47 O3
Tsagaannuur Mongolia 80 G2
Tsagaan-Uul Mongolia 80 I2
Tsagan Aman Russia 43 J7
Tsagan Nur Russia 43 J7
Tsaidam Basin China see Qaidam Pendi
Tsaka La pass China/India 82 D2
Ts'alenjikha Georgia 91 F2
Tsaratanana, Massif du mts Madag. 99 E5
Tsarevo Bulg. 59 L3
Tsaris Mountains Namibia 100 C3
Tsaritsyn Russia see Volgograd
Tsaukaib Namibia 100 B4
Tsavo East National Park Kenya 98 D4
Tsavo West National Park Africa 98 D3
Tsefat Israel see Ẕefat
Tselinograd Kazakh. see Astana
Tsenhermandal Mongolia 73 J3
Tsenogora Russia 42 J2
Tses Namibia 100 D3
Tsetseg Mongolia 80 H2
Tsetseng Botswana 100 F2
Tsetserleg Arhangay Mongolia 80 J2
Tsetserleg Hövsgöl Mongolia 80 I2
Tshabong Botswana 100 F4
Tshad country Africa see Chad
Tshane Botswana 100 E3
Tshela Dem. Rep. Congo 99 B4
Tshibala Dem. Rep. Congo 99 C4
Tshikapa Dem. Rep. Congo 99 C4
Tshing S. Africa 101 H4
Tshipise S. Africa 101 J2
Tshitanzu Dem. Rep. Congo 99 C4
Tshofa Dem. Rep. Congo 99 C4
Tshokwane S. Africa 101 J3
Tsholotsho Zimbabwe 99 C5
Tshootsha Botswana 100 E2
Tshuapa r. Dem. Rep. Congo 97 F5
Tshwane S. Africa see Pretoria
Tsil'ma r. Russia 42 K2
Tsimlyansk Russia 43 I7
Tsimlyanskoye Vodokhranilishche resr Russia 43 I7
Tsimmermanovka Russia 74 E2
Tsinan China see Jinan
Tsineng S. Africa 100 F4
Tsinghai prov. China see Qinghai
Tsingtao China see Qingdao
Tsing Yi i. H.K. China 77 [inset]
Tsining China see Ulan Qab
Tsiombe Madag. 99 E6
Tsiroanomandidy Madag. 99 E5
Tsitsihar China see Qiqihar
Tsitsutl Peak Canada 120 E4
Tsivil'sk Russia 42 J5
Tskhaltubo Georgia see Ts'q'alt'ubo

▶Tskhinvali Georgia 91 F2
Capital of South Ossetia.

Tsna r. Russia 43 I5
Ts'nori Georgia 91 G2
Tsokar Chumo l. India 82 D2
Tsolo S. Africa 101 I6
Tsomo S. Africa 101 H7
Tsona China see Cona
Ts'q'alt'ubo Georgia 91 F2
Tsu Japan 75 E6
Tsuchiura Japan 75 F5
Tsuen Wan H.K. China 77 [inset]
Tsugarū-kaikyō strait Japan 74 F4
Tsugaru Strait Japan see Tsugarū-kaikyō
Tsumeb Namibia 99 B5
Tsumis Park Namibia 100 C2
Tsumkwe Namibia 99 C5
Tsuruga Japan 75 E6
Tsurugi-san mt. Japan 75 D6
Tsurukhaytuy Russia see Priargunsk
Tsuruoka Japan 75 E5
Tsushima Japan 75 C6
Tsushima is Japan 75 C6
Tsushima-kaikyō strait Japan/S. Korea see Korea Strait
Tsuyama Japan 75 D6
Tswaane Botswana 100 E2
Tswaraganang S. Africa 101 G5
Tswelelang S. Africa 101 G4
Tsyelyakhany Belarus 45 N10
Tsypnavolok Russia 44 R2
Tsyurupyns'k Ukr. 59 O1
Tthenaagoo Canada see Nahanni Butte
Tu, Nam r. Myanmar 70 B2
Tua Dem. Rep. Congo 98 B4
Tual Indon. 69 I8
Tuam Ireland 51 D4
Tuamotu Archipelago is Fr. Polynesia see Tuamotu Islands
Tuamotu Islands Fr. Polynesia 151 K6
Tuần Giao Vietnam 70 C2
Tuangku i. Indon. 71 B7
Tuapse Russia 90 E1
Tuas Sing. 71 [inset]
Tuath, Loch a' b. U.K. 50 C2
Tuba City U.S.A. 129 H3
Tubarão Brazil 145 A5
Tubarjal Saudi Arabia 85 D4
Tübingen Germany 47 L6
Tubmanburg Liberia 96 B4
Tubruq Libya 90 A4
Tubuai i. Fr. Polynesia 151 K7
Tubuai Islands Fr. Polynesia 151 J7
Tucano Brazil 143 K6
Tucavaca Bol. 143 G7
Tüchen Germany 53 M1
Tuchheim Germany 53 M2
Tuchitua Canada 120 D2
Tuchodi r. Canada 120 F3
Tuckerton U.S.A. 135 H4
Tucopia i. Solomon Is see Tikopia
Tucson U.S.A. 129 H5
Tucson Mountains U.S.A. 129 H5
Tuctuc r. Canada 123 I2
Tucumán Arg. see San Miguel de Tucumán
Tucumcari U.S.A. 131 C5
Tucupita Venez. 142 F2
Tucuruí Brazil 143 I4
Tucuruí, Represa de resr Brazil 143 I4
Tudela Spain 57 F2
Tuder Italy see Todi
Tüdevtey Mongolia 80 I2
Tudun Wada Nigeria 96 D3
Tuela r. Port. 57 C3
Tuen Mun H.K. China 77 [inset]
Tuensang India 83 H4
Tufts Abyssal Plain sea feature N. Pacific Ocean 151 K2
Tuglung China 76 B2
Tuguegarao Phil. 69 G3
Tugur Russia 74 E1
Tuhemberua Indon. 71 B7
Tujiabu China see Yongxiu
Tukangbesi, Kepulauan is Indon. 69 G8
Tukarak Island Canada 122 F2
Ţukhmān, Banī reg. Saudi Arabia 88 C6
Tukituki r. N.Z. 113 F4
Tuktoyaktuk Canada 118 E3
Tuktut Nogait National Park Canada 118 F3
Tukums Latvia 45 M8
Tukuringra, Khrebet mts Russia 74 B1
Tukuyu Tanz. 99 D4
Tukzār Afgh. 89 G3
Tula Russia 43 H5
Tulach Mhór Ireland see Tullamore
Tulagt Ar Gol r. China 83 H1
Tülak Afgh. 89 F3
Tulameen Canada 120 F5
Tula Mountains Antarctica 152 D2
Tulancingo Mex. 136 E4
Tulare U.S.A. 128 D3
Tulare Lake Bed U.S.A. 128 D4
Tularosa Mountains U.S.A. 129 I5
Tulasi mt. India 84 D2
Tulbagh S. Africa 100 D7
Tulcán Ecuador 142 C3
Tulcea Romania 59 M2
Tule r. U.S.A. 131 C5
Tuléar Madag. see Toliara
Tulemalu Lake Canada 121 L2
Tule Springs Fossil Beds National Monument nat. park U.S.A. 129 F3
Tulia U.S.A. 131 C5
Tulihe China 74 A2
Tulita Canada 120 E1
Tulkarem West Bank see Ţūlkarm
Ţūlkarm West Bank 85 B3
Tulla Ireland 51 D5
Tullahoma U.S.A. 132 C5
Tullamore Australia 112 C4
Tullamore Ireland 51 E4
Tulle France 56 E4
Tulleråsen Sweden 44 I5
Tullibigeal Australia 112 C4
Tullow Ireland 51 F5
Tully Australia 110 D3
Tully r. Australia 110 D3
Tully U.K. 51 E3
Tulos Russia 44 Q5
Tulqarem West Bank see Ţūlkarm
Tulsa U.S.A. 131 E4
Tulsipur Nepal 83 E3
Tuluá Col. 142 C3
Tuluksak U.S.A. 153 B2
Tulūl al Ashāqif hills Jordan 85 C3
Tulun Russia 72 I2
Tulu-Tuloi, Serra hills Brazil 142 F3
Tulu Welel mt. Eth. 98 D3
Tuma Russia 43 I5
Tumaco Col. 142 C3
Tumahole S. Africa 101 H4
Tumain China 83 G2
Tumakuru India 84 C3
Tumannyy Russia 44 S2
Tumasik Sing. see Singapore
Tumba Dem. Rep. Congo 98 C4
Tumba Sweden 45 J7
Tumba, Lac l. Dem. Rep. Congo 98 B4
Tumbarumba Australia 112 D5
Tumbes Peru 142 B4
Tumbler Ridge Canada 120 F4
Tumby Bay Australia 111 B7
Tumen Jilin China 74 C4
Tumen Shaanxi China 77 F1
Tumereng Guyana 142 F2
Tumindao i. Phil. 68 F6
Tumiritinga Brazil 145 C2
Tumkur India see Tumakuru
Tummel r. U.K. 50 F4
Tummel, Loch l. U.K. 50 F4
Tumnin r. Russia 74 F2
Tump Pak. 89 F5
Tumpat Malaysia 71 C6
Tumpôr, Phnum mt. Cambodia 71 C4
Tumshuk Uzbek. 89 G2
Tumu Ghana 96 C3
Tumucumaque, Serra hills Brazil 143 G3
Tumudibandh India 84 D2
Tumut Australia 112 D5
Tuna India 82 B5
Ţunb al Kubrá i. The Gulf see Tonb-e Bozorg, Jazireh-ye
Ţunb aş Şughrá i. The Gulf see Tonb-e Küchek, Jazireh-ye
Tunceli Turkey 91 E3
Tunchang China 77 F5
Tuncurry Australia 112 F4
Tundi imp. l. Afgh. 89 F3
Tunduru Tanz. 99 D5
Tunes Tunisia see Tunis
Tunga Nigeria 96 D4
Tungabhadra Reservoir India 84 C3
Tungi Bangl. 83 G5
Tung Lung Island i. H.K. China 77 [inset]
Tungnaá r. Iceland 44 [inset 1]
Tungor Russia 74 F1
T'ung-shan China see Xuzhou
Tungsten (abandoned) Canada 120 D2
Tung Wan b. H.K. China 77 [inset]
Tuni India 84 D2
Tūnī, Chāh-e well Iran 88 E3
Tunica U.S.A. 131 F5
Tūnis country Africa see Tunisia

▶Tunis Tunisia 58 D6
Capital of Tunisia.

Tunis, Golfe de g. Tunisia 58 D6
Tunisia country Africa 54 F5
Tunja Col. 142 D2
Tunkhannock U.S.A. 135 H3
Tunnsjøen l. Norway 44 H4
Tunstall U.K. 49 I6
Tuntsa Fin. 44 P3
Tuntsajoki r. Fin./Russia see Tuntsayoki
Tuntsayoki r. Fin./Russia 44 Q3
also known as Tuntsajoki
Tunulic r. Canada 123 I2
Tununak U.S.A. 118 B3
Tunungayualok Island Canada 123 J2
Tunxi China see Huangshan
Tuodian China see Shuangbai
Tuojiang China see Fenghuang
Tuŏl Khpós Cambodia 71 D5
Tuoniang Jiang r. China 76 E3
Tuotuo He r. China see Togton He
Tuotuoheyan China see Tanggulashan
Tüp Kyrg. 80 E3
Tupã Brazil 145 A3
Tupelo U.S.A. 131 F5
Tupik Russia 73 L2
Tupinambarama, Ilha i. Brazil 143 G4
Tupiraçaba Brazil 145 A1
Tupiza Bol. 142 E8
Tupper Canada 120 F4
Tupper Lake U.S.A. 135 H1
Tupper Lake l. U.S.A. 135 H1

▶Tupungato, Cerro mt. Arg./Chile 144 C4
5th highest mountain in South America.

Tuqayyid well Iraq 88 B4
Tuquan China 73 M3
Tuqu Wan b. China see Lingshui Wan
Tura China 83 F1
Tura India 83 G4
Tura Russia 65 L3
Turabah Saudi Arabia 86 F5
Turakina N.Z. 113 E5
Turan Russia 72 G2
Turana, Khrebet mts Russia 74 C2
Turan Lowland Asia 80 A4
Turan Oypaty lowland Asia see Turan Lowland
Turan Pesligi lowland Asia see Turan Lowland
Turanskaya Nizmennost' lowland Asia see Turan Lowland
Ţurāq al 'Ilab hills Syria 85 D3
Turar Ryskulov Kazakh. 80 D3
Tura-Ryskulova Kazakh. see Turar Ryskulov
Ţurayf Saudi Arabia 85 D4
Ţurayf, Kutayfat vol. Saudi Arabia 85 D4
Turba Estonia 45 N7
Turbat Pak. 89 F5
Turbo Col. 142 C2
Turda Romania 59 J1
Türeh Iran 88 C3
Turfan China see Turpan
Turfan Basin depr. China see Turpan Pendi
Turfan Depression China see Turpan Pendi
Turgayskaya Dolina valley Kazakh. 80 B2
Turgutlu Turkey 59 L5
Turhal Turkey 90 E2
Türi Estonia 45 N7
Turia r. Spain 57 F4
Turin Canada 121 H5
Turin Italy 58 B2
Turiy Rog Russia 74 C3

▶Turkana, Lake salt l. Eth./Kenya 98 D3
5th largest lake in Africa.

Turkestan Range mts Asia 89 G2
Turkey country Asia/Europe 90 D3
Turkey U.S.A. 134 D5
Turkey r. U.S.A. 130 F3
Turki Russia 43 I6
Turkish Republic of Northern Cyprus disp. terr. Asia see Northern Cyprus
Turkistan Kazakh. 80 C3
Türkistan Kazakh. see Turkistan
Turkistān, Silsilah-ye Band-e mts Afgh. 89 F3
Türkiye country Asia/Europe see Turkey
Türkmenabat Turkm. 89 F2
Türkmen Adasy i. Turkm. see Ogurjaly Adasy
Türkmen Aylagy b. Turkm. see Türkmen Aýlagy
Türkmen Aýlagy b. Turkm. 88 D2
Türkmenbaşy Turkm. 88 D1
Türkmenbaşy Turkm. see Türkmenbaşy
Türkmenbaşy Aylagy b. Turkm. see Türkmenbaşy Aýlagy
Türkmenbaşy Aýlagy b. Turkm. 88 D2
Türkmenbaşy Döwlet Gorugy nature res. Turkm. 88 D2
Türkmen Dağı mt. Turkey 59 N5
Turkmenistan country Asia 87 I2
Turkmeniya country Asia see Turkmenistan
Türkmenostan country Asia see Turkmenistan
Turkmenskaya S.S.R. country Asia see Turkmenistan
Türkoğlu Turkey 90 E3

▶Turks and Caicos Islands terr. West Indies 137 J4
United Kingdom Overseas Territory.

Turks Island Passage Turks and Caicos Is 133 G8
Turks Islands Turks and Caicos Is 137 J4
Turku Fin. 45 M6
Turkwel watercourse Kenya 98 D3
Turlock U.S.A. 128 C3
Turlock Lake U.S.A. 128 C3
Turmalina Brazil 145 C2
Turnagain r. Canada 120 E3
Turnagain, Cape N.Z. 113 F5
Turnberry U.K. 50 E5
Turnbull, Mount U.S.A. 129 H5
Turneffe Islands atoll Belize 136 G5
Turner U.S.A. 134 D1
Turner Valley Canada 120 H5
Turnhout Belgium 52 E3
Turnor Lake Canada 121 I3
Tŭrnovo Bulg. see Veliko Tarnovo
Turnu Măgurele Romania 59 K3
Turnu Severin Romania see Drobeta-Turnu Severin
Turon r. Australia 112 D4
Turones France see Tours
Turon pasttekisligi lowland Asia see Turan Lowland
Turovets Russia 42 I4
Turpan China 80 G3

▶Turpan Pendi depr. China 80 G3
Lowest point in northern Asia.

Turquino, Pico mt. Cuba 137 I4
Turriff U.K. 50 G3
Turris Libisonis Sardinia Italy see Porto Torres
Tursāq Iraq 91 G4
Turtle Island Fiji see Vatoa
Turtle Lake Canada 121 I4
Turugart Pass China/Kyrg. 80 E3
Turugart Shankou pass China/Kyrg. see Turugart Pass
Turuvanur India 84 C3
Turvo r. Goiás Brazil 145 A2
Turvo r. São Paulo Brazil 145 A2
Tusayan U.S.A. 129 G4
Tuscaloosa U.S.A. 133 C5
Tuscarawas r. U.S.A. 134 E3
Tuscarora Mountains hills U.S.A. 135 G3
Tuscola IL U.S.A. 130 F4
Tuscola TX U.S.A. 131 D5
Tuscumbia U.S.A. 133 C5
Tuskegee U.S.A. 133 C5
Tussey Mountains hills U.S.A. 135 F3
Tustin U.S.A. 134 C1
Tutak Turkey 91 F3
Tutayev Russia 42 H4
Tutera Spain see Tudela
Tuticorin India 84 C4
Tutong Brunei 68 E6
Tuttle Creek Reservoir U.S.A. 130 D4
Tuttlingen Germany 47 L7
Tuttut Nunaat reg. Greenland 119 P2
Tutuala East Timor 108 D2
Tutubu P.N.G. 110 E1
Tutubu Tanz. 99 D4
Tutuila i. American Samoa 107 I3
Tutume Botswana 99 C6
Tutwiler U.S.A. 131 F5
Tuun-bong mt. N. Korea 74 B4
Tuupovaara Fin. 44 Q5
Tuusniemi Fin. 44 P5
Tuvalu country S. Pacific Ocean 107 H2
Tuwayq, Jabal hills Saudi Arabia 86 G4
Tuwayq, Jabal mts Saudi Arabia 86 G5
Ţuwayyil ash Shihāq mt. Jordan 85 C4
Tuwwal Saudi Arabia 86 E5
Tuxpan Mex. 136 E4
Tuxtla Gutiérrez Mex. 136 F5
Tuya Lake Canada 120 D3
Tuyên Quang Vietnam 70 D2
Tuy Hoa Vietnam 71 E4
Tuz, Lake salt l. Turkey 90 D3
Tuz Gölü salt l. Turkey see Tuz, Lake
Tuzha Russia 42 J4
Tuz Khurmātū Iraq 91 G4
Tuzla Bos. & Herz. 58 H2
Tuzla Turkey 85 B1
Tuzla Gölü lag. Turkey 59 L4
Tuzlov r. Russia 43 I7
Tuzu r. Myanmar 70 A1
Tvedestrand Norway 45 F7
Tver' Russia 42 G4
Twain Harte U.S.A. 128 C2
Tweed Canada 135 G1
Tweed r. U.K. 50 G5
Tweed Heads Australia 112 F2
Tweedie Canada 121 I4
Tweefontein S. Africa 100 D7
Twee Rivier Namibia 100 D3
Twentekanaal canal Neth. 52 G2
Twentynine Palms U.S.A. 128 E4
Twin Bridges CA U.S.A. 128 C2
Twin Bridges MT U.S.A. 126 E3
Twin Buttes Reservoir U.S.A. 131 C6
Twin Falls Canada 123 I3
Twin Falls U.S.A. 126 E4
Twin Heads hill Australia 108 D5
Twin Peak U.S.A. 128 C2
Twistringen Germany 53 I2
Twitchen Reservoir U.S.A. 128 C4
Twitya r. Canada 120 D1
Twizel N.Z. 113 C7
Twofold Bay Australia 112 D6
Two Harbors U.S.A. 130 F2
Two Hills Canada 121 I4
Two Rivers U.S.A. 134 B1
Tyan' Shan' mts China/Kyrg. see Tien Shan
Tyao r. India/Myanmar 76 B4
Tyatya, Vulkan vol. Russia 74 G3
Tydal Norway 44 G5
Tygart Valley U.S.A. 134 F4
Tygda Russia 74 B1
Tygda r. Russia 74 B1
Tyler U.S.A. 131 E5
Tylertown U.S.A. 131 F6
Tym' r. Russia 74 F2
Tymovskoye Russia 74 F2
Tynda Russia 73 M1
Tyndall U.S.A. 130 D3
Tyndinskiy Russia see Tynda
Tyne r. U.K. 50 G4
Tynemouth U.K. 48 F3
Tynset Norway 44 G5
Tyoploozyorsk Russia see Teploozersk
Tyoploye Ozero Russia see Teploozersk
Tyr Lebanon see Tyre
Tyras Ukr. see Bilhorod-Dnistrovs'kyy
Tyre Lebanon 85 B3
Tyree, Mount Antarctica 152 L1
Tyrma Russia 74 D2
Tyrma r. Russia 74 C2
Tyrnävä Fin. 44 N4
Tyrnavos Greece 59 J5
Tyrnyauz Russia 91 F2
Tyrone U.S.A. 135 F3
Tyrrell r. Australia 112 A5
Tyrrell, Lake dry lake Australia 111 C7
Tyrrell Lake Canada 121 J2
Tyrrhenian Sea France/Italy 58 D4
Tyrus Lebanon see Tyre
Tysa r. Serbia see Tisa
Tyukalinsk Russia 64 I4
Tyulen'i, Ostrova is Kazakh. 91 H1
Tyumen' Russia 64 H4
Tyup Kyrg. see Tüp
Tyuratam Kazakh. see Baykonyr
Tywi r. U.K. 49 C7
Tywyn U.K. 49 C6
Tzaneen S. Africa 101 J2
Tzia i. Greece 59 K6

U

Uaco Congo Angola see Waku-Kungo
Ualan atoll Micronesia see Kosrae
Uamanda Angola 99 C5
Uarc, Ras c. Morocco see Trois Fourches, Cap des
Uaroo Australia 109 A5
Uatumã r. Brazil 143 G4
Uauá Brazil 143 K5
Uaupés r. Brazil 142 E3
U'aylī, Wādī al watercourse Saudi Arabia 85 D4
U'aywij well Saudi Arabia 88 B4
U'aywij, Wādī al watercourse Saudi Arabia 91 F5
Ubá Brazil 145 C3
Ubaí Brazil 145 B2
Ubaitaba Brazil 145 D1
Ubangi r. Cent. Afr. Rep./Dem. Rep. Congo 98 B4
Ubangi-Shari country Africa see Central African Republic
Ubauro Pak. 89 H4
Ubayyiḍ, Wādī al watercourse Iraq/Saudi Arabia 91 F4
Ube Japan 75 C6
Úbeda Spain 57 E4
Uberaba Brazil 145 B2
Uberlândia Brazil 145 A2
Ubin, Pulau i. Sing. 71 [inset]
Ubiña, Peña mt. Spain 57 D2
Ubly U.S.A. 134 D2
Ubolratna, Ang Kep Nam Thai. 70 C3
Ubombo S. Africa 101 K4
Ubon Ratchathani Thai. 70 D4
Ubstadt-Weiher Germany 53 I5
Ubundu Dem. Rep. Congo 97 F5
Üçajy Turkm. 89 F2
Ucar Azer. 91 G2
Uçarı Turkey 85 A1
Ucayali r. Peru 142 D4
Uch Pak. 89 H4
Üchajy Turkm. see Üçajy
Üchān Iran 88 C2
Uchiura-wan b. Japan 74 F4
Uchkeken Russia 91 F2
Uchkuduk Uzbek. see Uchquduq
Uchquduq Uzbek. 80 B3
Uchte Germany 53 I2
Uchte r. Germany 53 L2
Uchur r. Russia 65 O4
Uckermark reg. Germany 53 N1
Uckfield U.K. 49 H8
Ucluelet Canada 120 E5
Ucross U.S.A. 126 G3
Uda r. Russia 73 J2
Uda r. Russia 74 D1
Udachnoye Russia 43 J7
Udachnyy Russia 153 E2
Udagamandalam India 84 C4
Udaipur Rajasthan India 82 C4
Udaipur Tripura India 83 G5
Udanti r. India/Myanmar 83 E5
Uday r. Ukr. 43 G6
'Udaynān well Saudi Arabia 88 C6
Uddevalla Sweden 45 G7
Uddingston U.K. 50 E5
Uddjaure l. Sweden 44 J4
'Udeid, Khōr al inlet Qatar 88 C5
Uden Neth. 52 F3
Udgir India 84 C2
Udhagamandalam India see Udagamandalam
Udhampur India 82 C2
Udia-Milai atoll Marshall Is see Bikini
Udimskiy Russia 42 J3
Udine Italy 58 E1
Udit India 89 I5
Udjuktok Bay Canada 123 J3
Udmalaippettai India see Udumalaippettai
Udomlya Russia 42 G4
Udon Thani Thai. 70 C3
Udskaya Guba b. Russia 65 O4
Udskoye Russia 74 D1
Udumalaippettai India 84 C4
Udupi India 84 B3
Udyl', Ozero l. Russia 74 E1
Udzhary Azer. see Ucar
Udzungwa Mountains National Park Tanz. 99 D4
Uéa atoll New Caledonia see Ouvéa
Ueckermünde Germany 47 O4
Ueda Japan 75 E5
Uele r. Dem. Rep. Congo 98 C3
Uelen Russia 65 U3
Uelzen Germany 53 K2
Uetersen Germany 53 J1
Uettingen Germany 53 J5
Uetze Germany 53 K2
Ufa Russia 41 R5
Ufa r. Russia 41 R5
Uffenheim Germany 53 K5
Uftyuga r. Russia 42 J3
Ugab watercourse Namibia 99 B6
Ugalla r. Tanz. 99 D4
Uganda country Africa 98 D3
Ugie S. Africa 101 I6
Üğinak Iran 89 F5
Uglegorsk Russia 74 F2
Uglich Russia 42 H4
Ugljan i. Croatia 58 F2
Uglovoye Russia 74 C2
Ugol'noye Russia 65 P3
Ugolnyy Russia see Beringovskiy
Ugol'nyye Kopi Russia 65 S3
Ugra Russia 43 G5
Uherské Hradiště Czechia 47 P6
Úhlava r. Czechia 53 N5
Uhrichsville U.S.A. 134 E3
Uibhist a' Deas i. U.K. see South Uist
Uibhist a' Tuath i. U.K. see North Uist
Uig U.K. 50 C3
Uíge Angola 99 B4
Uijeongbu S. Korea 75 B5
Ŭiju N. Korea 75 B4
Uimaharju Fin. 44 Q5
Uinta Mountains U.S.A. 129 H1
Uis Mine Namibia 99 B6
Uitenhage S. Africa 101 G7
Uithoorn Neth. 52 E2
Uithuizen Neth. 52 G1
Uivak, Cape Canada 123 J2
Ujhani India 82 D4
Uji Japan 75 D6
Uji-guntō is Japan 75 C7
Ujiyamada Japan see Ise
Ujjain India 82 C5
Ujung Pandang Indon. see Makassar
Újvidék Serbia see Novi Sad
Ukal Sagar l. India 82 C5
Ukata Nigeria 96 D3
'Ukayrishah well Saudi Arabia 88 B5
uKhahlamba-Drakensberg Park nat. park S. Africa 101 I5
Ukholovo Russia 43 I5
Ukhrul India 83 H4
Ukhta Respublika Kareliya Russia see Kalevala
Ukhta Respublika Komi Russia 42 L3
Ukiah CA U.S.A. 128 B2
Ukiah OR U.S.A. 126 D3
Ukkusiksalik National Park nat. park Canada 119 J3
Ukkusissat Greenland 119 M2
Ukmergė Lith. 45 N9

▶Ukraine country Europe 43 F6
2nd largest country in Europe.

Ukrainskaya S.S.R. country Europe see Ukraine
Ukrayina country Europe see Ukraine
Uku-jima i. Japan 75 C6
Ukwi Botswana 100 E2
Ukwi Pan salt pan Botswana 100 E2
Ulaanbaatar Mongolia see Ulan Bator
Ulaangom Mongolia 80 H2
Ulan Australia 112 D4

▶Ulan Bator Mongolia 72 J3
Capital of Mongolia.

Ulanbel' Kazakh. 80 D3
Ulan Erge Russia 43 J7
Ulanhad China see Chifeng
Ulanhot China 74 A3
Ulan Hua China 73 K4
Ulan-Khol Russia 43 J7
Ulan Qab China 73 K4
Ulan-Ude Russia 73 J2
Ulan Ul Hu l. China 83 G2
Ulaş Turkey 90 E3
Ulawa Island Solomon Is 107 G2
Ulayyah reg. Saudi Arabia 88 B6
Ul'banskiy Zaliv b. Russia 74 E1
Uldz Gol r. Mongolia 73 L3
Uleåborg Fin. see Oulu
Ulefoss Norway 45 F7
Ülenurme Estonia 45 O7
Ulety Russia 73 K2
Ulhasnagar India 84 B2
Uliastai China 73 L3
Uliastay Mongolia 80 I2
Uliatea i. Fr. Polynesia see Raiatea
Ulicoten Neth. 52 E3
Ulie atoll Micronesia see Woleai
Ulita r. Russia 44 R2
Ulithi atoll Micronesia 69 J4
Uljin S. Korea 75 C5
Ul'ken Naryn Kazakh. 80 F2
Ulladulla Australia 112 E5
Ullapool U.K. 50 D3
Ulla Ulla, Parque Nacional nat. park Bol. 142 E6
Ullava Fin. 44 M5
Ullersuaq c. Greenland 119 K2
Ulleung-do i. S. Korea 75 C5
Ullswater l. U.K. 48 E4

Ulm Germany 47 L6
Ulmarra Australia 112 F2
Ulmen Germany 52 G4
Uloowaranie, Lake salt flat Australia 111 B5
Ulricehamn Sweden 45 H8
Ulrum Neth. 52 G1
Ulsan S. Korea 75 C6
Ulsberg Norway 44 F5
Ulster reg. Ireland/U.K. 51 E3
Ulster U.S.A. 135 G3
Ulster Canal Ireland/U.K. 51 E3
Ultima Australia 112 A5
Ulubat Gölü l. Turkey 59 M4
Ulubey Turkey 59 M5
Uluborlu Turkey 59 N5
Uludağ mt. Turkey 59 M4
Uludağ Milli Parkı nat. park Turkey 59 M4
Ulugqat China 80 D4
Ulu Kali, Gunung mt. Malaysia 71 C7
Ulukhaktok Canada 118 G2
Ulukışla Turkey 90 D3
Ulundi S. Africa 101 J5
Ulungur Hu l. China 80 G2
Uluqsaqtuuq Canada see Ulukhaktok
Uluṟu hill Australia 109 E6
Uluṟu-Kata Tjuṯa National Park Australia 109 E6
Uluru National Park Australia see Uluṟu-Kata Tjuṯa National Park
Ulutau Kazakh. see Ulytau
Ulutau, Gory mts Kazakh. see Ulytau, Gory
Uluyatır Turkey 85 C1
Ulva i. U.K. 50 C4
Ulvenhout Neth. 52 E3
Ulverston U.K. 48 D4
Ulvsjön Sweden 45 I6
Ül'yanov Kazakh. see Botakara
Ul'yanovsk Russia 43 K5
Ul'yanovskoye Kazakh. see Botakara
Ulysses KS U.S.A. 130 C4
Ulysses KY U.S.A. 134 D5
Ulytau Kazakh. 80 C2
Ulytau, Gory mts Kazakh. 80 C2
Ulyunkhan Russia 73 K2
Uma Russia 74 A1
Umal'ta (abandoned) Russia 74 D2
'Umān country Asia see Oman
Uman' Ukr. 43 F6
Umarao Pak. 89 G4
'Umarī, Qā' al salt pan Jordan 85 C4
Umaria India 82 E5
Umarkhed India 84 C2
Umarkot India 84 D2
Umarkot Punjab Pak. 89 H4
Umarkot Sindh Pak. 89 H5
Umaroona, Lake salt flat Australia 111 B5
Umarpada India 82 C5
Umatilla U.S.A. 126 D3
Umba Russia 42 G2
Umbagog Lake U.S.A. 135 J1
Umbeara Australia 109 F6
Umboi i. P.N.G. 69 L8
Umeå Sweden 44 L5
Umeälven r. Sweden 44 L5
Umfreville Lake Canada 121 M5
uMhlanga S. Africa 101 J5
Umiiviip Kangertiva inlet Greenland 119 N3
Umingmaktok Canada 153 L2
Umiujaq Canada 122 F2
Umkomaas S. Africa 101 J6
Umlaiteng India 83 H4
Umlazi S. Africa 101 J5
Umm ad Daraj, Jabal mt. Jordan 85 B3
Umm al 'Amad Syria 85 C2
Umm al Jamājim well Saudi Arabia 88 B5
Umm al Qaiwain U.A.E. see Umm al Qaywayn
Umm al Qaywayn U.A.E. 88 D5
Umm al Qulbān Saudi Arabia 91 F6
Umm ar Raqabah, Khabrat imp. l. Saudi Arabia 85 C5
Umm az Zumūl well Oman 88 D6
Umm Bāb Qatar 88 C5
Umm Bel Sudan 86 C7
Umm Keddada Sudan 86 C7
Umm Lajj Saudi Arabia 86 E4
Umm Nukhaylah hill Saudi Arabia 85 D5
Umm Qaṣr Iraq 91 G5
Umm Quṣūr i. Saudi Arabia 90 D6
Umm Ruwaba Sudan 86 D7
Umm Sa'ad Libya 90 B5
Umm Sa'īd Qatar 88 C5
Umm Ṣalāl Muḥammad Qatar 88 C5
Umm Shugeira Sudan 86 C7
Umm Wa'āl hill Saudi Arabia 85 D4
Umm Wazīr well Saudi Arabia 88 B6
Umnak Island U.S.A. 118 B4
Um Phang Wildlife Reserve nature res. Thai. 70 B4
Umpqua r. U.S.A. 126 B4
Umpulo Angola 99 B5
Umraniye Turkey 59 N5
Umred India 84 C1
Umri India 82 D4
Umtali Zimbabwe see Mutare
Umtata S. Africa see Mthatha
Umtentweni S. Africa 101 J6
Umuahia Nigeria 96 D4
Umuarama Brazil 144 F2
Umvuma Zimbabwe see Mvuma
Umzimkulu S. Africa 101 I6
Una r. Bos. & Herz./Croatia 58 G2
Una Brazil 145 D1
Una India 82 D3
'Unāb, Jabal al hill Jordan 85 C5
'Unāb, Wādī al watercourse Jordan 85 C4
Unaí Brazil 145 B2
Unalaska Island U.S.A. 118 B4
Unapool U.K. 50 D2
'Unayzah Saudi Arabia 86 F4
'Unayzah, Jabal hill Iraq 91 E4
Uncia Bol. 142 E7
Uncompahgre Peak U.S.A. 129 J2
Uncompahgre Plateau U.S.A. 129 I2
Undara National Park Australia 110 D3
Underberg S. Africa 101 I5
Underbool Australia 111 C7
Underwood U.S.A. 134 C4
Undur Indon. 69 I7
Unecha Russia 43 G5
Ungama Bay Kenya see Ungwana Bay
Ungarie Australia 112 C4
Ungava, Baie d' b. Canada see Ungava Bay
Ungava, Péninsule d' pen. Canada 122 G1
Ungava Bay Canada 123 I2
Ungava Peninsula Canada see Ungava, Péninsule d'
Ungeny Moldova see Ungheni
Ungheni Moldova 59 L1
Unguana Moz. 101 L2
Unguja i. Tanz. see Zanzibar Island
Unguz, Solonchakovyye Vpadiny salt flat Turkm. 88 E2
Üngüz Angyrsyndaky Garagum des. Turkm. 88 E1
Ungvár Ukr. see Uzhhorod
Ungwana Bay Kenya 98 E4
Uni Russia 42 K4
União Brazil 143 J4
União da Vitória Brazil 145 A4
União dos Palmares Brazil 143 K5
Unimak Island U.S.A. 118 B4
Unini r. Brazil 142 F4
Union MO U.S.A. 130 F4
Union WV U.S.A. 134 E5
Union, Mount U.S.A. 129 G4
Union City OH U.S.A. 134 C3
Union City PA U.S.A. 134 F3
Union City TN U.S.A. 131 F4
Uniondale S. Africa 100 F7
Unión de Reyes Cuba 133 D8
▶Union of Soviet Socialist Republics
Divided in 1991 into 15 independent nations: Armenia, Azerbaijan, Belarus, Estonia, Georgia, Latvia, Kazakhstan, Kyrgyzstan, Lithuania, Moldova, Russia, Tajikistan, Turkmenistan, Ukraine and Uzbekistan.
Union Springs U.S.A. 133 C5
Uniontown U.S.A. 134 F4
Unionville U.S.A. 135 G3
United Arab Emirates country Asia 88 D6
United Arab Republic country Africa see Egypt
▶United Kingdom country Europe 46 G3
3rd most populous country in Europe.
United Provinces state India see Uttar Pradesh
▶United States of America country N. America 124 F3
Most populous country in North America and 3rd most populous in the world. Also 2nd largest country in North America and 3rd in the world.
United States Range mts Canada 119 L1
Unity Canada 121 I4
Unjha India 82 C5
Unna Germany 53 H3
Unnao India 82 E4
Ŭnp'a N. Korea 75 B5
Unsan N. Korea 75 B4
Ŭnsan N. Korea 75 B5
Unst i. U.K. 50 [inset]
Unstrut r. Germany 53 L3
Untor, Ozero l. Russia 41 T3
Unuk r. Canada/U.S.A. 120 D3
Unuli Horog China 83 G2
Unzen-dake vol. Japan 75 C6
Unzha Russia 42 J4
Upalco U.S.A. 129 H1
Upar Ghat reg. India 83 F5
Upemba, Lac l. Dem. Rep. Congo 99 C4
Upemba, Parc National de l' nat. park Dem. Rep. Congo 99 C4
Uperbada India 83 F5
Upernavik Greenland 119 M2
Upington S. Africa 100 E5
Upland U.S.A. 128 E4
Upleta India 82 B5
Upoloksha Russia 44 Q3
'Upolu i. Samoa 107 I3
Upper Arlington U.S.A. 134 D3
Upper Arrow Lake Canada 120 G5
Upper Chindwin Myanmar see Mawlaik
Upper Fraser Canada 120 F4
Upper Garry Lake Canada 121 K1
Upper Hutt N.Z. 113 E5
Upper Klamath Lake U.S.A. 126 C4
Upper Lough Erne l. U.K. 51 E3
Upper Marlboro U.S.A. 135 G4
Upper Mazinaw Lake Canada 135 G1
Upper Missouri Breaks National Monument nat. park U.S.A. 130 A2
Upper Peirce Reservoir Sing. 71 [inset]
Upper Red Lake U.S.A. 130 E1
Upper Sandusky U.S.A. 134 D3
Upper Saranac Lake U.S.A. 135 H1
Upper Seal Lake Canada see Iberville, Lac d'
Upper Tunguska r. Russia see Angara
Upper Volta country Africa see Burkina Faso
Upper Yarra Reservoir Australia 112 B6
Uppinangadi India 84 B3
Uppsala Sweden 45 J7
Upsala Canada 122 C4
Upshi India 82 D2
Upton U.S.A. 135 J2
'Uqayqah, Wādī watercourse Jordan 85 B4
'Uqayribāt Syria 85 C2
'Uqlat al 'Udhaybah well Iraq 91 G5
Uqturpan China see Wushi
Uracas vol. N. Mariana Is see Farallon de Pajaros
Urad Houqi China see Sain Us
Ūrāf Iran 88 E4
Urakawa Japan 74 F4
Ural hill Australia 112 C4
Ural r. Kazakh./Russia 78 E2
Uralla Australia 112 E3
Ural Mountains Russia 41 S2
Ural'sk Kazakh. 78 E1
Ural'skaya Oblast' admin. div. Kazakh. see Zapadnyy Kazakhstan
Ural'skiye Gory mts Russia see Ural Mountains
Ural'skiy Khrebet mts Russia see Ural Mountains
Urambo Tanz. 99 D4
Uran India 84 B2
Urana Australia 112 C5
Urana, Lake Australia 112 C5
Urandangi Australia 110 B4
Urandi Brazil 145 C1
Uranium City Canada 121 I3
Uranquinty Australia 112 C5
Uraricoera r. Brazil 142 F3
Urartu country Asia see Armenia
Ura-Tyube Tajik. see Istaravshan
Uravakonda India 84 C3
Uravan (abandoned) U.S.A. 129 I2
Urawa Japan 75 E6
'Urayf an Nāqah, Jabal hill Egypt 85 B4
Uray'irah Saudi Arabia 88 C5
'Urayq ad Duḥūl des. Saudi Arabia 88 B5
'Urayq Sāqān des. Saudi Arabia 88 B5
Urbana IL U.S.A. 130 F3
Urbana OH U.S.A. 134 D3
Urbino Italy 58 E3
Urbinum Italy see Urbino
Urbs Vetus Italy see Orvieto
Urdoma Russia 42 K3
Urdyuzhskoye, Ozero l. Russia 42 K2
Ure r. U.K. 48 F4
Urek'i Georgia 91 F2
Uren' Russia 42 J4
Urengoy Russia 64 I3
Uréparapara i. Vanuatu 107 G3
Urfa Turkey see Şanlıurfa
Urfa prov. Turkey see Şanlıurfa
Urga Mongolia see Ulan Bator
Urgal r. Russia 74 D2
Urganch Uzbek. 80 B3
Urgench Uzbek. see Urganch
Urgün-e Kalān Afgh. 89 H3
Ürgüp Turkey 90 D3
Urgut Uzbek. 89 G2
Urho China 80 G2
Urho Kekkosen kansallispuisto nat. park Fin. 44 O2
Urie r. U.K. 50 G3
Uril Russia 74 C2
Urisino Australia 112 A2
Urjala Fin. 45 M6
Urk Neth. 52 F2
Urkan Russia 74 B1
Urkan r. Russia 74 B1
Urla Turkey 59 L5
Urlingford Ireland 51 E5
Urluk Russia 73 J2
Ūrmā aş Şughrá Syria 85 C1
Urmai China 83 F3
Urmia Iran 88 B2
Urmia, Lake salt l. Iran 88 B2
Urmston Road sea chan. H.K. China 77 [inset]
Uromi Nigeria 96 D4
Uroševac Kosovo see Ferizaj
Urosozero Russia 42 G3
Urru Co salt l. China 83 F3
Urt Moron China 80 H4
Uruáchic Mex. 124 F6
Uruaçu Brazil 145 A1
Uruana Brazil 145 A1
Uruapan Baja California Mex. 127 D7
Uruapan Michoacán Mex. 136 D5
Urubamba r. Peru 142 D6
Urucará Brazil 143 G4
Urucu r. Brazil 142 F4
Uruçuca Brazil 145 D1
Uruçuí Brazil 143 J5
Uruçuí, Serra do hills Brazil 143 I5
Urucuia Brazil 145 B2
Urucurituba Brazil 143 G4
Uruguai r. Arg./Uruguay see Uruguay
Uruguaiana Brazil 144 E3
Uruguay r. Arg./Uruguay 144 E4
also known as Uruguai
Uruguay country S. America 144 E4
Uruhe China 74 B2
Urumchi China see Ürümqi
Ürümqi China 80 G3
Urundi country Africa see Burundi
Urup, Ostrov i. Russia 73 S3
Urusha Russia 74 A1
Urutaí Brazil 145 A2
Uruzgān Afgh. 89 G3
Uryupino Russia 73 M2
Uryupinsk Russia 43 I6
Ürzhar Kazakh. see Urzhar
Urzhar Kazakh. 80 F2
Urzhum Russia 42 K4
Urziceni Romania 59 L2
Usa Japan 75 C6
Usa r. Russia 42 M2
Uşak Turkey 59 M5
Usakos Namibia 100 B1
Usarp Mountains Antarctica 152 H2
Usborne, Mount hill Falkland Is 144 E8
Ushakova, Ostrov i. Russia 64 I1
Ushant i. France see Ouessant, Île d'
Üsharal Kazakh. see Usharal
Usharal Kazakh. 80 F2
Ush-Bel'dyr Russia 72 H2
Ushtobe Kazakh. 80 E2
Ush-Tyube Kazakh. see Ushtobe
Ushuaia Arg. 144 C8
Ushumun Russia 74 B1
Usingen Germany 53 I4
Usinsk Russia 41 R2
Usk U.K. 49 E7
Usk r. U.K. 49 E7
Uskhodni Belarus 45 O10
Uskoplje Bos. & Herz. see Gornji Vakuf
Üsküdar Turkey 59 M4
Uslar Germany 53 J3
Usman' Russia 43 H5
Usmanabad India see Osmanabad
Usmas ezers l. Latvia 45 M8
Usogorsk Russia 42 K3
Usol'ye-Sibirskoye Russia 72 I2
Ussel France 56 F4
Ussuri r. China/Russia 74 D2
Ussuriysk Russia 74 C4
Ust'-Abakanskoye Russia see Abakan
Usta Muhammad Pak. 89 H4
Ust'-Balyk Russia see Nefteyugansk
Ust'-Donetskiy Russia 43 I7
Ust'-Dzheguta Russia 91 F1
Ust'-Dzhegutinskaya Russia see Ust'-Dzheguta
Ustica, Isola di i. Sicily Italy 58 E5
Ust'-Ilimsk Russia 65 L4
Ust'-Ilimskoye Vodokhranilishche resr Russia 65 L4
Ust'-Ilych Russia 41 R3
Ústí nad Labem Czechia 47 O5
Ustinov Russia see Izhevsk
Üstirt plat. Kazakh./Uzbek. see Ustyurt Plateau
Ustka Poland 47 P3
Ust'-Kamchatsk Russia 65 R4
Ust'-Kamenogorsk Kazakh. 80 F2
Ust'-Kan Russia 80 F1
Ust'-Koksa Russia 80 G1
Ust'-Kulom Russia 42 L3
Ust'-Kut Russia 65 L4
Ust'-Kuyga Russia 65 O2
Ust'-Labinsk Russia 91 E1
Ust'-Labinskaya Russia see Ust'-Labinsk
Ust'-Lyzha Russia 42 M2
Ust'-Maya Russia 65 O3
Ust'-Nera Russia 65 P3
Ust'-Ocheya Russia 42 K3
Ust'-Olenek Russia 65 M2
Ust'-Omchug Russia 65 P3
Ust'-Ordynskiy Russia 72 I2
Ust'-Port Russia 64 J3
Ustrem Russia 41 T3
Ust'-Tsil'ma Russia 42 L2
Ust'-Uda Russia 72 I2
Ust'-Umalta (abandoned) Russia 74 D2
Ust'-Undurga Russia 73 L2
Ust'-Ura Russia 42 J3
Ust'-Urgal Russia 74 D2
Ust'-Usa Russia 42 M2
Ust'-Vayen'ga Russia 42 I3
Ust'-Voya Russia 41 R3
Ust'-Vyyskaya Russia 42 J3
Ust'ya r. Russia 42 I3
Ust'ye Russia 42 H4
Ustyurt, Plato plat. Kazakh./Uzbek. see Ustyurt Plateau
Ustyurt Plateau Kazakh./Uzbek. 78 E2
Ustyurt Platosi plat. Kazakh./Uzbek. see Ustyurt Plateau
Ustyuzhna Russia 42 H4
Usulután El Salvador 136 G6
Usumbura Burundi see Bujumbura
Usvyaty Russia 42 F5
Utah state U.S.A. 126 F5
Utah Lake U.S.A. 129 H1
Utajärvi Fin. 44 O4
Utashinai Russia see Yuzhno-Kuril'sk
'Utaybah, Buḥayrat al imp. l. Syria 85 C3
Utena Lith. 45 N9
Uterlai India 82 B4
Uthai Thani Thai. 70 C4
Uthal Pak. 89 G5
'Uthmānīyah Syria 85 C2
uThukela r. S. Africa 101 J5
Utiariti Brazil 143 G6
Utica NY U.S.A. 135 H2
Utica OH U.S.A. 134 D3
Utiel Spain 57 F4
Utikuma Lake Canada 120 H4
Utlwanang S. Africa 101 G4
Utrecht Neth. 52 F2
Utrecht S. Africa 101 J4
Utrera Spain 57 D5
Utsjoki Fin. 44 O2
Utsunomiya Japan 75 E5
Utta Russia 43 J7
Uttaradit Thai. 70 C3
Uttarakhand state India 82 D3
Uttaranchal state India see Uttarakhand
Uttarkashi India 82 D3
Uttar Kashi India see Uttarkashi
Uttar Pradesh state India 82 D4
Uttoxeter U.K. 49 F6
Uttranchal state India see Uttarakhand
Utubulak China 80 G2
Utupua i. Solomon Is 107 G3
Uturuncu, Cerro mt. Bol. 142 E8
Uummannaq Fjord inlet Greenland 153 J2
Uummannarsuaq c. Greenland see Farewell, Cape
Uurainen Fin. 44 N5
Uusikaarlepyy Fin. see Nykarleby
Uusikaupunki Fin. 45 L6
Uva Russia 42 L4
Uvalde U.S.A. 131 D6
Uvarovo Russia 43 I6
Uvéa atoll New Caledonia see Ouvéa
Uvinza Tanz. 99 D4
Uvs Nuur salt l. Mongolia 80 H1
Uwajima Japan 75 D6
'Uwayrid, Ḥarrat al lava field Saudi Arabia 86 E4
Uwaysiṭ well Saudi Arabia 85 D4
Uweinat, Jebel mt. Sudan 86 C5
Uwi i. Indon. 71 D7
Uxbridge Canada 134 F1
Uxbridge U.K. 49 G7
Uxin Qi China see Dabqig
Uyaly Kazakh. 80 B3
Uyar Russia 72 G1
Uyo Nigeria 96 D4
Uyu Chaung r. Myanmar 70 A1
Uyuni Bol. 142 E8
Uyuni, Salar de salt flat Bol. 142 E8
Uza r. Russia 43 J5
Uzbekistan country Asia 80 B3
Ŭzbekiston country Asia see Uzbekistan
Uzbekskaya S.S.R. country Asia see Uzbekistan
Uzbek S.S.R. country Asia see Uzbekistan
Uzboý Turkm. 88 D2
Uzen' Kazakh. see Kyzylsay
Uzhgorod Ukr. see Uzhhorod
Uzhhorod Ukr. 43 D6
Užhorod Ukr. see Uzhhorod
Užice Serbia 59 H3
Uzlovaya Russia 43 H5
Üzümlü Turkey 59 M6
Uzun Uzbek. 89 H2
Uzunköprü Turkey 59 L4
Uzynkair Kazakh. 80 B3

V

Vaajakoski Fin. 44 N5
Vaal r. S. Africa 101 F5
Vaala Fin. 44 O4
Vaalbos National Park S. Africa 100 G5
Vaal Dam S. Africa 101 I4
Vaalwater S. Africa 101 I3
Vaasa Fin. 44 L5
Vaavu Atoll Maldives see Felidhe Atholhu
Vác Hungary 47 Q7
Vacaria Brazil 145 A5
Vacaria, Campo da plain Brazil 145 A5
Vacaville U.S.A. 128 C2
Vachon r. Canada 123 H1
Vad Russia 42 J5
Vad r. Russia 43 I5
Vada India 84 B2
Vadakara India 84 B4
Vadla Norway 45 E7
Vadodara India 82 C5
Vadsø Norway 44 P1
▶Vaduz Liechtenstein 56 I3
Capital of Liechtenstein.
Værøy i. Norway 44 H3
Vaga r. Russia 42 I3
Vågåmo Norway 45 F6
Vaganski Vrh mt. Croatia 58 F2
Vágar i. Faroe Is 44 [inset 2]
Vagharshapat Armenia 91 G2
Vågsele Sweden 44 K4
Vágur Faroe Is 44 [inset 2]
Váh r. Slovakia 47 Q7
Vähäkyrö Fin. 44 M5
▶Vaiaku Tuvalu 107 H2
Capital of Tuvalu, on Funafuti atoll.
Vaida Estonia 45 N7
Vaiden U.S.A. 131 F5
Vail U.S.A. 124 F4
Vailly-sur-Aisne France 52 D5
Vaitupu i. Tuvalu 107 H2
Vajrakarur India see Kanur
Vakhsh Tajik. 89 H2
Vakhsh r. Tajik. 89 H2
Vakhstroy Tajik. see Vakhsh
Vakīlābād Iran 88 E4
Valbo Sweden 45 J6
Valcheta Arg. 144 C6
Valdai Hills Russia see Valdayskaya Vozvyshennost'
Valday Russia 42 G4
Valdayskaya Vozvyshennost' hills Russia 42 G4
Valdecañas, Embalse de resr Spain 57 D4
Valdemārpils Latvia 45 M8
Valdemarsvik Sweden 45 J7
Valdepeñas Spain 57 E4
Val-de-Reuil France 52 B5
Valdés, Península pen. Arg. 144 D6
Valdez U.S.A. 118 D3
Valdivia Chile 144 B5
Val-d'Or Canada 122 F4
Valdosta U.S.A. 133 D6
Valdres valley Norway 45 F6
Vale Georgia 91 F2
Vale U.S.A. 126 D3
Valemount Canada 120 G4
Valença Bahia Brazil 145 D1
Valença Rio de Janeiro Brazil 145 C3
Valence France 56 G4
Valencia Spain 57 F4
València Spain see Valencia
Valencia reg. Spain 57 F4
Valencia Venez. 142 E1
Valencia, Golfo de g. Spain 57 G4
Valencia de Don Juan Spain 57 D2
Valencia Island Ireland 51 B6
Valenciennes France 52 D4
Valensole, Plateau de France 56 H5
Valentia Spain see Valencia
Valentin Russia 74 D4
Valentine U.S.A. 130 C3
Våler Norway 45 G6
Valera Venez. 142 D2
Vale Verde Brazil 145 D2
Val Grande, Parco Nazionale della nat. park Italy 58 C1
Valiyakara, Suheli India 84 B4
Valjevo Serbia 59 H2
Valka Latvia 45 O8
Valkeakoski Fin. 45 N6
Valkenswaard Neth. 52 F3
Valky Ukr. 43 G6
Valkyrie Dome ice feature Antarctica 152 D1
Valladolid Mex. 136 G4
Valladolid Spain 57 D3
Vallard, Lac l. Canada 123 H3
Valle Norway 45 E7
Vallecillos Mex. 131 D7
Vallecito Reservoir U.S.A. 129 J3
Valle de la Pascua Venez. 142 E2
Valledupar Col. 142 D1
Vallée-Jonction Canada 123 H5
Valle Fértil, Sierra de mts Arg. 144 C4
Valle Grande Bol. 142 F7
Valle Hermoso Mex. 131 D7
Vallejo U.S.A. 128 B2
Vallenar Chile 144 B3
Valles Caldera National Preserve nat. park U.S.A. 127 G6
▶Valletta Malta 58 F7
Capital of Malta.
Valley r. Canada 121 L5
Valley U.K. 48 C5
Valley City U.S.A. 130 D2
Valleyview Canada 120 G4
Valls Spain 57 G3
Val Marie Canada 121 J5
Valmiera Latvia 45 N8
Valmy U.S.A. 128 E1
Valnera mt. Spain 57 E2
Valognes France 49 F9
Valona Albania see Vlorë
Valozhyn Belarus 45 O9
Val-Paradis Canada 122 F4
Valparai India 84 C4
Valparaíso Chile 144 B4
Valparaiso U.S.A. 134 B3
Valpoi India 84 B3
Valréas France 56 G4
Vals, Tanjung c. Indon. 69 J8
Valsad India 84 B1
Valspan S. Africa 100 G4
Valtimo Fin. 44 P5
Valuyevka Russia 43 I7
Valuyki Russia 43 H6
Vammala Fin. 45 M6
Van Turkey 91 F3
Van, Lake salt l. Turkey 91 F3
Vanadzor Armenia 91 G2
Van Buren AR U.S.A. 131 E5
Van Buren MO U.S.A. 131 F4
Van Buren OH U.S.A. see Kettering
Vanceburg U.S.A. 134 D4
Vanch Tajik. see Vanj
Vancleve U.S.A. 134 D5
Vancouver Canada 120 F5
Vancouver U.S.A. 126 C3
Vancouver, Mount Canada/U.S.A. 120 B2
Vancouver Island Canada 120 E5
Vanda Fin. see Vantaa
Vandalia IL U.S.A. 130 F4
Vandalia OH U.S.A. 134 C4
Vandekerckhove Lake Canada 121 K3
Vanderbijlpark S. Africa 101 H4
Vanderbilt U.S.A. 134 C1
Vandergrift U.S.A. 134 F3
Vanderhoof Canada 120 E4
Vanderkloof Dam resr S. Africa 100 G6
Vanderlin Island Australia 110 B2
Vanderwagen U.S.A. 129 I4
Van Diemen, Cape N.T. Australia 108 E2
Van Diemen, Cape Qld Australia 110 B3
Van Diemen Gulf Australia 108 F2
Vändra Estonia 45 N7
Väner, Lake Sweden see Vänern
▶Vänern l. Sweden 45 H7
4th largest lake in Europe.
Vänersborg Sweden 45 H7
Vangaindrano Madag. 99 E6
Van Gia Vietnam 71 E4
Van Gölü salt l. Turkey see Van, Lake
Van Horn U.S.A. 127 G7
Vanikoro Islands Solomon Is 107 G3
Vanimo P.N.G. 69 K7
Vanino Russia 74 F2
Vanivilasa Sagara resr India 84 C3
Vaniyambadi India 84 C3
Vanj Tajik. 89 H2
Vännäs Sweden 44 K5
Vannes France 56 C3
Vannes, Lac l. Canada 123 I3
Vannovka Kazakh. see Turar Ryskulov
Vannøya i. Norway 44 K1
Vanoise, Massif de la mts France 56 H4
Vanoise, Parc National de la nat. park France 56 H4
Van Rees, Pegunungan mts Indon. 69 J7
Vanrhynsdorp S. Africa 100 D6
Vansant U.S.A. 134 D5
Vansbro Sweden 45 I6
Vansittart Island Canada 119 J3
Van Starkenborgh Kanaal canal Neth. 52 G1
Vantaa Fin. 45 N6
Van Truer Tableland reg. Australia 109 C6
Vanua Lava i. Vanuatu 107 G3
Vanua Levu i. Fiji 107 H3
Vanuatu country S. Pacific Ocean 107 G3
Van Wert U.S.A. 134 C3
Van Wyksvlei S. Africa 100 E6
Van Wyksvlei Dam l. S. Africa 100 E6
Văn Yên Vietnam 70 D2
Van Zylsrus S. Africa 100 F4
Varadero Cuba 133 D8
Varahi India 82 B5
Varakļāni Latvia 45 O8
Varalé Côte d'Ivoire 96 C4
Varāmīn Iran 88 C3
Varanasi India 83 E4
Varandey Russia 42 M1
Varangerfjorden sea chan. Norway 44 P1
Varangerhalvøya pen. Norway 44 P1
Varaždin Croatia 58 G1
Varberg Sweden 45 H8
Vardar r. Macedonia 59 J4
Varde Denmark 45 F9
Vardenis Armenia 91 G2
Vardø Norway 44 Q1
Varel Germany 53 I1
Varėna Lith. 45 N9
Varese Italy 58 C2
Varfolomeyevka Russia 74 D3
Vårgårda Sweden 45 H7
Varginha Brazil 145 B3
Varik Neth. 52 F3
Varillas Chile 144 B2
Varkaus Fin. 44 O5
Varna Bulg. 59 L3
Värnamo Sweden 45 I8
Värnäs Sweden 45 H6
Varnavino Russia 42 J4
Várnjárg pen. Norway see Varangerhalvøya
Varpaisjärvi Fin. 44 O5
Várpalota Hungary 58 H1
Varsh, Ozero l. Russia 42 J2
Varto Turkey 91 F3
Várzea da Palma Brazil 145 B2
Várzea Grande Brazil 143 G7
Vasa Fin. see Vaasa
Vasai India 84 B2
Vashka r. Russia 42 J2
Vasht Iran see Khāsh
Vasilkov Ukr. see Vasyl'kiv
Vasknarva Estonia 45 O7
Vaslui Romania 59 L1
Vassar U.S.A. 134 D2
Vas-Soproni-síkság hills Hungary 58 G1
Vastan Turkey see Gevaş
Västerås Sweden 45 J7

Västerdalälven r. Sweden 45 I6
Västerfjäll Sweden 44 J3
Västerhaninge Sweden 45 K7
Västervik Sweden 45 J8
Vasto Italy 58 F3
Vasyl'kiv Ukr. 43 F6
Vatan France 56 E3
Vaté i. Vanuatu see Éfaté
Vatersay i. U.K. 50 B4
Vathar India 84 B2
Vathí Greece see Vathy
Vathy Greece 59 L6

▶Vatican City Europe 58 E4
Independent papal state, the smallest country in the world.

Vaticano, Città del Europe see Vatican City
Vatnajökull ice cap Iceland 44 [inset 1]
Vatnajökulsthjóðgarður nat. park Iceland 44 [inset 1]
Vatnajökulsþjóðgarður nat. park Iceland see Vatnajökulsthjóðgarður
Vatoa i. Fiji 107 I3
Vatra Dornei Romania 59 K1
Vätter, Lake Sweden see Vättern
Vättern l. Sweden 45 I7
Vaughn U.S.A. 127 G6
Vaupés r. Col. 142 E3
Vauquelin r. Canada 122 F3
Vauvert France 56 G5
Vauxhall Canada 121 H5
Vavatenina Madag. 99 E5
Vava'u Group is Tonga 107 I3
Vavitao i. Fr. Polynesia see Raivavae
Vavoua Côte d'Ivoire 96 C4
Vavozh Russia 42 K4
Vavuniya Sri Lanka 84 D4
Vawkavysk Belarus 45 N10
Växjö Sweden 45 I8
Vay, Đao i. Vietnam 71 C5
Vayenga Russia see Severomorsk
Vazante Brazil 145 B2
Vazáš Sweden see Vittangi
Veaikevárri Sweden see Svappavaara
Véal Rénh Cambodia 71 C5
Véal Vêng Cambodia 71 C4
Vecht r. Neth. 52 G2
also known as Vechte (Germany)
Vechta Germany 53 I2
Vechte r. Germany 53 G2
also known as Vecht (Netherlands)
Veckerhagen (Reinhardshagen) Germany 53 J3
Vedaranniyam India 84 C4
Vedasandur India 84 C4
Veddige Sweden 45 H8
Vedea r. Romania 59 K3
Veedersburg U.S.A. 134 B3
Veendam Neth. 52 G1
Veenendaal Neth. 52 F2
Vega i. Norway 44 G4
Vega U.S.A. 131 C5
Vegreville Canada 121 H4
Vehari Pak. 89 I4
Vehkalahti Fin. 45 O6
Vehowa Pak. 89 H4
Veinticinco de Mayo Buenos Aires Arg. see 25 de Mayo
Veinticinco de Mayo La Pampa Arg. see 25 de Mayo
Veirwaro Pak. 89 H5
Veitshöchheim Germany 53 J5
Vejle Denmark 45 F9
Vekil'bazar Turkm. see Wekilbazar
Velbert Germany 52 H3
Velbŭzhdki Prokhod pass Bulg./Macedonia 59 J3
Velddrif S. Africa 100 D7
Velebit mts Croatia 58 F2
Velen Germany 52 G3
Velenje Slovenia 58 F1
Veles Macedonia 59 I4
Vélez-Málaga Spain 57 D5
Vélez-Rubio Spain 57 E5
Velhas r. Brazil 145 B2
Velibaba Turkey see Aras
Velika Gorica Croatia 58 G2
Velika Plana Serbia 59 I2
Velikaya r. Russia 42 K4
Velikaya r. Russia 45 P8
Velikaya r. Russia 65 S3
Velikaya Kema Russia 74 E3
Veliki Preslav Bulg. 59 L3
Velikiye Luki Russia 42 F4
Velikiy Novgorod Russia 42 F4
Velikiy Ustyug Russia 42 J3
Velikonda Range hills India 84 C3
Veliko Tarnovo Bulg. 59 K3
Velikoye Russia 42 H4
Velikoye, Ozero l. Russia 43 I5
Veli Lošinj Croatia 58 F2
Velizh Russia 42 F5
Vella Lavella i. Solomon Is 107 F2
Vellar r. India 84 C4
Vellberg Germany 53 J5
Vellmar Germany 53 J3
Vellore India 84 C3
Velpke Germany 53 K2
Vel'sk Russia 42 I3
Velsuna Italy see Orvieto
Velten Germany 53 N2
Veluwezoom, Nationaal Park nat. park Neth. 52 F2
Velykyy Tokmak Ukr. see Tokmak
Vel'yu r. Russia 42 L3
Vemalwada India 84 C2
Vema Seamount sea feature S. Atlantic Ocean 148 I8
Vema Trench sea feature Indian Ocean 149 M6
Vempalle India 84 C3
Venado Tuerto Arg. 144 D4
Venafro Italy 58 F4
Vendinga Russia 42 J3
Vendôme France 56 E3
Venegas Mex. 131 C8
Venetia Italy see Venice
Venetie Landing U.S.A. 118 D3
Venev Russia 43 H5
Venezia Italy see Venice
Venezia, Golfo di g. Europe see Venice, Gulf of

▶Venezuela country S. America 142 E2
5th most populous country in South America.

Venezuela, Golfo de g. Venez. 142 D1
Venezuelan Basin sea feature S. Atlantic Ocean 148 D4
Vengurla India 84 B3
Veniaminof Volcano U.S.A. 118 C4
Venice Italy 58 E2
Venice U.S.A. 133 D7
Venice, Gulf of Europe 58 E2
Vénissieux France 56 G4
Venkatapalem India 84 D2
Venkatapuram India 84 D2
Venlo Neth. 52 G3
Vennesla Norway 45 E7
Venray Neth. 52 F3
Venta r. Latvia/Lith. 45 M8
Venta Lith. 45 M8
Ventersburg S. Africa 101 H5
Ventersdorp S. Africa 101 H4
Venterstad S. Africa 101 G6
Ventnor U.K. 49 F8
Ventotene, Isola i. Italy 58 E4
Ventoux, Mont mt. France 56 G4
Ventspils Latvia 45 L8
Ventura U.S.A. 128 D4
Venus Bay Australia 112 B7
Venustiano Carranza Mex. 131 C7
Venustiano Carranza, Presa resr Mex. 131 C7
Vera Arg. 144 D3
Vera Spain 57 F5
Vera Cruz Brazil 145 A3
Vera Cruz Mex. see Veracruz
Veracruz Mex. 136 E5
Veraval India 82 B5
Verbania Italy 58 C2
Vercelli Italy 58 C2
Vercors reg. France 56 G4
Verdalsøra Norway 44 G5
Verde r. Goiás Brazil 145 A2
Verde r. Goiás/Minas Gerais Brazil 145 B2
Verde r. Minas Gerais Brazil 145 A2
Verde r. Minas Gerais Brazil 145 A2
Verde r. Mex. 127 G8
Verde r. U.S.A. 129 H5
Verden (Aller) Germany 53 J2
Verde Pequeno r. Brazil 145 C1
Verdi U.S.A. 128 D2
Verdon r. France 56 G5
Verdun France 52 F5
Vereeniging S. Africa 101 H4
Vereshchagino Russia 41 Q4
Vergennes U.S.A. 135 I1
Véria Greece see Veroia
Verín Spain 57 C3
Veríssimo Brazil 145 A2
Verkhneimbatsk Russia 64 J3
Verkhnekolvinsk Russia 42 M2
Verkhnespasskoye Russia 42 J4
Verkhnetulomskiy Russia 44 Q2
Verkhnetulomskoye Vodokhranilishche res. Russia 44 Q2
Verkhnevilyuysk Russia 65 N3
Verkhneye Kuyto, Ozero l. Russia 44 Q4
Verkhnezeysk Russia 73 N2
Verkhniy Vyalozerskiy Russia 42 G2
Verkhnyaya Khava Russia 43 H6
Verkhnyaya Salda Russia 41 S4
Verkhnyaya Tunguska r. Russia see Angara
Verkhnyaya Tura Russia 41 R4
Verkhoshizhem'ye Russia 42 K4
Verkhovazh'ye Russia 42 I3
Verkhov'ye Russia 43 H5
Verkhoyansk Russia 65 O3
Verkhoyanskiy Khrebet mts Russia 65 N2
Vermand France 52 D5
Vermelho r. Brazil 145 A1
Vermilion Canada 121 I4
Vermilion Bay U.S.A. 131 F6
Vermilion Cliffs AZ U.S.A. 129 G3
Vermilion Cliffs UT U.S.A. 129 G3
Vermilion Cliffs National Monument nat. park U.S.A. 129 H3
Vermilion Lake U.S.A. 130 E2
Vermillion U.S.A. 130 D3
Vermillion Bay Canada 121 M5
Vermont state U.S.A. 135 I1
Vernadsky research station Antarctica 152 L2
Vernal U.S.A. 129 I1
Verner Canada 122 E5
Verneuk Pan salt pan S. Africa 100 E5
Vernon Canada 120 G5
Vernon France 52 B5
Vernon AL U.S.A. 131 F5
Vernon IN U.S.A. 134 C4
Vernon TX U.S.A. 131 D5
Vernon UT U.S.A. 129 G1
Vernon Islands Australia 108 E3
Vernoye Russia 74 C2
Vernyy Kazakh. see Almaty
Vero Beach U.S.A. 133 D7
Veroia Greece 59 J4
Verona Italy 58 D2
Verona U.S.A. 134 F4
Versailles France 52 C6
Versailles IN U.S.A. 134 C4
Versailles KY U.S.A. 134 C4
Versailles OH U.S.A. 134 C3
Versec Serbia see Vršac
Versmold Germany 53 I2
Vert, Île i. Canada 123 H4
Vertou France 56 D3
Verulam S. Africa 101 J5
Verulamium U.K. see St Albans
Verviers Belgium 52 F4
Vervins France 52 D5
Verwood Canada 121 J5
Verzy France 52 E5
Vescovato Corsica France 56 I5
Vesele Ukr. 43 G7
Veselyy Russia 43 I7
Veselyy Yar Russia 74 D4
Veshenskaya Russia 43 I6
Vesle r. France 52 D5
Veslyana r. Russia 42 L3
Vesontio France see Besançon
Vesoul France 56 H3
Vessem Neth. 52 F3
Vesterålen is Norway 44 H2
Vesterålsfjorden sea chan. Norway 44 H2
Vestertana Norway 44 O1
Vestfjorddalen valley Norway 45 F7
Vestfjorden sea chan. Norway 44 H3
Véstia Brazil 145 A3
Vestmanna Faroe Is 44 [inset 2]
Vestmannaeyjar Iceland 44 [inset 1]
Vestmannaeyjar is Iceland 44 [inset 1]
Vestnes Norway 44 E5
Vesturhorn hd Iceland 44 [inset 1]
Vesuvio vol. Italy see Vesuvius
Vesuvius vol. Italy 58 F4
Ves'yegonsk Russia 42 H4
Veszprém Hungary 58 G1
Veteli Fin. 44 M5
Veteran Canada 121 I4
Vetlanda Sweden 45 I8
Vetluga Russia 42 J4
Vetluga r. Russia 42 J4
Vetluzhskiy Kostromskaya Oblast' Russia 42 J4
Vetluzhskiy Nizhegorodskaya Oblast' Russia 42 J4
Vettore, Monte mt. Italy 58 E3
Veurne Belgium 52 C3
Vevay U.S.A. 134 C4
Vevey Switz. 56 H3
Vexin Normand reg. France 52 B5
Veyo U.S.A. 129 G3
Vézère r. France 56 E4
Vezirköprü Turkey 90 D2
Viajas, Isla de las i. Peru 142 C6
Vialar Alg. see Tissemsilt
Viamão Brazil 145 A5
Viana Espírito Santo Brazil 145 C3
Viana Maranhão Brazil 143 J4
Viana do Castelo Port. 57 B3
Vianen Neth. 52 F3
Viangchan Laos see Vientiane
Viangphoukha Laos 70 C2
Viannos Greece 59 K7
Vianópolis Brazil 145 A2
Viareggio Italy 58 D3
Viborg Denmark 45 F8
Viborg Russia see Vyborg
Vibo Valentia Italy 58 G5
Vic Spain 57 H3
Vicam Mex. 127 F8
Vicecomodoro Marambio research station Antarctica see Marambio
Vicente, Point U.S.A. 128 D5
Vicente Guerrero Mex. 127 D7
Vicenza Italy 58 D2
Vich Spain see Vic
Vichada r. Col. 142 E3
Vichadero Uruguay 144 F4
Vichy France 56 F3
Vicksburg AZ U.S.A. 129 G5
Vicksburg MS U.S.A. 131 F5
Viçosa Brazil 145 C3
Victor, Mount Antarctica 152 D2
Victor Harbor Australia 111 B7
Victoria Arg. 144 D4
Victoria r. Australia 108 E3
Victoria state Australia 112 B6

▶Victoria Canada 120 F5
Capital of British Columbia.

Victoria Chile 144 B5
Victoria Malaysia see Labuan
Victoria Malta 58 F6

▶Victoria Seychelles 149 L6
Capital of the Seychelles.

Victoria TX U.S.A. 131 D6
Victoria VA U.S.A. 135 F5
Victoria prov. Zimbabwe see Masvingo

▶Victoria, Lake Africa 98 D4
Largest lake in Africa and 3rd in the world.

Victoria, Lake Australia 111 C7
Victoria, Mount Fiji see Tomanivi
Victoria, Mount Myanmar 70 A2
Victoria, Mount P.N.G. 69 L8
Victoria and Albert Mountains Canada 119 K2
Victoria Falls Zambia/Zimbabwe 99 C5

▶Victoria Island Canada 118 H2
3rd largest island in North America and 9th in the world.

Victoria Land coastal area Antarctica 152 H2
Victoria Peak Belize 136 G5
Victoria Peak hill H.K. China 77 [inset]
Victoria Range mts N.Z. 113 D6
Victoria River Downs Australia 108 E4
Victoriaville Canada 123 H5
Victoria West S. Africa 100 F6
Victorica Arg. 144 C5
Victorville U.S.A. 128 E4
Victory Downs Australia 109 F6
Vidalia U.S.A. 131 F6
Vidal Junction U.S.A. 129 F4
Videle Romania 59 K2
Vidisha India 82 D5
Vidlin U.K. 50 [inset]
Vidlitsa Russia 42 G3
Viechtach Germany 53 M5
Viedma Arg. 144 D6
Viedma, Lago l. Arg. 144 B7
Viejo, Cerro mt. Mex. 127 E7
Vielank Germany 53 L1
Vielsalm Belgium 52 F4
Vienenburg Germany 53 K3

▶Vienna Austria 47 P6
Capital of Austria.

Vienna MO U.S.A. 130 F4
Vienna WV U.S.A. 134 E4
Vienne France 56 G4
Vienne r. France 56 E3

▶Vientiane Laos 70 C3
Capital of Laos.

Vieques i. Puerto Rico 137 K5
Vieremä Fin. 44 O5
Viersen Germany 52 G3
Vierzon France 56 F3
Viesca Mex. 131 C7
Viesīte Latvia 45 N8
Vieste Italy 58 G4
Vietas Sweden 44 K3
Vietnam country Asia 70 D3
Viêt Nam country Asia see Vietnam
Viêt Quang Vietnam 70 D2
Viêt Tri Vietnam 70 D2
Vieux Comptoir, Lac du l. Canada 122 F3
Vieux-Fort Canada 123 K4
Vieux Poste, Pointe du pt Canada 123 J4
Vigan Phil. 69 G3
Vigevano Italy 58 C2
Vigia Brazil 143 I4
Vignacourt France 52 C4
Vignemale mt. France 54 D3
Vignola Italy 58 D2
Vigo Spain 57 B2
Vihanti Fin. 44 N4
Vihti Fin. 45 N6
Viipuri Russia see Vyborg
Viitasaari Fin. 44 N5
Vijayadurg India 84 B2
Vijayanagaram India see Vizianagaram
Vijayapati India 84 C4
Vijayapura India 84 B2
Vijayawada India 84 D2
Vijayraghavgarh India 82 E5
Vík Iceland 44 [inset 1]
Vikajärvi Fin. 44 O3
Vikeke East Timor see Viqueque
Viking Canada 121 I4
Vikna i. Norway 44 G4
Vikøyri Norway 45 E6
Vila Vanuatu see Port Vila
Vila Alferes Chamusca Moz. see Guija
Vila Bela da Santíssima Trindade Brazil 142 G7
Vila Bittencourt Brazil 142 E4
Vila Bugaço Angola see Camanongue
Vila Cabral Moz. see Lichinga
Vila da Ponte Angola see Kuvango
Vila de Aljustrel Angola see Cangamba
Vila de Almoster Angola see Chiange
Vila de João Belo Moz. see Xai-Xai
Vila de María Arg. 144 D3
Vila de Trego Morais Moz. see Chókwè
Vila Fontes Moz. see Caia
Vila Franca de Xira Port. 57 B4
Vilagarcía de Arousa Spain 57 B2
Vila Gomes da Costa Moz. 101 K3
Vilalba Spain 57 C2
Vila Luísa Moz. see Marracuene
Vila Marechal Carmona Angola see Uíge
Vila Miranda Moz. see Macaloge
Vilanandro, Tanjona pt Madag. 99 E5
Vilanculos Moz. 101 L1
Vila Nova de Gaia Port. 57 B3
Vilanova i la Geltrú Spain 57 G3
Vila Pery Moz. see Chimoio
Vila Real Port. 57 C3
Vilar Formoso Port. 57 C3
Vila Salazar Angola see N'dalatando
Vila Salazar Zimbabwe see Sango
Vila Teixeira de Sousa Angola see Luau
Vila Velha Brazil 145 C3
Vilcabamba, Cordillera mts Peru 142 D6
Vil'cheka, Zemlya i. Russia 64 H1
Viled' r. Russia 42 J3
Vileyka Belarus see Vilyeyka
Vil'gort Russia 42 K3
Vilhelmina Sweden 44 J4
Vilhena Brazil 142 F6
Viliya r. Lith. see Neris
Viljandi Estonia 45 N7
Viljoenskroon S. Africa 101 H4
Vilkaviškis Lith. 45 M9
Vilkija Lith. 45 M9
Vil'kitskogo, Proliv strait Russia 65 K2
Vilkovo Ukr. see Vylkove
Villa Abecia Bol. 142 E8
Villa Ahumada Mex. 127 G7
Villa Ángela Arg. 144 D3
Villa Bella Bol. 142 E6
Villa Bens Morocco see Tarfaya
Villablino Spain 57 C2
Villacañas Spain 57 E4
Villach Austria 47 N7
Villacidro Sardinia Italy 58 C5
Villa Cisneros W. Sahara see Dakhla
Villa Constitución Mex. see Ciudad Constitución
Villa Dolores Arg. 144 C4
Villagarcía de Arosa Spain see Vilagarcía de Arousa
Villagrán Mex. 131 D7
Villaguay Arg. 144 E4
Villahermosa Mex. 136 F5
Villa Insurgentes Mex. 127 F8
Villajoyosa Spain see Villajoyosa-La Vila Joiosa
Villajoyosa-La Vila Joiosa Spain 57 F4
Villaldama Mex. 131 C7
Villa Mainero Mex. 131 D7
Villa María Arg. 144 D4
Villa Montes Bol. 142 F8
Villa Nora S. Africa 101 I2
Villanueva de la Serena Spain 57 D4
Villanueva de los Infantes Spain 57 E4
Villanueva-y-Geltrú Spain see Vilanova i la Geltrú
Villa Ocampo Arg. 144 E3
Villa Ocampo Mex. 131 B7
Villa Ojo de Agua Arg. 144 D3
Villaputzu Sardinia Italy 58 C5
Villa Regina Arg. 144 C5
Villarrica Para. 144 E3
Villarrica, Lago l. Chile 144 B5
Villarrica, Parque Nacional nat. park Chile 144 B5
Villarrobledo Spain 57 E4
Villas U.S.A. 135 H4
Villasalazar Zimbabwe see Sango
Villa San Giovanni Italy 58 F5
Villa Sanjurjo Morocco see Al Hoceima
Villa Unión Arg. 144 C3
Villa Unión Coahuila Mex. 131 C6
Villa Unión Durango Mex. 131 B8
Villa Unión Sinaloa Mex. 136 C4
Villa Valeria Arg. 144 D4
Villavicencio Col. 142 D3
Villazon Bol. 142 E8
Villefranche-sur-Saône France 56 G4
Ville-Marie Canada see Montréal
Villena Spain 57 F4
Villeneuve-sur-Lot France 56 E4
Villeneuve-sur-Yonne France 56 F2
Villers-Cotterêts France 52 D5
Villers-sur-Mer France 49 G9
Villerupt France 52 F5
Villeurbanne France 56 G4
Villiers S. Africa 101 I4
Villingen Germany 47 L6
Villuppuram India see Villupuram
Villupuram India 84 C4
Vilna Canada 121 I4
Vilna Lith. see Vilnius

▶Vilnius Lith. 45 N9
Capital of Lithuania.

Vil'nyans'k Ukr. 43 G7
Vilppula Fin. 44 N5
Vils r. Bayern Germany 53 L5
Vils r. Bayern Germany 53 N6
Vilvoorde Belgium 52 E4
Vilyeyka Belarus 45 O9
Vilyuy r. Russia 65 N3
Vilyuyskoye Vodokhranilishche resr Russia 65 M3
Vimmerby Sweden 45 I8
Vimy France 52 C4
Vina r. Cameroon 97 E4
Vina U.S.A. 128 B2
Viña del Mar Chile 144 B4
Vinalhaven Island U.S.A. 132 G2
Vinaròs Spain 57 G3
Vinaroz Spain see Vinaròs
Vincelotte, Lac l. Canada 123 G3
Vincennes U.S.A. 134 B4
Vincennes Bay Antarctica 152 F2
Vinchina Arg. 144 C3
Vindelälven r. Sweden 44 K5
Vindeln Sweden 44 K4
Vindhya Range hills India 82 C5
Vindobona Austria see Vienna
Vine Grove U.S.A. 134 C5
Vineland U.S.A. 135 H4
Vinh Vietnam 70 D3
Vinh Loc Vietnam 70 D2
Vinh Long Vietnam 71 D5
Vinh Thuc, Đao i. Vietnam 70 D2
Vinita U.S.A. 131 E4
Vinjhan India 82 B5
Vinland i. Canada see Newfoundland
Vinnitsa Ukr. see Vinnytsya
Vinnytsya Ukr. 43 F6
Vinogradov Ukr. see Vynohradiv

▶Vinson, Mount mt. Antarctica 152 L1
Highest mountain in Antarctica.

Vinstra Norway 45 F6
Vinton U.S.A. 130 E3
Vinukonda India 84 C2
Violeta Cuba see Primero de Enero
Vipperow Germany 53 M1
Viqueque East Timor 108 D2
Virac Phil. 69 G4
Viramgam India 82 C5
Virandozero Russia 42 H2
Viranşehir Turkey 91 E3
Virawah Pak. 89 H5
Virchow, Mount hill Australia 108 B5
Virdel India 82 C5
Virden Canada 121 K5
Virden U.S.A. 129 I5
Vire France 56 D2
Virei Angola 99 B5
Virgem da Lapa Brazil 145 C2
Virgilina U.S.A. 135 F5
Virgin r. U.S.A. 129 F3
Virginia Ireland 51 E4
Virginia S. Africa 101 H5
Virginia U.S.A. 130 F4
Virginia state U.S.A. 134 F5
Virginia Beach U.S.A. 135 H5
Virginia City MT U.S.A. 126 F3
Virginia City NV U.S.A. 128 D2
Virginia Falls Canada 120 E2

▶Virgin Islands (U.K.) terr. West Indies 137 L5
United Kingdom Overseas Territory.

▶Virgin Islands (U.S.A.) terr. West Indies 137 L5
United States Unincorporated Territory.

Virgin Mountains U.S.A. 129 F3
Virginópolis Brazil 145 C2
Virkkala Fin. 45 N6
Virôchey Cambodia 71 D4
Viroqua U.S.A. 130 F3
Virovitica Croatia 58 G2
Virrat Fin. 44 M5
Virton Belgium 52 F5
Virtsu Estonia 45 M7
Virudhunagar India 84 C4
Virudunagar India see Virudhunagar
Virunga, Parc National des nat. park Dem. Rep. Congo 98 C4
Vis i. Croatia 58 G3
Visaginas Lith. 45 O9
Visakhapatnam India see Vishakhapatnam
Visalia U.S.A. 128 D3
Visapur India 84 B2
Visayan Sea Phil. 69 G4
Visbek Germany 53 I2
Visby Sweden 45 K8
Viscount Melville Sound sea chan. Canada 119 G2
Visé Belgium 52 F4
Viseu Brazil 143 I4
Viseu Port. 57 C3
Vishakhapatnam India 84 D2
Vishera r. Russia 41 R4
Vishera r. Russia 42 L3
Vishwanath India 76 B3
Višķi Latvia 45 O8
Visnagar India 82 C5
Viso, Monte mt. Italy 58 B2
Visoko Bos. & Herz. 58 H3
Visp Switz. 56 H3
Visselhövede Germany 53 J2
Vista U.S.A. 128 E5
Vista Lake U.S.A. 128 D4
Vistonida, Limni lag. Greece 59 K4
Vistula r. Poland 47 Q3
Vitebsk Belarus see Vitsyebsk
Viterbo Italy 58 E3
Vitichi Bol. 142 E8
Vitigudino Spain 57 C3
Viti Levu i. Fiji 107 H3
Vitimskoye Ploskogor'ye plat. Russia 73 K2
Vitória Brazil 145 C3
Vitória da Conquista Brazil 145 C1
Vitoria-Gasteiz Spain 57 E2
Vitória Seamount sea feature S. Atlantic Ocean 148 F7
Vitré France 56 D2
Vitry-en-Artois France 52 C4
Vitry-le-François France 52 E6
Vitsyebsk Belarus 43 F5
Vittangi Sweden 44 L3
Vittel France 56 G2
Vittoria Sicily Italy 58 F6
Vittorio Veneto Italy 58 E2
Viveiro Spain 57 C2
Vivero Spain see Viveiro
Vivo S. Africa 101 I2
Vizagapatam India see Vishakhapatnam
Vizcaíno, Desierto de des. Mex. 127 E8
Vizcaíno, Sierra mts Mex. 127 E8
Vize Turkey 59 L4
Vize, Ostrov i. Russia 64 I2
Vizhas r. Russia 42 J2
Vizianagaram India 84 D2
Vizinga Russia 42 K3
Vlaardingen Neth. 52 E3
Vlădeasa, Vârful mt. Romania 59 J1
Vladikavkaz Russia 91 G2
Vladimir Primorskiy Kray Russia 74 D4
Vladimir Vladimirskaya Oblast' Russia 42 I4
Vladimiro-Aleksandrovskoye Russia 74 D4
Vladimir-Volynskiy Ukr. see Volodymyr-Volyns'kyy
Vladivostok Russia 74 C4
Vlakte S. Africa 101 I3
Vlasotince Serbia 59 J3
Vlas'yevo Russia 74 F1
Vlieland i. Neth. 52 E1
Vlissingen Neth. 52 D3
Vlora Albania see Vlorë
Vlorë Albania 59 H4
Vlotho Germany 53 I2
Vlotslavsk Poland see Włocławek
Vltava r. Czechia 47 O5
Vobkent Uzbek. 89 G1
Vöcklabruck Austria 47 N6
Vodlozero, Ozero l. Russia 42 H3
Voe U.K. 50 [inset]
Voerendaal Neth. 52 F4
Vogelkop pen. Indon. see Doberai, Jazirah
Vogelsberg hills Germany 53 I4
Voghera Italy 58 C2
Vohburg an der Donau Germany 53 L6
Vohémar Madag. see Iharaña
Vohenstrauß Germany 53 M5
Vohibinany Madag. see Ampasimanolotra
Vohimarina Madag. see Iharaña
Vohimena, Tanjona c. Madag. 99 E6
Vohipeno Madag. 99 E6
Vöhl Germany 53 I3
Võhma Estonia 45 N7
Voinjama Liberia 96 C4
Vojens Denmark 45 F9
Vojvodina prov. Serbia 59 H2
Vokhma Russia 42 J4
Voknavolok Russia 44 Q4
Vokre, Hosséré mt. Cameroon 96 E4
Vol' r. Russia 42 L3
Volcano Bay Japan see Uchiura-wan

▶Volcano Islands Japan 69 K2
Part of Japan.

Volda Norway 44 E5
Vol'dino Russia 42 L3
Volendam Neth. 52 F2
Volga Russia 42 H4

▶Volga r. Russia 43 J7
Longest river in Europe.

Volga Upland hills Russia see Privolzhskaya Vozvyshennost'
Volgodonsk Russia 43 I7
Volgograd Russia 43 J6
Volgogradskoye Vodokhranilishche resr Russia 43 J6
Völkermarkt Austria 47 O7
Volkhov Russia 42 G4
Volkhov r. Russia 42 G3
Völklingen Germany 52 G5
Volkovysk Belarus see Vawkavysk
Volksrust S. Africa 101 I4
Vol'no-Nadezhdinskoye Russia 74 C4
Volnovakha Ukr. 43 H7
Vol'nyansk Ukr. see Vil'nyans'k
Volochanka Russia 64 K2
Volochisk Ukr. see Volochys'k
Volochys'k Ukr. 43 E6
Volodars'ke Ukr. 43 H7
Volodarskoye Kazakh. see Saumalkol'
Volodymyr-Volyns'kyy Ukr. 43 E6
Vologda Russia 42 H4
Volokolamsk Russia 42 G4
Volokovaya Russia 42 K2

Volos Greece 59 J5
Volosovo Russia 45 P7
Volot Russia 42 F4
Volovo Russia 43 H5
Volozhin Belarus see Valozhyn
Volsinii Italy see Orvieto
Vol'sk Russia 43 J5

▶Volta, Lake resr Ghana 96 D4
4th largest lake in Africa.

Volta Blanche r. Burkina Faso/Ghana see White Volta
Voltaire, Cape Australia 108 D3
Volta Redonda Brazil 145 B3
Vol'tevo Russia 42 J2
Volturno r. Italy 58 E4
Volubilis tourist site Morocco 54 C5
Volvi, Limni l. Greece 59 J4
Volzhsk Russia 42 K5
Volzhskiy Samarskaya Oblast' Russia 43 K5
Volzhskiy Volgogradskaya Oblast' Russia 43 J6
Vondanka Russia 42 J4
Vontimitta India 84 C3
Vopnafjörður Iceland 44 [inset 1]
Vopnafjörður b. Iceland 44 [inset 1]
Vörå Fin. 44 M5
Voranava Belarus 45 N9
Voreies Sporades is Greece 59 J5
Voríai Sporádhes is Greece see Voreies Sporades
Voring Plateau sea feature N. Atlantic Ocean 148 I1
Vorjing mt. India 83 H3
Vorkuta Russia 64 H3
Vormsi i. Estonia 45 M7
Vorona r. Russia 43 I6
Voronezh Russia 43 H6
Voronezh r. Russia 43 H6
Voronov, Mys pt Russia 42 I2
Vorontsovo-Aleksandrovskoye Russia see Zelenokumsk
Voroshilov Russia see Ussuriysk
Voroshilovgrad Ukr. see Luhans'k
Voroshilovsk Russia see Stavropol'
Voroshilovsk Ukr. see Alchevs'k
Vorotynets Russia 42 J4
Vorozhba Ukr. 43 G6
Vorpommersche Boddenlandschaft, Nationalpark nat. park Germany 47 N3
Vorskla r. Russia 43 G6
Võrtsjärv l. Estonia 45 N7
Võru Estonia 45 O8
Vorukh Tajik. 89 H2
Vosburg S. Africa 100 F6
Vose' Tajik. 89 H2
Vosges mts France 56 H3
Voskresensk Russia 43 H5
Voskresenskoye Russia 42 H4
Voss Norway 45 E6
Vostochno-Sakhalinskiye Gory mts Russia 74 F2
Vostochno-Sibirskoye More sea Russia see East Siberian Sea
Vostochnyy Kirovskaya Oblast' Russia 42 L4
Vostochnyy Sakhalinskaya Oblast' Russia 74 F2
Vostochnyy Sayan mts Russia 72 G2

▶Vostok research station Antarctica 152 F1
Lowest recorded screen temperature in the world.

Vostok Primorskiy Kray Russia 74 D3
Vostok Sakhalinskaya Oblast' Russia see Neftegorsk (abandoned)
Vostok Island Kiribati 151 J6
Vostroye Russia 42 J3
Votkinsk Russia 41 Q4
Votkinskoye Vodokhranilishche resr Russia 41 R4
Votuporanga Brazil 145 A3
Vouziers France 52 E5
Voves France 56 E2
Voyageurs National Park U.S.A. 130 E1
Voynitsa Russia 44 Q4
Vöyri Fin. see Vörå
Voyvozh Russia 42 L3
Vozhayel' Russia 42 K3
Vozhe, Ozero l. Russia 42 H3
Vozhega Russia 42 I3
Vozhgaly Russia 42 K4
Voznesens'k Ukr. 43 F7
Vozonin Trough sea feature Arctic Ocean 153 F1
Vozrozhdenya Island i. Uzbek. 80 A3
Vozzhayevka Russia 74 C2
Vrangel' Russia 74 D4
Vrangelya, Mys pt Russia 74 E1
Vranje Serbia 59 I3
Vratnik pass Bulg. 59 L3
Vratsa Bulg. 59 J3
Vrbas Serbia 59 H2
Vrede S. Africa 101 I4
Vredefort S. Africa 101 H4
Vredenburg S. Africa 100 C7
Vredendal S. Africa 100 D6
Vresse-sur-Semois Belgium 52 E5
Vriddhachalam India 84 C4
Vries Neth. 52 G1
Vrigstad Sweden 45 I8
Vršac Serbia 59 I2
Vryburg S. Africa 100 G4
Vryheid S. Africa 101 J4
Vsevidof, Mount vol. U.S.A. 118 B4
Vsevolozhsk Russia 42 F3
Vu Ban Vietnam 70 D2
Vučitrn Kosovo see Vushtrri
Vukovar Croatia 59 H2
Vuktyl Russia 41 R3
Vukuzakhe S. Africa 101 I4
Vulcan Canada 120 H5
Vulcan Island P.N.G. see Manam Island
Vulcano, Isola i. Italy 58 F5
Vu Liêt Vietnam 70 D3
Vulkathunha-Gammon Ranges National Park Australia 111 B6
Vulture Mountains U.S.A. 129 G5
Vung Tau Vietnam 71 D5
Vuohijärvi Fin. 45 O6
Vuolijoki Fin. 44 O4
Vuollerim Sweden 44 L3
Vuostimo Fin. 44 O3
Vurnary Russia 42 J5
Vushtrri Kosovo 59 I3
Vvedenovka Russia 74 C2
Vyara India 82 C5
Vyarkhowye Belarus see Ruba
Vyatka Russia see Kirov
Vyatka r. Russia 42 K5
Vyatskiye Polyany Russia 42 K4
Vyazemskiy Russia 74 D3
Vyaz'ma Russia 43 G5
Vyazniki Russia 42 I4
Vyazovka Russia 43 J5
Vyborg Russia 45 P6
Vychegda r. Russia 42 J3
Vychegodskiy Russia 42 J3
Vyerkhnyadzvinsk Belarus 45 O9
Vyetryna Belarus 45 P9
Vygozero, Ozero l. Russia 42 G3
Vyksa Russia 43 I5
Vylkove Ukr. 59 M2
Vym' r. Russia 42 K3
Vynohradiv Ukr. 43 D6
Vypin Island India 84 C4
Vypolzovo Russia 42 G4
Vyritsa Russia 45 Q7
Vyrnwy, Lake U.K. 49 D6
Vyselki Russia 43 H7
Vysha Russia 43 I5
Vyshhorod Ukr. 43 F6
Vyshnevolotskaya Gryada ridge Russia 42 G4
Vyshniy-Volochek Russia 42 G4
Vyškov Czechia 47 P6
Vysokaya Gora Russia 42 K5
Vysokogorniy Russia 74 E2
Vystupovychi Ukr. 43 F6
Vytegra Russia 42 H3
Vyya r. Russia 42 J3
Vyžuona r. Lith. 45 N9

W

Wa Ghana 96 C3
Waal r. Neth. 52 E3
Waalwijk Neth. 52 F3
Waat South Sudan 86 D8
Wabag P.N.G. 69 K8
Wabakimi Lake Canada 122 C4
Wabasca r. Canada 120 H3
Wabasca-Desmarais Canada 120 H4
Wabash U.S.A. 134 C3
Wabash r. U.S.A. 134 A5
Wabasha U.S.A. 130 E2
Wabassi r. Canada 122 D4
Wabatongushi Lake Canada 122 D4
Wabigoon Lake Canada 121 M5
Wabowden Canada 121 L4
Wabrah well Saudi Arabia 88 B5
Wabu China 77 H1
Wabuk Point Canada 122 D3
Wabush Canada 123 I3
Waccasassa Bay U.S.A. 133 D6
Wächtersbach Germany 53 J4
Waco Canada 123 I4
Waco U.S.A. 131 D6
Waconda Lake U.S.A. 130 D4
Wadbilliga National Park Australia 112 D6
Waddān Libya 55 H6
Waddell Dam U.S.A. 129 G5
Waddeneilanden Neth. see West Frisian Islands
Waddenzee sea chan. Neth. 52 E2
Waddington, Mount Canada 120 E5
Waddinxveen Neth. 52 E2
Wadebridge U.K. 49 C8
Wadena Canada 121 K5
Wadena U.S.A. 130 E2
Wadern Germany 52 G5
Wadesville U.S.A. 134 B4
Wadeye Australia 108 E3
Wadgassen Germany 52 G5
Wadh Pak. 89 G5
Wadhwan India see Surendranagar
Wadi India 84 C2
Wādī as Sīr Jordan 85 B4
Wadi Halfa Sudan 86 D5
Wadi Howar National Park nat. park Sudan 98 C2
Wadi Rum Protected Area tourist site Jordan 85 B5
Wad Madani Sudan 86 D7
Wad Rawa Sudan 86 D6
Wadsworth U.S.A. 128 D2
Wafangdian China 73 M5
Wafra Kuwait see Al Wafrah
Wagenfeld Germany 53 I2
Wagenhoff Germany 53 K2
Wagga Wagga Australia 112 C5
Wagner U.S.A. 130 D3
Wagoner U.S.A. 131 E4
Wagon Mound U.S.A. 127 G5
Wah Pak. 89 I3
Wahai Indon. 69 H7
Wāḩāt Jālū Libya 97 F2
Wahemen, Lac l. Canada 123 H3
Wahiawā U.S.A. 127 [inset]
Wahlhausen Germany 53 J3
Wahpeton U.S.A. 130 D2
Wahran Alg. see Oran
Wah Wah Mountains U.S.A. 129 G2
Wai India 84 B2
Waialua U.S.A. 127 [inset]
Waiau N.Z. see Franz Josef Glacier
Waiau r. N.Z. 113 D6
Waiblingen Germany 53 J6
Waidhofen an der Ybbs Austria 47 O7
Waigeo i. Indon. 69 I7
Waiheke Island N.Z. 113 E3
Waikabubak Indon. 108 B2
Waikaia r. N.Z. 113 B7
Waikari N.Z. 113 D6
Waikerie Australia 111 B7
Waikouaiti N.Z. 113 C7
Wailuku U.S.A. 127 [inset]
Waimangaroa N.Z. 113 C5
Waimarama N.Z. 113 F4
Waimate N.Z. 113 C7
Waimea U.S.A. 127 [inset]
Wainganga r. India 84 C2
Waingapu Indon. 108 C2
Wainhouse Corner U.K. 49 C8
Waini Point Guyana 143 G2
Wainwright Canada 121 I4
Wainwright U.S.A. 118 C2
Waiouru N.Z. 113 E4
Waipahi N.Z. 113 B8
Waipaoa r. N.Z. 113 F4
Waipara N.Z. 113 D6
Waipawa N.Z. 113 F4
Waipukurau N.Z. 113 F4
Wairarapa, Lake N.Z. 113 E5
Wairau r. N.Z. 113 E5
Wairoa N.Z. 113 F4
Wairoa r. N.Z. 113 F4
Waitahanui N.Z. 113 F4
Waitahuna N.Z. 113 B7
Waitakaruru N.Z. 113 E3
Waitaki r. N.Z. 113 C7
Waitangi N.Z. 107 I6
Waite River Australia 108 F5
Waiuku N.Z. 113 E3
Waiwera South N.Z. 113 B8
Waiyang China 77 H3
Wajima Japan 75 E5
Wajir Kenya 98 E3
Waka Indon. 108 C2
Wakasa-wan b. Japan 75 D6
Wakatipu, Lake N.Z. 113 B7
Wakaw Canada 121 J4
Wakayama Japan 75 D6
Wake Atoll terr. N. Pacific Ocean see Wake Island
WaKeeney U.S.A. 130 D4
Wakefield N.Z. 113 D5
Wakefield U.K. 48 F5
Wakefield MI U.S.A. 130 F2
Wakefield RI U.S.A. 135 J3
Wakefield VA U.S.A. 135 G5

▶Wake Island terr. N. Pacific Ocean 150 H4
United States Unincorporated Territory.

Wakema Myanmar 70 A3
Wākhān reg. Afgh. 89 I2
Wakkanai Japan 74 F3
Wakkerstroom S. Africa 101 J4
Wakool Australia 112 B5
Wakool r. Australia 112 A5
Wakuach, Lac l. Canada 123 I3
Waku-Kungo Angola 99 B5
Wałbrzych Poland 47 P5
Walcha Australia 112 E3
Walcott U.S.A. 126 G4
Walcourt Belgium 52 E4
Wałcz Poland 47 P4
Waldburg Range mts Australia 109 B6
Walden U.S.A. 135 H3
Waldenbuch Germany 53 J6
Waldenburg Poland see Wałbrzych
Waldkraiburg Germany 47 N6
Waldo U.S.A. 134 D3
Waldoboro U.S.A. 135 K1
Waldorf U.S.A. 135 G4
Waldport U.S.A. 126 B3
Waldron U.S.A. 131 E5
Waldron, Cape Antarctica 152 F2
Walebing Australia 109 B7
Walêg China 76 D2
Wales admin. div. U.K. 49 D6
Walgaon India 82 D5
Walgett Australia 112 D3
Walgreen Coast Antarctica 152 K1
Walhalla MI U.S.A. 134 B2
Walhalla ND U.S.A. 130 D1
Walikale Dem. Rep. Congo 97 F5
Walingai P.N.G. 69 L8
Walker r. Australia 110 A2
Walker watercourse Australia 109 F6
Walker MI U.S.A. 134 C2
Walker MN U.S.A. 130 E2
Walker r. U.S.A. 128 D2
Walker Bay S. Africa 100 D8
Walker Creek r. Australia 110 C3
Walker Lake Canada 121 L4
Walker Lake U.S.A. 128 D2
Walker Pass U.S.A. 128 D4
Walkersville U.S.A. 135 G4
Walkerton Canada 134 E1
Walkerton U.S.A. 134 B3
Wall, Mount hill Australia 108 B5
Wallaby Island Australia 110 C2
Wallace ID U.S.A. 126 D3
Wallace NC U.S.A. 133 E5
Wallace VA U.S.A. 134 D5
Wallaceburg Canada 134 D2
Wallal Downs Australia 108 C4
Wallangarra Australia 112 E2
Wallaroo Australia 111 B7
Wallasey U.K. 48 D5
Walla Walla Australia 112 C5
Walla Walla U.S.A. 126 D3
Walldürn Germany 53 J5
Wallekraal S. Africa 100 C6
Wallendbeen Australia 112 D5
Wallingford U.K. 49 F7
Wallis, Îles is Wallis and Futuna 107 I3

▶Wallis and Futuna terr. S. Pacific Ocean 107 I3
French Overseas Collectivity.

Wallis et Futuna, Îles terr. S. Pacific Ocean see Wallis and Futuna
Wallis Islands Wallis and Futuna see Wallis, Îles
Wallis Lake inlet Australia 112 F4
Wall of Genghis Khan tourist site Asia 73 K3
Wallonia, Major Mining Sites of tourist site Belgium 52 E4
Wallops Island U.S.A. 135 H5
Wallowa Mountains U.S.A. 126 D3
Walls U.K. 50 [inset]
Walls of Jerusalem National Park Australia 111 [inset]
Wallumbilla Australia 111 E5
Walmsley Lake Canada 121 I2
Walney, Isle of i. U.K. 48 D4
Walnut Creek U.S.A. 128 B3
Walnut Grove U.S.A. 128 C2
Walnut Ridge U.S.A. 131 F4
Walong India 83 I3
Walpole U.S.A. 135 I2
Walsall U.K. 49 F6
Walsenburg U.S.A. 127 G5
Walsh U.S.A. 131 C4
Walsrode Germany 53 J2
Waltair India 84 D2
Walterboro U.S.A. 133 D5
Walters U.S.A. 131 D5
Walter's Range hills Australia 112 B2
Walthall U.S.A. 131 F5
Waltham U.S.A. 135 J2
Walton IN U.S.A. 134 B3
Walton KY U.S.A. 134 C4
Walton NY U.S.A. 135 H2
Walton WV U.S.A. 134 E4
Walvisbaai Namibia see Walvis Bay
Walvisbaai b. Namibia see Walvis Bay
Walvis Bay Namibia 100 B2
Walvis Bay b. Namibia 100 B2
Walvis Ridge sea feature S. Atlantic Ocean 148 H8
Wāmā Afgh. 89 H3
Wamba Équateur Dem. Rep. Congo 97 F5
Wamba Orientale Dem. Rep. Congo 98 C3
Wamba Nigeria 96 D4
Wampum U.S.A. 134 E3
Wampusirpi Hond. 137 H5
Wamsutter U.S.A. 126 G4
Wana Pak. 89 H3
Wanaaring Australia 112 B2
Wanaka N.Z. 113 B7
Wanaka, Lake N.Z. 113 B7
Wan'an China 77 G3
Wanapitei Lake Canada 122 E5
Wanbi Australia 111 C7
Wanbrow, Cape N.Z. 113 C7
Wanda Shan mts China 74 D3
Wandering River Canada 121 H4
Wandersleben Germany 53 K4
Wandlitz Germany 53 N2
Wando S. Korea 75 B6
Wandoan Australia 111 E5
Wanganui N.Z. 113 E4
Wanganui r. N.Z. 113 E4
Wangaratta Australia 112 C6
Wangcang China 76 E1
Wangda China see Zogang
Wangdain China 83 G3
Wangdue Phodrang Bhutan 83 G4
Wanggamet, Gunung mt. Indon. 108 C2
Wanggao China 77 F3
Wang Gaxun China 83 I1
Wangguan China 76 E1
Wangiwangi i. Indon. 69 G8
Wangkui China 74 B3
Wangmo China 76 E3
Wangqing China 74 C4
Wangwu Shan mts China 77 F1
Wangying China see Huaiyin
Wanham Canada 120 G4
Wan Hsa-la Myanmar 70 B2
Wanie-Rukula Dem. Rep. Congo 98 C3
Wankaner India 82 B5
Wankie Zimbabwe see Hwange
Wanlaweyn Somalia 98 E3
Wanna Germany 53 I1
Wanna Lakes salt flat Australia 109 E7
Wannian China 77 H2
Wanning China 77 F5
Wanroij Neth. 52 F3
Wanshan China 77 F3
Wanshan Qundao is China 77 G4
Wansheng China 76 E2
Wanshengchang China see Wansheng
Wantage U.K. 49 F7
Wanxian China see Wanzhou
Wanyuan China 77 F1
Wanzai China 77 G2
Wanze Belgium 52 F4
Wanzhou China 77 F2
Wapakoneta U.S.A. 134 C3
Wapawekka Lake Canada 121 J4
Wapello U.S.A. 130 F3
Wapikaimaski Lake Canada 122 C4
Wapikopa Lake Canada 122 C3
Wapiti r. Canada 120 G4
Wapusk National Park Canada 121 M3
Waqên China 76 D1
Waqf aş Şawwān, Jibāl hills Jordan 85 C4
War U.S.A. 134 E5
Warangal India 84 C2
Waranga Reservoir Australia 112 B6
Waratah Bay Australia 112 B7
Warbreccan Australia 110 C5
Warburg Germany 53 J3
Warburton Australia 109 D6
Warburton watercourse Australia 111 B5
Warburton Bay Canada 121 I2
Warche r. Belgium 52 F4
Ward, Mount N.Z. 113 B6
Warden S. Africa 101 I4
Wardenburg Germany 53 I1
Warder Eth. 98 E3
Wardha India 84 C1
Wardha r. India 84 C2
Ward Hill hill U.K. 50 F2
Ward Hunt, Cape P.N.G. 69 L8
Ware Canada 120 E3
Ware U.S.A. 135 I2
Wareham U.K. 49 E8
Waremme Belgium 52 F4
Waren (Müritz) Germany 53 M1
Warendorf Germany 53 H3
Warginburra Peninsula Australia 110 E4
Wargla Alg. see Ouargla
Warialda Australia 112 E2
Warin Chamrap Thai. 70 D4
Warkum Neth. see Workum
Warkworth U.K. 48 F3
Warli China see Walêg
Warloy-Baillon France 52 C4
Warman Canada 121 J4
Warmbad Namibia 100 D5
Warmbad S. Africa see Bela-Bela
Warmbaths S. Africa see Bela-Bela
Warminster U.K. 49 E7
Warminster U.S.A. 135 H3
Warmond Neth. 52 E2
Warm Springs NV U.S.A. 128 E2
Warm Springs VA U.S.A. 134 F4
Warmwaterberg mts S. Africa 100 E7
Warner Canada 121 H5
Warner Lakes U.S.A. 126 D4
Warner Mountains U.S.A. 126 C4
Warnes Bol. 142 F7
Warning, Mount Australia 112 F2
Waronda India 84 C2
Warora India 84 C1
Warra Australia 112 E1
Warragamba Reservoir Australia 112 E5
Warragul Australia 112 B7
Warrambool r. Australia 112 C3
Warrandirinna, Lake salt flat Australia 111 B5
Warrandyte Australia 112 B6
Warrap South Sudan 86 C8
Warrawagine Australia 108 C5
Warrego r. Australia 112 B3
Warrego Range hills Australia 110 D5
Warren Australia 112 C3
Warren AR U.S.A. 131 E5
Warren MI U.S.A. 134 D2
Warren MN U.S.A. 130 D1
Warren OH U.S.A. 134 E3
Warren PA U.S.A. 134 F3
Warren Hastings Island Palau see Merir
Warren Island U.S.A. 120 C4
Warrenpoint U.K. 51 F3
Warrensburg MO U.S.A. 130 E4
Warrensburg NY U.S.A. 135 I2
Warrenton S. Africa 100 G5
Warrenton GA U.S.A. 133 D5
Warrenton MO U.S.A. 130 F4
Warrenton VA U.S.A. 135 G4
Warri Nigeria 96 D4
Warriners Creek watercourse Australia 111 B6
Warrington N.Z. 113 C7
Warrington U.K. 48 E5
Warrington U.S.A. 133 C6
Warrnambool Australia 111 C8
Warroad U.S.A. 130 E1
Warrumbungle National Park Australia 112 D3
Warsaj 'Alāqahdārī Afgh. 89 H2

▶Warsaw Poland 47 R4
Capital of Poland.

Warsaw IN U.S.A. 134 C3
Warsaw KY U.S.A. 134 C4
Warsaw MO U.S.A. 130 E4
Warsaw NY U.S.A. 135 F2
Warsaw VA U.S.A. 135 G5
Warshiikh Somalia 98 E3
Warstein Germany 53 I3
Warszawa Poland see Warsaw
Warta r. Poland 47 O4
Wartburg, Schloss tourist site Germany 53 K3
Warwick Australia 112 F2
Warwick U.K. 49 F6
Warwick U.S.A. 135 J3
Warzhong China 76 D2
Wasaga Beach Canada 134 E1
Wasatch Range mts U.S.A. 126 F5
Wasbank S. Africa 101 J5
Wasco U.S.A. 128 D4
Washburn ND U.S.A. 130 C2
Washburn WI U.S.A. 130 F2
Wāshēr Afgh. 89 F3
Washim India 84 C1

▶Washington DC U.S.A. 135 G4
Capital of the United States of America.

Washington GA U.S.A. 133 D5
Washington IA U.S.A. 130 F3
Washington IN U.S.A. 134 B4
Washington MO U.S.A. 130 F4
Washington NC U.S.A. 132 E5
Washington NJ U.S.A. 135 H3
Washington PA U.S.A. 134 E3
Washington UT U.S.A. 129 G3
Washington state U.S.A. 126 C3
Washington, Cape Antarctica 152 H2
Washington, Mount U.S.A. 135 J1
Washington Court House U.S.A. 134 D4
Washington Island U.S.A. 132 C2
Washington Land reg. Greenland 119 L2
Washita r. U.S.A. 131 D5
Washpool National Park Australia 112 F2
Washtucna U.S.A. 126 D3
Washuk Pak. 89 G5
Wasi India 84 B2
Wasī' Saudi Arabia 88 B5
Wasī' well Saudi Arabia 88 C6
Waskaganish Canada 122 F4
Waskagheganish Canada see Waskaganish
Waskaiowaka Lake Canada 121 L3
Waskey, Mount U.S.A. 118 C4
Wassenaar Neth. 52 E2
Wasser Namibia 100 D4
Wasserkuppe hill Germany 53 J4
Wassertrüdingen Germany 53 K5
Wassuk Range mts U.S.A. 128 D2
Wasua P.N.G. 69 K8
Wasum P.N.G. 69 L8
Waswanipi r. Canada 122 F4
Waswanipi, Lac l. Canada 122 F4
Watam P.N.G. 69 K7
Watampone Indon. 69 G7
Watapi Lake Canada 121 I4
Watarrka National Park Australia 109 E6
Watenstadt-Salzgitter Germany see Salzgitter
Waterbury CT U.S.A. 135 I3
Waterbury VT U.S.A. 135 I1
Waterbury Lake Canada 121 J3
Water Cays i. Bahamas 133 E8
Waterdown Canada 134 F2
Wateree r. U.S.A. 133 D5
Waterfall U.S.A. 120 C4
Waterford Ireland 51 E5
Waterford PA U.S.A. 134 F3
Waterford WI U.S.A. 134 A2
Waterford Harbour Ireland 51 F5
Watergrasshill Ireland 51 D5
Waterhen Lake Canada 121 L4
Waterloo Australia 108 E4
Waterloo Belgium 52 E4
Waterloo Ont. Canada 134 E2
Waterloo Que. Canada 135 I1
Waterloo IA U.S.A. 130 E3
Waterloo IL U.S.A. 130 F4
Waterloo NY U.S.A. 135 G2
Waterlooville U.K. 49 F8
Waterton Lakes National Park Canada 120 H5
Watertown NY U.S.A. 135 H2
Watertown SD U.S.A. 130 D2
Watertown WI U.S.A. 130 F3
Water Valley U.S.A. 131 F5
Waterville ME U.S.A. 135 K1
Waterville WA U.S.A. 126 C3
Watford Canada 134 E2
Watford U.K. 49 G7
Watford City U.S.A. 130 C2
Wathaman r. Canada 121 K3
Wathaman Lake Canada 121 K3
Watheroo National Park Australia 109 A7
Wathlingen Germany 53 K2
Watino Canada 120 G4
Watīr, Wādī watercourse Egypt 85 B5
Watkins Glen U.S.A. 135 G2
Watling Island Bahamas see San Salvador
Watmuri Indon. 108 E1
Watonga U.S.A. 131 D5
Watrous Canada 121 J5
Watrous U.S.A. 127 G6
Watseka U.S.A. 134 B3
Watsi Kengo Dem. Rep. Congo 97 F5
Watson r. Australia 110 C2
Watson Canada 121 J4
Watson Lake Canada 120 D2
Watsontown U.S.A. 135 G3
Watsonville U.S.A. 128 C3
Watten U.K. 50 F2
Watterson Lake Canada 121 L2
Watton U.K. 49 H6
Watts Bar Lake resr U.S.A. 132 C5
Wattsburg U.S.A. 134 F2
Watubela, Kepulauan is Indon. 69 I7
Wau P.N.G. 69 L8
Wau South Sudan 86 C8
Waubay Lake U.S.A. 130 D2
Wauchope N.S.W. Australia 112 F3
Wauchope N.T. Australia 108 F5
Waukaringa (abandoned) Australia 111 B7
Waukarlycarly, Lake salt flat Australia 108 C5
Waukegan U.S.A. 134 B2
Waukesha U.S.A. 134 A2
Waupaca U.S.A. 130 F2
Waupun U.S.A. 130 F3
Waurika U.S.A. 131 D5
Wausau U.S.A. 130 F2
Wausaukee U.S.A. 132 C2
Wauseon U.S.A. 134 C3
Wautoma U.S.A. 130 F2
Wave Hill Australia 108 E4
Waveney r. U.K. 49 I6
Waverly IA U.S.A. 130 E3
Waverly NY U.S.A. 135 G2
Waverly OH U.S.A. 134 D4
Waverly TN U.S.A. 132 C4
Waverly VA U.S.A. 135 G5
Wavre Belgium 52 E4
Waw Myanmar 70 B3
Wawa Canada 122 D5
Wawalalindu Indon. 69 G7
Wāw al Kabīr Libya 97 E2
Wawasee, Lake U.S.A. 134 C3
Wawo Indon. 69 G7
Waxahachie U.S.A. 131 D5
Waxü China 76 D1
Waxxari China 80 G4
Way, Lake salt flat Australia 109 C6
Waycross U.S.A. 133 D6
Wayland KY U.S.A. 134 D5
Wayland MI U.S.A. 134 C2
Wayne NE U.S.A. 130 D3
Wayne WV U.S.A. 134 D4
Waynesboro GA U.S.A. 133 D5
Waynesboro MS U.S.A. 131 F6
Waynesboro TN U.S.A. 132 C5
Waynesboro VA U.S.A. 135 F4
Waynesburg U.S.A. 134 E4
Waynesville MO U.S.A. 130 E4
Waynesville NC U.S.A. 132 D5
Waynoka U.S.A. 131 D4
Waza, Parc National de nat. park Cameroon 97 E3
Wāzah Khwāh Afgh. see Mashōrêy
Wazirabad Pak. 89 I3
W du Niger, Parc National du nat. park Niger 96 D3
We, Pulau i. Indon. 71 A6
Weagamow Lake Canada 121 N4
Weam P.N.G. 69 K8
Wear r. U.K. 48 F4
Weare U.S.A. 135 J2
Weatherford U.S.A. 131 D5
Weaver Lake Canada 121 L4
Weaverville U.S.A. 126 C4
Webb, Mount hill Australia 108 E5
Webequie Canada 122 D3
Weber, Mount Canada 120 D4
Weber Basin sea feature Laut Banda 150 E6
Webster IN U.S.A. 134 C4
Webster MA U.S.A. 135 J2
Webster SD U.S.A. 130 D2
Webster City U.S.A. 130 E3
Webster Springs U.S.A. 134 E4
Wecho Lake Canada 120 H2
Wedau P.N.G. 110 E1
Weddell Abyssal Plain sea feature Southern Ocean 152 A2
Weddell Island Falkland Is 144 D8
Weddell Sea Antarctica 152 A2
Wedderburn Australia 112 A6

Weddin Mountains National Park Australia 112 D4
Wedel Germany 53 J1
Wedge Mountain Canada 120 F5
Wedowee U.S.A. 133 C5
Weedville U.S.A. 135 F3
Weenen S. Africa 101 J5
Weener Germany 53 H1
Weert Neth. 52 F3
Weethalle Australia 112 C4
Wee Waa Australia 112 D3
Wegberg Germany 52 G3
Węgorzewo Poland 47 R3
Weichang China 73 L4
Weida Germany 53 M4
Weidenberg Germany 53 L5
Weiden in der Oberpfalz Germany 53 M5
Weifang China 73 L5
Weihai China 73 M5
Wei He r. Henan China 77 G1
Wei He r. Shaanxi China 76 F1
Weilburg Germany 53 I4
Weilmoringle Australia 112 C2
Weimar Germany 53 L4
Weinan China 77 F1
Weinheim Germany 53 I5
Weining China 76 E3
Weinsberg Germany 53 J5
Weipa Australia 110 C2
Weiqu China see Chang'an
Weir r. Australia 112 D2
Weir River Canada 121 M3
Weirton U.S.A. 134 E3
Weiser U.S.A. 126 D3
Weishan China 76 D3
Weishan Hu l. China 77 H1
Weishi China 77 G1
Weiße Elster r. Germany 53 L3
Weißenburg in Bayern Germany 53 K5
Weißenfels Germany 53 L3
Weißkugel mt. Austria/Italy 47 M7
Weissrand Mountains Namibia 100 D3
Weiterstadt Germany 53 I5
Weitzel Lake Canada 121 J3
Weixi China 76 C3
Weixin China 76 E3
Weiya China 80 H3
Weiyuan Gansu China 76 E1
Weiyuan Sichuan China 76 E2
Weiyuan Yunnan China see Jinggu
Weiyuan Jiang r. China 76 D4
Weiz Austria 47 O7
Weizhou China see Wenchuan
Weizhou Dao i. China 77 F4
Wejherowo Poland 47 Q3
Wekilbazar Turkm. 89 F2
Wekusko Canada 121 L4
Wekusko Lake Canada 121 L4
Wekweètì Canada 120 H1
Welatam Myanmar 70 B1
Welbourn Hill Australia 109 F6
Welch U.S.A. 134 E5
Weld U.S.A. 135 J1
Weldiya Eth. 98 D2
Welford National Park Australia 110 C5
Welk'īt'ē Eth. 98 D3
Welkom S. Africa 101 H4
Welland Canada 134 F2
Welland r. U.K. 49 G6
Welland Canal Canada 134 F2
Wellesley Canada 134 E2
Wellesley Islands Australia 110 B3
Wellesley Lake Canada 120 B2
Wellfleet U.S.A. 135 J3
Wellin Belgium 52 F4
Wellingborough U.K. 49 G6
Wellington Australia 112 D4
Wellington Canada 135 G2

▶Wellington N.Z. 113 E5
Capital of New Zealand.

Wellington S. Africa 100 D7
Wellington England U.K. 49 D8
Wellington England U.K. 49 E6
Wellington CO U.S.A. 126 G4
Wellington IL U.S.A. 134 B3
Wellington KS U.S.A. 131 D4
Wellington NV U.S.A. 128 D2
Wellington OH U.S.A. 134 D3
Wellington TX U.S.A. 131 C5
Wellington UT U.S.A. 129 H2
Wellington, Isla i. Chile 144 B7
Wellington Range hills N.T. Australia 108 F3
Wellington Range hills W.A. Australia 109 C6
Wells Canada 120 F4
Wells U.K. 49 E7
Wells U.S.A. 126 E4
Wells, Lake salt flat Australia 109 C6
Wellsboro U.S.A. 135 G3
Wellsburg U.S.A. 134 E3
Wellsford N.Z. 113 E3
Wells-next-the-Sea U.K. 49 H6
Wellston U.S.A. 134 C1
Wellsville U.S.A. 135 G2
Wellton U.S.A. 129 F5
Wels Austria 47 O6
Welshpool U.K. 49 D6
Welsickendorf Germany 53 N3
Welwitschia Namibia see Khorixas
Welwyn Garden City U.K. 49 G7
Welzheim Germany 53 J6
Wem U.K. 49 E6
Wembesi S. Africa 101 I5
Wembley Canada 120 G4
Wemindji Canada 122 F3
Wenatchee U.S.A. 126 C3
Wenatchee Mountains U.S.A. 126 C3
Wenbu China see Cozhê
Wenceslau Braz Brazil 145 A3
Wenchang China see Zitong
Wencheng China 77 F5
Wenchow China see Wenzhou
Wenchuan China 76 D2
Wendelstein Germany 53 L5
Wenden Germany 53 H4
Wenden Latvia see Cēsis
Wenden U.S.A. 129 G5
Wendover U.S.A. 129 F1
Weng'an China 76 E3
Wengda China 76 D2
Wengshui China 76 C2
Wengyuan China 77 G3
Wenhua China see Weishan
Wenlan China see Mengzi
Wenling China 77 I2
Wenlock r. Australia 110 C2
Wenping China see Ludian
Wenquan Guizhou China 76 E2
Wenquan Henan China see Wenxian
Wenquan Hubei China see Yingshan

▶Wenquan Qinghai China 83 G2
Highest settlement in the world.

Wenquan Xinjiang China 80 F3
Wenshan China 76 E4
Wenshui China 76 E2
Wensum r. U.K. 49 I6
Wentorf bei Hamburg Germany 53 K1
Wentworth Australia 111 C7
Wenxi China 77 F1
Wenxian Gansu China 76 E1
Wenxian Henan China 77 G1
Wenxing China see Xiangyin
Wenzhou China 77 I3
Wenzlow Germany 53 M2
Wepener S. Africa 101 H5
Wer India 82 D4
Werben (Elbe) Germany 53 L2
Werda Botswana 100 F3
Werdau Germany 53 M4
Werder (Havel) Germany 53 M2
Werdohl Germany 53 H3
Werl Germany 53 H3
Wernberg-Köblitz Germany 53 M5
Werne Germany 53 H3
Wernecke Mountains Canada 120 B1
Wernigerode Germany 53 K3
Werra r. Germany 53 J3
Werris Creek Australia 112 E3
Wertheim Germany 53 J5
Wervik Belgium 52 D4
Wesel Germany 52 G3
Wesel-Datteln-Kanal canal Germany 52 G3
Wesenberg Germany 53 M1
Wesendorf Germany 53 K2
Weser r. Germany 53 I1
Weser sea chan. Germany 53 I1
Wesergebirge hills Germany 53 I2
Weslaco U.S.A. 131 D7
Weslemkoon Lake Canada 135 G1
Wesleyville Canada 123 L4
Wessel, Cape Australia 110 B1
Wessel Islands Australia 110 B1
Wesselsbron S. Africa 101 H4
Wesselton S. Africa 101 I4
Wessington Springs U.S.A. 130 D2
Westall, Point Australia 109 F8
West Allis U.S.A. 134 A2
West Antarctica reg. Antarctica 152 J1
West Australian Basin sea feature Indian Ocean 149 O7
West Bank disp. terr. Asia 85 B3
West Bay Canada 123 K3
West Bay inlet U.S.A. 133 C6
West Bend U.S.A. 134 A2
West Bengal state India 83 F5
West Branch U.S.A. 134 C1
West Bromwich U.K. 49 F6
Westbrook U.S.A. 135 J2
West Burke U.S.A. 135 J1
Westbury U.K. 49 E7
West Caicos i. Turks and Caicos Is 133 F8
West Cape Howe Australia 109 B8
West Caroline Basin sea feature N. Pacific Ocean 150 F5
West Chester U.S.A. 135 H4
Westcliffe U.S.A. 127 G5
West Coast National Park S. Africa 100 D7
West End Bahamas 133 E7
Westerburg Germany 53 H4
Westerholt Germany 53 H1
Westerland Germany 47 L3
Westerlo Belgium 52 E3
Westerly U.S.A. 135 J3
Western r. Canada 121 J1
Western Australia state Australia 109 C6
Western Cape prov. S. Africa 100 E7
Western Desert Egypt 90 C6
Western Dvina r. Europe see Zapadnaya Dvina
Western Ghats mts India 84 B3
Western Port b. Australia 112 B7
Western Sahara disp. terr. Africa 96 B2
Western Samoa country S. Pacific Ocean see Samoa
Western Sayan Mountains reg. Russia see Zapadnyy Sayan
Westerschelde est. Neth. 52 D3
Westerstede Germany 53 H1
Westerville U.S.A. 134 D3
Westerwald hills Germany 53 H4
West Falkland i. Falkland Is 144 D8
West Fargo U.S.A. 130 D2
West Fayu atoll Micronesia 69 L5
Westfield IN U.S.A. 134 B3
Westfield MA U.S.A. 135 I2
Westfield NY U.S.A. 134 F2
Westfield PA U.S.A. 135 G3
West Frisian Islands Neth. 52 E1
Westgat sea chan. Neth. 52 G1
Westgate Australia 112 C1
West Glacier U.S.A. 126 E2
West Grand Lake U.S.A. 132 H2
West Hartford U.S.A. 135 I3
Westhausen Germany 53 K6
West Haven U.S.A. 135 I3
Westhill U.K. 50 G3
Westhope U.S.A. 130 C1
West Ice Shelf Antarctica 152 E2
West Indies is Caribbean Sea 137 J4
West Island India 71 A4
Westkapelle Neth. 52 D3
West Kazakhstan Oblast admin. div. Kazakh. see Zapadnyy Kazakhstan
West Kelowna Canada 120 F5
West Kingston U.S.A. 135 J3
West Lafayette U.S.A. 134 B3
West Lamma Channel H.K. China 77 [inset]
Westland Australia 110 C4
Westland Tai Poutini National Park N.Z. 113 C6
Westleigh S. Africa 101 H4
Westleton U.K. 49 I6
West Liberty U.S.A. 134 D5
West Linton U.K. 50 F5
West Loch Roag b. U.K. 50 C2
Westlock Canada 120 H4
West Lorne Canada 134 E2
West Lunga National Park Zambia 99 C5
West MacDonnell National Park Australia 109 F5
West Malaysia pen. Malaysia see Peninsular Malaysia
Westmalle Belgium 52 E3
Westman Islands Iceland see Vestmannaeyjar
Westmar Australia 112 D1
West Mariana Basin sea feature N. Pacific Ocean 150 F4
West Memphis U.S.A. 131 F5
Westminster U.S.A. 135 G4
Westmoreland Australia 110 B3
Westmoreland U.S.A. 134 B5
Westmorland U.S.A. 129 F5
Weston OH U.S.A. 134 D3
Weston WV U.S.A. 134 E4
Weston-super-Mare U.K. 49 E7
West Palm Beach U.S.A. 133 D7
West Plains U.S.A. 131 F4
West Point pt Australia 111 [inset]
West Point CA U.S.A. 128 C2
West Point KY U.S.A. 134 C5
West Point MS U.S.A. 131 F5
West Point NE U.S.A. 130 D3
West Point VA U.S.A. 135 G5
West Point Lake resr U.S.A. 133 C5
Westport Canada 135 G1
Westport Ireland 51 C4
Westport N.Z. 113 C5
Westport CA U.S.A. 128 B2
Westport KY U.S.A. 134 C4
Westport NY U.S.A. 135 I1
Westray Canada 121 K4
Westray i. U.K. 50 F1
Westray Firth sea chan. U.K. 50 F1
Westree Canada 122 E5
West Rutland U.S.A. 135 I2
West Salem U.S.A. 134 D3
West Siberian Plain Russia 64 J3
West-Skylge Neth. see West-Terschelling
West Stewartstown U.S.A. 135 J1
West-Terschelling Neth. 52 F1
West Topsham U.S.A. 135 I1
West Union IA U.S.A. 130 F3
West Union IL U.S.A. 134 B4
West Union OH U.S.A. 134 D4
West Union WV U.S.A. 134 E4
West Valley City U.S.A. 129 H1
Westville U.S.A. 134 B3
West Virginia state U.S.A. 134 E4
Westwood U.S.A. 128 C1
West Wyalong Australia 112 C4
West York U.S.A. 135 G4
Westzaan Neth. 52 E2
Wetar i. Indon. 108 D1
Wetar, Selat sea chan. Indon. 108 D2
Wetaskiwin Canada 120 H4
Wete Tanz. 99 D4
Wetter r. Germany 53 I4
Wettin Germany 53 L3
Wetumpka U.S.A. 133 C5
Wetwun Myanmar 70 B2
Wetzlar Germany 53 I4
Wewahitchka U.S.A. 133 C6
Wewak P.N.G. 69 K7
Wewoka U.S.A. 131 D5
Wexford Ireland 51 F5
Wexford Harbour b. Ireland 51 F5
Weyakwin Canada 121 J4
Weybridge U.K. 49 G7
Weyburn Canada 121 K5
Weyhe Germany 53 I2
Weymouth U.K. 49 E8
Weymouth U.S.A. 135 J2
Wezep Neth. 52 G2
Whakaari i. N.Z. 113 F3
Whakatane N.Z. 113 F3
Whalan Creek r. Australia 112 D2
Whale r. Canada see Baleine, Rivière à la
Whalsay i. U.K. 50 [inset]
Whampoa China see Huangpu
Whangamata N.Z. 113 E3
Whanganui National Park N.Z. 113 E4
Whangarei N.Z. 113 E2
Whapmagoostui Canada 122 F3
Wharfe r. U.K. 48 F5
Wharfedale valley U.K. 48 F4
Wharton U.S.A. 131 D6
Wharton Lake Canada 121 L1
Whatì Canada 120 G2
Wheatland IN U.S.A. 134 B4
Wheatland WY U.S.A. 126 G4
Wheaton IL U.S.A. 134 A3
Wheaton MD U.S.A. 135 G4
Wheaton MN U.S.A. 130 D2
Wheeler U.S.A. 131 C5
Wheeler Lake Canada 120 H2
Wheeler Lake resr U.S.A. 133 C5
Wheeler Peak NM U.S.A. 127 G5
Wheeler Peak NV U.S.A. 129 F2
Wheelersburg U.S.A. 134 D4
Wheeling U.S.A. 134 E3
Whernside hill U.K. 48 E4
Whinham, Mount Australia 109 E6
Whiskey Jack Lake Canada 121 K3
Whitburn U.K. 50 F5
Whitby Canada 135 F2
Whitby U.K. 48 G4
Whitchurch U.K. 49 E6
Whitchurch-Stouffville Canada 134 F2
White r. Canada 122 D4
White r. Canada/U.S.A. 120 B2
White r. AR U.S.A. 131 F5
White r. CO U.S.A. 129 I1
White r. IN U.S.A. 134 B4
White r. MI U.S.A. 134 B2
White r. NV U.S.A. 129 F3
White r. SD U.S.A. 130 D3
White r. VT U.S.A. 135 I2
White watercourse U.S.A. 129 H5
White, Lake salt flat Australia 108 E5
White Bay Canada 123 K4
White Butte mt. U.S.A. 130 C2
White Canyon U.S.A. 129 H3
White Cloud U.S.A. 134 C2
Whitecourt Canada 120 H4
Whiteface Mountain U.S.A. 135 I1
Whitefield U.S.A. 135 J1
Whitefish r. Canada 120 E1
Whitefish U.S.A. 126 E2
Whitefish Bay U.S.A. 134 B1
Whitefish Lake Canada 121 J2
Whitefish Point U.S.A. 132 C2
Whitehall U.K. 50 G1
Whitehall NY U.S.A. 135 I2
Whitehall WI U.S.A. 130 F2
Whitehaven U.K. 48 D4
Whitehead U.K. 51 G3
White Hill hill Canada 123 J5
Whitehill U.K. 49 G7

▶Whitehorse Canada 120 C2
Capital of Yukon.

Whitehorse U.S.A. 129 J4
White Horse, Vale of valley U.K. 49 F7
White Horse Pass U.S.A. 129 F1
White House U.S.A. 134 B5
White Island Antarctica 152 D2
White Island N.Z. see Whakaari
White Lake Ont. Canada 122 D4
White Lake Ont. Canada 135 G1
White Lake LA U.S.A. 131 E6
White Lake MI U.S.A. 134 B2
Whitemark Australia 111 [inset]
White Mountain Peak U.S.A. 128 D3
White Mountains U.S.A. 135 J1
White Mountains National Park Australia 110 D4
Whitemouth Lake Canada 121 M5
Whitemud r. Canada 120 G3
White Nile r. Africa 86 D6
also known as Bahr el Abiad or Bahr el Jebel
White Nossob watercourse Namibia 100 D2
White Oak U.S.A. 134 D5
White Otter Lake Canada 121 N5
White Pass Canada/U.S.A. 120 C3
White Pine Range mts U.S.A. 129 F2
White Plains U.S.A. 135 I3
White River Canada 122 D4
Whiteriver U.S.A. 129 I5
White River U.S.A. 130 C3
White River Valley U.S.A. 129 F2
White Rock Peak U.S.A. 129 F2
White Russia country Europe see Belarus
Whitesail Lake Canada 120 E4
White Salmon U.S.A. 126 C3
Whitesand r. Canada 120 H2
White Sands National Monument nat. park U.S.A. 127 G6
Whitesburg U.S.A. 134 D5
White Sea Russia 42 H2
White Stone U.S.A. 135 G5
White Sulphur Springs MT U.S.A. 126 F3
White Sulphur Springs WV U.S.A. 134 E5
Whitesville U.S.A. 134 E5
Whiteville U.S.A. 133 E5
White Volta r. Burkina Faso/Ghana 96 C4
also known as Nakambé or Nakanbe or Volta Blanche
Whitewater U.S.A. 129 I2
Whitewater Baldy mt. U.S.A. 129 I5
Whitewater Lake Canada 122 C4
Whitewood Australia 110 C4
Whitewood Canada 121 K5
Whitfield U.K. 49 I7
Whithorn U.K. 50 E6
Whitianga N.Z. 113 E3
Whitland U.K. 49 C7
Whitley Bay U.K. 48 F3
Whitmore Mountains Antarctica 152 K1
Whitney Canada 135 F1
Whitney, Mount U.S.A. 128 D3
Whitney Point U.S.A. 135 H2
Whitstable U.K. 49 I7
Whitsunday Group is Australia 110 E4
Whitsunday Island National Park Australia 110 E4
Whitsun Island Vanuatu see Pentecost Island
Whittemore U.S.A. 134 D1
Whittlesea Australia 112 B6
Whittlesey U.K. 49 G6
Whitton Australia 112 C5
Wholdaia Lake Canada 121 J2
Why U.S.A. 129 G5
Whyalla Australia 111 B7
Wiang Sa Thai. 70 C3
Wiarton Canada 134 E1
Wibaux U.S.A. 126 G3
Wichelen Belgium 52 D3
Wichita U.S.A. 130 D4
Wichita r. U.S.A. 131 D5
Wichita Falls U.S.A. 131 D5
Wichita Mountains U.S.A. 131 D5
Wick U.K. 50 F2
Wick r. U.K. 50 F2
Wickenburg U.S.A. 129 G5
Wickes U.S.A. 131 E5
Wickford U.K. 49 H7
Wickham r. Australia 108 E4
Wickham, Cape Australia 111 [inset]
Wickham, Mount hill Australia 108 E4
Wickliffe U.S.A. 131 F4
Wicklow Ireland 51 F5
Wicklow Head hd Ireland 51 G5
Wicklow Mountains Ireland 51 F5
Wicklow Mountains National Park Ireland 51 F4
Widerøe, Mount Antarctica 152 C2
Widerøefjellet mt. Antarctica see Widerøe, Mount
Widgeegoara watercourse Australia 112 B1
Widgiemooltha (abandoned) Australia 109 C7
Widnes U.K. 48 E5
Wi-do i. S. Korea 75 B6
Wied r. Germany 53 H4
Wiehengebirge hills Germany 53 I2
Wiehl Germany 53 H4
Wielkopolskie, Pojezierze reg. Poland 47 O4
Wielkopolski Park Narodowy nat. park Poland 47 P4
Wieluń Poland 47 Q5
Wien Austria see Vienna
Wiener Neustadt Austria 47 P7
Wierden Neth. 52 G2
Wieren Germany 53 K2
Wieringerwerf Neth. 52 F2
Wiesbaden Germany 53 I4
Wiesenfelden Germany 53 M5
Wiesentheid Germany 53 K5
Wiesloch Germany 53 I5
Wiesmoor Germany 53 H1
Wietze Germany 53 J2
Wietzendorf Germany 53 J2
Wieżyca hill Poland 47 Q3
Wigan U.K. 48 E5
Wiggins U.S.A. 131 F6
Wight, Isle of i. U.K. 49 F8
Wigierski Park Narodowy nat. park Poland 45 M9
Wignes Lake Canada 121 J2
Wigston U.K. 49 F6
Wigton U.K. 48 D4
Wigtown U.K. 50 E6
Wigtown Bay U.K. 50 E6
Wijchen Neth. 52 F3
Wijhe Neth. 52 G2
Wilberforce, Cape Australia 110 B1
Wilbur U.S.A. 126 D3
Wilburton U.S.A. 131 E5
Wilcannia Australia 112 A3
Wilcox U.S.A. 135 F3
Wilczek Land i. Russia see Vil'cheka, Zemlya
Wildberg Germany 53 M2
Wildcat Peak U.S.A. 128 E2
Wild Coast S. Africa 101 I6
Wildeshausen Germany 53 I2
Wild Horse Hill mt. U.S.A. 130 C3
Wildspitze mt. Austria 47 M7
Wildwood FL U.S.A. 133 D6
Wildwood NJ U.S.A. 135 H4
Wilge r. Free State S. Africa 101 I4
Wilge r. Gauteng/Mpumalanga S. Africa 101 I3
Wilgena Australia 109 F7

▶Wilhelm, Mount P.N.G. 69 L8
5th highest mountain in Oceania.

Wilhelm II Land reg. Antarctica see Kaiser Wilhelm II Land
Wilhelmina Gebergte mts Suriname 143 G3
Wilhelmina Kanaal canal Neth. 52 F3
Wilhelmshaven Germany 53 I1
Wilhelmshöhe, Bergpark tourist site Germany 53 J3
Wilhelmstal Namibia 100 C1
Wilkes-Barre U.S.A. 135 H3
Wilkesboro U.S.A. 132 D4
Wilkes Coast Antarctica 152 G2
Wilkes Land reg. Antarctica 152 G2
Wilkie Canada 121 I4
Wilkins Coast Antarctica 152 L2
Wilkins Ice Shelf Antarctica 152 L2
Wilkinson Lakes salt flat Australia 109 F7
Will, Mount Canada 120 D3
Willand U.K. 49 D8
Willandra Billabong watercourse Australia 112 B4
Willandra National Park Australia 112 B4
Willapa Bay U.S.A. 126 B3
Willard Mex. 127 F7
Willard NM U.S.A. 127 G6
Willard OH U.S.A. 134 D3
Willcox U.S.A. 129 I5
Willcox Playa salt flat U.S.A. 129 I5
Willebadessen Germany 53 J3
Willebroek Belgium 52 E3
Willemstad Curaçao 137 K6
Willeroo Australia 108 E3
Willette U.S.A. 134 C5
William, Mount Australia 111 C8
William Creek Australia 111 B6
William Lake Canada 121 L4
Williams AZ U.S.A. 129 G4
Williams CA U.S.A. 128 B2
Williamsburg KY U.S.A. 134 C5
Williamsburg OH U.S.A. 134 C4
Williamsburg VA U.S.A. 135 G5
Williams Lake Canada 120 F4
William Smith, Cap c. Canada 123 I1
Williamson NY U.S.A. 135 G2
Williamson WV U.S.A. 134 D5
Williamsport IN U.S.A. 134 B3
Williamsport PA U.S.A. 135 G3
Williamston U.S.A. 132 E5
Williamstown KY U.S.A. 134 C4
Williamstown NJ U.S.A. 135 H4
Willimantic U.S.A. 135 I3
Willis Group atolls Australia 110 E3
Williston S. Africa 100 E6
Williston ND U.S.A. 130 C1
Williston SC U.S.A. 133 D5
Williston Lake Canada 120 F4
Williton U.K. 49 D7
Willits U.S.A. 128 B2
Willmar U.S.A. 130 E2
Willoughby, Lake U.S.A. 135 I1
Willow Beach U.S.A. 129 F4
Willow Bunch Canada 121 J5
Willow Hill U.S.A. 135 G3
Willow Lake Canada 120 G2
Willowlake r. Canada 120 F2
Willowmore S. Africa 100 F7
Willowra Australia 108 F5
Willows U.S.A. 128 B2
Willow Springs U.S.A. 131 F4
Willowvale S. Africa 101 I7
Wills, Lake salt flat Australia 108 E5
Wilma U.S.A. 133 C6
Wilmington DE U.S.A. 135 H4
Wilmington NC U.S.A. 133 E5
Wilmington OH U.S.A. 134 D4
Wilmore U.S.A. 134 C5
Wilmslow U.K. 48 E5
Wilno Lith. see Vilnius
Wilnsdorf Germany 53 I4
Wilpattu National Park Sri Lanka 84 D4
Wilseder Berg hill Germany 53 J1
Wilson watercourse Australia 111 C5
Wilson atoll Micronesia see Ifalik
Wilson KS U.S.A. 130 D4
Wilson NC U.S.A. 132 E5
Wilson NY U.S.A. 135 F2
Wilson, Mount CO U.S.A. 129 J3
Wilson, Mount NV U.S.A. 129 F2
Wilson, Mount OR U.S.A. 126 C3
Wilsonia U.S.A. 128 D3
Wilson's Promontory pen. Australia 112 C7
Wilson's Promontory National Park Australia 112 C7
Wilsum Germany 52 G2
Wilton r. Australia 108 F3
Wilton U.S.A. 135 J1
Wiltz Lux. 52 F5
Wiluna Australia 109 C6
Wimereux France 52 B4
Wina r. Cameroon see Vina
Winamac U.S.A. 134 B3
Winbin watercourse Australia 111 D5
Winburg S. Africa 101 H5
Wincanton U.K. 49 E7
Winchester Canada 135 H1
Winchester U.K. 49 F7
Winchester IN U.S.A. 134 C3
Winchester KY U.S.A. 134 C5
Winchester NH U.S.A. 135 I2
Winchester TN U.S.A. 133 C5
Winchester VA U.S.A. 135 F4
Wind r. Canada 120 C1
Wind r. U.S.A. 126 F4
Windau Latvia see Ventspils
Windber U.S.A. 135 F3
Wind Cave National Park U.S.A. 130 C3
Windermere U.K. 48 E4
Windermere l. U.K. 48 E4
Windham U.S.A. 120 C3

▶Windhoek Namibia 100 C2
Capital of Namibia.

Windigo Lake Canada 121 N4
Windlestraw Law hill U.K. 50 G5
Wind Mountain U.S.A. 127 G6
Windom U.S.A. 130 E3
Windom Peak U.S.A. 129 J3
Windorah Australia 110 C5
Window Rock U.S.A. 129 I4
Wind Point U.S.A. 134 B2
Wind River Range mts U.S.A. 126 F4
Windrush r. U.K. 49 F7
Windsbach Germany 53 K5
Windsor Australia 112 E4
Windsor N.S. Canada 123 I5
Windsor Ont. Canada 134 D2
Windsor U.K. 49 G7
Windsor NC U.S.A. 132 E4
Windsor NY U.S.A. 135 H2
Windsor VA U.S.A. 135 G5
Windsor VT U.S.A. 135 I2
Windsor Locks U.S.A. 135 I3
Windward Islands Caribbean Sea 137 L5
Windward Passage Cuba/Haiti 137 J5
Windy U.S.A. 118 D3
Winefred Lake Canada 121 I4
Winfield KS U.S.A. 131 D4
Winfield WV U.S.A. 134 E4
Wingate U.K. 48 F4
Wingen Australia 112 E3
Wingene Belgium 52 D3
Wingen-sur-Moder France 53 H6
Wingham Australia 112 F3
Wingham Canada 134 E2
Winisk r. Canada 122 D3
Winisk (abandoned) Canada 122 D3
Winisk Lake Canada 122 D3
Winkana Myanmar 70 B4
Winkelman U.S.A. 129 H5
Winkler Canada 121 L5
Winlock U.S.A. 126 C3
Winneba Ghana 96 C4
Winnebago, Lake U.S.A. 134 A1
Winnecke Creek watercourse Australia 108 E4
Winnemucca U.S.A. 128 E1
Winnemucca Lake U.S.A. 128 D1
Winner U.S.A. 130 C3
Winnett U.S.A. 126 F3
Winnfield U.S.A. 131 E6
Winnibigoshish, Lake U.S.A. 130 E2
Winnie U.S.A. 131 E6
Winning Australia 109 A5

▶Winnipeg Canada 121 L5
Capital of Manitoba.

Winnipeg r. Canada 121 L5
Winnipeg, Lake Canada 121 L5
Winnipegosis Canada 121 L5
Winnipegosis, Lake Canada 121 K4
Winnipesaukee, Lake U.S.A. 135 J2
Winona AZ U.S.A. 129 H4
Winona MN U.S.A. 130 F2
Winona MO U.S.A. 131 F4
Winona MS U.S.A. 131 F5
Winschoten Neth. 52 H1
Winsen (Aller) Germany 53 J2
Winsen (Luhe) Germany 53 K1
Winsford U.K. 48 E5
Winslow AZ U.S.A. 129 H4
Winslow ME U.S.A. 135 K1
Winsop, Tanjung pt Indon. 69 I7
Winsted U.S.A. 135 I3
Winston-Salem U.S.A. 132 D4
Winterberg Germany 53 I3
Winter Haven U.S.A. 133 D6
Winters CA U.S.A. 128 C2
Winters TX U.S.A. 131 D6
Wintersville U.S.A. 134 E3
Winterswijk Neth. 52 G3
Winterthur Switz. 56 I3
Winterton S. Africa 101 I5
Winthrop U.S.A. 135 K1
Winton Australia 110 C4
Winton N.Z. 113 B8
Winton U.S.A. 132 E4

Winwick U.K. 49 G6
Wirral pen. U.K. 48 D5
Wirrulla Australia 111 A7
Wisbech U.K. 49 H6
Wiscasset U.S.A. 135 K1
Wisconsin r. U.S.A. 130 F3
Wisconsin state U.S.A. 134 A1
Wisconsin Rapids U.S.A. 130 F2
Wise U.S.A. 134 D5
Wiseman U.S.A. 118 C3
Wishaw U.K. 50 F5
Wishek U.S.A. 130 D2
Wisil Dabarow Somalia 98 E3
Wisła r. Poland see Vistula
Wismar Germany 47 M4
Wistaria Canada 120 E4
Witbank S. Africa see eMalahleni
Witbooisvlei Namibia 100 D3
Witham U.K. 49 H7
Witham r. U.K. 49 H6
Witherbee U.S.A. 135 I1
Withernsea U.K. 48 H5
Witjira National Park Australia 111 A5
Witmarsum Neth. 52 F1
Witney U.K. 49 F7
Witrivier S. Africa 101 J3
Witry-lès-Reims France 52 E5
Witteberg mts S. Africa 101 H6
Wittenberg Germany see Wittenberg, Lutherstadt
Wittenberg, Lutherstadt Germany 53 M3
Wittenberge Germany 53 L2
Wittenburg Germany 53 L1
Wittingen Germany 53 K2
Wittlich Germany 52 G5
Wittmund Germany 53 H1
Wittstock/Dosse Germany 53 M1
Witu Islands P.N.G. 69 L7
Witvlei Namibia 100 D2
Witzenhausen Germany 53 J3
Wivenhoe, Lake Australia 112 F1
Władysławowo Poland 47 Q3
Włocławek Poland 47 Q4
Wobkent Uzbek. see Vobkent
Wodonga Australia 112 C6
Wœrth France 53 H6
Woëvre, Plaine de la plain France 52 F5
Wohlthat Mountains Antarctica 152 C2
Woippy France 52 G5
Wōjjā atoll Marshall Is see Wotje
Wokam i. Indon. 69 I8
Woken He r. China 74 C3
Wokha India 83 H4
Woking U.K. 49 G7
Wokingham watercourse Australia 110 C4
Wokingham U.K. 49 G7
Woko National Park Australia 112 E3
Wolcott IN U.S.A. 134 B3
Wolcott NY U.S.A. 135 G2
Woldegk Germany 53 N1
Wolea atoll Micronesia see Woleai
Woleai atoll Micronesia 69 K5
Wolf r. Canada 120 C2
Wolf r. TN U.S.A. 131 F5
Wolf r. WI U.S.A. 130 F2
Wolf Creek MT U.S.A. 126 E3
Wolf Creek OR U.S.A. 126 C4
Wolf Creek Pass U.S.A. 127 G5
Wolfen Germany 53 M3
Wolfenbüttel Germany 53 K2
Wolfhagen Germany 53 J3
Wolf Lake Canada 120 D2
Wolf Point U.S.A. 126 G2
Wolfsberg Austria 47 O7
Wolfsburg Germany 53 K2
Wolfstein Germany 53 H5
Wolfville Canada 123 I5
Wolgast Germany 47 N3
Wolin Poland 47 O4
Wollaston Lake Canada 121 K3
Wollaston Lake l. Canada 121 K3
Wollaston Peninsula Canada 118 G3
Wollemi National Park Australia 112 E4
Wollongong Australia 112 E5
Wolmaransstad S. Africa 101 G4
Wolmirstedt Germany 53 L2
Wolong Natural Reserve nature res. China 76 D2
Wolseley Australia 111 C8
Wolseley S. Africa 100 D7
Wolsey U.S.A. 130 D2
Wolsingham U.K. 48 F4
Wolvega Neth. 52 G2
Wolvegea Neth. see Wolvega
Wolverhampton U.K. 49 E6
Wolverine U.S.A. 134 C1
Wommelgem Belgium 52 E3
Womrather Höhe hill Germany 53 H5
Wonarah Australia 110 B3
Wondai Australia 111 E5
Wongalarroo Lake salt l. Australia 112 B3
Wongarbon Australia 112 D4
Wong Chuk Hang H.K. China 77 [inset]
Wong Leng hill H.K. China 77 [inset]
Wonju S. Korea 75 B5
Wonowon Canada 120 F3
Wŏnsan N. Korea 75 B5
Wonthaggi Australia 112 B7
Wonyulgunna, Mount hill Australia 109 B6
Woocalla Australia 111 B6
Wood, Mount Canada 120 A2
Woodbine GA U.S.A. 133 D6
Woodbine NJ U.S.A. 135 H4
Woodbridge U.K. 49 I6
Woodbridge U.S.A. 135 G4
Wood Buffalo National Park Canada 120 H3
Woodburn U.S.A. 126 C3
Woodbury NJ U.S.A. 135 H4
Woodbury TN U.S.A. 131 G5
Wooded Bluff hd Australia 112 F2
Wood Lake Canada 121 K4
Woodlake U.S.A. 128 D3
Woodland CA U.S.A. 128 C2
Woodland PA U.S.A. 135 F3
Woodland WA U.S.A. 126 C3
Woodlands Sing. 71 [inset]
Woodlark Island P.N.G. 106 F2
Woodridge Canada 121 L5
Woodroffe watercourse Australia 110 B4
Woodroffe, Mount Australia 109 E6
Woodruff UT U.S.A. 126 F4
Woodruff WI U.S.A. 130 F2
Woods, Lake salt flat Australia 108 F4
Woods, Lake of the Canada/U.S.A. 125 I2
Woodsfield U.S.A. 134 E4
Woodside Australia 112 C7
Woodstock N.B. Canada 123 I5
Woodstock Ont. Canada 134 E2
Woodstock IL U.S.A. 130 F3
Woodstock VA U.S.A. 135 F4
Woodstock VT U.S.A. 135 I2
Woodsville U.S.A. 135 I1
Woodville Canada 135 F1
Woodville MS U.S.A. 131 F6
Woodville OH U.S.A. 134 D3
Woodville TX U.S.A. 131 E6
Woodward U.S.A. 131 D4
Woody U.S.A. 128 D4
Wooler U.K. 48 E3
Woolgoolga Australia 112 F3
Wooli Australia 112 F2
Woollard, Mount Antarctica 152 K1
Woollett, Lac l. Canada 122 G4
Woolyeenyer Hill hill Australia 109 C8
Woomera Australia 111 B6
Woomera Prohibited Area Australia 109 F7
Woonsocket RI U.S.A. 135 J2
Woonsocket SD U.S.A. 130 D2
Woorabinda Australia 110 E5
Wooramel r. Australia 109 A6
Wooster U.S.A. 134 E3
Wootton Bassett U.K. see Royal Wootton Bassett
Worbis Germany 53 K3
Worbody Point Australia 110 C2
Worcester S. Africa 100 D7
Worcester U.K. 49 E6
Worcester MA U.S.A. 135 J2
Worcester NY U.S.A. 135 H2
Wörgl Austria 47 N7
Workai i. Indon. 69 I8
Workington U.K. 48 D4
Worksop U.K. 48 F5
Workum Neth. 52 F2
Worland U.S.A. 126 G3
Wörlitz Germany 53 M3
Wormerveer Neth. 52 E2
Worms Germany 53 I5
Worms Head hd U.K. 49 C7
Wortel Namibia 100 C2
Wörth am Rhein Germany 53 I5
Worthing U.K. 49 G8
Worthington IN U.S.A. 134 B4
Worthington MN U.S.A. 130 E3
Wotje atoll Marshall Is 150 H5
Wotu Indon. 69 G7
Woudrichem Neth. 52 E3
Woustviller France 52 H5
Wowoni i. Indon. 69 G7
Wozrojdeniye oroli i. Uzbek. see Vozrozhdenya Island
Wrangel Island Russia 65 T2
Wrangell Island U.S.A. 120 C3
Wrangell Mountains U.S.A. 153 B3
Wrangell-St Elias National Park and Preserve U.S.A. 120 A2
Wrath, Cape U.K. 50 D2
Wray U.S.A. 130 C3
Wreake r. U.K. 49 F6
Wreck Point S. Africa 100 C5
Wreck Reef Australia 110 F4
Wrecsam U.K. see Wrexham
Wrestedt Germany 53 K2
Wrexham U.K. 49 E5
Wrightmyo India 71 A5
Wrightson, Mount U.S.A. 127 F7
Wrightwood U.S.A. 128 E4
Wrigley Canada 120 F2
Wrigley U.S.A. 134 D4
Wrigley Gulf Antarctica 152 J2
Wrocław Poland 47 P5
Września Poland 47 P4
Wu'an China see Changtai
Wubin Australia 109 B7
Wuchang Heilong. China 74 B3
Wuchang Hubei China see Jiangxia
Wuchow China see Wuzhou
Wuchuan Guangdong China 77 F4
Wuchuan Guizhou China 76 E2
Wudalianchi China 74 B2
Wuḍām 'Alwā Oman 88 E6
Wudang Shan mt. China 77 F1
Wudaoliang China 76 B1
Wuding China 76 D3
Wudinna Australia 109 F8
Wufeng Hubei China 77 F2
Wufeng Yunnan China see Zhenxiong
Wugang China 77 F3
Wuhai China 72 J5
Wuhan China 77 G2
Wuhe China 77 H1
Wuhu China 77 H2
Wuhua China 77 G4
Wuhubei China 77 H2
Wüjang China 82 D2
Wu Jiang r. China 76 E2
Wujin Jiangsu China see Changzhou
Wujin Sichuan China see Xinjin
Wukari Nigeria 96 D4
Wulang China 76 B2
Wulêswālī Bihsūd Afgh. 89 G3
Wuli China 76 B1
Wulian Feng mts China 76 D2
Wuliang Shan mts China 76 D3
Wuliaru i. Indon. 108 E1
Wuli Jiang r. China 77 F4
Wuling Shan mts China 77 F2
Wulong China 76 E2
Wulongji China see Huaibin
Wulur Indon. 108 E1
Wumeng Shan mts China 76 D3
Wuming China 77 F4
Wümme r. Germany 53 I1
Wundwin Myanmar 70 B2
Wuning China 77 G2
Wünnenberg Germany 53 I3
Wunnummin Lake Canada 119 J4
Wunsiedel Germany 53 M4
Wunstorf Germany 53 J2
Wupatki National Monument nat. park U.S.A. 129 H4
Wuping China 77 H3
Wuppertal Germany 53 H3
Wuppertal S. Africa 100 D7
Wuqi China 73 J5
Wuquan China see Wuyang
Wuranga Australia 109 B7
Wurno Nigeria 96 D3
Würzburg Germany 53 J5
Wurzen Germany 53 M3
Wushan Chongqing China 77 F2
Wushan Gansu China 76 E1
Wu Shan mts China 77 F2
Wushi Guangdong China 77 F4
Wushi Xinjiang China 80 E3
Wüstegarten hill Germany 53 J3
Wusuli Jiang r. China/Russia see Ussuri
Wuvulu Island P.N.G. 69 K7
Wuwei China 72 I5
Wuxi Chongqing China 77 F2
Wuxi Hunan China 77 F2
Wuxi Hunan China see Qiyang
Wuxi Jiangsu China 77 I2
Wuxia China see Wushan
Wuxian China see Suzhou
Wuxing China see Huzhou
Wuxu China 77 F4
Wuxuan China 77 F4
Wuxue China 77 G2
Wuyang Guizhou China see Zhenyuan
Wuyang Henan China 77 G1
Wuyang Zhejiang China see Wuyi
Wuyi China 77 H2
Wuyiling China 74 C2
Wuyi Shan mts China 77 H3
Wuyuan Jiangxi China 77 H2
Wuyuan Nei Mongol China 73 J4
Wuyuan Zhejiang China see Haiyan
Wuyun China see Jinyun
Wuzhishan China 77 F5
Wuzhi Shan mts China 77 F5
Wuzhong China 72 J5
Wuzhou China 77 F4
Wyalkatchem Australia 109 B7
Wyalong Australia 112 C4
Wyandra Australia 112 B1
Wyangala Reservoir Australia 112 D4
Wyara, Lake salt flat Australia 112 B2
Wycheproof Australia 112 A6
Wylliesburg U.S.A. 135 F5
Wyloo Australia 108 B5
Wylye r. U.K. 49 F7
Wymondham U.K. 49 I6
Wymore U.S.A. 130 D3
Wynbring Australia 109 F7
Wyndham Australia 108 E3
Wyndham-Werribee Australia 112 B6
Wynne U.S.A. 131 F5
Wynyard Canada 121 J5
Wyola Lake salt flat Australia 109 E7
Wyoming U.S.A. 134 C2
Wyoming state U.S.A. 126 G4
Wyoming Peak U.S.A. 126 F4
Wyoming Range mts U.S.A. 126 F4
Wyong Australia 112 E4
Wyperfeld National Park Australia 111 C7
Wysox U.S.A. 135 G3
Wyszków Poland 47 R4
Wythall U.K. 49 F6
Wytheville U.S.A. 134 E5
Wytmarsum Neth. see Witmarsum

X

Xaafuun Somalia 98 F2
▶Xaafuun, Raas pt Somalia 86 H7
Most easterly point of Africa.
Xabyaisamba China 76 C2
Xaçmaz Azer. 91 H2
Xago China 83 G3
Xagquka China 76 B2
Xaidulla China 82 D1
Xaignabouli Laos 70 C3
Xaignabouri Laos see Xaignabouli
Xainza China 83 G3
Xai-Xai Moz. 101 K3
Xalapa Mex. 136 E5
Xaltan Aşırımı Azer. 91 H2
Xambioá Brazil 143 I5
Xamgyi'nyilha China 76 C3
Xam Nua Laos 70 D2
Xá-Muteba Angola 99 B4
Xan r. Laos 70 C3
Xanagas Botswana 100 E2
Xangda China see Nangqên
Xangdin Hural China 73 K4
Xangdoring China see Xungba
Xangongo Angola 99 B5
Xanh, Cu Lao i. Vietnam 71 E4
▶Xankändi Azer. 91 G3
Capital of Nagorno-Karabakh.
Xanthi Greece 59 K4
Xarag China 83 I1
Xarardheere Somalia 98 E3
Xàtiva Spain 57 F4
Xavantes, Serra dos hills Brazil 143 I6
Xaxa China 83 E2
Xayar China 80 F3
Xékong Laos 70 D4
Xela Guat. see Quetzaltenango
Xelva Spain see Chelva
Xenia U.S.A. 134 D4
Xero Potamos r. Cyprus see Xeros
Xeros r. Cyprus 85 A2
Xhora S. Africa see Elliotdale
Xiabole Shan mt. China 74 B2
Xiachuan Dao i. China 77 G4
Xiaguan China see Dali
Xiahe China 76 D1
Xiamen China 77 H3
Xi'an China 77 F1
Xianfeng China 77 F2
Xiangcheng Sichuan China 76 C2
Xiangcheng Yunnan China see Xiangyun
Xiangfan China see Xiangyang
Xiangfeng China see Laifeng
Xianggang H.K. China see Hong Kong
Xianggang Tebie Xingzhengqu aut. reg. China see Hong Kong
Xiangkou China see Wulong
Xiangning China 73 K5
Xiangquan He r. China see Langqên Zangbo
Xiangride China 83 I2
Xiangshan China see Menghai
Xiangshui China 77 H1
Xiangshuiba China 77 F3
Xiangtan China 77 G3
Xiangxiang China 77 G3
Xiangyang China 77 G1
Xiangyang Hu l. China 83 G2
Xiangyin China 77 G2
Xiangyun China 76 D3
Xianju China 77 I2
Xianning China 77 G2
Xiannümiao China see Jiangdu
Xianshui He r. China 76 D2
Xiantao China 77 G2
Xianxia Ling mts China 77 H3
Xianyang China 77 F1
Xiaocaohu China 80 G3
Xiaodong China 77 F4
Xiaodongliang China 76 C1
Xiao'ergou China 74 A2
Xiaogan China 77 G2
Xiaogang China see Dongxiang
Xiao Hinggan Ling mts China 74 B2
Xiaojin China 76 D2
Xiaonanchuan China 83 H2
Xiaosanjiang China 77 G3
Xiaoshan China 77 I2
Xiao Shan mts China 77 F1
Xiaoshi China see Benxi
Xiao Surmang China 76 C1
Xiaotao China 77 H3
Xiaoxi China see Pinghe
Xiaoxian China 77 H1
Xiaoxiang Ling mts China 76 D2
Xiaoxita China see Yiling
Xiapu China 77 I3
Xiaqiong China see Batang
Xiashan China see Zhanjiang
Xiayang China see Yanling
Xiayingpan China see Liuzhi
Xiayukou China 77 F1
Xiazhuang China see Linshu
Xibdê China 76 C2
Xibing China 77 H3
Xibu China see Dongshan
Xichang China 76 D3
Xichou China 76 E4
Xichuan China 77 F1
Xide China 76 D2
Xidu China see Hengyang
Xiema China 77 F2
Xiêng Lam Vietnam 70 D3
Xieyang Dao i. China 77 F4
Xifeng Guizhou China 76 E3
Xifeng Liaoning China 74 B4
Xifengzhen China see Qingyang
Xigazê China 83 G3
Xihan Shui r. China 76 E1
Xi He r. China 76 E2
Xi Jiang r. China 77 G4
Xijir China 83 G2
Xijir Ulan Hu salt l. China 83 G2
Xiliao He r. China 74 A4
Xilin China 76 E3
Xilinhot China 73 L4
Ximiao China 80 J3
Xin'an Anhui China see Lai'an
Xin'an Guizhou China see Anlong
Xin'an Henan China 77 G1
Xinavane Moz. 101 K3
Xin Barag Zuoqi China see Amgalang
Xincai China 77 G1
Xinchang Jiangxi China see Yifeng
Xinchang Zhejiang China 77 I2
Xincheng Fujian China see Gutian
Xincheng Guangdong China see Xinxing
Xincheng Guangxi China 77 F3
Xincheng Sichuan China see Zhaojue
Xincun China see Dongchuan
Xindi Guangxi China 77 F4
Xindi Hubei China see Honghu
Xindian China 74 B3
Xindu Guangxi China 77 F4
Xindu Sichuan China see Luhuo
Xindu Sichuan China 76 E2
Xinduqiao China 76 D2
Xinfeng Guangdong China 77 G3
Xinfeng Jiangxi China 77 G3
Xinfengjiang Shuiku resr China 77 G4
Xing'an Guangxi China 77 F3
Xingan China 77 G3
Xing'an Shaanxi China see Ankang
Xingba China see Lhünzê
Xingguo Gansu China see Qin'an
Xingguo Hubei China see Yangxin
Xingguo Jiangxi China 77 G3
Xinghai China 80 I4
Xinghua China 77 H1
Xinghua Wan b. China 77 H3
Xingkai China 74 D3
Xingkai Hu l. China/Russia see Khanka, Lake
Xinglong Heilong. China 74 B2
Xinglong Heilong. China 74 B3
Xinglongzhen China 76 E1
Xingning Guangdong China 77 G3
Xingning Hunan China 77 G3
Xingou China 77 G2
Xingping China 77 F1
Xingqêngoin China 76 D2
Xingren China 76 E3
Xingsagoinba China 76 D1
Xingshan Guizhou China see Majiang
Xingshan Hubei China 77 F2
Xingtai China 73 K5
Xingu r. Brazil 143 H4
Xingu, Parque Indígena do res. Brazil 143 H6
Xinguara Brazil 143 H5
Xingye China 77 F4
Xingyi China 76 E3
Xinhua Guangdong China see Huadu
Xinhua Hunan China 77 F3
Xinhua Yunnan China see Qiaojia
Xinhua Yunnan China see Funing
Xinhuang China 77 F3
Xinhui China 77 G4
Xining China 72 I5
Xinjian China 77 G2
Xinjiang China 77 F1
Xinjiang aut. reg. China see Xinjiang Uygur Zizhiqu
Xinjiangkou China see Songzi
Xinjiang Uygur Zizhiqu aut. reg. China 82 E1
Xinjie Qinghai China 76 D1
Xinjie Yunnan China 76 C3
Xinjie Yunnan China 76 D4
Xinjin China 76 D2
Xinjing China see Jingxi
Xinkai He r. China 74 A4
Xinkou China 73 K5
Xinling China see Badong
Xinlitun China 74 B2
Xinlong China 76 D2
Xinmi China 77 G1
Xinmin China 74 B2
Xinning Gansu China see Ningxian
Xinning Hunan China 77 F3
Xinning Jiangxi China see Wuning
Xinning Sichuan China see Kaijiang
Xinping China 76 D3
Xinqiao China 77 G1
Xinqing China 74 C2
Xinquan China 77 H3
Xinshan China see Anyuan
Xinshiba China see Ganluo
Xinsi China 76 E1
Xintai China 73 L5
Xintanpu China 77 G2
Xintian China 77 G3
Xinxiang China 77 G1
Xinxing China 77 G4
Xinyang Henan China see Pingqiao
Xinyang Henan China 77 G1
Xinye China 77 G1
Xinyi Guangdong China 77 F4
Xinyi Jiangsu China 77 H1
Xinying China 77 F5
Xinying Taiwan 77 I4
Xinyu China 77 G3
Xinyuan Qinghai China see Tianjun
Xinyuan Xinjiang China 80 F3
Xinzhangfang China 74 A2
Xinzhou Guangxi China see Longlin
Xinzhou Hubei China 77 G2
Xinzhu Taiwan see Hsinchu
Xinzo de Limia Spain 57 C2
Xiongshan China see Zhenghe
Xiongshi China see Guixi
Xiongzhou China see Nanxiong
Xiping Henan China 77 F1
Xiping Henan China 77 G1
Xiqing Shan mts China 76 D1
Xique-Xique Brazil 143 J6
Xisa China see Xichou
Xisha Qundao is S. China Sea see Paracel Islands
Xishuangbanna reg. China 76 D4
Xishui Guizhou China 76 E2
Xishui Hubei China 77 G2
Xitianmu Shan mt. China 77 H2
Xiugu China see Jinxi
Xi Ujimqin Qi China see Bayan Ul
Xiuning China 77 H2
Xiushan Chongqing China 77 F2
Xiushan Yunnan China see Tonghai
Xiushui China 77 G2
Xiuwen China 76 E3
Xiuwu China 77 G1
Xiuying China 77 F4
Xiwol China 82 E1
Xiwu China 76 C1
Xixabangma Feng mt. China 83 F3
Xixia China 77 F1
Xixiang China 76 E1
Xixiu China see Anshun
Xixón Spain see Gijón/Xixón
Xiyang Dao i. China 77 I3
Xiyang Jiang r. China 76 E3
Xiyuping Yu i. Taiwan 77 H4
Xizang aut. reg. China see Xizang Zizhiqu
Xizang Gaoyuan plat. China see Tibet, Plateau of
Xizang Zizhiqu aut. reg. China 83 G3
Xo'japiryox tog'i mt. Uzbek. 89 G2
Xo'jayli Uzbek. 80 A3
Xorkol China 80 H4
Xuancheng China 77 H2
Xuande Qundao is Paracel Is see Amphitrite Group
Xuan'en China 77 F2
Xuanhua China 73 L4
Xuân Lôc Vietnam 71 D5
Xuanwei China 76 E3
Xuanzhou China see Xuancheng
Xuchang China 77 G1
Xucheng China see Xuwen
Xuddur Somalia 98 E3
Xuefeng China see Mingxi
Xuefeng Shan mts China 77 F3
Xue Shan mts China 76 C3
Xue Shan mt. Taiwan 77 I3
Xugui China 80 I4
Xuguit Qi China see Yakeshi
Xujiang China see Guangchang
Xümatang China 76 C1
Xungba China 83 E2
Xungmai China 83 G3
Xunhe China 74 B2
Xun He r. China 74 C2
Xun Jiang r. China 77 F4
Xunwu China 77 G3
Xunyi China 77 F1
Xúquer, Riu r. Spain 57 F4
Xuru Co salt l. China 83 F3
Xuwen China 68 E2
Xuyi China 77 H1
Xuyong China 76 E2
Xuzhou China 77 H1

Y

Ya'an China 76 D2
Yabanabat Turkey see Kızılcahamam
Yabēlo Eth. 98 D3
Yablonovyy Khrebet mts Russia 73 J2
Yabrīn reg. Saudi Arabia 88 C6
Yabuli China 74 C3
Yacha China see Baisha
Yacheng China 77 F5
Yachi He r. China 76 E3
Yacuma r. Bol. 142 E6
Yadgir India 84 C2
Yadrin Russia 42 J5
Yaeyama-rettō is Japan 73 M8
Yafa Israel see Tel Aviv-Yafo
Yagaba Ghana 96 C3
Yagan China 72 I4
Yağda Turkey see Erdemli
Yaghan Basin sea feature S. Atlantic Ocean 148 D9
Yagman Turkm. 88 D2
Yagmo China 83 F3
Yagodnoye Russia 65 P3
Yagodnyy Russia 74 E2
Yagoua Cameroon 97 E3
Yagra China 83 E3
Yagradagzê Feng mt. China 76 B1
Yaguajay Cuba 133 E8
Yagul and Mitla, Prehistoric Caves of tourist site Mex. 136 E5
Yaha Thai. 71 C6
Yahk Canada 120 G5
Yahualica Mex. 136 D4
Yahyalı Turkey 55 L4
Yai Myanmar see Ye
Yai, Khao mt. Thai. 71 B4
Yaizu Japan 75 E6
Yajiang China 76 D2
Yakacık Turkey 85 C1
Yakeshi China 73 M3
Yakhab waterhole Iran 88 E3
Yakhchāl Afgh. 89 G4
Yakima U.S.A. 126 C3
Yakima r. U.S.A. 126 D3
Yakmach Pak. 89 F4
Yako Burkina Faso 96 C3
Yakovlevka Russia 74 D3
Yaku-shima i. Japan 75 C7
Yakutat U.S.A. 120 B3
Yakutat Bay U.S.A. 120 A3
Yakutsk Russia 65 N3
Yakymivka Ukr. 43 G7
Yala Thai. 71 C6
Yala National Park Sri Lanka 84 D5
Yalan Dünya Mağarası tourist site Turkey 85 A1
Yale Canada 120 F5
Yale U.S.A. 134 D2
Yalgoo Australia 109 B7
Yalleroi Australia 110 D5
Yaloké Cent. Afr. Rep. 98 B3
Yalova Turkey 59 M4
Yalta Crimea 90 D1
Yalu Jiang r. China/N. Korea 74 B4
Yalujiang Kou r. mouth China/N. Korea 75 B5
Yalvaç Turkey 59 N5
Yamagata Japan 75 F5
Yamaguchi Japan 75 C6
Yamal, Poluostrov pen. Russia see Yamal Peninsula
Yam-Alin', Khrebet mts Russia 74 D1
Yamal Peninsula Russia 64 H2
Yamanie Falls National Park Australia 110 D3
Yamba Australia 112 F2
Yamba Lake Canada 121 I1
Yambarran Range hills Australia 108 E3
Yambi, Mesa de hills Col. 142 D3
Yambio South Sudan 97 F4
Yambol Bulg. 59 L3
Yamdena i. Indon. 108 E1
Yamethin Myanmar 70 B2
▶Yamin, Puncak mt. Indon. 69 J7
4th highest mountain in Oceania.
Yamkanmardi India 84 B2
Yamkhad Syria see Aleppo
Yamm Russia 45 P7
Yamma Yamma, Lake salt flat Australia 111 C5
▶Yamoussoukro Côte d'Ivoire 96 C4
Capital of Côte d'Ivoire (Ivory Coast).
Yampa r. U.S.A. 129 I1
Yampil' Ukr. 43 F6
Yampol' Ukr. see Yampil'
Yamuna r. India 82 E4
Yamunanagar India 82 D3
Yamzho Yumco l. China 83 G3
Yana r. Russia 65 O2
Yanam India 84 D2
Yan'an China 73 J5
Yanaoca Peru 142 D6
Yanaon India see Yanam
Yanaul Russia 41 Q4
Yanbu' al Baḥr Saudi Arabia 86 E5
Yanceyville U.S.A. 132 E4
Yancheng Henan China 77 G1
Yancheng Jiangsu China 77 I1
Yanchep Australia 109 A7
Yanco Australia 112 C5
Yanco Creek r. Australia 112 B5
Yanco Glen Australia 111 C6
Yanda watercourse Australia 112 B3
Yandama Creek watercourse Australia 111 C6
Yandao China see Yingjing
Yandoon Myanmar 70 A3
Yandun China 80 H3
Yanfolila Mali 96 C3
Ya'ngamdo China 76 B2
Yangbi China 76 C3
Yangcheng China 76 E3
Yangcheng Guangdong China see Yangshan

Yangcheng *Shanxi* China 77 G1
Yangchuan China *see* Suiyang
Yangchun China 77 F4
Yangcun China 77 G4
Yangdok N. Korea 75 B5
Yang Hu *l.* China 83 F2
Yangi Nishon Uzbek. 89 G2
Yangī Qal'ah Afgh. 89 H2
Yangiqishloq Uzbek. 80 C3
Yangirabot Uzbek. 89 G1
Yangiyo'l Uzbek. 80 C3
Yangjiajiang China 77 G2
Yangjiang China 77 F4
Yangming China *see* Heping
Yangôn Myanmar *see* Rangoon
Yangping China 77 F2
Yangquan China 73 K5
Yangshan China 77 G3
Yang Sin, Chư *mt.* Vietnam 71 E4
Yang Talat Thai. 70 C3
Yangtouyan China 76 D3

▶Yangtze *r.* China 76 E2
Longest river in Asia and 3rd in the world. Also known as Chang Jiang or Jinsha Jiang or Tongtian He or Yangtze Kiang or Zhi Qu.

Yangtze Kiang *r.* China *see* Yangtze
Yangudi Rassa National Park Eth. 98 E2
Yangxi China 77 F4
Yangxian China 76 E1
Yangxin China 77 G2
Yangyang S. Korea 75 C5
Yangzhou *Jiangsu* China 77 H1
Yangzhou *Shaanxi* China *see* Yangxian
Yanhe China 77 F2
Yanhuqu China 83 E2
Yanishpole Russia 42 G3
Yanis''yarvi, Ozero *l.* Russia 44 Q5
Yanji China 74 C4
Yanjiang China *see* Ziyang
Yanjin *Henan* China 77 G1
Yanjin *Yunnan* China 76 E2
Yanjing *Sichuan* China *see* Yanyuan
Yanjing *Yunnan* China *see* Yanjin
Yankari National Park Nigeria 96 E4
Yankton U.S.A. 130 D3
Yanling *Hunan* China 77 G3
Yanling *Sichuan* China *see* Weiyuan
Yannina Greece *see* Ioannina
Yano-Indigirskaya Nizmennost' *lowland* Russia 65 P2
Yanovski, Mount U.S.A. 120 C3
Yanrey *r.* Australia 109 A5
Yanshan *Jiangxi* China 77 H2
Yanshan *Yunnan* China 76 E4
Yanshi China 77 G1
Yanshiping China 76 B1
Yanskiy Zaliv *g.* Russia 65 O2
Yantabulla Australia 112 B2
Yantai China 73 M5
Yanting China 76 E2
Yantongshan China 74 B4
Yantou China 77 I2
Yanwa China 76 C3
Yanweigang China 77 H1
Yany-Kurgan Kazakh. *see* Zhanakorgan
Yanyuan China 76 D3
Yao Chad 97 E3
Yao'an China 76 D3
Yaodu China *see* Dongzhi
Yaoli China 77 H2

▶Yaoundé Cameroon 96 E4
Capital of Cameroon.

Yaoxian China *see* Yaozhou
Yaoxiaoling China 74 B2
Yao Yai, Ko *i.* Thai. 71 B6
Yaozhou China 77 F1
Yap *i.* Micronesia 69 J5
Yapen *i.* Indon. 69 J7
Yappar *r.* Australia 110 C3
Yap Trench *sea feature* N. Pacific Ocean 150 F5
Yaqui *r.* Mex. 127 F8
Yar Russia 42 L4
Yaradzha Turkm. *see* Ýarajy
Ýarajy Turkm. 88 E2
Yaraka Australia 110 D5
Yarangüme Turkey *see* Tavas
Yaransk Russia 42 J4
Yardea Australia 111 A7
Yardımcı Burnu *pt* Turkey 59 N6
Yardımlı Azer. 91 H3
Yardymly Azer. *see* Yardımlı
Yare *r.* U.K. 49 I6
Yarega Russia 42 L3

▶Yaren Nauru 107 G2
De facto capital of Nauru.

Yarensk Russia 42 K3
Yariga-take *mt.* Japan 75 E5
Yarīm Yemen 86 F7
Yarımca Turkey *see* Körfez
Yarkand China *see* Shache
Yarkant China *see* Shache
Yarkant He *r.* China 80 E4
Yarker Canada 135 G1
Yarkhun *r.* Pak. 89 I2
Yarlêb China 83 F3
Yarlung Zangbo *r.* China *see* Brahmaputra
Yarmouth Canada 123 I6
Yarmouth *England* U.K. 49 F8
Yarmouth *England* U.K. *see* Great Yarmouth
Yarmouth U.S.A. 135 J2
Yarmuk *r.* Asia 85 B3
Yarnell U.S.A. 129 G4
Yaroslavl' Russia 42 H4
Yaroslavskiy Russia 74 D3
Yarra *r.* Australia 112 B6
Yarra Junction Australia 112 B6
Yarram Australia 112 C7
Yarraman Australia 112 E1
Yarrawonga Australia 112 B6
Yarra Yarra Lakes *salt flat* Australia 109 A7
Yarronvale Australia 112 B1
Yarrowmere Australia 110 D4
Yartö Tra La *pass* China 83 H3
Yartsevo *Krasnoyarskiy Kray* Russia 64 J3
Yartsevo *Smolenskaya Oblast'* Russia 43 G5
Yarumal Col. 142 C2
Yarwa China 76 C2
Yarzhong China 76 C2
Yaş Romania *see* Iaşi
Yasawa Group *is* Fiji 107 H3
Yashilkŭl *l.* Tajik. 89 I2
Yashkul' Russia 43 J7
Yasin Pak. 82 C1
Yasnogorsk Russia 43 H5
Yasnyy Russia 74 C1
Yasothon Thai. 70 D4
Yass Australia 112 D5
Yass *r.* Australia 112 D5
Yassı Burnu *c.* Cyprus *see* Plakoti, Cape
Yāsūj Iran 88 C4
Yasuní, Parque Nacional *nat. park* Ecuador 142 C4
Yatağan Turkey 59 M6
Yaté New Caledonia 107 G4
Yates *r.* Canada 120 H2
Yates Center U.S.A. 130 E4
Yathkyed Lake Canada 121 L2
Yatsushiro Japan 75 C6
Yaṭṭah West Bank 85 B4
Yatton U.K. 49 E7
Yauca Peru 142 D7
Yau Tong *b.* H.K. China 77 [inset]
Yavan Tajik. *see* Yovon
Yavarí *r.* Brazil/Peru 142 E4
also known as Javari (Brazil/Peru)
Yávaros Mex. 127 F8
Yavatmal India 84 C1
Yavi Turkey 91 F3
Yaví, Cerro *mt.* Venez. 142 E2
Yavoriv Ukr. 43 D6
Yavuzlu Turkey 85 C1
Yawatongguzlangar China 83 E1
Yaw Chaung *r.* Myanmar 76 B4
Yaxian China *see* Sanya
Yay Myanmar *see* Ye
Yayladağı Turkey 85 C2
Yazd Iran 88 D4
Yazdān Iran 89 F3
Yazd-e Khvāst Iran *see* Shāhīn Dezh
Yazıhan Turkey 90 E3
Yazoo City U.S.A. 131 F5
Y Bala U.K. *see* Bala
Yding Skovhøj *hill* Denmark 47 L3
Ydra *i.* Greece 59 J6
Y Drenewydd U.K. *see* Newtown
Ye Myanmar 70 B4
Yea Australia 112 B6
Yealmpton U.K. 49 D8
Yebawmi Myanmar 70 A1
Yebbi-Bou Chad 97 E2
Yecheng China 80 E4
Yécora Mex. 127 F7
Yedashe Myanmar 70 B3
Yedi Burun Başı *pt* Turkey 59 M6
Yeeda River Australia 108 C4
Yefremov Russia 43 H5
Yêgainnyin China *see* Henan
Yeghegnadzor Armenia 91 G3
Yegindykol' Kazakh. 80 C1
Yegorlykskaya Russia 43 I7
Yegorova, Mys *pt* Russia 74 E3
Yegor'yevsk Russia 43 H5
Yei South Sudan 97 G4
Yei *r.* South Sudan 97 G4
Yeji China 77 G2
Yejiaji China *see* Yeji
Yekaterinburg Russia 64 H4
Yekaterinodar Russia *see* Krasnodar
Yekaterinoslav Ukr. *see* Dnipropetrovs'k
Yekaterinoslavka Russia 74 C2
Yekhegnadzor Armenia *see* Yeghegnadzor
Yekibastuz Kazakh. 80 E1
Ye Kyun *i.* Myanmar 70 A3
Yelabuga *Khabarovskiy Kray* Russia 74 D2
Yelabuga *Respublika Tatarstan* Russia 42 K5
Yelan' Russia 43 I6
Yelan' *r.* Russia 43 I6
Yelandur India 84 C3
Yelantsy Russia 72 J2
Yelarbon Australia 112 E2
Yelbarsli Turkm. 89 F2
Yelenovskiye Kar'yery Ukr. *see* Dokuchayevs'k
Yelets Russia 43 H5
Yélimané Mali 96 B3
Yelizavetgrad Ukr. *see* Kirovohrad
Yelkhovka Russia 43 K5
Yell *i.* U.K. 50 [inset]
Yellabina Regional Reserve *nature res.* Australia 109 F7
Yellandu India 84 D2
Yellapur India 84 B3
Yellowhead Pass Canada 120 G4

▶Yellowknife Canada 120 H2
Capital of the Northwest Territories.

Yellowknife *r.* Canada 120 H2
Yellow Mountain *hill* Australia 112 C4

▶Yellow River *r.* China 77 G1
4th longest river in Asia and 7th in the world.

Yellow Sea N. Pacific Ocean 73 N5
Yellowstone *r.* U.S.A. 130 C2
Yellowstone Lake U.S.A. 126 F3
Yellowstone National Park U.S.A. 126 F3
Yell Sound *strait* U.K. 50 [inset]
Yeloten Turkm. *see* Ýolöten
Yelovo Russia 41 Q4
Yel'sk Belarus 43 F6
Yelva *r.* Russia 42 K3
Yematan China 76 C1
Yemen *country* Asia 86 G6
Yemetsk Russia 42 I3
Yemişenbükü Turkey *see* Taşova
Yemmiganur India *see* Emmiganuru
Yemtsa Russia 42 I3
Yemva Russia 42 K3
Yena Russia 44 Q3
Yenagoa Nigeria 96 D4
Yenakiyeve Ukr. 43 H6
Yenakiyevo Ukr. *see* Yenakiyeve
Yenangyat Myanmar 70 A2
Yenangyaung Myanmar 70 A2
Yenanma Myanmar 70 A3
Yenda Australia 112 C5
Yêndum China *see* Zhag'yab
Yengisar China 80 E4
Yengo National Park Australia 112 E4
Yenice Turkey 59 L5
Yenidamlar Turkey *see* Demirtaş
Yenihan Turkey *see* Yıldızeli
Yenije-i-Vardar Greece *see* Giannitsa
Yenişehir Greece *see* Larisa
Yenişehir Turkey 59 M4

▶Yenisey *r.* Russia 64 J2
Part of the Yenisey-Angara-Selenga, 3rd longest river in Asia.

▶Yenisey-Angara-Selenga *r.* Russia 64 J2
3rd longest river in Asia and 6th in the world.

Yeniseysk Russia 64 K4
Yeniseyskaya Ravnina *ridge* Russia 64 K4
Yeniseyskiy Zaliv *inlet* Russia 153 F2
Yeniyol Turkey *see* Borçka
Yên Minh Vietnam 70 D2
Yenotayevka Russia 43 J7
Yeola India 84 B1
Yeo Lake *salt flat* Australia 109 D6
Yeongil-man *b.* S. Korea 75 C6
Yeongju S. Korea 75 C5
Yeosu S. Korea 75 B6
Yeotmal India *see* Yavatmal
Yeoval Australia 112 D4
Yeovil U.K. 49 E8
Yeo Yeo *r.* Australia *see* Bland
Yeppoon Australia 110 E4
Yeraliyev Kazakh. *see* Kuryk
Yerbent Turkm. 88 E2
Yerbogachen Russia 65 L3
Yercaud India 84 C4

▶Yerevan Armenia 91 G2
Capital of Armenia.

Yereymentau Kazakh. 80 D1
Yergara India 84 C2
Yergeni *hills* Russia 43 J7
Yergoğu Romania *see* Giurgiu
Yeriho West Bank *see* Jericho
Yerilla Australia 109 C7
Yerington U.S.A. 128 D2
Yerköy Turkey 90 D3
Yerla *r.* India 84 B2
Yermak Kazakh. *see* Aksu
Yermakovo Russia 74 B1
Yermak Plateau *sea feature* Arctic Ocean 153 H1
Yermentau Kazakh. *see* Yereymentau
Yermo Mex. 131 B7
Yermo U.S.A. 128 E4
Yerofey Pavlovich Russia 74 A1
Yerres *r.* France 52 C6
Yërsha *r.* Russia 42 L2
Yershov Russia 43 K6
Yertsevo Russia 42 I3
Yeruḥam Israel 85 B4
Yerupaja *mt.* Peru 142 C6
Yerushalayim Israel/West Bank *see* Jerusalem
Yeruslan *r.* Russia 43 J6
Yesagyo Myanmar 70 A2
Yesan S. Korea 75 B5
Yesil' Kazakh. 78 F1
Yesil' *r.* Kazakh./Russia 80 D1
Yeşilhisar Turkey 90 D3
Yeşilırmak *r.* Turkey 90 E2
Yeşilova *Burdur* Turkey 59 M6
Yeşilova *Yozgat* Turkey *see* Sorgun
Yessentuki Russia 91 F1
Yessey Russia 65 L3
Yes Tor *hill* U.K. 49 C8
Yêtatang China *see* Baqên
Yetman Australia 112 E2
Ye-U Myanmar 70 A2
Yeu, Île d' *i.* France 56 C3
Yevdokimovskoye Russia *see* Krasnogvardeyskoye
Yevlakh Azer. *see* Yevlax
Yevlax Azer. 91 G2
Yevpatoriya Crimea 90 D1
Yevreyskaya Avtonomnaya Oblast' *admin. div.* Russia 74 D2
Yexian China *see* Laizhou
Yeyik China 83 E1
Yeysk Russia 43 H7
Yeyungou China 80 G3
Yezhou China *see* Jianshi
Yezhuga *r.* Russia 42 J2
Yezo *i.* Japan *see* Hokkaidō
Yezyaryshcha Belarus 42 F5
Y Fali U.K. *see* Valley
Y Fenni U.K. *see* Abergavenny
Y Fflint U.K. *see* Flint
Y Gelli Gandryll U.K. *see* Hay-on-Wye
Yialí *i.* Greece *see* Gyali
Yi'allaq, Gebel *mt.* Egypt *see* Yu'alliq, Jabal
Yialousa Cyprus *see* Aigialousa
Yi'an China 74 B3
Yianisádha *i.* Greece *see* Gianisada
Yiannitsá Greece *see* Giannitsa
Yibin *Sichuan* China 76 E2
Yibin *Sichuan* China 76 E2
Yibug Caka *salt l.* China 83 F2
Yichang China 77 F2
Yicheng *Henan* China *see* Zhumadian
Yicheng *Hubei* China 77 G2
Yicheng *Shanxi* China 77 F1
Yichun *Heilong.* China 74 C3
Yichun *Jiangxi* China 77 G3
Yidu China *see* Zhicheng
Yidun China 76 C2
Yifeng China 77 G2
Yiftaḥ Israel 85 B3
Yi He *r.* *Henan* China 77 G1
Yi He *r.* *Shandong* China 77 H1
Yihuang China 77 H3
Yijun China 77 F1
Yilaha China 74 B2
Yilan China 74 C3
Yilan Taiwan 77 I3
Yıldız Dağları *mts* Turkey 59 L4
Yıldızeli Turkey 90 E3
Yilehuli Shan *mts* China 74 A2
Yiliang China 76 E3
Yiling China 77 F2
Yilong *Heilong.* China 74 B3
Yilong *Sichuan* China *see* Jincheng
Yilong *Yunnan* China *see* Shiping
Yilong Hu *l.* China 76 D4
Yimianpo China 74 C3
Yinbaing Myanmar 70 B3
Yincheng China *see* Dexing
Yinchuan China 72 J5
Yindarlgooda, Lake *salt flat* Australia 109 C7
Yingcheng China 77 G2
Yingde China 77 G3
Yinggehai China 77 F5
Yinggen China *see* Qiongzhong
Ying He *r.* China 77 H1
Yingjing China 76 D2
Yingkiong India 83 H3
Yingkou China 73 M4
Yingshan China 77 G2
Yingtan China 77 H2
Yining *Jiangxi* China *see* Xiushui
Yining *Xinjiang* China 80 F3
Yinjiang China 77 F3
Yinkeng China 77 G3
Yinkengxu China *see* Yinkeng
Yinmabin Myanmar 70 A2
Yinnyein Myanmar 70 B3
Yin Shan *mts* China 73 J4
Yinxian China *see* Ningbo
Yipinglang China 76 D3
Yiquan China *see* Meitan
Yirga Alem Eth. 98 D3
Yirol South Sudan 97 G4
Yisa China *see* Honghe
Yishan *Guangxi* China *see* Yizhou
Yishan *Jiangsu* China *see* Guanyun
Yishui China 73 L5
Yishun Sing. 71 [inset]
Yíthion Greece *see* Gytheio
Yitiaoshan China *see* Jingtai
Yitong He *r.* China 74 B3
Yiwu China 76 D4
Yixing China 77 H2
Yiyang China 77 G2
Yizheng China 77 H1
Yizhou China 77 F3
Yizra'el *country* Asia *see* Israel
Ylāne Fin. 45 M6
Ylihärmä Fin. 44 M5
Yli-Ii Fin. 44 N4
Yli-Kärppä Fin. 44 N4
Ylikiiminki Fin. 44 O4
Yli-Kitka *l.* Fin. 44 P3
Ylistaro Fin. 44 M5
Ylitornio Fin. 44 M3
Ylivieska Fin. 44 N4
Ylöjärvi Fin. 45 M6
Ymer Ø *i.* Greenland 119 P2
Ynys Enlli *i.* U.K. *see* Bardsey Island
Ynys Môn *i.* U.K. *see* Anglesey
Yoakum U.S.A. 131 D6
Yoder U.S.A. 134 C3
Yogan, Cerro *mt.* Chile 144 B8
Yogyakarta Indon. 68 E8
Yoho National Park Canada 120 G5
Yokadouma Cameroon 97 E4
Yokkaichi Japan 75 E6
Yoko Cameroon 96 E4
Yokohama Japan 75 E6
Yokosuka Japan 75 E6
Yokote Japan 75 F5
Yola Nigeria 96 E4
Yolo U.S.A. 128 C2
Yolombo Dem. Rep. Congo 98 C4
Ýolöten Turkm. 89 F2
Yoluk Mex. 133 C8
Yom, Mae Nam *r.* Thai. 70 C4
Yomou Guinea 96 C4
Yomuka Indon. 69 J8
Yonaguni-jima *i.* Japan 77 I3
Yŏnan N. Korea 75 B5
Yonezawa Japan 75 F5
Yong'an *Chongqing* China *see* Fengjie
Yong'an *Fujian* China 77 H3
Yongbei China *see* Yongsheng
Yongcong China 77 F3
Yongding *Fujian* China 77 H3
Yongding *Yunnan* China *see* Yongren
Yongding *Yunnan* China *see* Fumin
Yongfeng China 77 G3
Yongfu China 77 F3
Yŏnghŭng N. Korea 75 B5
Yŏnghŭng-man *b.* N. Korea 75 B5
Yongjing China *see* Xifeng
Yongkang *Yunnan* China 76 C3
Yongkang *Zhejiang* China 77 I2
Yongle China *see* Zhen'an
Yongning *Guangxi* China 77 F4
Yongning *Jiangxi* China *see* Tonggu
Yongning *Sichuan* China *see* Xuyong
Yongping China 76 C3
Yongqing China *see* Qingshui
Yongren China 76 D3
Yongsheng China 76 D3
Yongshou China 77 F1
Yongshun China 77 F2
Yongtai China 77 H3
Yongxi China *see* Nayong
Yongxin China 77 G3
Yongxing China 77 G3
Yongxiu China 77 G2
Yongyang China *see* Weng'an
Yongzhou China 77 F3
Yonkers U.S.A. 135 I3
Yopal Col. 142 D2
Yopurga China 80 E4
Yordu India 82 C2
York Australia 109 B7
York Canada 134 F2
York U.K. 48 F5
York *AL* U.S.A. 131 F5
York *NE* U.S.A. 130 D3
York *PA* U.S.A. 135 G4
York, Cape Australia 110 C1
York, Kap *c.* Greenland *see* Innaanganeq
York, Vale of *valley* U.K. 48 F4
Yorke Peninsula Australia 111 B7
Yorkshire Dales National Park U.K. 48 E4
Yorkshire Wolds *hills* U.K. 48 G5
Yorkton Canada 121 K5
Yorktown U.S.A. 135 G5
Yorkville U.S.A. 130 F3
Yorosso Mali 96 C3
Yosemite U.S.A. 134 C5
Yosemite National Park U.S.A. 128 D3
Yoshkar-Ola Russia 42 J4
Yos Sudarso *i.* Indon. *see* Dolok, Pulau
Yotvata Israel 85 B5
Youbou Canada 120 E5
Youghal Ireland 51 E6
Young Australia 112 D5
Young U.S.A. 129 H4
Younghusband, Lake *salt flat* Australia 111 B6
Younghusband Peninsula Australia 111 B7
Young Island Antarctica 152 H2
Youngstown Canada 121 I5
Youngstown U.S.A. 134 E3
You Shui *r.* China 77 F2
Youssoufia Morocco 54 C5
Youvarou Mali 96 C3
Youxi China 77 H3
Youxian China 77 G3
Youyang China 77 F2
Youyi China 74 C3
Youyi Feng *mt.* China/Russia 80 G2
Yovon Tajik. 89 H2
Yowah *watercourse* Australia 112 B2
Yozgat Turkey 90 D3
Ypres Belgium *see* Ieper
Yreka U.S.A. 126 C4
Yrghyz Kazakh. *see* Yrgyz
Yrgyz Kazakh. 80 B2
Yrgyz *r.* Kazakh. 80 B2
Yr Wyddfa *mt.* U.K. *see* Snowdon
Yser *r.* France 52 C4
also known as IJzer (Belgium)
Ysselsteyn Neth. 52 F3
Ystad Sweden 45 H9
Ystwyth *r.* U.K. 49 C6
Ysyk-Köl Kyrg. *see* Balykchy

▶Ysyk-Köl *salt l.* Kyrg. 80 E3
5th largest lake in Asia.

Ythan *r.* U.K. 50 G3
Y Trallwng U.K. *see* Welshpool
Ytyk-Kyuyel' Russia 65 O3
Yu'alliq, Jabal *mt.* Egypt 85 A4
Yuan'an China 77 F2
Yuanbao Shan *mt.* China 77 F3
Yuanjiang *Hunan* China 77 G2
Yuanjiang *Yunnan* China 76 D4
Yuan Jiang *r.* *Hunan* China 77 F2
Yuan Jiang *r.* *Yunnan* China 76 D4
Yuanjiazhuang China *see* Foping
Yuanlin China 74 A2
Yuanling China 77 F2
Yuanma China *see* Yuanmou
Yuanmou China 76 D3
Yuanquan China *see* Guazhou
Yuanshan China *see* Lianping
Yuanyang China *see* Xinjie
Yub'ā *i.* Saudi Arabia 90 D6
Yuba City U.S.A. 128 C2
Yubei China 76 E2
Yuben' Tajik. 89 I2
Yucatán *pen.* Mex. 136 F5
Yucatan Channel Cuba/Mex. 137 G4
Yucca U.S.A. 129 F4
Yucca Lake U.S.A. 128 E3
Yucca Valley U.S.A. 128 E4
Yucheng *Henan* China 77 G1
Yucheng *Sichuan* China *see* Ya'an
Yuci China *see* Jinzhong
Yudi Shan *mt.* China 74 A1
Yudu China 77 G3
Yuelai China *see* Huachuan
Yueliang Pao *l.* China 74 A3
Yuendumu Australia 108 E5
Yuen Long *H.K.* China 77 [inset]
Yueqing China 77 I2
Yuexi China 77 H2
Yueyang *Hunan* China 77 G2
Yueyang *Hunan* China 77 G2
Yueyang *Sichuan* China *see* Anyue
Yug *r.* Russia 42 J3
Yugan China 77 H2
Yugorsk Russia 41 S3
Yuhang China 77 I2
Yuhu China *see* Eryuan
Yuhuan China 77 I2
Yuin Australia 109 B6
Yu Jiang *r.* China 77 F4
Yukagirskoye Ploskogor'ye *plat.* Russia 65 Q3
Yukamenskoye Russia 42 L4
Yukarı Sakarya Ovaları *plain* Turkey 59 N5
Yukarısarıkaya Turkey 90 D3
Yukon *admin. div.* Canada 120 C2

▶Yukon *r.* Canada/U.S.A. 120 B2
5th longest river in North America.

Yukon Crossing (abandoned) Canada 120 B2
Yüksekova Turkey 91 G3
Yulara Australia 109 E6
Yule *r.* Australia 108 B5
Yuleba Australia 112 D1
Yulee U.S.A. 133 D6
Yulin *Guangxi* China 77 F4
Yulin *Shaanxi* China 73 J5
Yulong Xueshan *mt.* China 76 D3
Yuma *AZ* U.S.A. 129 F5
Yuma *CO* U.S.A. 130 C3
Yuma Desert U.S.A. 129 F5
Yumen China *see* Laojunmiao
Yumenguan China 80 H3
Yumurtalık Turkey 85 B1
Yuna Australia 109 A7
Yunak Turkey 90 C3
Yunan China 77 F4
Yunaska Island U.S.A. 118 A4
Yuncheng China 77 F1
Yundamindera Australia 109 C7
Yunfu China 77 G4
Yungas *reg.* Bol. 142 E7
Yungui Gaoyuan *plat.* China 76 D3
Yunhe *Jiangsu* China *see* Pizhou
Yunhe *Yunnan* China *see* Heqing
Yunhe *Zhejiang* China 77 H2
Yunjinghong China *see* Jinghong
Yunkai Dashan *mts* China 77 F4
Yünlin Taiwan *see* Douliu
Yunling China *see* Yunxiao
Yun Ling *mts* China 76 C3
Yunlong China 76 C3
Yunmeng China 77 G2
Yunmenling China *see* Junmenling
Yunnan *prov.* China 76 D3
Yunta Australia 111 B7
Yunt Dağı *mt.* Turkey 85 A1
Yunxi *Hubei* China 77 F1
Yunxi *Sichuan* China *see* Yanting
Yunxian *Hubei* China 77 F1
Yunxian *Yunnan* China 76 D3
Yunxiao China 77 H4
Yunyang *Chongqing* China 77 F2
Yunyang *Henan* China 77 G1
Yuping *Guizhou* China *see* Libo
Yuping *Guizhou* China 77 F3
Yuping *Yunnan* China *see* Pingbian
Yuqing China 76 E3
Yuraygir National Park Australia 112 F2
Yurba Co *l.* China 83 F2
Yürekli Turkey 85 B1
Yurga Russia 64 J4
Yurihonjō Japan 75 F5
Yuriria Mex. 136 D4
Yurungkax He *r.* China 82 E1
Yur'ya Russia 42 K4
Yur'yakha *r.* Russia 42 L2
Yuryev Estonia *see* Tartu
Yur'yevets Russia 42 I4
Yur'yev-Pol'skiy Russia 42 H4
Yushan China 77 H2
Yu Shan *mt.* Taiwan 77 I4
Yushino (abandoned) Russia 42 L1
Yushkozero Russia 44 R4
Yushu *Jilin* China 74 B3
Yushu *Qinghai* China 76 C1
Yushuwan China *see* Huaihua
Yusufeli Turkey 91 F2
Yus'va Russia 41 Q4
Yuta West Bank *see* Yaṭṭah
Yutai China 77 H1
Yutan China *see* Ningxiang
Yuxi *Guizhou* China *see* Daozhen
Yuxi *Hubei* China 77 F2
Yuxi *Yunnan* China 76 D3
Yuyangguan China 77 F2
Yuyao China 77 I2
Yuzawa Japan 75 F5
Yuzha Russia 42 I4
Yuzhno-Kamyshovyy Khrebet *ridge* Russia 74 F3
Yuzhno-Kuril'sk Russia 74 G3
Yuzhno-Muyskiy Khrebet *mts* Russia 73 K1
Yuzhno-Sakhalinsk Russia 74 F3
Yuzhno-Sukhokumsk Russia 91 G1
Yuzhnoukrayins'k Ukr. 43 F7
Yuzhnyy Russia *see* Adyk
Yuzhnyy, Ostrov *i.* Russia 64 G2
Yuzhou *Chongqing* China *see* Chongqing
Yuzhou *Henan* China 77 G1
Yuzovka Ukr. *see* Donets'k
Yverdon-les-Bains Switz. 56 H3
Yvetot France 56 E2
Ywamun Myanmar 70 A2

Z

Zaamin Uzbek. *see* Zomin
Zaandam Neth. 52 E2
Zaatari Jordan *see* Az Za'tarī
Zab, Monts du *mts* Alg. 57 I6
Zabānābād Iran 88 E3
Zabaykal'sk Russia 73 L3
Zabīd Yemen 86 F7
Zābolī Iran *see* Mehrestān
Zacapa Guat. 136 G5
Zacatecas Mex. 136 D4
Zacatecas *state* Mex. 131 C8
Zacharo Greece 59 I6
Zacoalco Mex. 136 D4
Zacynthus *i.* Greece *see* Zakynthos
Zadar Croatia 58 F2
Zadetkale Kyun *i.* Myanmar 71 B5
Zadetkyi Kyun *i.* Myanmar 71 B5
Zadi Myanmar 71 B4
Zadoi China 76 B1
Zadonsk Russia 43 H5
Za'farâna Egypt *see* Za'farānah
Za'farānah Egypt 90 D5
Zafer Adaları *is* Cyprus *see* Kleides Islands
Zafer Burnu *c.* Cyprus *see* Apostolos Andreas, Cape
Zafora *i.* Greece *see* Sofrana
Zafra Spain 57 C4
Zagazig Egypt *see* Az Zaqāzīq
Zaghdeh *well* Iran 88 E3
Zaghouan Tunisia 58 D6
Zagorsk Russia *see* Sergiyev Posad

▶Zagreb Croatia 58 F2
Capital of Croatia.

Zagros, Kūhhā-ye *mts* Iran *see* Zagros Mountains
Zagros Mountains Iran 88 B3
Zagunao China *see* Lixian
Za'gya Zangbo *r.* China 83 G3
Zāhedān Iran 89 F4
Zahir Pir Pak. 89 H4
Zaḥlah Lebanon *see* Zahlé
Zahlé Lebanon 85 B3
Zähmet Turkm. 89 F2
Ẓahrān Saudi Arabia 86 F6

Acknowledgements

Maps and data

Maps, design and origination by Collins Bartholomew Ltd, Westerhill Road, Bishopbriggs, Glasgow G64 2QT
Illustrations created by HarperCollins Publishers unless otherwise stated.

General/Various themes:
World Bank World Development Indicators
http://data.worldbank.org/data-catalog/world-development-indicators

Earthquake data (pp14–15): United States Geological Survey (USGS) National Earthquakes Information Center, Denver, USA.

Tropical Storms (pp16–17): National Oceanic and Atmospheric Administration (NOAA) National Hurricane Centre

Population map (pp20–21): 2005. Gridded Population of the World Version 3 (GPWv3). Palisades, NY: Socioeconomic Data and Applications Center (SEDAC), Columbia University. Available at: http://sedac.ciesn.columbia.edu/plue/gpw
http://www.ciesin.columbia.edu
United Nations Department of Economic and Social Affairs (UN DESA) World Population Prospects
http://esa.un.org/wpp/

Urbanization (pp22–23): United Nations Department of Economic and Social Affairs (UN DESA) World Urbanization Prospects http://esa.un.org/unpd/wup/

Communications (pp24-25): International Telecommunication Union (ITU), ICT ststistics
http://www.itu.int/en/ITU-D/Statistics/Pages/stat/default.aspx

Conflict (pp30–31): National Consortium for the Study of Terrorism and Responses to Terrorism (START). (2013). Global Terrorism Database (GTD).
http://www.start.umd.edu/gtd

Global Issues (pp32-33):International drugs trade - United Nations Office on Drugs and Crime (UNODC)
http://www.unodc.org/

HIV/AIDS - UNAIDS
http://www.unaids.org/

Environment (pp34–35): United Nations Environment Programme's World Conservation Monitoring Centre (UNEP-WCMC) http://unep-wcmc.org/ United Nations List of Protected Areas 2014

Coral reefs data (p35): World Resources Institute (WRI), Washington D.C., USA.

Desertification data (p35): U.S. Department of Agriculture Natural Resources Conservation Service.

Antarctica (p152): Antarctic Digital Database (versions1 and 2), ©Scientific Committee on Antarctic research (SCAR), Cambridge, UK.

Photographs and images

Page	Image	Credit
5	The Alps	MODIS/NASA
	Paris	Antonio Gravante/Shutterstock
6	Cyprus	MODIS/NASA
	Angkor	Amnartk/Shutterstock
7	Victoria Falls	Jan Zoetekouw/Shutterstock
8	Mataiva Atoll	NASA/JSC Gateway to Astronaut Photography of Earth
	Uluru (Ayers Rock)	Stanislav Fosenbauer/Shutterstock.com
	Queenstown and Lake Wakatipu	skyearth/Shutterstock
9	Liberty Island	Yuri Arcurs/Shutterstock
	Cuba	MODIS/NASA
10–11	Vatican City	SF photo/Shutterstock
12–13	Greenland	MODIS/NASA
16–17	Hurricane Sandy	NASA Earth Observatory image by Robert Simmon with data courtesy of the NASA/NOAA GOES Project Science team.
18–19	Tokyo	NASA Earth Observatory image courtesy Ron Beck, USGS Eros Data Center Satellite Systems Branch
	Cropland, Consuegra	Rick Barrentine/Corbis
	Mojave Desert	Keith Moore
	Larsen Ice Shelf	MODIS/NASA
20–21	Singapore	Wikipedia: CC by 1.0
	Kuna Indians	Danny Lehman/Corbis
22–23	Hong Kong	Exploring life: CC by SA-4.0
28–29	London	QQ7/Shutterstock
	Malawi village	Magdanatka/Shutterstock
30–31	Refugee camp in Thailand	Liewluck/Shutterstock
32–33	Opium poppy	forbis/Shutterstock
	Ganga river, Varanasi	OlegD/Shutterstock
34–35	Deforestation, Itaipu	Images reproduced by kind permission of UNEP
	Aral Sea 1973, 1986, 2001	Images reproduced by kind permission of UNEP
	Aral Sea 2014	MODIS/NASA
	Great Barrier Reef	MODIS/NASA
36–37	Iceland	MODIS/NASA
38–39	Bosporus	NASA/Johnson Space Center
60–61	Yangtze	MODIS/NASA
	Caspian Sea	MODIS/NASA
62–63	Timor	MODIS/NASA
	Beijing	NASA GSFC Landsat/LDCM EPO Team
92–93	Congo River	European Space Agency
	Lake Victoria	MODIS/NASA
94–95	Cape Town	esinel/Shutterstock
102–103	Princess Charlotte Bay	Earth Observatory images by Jesse Allen and Robert Simmon, using data provided by the U.S. Geological Survey.
	Banks Peninsula	NASA
104–105	Nouméa	NASA/Johnson Space Center
	Wellington	NASA/Johnson Space Center
114–115	Mississippi	ASTER/NASA
	Panama Canal	dazgee/Shutterstock
116–117	Mexicali	NASA
	The Bahamas	MODIS/NASA
138–139	Amazon / Rio Negro	NASA
	Tierra del Fuego	MODIS/NASA
140–141	Galapagos Islands	MODIS/NASA
	Falkland Islands	MODIS/NASA
146–147	Pacific Ocean globe	Anton Balazh/Shutterstock
	Atlantic Ocean globe	Anton Balazh/Shutterstock
	Indian Ocean globe	Anton Balazh/Shutterstock
	Antarctic Peninsula	MODIS/NASA

Published by **Collins**
An imprint of HarperCollins Publishers
Westerhill Road
Bishopbriggs
Glasgow
G64 2QT
www.harpercollins.co.uk

First published 2010
Second edition 2012
Third edition 2014
Reprinted 2015
Reprinted with revisions 2016
Fourth edition 2016

A catalogue record for this book is available from the British Library.

ISBN 978-0-00-820976-6
10 9 8 7 6 5 4 3 2 1

Printed in Hong Kong

All mapping in this atlas is generated from Collins Bartholomew™ digital databases. Collins Bartholomew™, the UK's leading independent geographical information supplier, can provide a digital, custom, and premium mapping service to a variety of markets.
For further information:
Tel: +44 (0) 208 307 4515
e-mail: collinsbartholomew@harpercollins.co.uk
or visit our website at: www.collinsbartholomew.com

If you would like to comment on any aspect of this atlas, please contact us at the above address or online.
e-mail: collinsmaps@harpercollins.co.uk
facebook.com/collinsmaps
@collinsmaps

Zahrez Chergui *salt pan* Alg. **57** H6
Zahrez Rharbi *salt pan* Alg. **57** H6
Zainlha China *see* **Xiaojin**
Zainsk Russia **42** L5
Zaire *country* Africa *see* **Congo, Democratic Republic of the**
Zaïre *r.* Congo/Dem. Rep. Congo *see* **Congo**
Zaječar Serbia **59** J3
Zaka Zimbabwe **99** D6
Zakamensk Russia **80** J1
Zakataly Azer. *see* **Zaqatala**
Zakháro Greece *see* **Zacharo**
Zakhmet Turkm. *see* **Zähmet**
Zakhodnyaya Dzvina *r.* Europe *see* **Zapadnaya Dvina**
Zākhū/Zaxo Iraq **91** F3
Zákinthos *i.* Greece *see* **Zakynthos**
Zakopane Poland **47** Q6
Zakouma, Parc National de *nat. park* Chad **97** E3
Zakwaski, Mount Canada **120** F5
Zakynthos Greece **59** I6
Zakynthos *i.* Greece **59** I6
Zala China **76** B2
Zalaegerszeg Hungary **58** G1
Zalai-domsag *hills* Hungary **58** G1
Zalamea de la Serena Spain **57** D4
Zalantun China **74** A3
Zalari Russia **72** I2
Zalău Romania **59** J1
Zaleski U.S.A. **134** D4
Ẕalim Saudi Arabia **86** F5
Zalingei Sudan **97** F3
Ẕalmā, Jabal aẓ *mt.* Saudi Arabia **86** E4
Zama City Canada **120** G3
Zambeze *r.* Africa *see* **Zambezi**

►**Zambezi** *r.* Africa **99** C5
4th longest river in Africa.
Also known as Zambeze.

Zambezi Zambia **99** C5
Zambia *country* Africa **99** C5
Zamboanga Phil. **69** G5
Zamfara *watercourse* Nigeria **96** D3
Zamīndāwar *reg.* Afgh. **89** F4
Zamkog China *see* **Zamtang**
Zamora Ecuador **142** C4
Zamora Spain **57** D3
Zamora de Hidalgo Mex. **136** D5
Zamość Poland **43** D6
Zamost'ye Poland *see* **Zamość**
Zamtang China **76** D1
Zamuro, Sierra del *mts* Venez. **142** F3
Zanaga Congo **98** B4
Zancle *Sicily* Italy *see* **Messina**
Zandamela Moz. **101** L3
Zandvliet Belgium **52** E3
Zanesville U.S.A. **134** D4
Zangguy China **82** D1
Zangsêr Kangri *mt.* China **83** F2
Zangskar *reg.* India *see* **Zanskar**
Zangskar Mountains India *see* **Zanskar Mountains**
Zanjān Iran **88** C2
Zanjān Rūd *r.* Iran **88** B2
Ẕannah, Jabal aẓ *hill* U.A.E. **88** D5
Zanskar *reg.* India **82** D2
Zanskar Mountains India **82** D2
Zante *i.* Greece *see* **Zakynthos**
Zanthus Australia **109** C7
Zanūghān Iran **88** E3
Zanzibar Tanz. **99** D4
Zanzibar Island Tanz. **99** D4
Zaoshi *Hubei* China **77** G2
Zaoshi *Hunan* China **77** G3
Zaouatallaz Alg. **96** D2
Zaouet el Kahla Alg. *see* **Bordj Omer Driss**
Zaoyang China **77** G1
Zaoyangzhan China **77** G1
Zaozernyy Russia **65** K4
Zapadnaya Dvina *r.* Europe **42** F5
also known as Dvina or Zakhodnyaya Dzvina. English form Western Dvina
Zapadnaya Dvina Russia **42** G4
Zapadni Rodopi *mts* Bulg. **59** J4
Zapadno-Kazakhstanskaya Oblast' *admin. div.* Kazakh. *see* **Zapadnyy Kazakhstan**
Zapadno-Sakhalinskiye Gory *mts* Russia **74** F2
Zapadno-Sibirskaya Nizmennost' *plain* Russia *see* **West Siberian Plain**
Zapadno-Sibirskaya Ravnina *plain* Russia *see* **West Siberian Plain**
Zapadnyy Chink Ustyurta *esc.* Kazakh. **91** I2
Zapadnyy Kazakhstan *admin. div.* Kazakh. **41** Q6
Zapadnyy Kil'din Russia **44** S2
Zapadnyy Sayan *reg.* Russia **72** F2
Zapata U.S.A. **131** D7
Zapata, Península de *pen.* Cuba **133** D8
Zapiga Chile **142** E7
Zapolyarnyy Russia **44** Q2
Zapol'ye Russia **42** H4
Zaporizhzhya Ukr. **43** G7
Zaporozh'ye Ukr. *see* **Zaporizhzhya**
Zapug China **82** E2
Zaqatala Azer. **91** G2
Zaqên China **76** B1
Za Qu *r.* China **76** C2
Zaqungngomar *mt.* China **83** G2
Zara China *see* **Zari**
Zara Croatia *see* **Zadar**
Zara Turkey **90** E3
Zarābād Iran **88** B2
Zarafshan Uzbek. *see* **Zarafshon**
Zarafshon Uzbek. **80** B3
Zarafshon, Qatorkŭhi *mts* Tajik. **89** G2
Zaragoza Spain **57** F3
Zaṟah Sharan Afgh. **89** H3
Zarand Iran **88** E4
Zarang China **82** D3
Zaranikh Protected Area *nature res.* Egypt **85** B4
Zaranj Afgh. **89** F4
Zarasai Lith. **45** O9
Zárate Arg. **144** E4
Zaraysk Russia **43** H5
Zaraza Venez. **142** E2
Zarbdor Uzbek. **89** H1
Zärdab Azer. **43** J8
Zarechensk Russia **44** Q3
Zāreh Iran **88** C3
Zarembo Island U.S.A. **120** C3
Zargun *mt.* Pak. **89** G4
Zari China **83** G3
Zaria Nigeria **96** D3
Zarichne Ukr. **43** E6
Zarifète, Col des *pass* Alg. **57** F6
Zaring China **83** G3
Zarinsk Russia **72** E2
Zarmardān Afgh. **89** F3
Zarneh Iran **88** B3
Zărnești Romania **59** K2
Zarqā' Jordan *see* **Az Zarqā'**
Zarqā', Nahr az *r.* Jordan **85** B3
Zarubino Russia **74** C4
Żary Poland **47** O5
Zarya Russia **43** H5
Zarzis Tunisia **54** G5
Zasheyek Russia **44** Q3
Zaskar *reg.* India *see* **Zanskar**
Zaskar Range *mts* India *see* **Zanskar Mountains**
Zaslawye Belarus **45** O9
Zastron S. Africa **101** H6
Za'tarī, Wādī az *watercourse* Jordan **85** C3
Zaterechnyy Russia **43** J7
Zauche *reg.* Germany **53** M2
Zaunguzskiye Karakumy *des.* Turkm. *see* **Üngüz Angyrsyndaky Garagum**
Zavala Moz. **101** L3
Zavalla U.S.A. **131** E6
Zavetnoye Russia **43** I7
Zavety Il'icha Russia **74** F2
Zavidovići Bos. & Herz. **58** H2
Zavitaya Russia *see* **Zavitinsk**
Zavitinsk Russia **74** C2
Zavolzhsk Russia **42** I4
Zavolzh'ye Russia *see* **Zavolzhsk**
Závora, Ponta *pt* Moz. **101** L3
Zawiercie Poland **47** Q5
Zawīlah Libya **97** E2
Zāwīyah, Jabal az *hills* Syria **85** C2
Zawr, Ra's az *pt* Saudi Arabia **91** H6
Zaybāk Afgh. **82** B1
Zaydī, Wādī az *watercourse* Syria **85** C3
Zaysan Kazakh. **80** F2
Zaysan, Lake Kazakh. **80** F2
Zaysan, Ozero *l.* Kazakh. *see* **Zaysan, Lake**
Zayü China *see* **Zhigang**
Zayü Qu *r.* China/India **83** I3
Žďár nad Sázavou Czechia **47** O6
Zdolbuniv Ukr. **43** E6
Zdolbunov Ukr. *see* **Zdolbuniv**
Zealand *i.* Denmark **45** G9
Zebulon U.S.A. **134** D5
Zedelgem Belgium **52** D3
Zeebrugge Belgium **52** D3
Zeeland U.S.A. **134** B2
Zeerust S. Africa **101** H3
Ẕefat Israel **85** B3
Zehdenick Germany **53** N2
Zeil, Mount Australia **109** F5
Zeil am Main Germany **53** K4
Zeist Neth. **52** F2
Zeitz Germany **53** M3
Zêkog China **76** D1
Zela Turkey *see* **Zile**
Zelennik Russia **42** J3
Zelenoborsk Russia **41** S3
Zelenoborskiy Russia **44** R3
Zelenodol'sk Russia **42** K5
Zelenogorsk Russia **45** P6
Zelenograd Russia **42** H4
Zelenogradsk Russia **45** L9
Zelenokumsk Russia **91** F1
Zelentsovo Russia **42** J4
Zelenyy, Ostrov *i.* Russia **74** G4
Zell am See Austria **47** N7
Zellingen Germany **53** J5
Zelzate Belgium **52** D3
Žemaitijos nacionalinis parkas *nat. park* Lith. **45** L8
Zêmdasam China **76** D1
Zemetchino Russia **43** I5
Zémio Cent. Afr. Rep. **98** C3
Zemmora Alg. **57** G6
Zempoaltépetl, Nudo de *mt.* Mex. **136** E5
Zengcheng China **77** G4
Zenica Bos. & Herz. **58** G2
Ẕenifim, Naḥal *watercourse* Israel **85** B4
Zennor U.K. **49** B8
Zenta Serbia *see* **Senta**
Zenzach Alg. **57** H6
Zerah, Gowd-e *plain* Afgh. **89** F4
Zeravshanskiy Khrebet *mts* Tajik. *see* **Zarafshon, Qatorkŭhi**
Zerbst/Anhalt Germany **53** M3
Zerenike Reserve *nature res.* Egypt *see* **Zaranikh Protected Area**
Zerf Germany **52** G5
Zernien Germany **53** K1
Zernitz Germany **53** M2
Zernograd Russia **43** I7
Zernovoy Russia *see* **Zernograd**
Zêtang China *see* **Nêdong**
Zetel Germany **53** H1
Zeulenroda Germany **53** L4
Zeven Germany **53** J1
Zevenaar Neth. **52** G3
Zevgari, Cape Cyprus **85** A2
Zeya Russia **74** B1
Zeya *r.* Russia **74** B2
Zeydar Iran **88** E2
Zeydī Iran **89** F5
Zeyskiy Zapovednik *nature res.* Russia **74** B1
Zeysko-Bureinskaya Vpadina *depr.* Russia **74** C2
Zeyskoye Vodokhranilishche *resr* Russia **74** B1
Zeytin Burnu *c.* Cyprus *see* **Elaia, Cape**
Zêzere *r.* Port. **57** B4
Zgharta Lebanon **85** B2
Zghorta Lebanon *see* **Zgharta**
Zgierz Poland **47** Q5
Zhabdün China *see* **Zhongba**
Zhabinka Belarus **45** N10
Zhaggo China *see* **Luhuo**
Zhaglag China **76** C1
Zhag'yab China **76** C2
Zhaksy Sarysu *watercourse* Kazakh. *see* **Sarysu**
Zhalanash Kazakh. *see* **Damdy**
Zhalpaktal Kazakh. **41** P6
Zhalpaqtal Kazakh. *see* **Zhalpaktal**
Zhaltyr Kazakh. **80** C1
Zhambyl *Karagandinskaya Oblast'* Kazakh. **80** D2
Zhambyl *Zhambylskaya Oblast'* Kazakh. *see* **Taraz**
Zhamo China *see* **Bomi**
Zhanakala Kazakh. **41** Q6
Zhanakazan Kazakh. **41** P6
Zhanakorgan Kazakh. **80** C3
Zhanaozen Kazakh. **78** E2
Zhanatas Kazakh. **80** C3
Zhanbei China **74** B2
Zhangaözen Kazakh. *see* **Zhanaozen**
Zhanga Qazan Kazakh. *see* **Zhanakazan**
Zhangaqorghan Kazakh. *see* **Zhanakorgan**
Zhangatas Kazakh. *see* **Zhanatas**
Zhangbang China **77** G2
Zhangbei China **73** K4
Zhangcheng China *see* **Yongtai**
Zhangcun China **77** H1
Zhangde China *see* **Anyang**
Zhangdian China *see* **Zibo**
Zhanggu China *see* **Danba**
Zhangguangcai Ling *mts* China **74** C3
Zhanghua Taiwan *see* **Changhua**
Zhangjiajie China **77** F2
Zhangjiakou China **73** K4
Zhangjiang China *see* **Taoyuan**
Zhangjiapan China *see* **Jingbian**
Zhangla China **76** D1
Zhangling China **74** A1
Zhanglou China **77** H1
Zhangping China **77** H3
Zhangqiang China **74** A4
Zhangqiao China **77** H1
Zhangshu China **77** G2
Zhangxian China **76** E1
Zhangye China **80** J4
Zhangzhou China **77** H3
Zhanhe China *see* **Zhanbei**
Zhanibek Kazakh. **41** P6
Zhanjiang China **77** F4
Zhao'an China **77** H4
Zhaodong China **74** B3
Zhaojue China **76** D2
Zhaoliqiao China **77** G2
Zhaoping China **77** F3
Zhaoqing China **77** G4
Zhaotong China **76** D3
Zhaoyuan China **74** B3
Zhaozhou China **74** B3
Zhari Namco *salt l.* China **83** F3
Zharkamys Kazakh. **80** A2
Zharkent Kazakh. **80** F3
Zharkovskiy Russia **42** G5
Zharma Kazakh. **80** F2
Zhashkiv Ukr. **43** F6
Zhashkov Ukr. *see* **Zhashkiv**
Zhaslyk Uzbek. *see* **Jasliq**
Zhaxi China *see* **Weixin**
Zhaxi Co *salt l.* China **83** F2
Zhaxigang China **82** D2
Zhaxizê China **76** C2
Zhaxizom China **83** F3
Zhayyq *r.* Kazakh./Russia *see* **Ural**
Zhdanov Ukr. *see* **Mariupol'**
Zhdanovsk Azer. *see* **Beyläqan**
Zhedao China *see* **Lianghe**
Zhêhor China **76** D2
Zhejiang *prov.* China **77** I2
Zhelaniya, Mys *c.* Russia **64** H2
Zheleznodorozhnyy Russia *see* **Yemva**
Zheleznodorozhnyy Uzbek. *see* **Qo'ng'irot**
Zheleznogorsk Russia **43** G5
Zhelou China *see* **Ceheng**
Zheltyye Vody Ukr. *see* **Zhovti Vody**
Zhem Kazakh. *see* **Emba**
Zhem *r.* Kazakh. **80** A2
Zhemgang Bhutan **83** G4
Zhen'an China **77** F1
Zhenba China **76** E1
Zhenghe China **77** H3
Zhengjiatun China *see* **Shuangliao**
Zhengning China **77** F1
Zhengyang China **77** G1
Zhengyangguan China **77** H1
Zhengzhou China **77** G1
Zhenhai China **77** I2
Zhenjiang China **77** H1
Zhenjiangguan China **76** D1
Zhenlai China **74** A3
Zhenning China **76** E3
Zhenping China **77** F2
Zhenxiong China **76** E3
Zhenyang China *see* **Zhengyang**
Zhenyuan China **77** F3
Zherdevka Russia **43** I6
Zherong China **77** H3
Zheshart Russia **42** K3
Zhetysuskiy Alatau *mts* China/Kazakh. **80** E3
Zhêxam China **83** F3
Zhexi Shuiku *resr* China **77** F2
Zhezkazgan Kazakh. **80** C2
Zhezqazghan Kazakh. *see* **Zhezkazgan**
Zhicheng *Hubei* China **77** F2
Zhicheng *Zhejiang* China *see* **Changxing**
Zhidoi China **76** B1
Zhifang China *see* **Jiangxia**
Zhigalovo Russia **72** J2
Zhigang China **76** C2
Zhigansk Russia **65** N3
Zhigong China *see* **Yangxi**
Zhigung China **83** G3
Zhijiang *Hubei* China **77** F2
Zhijiang *Hunan* China **70** E1
Zhijin China **76** E3
Zhi Qu *r.* China *see* **Yangtze**
Zhishan China *see* **Lingling**
Zhitikara Kazakh. **78** F1
Zhitkovichi Belarus *see* **Zhytkavichy**
Zhitkur Russia **43** J6
Zhitomir Ukr. *see* **Zhytomyr**
Zhīvār Iran **88** B3
Zhiziluo China **76** C3
Zhlobin Belarus **43** F5
Zhmerinka Ukr. *see* **Zhmerynka**
Zhmerynka Ukr. **43** F6
Zhob Pak. **89** H4
Zhob *r.* Pak. **89** H3
Zhong'an China *see* **Fuyuan**
Zhongba *Guangdong* China **77** G4
Zhongba *Sichuan* China *see* **Jiangyou**
Zhongba *Xizang* China **83** F3
Zhongduo China *see* **Youyang**
Zhongguo *country* Asia *see* **China**
Zhongguo Renmin Gongheguo *country* Asia *see* **China**
Zhonghe China *see* **Xiushan**
Zhongping China *see* **Huize**
Zhongshan *research station* Antarctica **152** E2
Zhongshan *Guangdong* China **77** G4
Zhongshan *Guangxi* China **77** F3
Zhongshan *Guizhou* China *see* **Liupanshui**
Zhongshu *Yunnan* China *see* **Luxi**
Zhongshu *Yunnan* China *see* **Luliang**
Zhongtai China *see* **Lingtai**
Zhongtiao Shan *mts* China **77** F1
Zhongwei China **72** J5
Zhongxin *Guangdong* China **77** G3
Zhongxin *Yunnan* China *see* **Xamgyi'nyilha**
Zhongxin *Yunnan* China *see* **Huaping**
Zhongxing China **77** H2
Zhongyang Shanmo *mts* Taiwan **77** I4
Zhongyaozhan China **74** B2
Zhongyicun China *see* **Gucheng**
Zhongyuan China **77** F5
Zhongzhai China **76** E1
Zhosaly Kazakh. **80** B2
Zhoujiajing China **72** I5
Zhoukou *Henan* China **77** G1
Zhoukou *Sichuan* China *see* **Peng'an**
Zhouning China **77** H3
Zhoushan China **77** I2
Zhoushan Dao *i.* China **77** I2
Zhoushan Qundao *is* China **77** I2
Zhouzhi China **77** F1
Zhovti Vody Ukr. **43** G6
Zhuanghe China **75** A5
Zhuanglang China **76** E1
Zhubgyügoin China **76** C1
Zhuchengzi China **74** B3
Zhudong Taiwan **77** I3
Zhugla China **76** B2
Zhugqu China **76** E1
Zhuhai China **77** G4
Zhuji *Henan* China *see* **Shangqiu**
Zhuji *Zhejiang* China **77** I2
Zhujing China **77** I2
Zhukeng China **77** G4
Zhukovka Russia **43** G5
Zhukovskiy Russia **43** H5
Zhumadian China **77** G1
Zhuokeji China **76** D2
Zhushan *Hubei* China **77** F1
Zhushan *Hubei* China *see* **Xuan'en**
Zhuxi China **77** F1
Zhuxiang China **77** H1
Zhuyang China *see* **Dazhu**
Zhuzhou *Hunan* China **77** G3
Zhuzhou *Hunan* China **77** G3
Zhydachiv Ukr. **43** E6
Zhympity Kazakh. **41** Q5
Zhytkavichy Belarus **45** O10
Zhytomyr Ukr. **43** F6
Ẕīā'ābād Iran **88** C3
Žiar nad Hronom Slovakia **47** Q6
Zibā *salt pan* Saudi Arabia **85** D4
Zibo China **73** L5
Zicheng China *see* **Zijin**
Zidi Pak. **89** G5
Ziel, Mount Australia *see* **Zeil, Mount**
Zielona Góra Poland **47** O5
Ziemelkursas augstiene *hills* Latvia **45** M8
Zierenberg Germany **53** J3
Ziesar Germany **53** M2
Ziftá Egypt **90** C5
Zīghan Libya **97** F2
Zigong China **76** E2
Ziguey Chad **97** E3
Ziguinchor Senegal **96** B3
Žīguri Latvia **45** O8
Zihuatanejo Mex. **136** D5
Zijin China **77** G4
Zijpenberg *hill* Neth. **52** G2
Ziketan China *see* **Xinghai**
Zile Turkey **90** D2
Žilina Slovakia **47** Q6
Zillah Libya **97** E2
Zima Russia **72** I2
Zimba Zambia **99** C5
Zimbabwe *country* Africa **99** C5
Zimi Sierra Leone *see* **Zimmi**
Zimmerbude Russia *see* **Svetlyy**
Zimmi Sierra Leone **96** B4
Zimnicea Romania **59** K3
Zimniy Bereg *coastal area* Russia **42** H2
Zimovniki Russia **43** I7
Zimrīn Syria **85** B2
Zin Pak. **89** H4
Ẕin, Naḥal *watercourse* Israel **85** B4
Zinave, Parque Nacional do *nat. park* Moz. **99** D6
Zinder Niger **96** D3
Zindo China **76** D2
Ziniaré Burkina Faso **96** C3
Zinjibār Yemen **86** G7
Zinoyevsk Ukr. *see* **Kirovohrad**
Zion U.S.A. **134** B2
Zion National Park U.S.A. **129** G3
Zionz Lake Canada **121** N5
Zippori Israel **85** B3
Ziqudukou China **76** B1
Zirc Hungary **58** G1
Zirkel, Mount U.S.A. **126** G4
Zirkūh *i.* U.A.E. **88** D5
Zirndorf Germany **53** K5
Ziro India **83** H4
Zirreh Afgh. **89** F4
Zīr Rūd Iran **88** C4
Zi Shui *r.* China **73** K7
Zistersdorf Austria **47** P6
Zitácuaro Mex. **136** D5
Zito China *see* **Lhorong**
Zitong China **76** E2
Zittau Germany **47** O5
Zixi China **77** H3
Zixing China *see* **Xingning**
Ziyang *Jiangxi* China *see* **Wuyuan**
Ziyang *Shaanxi* China **77** F1
Ziyang *Sichuan* China **76** E2
Ziyaret Dağı *hill* Turkey **85** B1
Ziyuan China **77** F3
Ziyun China **76** E3
Ziz, Oued *watercourse* Morocco **54** D5
Zizhong China **76** E2
Zlatitsa Bulg. **59** K3
Zlatoustovsk Russia **74** D1
Zlín Czechia **47** P6
Zmeinogorsk Russia **80** F1
Zmiyevka Russia **43** H5
Znamenka Russia **43** I5
Znamenka Ukr. *see* **Znam"yanka**
Znam"yanka Ukr. **43** G6
Znojmo Czechia **47** P6
Zoar S. Africa **100** E7
Zoetermeer Neth. **52** E2
Zogainrawar China *see* **Huashixia**
Zogang China **76** C2
Zogqên China **76** C1
Zoigê China **76** D1
Zoji La *pass* India **82** C2
Zola S. Africa **101** H7
Zolder Belgium **52** F3
Zolochev *Kharkivs'ka Oblast'* Ukr. *see* **Zolochiv**
Zolochev *L'vivs'ka Oblast'* Ukr. *see* **Zolochiv**
Zolochiv *Kharkivs'ka Oblast'* Ukr. **43** G6
Zolochiv *L'vivs'ka Oblast'* Ukr. **43** E6
Zolotonosha Ukr. **43** G6
Zolotoye Russia **43** J6
Zolotukhino Russia **43** H5

►**Zomba** Malawi **99** D5
Former capital of Malawi.

Zombor Serbia *see* **Sombor**
Zomin Uzbek. **89** H2
Zongga China *see* **Gyirong**
Zonguldak Turkey **59** N4
Zongxoi China **83** G3
Zörbig Germany **53** M3
Zorgho Burkina Faso **96** C3
Zorgo Burkina Faso *see* **Zorgho**
Zorn *r.* France **53** I6
Żory Poland **47** Q5
Zossen Germany **53** N2
Zottegem Belgium **52** D4
Zouar Chad **97** E2
Zoucheng China **77** H1
Zouérat Mauritania **96** B2
Zousfana, Oued *watercourse* Alg. **54** D5
Zoushi China **77** F2
Zouxian China *see* **Zoucheng**
Zrenjanin Serbia **59** I2
Zschopau Germany **53** N4
Zschopau *r.* Germany **53** N3
Zschornewitz Germany **53** M3
Ẕuayyinī, Mishāsh aẓ *well* Saudi Arabia **88** C5
Zubālah, Birkat *waterhole* Saudi Arabia **91** F5
Zubillaga Arg. **144** D5
Zubova Polyana Russia **43** I5
Zubtsov Russia **42** G4
Zuénoula Côte d'Ivoire **96** C4
Zug Switz. **56** I3
Zugdidi Georgia **91** F2
Zugspitze *mt.* Austria/Germany **47** M7
Zugu Nigeria **96** D3
Zuider Zee *l.* Neth. *see* **IJsselmeer**
Zuidhorn Neth. **52** G1
Zuid-Kennemerland, Nationaal Park *nat. park* Neth. **52** E2
Zuitai China *see* **Kangxian**
Zuitaizi China *see* **Kangxian**
Zuitou China *see* **Taibai**
Zújar *r.* Spain **57** D4
Zülpich Germany **52** G4
Zumba Ecuador **142** C4
Zunheboto India **83** H4
Zuni U.S.A. **129** I4
Zuni *watercourse* U.S.A. **129** I4
Zuni Mountains U.S.A. **129** I4
Zunyi *Guizhou* China **76** E3
Zunyi *Guizhou* China **76** E3
Zuo Jiang *r.* China/Vietnam **70** E2
Županja Croatia **58** H2
Zūrābād Iran **89** F3
Zürich Switz. **56** I3
Zurmat *reg.* Afgh. **89** H3
Zuru Nigeria **96** D3
Zurzuna Turkey *see* **Çıldır**
Zutphen Neth. **52** G2
Zuwārah Libya **96** E1
Zuyevka Russia **42** K4
Zūzan Iran **89** E3
Zvishavane Zimbabwe **99** D6
Zvolen Slovakia **47** Q6
Zvornik Bos. & Herz. **59** H2
Zwedru Liberia **96** C4
Zweeloo Neth. **52** G2
Zweibrücken Germany **53** H5
Zweletemba S. Africa **100** D7
Zwelitsha S. Africa **101** H7
Zwethau Germany **53** N3
Zwettl Austria **47** O6
Zwickau Germany **53** M4
Zwochau Germany **53** M3
Zwolle Neth. **52** G2
Zwönitz Germany **53** M4
Zyablovo Russia **42** L4
Zygi Cyprus **85** A2
Zyryan Kazakh. *see* **Zyryanovsk**
Zyryanka Russia **65** Q3
Zyryanovsk Kazakh. **80** F2
Zyyi Cyprus *see* **Zygi**

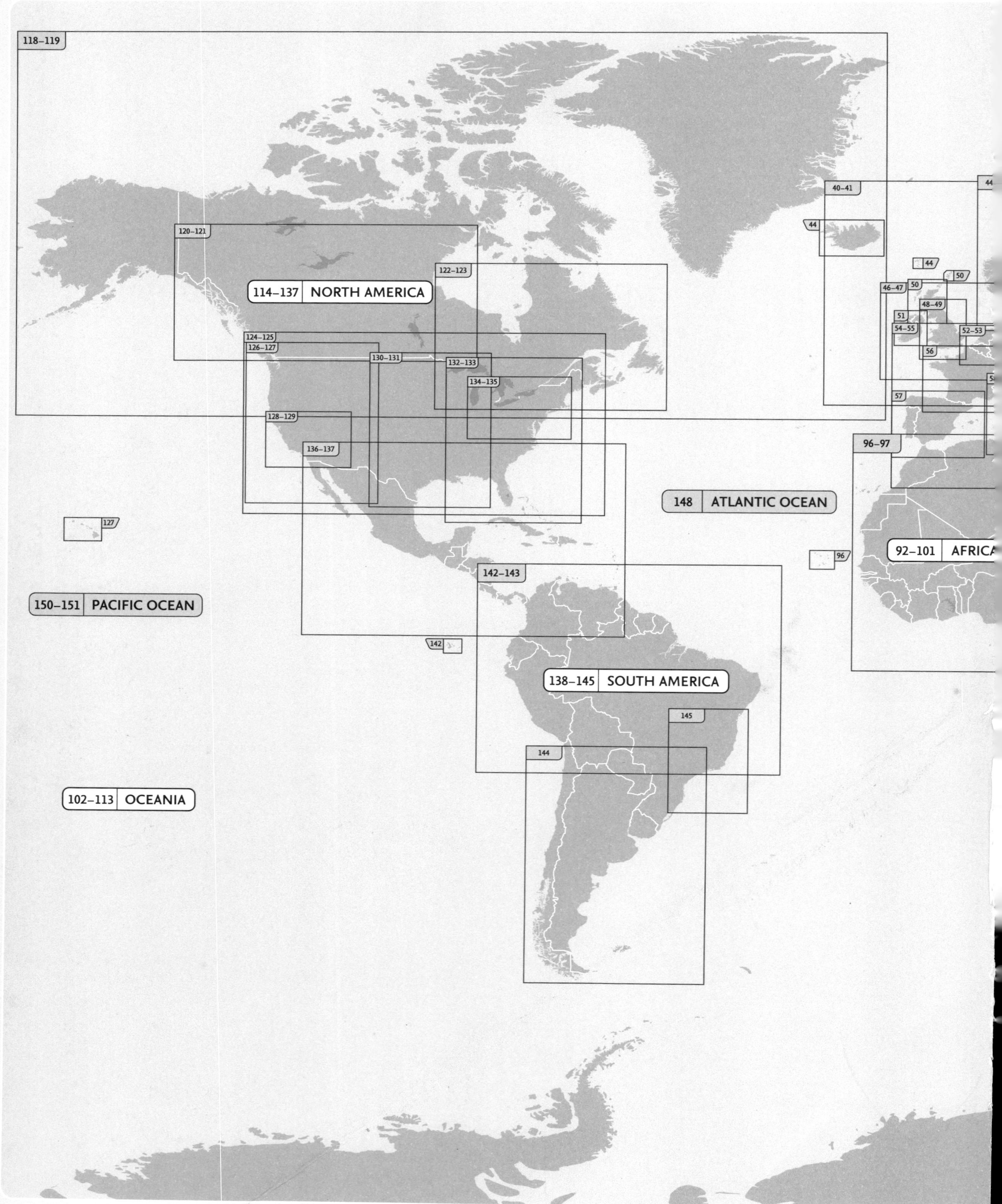
118–119
120–121
114–137 NORTH AMERICA
122–123
124–125
126–127
130–131
132–133
134–135
128–129
136–137
127
148 ATLANTIC OCEAN
150–151 PACIFIC OCEAN
142–143
142
138–145 SOUTH AMERICA
145
144
102–113 OCEANIA
40–41
44
44
50
46–47
50
48–49
51
54–55
52–53
56
57
96–97
96
92–101

Find your map